MW00913028

Volume Two

Volume One

AAAI–96 Technical Papers

Agents
AI in Art and Entertainment
Constraint Satisfaction
Education
Information Retrieval & Natural Language Processing
Knowledge-Based Systems
Knowledge Compilation
Knowledge Representation
Learning

Volume Two

AAAI–96 Technical Papers

Mobile Robots
Model-Based Reasoning
Perception
Planning
Rule-Based Reasoning & Connectionism
Uncertainty

AAAI–96 Invited Talks

AAAI–96 Robot Competition & Exhibition Abstracts

SIGART/AAAI Doctoral Consortium Abstracts

AAAI–96 Student Abstracts

Innovative Applications of Artificial Intelligence

Case Studies
Invited Talks

Proceedings *of the* Thirteenth National Conference on Artificial Intelligence and the Eighth Innovative Applications of Artificial Intelligence Conference

Volume Two

Sponsored by the American Association for Artificial Intelligence

AAAI Press / The MIT Press

Menlo Park • Cambridge • London

Copublished and distributed by The MIT Press,
Massachusetts Institute of Technology
Cambridge, Massachusetts and London, England

ISBN 0-262-51091-X

Manufactured in the United States of America on acid-free paper.

Contents, Volume Two

Natural Language

Learning

Semantics & Discourse

Perception

Perception

Vision

Planning

The Environment

AAAI–96 INVITED TALKS

AAAI–96 ROBOT COMPETITION & EXHIBITION ABSTRACTS

SIGART/AAAI DOCTORAL CONSORTIUM ABSTRACTS

AAAI-96 STUDENT ABSTRACTS

INNOVATIVE APPLICATIONS OF ARTIFICIAL INTELLIGENCE CONFERENCE

Case Studies

Invited Talks

Mobile Robots

Estimating the Absolute Position of a Mobile Robot Using Position Probability Grids

Wolfram Burgard and **Dieter Fox** and **Daniel Hennig** and **Timo Schmidt**

Institut für Informatik III, Universtiät Bonn
Römerstr. 164
D-53117 Bonn, Germany
{wolfram,fox,hennig,schmidt1}@uran.cs.uni-bonn.de

Abstract

In order to re-use existing models of the environment mobile robots must be able to estimate their position and orientation in such models. Most of the existing methods for position estimation are based on special purpose sensors or aim at tracking the robot's position relative to the known starting point. This paper describes the position probability grid approach to estimating the robot's absolute position and orientation in a metric model of the environment. Our method is designed to work with standard sensors and is independent of any knowledge about the starting point. It is a Bayesian approach based on certainty grids. In each cell of such a grid we store the probability that this cell refers to the current position of the robot. These probabilities are obtained by integrating the likelihoods of sensor readings over time. Results described in this paper show that our technique is able to reliably estimate the position of a robot in complex environments. Our approach has proven to be robust with respect to inaccurate environmental models, noisy sensors, and ambiguous situations.

Introduction

In order to make use of environmental models mobile robots always must know their current position and orientation[1] in their environment. Therefore, the ability of estimating their position is one of the basic preconditions for the autonomy of mobile robots. The methods for position estimation can be roughly divided into two classes: *relative* and *absolute* position estimation techniques (Feng, Borenstein, & Everett 1994). Members of the first class track the robot's relative position according to a known starting point. The problem solved by these methods is the correction of accumulated dead reckoning errors coming from the inherent inaccuracy of the wheel encoders and other factors such as slipping. Absolute position estimation techniques attempt to determine the robot's position without a priori information about the starting position. These approaches of the second class can be used to initialize the tracking techniques belonging to the first class.

[1] In the remainder of this paper we use the notion "position" to refer to "position and orientation" if not stated otherwise.

This paper addresses the problem of estimating the absolute position of a mobile robot operating in a known environment. There are two reasons why we consider this problem as relevant:

1. Whenever the robot is switched on, it should be able to re-use its model of the environment. For this purpose, it first has to localize itself in this model.

2. If the position tracking has failed, i.e. the robot has lost its position in the environment, it should be able to perform a repositioning.

To avoid modifications of the environment and expensive special purpose sensors we are interested in map-matching techniques, which match measurements of standard sensors against the given model of the environment. We have the following requirements to such a method:

1. **The method should be able to deal with uncertain information.** This is important because sensors are generally imperfect. This concerns wheel encoders as well as proximity sensors such as ultrasonic sensors or laser range-finders. Moreover, models of the environment are generally inaccurate. Possible reasons for deviations of the map from the real world come from imperfect sensors, measuring errors, simplifications, open or closed doors, or even moving objects such as humans or other mobile robots.

2. **The method should be able to deal with ambiguities.** Typical office environments contain several places which cannot be distinguished with a single measurement. As example consider a long corridor, where changes of the position due to the limited range of the sensors do not necessarily result in changes of the measured values. Thus, the set of possible positions of the robot is a region in that corridor.

3. **The method should allow the integration of sensor readings from different types of sensors over time.** Sensor fusion improves reliability while the integration

over time compensates noise and is necessary to resolve ambiguities.

Position probability grids simultaneously address all these desiderata. They allow a mobile robot to determine its position in typical office environments within a short time. Moreover, our method is able to deal with uncertain sensor information and ambiguous situations.

The approach described in this paper is based on the construction of certainty grid maps described in (Moravec & Elfes 1985). Certainty grid maps have been proven to be a powerful means for the solution of different problems. Originally, they were designed to provide a probabilistic model of the robot's environment. In the past such occupancy probability maps or variants of them have been successfully used for collision avoidance (Borenstein & Koren 1990; 1991) and path planning (Buhmann *et al.* 1995; Moravec 1988). This paper issues a further application area of this technique, namely the estimation of the absolute position of a robot. The principle of our approach is to accumulate in each cell of the position probability grid the posterior probability of this cell referring to the current position of the robot. Because we have to consider a discrete set of possible orientations in addition to the discretization of the two-dimensional environment, position estimation is a three-dimensional problem. This extension, however, does not result in any principle problems, because the certainty grid concept can easily be extended to problems with higher dimensionality (Moravec & Martin 1994).

Related work

Various techniques for the estimation of the position of mobile vehicles by matching sensor readings against a given model of the environment have been developed in the past (Cox & Wilfong 1990; Feng, Borenstein, & Everett 1994). Most of them address the problem of tracking the current position and orientation of the robot given its initial configuration. Recently, more and more probabilistic techniques are applied to position estimation problems. These approaches can be distinguished by the type of maps they rely on.

Techniques based on metric or grid-based representations of the environment generally generate unimodal or Gaussian distributions representing the estimation of the robot's position. (Weiß, Wetzler, & von Puttkamer 1994) store angle histograms constructed out of range-finder scans taken at different locations of the environment. The position and orientation of the robot is calculated by maximizing the correlation between histograms of new measurements and the stored histograms. (Schiele & Crowley 1994) compare different strategies to track the robot's position based on occupancy grid maps. They use two different maps: a local grid computed using the most recent sensor readings, and a global map built during a previous exploration of the environment or by an appropriate CAD-tool. The local map is matched against the global map to produce a position and orientation estimate. This estimate is combined with the previous estimate using a Kalman filter (Maybeck 1990), where the uncertainty is represented by the width of the Gaussian distribution. Compared to the approach of Weiß et al., this technique allows an integration of different measurements over time rather than taking the optimum match of the most recent sensing as a guess for the current position.

Other researchers developed positioning techniques based on topological maps. (Nourbakhsh, Powers, & Birchfield 1995) apply Markov Models to determine the node of the topological map which contains the current position of the robot. Different nodes of the topological map are distinguished by walls, doors or hallway openings. Such items are detected using ultrasonic sensors, and the position of the robot is determined by a "state-set progression technique", where each state represents a node in the topological map. This technique is augmented by certainty factors which are computed out of the likelihoods that the items mentioned above will be detected by the ultrasonic sensors. (Simmons & Koenig 1995) describe a similar approach to position estimation. They additionally utilize metric information coming from the wheel encoders to compute state transition probabilities. This metric information puts additional constraints on the robot's location and results in more reliable position estimates. (Kortenkamp & Weymouth 1994) combine information obtained from sonar sensors and cameras using a Bayesian network to detect gateways between nodes of the topological map. The integration of sonar and vision information results in a much better place recognition which reduces the number of necessary robot movements respectively transitions between different nodes of the topological map.

Due to the separation of the environment into different nodes the methods based on topological maps, in contrast to the methods based on metric maps described above, allow to deal with ambiguous situations. Such ambiguities are represented by different nodes having high position probabilities. However, the techniques based on topological maps provide a limited accuracy because of the low granularity of the discretization. This restricted precision is disadvantageous if the robot has to navigate fast through its environment or even grasp for objects.

The position probability grid method described here allows to estimate the robot's position up to a few centimeters. This is achieved by approximating a position probability function over a discrete metric space defining possible positions in the environment. It therefore can be used to provide an initial estimate for the tracking techniques. But even the methods based on topological maps could be augmented by our approach. If the nodes of the topological map additionally contain metric information, our approach could be used to position the robot within a node.

Building position probability grids

The certainty grid approach was originally designed by Elfes and Moravec as a probabilistic grid model for the representation of obstacles. The basic idea is to accumulate in each cell of a rectangular grid field the probability that this cell is occupied by an obstacle. Whereas Moravec and Elfes construct a model of the environment given the position of the robot and sensor readings, we go the opposite direction estimating the position given the environmental model and the sensor readings. For this purpose, we construct a *position probability grid* P containing in each field the posterior probability that this field includes the current position of the robot. For a grid field x this certainty value is obtained by repeatedly firing the robot's sensors and accumulating in x the likelihoods of the sensed values supposed the center of x currently is the position of the robot in the environment model m. Each time the robot's sensors are fired, the following two steps are carried out:

1. Update P according to the movement of the robot since the last update. This includes a processing of P to deal with possible dead-reckoning errors.

2. For each grid field x of P and each reading s, compute the likelihood of s supposed x is the current position of the robot in m, and combine this likelihood with the probability stored in x to obtain a new probability for x.

The basic assumptions for our approach are:

- *The robot must have a model m of the world the sensor readings can be matched against.* Such models can either come from CAD-drawings of the environment or can themselves be grid representations of occupancy probabilities.

- *The robot does not leave the environmental model.* This assumption allows us to use the same size for the position probability grid P as for the environmental model m, and to set the probability for positions outside of P to 0.

In the remainder of this section we describe how to integrate different sensor readings into position probabilities. Furthermore we show how to keep track of the robot's movements with explicit consideration of possible dead-reckoning errors.

Integrating multiple sensor readings

In order to give reliable position estimates we have to integrate the information of consecutive sensor readings. Suppose m is the model of the environment, and $p(x \mid s_1 \wedge \ldots \wedge s_{n-1} \wedge m)$ is the (posterior) probability that x refers to the current position of the robot, given m and the sensor readings $s_1, \ldots, s_{n-1}$. Then, to update the probability for x given new sensory input s_n we use the following update formula (Pearl 1988):

$$p(x \mid s_1 \wedge \ldots \wedge s_{n-1} \wedge s_n \wedge m) = \alpha \cdot p(x \mid s_1 \wedge \ldots \wedge s_{n-1} \wedge m) \cdot p(s_n \mid x \wedge m) \quad (1)$$

The term $p(s_n \mid x \wedge m)$ is the likelihood of measuring the sensory input s_n given the world model m and assuming that x refers to the current position of the robot. The constant α simply normalizes the sum of the position probabilities over all x up to 1.

To initialize the grid we use the a priori probability $p(x \mid m)$ of x referring to the actual position of the robot given m. The estimation of $p(x \mid m)$ and $p(s_n \mid x \wedge m)$ depends on the given world model and the type of the sensors used for position estimation. Below we demonstrate how to use occupancy probability maps for position estimation and how sensor readings of ultrasonic sensors are matched against such maps.

Integrating the movements of the robot

In order to update the grid according to the robot's movements and to deal with possible dead reckoning errors we use a general formula coming from the domain of Markov chains. We regard each cell in P as one possible state of the robot, and determine a state transition probability $p(x \mid \tilde{x} \wedge \tau \wedge t)$ for each pair x, $\tilde{x}$ of cells in P, which depends on the trajectory τ taken by the robot and the time t elapsed since the previous update. This transition probability should also model how the trajectory τ fits into the environment. For example, a trajectory leading the robot through free space has a higher probability than a trajectory blocked by an obstacle. Thus, the new probability of a grid field after a movement of the robot is:

$$P[x] \ := \ \alpha \cdot \sum_{\tilde{x} \in P} P[\tilde{x}] \cdot p(x \mid \tilde{x} \wedge \tau \wedge t) \quad (2)$$

where α is a normalizing constant. At any time the field of P with the highest probability represents the best estimation for the current position of the robot. The confidence in this estimation depends on the absolute value of the probability and on the difference to the probabilities in the remaining fields of the grid. Thus, ambiguities are represented by different fields having a similar high probability.

Position estimation with occupancy probability maps as world model

In this section we describe the application of this approach by matching ultrasonic sensors against occupancy grid maps.

Matching sonar sensor readings against occupancy grids

To compute the likelihood $p(s \mid x \wedge m)$ that a sensor reading s is received given the position x and an occupancy grid map m we use a similar approach as described in (Moravec 1988). We consider a discretization $R_1, \ldots, R_k$ of possible distances measured by the sensor. Consequently, $p(R_i \mid x \wedge m)$ is the likelihood that the sonar beam is reflected in R_i.

Suppose $p(r(\tilde{x}) \mid x \wedge m)$ is the likelihood that the cell $\tilde{x}$ reflects a sonar beam, given the position x of the robot and the map m. Furthermore suppose that $\tilde{x}$ belongs to R_i. Assuming the reflection of the sonar beam by $\tilde{x}$ being conditionally independent of the reflection of the other cells in R_i, the likelihood that R_i reflects a sonar beam is

$$p(R_i \mid x \wedge m) = 1 - \prod_{\tilde{x} \in R_i} (1 - p(r(\tilde{x}) \mid x \wedge m)) \qquad (3)$$

Before the beam reaches R_i, it traverses $R_1, \ldots, R_{i-1}$. Supposed that the sonar reading s is included by range R_i, the likelihood $p(s \mid x \wedge m)$ equals the likelihood that R_i reflects the sonar beam given that none of the ranges $R_{<i}$ reflects it. Thus, we have

$$p(s \mid x \wedge m) = p(R_i \mid x \wedge m) \cdot \prod_{j=1}^{i-1} (1 - p(R_j \mid x \wedge m)) \qquad (4)$$

Computing position estimates using occupancy grids

It remains to estimate the initial probability $p(x \mid m)$ that the field x of m contains the current position of the robot. We assume that this probability directly depends on the occupancy probability $m(x)$ of the field x in m: the higher the occupancy probability, the lower is the position probability and vice versa. Therefore, the value $p(x \mid m)$ is computed as follows:

$$p(x \mid m) \quad = \quad \frac{1 - m(x)}{\sum_{\tilde{x} \in m} (1 - m(\tilde{x}))} \qquad (5)$$

Experiments

In this section we show the results from experiments carried out with our robot *RHINO* in real world environments such as typical offices and the AAAI '94 mobile robot competition arena. For the position estimation we match sensor readings coming from ultrasonic sensors against occupancy grid maps.

Implementation aspects

For the sake of efficiency we implemented a simplified model of sonar sensors to compute the likelihood of a reading: instead of considering all cells of the grid covered by the sonar wedge as done in (Moravec 1988) we only consider the cells on the acoustic axis of the sensor. This rough simplification has already been applied successfully in (Borenstein & Koren 1991) to realize a fast collision avoidance technique for mobile robots.

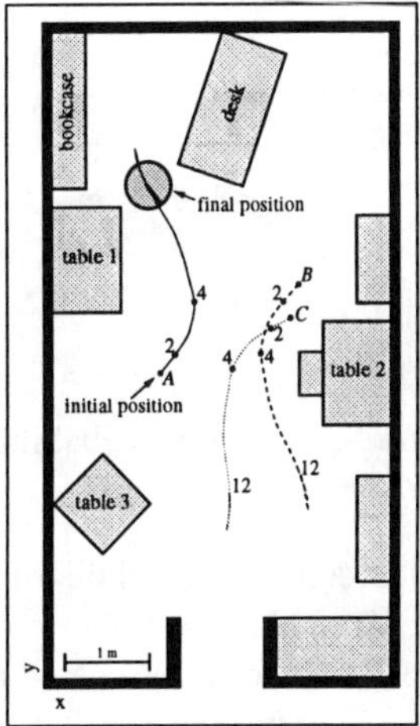

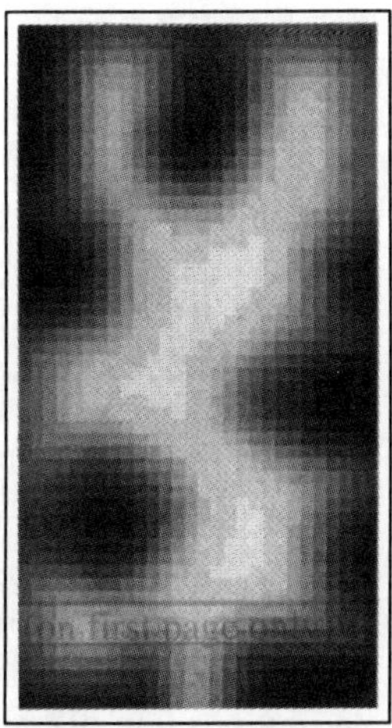

Figure 1: Outline and occupancy grid map of the office

To compute the transition probability $p(x \mid \tilde{x} \wedge \tau \wedge t)$ we assume the dead reckoning errors to be normally distributed. Supposing frequent updates of the position information we simply approximate the probability of the robot's trajectory τ by $p(y|m)$ where y is the position corresponding to x. Thus we have

$$p(x \mid \tilde{x} \wedge \tau \wedge t) \quad = \quad \omega_{x,\tau,t}(\tilde{x}) \cdot p(y \mid m) \qquad (6)$$

where $\omega_{x,\tau,t}$ is a Gaussian distribution.

Position estimation in a typical office

To evaluate the capabilities of our approach we used the task of estimating the position in a typical office of our department. Figure 1 shows an outline of this office, which has a size of $4 \times 7m^2$ and the occupancy grid map used to compute the likelihoods of the sensor readings. For the position estimation we used only 8 of the 24 ultrasonic sensors our robot is equipped with. The size of one grid field is 15×15 cm^2, while we consider 180 possible orientations. For this grid and 8 sensor readings per step, the update of the grid takes about 6 seconds on a Pentium 90 computer.

Figure 1 also shows the initial and final position of the path taken by the robot. At the beginning the robot turned to the left and moved between the bookcase and the desk. At the end of the trajectory the robot turned and started to leave the corner. On this trajectory, which is illustrated by the solid line, 12 sweeps of sonar readings were taken for the position estimation. In addition to the real trajectory *A* two alternative paths *B* and *C* are shown. Figure 2 shows plots of the maximum probabilities for the first, second, fourth, and twelfth reading sets for each position of the map. For the sake of simplicity only the maximal probability over all orientations at each position is shown. Note that the z-axes of the four figures have different scales. The probabilities of the corresponding points belonging to the trajectories *A*, *B*, and *C* are highlighted by vertical lines.

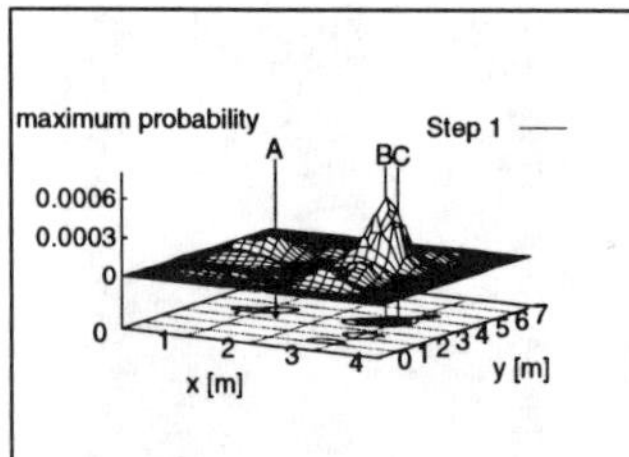

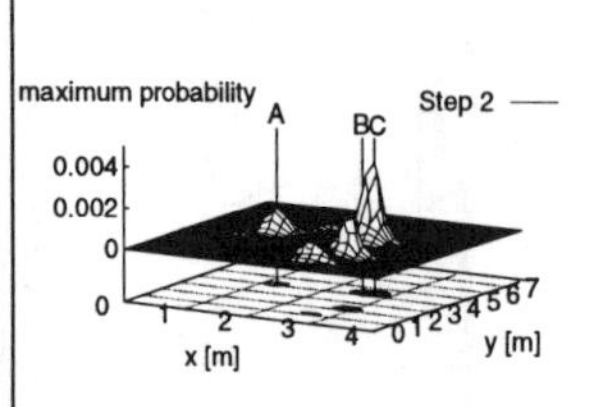

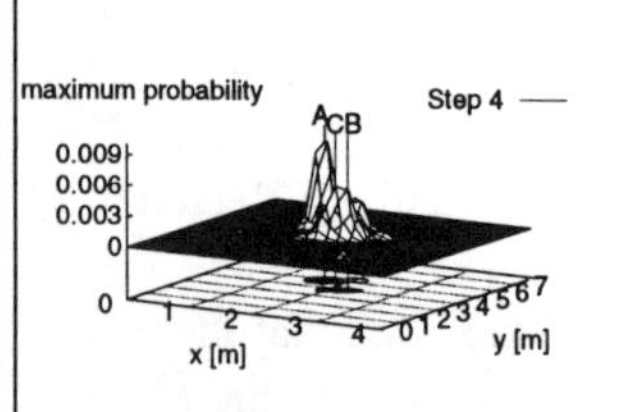

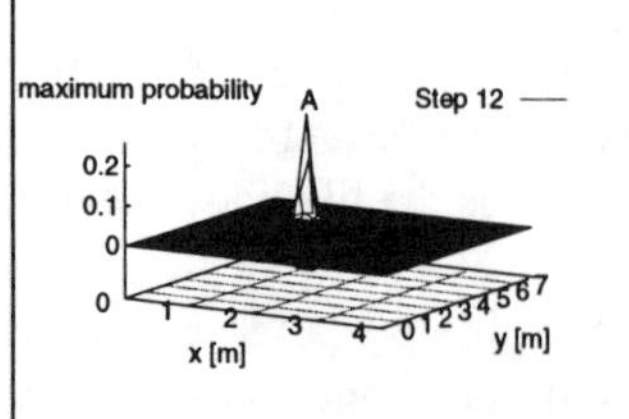

Figure 2: Position probability distribution after 1, 2, 4, and 12 steps

After the first reading we obtain a multi-modal distribution with several small local maxima. At the correct position we observe only a small peak, which is dominated by the starting position of trajectory *B*. After interpreting the second set of readings the probabilities become more concentrated. We observe four small peaks which now have their maximum in position 2 of trajectory *C*. The third and fourth reading sets support the initial position so that the position on trajectory *A* gets the maximum probability. There are two peaks where the smaller one is a super-imposition of two different peaks for the trajectories *B* and *C*. After evaluating 12 sonar sweeps all ambiguities are resolved, and the result is a significant and unique peak with probability 0.26 for the final point of trajectory *A*. This position in fact refers to the real position of the robot.

Dealing with large environments

In the previous example ambiguities appeared as several peaks in the position probability distribution. In large environments we have to expect that due to the limited range of the proximity sensors ambiguities spread out over complete regions. In order to demonstrate the capability of our approach to deal with such complex situations we applied it to the arena of the AAAI '94 mobile robot competition (Simmons 1995). The size of this arena amounts $20 \times 30m^2$. Figure 3 shows the occupancy grid map of this arena constructed with the map-building tool described in (Thrun 1993). The sonar sensor measurements were recorded during an exploration run in this arena. The trajectory of the robot and the 12 positions at which the sensors were fired are included in Figure 3. Again we only used 8 of the 24 sonar sensors and the same resolution for the position probability grid as in the previous example.

Figures 4 and 5 show logarithmic density plots of the maximum position probabilities for all directions after interpreting 6 and 12 sets of sensor readings. Although the information obtained after the first 6 sensor readings does not suffice to definitely determine the current position of the robot, it is obvious that the robot must be in a long corridor. After 12 steps the position of the robot is uniquely determined. The corresponding grid cell has a probability of 0.96 while the small peak at the bottom of Figure 5 has a maximum of 8e-6.

Conclusions

We presented the position probability grid approach as a robust Bayesian technique to estimate the position of a mobile robot. Our method allows the integration of sensor readings from different types of sensors over time. We showed that this method is able to find the position of a robot even if noisy sensors such as ultrasonic sensors and approximative environmental models like occupancy grid maps are used. Our approach has any-time characteristic, because it is able to give an estimation for the current position of the robot already after interpreting the first sensor reading. By incorporating new input this estimation is continuously improved. Position probability grids allow to represent and to deal with ambiguous situations. These ambiguities are resolved if sufficient sensory information is provided. Our technique has been implemented and tested in several complex real-world experiments.

The only precondition for the applicability of the position probability grid approach is an environmental model which allows to determine the likelihood of a sensor reading at a certain position in the environment. In our implementation we used occupancy probability grids as world model in combination with ultrasonic sensors. Alternatively one could use a CAD-model of the environment and cameras for edge detection or integrate simple features like the color of the floor.

Using the currently implemented system our robot needs about one minute to determine its position in a typical office. Although the computation time depends linearly on the grid size, very large environments such as the $600m^2$ wide AAAI '94 robot competition arena do not impose any principle limitations on the algorithm. We are convinced that different optimizations will make our approach applicable online even in such large environments. The most important source for speed-up lies in the pre-analysis of the environmental model. This includes computing and storing the likelihoods of all possible sensor readings for all positions. Additionally, in orthogonal environments the reduction of possible orientations to the alignment of the walls drastically reduces the complexity of the overall problem. Furthermore, the application of a map resolution hierarchy as proposed in (Moravec 1988) can be used to produce rough po-

Figure 3: Occupancy grid map of the AAAI '94 mobile robot competition

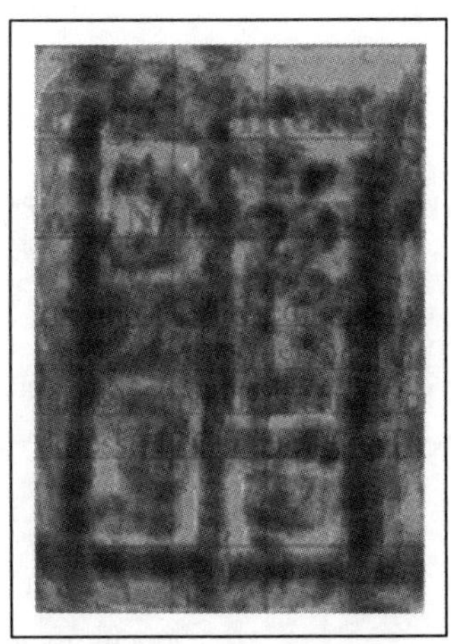

Figure 4: Density plot after 6 steps

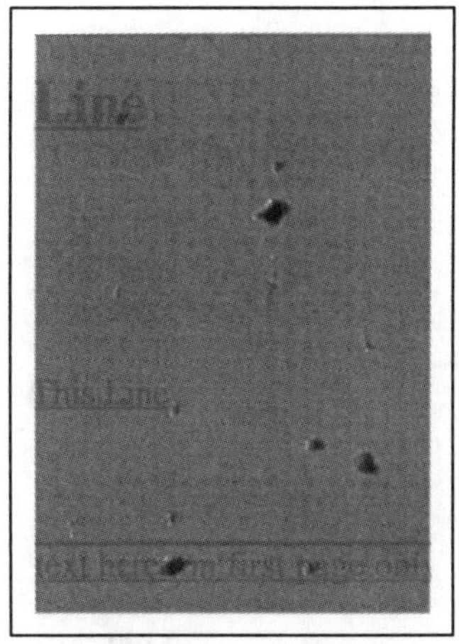

Figure 5: Density plot after 12 steps

sition estimates which are refined subsequently.

Despite these encouraging results there are several warrants for future research. This concerns optimizations as described above as well as active exploration strategies. Such strategies will guide the robot to points in the environment, which provide the maximum information gain with respect to the current knowledge.

References

Borenstein, J., and Koren, Y. 1990. Real-time obstacle avoidance for fast mobile robots in cluttered environments. In *Proc. of the IEEE International Conference on Robotics and Automation*, 572–577.

Borenstein, J., and Koren, Y. 1991. The vector field histogram - fast obstacle avoidance for mobile robots. *IEEE Transactions on Robotics and Automation* 7(3):278–288.

Buhmann, J.; Burgard, W.; Cremers, A. B.; Fox, D.; Hofmann, T.; Schneider, F.; Strikos, J.; and Thrun, S. 1995. The mobile robot Rhino. *AI Magazine* 16(2):31–38.

Cox, I., and Wilfong, G., eds. 1990. *Autonomous Robot Vehicles*. Springer Verlag.

Feng, L.; Borenstein, J.; and Everett, H. 1994. "Where am I?" Sensors and Methods for Autonomous Mobile Robot Positioning. Technical Report UM-MEAM-94-21, University of Michigan.

Kortenkamp, D., and Weymouth, T. 1994. Topological mapping for mobile robots using a combination of sonar and vision sensing. In *Proc. of the Twelfth National Conference on Artificial Intelligence*, 979–984.

Maybeck, P. S. 1990. The Kalman filter: An introduction to concepts. In Cox and Wilfong (1990).

Moravec, H. P., and Elfes, A. 1985. High resolution maps from wide angle sonar. In *Proc. IEEE Int. Conf. Robotics and Automation*, 116–121.

Moravec, H. P., and Martin, M. C. 1994. Robot navigation by 3D spatial evidence grids. Mobile Robot Laboratory, Robotics Institute, Carnegie Mellon University.

Moravec, H. P. 1988. Sensor fusion in certainty grids for mobile robots. *AI Magazine* 61–74.

Nourbakhsh, I.; Powers, R.; and Birchfield, S. 1995. DERVISH an office-navigating robot. *AI Magazine* 16(2):53–60.

Pearl, J. 1988. *Probabilistic Reasoning in Intelligent Systems: Networks of Plausible Inference*. Morgan Kaufmann Publishers, Inc.

Schiele, B., and Crowley, J. L. 1994. A comparison of position estimation techniques using occupancy grids. In *Proc. of the IEEE International Conference on Robotics and Automation*, 1628–1634.

Simmons, R., and Koenig, S. 1995. Probabilistic robot navigation in partially observable environments. In *Proc. International Joint Conference on Artificial Intelligence*.

Simmons, R. 1995. The 1994 AAAI robot competition and exhibition. *AI Magazine* 16(2):19–29.

Thrun, S. 1993. Exploration and model building in mobile robot domains. In *Proceedings of the ICNN-93*, 175–180. San Francisco, CA: IEEE Neural Network Council.

Weiß, G.; Wetzler, C.; and von Puttkamer, E. 1994. Keeping track of position and orientation of moving indoor systems by correlation of range-finder scans. In *Proceedings of the International Conference on Intelligent Robots and Systems*, 595–601.

Navigation for Everyday Life

Daniel D. Fu and Kristian J. Hammond and Michael J. Swain
Department of Computer Science, University of Chicago
1100 East 58th Street, Chicago, Illinois 60637

Abstract

Past work in navigation has worked toward the goal of producing an accurate map of the environment. While no one can deny the usefulness of such a map, the ideal of producing a complete map becomes unrealistic when an agent is faced with performing real tasks. And yet an agent accomplishing recurring tasks should navigate more efficiently as time goes by. We present a system which integrates navigation, planning, and vision. In this view, navigation supports the needs of a larger system as opposed to being a task in its own right. Whereas previous approaches assume an unknown and unstructured environment, we assume a structured environment whose organization is known, but whose specifics are unknown. The system is endowed with a wide range of visual capabilities as well as search plans for informed exploration of a simulated store constructed from real visual data. We demonstrate the agent finding items while mapping the world. In repeatedly retrieving items, the agent's performance improves as the learned map becomes more useful.

Introduction

Past work in navigation has generally assumed that the purpose of navigation is to endow a robot with the ability to navigate reliably from place to place. However, in focusing on this specific problem, researchers have ignored a more fundamental question: What is the robot's purpose in moving from place to place? Presumably the robot will perform some later-to-be-named task: The point of navigation is only to get the robot to the intended destination. What happens afterwards is not a concern. This notion has led researchers toward building systems whose sensing ultimately relies on the lowest common denominator (e.g., sonar, dead reckoning). We believe that: (1) Robots will use navigation as a store of knowledge in service of tasks, and (2) Robots will have semantically rich perception in order to perform a wide range of tasks. Given these two beliefs we suggest first that: Navigation must coexist with a robot's planning and action mechanisms instead of being a task in and of itself, and second that: Rich perception, used for tasks, can also be used for constructing a map to make route following and place recognition more tractable.

In this paper we present a system which embodies these two notions as they apply to these five areas: run-time planning, context-based vision, passive mapping, path planning, and route following. This system differs from past navigation research in several ways - the principal difference being the integration of a passive mapper with a planning system. This notion was introduced by Engelson and McDermott (1992). They view a mapping system as a resource for a planner: A mapping subsystem maintains a map of the world as the planner accomplishes tasks. When applicable, the planner uses the acquired map information for achieving goals.

In contrast, traditional research has viewed the mapping subsystem as an independent program which explores and maps its environment. Eventually the program produces a complete map. While no one can doubt the usefulness of such a map, we believe that this mapping may be neither realistic nor necessary. Previously, we showed that an agent can instead use its knowledge of a domain's organization in order to accomplish tasks (Fu *et al.* 1995). This was shown to be effective in a man-made domain - a grocery store. Whereas past approaches have assumed an unknown and unstructured environment, e.g. (Elfes 1987), our approach assumes an environment whose structure is known, but whose specifics are unknown.

For common tasks such as shopping in a grocery store, finding a book in a library, or going to an airport gate, there is much known about each setting which allows the average person to achieve his goals without possessing prior knowledge of each specific setting. For example, people know that: managers of grocery stores organize items by their type, how they're used, etc; librarians shelve books according to category; airport architects account for typical needs of travelers by putting signs in relevant areas. People count on these regularities in order to act appropriately and efficiently without first completely mapping the environment. In this sense, the domains are known. Moreover, the domains are actively structured by someone else so we can depend on regularities being maintained.

We can also rely on certain stable physical properties. Previously we showed that grocery stores exhibit several useful physical properties allowing us to build fast and reliable vision sensing routines. For example, light comes from above, shelves always stock items, items are always displayed facing forward, etc. This work is similar to recent research done in the areas of context-based (Strat and Fischler 1991; Firby *et al.* 1995) and lightweight (Horswill 1993) vision. These paradigms have produced perceptual algorithms which compute useful information reasonably fast so long as the reliability conditions for each perceptual algorithm are known. An immediate consequence of these conditions is that at least some of the sensing routines don't have to be run continuously. If these routines are used in the navigation process, the map must represent the different conditions and results of running a sensing routine. In contrast, previous research has often committed to using uniform fixed-cost sensing (e.g., sonar). This commitment allows the same sensing to be used for both map learning and route following. However, since we use conditional sensing routines, the map learning and route-following methods are markedly different.

In summary, the research presented here differs from traditional research in two major ways. First, we view map learning and route-following in the context of a larger system which performs a wide range of tasks in addition to navigation. We present a framework from which existing planners can integrate navigation. Second, we assume a known and structured environment which enables us to write effective search plans as well as to build a wide range of visual capabilities. We describe a method for using these capabilities in the navigation task.

Shopper

In order to study some of the types of knowledge and underlying mechanisms involved in everyday tasks, we selected grocery store shopping. Shopping is a common activity which takes place in a completely man-made environment. Previously, we showed how our system, SHOPPER, used structural knowledge of the environment to quickly find items using a small set of regularities: items of a similar nature are clustered together (e.g., cereals) as well as items which are often used together (e.g., pancake mix and maple syrup). Several regularities were then encoded into search plans for finding items. For example, if SHOPPER is looking for Aunt Jemima's pancake mix and it sees a "syrup" sign at the head of an aisle, it executes a plan to search an aisle for syrup. After locating the syrup, it executes another search plan for finding the pancake mix in the local area close to the syrup.

These plans were tested in GROCERYWORLD; a simulator of a real grocery store. GROCERYWORLD provides range information from eight sonars plus compass information. SHOPPER is cylindrical with sonars placed equidistant along the circumference. SHOPPER also possesses a panning head. Figure 1 shows the GROCERYWORLD user interface. The top left pane shows SHOPPER in the grocery store with both head and body orientations. The top right pane shows the body-relative sonar readings while the bottom pane shows the sign information available to the agent. If the agent is located at the head of an aisle and is facing the aisle, GROCERYWORLD can supply sign data.

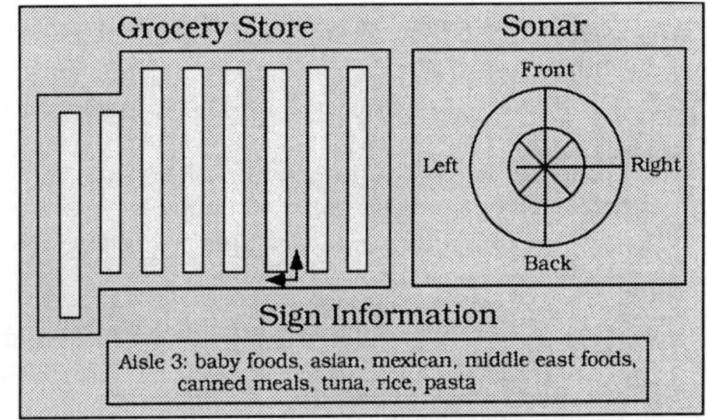

Figure 1: User Interface

GROCERYWORLD differs from most robot simulators in that it supplies real color images taken from a local grocery store. Camera views are restricted to four cardinal directions at each point in the store. Altogether, the domain consists of 75,000 images. Figure 2 shows example views.

GROCERYWORLD also differs from past simulators in that travel is limited to moving along one dimension, except at intersections. However, stores, like office environments, don't have much free space; in fact, hallways and store aisles constrain movement to be in two obvious directions. Kortenkamp and Weymouth (1994) showed that a robot could stay centered in an office hallway with less than 3.5 degrees of orientation error. In light of this fact, we do not believe the one-dimensional travel restriction is a serious shortcoming since we actually prefer SHOPPER to stay centered in an aisle for consistent vision perception.

Figure 2: Example views. Left: A typical view down an aisle. Right: A view to the side. Two horizontal lines denote shelf locations. Color regions are enclosed by the larger rectangle. The smaller rectangle around Corn Pops denotes identification.

SHOPPER's perceptual apparatus is primarily suited towards moving around and identifying objects in an image. Below we outline the various sensing routines and explain their use.

Compass: SHOPPER moves and looks in four cardinal directions. We use a compass as an aid to mapping the environment. For example, if SHOPPER knows there is a "soup" sign in view at a particular intersection, it can turn to that direction and attempt to sense the sign.

Sonar: We have sonar sensing continuously for classifying intersections and verifying proximity to shelves.

Signs: When SHOPPER is looking down an aisle and attempts to detect signs, GROCERYWORLD supplies the text of the signs. In Figure 2 a diamond-like sign can be seen above the aisle. However, the image resolution, sign transparency, and specularity prohibit any useful reading.

Shelf Detection: This sensor finds the vertical location of steep gradient changes in an image by smoothing and thresholding for large gradients.

Color Histogram Intersection: Sample color histograms (Swain and Ballard 1991) are taken successively above a shelf and compared to a sought object's histogram in order to identify potential regions according to the intersection response.

Edge Template Matcher: Given an image of object, we use an edge image template matching routine using the Hausdorff distance (Rucklidge 1994) as a similarity metric. This sensor is the most expensive, so it processes areas first filtered by the shelf and color histogram detectors.

All of the above vision algorithms have been implemented and are used by SHOPPER.

Navigation

SHOPPER's navigation system is comprised of four subsystems: RETRIEVER, PATH PLANNER, FOLLOWER, and PASSIVE MAPPER. These subsystems are shown in Figure 3. Initially a goal item is given to the RETRIEVER which uses similarity metrics and the current map to select a destination and a search plan to execute on arrival. The PATH PLANNER replaces the destination with a sequence of nodes (created on previous visits) leading from the current location to the destination. The nodes denote intersections and places of interest. Each node is annotated with accumulated sensor information associated from past visits. Next, the FOLLOWER uses the sequence to follow the path. Vision algorithms are selected and run to ensure correspondence between the predicted sensor information and the current perception. Once the path has been followed, the PLAN INTERPRETER executes the search plan. The PASSIVE MAPPER updates the map during the time the search plan is executed.

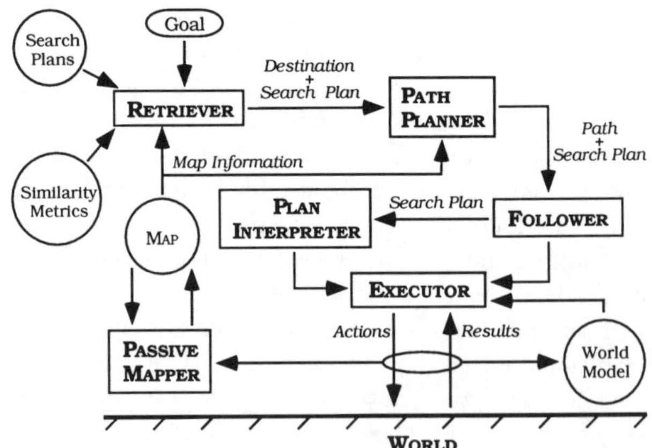

Figure 3: SHOPPER's Architecture. Arrows indicate data flow from one module to another.

In the following sections we describe the four subsystems. Later, using examples, we explain how they interact with each other as well as with the rest of the system.

Passive Mapping

The purpose of the PASSIVE MAPPER subsystem is to maintain a topological map of the world. This subsystem is active when the agent is exploring the world via search plans by monitoring the EXECUTOR as it performs visual and physical actions. The actions and results are used for creating the map. For each physical action the agent performs, it commits, as a policy, to perform a fixed-cost sensing procedure consisting of a compass reading and sonar readings. When the agent knows where it is and exactly where it's going, the PASSIVE MAPPER is disabled since the current map will suffice for route following.

Map Representation. Our map representation draws from previous navigation work using topological maps (Brooks 1985; Engelson and McDermott 1992; Kortenkamp and Weymouth 1994; Kuipers and Byun 1988; Mataric 1992). These maps use relations between places (aka landmarks, distinctive places, gateways, waypoints) for navigation. These methods require the robot be able to recognize a place, and travel from place to place.

We use a topological map consisting of distinctive places and connecting edges. In Kuipers and Byun's NX model, distinctive places are local maxima according to a geometric criterion. Examples of these can be: beginnings of open space, transitions from different spaces, dead ends, etc. Essentially, a distinctive place is a landmark which a robot can recognize and use for map learning and route following. In contrast, our notion of a distinctive place is closely coupled to a place's usefulness to the agent, either as a navigation point where an agent may move into a different space, or a location that is somehow relevant to the agent. In the GROCERYWORLD domain these places are, respectively, *intersections* (INTER's) and *places of interest* (POI's).

Recall that SHOPPER is constrained to move along one dimension at a time. It can move in another dimension only at intersections. One example of a distinctive place is an intersection. Similar to Kortenkamp and Weymouth, we categorize intersections qualitatively as T-SHAPE, CROSS, and CORNER. These descriptions of space are based only on sonar readings. Examples are illustrated in Figure 4. The other example of a distinctive place is a place of interest. These places denote locations important to the agent's goals. For SHOPPER, each place of interest corresponds to a location where SHOPPER found a sought item.

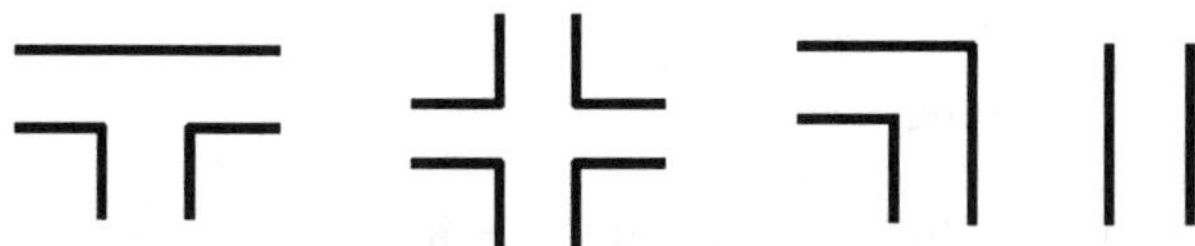

Figure 4: Qualitative descriptions of space: T-SHAPE, CROSS, CORNER, and CORRIDOR.

As SHOPPER encounters new distinctive places, it updates its map by storing perceptual information associated with the distinctive place. The distinctive place description, describing both intersections and places of interest, is a set of tuples $\langle T, S \times C, A, R \rangle$ where:

- $C \in \{0, 1, 2, 3\}$ is a compass direction.
- $T \in$ {T-SHAPE, CROSS, CORNER, CORRIDOR} $\times$ C is the distinctive place type and orientation.
- $S \in$ {sign, shelf, color, template matcher} is a sensing routine. $S \times C$ also accounts for the head's direction at the time the routine was executed.
- A is a set of parameter arguments supplied to the sensing routine.
- R is the output of the routine.

Note that fixed-cost sensors compass and sonar are automatically associated with each distinctive place. For the agent's location in Figure 1, an example sign sensing tuple is: $\langle$(T-SHAPE, 2), (sign, 0), $\emptyset$, { Aisle-3, Baby-foods, Asian, Mexican, Middle-east-foods, Canned-meals, Tuna, Rice, Pasta}$\rangle$.

Landmark Disambiguation. As the PASSIVE MAPPER encounters a new distinctive place, it attempts to determine whether or not it's been there before. For passive mapping, there are two problems to landmark disambiguation: passivity and disparate sensing.

A tension exists between keeping a mapper passive (so as not to interfere with plan execution) and supplying enough information to the mapper for dependable navigation. There are two ways to alleviate this tension:

1. Maintain possible distinctive places. This method, proposed by Engelson and McDermott, requires possibilities to be eventually culled as the agent moves about in the world. Map updates are delayed until the agent has disambiguated its position.

2. Assume rich sensing. The only reason the PASSIVE MAPPER is activated is precisely because it's exploring the environment. If the agent knows where it is, it would be following a route instead. Basically, if SHOPPER doesn't know where it is, assume it will "look around" (Ishiguro *et al.* 1994). Since the PASSIVE MAPPER is active when SHOPPER executes a search plan, we adopt this assumption in the PASSIVE MAPPER as it appears tenable for the time being.

A related problem surfaces when a passive mapper uses a wider range of sensing routines. Since SHOPPER does not run all its sensing routines all the time, we can't guarantee any other sensing routines were run except for the fixed costs of compass and sonar. For

SHOPPER, the plans that are run are search plans. Consequently, we depend on there being additional sensing information as the agent explores the environment. If the agent were executing a different set of plans which involve movement, there might be an altogether different set of sensing routines run. If, however, we commit to changing the agent's location only through search plans or route following, distinctive places will not be confused with each other.

Retriever

Given a goal item, search plans, and similarity metrics, the RETRIEVER selects a target destination and search plan to execute once SHOPPER arrives. Table 1 lists conditions for selecting a particular destination and search plan.

Recall earlier that SHOPPER uses regularities of a domain in order to find items via its search plans. Regularities are also used for deciding on a destination. For the examples discussed later, we use two regularities: *type* and *counterpart*. The type relationship denotes a category made up of items of the same type. The counterpart relation denotes a category of items that are often used together; e.g., pancake mix and maple syrup.

As an example of how the type relationship is used, Surf and CheerFree are types of laundry detergents. Items of the same type are likely to be physically close. If, in a previous visit, SHOPPER found Surf and now wants to find CheerFree, it selects a place of interest (Surf) as the destination as well as a LOCAL SAME-SIDE search plan. This particular search plan looks for an item hypothesized to be nearby on the same side of the aisle as the previously found item.

Path Planning

Given a target destination from the RETRIEVER and the current location from the map, the PATH PLANNER plans a route that will get the agent from the current location to the destination. Because the map is organized in terms of nodes and edges, the path planner uses Dijkstra's algorithm for finding a shortest path. No metrical information is stored, so each edge is of equal cost. After the nodes along the route have been selected, the PATH PLANNER then annotates each node with all the sensing information gathered from past visits. These annotations are used by the FOLLOWER.

Route Following

The FOLLOWER receives a path and search plan from the PATH PLANNER. The FOLLOWER's purpose is to follow the path and then pass the search plan to the PLAN INTERPRETER. In order to follow a path the FOLLOWER must verify that the current sensing is consistent with the predicted sensing. The stored sensing is processed according to the particular place prediction. Recall these are a set of tuples $\langle T, S \times C, A, R\rangle$.

The consistency check is based on a match function for each sensing routine:

$$\forall s \epsilon S \exists m_s : A \times R \times A \times R \rightarrow \{True, False\}$$

where m_s is the match function for sensing routine s. The match functions compare the arguments and results of the past and current sensing routine to ensure the agent is on course. If the results are consistent, the match function returns a match (True), otherwise no match (False). For example, suppose SHOPPER is checking if shelf positions match. After the Shelf Detector is run on the current image, the arguments (horizontal subsampling) and currently found shelves (vertical image positions) are passed to the shelf match function as well as the stored shelf information composed of the same arguments and vertical image positions. For this particular match function, we require one-third of the shelf positions in the current image be within twenty pixels of the stored shelf positions, and vice versa. If both match correctly, the shelf match function returns True otherwise False.

The consistency check is done by using the match functions over the sensing routines common to both the past and current perception. Let P be the set of stored perception at a place, and let Q be the set of current perception. Place consistency is defined to be equivalent distinctive place types and a match on all the common sensing between P and Q. Figure 5 illustrates this method as a procedure. If the procedure returns True, the two locations are consistent. If False, the two locations are different.

procedure Consistency-Check(P, Q)
  for all sensors $s \in S$
    for all compass directions $c \in C$
      if $\langle t, (s, c), a, r\rangle \in P$ **and**
        $\langle t', (s, c), a', r'\rangle \in Q$ **and**
        $m_s(a, r, a', r') =$ False **then**
        return False
  return $t \stackrel{?}{=} t'$

Figure 5: Procedure for determining consistency between places P and Q.

This procedure is at the heart of the PASSIVE MAPPER. The FOLLOWER performs the stored sensing routines, and then makes use of the procedure to ensure it is on course. At an intersection the FOLLOWER checks for consistency by alternating between a consistency check and executing a sensing routine. After the intersection matches, the FOLLOWER orients the agent

Strategy Name	Conditions	Destination	Search Plan
EXACT	I_1 was found before.	POI with I_1	None
TYPE	Similar item I_2 was found before.	POI with I_2	LOCAL SAME-SIDE
COUNTERPART	I_1 and I_2 are counterparts. I_2 previously found.	POI with I_2	LOCAL
SIGN-TYPE	Sign S seen. I_1 is a type of S.	INTER with S	AISLE
SIGN-COUNTERPART	Sign S seen. I_1 and S are counterparts.	INTER with S	AISLE
DEFAULT	None	None	BASIC

Table 1: In order of preference: strategy names, their conditions, destination, and search plan for locating item I_1.

to move toward the next distinctive place. A similar method is employed for finding a place of interest, except that a consistency check failure is allowed owing to the agent not being in the right place yet. Currently SHOPPER does not handle the case when it fails to find a place of interest.

Examples

We select three items to demonstrate SHOPPER's navigation capabilities: Solo laundry detergent, Corn Pops cereal, and Downy fabric softener.

Solo Initially in first coming to the store, SHOPPER's map is empty. Given an empty map, Solo laundry detergent, and preferences shown in Table 1, the RETRIEVER picks a null destination and BASIC search plan as the DEFAULT strategy. The BASIC search plan is simple: go to the beginning of an aisle, move across aisles until a relevant sign is seen, go into that aisle, look left and right until the item is found.

On receiving the null destination with search plan, the PATH PLANNER outputs a null path and BASIC search plan. The FOLLOWER has no path to follow, so it passes control and the search plan to the PLAN INTERPRETERstarts executing the search plan starting at the store entrance in front of Aisle 1. The BASIC search plan instructs SHOPPER to move around the outside perimeter of the store reading signs and moving until it finds a relevant sign. For example, in Aisle 4, the sign reads: Aisle-4 Salad-dressing Canned-soup Sauce Nut Cereal Jam Jelly Candy. Eventually Solo is found on the left side of Aisle 6 since there is a "laundry aid" sign in front of that aisle. During the time this search was done, the PASSIVE MAPPER recorded the intersection types of Aisles 1 through 6 plus visual (sign) information. A place of interest is created where Solo was found. The POI is defined according to the shelf positions, color region, and item identification as output by the sensing routines.

Corn Pops Next, we give SHOPPER the goal of finding Corn Pops. The RETRIEVER recalls that a "cereal" sign was seen in front of Aisle 4 and selects the SIGN-TYPE strategy. The target destination is now the beginning of Aisle 4, and the search plan is AISLE. The PATH PLANNER plans a path from the current location (a POI) to Aisle 4 (an INTER). The FOLLOWER starts by verifying it's at the current place. The current accumulated sensor information is a match to the stored perception. SHOPPER now orients its body to the beginning of Aisle 6 and goes there. Once it reaches the beginning, the intersection is verified to be Aisle 6 by matching the intersection type and turning the head around to match sign information. Using a similar method, SHOPPER continues to the beginnings of Aisle 5, then Aisle 4. The AISLE search plan and control is now passed to the PLAN INTERPRETER. The PLAN INTERPRETER searches Aisle 4 and eventually finds Corn Pops where it creates a POI similar to Solo.

Downy Finally, we give SHOPPER the goal of finding Downy fabric softener. Since fabric softener is used with laundry detergent, SHOPPER uses the COUNTERPART strategy. The intended destination now becomes the POI containing Solo, with the search plan as LOCAL. In a similar fashion, the FOLLOWER follows a route from the current POI to the intended POI. When the agent is at the beginning of Aisle 6, the FOLLOWER then runs the POI sensing routines and compares results associated with Solo while moving down the aisle. Once Solo is reached, a LOCAL search plan is executed. This plan allows SHOPPER to search on the left and right of Solo as well as the other side of the aisle as tries to find Downy. In this instance, Downy is on the other side. SHOPPER finds Downy and creates a new POI.

Status

SHOPPER has been tested successfully on fourteen items ranging over cereals, laundry aids, cake mixes, cleaning materials, and storage supplies. SHOPPER can quickly compute routes to likely areas and reliably arrive there. For the items SHOPPER cannot find – and there are many – it has been the case that its sensors failed to detect the item. So long as SHOPPER reaches a close enough proximity to point the camera at an item, we do not consider the navigation system faulty.

Currently the FOLLOWER uses a static procedure for following routes. Because our search plans are declarative and can account for opportunistic types of behavior (e.g., recognizing a sought item unexpectedly), we would like the FOLLOWER to use a similar representation for coping with contingencies during the navigation process, c.f. (Simmons 1994).

Earlier we cited the possibility of the system using different or new sensing routines, not necessarily having any overlap with previously stored sensing. We believe that landmark disambiguation is simpler if the PASSIVE MAPPER is sometimes active by signaling an ambiguity before the agent moves away. Then it duplicates perceptual actions and compares the results to past perception. This method appears to be promising since Kortenkamp and Weymouth, in using a visual representation of vertical lines, were able to successfully disambiguate locations without traveling away from the location.

Another possible way to disambiguate position is to use dead reckoning. Currently SHOPPER's map data does not indicate relative distances between places. So when sensor data alone indicates that SHOPPER could be in one of several places, dead reckoning allows SHOPPER to reject many places before needing more information.

The navigation method we have presented here assumes that major errors in sensing will not happen. For a specific set of items, our sensing routines have empirically shown to be sufficient and reliable in our particular domain. For integration with existing robots, this may not be a realistic assumption. However, we view errors in sensing as being just that: errors in sensing. We do not believe a mapper should bear the burden of coping with an incorrect map because of error-prone and/or semantic-poor data. Surely there are instances in real life where one can become genuinely lost because of sheer size, or absence of distinguishable cues. Although every navigation system must handle those inevitable situations, we believe those instances are rare simply because we live and depend on a culturally rich world (Agre and Horswill 1992) full of distinguishing cues to support everyday activity - one of them being navigation.

Acknowledgments

The research reported here has benefited from discussions with Charles Earl, Mark Fasciano, Jim Firby, and Val Kulyukin as well as from helpful comments from reviewers. This work was supported in part by Office of Naval Research grant number N00014-91-J-1185.

References

Philip E. Agre and Ian Horswill. Cultural support for improvisation. In *The Proceedings of the Tenth National Conference on Artificial Intelligence*, pages 363–368, 1992.

Rodney A. Brooks. Visual map making for a mobile robot. In *Proceedings IEEE International Conference on Robotics and Automation*, 1985.

Alberto Elfes. Sonar-based real-world mapping and navigation. *IEEE Journal of Robotics and Automation*, RA-3(3):249–265, 1987.

Sean P. Engelson and Drew V. McDermott. Maps considered as adaptive planning resources. In *AAAI Fall Symposium on Applications of Artificial Intelligence to Real-World Autonomous Mobile Robots*, pages 36–44, 1992.

R. James Firby, Roger E. Kahn, Peter N. Prokopowicz, and Michael J. Swain. An architecture for vision and action. In *The Proceedings of the Fourteenth International Joint Conference on Artificial Intelligence*, pages 72–79, 1995.

Daniel D. Fu, Kristian J. Hammond, and Michael J. Swain. Action and perception in man-made environments. In *The Proceedings of the Fourteenth International Joint Conference on Artificial Intelligence*, pages 464–469, 1995.

Ian Horswill. Polly: A vision-based artificial agent. In *The Proceedings of the Eleventh National Conference on Artificial Intelligence*, 1993.

Hiroshi Ishiguro, Takeshi Maeda, Takahiro Miyashita, and Saburo Tsuji. A strategy for acquiring an environmental model with panoramic sensing by a mobile robot. In *Proceedings IEEE International Conference on Robotics and Automation*, volume 1, pages 724–729, 1994.

David Kortenkamp and Terry Weymouth. Topological mapping for mobile robots using a combination of sonar and vision sensing. In *The Proceedings of the Twelfth National Conference on Artificial Intelligence*, 1994.

Benjamin J. Kuipers and Yung-Tai Byun. A robust, qualitative method for robot spatial learning. In *The Proceedings of the Seventh National Conference on Artificial Intelligence*, 1988.

Maja J. Mataric. Integration of representation into goal-driven behavior-based robots. *IEEE Transactions on Robotics and Automation*, 8(3):304–312, June 1992.

William Rucklidge. *Efficient Computation of the Minimum Hausdorff Distance for Visual Recognition.* PhD thesis, Cornell University Department of Computer Science, 1994. Technical Report TR94-1454.

Reid Simmons. Becoming increasingly reliable. In *Proceedings, The Second International Conference on Artificial Intelligence Planning Systems*, pages 152–157, 1994.

Thomas M. Strat and Martin A. Fischler. Context-based vision: Recognizing objects using both 2-d and 3-d imagery. *IEEE Transactions on Pattern Analysis and Machine Intelligence*, 13(10):1050–1065, 1991.

Michael J. Swain and Dana H. Ballard. Color indexing. *International Journal of Computer Vision*, 7:11–32, 1991.

Guaranteeing Safety in Spatially Situated Agents

Robert C. Kohout and **James A. Hendler**
Department of Computer Science and
Institute for Advanced Computer Studies
University of Maryland
College Park, MD 20742
kohout,hendler@cs.umd.edu
phone: (301) 405-7027
fax: (301) 405-6707

David J. Musliner
Honeywell Technology Center
MN65-2200
3660 Technology Drive
Minneapolis, MN 55418
musliner@src.honeywell.com
phone: (612) 951-7599

Abstract

"Mission-critical" systems, which include such diverse applications as nuclear power plant controllers, "fly-by-wire" airplanes, medical care and monitoring systems, and autonomous mobile vehicles, are characterized by the fact that system failure is potentially catastrophic. The high cost of failure justifies the expenditure of considerable effort at design-time in order to guarantee the correctness of system behavior. This paper examines the problem of guaranteeing safety in a well studied class of robot motion problems known as the "asteroid avoidance problem." We establish necessary and sufficient conditions for ensuring safety in the simple version of this problem which occurs most frequently in the literature, as well as sufficient conditions for a more general and realistic case. In doing so, we establish functional relationships between the number, size and speed of obstacles, the robot's maximum speed and the conditions which must be maintained in order to ensure safety.

Introduction

Applications in which the failure of a system to perform correctly can result in catastrophe are known as *mission-critical* systems. The reliability requirements of such applications, which include nuclear power plant controllers, "fly-by-wire" airplanes, medical care and monitoring systems, and autonomous mobile vehicles, have motivated extensive research into the development of highly reliable software systems. Research into the development of systems-level support for mission-critical systems focuses upon "hard" real-time operating systems, which can *guarantee* that the system can deliver resources stipulated by some externally generated set of timing constraints. Similarly, the programming language community has developed technologies to ensure that programs will *always* behave correctly, with respect to some externally provided performance specification.

In contrast to the effort in the systems and programming languages communities, there is not a large body of research into the problem of *generating the specifications* which will ensure the correct and timely operation of a deployed mission-critical system. Determining a correct plan of action is the focus of AI Planning research. However, the high-variance time requirements of current techniques make it difficult to guarantee that they will produce a correct solution in time to actually use it. CIRCA (Musliner, Durfee, & Shin 1995) was developed to address this problem: by modeling the world as a finite set of situation-states, with well defined transitions between them, CIRCA is able to search the situation space "offline" (i.e. before the system is actually deployed), in an effort to find a closed set of safe states such that, for any possible combination of external events, it will always be possible for the control system to take an action that will keep the current situation-state within the closed set of safe states. When the situation space includes continuous dimensions, this technique can only be used if we can somehow discretize the continuous space. When the dimension is time, it is usually straightforward to meaningfully distinguish between times before and after a deadline, as well as some small set of "deadline approaching" intervals. However, when the dimensions are spatial, there is often no simple partitioning which will allow us to reason about a finite set of discrete states. This paper examines the problem of guaranteeing safety in a well-studied class of robot motion problems. By establishing sufficient conditions for ensuring safety, we provide the basis for automatic reasoning about maintaining safety in spatial domains.

The "Asteroid Avoidance Problem"

Consider one of the simplest natural problems in dynamic motion planning: how can we find a path for a robot, R, which travels from some initial location l_0 to some goal location l_G, while avoiding each of n obstacles, $O_1, \ldots, O_n$, where each of the O_i is moving at a known, constant velocity? We are making three simplifying assumptions that would rarely occur in a real-world application:

1. The trajectories of the obstacles are *known* to the system in advance.
2. The obstacles move linearly.

3. The speed of the obstacles is fixed.

(Reif & Sharir 1985) named this class of problems the *asteroid avoidance problem*, and they showed that, for the three-dimensional case, the problem is $\mathcal{PSPACE}$-hard when the velocity of the robot is bounded, and $\mathcal{NP}$-hard even when the robot's velocity is unbounded. (Canny & Reif 1987) showed that the 2-dimensional case is $\mathcal{NP}$-hard. This has strong implications for any mission-critical application, such as a fly-by-wire or autonomous vehicle system, for which the failure to avoid obstacles could be catastrophic: *in the general case*, we will only be able to find timely results for problems of very small size, even under the strong simplifying assumptions listed above. Additionally, one should note that these results are for the problem of finding a path *if it exists*; there is no guarantee that such a path will in fact exist.

This paper focuses upon finding restrictions to the problem for which we can guarantee that some safety-preserving path exists, and for which the problem of computing the solution is tractable. For instance (Fujimura & Samet 1989) give an $O(n^2 logn)$ algorithm for solving the asteroid avoidance problem, under the assumption that the robot can move faster than all of the obstacles. (Reif & Sharir 1985) claim that under such an assumption, it is always possible to find such a path, *as long as the initial position of the robot is not in the "shadow" of any obstacle*, where the shadow of an obstacle is defined to be all those locations from which escape from that obstacle is impossible. The proofs that 1) a safety-preserving path always exists, and that 2) we have a relatively efficient way of finding it, are the two most important criteria for guaranteeing that under these conditions obstacles will always be avoided. We shall refer to these as the *existence* and *ability* criteria, respectively.

If we have the luxury of knowing well in advance what the initial positions and trajectories of the robot and obstacles are, so that we can compute the solution "offline", and use it at the appropriate time, the existence and ability criteria are all we need to satisfy to ensure the robot's safety. However, this situation rarely occurs in practice. Normally, the relevant data become available at some time, t_0, and we must have the appropriate solution by some later deadline, t_d, or the solution will be obsolete by the time we begin to execute it. We call the requirement that a solution be produced before it is obsolete the *timeliness* criteria. In the case where the speed of a robot is greater than that of any object, we can establish timeliness by expanding the shadow of each obstacle to account for the (worst-case) time required to compute a solution to the problem.

In this section, we will consider the following variant of the asteroid problem: we have a single robot, R, and a set of n obstacles $O_1, \ldots, O_n$ moving at constant speeds $v_1, \ldots, v_n$ along linear trajectories. The robot is capable of instantaneous, unbounded acceleration, up to some maximum speed V_r. Under what conditions can we guarantee that 1) a safety-preserving path exists which will allow the robot to avoid being hit by any obstacle and 2) we can compute the path in time to execute it? We shall model the robot as a single point and the obstacles as circles with diameters $d_1, \ldots, d_n$. Most path planning literature assumes we can bound the robot and obstacles by polygons. Reducing the robot to a point is a standard technique introduced in (Lozano-Pérez & Wesley 1979) : it turns out that a solution in the case where the robot is a convex polygon is equivalent to the case where the robot is a point and the sizes of the obstacles have been increased by the size of the robot. However, this technique can only be used when the obstacles do not rotate. Since a polygon that does not rotate can be bounded by a circle, and a polygon that does rotate can also be bounded by a (possibly larger) circle, centered at the center of rotation, we use circles to represent obstacles in order to simplify our presentation, and actually gain some generality. In this paper, we are concerned only with avoiding the obstacles: there is no goal position to which we are trying to move the robot. Finally, though the concepts we present do generalize to higher dimensions, we will limit our treatment to the two-dimensional case for ease of presentation.

The Threat Horizon

The central insight of this section is that, once we fix the number, speed and sizes of the obstacles, and the maximum speed of the robot, the obstacles can always be avoided, so long as they are each initially some minimum distance away from the robot. We call this distance the *threat horizon*, H. It should be obvious that, if we make H extremely large relative to the speeds of the obstacles, some safety-preserving path must exist. However, we would like to make H as small as possible. We also need to satisfy the ability criteria, i.e., it is not enough to know a path exists, we must be able to find it. We address these issues in the proof of the following theorem:

Theorem 1 *Let R be a point in a 2-dimensional Euclidean plane, which represents the location of a robot at time t_0. Assume that the robot can rotate and accelerate instantaneously, but is limited by a maximum speed V_r. Let $O_1, \ldots, O_n$ be a set of n circular obstacles with diameters $d_1, \ldots, d_n$ which move at known, constant velocities $v_1, \ldots, v_n$. Let V_o be the largest of the v_i. Let W be the sum of the widths of the obstacles, i.e., $W = \sum_{i=1}^{n} d_i$. If each of the obstacles is initially a distance greater than*

$$\frac{W(V_o + V_r)}{2V_r}$$

from R, then there exists a "safe harbor" point S such that none of the O_i will touch S at any time, and the robot can move from R to S without intersecting any of the O_i.

Proof: Let Φ_i be the space occupied by obstacle O_i, from time t_0 to t_∞. Since the obstacles move along linear paths, Φ_i is comprised of all of the space between two parallel rays, separated by a width of d_i. Since the space which lies between two parallel lines has been named a *plank*, we shall call this region a *half-plank* of width d_i.

If each of the obstacles begins at a distance greater than $W(V_o + V_r)/2V_r$ from R, then for each obstacle O_i, there must exist a positive number $\hat{\epsilon}_i$, such that O_i begins *exactly* $W(V_o + V_r)/2V_r + \hat{\epsilon}_i$ from R. Let $\epsilon = 2V_r\hat{\epsilon}_i/(V_o+V_r)$. Then ϵ is positive, $\hat{\epsilon}_i = \epsilon(V_o+V_r)/2V_r$, and O_i begins a distance $(W + \epsilon)(V_o + V_r)/2V_r$ from R.

The earliest time that one of the obstacles could intersect the robot would be in the case that the obstacle O_n for which $\hat{\epsilon}_n$ is the smallest of the $\hat{\epsilon}_i$, travels at speed V_o and heads directly towards R, while the robot travels a straight-line path towards O_n, at its maximum speed V_r. In this case, O_n and the robot would collide at time $t_0 + ((W + \epsilon)(V_o + V_r)/2V_r(V_o + V_r))$, which is just $t_0 + (W + \epsilon)/2V_r$.

Now consider the region which comprises all of the points to which the robot could move by time $t_j > t_0$, while never moving at a speed greater than V_r. This area is just a circle, with radius $V_r(t_j - t_0)$. It follows that the area which comprises the locations to which the robot could travel before it could possibly be hit is a circle centered at R, with radius $V_r(t_0 + (W + \epsilon)/2V_r - t_0)$, which simplifies to $(W + \epsilon)/2$. We shall call the distance $(W + \epsilon)/2$ the *safety radius*, and the circle of this radius centered at R the *safety region*.

Now we need to show that the n half-planks, $\Phi_1, \ldots, \Phi_n$, cannot completely cover the safety region. To do this, we use the 2-dimensional version of Bang's solution to Tarski's "plank problem" (Bang 1951), which states[1]:

Theorem 2 (Bang) *If L is a convex body of minimal width l in a 2-dimensional Euclidean plane, and L is contained in the union of p planks of widths $h_1, \ldots, h_p$, then $h_1 + \cdots + h_p \geq l$.*

Clearly, the set of objects which can be covered by planks is a superset of the set of objects which can covered by half-planks. Since the safety region is a convex body of width $W + 2\epsilon$, by Bang's theorem, in order for the n half-planks to cover the safety region, $\sum_{i=1}^{n} d_i$ must be greater than or equal to $W + 2\epsilon$. But, by definition, $W = \sum_{i=1}^{n} d_i$, and ϵ is positive, so there must be some area within the safety region which is not covered by the Φ_i. This proves the existence of S. To see that the robot can move from R to S without being hit, one only need remember that the safety radius was defined so that it is possible for the robot to move anywhere in the safety region by the time the first obstacle reaches its perimeter. **Q.E.D.**

[1] This theorem generalizes to n-dimensions.

This proof satisfies the existence criteria. In order to compute the solution, we need to compute the intersection of the n half-planks with the safety region. If k is the number of intersections of the half-planks, this can be done in $O((k + n)logn)$ using a modification of (Bentley & Ottmann 1979) algorithm for reporting the intersection of line segments, as elaborated in (Melhorn 1984, pp. 154–160). (Chazelle & Edelsbrunner 1992) describe an $O(nlogn + k)$ algorithm which could also be modified to find safe harbors within the safety region. Either of these solutions satisfies the ability criterion.

In order to establish timeliness, for a fixed number of obstacles n, we need to know the *actual* worst-case time required to compute the solution. Call this time t_s. If we increase H by the maximum distance an obstacle can travel in t_s, then we ensure that the system will have sufficient time to compute and execute the solution. Thus, the threat horizon, H should be

$$V_o * t_s + W(V_o + V_r)/2V_r$$

in order to guarantee timeliness. Note that we can use a similar argument to account for robot rotation and acceleration times, in the more realistic cases where acceleration and rotation are not assumed to be instantaneous.

The Necessity of the Threat Horizon

In the previous subsection, we showed that constraining obstacles to begin their travels outside of the threat horizon H was sufficient to ensure the safety of the robot. In this subsection, we show that the bound is tight. Note that the size of the safety region depends only upon the sizes of the obstacles, while H also depends upon the ratio of V_o to V_r. This leads to the following theorem:

Theorem 3 *Let R be a point in a 2-dimensional Euclidean plane, which represents the location of a robot at time t_0. Assume that the robot can rotate and accelerate instantaneously, but is capable of only a maximum speed V_r. Let $O_1, \ldots, O_n$ be a set of n circular obstacles with diameters $d_1, \ldots, d_n$, which move at known, constant velocities $v_1, \ldots, v_n$. Let $W = \sum_{i=1}^{n} d_i$, and let δ be a positive constant, such that $\delta > 2WV_r/V_o$. If at time t_0 obstacles are allowed to start a distance*

$$(W - \delta)(V_o + V_r)/2V_r$$

from the robot, then there exist configurations for which it is not possible for the robot to avoid collision.

Proof: It suffices to show a single configuration for which it is not possible to avoid the obstacles. Let all the obstacles O_i have the same diameter D. Assume that the O_i start in the configuration depicted in Figure 1, where the obstacles are just touching (i.e. for $i < n$ the distance from the center of O_i to the center of O_{i+1} is D), and they are all traveling at speed V_o, along parallel courses as indicted in the figure. Let l_t

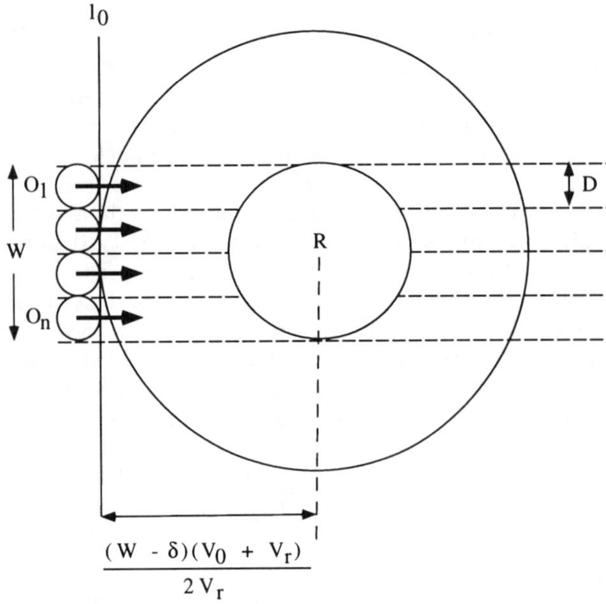

Figure 1: Necessity of the Threat Horizon

be the line which is tangent to all of the obstacles at time t, and which is on the same side of the obstacles as it is at time t_0, when it is on the side of the obstacles nearest the robot. Let the distance from R to the line l_0 be $(W-\delta)(V_o+V_r)/2V_r$. Clearly, all of the obstacles are initially at least this distance from R at time t_0. The robot can travel the distance $(W-\delta)/2$ in time $(W-\delta)/2V_r$. When it has done so, the line $l_{(W-\delta)/2V_r}$ will be a distance $(W-\delta)/2$ away from the (original) point R. If the obstacles can travel the distance W before the robot can move $\delta/2$, then they will completely traverse the circle of radius $W/2$ centered at R before the robot is able to have moved outside of this circle. That is, if $W/V_o < \delta/2V_r$, the robot will be hit by at least one obstacle. Since, by definition $\delta > 2WV_r/V_o$, this completes the proof.

In cases where V_o is large relative to W and V_r, δ approaches arbitrarily close to 0. Consequently, $H = W(V_o+V_r)/2V_r$ is the minimum distance for which we can guarantee that a safety-preserving path exists, in the general case.

The Dynamic Asteroid Avoidance Problem

In the previous section, we presented a necessary and sufficient criterion for guaranteeing safety in the asteroid avoidance problem. In doing so, we have established a functional relationship between the number, size and speed of the obstacles, the maximum speed of the robot and the distance which obstacles must initially be from a robot in order to ensure that the robot will never collide with any of the obstacles. We have also shown that, in those cases where we can guarantee safety, there is a simple and efficient means of finding the safety-preserving path. The problem we have addressed thus far makes the same simplifying assumption as in made in, e.g., (Fujimura & Samet 1989; Kant & Zucker 1986; Reif & Sharir 1985) : the position and the trajectories of the obstacles are known *prior* to execution time. While this formulation has proven challenging, it is overly optimistic. Normally, we can expect the existence, location and trajectories of obstacles to become known during execution, perhaps while the robot is already in the process of avoiding previously detected obstacles. In this section, we examine the problem of guaranteeing safety when the location of obstacles must be sensed at execution time, which we have named the "dynamic" asteroid problem. Using Theorem 1, we develop a sufficient condition for ensuring the existence of a safety-preserving path in this problem.

Obstacles with Uniform Velocity

Consider the asteroids problem described above, where we know there are at most n circular obstacles $O_1, \ldots, O_n$, traveling along linear trajectories at constant speeds. For simplicity, we will assume that all of the obstacles are of the same diameter, D. In addition, assume that all of the O_i move at the same speed, V_o. Unlike the previous section, we do not assume that we know the location of the obstacles in advance. Instead, the obstacles are allowed to appear, one or more at a time, up to a maximum of n obstacles. We wish to determine a safety horizon, $\bar{H}$, such that we know that a safety-preserving path exists as long as all of the obstacles initially appear at a distance of at least $\bar{H}$ from the robot. The following is a corollary of Theorem 1 above:

Corollary 1 *Let H be $W(V_o+V_r)/2V_r$, where $W = nD$, V_r is the maximum speed of the robot, and V_o is the (uniform) speed of the obstacles. If each of the obstacles O_i appears at some time $t_{a(i)} \geq t_0$, at a distance greater than $\bar{H} = nH + W$ from the position of the robot at that time, then there exists a collision-free path from the starting point R to some point S such that none of the O_i will touch S at any time.*

Proof (by induction on m, the number of obstacles which have already appeared[2]): The base case is handled by Theorem 1, since $nH + W \geq H$, and we can assume that $t_{a(1)} = t_0$.

Assume, by induction, that after the first $m < n$ of the obstacles have appeared, there exists a safety preserving path to some point S_m which is safe from all of the obstacles $O_1, \ldots, O_m$. Let R_x be the location of the robot at time t_x. If at time $t_{a(m+1)}$ all of the obstacles $O_1, \ldots, O_m$ are farther than H from $R_{a(m+1)}$, then

[2]This is not induction on n, the maximum number of obstacles which can appear.

once again Theorem 1 holds, and a safety preserving path exists from $R_{a(m+1)}$ to some point S_{m+1}. If one (or more) of the O_i is within H of the robot, then the robot can wait at S_m until those obstacles have traveled at least a distance H from S_m. In the worst case, this time is $(H + D)/V_o$. Of course, another obstacle could move to within H of S_m in this time. Since there are only $m < n$ obstacles, the longest we would have to wait would be $m(H + D)/V_o$ before we can be assured that all of the obstacles are at least H from S_m. In this worst-case, the most recent obstacle, O_{m+1} will still be a distance greater than $(nH+W)-m(H+D) = n(H + D) - m(H + D) = (n - m)(H + D)$ from S_m, and since $m < n$, we know that this distance is greater than H. Thus we know that at some time, all of the $m + 1$ obstacles will be outside of the safety region, and so Theorem 1 applies. Thus there exists a (linear) path from S_m to some new point S_{m+1}. **Q.E.D.**

Since by definition $W = nD$, it follows that $\bar{H} = n^2D((V_o + V_r)/V_r + 1)$, and thus this corollary gives an $O(n^2)$ upper bound for the threat horizon in the dynamic asteroids problem. It is also easy to see that $\bar{H}$ is sufficient to guarantee safety so long as there are never more than n obstacles within $\bar{H}$ of the robot R at any single time, even if many more than n obstacles appear over time.

Allowing the speed of Obstacles to Range from V_l to V_o

There is a straightforward generalization of the above theorem in cases where the obstacles are constrained to have constant positive velocities ranging from a lower bound of V_l to a maximum speed of V_o.

Corollary 2 *Let $O_1, \ldots, O_n$ be n circular obstacles of fixed diameter D, each constrained to move at a constant velocity, V_i, such that $\forall i\ V_l \leq V_i \leq V_o$, where V_l and V_o are fixed positive constants. Let $W = nD$, and H be $W(V_o + V_r)/2V_r$, where V_r is the maximum speed of the robot. If each of the obstacles O_i appears at some time $t_{a(i)} \geq t_0$, at a distance greater than*

$$\bar{H} = \frac{V_o(nH + W)}{V_l}$$

from the position of the robot at that time, then there exists a collision-free path from the starting point R to some point S such that none of the O_i will touch S at any time.

Proof (by induction on m, the number of obstacles which have already appeared): The base case is again handled by Theorem 1, since that theorem applies whenever obstacle velocities are constrained by some maximum, V_o, and obstacles occur outside the threat horizon H. Since $V_o \geq V_l$, it follows that, for all values of n, $V_o n/V_l \geq 1$, and thus $\bar{H} > H$.

The inductive step is very similar to that for Corollary 1: Assume, by induction, that after the first $m < n$ of the obstacles have appeared, there exists a safety preserving path to some point S_m which is safe from all of the obstacles $O_1, \ldots, O_m$. Let R_x be the location of the robot at time t_x. If at time $t_{a(m+1)}$ all of the obstacles $O_1, \ldots, O_m$ are farther than H from $R_{a(m+1)}$, then once again Theorem 1 holds, and a safety preserving path exists from $R_{a(m+1)}$ to some point S_{m+1}. If one (or more) of the O_i is within H of the robot, then the robot can wait at S_m until those obstacles have traveled at least a distance H from S_m.

In the following, we have to change the earlier proof to account for the fact that slower moving obstacles may remain near the robot for longer periods of time: In the worst case, this time is $(H + D)/V_l$ (note that $(H + D)/V_l \leq (H + D)/V_o$, which was the worst case in the previous proof). Again, another obstacle could move to within H of S_m in this time. Since there are only $m < n$ obstacles, the longest we would have to wait would be $m(H + D)/V_l$ before we can be assured that all of the obstacles are at least H from S_m. In this worst-case, the most recent obstacle, O_{m+1} can travel a distance of up to

$$V_o * m(H + D)/V_l$$

(if it happens to have the maximum speed, V_o). In any case, then, this will still be a distance greater than $V_o * (nH+W)/V_l - V_o * m(H+D)/V_l = (n-m)V_o(H+D)/V_l$ from S_m, and since $n > m$, and $V_o \geq V_l$, we know that this distance is greater than H, and Theorem 1 applies. Thus there exists a (linear) path from S_m to some new point S_{m+1}, which is safe with respect to all of the currently visible obstacles. **Q.E.D.**

Note that this threat horizon grows with the ratio of the maximum speed to the minimum speed of obstacles, V_o/V_l. If this number is large, the horizon becomes prohibitive. Intuitively, slower moving obstacles should be easier to avoid, but in the context of this result, allowing the speed of obstacles to approach zero will make the threat horizon approach infinity. This is a clear indication that the bound is not tight. Even in the case where $V_o = V_l$, we choose H to account for the case when all n obstacles are a distance H from the obstacle, but we choose $\bar{H} = nH + W$ to account for the times when the n obstacles are "evenly" spaced. But when all the O_i are visible H alone is sufficient, and when the obstacles are evenly spaced, so that exactly one is within H or the robot at any given time, then a horizon of $H' = \bar{H}/n = H + D$ will suffice. With this insight, it is possible to reduce $\bar{H}$ by a factor of 4, but the resulting horizon is still $O(n^2)$. We are currently trying to prove the conjecture that a threat horizon which is linear in the number of obstacles exists.

Goals of Achievement

In mission-critical applications, we can distinguish two components to the planning problem:

1. **Achieving Goals** - in most applications, the agent will be charged with satisfying (or perhaps optimizing) some goal function, where the successful

achievement of a goal has some positive utility, and the failure to achieve a goal is not considered catastrophic (i.e. the utility in negative, but small compared to the cost incurred by a failure to maintain safety).

2. **Maintaining Safety** - avoiding catastrophic failure is the primary consideration of MC control systems. For our purposes, all catastrophes are equivalent, in the sense that none is considered more or less desirable than any other. Since the cost of failure is extremely high, we seek problem solutions which will guarantee that the agent remains appropriately distant from any and all threats.

In these domains, the constraints imposed by the second component absolutely dominate the influences of the first. So, for example, a mission-critical system will not attempt to achieve a non-critical goal, no matter what its utility is, unless it can assure itself that it is possible to maintain safety. This dominance allows us to effectively decouple the two components, and to consider the problem of maintaining safety independently of the influences of goals-of-achievement. This has allowed us to develop and implement a simulation in which a robot can achieve goals while avoiding moving obstacles. (Reif & Sharir 1985) present a search-based solution to the asteroids problem which is exponential in the number of moving obstacles. The high-variance time requirements of this algorithm make it unsuitable for ensuring that obstacles are avoided, but we are using a version of it to determine non-critical, safety-preserving paths to goals, while using a much faster algorithm based upon the results above to ensure safety. Using the Maruti hard real-time operating system (Saksena, da Silva, & Agrawala 1993), we are able to guarantee processing time to the safety-critical routines, and allow the search to use the processor time that is left over when the critical routines have finished. If the search algorithm is able to find a path to a goal quickly, then the system can use it without compromising safety. Otherwise, the lower-level competences for finding and reaching a safe-harbor will ensure that the robot remains safe while it searches for a way to achieve its goals.

Conclusions

It is easy to see the limitations of this work in its current form. However, without similar, albeit more comprehensive, results, we cannot deploy mission-critical systems in spatially-situated domains. The time and expense involved in developing hard real-time operating systems running provably correct software is wasted if the system specifications are not sufficient to ensure that catastrophe will be avoided. Presumably, the application domains will have sufficient restrictions and regularities to allow the development of provably correct behavioral competences. We believe the techniques introduced in this paper provide a basis for reasoning about safety maintenance in spatial domains in particular, and continuous domains in general.

Acknowledgements

This research was supported in part by grants from NSF(IRI-9306580), ONR (N00014-J-91-1451), AFOSR (F49620-93-1-0065), the ARPA/Rome Laboratory Planning Initiative (F30602-93-C-0039), the ARPA I3 Initiative (N00014-94-10907) and ARPA contract DAST-95-C0037. Dr. Hendler is also affiliated with the UM Institute for Systems Research (NSF Grant NSF EEC 94-02384). Thanks to V.S. Subrahmanian for additional support.

References

Bang, T. 1951. A solution of the "plank problem". In *Proceedings of the American Mathematical Society*, volume 2, 990–993.

Bentley, J. L., and Ottmann, T. A. 1979. Algorithms for reporting and counting geometric intersections. *IEEE Transactions on Computers* C-28(9):643–647.

Canny, J., and Reif, J. 1987. New lower bound techniques for robot motion planning problems. In *Proceedings of the 28th IEEE Symposium of Foundations of Computer Science*, 49–60.

Chazelle, B., and Edelsbrunner, H. 1992. An optimal algorithm for intersecting line segments in the plane. *Journal of the Association for Computing Machinery* 39(1):1 – 54.

Fujimura, K., and Samet, H. 1989. A hierarchical strategy for path planning among moving obstacles. *IEEE Transactions on Robots and Automation* 5(1):61–69.

Kant, K., and Zucker, S. 1986. Towards efficient trajectory planning: Path velocity decomposition. *International Journal of Robotics Research* 5:72–89.

Lozano-Pérez, T., and Wesley, M. 1979. An algorithm for planning collision-free paths among polyhedral obstacles. *Communications of the ACM* 22(10):560–570.

Melhorn, K. 1984. *Multi-dimensional Searching and Computational Geometry*, volume 3. New York, Berlin, Heidelberg: Springer-Verlag.

Musliner, D. J.; Durfee, E. H.; and Shin, K. G. 1995. World modeling for the dynamic construction of real-time control plans. *Artificial Intelligence* 74(1):83–127.

Reif, J., and Sharir, M. 1985. Motion planning in the presense of moving obstacles. In *Proceedings of the 25th IEEE Symposium of Foundations of Computer Science*, 144–154.

Saksena, M.; da Silva, J.; and Agrawala, A. 1993. Design and implementation of Maruti. Technical Report CS-TR-3181, University of Maryland Department of Computer Science.

Recognizing and interpreting gestures on a mobile robot

David Kortenkamp, Eric Huber, and R. Peter Bonasso
Metrica, Inc.
Robotics and Automation Group
NASA Johnson Space Center - ER2
Houston, TX 77058
korten@mickey.jsc.nasa.gov

Abstract

Gesture recognition is an important skill for robots that work closely with humans. Gestures help to clarify spoken commands and are a compact means of relaying geometric information. We have developed a real-time, three-dimensional gesture recognition system that resides on-board a mobile robot. Using a coarse three-dimensional model of a human to guide stereo measurements of body parts, the system is capable of recognizing six distinct gestures made by an unadorned human in an unaltered environment. An active vision approach focuses the vision system's attention on small, moving areas of space to allow for frame rate processing even when the person and/or the robot are moving. This paper describes the gesture recognition system, including the coarse model and the active vision approach. This paper also describes how the gesture recognition system is integrated with an intelligent control architecture to allow for complex gesture interpretation and complex robot action. Results from experiments with an actual mobile robot are given.

Introduction

In order to work effectively with humans, robots will need to track and recognize human gestures. Gestures are an integral part of communication. They provide clarity in situations where speech is ambiguous or noisy (Cassell 1995). Gestures are also a compact means of relaying geometric information. For example, in robotics, gestures can tell the robot where to go, where to look and when to stop. We have implemented a real-time, three-dimensional gesture recognition system on a mobile robot. Our robot uses a stereo vision system to recognize natural gestures such as pointing and hand signals and then interprets these gestures within the context of an intelligent agent architecture. The entire system is contained on-board the mobile robot, tracks gestures at frame-rate (30 hz), and identifies gestures in three-dimensional space at speeds natural to a human.

Gestures for mobile robots

Gesture recognition is especially valuable in mobile robot applications for several reasons. First, it provides a redundant form of communication between the user and the robot. For example, the user may say "Halt" at the same time that they are giving a halting gesture. The robot need only recognize one of the two commands, which is crucial in situations where speech may be garbled or drowned out (e.g., in space, underwater, on the battlefield). Second, gestures are an easy way to give geometrical information to the robot. Rather than give coordinates to where the robot should move, the user can simply point to a spot on the floor. Or, rather than try to describe which of many objects the user wants the robot to grasp, they can simply point. Finally, gestures allow for more effective communication when combined with speech recognition by grounding words such as "there" and "it" with recognizable objects.

However, mobile robot applications of gesture recognition impose several difficult requirements on the system. First, the gesture recognition system needs to be small enough to fit onto the mobile robot. This means that processing power is limited and care must be taken to design efficient algorithms. Second, the system needs to work when the robot and the user are moving, when the precise location of either is unknown and when the user may be at different distances from the robot. It is also likely that objects will be moving in the background of the image. Third, precise calibration of cameras is difficult if not impossible on a mobile platform that is accelerating and decelerating as it moves around. Finally, the system needs to work at a speed that is comfortable for human tasks, for example the halting gesture needs to be recognized quickly enough to halt the robot within a reasonable time. In this paper we present a gesture recognition system that meets these requirements.

Figure 1: A mobile robot with on-board vision system.

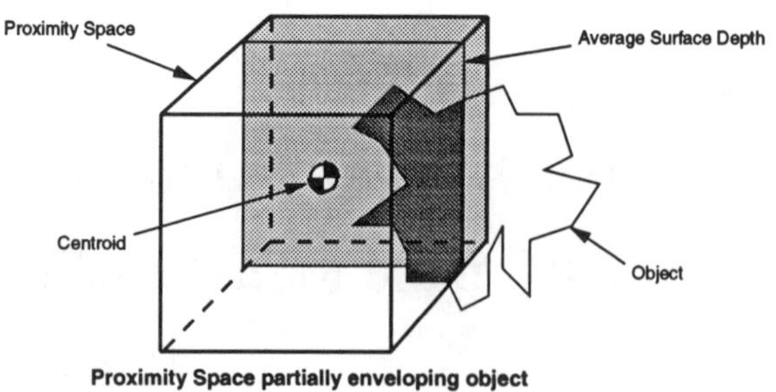

Figure 2: A proximity space.

Related work

Gesture recognition has become a very important research area in recent years and there are several mature implementations. The ALIVE system (Darrell *et al.* 1994) allows people to interact with virtual agents via gestures. The ALIVE system differs from ours in that the cameras are fixed (i.e., not on a mobile platform as ours are) and that it requires a known background. Similar restrictions hold for a system by Gavrila and Davis (Gavrila & Davis 1995). The Perseus system (Kahn *et al.* 1996) uses a variety of techniques (e.g., motion, color, edge detection) to segment a person and their body parts. Based on this segmentation the Perseus system can detect pointing vectors. This system is very similar to ours in that it is mounted on a mobile robot and integrated with robot tasks. The Perseus system differs from ours in that it requires a static background, doesn't detect gestures in three dimensions and relies on off-board computation, which can cause delays in recognition of gestures. Wilson and Bobick (Wilson & Bobick 1995) use a hidden Markov model to learn repeatable patterns of human gestures. Their system differs from ours in that it requires people to maintain strict constraints on their orientation with respect to the cameras.

Recognizing gestures

Our gesture recognition system consists of a stereo pair of black and white cameras mounted on a pan/tilt/verge head that is, in turn, mounted on the mobile robot (see Figure 1). The basis of our stereo vision work is the PRISM-3 system developed by Keith Nishihara (Nishihara 1984). The PRISM-3 system provides us with low-level spatial and temporal disparity measurements. We use these measurements as input to our algorithms for gesture recognition.

Our gesture recognition process has two components. First, we concentrate our vision system's attention on small regions of 3-D visual space. We call these regions *proximity spaces.* These spaces are designed to react to the visual input much as a robot reacts to its sensory input. Second, we spawn multiple proximity spaces that attach themselves to various parts of the agent and are guided by a coarse, three-dimensional model of the agent. The relationships among these proximity spaces gives rise to gesture recognition. Each of these two components is described in the following two subsections and then their application to gesture recognition.

The proximity space method

The active vision philosophy emphasizes concentrating measurements where they are most needed. An important aspect of this approach is that it helps limit the number of measurements necessary while remaining attentive to artifacts in the environment most significant to the task at hand. We abide by this philosophy by limiting all our measurements in and about cubic volumes of space called proximity spaces.

Within the bounds of a proximity space, an array of stereo and motion measurements are made in order to determine which regions of the space (measurement cells) are occupied by significant proportions of surface material, and what the spatial and temporal disparities are within those regions. Surface material is identified by detecting visual texture, i.e., variations in pixel values across regions of the LOG (Laplacian of Gaussian) filtered stereo pair (see Figure 2).

The location of a proximity space is controlled by behaviors generating vectors that influence its motion from frame to frame. Behaviors generate motion vectors by assessing the visual information within the proximity space. There are behaviors for following, clinging, pulling, migrating to a boundary and resiz-

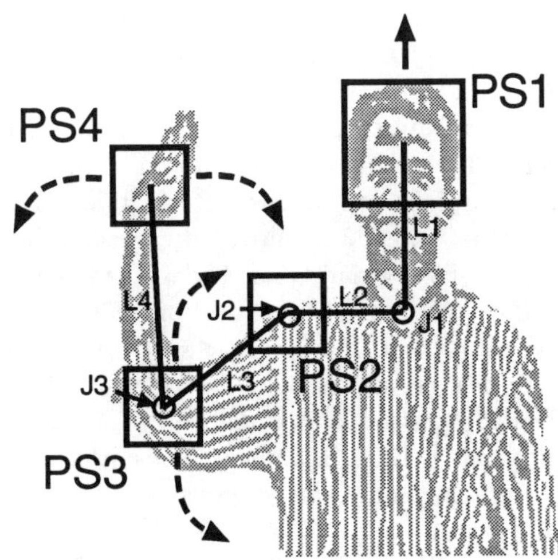

Figure 3: Coarse 3-D model of a human used for gesture recognition.

ing (which does not generate a motion vector, but a size for the proximity space). Patterned after the subsumption architecture (Brooks 1986), these behaviors compete for control of the proximity space. In dynamic terms, the proximity space acts as an inertial mass and the behaviors as forces acting to accelerate that mass (see (Huber & Kortenkamp 1995) for a more detailed description).

Chaining multiple proximity spaces using a human model

In order to recognize gestures, multiple proximity spaces are spawned, which attach themselves to various body parts in the image of the gesturing person. Each of these proximity spaces has its own set of behaviors independently controlling its location in space. However, these behaviors are constrained by a coarse three-dimensional, kinematic model of a human that limits their range of motion. With perfect tracking there would be no need for a model as the proximity spaces would track the body parts in an unconstrained manner. However, real-world noise may sometimes cause the proximity space to wander off of their body parts and begin tracking something in the background or another part on the body. While the behaviors acting on the proximity spaces continue to generate motion vectors independent of the model, the final movement of the proximity spaces is overridden by the model if the generated vectors are not consistent with the model.

We have chosen a model that resembles the human skeleton, with similar limitations on joint motion. The model, shown in Figure 3, consists of a head connected to two shoulder joints. There are four proximity spaces that are tracking various parts of the body. The first proximity space (PS1) is tracking the head. Its behaviors allow it to move freely, but are also biased to migrate it upward. The second proximity space (PS2) tracks the shoulder. PS1 and PS2 are connected by two links, L1 and L2. These links are stiff springs that allow very little movement along their axes. The lengths of L1 and L2 are set at the start of tracking and do not change during tracking. We have a procedure for automatically determining the lengths of the links from the height of the person being tracked, which is described later in the paper. The connection between L1 and L2 (J1) acts as a ball joint. The motion of L2 relative to L1 (and thus, PS2 relative to PS1) is constrained by this joint to be 0 deg in the up-down direction (i.e., shrugging of the shoulders will not affect the location of the proximity space). The joint J1 also constrains the movements of L2 relative to L1 by ±38 deg in the in-out direction (i.e., towards and away from the camera). This means that the person must be facing the cameras to within 38 deg for the gesture recognition system to work correctly.

The third proximity space (PS3) is tracking the end of the upper arm and is connected to PS2 by the link L3. Again, L3 is modeled as a very stiff spring with a length fixed at the start of tracking. L3 is connected to L2 with a ball joint (J2). L3 can move relative to L2 up at most 75 deg and down at most 70 deg. It can move into or out-of perpendicular to the camera by at most ±45 deg. This means that a pointing gesture that is towards or away from the robot by more than 45 deg will not be recognized. Finally, the fourth proximity space (PS4) tracks the end of the lower arm (essentially the hand) and is connected to PS3 with link L4 at joint J3. The range of motion of L4 relative to L3 at J3 is up at most 110 deg, down at most −10 deg and into or out-of perpendicular with the camera by at most ±45 deg. All of the links in the model are continuously scaled based on the person's distance from the cameras.

One limitation of our gesture recognition system is that it can only track one arm at a time. There are two reasons for this limitation. First, we do not have enough processing power to calculate the locations of seven proximity spaces at frame rate. Second, when both arms are fully extended the hands fall out of the field of view of the cameras. If the person backs up to fit both hands into the field of view of the cameras then the pixel regions of arms are too small for tracking. The arm to be tracked can be specified at the start of the tracking process and can be switched by the user. While Figure 3 only shows the model of the right arm for simplicity, the model for the left arm is simply a

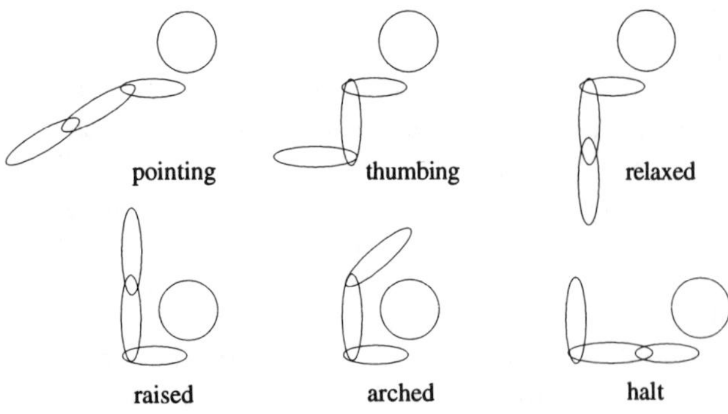

Figure 4: Recognizable gestures.

mirror image of the right.

Experiments, which are described in more detail later, show that our system can recognize gestures from distances as close as 1.25 meters from the camera (at which point the person's arm extends out of the field of view of the cameras) to as far as 5 meters away from the robot. The system can track a fully extended arm as it moves at speeds up to approximately 36 deg per second (i.e., a person can move their arm in an arc from straight up to straight down in about five seconds without the system losing track).

Acquisition and reacquistion using the model Gesture recognition is initiated by giving the system a camera-to-person starting distance and a starting arm. Four proximity spaces are spawned and lay dormant waiting for some texture to which to attach themselves. As a person steps into the camera at approximately the starting distance the head proximity space will attach itself to the person and begin migrating towards the top, stopping when it reaches the boundary of the person. The other three proximity spaces are pulled by their links up along with the head. While the person's arm is at their side, these proximity spaces are continually sweeping arcs along the dashed arrows shown in Figure 3 looking for texture to which to attach themselves. When the arm is extended the three proximity spaces "lock onto" the arm and begin tracking it. If they lose track (e.g., the arm moves to fast or is occluded) they begin searching again along the dashed arcs shown in Figure 3. If the head proximity space loses track it begins an active search starting at the last known location of the head and spiraling outward. Many times this re-acquisition process works so quickly that the user never realizes that tracking was lost.

Defining gestures

Figure 4 shows the gestures that are currently recognized by the system. These gestures are very easily determined by looking at the relative angles between the links L2, L3 and L4 at the joints J2 and J3 (see Figure 3). Let's call the angle between L2 and L3 (i.e., the upper arm angle) $\Theta 1$ and the angle between L3 and L4 (i.e., the lower arm angle) $\Theta 2$. 0 deg is straight out to the left or right. Then, if $\Theta 1 < -50$ deg and $\Theta 2 < 45$ deg the gesture is *relaxed.* If $\Theta 1 < -50$ deg and $\Theta 2 > 45$ deg the gesture is *thumbing.* If -50 deg $< \Theta 1 < 45$ deg and $\Theta 2 < 45$ deg the gesture is *pointing.* If -50 deg $< \Theta 1 < 45$ deg and $\Theta 2 > 45$ deg the gesture is *halt.* If $\Theta 1 > 45$ deg and $\Theta 2 < 45$ deg the gesture is *raised.* If $\Theta 1 > 45$ deg and $\Theta 2 > 45$ deg the gesture is *arched.* Thus, the person is always producing some kind of gesture based on the joint angles.

Gesture recognition is not immediate as that may lead to many spurious gestures. Confidence in a gesture is built up logarithmically over time as the angles stay within the limits for the gesture. When the logarithmic confidence passes a threshold (0.8 in our experiments) then the gesture is reported by the system. That gesture continues to be reported until the confidence drops below the threshold.

This gesture recognition technique does not currently support recognizing gestures that occur over time (e.g., a waving gesture). We believe that our approach, because it is active, lends itself to this and we are working towards implementing it.

Connecting gestures to robot action

Simply recognizing gestures is not enough for them to be useful; they need to be connected to a specific robot actions. For the last several years we have been working on an intelligent control architecture, known as 3T, which can integrate reactive vision and robot processes with more deliberative reasoning techniques to produce intelligent, reactive robot behavior (Bonasso *et al.* 1995). The architecture consists of three layers of control: skills, sequencing and planning. Only the first two layers (skills and sequencing) have been used in the system described in this paper. The next two subsections will describe the skills of our robot and how those skills can be intelligently sequenced to perform tasks.

Visual skills

Skills are the way in which the robot interacts with the world. They are tight loops of sensing and acting that seek to achieve or maintain some state. Skills can be enabled or disabled depending on the situation and the set of enabled skills forms a network in which information passes from skill to skill. Figure 5 shows the skill network for our work in gesture recognition. The

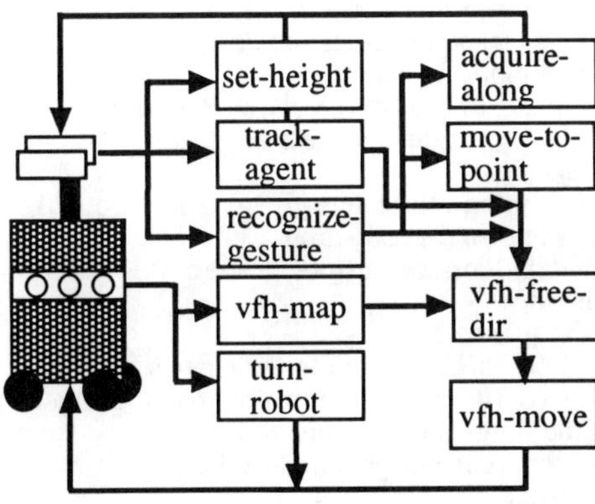

Figure 5: Mobile robot skills for gesture recognition.

skills labeled `vfh` are obstacle avoidance and robot motion skills base on the Vector Field Histogram method (Borenstein & Koren 1991). They take a goal location, generated from any skill, and move the robot to that goal location. The `move-to-point`, the `track-agent` and the `recognize-gesture` skills allow can provide goal locations to the `vfh` skills.

The `recognize-gesture` skill encapsulates the processes described in the previous section and produces one of the five gestures or no gesture as output. It also generates as output the (x,y,z) locations of the four proximity spaces when the gesture was recognized. The next several subsections described the more interesting gesture recognition skills in detail.

Moving to a point This skill produces an (x,y) goal for the robot corresponding to the location at which the person is pointing. This skill takes the (x,y,z) location of the centroid of the shoulder proximity space (PS2 in Figure 3) and the hand proximity space (PS4 in Figure 3) and computes a three-dimensional vector. It then determines the intersection point of this vector with the floor. Assuming the vector does intersect with the floor, the skill begins generating a goal for the robot and the motion control and obstacle avoidance skills move the robot to that point.

We conducted a number of experiments to determine the accuracy of the pointing gesture. The experimental set-up was to have a person point to a marked point on the floor. The vision system would recognize the pointing gesture and the `move-to-point` skill would determine the intersection of the pointing vector with the floor. We would then compare this point with the actual location of the target. We choose eight different target points on the floor in various directions and at various distances. We pointed five times at each target point. Two different people did the point, both of them familiar with the system. No feedback was given to the

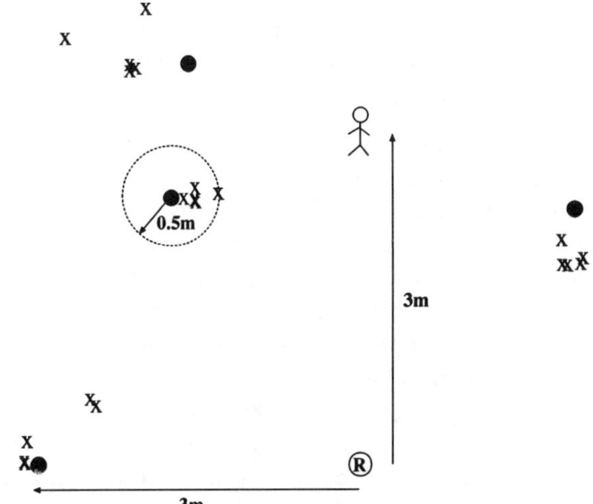

Figure 6: A sample of experimental results. The person is standing directly in front of the robot and pointing at different points on the floor (black circles). The 'X' is the point that the robot calculated as the intersection between the pointing gesture and the floor.

user between trials. Figure 6 shows a sample of those points and the system's performance.

For the five points that were between 2.5 and 4.5 meters away from the person, the mean error distance from the target to the vector intersection was 0.41 meters, with a standard deviation of 0.17. As the distance from the person to the target grew the error also grew rapidly, up to a mean error of over 3 meters at 5.5 meters away.

These results need to be taken with a grain of salt. There are several factors that can introduce errors into the system and that cannot be accounted for, including: how accurately a person can actually point at a spot; the initial accuracy of the robot both in position and orientation; and the tilt of the robot due to an uneven floor.

Acquiring along a vector When this skill is enabled, a pointing gesture will result in the vision system searching along the pointing vector and stopping if it acquires a distinct object. The vision system then begins tracking that object. This skill takes the (x,y,z) location of the centroid of the shoulder proximity space and the hand proximity and computes a three dimensional vector. The skill then causes the vision system to search along through a tube of space surrounding that vector until a patch of significant texture is encountered. The skill stops searching after a certain distance, which is passed to the skill as a parameter at run time. Informal experiments allowed two people standing about 2 meters apart to "pass control" of the system back and forth by pointing at each other. The system successfully moved from person to person over 10 consecutive times.

Tracking an agent While the vision system is recognizing gestures it tracks the person's head. The position of the person's head is converted to a goal for the robot and the robot moves, under local obstacle avoidance towards that goal. The speed of the robot is set at a maximum of 0.4 meters per second, but the robot moves more slowly as it approaches the person it is tracking or as it maneuvers to avoid obstacles. We have successfully tracked people for periods of twenty to thirty minutes in previous work (Huber & Kortenkamp 1995). For this work we added gesture recognition and allowed the person to stop the robot by giving the "halting" gesture. When the robot detects this gesture it stops moving, but the robot's head continues to track the person and the vision system continues to perform gesture recognition. The robot resumes moving when the person gives a "raised" gesture.

Determining tracking height The coarse 3-D model used for gesture recognition requires a rough estimate of the height of the person. For this reason we have implemented a skill that will automatically acquire the height of a person being tracked and reset the 3-D model on-the-run. This skill uses height of the centroid of the head proximity space as the height of the person. Experiments on five people ranging from 1.60m to 1.90m tall showed that the system estimated their height to within an average error of 0.07m. This is well within the gesture recognition system's tolerance for tracking based on a fixed model.

Interpreting gestures in task contexts

Our target environments involve robots working with astronauts in space or on planetary surfaces. Recently, in support of these environments, we have begun to investigate human-robot interaction through gesturing. Wanting to exploit the skills described above in as many situations as possible, we have observed that in many tasks a human pointing gesture can have a wide range of interpretations depending on the task. The middle layer of our 3T architecture is the RAPs system (Firby 1994). A reactive action package (RAP) specifies how and when to carry out routine procedures through conditional sequencing. As such, a RAP provides a way to interpret gestures through context limiting procedures of action.

Finding an agent to track One example of interpreting the same gesture in two different contexts can be shown in the task of pointing out an agent to be tracked. In our research we have noted that the designator agent can simply point to the designated agent's feet and the robot can use the `move-to-point` skill. But when the designated agent is some distance away from the designator, the `acquire-along-vector` skill, while slower, is less error prone. We devised a two step gesture approach wherein the first gesture tells the robot the method to be used to designate the agent to be tracked, and the second gesture would be the pointing gesture itself. Figure 7 shows this RAP (simplified for the purposes of this paper).

```
(define-rap (respond-to-gesture ?agent)
  (method motion-gesture
     (context (or (current-gesture "Pointing")
                  (current-gesture "Halting")))
     (task-net
        (t1 (interpret-gesture-for-motion ?agent))))
  (method normal-acquisition
     (context (current-gesture "Raised"))
     (task-net
        (sequence
           (t1 (speak "Point to the agent's feet"))
           (t2 (interpret-gesture-for-tracking ?agent)))))
  (method long-range-acquisition
     (context (current-gesture "Arched"))
     (task-net
        (sequence
           (t1 (speak "Point at the agent"))
           (t2 (find-agent-along-vector ?agent))))))
```

Figure 7: RAP that uses task context to interpret a gesture.

This RAP assumes a gesture has been received. If it is a pointing or halting gesture, a lower level RAP is called to stop the robot or to move to a point on the floor. If the gesture received is "raised", the usual tracking RAP will be invoked (*interpret-gesture-for-tracking*) which gets a pointing gesture, computes the point on the floor, and then looks for an agent at the appropriate height above that point. If, on the other hand, the arched gesture is detected, the *find-agent-along-vector* RAP will be invoked to get a pointing gesture and find an agent somewhere along the indicated vector. That RAP also enables the tracking skill.

The higher level RAP in Figure 8 sets up a single gesture (such as go to place) or the first of a two gesture sequence. This RAP has three methods depending on whether there is a gesture stored in the RAP memory. Normally, there is no current gesture and the robot must look for the designating agent, get a gesture, and respond appropriately (as described in the previous RAP). Once a gesture task is completed, memory rules associated with lower level RAPs will remove the

```
(define-rap (get-and-respond-to-gesture ?agent)
  (succeed (or (last-result timeout) (last-result succeed)))
  (method no-current-gesture
    (context (not (current-gesture ?g)))
    (task-net
      (sequence
        (t1 (find-agent ?agent))
        (t2 (get-gesture ?agent))
        (t3 (respond-to-gesture ?agent)))))
  (method useful-current-gesture
    (context (and (current-gesture ?g) (not (= ?g "Halting"))))
    (task-net
      (sequence
        (t1 (recognize-gesture ?agent))
        (t2 (respond-to-gesture ?agent)))))
  (method current-halt-gesture
    (context (and (current-gesture ?g) (= ?g "Halting")))
    (task-net
      (sequence
        (t1 (speak "I need another gesture"))
        (t2 (find-agent-at ?agent))
        (t3 (get-gesture ?agent))
        (t4 (respond-to-gesture ?agent))))))
```

Figure 8: RAP that sets up the gesture recognition process.

used gestures from the RAP memory.

But sometimes a lower level RAP will fail, e.g., when the designated agent can't be found, and a gesture such as "Raised" will remain in the RAP memory. Thus, in the second method, an other than halting gesture is current and the robot will turn on the `recognize-gesture` skill (for subsequent gestures) and attempt to carry out (retry) the task indicated by the current gesture.

In some cases, the robot will receive an emergency halting gesture before a lower level RAP is completed such as in the middle of a movement. If this happens the robot's last recollection of a gesture will be "Halting." In these cases, the robot tells the designating agent that they need to start over, and continues as in the first method. These RAPs do not show the details of enabling actual skills, see (Bonasso *et al.* 1995) for details of how this works.

Conclusions

Our goal is to develop technologies that allow for effective human/robot teams in dynamic environments. The ability to use the human's natural communication tendencies allows the robot to be more effective and safer when working among humans. The contributions of our system include a demonstration of gesture recognition in real-time while on-board a mobile robot. The system does not require the user to wear any special equipment nor does it require that the robot, user or background be static. Our contributions also include integrating the gesture recognition system with an intelligent agent architecture that can interpret complex gestures within tasks contexts. This complete system is a first step towards realizing effective human/robot teams. In the future we hope to extend the system by recognizing gestures over time and by integrating gesture recognition with speech recognition.

References

Bonasso, R. P.; Kortenkamp, D.; Miller, D. P.; and Slack, M. 1995. Experiences with an architecture for intelligent, reactive agents. In *Proceedings 1995 IJCAI Workshop on Agent Theories, Architectures, and Languages.*

Borenstein, J., and Koren, Y. 1991. The Vector Field Histogram for fast obstacle-avoidance for mobile robots. *IEEE Journal of Robotics and Automation* 7(3).

Brooks, R. A. 1986. A Robust Layered Control System for a Mobile Robot. *IEEE Journal of Robotics and Automation* 2(1).

Cassell, J. 1995. Speech, action and gestures as context for on-going task-oriented talk. In *Working Notes of the 1995 AAAI Fall Symposium on Embodied Language and Action.*

Darrell, T. J.; Maes, P.; Blumberg, B.; and Pentland, A. 1994. A novel environment for situated vision and behavior. In *Workshop on Visual Behaviors: Computer Vision and Pattern Recognition.*

Firby, R. J. 1994. Task networks for controlling continuous processes. In *Proceedings of the Second International Conference on AI Planning Systems.*

Gavrila, D. M., and Davis, L. 1995. 3-D model-based tracking of human upper body movement: A multiview approach. In *IEEE Symposium on Computer Vision.*

Huber, E., and Kortenkamp, D. 1995. Using stereo vision to pursue moving agents with a mobile robot. In *1995 IEEE International Conference on Robotics and Automation.*

Kahn, R. E.; Swain, M. J.; Prokopowicz, P. N.; and Firby, R. J. 1996. Gesture recognition using the perseus architecture. *Computer Vision and Pattern Recognition.*

Nishihara, H. 1984. Practical real-time imaging stereo matcher. *Optical Engineering* 23(5).

Wilson, A., and Bobick, A. 1995. Configuration states for the representation and recognition of gesture. In *International Workshop on Automatic Face and Gesture Recognition.*

Classifying and Recovering from Sensing Failures in Autonomous Mobile Robots

Robin R. Murphy David Hershberger
Center for Robotics and Intelligent Systems
Colorado School of Mines
Golden, CO 80401-1887
phone: (303) 273-3874 fax: (303) 273-3975
{rmurphy,dhershbe}@mines.edu

Abstract

This paper presents a characterization of sensing failures in autonomous mobile robots, a methodology for classification and recovery, and a demonstration of this approach on a mobile robot performing landmark navigation. A sensing failure is any event leading to defective perception, including sensor malfunctions, software errors, environmental changes, and errant expectations. The approach demonstrated in this paper exploits the ability of the robot to interact with its environment to acquire additional information for classification (i.e., active perception). A Generate and Test strategy is used to generate hypotheses to explain the symptom resulting from the sensing failure. The recovery scheme replaces the affected sensing processes with an alternative logical sensor. The approach is implemented as the Sensor Fusion Effects Exception Handling (SFX-EH) architecture. The advantages of SFX-EH are that it requires only a partial causal model of sensing failure, the control scheme strives for a fast response, tests are constructed so as to prevent confounding from collaborating sensors which have also failed, and the logical sensor organization allows SFX-EH to be interfaced with the behavioral level of existing robot architectures.

Introduction

The transfer of autonomous mobile robot (AMR) technology to applications in manufacturing, defense, space, hazardous waste cleanup, and search and rescue missions has been impeded by a lack of mechanisms to ensure robust and certain sensing. The actions of an AMR depend on its perception; if perception is faulty and goes unnoticed, the robot may "hallucinate" and act incorrectly. One key mechanism for robust sensing is fault-tolerance: the ability to detect sensing failures and either recover from them in such a way as to allow the robot to resume performance of its task(s) or to gracefully degrade.

Previous work in robotic sensing has demonstrated how certain types of sensing failures can be detected either at the behavioral (i.e., self-monitoring) (Ferrell 1993; Murphy & Arkin 1992) and/or deliberative layer (i.e., global monitoring) (Hughes 1993; Noreils & Chatila 1995). An open research question is how to recover from these failures. In the general case, recovery requires identification of the source of the problem; *if the cause is not known, the wrong response may be employed.* Detection of a failure does not necessarily mean that the cause is known. For example, in (Murphy 1992), three different problems which interfered with sensing in a security robot (sensor drift, incorrect placement of the robot, sensor malfunction) evinced that same symptom: a lack of consensus between the observations. The appropriate response to each problem was significantly different (recalibrate the offending sensor, rotate the robot until it reached the correct view, and replace the damaged sensor with an alternative, respectively). However, the correct response was known once the cause was identified. While classification is essential for the general case, it may be unnecessary in situations where the recovery options are limited, i.e. "do whatever works" (Payton *et al.* 1992).

This paper presents a symbolic AI approach to classifying and recovering from sensing failures. The characteristics of the AMR domain is differentiated from typical diagnosis applications (e.g., medicine, geological interpretation) in the next section. Related work in problem solving and diagnosis for robotic sensing follows. An overview of the approach taken in this paper is given next. Classification of errors is done with a novel extension of the basic Generate and Test strategy developed for Dendral (Lindsay *et al.* 1980), with contributions from Generate, Test, Debug (Simmons & Davis 1987). This classification scheme takes advantage of the robot's ability to actively use other sensors and feature extraction algorithms to test hypotheses about the sensing failure; it can be considered a form of active perception (Bajcsy 1988). The classification and recovery scheme is implemented as the exception handling (EH) portion of the Sensor Fusion Effects (SFX) architecture. Demonstrations of SFX-EH on a mobile robot with a landmark navigation behavior are reviewed. The paper concludes with a summary and brief discussion, including on-going research efforts.

Sensing Failures in AMR

A characterization of sensing failures in AMRs is useful at this point for two reasons. First, it provides the context for justifying the approach taken in this paper. Second, it will distinguish classifying and recovering from sensing failures for AMRs from the connotations associated with general diagnosis in other domains such as medicine and the identification of geological features. The unique attributes of this domain are:

The class of sensing failures includes more than sensor failures. For the purposes of this paper, a *sensing failure* is defined as any event leading to defective perception. These events may stem from sensor hardware malfunctions, bugs in the perceptual processing software (e.g., does not work in a particular situation), changes in the environment which negatively impact sensing either at the hardware or software level (e.g., turning the lights off), or errant expectations (e.g., looking for the wrong thing at the wrong time).

The inclusion of software defects, environmental change, and errant expectations as sources of sensing failures makes classification particularly challenging. Indeed, one of the motivations for (Payton *et al.* 1992) is to avoid having to attempt to identify software defects. These sources of faulty sensing have the potential to interrupt progress, especially changes in the environment. Exploiting the environment is a fundamental principle of behavioral robotics. However, (Howe & Cohen 1990) note the difficulty of designing agents that can tolerate environmental change. Since AMRs function in an open world, this suggests that this difficulty will be exacerbated and environmental change will be a significant source of problems as robots are deployed in more demanding settings.

Sensing failures occur frequently, but different types occur infrequently. (Ferrell 1993) noted that in experiments with Hannibal, a hexapod robot with over 100 sensors, a hardware sensor failure occurred approximately once every two weeks. Our experience with two different mobile robots is consistent.

It is unrealistic and undesirable to attempt to explicitly model all possible failure modes. (Velde & Carignan 1984) devised one such explicit modeling scheme. However, this scheme assumed that all sensors were of the same type and their observations could be correlated statistically. But it begs the issue of how to acquire statistical data about a set of events, when, by definition, the very members of that set may not be known *a priori*. The difficulties are increased as roboticists turn to multiple sensors (sensor fusion). Modeling the interactions between sensors for the environment and the task leads to a combinatorial explosion with a statistical method such as (Velde & Carignan 1984; Weller, Groen, & Hertzberger 1989), again ignoring that a sensing failure may result from a never encountered or unanticipated event. Even if multi-sensor modeling could be done satisfactorily, the causal models are unlikely to be portable to new sensor configurations and application domains.

An AMR can actively perceive. One advantage that an AMR has is that it can acquire new information by deliberately engaging its environment as per *active perception* (Bajcsy 1988), and/or by extracting new meanings from previous observations (e.g., examines the recent history of measurements).

An AMR may have both redundant and complementary sensing modalities. The trend in robotic sensing is to use a small set of general purpose sensors. Some sensors may be redundant (i.e., two or more of the same sensor). However, the majority of sensors are likely to be complementary. For example, at the AAAI Mobile Robot Competitions, the entries are invariably equipped with vision and sonar. This makes classification challenging because the scheme cannot assume that there is an alternative sensor which can directly collaborate a suspect sensor; instead, inferences from the behaviors of other sensors will have to be made.

Exception handling is a secondary function in an AMR. In other domains, diagnosis is their primary task. In an AMR, sensing failures can be viewed as *exceptions* which cause the robot's progress to be suspended. Reliable sensing must be reestablished before the robot can resume the behavior and complete the intended task. However, an AMR may have only a finite time to spend on exception handling. It can't remain indefinitely in a hostile environment such as Three Mile Island or an outgassing Near Earth Object without increasing the risk of a hardware failure from radiation or catastrophe. Therefore, the time dedicated to exception handling is an important consideration in the development of any classification and recovery scheme.

Exception handling must be integrated with the whole system. To see how sensing failures impact the whole system, consider the following examples. First, because the robot cannot act correctly without adequate sensing, an AMR must cease execution of the failed behavior and possibly revert to a stand-by, defensive mode if it cannot continue other behaviors. This requires information about sensing failures to be propagated to the behavioral or task manager. If the behavior cannot recover quickly, the mission planner aspect of the robot must be informed so that it can replan or abort the mission. Second, since classification and recovery may involve active perception, contention for sensing resources may occur, e.g., is it safe to take away sensor X from behavior Y and point it in a different direction? Contention resolution requires knowledge about the robot's goals, interchangeability of sensors, etc., making exception handling a process which must communicate with other modules in the robot architecture. Third, if the source of a sensing failure is used by other behaviors, the recovery scheme should include replacing the failed component in the other behaviors which may be hallucinating, as well as the behavior that first detected the problem.

The attributes of the classification and recovery task for AMR itemized above lead to a characterization of a desirable exception handling mechanism and an appropriate problem solving strategy. This exception handler is intended to be applicable to any AMR sensing configuration. Because sensor failures occur frequently and suspend progress of the robot, exception handling must attempt to effect a timely recovery. The exception handler must interact with the task manager to prevent unsafe actions from occurring during classification and recovery. The exception handling scheme can reduce the down time by exploiting any situations where a recovery scheme can be directly invoked, either because the symptom clearly defines the cause or because all possible causes result in the same response. It should continue to attempt to identify the source of the sensing failure in a background mode if it invokes a direct recovery scheme. The exception handler can use active perception to overcome the open world assumption and the resultant difficulty in constructing a complete model of failure modes. But active perception leads to a new issue of how to safely reallocate sensing resources from other behaviors (if needed) to identify the source of the problem. Therefore, the exception handling mechanism must be a global, or deliberative, process in order to reason about possible corroborating sensors which may not be allocated to it. These sensors may or may not be redundant. The mechanism must be able to handle contention resolution or communicate its needs to the appropriate sensor allocation process. When the exception handler identifies the source of the failure, it propagates the information to other behaviors so they don't hallucinate or go into a redundant classification and recovery cycle.

Related Work

As noted in the introduction, detection, classification, and recovery from sensing failures in mobile robots has been addressed by (Noreils & Chatila 1995), (Ferrell 1993) and (Payton *et al.* 1992). Other noteworthy efforts are those by (Weller, Groen, & Hertzberger 1989), (Velde & Carignan 1984), (Hanks & Firby 1990), and (Chavez & Murphy 1993).

(Weller, Groen, & Hertzberger 1989) and (Velde & Carignan 1984) deal with sensor errors in general. (Weller, Groen, & Hertzberger 1989) create modules for each sensor containing tests to verify the input based on local expert knowledge. Environmental conditions determine whether a test can be performed or not. The partitioning of problem space by symptom is based on these modules. The approach taken in this paper follows (Weller, Groen, & Hertzberger 1989), testing corroborating sensors before using them for error classification.

(Hanks & Firby 1990) propose a planning architecture suitable for mobile robots. As with (Noreils & Chatila 1995), a plan failure triggers exception handling. The system recovers by either choosing another method randomly whose pre-conditions are currently satisfied (similar in concept to logical sensors (Henderson & Shilcrat 1984) and behaviors (Henderson & Grupen 1990)), or by running the same method again (similar to the retesting strategy used by (Ferrell 1993)). As with (Payton *et al.* 1992), there is no formal error classification scheme. No check is performed to confirm that the sensors providing information about the pre-conditions are still functioning themselves. If they are not, the recovery scheme may pick a method that will either fail, or, more significantly, hallucinate and act incorrectly.

An earlier version of SFX-EH was presented in (Chavez & Murphy 1993). This article builds on that work, with two significant advances. The control scheme is now a global, deliberative process with the ability to access information from sensors not allocated to the behavior. The original was restricted to using only information directly available to the behavior. This was intended to provide fault tolerance entirely within a behavior; in practice with landmark navigation and hall-following this proved to be too severe.

Approach

This paper concentrates on the exception handling strategy needed to classify a sensing failure. It assumes that an AMR accomplishes a task via independent behaviors which have no knowledge about sensing processes being used by the other behaviors. A behavior is assumed to consist of two parts: a motor process or schema, which defines the pattern of activity for the behavior, and a perceptual process or schema, which supplies the motor process with the necessary perception to guide the next action. This assumption allows the perceptual process to be treated as a logical sensor. Alternative logical sensors may exist for the percept. The sensor and feature extraction algorithms used to compute the percept are referred to as a *description* of the percept, synonymous with a logical sensor. There may be more than one description of a percept using the same sensor. For example, a hazardous waste container can be modeled in terms of 2D visual features or 3D visual features; each set would form a unique description even though they were extracted from the same camera. A logical sensor may fuse the evidence from than one description; this is generally referred to as sensor fusion of multiple logical sensors.

A description is the smallest granularity for identifying a sensing failure; therefore, the difference between a software defect (e.g., the algorithm fails after the 100th iteration) and errant instantiation (e.g., the algorithm is triggered with the wrong parameters) is indistinguishable. However, the exception handler should not assume that a failed logical sensor means that the physical sensor is "bad." Instead, it should attempt to isolate and test the physical sensor separately where possible.

Either the behavior or a global supervisory monitor is assumed to detect a sensing failure and supply the exception handler with the symptom and relevant information. The symptom may provide an explicit classification of the source of the problem, i.e., serves as a complete causal model; for example, upon malfunctioning, the hardware returns a failure code. The symptom may only be a partial causal model (e.g., lack of consensus between observations), thereby necessitating further investigation. The exception handler assumes that there is only one sensing failure at a time. This simplifies classification. By solving one sensing failure, it is hoped that any additional failures would be taken care of. If not, the new logical sensor will fail and exception handling reinvoked. It is worth emphasizing that the system does not assume that any additional sensors used for classification or recovery are operational; therefore any sensors used for corroboration must be validated as functional in advance. Also, the exception handling approach supports graceful degradation by acknowledging when it can't solve the problem and turning control over to whatever mission planning arrangement is used by the robot.

The exception handling strategy is divided into two steps: *error classification* and *error recovery*. The error classification module uses a variation of Generate and Test (Lindsay *et al.* 1980) to generate hypotheses about the underlying cause of the failure. There are three advantages to using Generate and Test. First, since it is an exhaustive search, it catches errors that occur infrequently. Second, Generate and Test allows the robot to actively collect additional information. Because robotic behaviors generally are reactive in the sense of (Brooks 1986), their perception is limited to local representations focused solely on the motor action. As a result, there is usually not enough information available to a behavior to isolate the cause locally. Active acquisition of additional information is critical to the success of error classification. Three, the tests do not require redundant sensors, instead information from other modalities can be used. A Generate and Test strategy does have one disadvantage; because it performs an exhaustive search, it can be time consuming. However, this disadvantage has not been encountered in practice to date because of the small search space for the set of sensors typically used by mobile robots.

Error classification follows the same basic procedure as Generate and Test (Lindsay *et al.* 1980):

1. Generate all possible causes based on the symptom.
2. Order the list of associated tests and execute the tests to confirm any of these causes.
3. Terminate classification when all tests have been performed or an environmental change has been confirmed. Testing does not terminate upon the first confirmed sensor failure because an environmental change can cause a sensor diagnostic test to report a false positive. This can be determined by examining the results of all tests. If the list of tests is exhausted and no source of the failure can be identified, an errant expectation (i.e., planner failure) is assumed to be the cause.

There are five novel extensions to Generate and Test for classifying sensor failures in AMRs. One, the problem space is constrained by the symptom (e.g., missing observation, lack of consensus between multiple observations, highly uncertain evidence, etc.) in order to reduce search. Two, the exception handler generates all possible hypotheses and tests associated with that symptom at one time in order to reduce testing time and resources, and to prevent cycles in testing. Portions of the tests associated with the hypotheses may be redundant; this prevents them from being rerun. Three, the list of hypothetical causes always includes violations of the pre-conditions for each description (sub-logical sensor) in the logical sensor. This is similar in philosophy to GTD (Simmons & Davis 1987) where the debugger challenges the pre-conditions of nodes in the dependency structure. Note that in this application, the challenge is part of the initial hypothesis generation step rather than a debugging step. Example pre-conditions are sufficient ambient light and adequate power supply. Four, the tests are ordered to ensure correctness. If additional sensors are being used in the tests to corroborate observations or verify the condition of the environment, they must first be tested (if possible) to confirm that they are operational. Five, the list of tests is examined and redundant tests removed in order to speed up testing.

Once the sensing failure is classified, recovery is straightforward since the logical sensor scheme explicitly represents equivalences between sensing processes. The search for an alternative degenerates to a table look-up. If the sensing failure is due to either a malfunction or an environmental change, error recovery attempts to replace the logical sensor with an alternative. The alternative must satisfy any new pre-conditions discovered by the classification process. For example, if the reason for a sensing failure with a video camera is because the ambient lighting is extremely low, then a logical sensor using a redundant video camera is not considered. If there is no viable alternative logical sensor, the error recovery process declares a mission failure and passes control to the planner portion of the robot.

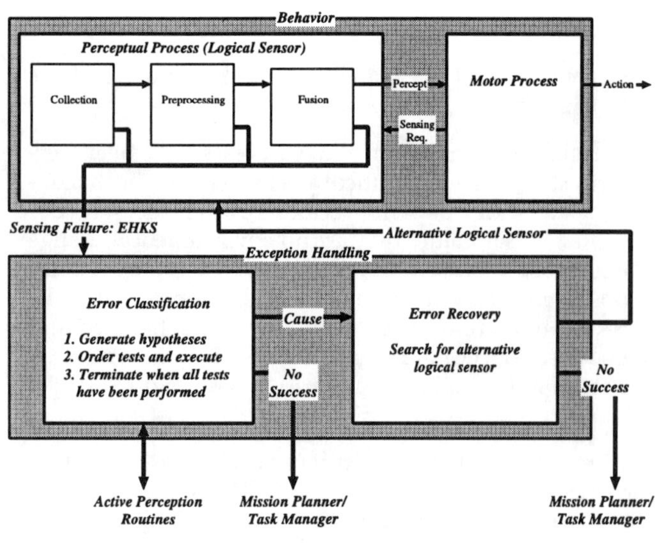

Figure 1: Overview of SFX-EH.

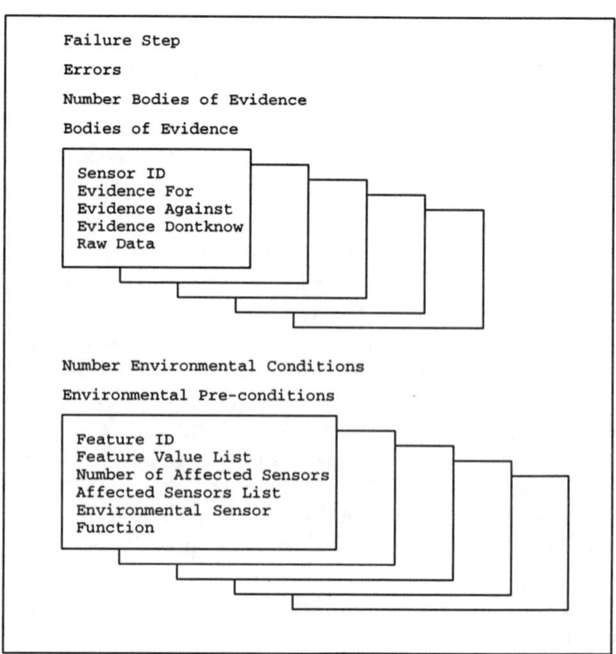

Figure 2: Diagram of the Exception Handling Knowledge Structure (EHKS)

Implementation: SFX-EH

The exception handling strategy described above has been implemented as an extension to the Sensor Fusion Architecture (SFX) (Murphy & Arkin 1992), called SFX-EH (SFX Exception Handling). Figure 1 shows a conceptual layout of sensing activities in SFX-EH. The perceptual process component of a behavior executes in three steps, as per SFX. First, observations are *collected* from each description in the logical sensor, e.g., grab an image, run feature extraction algorithms on it. Next, the descriptions are *preprocessed* to compensate for asynchronous observations, etc. The *fusion* step integrates the evidence for the percept from each description and passes it to the motor process. Situations where the logical sensor consists of a single description are treated as a degenerate case of sensor fusion and the fusion step is null.

At this time, self-monitoring perceptual processes within a behavior are the only mechanisms for detecting sensing failures, but behavioral and planning level monitoring is not precluded. SFX examines the data for a failure after each step. The four symptoms currently recognized by SFX are: *missing data* (the description has not been updated with a new reading), *highly uncertain data* (the observation of a description is vague or ambiguous), *highly conflicting observations* (the observations from multiple descriptions do not show a consensus), and *below minimum certainty in the percept* (the evidence that the percept is correct is too low for the motor process to safely use). Hardware or dedicated diagnostic software can short-circuit the detection process. If an explicit error is detected, perceptual processing for the behavior is immediately suspended, and the associated recovery scheme implemented (if any) or control is passed to the exception handler.

The exception handling module is global. It relies on the Exception Handling Knowledge Structure (EHKS) to provide it with the relevant data about the sensing failure and the task. The EHKS, shown in Figure 2, is a frame with six slots. The **failure step slot** is a flag that describes whether the failure occurred at what stage of execution. The **errors** slot gives the failure condition encountered. The **bodies of evidence** slot is list of frames, each of which holds data from each description in the logical sensor. The **environmental pre-conditions** slot also holds a list of frames, each of which describe the attribute of the environment (if any) which serves as a pre-condition for using that sensor, the expected value of the environmental attribute for acceptable performance of the sensors, and pointers to other sensors which share the same environmental pre-condition. The EKHS contains this so it can challenge the environmental pre-conditions.

The hypotheses take the form that a particular description or logical sensor has failed. The failure conditions describe if the failure occurred during the collection step, the pre-processing step, or the fusion step, along with what type of failure occurred. If the failure occurred during the collection step or the pre-processing step, then individual suspect bodies of evidence are directly known; otherwise, all bodies of evidence are considered suspect.

Once the suspect descriptions have been identified, the actual list of tests is generated. The tests are used to determine the specific cause of the error by investigating potential sensor malfunctions and environmental changes. Generating the test list requires deciding which environmental conditions need to be tested, based on which descriptions are suspect. Because the environmental pre-conditions may hold different attribute values for each sensor, an environmental change can affect some sensors, but not others. Also, because challenging environmental pre-conditions may require additional sensing, the system must be certain that the sensor to be used for additional sensing is operating nominally. Thus, a sensor diagnostic must be run before collecting additional sensor data.

The test list is generated by initially checking if any descriptions in the **Affected Sensors** slot of an environmental frame and in the sensing plan contribute a suspect body of evidence. If so, and no sensing is required to acquire data to determine the value of the desired environmental attribute, then the environmental pre-condition challenge is added to the test list. If additional sensing is required to challenge an environmental pre-condition, then a diagnostic for the sensor which performs the additional sensing is added to the test list *in front of* the environmental pre-condition challenge. Finally, duplicate sensor diagnostic routines are removed from the list, if present. Each test list item contains identification of the test and indicates if the test is for an environmental change, a sensor diagnostic for a sensor contributing a body of evidence, or a sensor diagnostic for an environmental sensor.

Demonstrations

The current version of SFX-EH has been transferred to *Clementine*, a Denning MRV-4 mobile robot, shown in Figure 3 and demonstrated for landmark navigation using redundant sensors. The objective was to show the operation of the classification and recovery scheme for all types of failures in a realistic setting.

The behavior used for this demonstration was **move-to-goal(goal=purple-square)**, where the goal was a purple square landmark. The behavior was purely reactive; the robot had no a priori knowledge of its relative position. The presence of the landmark in the image elicited a constant attraction potential field. Two logical sensors were available for perceiving the purple square. The default logical sensor consisted of one description taken from the color video camera mounted on front of the robot (camera 0). The landmark was represented by two features: the intensity values in HSV space corresponding to that shade of "purple", and shape via the Hu invariant spatial moments (Pratt 1991). The belief in the landmark was computed as how well the Hu spatial moments of a candidate "purple" region matched the

a.

b.

c.

Figure 3: Landmark navigation: a.) Initiating sensor malfunction by covering camera b.) Recovery by turning to alternative sensor (shown in mid turn) c.) Resumption of behavior and completion of task.

```
** STARTING ERROR CLASSIFICATION **
Body of evidence 0: Sensor type is color camcorder

STEP 1: Identification of suspect bodies of evidence
Pre-processing errors discovered
Suspect body of evidence: 0
This BOE did not report missing data

STEP 2: Generation of candidate hypotheses (tests)
Building test list.
        Color camera diagnostic:
        This is an environmental sensor diagnostic.
        Check intensity:
        This test challenges an environmental pre'cond.
        Color camera diagnostic:
        This is a suspect sensor diagnostic for sensor number 0.
        Check intensity:
        This is a suspect sensor diagnostic for sensor number 0.
Done building test list.

STEP 3: Execution of tests

        Test 1: This is a color video hardware diagnostic function.
                to see if any good color cameras exist.
                Testing color sensor number 0 which was marked good...
                Found a good color sensor, number 0. Ok to run other tests.

        Test 2: This is to find out if any color sensor reports good intensity.
                Color sensor 0 reports below minimum intensity threshold.
                Environmental intensity is ok, detected with sensor 1.

== CONFIRMED TEST LIST ======
Color camera error
==============================
** ERROR CLASSIFICATION COMPLETE **
** STARTING ERROR RECOVERY ********
Recovery 1
   Original sensing plan:
      description 0: sensor number 0, named Sony- Videocam

Performing color video hardware error recovery.
  REPLACING sensor number 0 with sensor number 1

Repaired sensing plan
Description 0: sensor number 1, named Sony- Videocam
** ERROR RECOVERY COMPLETE **
```

Figure 4: Abbreviated output from SFX-EH.

landmark model. The alternative logical sensor applied the same algorithms but used the color video camera mounted on the rear of the robot (camera 1). While the logical sensors are redundant in terms of the type of information they produce, the robot must face backwards in order to use camera 1 for landmark navigation.

In each run, the robot was placed in an open area within 25 feet of the purple-square landmark. Depending on the purpose of the demonstration, the robot may or may not have been placed facing the landmark. As the robot made progress towards the landmark, a failure would be introduced. Sensor malfunctions were introduced by pulling the video cable out of a camera and putting a box over one camera to simulate a problem with the optics. Turning out the lights, an environmental change, was simulated by putting boxes over both cameras simultaneously. An errant expectation was generated by moving the landmark in the middle of a run or orienting the robot where it was not seeing the landmark.

Figure 3 shows instances from a typical sequence; the corresponding output of SFX-EH is in Figure 4. In Fig. 3a. the robot is making normal progress towards the landmark using the default logical sensor as a graduate student is about to place a box over the camera to simulate a sensor malfunction (e.g., dirt on the lens). In Fig. 3b. the robot has halted while it generates hypotheses and tests them. It uses the video camera in the rear to attempt to establish whether an environmental change has occurred. If so, both cameras should report images with a high average intensity level. The output of the two cameras does not agree; camera 1 shows no indication of an environmental change but camera 0 does. Since the cameras are mounted on the same small robot, it is unlikely that only one camera would be affected by an environmental change. Therefore, SFX-EH concludes that camera 0, or its software, has become defective and must be replaced. Fig. 3c. shows the robot resuming progress towards the landmark, but turned 180° in order to use the alternative logical sensor. The sign of the motor commands are automatically reversed when camera 1 is the "leader;" other behaviors which depend on the direction of motion receive the reversed commands.

Conclusions and On-going Work

The Generate and Test approach taken by SFX-EH has several advantages. It requires only a partial causal model of sensing failure, and that partial causal model is based on interactions between physical sensors and the environment, rather than limited to models of how the sensors respond for a task, which are difficult to acquire. This is expected to allow the problem solving knowledge associated with a specific physical sensor configuration to be portable to other tasks. The classification process can be short-circuited when all causes of a symptom have the same recovery scheme. The construction of tests takes into account possible confounding from other failed sensors, adding more reliability to the classification and recovery process, plus preventing cycles in testing. Unlike previous systems, the tests themselves can extract information from complementary sensors. The logical sensor organization allows exception handling to be interfaced with the behavioral level of existing robot architectures.

SFX-EH has two disadvantages. The most significant is that the hypotheses and tests are based on domain-dependent knowledge, not purely general purpose problem solving skills. The basic structure can be ported to new applications, but new knowledge will have to be added. However, most of the domain-dependent knowledge is portable because the knowledge base is organized around sensor interactions, not a casual model of the sensors for a specific behavior. For example, a change in the environment can be confirmed with a redundant sensor regardless of what the robot was attempting to perceive prior to the failure. The addition of general problem solving strategies and a learning mechanism, such as

Case-Based Learning, is being considered. Second, the logical sensor representation allows rapid generation of a small set of tests and ease of generation, but introduces other problems due to coarse granularity and a possible lack of available alternate logical sensors. However, these problems, especially the issue of when to re-consider a "bad" physical sensor, appear to be tractable and will be addressed in future refinements of SFX-EH.

The demonstrations provided additional insights and directions for future research. A practical issue is when to retry a sensor that has been identified as "bad." It should also be noted that experience with SFX-EH has shown that the testing, not the problem space search needed for hypothesis generation, is the bottleneck in recovering from a sensing failure. Part of this experience is due to the small set of possible hypotheses implemented at this time. But a large part of the rapid generation of hypotheses is due to a) the category of sensing failure indexing the classifier into the subspace of potentially applicable hypotheses and b) the coarse granularity of the failure modes.

SFX-EH currently lacks the ability to resolve resource contention due to active perception demands and does not update the sensing status to other behaviors. These issues are being actively addressed by the addition of a global event-driven sensing manager. The utility of the SFX-EH style of classification and recovery is not limited to AMR; SFX-EH is currently being applied to intelligent process control for power generation as well.

Acknowledgments

This research is supported in part by NSF Grant IRI-9320318, ARPA Grant AO#B460, and NASA/JSC Contract NAS.9-19040. The authors would like to thank Greg Chavez for his original research efforts, Elizabeth Nitz for coding a previous version of SFX-EH and the Hu moments, and the anonymous reviewers.

References

Bajcsy, R. 1988. Active perception. *Proceedings of IEEE* 76(8):886–1005.

Brooks, R. A. 1986. A robust layered control system for a mobile robot. *IEEE Journal of Robotics and Automation* RA-1(1):1–10.

Chavez, G., and Murphy, R. 1993. Exception handling for sensor fusion. In *SPIE Sensor Fusion VI*, 142–153.

Ferrell, C. 1993. *Robust Agent Control of an Autonomous Robot with Many Sensors and Actuators.* M.S. Dissertation, Department of Electrical Engineering and Computer Science, MIT.

Hanks, S., and Firby, R. 1990. Issues and architectures for planning and execution. In *Proceedings of a Workshop on Innovative Approaches to Planning, Scheduling and Control*, 59–70.

Henderson, T., and Grupen, R. 1990. Logical behaviors. *Journal of Robotic Systems* 7(3):309–336.

Henderson, T., and Shilcrat, E. 1984. Logical sensor systems. *Journal of Robotic Systems* 1(2):169–193.

Howe, A., and Cohen, P. 1990. Responding to environmental change. In *Proceedings of a Workshop on Innovative Approaches to Planning, Scheduling and Control*, 85–92.

Hughes, K. 1993. Sensor confidence in sensor integration tasks: A model for sensor performance measurement. In *SPIE Applications of Artificial Intelligence XI: Machine Vision and Robotics*, 169–193.

Lindsay, R.; Buchanan, E.; Feigenbaum, E.; and Lederberg, J. 1980. *Applications of Artificial Intelligence for Organic Chemistry: The Dendral Project.* New York: McGraw-Hill.

Murphy, R., and Arkin, R. 1992. Sfx: An architecture for action-oriented sensor fusion. In *1992 IEEE/RSJ International Conference on Intelligent Robots and Systems (IROS)*, 225–250.

Murphy, R. 1992. *An Architecture for Intelligent Robotic Sensor Fusion.* Ph.D. Dissertation, College of Computing, Georgia Institute of Technology. GIT-ICS-92/42.

Noreils, F., and Chatila, R. 1995. Plan execution monitoring and control architecture for mobile robots. *IEEE Transactions on Robotics and Automation* 11(2):255–266.

Payton, D.; Keirsey, D.; Kimble, D.; Krozel, J.; and Rosenblat, J. 1992. Do whatever works: A robust approach to fault-tolerant autonomous control. *Journal of Applied Intelligence* 2:225–250.

Pratt, W. 1991. *Digital Image Processing, 2nd ed.* New York: Wiley.

Simmons, R., and Davis, R. 1987. Generate test and debug: Combining associational rules and causal models. In *Proceedings of 10th International Joint Conference on Artificial Intelligence*, 1071–1078.

Velde, W. V., and Carignan, C. 1984. Number and placement of control system components considering possible failures. *Journal of Guidance and Control* 7(6):703–709.

Weller, G.; Groen, F.; and Hertzberger, L. 1989. A sensor processing model incorporating error detection and recovery. In Henderson, T., ed., *Traditional and Non-traditional Robotic Sensors.* Maratea, Italy: Springer-Verlag. 225–250.

GARGOYLE: An Environment for Real-Time, Context-Sensitive Active Vision

Peter N. Prokopowicz, Michael J. Swain, R. James Firby, and Roger E. Kahn

Department of Computer Science
University of Chicago
1100 East 58th Street
Chicago, IL 60637
peterp@cs.uchicago.edu, swain@cs.uchicago.edu, firby@cs.uchicago.edu, kahn@cs.uchicago.edu

Abstract

Researchers in robot vision have access to several excellent image processing packages (e.g., Khoros, Vista, Susan, MIL, and XVision to name only a few) as a base for any new vision software needed in most navigation and recognition tasks. Our work in automonous robot control and human-robot interaction, however, has demanded a new level of run-time flexibility and performance: on-the-fly configuration of visual routines that exploit up-to-the-second context from the task, image, and environment. The result is Gargoyle: an extendible, on-board, real-time vision software package that allows a robot to configure, parameterize, and execute image-processing pipelines at run-time. Each operator in a pipeline works at a level of resolution and over regions of interest that are computed by upstream operators or set by the robot according to task constraints. Pipeline configurations and operator parameters can be stored as a library of visual methods appropriate for different sensing tasks and environmental conditions. Beyond this, a robot may reason about the current task and environmental constraints to construct novel visual routines that are too specialized to work under general conditions, but that are well-suited to the immediate environment and task. We use the RAP reactive plan-execution system to select and configure pre-compiled processing pipelines, and to modify them for specific constraints determined at run-time.

Introduction

The Animate Agent Project at the University of Chicago is an on-going effort to explore the mechanisms underlying intelligent, goal-directed behavior. Our research strategy is centered on the development of an autonomous robot that performs useful tasks in a real environment, with natural human instruction and feedback, as a way of researching the links between perception, action, and intelligent control. Robust and timely perception is fundamental to the intelligent behavior we are working to achieve.

As others have done before us (Bajcsy 1988; Ullman 1984; Chapman 1991; Ballard 1991; Aloimonos 1990), we have observed that a tight link between the perceptual and control systems enables perception to be well tuned to the context: the task, environment, and state of the perceiving agent (or robot in our case). As a result, perception can be more robust and efficient, and in addition these links can provide elegant solutions to issues such as grounding symbols in plans of the control system.

Our computer vision research concerns the problems of *identifying* relevant contextual constraints that can be brought to bear on our more or less traditional computer vision problems, and *applying* these constraints effectively in a real-time system. We have demonstrated that certain vision problems which have proven difficult or intractable can be solved robustly and efficiently if enough is known about the specific contexts in which they occur (Prokopowicz, Swain, & Kahn 1994; Firby *et al.* 1995). This context includes what the robot is trying to do, its current state, and its knowledge of what it expects to see in this situation. The difficulty lies not so much identifying the types of knowledge that can be used in different situations, but in applying that knowledge to the quick and accurate interpretation of images.

Our most important techniques in this regard so far have been the use of several low-level image cues to select regions of interest before applying expensive operators, and the ability of the robot to tune its vision software parameters during execution, according to what it knows about the difficulty or time-constraints of the problem. For example, one of the visual routines for object search that we have developed (Firby *et al.* 1995) can use a color model of the object to restrict search to areas where it is more likely to be found, prior to edge matching. The edge matcher is restricted by knowledge of the size of the object, and what is known about its likely orientations and locations. As another example, when tracking an object, the robot lowers the level of resolution at which images are processed to speed processing and thereby improve eye-body or eye-hand coordination. The loss of acuity is acceptable because the improved focus of attention created by tight tracking greatly reduces the number of false matches that might otherwise result from degraded inputs.

We would like to push the use of context much further. For example, as the robot moves closer to an object that it is tracking, it should be able to adjust the level of resolution downward. Also, if the robot needs to do a number of visual tasks at once (e.g., "free-space" obstacle avoidance and target tracking) it could tune each algorithm for improved speed, at the cost of some accuracy. These are two examples of using *task context* to improve visual performance. We can also gain from using *environmental context.* For example, the robot could decide which low-level cues it will use for determining regions of interest, according to feedback from the visual routines about the usefulness of the cues in a previous scene, or perhaps from long-term knowledge or short term memory of what is likely to be around it. The visual interest cues provide *image context* that not only can be used to limit computation to a part of the scene, but that places geometric constraints about how an object can appear if it is to be in a certain region of the image. In general, careful restriction of viewpoint search based on image location may ameliorate the inherent combinatorics of most general purpose model-matching algorithms.

We want to make it possible for a robot to construct, at run time, from a fixed set of visual operators, a visual routine appropriate for the current goal, and adapt it on-the-fly to the state of the task and environment. The routine itself would exploit appropriate low-level cues to reduce the aspects of the scene under consideration.

Gargoyle: Run-time configurable pipelines for active vision

In developing Gargoyle, one of our aims is to provide *composability* that is available in most vision software packages, but not at the overhead required by these packages. For example, Khoros' Cantata is an interpreter that can combine operators into new routines at run-time. Unfortunately Cantata's design is not suited for real-time processing, mainly because it uses expensive inter-process communication to pass copies of images from one module to another. Xvision (Hager & Toyama 1994) allows new operators to be derived very flexibly from others, but requires new C++ classes and recompilation to use them.

Although no vision software package provides the performance and run-time flexibility we seek, we don't want to write an entirely new system if there is one that provides an adequate base. We have chosen the Teleos AVP vision system[1], which provides low-level real-time image processing, because it is designed for high performance, and is supported on a standard Windows NT platform.

Gargoyle is a multithreaded, multiprocessing Java program that calls external C or C++ functions for most image processing. It augments the Teleos AVP vision library to provide the kinds of visual routines an autonomous mobile robot needs for navigation, target recognition and manipulation, and human-computer interaction, and is extendible to other tasks.

Gargoyle provides a run-time interpreter that allows dynamic configuration of image-processing pipelines. The pipelines constitute visual routines for accomplishing specific visual goals. Gargoyle includes a set of visual operator modules that are composed into pipelines, and it can be extended with new modules.

The pipelines are constructed out of linked image-processing and computer vision modules. In a graphical representation of a visual routine in Gargoyle such as is shown in Figure 1, images and regions of interest (ROI) can be thought of as flowing one-way along the links. A feature of the Gargoyle runtime system is that no unnecessary copying is done when executing these pipelines. Images can be tagged with viewer state information that can be used to translate from image to world coordinates.

Gargoyle communicates with a robot control system (we use the RAP reactive plan-execution system (Firby *et al.* 1995)) via string messages. There are command messages sent to Gargoyle for constructing, reconfiguring, and executing pipelines. Gargoyle returns messages that contain the results from pipeline execution, and error conditions from modules within a pipeline.

Data structures and processing modules

Gargoyle defines two basic data structures, images and regions of interest, and provides a set of vision modules that process images within regions of interest. This section describes the image and ROI data structures, and the vision modules we provide.

ROI: Regions of Interest

The **ROI** defines a rectangular area in an image, and specifies a level of resolution as an integer subsampling factor. Optionally, individual pixels with the region may be masked out. ROIs are used to restrict subsequent image processing to the given area. They are

[1] http://www.teleos.com

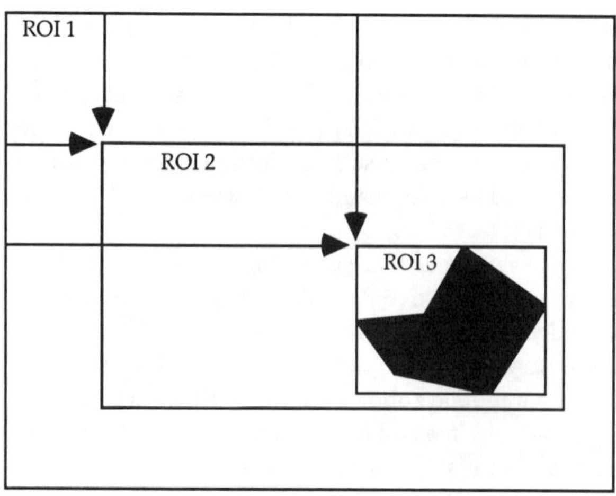

Figure 1: Region and sub-region of interest within full field of view. Offsets defining a region are always with respect to full field of view. Regions are rectangles with optional binary masks.

also used to annotate image buffers with information about the source of the data in the image.

A ROI is specified with respect to a full size, high-resolution image area, whose upper left pixel is indexed at $(0,0)$ (Figure 1). A region is defined by its offsets, measured in pixels from the upper left corner of the full field of view, and its width and height. Regions of interest are created from other regions by specifying the offset and size of the subregion within the larger region. If the larger region was itself a subregion, *its* offsets are added to the new offsets, so that all ROIs remain in a canonical coordinate system.

ROIs may also include a binary 2-D mask for defining regions that are not rectangular. There are methods to initialize the mask to the entire region or to a pre-defined mask, empty it, and add or remove pixels from it. ROI objects also provide iterators that sequentially return each location in the region, whether it is a simple rectangular region or an arbitrary set of pixels in a mask.

Calibrated regions of interest

Regions of interest can be calibrated with an object that describes the viewer's (i.e., camera's) location and pose in a world coordinate system. The calibrated ROI class is derived from the ROI class and adds camera height, location, viewing angles, magnification, real clock time, and a flag to indicate if the camera is in motion. To get this information, Gargoyle calls a global function called **viewerState**, with a single parameter for the camera number in a multiple camera system,

From	To
monocular image point	3D line of sight
stereo image point pair	3D world location
3D world location	image point
3D world volume or plane	image region

Table 1: Calibration functions

whenever image data is created (see Feature Maps, below). The Gargoyle user must replace this function with one that can query the robot control system for its current location, bearing, and the position and magnification of the camera if these are adjustable. The values are simply stored with the region of interest. Since images also define regions of interest, any image can be annotated with viewer state information.

Gargoyle includes a camera model class that can be parameterized for different cameras. The model can convert from image coordinates into lines of sight and back, and, if an image is annotated with viewer state information, image locations and regions can be converted into real world locations and regions, as listed in table 1. Finally, Gargoyle can generate image ROIs corresponding to volumes in real-world coordinates, using the current viewer state. This is needed in order for the robot to give hints about where the visual system should look for an object. For example, if the task is to clean up trash from the floor, then the visual system only needs to look in the parts of the image that correspond to the floor and some small height above it. If the cameras are tilted down so that only the floor is visible, the ROI generated will include the entire image, but if the camera needs to be raised slightly for some other purpose, or can't be moved, image processing will still take place only where it makes sense for the current task.

Image buffers

Image buffers hold one or three-band images, and are defined as a C++ template class. The class provides methods only for pixel access, reading and writing to disk, and setting a color space tag. A visual processing module is available to convert images from one color space to another.

Image buffers inherit from the calibrated region of interest class, above. The ROI defines the source region of the image with respect to the maximum field of view. It also indicates if the pixel data represents a subsampling of full-resolution data. If the viewer state global function is redefined for the robot, the image will be annotated with the camera's position. If this information is not available, the image is simply

Map	Output	Parameters
Color	3bnd int.	color space
Gray scale	1bnd int.	none
Contrast	1bnd signed	filter size
Edge	1bnd binary	filter size
Motion	1bnd int.	max. movement
Disparity	1bnd int.	max. disp.
Frame diff.	1bnd signed	interval

Table 2: Gargoyle input modules or feature maps. Outputs (1 or 3 band images) are processed as inputs by other modules in a pipeline.

stamped with the time it was taken and the camera number. Images, including viewer state information, can be written to disk, so that real experiments can be replayed later. This makes it possible to debug an experiment any time after it takes place.

Visual processing operators

The processing modules which comprise every visual routine fall into three general categories, based on the type of links into and out of the operators. *Feature maps* provide system input. In a pipeline they take no image input, but have an optional ROI input, and produce an image buffer as output. *Segmenters* take an image and optional ROI input, and produce an ROI output. *Processors* take image and ROI inputs, and may produce an image output. They also may send result messages to the robot control system. The bulk of image processing and computer vision modules are processors in this scheme.

Feature Map Modules Feature maps get input from the cameras. For efficiency and programming simplicity, Gargoyle provides a small set of modules that interface to the underlying image processing system (Teleos AVP). These modules provide the input to all pipelines, and are often used by several visual routines that execute simultaneously. To efficiently share information about features, and to keep inputs to separately executing routines in synchronization, the lowest level of the Gargoyle system is a fixed set of image feature map modules. Since these modules include color and grayscale images, users can perform any type of image processing by starting with these, and adding new processing modules (see below).

The set of feature maps is determined by the underlying AVP hardware and libraries. The Gargoyle user is not expected to add new feature maps. The feature maps available are shown in table 2. Figure 2 shows the contents of an edge feature map.

Figure 2: top: gray-scale image; second: binary edge image; third: color histogram back-projection of a picture of a brown trash can, bottom: rectangular regions-of-interest around local peaks

Segmentation and Region of Interest Modules These modules split an image into one or more regions for further processing. The output is a *stream* of ROIs. Some modules may use the optional image mask to define nonrectangular ROIs. Typically, the ROI stream is passed to a cropping module which produces a stream of sub-images corresponding to the ROIs. This image stream is then piped into other modules for processing. The segmentation and ROI-generating modules standard in Gargoyle are listed in table 3.

In figure 2, the local peak segmenter finds local peaks in an intensity image, which in this case is a color histogram back-projection image. The peaks must be separated by a minimum distance, which is a parameter of the module. The peaks are bounded with rectangles whose edges are determined by where the intensity image falls below a threshold fraction of the local peak value, measured along horizontal and vertical lines through the local peak point. The threshold fraction is another parameter of the module.

The connected component segmenter uses image morphology operations to find connected or nearly connected binary image segments of sufficient size. Each connected component generates a rectangular ROI with a binary mask that gives the exact shape of the segment. Subsequent image processing would normally use the ROI pixel iterator to step through only the pixels in the segment. This is how, for example, the average intensity of an arbitrary segment would be computed.

The tracker module tracks the location defined by ROIs as they come into the module, and generates a prediction of the next ROI it will see. Since each ROI is stamped with the time that it was produced (from a feature map, originally), the tracker knows how fast the ROI is moving in image coordinates. It also can compute when the next ROI will likely be produced, because it tracks the time intervals between successive inputs. The output is a predicted ROI which can be used to direct perception toward where a moving object will likely be next.

The world volume ROI module produces an image ROI corresponding to a rectangular volume in the world. The volume is set from the robot control system as parameters of the module. The module does not take any input from the pipeline. This module requires a user supplied viewer state function, and camera parameters (see Calibrated ROIs, above). If the world volume described does not project into image based on the current viewer state, an empty stream of ROIs will be generated.

The set operation module combines two ROIs into one, using the intersection, union, and subtraction operators.

ROI module	Pipe In	Parameters
Local peaks	scalar img	thr, min sep
Conn comp	bin img	max gap, min area
Tracker	ROI	smoothing rate
World vol	calib. ROI	rect vol
ROI comb	ROI a, b	set op ($\cap, \cup, -$)

Table 3: Region of interest and segmentation modules. Each module produces a ROI or stream of ROIs for further processing.

Filter module	Input	Output	Parameters
Threshold	img	bin img	thr
Convolution	img	img	kernel
Warp	img	img	interp func
Frame avg.	img	img	interval
Color conv.	img	img	color space
Back-proj.	3bnd img	img	color hist
Cropper	img	img	none
Lines	img	bin img	thr, min seg

Table 4: Image filtering modules. Outputs from these modules are images that are processed as pipeline inputs by other modules.

Processing modules The processing modules comprise the bulk of the Gargoyle system. There are filtering modules for processing images into other images, and recognition and measurement modules for finding objects or calculating properties of the scene. The filter modules currently in use are shown in table 4. These are largely self-explanatory. The color back-projection module produces an intensity image whose pixel values indicate the "saliency" of the corresponding color image's pixel as an indicator of the presence of a known colored object (Swain & Ballard 1991). New filters are easily added using a C++ template class.

Recognition and measurement modules implement computer vision algorithms, which can be very complex. In keeping with our research strategy we have tried to use well-established algorithms and software when possible. The modules we have incorporated so far are listed in table 5. These modules normally produce results that need to be returned to the robot control system, rather than an image that is sent further along the pipeline. Table 5 shows the messages that are sent back to the control system.

New algorithms can be added using a template class. The programmer has access to an input image with a pixel-access iterator that will step through the image.

Module	Input	Signal	Params
templ match	bin img	target loc	model, thr
pat match	bin img	target loc	model, thr
free-space	bin img	ranges	resolution

Table 5: Computer vision modules. The outputs of these modules encode answers to perceptual queries and are transmitted as signals to the RAP system

If the image is calibrated with viewer state information, the algorithm can use image point-to-world-line functions (table 1) to get information about where the image points may come from. For example, we find the lines of sight corresponding to the highest and lowest parts of the image, and intersect those lines with the plane of the floor to determine how far away an object in the image could be if it is assumed to be on the floor. This is used to control the viewpoint search in the Hausdorff template matching algorithm.

Visual routines as pipelined processes

Consider a visual routine for finding objects that we use frequently in our research. This routine searches for an object by shape, matching a library of edge models against an edge image. Other binary models and images could be used instead of edges. The model database contains different views of the object, which are needed to the extent that the object's surface is not planar or circularly symmetric. The search algorithm (Huttenlocher & Rucklidge 1992) translates, scales, and skews the models as it searches through the space of possible viewpoints. The viewpoint space can be controlled through parameters depending on the task context and knowledge of where the object might be, as well as through calibrated image context as described above.

Searching across a large space of viewpoints is expensive; with a cluttered, high resolution (roughly .25 megapixel) image, searching from all frontal viewpoints between, for example, 0.5 to 5 meters, for a single model, takes over a minute on Sun Sparcstation 20. To reduce the space of possible viewpoints, we restrict the search to areas of the scene containing colors found in the model. This requires a color model of the object, which is represented as a 256 bin histogram of an 8-bit color-resolution image of the object. The 8-bits could represent, for example, 4 bits of hue, 4 bits of saturation, and 0 bits of value (a distribution we have found effective).

Figure 3 shows the processing pipeline that implements the routine. Two feature maps generate input simultaneously, or as close together as the underlying

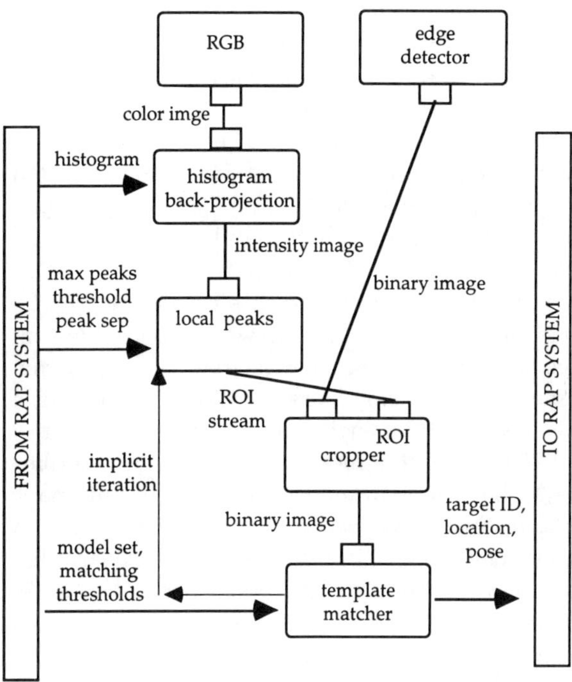

Figure 3: An image processing pipeline for finding objects by shape, using color as an interest cue.

hardware allows. The RGB map is piped into a color histogram back-projection module. The RGB map can be parameterized with a low-resolution (subsampled) ROI so that the output image is very small and later segmentation is fast. The edge detector can also be operated at different levels of resolution according to how large and nearby the object is expected to be. The modules need not operate at the same resolution.

The color histogram back-projection output is piped into the local peak segmenter to generate regions of interest where the object could possibly be found. The output of the local peak module is a stream of ROIs. The interpreter processes the stream by marking the module as the head of an *implicit iteration loop*. Each ROI in the stream is then processed separately by the next module. When the pipeline bottoms out, that is, no more links exist, or a module finishes processing without generating an output image, the interpreter returns to the nearest upstream iteration head, and continues processing with the next ROI. After the last ROI is processed, a special end-of-stream ROI is sent to the next module and the interpreter notes not to return for processing. Most modules do nothing but pass the end-of-stream markers on. Others may process a stream of ROIs and wait for the end-of-stream indicator to perform a calculation based on the entire stream of inputs. The hausdorff template matcher is one such module, as we will see.

The ROI stream from the local peak segmenter passes into the cropper, which also receives an image input from the edge detector. The cropper produces a binary subimage from the edge image for each ROI passed in. The resolution of the binary image is preserved, even though the ROI may be at a lower resolution.

The template matcher searches each image for instances of its models. The viewpoint search is controlled according to parameters from the robot control system, which may know how far away the object should be, and by inferring the possible viewpoint of the object if it is to appear in the image, as described earlier. The template matcher runs in several search modes, in that it can report an answer as soon as it finds any match, or wait until the stream of images has been processed to return the best match. When the robot receives an answer from the module, it can tell the interpreter to halt further execution of the pipeline.

Toward more flexible visual routines

Pipeline configurations and the parameters for their operators can be stored as a library of visual methods appropriate for different sensing tasks and environmental conditions. We use the RAP system to store the configuration commands for constructing pipelines. Visual routines, then, are represented as RAP plans for achieving particular perceptual goals.

On-the-fly pipeline reconfiguration

One somewhat more flexible routine we are developing uses two low-level cues, motion and color, for following a person (Prokopowicz, Swain, & Kahn 1994). A RAP encodes the connections for a simple pipeline to track an object by motion or color. The encoding is sent to GARGOYLE to build the pipeline. The pipeline is very simple to begin with: a motion map is piped into the local peak segmenter, which finds sufficiently large areas of motion. These are piped into a ROI tracker module. A color feature map is also created and piped into a histogram backprojector. This feature map is initially turned off to save processing power. GARGOYLE will not execute a pipeline whose input is off. The RAP is sketched in Figure 4.

If more than one moving area is segmented, the tracker module will follow the largest one, but will also send a warning message (:no-target or :multiple-target), which the GARGOYLE interpreter sends to the RAP system. Likewise, if no region is found, a warning is sent. The RAP level is where the knowledge for how to track an object under different conditions is encoded. In this case, the RAP responds to the warning by instructing the GARGOYLE interpreter to reconfigure the pipeline so that a different module is used as input to the segmenter. If the RAP used the motion map the last time, it will use color and histogram backprojection. Of course, flipping between two modes of segmentation is only the simplest example of run-time flexibility. We feel that GARGOYLE provides the basis for flexible real-time vision, and that a high-level planning system like RAPs provides the reasoning and knowledge representation capacity needed to exploit that flexibility in much more interesting and powerful ways.

```
(define-rap
 (track-motion-or-color ?target-name ?color-model)

 (init (pipeline-create 1
    (1 motion-feature-map RESLEVEL1)
    (2 local-peak-segment MINPEAK MINSEP)
    (3 ROI-tracker)
    (4 RGB-feature-map)
    (5 histogram-BP ?color-model RESLEVEL2)
    (1 into 2)
    (2 into 3)
    (4 into 5)
    (4 off)
    (1 off)))

// track by motion
 (method (context (not track-by color))
    (pipeline-config 1 (1 into 2) (1 on))
    (pipeline-execute 1)
    (wait-for (:object-at ?x ?y)
      (mem-set target-at ?target-name ?x ?y))
    (wait-for (or (:no-target) (:multiple-target))
      (pipeline-config 1 (1 off))    // stop pipe
      (mem-del track-by motion)      // use color
      (mem-add track-by color)))     // next time

      // track by color
 (method (context (track-by color))
   (pipeline-config 1 (5 into 2) (4 on))
   (pipeline-execute 1)
   (wait-for (:object-at ?x ?y)
     (mem-set target-at ?target-name ?x ?y))
   (wait-for (or (:no-target) (:multiple-target))
   (pipeline-config 1 (4 off))       // stop pipe
     (mem-del track-by color)        // use motion
     (mem-add track-by motion))))    // next time
```

Figure 4: RAP that constructs and modifies visual routine for flexible tracking using color and motion cues.

Because Gargoyle is a single process, creating and linking a module into a pipeline only involves adding an entry to the current configuration graph in memory. Executing a module requires spawning a new thread, which is also a very fast operation. The interpreter runs as a separate thread and accepts messages from the skill processes asynchronously, so it can respond immediately to requests to reconfigure, reparameterize, or control execution, even during image processing.

Related work

Ullman proposed that visual routines (Ullman 1984) which answer specific perceptual questions concerning shape and geometric relationships can be constructed out of elemental visual operators and control structures. Our work is fundamentally similar, but explores the issues that come up when these ideas are extended to a real-time active system that is interacting with its environment. In particular, it emphasizes the need for different ways to compute the same result, depending on the immediate context.

The Perseus vision system (Kahn & Swain 1995) is being developed at the University of Chicago to augment human-computer interaction through gestures such as pointing. Perseus is currently implemented with the DataCube server as the underlying visual processor. Perseus is based on the notion of active visual objects, or markers, that are spawned to recognize and track relevant parts of a scene, such as a person's head and hands. One of the Gargoyle design goals was to provide a platform to support Perseus on a visual robot. The markers will be implemented as RAPs that construct image pipelines for recognition and tracking. Gesture recognition is carried out by a higher-level visual routine that spawns markers and monitors their locations, looking for certain configurations that indicate human gestures.

Horswill has shown that it is possible to translate a Horn clause into a custom program, written in a "visual-computer assembly language", that attempts to satisfy the clause. The operators of this assembly language are much more primitive than what most robot researchers would like to use, and the underlying hardware (the Polly robot) is not in widespread use. Gargoyle will provide ourselves and other robotic researchers with the means for writing visual programs in a high-level language, using the best computer vision algorithms and software as operators, on standard PC hardware.

Conclusion

Gargoyle will provide us with a tool that is sufficiently flexible to create much more specialized and efficient visual routines that are adapted to solve specific tasks, and fully exploit run-time context, with no significant cost in run-time efficiency. Because Gargoyle will run on a standard, multi-platform operating system, it can be easily and affordably ported to other systems, and will benefit from further advances in these platforms. Gargoyle's extendibility will allow it to be useful for other domains besides the mobile robot domain described here – we are already working towards its use in creating a human-computer interface for a virtual reality environment.

References

Aloimonos, J. 1990. Purposive and qualitative active vision. In *International Conference on Pattern Recognition*, 346–360.

Bajcsy, R. 1988. Active perception. *Proceedings of the IEEE* 76:996–1005.

Ballard, D. H. 1991. Animate vision. *Artificial Intelligence* 48:57–86.

Chapman, D. 1991. *Vision, Instruction, and Action.* MIT Press.

Firby, R. J.; Kahn, R. E.; Prokopowicz, P. N.; and Swain, M. J. 1995. An architecture for vision and action. In *Proceedings of the International Joint Conference on Artificial Intelligence.*

Hager, G. D., and Toyama, K. 1994. A framework for real-time window-based tracking using off-the-shelf hardware. Technical Report 0.95 Alpha, Yale University Computer Science Dept.

Huttenlocher, D. P., and Rucklidge, W. J. 1992. A multi-resolution technique for comparing images using the hausdorff distance. Technical Report CUCS TR 92-1321, Department of Computer Science, Cornell University.

Kahn, R. E., and Swain, M. J. 1995. Understanding people pointing: The Perseus system. In *Proceedings of the IEEE International Symposium on Computer Vision.*

Prokopowicz, P. N.; Swain, M. J.; and Kahn, R. E. 1994. Task and environment-sensitive tracking. In *Proceedings of the IAPR/IEEE Workshop on Visual Behaviors.*

Swain, M. J., and Ballard, D. H. 1991. Color indexing. *International Journal of Computer Vision* 7:11–32.

Ullman, S. 1984. Visual routines. *Cognition* 18:97–159.

Robot Navigation Using Image Sequences

Christopher Rasmussen and **Gregory D. Hager**

Department of Computer Science, Yale University
51 Prospect Street
New Haven, CT 06520-8285
rasmuss@powered.cs.yale.edu, hager@cs.yale.edu

Abstract

We describe a framework for robot navigation that exploits the continuity of image sequences. Tracked visual features both guide the robot and provide predictive information about subsequent features to track. Our hypothesis is that image-based techniques will allow accurate motion without a precise geometric model of the world, while using predictive information will add speed and robustness.

A basic component of our framework is called a *scene*, which is the set of image features stable over some segment of motion. When the scene changes, it is appended to a stored sequence. As the robot moves, correspondences and dissimilarities between current, remembered, and expected scenes provide cues to join and split scene sequences, forming a map-like directed graph. Visual servoing on features in successive scenes is used to traverse a path between robot and goal map locations.

In our framework, a human guide serves as a scene recognition oracle during a map-learning phase; thereafter, assuming a known starting position, the robot can independently determine its location without general scene recognition ability. A prototype implementation of this framework uses as features color patches, sum-of-squared differences (SSD) subimages, or image projections of rectangles.

Introduction

A robot whose duties include navigation may be called upon to perform them in many different environments. In such fluid situations, it is unlikely that a geometric model will always be available, and arranging and testing fiducial markers may be onerous or impossible. An attractive way to alter the job description of a navigating robot would be to simply "show" it the path(s) it should follow, and have it rely on its own sensing systems to develop an internal representation sufficient to allow repetition of the path within some bounds. Specific points of interest should be easy to indicate, although special locations (*e.g.* a delivery site) may be adorned with guide markers which can be used for precise position control once they are approached. Our aim is to develop a vision-based navigation system capable of such performance. Our choice of vision is based on the necessity of observing large areas to find useful landmarks for defining the path, and the need to distinguish them from one another as easily as possible.

Navigation depends on the notion of location, which can be characterized in a number of ways. Strictly metrical approaches describe it as a position in a fixed world coordinate system. The system in (Kosaka & Kak 1992) knows the environment's three-dimensional geometry and its initial position and orientation; the navigation task is to find a path to a goal position and orientation. Kalman filtering is used to reconstruct and predict the coordinates of model features, which are matched at regular intervals during motion. The sonar-based algorithm of (Leonard, Durrant-Whyte, & Cox 1990) builds its own map of beacons' absolute positions using Kalman filtering to account for uncertainty. Their mapping process is dynamic in that the robot constantly compares sensory evidence with expectations, and updates its map and/or position estimate when the two disagree. Prediction allows directed sensing: "knowing where to look" can improve the speed and reliability of the mapping process.

Graph-based techniques smear out exactness somewhat by relating position regions to nodes or "places" in a connectivity graph, and rely on closed-loop feedback to guide the robot from place to place. In (Taylor & Kriegman 1994) the model of the environment is a graph constructed while exploring, based on visibility of barcode landmarks. Similarly, in (Kortenkamp et al. 1992), (Kuipers & Byun 1981), and (Engelson 1994), the robot learns a model of the environment by building a graph based on topological connectivity of interesting locations, but it attempts to decide what constitute landmarks on its own. The robot in (Kortenkamp et al. 1992) learns the environment's topology from doorways detected by sonar while storing images for place recognition. The robot in (Kuipers & Byun 1981) uses sonar to detect places that maximize a distinctiveness function and to match or add them to its map. A disadvantage of graph-based approaches is their tendency to rely on a solution to the difficult problem of general place recognition.

We avoid reference to absolute coordinates by taking advantage of vision to define locations by the notion of view. A robot is at place A if what it sees corresponds to what can be seen at place A. Given that we know where we are, we use visual tracking to extend the definition of place to a range of motions, and require that all (or nearly all) of the world corresponds to some place. We then utilize the continuity of our representation to predict changes of view between places, thereby eliminating the need for a strong notion of recognition. Navigation then becomes a problem of moving from view to view. The desired motion is computed using visual feedback between what the robot currently sees, and what it saw when it was at the goal location before.

The work described in (Fennema et al. 1990) is similar to ours. They use a servoing approach to navigation, but with reference to an accurate geometric model of the environment which we do not assume. Navigation proceeds by identifying landmarks along a path through the graph that are visible from their predecessors, and servoing on them in succession via visual feedback. Recognizing landmarks is a matching problem between 2-D image data and the 3-D world model. Other route-based approaches to navigation are described in (Hong et al. 1992) and (Zheng & Tsuji 1992). The robots in these papers are guided in a learning stage through the environment, periodically storing whole panoramic images. A graph is built up by matching new images with the known corpus; paths can be planned in the completed graph with a standard algorithm. When executing a path, image-based servoing is used to traverse individual edge segments. (Kortenkamp et al. 1992) argue that taking snapshots at regular intervals leads to the storage of much unnecessary information. Moreover, new scenes must be matched against all remembered ones, an inefficient process. Our system addresses the first of these issues by finding image features and storing them only as frequently as necessary for servoing. We sidestep the place recognition problem with human assistance during a learning phase; general recognition ability is not needed during navigation.

Map Construction

In order to present our navigation system it is useful to first define some terminology and to sketch the procedure used to create the internal map used by the robot.

Terms

We use the term *marker* to denote any visual entity that is in some way distinctive or meaningful to the system. A marker is characterized by a set of relatively invariant properties (color, shape, texture, function) and a dynamic state (image location and size). Within most images there are many potential markers that can be discovered and analyzed; the current *scene* is the set of markers upon which the robot is currently focusing its attention. The question of what kind of visual entities will gain attention is left to the implementation, but these can run the gamut of complexity from chairs, doors, and trees to lines, points, and splotches of color. The limiting factors of the recognition process are sophistication and speed; these must be traded against the distinctiveness, trackability, and rarity of the markers thus found.

As an additional consideration, to successfully servo from one scene to another certain geometric constraints on the number and configuration of the markers in them must be met. These constraints vary according to what kinds of markers are used. As a shorthand, we will say that an evaluation function $C(s)$ returns a truth value T if scene s meets these criteria and F otherwise. Likewise, we shall say that two scenes, s_1 and s_2 are *equivalent*, $s_1 \equiv s_2$, if an abstract comparison function returns true. Intuitively, equivalency is measured by some matching function which is invariant over small changes in viewpoint caused by the motion of the robot. Furthermore, we say that the robot is viewing a previously stored scene s_i if $s_{viewed} \equiv s_i$, where s_{viewed} is the scene currently being viewed.

A *sequence* is an ordered list of scenes stored as the viewer moves through an environment. The currently-viewed scene is added to the current sequence when there is a *scene change*: here we use the occurrence of a marker appearing or disappearing to signal this. When a marker appears, the current scene is added. When a marker disappears, the last scene containing the disappearing marker is added. In essence, scenes serve as key frames for reconstructing movement later through visual servoing (Hutchinson, Hager, & Corke 1995).

A *location* is a set of two or more scenes from different sequences that are the same under the equivalency function; this is where sequences intersect. There are two kinds of locations: *divergences* and *convergences*.

A divergence is a choice point: multiple possible sequences can be followed away from a single scene. Convergences are scenes at which multiple sequences terminate. Since a scene can satisfy both of these definitions (where two corridors cross each other, for instance), the type assigned to a location can vary according to its place in the order of scenes encountered by the robot. The key quality of locations is that they are topologically meaningful events that can be recognized by the robot simply by keeping track of what it is seeing and what it remembers. A *map* is the directed graph consisting of all sequences recorded and all locations noted by the robot as it moves.

Map-Building

The state of the robot as it makes a map is described by the following variables: $\{S\}$, the set of sequences recorded so far; $\{L\}$, the set of known locations; S_{new}, the sequence the robot is in; $\{s_{possible}\}$, the set of scenes that the robot could be viewing; and s_{viewed}. s_i^* denotes the set of scenes reachable in one scene-step from s_i via the current map graph. Map-making begins with $\{S\} = \emptyset$; $\{L\} = \emptyset$; $S_{new} = ()$, the empty list; and $\{s_{possible}\} = \infty$, the set of all possible scenes. This corresponds to seeing *unfamiliar* scenery; *familiar* scenery is indicated when $\{s_{possible}\}$ has a finite number of members. When the robot is instructed to cease mapping, s_{viewed} is added to S_{new} and exploration halts. It is assumed that an exploration process that drives movement is running in the background. This could be the human guide suggested, a sonar-based obstacle avoidance routine, or any other desired program. While not finished, s_{viewed} is updated continually until $C(s_{viewed}) = F$; whenever s_{viewed} changes the steps in Figure 1 are executed.

The key question in this algorithm is the nature of the scene comparison function, with the additional problem of efficient image indexing to determine the confluence of sequences. We describe the current instantiation of equivalency in the Implementation section. For the moment, we rely on a human guide to inform the robot when a convergence or divergence has occurred, and hence do not need to solve the general indexing problem.

In Figure 2 the map-making process is illustrated for a sample environment. By continuing this process of exploration, the robot would eventually arrive at a complete map of the floor, but even in its intermediate forms it has partial usefulness. A more complete exposition is given in (Rasmussen & Hager 1996).

1. If unfamiliar, does $\exists\, s_i \in S_j = (s_0, \ldots, s_n)$ s.t. $s_{viewed} \equiv s_i$?
   (a) Yes (convergence):
      i. Add location $\{s_{viewed}, s_i\}$ to $\{L\}$
      ii. If $S_{new} \neq S_j$, then replace S_j in $\{S\}$ with $S_{j_1} = (s_0, \ldots, s_i)$ and $S_{j_2} = (s_i, \ldots, s_n)$
      iii. Set $\{s_{possible}\} = s_i^*$
   (b) No: Append s_{viewed} to S_{new} in $\{S\}$
2. If familiar, does $\exists\, s_i \in \{s_{possible}\}$ s.t. $s_{viewed} \equiv s_i$?
   (a) Yes: Set $\{s_{possible}\} = s_i^*$
   (b) No (divergence):
      i. Add $S_{new_1} = (s_0, \ldots, s_i)$, $S_{new_2} = (s_i, \ldots, s_n)$ to $\{S\}$, and add location $\{s_i\}$ to $\{L\}$
      ii. Replace S_{new} in $\{S\}$ with $S_{new} = (s_i, s_{viewed})$
      iii. Set $\{s_{possible}\} = \infty$

Figure 1: Decision process for map-building

Using the Map

During and after map-building, the robot can navigate between any two scenes in the map that are connected by a *traversable* path. A traversable path is a series of sequences or partial sequences in the map, all directed head to tail, from the robot's current scene to the goal scene. As the learning process progresses, more places in the environment will become represented in the map by scenes, and more pairs of scenes will be traversable. In order to initialize this process, the robot must analyze the current scene, identifying markers, and then match them to the markers it expects to see given its current location.

The basic building block of navigation is the *traversal.* Let s_i and s_j be scenes in the map such that the robot is viewing s_i and there is a traversable path from s_i to s_j. Let $M_{ij} = s_i \cap s_j$ and define s_j' to be s_j restricted to the markers in M_{ij}. If M_{ij} is not empty and $C(M_{ij}) = T$ (always the case if $j = i + 1$), then by using some variant of visual servoing the robot can move until $s_{viewed} = s_j'$ within an arbitrary tolerance. In the limit, this movement will bring the robot to the absolute position and angle that it was at when it recorded s_j.

In many cases, M_{ij} is empty, meaning that the goal scene is not even partially visible from the initial scene. This necessitates traversing intermediate scenes and performing a *handoff* between each. Let s_i, s_j, and s_k be scenes in the map such that the robot is currently s_i and there is a traversable path from s_i to s_k through s_j. Let M_{ij} and M_{jk} be defined as above such that both are non-empty, but $M_{ik} = M_{ij} \cap M_{jk}$ is empty. The robot cannot traverse directly from s_i to s_k; instead it must first servo to s_j using markers in M_{ij}

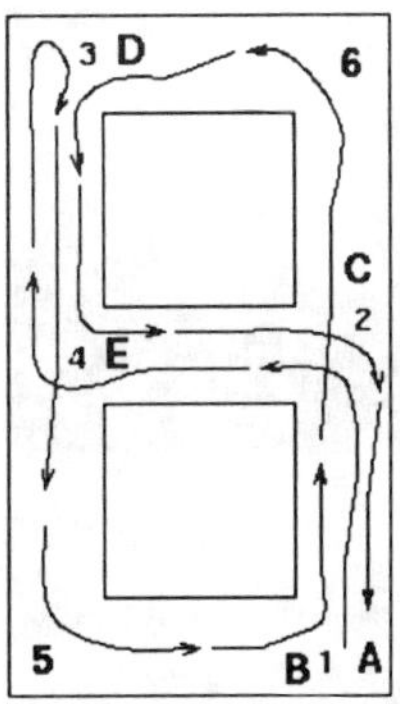

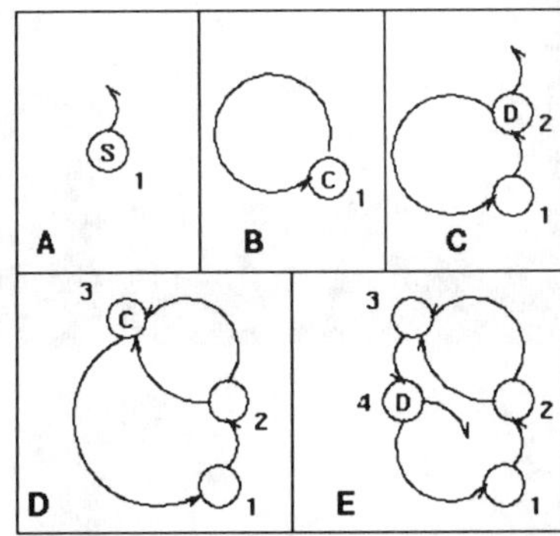

Figure 2: Hypothetical exploration. The path the robot follows is shown schematically on the left, starting at 1 (numbers are for spatial reference only); successive updates of the map occurring at steps A-E are shown on the right. Location nodes are marked to indicate why they were created: S = start event, C = convergence, and D = divergence.

until the markers in M_{jk} are found, and then "hand off" and servo on those markers to the destination.

The simplest way of implementing a handoff is to rely on the default marker search technique used for mapping. As the robot servos toward s_j and searches for new markers concurrently, it may find all of M_{jk} before it ceases movement, allowing it to smoothly switch servoing control at the appropriate moment. If not all of M_{jk} is found before stopping, the robot can continue searching until it acquires the markers, then change control to the next servoing phase. In practice, though, the time needed to find the markers can be quite long, and the matching process is likely to be error-prone. Furthermore, if a significant location discrepancy exists between s_{viewed} and s'_j at the end of servoing, not all of the desired features for s'_k may be in view. Angular errors are especially significant because they often cause more distant markers in M_{jk} to be partially or completely out of view.

Correcting such errors is critical, so we have investigated a predictive mode for marker location in which the robot dynamically estimates the image locations of M_{jk} as it moves (Rasmussen & Hager 1996). Since we do not have an underlying geometric map, all feature prediction must operate directly from image information. Thus, we have adapted a result from the theory of geometric invariance (Barrett et al. 1992) to vehicles moving in a plane. We have found that when the image projections of four three-dimensional points p_0, p_1, p_2, p_3 are known in two different views v_1 and v_2, knowledge of the image projections of p_0, p_1, and p_2 in a third view v_3 is sufficient to predict the image location of p_3 modulo certain geometric constraints on the points and the transformations between views.

This result means that if three points in M_{ij} and one in M_{jk} are simultaneously visible in two frames during map-building, then during servoing on the markers in M_{ij}, any points that were visible in M_{jk} have predictable locations. The predictions are somewhat noisy, but they are reasonable hints for initializing and limiting search procedures. Furthermore, if the predicted point locations fall consistently outside the image, the robot can make an open-loop adjustment to bring them into view.

Putting this together, a navigational directive is issued as a pair of scenes (s_{start}, s_{finish}), where the robot is assumed to be currently viewing s_{start}. A path-planning algorithm returns an ordered list of scenes constituting a traversable path to the goal. This list is input to a greedy scheduling algorithm that selects which set of markers can be servoed on for the most consecutive scenes before the robot must switch to a new target set. This approach is based on a desire to minimize the number of handoffs.

Implementation

We have implemented most of the architecture described above on a tethered Nomad 200 robot (lack of an onboard digitizer has limited movement to one lab and an adjoining hallway). In this section, we describe the implementation of various system modules.

3-D Rectangles

One type of marker we have tested is image rectangles, defined by two approximately horizontal image edges and two approximately vertical image edges at least 20 pixels in length meeting at four distinct corners. We are using the XVision system (Hager 1995) for real-time visual tracking as the basis for our marker identification and tracking algorithms, which are described in detail in (Rasmussen & Hager 1996). Rectangles were chosen primarily because they are simple to detect and track, and in an indoor environment they are relatively common. The default marker-finding method is random search over the entire image. When traversing a previously known area, the same search procedure is used, but the markers found are matched to those previously located in the scene. For our limited experiments, we have found matching rectangles by aspect ratio alone satisfactory, although we have also experimented with using statistics on the gray value distribution of the interior of the rectangle as well. Based on the techniques described in (Chaumette, Rives, & Espian 1991), the four corners of one rectangle are sufficient to servo on. Thus, the scene evaluation function $C(s)$ is simply that $s \neq \emptyset$. To maintain this condition, the robot must block movement whenever it loses track

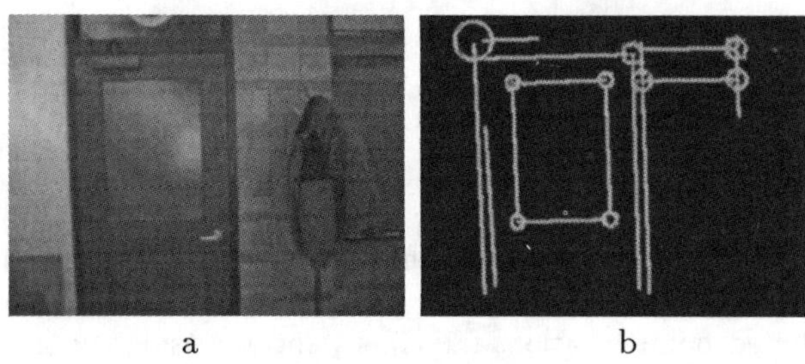

a b

Figure 3: Rectangle-finding. Corners are marked with circles of radius inversely proportional to the confidence of correctness. The door window was the only rectangle found here.

of the only marker it has until it finds another one.

Experimental Results

We have tested the above modules on a variety of indoor scenes. This section briefly describes our experimental results.

Marker Finding When not using prediction, the performance of our rectangle-finding algorithm varied. In particular, it performed poorly on cluttered scenes, due to the combinatorics of testing many pairs of edges as possible corners and many groups of corners as possibly belonging to rectangles. It performed roughly as well at locating lines when moving slowly as when immobile. A sample image and the rectangle found in it is shown in Figure 3.

One central issue is the ability of the algorithm to find markers quickly, and to consistently find roughly the same set of markers in an image. On a SPARC 10/40, over twenty runs of the algorithm on the door view in Figure 3, it found the window rectangle 11 times within 60 seconds (for those times, in an average of 29 seconds). Four other times it found another rectangle in the tile pattern on the wall above the coat rack. In the other five trials it did not find any rectangle in less than 60 seconds. Slight variations in robot position and viewing angle did not affect performance.

As described above, our goal is to use prediction to improve performance when attempting to refind markers. Searching the entire 640 x 480 image is cumbersome and slow. Our view is that prediction provides a seed about which a local search can be centered. If we are looking specifically for the door window rectangle of Figure 3.a and assume that prediction has yielded a seed approximately in its center, we can constrain search to a smaller window tailored to the remembered area of the rectangle. Accordingly, another 20 runs were done with random search limited to a 300 x 300 square uniform distribution about the door window. The door window rectangle and only the window rectangle was found for all 20 trials. Furthermore, the average time to find it was reduced to only 12 seconds. In this manner distracting lines elsewhere in the image were effectively ignored.

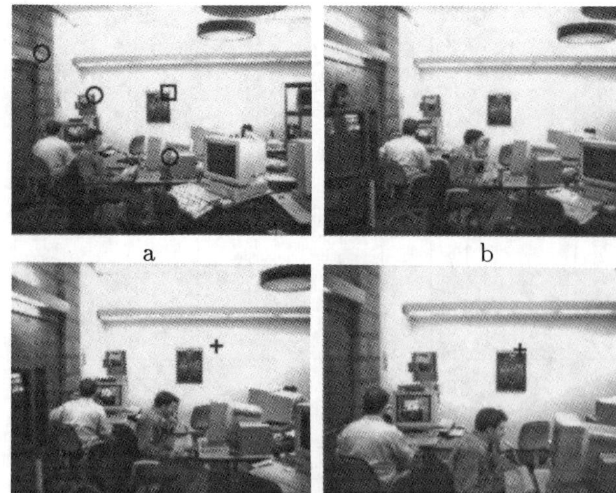

a b c d

Figure 4: Prediction. (a) and (b) are calibration views taken at the start and finish of a three-foot leftward translation of the robot, with four tracked SSD features marked. (c) and (d) are the first and last images in a sequence of six taken at equal intervals along a ten-foot forward translation from (b). In them, only the image location of the feature marked with a square in (a) is unknown to the robot. The crosses indicate the predicted locations of this feature.

Prediction In Figure 4 the performance of our prediction scheme is illustrated. We must imagine that the first two images were taken during learning, and the other two (along with the four not pictured) were taken later as the robot consulted its map. The predicted feature is one that it wants to pick up while moving in order to effect a smooth handoff.The mean error magnitude over the six images of the sequence between the predicted and actual x coordinate of the feature was 14.1 pixels, and for the y coordinate it was 2.1 pixels; yielding a mean distance error of about 14.3 pixels. This is close enough that the robot could find it very quickly with a local search.

Servoing Traversal-type servoing has been successfully done in a number of situations (such as approaching the door in Figure 3). We are working to improve the reliability of handoffs by addressing the angular error problem described above.

Discussion

One vulnerability of the scene-based framework is its assumption that an acceptable group of markers will always be in view. For any kind of markers chosen, in a real-world environment there will be gaps. In the indoor environment expected by our implementation, for instance, there are not enough closely-spaced rectangles for the robot to handoff its way around a ninety-degree corner. Even straight corridors may be relatively featureless for long stretches, rendering them impassable. Clearly, we can use odometry locally as a second source of predictive information. Open-loop movements based on saved odometric information could be useful on a limited basis—say, to negotiate corners. The system we have presented is fairly robust with respect to slight angular and positional errors, and errors would not be cumulative.

Another possible solution is to consider a different kind of servoing. The servoing we have focused on so far is *transformational*, insofar as the robot tries, by moving, to make a tracked object change appearance to look like a target object. A different, *homeostatic* paradigm is suggested by road-following and wall-following systems (Turk et al. 1988). In them, the goal is not to change one sensory entity into another through movement, but rather to move while maintaining a certain constancy of sensory input. Road-followers seek to move forward while keeping the sides of the road centered. Something like this could be used to guide movement while no target is visible. If the robot can discern situations in which the maintenance of a visual constraint—e.g., staying centered in a hallway, keeping a building in front of it, etc.—can provide appropriate cues for movement, then it can bridge gaps between homing-type targets. The difficulty of this approach is that the robot does not know accurately, as with our framework, when something should be visible. Rather, it must be vigilant for the appearance of a marker signalling that it has arrived. Some odometry, either in distance traveled or time spent, would help limit the time it spends looking for such a signal.

With multiple markers in one scene, joining these individual discrimination criteria to constraints imposed by spatial relationships (above, next-to, etc.) as well as the invariant relationship used for prediction would lead to still greater confidence in matching. Finally, an important area of additional research is dynamically updating the map during motion. In particular, it is likely that certain markers are stable and easy to find, while others occasionally appear and disappear. Ideally, as the robot moves around it should modify its internal representation to more heavily weight more reliable markers, and possibly add new markers.

In conclusion, we have presented a vision-based navigation framework for mobile robots that requires no *a priori* environmental model and very little odometry, and implemented most of its fundamental components. The notion of the environment that it builds remains on the image level, both as stored and when generating movement. It is also modular, permitting easy modification, especially to its recognition and matching capabilities and its task description.

Acknowledgments

This research was supported by ARPA grant N00014-93-1-1235, Army DURIP grant DAAH04-95-1-0058, by NSF grant IRI-9420982, and Yale University.

References

Barrett, E.; Brill, M.; Haag, N.; and Payton, P. 1992. Invariant Linear Methods in Photogrammetry and Model-matching. In *Geometric Invariance in Computer Vision*, Mundy, J., and Zisserman, A. eds., Cambridge, Mass.: MIT Press.

Chaumette, F.; Rives, P.; and Espian, B. 1991. Positioning of a Robot with respect to an Object, Tracking it, and Estimating its Velocity by Visual Servoing. In Proc. IEEE Inter. Conf. Robotics and Automation, 2248-53. Sacramento, CA, April.

Engelson, S. P. 1994. Passive Map Learning and Visual Place Recognition. Ph.D. diss., Dept. of Comp. Sci., Yale Univ.

Fennema, C.; Hanson, A.; Riseman, E.; Beveridge, J.; and Kumar, R. 1990. Model-Directed Mobile Robot Navigation. *IEEE Trans. Systems, Man, and Cybernetics* 20(6): 1352-69.

Hager, G. 1995. The 'X-Vision' System: A General-Purpose Substrate for Vision-Based Robotics. *Workshop on Vision for Robotics.*

Hong, J.; Tan, X.; Pinette, B.; Weiss, R.; and Riseman, E. 1992. Image-Based Homing. *IEEE Control Systems*: 38-44.

Hutchinson, S.; Hager, G.; and Corke, P. 1995. A Tutorial Introduction to Visual Servo Control. *IEEE Trans. Robotics and Automation.*

Kortenkamp, D.; Weymouth, T.; Chown, E.; and Kaplan, S. 1992. A scene-based, multi-level representation for mobile robot spatial mapping and navigation. Technical Report, CSE-TR-119-92, Univ. of Michigan.

Kosaka, A., and Kak, A. C. 1992. Fast Vision-Guided Mobile Robot Navigation Using Model-Based Reasoning and Prediction of Uncertainties. *CVGIP: Image Understanding* 56(3): 271-329.

Kuipers, B., and Byun, Y. T. 1981. A robot exploration and mapping strategy based on a semantic hierarchy of spatial representations. *Robotics and Autonomous Systems* 8: 47-63.

Leonard, J.; Durrant-Whyte, H.; and Cox, I. 1990. Dynamic Map Building for an Autonomous Mobile Robot. *IEEE Inter. Workshop on Intelligent Robots and Systems*: 89-95.

Rasmussen, C., and Hager, G. 1996. Robot Navigation Using Image Sequences. Technical Report, DCS-TR-1103, Yale Univ.

Taylor, C., and Kriegman, D. 1994. Vision-Based Motion Planning and Exploration Algorithms for Mobile Robots. *Workshop on the Algorithmic Foundations of Robotics.*

Turk, M.; Morgenthaler, D.; Gremban, K.; and Marra, M. 1988. VITS—A Vision System for Autonomous Land Vehicle Navigation. *IEEE Trans. Pattern Analysis and Machine Intelligence* 10(3): 342-61.

Zheng, Z., and Tsuji, S. 1992. Panoramic Representation for Route Recognition by a Mobile Robot. *Inter. Journal of Computer Vision* 9(1): 55-76.

Integrating Grid-Based and Topological Maps for Mobile Robot Navigation

Sebastian Thrun†‡

†Computer Science Department
Carnegie Mellon University
Pittsburgh, PA 15213

Arno Bücken‡

‡Institut für Informatik
Universität Bonn
D-53117 Bonn, Germany

Abstract

Research on mobile robot navigation has produced two major paradigms for mapping indoor environments: grid-based and topological. While grid-based methods produce accurate metric maps, their complexity often prohibits efficient planning and problem solving in large-scale indoor environments. Topological maps, on the other hand, can be used much more efficiently, yet accurate and consistent topological maps are considerably difficult to learn in large-scale environments.

This paper describes an approach that integrates both paradigms: grid-based and topological. Grid-based maps are learned using artificial neural networks and Bayesian integration. Topological maps are generated on top of the grid-based maps, by partitioning the latter into coherent regions. By combining both paradigms—grid-based and topological—, the approach presented here gains the best of both worlds: accuracy/consistency and efficiency. The paper gives results for autonomously operating a mobile robot equipped with sonar sensors in populated multi-room environments.

Introduction

To efficiently carry out complex missions in indoor environments, autonomous mobile robots must be able to acquire and maintain models of their environments. The task of acquiring models is difficult and far from being solved. The following factors impose practical limitations on a robot's ability to learn and use accurate models:

1. **Sensors.** Sensors often are not capable to directly measure the quantity of interest (such as the exact location of obstacles).
2. **Perceptual limitations.** The perceptual range of most sensors is limited to a small range close to the robot. To acquire global information, the robot has to actively explore its environment.
3. **Sensor noise.** Sensor measurements are typically corrupted by noise, the distribution of which is often unknown (it is rarely Gaussian).
4. **Drift/slippage.** Robot motion is inaccurate. Odometric errors accumulate over time.
5. **Complexity and dynamics.** Robot environments are complex and dynamic, making it principally impossible to maintain exact models.
6. **Real-time requirements.** Time requirements often demand that the internal model must be simple and easily accessible. For example, fine-grain CAD models are often disadvantageous if actions must be generated in real-time.

Recent research has produced two fundamental paradigms for modeling indoor robot environments: the *grid-based (metric) paradigm* and the *topological paradigm.* Grid-based approaches, such as those proposed by Moravec/Elfes (Moravec 1988) and many others, represent environments by evenly-spaced grids. Each grid cell may, for example, indicate the presence of an obstacle in the corresponding region of the environment. Topological approaches, such a those described in (Engelson & McDermott 1992; Kortenkamp & Weymouth 1994; Kuipers & Byun 1990; Matarić 1994; Pierce & Kuipers 1994), represent robot environments by graphs. Nodes in such graphs correspond to distinct situations, places, or landmarks (such as doorways). They are connected by arcs if there exists a direct path between them.

Both approaches to robot mapping exhibit orthogonal strengths and weaknesses. Occupancy grids are considerably easy to construct and to maintain even in large-scale environments (Buhmann *et al.* 1995; Thrun & Bücken 1996). Since the intrinsic geometry of a grid corresponds directly to the geometry of the environment, the robot's position within its model can be determined by its position and orientation in the real world—which, as shown below, can be determined sufficiently accurately using only sonar sensors, in environments of moderate size. As a pleasing consequence, different positions for which sensors measure the same values (*i.e.*, situations that look alike) are naturally disambiguated in grid-based approaches. This is not the case for topological approaches, which determine the position of the robot relative to the model based on landmarks or distinct sensory features. For example, if the robot traverses two places that look alike, topological approaches often have difficulty determining if these places are the same or not (particularly if these places have been reached via different paths). Also, since sensory input usually depends strongly on the view-point of the robot, topological approaches may fail to recognize geometrically nearby places.

On the other hand, grid-based approaches suffer from their enormous space and time complexity. This is because the resolution of a grid must be fine enough to capture every important detail of the world. Compactness in a key advantage of topological representations. Topological maps are usually more compact, since their resolution is determined by the complexity of the environment. Consequently, they permit fast planning, facilitate interfacing to symbolic planners and problem-solvers, and provide more natural interfaces for human instructions. Since topological approaches usually

Grid-based approaches	Topological approaches
+ easy to build, represent, and maintain + recognition of places (based on geometry) is non-ambiguous and view point-independent + facilitates computation of shortest paths	+ permits efficient planning, low space complexity (resolution depends on the complexity of the environment) + does not require accurate determination of the robot's position + convenient representation for symbolic planners, problem solvers, natural language interfaces
– planning inefficient, space-consuming (resolution does not depend on the complexity of the environment) – requires accurate determination of the robot's position – poor interface for most symbolic problem solvers	– difficult to construct and maintain in larger environments – recognition of places (based on landmarks) often ambiguous, sensitive to the point of view – may yield suboptimal paths

Table 1: Comparison of grid-based and topological approaches to map building.

do not require the exact determination of the geometric position of the robot, they often recover better from drift and slippage—phenomena that must constantly be monitored and compensated in grid-based approaches. To summarize, both paradigms have orthogonal strengths and weaknesses, which are summarized in Table 1.

This paper advocates to integrate both paradigms, to gain the best of both worlds. The approach presented here combines both grid-based (metric) and topological representations. To construct a grid-based model of the environment, sensor values are interpreted by an artificial neural network and mapped into probabilities for occupancy. Multiple interpretations are integrated over time using Bayes' rule. On top of the grid representation, more compact topological maps are generated by splitting the metric map into coherent regions, separated through *critical lines*. Critical lines correspond to narrow passages such as doorways. By partitioning the metric map into a small number of regions, the number of topological entities is several orders of magnitude smaller than the number of cells in the grid representation. Therefore, the integration of both representations has unique advantages that cannot be found for either approach in isolation: the grid-based representation, which is considerably easy to construct and maintain in environments of moderate complexity (e.g., 20 by 30 meters), models the world consistently and disambiguates different positions. The topological representation, which is grounded in the metric representation, facilitates fast planning and problem solving.

The robots used in our research are shown in Figure 1. All robots are equipped with an array of 24 sonar sensors. Throughout this paper, we will restrict ourselves to the interpretation of sonar sensors, although the methods described here have (in a prototype version) also been operated using cameras and infrared light sensors in addition to sonar sensors, using the image segmentation approach described in (Buhmann *et al.* 1995). The approach proposed here has extensively been tested in various indoor environments, and is now distributed commercially by a leading mobile robot manufacturer (Real World Interface, Inc.) as part of the regular navigation software.

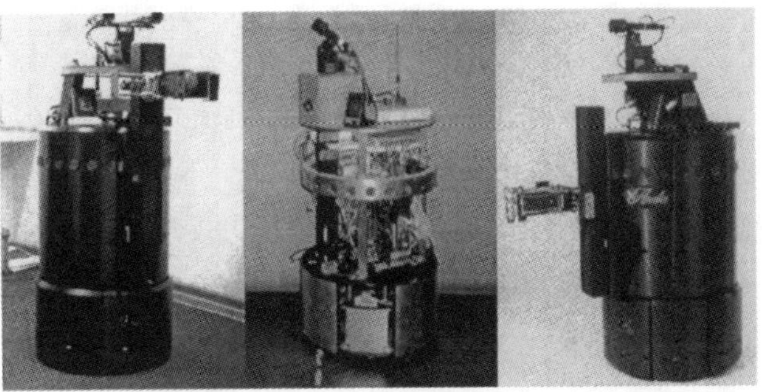

Figure 1: The robots used in our research: RHINO (University of Bonn), XAVIER, and AMELIA (both CMU).

Grid-Based Maps

The metric maps considered here are two-dimensional, discrete occupancy grids, as originally proposed in (Elfes 1987; Moravec 1988) and since implemented successfully in various systems. Each grid-cell $\langle x, y\rangle$ in the map has an *occupancy value* attached, which measures the subjective belief whether or not the center of the robot can be moved to the center of that cell (*i.e.*, the occupancy map models the *configuration space* of the robot, see *e.g.*, (Latombe 1991)). This section describes the four major components of our approach to building grid-based maps (see also (Thrun 1993)): (1) *sensor interpretation*, (2) *integration*, (3) *position estimation*, and (4) *exploration*. Examples of metric maps are shown in various places in this paper.

Sensor Interpretation

To build metric maps, sensor reading must be "translated" into occupancy values $occ_{x,y}$ for each grid cell $\langle x, y\rangle$. The idea here is to train an artificial neural network using Back-Propagation to map sonar measurements to occupancy values. The input to the network consists of the four sensor readings closest to $\langle x, y\rangle$, along with two values that encode $\langle x, y\rangle$ in polar coordinates relative to the robot (angle to the first of the four sensors, and distance). The output target for the network is 1, if $\langle x, y\rangle$ is occupied, and 0 otherwise. Training examples can be obtained by operating a robot in a known environment and recording its sensor readings; notice that each sonar scan can be used to construct many training examples for different x-y coordinates. In our implementation, training examples are generated with a mobile robot simulator.

Figure 2 shows three examples of sonar scans along with their neural network interpretation. The darker a value in the circular region around the robot, the larger the occupancy value computed by the network. Figures 2a&b depict situations in a corridor. Situations such as the one shown in Figure 2c—that defy simple interpretation—are typical for cluttered indoor environments.

Integration Over Time

Sonar interpretations must be integrated over time, to yield a single, consistent map. To do so, it is convenient to interpret

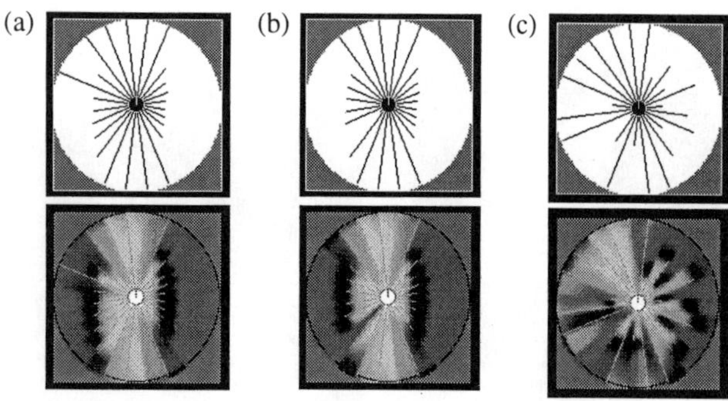

Figure 2: Sensor interpretation: Three example sonar scans (top row) and local occupancy maps (bottom row), generated by the neural network.

the network's output for the t-th sensor reading (denoted by $s^{(t)}$) as the *probability* that a grid cell $\langle x, y\rangle$ is occupied, conditioned on the sensor reading $s^{(t)}$:

$$Pr(occ_{x,y}|s^{(t)})$$

A map is obtained by integrating these probabilities for all available sensor readings, denoted by $s^{(1)}, s^{(2)}, \ldots, s^{(T)}$. In other words, the desired occupancy value for each grid call$\langle x, y\rangle$ can be expressed as the probability

$$Pr(occ_{x,y}|s^{(1)}, s^{(2)}, \ldots, s^{(T)}),$$

which is conditioned on *all* sensor reading. A straightforward approach to estimating this quantity is to apply Bayes' rule (Moravec 1988; Pearl 1988). To do so, one has to assume independence of the noise in different readings. More specifically, given the true occupancy of a grid cell $\langle x, y\rangle$, the conditional probability $Pr(s^{(t)}|occ_{x,y})$ must be assumed to be independent of $Pr(s^{(t')}|occ_{x,y})$ for $t \neq t'$. This assumption is not implausible—in fact, it is commonly made in approaches to building occupancy grids. The desired probability can now be computed as follows:

$$Pr(occ_{x,y}|s^{(1)}, s^{(2)}, \ldots, s^{(T)}) =$$

$$1 - \left(1 + \frac{Pr(x)}{1-Pr(x)} \prod_{\tau=1}^{T} \frac{Pr(occ_{x,y}|s^{(\tau)})}{1-Pr(occ_{x,y}|s^{(\tau)})} \frac{1-Pr(x)}{Pr(x)}\right)^{-1}$$

Here $Pr(x)$ denotes the prior probability for occupancy (which, if set to 0.5, can be omitted in this equation). Notice that this formula can be used to update occupancy values *incrementally*. An example map of a competition ring constructed at the 1994 AAAI autonomous robot competition is shown in Figure 3.

Position Estimation

The accuracy of the metric map depends crucially on the alignment of the robot with its map. Unfortunately, slippage and drift can have devastating effects on the estimation of the robot position. Identifying and correcting for slippage and drift is therefore imperative for grid-based approaches to robot navigation (Feng, Borenstein, & Everett 1994; Rencken 1993).

Figure 4 gives an example that illustrates the importance of position estimation in grid-based robot mapping. In Figure 4a, the position is determined solely based on dead-

Figure 3: Grid-based map, constructed at the 1994 AAAI autonomous mobile robot competition.

reckoning. After approximately 15 minutes of robot operation, the position error is approximately 11.5 meters. Obviously, the resulting map is too erroneous to be of practical use. Figure 4b is the result of exploiting and integrating three sources of information:

1. **Wheel encoders.** Wheel encoders measure the revolution of the robot's wheels. Based on their measurements, odometry yields an estimate of the robot's position at any point in time. Odometry is very accurate over short time intervals.
2. **Map correlation.** Whenever the robot interprets an actual sensor reading, it constructs a "local" map (such as the ones shown in Figure 2). The *correlation* of the local and the corresponding section of the global map is a measure of their correspondence (Schiele & Crowley 1994). Thus, the correlation—which is a function of the robot position—gives a second source of information for estimating the robot's position.
3. **Wall orientation.** The third source of information estimates and memorizes the *global wall orientation* (Crowley 1989; Hinkel & Knieriemen 1988). This approach rests on the restrictive assumption that walls are either parallel or orthogonal to each other, or differ by more than 15 degrees from these canonical wall directions. In the beginning of robot operation, the global orientation of walls is estimated by searching straight line segments in consecutive sonar measurements. Once the global wall orientation has been estimated, it is used to readjust the robot's orientation based on future sonar measurements.

All three mechanisms basically provide a probability density for the robot's position (Thrun & Bücken 1996). Gradient descent is then iterated to determine the most likely robot position (in an any-time fashion). Notice that position control based on odometry and map correlation alone (items 1 and 2 above) works well if the robot travels through mapped terrain, but seizes to function if the robot explores and maps unknown terrain. The third mechanism, which arguably relies on a restrictive assumption concerning the nature of indoor environments, has proven extremely valuable when autonomously exploring and mapping large-scale indoor environments.

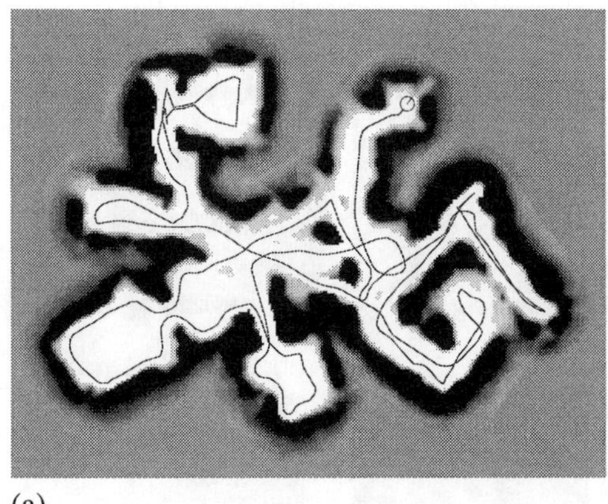

(a)

(b)

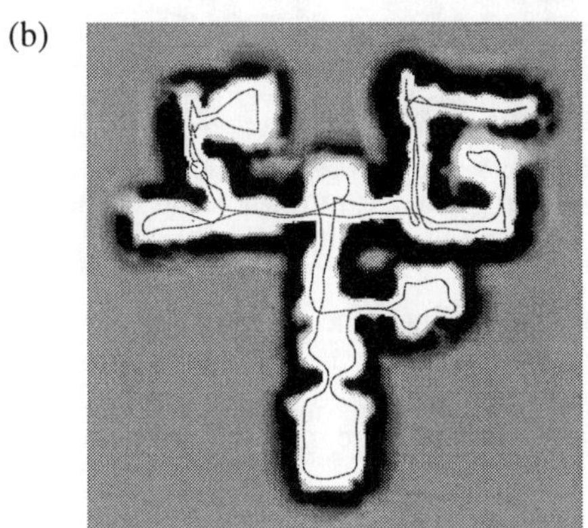

Figure 4: Map constructed without (a) and with (b) the position estimation mechanism described in this paper.

Exploration

To autonomously acquire maps, the robot has to explore. The idea for (greedy) exploration is to let the robot always move on a minimum-cost path to the nearest unexplored grid cell; The cost for traversing a grid cell is determined by its occupancy value. The minimum-cost path is computed using a modified version of *value iteration*, a popular dynamic programming algorithm (Howard 1960) (which bears similarities to A* (Nilsson 1982)).

In a nutshell, starting at each unexplored grid-cell, value iteration propagates values through the map. After convergence, each value measures the cumulative costs for moving to the cost-nearest unexplored grid cell. Figure 5a shows a value function after convergence. All white regions are unexplored, and the grey-level indicates the cumulative costs for moving towards the nearest unexplored point. Notice that the all minima of the value function correspond to unexplored regions—there are no local minima. Once value iteration converges, greedy exploration simply amounts to steepest descent in the value function, which can be done very efficiently. Figure 5b, sketches the path taken during approximately 15 minutes of autonomous exploration. The value function can, however, be used to generate motion control at any time (Dean & Boddy 1988), long before dynamic programming converges. Value iteration has the nice property that values are generated for *all* cells in the grid, not just the current robot position.

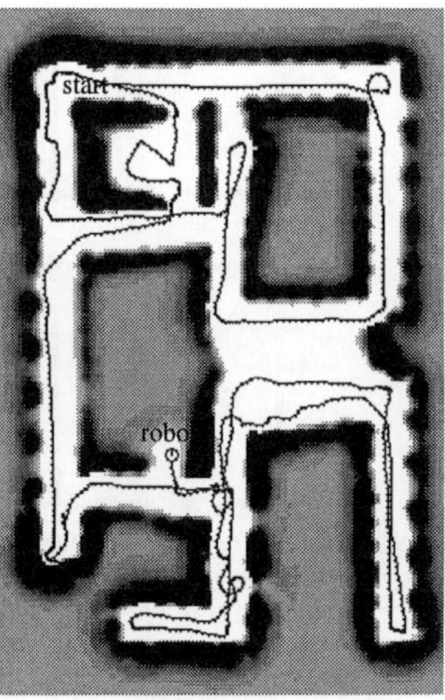

Figure 5: **Autonomous exploration.** (a) Exploration values, computed by value iteration. White regions are completely unexplored. By following the grey-scale gradient, the robot moves to the next unexplored area on a minimum-cost path. (b) Actual path traveled during autonomous exploration, along with the resulting metric map. The large black rectangle in (a) indicates the global wall orientation θ_{wall}.

Thus, if the robot has to change its path to avoid a collision with an unexpected obstacle, it can directly continue exploration without further planning. During exploration, the robot moves constantly, and frequently reaches a velocity of 80 to 90 cm/sec (see also (Buhmann *et al.* 1995; Fox, Burgard, & Thrun 1995)).

In grid maps of size 30 by 30 meters, optimized value iteration, done from scratch, requires approximately 2 to 10 seconds on a SUN Sparc station. For example, the planning time in the map shown in Fig. 3 is typically under 2 seconds, and re-planning (which becomes necessary when the map is updated) is performed usually in a tenth of a second. In the light of these results, one might be inclined to think that grid-based maps are sufficient for autonomous robot navigation. However, value iteration (and similar planning approaches) require time quadratic in the number of grid cells, imposing intrinsic scaling limitations that prohibit efficient planning in large-scale domains. Due to their compactness, topological maps scale much better to large environments. In what follows we will describe our approach for deriving topological graphs from grid maps.

Topological Maps

Topological maps are built on top of the grid-based maps. The key idea is simple but very effective: The free-space of a grid-based map is partitioned into a small number of regions, separated by *critical lines*. Critical lines correspond to narrow passages such as doorways. The partitioned map is then mapped into a isomorphic graph. The precise algorithm is illustrated in Figure 6, and works as follows:

1. **Thresholding.** Initially, each occupancy value in the occupancy grid is thresholded. Cells whose occupancy value is below the threshold are considered free-space (denoted by C). All other points are considered occupied (denoted by $\bar{C}$).

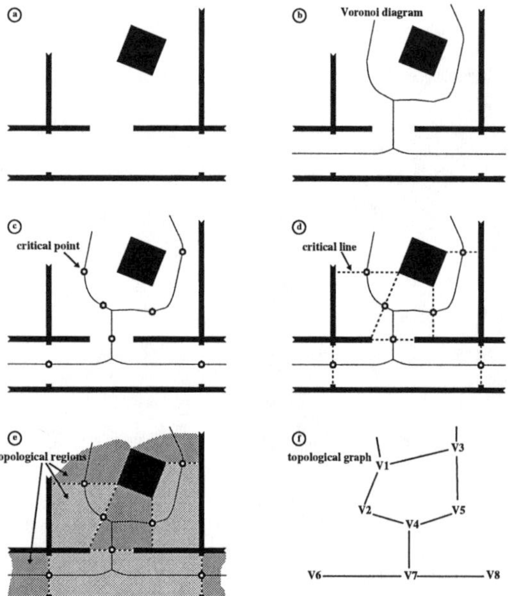

Figure 6: **Extracting topological maps.** (a) Metric map, (b) Voronoi diagram, (c) critical points, (d) critical lines, (e) topological regions, and (f) the topological graph.

2. **Voronoi diagram.** For each point in free-space $\langle x, y\rangle \in C$, there is one or more *nearest point(s)* in the occupied space $\bar{C}$. We will call these points the *basis points of* $\langle x, y\rangle$, and the distance between $\langle x, y\rangle$ and its basis points the *clearance of* $\langle x, y\rangle$. The Voronoi diagram (Latombe 1991) is the set of points in free-space that have at least two different (equidistant) basis-points (see Figure 6b).
3. **Critical points.** The key idea for partitioning the free-space is to find *"critical points."* Critical points $\langle x, y\rangle$ are points on the Voronoi diagram that minimize clearance locally. In other words, each critical point $\langle x, y\rangle$ has the following two properties: (a) it is part of the Voronoi diagram, and (b) the clearance of all points in an ε-neighborhood of $\langle x, y\rangle$ is *not* smaller. Figure 6c illustrates critical points.
4. **Critical lines.** Critical lines are obtained by connecting each critical point with its basis points (*cf.* Figure 6d). Critical points have exactly two basis points (otherwise they would not be local minima of the clearance function). Critical lines partition the free-space into disjoint regions (see Figure 6e).
5. **Topological graph**. The partitioning is mapped into an isomorphic graph. Each region corresponds to a node in the topological graph, and each critical line to an arc. Figure 6f shows an example of a topological graph.

Critical lines are motivated by two observations. Firstly, when passing through a critical line, the robot is forced to move in a considerably small region. Hence, the loss in performance inferred by planning using the topological map (as opposed to the grid-based map) is considerably small. Secondly, narrow regions are more likely blocked by obstacles (such as doors, which can be open or closed).

Figure 7 illustrates the process of extracting a topological map from the grid-based map depicted in Figure 3. Figure 7a shows the Voronoi diagram of the thresholded map, and Figure 7b depicts the critical lines (the critical points are on the intersections of critical lines and the Voronoi diagram). The resulting partitioning and the topological graph are shown in Figure 7c&d. As can be seen, the map has been partitioned into 67 regions.

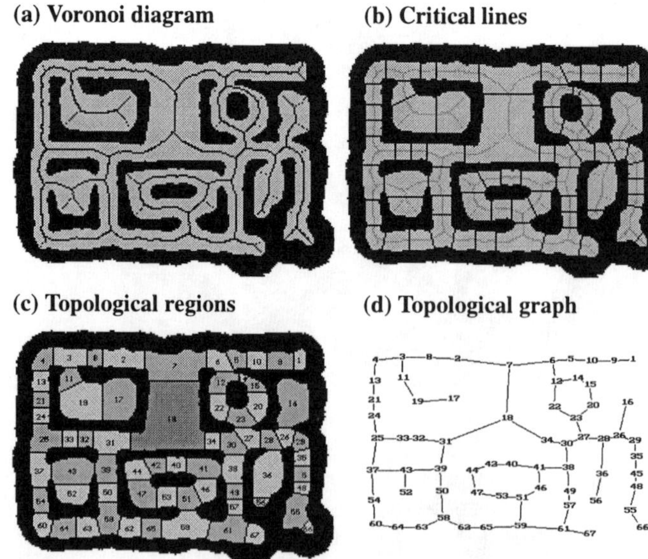

Figure 7: Extracting the topological graph from the map depicted in Figure 3: (a) Voronoi diagram, (b) Critical points and lines, (c) regions, and (d) the final graph.

Performance Results

Topological maps are abstract representations of metric maps. As is generally the case for abstract representations and abstract problem solving, there are three criteria for assessing the appropriateness of the abstraction: *consistency*, *loss*, and *efficiency*. Two maps are *consistent* with each other if every solution (plan) in one of the maps can be represented as a solution in the other map. The *loss* measures the loss in performance (path length), if paths are planned in the more abstract, topological map as opposed to the grid-based map. *Efficiency* measures the relative time complexity of problem solving (planning). Typically, when using abstract models, efficiency is traded off with consistency and performance loss.

Consistency

The topological map is always consistent with the grid-based map. For every abstract plan generated using the topological map, there exists a corresponding plan in the grid-based map (in other words, the abstraction has the *downward solution property* (Russell & Norvig 1995)). Conversely, every path that can be found in the grid-based map has an abstract representation which is a admissible plan in the topological map (*upward solution property*). Notice that although consistency appears to be a trivial property of the topological maps, not every topological approach proposed in the literature generates maps that would be consistent with their corresponding metric representation.

(a) Grid-based map **(b) Topological regions**

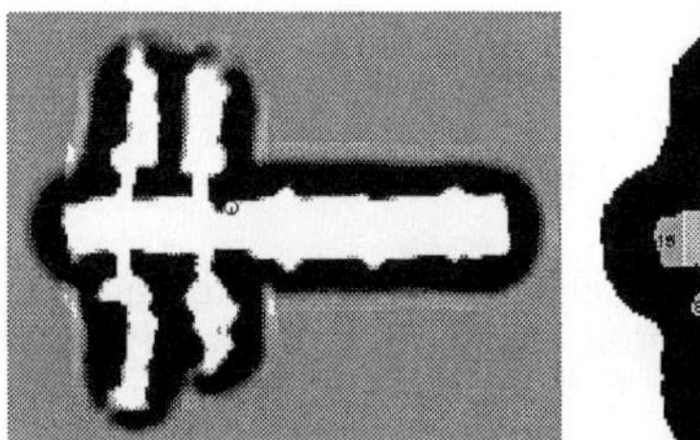

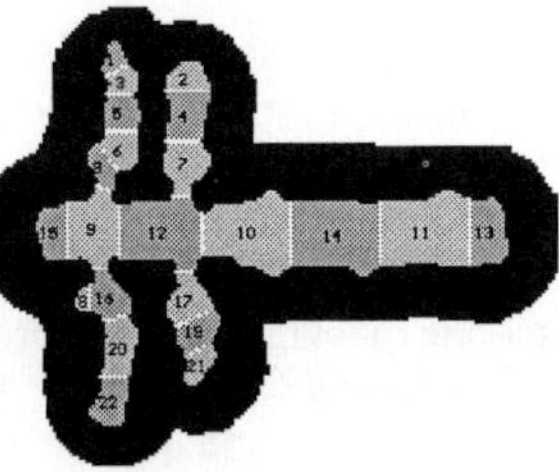

Figure 8: Another example of a map.

Loss

Abstract representations—such as topological maps—lack detail. Consequently, paths found in the topological map may not be as short as paths found using the metric representation. To measure performance loss, we empirically compared paths generated using the metric map shown in Figure 3 with those generated using the corresponding topological map, shown in Figures 7d. Value iteration can be applied using both representations. In grid-based maps, value iteration is applied just as described above. However, instead of planning paths to unexplored regions, paths were planned from a particular start point to a particular goal point. To compare the results to those obtained using topological representations, first the corresponding shortest path in the topological graph was determined. Subsequently, the shortest path was determined that followed exactly this topological plan. As a result, the quality of topological plans can directly be compared to those derived using the metric map.

We conducted a total of 23,881,062 experiments, each using a different starting and goal position that were generated systematically with an evenly-spaced grid. The results are intriguing. The average length of the shortest path is 15.88 meters. If robot motion is planned using the topological map, this path length increases on average only by 0.29 meters, which is only 1.82% of the total path length. It is remarkable that in 83.4% of all experiments, the topological planner returns a loss-free plan. The largest loss that we found in our experiments was 11.98 meters, which occurred in 6 of the 23,881,062 experiments. Figure 9a shows the average loss as a function of the length of the shortest path. Figure 8 depicts a different map. Here the loss is zero, since both maps are free of cycles.

Efficiency

The most important advantage of topological planning lies in its efficiency. Dynamic programming is quadratic in the number of grid cells. The map shown in Figure 3 happens to possess 27,280 explored cells. In the average case, the number of iterations of value iteration is roughly equivalent to the length of the shortest path, which in our example map is 94.2 cells. Thus, in this example map, value iteration requires on average $2.6 \cdot 10^6$ backups. Planning using the topological representation is several orders of magnitudes more efficient. The average topological path length is 7.84. Since the topological graph shown in Figure 7d has 67 nodes, topological planning requires on average 525 backups. Notice the enormous gain in efficiency! Planning using the metric map is $4.9 \cdot 10^3$ more expensive than planning with the topological

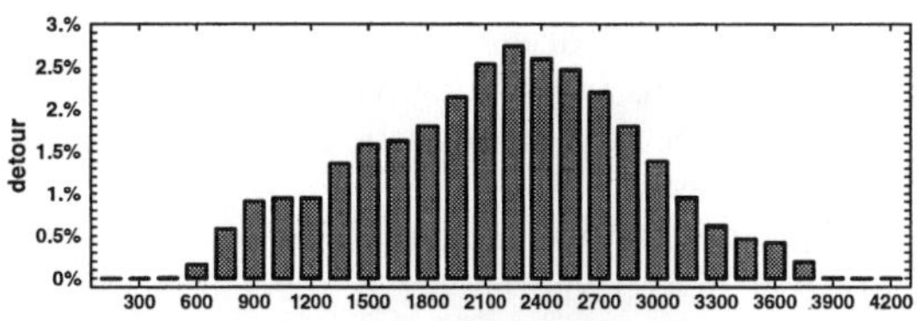

Figure 9: Loss, as a function of optimal path length.

map. In other words, planning on the topological level increases the efficiency by more than three orders of magnitude, while inducing a performance loss of only 1.82%.

The map shown in Figure 8, which is smaller but was recoded with a higher resolution, consists of 20,535 explored grid cells and 22 topological regions. On average, paths in the grid-based map lead through 84.8 cells, while the average length of a topological plan is 4.82 (averaged over 1,928,540 systematically generated pairs of points). Here the complexity reduction is even larger. Planning using the metric map is $1.6 \cdot 10^4$ more expensive than planning with the topological map. While these numbers are empirical and only correct for the particular maps investigated here, we conjecture that the relative quotient is roughly correct for other maps as well.

It should be noted that the compactness topological maps allows us to exhaustively pre-compute and memorize all plans connecting two nodes. Our example maps contain 67 (22) nodes, hence there are only 2,211 (231) different plans that are easily generated and memorized. If a new path planning problem arrives, topological planning amounts to looking up the correct plan.

The reader may also notice that topological plans often do not directly translate into motion commands. In (Thrun & Bücken 1996), a local "triplet planner" is described, which generates cost-optimal plans for triplets of adjacent topological regions. As shown there, triplet plans can also be pre-computed exhaustively, but they are not necessarily optimal, hence cause some small additional performance loss (1.42% and 1.19% for the maps investigated here).

Discussion

This paper proposes an integrated approach to mapping indoor robot environments. It combines the two major existing paradigms: grid-based and topological. Grid-based maps are learned using artificial neural networks and Bayes' rule. Topological maps are generated by partitioning the grid-based map into critical regions.

Building occupancy maps is a fairly standard procedure, which has proven to yield robust maps at various research sites. To the best of our knowledge, the maps exhibited in this paper are significantly larger than maps constructed from sonar sensors by other researchers. The most important aspect of this research, however, is the way topological graphs are constructed. Previous approaches have constructed topological maps from scratch, memorizing only partial metric information along the way. This often led to problems of disambiguation (*e.g.*, different places that look alike), and problems of establishing correspondence (*e.g.*, different views of the same place). This paper advocates to integrate both, grid-based and topological maps. As a direct consequence, different places are naturally disambiguated, and nearby locations are detected as such. In the integrated approach, landmarks play only an indirect role, through the grid-based position estimation mechanisms. Integration of landmark information over multiple measurements at multiple locations is automatically done in a consistent way. Visual landmarks, which often come to bear in topological approaches, can certainly be incorporated into the current approach, to further improve the accuracy of position estimation. In fact, sonar sensors can be understood as landmark detectors that indirectly—through the grid-based map—help determine the actual position in the topological map (*cf.* (Simmons & Koenig 1995)).

One of the key empirical results of this research concerns the cost-benefit analysis of topological representations. While grid-based maps yield more accurate control, planning with more abstract topological maps is several orders of magnitude more efficient. A large series of experiments showed that in a map of moderate size, the efficiency of planning can be increased by three to four orders of magnitude, while the loss in performance is negligible (*e.g.*, 1.82%). We believe that the topological maps described here will enable us to control an autonomous robot in multiple floors in our university building—complex mission planning in environments of that size was completely intractable with our previous methods.

A key disadvantage of grid-based methods, which is inherited by the approach presented here, is the need for accurately determining the robot's position. Since the difficulty of position control increases with the size of the environment, one might be inclined to think that grid-based approaches generally scale poorly to large-scale environments (unless they are provided with an accurate map). Although this argument is convincing, we are optimistic concerning the scaling properties of the approach taken here. The largest cycle-free map that was generated with this approach was approximately 100 meters long; the largest single cycle measured approximately 58 by 20 meters. We are not aware of any purely topological approach to robot mapping that would have been demonstrated to be capable of producing consistent maps of comparable size. Moreover, by using more accurate sensors (such as laser range finders), and by re-estimating robot positions backwards in time (which would be mathematically straightforward, but is currently not implemented because of its enormous computational complexity), we believe that maps can be learned and maintained for environments that are an order of magnitude larger than those investigated here.

Acknowledgment

The authors wish to thank the RHINO mobile robot group at the University of Bonn, in particular W. Burgard, A. Cremers, D. Fox, M. Giesenschlag, T. Hofmann, and W. Steiner, and the XAVIER mobile robot group at CMU. We also thank T. Ihle for pointing out an error in a previous version of this paper.

This research is sponsored in part by the National Science Foundation under award IRI-9313367, and by the Wright Laboratory, Aeronautical Systems Center, Air Force Materiel Command, USAF, and the Advanced Research Projects Agency (ARPA) under grant number F33615-93-1-1330. The views and conclusions contained in this document are those of the author and should not be interpreted as necessarily representing official policies or endorsements, either expressed or implied, of NSF, Wright Laboratory or the United States Government.

References

Buhmann, J.; Burgard, W.; Cremers, A. B.; Fox, D.; Hofmann, T.; Schneider, F.; Strikos, J.; and Thrun, S. 1995. The mobile robot Rhino. *AI Magazine* 16(1).

Crowley, J. 1989. World modeling and position estimation for a mobile robot using ultrasonic ranging. In *Proceedings 1989 IEEE International Conference on Robotics and Automation.*

Dean, T. L., and Boddy, M. 1988. An analysis of time-dependent planning. In *Proceeding Seventh NCAI*, AAAI.

Elfes, A. 1987. Sonar-based real-world mapping and navigation. *IEEE Journal of Robotics and Automation* 3(3):249–265.

Engelson, S., and McDermott, D. 1992. Error correction in mobile robot map learning. In *Proceedings 1992 IEEE International Conference on Robotics and Automation.*

Feng, L.; Borenstein, J.; and Everett, H. 1994. "where am I?" sensors and methods for autonomous mobile robot positioning. TR UM-MEAM-94-12, University of Michigan at Ann Arbor.

Fox, D.; Burgard, W.; and Thrun, S. 1995. The dynamic window approach to collision avoidance. TR IAI-TR-95-13, University of Bonn.

Hinkel, R., and Knieriemen, T. 1988. Environment perception with a laser radar in a fast moving robot. In *Proceedings Symposium on Robot Control.*

Howard, R. A. 1960. *Dynamic Programming and Markov Processes.* MIT Press.

Kortenkamp, D., and Weymouth, T. 1994. Topological mapping for mobile robots using a combination of sonar and vision sensing. In *Proceedings Twelfth NCAI*, AAAI.

Kuipers, B., and Byun, Y.-T. 1990. A robot exploration and mapping strategy based on a semantic hierarchy of spatial representations. TR, University of Texas at Austin.

Latombe, J.-C. 1991. *Robot Motion Planning.* Kluwer Academic Publishers.

Matarić, M. J. 1994. Interaction and intelligent behavior. Technical Report AI-TR-1495, MIT, AI-Lab.

Moravec, H. P. 1988. Sensor fusion in certainty grids for mobile robots. *AI Magazine* 61–74.

Nilsson, N. J. 1982. *Principles of Artificial Intelligence.* Springer Publisher.

Pearl, J. 1988. *Probabilistic reasoning in intelligent systems: networks of plausible inference.* Morgan Kaufmann Publishers.

Pierce, D., and Kuipers, B. 1994. Learning to explore and build maps. In *Proceedings Twelfth NCAI*, AAAI.

Rencken, W. 1993. Concurrent localisation and map building for mobile robots using ultrasonic sensors. In *Proceedings IEEE/RSJ International Conference on Intelligent Robots and Systems.*

Russell, S., and Norvig, P. 1995. *Artificial Intelligence: A Modern Approach.* Prentice Hall.

Schiele, B., and Crowley, J. 1994. A comparison of position estimation techniques using occupancy grids. In *Proceedings IEEE International Conference on Robotics and Automation.*

Simmons, R., and Koenig, S. 1995. Probabilistic robot navigation in partially observable environments. In *Proceedings IJCAI-95.*

Thrun, S., and Bücken, A. 1996. Learning maps for indoor mobile robot navigation. TR CMU-CS-96-121, Carnegie Mellon University.

Thrun, S. 1993. Exploration and model building in mobile robot domains. In *Proceedings ICNN-93*, IEEE NN Council.

Model-Based Reasoning

Improving Model-Based Diagnosis through Algebraic Analysis: the Petri Net Challenge

Luigi Portinale
Dipartimento di Informatica - Universita' di Torino
C.so Svizzera 185 - 10149 Torino (Italy)
e-mail: portinal@di.unito.it

Abstract

The present paper describes the empirical evaluation of a linear algebra approach to model-based diagnosis, in case the behavioral model of the device under examination is described through a Petri net model. In particular, we show that algebraic analysis based on P-invariants of the net model, can significantly improve the performance of a model-based diagnostic system, while keeping the integrity of a general framework defined from a formal logical theory. A system called INVADS is described and experimental results, performed on a car fault domain and involving the comparison of different implementations of P-invariant based diagnosis, are then discussed.

Introduction

In some recent papers (Portinale 1993), we have shown that Petri nets (PNs) (Murata 1989) can be fruitfully employed to face the problem of model-based diagnosis. This is accomplished by taking into account a formal logical framework of reference, defining classical notions (from the AI point of view) concerning the characterization of a diagnostic problem. In particular, it is shown that classical reachability analysis of PNs can naturally be exploited in order to realize "formally correct" (with respect to the logical framework of reference) diagnostic inference procedures. In the present paper, we focus on the empirical evaluation of a particular reachability analysis technique, namely P-invariant analysis, in order to show its practical usefulness and its possible advantages with respect to a logical inference mechanism. This analysis exploits a matrix representation of the net model and it is grounded on a linear algebra algorithm able to compute the so-called P-invariants of the net. They informally represent the correspondent of logical derivations and form the basis for the computation of the diagnoses. We will report on the empirical results obtained from some tests performed on a car fault domain, by comparing different implementations of P-invariant diagnosis and a classical abductive approach.

Petri Nets: Outline

A Petri net is a directed bipartite graph $N = \langle P, T, F\rangle$ whose vertices are called *places* (the elements of P represented as small circles) and *transitions* (the element of T represented as bars). The set of arcs is represented by F. In case the transitive closure F^+ of the arcs is irreflexive, the net is said to be *acyclic*. In a Petri net, an arc multiplicity function is usually defined as $W : (P \times T) \cup (T \times P) \rightarrow I\!N$; in case W is such that $W(f) = 1$ if $f \in F$ and $W(f) = 0$ if $f \notin F$, the net is said to be an *ordinary Petri net.* We will mainly be interested in such a kind of nets. For each $x \in P \cup T$ we use the classical notations ${}^\bullet x = \{y/yFx\}$ and $x^\bullet = \{y/xFy\}$. If ${}^\bullet x = \emptyset$, x is said to be a *source*, while if $x^\bullet = \emptyset$, x is said to be a *sink*. A *marking* is a function from the set of places to nonnegative integers, represented by means of *tokens* into places; a place containing a token is said to be *marked.* A *marked Petri net* is a pair (N, μ) where N is a Petri net and μ is a marking. The dynamics of the net is described by moving tokens from places to places according to the *concession* and *firing rules.* In ordinary Petri nets we say that a transition t *has concession* at a marking μ if and only if $\forall p \in^\bullet t\ \mu(p) \geq 1$. If a transition t has concession in a marking μ, it may *fire* (execute) producing a new marking μ' such that $\forall p \in P\ \ \mu'(p) = \mu(p) - W(p,t) + W(t,p)$. A marking μ' is *reachable* from a marking μ in a net N ($\mu' \in R(N, \mu)$) if and only if there exists a sequence of transitions producing μ' from μ in N. If a place of a marked net cannot be marked with more than one token, the place is said to be *safe*; if the property holds for every place, the net itself and every marking are said to be *safe.* Given a Petri net $N = \langle P, T, F\rangle$, if $n = |T|$ and $m = |P|$, the *incidence matrix* of N is the $n \times m$ matrix of integers A=$[a_{ij}]$ such that $a_{ij} = W(i,j) - W(j,i) (i \in T, j \in P)$ An m-vector of integers Y such that $A \cdot Y = 0$ is said to be a *P-invariant* of the net represented by A, the entry $Y(j)$ corresponding to place j. The *support* σ_Y of a P-invariant Y is the subset of places corresponding to nonzero entries of Y. In a dual way, if A^T is the transpose matrix of A, an n-vector of integers X such that $A^T \cdot X = 0$ is said to be a *T-invariant* (entries corresponding to transitions). It is well known that any invariant can be obtained as a linear combination of invariants having minimal (with respect to set inclusion) supports (Murata 1989).

Petri nets and Model-based Diagnosis

Model-based diagnosis deals with the problem of determining the explanation of the abnormal behavior of a given device, by reasoning on a model (usually a behavioral model) of such a device (Hamscher, Console, & de Kleer 1992). Approaches based on "consistency" between the observed and the predicted system behavior (with some components assumed to be faulty) are usually considered when the model represents the expected behavior of the system; however, when also the faulty behavior is taken into account, approaches based on "abduction" can be more adequately adopted.

Since both purely consistency based and purely abductive approaches suffer from some drawbacks, some effort has been done in order to combine them (Poole 1989; Console & Torasso 1991). In the present paper, we will refer to the framework defined in (Console & Torasso 1991).

Definition 1 *A model-based diagnostic problem is a tuple $DP = \langle M, H, CXT, \langle \Psi^+, \Psi^- \rangle \rangle$ where:*
- M is a logical theory representing the model of the system to be diagnosed;
*- H is a set of ground atoms of M identified as possible diagnostic hypotheses (*abducibles*);*
- CXT is a set of ground atoms of M representing contextual information;
- Ψ^+ is a set of ground atoms of M representing the observations to be covered in the current case;
- Ψ^- is a set of ground atoms of M representing the values of observable parameters conflicting with the observations.

We assume that M is represented by a set of definite clauses. This allows us to focus on a simple kind of model that is however representationally adequate for significant classes of behavioral models (see (Console *et al.* 1993)). If OBS is the set of current observations, the set Ψ^+ is in general a subset of OBS ($\Psi^+ \subseteq OBS$), while $\Psi^- = \{m(x)/m(y) \in OBS, x \neq y\}$. In a similar way, given the set CXT we define the set $CXT^- = \{c(x)/c(y) \in CXT\}$. The framework has the implicit assumption of abstracting from time; this allows us to further simplify the logical model by assuming M to be a set of definite clauses without recursion (i.e. a hierarchical definite logic program). We also assume the set OBS be composed by ground atoms having no consequences. Similarly, atoms in H cannot appear in the head of any clause (i.e. diagnostic hypotheses are independent) and so atoms in CXT.

Definition 2 *Given a diagnostic problem DP a diagnosis to DP is a set $E \subseteq H$ such that*
$\forall m(x) \in \Psi^+ \; M \cup CXT \cup E \vdash m(x)$
$\forall m(y) \in \Psi^- \; M \cup CXT \cup E \not\vdash m(y)$

We will refer to a diagnostic problem defined in this way as a *logic-based diagnostic problem.* Notice that definition 2 does not require the set E to mention every abducible predicate of M; however, E could not be a *partial diagnosis* in the sense of (de Kleer, Mackworth, & Reiter 1992), since there could be an extension of E to unmentioned abducible predicates such that some atoms in the set Ψ^- are derived. However, in the following we will consider only fault models (i.e. models describing only the consequences of the faulty behavior of the device under examination); in this case, a diagnosis E is interpreted as assigning a "normal" or "correct" value to abducible predicates not mentioned in E. The capability of dealing with models mixing the correct and the faulty behavior of the system requires a slight revision of the definition of diagnosis, by considering the set Ψ^- to be a set of denials, to be used in a contrapositive way. This would allows us to get the equivalent of the *kernel diagnoses* defined in (de Kleer, Mackworth, & Reiter 1992)[1].

In (Portinale 1993) a simple Petri net model, called Behavioral Petri Net (BPN), has been introduced, in order to capture the representational issues discussed above.

Definition 3 *A Behavioral Petri Net (BPN) is a 4-tuple $M = \langle P, T_N, T_{OR}, F \rangle$ such that $(P, T_N \cup T_{OR}, F)$ is an acyclic ordinary Petri net that satisfies the following axioms:*
1. $\forall p \in P (|{}^\bullet p| \leq 1 \wedge |p^\bullet| \leq 1)$
2. $\forall p_1, p_2 \in P \; (({}^\bullet p_1 = {}^\bullet p_2) \wedge (p_1^\bullet = p_2^\bullet) \rightarrow p_1 = p_2)$
3. $\forall t \in T_N \; (|{}^\bullet t| = 1 \wedge |t^\bullet| > 0) \vee (|{}^\bullet t| > 0 \wedge |t^\bullet| = 1)$
4. $\forall t \in T_{OR} (|{}^\bullet t| \geq 2 \wedge |t^\bullet| = 1)$

The set of transitions is partitioned into two subset T_N and T_{OR}; those in the former set are the usual kind of transitions of ordinary Petri nets while a transition $t \in T_{OR}$ has concession in a marking iff at least one of its input places is marked. They are actually "macro-transitions" that can be obtained by means of a set of classical transitions (see (Portinale 1993)). It can be shown that a BPN models the same kind of knowledge of a hierarchical definite logic program. Figure 1 shows an example of a BPN corresponding to the following set of clauses (OR transitions are represented as empty thick bars):

$grcl(low) \wedge roco(poor) \rightarrow oils(holed) \qquad oils(holed) \rightarrow obca(huge\_am)$

[1] Notice that definition 2 can be directly used if we consider E to contain exactly one ground instance for each abducible predicate.

$roco(poor) \rightarrow jerk(very\_strong)$ $osga(worn) \rightarrow oils(leaking)$
$oils(leaking) \rightarrow obca(small\_am)$ $piws(worn) \rightarrow laoi(severe)$
$jerk(very\_strong) \rightarrow vibr(very\_strong)$ $ente(incr) \rightarrow htin(red)$
$engi(run) \wedge laoi(severe) \rightarrow ente(incr)$ $oils(holed) \rightarrow laoi(severe)$
$jerk(very\_strong) \wedge oils(leaking) \rightarrow laoi(severe)$

Table 1 shows the key for acronyms used. The net of figure 1 is just for explanatory purposes, corresponding to a simplified part of a more general model, describing the faulty behavior of a car engine. Notice that the BPN contains some "dummy places" (labeled in figure 1 with capital letters) used to split places representing ground atoms involved in the body of more than one clause. This allows us to identify the token flow on the net with logical derivations in the logical model. OR-transitions model alternative way of obtaining a given atom.

Since a BPN is acyclic, a partial order $\prec$ over transitions is defined as $t_1 \prec t_2 \leftrightarrow t_1 F^+ t_2$. A concession rule with priority for transitions can then be introduced, resulting in the *enabling rule* of a BPN.

Definition 4 *Given a BPN, a transition t is* enabled *(i.e. it may fire) in a given marking μ if and only if it has concession at μ and $\not\exists t' \prec t$ such that t' has concession at μ.*

For example, in the net of figure 1, if both places $piws(worn)$ and $oils(holed)$ are marked, transition t_{27} is not enabled, since there is transition t_2 having concession and such that $t_2 \prec t_{27}$.

Definition 5 *An initial marking of a BPN is a safe marking μ_0 such that $\mu_0(p) = 1 \rightarrow^{\bullet} p = \emptyset$.*

A marked BPN is always considered with respect to a marking reachable from an initial marking. As shown in (Portinale 1993), every marked BPN is *safe* and in a marked BPN there is a unique marking, called the *final marking*, from which no transition can fire.

Given a BPN $N = \langle P, T_N, T_{OR}, F\rangle$ corresponding to a hierarchical definite logic program M, if B_M is

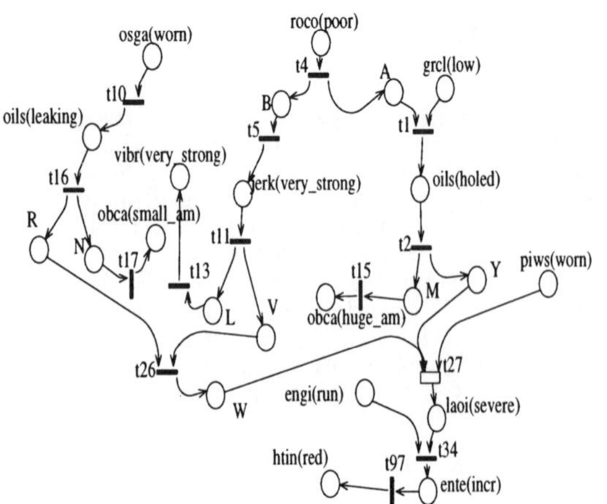

Figure 1: Example of a BPN

ENTITY	ACRONYM	ENTITY	ACRONYM
engine status	engi	engine temper.	ente
ground clear.	grcl	high temp. ind.	htin
jerks	jerk	lack of oil	laoi
oil below car	obca	oil sump gasket	osga
oil sump status	oils	piston wear	piws
road conditions	roco	vibrations	vibr

Table 1: Acronyms used in the BPN of fig. 1 and in the corresponding logical model

the Herbrand base of M, an *interpretation function* $\Phi : P \rightarrow B_M$ associating places of N with ground atoms of M can be defined. The function is in general a partial function; for example, in figure 1 the function Φ is considered undefined ($\perp$) for places labeled with capital letters (dummy places having no direct correspondence with ground atoms of M), while for the other places the label itself shows the value of Φ.

Given a conjunction of ground atoms J (represented as a set) we can determine a corresponding marking μ_J such that $\mu_J(p) = 1$ if $\Phi(p) \in J$ and $\mu_J(p) = 0$ otherwise.

Definition 6 *Given a logic-based diagnostic problem $DP = \langle M, H, CXT, \langle\Psi^+, \Psi^-\rangle\rangle$ and a BPN N_M corresponding to M, we can define the diagnostic problem in terms of the BPN model in the following way: BPN-DP= $\langle N, P_H, P_C, \langle P^+, P^-\rangle\rangle$ where $P_H = \{p \in P/\Phi(p) \in H\}$, $P_C = \{p \in P/\Phi(p) \in CXT\}$, $P^+ = \{p \in P/\Phi(p) \in \Psi^+\}$ and $P^- = \{p \in P/\Phi(p) \in \Psi^-\}$.*

Notice that, $\forall p \in P^+ \cup P^- \rightarrow p^{\bullet} = \emptyset$ (i.e. p is a sink place); similarly, $\forall p \in P_H \cup P_C \rightarrow^{\bullet} p = \emptyset$ (i.e. p is a source place). The formal connection between logic-based and BPN-based characterizations is established by means of the following theorem whose proof can be found in (Portinale 1993):

Theorem 1 *Given a logic-based diagnostic problem $DP = \langle M, H, CXT, \langle\Psi^+, \Psi^-\rangle\rangle$, let N_M be the BPN corresponding to M and μ_E^{CXT} be the marking corresponding to $E \cup CXT$ ($E \subseteq H$); if*
$(N_M, \mu_E^{CXT}) \vdash \alpha(c) \equiv$
$\exists \mu \in R(N_M, \mu_E^{CXT}) / \mu(p) = 1 \wedge \Phi(p) = \alpha(c)$
then $M \cup E \cup CXT \vdash \alpha(c) \leftrightarrow (N_M, \mu_E^{CXT}) \vdash \alpha(c)$

Definition 7 *Given a diagnostic problem BPN-DP= $\langle N_M, P_H, P_C, \langle P^+, P^-\rangle\rangle$, a* candidate diagnosis *is a marking μ_0 such that $\mu_0(p) = 1 \rightarrow p \in P_H$.*

We indicate with μ_C the marking corresponding to contextual information (i.e. $\mu_C(p) = 1 \leftrightarrow p \in P_C$) and with P_C^- the set of places corresponding to CXT^- (i.e. $P_C^- = \{p \in P/\Phi(p) \in CXT^-\}$).

Definition 8 *Given a diagnostic problem BPN-DP= $\langle N_M, P_H, P_C, \langle P^+, P^-\rangle\rangle$ a candidate diagnosis μ_0 is a solution to BPN-DP (i.e. is a diagnosis) if and only if*
$\forall p \in P^+ \quad (N_M, \mu_0 \cup \mu_C) \vdash \Phi(p)$
$\forall q \in P^- \quad (N_M, \mu_0 \cup \mu_C) \not\vdash \Phi(q)$

Definition 9 *A marking μ of a Behavioral Petri Net* covers *a set of places Q if and only if $\forall p \in Q \rightarrow \mu(p) = 1$, while it* zero-covers *Q if and only if $\forall p \in Q \rightarrow \mu(p) = 0$.*

The following theorem provides us with an operational notion of diagnosis in a BPN framework (see (Portinale 1993) for the proof):

Theorem 2 *A candidate diagnosis μ_0 is a solution to BPN-DP= $\langle N_M, P_H, P_C, \langle P^+, P^- \rangle \rangle$ (i.e. is a diagnosis) if and only if the final marking μ of $(N_M, \mu_0 \cup \mu_C)$* covers *P^+ and* zero-covers *P^-.*

This means that the problem of finding the solutions to a diagnostic problem can be re-formulated as a reachability problem on the net model; this can classically be tackled in two different ways, with a *reachability graph approach* (as shown in (Anglano & Portinale 1994)) or with an *algebraic (invariant-based) approach.* The aim of this paper is to concentrate on invariant analysis and to discuss the performance of a diagnostic algorithm based on such a principle, with respect to a classical approach based on symbolic manipulation.

Diagnostic Reasoning by Computing P-Invariants

In this section, we will show how to generate an initial marking satisfying the condition of theorem 2 from a set of P-invariant supports. By definition, P-invariants of a net $N = \langle P, T, F \rangle$ correspond to T-invariants of its dual net $N_D = \langle T, P, F \rangle$. The following lemma has been proved in (Peterka & Murata 1989).

Lemma 1 *Let $N = \langle P, T, F \rangle$ be a Petri net such that $\forall t \in T |t^\bullet| \leq 1$ and $t \in T$ be a sink transition; there exists a T-invariant X of N such that $X(t) \neq 0$ if and only if t is firable from the empty marking.*

This means that in N there are some source transitions firing from the empty marking, eventually leading to the firing of t. Consider now an ordinary Petri net: in order a place p to be marked, there must be a transition $t \in^\bullet p$ that fire, while in order a transition t to fire, every place $p \in^\bullet t$ must be marked. If every transition of a Petri net has exactly one input place, the sentence "a place is marked" corresponds to the sentence "a transition can fire" in the dual net. Let us then consider the following transformation on a BPN:

$\wedge$-fusion. Given a BPN $N = \langle P, T_N, T_{OR}, F \rangle$, produce the ordinary Petri net $N' = \langle P', \{T_N \cup T_{OR}\}, F' \rangle$ as follows: for each $t \in T_N$ such that $^\bullet t = \{p_1, \ldots p_k\}$ $(k > 1)$ substitute in P the set $\{p_1, \ldots p_k\}$ with the place $p_{1,k}$ such that $^\bullet p_{1,k} = \bigcup_{i=1}^{k} {}^\bullet p_i$ and $p_{1,k}^\bullet = \{t\}$

This transformation simply collapses places that are "AND-ed" into a single place representing their conjunction; even if the resulting net is no longer a BPN, it encodes the same kind of knowledge of the original BPN. In fact, let us consider the interpretation function Φ of N and the following operator $\oplus$ on it:

$$\Phi(p) \oplus \Phi(q) = \Phi(p) \cup \Phi(q)$$

With $\Phi(p) \oplus \perp = \perp \oplus \Phi(p) = \Phi(p)$

We can define an interpretation function Φ' for N' from the interpretation function Φ of N as follows:

$$\Phi'(p) = \begin{cases} \Phi(p) & \text{if } p \in P \cap P' \\ \bigoplus_{i=1}^{k} \Phi(p_i) & \text{if } p = p_{1,k} \in P' - P \end{cases}$$

Figure 2 shows the net obtained from the BPN of figure 1 by means of the $\wedge$-fusion. Places $grcl(low)$ and A are collapsed into place "$grcl(low) + A$", V and R into place "$V + R$", $laoi(severe)$ and $engi(run)$ into place "$laoi(moder) + engi(run)$". The interpretation function Φ' is such that $\Phi'(grcl(low) + A) = \{grcl(low)\}$, $\Phi'(V + R) = \perp$, $\Phi'(laoi(severe) + engi(run)) = \{laoi(severe), engi(run)\}$, $\Phi' \equiv \Phi$ for remaining places.

Theorem 3 *Given a BPN N_M corresponding to a hierarchical definite logic program M, let N'_M be the net obtained from N_M through the $\wedge$-fusion transformation, Φ' the interpretation function of N'_M and p a sink place; the following are equivalent propositions:*
1) there is a P-invariant Y of N'_M such that $Y(p) \neq 0$;
2) by marking source places p_s such that $Y(p_s) \neq 0$, the place p can eventually be marked;
3) $\bigcup_{p_s} \Phi'(p_s) \cup M \vdash \Phi'(p)$

Proof. 1) $\equiv$ 2) is a consequence of lemma 1 and of the fact that T-invariants of a net are P-invariants for

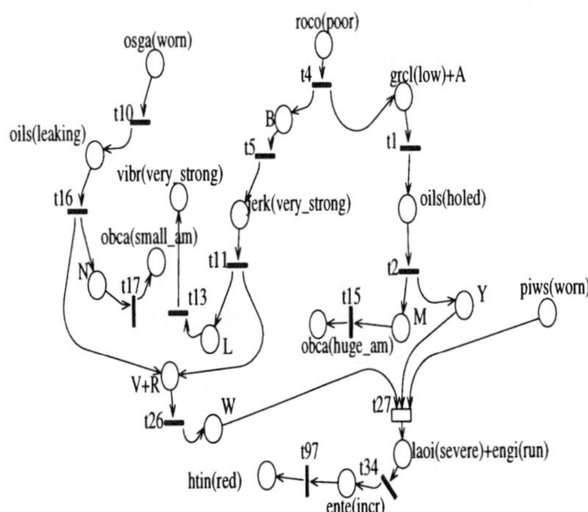

Figure 2: BPN for P-invariant Computation

its dual net. 2) $\equiv$ 3) is a consequence of theorem 1. □ From theorem 3 we conclude that the supports of the P-invariants of N'_M characterize the logical derivations from atoms representing diagnostic hypotheses and contexts, to atoms representing observable parameters. Consider for instance the following diagnostic problem BPN-DP= $\langle N_M, P_H, , P_C, \langle P^+, P^- \rangle \rangle$ where N_M is the net of figure 1 (we remember that such a net is intended to represent a fault model). Let us suppose to have the following set of observations:

$OBS = \{htin(red), obca(small\_am), vibr(normal)\}$ (i.e. the temperature indicator is red, there is a small amount of oil below the car and vibrations are normal). Contextual information are $CXT = \{grcl(normal), engi(run)\}$ (i.e. we are considering a car with a normal ground clearance and in the context of the engine being running). Let us also suppose that all the "abnormal" observations have to covered, then:

$P_H = \{piws(worn), osga(worn), roco(poor)\}$,
$P_C = \{engi(run)\}$ $\quad P_C^- = \{grcl(low)\}$
$P^+ = \{htin(red), obca(small\_am)\}$,
$P^- = \{vibr(very\_strong), obca(huge\_am)\}$.

The net of figure 2 is the result of the $\wedge$-fusion of N_M; the minimal supports of its P-invariants are:

$\sigma_1 = \{grcl(low) + A, oils(holed), roco(poor), M, obca(huge\_am)\}$
$\sigma_2 = \{grcl(low) + A, oils(holed), roco(poor), Y, ente(incr)$
$laoi(severe) + engi(run), htin(red)\}$
$\sigma_3 = \{B, roco(poor), jerk(very\_strong), osga(worn), V + R, W,$
$oils(leaking), laoi(severe) + engi(run), ente(incr), htin(red)\}$
$\sigma_4 = \{B, roco(poor), jerk(very\_strong), L, vibr(very\_strong)\}$
$\sigma_5 = \{obca(small\_am), osga(worn), oils(leaking), N\}$
$\sigma_6 = \{piws(worn), laoi(severe)+engi(run), ente(incr), htin(red)\}$

Consider for instance σ_4: we notice that the support contains the source place *roco(poor)* $\in P_H$ and the sink place $vibr(very\_strong) \in P^-$. From theorem 3 we conclude that $M \cup \{roco(poor)\} \vdash vibr(very\_strong)$; this means that any initial marking having place *roco(poor)* marked is not a diagnosis, since it will eventually produce a final marking having place $vibr(very\_strong) \in P^-$ marked.

From these considerations, we can devise a P-invariant based diagnostic algorithm: after having computed the minimal supports of P-invariants, (efficient algorithms exist for this task (Martinez & Silva 1982)) those related to predictions corresponding to places in P^- are eliminated by taking into account the fact that if $\hat{\sigma}$ and $\hat{\sigma}'$ are two sets of ground atoms such that $\hat{\sigma} \subseteq \hat{\sigma}'$, if $\hat{\sigma} \vdash \alpha$ then $\hat{\sigma}' \vdash \alpha$; at the same way, supports containing places belonging to P_C^- are also eliminated. We have then to consider the coverability of P^+; for each place $p \in P^+$, we build from remaining supports the list of places having interpretation function corresponding to a diagnostic hypothesis and supporting p (i.e. contained in a P-invariant support containing p). Final diagnoses are obtained by combining such lists.

Let us consider again the diagnostic problem introduced above; supports σ_1, σ_2 are discarded since they contain place $grcl(low) + A$ such that $\Phi'(grcl(low) + A) = grcl(low) \in CXT^-$ (σ_1 also contains $obca(huge\_am) \in P^-$) and support σ_4 because it contains place $vibr(very\_strong) \in P^-$, Moreover, also support σ_3 is discarded because of the pruning of σ_4; indeed, $\hat{\sigma}_4 = \{roco(poor)\}$ and $\hat{\sigma}_3 = \{roco(poor), osga(worn), engi(run)\}$. Since $\hat{\sigma}_4 \subset \hat{\sigma}_3$, we need to prune also σ_3. Only supports σ_5 and σ_6 survive to the pruning phase and we then obtain:

$\hat{\sigma}_6 = \{osga(worn)\}$ for $obca(small\_am) \in P^+$
$\hat{\sigma}_9 = \{piws(worn), engi(run)\}$ for $htin(red) \in P^+$

The only possible combination in this case is $\hat{\sigma}_6 \cup \hat{\sigma}_9 = \{piws(worn), engi(run), osga(worn)\}$ representing the diagnosis "$piws(worn) \wedge osga(worn)$" in the context "$engi(run) \wedge grcl(normal)$" (i.e. if the engine is running and the car has a normal ground clearance, the normal intensity of vibrations, the red temperature indicator and the small amount of oil below the car are explained by the fact that both the state of the pistons and the oil sump gasket are worn).

Experimental Results

We implemented the P-invariant approach to diagnosis in a system called INVADS (INVAriant based Diagnostic System) and we performed different series of experiments addressing the following two issues:

1. comparison of different implementations of invariant-based diagnosis;
2. comparison between invariant-based diagnosis and logical-abductive diagnosis.

Both types of experiments have been done on a BPN relative to a knowledge base describing the fault "causal" model of a car engine and consisting in more than 100 places and more than 100 transitions. We ran the experiments on a SUN Sparc station Classic with 32 Mbytes of memory; the software environment has been realized in SICStus prolog, with an embedded module for invariant computation written in C. We considered 48 different cases of car engine malfunctions in such a way to consider all the main fault evolutions described in the model. Different running of the same batch of cases have been considered for each implementation; results about the running time showed a quite low variance between different runs, so they have been simply averaged.

Implementation Testing

We tested three different kinds of implementation of P-invariant based diagnosis that we classified as follows:

off-line invariant computation (OFF); net simplification (SIM); observation addition (ADD).
The first kind of implementation (OFF) simply consists in the off-line computation of all the P-invariants of the net obtained from the $\wedge$-fusion on the BPN under examination; this approach makes explicit the information related to the P-invariants once for all and any diagnostic case that will be provided to the system, will use the same set of P-invariants. However, we have to search the solution in a search space (the set of P-invariants supports) that contains information that is not relevant to the current case. The complexity of a diagnostic algorithm based on this principle is just the complexity of the phase concerning the generation of diagnoses from P-invariant supports.

The SIM approach consists in simplifying the net with respect to the observations made in the case to be solved. This can be done by considering the sets P^+ and P^- from the current diagnostic problem, iteratively repeating the following actions, until no transition is removed.
for each place $p \notin P^+ \cup P^-$ **do remove** p;
for each transition $t/t^\bullet = \emptyset$ **do remove** t;
This allows us to consider only the part of the net relevant to the current set of observations and to compute the P-invariants only for this reduced net. A diagnostic algorithm based on SIM must take into account three different phases for each case to be solved: *net simplification*, *P-invariant computation* and *diagnosis generation*. Since the set of P-invariant supports from which to generate diagnoses is reduced with respect to the previous approach, diagnosis generation could result much faster than in OFF.

The ADD approach is conceptually similar to SIM; we consider the net obtained from the $\wedge$-fusion on the current BPN, by deleting all the sink places representing observable parameters. Given the current set of observations, we then add to N the sink places corresponding to sets P^+ and P^-. Also in this case we have to consider three distinct phases namely *observation addition*, *P-invariant computation* and *diagnosis generation* and, as in the previous case, the set of P-invariant supports we get does not contain information irrelevant to current observations.
Results concerning the comparison of the three proposed strategies are summarized in figure 3, where the average computation times of the above strategies are reported for the 48 sample cases we used. The SIM approach resulted in very high execution times, essentially because of the expensiveness of the net simplification phase. This can be see in figure 4 where cpu times of net simplification and observation addition phases are plotted. Notice also that the basic pattern of the SIM strategy in figure 3 is essentially determined by the net simplification phase. We did not investigate the possibility of directly performing the simplification on the incidence matrix of the net; our claim is that a matrix simplification will be less expensive, but it would not improve to much the result.
Between OFF and ADD, the latter strategy resulted to be better in terms of global execution time, even if without showing the huge difference of the SIM strategy. Obviously, the OFF strategy resulted in the higher computation time (with respect to both SIM and ADD strategies) for the diagnosis generation phase and for the invariant computation phase, but the fact that the latter phase is done off-line, determined the situation depicted in figure 3.

Logical and P-invariant Diagnosis Comparison

To test the performance of a P-invariant diagnostic algorithm against a classical logical approach, we chose to compare the INVADS system using the ADD strategy with an abductive diagnostic system called AID (Console *et al.* 1993). The reasons for such a direct comparison are twofold:
1. both systems rely on the same formal framework of reference we previously discussed;

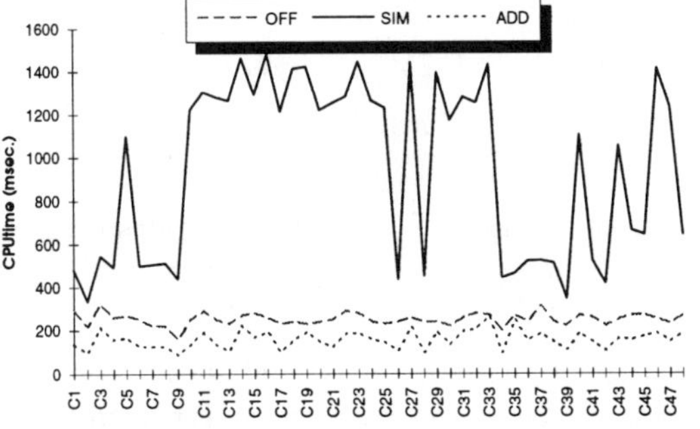

Figure 3: Comparison of different strategies for P-invariant diagnosis

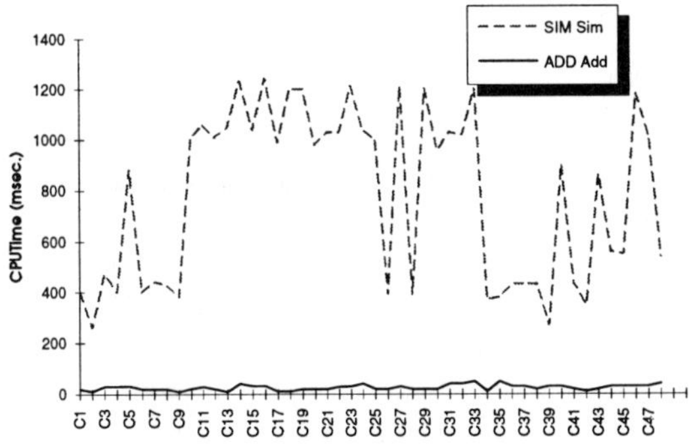

Figure 4: Net Simplification vs Observation Addition

2. both systems share the same implementation environment (a SICStus prolog implementation for SUN sparc stations).

Also for this experiment, we tested different runs of the batch of our sample cases. In particular, we measured for each case C the percentage gain of INVADS vs AID, defined as follows:

$$G(C) = \frac{T^C_{AID} - T^C_{INVADS}}{T^C_{INVADS}}$$

where T^C_{AID} and T^C_{INVADS} represent the execution times on case C of AID and INVADS respectively. Results on our car engine fault domain showed a quite good behavior of P-invariant based approach (see figure 5); the average gain resulted to be of 34.41% with some peaks of about (or even more then) 100%.

Conclusions

In the present paper, we have shown how Petri net reachability analysis could be used as a formal basis for explaining the misbehavior of a given device. We briefly discussed a net model called BPN, used to describe the behavior of the device under examination. The BPN model is not proposed as a direct tool of diagnostic knowledge representation, but rather as an analysis formalism that can be derived from other forms of knowledge representation, like for instance causal networks as described in (Portinale 1992). We concentrated on P-invariant reachability analysis, representing the starting point for the definition of an innovative approach to model-based diagnosis.

We tested the different implementation of the approach on a car engine fault domain, by getting an encouraging comparison with a classical logical approach to diagnosis. Notice also that, besides the fact that P-invariants are obtained through a linear algebra based computation (that can result more efficient than symbolic computation), parallel algorithms can be devised for this kind of approach (Marinescu, Beaven, & Stansifer 1991; Lin *et al.* 1993)). This clearly adds more interest to the net invariant approach to diagnosis, by also taking into account the fact that its complementary approach (i.e. the diagnosis based on reachability graph analysis) has been shown to be very adequate to a parallel implementation (Anglano & Portinale 1994). Future works are planned in order to compare P-invariant diagnosis also with this approach.

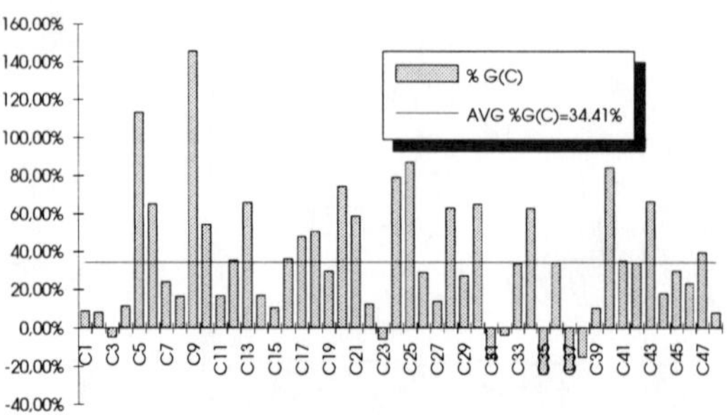

Figure 5: Percentage Gain INVADS vs AID

References

Anglano, C., and Portinale, L. 1994. B-W analysis: a backward reachability analysis for diagnostic problem solving suitable to parallel implementation. In *LNCS 815*, 39–58. Springer Verlag.

Console, L., and Torasso, P. 1991. A spectrum of logical definitions of model-based diagnosis. *Computational Intelligence* 7(3):133–141.

Console, L.; Portinale, L.; Theseider Dupré, D.; and Torasso, P. 1993. Combining heuristic and causal reasoning in diagnostic problem solving. In *Second Generation Expert Systems.* Springer Verlag. 46,68.

de Kleer, J.; Mackworth, A.; and Reiter, R. 1992. Characterizing diagnoses and systems. *Artificial Intelligence* 56(2–3):197–222.

Hamscher, W.; Console, L.; and de Kleer, J. 1992. *Readings in Model-Based Diagnosis.* Morgan Kaufmann.

Lin, C.; Chaundhury, A.; Whinston, A.; and Marinescu, D. 1993. Logical inference of Horn clauses in Petri net models. *IEEE TKDE* 5(3):416–425.

Marinescu, D.; Beaven, M.; and Stansifer, R. 1991. A parallel algorithm for computing invariants of a Petri net model. In *Proc. 4th PNPM*, 136–143.

Martinez, J., and Silva, M. 1982. A simple and fast algorithm to obtain all invariants of a generalized Petri net. In *Applications and Theory of Petri Nets.* Springer Verlag. 301–310.

Murata, T. 1989. Petri nets: Properties, analysis and applications. *Proceedings of the IEEE* 77(4):541–580.

Peterka, G., and Murata, T. 1989. Proof procedure and answer extraction in Petri net model of logic programs. *IEEE TSE* 15(2):209–217.

Poole, D. 1989. Normality and faults in logic-based diagnosis. In *Proc. 11th IJCAI*, 1304–1310.

Portinale, L. 1992. Verification of causal models using Petri nets. *International Journal of Intelligent Systems* 7(8):715–742.

Portinale, L. 1993. *Petri net models for diagnostic knowledge representation and reasoning.* PhD Thesis, Dip. Informatica, Universita' di Torino. `ftp://ftp.di.unito.it/pub/portinal`.

A Model-Based Approach to Blame Assignment: Revising the Reasoning Steps of Problem Solvers

Eleni Stroulia
Center for Applied Knowledge Processing
Helmholtzstr. 16
89081 Ulm, Germany
stroulia@faw.uni-ulm.de

Ashok K. Goel
College of Computing
Georgia Institute of Technology
Atlanta, GA 30332-0280
goel@cc.gatech.edu

Abstract

Blame assignment is a classical problem in learning and adaptation. Given a problem solver that fails to deliver the behaviors desired of it, the blame-assignment task has the goal of identifying the cause(s) of the failure. Broadly categorized, these causes can be knowledge faults (errors in the organization, content, and representation of the problem-solver's domain knowledge) or processing faults (errors in the content, and control of the problem-solving process). Much of AI research on blame assignment has focused on identifying knowledge and control–of–processing faults based on the trace of the failed problem-solving episode. In this paper, we describe a blame-assignment method for identifying content–of–processing faults, i.e., faults in the specification of the problem-solving operators. This method uses a structure–behavior–function (SBF) model of the problem-solving process, which captures the functional semantics of the overall task and the operators of the problem solver, the compositional semantics of its problem-solving methods that combine the operators' inferences into the outputs of the overall task, and the "causal" inter-dependencies between its tasks, methods and domain knowledge. We illustrate this model-based blame-assignment method with examples from AUTOGNOSTIC.

Introduction

Blame assignment is a classical problem in learning and adaptation (Samuel 1959). Given a problem solver that fails to deliver the behaviors desired of it, the general blame-assignment task has the goal of identifying the cause(s) of the failure. The types of the identified cause(s) can then be used as indices to appropriate learning strategies which can eliminate the causes of the failure and thus improve the problem solver.

A problem solver may fail due to a wide variety of causes that may be broadly categorized into knowledge faults and processing faults. The former (Davis 1980; Weintraub 1991) pertain to errors in the organization, content, and representation of the problem-solver's domain knowledge, while the latter refer to errors in the content of, and control over the steps of its processing. Much of AI research on blame assignment has focused on the identification of knowledge faults. In this paper, we focus on the identification of processing faults.

AI work on identification of processing faults itself has focused on faults in the control of processing. For example, both Lex (Mitchell et. al 1981) and Prodigy (Carbonell et. al 1989) assume that the causes of the failures of their problem solvers lie in their incorrect operator-selection heuristics. Their blame-assignment methods assume that the set of available operators is both complete and correctly specified. This assumes that the exact same operators used in the failed problem-solving episode can be in some way combined to produce a correct solution. In contrast, in this paper, we are interested in the issue of identifying faults in the specification of the operators. While we too assume that the set of available problem-solving operators is complete relative to the problem-solver's task, we admit the possibility that they may be incorrectly specified. That is, the information transformations the operators are designed to perform may not be sufficient for delivering a solution to (all of) the problems presented to the problem solver. Thus, the research issue becomes, given a problem-solver that fails to deliver the overall behavior desired of it, to specify a combination of knowledge and processing that enables the failing problem solver to identify faults in the specification of its operators.

Traditional blame-assignment methods for identifying faults in the control of processing are based on problem-solving traces. For example, both Lex and Prodigy require the trace of the processing in the failed problem-solving episode as well as a trace of the processing that would have led to problem-solving success. Under the assumption that the cause of the failure is that the problem solver does not know the exact conditions under which each of the operators should be used, both these systems compare the failed trace against the successful one to identify situations where operators were incorrectly used. In contrast, we describe a method which, in addition to the trace of the failed problem solving, uses a model of the problem-solver's processing and knowledge to identify faults in the specification of the problem-solving operators. We posit that the identification of faults in operator specification is facilitated by knowledge of (i) the functional semantics of the overall task of the problem solver, (ii) the functional semantics of its operators, (iii) the compositional semantics of the problem-solving methods that recursively synthesize the inferences carried out by the available operators into the outputs of its overall task, and (iv) the "causal" inter-dependencies between (sub)tasks, methods and domain knowledge. We use structure–behavior–function (SBF) models to capture this semantics of problem solving.

This model-based method for blame assignment is implemented in AUTOGNOSTIC, a "shell" which provides (i) a language for representing SBF models of problem solvers, and (ii) mechanisms for monitoring the problem solving, receiving and assimilating feedback on the result, assigning blame in case of failure, and repairing the problem solver. In this paper, we illustrate AUTOGNOSTIC's blame-assignment method for processing faults with examples from AUTOGNOSTIC's integration with ROUTER (Goel et. al 1994), a path-planning system.

SBF Models of Problem Solving

SBF models of problem solving analyze the problem-solver's task structure, its domain knowledge and their inter-dependencies. In this model, the problem-solver's tasks constitute the building blocks of its problem-solving mechanism. The problem-solving methods that it employs decompose its complex overall tasks into simpler subtasks. These, in turn, get recursively decomposed into even simpler subtasks until they become elementary reasoning steps, i.e., *"leaf" tasks*. These leaf tasks are directly accomplished by the problem-solver's domain operators.

A task is specified as a transformation from an input to an output information state. It is characterized by the type(s) of information it consumes as input and produces as output, and the nature of the transformation it performs between the two. The functional semantics of a task describes the nature of the information transformation this task is intended to perform, and thus, constitutes a partial description of its expected, correct behavior. It is expressed in terms of specific domain relations that hold true among the task's inputs and outputs. For a non-leaf task, the functional semantics of the subtasks into which the task is recursively decomposed, and the ordering relations that the decomposing methods impose over them, constitute a partial description of a correct reasoning strategy for this task. Henceforth, we will use the term *strategy* to refer to the task tree that results from a task's decomposition by a particular method.

Methods can be thought of as general plans for how the solutions to different low-level subtasks get combined to deliver the output desired of higher-level tasks. They specify compositions of the problem-solver's domain operators into its higher-level tasks. Each method captures the semantics of the composition of a set of lower-level subtasks into a higher-level task in terms of control inter-dependencies (that is, a set of ordering relations), and information inter-dependencies, (that is, a set of information producer-consumer relations), among these subtasks.

In addition to the task structure, the SBF model of a problem solver specifies its domain knowledge in terms of the types of domain objects that the problem solver knows about, and the relations applicable to them. This specification of object types and relations captures the problem-solver's ontology of its domain. In addition, the information types flowing through the task structure are specified as instances of domain-object types, and thus each particular task input or output is related to the ontological commitments associated with the object type of which it is an instance. Finally, the specification of the tasks' functional semantics in terms of domain relations, that must hold between their inputs and outputs, captures the "causal" inter-dependencies of the inferences drawn to accomplish the tasks with the problem-solver's domain knowledge, where each inference is based on some specific domain knowledge. The assumption here is that if the semantics of a task is specified in terms of a particular domain relation, then in order to meet its semantics, the set of inferences drawn in service of this task will use the knowledge of the problem solver about this domain relation.

The Case Study: ROUTER is a multistrategy navigational planner which will be used in this paper to illustrate AUTOGNOSTIC's model-based method for blame assignment. ROUTER's task, `path-planning`, is to find a path from an initial location to a goal location in a physical space. Its spatial model of the navigation world is organized in a neighborhood-subneighborhood hierarchy. High-level neighborhoods describe large spaces in terms of major streets and their intersections. They get refined into lower-level neighborhoods which describe both major and minor streets and their intersections but over smaller spaces. Figure 1 diagrammatically depicts ROUTER's task structure and gives part of the SBF specification of some of its tasks and types of domain knowledge. In addition to the spatial model, Router contains a memory of past path-planning cases; the case memory is organized around the neighborhood-subneighborhood hierarchy.

AUTOGNOSTIC's SBF model of ROUTER's problem solving specifies that its overall task, `path-planning`, is decomposed into the subtasks `elaboration`, `retrieval`, `search` and `storage`. The elaboration subtask classifies the initial and goal locations into the neighborhood-subneighborhood hierarchy; it identifies the neighborhoods to which the two locations belong. This is a leaf task, i.e., it is directly solved by the domain operator `elaboration-op`. The `retrieval` subtask recalls from ROUTER's memory a similar path which connects locations spatially close to the current initial and goal locations. Next, the `search` subtask produces the desired path, and, subsequently, the `storage` subtask stores it in memory for future reuse. The search task can be accomplished by three different methods, the `intrazonal`, the `interzonal`, and the `case-based` method. The first two methods are model-based, that is, the semantics of the subtasks resulting from the use of these methods refer to model relations. In analogy, the semantics of the subtasks resulting from the use of the case-based method refer to case-memory relations.

The first method is applicable only under the condition that the initial and the goal problem locations belong in the same neighborhood. It decomposes the `search` task into the subtasks `search-initialization`, `temp-path-selection` and `path-increase`. The first of these subtasks initializes the set of paths already explored by ROUTER to contain only a path consisting of a single location, i.e., the initial location. The `temp-path-selection` subtask takes as input this set of explored paths and selects from it a particular temporary path which feeds as input to the `path-increase` subtask. The latter task extends the temporary path to reach its neighboring points, i.e., all the

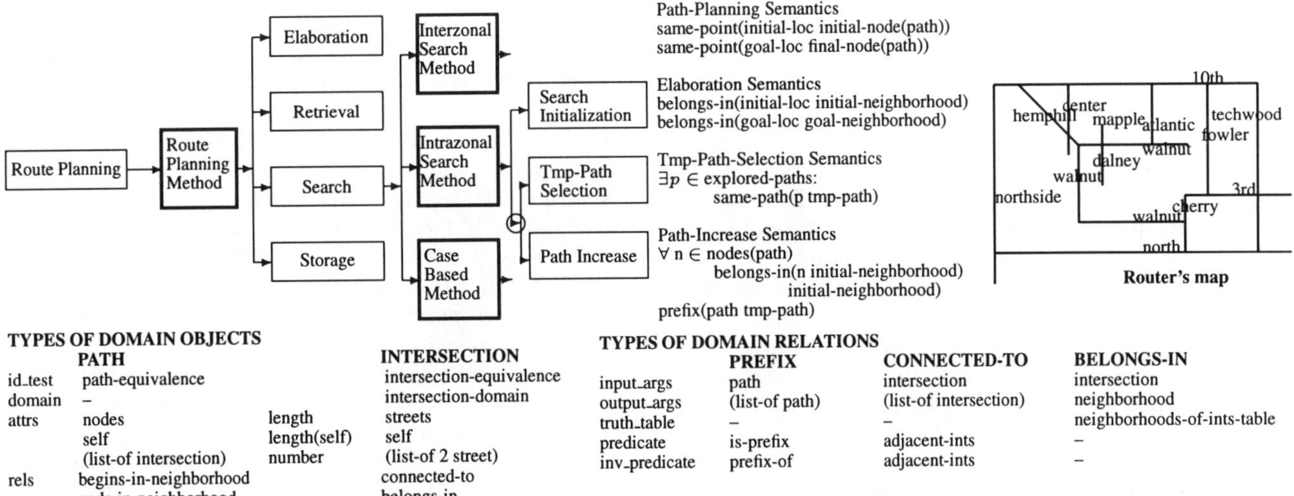

Figure 1: Fragment of ROUTER's planning task structure and part of the SBF specification of some of ROUTER's domain objects and relations.

intersections that belong in the common initial- and goal-neighborhood and are immediately adjacent to its last node. These extended paths are all added to the set of explored paths. The last two subtasks are repeatedly performed (as denoted by the small circle in the illustration of ROUTER's task structure in Figure 1), until one of the explored paths reaches the goal location, in which case, it is returned as the desired output of the overall task.

As shown in the bottom of Figure 1, ROUTER's world is described in terms of several different object types, such as `intersections`, `neighborhoods`, `streets` and `paths`. For each type of these domain objects, the SBF model specifies the set of values that specific instances of objects may take, the attributes of the object type, the predicate that evaluates whether two instances of this object type are identical, and the domain relations that relate it to other domain objects. The objects in ROUTER's world are related through `relations`, such as `belongs-in` which relates intersections to neighborhoods. For each type of domain relation the SBF model specifies the types of domain objects it applies to, and its truth table or the predicate that evaluates whether a tuple belongs in this relation or not.

Model-based Blame Assignment

In this paper, we focus on the blame-assignment task that arises when the problem solver is given as feedback information that a value desired for one of its outputs is different from the value actually produced. More specifically, the symptom of the failure is a divergence between the actual and the desired problem-solving behavior, although the actual behavior may be consistent with the range of behaviors intended of the problem solver. We will illustrate the model-based method for addressing this task with an example from ROUTER, which given the problem of going from *(10th center)* to *(walnut dalney)*, produces the path *((center 10th) (10th atlantic) (atlantic walnut) (walnut dalney))*, for which AUTOGNOSTIC receives the shorter path *((center 10th) (center mapple) (mapple dalney) (dalney walnut))* as feedback (see Figure 1 right for a map of ROUTER's navigational domain).

Before localizing the cause of the failure into a specific operator or piece of domain knowledge, the blame-assignment method evaluates whether the feedback is within the class of values the overall problem-solver's task was intended to produce; otherwise it would be meaningless to examine why it was not actually produced. To this end, it evaluates whether the feedback conforms with the overall task's expected correct behavior as specified by the task's functional semantics. As mentioned above, the SBF specification of a task's semantics consists of task's input and output information types and a domain relation. For each domain relation, the SBF model specifies a predicate (or, a truth table), which makes it possible to evaluate whether or not the specific values of input and output information in the episode belong to the domain relation. The tuple formed by the specific values of the input and output information in a particular problem-solving episode should belong in the domain relation.

In our example, AUTOGNOSTIC's first step is to establish, based on the semantics of the overall `path-planning` task (see Figure 1), whether the feedback path belongs in the class of paths that ROUTER was intended to produce given its actual input initial and goal locations. The feedback path begins at the initial and ends at the goal location, therefore, AUTOGNOSTIC infers that the feedback is indeed a valid output for ROUTER's current problem.

If the feedback belongs indeed in the class of intended correct outputs for the current problem input (see Figure 2[1]), then the strategy employed to accomplish this task should have produced it. Thus, the blame-assignment method postulates that the cause of the failure must lie within this strategy, that is, within some of its subtasks. From the trace of the failed problem-solving episode, it identifies the method which was used for the task in question, and focuses the search for the cause of the failure to the last subtask of this method producing the erroneous output (see Figure 2[1.2]).

Having established that the feedback belongs in the class of paths that `path-planning` could have produced for this problem, AUTOGNOSTIC postulates that the cause of the failure must lie within the strategy used to accomplish this task. Thus, it successively refines the focus of its investigation to the subtasks involved in the production of the path, i.e., `search` and next `path-increase`.

If at some point, the semantics of some task is not validated by its actual input and the feedback (see Figure 2[2]), then the blame-assignment method attempts to infer alternative inputs which would satisfy it. This is meaningful only when the task's input is not part of the overall problem specification, otherwise it would be an attempt to redefine the problem in order to fit the desired solution. If, however, the input of the task in question is produced by some earlier subtask, and, if alternative values can be found for it such that the current task's semantics is satisfied (see Figure 2[2.1]), then the blame-assignment method infers that the fault must lie within this earlier subtask which produced the "wrong" input for the task currently under examination. Therefore, it identifies the highest earlier subtask producing the information in question, and shifts its focus to assigning blame for its failure to produce the alternative desired value. To identify the producing subtask, the method uses the compositional semantics of the methods that gave rise to the subtask under examination. Had this knowledge not been available in the SBF model, the method would have to examine all the subtasks performed before the current subtask with failing semantics.

AB-undesired-value(*task info feedback*)
IF *feedback* belongs in the class of values *task* produces for *info*
THEN **[1]**
  IF *task* is accomplished by an operator
  THEN **under-specified-task-semantics** **[1.1]**
    IF the task semantics is an enumerated domain relation
    THEN **incorrect-domain-relation** **[1.1.a]**
  IF *task* is accomplished by a method *M*
  THEN AB-undesired-value(*task-i info feedback*) **[1.2]**
    where *task-i* ∈ subtasks(*task M*) and *info* ∈ output(task-i)
ELSE **[2]**
  IF there is alternative value, *v*, for info *i*, where *i* ∈ input(task)
    for which *task* could have produced *feedback* for *info*
  THEN AB-undesired-value(task-i i v) **[2.1]**
    where *i* ∈ output(task-i) ∩
    ∄ *task-j*: *i* ∈ output(task-j) ∩ *task-i* ∈ subtasks(task-j)
  ELSE **over-constrained-task-semantics** **[2.2]**
    IF the violated semantics is an enumerated domain relation
    THEN **incomplete-domain-relation** **[2.2.a]**

Figure 2: The blame-assignment algorithm. The different diagnostic hypotheses that can be postulated are shown in boldface.

The ability to infer possible alternative values for types of information produced by the problem-solver's intermediate subtasks is based on the SBF specification first, of the functional semantics of the task under inspection, and second, of the domain relations on which this semantics is based. As we have already described, based on these types of knowledge, the blame-assignment method is able to evaluate whether or not a particular value tuple validates a task's semantics. In addition, given a partially specified tuple, the blame-assignment method is potentially able to identify possible values for the unspecified tuple members such that the tuple belongs in the relation and satisfies the semantics. If the domain relation is exhaustively described in a truth table, then the possible values are inferred through a search of this table for all the tuples that match the partially specified one. If it is evaluated by a predicate, then there are two possibilities. Either an inverse predicate is also specified in the SBF model, such that it maps the task's output to its possible inputs, or the task's input is an instance of an object type with an exhaustively described domain. In the former case, the inverse predicate is applied to the task's desired output to produce the possible values for the alternative input which could lead to its production. In the latter case, the input domain is searched for these values which, together with the desired output, would satisfy the semantics of the task. Thus, given the output desired of a task, and based on the SBF specification of its semantics the blame-assignment method is potentially able to infer the input which could possibly lead the task to produce it. Clearly, if none of the above conditions is true, then no alternative inputs can be inferred.

The semantics of `path-increase`, which specify that the produced path must be a extension of the path selected by `tmp-path-selection` (*prefix(tmp-path path)*), fails for the feedback path. The path selected in the last repetition of the loop was *((center 10th) (10th atlantic) (atlantic walnut))* and it is not a prefix of the feedback, therefore the desired path could not possibly have been produced by the `path-increase` task given the temporary path it received as input. Thus, AUTOGNOSTIC attempts to infer alternative values for the input temporary path which could enable `path-increase` to produce the desired path. The relation `prefix` is evaluated by a predicate, and the SBF model also specifies an inverse predicate for it which, given a path, produces all its possible prefixes. Given the possible prefixes of the desired path, AUTOGNOSTIC infers that if *((center 10th) (center mapple) (mapple dalney))* had been selected, the `path-increase` subtask could, in principle, have produced the feedback. Thus, the cause of the failure must lie within the subtask which selected the "wrong" path, `tmp-path-selection`. Therefore, it focuses the investigation towards identifying why this earlier subtask did not select the right path.

The blame-assignment method may reach a leaf task whose semantics is validated by both the feedback and the value actually produced for its output (see Figure 2[1.1]). This situation implies that the problem-solver's task structure is not sufficiently tailored to producing the right kind of solutions. In such situations the blame-assignment method postulates the following two types of errors as possible causes for the failure. First, the *task's semantics may be under-specified* and they allow both the actual and feedback values to be produced, when only the latter conforms with the requirements of the problem-solver's environment.

In such cases, the function of this subtask should be refined (i.e., more domain relations should be added to its functional semantics), so that the overall problem-solving process becomes more selective. Second, if the task semantics refer to domain relations exhaustively described in truth tables, the blame-assignment method hypothesizes as an additional cause of the failure the *incorrect domain knowledge* of the problem solver regarding this relation which allows the mapping from its actual input to its actual output (see Figure 2[1.1.a]). This mapping could potentially be incorrect, in which case the task should have never produced the undesired actual value, and it should have preferred the feedback. Among these two hypotheses, the subsequent repair step will first attempt to address the former one, which is the more grave one, by identifying new semantics for the under-specified operator. If this is not possible, it will attempt to address the latter one.

AUTOGNOSTIC evaluates the functional semantics of `tmp-path-selection` and notices that it is satisfied by the desired temporary path. Indeed, this path belongs in the set of paths that ROUTER has already explored. Thus, AUTOGNOSTIC infers that this desired value could have been produced by `tmp-path-selection`. This task is a leaf task, and therefore, the error must lie within the operator that accomplishes it (notice, the task's semantics does not depend on any truth-table defined domain relations). That is, the specification of the `tmp-path-selection` operator is incomplete with respect to quality of solutions that is desired of the overall `path-planning` task. Indeed, the `intrazonal-search-method` performs a breadth-first search in the space of possible paths with no particular quality criterion to guide it. If there is a quality desired of ROUTER's paths, then a "best"-first search method would be more appropriate. By postulating the under-specification of the `tmp-path-selection` operator as cause for this failure of ROUTER, AUTOGNOSTIC's subsequent repair step is able to search for additional semantics with which to characterize the information transformation of this operator. As a result, it modifies this operator so as to select the shortest of the available explored paths, thus transforming the `intrazonal-search method` into a greedy, shortest-path first search.

Alternatively, the blame-assignment method may reach a task whose semantics is violated by the feedback, and no alternative values can be found for its input which can satisfy it (see Figure 2[2.2]). Under these circumstances, it postulates that the cause of the failure may be the *over-constrained task semantics* which does not allow it to produce the feedback as its output, although this value is acceptable given the information transformation intended of the overall task. In such cases the function of this subtask should be respecified in terms of other domain relations, in order to extend the class of its output values to include in it the feedback value. In addition, if the domain relations defining its semantics are exhaustively described by truth tables, the blame-assignment method postulates that the cause of the failure may be the *incomplete domain knowledge* of the problem solver regarding this relation which does not include the a tuple relating the task's actual input with its desired output, although it belongs in this relation (see Figure 2[2.2.a]).

This could have been the case in our example, if the `tmp-path-selection` semantics specified that the selected temporary path had to be the most scenic (or, for that matter, any other property that the desired temporary path does not satisfy) of the already explored paths. In this case, the blame-assignment method would have postulated that this operator was over-constrained.

Evaluation

Assigning blame is pointless unless it results in repairing the error and improving the problem solving. Indeed, whether or not repair of the fault identified by blame assignment results in improvement in problem-solving performance provides a good measure of the efficacy of the blame-assignment method. The repair of an incorrectly specified operator in AUTOGNOSTIC involves the discovery of relations that characterize the examples of behavior desired of the operator, and that differentiate them from the examples of its actual undesired behavior. As described in (Stroulia 1995), these discovered relations are used to re-specify the operator's functional semantics.

In addition to ROUTER, AUTOGNOSTIC to date has been integrated with KRITIK2 (Goel 1989; Goel 1991), a design system, and REFLECS a reactive robot. In one set of experiments, AUTOGNOSTIC was tested with 8, 4, and 1 individual problems with ROUTER, KRITIK2, and REFLECS respectively. Each experiment in this set addressed a different learning task in that blame assignment identified a different kind of fault. We found that after repair the problem-solver's performance improved in each experiment. The differences among the three problem solvers (paradigm: deliberative vs. reactive; task: planning, design, navigation) provide some evidence for the generality of the SBF language and the model-based blame-assignment method.

Also, to evaluate long-term learning, in another set of experiments, AUTOGNOSTIC's integration with ROUTER was tested twice with 3 sequences of 40 randomly generated problems. For each problem, a different kind of "better" path was given as feedback. In this set of experiments, we found that AUTOGNOSTIC converged to a modified task structure of ROUTER after modifying the same three or four operators. The modified task structure was significantly superior to the original one in terms of problem-solving performance (Stroulia 1995). Collectively these experiments appear to indicate that the SBF language and the model-based method for blame assignment are appropriate for problem solvers whose behaviors can be described in terms of the interactions among a set of identifiable design elements with well-defined functionalities.

Related Research

The analysis of problem solving in terms of task structures builds on Chandrasekaran (1989). The representation language of SBF models is based on another type of SBF models that describe how physical devices work (Goel 1989). KRITIK2 uses SBF models of physical devices for diagnosis

(Stroulia et. al 1992; Goel & Stroulia 1996) and for design adaptation (Goel 1991). In formulating AUTOGNOSTIC's SBF language for modeling problem solvers, we needed to make many changes to KRITIK2's SBF models. For example, we had to significantly enhance the SBF language for capturing the functional semantics of tasks.

Teiresias (Davis 1980), Gordius (Simmons 1988), Cream (Weintraub 1991), and Meta-Aqua (Ram & Cox 1994) identify knowledge faults. In addition to Lex (Mitchell et. al 1981) and Prodigy (Carbonell et. al 1989), which we have already discussed, Castle (Freed at. al 1992) too identifies processing faults. It uses a model of the problem solver that specifies the behavior expected of it, the interacting components of the problem solver, and the assumptions underlying their correct behavior. This is similar to the SBF specification of functional semantics of the tasks and subtasks of the problem solver. Like AUTOGNOSTIC, Castle's model provides a justification structure for the expected problem-solving behavior. But Castle's models lack the hierarchical organization and compositional semantics of SBF models, thus, they do not provide any guidance in searching through the inter-dependencies of the problem-solver's components. The blame assignment task in Castle is also different: given the failure of an explicitly stated assumption about the problem-solver's behavior, it identifies the component whose design assumptions support the failed expectation and postulates errors in its functioning. In contrast, given a behavior desired of the problem solver, AUTOGNOSTIC uses the functional semantics of tasks and subtasks to postulate alternative behaviors desired of them.

Conclusions

In this paper, we have described a blame-assignment method, able to identify faults in the specification of a problem-solver's operators, based on the problem-solver's SBF model. The SBF model of a problem solver captures (i) the functional semantics of the problem-solver's tasks, (ii) the compositional semantics of the methods that recursively synthesize the inferences drawn by its operators into the outputs of its overall task, and (iii) the "causal" inter-dependencies between its tasks and domain knowledge.

The SBF specification of the tasks' functional semantics plays a variety of roles in this blame-assignment method. First, the functional semantics of the problem-solver's overall task establishes the range of behaviors that the problem solver is intended to deliver, irrespective of whether or not it is explicitly designed to do so. Second, based on the functional semantics of the problem-solver's intermediate subtasks and the overall behavior desired of it, the blame-assignment method infers the behaviors desired of these subtasks. Third, by comparing the functional semantics of the problem-solver's operators with the behaviors desired of them, it identifies when the functions originally designed in these operators are incorrect (under-specified or over-constrained) with respect to the behaviors desired of the problem-solver.

The SBF specification of the compositional semantics of the methods that the problem solver uses to accomplish its overall task enables the blame-assignment method to investigate only the tasks involved in the production of the output for which an undesired value was produced. The blame-assignment method focuses the investigation from higher- to lower- level tasks and from one type of information to another, and thus, limits the number of information inter-dependencies that it examines.

Finally, based on the "causal" inter-dependencies between the tasks' functional semantics with the problem-solver's domain knowledge, the blame-assignment method is able to identify incorrect uses of this knowledge in the specification of the problem-solver's operators, and errors in this domain knowledge.

References

Carbonell, J.G.; Knoblock, C.A.; and Minton, S. 1989. Prodigy: An Integrated Architecture for Planning and Learning. *Architectures for Intelligence*, Hillsdale, NJ: LEA.

Chandrasekaran, B. 1989. Task Structures, Knowledge Acquisition and Machine Learning. *Machine Learning* 4: 341-347.

Davis, R. 1980. Meta-Rules: Reasoning about Control. *Artificial Intelligence* 15: 179-222.

Freed, M.; Krulwich, B.; Birnbaum, L.; and Collins, G. 1992. Reasoning about performance intentions. In *Proc. of the Fourteenth Annual Conference of Cognitive Science Society*, 7-12.

Goel, A. 1989. Integration of Case-Based Reasoning and Model-Based Reasoning for Adaptive Design Problem Solving, Ph.D. diss, The Ohio State University.

Goel, A. 1991. A Model-Based Approach to Case Adaptation, In *Proceedings of the Thirteenth Annual Conference of the Cognitive Science Society*, 143-148.

Goel, A.; Ali, K.; Donnellan, M.; Gomez, A.; and Callantine, T. 1994. Multistrategy Adaptive Navigational Path Planning. *IEEE Expert*, 9(6):57-65.

Goel, A. and Stroulia, E. 1996. Functional Representation and Functional Device Models and Model-Based Diagnosis in Adaptive Design. In *Artificial Intelligence in Design, Engineering and Manufacturing* (to appear).

Mitchell, T.M.; Utgoff, P.E.; Nudel, B.; and Banerji, R.B. 1981. Learning problem-solving heuristics through practice. In *Proc. of the Seventh International Joint Conference on Artificial Intelligence*, 127-134.

Ram, A.; and Cox M.T. 1994. Introspective Reasoning Using Meta-Explanations for Multistrategy Learning. Machine Learning: A Multistrategy Approach IV. (eds.) R.S. Michalski and G. Tecuci, 349-377. San Mateo, CA: Morgan Kaufmann,

Samuel, A. 1959. Some studies in machine learning using the game of checkers. IBM Journal of R&D. Reprinted in Feigenbaum and Feldman (eds): *Computers and Thought*, McGraw-Hill, New York.

Simmons, R.G. 1988. Combining Associational Causal Reasoning to Solve Interpretation and Planning Problems, Ph.D. diss, MIT.

Stroulia, E.; Shankar, M.; Goel, A.; and Penberthy, L. 1992. A Model-Based Approach to Blame Assignment in Design. In J.S. Gero (ed.) *Proc. of the Second International Conference on AI in Design*, 519-537. Kluwer Academic Publishers.

Stroulia, E. 1995. Failure-Driven Learning as Model-Based Self-Redesign, Ph.D. diss, Georgia Inst. of Technology.

Weintraub, M. 1991. An Explanation-Based Approach to Assigning Credit, Ph.D. diss, The Ohio State University.

Qualitative Multiple-Fault Diagnosis of Continuous Dynamic Systems Using Behavioral Modes

Siddarth Subramanian
National Instruments - Georgetown
1978 S. Austin Ave.
Georgetown, Texas 78626
sid@georgetown.com

Raymond J. Mooney
Dept. of Computer Sciences
University of Texas at Austin
Austin, Texas 78712
mooney@cs.utexas.edu

Abstract

Most model-based diagnosis systems, such as GDE and Sherlock, have concerned discrete, static systems such as logic circuits and use simple constraint propagation to detect inconsistencies. However, sophisticated systems such as QSIM and QPE have been developed for qualitative modeling and simulation of continuous dynamic systems. We present an integration of these two lines of research as implemented in a system called QDOCS for multiple-fault diagnosis of continuous dynamic systems using QSIM models. The main contributions of the algorithm include a method for propagating dependencies while solving a general constraint satisfaction problem and a method for verifying the consistency of a behavior with a model across time. Through systematic experiments on two realistic engineering systems, we demonstrate that QDOCS demonstrates a better balance of generality, accuracy, and efficiency than competing methods.

Introduction

In a world increasingly filled with devices that exhibit complex dynamic behavior, online diagnostic systems are becoming increasingly important. To address this problem, researchers have devised various solutions over the last two decades (Shortliffe & Buchanan 1975; de Kleer & Williams 1987). These systems have been applied to the problems of medical diagnosis, as well as to combinational circuit diagnosis and similar domains. However, as we shall see, these diagnosis approaches are not directly suited to the kinds of continuous dynamic systems that we are interested in.

Traditional modes of reasoning about physical systems use differential equations to model their dynamics. However, these techniques are limited in their ability to usefully model large systems because of the difficulties in constructing accurate formulations of large systems, and because of the computational complexities involved in solving large systems of differential equations. One solution to this problem is to use *Qualitative Reasoning* (Forbus 1984; Kuipers 1984). Our work uses QSIM (Kuipers 1994) as the modelling language and applies a very general diagnostic technique to models described in this language.

Previous approaches to diagnosing faults in systems described with QSIM models have been limited in scope and have been unable to work with fault modes (Ng 1990; Lackinger & Nejdl 1991) or have made a single-fault assumption (Dvorak 1992). Most previous work on model-based diagnosis (Reiter 1987; de Kleer & Williams 1987) has concentrated on static systems and is generally insufficient to diagnose continuous dynamic systems. Few of the other approaches to diagnosis of continuous systems (Oyeleye, Finch, & Kramer 1990; Dague *et al.* 1991) have made use of a general modelling language such as that provided by QSIM or used any of the general diagnostic formalisms introduced by Reiter or DeKleer.

This work[1] is an integration of the two paradigms of model-based diagnosis and qualitative reasoning into a general, multiple-fault diagnosis system for continuous dynamic systems using behavioral modes with *a priori* probabilities. The diagnostic architecture is similar to SHERLOCK (de Kleer & Williams 1989) and the algorithm builds on INC-DIAGNOSE (Ng 1990). The system uses a general constraint-satisfaction technique to detect faults and trace dependencies in order to generate conflicts and diagnoses. A QSIM-based simulation component is used to verify hypotheses and detect additional inconsistencies. The implemented system, QDOCS (Qualitative Diagnosis Of Continuous Systems), is powerful enough to accurately diagnose a number of different faults in the Space Shuttle's Reaction Control System and a simple chemical reaction tank.

An Example

An example used to illustrate the algorithm consists of a simple bathtub with a drain. It is assumed that the bathtub is monitored by sensors measuring the

[1] A much more detailed account of this work can be found in (Subramanian 1995).

amount of water in the tub and the flow rate of the water through the drain. Some of the faults that can be posited about this system include a blocked drain, leaks in the tank, and sensors stuck at various levels.

This system is described using a qualitative differential equation or a QDE. A QDE is a set of constraints, each of which describes the relationship between two or more variables. For instance, an M+ relation is said to exist between two variables if one is a monotonically increasing function of the other. So, in our normal bathtub model, there is an M+ relation between the amount and the level of water in the bathtub and also between the the level and pressure, and the pressure and outflow rate. However, in a model of a blocked bathtub, the outflow rate is zero, and it is described by the constraint ZERO-STD.

The use of discrete mode variables in QSIM allows us to combine normal and faulty models of a system into a single description as shown here:

```
(M+ amount level)
(M+ level pressure)
(mode (drain-mode normal) (M+ pressure outflow))
(mode (drain-mode blocked) (ZERO-STD outflow))
(ADD netflow outflow inflow)
(D/DT amount netflow)
(CONSTANT inflow if*)
```

Here, the variable drain-mode takes on the possible values of *normal*, *blocked*, or *unknown* and the constraints shown above correspond to the two known modes of the bathtub's behavior.

For the purposes of diagnosis, these mode variables can then be associated with components of the system and their different values with behavioral modes of the component. Each of these behavioral modes has an *a priori* probability specified by the model-builder. The component structure used to represent the bathtub looks like this:

```
(defcomponents bathtub
 (drain drain-mode (normal 0.89)(blocked 0.1)
   (unknown 0.01))
 (levelsensor levelsensor-mode (normal 0.79)
  (stuck-at-0 0.1)(stuck-at-top 0.1)
  (unknown 0.01))
 (flowsensor flowsensor-mode (normal 0.79)
  (stuck-high 0.1)(stuck-at-0 0.1)(unknown 0.01))
 (inletvalve inletvalve-mode (normal 0.79)
  (stuck-closed 0.1)(unknown 0.01)))
```

Here, each entry consists of the component name (e.g., drain), the mode variable (drain-mode) and a list of behavioral modes with their *a priori* probabilities ((normal 0.89) (blocked 0.1) (unknown 0.01)).

The input to the diagnostic algorithm consists of a behavior, which is a sequence of qualitative values for a subset of the variables corresponding to sensor readings. The output of the algorithm is an assignment of values to the mode variables such that the resulting model is consistent with the observed behavior, i.e., the behavior corresponds to a QSIM simulation of the model.

As an example, suppose QDOCS is given the following single set of sensor readings from a behavior of the bathtub: (level-sensed (0 top)), (outflow-sensed 0) (i.e., the level sensed is somewhere between 0 and top and the outflow sensed is 0). This is clearly inconsistent with the normal model of the system which would predict a flow through the drain. Some of the valid diagnoses for this behavior include [(drain-mode blocked)], [(flowsensor-mode stuck-at-0)] and [(drain-mode blocked) (flowsensor-mode stuck-at-0)].

The above example motivates an approach of applying QSIM's constraint satisfaction techniques to detect inconsistencies between the sensor readings and the model. However, since the systems under study are dynamic systems that maintain temporal consistency, satisfying the constraints for a given set of sensor readings does not guarantee that the sequence of readings is consistent. The approach we discuss in the next section includes using the continuity checking of QSIM to check this temporal consistency.

QDOCS's Diagnostic Approach

QDOCS uses a standard diagnostic approach similar to that of (de Kleer & Williams 1989) and combines it with a hypothesis checker (and conflict generator) based on the QSIM algorithm of (Kuipers 1994).

Diagnosis Construction: Like SHERLOCK's technique for constructing diagnoses, QDOCS uses a best-first search mechanism and focusses its search on the leading candidate diagnoses as determined by their *a priori* probabilities. QDOCS maintains an *agenda* of hypotheses to be tested and a list of conflict sets. The former is initialized to the single hypothesis that everything is functioning normally while the latter is initialized to the null set.

The hypothesis checker is first called with the initial hypothesis of all the components being normal. If it returns a null value, the given behavior is consistent with the hypothesis; in other words, the given behavior is a possible result of running QSIM on the model assuming all component mode variables are in the normal mode. If there is no QSIM simulation that results in the given behavior, the checker returns a conflict set of component mode variable values. This conflict set is then added to the set of conflict sets, and the agenda is expanded by adding all hypotheses generated by changing the mode value of a single component in such a way that it *hits*[2] all the conflict sets. This process is repeated until one or more hypotheses are found to be consistent with the observations.

Checking Hypotheses: Most diagnostic systems like GDE (de Kleer & Williams 1987) use simple constraint propagation to determine conflict sets. However, QSIM requires a more complete constraint sat-

[2] A conflict is *hit* by a hypothesis if some literal in the diagnosis contradicts a literal in the conflict.

isfaction algorithm since a qualitative constraint typically does not entail a unique value for a remaining variable when all its other variables have been assigned. An earlier attempt to use QSIM to track dependencies for diagnosis (Ng 1990) only used a simple propagator. Since the propagator alone is not complete, Ng's program, INC-DIAGNOSE is not guaranteed to detect all inconsistencies.

QSIM takes a set of initial qualitative values for some or all of the variables of a model and produces a representation of all the possible behaviors of the system. The inputs to QSIM are 1) a qualitative differential equation (QDE) represented as a set of variables and constraints between them, and 2) an initial state represented by qualitative magnitudes and directions of change for some of these variables. QSIM first completes the state by solving the constraint satisfaction problem (CSP) defined by the initial set of values and the QDE. For each of the completed states satisfying the constraints, QSIM finds qualitative states that are possible successors and uses constraint satisfaction to determine which of these are consistent. The process of finding successors to states and filtering on constraints continues as QSIM builds a tree of states called a behavior tree.

There are two possible ways in which the QDE corresponding to a hypothesis can be inconsistent with a given set of sensor readings: 1) a particular set of readings may be incompatible with the QDE, or 2) all the sets of readings may be compatible with the QDE but the sequence may not correspond to any particular behavior in a QSIM behavior tree. QDOCS's approach is to first test for consistency between individual sets of readings and the QDE by using QSIM's CSP algorithms, and then, test to see if the model fits the sequence, i.e., if the sequence of readings corresponds to a behavior generated by QSIM.

For the first step, QDOCS modifies QSIM's constraint satisfier to keep track of mode-variables whose values played a role in reducing the set of possible values for a variable. Each variable and constraint is associated with an initially empty dependency set of mode variables. Whenever a constraint causes a variable's set of possible values to decrease, the dependency set of the variable is updated with the union of its old dependency set, the dependency set associated with the constraint, and the mode variable, if any, that is associated with the constraint. When a variable reduces the set of possible tuples associated with the constraint, the constraint's dependency set is similarly updated with the union. When a variable is left with no possible values, its current dependency set is returned as a conflict set.

QDOCS's approach to solving the CSP, based on QSIM's, is to first establish node consistency by ensuring that each constraint is satisfied by the possible values of the variables it acts upon, and then use Waltz filtering (Waltz 1975) to establish arc consistency, by propagating the results of the node consistency checker to other variables and constraints. Finally, QDOCS uses backtracking to assign values to variables. The first step above is a standard constraint propagation algorithm as used in traditional diagnostic systems while the last two steps will be referred to as the constraint satisfaction algorithm of QDOCS. Mode variable dependencies are maintained at each stage of this process so that the procedure can stop if an inconsistency is detected at any step. The Waltz filtering step is performed incrementally and at each point selects the most restrictive constraint (i.e., the one most likely to fail) to process and propagates its effect on the rest of the network. This heuristic of first filtering on the most restrictive constraints helps reduce the size of conflict sets since the most restrictive constraints are those with the least number of initial possible tuples, and therefore are more likely to lead to an inconsistency.

For the second part of the algorithm, QDOCS must track a QSIM simulation and match all possible successors at each stage of the simulation with the given sensor readings. Successors that do not either match the current set of sensor readings or the next set of sensor readings in the observed sequence are pruned out. Whenever the computed states corresponding to a particular set of sensor readings fail to have any successors matching the next set of sensor readings, an inconsistency is noted and the entire hypothesis is returned as a conflict.

This last step differs from the general QDOCS approach of trying to isolate the individual mode variable values responsible for an inconsistency. We discovered through our experiments (Subramanian 1995) that keeping track of the dependencies of variable values on mode variables across time was computationally expensive while giving us little benefit as most conflict sets were still almost as large as the entire hypothesis set. This kind of inconsistency was much rarer than inconsistencies in individual states detected through either the propagation or constraint satisfaction phases of the hypothesis checker.

Experiments

The experiments presented in this section test three primary claims about QDOCS. First, because it can detect inconsistencies and generate conflicts when propagation is blocked, QDOCS is more accurate than an approach that only uses propagation such as INC-DIAGNOSE. Second, because it uses dependencies and conflict sets to focus diagnosis, QDOCS is more efficient than a baseline generate-and-test approach. Third, each of the phases of QDOCS's hypothesis checking algorithm contributes to improving its accuracy or efficiency.

Experimental Methodology: In each of our domains, the *a priori* probabilities in the model were used to randomly generate sets of multiple faults. QSIM was used to simulate the model corresponding to these multiple fault hypotheses, and a behavior randomly chosen from the resulting behavior tree was used to test QDOCS.

QDOCS was compared to various different techniques and for each of these we collected data on the efficiency and accuracy of the methods. First, a generate-and-test method was used as a baseline comparison. This technique used the same hypothesis checker as QDOCS, and simply tests hypotheses generated in most-probable-first order until one or more hypotheses are found to be consistent with the observations. Note that given the fact that QSIM makes acausal inferences, a generate-and-test procedure is the best we can do without using QDOCS-style dependency propagation.

We also compared QDOCS with a number of ablated versions in order to justify all the different parts of the hypothesis checker. First, it was compared against a system that simply used QDOCS's constraint propagation procedure which is equivalent to INC-DIAGNOSE (enhanced to handle behavioral modes). Another ablated version of QDOCS we test against is one with both the propagation and constraint satisfaction parts of the code but without across-time verification. This test is to determine if the across-time verifier (which is one of the most computationally expensive parts of QDOCS) is worthwhile in improving the accuracy of the system. Finally, we test a version of QDOCS that used the constraint satisfaction and across-time verification portions of the hypothesis checker but skipped the constraint propagation portion. This comparison was run to verify that that the constraint propagation algorithm speeds up the constraint satisfaction process even though the constraint satisfaction and across-time verification algorithms together are just as powerful (in terms of accuracy of diagnoses) as the complete QDOCS hypothesis checker.

On each problem, the tested technique was run until the best remaining hypothesis had a probability of less than a tenth of the probability of the best (i.e., most probable) hypothesis that was found to be consistent with the observations thus far. This would give us a range of all the consistent hypotheses that were within an order of magnitude of each other in *a priori* probability and would provide a termination condition for the top-level procedure of QDOCS. In each of our domains, we first generated a test suite of 100 examples and ran the above experiments on all of them.

Reaction Control System: The first problem we look at is that of diagnosing faults in the Reaction Control System (RCS) of the Space Shuttle. The RCS is a collection of jets that provides motion control for the orbiter when it is in space. These jets are fired appropriately whenever changes need to be made to the orientation or position of the craft. Detailed descriptions of this problem domain and our approaches to it can be found in (Subramanian 1995).

A QSIM model for this system was first built by (Kay

Method	Avg. # Hyps.	Most Prob. Corr.%	Member Subs.%	Run Time (sec)	Hyps. Tested
Gen & Test	1.39	77.00	100.00	1288.77	456.55
Prop. only	2.91	29.00	85.00	44.39	19.71
No Across	1.71	42.00	84.00	85.68	25.29
No Prop.	1.39	77.00	100.00	647.95	52.62
QDOCS	1.39	77.00	100.00	454.02	52.70

Figure 1: Results in the RCS domain

1992). This model has been extended and modified by us for the purposes of diagnosis. The complete QSIM model contains 135 constraints and 23 components, each with multiple behavioral modes. Some of the kinds of faults modeled include pressure regulators stuck open and closed, leaks in the helium tank, the fuel tank, or the fuel line, and sensors being stuck low or high.

Since the actual probabilities of the faults were unknown, they were assigned by us with normal modes being much more common than the fault modes. As with all QDOCS models, we make the assumption that the faults are independent of each other.

We ran the series of experiments described above on the RCS system. The results are summarized in Figure 1. The first column reports the average number of hypotheses generated per diagnosis problem for each of the tests. The second and third columns show different measures of accuracy for each method, while the last two columns show different measures of efficiency.

For each method we separated out the most probable hypotheses (often more than one if there were a few equally probable hypotheses) and compared these to the correct hypothesis. The percentage of cases where the correct hypothesis was among these is reported in the second column. In many cases, a subset of the correct faults is sufficient to model the given behavior. The third column shows the percentage of cases in which some hypothesis is a subset of the faults of the correct hypothesis. The last two columns show respectively the average time taken for each problem on a Sparc 5 workstation running Lucid Common Lisp and the number of hypotheses the hypothesis checker actually had to test.

When we compare the generate-and-test method (first line) to the complete QDOCS algorithm (last line), we see that they both have identical accuracies – in 77% of the cases the correct solution was among the most probable. This result is as expected since a systematic elimination of hypotheses as in the generate and test method is guaranteed to reach the right hypotheses eventually. The big difference appears in the average number of hypotheses tested – the generate and test method tests 8.7 times more hypotheses than QDOCS. This shows that QDOCS is able to narrow the search space considerably using its dependency propagation algorithms but the ratio of run times, which is 2.8 to 1 in favor of QDOCS, indicates that there is a

Method	Avg. # Hyps.	Most Prob. Corr.%	Member Subs.%	Run Time (sec)	Hyps. Tested
Gen & Test	4.96	50.00	98.00	59.21	215.14
Prop. only	4.63	39.00	99.00	6.63	26.60
No Across	4.65	39.00	99.00	7.69	26.83
No Prop.	4.96	50.00	98.00	31.50	24.31
QDOCS	4.96	50.00	98.00	27.39	33.95

Figure 2: Results in the Level-Controller domain

cost to be paid for this. This is still a substantial advantage for QDOCS over the simpler generate and test method.

Figure 1 also shows the results of the ablation tests. We find that using just propagation or propagation and constraint satisfaction reduces the accuracy of the method since we are not verifying the hypotheses across time, while leaving out propagation has no effect on accuracy (compared to QDOCS) but the propagation step does speed up the process of finding contradictions and hence the overall computation time.

Another interesting experiment we conducted regarding run time comparisons between QDOCS and the generate and test method was a study of a part of the RCS subsystem consisting of a single propellant flow path to the thruster. The model for this system is almost exactly half the size of the full RCS subsystem model. We generated problems in the same way as for the experiments reported on in Figure 1, and ran 100 problems through the generate and test and QDOCS algorithms. The accuracies were identical (86% correct, 100% subset) between the two methods. However, the run times averaged 264 seconds for the generate and test and 221 for QDOCS. This is a ratio of only 1.2 to 1 even though the ratio of hypotheses tested was 4.4 to 1. The corresponding ratios for the complete system are 2.9 to 1 and 8.7 to 1. This suggests that for similar problems, the larger the problem size, the greater the advantage of using a dependency propagation algorithm like QDOCS to generate conflict sets. We therefore expect the advantages of QDOCS to be greater for even larger problem sizes.

Level-Controlled Tank: We studied one other system, a level controller for a reaction tank, taken from a standard control systems textbook, (Kuo 1991). The main reason this system is of interest is to show that the QDOCS mode of dependency propagation is useful even for feedback systems. Some researchers (e.g., (Dvorak & Kuipers 1992)) have held that such an algorithm would not be useful in dynamic systems with feedback loops because variable values are usually dependent on all constraints.

The level-controlled tank is modeled using a QSIM model with 45 constraints and a component structure with 14 components. We ran all the experiments described in the methodology section on this model of the controlled tank. The results are summarized in Figure 2.

As in the equivalent experiments with the RCS, QDOCS does better than the other techniques. It is about 2.2 times faster and tests 6.3 times fewer hypotheses than the generate and test method. QDOCS is also more accurate than either propagation alone or propagation and constraint satisfaction.

Future Work

This work needs to be further extended and applied to a variety of different engineering systems. One important first step towards applying such a system is to integrate it with a monitoring system such as MIMIC (Dvorak 1992). This would require the use of semi-quantitative information which is likely to add more power to QDOCS.

One area we have investigated but which could use further research is that of efficient caching of possible values of different variables during the constraint satisfaction phase of the algorithm. Traditional truth maintenance systems like the ATMS(de Kleer 1986) are not useful for this purpose since the range of possible values for a variable is rarely narrowed to a single one. Initial results on our attempt at implementing a more general caching mechanism are reported in (Subramanian 1995) but these are somewhat discouraging in that the overheads required to maintain the caches in our implementation are often higher than the computational savings. Further investigation will be required to formulate a truly efficient caching scheme.

Related Work

Compared to QDOCS, the previous diagnosis systems for QSIM models all have important limitations. INC-DIAGNOSE (Ng 1990) was an application of Reiter's theory of diagnosis (Reiter 1987) to QSIM models. Its main limitations were that first, like Reiter's theory, it was restricted to models where no fault mode information was known, and second, it used a constraint propagator that was not guaranteed to detect all inconsistencies. Another system that used the INC-DIAGNOSE approach in the context of a monitoring system is DIAMON(Lackinger & Nejdl 1991). Again, due to its dependence on the simple constraint propagation in INC-DIAGNOSE, it is only able to detect a small subset of possible faults which QDOCS can diagnose.

The other previous diagnosis work on QSIM models, MIMIC (Dvorak 1992), has several limitations. First, MIMIC requires the model builder to provide a structural model of the system in addition to the QSIM constraint model. This structural model was fixed and could not change under different fault models. QDOCS does not require this since it uses a constraint-satisfaction algorithm to determine the causes for inconsistencies. Second, MIMIC uses a very simple dependency tracing algorithm to generate potential single-fault diagnoses. This algorithm looks at the structural graph from the point at which the fault is detected and considers all components it finds upstream as possible candidates for failure and thus generates a larger set of possible component failures.

A number of other researchers have looked at diagnosis in the context of monitoring continuous systems (Oyeleye, Finch, & Kramer 1990; Doyle & Fayyad 1991). Each of these systems concentrates on different aspects of the monitoring process, but none performs multiple-fault diagnosis using behavioral modes.

Some recent work by Dressler (Dressler 1994) performs model-based diagnosis on a dynamical system (a ballast tank system) using a variant of GDE. It first reduces the model to a version suitable for constraint propagation, and then considers only conflicts generated by constraints acting at a particular time. While this is an efficient technique that apparently works well for their application, it is not a general method since some systems may have faults which can only be detected using information gathered across time.

Conclusion

We have described an architecture for diagnosing systems described by qualitative differential equations that performs multiple-fault diagnosis using behavioral modes. An implemented system, QDOCS, has been shown to be powerful enough to accurately generate diagnoses from qualitative behaviors of a fairly complex system – the Reaction Control System of the Space Shuttle. The approach is more powerful than previous methods in that it uses 1) a general modelling framework (QSIM), 2) a more complete diagnostic architecture and 3) a more complete constraint-satisfaction algorithm as opposed to simple propagation.

References

Dague, P.; Jehl, O.; Deves, P.; Luciani, P.; and Taillibert, P. 1991. When oscillators stop oscillating. In *Proceedings of the Twelfth International Joint Conference on Artificial Intelligence*, 1109–1115.

de Kleer, J., and Williams, B. C. 1987. Diagnosing multiple faults. *Artificial Intelligence* 32:97–130.

de Kleer, J., and Williams, B. C. 1989. Diagnosis with behavioral modes. In *Proceedings of the Eleventh International Joint Conference on Artificial Intelligence*, 1324–1330.

de Kleer, J. 1986. An assumption-based TMS. *Artificial Intelligence* 28:127–162.

Doyle, R. J., and Fayyad, U. M. 1991. Sensor selection techniques in device monitoring. In *Proceedings of the Second Annual Conference on AI, Simulation and Planning in High Autonomy Systems*, 154–163. IEEE Computer Society Press.

Dressler, O. 1994. Model-based diagnosis on board: Magellan-MT inside. In *Fifth International Workshop on Principles of Diagnosis*, 87–92.

Dvorak, D., and Kuipers, B. 1992. Model-based monitoring of dynamic systems. In Hamscher, W.; Console, L.; and de Kleer, J., eds., *Readings in Model-Based Diagnosis.* San Mateo, CA: Morgan Kaufmann. 249–254.

Dvorak, D. 1992. *Monitoring and Diagnosis of Continuous Dynamic Systems Using Semiquantitative Simulation.* Ph.D. Dissertation, University of Texas, Austin, TX.

Forbus, K. D. 1984. Qualitative process theory. *Artificial Intelligence* 24:85–168.

Kay, H. 1992. A qualitative model of the space shuttle reaction control system. Technical Report AI92-188, Artificial Intelligence Laboratory, University of Texas, Austin, TX.

Kuipers, B. J. 1984. Commonsense reasoning about causality: Deriving behavior from structure. *Artificial Intelligence* 24:169–203.

Kuipers, B. J. 1994. *Qualitative Reasoning: Modeling and Simulation with Incomplete Knowledge.* Cambridge, MA: MIT Press.

Kuo, B. C. 1991. *Automatic Control Systems.* Engelwood Cliffs, New Jersey: Prentice Hall.

Lackinger, F., and Nejdl, W. 1991. Integrating model-based monitoring and diagnosis of complex dynamic systems. In *Proceedings of the Twelfth International Joint Conference on Artificial Intelligence*, 1123–1128.

Ng, H. T. 1990. Model-based, multiple fault diagnosis of time-varying, continuous physical devices. In *Proceedings of the Sixth IEEE Conference on Artificial Intelligence Applications*, 9–15.

Oyeleye, O. O.; Finch, F. E.; and Kramer, M. A. 1990. Qualitative modeling and fault diagnosis of dynamic processes by Midas. *Chemical Engineering Communications* 96:205–228.

Reiter, R. 1987. A theory of diagnosis from first principles. *Artificial Intelligence* 32:57–95.

Shortliffe, E., and Buchanan, B. 1975. A model of inexact reasoning in medicine. *Mathematical Biosciences* 23:351–379.

Subramanian, S., and Mooney, R. J. 1995. Multiple-fault diagnosis using qualitative models and fault modes. In *IJCAI-95 Workshop on Engineering Problems in Qualitative Reasoning.*

Subramanian, S. 1995. *Qualitative Multiple-Fault Diagnosis of Continuous Dynamic Systems Using Behavioral Modes.* Ph.D. Dissertation, Department of Computer Science, University of Texas, Austin, TX. Also appears as Artificial Intelligence Laboratory Technical Report AI 95-239 and at URL ftp://ftp.cs.utexas.edu/pub/mooney/papers/qdocs-dissertation-95.ps.Z.

Waltz, D. 1975. Understanding line drawings of scenes with shadows. In Winston, P. H., ed., *The Psychology of Computer Vision.* Cambridge, Mass.: McGraw Hill. 19–91.

A Model-based Approach to Reactive Self-Configuring Systems*

Brian C. Williams and P. Pandurang Nayak
Recom Technologies, NASA Ames Research Center, MS 269-2
Moffett Field, CA 94305 USA
E-mail: `williams,nayak@ptolemy.arc.nasa.gov`

Abstract

This paper describes Livingstone, an implemented kernel for a model-based reactive self-configuring autonomous system. It presents a formal characterization of Livingstone's representation formalism, and reports on our experience with the implementation in a variety of domains. Livingstone provides a reactive system that performs significant deduction in the sense/response loop by drawing on our past experience at building fast propositional conflict-based algorithms for model-based diagnosis, and by framing a model-based configuration manager as a propositional feedback controller that generates focused, optimal responses. Livingstone's representation formalism achieves broad coverage of hybrid hardware/software systems by coupling the transition system models underlying concurrent reactive languages with the qualitative representations developed in model-based reasoning. Livingstone automates a wide variety of tasks using a single model and a single core algorithm, thus making significant progress towards achieving a central goal of model-based reasoning. Livingstone, together with the HSTS planning and scheduling engine and the RAPS executive, has been selected as part of the core autonomy architecture for NASA's first New Millennium spacecraft.

Introduction and Desiderata

NASA has put forth the challenge of establishing a "virtual presence" in space through a fleet of intelligent space probes that autonomously explore the nooks and crannies of the solar system. This "presence" is to be established at an Apollo-era pace, with software for the first probe to be completed in 1997 and the probe (Deep Space 1) to be launched in 1998. The final pressure, low cost, is of an equal magnitude. Together this poses an extraordinary challenge and opportunity for AI. To achieve robustness during years in the harsh environs of space the spacecraft will need to radically reconfigure itself in response to failures, and then navigate around these failures during its remaining days. To achieve low cost and fast deployment, one-of-a-kind space probes will need to be plugged together quickly, using component-based models wherever possible to automatically generate flight software. Finally, the space of failure scenarios and associated responses will be far too large to use software that requires prelaunch enumeration of all contingencies. Instead, the spacecraft will have to reactively think through the consequences of its reconfiguration options.

We made substantial progress on each of these fronts through a system called *Livingstone*, an implemented kernel for a model-based reactive self-configuring autonomous system. This paper presents a formalization of the reactive, model-based configuration manager underlying Livingstone. Several contributions are key. First, the approach unifies the dichotomy within AI between deduction and reactivity (Agre & Chapman 1987; Brooks 1991). We achieve a reactive system that performs significant deduction in the sense/response loop by drawing on our past experience at building fast propositional conflict-based algorithms for model-based diagnosis, and by framing a model-based configuration manager as a propositional feedback controller that generates focused, optimal responses. Second, our modeling formalism represents a radical shift from first order logic, traditionally used to characterize model-based diagnostic systems. It achieves broad coverage of hybrid hardware/software systems by coupling the transition system models underlying concurrent reactive languages (Manna & Pnueli 1992) with the qualitative representations developed in model-based reasoning. Reactivity is respected by restricting the model to concurrent propositional transition systems that are synchronous. Third, the long held vision of model-based reasoning has been to use a single central model to support a diversity of engineering tasks. For model-based autonomous systems this means using a single model to support a variety of execution tasks including tracking planner goals, confirming hardware modes, reconfiguring hardware, detecting anomalies, isolating faults, diagnosis, fault recovery, and safing. Livingstone automates all these tasks using a single model and a single core algorithm, thus making significant progress towards achieving the model-based vision.

Livingstone, integrated with the HSTS planning and

*Authors listed in reverse alphabetical order.

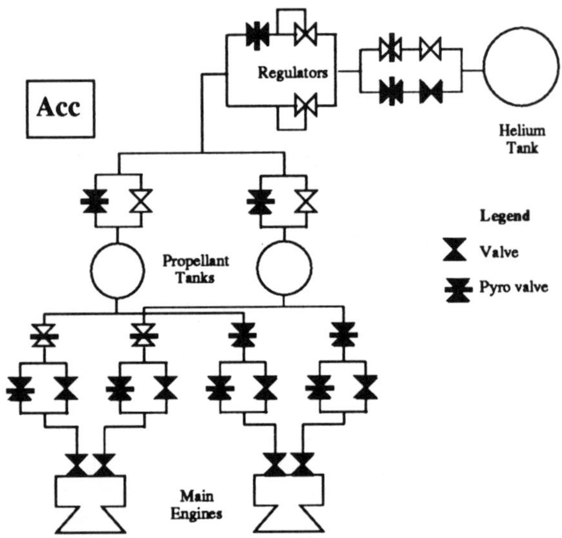

Figure 1: Engine schematic. Valves in solid black are closed, while the others are open.

scheduling system (Muscettola 1994) and the RAPS executive (Firby 1995), was demonstrated to successfully navigate the simulated NewMaap spacecraft into Saturn orbit during its one hour insertion window, despite about half a dozen failures. Consequently, Livingstone, RAPS, and HSTS have been selected to fly Deep Space 1, forming the core autonomy architecture of NASA's New Millennium program. In this architecture (Pell *et al.* 1996) HSTS translates high-level goals into partially-ordered tokens on resource timelines. RAPS executes planner tokens by translating them into low-level spacecraft commands while enforcing temporal constraints between tokens. Livingstone tracks spacecraft state and planner tokens, and reconfigures for failed tokens.

The rest of the paper is organized as follows. In the next section we introduce the spacecraft domain and the problem of configuration management. We then introduce transition systems, the key formalism for modeling hybrid concurrent systems, and a formalization of configuration management. Next, we discuss model-based configuration management and its key components: mode identification and mode reconfiguration. We then introduce algorithms for statistically optimal model-based configuration management using conflict-directed best-first search, followed by an empirical evaluation of Livingstone.

Example: Autonomous Space Exploration

Figure 1 shows an idealized schematic of the main engine subsystem of Cassini, the most complex spacecraft built to date. It consists of a helium tank, a fuel tank, an oxidizer tank, a pair of main engines, regulators, latch valves, pyro valves, and pipes. The helium tank pressurizes the two propellant tanks, with the regulators acting to reduce the high helium pressure to a lower working pressure. When propellant paths to a main engine are open, the pressurized tanks forces fuel and oxidizer into the main engine, where they combine and spontaneously ignite, producing thrust. The pyro valves can be fired exactly once, i.e., they can change state exactly once, either from open to closed or vice versa. Their function is to isolate parts of the main engine subsystem until needed, or to isolate failed parts. The latch valves are controlled using valve drivers (not shown), and the accelerometer (Acc) senses the thrust generated by the main engines.

Starting from the configuration shown in the figure, the high-level goal of producing thrust can be achieved using a variety of different configurations: thrust can be provided by either main engine, and there are a number of ways of opening propellant paths to either main engine. For example, thrust can be provided by opening the latch valves leading to the engine on the left, or by firing a pair of pyros and opening a set of latch valves leading to the engine on the right. Other configurations correspond to various combinations of pyro firings. The different configurations have different characteristics since pyro firings are irreversible actions and since firing pyro valves requires significantly more power than opening or closing latch valves.

Suppose that the main engine subsystem has been configured to provide thrust from the left main engine by opening the latch valves leading to it. Suppose that this engine fails, e.g., by overheating, so that it fails to provide the desired thrust. To ensure that the desired thrust is provided even in this situation, the spacecraft must be transitioned to a new configuration in which thrust is now provided by the main engine on the right. Ideally, this is achieved by firing the two pyro valves leading to the right side, and opening the remaining latch valves (rather than firing additional pyro valves).

A configuration manager constantly attempts to move the spacecraft into lowest cost configurations that achieve a set of high-level dynamically changing goals. When the spacecraft strays from the chosen configuration due to failures, the configuration manager analyzes sensor data to identify the current configuration of the spacecraft, and then moves the spacecraft to a new configuration which, once again, achieves the desired configuration goals. In this sense a configuration manager is a discrete control system that ensures that the spacecraft's configuration always achieves the set point defined by the configuration goals.

Models of Concurrent Processes

Reasoning about a system's configurations and autonomous reconfiguration requires the concepts of operating and failure modes, repairable failures, and configuration changes. These concepts can be expressed in a state diagram: repairable failures are transitions from a failure state to a nominal state; configuration changes are between nominal states; and failures are transitions from a nominal to a failure state.

Selecting a restricted, but adequately expressive, formalism for describing the configurations of a hybrid hardware/software system is essential to achieving the competing goals of reactivity and expressivity. First-order formulations, though expressive, are overly general and do not lend themselves to efficient reasoning. Propositional formulations lend themselves to efficient reasoning, but are inadequate for representing concepts such as state change. Hence, we use a concurrent transition system formulation and a temporal logic specification (Manna & Pnueli 1992) as a starting point for modeling hardware and software. Components operate concurrently, communicating over "wires," and hence can be modeled as concurrent communicating transition systems. Likewise, for software routines, a broad class of reactive languages can be represented naturally as concurrent transition systems communicating through shared variables.

Where our model differs from that of Manna & Pnueli, is that reactive software procedurally modifies its state through explicit variable assignments. On the other hand, a hardware component's behavior in a state is governed by a set of discrete and continuous declarative constraints. These constraints can be computationally expensive to reason about in all their detail. However, experience applying qualitative modeling to diagnostic tasks for digital systems, copiers, and spacecraft propulsion, suggests that simple qualitative representations over small finite domains are quite adequate for modeling continuous and discrete systems. The added advantage of using qualitative models is that they are extremely robust to changes in the details of the underlying model. Hence behaviors within states are represented by constraints over finite domains, and are encoded as propositional formulae which can be reasoned with efficiently.

Other authors such as (Kuipers & Astrom 1994; Nerode & Kohn 1993; Poole 1995; Zhang & Mackworth 1995) have been developing formal methods for representing and reasoning about reactive autonomous systems. The major difference between their work and ours is our focus on fast reactive inference using propositional encodings over finite domains.

Transition systems

We model a concurrent process as a *transition system*. Intuitively, a transition system consists of a set of state variables defining the system's state space and a set of transitions between the states in the state space.

Definition 1 A *transition system* $\mathcal{S}$ is a tuple $\langle \Pi, \Sigma, \mathcal{T} \rangle$, where

- Π is a finite set of *state variables*. Each state variable ranges over a finite domain.
- Σ is the *feasible* subset of the *state space*. Each state in the state space assigns to each variable in Π a value from its domain.
- $\mathcal{T}$ is a finite set of *transitions* between states. Each transition $\tau \in \mathcal{T}$ is a function $\tau : \Sigma \rightarrow 2^{\Sigma}$ representing a state transforming action, where $\tau(s)$ denotes the set of possible states obtained by applying transition τ in state s.

A *trajectory* for $\mathcal{S}$ is a sequence of feasible states $\sigma : s_0, s_1, \ldots$ such that for all $i \geq 0$, $s_{i+1} \in \tau(s_i)$ for some $\tau \in \mathcal{T}$. In this paper we assume that one of the transitions of $\mathcal{S}$, called τ_n, is designated the *nominal* transition, with all other transitions being *failure* transitions. Hence in any state a component may nondeterministically choose to perform either its nominal transition, corresponding to correct functioning, or a failure transition, corresponding to a component failure. Furthermore in response to a successful repair action, the nominal transition will move the system from a failure state to a nominal state.

A transition system $\mathcal{S} = \langle \Pi, \Sigma, \mathcal{T} \rangle$ is specified using a propositional temporal logic. Such specifications are built using *state formulae* and the $\bigcirc$ operator. A state formula is an ordinary propositional formula in which all propositions are of the form $y_k = e_k$, where y_k is a state variable and e_k is an element of y_k's domain. $\bigcirc$ is the *next* operator of temporal logic denoting truth in the next state in a trajectory.

A state s defines a truth assignment in the natural way: proposition $y_k = e_k$ is true iff the value of y_k is e_k in s. A state s satisfies a state formula ϕ precisely when the truth assignment corresponding to s satisfies ϕ. The set of states characterized by a state formula ϕ is the set of all states that satisfy ϕ. Hence, we specify the set of feasible states of $\mathcal{S}$ by a state formula $\rho_{\mathcal{S}}$.

A transition τ is specified by a formula ρ_τ, which is a conjunction of formulae ρ_{τ_i} of the form $\Phi_i \Rightarrow \bigcirc\Psi_i$, where Φ_i and Ψ_i are state formulae. A feasible state s_k can follow a feasible state s_j in a trajectory of $\mathcal{S}$ using transition τ iff for all formulae ρ_{τ_i}, if s_j satisfies the antecedent of ρ_{τ_i}, then s_k satisfies the consequent of ρ_{τ_i}. A transition τ_i that models a formula ρ_{τ_i} is called a *subtransition*. Hence taking a transition τ corresponds to taking all its subtransitions τ_i.

Note that this specification only adds the $\bigcirc$ operator to standard propositional logic. This severely constrained use of temporal logic is an essential property that allows us to perform deductions reactively.

Example 1 The transition system corresponding to a valve driver consists of 3 state variables $\{mode, cmdin, cmdout\}$, where *mode* represents the driver's mode (*on*, *off*, *resettable* or *failed*), *cmdin* represents commands to the driver and its associated valve (*on*, *off*, *reset*, *open*, *close*, *none*), and *cmdout* represents the commands output to its valve (*open*, *close*, or *none*). The feasible states of the driver are specified by the formula

$$\begin{aligned} mode = on \quad \Rightarrow \quad & (cmdin = open \Rightarrow cmdout = open) \\ & \wedge (cmdin = close \Rightarrow cmdout = close) \\ & \wedge ((cmdin \neq open \wedge cmdin \neq close) \\ & \quad \Rightarrow cmdout = none) \\ mode = off \quad \Rightarrow \quad & cmdout = none \end{aligned}$$

together with formulae like $(mode \neq on) \vee (mode \neq off)$, ...that assert that variables have unique values. The driver's nominal transition is specified by the following set of formulae:

$$((mode = on) \vee (mode = off)) \wedge (cmdin = off) \Rightarrow \bigcirc(mode = off)$$
$$((mode = on) \vee (mode = off)) \wedge (cmdin = on) \Rightarrow \bigcirc(mode = on)$$
$$(mode \neq failed) \wedge (cmdin = reset) \Rightarrow \bigcirc(mode = on)$$
$$(mode = resettable) \wedge (cmdin \neq reset) \Rightarrow \bigcirc(mode = resettable)$$
$$(mode = failed) \Rightarrow \bigcirc(mode = failed)$$

The driver also has two failure transitions specified by the formulae $\bigcirc(mode = failed)$ and $\bigcirc(mode = resettable)$, respectively.

Configuration management

We view an autonomous system as a combination of a high-level *planner* and a reactive *configuration manager* that controls a plant (Figure 2). The planner generates a sequence of hardware configuration goals. The configuration manager evolves the plant transition system along the desired trajectory. The combination of a transition system and a configuration manager is called a *configuration system*. More precisely,

Definition 2 A *configuration system* is a tuple $\langle \mathcal{S}, \Theta, \sigma \rangle$, where $\mathcal{S}$ is a transition system, Θ is a feasible state of $\mathcal{S}$ representing its initial state, and $\sigma : g_0, g_1, \ldots$ is a sequence of state formulae called *goal configurations*. A configuration system generates a *configuration* trajectory $\sigma : s_0, s_1 \ldots$ for $\mathcal{S}$ such that s_0 is Θ and either s_{i+1} satisfies g_i or $s_{i+1} \in \tau(s_i)$ for some failure transition τ.

Configuration management is achieved by sensing and controlling the state of a transition system. The state of a transition system is (partially) observable through a set of variables $\mathcal{O} \subseteq \Pi$. The next state of a transition system can be controlled through an exogenous set of variables $\mu \subseteq \Pi$. We assume that μ are exogenous so that the transitions of the system do not determine the values of variables in μ. We also assume that the values of $\mathcal{O}$ in a given state are independent of the values of μ at that state, though they may depend on the values of μ at the previous state.

Definition 3 A *configuration manager* $\mathcal{C}$ for a transition system $\mathcal{S}$ is an online controller that takes as input an initial state, a sequence of goal configurations, and a sequence of values for sensed variables $\mathcal{O}$, and incrementally generates a sequence of values for control variables μ such that the combination of $\mathcal{C}$ and $\mathcal{S}$ is a configuration system.

A *model-based configuration manager* is a configuration manager that uses a specification of the transition system to compute the desired sequence of control values. We discuss this in detail shortly.

Plant transition system

We model a plant as a transition system composed of a set of concurrent component transition systems that communicate through shared variables. The component transition systems of a plant operate synchronously, that is, at each plant transition every component performs a state transition. The motivation for imposing synchrony is given in the next section. We require the plant's specification to be composed out of its components' specification as follows:

Definition 4 A plant transition system $\mathcal{S} = \langle \Pi, \Sigma, \mathcal{T} \rangle$ composed of a set $\mathcal{CD}$ of component transition systems is a transition system such that;

- The set of state variables of each transition system in $\mathcal{CD}$ is a subset of Π. The plant transition system may introduce additional variables not in any of its component transition systems.
- Each state in Σ, when restricted to the appropriate subset of variables, is feasible for each transition system in $\mathcal{CD}$, i.e.., for each $C \in CD$, $\rho_{\mathcal{S}} \models \rho_C$, though $\rho_{\mathcal{S}}$ can be stronger than the conjunction of the ρ_C.
- Each transition $\tau \in \mathcal{T}$ performs one transition τ_C for each transition system $C \in \mathcal{CD}$. This means that

$$\rho_\tau \Leftrightarrow \bigwedge_{C \in \mathcal{CD}} \rho_{\tau_C}$$

The concept of synchronous, concurrent actions is captured by requiring that each component performs a transition for each state change. Nondeterminism lies in the fact that each component can traverse either its nominal transition or any of its failure transitions. The nominal transition of a plant performs the nominal transition for each of its components. Multiple simultaneous failures correspond to traversing multiple component failure transitions.

Returning to the example, each hardware component in Figure 1 is modeled by a component transition system. Component communication, denoted by wires in the figure, is modeled by shared variables between the corresponding component transition systems.

Model-based configuration management

We now introduce configuration managers that make extensive use of a model to infer a plant's current state and to select optimal control actions to meet configuration goals. This is essential in situations where mistakes may lead to disaster, ruling out simple trial-and-error approaches. A *model-based* configuration manager uses a plant transition model $\mathcal{M}$ to determine the desired control sequence in two stages—*mode identification* (MI) and *mode reconfiguration* (MR). MI incrementally generates the set of all plant trajectories consistent with the plant transition model and the sequence of plant control and sensed values. MR uses a plant transition model and the partial trajectories

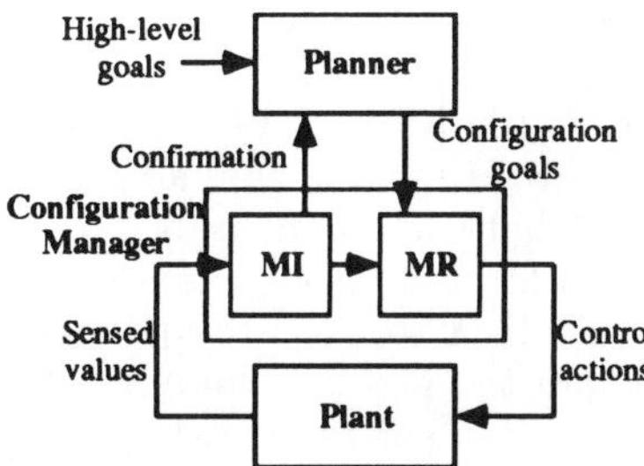

Figure 2: Model-based configuration management

generated by MI up to the current state to determine a set of control values such that all predicted trajectories achieve the configuration goal in the next state.

Both MI and MR are reactive. MI infers the current state from knowledge of the previous state and observations within the current state. MR only considers actions that achieve the configuration goal within the next state. Given these commitments, the decision to model component transitions as synchronous is key. An alternative is to model multiple transitions through interleaving. This, however, places an arbitrary distance between the current state and the state in which the goal is achieved, defeating a desire to limit inference to a small number of states. Hence we use an abstraction in which component transitions occur synchronously, even though the underlying hardware may interleave the transitions. The abstraction is correct if different interleavings produce the same final result.

We now formally characterize MI and MR. Recall that taking a transition τ_i corresponds to taking all subtransitions τ_{ij}. A transition τ_i can be defined to apply over a set of states S in the natural way:

$$\tau_i(S) = \bigcup_{s \in S} \tau_i(s)$$

Similarly we define $\tau_{ij}(S)$ for each subtransition τ_{ij} of τ_i. We can show that

$$\tau_i(S) \subseteq \bigcap_j \tau_{ij}(S) \tag{1}$$

In the following, S_i is the set of possible states at time i before any control values are asserted by MR, μ_i is the control values asserted at time i, $\mathcal{O}_i$ is the observations at time i, and S_{μ_i} and $S_{\mathcal{O}_i}$ is the set of states in which control and sensed variables have values specified in μ_i and $\mathcal{O}_i$, respectively. Hence, $S_i \cap S_{\mu_i}$ is the set of possible states at time i.

We characterize both MI and MR in two ways—first model theoretically and then using state formulas.

Mode Identification

MI incrementally generate the sequence $S_0, S_1, \ldots$ using a model of the transitions and knowledge of the control actions μ_i as follows:

$$S_0 = \{\Theta\} \tag{2}$$

$$S_{i+1} = \left(\bigcup_j \tau_j(S_i \cap S_{\mu_i})\right) \cap \Sigma \cap S_{\mathcal{O}_{i+1}} \tag{3}$$

$$\subseteq \bigcup_j \left(\bigcap_k \tau_{jk}(S_i \cap S_{\mu_i})\right) \cap \Sigma \cap S_{\mathcal{O}_{i+1}} \tag{4}$$

where the final inclusion follows from Equation 1. Equation 4 is useful because it is a characterization of S_{i+1} in terms of the subtransitions τ_{jk}. This allows us to develop the following characterization of S_{i+1} in terms of state formulae:

$$\rho_{S_{i+1}} \equiv \bigvee_{\tau_j} \left(\bigwedge_{\rho_{S_i} \wedge \rho_{S_{\mu_i}} \models \Phi_{jk}} \Psi_{jk} \right) \wedge \rho_\Sigma \wedge \rho_{\mathcal{O}_{i+1}} \tag{5}$$

This is a sound but potentially incomplete characterization of S_{i+1}, i.e., every state in S_{i+1} satisfies $\rho_{S_{i+1}}$ but not all states that satisfy $\rho_{S_{i+1}}$ are necessarily in S_{i+1}. However, generating $\rho_{S_{i+1}}$ requires only that the entailment of the antecedent of each subtransition be checked. On the other hand, generating a complete characterization based on Equation 3 would require enumerating all the states in S_i, which can be computationally expensive if S_i contains many states.

Mode Reconfiguration

MR incrementally generates the next set of control values μ_i using a model of the nominal transition τ_n, the desired goal configuration g_i, and the current set of possible states S_i. The model-theoretic characterization of $\mathcal{M}_i$, the set of possible control actions that MR can take at time i, is as follows:

$$\mathcal{M}_i = \{\mu_j | \tau_n(S_i \cap S_{\mu_j}) \cap \Sigma \subseteq g_i\} \tag{6}$$

$$\supseteq \{\mu_j | \bigcap_k \tau_{nk}(S_i \cap S_{\mu_j}) \cap \Sigma \subseteq g_i\} \tag{7}$$

where, once again, the latter inclusion follows from Equation 1. As with MI, this weaker characterization of $\mathcal{M}_i$ is useful because it is in terms of the subtransitions τ_{nk}. This allows us to develop the following characterization of $\mathcal{M}_i$ in terms of state formulae:

$$\mathcal{M}_i \supseteq \{\mu_j | \ \rho_{S_i} \wedge \rho_{\mu_j} \text{is consistent and} \bigwedge_{\rho_{S_i} \wedge \rho_{\mu_j} \models \Phi_{nk}} \Psi_{nk} \wedge \rho_\Sigma \models \rho_{g_i}\} \tag{8}$$

The first part says that the control actions must be consistent with the current state, since without this condition the goals can be simply achieved by making the world inconsistent. Equation 8 is a sound but potentially incomplete characterization of the set of control actions in $\mathcal{M}_i$, i.e., every control action that satisfies the condition on the right hand side is in $\mathcal{M}_i$, but not necessarily vice versa. However, checking whether a given μ_j is an adequate control action only requires that the entailment of the antecedent of each subtransition be checked. On the other hand, generating a complete characterization based on Equation 6 would require enumerating all the states in S_i, which can be computationally expensive if S_i contains many states.

If $\mathcal{M}_i$ is empty, no actions achieve the required goal. The planner then initiates replanning to dynamically change the sequence of configuration goals.

Statistically optimal configuration management

The previous section characterized the set of all feasible trajectories and control actions. However, in practice, not all such trajectories and control actions need to be generated. Rather, just the likely trajectories and an optimal control action need to be generated. We efficiently generate these by recasting MI and MR as *combinatorial optimization problems*.

A combinatorial optimization problem is a tuple (X, C, f), where X is a finite set of variables with finite domains, C is set of constraints over X, and f is an objective function. A feasible solution is an assignment to each variable in X a value from its domain such that all constraints in C are satisfied. The problem is to find one or more of the leading feasible solutions, i.e., to generate a prefix of the sequence of feasible solutions ordered in decreasing order of f.

Mode Identification

Equation 3 characterizes the trajectory generation problem as identifying the set of all transitions from the previous state that yield current states consistent with the current observations. Recall that a transition system has one nominal transition and a set of failure transitions. In any state, the transition system non-deterministically selects exactly one of these transitions to evolve to the next state. We quantify this non-deterministic choice by associating a probability with each transition: $p(\tau)$ is the probability that the plant selects transition τ.[1]

With this viewpoint, we recast MI's task to be one of identifying the likely trajectories of the plant. In keeping with the reactive nature of configuration management, MI incrementally tracks likely trajectories by extending the current set of trajectories by the likely transitions. The only change required in Equation 5 is that, rather than the disjunct ranging over all transitions τ_j, it ranges over the subset of likely transitions.

The likelihood of a transition is its posterior probability $p(\tau|\mathcal{O}_i)$. This posterior is estimated in the standard way using Bayes Rule:

$$p(\tau|\mathcal{O}_i) = \frac{p(\mathcal{O}_i|\tau)p(\tau)}{p(\mathcal{O}_i)} \propto p(\mathcal{O}_i|\tau)p(\tau)$$

If $\tau(S_{i-1})$ and $\mathcal{O}_i$ are disjoint sets then clearly $p(\mathcal{O}_i|\tau) = 0$. Similarly, if $\tau(S_{i-1}) \subseteq \mathcal{O}_i$ then $\mathcal{O}_i$ is entailed and $p(\mathcal{O}_i|\tau) = 1$, and hence the posterior probability of τ is proportional to the prior. If neither of the above two situations arises then $p(\mathcal{O}_i|\tau) \leq 1$. Estimating this probability is difficult and requires more research, but see (de Kleer & Williams 1987).

Finally, to view MI as a combinatorial optimization problem, recall that each plant transition consists of a single transition for each of its components. We introduce a variable into X for each component in the plant whose values are the possible component transitions. Each plant transition corresponds to an assignment of values to variables in X. C is the constraint that the states resulting from taking a plant transition is consistent with the observed values. The objective function f is the probability of a plant transition. The resulting combinatorial optimization problem hence identifies the leading transitions at each state, allowing MI to track the set of likely trajectories.

[1] We make the simplifying assumption that the probability of a transition is independent of the current state.

Mode reconfiguration

Equation 6 characterizes the reconfiguration problem as one of identifying a control action that ensures that the result of taking the nominal transition yields states in which the configuration goal is satisfied. Recasting MR as a combinatorial optimization problem is straightforward. The variables X are just the control variables μ with identical domains. C is the constraint in Equation 5 that μ_j must satisfy to be in $\mathcal{M}_i$. Finally, as noted earlier, different control actions can have different costs that reflect differing resource requirements. We take f to be negative of the cost of a control action. The resulting combinatorial optimization problem hence identifies the lowest cost control action that achieves the goal configuration in the next state.

Conflict-directed best first search

We solve the above combinatorial optimization problems using a *conflict directed best first search*, similar in spirit to (de Kleer & Williams 1989; Dressler & Struss 1994). A conflict is a partial solution such that any solution containing the conflict is guaranteed to be infeasible. Hence, a single conflict can rule out the feasibility of a large number of solutions, thereby focusing the search. Conflicts are generated while checking to see if a solution X_i satisfies the constraints C.

Our conflict-directed best-first search algorithm, *CBFS*, is shown in in Figure 3. It has two major components: (a) an agenda that holds unprocessed solutions in decreasing order of f; and (b) a procedure to generate the *immediate successors* of a solution. The main loop removes the first solution from the agenda, checks its feasibility, and adds in the solution's immediate successors to the agenda. When a solution X_i is infeasible, we assume that the process of checking the constraints C returns a part of X_i as a conflict N_i. We focus the search by generating only those immediate successors of X_i that are not subsumed by N_i, i.e., do not agree with N_i on all variables.

Intuitively, solution X_j is an immediate successor of solution X_i only if $f(X_i) \geq f(X_j)$ and X_i and X_j differ

```
function CBFS(X, C, f)
  Agenda = {{best-solution(X)}}; Result = ∅;
  while Agenda is not empty do
    Soln = pop(Agenda);
    if Soln satisfies C then
      Add Soln to Result;
      if enough solutions have been found then
        return Result;
      else Succs = immediate successors Soln;
    else
      Conf = a conflict that subsumes Soln;
      Succs = immediate successors of Soln not
        subsumed by Conf;
    endif
    Insert each solution in Succs into Agenda
      in decreasing f order;
  endwhile
  return Result;
end CBFS
```

Figure 3: Conflict directed best first search algorithm for combinatorial optimization

only in the value assigned to a single variable (ties are broken consistently to prevent loops in the successor graph). One can show this definition of the immediate successors of a solution suffices to prove the correctness of *CBFS*, i.e., to show that all feasible solutions are generated in decreasing order of f.

Our implemented algorithm further refines the notion of an immediate successor. The major benefit of this refinement is that each time a solution is removed from the agenda, at most two new solutions are added on, so that the size of the agenda is bounded by the total number of solutions that have been checked for feasibility, thus preserving reactivity (details are beyond the scope of this paper). For MI, we use full propositional satisfiability to check C (transition consistency). Interestingly, reactivity is preserved since the causal nature of a plant's state constraints means that full satisfiability requires little search. For MR, we preserve reactivity by using unit propagation to check C (entailment of goals), reflecting the fact that entailment is usually harder than satisfiability. Finally, note that *CBFS* does not require minimal conflicts. Empirically, the first conflict found by the constraint checker provides enough focusing, so that the extra effort to find minimal conflicts is unnecessary.

Implementation and experiments

We have implemented Livingstone based on the ideas described in this paper. Livingstone was part of a rapid prototyping demonstration of an autonomous architecture for spacecraft control, together with the HSTS planning/scheduling engine and the RAPS executive (Pell *et al.* 1996). In this architecture, RAPS further decomposes and orders HSTS output before handing goals to Livingstone. To evaluate the architecture, spacecraft engineers at JPL defined the Newmaap spacecraft and scenario. The Newmaap spacecraft is a scaled down version of the Cassini spacecraft that retains the most challenging aspects of spacecraft control. The Newmaap scenario was based on the most complex mission phase of the Cassini spacecraft—successful insertion into Saturn's orbit even in the event of any single point of failure. Table 1 provides summary information about Livingstone's model of the Newmaap spacecraft, demonstrating its complexity.

Number of components	80
Average modes/component	3.5
Number of propositions	3424
Number of clauses	11101

Table 1: NewMaap spacecraft model properties

Failure Scenario	MI			MR	
	Chck	Accpt	Time	Chck	Time
EGA preaim	7	2	2.2	4	1.7
BPLVD	5	2	2.7	8	2.9
IRU	4	2	1.5	4	1.6
EGA burn	7	2	2.2	11	3.6
ACC	4	2	2.5	5	1.9
ME hot	6	2	2.4	13	3.8
Acc low	16	3	5.5	20	6.1

Table 2: Results from the seven Newmaap failure recovery scenarios

The Newmaap scenario included seven failure scenarios. From Livingstone's viewpoint, each scenario required identifying the failure transitions using MI and deciding on a set of control actions to recover from the failure using MR. Table 2 shows the results of running Livingstone on these scenarios. The first column names each of the scenarios; a discussion of the details of these scenarios is beyond the scope of this paper. The second and fifth columns show the number of solutions checked by algorithm *CBFS* when applied to MI and MR, respectively. On can see that even though the spacecraft model is large, the use of conflicts dramatically focuses the search. The third column shows the number of leading trajectory extensions identified by MI. The limited sensing available on the Newmaap spacecraft often makes it impossible to identify unique trajectories. This is generally true on spacecraft, since adding sensors increases spacecraft weight. The fourth and sixth columns show the time in seconds on a Sparc 5 spent by MI and MR on each scenario, once again demonstrating the efficiency of our approach.

Livingstone's MI component was also tested on ten combinational circuits from a standard test suite (Brglez & Fujiwara 1985). Each component in these circuits was assumed to be in one of four modes: ok, stuck-at-1, stuck-at-0, unknown. The probability of transitioning to the stuck-at modes was set at 0.099 and to the unknown mode was set at 0.002. We ran 20

Devices	# of components	# of clauses	Checked	Time
c17	6	18	18	0.1
c432	160	514	58	4.7
c499	202	714	43	4.5
c880	383	1112	36	4.0
c1355	546	1610	52	12.3
c1908	880	2378	64	22.8
c2670	1193	3269	93	28.8
c3540	1669	4608	140	113.3
c5315	2307	6693	84	61.2
c7552	3512	9656	71	61.5

Table 3: Testing MI on a standard suite of circuits

experiments on each circuit using a random fault and a random input vector sensitive to this fault. MI stopped generating trajectories after either 10 leading trajectories had been generated, or when the next trajectory was 100 times more unlikely than the most likely trajectory. Table 3 shows the results of our experiments. The columns are self-explanatory, except that the time is the number of seconds on a Sparc 2. Note once again the power of conflict-directed search to dramatically focus search. Interestingly, these results are comparable to the results from the very best ATMS-based implementations, even though Livingstone uses no ATMS. Furthermore, initial experiments with a partial LTMS have demonstrated an order of magnitude speed-up.

Livingstone is also being applied to the autonomous real-time control of a scientific instrument called a Bioreactor. This project is still underway, and final results are forthcoming. More excitingly, the success of the Newmaap demonstration has launched Livingstone to new heights: Livingstone, together with HSTS and RAPS, is going to be part of the flight software of the first New Millennium mission, called Deep Space One, to be launched in 1998. We expect final delivery of Livingstone to this project in 1997.

Conclusions

In this paper we introduced Livingstone, a reactive, model-based self-configuring system, which provides a kernel for model-based autonomy. It represents an important step toward our goal of developing a fully model-based autonomous system (Williams 1996).

Three technical features of Livingstone are particularly worth highlighting. First, our modeling formalism achieves broad coverage of hybrid hardware/software systems by coupling the transition system models underlying concurrent reactive languages (Manna & Pnueli 1992) with the qualitative representations developed in model-based reasoning. Second, we achieve a reactive system that performs significant deduction in the sense/response loop by using propositional transition systems, qualitative models, and synchronous components transitions. The interesting and important result of Newmaap, Deep Space One, and the Bioreactor is that Livingstone's models and restricted inference are still expressive enough to solve important problems in a diverse set of domains. Third, Livingstone casts mode identification and mode reconfiguration as combinatorial optimization problems, and uses a core conflict-directed best-first search to solve them. The ubiquity of combinatorial optimization problems and the power of conflict-directed search are central themes in Livingstone.

Livingstone, the HSTS planning/scheduling system, and the RAPS executive, have been selected to form the core autonomy architecture of Deep Space One, the first flight of NASA's New Millennium program.

Acknowledgements: We would like to thank Nicola Muscettola and Barney Pell for valuable discussions and comments on the paper.

References

Agre, P., and Chapman, D. 1987. Pengi: An implementation of a theory of activity. In *Procs. of AAAI-87.*

Brglez, F., and Fujiwara, H. 1985. A neutral netlist of 10 combinational benchmark circuits. In *Int. Symp. on Circuits and Systems.*

Brooks, R. A. 1991. Intelligence without reason. In *Procs. of IJCAI-91*, 569–595.

de Kleer, J., and Williams, B. C. 1987. Diagnosing multiple faults. *Artificial Intelligence* 32(1):97–130.

de Kleer, J., and Williams, B. C. 1989. Diagnosis with behavioral modes. In *Procs. of IJCAI-89*, 1324–1330.

Dressler, O., and Struss, P. 1994. Model-based diagnosis with the default-based diagnosis engine: Effective control strategies that work in practice. In *Procs. of ECAI-94.*

Firby, R. J. 1995. The RAP language manual. Working Note AAP-6, University of Chicago.

Kuipers, B., and Astrom, K. 1994. The composition and validation of heterogenous control laws. *Automatica* 30(2):233–249.

Manna, Z., and Pnueli, A. 1992. *The Temporal Logic of Reactive and Concurrent Systems: Specification.* Springer-Verlag.

Muscettola, N. 1994. HSTS: Integrating planning and scheduling. In Fox, M., and Zweben, M., eds., *Intelligent Scheduling.* Morgan Kaufmann.

Nerode, A., and Kohn, W. 1993. Models for hybrid systems. In Grossman, R. L. *et al*, eds., *Hybrid Systems.* Springer-Verlag. 317–356.

Pell, B.; Bernard, D. E.; Chien, S. A.; Gat, E.; Muscettola, N.; Nayak, P. P.; Wagner, M. D.; and Williams, B. C. 1996. A remote agent prototype for spacecraft autonomy In *Procs. of SPIE Conf. on Optical Science, Engineering, and Instrumentation.*

Poole, D. 1995. Sensing and acting in the independent choice logic. In *Procs. of the AAAI Spring Symp. on Extending Theories of Action*, 163–168.

Williams, B. C. 1996. Model-based autonomous systems in the new millennium. In *Procs. of AIPS-96.*

Zhang, Y., and Mackworth, A. K. 1995. Constraint nets: A semantic model for hybrid dynamic systems. *Journal of Theoretical Computer Science* 138(1):211–239.

Trajectory Constraints in Qualitative Simulation

Giorgio Brajnik*
Dip. di Matematica e Informatica
Università di Udine
Udine — Italy
giorgio@dimi.uniud.it

Daniel J. Clancy
Department of Computer Sciences
University of Texas at Austin
Austin, Texas 78712
clancy@cs.utexas.edu

Abstract

We present a method for specifying temporal constraints on trajectories of dynamical systems and enforcing them during qualitative simulation. This capability can be used to focus a simulation, simulate non–autonomous and piecewise–continuous systems, reason about boundary condition problems and incorporate observations into the simulation. The method has been implemented in TeQSIM, a qualitative simulator that combines the expressive power of qualitative differential equations with temporal logic. It interleaves temporal logic model checking with the simulation to constrain and refine the resulting predicted behaviors and to inject discontinuous changes into the simulation.

Introduction

State space descriptions, such as differential equations, constrain the values of related variables within individual states and are often used in models of continuous dynamical systems. Besides continuity, which is implicit, these models cannot represent non–local information constraining the behavior of the system across time. Because qualitative simulation (Kuipers 1994; Forbus 1984) uses an abstraction of ordinary differential equations, it is based on a state space description too. The discretization of system trajectories into abstract qualitative states, however, makes the representation used by qualitative simulation amenable to the application of temporal formalisms to specify explicit across–time constraints. In general, these trajectory constraints can be used to restrict the simulation to a region of the state space in order to focus the simulation, simulate non–autonomous systems, reason about boundary condition problems and incorporate observations into the simulation.

TeQSIM (Temporally Constrained QSIM, pronounced *tek'sim*) restricts the simulation generated by QSIM (Kuipers 1994) to behaviors (*i.e.* sequences of qualitative states) that satisfy continuous and discontinuous behavioral requirements specified via *trajectory constraints*[1]. Figure 1 describes the relationship between the sources of constraining power within TeQSIM.

Trajectory constraints are formulated using a combination of temporal logic expressions, a specification of discontinuous changes and a declaration of external events. Temporal logic expressions are written using a variation of a propositional linear–time temporal logic (Emerson 1990) that combines state formulæ specifying both qualitative and quantitative information about a qualitative state with temporal operators, such as *until*, *always*, and *eventually*, that quantify such properties over a sequence of states. Temporal logic model checking is interleaved with the simulation to ensure that all and only the behaviors satisfying temporal logic expressions are included within the resulting description. Our logic extends the work done by Shults and Kuipers (Kuipers & Shults 1994; Shults & Kuipers 1996) in two ways. A three–valued logic is used to allow an expression to be conditionally entailed when quantitative information contained within the expression can be applied to a behavior to refine it. In addition, the model checking algorithm is designed to handle the incremental nature of a qualitative simulation. An undetermined result occurs whenever the behavior is not sufficiently determined to evaluate the truth of a temporal logic expression.

Discontinuous change expressions define when a particular discontinuity can occur and specify the new values for the variables that change discontinuously. This information is propagated through the model to determine the variables that are indirectly affected by the change.

Finally, *external events* enable the modeler to refer to otherwise unpredictable events and to provide a quantitatively bounded temporal correlation between the occurrence of these events and distinctions pre-

*The research reported in this paper has been performed while visiting the Qualitative Reasoning Group at the University of Texas at Austin.

[1] A *trajectory* for a tuple of variables $<v_1, \ldots, v_n>$ over a time interval $[a,b] \subseteq \Re^+ \cup \{0, +\infty\}$ is defined as a function τ mapping time to variable values defined over the set of the extended reals, *i.e.* $\tau : [a,b] \rightarrow (\Re \cup \{-\infty, +\infty\})^n$.

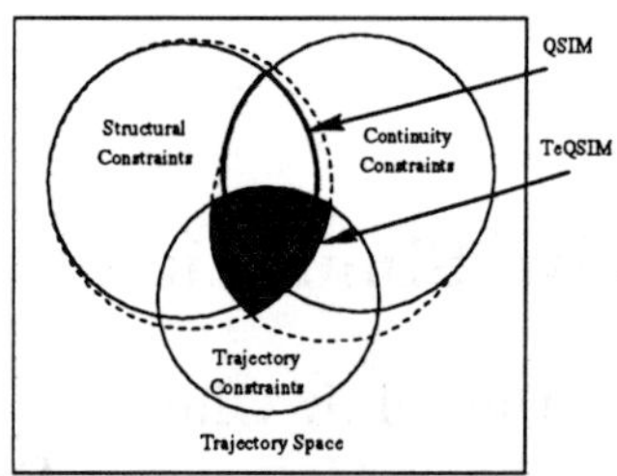

TeQSIM uses three sources of information to constrain a simulation: **structural constraints** are specified as equations relating model variables within individual states; implicit **continuity constraints** restrict the relationship between variable values across time to ensure the continuity of each variable; and **trajectory constraints** restrict the behavior of individual variables and the interactions between variables.

- Each point in the above diagram represents a real valued trajectory. A qualitative behavior corresponds to a region within this space of trajectories.
- Discontinuous changes specified by the user cause a relaxation of the continuity constraints applied during simulation (dotted line surrounding the continuity constraints). Incorporating external events into the simulation extends the set of trajectories consistent with the structural constraints (dotted line surrounding the structural constraints).
- The qualitative behaviors generated by QSIM correspond to the trajectories consistent with both the unextended structural constraints and the unrelaxed continuity constraints (thick boundary region), while the set of behaviors generated by TeQSIM corresponds to those trajectories consistent with all three constraint types (shaded region).

Figure 1: TeQSIM constraint interaction.

dicted by the model.

A Control Problem

TeQSIM has been applied to a variety of problems to address a range of tasks (Brajnik & Clancy 1996b). This section provides a simple example to demonstrate how trajectory information can be used to constrain a qualitative simulation in a realistic setting. Suppose that operators of a dam are told of a forecasted perturbation to the flow of water into the lake. When involved in risk assessment decision making, they face the control problem of determining how to react, in terms of operations on gates and turbines, in order to avoid flooding neither the lake nor the downstream areas.

To show some of TeQSIM's capabilities, we use a simple model of a lake, consisting of a reservoir, an incoming river and an outgoing river; lake level and outflow are regulated through a dam that includes a single floodgate. The implemented model uses quantitative information concerning Lake Travis, near Austin (TX), obtained from the Lower Colorado River Authority. Quantitative information is provided by numerical tables which, in this specific case, are interpolated in a step–wise manner to provide lower and upper bounds for any intermediate point. Table 2 shows a portion of the rating table of a floodgate of Lake Travis. Its columns indicate the lake *stage*, *i.e.* level with respect to the mean sea level, the gate *opening*, and the gate *discharge rate*. A similar table correlates the lake stage with its volume.

Stage (ft)	Opening (ft)	Discharge rate (cfs)
665.00	1.00	638.82
665.00	2.00	1277.65
...		
720.00	8.50	6200.00

Figure 2: Rating table for floodgates of Lake Travis.

The simulation starts from a state with initial values for stage and gate opening that guarantee a steady outflow in the downstream leg of the river. It is forecasted that in 2–3 days the inflow will increase and that for the subsequent 15–21 days there will be no substantial change. The task is to determine if there is any risk of overflowing the dam and, if so, what actions can be taken to prevent this.

We use TeQSIM to specify trajectory constraints on input variables: input flow rate and gate opening. The following trajectory constraints specify the perturbation to the inflow rate (`Colorado-up`).

```
(EVENT step-up :time (2 3))
(EVENT step-down :time (17 24))
(DISC-CHANGE (event step-up) ((Colorado-up (if* inf)
                                           :range (1500 1800))))
(DISC-CHANGE (event step-down) ((Colorado-up if*)))
```

The declaration of an event (*e.g.* `(EVENT step-up :time (2 3))`) defines a name for a time–point and provides quantitative bounds (*i.e.* between days 2 and 3 from the start of the simulation). The expression `(DISC-CHANGE (event step-up ((Colorado-up (if* inf):range (1500 1800))))` states that when event `step-up` occurs, the qualitative magnitude of `Colorado-up` will instantaneously change into the interval `(if* inf)` and its value will be bounded by the range [1500, 1800].

A simulation using these trajectory constraints shows that an overflow of the lake is indeed possible if no intervening action is taken. To guarantee that no overflow occurs, a significant opening action is required. To this end, we postulate that an opening action to at least 4 feet occurs after `Stage` reaches the `top-of-pool` threshold. We are interested in knowing the latest time at which such an action can occur to prevent an overflow. The previous trajectory specification is extended by including an additional event (corresponding to the opening of the gate), the corresponding discontinuous action (the gate opening changes from its initial value `op*`=1 to an intermediate value within (`op* max`) constrained to be greater than or equal to 4) and the ordering with respect to the threshold (using the temporal operator `BEFORE` applied to a state formula referring to the qualitative value of `Stage` and the external event). By focusing the simulation on behaviors that lead to an overflow condition (using the `EVENTUALLY` temporal operator applied to a state formula stating that `Stage` reaches the value `Top`), TeQSIM determines a lower bound for the temporal occurrence of actions leading to an overflow.

```
(EVENT open)
(DISC-CHANGE (event open)
        ((opening (op* max) :range (4 NIL))))
```

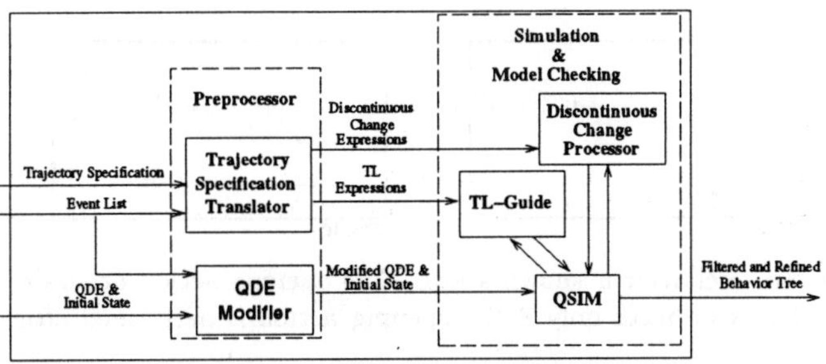

Figure 4: TeQSIM architecture.

```
(BEFORE (qvalue stage (top-of-pool NIL)) (event open))
(EVENTUALLY (qvalue stage (top NIL)))
```

This simulation tells us (figure 3) that if the gate is opened to at least 4 feet *after* 15.5 days then an overflow may occur. Taking the action *before* 15.5 days, however, will prevent such an outcome. After constraining the action to occur before 15.5 days and removing the `eventually` constraint, a third simulation produces only two behaviors, verifying that an overflow cannot occur. In a similar manner, we infer an upper bound of 6 ft for the size of the opening action, given a restriction on the outflow rate expressed via the temporal logic expression `(always (value-<= Colorado-dn 350))`.

It is worth noting the amount of uncertainty present in even such a simple problem: functions (especially the discharge rate) may be non–linear, numeric envelopes are based on a rough step–wise interpolation of tables, and the specification of input trajectories is uncertain (*i.e.* ranges for times and values). Nevertheless, with a few simple simulations a reasonably useful and reliable result has been achieved.

TeQSIM Architecture and Theory

TeQSIM can be divided into two main components. The *preprocessor* modifies the qualitative differential model and decomposes the trajectory specification into temporal logic and discontinuous change expressions. The *simulation and model checking* component integrates temporal logic model checking into the simulation performed by QSIM by filtering and refining qualitative behaviors according to a set of temporal logic expressions; it also injects discontinuous changes into the simulation. Figure 4 provides an overview of the system architecture.

The user provides trajectory constraints to TeQSIM in the form of a trajectory specification that consists of an external event list and a set of extended temporal logic and discontinuous change expressions. The external event list is a totally ordered sequence of named, quantitatively bound time points. Events are represented as landmarks of an auxiliary variable added to the model. The additional variable causes QSIM to branch on different orderings between external events and internal qualitative events identified during the simulation. The occurrence of external events is restricted by their quantitative bounds and the trajectory constraints specified by the modeler.

The following subsections include a summary of the formal framework developed for the trajectory specification language. A more detailed treatment of the language and main theorems, along with proofs and additional lemmas, is given in (Brajnik & Clancy 1996a; 1996b).

Guiding and refining the simulation

Model checking and behavior refinement are performed by the *Temporal Logic Guide* (TL–Guide). Each time QSIM extends a behavior by adding a new state, the behavior is passed to the TL–Guide. The behavior is refuted if it contains sufficient information to determine that each of its completions fail to satisfy the set of TL expressions. If the behavior conditionally models the TL expressions, then it is refined by incorporating relevant quantitative information contained within the TL expressions. Otherwise, the behavior is retained unchanged.

The trajectory specification language includes propositional state formulæ that can refer to qualitative and quantitative values of variables within states. Qualitative value information is specified using (`qvalue` v ($qmag$ $qdir$)) where v is a model variable, $qmag$ is a qualitative magnitude, and $qdir$ is one of {`inc`, `std`, `dec`}. `NIL` can be used anywhere to match anything. Such a proposition is true for a state exactly when the qualitative value of v in the state matches the description ($qmag$ $qdir$).

Path formulæ are defined recursively as either state formulæ or combinations of path formulæ using temporal and boolean operators. A state formula is true of a behavior if it is true for the first state in the behavior. The path formula (`until` p q), where both p and q are path formulæ, is true for a behavior if p holds for all suffixes of the behavior preceding the first one where q holds, while (`strong-next` p) is true for a behavior if it contains at least two states and p holds in the behavior starting at the second state. Other temporal operators can be defined as abbreviations from these two. We have extended those defined in (Shults & Kuipers 1996) to provide a more abstract language to simplify the specification of assertions.

Temporal logic formulæ are given meaning with respect to linear–time interpretation structures. These structures are extended from their typical definition (*e.g.* (Emerson 1990)) in order to accommodate the refinement of behaviors with quantitative information. In addition to defining a sequence of states and a propositional interpretation function, means for representing, generating and applying refinement conditions are provided. Refinement conditions are needed because the language provides quantitative propositions whose truth value cannot always be determined. When ambiguity occurs for a formula, then the interpretation is required to provide necessary and sufficient re-

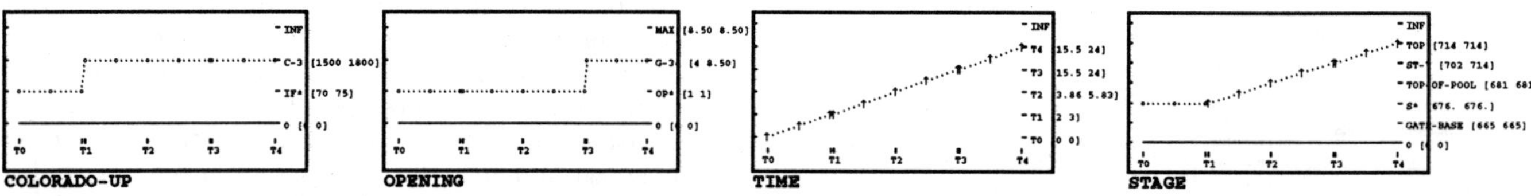

TeQSIM produces two behaviors where `Stage` reaches `Top`. The first behavior is shown above. The opening action occurs at `T3`. The numeric bounds on this time–point shows that an overflow can occur only if the opening action is performed after 15.5 days. The second behavior provides similar results.

Figure 3: Lake simulation with opening actions leading to overflow.

finement conditions on quantitative ranges to disambiguate the truth value of the formula. A *refinement condition* is a boolean combination of inequalities between the partially known numeric value of a variable in a state and an extended real number.

The trajectory specification language contains potentially ambiguous state formulæ like (`value-<=` v n), where v is a variable and $n \in \Re \cup \{-\infty, +\infty\}$. The formula is true in a state s iff $\forall x \in \mathcal{R}(v,s) : x \leq n$, where $\mathcal{R}(v,s)$ denotes the range of possible numeric values for variable v in state s; it is false iff $\forall x \in \mathcal{R}(v,s) : n < x$; otherwise, it is conditionally true. In such a case, the refinement condition is that the least upper bound of the possible numeric values of v is equal to n (*i.e.* $v_s \leq n$, where v_s is the unknown value of v in s).

Applying a refinement condition to a state yields a new, more refined state. For example, the formula (`value-<= X 0.3`) generates the condition $X_s \leq 0.3$ when interpreted on a state s where $\mathcal{R}(X,s) = [0, 1.0]$. Applying the condition to s leads to a new state s' where $\mathcal{R}(X,s') = [0, 0.3]$.

Notice that ambiguity is not a purely syntactic property, but rather it depends on state information. For example, (`value-<= X 0.3`) is (unconditionally) true on a state where $\mathcal{R}(X,s) = [0, 0.25]$, but only conditionally true if $\mathcal{R}(X,s) = [0, 1.0]$. Due to potential ambiguity, two entailment relations are used to define the semantics of formulæ. The first one, called *models*, characterizes non–ambiguous true formulæ while the second one, called *conditionally models*, characterizes ambiguous formulæ.

To avoid hindering the simulation process, the usage of ambiguous formulæ must be restricted. The problem is that an arbitrary formula may yield several alternative refinement conditions. A disjunction of refinement conditions can be applied to states, but it requires the introduction of a new behavior that is qualitatively identical to the original behavior. For example, when interpreted on a particular state (`or (value-<= X 0.5) (value-<= Y 15)`) may yield the condition $(X_s \leq 0.5 \vee Y_s \leq 15)$. Applying such a condition yields a state s' in which $\mathcal{R}(X,s') = [\ldots, 0.5]$ and a state s'' where $\mathcal{R}(Y,s'') = [\ldots, 15]$. A similar, more severe problem occurs with path formulæ.

The set of *admissible formulæ* is a syntactic restriction that excludes formulæ that may result in disjunctive conditions. Even though such a restriction reduces the expressiveness of the language, it does not have an important impact from a practical point. If the modeler adheres to the general principle that all important distinctions are made explicit in the qualitative model (*i.e.* introduces appropriate landmarks with associated numerical bounds instead of using quantitative bounds), then the restriction to admissible formulæ does not reduce the applicability of TeQSIM.

Discontinuous Changes

The injection of discontinuous changes into qualitative simulation consists of identifying when the change occurs and then propagating its effects through the model to determine which variables inherit their values across the change and which don't.

A discontinuous change is specified by (`disc-change` *precond effect*), where *precond* is a boolean combination of `qvalue` propositions and *effect* is a list of expressions of the form (*variable qmag* [`:range` *range*]). This expression is translated into the temporal logic path formula (`occurs-at` *precond* (`strong-next` *effect'*)) where *effect'* is a conjunction of `qvalue`, `value-<=` and `value->=` formulæ derived from *effect*. This formula is true for a behavior iff *effect'* is true for the state immediately following the first state in which *precond* is true.

The Discontinuous Change Processor monitors states as they are created and tests them against the preconditions of applicable discontinuous change expressions. A new state is inserted into the simulation following state s if the preconditions are satisfied and a discontinuous change is required to assert the effects in the successor states. A new, possibly incomplete state s' is created by asserting the qualitative values specified within the effects and inheriting values from s for variables not affected by the discontinuous change via continuity relaxation (see below). All consistent completions of s' are computed and installed as successors of s.

Continuity relaxation propagates the effects of a discontinuous change through the model by identifying potentially affected variables. The following assumptions are made: (i) *state* variables (variables whose time derivative is included in the model) are *piecewise–*C^1 (*i.e.* continuous everywhere, and differentiable everywhere except at isolated points); (ii) *non–state* variables are at least *piecewise-*C^0 (*i.e.* continuous everywhere except at isolated points); (iii) all discontinuous changes in input variables are explicitly specified; and (iv) the model is valid during the transient caused by a discontinuous change. These assumptions suffice to support an effective criterion, proven to be sound, for automatically identifying all the variables that are potentially affected by the simultaneous discontinuity of variables in a set $\Delta = \{V_1 \ldots V_n\}$.

Given a qualitative differential model $\mathcal{M}$, a variable Z is *totally dependent* on a set of variables $\mathcal{A}$ (written $\mathcal{A} \rightsquigarrow Z$) iff $\mathcal{M}$ includes a non-differential, continuous relation $R(X_1 \ldots X_i, Z, X_{i+1} \ldots X_n)$ with $n \geq 1$ such that $\forall i$: $X_i \in \mathcal{A}$ or $\mathcal{A} \rightsquigarrow X_i$. For example, if $\mathcal{M}$ includes the constraint (add X Y Z) then $\{Y, Z\} \rightsquigarrow X$. Furthermore, let $TD(\mathcal{A})$ represent the set of variables totally dependent on $\mathcal{A}$ (i.e. $TD(\mathcal{A}) = \{X | \mathcal{A} \rightsquigarrow X\}$).

Let $\mathcal{E}$ be the set of input variables and $\mathcal{S}$ the set of state variables of $\mathcal{M}$. Then define $\mathcal{PD}_\Delta$ (the set of variables that are potentially affected by the discontinuity of variables in Δ) as the maximum set of variables of $\mathcal{M}$ that satisfies:

1. $\Delta \subseteq \mathcal{PD}_\Delta$ (by definition of Δ);
2. $\mathcal{S} \cap \mathcal{PD}_\Delta = \emptyset$ (by assumption (i));
3. $\mathcal{E} \cap \mathcal{PD}_\Delta = \Delta$ (by assumption (iii));
4. $TD(\mathcal{S} \cup \mathcal{E} - \Delta) \cap \mathcal{PD}_\Delta = \emptyset$ (by definition of total dependency, if Z totally depends on a set of continuous variables, then Z must be continuous too and cannot belong to $\mathcal{PD}_\Delta$).

Continuity relaxation handles discontinuous changes of variables in Δ by computing the set $\mathcal{PD}_\Delta$ so that, during a transient, variables in $\mathcal{PD}_\Delta$ are unconstrained and can change arbitrarily, whereas those not in $\mathcal{PD}_\Delta$ retain their previous qualitative magnitude. The direction of change (*i.e. qdir*) for all variables is assumed to be potentially discontinuous.

In the simulation shown in figure 3, the discontinuity occurring to `Opening` at `T3` cannot affect `Stage` because the latter is totally dependent on the state variable `Volume`. On the other hand, the discontinuity affects the magnitude of `Discharge-rate` (not shown in the figure) because none of the conditions above apply. Notice also how the discontinuities affect the *qdir* of variables.

Model Checking

The temporal logic model checking algorithm is designed to evaluate a QSIM behavior with respect to a set of temporal logic formulæ as the behavior is incrementally developed. This allows behaviors to be filtered and refined as early as possible *during* the simulation. Kuipers and Shults (1994) developed a model checking algorithm to prove properties about continuous dynamical systems by testing a *completed* simulation against temporal logic expressions. We have extended this work to deal with conditionally true formulæ and with behaviors that are not closed, *i.e.* still being extended by the simulator.

The model checking algorithm, described in (Brajnik & Clancy 1996b), computes the function τ: *Formulæ* $\times$ *Behaviors* $\rightarrow \{\mathtt{T}, \mathtt{F}, \mathtt{U}\} \times \mathcal{C}$, where $\mathcal{C}$ is the set of all possible refinement conditions, including the trivial condition `TRUE`. A definite answer (*i.e.* `T` or `F`) is provided when the behavior contains sufficient information to determine the truth value of the formula. For example, a non-closed behavior b will *not* be sufficiently determined with respect to the formula (**`eventually`** p) if p is false for all suffixes of b, since p may become true anytime in the future.

A behavior b is *sufficiently determined* with respect to a temporal logic formula φ (written $b \rhd \varphi$) whenever there is enough information within the behavior to determine a single truth value for all of its completions. If a behavior is not sufficiently determined for a formula, then `U` is returned by the algorithm. The definition of *sufficiently determined* (omitted due to space restrictions) is given recursively on the basis of the syntactic structure of the formula. We will write $b \not\rhd \varphi$ to signify that b is not sufficiently determined for φ.

Notice that indeterminacy is a property independent from ambiguity: the former is related to incomplete behaviors, whereas the latter deals with ambiguous information present in states of a behavior.

The following theorem supports our use of temporal logic model checking for guiding and refining the simulation.

Theorem 1 (TL–guide is sound and complete) *Given a QSIM behavior b and an admissible formula φ then TL-guide:*

1. *refutes b iff $b \rhd \varphi$ and there is no way to extend b to make it a model for φ.*
2. *retains b without modifying it iff*
   (a) *$b \rhd \varphi$ and b is a model for φ; or*
   (b) *$b \not\rhd \varphi$ and there is no necessary refinement condition C for refining b into a model for φ.*
3. *replaces b with b' iff*
   (a) *$b \rhd \varphi$ and b conditionally models φ and there exists C that is necessary and sufficient for refining b into a model for φ; or*
   (b) *$b \not\rhd \varphi$ and there is a necessary condition C for refining b into a model for φ.*

Proof. By induction on the length of φ; see (Brajnik & Clancy 1996b).

Discussion and Conclusions

We are currently exploring several directions to extend the expressiveness of the trajectory specification language. Enabling the comparison of magnitudes of variables across states (*e.g.* to specify a decreasing oscillation) requires a move from a propositional logic to some sort of first order logic. Expressing the *possibility* of a discontinuous change requires a more complex relationship between preconditions and effects of a discontinuous change. Addressing discontinuous feed–forward control problems requires that preconditions are specified using arbitrary temporal logic expressions, not simply state formulæ. Simulating hybrid discrete–continuous systems calls for a more flexible specification of partially ordered external events.

While the practical time–complexity of a TeQSIM simulation is dominated by quantitative inferences performed by QSIM, we are still investigating improvements to our algorithm with respect to complexity.

The incorporation of trajectory information into a qualitative simulation has been explored by DeCoste (1994), who introduces *sufficient discriminatory envisionments* to determine whether a goal region is possible, impossible or inevitable from each state of the space. Washio and Kitamura (1995) also present a technique that uses temporal logic to perform a *history oriented envisionment* to filter predictions. TeQSIM, within a rigorously formalized framework, provides a more expressive language not limited to reachability problems, refines behaviors as opposed to just filtering them, and incorporates discontinuous changes into behaviors.

Discontinuities have been investigated by Nishida and Doshita (1987), Forbus (1989), Iwasaki and colleagues (1995), and others. The continuity relaxation method adopted in TeQSIM is conceptually simpler, sound, widely applicable and practically effective.

Our trajectory specification language is similar in expressiveness to both Allen's *interval algebra* (Allen 1984) and Dechter, Meiri and Pearl's *temporal constraint networks* (Dechter, Meiri, & Pearl 1991). The usage of the language in TeQSIM, however, is quite different from these two formalisms. Instead of asserting temporal constraints in a database of assertions and querying if certain combinations of facts are consistent, TeQSIM checks that a database of temporally related facts generated by QSIM satisfy a set of temporal logic constraints.

TeQSIM supports a general methodology for incorporating otherwise inexpressible trajectory information into the qualitative simulation process. The correctness of TL–Guide, of the Discontinuous Change Processor, and of QSIM guarantee that all possible trajectories of the modeled system that are compatible with the model, the initial state and the trajectory constraints are included in the generated behaviors. In addition, the completeness of TL–Guide ensures that all behaviors generated by TeQSIM are potential models of the trajectory constraints specified by the modeler. For these reasons, and its limited complexity, TeQSIM can be applied to problems where QSIM alone would not be appropriate.

Acknowledgments

We thank Benjamin Shults for letting us use his TL program to implement TeQSIM. This work has taken place in the Qualitative Reasoning Group at the Artificial Intelligence Laboratory, The University of Texas at Austin. Research of the Qualitative Reasoning Group is supported in part by NSF grants IRI–9216584 and IRI–9504138, by NASA grants NCC 2–760 and NAG 2–994, and by the Texas Advanced Research Program under grant no. 003658–242.

QSIM and TeQSIM are available for research purposes via `http://www.cs.utexas.edu/users/qr`.

References

Allen, J. F. 1984. Towards a general theory of action and time. *Artificial Intelligence* 23:123–154.

Brajnik, G., and Clancy, D. J. 1996a. Guiding and refining simulation using temporal logic. In *Proc. of the Third International Workshop on Temporal Representation and Reasoning (TIME'96)*. Key West, Florida: IEEE Computer Society Press. To appear.

Brajnik, G., and Clancy, D. J. 1996b. Temporal constraints on trajectories in qualitative simulation. Technical Report UDMI–RT–01–96, Dip. di Matematica e Informatica, University of Udine, Udine, Italy.

Dechter, R.; Meiri, I.; and Pearl, J. 1991. Temporal constraint networks. *Artificial Intelligence* 49:61–95.

DeCoste, D. 1994. Goal–directed qualitative reasoning with partial states. Technical Report 57, The Institute for the Learning Sciences, University of Illinois at Urbana–Champaign.

Emerson, E. 1990. Temporal and modal logic. In van Leeuwen, J., ed., *Handbook of Theoretical Computer Science*. Elsevier Science Publishers/MIT Press. 995–1072. Chap. 16.

Forbus, K. 1984. Qualitative process theory. *Artificial Intelligence* 24:85–168.

Forbus, K. 1989. Introducing actions into qualitative simulation. In *IJCAI–89*, 1273–1278.

Iwasaki, Y.; Farquhar, A.; Saraswat, V.; Bobrow, D.; and Gupta, V. 1995. Modeling time in hybrid systems: how fast is "instantaneous"? In *IJCAI–95*, 1773–1780. Montréal, Canada: Morgan Kaufmann Publishers, Inc.

Kuipers, B., and Shults, B. 1994. Reasoning in logic about continuous change. In *Principles of Knowledge Representation and Reasoning (KR–94)*. Morgan Kaufmann Publishers, Inc.

Kuipers, B. 1994. *Qualitative Reasoning: modeling and simulation with incomplete knowledge*. Cambridge, Massachusetts: MIT Press.

Nishida, T., and Doshita, S. 1987. Reasoning about discontinuous change. In *AAAI–87*, 643–648.

Shults, B., and Kuipers, B. J. 1996. Qualitative simulation and temporal logic: proving properties of continuous systems. Technical Report TR AI96–244, University of Texas at Austin, Dept. of Computer Sciences.

Washio, T., and Kitamura, M. 1995. A fast history–oriented envisioning method introducing temporal logic. In *Ninth International Workshop on Qualitative Reasoning (QR–95)*, 279–288.

A Formal Hybrid Modeling Scheme for Handling Discontinuities in Physical System Models

Pieter J. Mosterman and **Gautam Biswas**
Center for Intelligent Systems
Box 1679, Sta B
Vanderbilt University
Nashville, Tennessee 37235
`pjm, biswas@vuse.vanderbilt.edu`

Abstract

Physical systems are by nature continuous, but often exhibit nonlinearities that make behavior generation complex and hard to analyze. Complexity is often reduced by linearizing model constraints and by abstracting the time scale for behavior generation. In either case, the physical components are modeled to operate in *multiple modes*, with abrupt changes between modes. This paper discusses a *hybrid* modeling methodology and analysis algorithms that combine continuous energy flow modeling and localized discrete signal flow modeling to generate complex, multi-mode behavior in a consistent and correct manner. Energy phase space analysis is employed to demonstrate the correctness of the algorithm, and the reachability of a continuous mode.

Introduction

Recent advances in model-based and qualitative reasoning have led to researchers developing large scale models of complex, continuous systems, such as power plants and space station sub-systems. System complexity is handled by replacing nonlinear component behaviors by simpler piecewise linear behaviors, causing the system to exhibit multi-mode behavior[11]. For example, the Airbus A-320 fly-by-wire system includes the *take off*, *cruise*, *approach*, and *go-around* operational modes[13].

Quantitative and qualitative simulation methods (e.g., [6, 12]) typically impose *continuity constraints* to ensure generated behaviors are meaningful. However, system models that accommodate configuration changes and multi-mode components can exhibit discontinuous behavior. Consider the diode-inductor circuit in Fig. 1. When closed switch S_w is opened, and the voltage drop across the diode exceeds $0.6V$ it comes on and *abruptly* enforces this voltage across the inductor. Computational complexity is reduced by modeling the diode as an ideal switch with on and off modes. In reality, parasitic resistive and capacitive effects in the diode would force the *on/off* changes to be continuous with a very fast time constant.

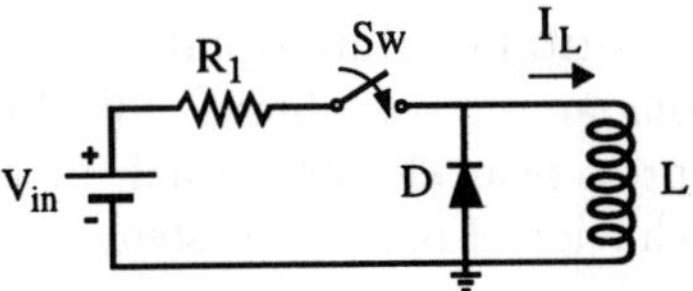

Figure 1: **Physical system with discontinuities.**

Our goal is to derive a uniform approach to analyzing continuous and discontinuous system behavior without violating fundamental physical principles of conservation of energy and momentum. The solution is a hybrid modeling scheme that combines traditional energy-related bond graph elements to model the physical components and finite state automata controlled junctions to model configuration changes.

Characteristics of Physical Systems

A physical system can be regarded as a configuration of connected physical elements. The energy distribution in the system reflects its behavioral history up to that time and defines the traditional notion of system *state*. Future behavior of the system is a function of its current state and input to the system from the present time. State changes are caused by energy exchange between system components, expressed as *power*, the time derivative or flow of energy. Independent of the physical domain (mechanical, electrical, hydraulic, etc.), power is defined as the product of two conjugate *power variables*, *effort*, e, and *flow*, f. Correspondingly, energy comes in two forms: stored effort and flow, called *generalized momentum*, p, and *generalized displacement*, q, respectively. The variables p and q are called *state variables*.

Bond graphs capture continuous energy-related physical system behavior[12]. Its constituent elements are energy storage elements *inductors*, I, and *capaci-*

tors, C, dissipators, R and sources/sinks of effort and flow, S_e and S_f. Sources define interaction with the environment. Idealized, lossless 0- (*common effort*) and 1- (*common flow*) *junctions* connect sets of elements and define the system configuration. Two special junctions called signal transformers complete the set of bond graph primitive elements, the transformer, TF, and the gyrator, GY.

Bond graph models describe system behavior by energy exchange among components. Depending on the type of stored energy, buffer elements impose either effort or flow on their respective junctions. This imposes a causal structure on the system effort and flow variables which is exploited to generate system behavior in the form of quantitative state equations[12] and qualitative relations among variables [1, 8]. In summary, bond graphs provide an elegant formalism to model the continuous behavior of physical systems.

Nature and Effects of Discontinuities

Conservation of energy enforces a time integral relation between energy and power variables which implies *continuity* of power, therefore, effort and flow. Discontinuities in behavior generation can be attributed to simplifying model descriptions[2, 11]. We contend that all discontinuities in the modeling of physical systems can be attributed to *abstracting* component behavior to simplify (i) the time-scale of the interactions, or (ii) the relations among parameters.

Often the time scale of nonlinear behavior in components is significantly less than the time scale at which overall system behavior is studied. Explicit modeling of system behavior at the smaller time scale may greatly increase the time complexity of behavior simulation and introduce numerical stiffness. To avoid this, components like electric switches, valves, and diodes are modeled to have abrupt or discontinuous changes in behavior.

Another cause for discontinuities in models stems from component parameter abstractions. The detailed effects of particular component characteristics, such as fast nonlinear behaviors of transistors and oscillators, are usually not important except for their gross effects on overall system behavior. Behavior generation is simplified by approximating nonlinear behavior as a series of *piecewise* linear behaviors. In other situations certain parameter effects that have negligible effects on gross behavior are omitted from system models.

Since all changes in the state of any physical system are brought about by energy exchange or power, the constraint on power continuity plays an important role in meaningful behavior generation. However, in models with discontinuities, behavior generation schemes have to deal with discontinuities in power variables[9].

The Hybrid Modeling Scheme

In qualitative simulation systems, such as QSIM[6], a higher level global control structure (meta-model) determines when to switch QDE sets during behavior generation. In other approaches[2, 6], transition functions between configurations are specified as rules or state transition tables. In work based on bond graph schemes, researchers have introduced switching bonds[2] controlled by global *finite state automata* to connect and disconnect subsystem models. All these methods fail for systems whose range of behaviors have not been pre-enumerated. Compositional modeling approaches that build system models *dynamically* by composing model fragments[1, 10] overcome this problem. We adopt this methodology and implement a dynamic model switching methodology in the bond graph modeling framework.

We avoid global control structures and pre-enumerated bond graph models. Instead we translate the overall physical model to one bond graph model that covers the energy flow relations within the system. Next, the discontinuous mechanisms and components in the system are modeled locally as *controlled junctions* which can assume one of two states – *on* and *off*. Local *finite state automata* which control each junction constitute the *signal flow model* of the system. It is distinct from the bond graph model that deals with the energy-related behavior of the physical system variables. Signal flow models describe the *transitional*, mode-switching behavior of the system. A *mode* of a system is determined by the combination of the *on/off states* of all the controlled junctions in its bond graph model.

Controlled Junctions

When active (*on*), controlled junctions behave like normal 0- or 1-junctions. Deactivated 0-junctions force the effort and deactivated 1-junctions force the flow at adjoining bonds to become 0, thus inhibiting energy flow. In both cases, the controlled junction exhibits *ideal switch* behavior, and modeling discontinuous behavior in this way is consistent with bond graph theory[12]. Deactivating controlled junctions can affect the behaviors at adjoining junctions, and, therefore, the causal relations among system variables.

Controlled junctions are marked with subscripts (e.g., 1_1, 0_2) in the hybrid bond graph representation (Fig. 2). Each controlled junction has an associated finite state automata that generates the *on/off* signals for the controlled junction. This is called a junction's *control specification* (CSPEC). CSPEC input consists

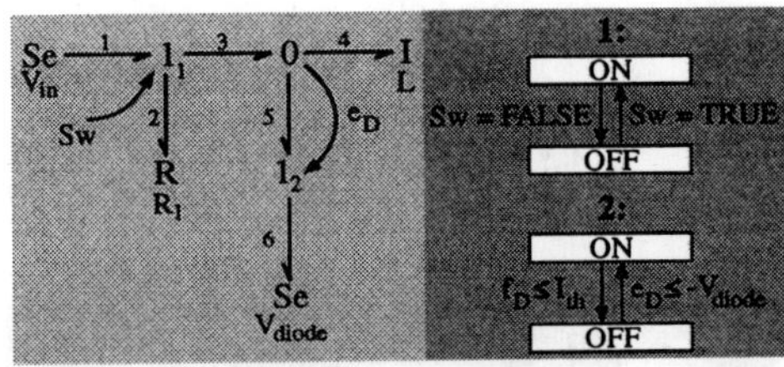

Figure 2: **Hybrid bond graph model.**

of power variables from the bond graph and external control signals. Its output is the *on/off* signal for the controlled junction. In every CSPEC transition sequence, *on/off* signals have to alternate.

Mode Switching in the Hybrid Model

Discontinuous effects establish or break energetic connections in the model when threshold values are crossed. As a consequence, signals associated with bonds at the junction may change discontinuously. Also, when junctions become active, buffers may become dependent, causing an apparent instantaneous change in the energy distribution of the system[9].

The use of controlled junctions is illustrated for the diode-inductor circuit (Fig. 1) in Fig. 2. The manual switch turns *on* or *off* based on an external control signal as shown in CSPEC **1**, and the diode switches *on* or *off* based on CSPEC **2**. Fig. 3 shows a simulation run of this system with parameter values $V_{in} = 10V, R_1 = 330\Omega, L = 5mH, p(0) = 0$. When the switch is closed ($t = 10$), the inductor is connected to the source and builds up a flux, p, by drawing a current. The diode is not active in this mode of operation (10). When the switch is opened ($t = 100$), the current drawn by the inductor drops to 0, causing its flux to discharge instantaneously. Because of the derivative nature of the constituent relation $V_L = L\frac{dp}{dt}$, the result is an infinite negative (the flux changes from a positive value to 0) voltage across the diode (Fig. 4). Because its threshold value, V_{diode}, is exceeded, the diode comes on instantaneously and the mode of operation where the switch was open and the diode inactive (00) is never realized in real time. If it were, the stored energy of the inductor would be released instantaneously in a mythical mode where the model has no real representation, producing an incorrect energy balance in the overall system. Consequently, there would be no flow of current after the diode becomes active. In real time the system switches from mode 10 to 01 directly.

At $t = 350$ the diode turns *off* because its current falls below $I_{th} = 0$. Since there is no stored energy in the system, 00 becomes the final mode. The spike observed is a simulation artifact caused by the simu-

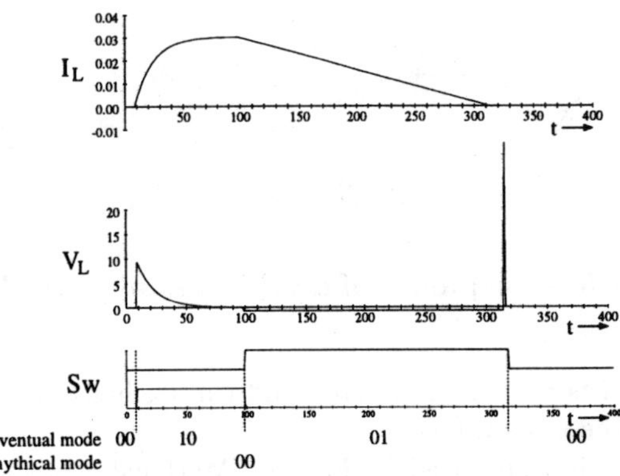

Figure 3: **Diode-inductor simulation.**

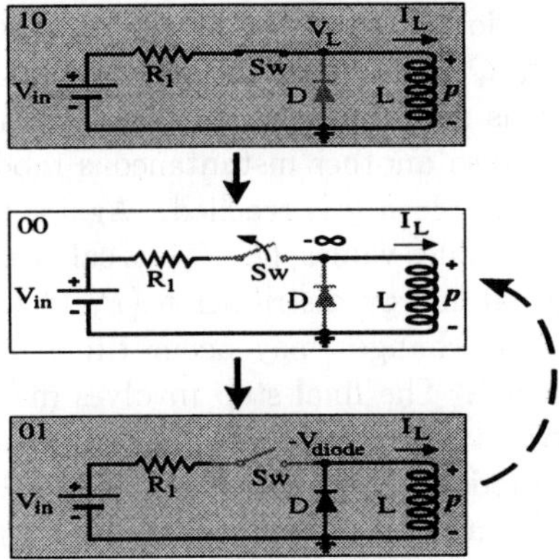

Figure 4: **A series of mode switches may occur.**

lation time step. The diode was inferred to switch *off* when the current had a small negative value, rather than 0. This small current in the inductor went to 0 instantaneously, which resulted in the spike shown.

A model that undergoes a sequence of instantaneous mode changes has no physical manifestation during these changes, therefore, these modes are termed *mythical*. Thermodynamically, the system is considered to be *isolated*[3] during mythical modes, i.e., there is no energy exchange with the environment. This establishes the energy distribution of the system as a switching invariant. Because the energy distribution in the system defines its state vector, it is referred to as the principle of *invariance of state*. In the diode-inductor example, the flux, p, of the inductor is invariant during switching. The invariance of state principle applies only if the state variables represent the energy distribution (buffer energy values) in the system.

Energy redistribution can occur in the real mode, and the challenge is to compute the initial energy distribution when a real mode is reached after a series of discontinuous mythical changes. At this point, the

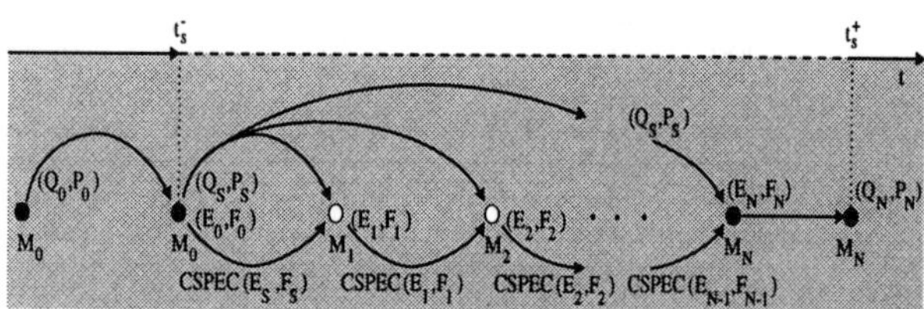

Figure 5: **A sequence of mythical mode switches.**

system is no longer isolated and can exchange energy with the environment.

This is illustrated in Fig. 5. Mythical modes are depicted as open circles and real modes are shown by solid circles. In real mode M_0 a signal value crosses a threshold at time t_s^-, which causes a discontinuous change to mode M_1. Based on the original energy distribution (P_s, Q_s) values for the set of power variables (E_i, F_i) in this new configuration are calculated. The new values cause another instantaneous mode change and the new mode M_2 is reached. Again, the set of new power variables values, (E_i, F_i), is calculated based on the original energy distribution (P_s, Q_s). Further mythical mode changes may occur till a real mode, M_N, is reached. The final step involves mapping the energy distribution, or state variable values, of the departed real mode to the eventual real mode. Real time continuous simulation resumes at t_s^+ so system behavior in real time implies mode M_N follows M_0. The formal *Mythical Mode Algorithm* (MMA) is outlined below.

1. Calculate the energy values (Q_s, P_s) and signal values (E_s, F_s) for bond graph model M_0 using (Q_0, P_0), at the previous simulation step as initial values.

2. Use *CSPEC* to infer a new mode given (E_s, F_s).

3. If one or more controlled junctions switch states:
   (a) Derive the bond graph for this configuration.
   (b) Assign causal directions to bonds[12].
   (c) Calculate the signals (E_i, F_i) for the new mode, M_i, based on the initial values (Q_s, P_s).
   (d) Use *CSPEC* again to infer a possible new mode based on (E_i, F_i) for the new mode, M_i.
   (e) Repeat step 3 till no more mode changes occur.

4. Establish the final mode, M_N, as the new system configuration.

5. Map (Q_0, P_0) to the energy distribution (Q_N, P_N).

Details of the complete simulation algorithm and software for modeling hybrid system behavior are described elsewhere[7].

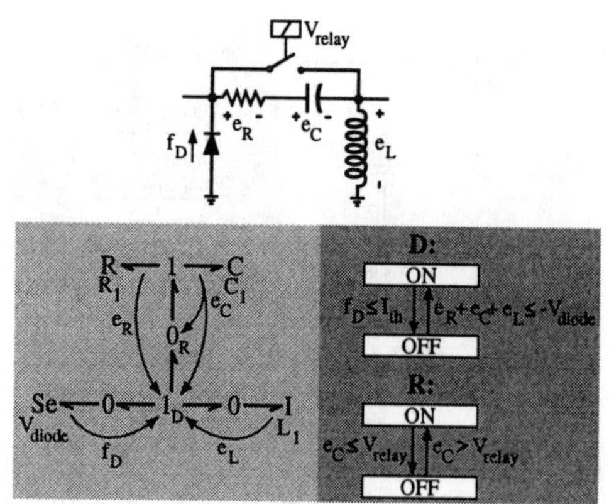

Figure 6: **Diode-relay circuit.**

Divergence of Time

Consider a scenario where the diode requires a threshold current $I_{th} > 0$ to maintain its *on* state. If the inductor has built up a positive flux, the diode comes *on* when the switch opens. However, if the flux in the inductor is too low to maintain the threshold current, the diode goes *off* instantaneously, but in its *off* state the voltage drop exceeds the threshold voltage again. The model goes into a loop of instantaneous changes (see Fig. 4). For instantaneous changes, real time does not progress or diverge, but this violates the physical principle of *divergence of time*[4]. Checking for divergence of time in model behavior is accomplished by a multiple energy phase plot method. Failure to diverge is linked back to the initial values of associated state variables.

Consider the electrical circuit in Fig. 6. The three branches where voltage drops occur in this circuit are represented by 0-junctions. The diode is modeled as an ideal voltage sink and the three branches and elements are connected using 1-junctions. Two switches make up the control flow model

1. The diode switches *on/off* depending on its voltage drop or current. The corresponding controlled junction is 1_D with CSPEC **D**. The input to **D** are the power signals e_R, e_C, e_L, and f_D.

2. The relay is *closed/open* depending on the voltage drop across the capacitor, modeled by controlled junction 0_R with the controlling power variable e_C. A closed relay implies that 0_R is *off* and an open relay implies 0_R is *on*.

To avoid discontinuous changes in power variables during analysis, CSPEC transition conditions are rewritten in terms of the energy variables which are invariant across mythical modes. Since discontinuities

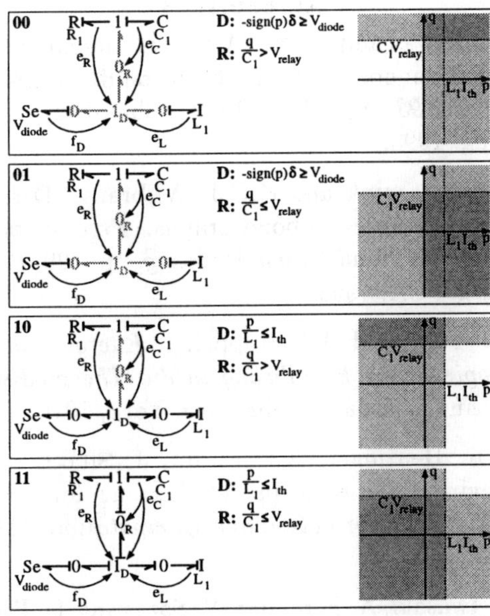

Figure 7: **Multiple energy phase space analysis.**

can cause changes in system configuration, and the relation between power and energy variables, an energy phase space diagram has to be constructed for each switch configuration.

The energy phase space is k-dimensional, where k is the total number of independent buffers in the system. For example, the circuit in Fig. 6 has two energy buffers implying a two dimensional phase space with axes p, the flux in inductor L_1, and q, the charge on capacitor C_1 (Fig. 7). The four modes for the two switches are 00, 01, 10, and 11. The first digit indicates the open/closed state of the diode, and the second digit defines the on/off state of the relay. For each mode, the transition conditions based on the energy variables are grayed out in the phase spaces. For example, in mode 00 the relay turns on if $e_C > V_{relay}$.[1] Substituting $e_C = \frac{q}{C_1}$ generates $q > C_1 V_{relay}$, which is grayed out in the phase space.

The conditions under which the diode turns on are harder to derive because L_1 induces a Dirac pulse, δ.[2] CSPEC **D** switches *on* if $e_R + e_C + e_L \leq -V_{diode}$. When the diode is off, $e_R = e_C = \frac{q}{C_1}$. A deactivated 1-junction has 0 flow so the stored flux in the inductor becomes 0 instantaneously and because $e_L = \frac{dp}{dt}$, this causes e_L to be a Dirac pulse which approaches positive

[1] As part of a larger system (e.g., automobile ignitions), this circuit discharges the inductor through the diode and capacitor. The relay keeps the charge in the capacitor above a small threshold value so that the flux in the inductor does not increase first when it is switched to discharge.

[2] This is a pulse of finite area but infinitesimal width that occurs at a time point.

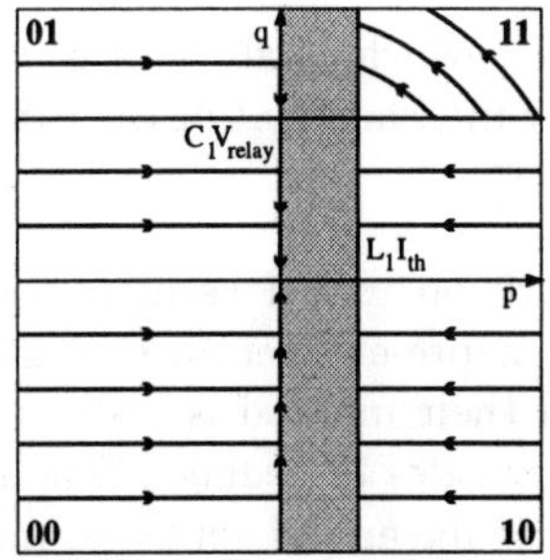

Figure 8: **One energy phase space.**

or negative infinity, depending on whether the stored flux was negative or positive, respectively. If the flux was 0, e_L equals 0. Using the function *sign*

$$sign(x) = \begin{cases} -1 & \text{if } x < 0 \\ 0 & \text{if } x = 0 \\ 1 & \text{if } x > 0 \end{cases} \tag{1}$$

we derive $e_L = -sign(p)\delta \leq -V_{diode}$. The minus signs cancel and e_R and e_C can be neglected, so the condition for switching of the diode becomes $sign(p)\delta \geq V_{diode}$. Assuming the voltage enforced by the diode is 0.6V, this inequality holds for all values of $p > 0$. This area is grayed out in the phase space.

The phase space representation for the four modes (Fig. 7) are superimposed (Fig. 8) to study possible divergence of time violations. If an energy distribution does not have a real energy phase space component, the state vector can never lead to a real mode and time does not diverge for this behavior.

In this example, divergence of time is violated if $I_{th} > 0$ for the diode. This area will be reached for all energy distributions with positive initial flux, p. When $p = 0$ in the 00 and 01 modes, time does diverge. If the flux has a negative initial value, both the flux and capacitor charge converge asymptotically to 0.

Discussion and Conclusions

Hybrid models of physical systems may undergo a series of discontinuous changes. These discontinuities are a result of abstracting the time scale and component parameters in system models. The Mythical Mode Algorithm uses the principle of invariance of state to correctly infer new modes of continuous operation and their state variable values. In pathological cases, system models result in mythical loops, implying the model is physically incorrect. Using the principle of invariance of state, a systematic energy phase space analysis method is developed to verify the correctness of system models. Note that our work verifies the correctness of models, i.e., it ensures that these models do not violate physical principles. This is different from *model validation* which establishes how well a system model behavior matches that of the exact physical situation of interest.

Previous work on model verification by Henzinger *et al*[4] relies on pre-enumeration of global modes of operation, and their method is restricted to variables that have *linear rates of change*. Our method applies more generally to linear and nonlinear models. In other work, Iwasaki *et al.*[5], introduce the concept of *hypertime* to represent the instantaneous switching as an infinitesimal interval. A sequence of switches can be analyzed in hypertime to determine state changes. This approach emulates physical effects of small time constants (e.g., parasitic dissipation) which can greatly increase simulation complexity. Moreover, the modeler often chooses to simplify the model by ignoring parasitic effects. If physical inconsistencies, e.g., non divergence of time arise in behavior generation, the modeler has to add more details in the model increasing its complexity, or adjust landmark values to establish a physically correct but more simple and abstract model. Adding detail may not increase the accuracy of behavior generation because the additional parameters required may be hard to estimate. Also, increasing the computational complexity of models and simulation engines does not guarantee correct models. In the diode-inductor example, an infinitesimal change of time when both the switch and diode are *off* discharges the stored flux and generates incorrect behavior. On the other hand, explicit incorporation of invariance of state ensures that physical consistency of the chosen models can be determined.

Another insight gained is that mythical modes arise from combinations of consistent switching elements, i.e., a single switch cannot cause mythical mode changes. When a number of switches interact via instantaneous relations with no intervening buffers, sequential behavior may ensue. Although these modes are modeling artifacts, they result from justifiable modeling decisions, which have to be dealt with appropriately. In future work we will attempt to demonstrate that reachability analysis can be applied in the multiple energy phase space approach by taking the cross product of all interacting local finite state automata. These sets of interacting automata represent *local modes* of operation. To avoid the computational complexity of the cross product of a number of automata, we will have to develop schemes that efficiently decompose the model into parts that are not instantaneously connected because of intervening energy buffers.

References

[1] G. Biswas and X. Yu. A formal modeling scheme for continuous systems: Focus on diagnosis. *Proc. IJCAI-93*, pp. 1474–1479, Chambery, France, Aug. 1993.

[2] J.F. Broenink and K.C.J. Wijbrans. Describing discontinuities in bond graphs. *Proc. of the Intl. Conf. on Bond Graph Modeling*, pp. 120–125, San Diego, CA, 1993.

[3] G. Falk and W. Ruppel. *Energie und Entropie: Eine Einführung in die Thermodynamik.* Springer-Verlag, Berlin, New York, 1976.

[4] T.A. Henzinger, X. Nicollin, J. Sifakis, and S. Yovine. Symbolic model checking for real-time systems. *Information and Computation*, 111:193–244, 1994.

[5] Y. Iwasaki, A. Farquhar, V. Saraswat, D. Bobrow, and V. Gupta. Modeling time in hybrid systems: How fast is "instantaneous"? *Qualitative Reasoning Workshop*, pp. 94–103, Amsterdam, The Netherlands, 1995.

[6] B. Kuipers. Qualitative simulation. *Artificial Intelligence*, 29:289–338, 1986.

[7] P.J. Mosterman and G. Biswas. Modeling discontinuous behavior with hybrid bond graphs. *Qualitative Reasoning Workshop*, pp. 139–147, Amsterdam, The Netherlands, 1995.

[8] P.J. Mosterman, R. Kapadia, and G. Biswas. Using bond graphs for diagnosis of dynamic physical systems. *Sixth Intl. Workshop on Principles of Diagnosis*, pp. 81–85, Goslar, Germany, 1995.

[9] P.J. Mosterman and G. Biswas. Analyzing discontinuities in physical system models. *Qualitative Reasoning Workshop*, Fallen Leaf Lake, CA, 1996.

[10] P.P. Nayak, L. Joscowicz, and S. Addanki. Automated model selection using context-dependent behaviors. *Proc. AAAI-91*, pp. 710–716, Menlo Park, CA, 1991.

[11] T. Nishida and S. Doshita. Reasoning about discontinuous change. *Proc. AAAI-87*, pp. 643–648, Seattle, WA, 1987.

[12] R.C. Rosenberg and D. Karnopp. *Introduction to Physical System Dynamics.* McGraw-Hill Publishing Company, New York, NY, 1983.

[13] W. Sweet. The glass cockpit. *IEEE Spectrum*, pp. 30–38, Sept. 1995.

Building steady-state simulators via hierarchical feedback decomposition

Nicolas Rouquette
Jet Propulsion Laboratory
California Institute of Technology
4800 Oak Grove Drive, M/S 525-3660
Pasadena, CA 91109
Nicolas.Rouquette@jpl.nasa.gov

Abstract

In recent years, compositional modeling and self-explanatory simulation techniques have simplified the process of building dynamic simulators of physical systems. Building steady-state simulators is, conceptually, a simpler task consisting in solving a set algebraic equations. This simplicity hides delicate technical issues of convergence and search-space size due to the potentially large number of unknown parameters. We present an automated technique for reducing the dimensionality of the problem by 1) automatically identifying feedback loops (a generally NP-complete problem), 2) hierarchically decomposing the set of equations in terms of feedback loops, and 3) structuring a simulator where equations are solved either serially without search or in isolation within a feedback loop. This paper describes the key algorithms and the results of their implementation on building simulators for a two-phase evaporator loop system across multiple combinations of causal and non-causal approximations.

Introduction

Recent advances in model-based reasoning have greatly simplified the task of building and using dynamic simulators of physical systems (Nayak 1993; Forbus & Falkenhainer 1995; Amador, Finkelstein, & Weld 1993). While the usefulness of dynamic simulators is well established in various fields from teaching to high-fidelity simulation, steady-state simulators are characterized by low computational requirements (i.e., that of solving a set of equations only once) which makes them attractive for a wide range of engineering analyses such as stress tolerance, sensitivity, and diagnosis (Biswas & Yu 1993). However, building steady-state simulators can be a challenging task dominated by issues related to the existence of numerical solutions, the physical interpretability of the solutions found and the convergence properties of the simulator (Manocha 1994).

Building a steady-state simulators is conceptually a simple task, that of solving N algebraic equations in $M < N$ unknown parameters with respect to $N - M$ known parameter values. This simplicity hides the computational and numerical task of efficiently and accurately searching a solution in a space as large as M dimensions. There are two extreme approaches for solving a set of algebraic equations: the brute-force approach uses an algorithm to search the numerical solution in the M-dimensional space of possible values; the clever approach seeks to identify closed-form algebraic formulae for computing the unknown parameters in terms of the known values. This paper presents an intermediate approach relying on an automated technique for reducing the dimensionality of the original search space thereby greatly simplifying the task of selecting numerical algorithms and initial solution estimates. This is achieved by 1) automatically identifying feedback loops, 2) hierarchically structuring a equation solver where groups of equations are solved either serially or independently from each other and 3) structurally merging the modeler's choice of algorithms and initial estimates with the feedback decomposition to build the steady-state simulator.

The construction of high-performance hierarchical steady-state simulators is organized as an operationalization process transforming the steady-state model into numerical simulation software. The former is a non-computable, unstructured, conceptual specification of the latter which is is a computable, structured, pragmatic description of the former. In doing so, we elicit engineering understanding of feedback loops related to closed-loop circuits (physical loops) or interdependent equations (algebraic loops). In varying modeling assumptions, we earnmark conceptual progress in tuning modeling assumptions not only to the purpose of the model and the conditions of the physical system but to the various numerical and physical aspects of the simulator (initial estimates, speed of convergence, and physical interpretability of solutions). Therefore this approach enables modelers to progress on conceptual and cognitive fronts; the alternance of which is characteristic of the cyclic nature of the modeling process from theory formation and revision, to experimentation, evaluation and interpretation as described in (Aris 1978). Like all modeling tools, efficiency is a practical concern. Consequently, we have limited the hierarchical feedback decomposition technique to a tractable domain of models where the algorithms have polynomial-time complexity and efficient implementations.

As an unstructured collection of equations, a model is computationally unoperational for there is no indication of which values must be computed when. The first step of operationalization consists in determining a partial ordering of computations; a process we call algebraic ordering whose emphasis on numerical computability distinguishes it from a physical notion of causation behind the process of causal ordering. We first presents a very efficient algorithm for computing algebraic orderings as a maximum flow problem through a network. This ordering produces a graph of algebraic dependencies among parameters. The key contribution of this paper is in an algorithm that decomposes parameter dependency graphs to elucidate the hierarchical feedback structure of the equation model. Knowledge of this structure can be exploited in many ways; we show here how it serves the purposes of constructing low-cost, high-performance steady-state simulators.

Algebraic ordering

In numerical analysis, it is well known that there is no general-purpose, universally good numerical equation solving algorithm (Press *et al.* 1992), there is only an ever-growing multitude of algorithms with various abilities in specific domains and for specific types of equations. For steady-state simulation, this variety poses a pragmatic problem; choosing the right algorithm for the job becomes more and more difficult as the size of the model grows. To efficiently reason about the possible ways to construct a simulation program for a given set of algebraic equations, we define the notion of an *algebraic ordering graph* that captures how each parameter of the model algebraically depends on the values of other model parameters via the algebraic model equations. Our notion of algebraic ordering bears close resemblance to that of causal ordering (Nayak 1993; Iwasaki & Simon 1993) and relevance in modeling (Levy 1993). These three notions of ordering share a common representation where an equation, E: $PV = nRT$, yields the following parameter-equation graph (left):

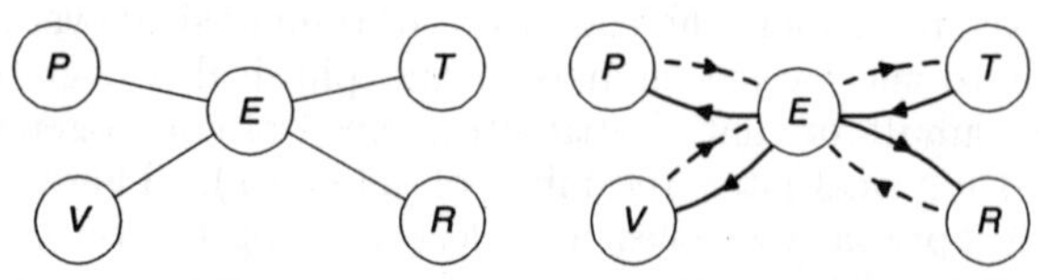

where edges indicate possible relations of physical causality and algebraic relevance between parameters and equations. Here, we focus on algebraic computation instead of physical causality and we explicitly distinguish two types of relations (above right). One where an equation can compute a parameter value (solid edges) and another where an equation needs other parameter values to perform such computations (dashed edges).

This allows us to distinguish several ways to numerically compute parameter values. An equation e can *directly* constrain a parameter value p if e is algebraically solvable with respect to p. An equation e *indirectly* constrains a parameter value p if e is not algebraically solvable with respect to p. For example, the equation: $y = \sqrt{x}$ can directly constrain y for a given x since the solution is unique. This equation indirectly constrains x for a given y since there two possible solutions in x.

Although, it is preferable to compute all model parameters through direct constrainment, it is not always possible to do so. The combinations of possible direct and indirect constrainment relationships lead to three categories of parameter constrainment: 1) A parameter may not have any equation directly constraining it; we say it is *under constrained* because its solution value must be guessed as there is no way to directly compute it. 2) When a parameter is directly constrained by exactly one equation, we say it is *properly constrained* because its value is unambiguously computed by solving a unique equation. 3) When multiple equations directly constrain the same parameter, we say it is *over constrained* because there is no guarantee that all such equations yield the same numerical value unless other parameters of these equations can be adjusted.

An equation can only be solved with respect to a single parameter; thus, there are only two possible constrainment categories: 1) A *properly constrained* equation e of n parameters properly constrains exactly one parameter p if p is computed numerically or analytically by solving e with respect to values for the other $n-1$ parameters. 2) An equation e of n parameters which constrains no parameter is said to be *over constrained*: there is no guarantee that the values given to the n parameters satisfy e unless some of the parameter values can be adjusted.

We have established a validity test for a set of equations and parameters which determines when a set of indirect and direct constrainment relationships is solvable (See Ch. 4 in (Rouquette 1995)). If all parameters and equations were properly constrainable, then a bipartite matching approach (e.g., (Nayak 1993; Serrano & Gossard 1987)) would suffice to establish a valid order of computations. To account for possible over and under constrainment, we defined an extended bipartite matching algorithm which ensures that each case of over constrainment is balanced by an adequate number of adjustable under-constrained parameters thereby resulting in a valid, computable ordering.

Extended bipartite matching

Algorithm 1 constructs a network flow graph F to match parameters and equations (Step 1 and 2). Step

3 creates paths between s and t for each exogenous parameter. The key difference with Nayak's algorithm is in the construction of paths corresponding to the possible constrainment relationships among equations and parameters. By default, equation e_j could be solved iteratively to find the value of one of its parameters $p_i \in P(e_j)$ $(p_i \rightarrow e_j^{\text{indirect}} \rightarrow e_j)$. For a given e_j, at most one $p_i \in P(e_j)$ can be computed in this manner. If an equation e_j can properly constrain a parameter p_i, then there is a path: $p_i \rightarrow e_j^{\text{direct}} \rightarrow e_j$ in F (Step 4). Since all paths have unit capacity, the paths $p_i \rightarrow e_j^{\text{direct}} \rightarrow e_j$ and $p_i \rightarrow e_j^{\text{indirect}} \rightarrow e_j$ for all p_i's and e_j's are mutually exclusive. This property confers to a maximum flow the meaning of a bipartite matching between the set of equations and parameters (step 5) as is also used in Nayak's causal ordering algorithm. Further, the costs associated to paths allow a maximum flow, minimum cost algorithim to optimize the use of direct computations as much as possible. Finally, the results of the matching are used to define the edges of the algebraic ordering graph (step 7). For models where the equations are causal, it follows that an algebraic ordering is identical to a causal ordering when every non-exogenous parameter is directly computed.

As an example, we consider the following hypothetical set of algebraic equations:

$$\begin{array}{llll}
e_1 & f_1(P_1, P_2, P_3, P_8) = 0 & ex_5 & \text{exogenous}(P_5) \\
e_2 & f_2(P_2, P_7) = 0 & ex_6 & \text{exogenous}(P_6) \\
e_3 & f_3(P_3, P_4) = 0 & e_7 & f_7(P_4, P_6, P_7) = 0 \\
e_4 & f_4(P_4, P_5) = 0 & e_8 & f_8(P_5, P_8) = 0
\end{array}$$

Suppose that e_2 is solvable in P_7 but not P_2 and that e_4 is solvable in P_5 but not P_4. The extended bipartite matching graph for this example is shown in Fig. 1.

Intuitively, Alg. 1 combines the idea of using a perfect matching as a validity criteria and the flexibility of both direct and indirect computations. Edges of the form (e, p) represent direct computations where the value of p is computed by e as a function of some arguments. Edges of the form (p, e) represent indirect computations where the value of p is constrained by e: the solution value of p is computed by search.

If the algebraic ordering graph were acyclic, a topological ordering would define an adequate order of computations. With cycles, the key to globally order computations is to relate the topological structure of the graph to feedback loops.

Feedback

Feedback is a property of the topological interdependencies among parameters.

Parameter Dependency Graph

Definition 1 (Algebraic dependency) *A parameter p' depends on p, noted by $p \rightsquigarrow p'$, iff there exists an equation e such that $p \in P(e)$ and $p' \in P(e)$*

Input: A parameter-equation graph $G = (V, A)$
Output: A predicate: $EBM(e, p)$ for $e \in E$ and $p \in P(e)$.
1) Create a network flow graph $F = (V_f, A_f)$.
2) $V_f = V \bigcup \{e^{\text{direct}}, e^{\text{indirect}} \mid e \in E\} \bigcup \{s, t\}$
(s and t are respectively the source and sink vertices)
3) $A_f = P_f \bigcup E_f$ where:
$P_f = \{(s, p) \mid p \in P\} \bigcup$
$\{(p, ex_p), (ex_p, t) \mid p \in P \wedge \text{exogenous}(p)\}$
$E_f = \{(e^{\text{direct}}, e), (e^{\text{indirect}}, e), (e, t) \mid e \in E\}$
Each path $s \rightarrow p \rightarrow ex_p \rightarrow t$ (p exogenous) has unit flow capacity and zero cost.
4) Edges between p_j and $e_{ic} = e_i^{\text{direct}}$ and $e_{ir} = e_i^{\text{indirect}}$ are defined as follows:

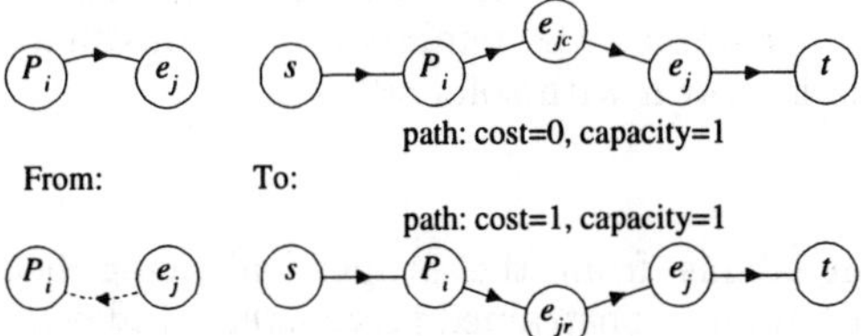

5) Apply a min. cost, max. flow algorithm on F
Nonzero transhipment nodes are:
- the source, s, with $b(s) = |P|$
- the sink, t, with $b(t) = -|P|$.
6) If $f(s, t) < |P|$ then return $\emptyset$
7) Define $EBM()$ from the maximum flow topology:
7a) $EBM(P_i, e_j, \text{indirect})$ holds iff $f(P_i, e_j^{\text{indirect}}) = 1$
7b) $EBM(P_i, e_j, \text{direct})$ holds iff $f(P_i, e_j^{\text{direct}}) = 1$
8) Return $EBM()$

Algorithm 1: Extended bipartite matching for constructing an algebraic ordering.

(i.e., p and p' are parameters of e) and $EBM(p', e, \text{direct})$ holds.

The dependency digraph $Gd = (Pd, Ed)$ corresponding to an algebraic ordering digraph $G' = (V = P \bigcup E, A')$ is defined as follows:

- $Pd = \{p \mid p \in P \wedge \neg \text{exogenous}(p)\}$
- $Ad = \{(p, p') \mid p, p' \in Pd \wedge p \rightsquigarrow p'\}$

For notation convenience, we say that $p \rightsquigarrow^* p'$ when there exists a sequence of parameters, $p = p_1, \ldots, p_n = p'$ such that

$$p = p_1 \rightsquigarrow p_2 \cdots p_{n-1} \rightsquigarrow p_n.$$

For the 7-equation example, we have the following parameter-dependency graph:

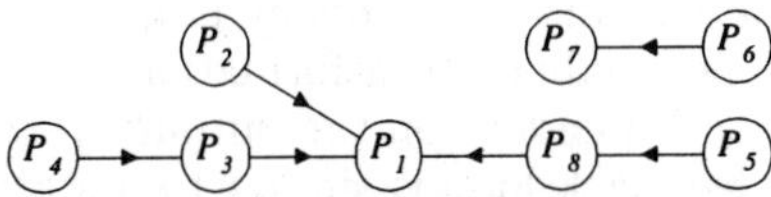

where parameters P_4 and P_2 are under-constrained while P_1 is over constrained. The validity of this

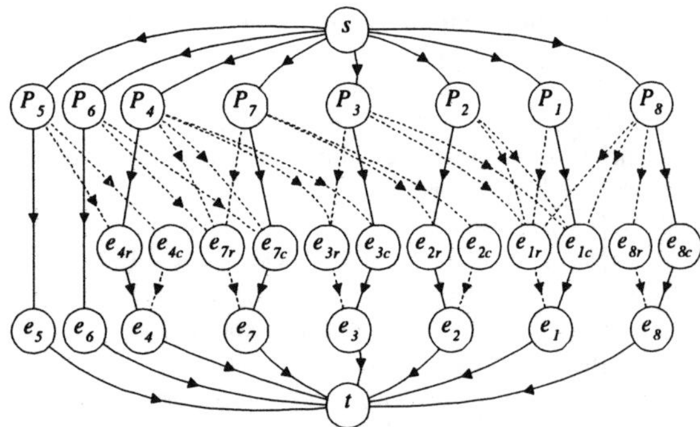

Figure 1: Extended bipartite matching for the 7-equation example. The minimum cost, maximum flow solution is drawn with solid edges.

ordering stems from the proper balancing between over and under-constrained parameters. Indeed, there are 3 ways to compute a value of P_1, two of which ($P_4 \rightarrow P_3 \rightarrow P_1$, $P2 \rightarrow P_1$) can be relaxed to match the value derived from the exogenous parameter P_5 ($P_5 \rightarrow P_8 \rightarrow P_1$).

Hierarchical Feedback Decomposition

Intuitively, feedback occurs when there exists at least two parameters p and p' in the dependency graph Gd such that $p \leadsto^* p'$ and $p' \leadsto^* p$ hold in Gd. Feedback is described by various terms in various scientific disciplines and engineering fields. Terms such as closed-loop circuit (as opposed to an open-loop circuit), circular dependencies, closed-loop control, circular state dependencies, and state or control feedback are commonly used. Here, we follow some basic ideas of system theory (Padulo & Arbib 1974) and concepts of connectedness of graph theory (Even 1979) to distinguish two types of feedback structures, namely state (left) and control (right) as shown below:

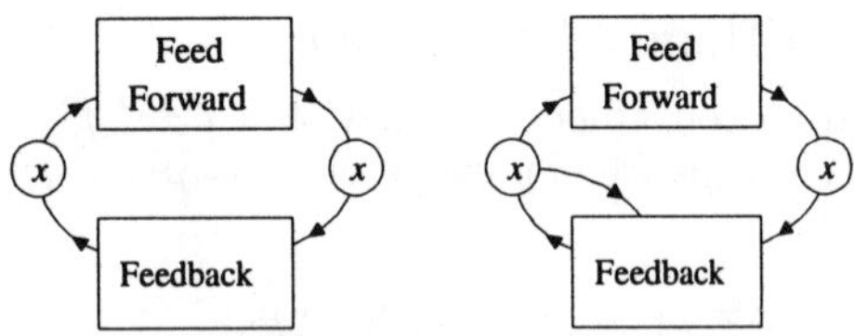

In a state feedback loop, input parameters, x, affect the output parameters, y, through a feedforward transformation. In a dependency graph, we will have: $x \leadsto^* y$. The feedback transformation in turns makes the inputs x dependent on the outputs y, or: $y \leadsto^* x$. A control feedback loop is similar to a state feedback loop except that the feedback transformation (usually the controller) uses both inputs x and outputs y inputs, i.e., $x, y \leadsto^* x$.

Operationalizing Feedback

Except for degenerate cases, a feedback loop must be solved iteratively for it corresponds to a system of $N \geq 2$ equations in N unknown parameters. Optimizing the solution quality and its computational cost requires making a number of choices for each feedback loop in terms of numerical algorithms, initial solution estimates, and convergence criteria. Addressing these issues globally can be very difficult. With a decomposition of the model in terms of a hierarchy of feedback loops, we can address these issues in two phases: one for the model subset corresponding to a given feedback loop and another for the structure of the model encompassing this loop. Typically, the former focuses on finding a solution for the feedback loop while the latter addresses convergence issues at a global level.

Unfortunately, identifying feedback in an arbitrary graph is an NP-complete problem. Fortunately, lumped-parameter algebraic models of physical systems are typically sparse (due to lumping) and have a low degree of connectivity (because most physical components have limited interactions with neighbor components). Combined with the fact that most man-made devices are often engineered with closed-loop control designs, it is quite common for the corresponding dependency graphs of such models to be decomposable in terms of feedback loops.

Breaking feedback loops apart

The algebraic dependency relation defined for Gd induces an equivalence relation. By definition, two parameters p_1 and p_2 are in the same equivalence class iff $p_1 \leadsto^* p_2$ and $p_2 \leadsto^* p_1$. These relations are characteristic of state and control feedback loops. Thus, feedback loops are strongly-connected subgraphs of Gd; the converse is not true[1]. Thus, we now define a structural criterion for recognizing feedback loops. In (Even 1979), a set of edges, T, is an (a, b) *edge separator* iff every directed path from a to b passes through at least one edge of T. Then for a strongly-connected component C, consider the smallest T such that, $C - T$ is either unconnected or broken into two or more strongly-connected subcomponents. For a given pair, a, b, we call such a subset T a *one-step optimal edge separator.*[2]

With the one-step optimal edge separator, we can solve a restricted version of the feedback vertex problem in polynomial time. Algorithm 2 shows how to remove optimal edge separators to analyze the topological structure of a graph G. The algorithm stops if G is not separable with the optimal edge separator (step 1). Consider $G' = (V, A - T)$. By definition of an optimal edge separator, T will break

[1] A fully-connected graph is not a feedback loop.

[2] One-step because we make a single analysis of how removing T affects the strong connectivity of the given subgraph. See (Rouquette 1995, Ch. 6) for a polynomial-time algorithm.

apart the strongly-connectedness of G. If G' is no longer strongly-connected, G is in fact a simple feedback loop (step 3). If G' is still strongly-connected, we need to analyze the remaining structure of G'. First, we remove the strongly-connected components already found (step 4).[3] Let G'' be the remaining subgraph (step 5). We consider two cases according to the connectivity of G''. If G'' is not strongly connected, G has a 2-level hierarchical structure (if there are 2 or more sub-components) or a 2-level nested structure (if there is only one sub-component) (step 7).

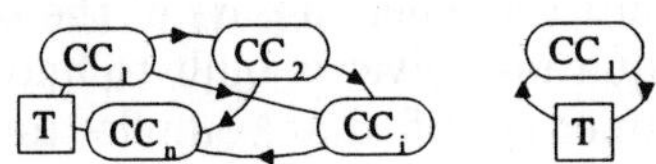

If G'' is strongly connected, it must have a single component, RCC[4]. Topologically, either RCC only shares vertices with the other sub-components already found (i.e.,CCS) (step 8) or it is distinct from them.

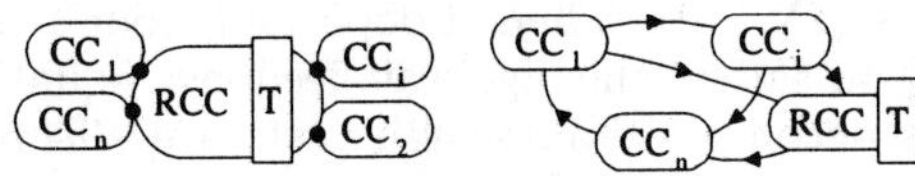

In the latter case, we need to abstract the sub-component already found $CC_1, \ldots, CC_n, RCC$ into equivalence class vertices $\widetilde{C_1}, \ldots, \widetilde{C_n}, \widetilde{R}$ so that we can further analyze the remaining structure of G'' (step 9). Since G was strongly-connected, $\widetilde{G}$ is also strongly-connected (step 10). The algorithm stops if this abstract component, $\widetilde{K}$, is not decomposable (step 12). Otherwise, we map to the base level graph G the optimal edge separator $\widetilde{S}$ that breaks apart $\widetilde{K}$ (step 13).

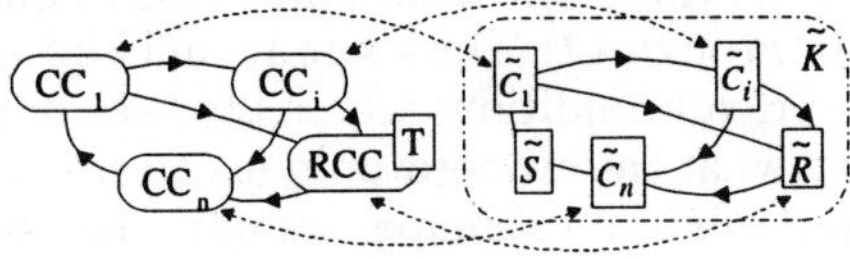

Note that the DAD algorithm is recursive for we also need to analyze the structure of the strongly-connected sub-components of G found (steps 7,8,14). The recursion stops if a strongly-connected component has either 1) the structure of a state or control feedback loop (step 3) or 2) a more complex structure than that of a feedback loop (steps 1,12).

Hierarchical Feedback Example

[3]We use the notation $A(X)$ to mean 'the set of edges of the subgraph X'.

[4]This follows from having removed all components found earlier (step 5) and from the nature of an optimal edge separator.

Input: $G = (V, A)$, a strongly-connected digraph
Output: The hierarchical feedback tree (HFT) decomposition of G

1) Let T be a one-step optimal edge separator of G; HFT=**ComplexFeedback**(G) if $T = \emptyset$.
2) $G' = (V, A - T)$ (remove T from G).
3) HFT=**Feedback(**G,T**)** if G' is not strongly connected.
4) Let $CCS = \{CC_1, \ldots, CC_n\}$ be the remaining strongly-connected components of G'
5) $G'' = \left(V, A - \left(\bigcup_{cc \in CCS} A(cc)\right)\right)$ (remove CCS from G)
6) If G'' is strongly-connected, go to step 8.
7) HFT= $\begin{cases} \textbf{Agg}(G, T, \bigcup_{cc \in CCS} DAD(cc)) & \text{if } n > 1 \\ \textbf{Nested}(G, T, DAD(CC_1)) & \text{if } n = 1 \end{cases}$
8) G'' has a single strongly-connected component RCC. HFT= **Agg**$(G, T, DAD(RCC) \bigcup \bigcup_{cc \in CCS} DAD(cc)))$ if $A(G'') - A(RCC) = \emptyset$.
9) Let $\widetilde{C}_i$ be an abstract vertex representing CC_i.
   Let $\widetilde{R}$ be an abstract vertex representing RCC.
   Let $\widetilde{G} = (\widetilde{V}, \widetilde{A})$ the abstract graph of G
   $\widetilde{V} = \{\widetilde{C}_1, \ldots, \widetilde{C}_n, \widetilde{R}\}$.
   $\widetilde{A}$ is defined according to paths among $CCS \bigcup \{RCC\}$.
10) Let $\widetilde{K}$ be the strongly-connected component of $\widetilde{G}$.
   Let $\widetilde{S}$ be the optimal edge separator of $\widetilde{K}$
12) HFT=**ComplexFeedback(**G**)** if $\widetilde{S} = \emptyset$.
13) Let $S \subset A$ be the base edges corresponding to $\widetilde{S}$.
14) HFT= **Aggr**$(G, S, \bigcup_{cc \in CCS} DAD(cc) \bigcup DAD(RCC))$

Algorithm 2: DAD: Decomposition and Aggregation of Dependencies

As an illustration example, we show in Fig 2 a schematic diagram of the evaporator loop of a two-phase, External-Active Thermal Control System (EATCS) designed at McDonnell Douglas. Liquid ammonia captures heat by evaporation from hot sources and releases it by condensation to cold sinks. The venturis maintain a sufficiently large liquid ammonia flow to prevent complete vaporization and superheating at the evaporators. The RFMD pump transfers heat between the two-phase evaporator return and the condenser loop (not shown). A model of the EATCS presented in (Rouquette 1995) yields a parameter-dependency graph of 55 parameters, 18 exogenous and

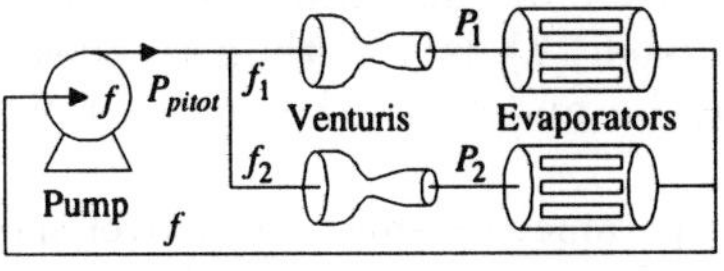

Figure 2: The evaporator loop of the External-Active Thermal Control System.

37 unknowns paired to 37 equations. A brute-force simulation approach consists in solving the 37 equations for the 37 unknown parameters at the cost of finding 37 initial value estimators for each unknown. The DAD algorithm finds a 2-level feedback decomposition shown in Fig. 3.

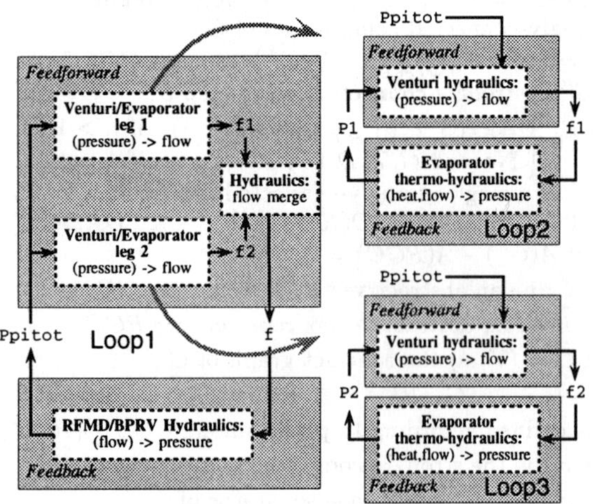

Figure 3: Physical and nested algebraic feedback loops.

With this feedback hierarchy, we now turn to producing a steady-state simulation, i.e., an equation solver for all the model equations. The modeler needs to choose for each feedback loop which subset of parameters will characterize its state[5] with the constraint that state parameters must be a graph cutset of the feedback loop[6]. Other issues influence the choice of a feedback cutset as a state vector: numerical convergence, stability and speed. For example, in Fig. 3, the modeler chose the pressures at each loop, namely, P_1, P_2, and P_{pitot}, because the pressures have the widest range of behavior across possible states. Flow rates would be a poor choice because they are mostly constant during nominal circumstances.

To produce the final hierarchical equation solver, the modeler must provide for each feedback loop the following information: 1) a state vector of parameters; 2) an initial function to compute the initial state vector values (this function can only use the exogenous parameters relative to the feedback loop.) and 3) a numerical algorithm to find the final feedback parameter values from any state vector estimate[7] Without decomposition, the equation solver has all unknown parameters to handle simultaneously. The gradient-descent approach (?) is a method to guess where the solution may be and focus the search towards there. This essentially amounts to determining, at problem-solving time, how to prioritize the unknown parameters to work on. In contrast, the hierarchical decomposition determines these priorities once and for all at compile time. With hierarchical decomposition, higher-level feedback loops effectively act as constraints on the possible values lower-level feedback parameters can take. This process is similar to the gradient-descent techniques used in numerical algorithms. The key difference is that a gradient-descent algorithm is continuously guessing the direction where the solution is. With hierarchical-feedback decomposition, there is no guesswork about the whereabouts of the solution; the hierarchical equation solver is built to find it in a very organized manner specified at compile-time instead of run-time.

For the EATCS, we start at Loop1. From P_{pitot} we compute new estimates of the lower-level feedback loop states (P_1, P_2). Then, Loop2 and Loop3 refine P_1 and P_2 to satisfy the algebraic feedback equations. With this decomposition, search costs are effectively divided among multiple feedback loops. Furthermore, we are spared from continuously evaluating the next-best direction to go as is done with gradient descent. The charts below show experimental results demonstrating that despite the lack of flexibility in determining the next-best parameters to adjust, the decomposition approach finds solutions of equal quality at much lower computational cost, even for difficult solutions. For each chart, we considered a series of 21 exogenous conditions defined by pump speed, venturi diameters (to analyze clogging conditions) and evaporator load. As long as the model converges to a nominal state for the EATCS, all three solvers are practically equivalent (data sets 0 through 12). Data sets 13 and above correspond to overload conditions where the heat applied is greater than what the evaporator loop can circulate. In such cases, the initial estimates are quite far from the actual abnormal solutions which implies more search. In fact, the brute-force and intermediate solvers spend several orders of magnitude more time searching only to find wrong solutions. Only the hierarchical solver managed to predict the temperature increase at the evaporator outlet due to the overheating condition.

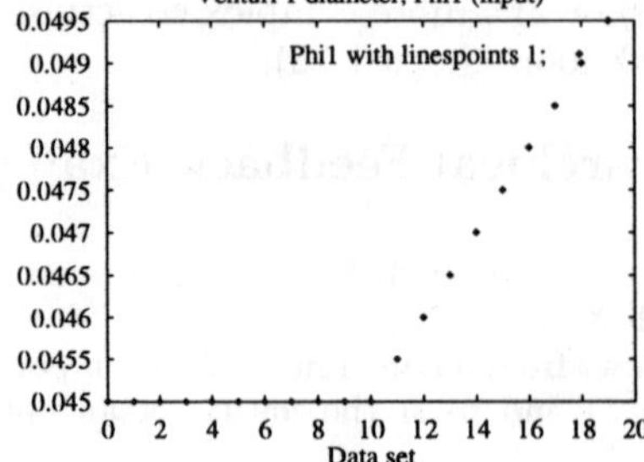

[5]The state parameter common to control and state feedback structures is a good candidate.

[6]i.e.,if state parameters are removed, the connectivity of the loop is broken.

[7]See (Rouquette 1995) for algorithms to generate C hierarchical equation solvers based on the above information.

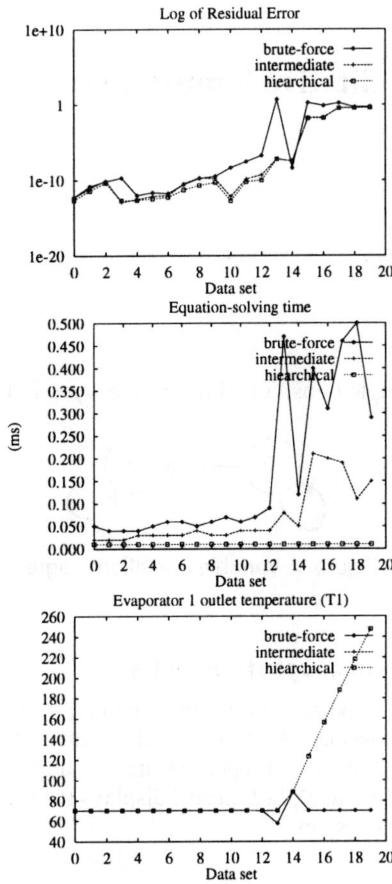

Conclusion

To describe the possible ways for solving a set of parameters from a set of algebraic equations, we presented the notion of algebraic ordering which is equivalent to causal ordering if all equations are believed to be causal. From an algebraic ordering, we constructed a parameter-dependency graph and described a decomposition algorithm based on analyzing the topological structure of the dependencies in terms of its strongly-connected components. By carefully choosing how to break apart such components, we showed how to construct the hierarchical decomposition of the dependency graph in terms of state and control feedback structures. Once the modeler chooses state feedback parameters and initial estimators for them, the set of all equations is solved bottom-up by applying a chosen equation solver according to the hierarchical feedback decomposition found. Compared to knowledge-free gradient-descent approaches to equation solving, our knowledge-intensive approach seeks to elucidate knowledge about feedback from the model itself to help the modeler provide as much relevant equation-solving knowledge as possible in terms of initial solution estimates and convergence metrics. Experimentally, this produced faster, better, and cheaper simulation programs trading off an expansive and broad search space (brute force approach) for a narrow, structured search space (fewer independent parameters) thereby achieving greater computational efficiency without loss of accuracy.

References

Amador, F.; Finkelstein, A.; and Weld, D. 1993. Real-time self-explanatory simulation. In *Proceedings of the Eleventh National Conference on Artificial Intelligence.* The AAAI Press.

Aris, R. 1978. *Mathematical Modeling Techniques,* volume 24 of *Research notes in mathematics.* Pitman.

Biswas, G., and Yu, X. 1993. A formal modeling scheme for continuous systems: Focus on diagnosis. In *International Joint Conference on Artificial Intelligence,* 1474–1479.

Even, S. 1979. *Graph Algorithms.* Computer Science Press.

Forbus, K., and Falkenhainer, B. 1995. Scaling up self-explanatory simulators: Polynomial-time compilation. In *International Joint Conference on Artificial Intelligence,* 1798–1805.

Iwasaki, Y., and Simon, H. A. 1993. Retrospective on čausality in device behavior. *Artificial Intelligence Journal* 141–146.

Levy, A. 1993. *Irrelevance Reasoning in Knowledge Based Systems.* Ph.D. Dissertation, Department of Computer Science, Stanford University.

Manocha, D. 1994. Algorithms for computing selected solutions of polynomial equations. *J. Symbolic Computation* 11:1–20.

Nayak, P. 1993. *Automated Modeling of Physical Systems.* Ph.D. Dissertation, Department of Computer Science.

Padulo, L., and Arbib, M. A. 1974. *System Theory.* W. B. Saunders Company.

Press, H.; Teukolsky, S.; W.Vetterling; and Flannery, B. 1992. *Numerical Recipes in C.* Cambridge University Press.

Rouquette, N. 1995. *Operationalizing Engineering Models of Steady-State Equations.* Ph.D. Dissertation, Dept. of Computer Science, Univ. of S. California.

Serrano, D., and Gossard, D. 1987. Constraint management in conceptual design. In Sriram, D., and Adey, R., eds., *Knowledge Based Expert SYstems in Engineering: Planning and Design.* Computational Mechanics Publications. 211–224.

Managing Occurrence Branching in Qualitative Simulation

Lance Tokuda

University of Texas at Austin
Department of Computer Sciences
Austin, Texas 78712-1188
unicron@cs.utexas.edu

Abstract

Qualitative simulators can produce common sense abstractions of complex behaviors given only partial knowledge about a system. One of the problems which limits the applicability of qualitative simulators is the intractable branching of successor states encountered with model of even modest size. Some branches may be unavoidable due to the complex nature of a system. Other branches may be accidental results of the model chosen.

A common source of intractability is occurrence branching. Occurrence branching occurs when the state transitions of two variables are unordered with respect to each other. This paper extends the QSIM model to distinguish between interesting occurrence branching and uninteresting occurrence branching. A representation, algorithm, and simulator for efficiently handling uninteresting branching is presented.

Introduction

Qualitative simulators can produce common sense abstractions of complex behaviors, however, they can also produce an intractable explosion of meaningless behaviors because they attempt to combinatorially order uncorrelated events. People who build brick walls obtain bricks, cement, and tools, and proceed to lay the wall. They don't worry about whether they obtain bricks then tools then cement, or cement, then tools, then bricks, or cement, then bricks, then tools, or cement *and* bricks, then tools, etc. Common sense tell them that the order in which the events are completed does not matter, what matters is that the events are completed before the wall is laid.

Qualitative simulators fail the common sense challenge when confronted with similar problems. Simulators such as QSIM (Kuipers 1994) attempt to calculate all possible orderings of inherently unordered events which can lead to intractable branching in models of even modest size. This paper presents a representation (L-behavior diagrams), an algorithm (L-filter), and a simulator (LSIM) which manages this complexity.

Occurrence branching problems

To explore the problems associated with occurrence branching, we examine systems with variables defined to have the simple transition diagram displayed in Figure 1.

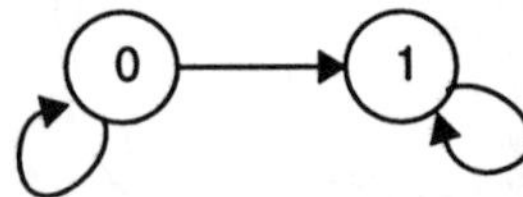

Figure 1: Variable transition diagram

Systems of uncoupled variables

First consider the behaviors generated in a system with two uncoupled variables A and B. Let the initial value for both variables is 0 so we can represent the initial state of the system as the 2-tuple (0,0). Figure 2 displays the transition diagram for this system.

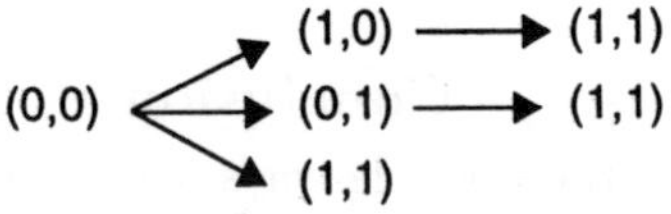

Figure 2: Transition diagram for 2 uncoupled variables (A,B)

Note that there are 3 possible behaviors for this system. Next consider the behavior tree when a third independent variable C is added. This system produces 13 possible behaviors (Figure 3).

Note that for a system with n variables, the number of behaviors is greater than 2^n. This intractable explosion of behaviors arises due to the combinatorial ordering of variables transitioning from 0 to 1. The phenomenon of creating branches due to the ordering of variables attaining landmarks is known as *occurrence branching*. In the example systems, variables transition from 0 to 1. In systems where variables transition between three or more values or are allowed to transition back and forth between values, the number of behaviors would grow even more rapidly. This is the nature of qualitative models.

Systems of coupled variables

Models of physical systems do not experience the explosion of behaviors demonstrated in the previous section. Vari-

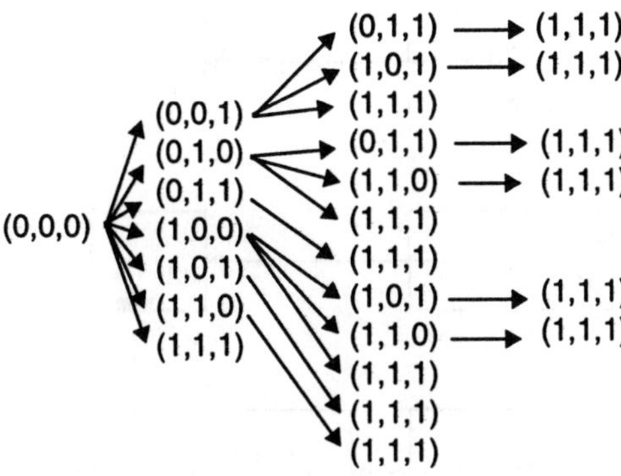

Figure 3: Transition diagram for 3 uncoupled variables (A,B,C)

ables in these models are often based on physical properties such as position, velocity and acceleration. The velocity of an object over time is related to both its acceleration and position. Properties of physical systems are captured through *constraints*. A constraint serves to prune the variable transition graph. A constraint may apply to a single variable (e.g the variable is constant) or it may apply to multiple variables (e.g. A = B + C).

Consider the simple model in Figure 4 which we will refer to as a *wishbone*. The wishbone has four nodes labeled A, B, C, and D.

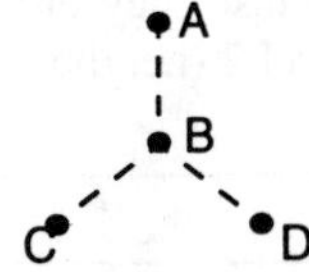

Figure 4: Wishbone

The lines connecting nodes represent constraints between nodes. The system has the following constraints:

A is in state 1 if and only if B is in state 1.

B is in state 1 if and only if C and D are in state 1.

The wishbone can experience three possible behaviors displayed in Figure 5.

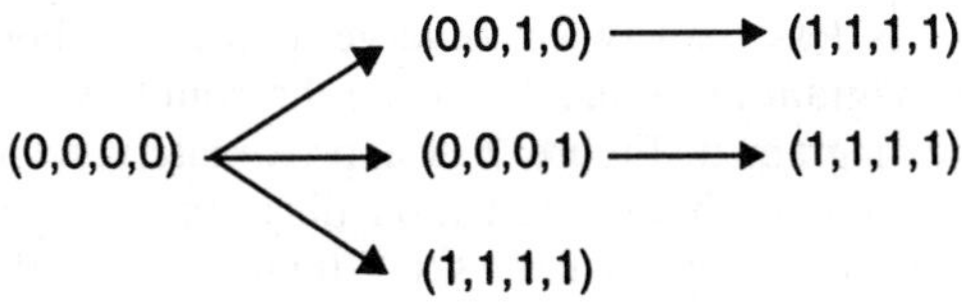

Figure 5: Transition diagram for wishbone (A,B,C,D)

The wishbone exhibits traces of occurrence branching since C can transition before, after, or at the same time as D.

Next consider a double-wishbone system composed of two wishbones connected through node A (Figure 6).

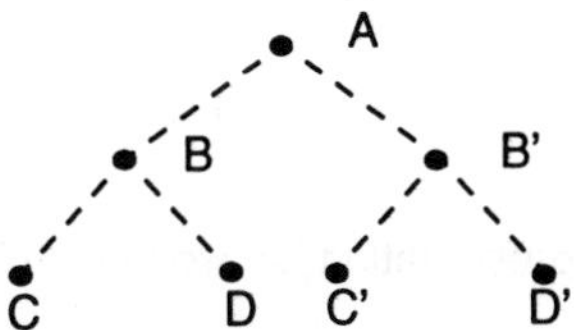

Figure 6: Double-wishbone

The number of possible behaviors resulting from this composite system is 17 (Figure 7).

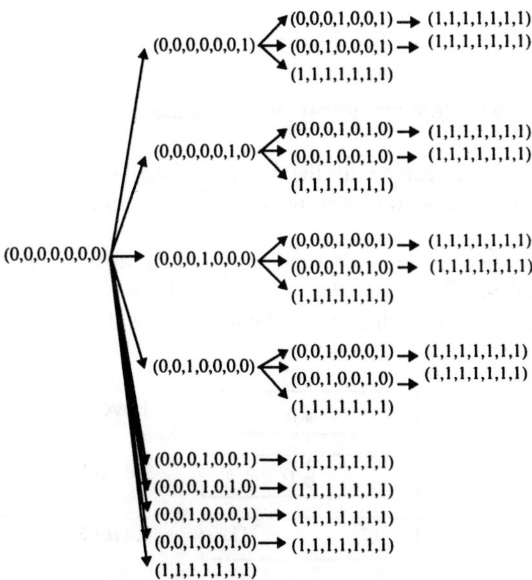

Figure 7: Transition diagram for double-wishbone (A,B,C,D,B',C',D')

The large number of behaviors is due to occurrence branching among variables C, D, C', and D'. For a system with m wishbone components (m > 1) joined at node A, the number of behaviors is greater than 3^m.

L-behavior diagrams

The C-filter algorithm employed by QSIM maintains a distinct tuple for each state of each behavior. This work proposes a compact representation which shares states among multiple behaviors. Consider the system of two uncoupled variables in Figure 1. The states for the behaviors of independent variables are tracked separately (Figure 8).

This representation asserts that there is no ordering specified as A and B transition from 0 to 1. Given the requirement that at least one variable must make a transition to create a new state, Figure 8 represents the same set of behaviors as Figure 2. Figure 9 displays the representation for three independent variables. The cost of this representa-

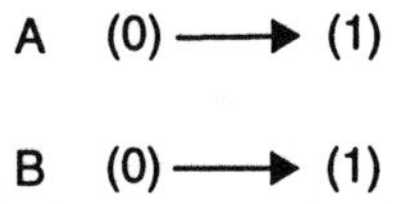

A (0) → (1)

B (0) → (1)

Figure 8: Representation for two uncoupled variables

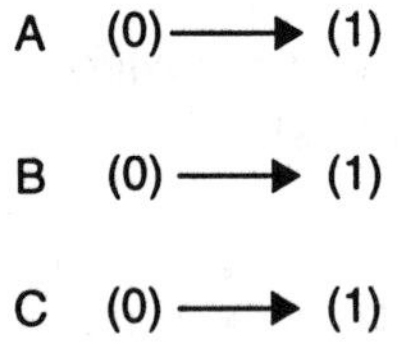

A (0) → (1)

B (0) → (1)

C (0) → (1)

Figure 9: Representation for three uncoupled variables

tion grows linearly with the number of variables versus the exponential cost of the transition diagrams in Figure 2 and Figure 3.

Next we extend this representation to support coupled variables. Consider the wishbone from the previous section. The system is divided into three levels (Figure 10).

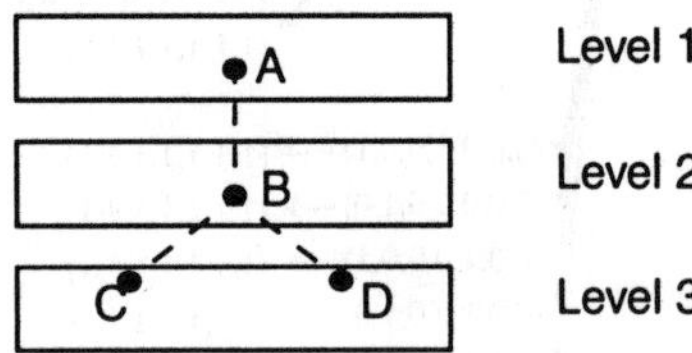

Figure 10: Wishbone layering

Based on this layering, a new representation called an *L-behavior diagram* is constructed. The L-behavior diagram for a wishbone is displayed in Figure 11.

The boxes around values represent *aggregate states*. Aggregate states store the behaviors of coupled variables within the same level. The check for coupling is made with respect to the next higher level, the current level, and all lower levels. For the wishbone, behaviors for C and D are placed in an aggregate state because C and D are jointly constrained by B. The dashed lines connecting an aggregate state to a single state represent *corresponding* states[1]. Corresponding states co-occur in some branch of the simulation. In Figure 11, the states (0,0), (0,1), and (1,0) in cd1 co-occur with state (0) in b1. The L-behavior diagram in Figure 11 is equivalent to the transition diagram presented in Figure 5. The Figure 5 representation

1.QSIM states refer to a tuple which stores the value of all model variables at a time-point or time-interval. States in this paper refer to individual variable states or aggregate variable states — all variable values are not tracked in a single tuple.

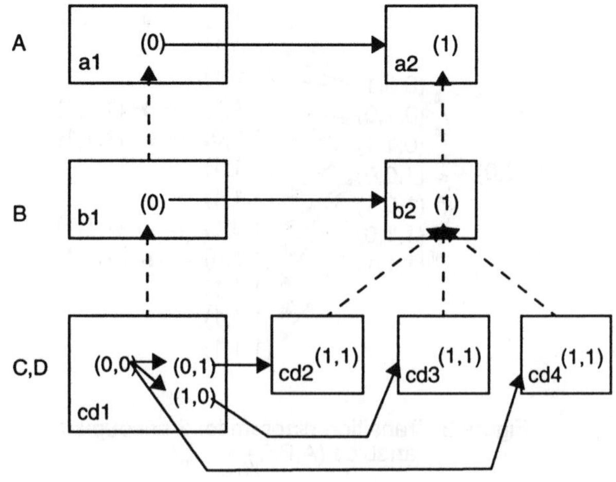

Figure 11: L-behavior diagram for wishbone

uses six 4-tuples for a total of 24 variable states. The L-behavior representation uses four 1-tuples and six 2-tuples for a total of 16 variable states. The L-behavior representation is more compact because the states for A and B are shared for different behaviors of C and D.

Figure 12 presents a layering for the double-wishbone. In this system there are two sets of aggregate states produced for level 3. One set of aggregate states contains C and D pairs and the other contains C' and D' pairs. The pairs are separated because they are not constrained by a common ancestor in level 2 (i.e. they are decoupled).

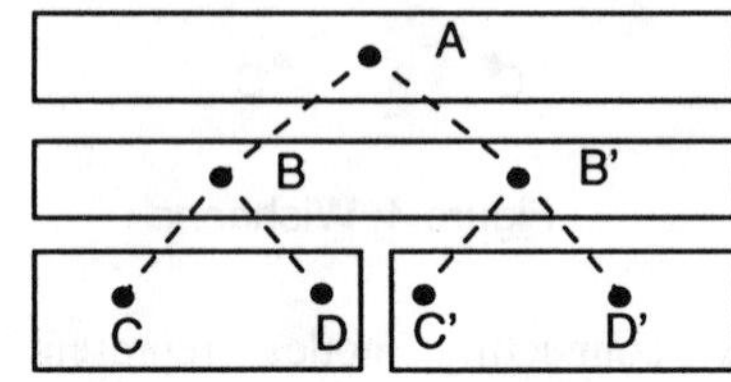

Figure 12: Double-wishbone layering

The L-behavior diagram for the double-wishbone is displayed in Figure 13.

Note that the double-wishbone L-behavior diagram in Figure 13 is less than twice as large as the wishbone L-behavior diagram in Figure 11, while the double-wishbone transition diagram in Figure 7 is approximately six times larger than the wishbone transition diagram in Figure 5. The L-behavior diagram uses six 1-tuples and twelve 2-tuples for a total of 30 variable states. The transition diagram in Figure 7 uses thirty-four 7-tuples for a total of 238 variable states. This is an order of magnitude difference.

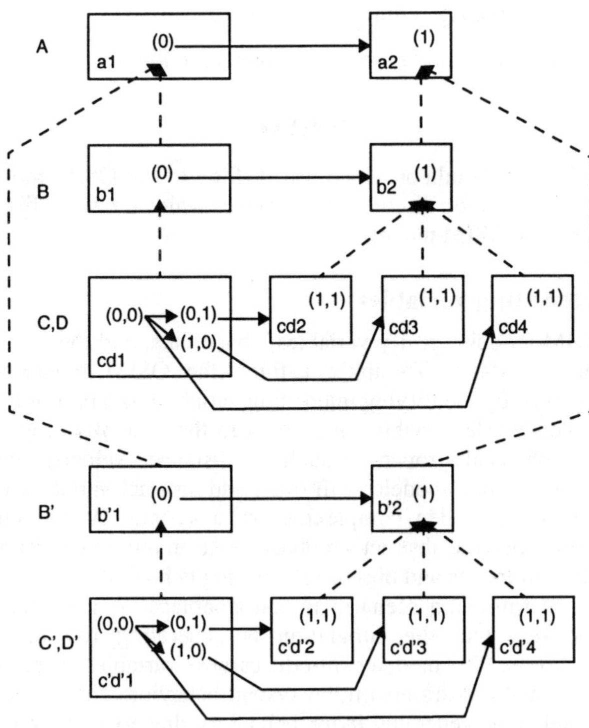

Figure 13: L-behavior diagram for double-wishbone

L-Filter

QSIM uses the C-filter algorithm (Kuipers 1994) to generate a behavior tree. C-filter, like the transition diagrams, attempts to assign an ordering to all variables as they attain landmarks. Thus, C-filter is subject to intractable occurrence branching.

L-behavior diagrams offer an implicit representation for unordered events and avoid the problems associated with occurrence branching. This section presents the *L-filter* algorithm for efficiently computing L-behavior diagrams.

I-Branching and U-Branching

L-filter distinguishes between interesting occurrence branching (*I-branching*) and uninteresting occurrence branching (*U-branching*). What is interesting or uninteresting depends on the user's perspective. The owner of a hydraulic power plant may want to know whether the warning light flashed red before or after the dam overflowed (I-branching). The stray dog downstream is more concerned with its own swimming ability than the ordering of the two events (U-branching).

L-filter is given a list of interesting variables as a part of the system model. I-branching is defined to be the occurrence branching involving interesting variables. U-branching is defined to be the branching involving uninteresting variables.

Currently, QSIM does not distinguish between interesting and uninteresting variables in the qualitative model. The result is that many uninteresting states are calculated and displayed. Clancy was the first to address this problem by eliminating branches off of uninteresting variables as a post-process (Clancy & Kuipers 1993). This solves the display problem but it does not reduce the computational complexity of the model.

L-Filter algorithm

L-filter requires the following five elements:

1 Variable transition diagram
2 Model variables
3 Model constraints
4 Identification of interesting variables
5 Initial state of variables

Given a system model, L-filter proceeds with the following steps:

1 The system diagram is constructed. All variables are identified and constraints between variables are connected with arcs (e.g. Figure 4).
2 Layering is added to the diagram. All interesting variables are placed in level 1. Other levels are identified by performing a breadth first search. Variables at depth 1 are placed in level 2, variables at depth 2 are placed in level 3, etc. (e.g. Figure 10). Let the number of levels be n. The highest level refers to level 1 and the lowest level refers to level n.
3 Aggregates within each level are identified (e.g. Figure 12). Aggregates are constructed by grouping variables which are coupled given that variables in the next higher level remain unchanged.[1]
4 Initialize all variables and freeze all levels.
5 Set CL = lowest frozen level. Thaw(CL).
6 Advance(CL). ApplyConstraints(CL).[2]
7 If no new states are created and CL = 1, then end the simulation.
8 If no new states are created then goto step 5.
9 If CL < n, then Freeze(CL) and set CL = CL+1. Goto step 6.

Freeze(level) blocks any transitions of variables in level.

Thaw(level) removes the transition block imposed by Freeze(level).

Advance(CL) generates successor states for all aggregates in level CL. The successor states are obtained by advancing each variable in each aggregate one step in the variable

1. Two variables in level 2 may be coupled by a constraint on a variable in level 1. For example if A = B + C where A is in level 1 and B and C are in level 2, B and C are coupled given a constant A. For cyclic models, variables are coupled if they share a common descendant.

2. This step is analogous to running one iteration of C-filter on level CL with the additional constraint that all variable values in levels higher than CL do not change and all variables in lower levels are ignored.

transition diagram (see Figure 1). All possible transition combinations are generated.

ApplyConstraints(CL) checks constraints among variables in levels CL and CL-1. States which do not satisfy the constraints are pruned. If all of an aggregate's states are deleted then the aggregate is deleted. If all aggregates for some set of variables corresponding to a state are deleted, then the state is deleted.

L-Filter applied to double-wishbone

For the double-wishbone, the variable transition diagram, model variables, model constraints, and initial variable values were given previously. The next step is to identify the interesting variables. If all variables were interesting, then the occurrence branching due to the ordering of variable transitions would be I-branching. C-filter would be an appropriate algorithm for this case since it explicitly calculates every possible ordering.

Suppose instead that the only interesting variable was A. For this system, the ordering of variable transitions for C, D, C', and D' constitutes U-branching. Given this knowledge, one would not need to unroll the L-behavior diagram to produce all possible transition orderings. Level 1 would be the only level of interest. This is the advantage of L-filter — I-branching is calculated explicitly while U-branching is implicit in the representation. To illustrate the advantage of L-filter, A is chosen as the only interesting variable.

Given the double-wishbone system model, L-filter proceeds in the following steps:

1 Construct the system diagram (Figure 6).
2 Divide the diagram into levels.
3 Identify aggregates within each level (Figure 12).
4 Set CL = 3. Thaw(3).
5 Advance(3). ApplyConstraints(3). This produces cd1 and c'd'1[1].
6 Since there are no lower levels, level 3 is advanced again. This time, no states which satisfy the constraints are produced.
7 Thaw(2). Advance(2). ApplyConstraints(2). B transitions from 0 to 1 and constraints are checked between B and A. No states are possible since A and B must have the same value.
8 Thaw(1). Advance(1). ApplyConstraints(1). This produces a2. Freeze(1).
9 Advance(2). ApplyConstraints(2). This produces b2 and b'2. Freeze(2).
10 Advance(3). ApplyConstraints(3). This produces cd2, cd3, cd4, c'd'2, c'd'3, and c'd'4.
11 Since there are no lower levels, level 3 is advanced again. This time, no states which satisfy the constraints are produced.
12 Thaw(2). Advance(2). ApplyConstraints(2). No new states are possible since B is in a terminal state.
13 Thaw(1). Advance(1). ApplyConstraints(1). No new states are possible since A is in a terminal state. At this point, the algorithm terminates.

The result is the L-behavior diagram in Figure 13.

1.Note that states cd1 and c'd'1 can be computed independently.

LSIM

LSIM is a simulator which uses L-filter to run QSIM models. This section discusses the changes which enable L-filter to run on QSIM models.

Interesting variables

QSIM models specify variables, constraints, and the initial variable state[2]. To apply L-filter, the QSIM model is extended by identifying interesting variables as a part of the model. While variables of interest to the user often represent physical properties such as distance, velocity and acceleration, a modeler will often add abstract variables to model the hidden complexities of a system. A problem arises when the abstract variables create an intractable number of branches and obscure interesting behaviors.

The following scenario is commonplace — a modeler discovers that the simulation is generating too many behaviors. The modeler introduces new variables to place additional constraints on the system behavior. The revised model now generates *more* behaviors due to occurrence branching caused by the newly introduced variables. For example, a user may be interested in the velocity v and height h of a bouncing ball but the modeler may add variables $KE = K * v^2$ and $PE = L * h$ to model the kinetic and potential energy of the ball. Depending on the model, C-filter may generate more behaviors when KE and PE are added. By identifying v and h as the only interesting variables, L-filter attempts to reduce the cost of U-branching due to KE and PE by not explicitly ordering uncoupled changes in the two variables[3].

Variable transition diagrams

Variables values in QSIM are a 2-tuple consisting of a magnitude and a direction. Magnitudes transition between landmarks and intervals and directions transition between increasing, steady, and decreasing. Variable transitions in QSIM are constrained by continuity (all variables in QSIM are continuous).

The transition of a continuous variable from a landmark to an interval is instantaneous. This instantaneous change restricts the possible transitions that other variables in corresponding states can make. For example, if a variable A transitions from (0,inc) to ((0,inf),inc), then a variable B

2.QIM generates all possible starting states given incomplete initial state information. L-filter assumes a single initial state but could be extended to generate all possible starting states.

3.This would be true if KE and PE were uncoupled. A modeler is likely to define KE + PE to be constant, thus, KE and PE would be coupled.

in corresponding state ((0,inf),dec) cannot transition to (0,dec). If a variable transitions from a landmark to an interval, then all corresponding states in the same and lower levels must obey the time-point to time-interval transition rules.

When a variable transitions from an interval to a landmark, all corresponding states in the same and lower levels cannot transition from a steady value to a non-steady value (analytic function constraint). Other transitions are possible since a time-interval to time-point transition is not instantaneous. A set of transition rules is given in Kuipers 1994. LSIM adds time-point and time-interval transition rules to support continuous variables.

Other Global Constraints

QSIM has a number of global constraints which should be detected and enforced — infinite time/infinite value, non-intersection, energy, analytic function, etc. Only the infinite time/infinite value and the analytic function constraints are enforced at the current time, however, L-filter does not preclude the implementation of other global constraints.

LSIM applied to a QSIM model

The current implementation of LSIM is severely limited because it does not support the full complement of local and global constraints available in QSIM. A very simple QSIM model which exhibits occurrence branching was chosen to illustrate that LSIM can provide an advantage over QSIM. The system contains two objects traveling on a line at increasing speeds in opposite directions. Branching is introduced as the object velocities attain unevenly spaced landmarks (Figure 14).

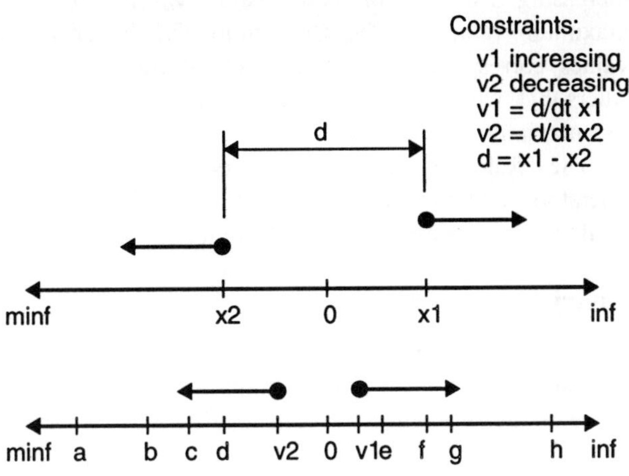

Figure 14: Two accelerating objects moving in opposite directions

The interesting variable is chosen to be d — the distance between the two objects. The system diagram is displayed in Figure 15.

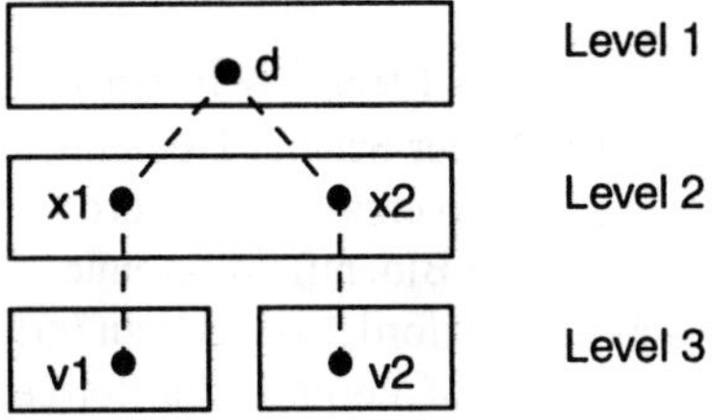

Figure 15: System layering

Both LSIM and QSIM are capable of producing the desired behavior for d (d is positive and increasing). LSIM used 28 variable states while QSIM was unable to solve the problem with 400 5-tuples (over 2000 variable states). When the QSIM state limit was set to 800, the simulator consumed over nine megabytes of memory before crashing.

This example shows that LSIM can produce efficiency gains for QSIM models. It also demonstrates the U-branching problem for two variables with more than two landmarks.

Conclusions

This paper establishes the intractable nature of attempting to order uncorrelated events. The unordered transition of only three variables is shown to produce an order of magnitude increase in the complexity for QSIM-style systems which use single tuples to represent system states. The L-behavior representation distinguishes between coupled and decoupled states is shown to be potentially more efficient that the QSIM approach. L-filter computes L-behavior diagrams and LSIM uses L-filter and additional qualitative reasoning constraints to simulate QSIM models. For a simple model where U-branching is prevalent, LSIM demonstrates a two orders of magnitude benefit over QSIM.

The hope is that this work will inspire a mature version of LSIM which supports the full complement of QSIM constraints and features. LSIM can then attempt to simulate models which where previously thought to be intractable.

References

Kuipers, B. J., 1994. *Qualitative Reasoning: Modeling and Simulation with Incomplete Knowledge*, Cambridge, MA: MIT Press.

Clancy, D., and Kuipers, B. J. 1993. Behavior Abstraction for Tractable Simulation. In Proceedings of the Seventh International Workshop on Qualitative Reasoning, 57-64.

Diagrammatic Reasoning and Cases

Michael Anderson
Computer Science Department
University of Hartford
200 Bloomfield Avenue
West Hartford, Connecticut 06117
anderson@morpheus.hartford.edu

Robert McCartney
Department of Computer Science and Engineering
University of Connecticut
191 Auditorium Road
Storrs, Connecticut 06269-315
robert@cse.uconn.edu

Abstract

We believe that many problem domains that lend themselves to a case-based reasoning solution can benefit from an diagrammatic implementation and propose a diagrammatic case-based solution to what we term the n-queens best solution problem where the best solution is defined as that which solves the problem moving the fewest queens. A working system, based on a novel combination of diagrammatic and case-based reasoning, is described.

Introduction

Interest in computing with analogical representations is on the rise. This is evidenced by the attention given to them in recent symposia (e.g. [Narayanan 1992]), journals (e.g. [Narayanan 1993]), and books (e.g. [Glasgow, Narayanan, & Chandrasekaran 1995]). We believe that such attention is the natural outgrowth of the evolution of the currency of computing, the first two generations of which were numeric and symbolic.

Our particular interest lies in developing a general set of operators that can be used to reason with sets of related diagrams— *inter-diagrammatic reasoning.* This concept has been explored in [Anderson 1994; Anderson & McCartney 1995a; Anderson & McCartney 1995b] in which a heuristic for a game has been developed, musical notation and Venn diagrams have been reasoned with, and information from cartograms and various type of charts has been inferred using a general set of operators. Along these lines, we have been investigating the integration of inter-diagrammatic reasoning with case-based reasoning.

We contend that many problem domains that lend themselves to a case-based reasoning solution can benefit from an inter-diagrammatic implementation. For example, domains that deal with spatial configuration, navigation [Goel et al. 1994], and perception all might benefit from explicit representation of cases stored as diagrams, retrieved via a diagrammatic match, and modified diagrammatically.

We propose a diagrammatic case-based solution to what we term the *n-queens best solution problem* where the best solution is defined as that which solves the problem moving the fewest queens, leaving queens that are already in place untouched (versus a solution that solves the problem in the fewest moves). Further, we develop an inter-diagrammatic implementation of the *min-conflicts heuristic* [Gu 1989] to find solutions to randomly chosen *n-queens problems* [Stone & Stone 1986] themselves.

We present a syntax and semantics of inter-diagrammatic reasoning and then introduce the inter-diagrammatic operators and functions. Next, case-based reasoning is briefly overviewed. This is followed by a description of the diagrammatic solution of the *n*-queens problem and the diagrammatic case-based solution of the *n*-queens best solution problem. A brief discussion of related work follows and, finally, we offer our conclusions.

Inter-diagrammatic Reasoning

Most generally, one can syntactically define a *diagram* to be a tessellation of a planar area such that it is completely covered by atomic two dimensional regions or tesserae. The semantic domain will be defined as $\{v_0, \ldots, v_{i-1}\}$ denoting an i valued, additive gray scale incrementally increasing from a minimum value v_0 ,WHITE, to a maximum value v_{i-1} , BLACK. Intuitively, the gray scale values correspond to a discrete set of transparent gray filters that, when overlaid, combine to create a darker filter to a maximum of BLACK.

The following primitive unary operators, binary operators, and functions provide a set of basic tools to facilitate the process of inter-diagrammatic reasoning.

Unary Operators

NOT, denoted $\neg d$, is a unary operator taking a single diagram that returns a new diagram where each tessera's value is the difference between BLACK and its previous value.

Binary Operators

Binary operators take two diagrams, d_1 and d_2, of equal dimension and tessellation and return a new diagram where each tessera has a new value that is some function of the two corresponding tesserae in the operands.

OR, denoted $d_1 \vee d_2$, returns the *maximum* of each pair of tesserae where the maximum of two corresponding tesserae is defined as the tessera whose value is closest to BLACK.

AND, denoted $d_1 \wedge d_2$, returns the *minimum* of each pair of tesserae where the minimum of two corresponding tesserae is defined as the tessera whose value is closest to WHITE.

OVERLAY, denoted $d_1 + d_2$, returns the *sum* of each pair of tesserae (to a maximum of BLACK) where the sum of values of corresponding tesserae is defined as the sum of their respective values' subscripts.

PEEL, denoted $d_1 - d_2$, returns the *difference* of each pair of tesserae (to a minimum of WHITE) where the difference of values of corresponding tesserae is defined as the difference of their respective values' subscripts.

ASSIGNMENT, denoted $d_1 \Leftarrow d_2$, modifies d_1 such that each tessera has the value of the corresponding tessera in d_2. (Note that non-diagrammatic assignment will be symbolized as := and the equality relation as =.)

Functions Over Diagrams

NULL, denoted NULL(d), is a one place Boolean function taking a single diagram that returns TRUE if all tesserae of d are WHITE else it returns FALSE.

NONNULL, denoted NONNULL(d), is a one place Boolean function taking a single diagram that returns FALSE if all tesserae of d are WHITE else it returns TRUE.

Functions Over Sets of Diagrams

ACCUMULATE, denoted ACCUMULATE (d, ds, o), is a three place function taking an initial diagram, d, a set of diagrams of equal dimension and tessellation, ds, and the name of a binary diagrammatic operator, o, that returns a new diagram which is the accumulation of the results of successively applying o to d and each diagram in ds.

MAP, denoted MAP(f, ds), is a two place function taking a function f and a set of diagrams of equal dimension and tessellation, ds, that returns a new set of diagrams comprised of all diagrams resulting from application of f to each diagram in ds.

FILTER, denoted FILTER(f, ds), is a two place function taking a Boolean function, f and a set of diagrams of equal dimension and tessellation, ds, that returns a new set of diagrams comprised of all diagrams in ds for which f returns TRUE.

RANDOM, denoted RANDOM([x,]s), is a one or two place function that returns a set of x unique elements of s at random, x defaulting to 1 if not present.

CARDINALITY, denoted CARDINALITY(s), is a one place function taking a finite set that returns the number of elements in s.

Case-based Reasoning

Case-based reasoning [Kolodner 1993] is the use of previous problem solving episodes (with solutions) to solve a new problem. Cases can be used for two purposes: 1) to support plausible inferencing in the absence of a complete domain theory [McCartney 1993], and 2) to increase efficiency by either providing partial solutions or providing focus and direction to problem solving efforts [Kambhampati & Hendler 1992]. For both of these purposes, case-based reasoning provides an obvious learning mechanism: as problems are solved, new episodes are incorporated into the case base, which can later be used in future problem solving.

Implementing a case-based reasoning system requires answering a number of fundamental questions.

- *representation*: What is a case and how is it represented?
- *indexing*: How is a case stored and retrieved?
- *similarity*: How do we determine which case is most appropriate to use in solving a given problem?
- *adaptation*: How do we use an appropriate case once we get it?

These questions have obvious general answers given our interest in diagrammatic reasoning. Cases will be diagrams, represented in a way consistent with the proposed syntax and semantics, and algorithms used for indexing, similarity, and adaptation of a case will be defined in terms of diagrammatic operators. As we are working with a complete domain theory and no uncertainty, we are using case-based reasoning to increase efficiency and provide a mechanism to improve performance over time.

Diagrammatic Constraint Satisfaction

Diagrammatic reasoning can be used to solve *constraint satisfaction problems*— problems in the form of a set of variables that must satisfy some set of constraints. The n-queens problem, for example, can be viewed as a constraint satisfaction problem that can be solved diagrammatically.

A solution to the n-queens problem is any configuration of n queens on an n by n chessboard in which no queen is being attacked by any other queen. Figure 1 shows a diagram of a solution to the problem when $n = 8$. When the location of each queen is considered a variable that must meet the constraint that no other queen can attack that location, a constraint satisfaction perspective of the problem arises. The min-conflicts heuristic, which advocates selecting a value for a variable that results in the minimum number of conflicts with other variables, can be

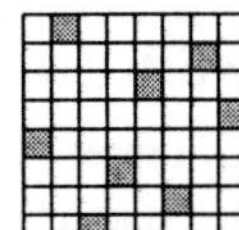

Figure 1: n-queen solution where $n = 8$

implemented diagrammatically to solve the n-queens problem.

A diagram in the n-queens domain is represented as an n by n tessellation of gray-scale valued tesserae. A set of n by n diagrams comprised of all possible single queen positions (denoted *Queens*) must be defined. Each of these diagrams represents one possible position of a queen (in a medium level gray) and the extent of its attack (in GRAY1). Figure 2 shows a diagram of n OVERLAYed queen diagrams and each of the corresponding diagrams from *Queens* that represent the individual queens in question where $n = 8$. Given a random selection of queen positions, the strategy is to move iteratively the most attacked queen to a position on the board that currently is the least attacked until a solution is discovered.

Discovering a Solution

After a random selection of queens is made, all the corresponding diagrams from *Queens* (denoted *SelectedQueens*) are OVERLAYed onto a single diagram (denoted *CurrentBoard*). This process can be more formally represented using the proposed diagrammatic operators as

CurrentBoard⇐
ACCUMULATE (∅, *SelectedQueens*, +)

The *CurrentBoard* is checked to see if it is a solution by PEELing from it a diagram that is completely covered in the same gray level that represents a queen (denoted *QueenGrayBoard*). Only if the result of this operation is a diagram with all WHITE tesserae (denoted *NullDiagram*) has a solution been found. More formally stated, a solution will return TRUE for

NULL (*CurrentBoard* - *QueenGrayBoard*)

As long as the gray level representing queens is greater than any gray level achievable by simply OVERLAYing the GRAY1 tesserae representing queen attack extents, a tessera will only take on a gray level greater than that representing queens if one or more GRAY1 tesserae is OVERLAYed upon a queen. If such a level of gray is found, a queen is under attack. Therefore, if the previous PEEL operation does not remove all gray from a diagram, it cannot be a solution. If a solution has yet to be found, an attacked queen is PEELed from the current diagram and a new queen is OVERLAYed at a minimally attacked location.

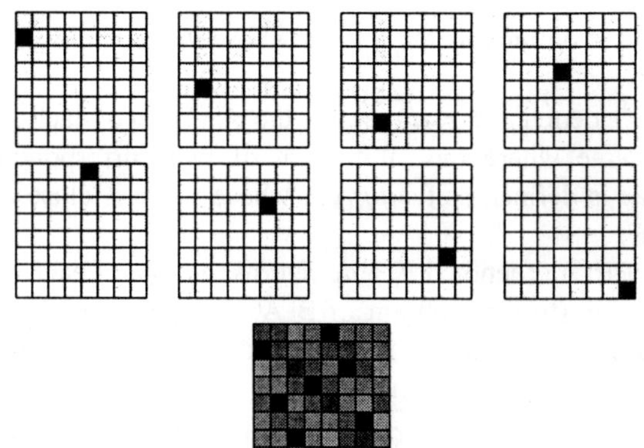

Figure 2: OVERLAYing 8 queen diagrams

An attacked queen (denoted *AttackedQueen*) is found by ANDing a GRAY1-PEELed version of all diagrams from *SelectedQueens* with the results of the solution test and randomly selecting from those queens that do not produce the *NullDiagram* (i.e. those queens that correspond with NON-WHITE tesserae in the diagram resulting from the solution test). More formally:

```
AttackedQueen⇐
    RANDOM
        (FILTER
            (NULL,
                MAP (λ(x) ((x - Gray1Board)
                                ∧
                        (CurrentBoard - QueenGrayBoard)),
                    SelectedQueens)))
```

AttackedQueen is PEELed from the *CurrentBoard* and a minimally attacked queen is OVERLAYed in its place. By definition, the minimally attacked queen (denoted *MinimalQueen*) on the current diagram will be the queen at the location that is the lightest gray level. These locations are found by ANDing a GRAY1-PEELed version of all unused diagrams from *Queens* (denoted *UnusedQueens*) with the current diagram and randomly selecting from those queens that produce the *NullDiagram* (i.e. those queens that correspond with WHITE tesserae in *CurrentBoard*). More formally:

```
MinimalQueen⇐
    RANDOM
        (FILTER
            (NONNULL,
                MAP (λ(x) ((x - Gray1Board)
                                ∧
                        (CurrentBoard - AttackedQueen)),
                    UnusedQueens)))
```

If no such queen is found, a diagram that is completely covered in GRAY1 (denoted *Gray1Board*) is iteratively PEELed from the current diagram, making all tesserae one gray level lighter, and the process repeated. More formally:

CurrentBoard ⇐ *CurrentBoard* - *Gray1Board*

MinimalQueen is then OVERLAYed upon the current diagram. More formally:

CurrentBoard ⇐
CurrentBoard - *AttackedQueen* + *MinimalQueen*

This new diagram is checked to see if it is a solution and the process continues until such a solution is discovered.

An Example

Figures 2 through 4 graphically display an example of the solution finding process where $n = 8$. Figure 2 shows the queen diagrams selected from *Queens* as well as the diagram that results from OVERLAYing these diagrams.

Figure 3 displays one iteration of this process. 3a shows the solution check, *QueenGrayBoard* is PEELed from the current diagram. This diagram is not a solution because the result is not the *NullDiagram*. In 3b, one of the attacked queens is selected and PEELed from the current diagram. Since there are no WHITE tesserae, *Gray1Board* is PEELed from the result in 3c. In 3d, a queen diagram is randomly selected from the set of queen diagrams that correspond to the WHITE tesserae in the result and OVERLAYed on the current diagram.

Figure 4 shows the next two iterations of the solution finding process. 4a displays the solution check for the current diagram created by the last iteration. This is also found not to be a solution, so an attacked queen's diagram is PEELed from the current diagram in 4b. Since there is a WHITE tesserae in the result, PEELing *Gray1Board* from it is not required. The only possible new queen diagram is then OVERLAYed on the current diagram in 4c. 4d shows the solution check for the third iteration and, as this is found to be a solution (i.e. the check results in the *NullDiagram*), processing stops. The result of the entire process is the 8-queen problem solution presented in 4e.

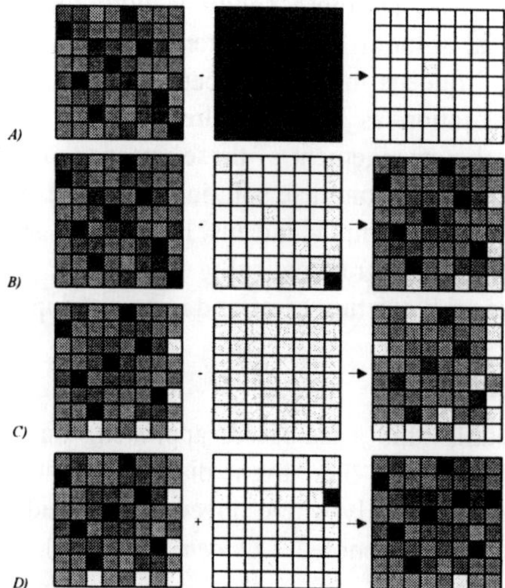

Figure 3: 8-queens example, 1st iteration

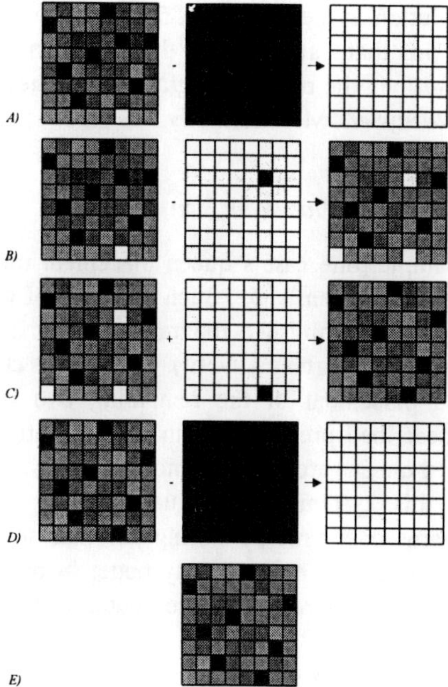

Figure 4: 8-queens example, 2nd and 3rd iterations

Diagrammatic Case-based Best Solution

A solution to an *n-queens best solution problem* is an n-queens placement obtained by moving the fewest queens from some initial placement. Although finding this minimal solution can only be achieved at great computational cost, we have implemented a system that improves its performance at this task by making use of previous solutions it has developed. Solutions to previous problems can be used to provide partial solutions to the current problem.

These previous solutions form the *cases* of our case-based reasoning solution. Case *representation* is defined diagrammatically as an OVERLAYed solution set of *n* queens without attack extent information. Case *similarity* is defined as cases that have the most number of queens in common with the current problem. This matching is accomplished diagrammatically by ANDing the current problem board (PEELed with *QueenGrayBoard*) with each of the stored solutions, counting all non-WHITE tesserae and retrieving those solutions with the highest count. A partial solution to the current problem has then been found; all queens in common can be exempted from further consideration as they are already in place. Case *adaptation* is the arrangement of those queens that are not yet in place to form a complete solution without disturbing the positions of the exempted queens. Lastly, case *indexing* is expedited by diagrammatically comparing a new candidate case with existing cases and rejecting duplicates.

An Example

Figure 5 details this case-based approach. 5a PEELs *QueenGrayBoard* from the current diagram resulting in a diagram that is gray only where queens are placed on the current diagram (denoted *QueenPlacement*). More formally:

$$QueenPlacement \Leftarrow CurrentBoard - QueenGrayBoard$$

5b shows the process of ANDing *QueenPlacement* with each stored solution in the *CaseBase*, 5c, resulting in a set of diagrams, 5d, that each display their similarity with *QueenPlacement* via the number of gray tessera they have (denoted *SimilaritySet*). More formally:

$$SimilaritySet := \text{MAP}(\lambda(x)\ (QueenPlacement \wedge x), CaseBase)$$

In this example, one case's queen placement matches six of the current diagram's, 5e. Such counting of certain valued tessera is accomplished diagrammatically as well (see [Anderson & McCartney 1995b]). This case is chosen, then, and the placement of the remaining two queens proceeds as described previously with the stipulation that the six matched queens are not to be moved.

Although this system cannot guarantee an optimal solution, it learns over time by storing previous solutions and, therefore, becomes progressively better at providing near optimal solutions at reasonable computational cost.

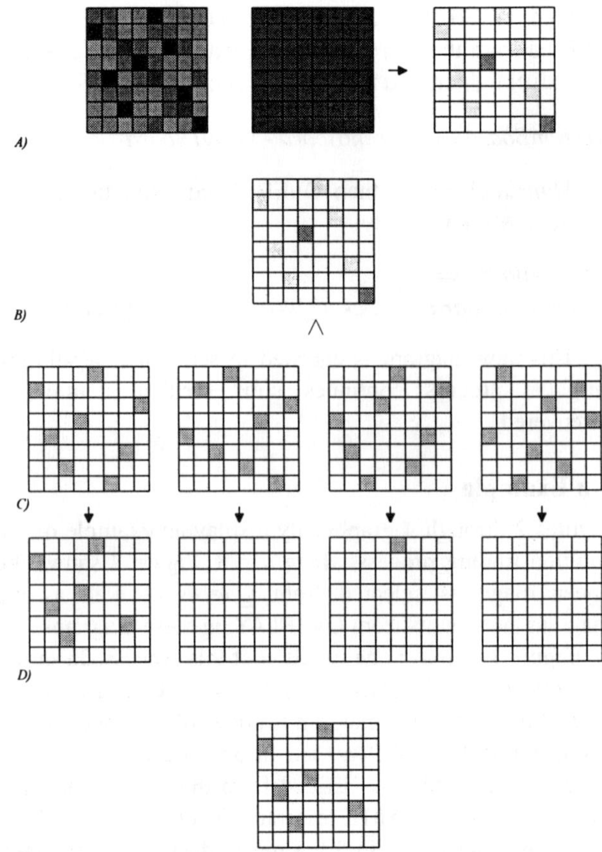

Figure 5: 8-queens example, case matching

Related Research

Research in diagrammatic reasoning is just beginning to flourish after a long dormancy it experienced being virtually abandoned after a brief flirtation in the early days of AI (e.g. [Gelernter 1959; Evans 1962]). See, for instance, [Larkin & Simon 1987; Narayanan & Chandrasekaran 1991; Narayanan 1992; Chandrasekaran, Narayanan, & Iwasaki 1993; Narayanan 1993; Glasgow 1993; Glasgow, Narayanan, & Chandrasekaran 1995] for a representative sample of this work. We have previously proposed inter-diagrammatic reasoning as one way of using diagrammatic representations to solve problems [Anderson 1994; Anderson & McCartney 1995a; Anderson & McCartney 1995b]. The earliest work in diagrammatic reasoning can be considered the first example of inter-diagrammatic reasoning as well [Evans 1962]. Bieger and Glock [1985; 1986] and Willows and Houghton [1987] have done work in human use of sets of related diagrams.

Case-based reasoning has generated a good deal of interest: much work has been and is being done in this area. See [Kolodner 1993] for an overview. Interestingly, case-based reasoning has been previously used to increase efficiency in solving constraint satisfaction problems in [Purvis 1995].

[Narayanan & Chandrasekaran 1991] discuss what they term "visual cases" for diagrammatic spatial reasoning but we believe that we are the first to successfully integrate diagrammatic and case-based reasoning.

Conclusion

We have shown how a diagrammatic cased-based approach is useful in providing near optimal solutions to the

n-queens problem. It is straight forward to generalize our approach to involve objects of various sizes and extents. This is the first step towards applying this approach to spatial configuration problems and other domains.

We believe that, in general, a diagrammatic approach to case-based reasoning can help provide answers to the questions of case representation, similarity, indexing, and adaptation in many interesting real world domains. Further, a case-based reasoning approach to diagrammatic reasoning provides a framework that enables the effectiveness of diagrammatic operators to emerge.

References

Anderson, M. 1994. Reasoning with Diagram Sequences. In Proceedings of the Conference on Information-Oriented Approaches to Logic, Language and Computation (Fourth Conference on Situation Theory and its Applications).

Anderson, M. and McCartney, R. 1995a. Developing a Heuristic via Diagrammatic Reasoning. In Proceedings of the Tenth Annual ACM Symposium on Applied Computing.

Anderson, M. and McCartney, R. 1995b. Inter-diagrammatic Reasoning. In Proceedings of the 14th International Joint Conference on Artificial Intelligence.

Bieger, G. and Glock, M. 1985. The Information Content of Picture-Text Instructions. *The Journal of Experimental Education*, 53(2), 68-76.

Bieger, G. and Glock, M. 1986. Comprehending Spatial and Contextual Information in Picture-Text Instructions. *The Journal of Experimental Education*, 54(4), 181-188.

Chandrasekaran, B., Narayanan, N. and Iwasaki, Y. 1993. Reasoning with Diagrammatic Representations, *AI Magazine*, 14(2).

Evans, T. G. 1962. A Heuristic Program to Solve Geometry Analogy Problems. MIT AI Memo 46. (also in *Semantic Information Processing* as "A Program for the Solution of a Class of Geometric-analogy Intelligence-test Questions", 271-353, Minsky, M. L., ed. MIT Press, 1968).

Feigenbaum, E. A. and Feldman, J., eds. 1963. *Computers and Thought*, McGraw-Hill.

Gelernter, H. 1959. Realization of a Geometry Theorem Proving Machine. In Proceedings of an International Conference on Information Processing, 273-282. UNESCO House. (also in [Feigenbaum & Feldman 1963]).

Glasgow, J. 1993. The Imagery Debate Revisited: A Computational Perspective in [Narayanan 1993].

Glasgow, J., Narayanan, N., and Chandrasekaran, B. 1995. *Diagrammatic Reasoning: Cognitive and Computational Perspectives*, AAAI Press.

Goel, A., Ali, K., Donnellan, M., de Silva Garza, A., and Callantine, T. 1994. Multistrategy Adaptive Path Planning, *IEEE Expert*, 9:6, 57-65.

Gu, J. 1989. Parallel Algorithms and Architectures for Very Fast AI Search, Ph.D. diss., University of Utah.

Kambhampati, S., and Hendler, J. 1992. A Validation Structure Based Theory of Plan Modification and Reuse. *Artificial Intelligence*, 55: 193-258.

Kolodner, J. L. 1993. *Case-based Reasoning*. Morgan Kaufmann, San Mateo.

Larkin, J. and Simon, H. 1987. Why a Diagram is (Sometimes) Worth Ten Thousand Words. *Cognitive Science*, 11, 65-99.

McCartney, R. 1993. Episodic Cases and Real-time Performance in a Case-based Planning System. *Expert Systems with Applications*, 6:9-22.

Narayanan, N., ed. 1992. Working Notes of AAAI Spring Symposium on Reasoning with Diagrammatic Representations.

Narayanan, N., ed. 1993. Taking Issue/Forum: The Imagery Debate Revisited. *Computational Intelligence*, 9(4).

Narayanan, N. H. and Chandrasekaran, B. 1991. Reasoning Visually about Spatial Interactions. In Proceedings of the 12th International Joint Conference on Artificial Intelligence.

Purvis, L. 1995. Constraint Satisfaction Combined with Case-Based Reasoning for Assembly Sequence Planning, Technical Report CSE-TR-93-20, University of Connecticut.

Stone, H. S. and Stone, J. 1986. Efficient Search Techniques: an Empirical Study of the n-Queens Problem, Technical Report RC 12057, IBM Thomas J. Watson Research Center, Yorktown Heights, New York.

Willows, D. and Houghton, H. 1987. *The Psychology of Illustration*, Springer-Verlag.

Augmenting the diagnostic power of flow-based approaches to functional reasoning

Luca Chittaro and Roberto Ranon

Dipartimento di Matematica e Informatica
Università di Udine
Via delle Scienze 206, 33100 Udine, ITALY
chittaro@dimi.uniud.it

Abstract

In this paper, we consider flow-based approaches to functional diagnosis. First, we contrast the existing approaches, pointing out the major limitations of each. Then, we choose one of them and extend it in order to overcome the identified limitations. Finally, we show how the proposed extension can be introduced into the other flow-based approaches.

Introduction

Reasoning about function for diagnostic purposes has been recently investigated by several research groups (Chandrasekaran 1994; Chittaro 1995; Hawkins et al. 1994; Hunt, Pugh, & Price 1995; Kumar & Upadhyaya 1995; Larsson 1996). Nevertheless, a lot of work has still to be done on the functional diagnosis of real complex systems. In this paper, we take into consideration *flow-based approaches* (Chittaro 1995; Kumar & Upadhyaya 1995; Larsson 1996) to functional diagnosis. These approaches propose to model a system by focusing on the flows (of mass, energy, or information) in the system and on the actions performed by components on the considered flows. From a diagnostic point of view, they typically implement diagnosis as a search in a graph structure and claim to perform diagnostic reasoning very efficiently. In this paper, we initially show that this claim is achieved at the expense of diagnostic power. Indeed, each approach exhibits at least one of the following limitations: (i) easy availability of measurements is assumed, while in real-world cases measurements are often difficult to take or too expensive, or too unreliable, (ii) a single-fault assumption is adopted, and it is thus not possible to handle multiple faults, (iii) the modeling of interactions among different physical domains is not easy or impossible.

Since we are dealing with the application of flow-based techniques to a real-world problem in the domain of marine engineering (Chittaro, Fabbri & Lopez Cortes 1996), we need to overcome these limitations. To this purpose, this paper: (i) compares the existing flow-based diagnostic engines, pointing out the major limitations of each, (ii) chooses one of them (i.e., FDef (Chittaro 1995)) and extends it in order to overcome the identified limitations, and (iii) shows how the proposed extension can be introduced into the other flow-based approaches.

Comparing flow-based approaches

This section contrasts the three main flow-based approaches to functional diagnosis. The considered approaches are MFM (Multilevel Flow Modeling) (Larsson 1996), Classes (Kumar & Upadhyaya 1995), and FDef (Functional Diagnosis with efforts and flows) (Chittaro 1995).

Flow-based approaches: a short overview

Flow-based approaches to functional representation are founded on the general concept of *flow* (Paynter 1961). Some specific instances of flow are electrical current, mechanical velocity, hydraulic volume flow rate, and thermal heat flow. Some approaches also support the general notion of *effort* (Paynter 1961), i.e., the force responsible for the flow. Specific instances of effort are voltage, force, pressure, and temperature. In flow-based approaches, function is represented by means of a set of primitives, which are interpretations of actions frequently performed on the substances flowing through physical systems. These approaches generally aim at representing function in isolation, separating it from other types of knowledge, such as behavioral or teleological, in order to increase the clarity and the reusability of models.

MFM. In MFM, functions are expressed in terms of primitives such as source, sink, storage, transport, barrier and balance. Instances of these primitives are connected together to build *flow-structures*. Functions are linked to goals (i.e., purposes of the system) by two types of means-ends relations: *achieve* and *condition*. An achieve relation connects a set of functions to the goal they are meant to achieve. A condition relation connects a goal to a function: the goal must be fulfilled in order for the function to be available.

In the diagnostic algorithm proposed by (Larsson 1996), the user starts the diagnostic process by choosing an unachieved goal. The search proceeds downwards from the goal, via achieve relations, into the connected network of functional primitives, each of which has to be investigated (by questioning the user or by sensor readings) to find if the associated function is available or not. If a functional primitive conditioned by a goal is found to be at fault (or has no means of being checked), then the connected goal is recursively investigated; if it is found to be working, the goal is skipped.

Classes. Classes represents function of a component in terms of the ports of the component, i.e., function is a relation between input and output of energy, matter or information. A set of functional primitives, called *classes* (producer, consumer, data, store, control, and address) is defined. Every causal flow in the system is called a *signal*; a *signal-line* is the sequence of components along the path from the origin to the use of a signal. Signal-lines can be of different types (power, clock, control, address, and data) with respect to the port of the component to which they provide input.

The diagnostic technique proposed by (Kumar & Upadhyaya 1995) starts from an incorrect system output S. Signal-lines that merge at output S are chosen for investigation, and ordered using heuristic criteria. Signal-lines are investigated following the order until a signal-line that contains a fault is found. Components in the currently investigated signal-line are ordered exploiting heuristic criteria, and tested in the obtained order until the faulty one is found. If a suspect component is connected to another signal-line, that signal-line is recursively investigated.

FDef. FDef (Chittaro 1995) adopts a limited version of the functional model proposed in Multimodeling (Chittaro et al. 1993), where functional primitives (called *roles*) are defined as interpretations of the physical equations describing the behavior of components. This interpretation is carried out using the Tetrahedron of State (TOS) (Paynter 1961), an abstract framework that describes a set of generalized equations which are common to a wide variety of physical domains. When the TOS is instantiated in a specific domain, the ordinary physical variables and equations are obtained. Functional roles are interpretations of the generalized equations of the TOS, and are of four types: generator, conduit, barrier, and reservoir.

The FDef diagnostic technique is based on the identification of the so called *enabling sets* and *disabling sets*. An enabling set is a set of roles which are all allowing the passage of flow or effort. A disabling set is a set of roles where there is at least one impediment to the passage of flow or effort. These sets are derived starting from the given measurements, using general axioms as those provided in (Chittaro 1995). They are then used both for exoneration purposes (identify normal roles), and to generate conflicts (i.e., sets of roles, each one containing at least a faulty role). A simple candidate generation algorithm (de Kleer & Williams 1987) uses the set of conflicts to produce the minimal diagnoses, and a minimum entropy (de Kleer & Williams 1987) prescription mechanism suggests the best measurement to discriminate among them.

Comparison

This section compares the three flow-based approaches in terms of the assumptions they make on the availability of measurements, their diagnostic output, and how they represent interactions among different physical domains.

Required availability of measurements. (Larsson 1996) uses questions (or sensor readings) in order to find if the currently investigated MFM functional primitive is faulty (or not), and in order to decide which further parts of the model have (or have not) to be investigated by the search algorithm. In order to guarantee the progress of the diagnostic algorithm, it is thus necessary that the highest number (possibly all) of the functions in the system is measurable (by diagnostic question or sensor readings). On the contrary, the scarce availability of measurements is a typical problem in real-world systems (e.g., because some of them are too costly, or too unreliable, or it is physically impossible to take them). In these cases, the diagnostic capability of the approach is impaired, leading to a partial, incomplete diagnosis or to a stuck reasoning process. It should also be noted that since MFM handles only flows, observations about efforts cannot be represented.

In Classes (Kumar & Upadhyaya 1995), components have to be testable in order to proceed in the investigation of signal-lines. This can lead again to a stuck reasoning process, when it is not possible to test some inputs and outputs of components. Unlike MFM, Classes tries to focus first on most probable diagnoses, by applying its heuristic ordering rules (e.g., a power signal-line has precedence over a control signal-line) to determine an order of investigation for signal-lines, and an order of testing for components inside the currently investigated signal-line.

FDef (Chittaro 1995) fully performs its diagnostic activity, regardless of the number of measurements given, returning the complete set of minimal diagnoses that are physically consistent with the given measurements. After generating this set, it ranks all the possible additional measurements from the most to the least informative, following an entropy-based strategy (de Kleer & Williams 1987). In this way, it aims at isolating the real diagnosis, using the least number of measurements.

Diagnostic output. The three approaches differ also in the type of diagnoses they produce. MFM produces just one diagnosis, including all the functions which have been measured to be faulty in the parts of model which have been explored. In order to help the user in the interpretation of this output, it classifies faulty functions into primary and secondary (the secondary could be an effect of the primary). Fault masking cases can thus be identified only if specific evidence is obtained, i.e., after a measurement pinpoints that a function involved in the masking is faulty.

Classes relies on the single-fault assumption, and produces an ordered set of single faults, which depend on the signal-line that has been currently reached by the investigation process. Multiple faults and fault masking cases are thus not covered.

FDef produces the set of all the minimal diagnoses that are physically consistent with the given measurements. It does not rely on the single-fault assumption, and each diagnosis is a minimal explanation of the observations. In this way, it covers also all the minimal fault masking cases consistent with the observations, without needing to obtain

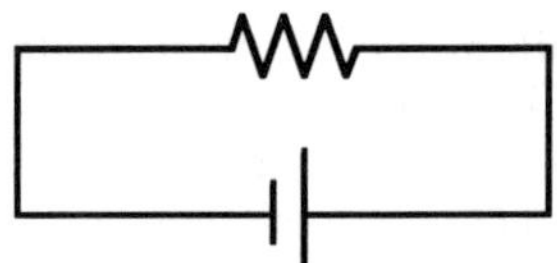

Figure 1. A simple circuit.

specific evidence first. However, producing this more detailed and complete diagnostic output causes FDef to be less efficient than MFM and Classes.

Representation of influences. All flow-based approaches aim at modeling separately the different flows in a system, by organizing the model into different networks (often called *flow-structures*) of functional primitives. Each flow-structure operates in a single physical domain (e.g., electrical, thermal,...). This modeling strategy is meant to allow: (i) the production of clear, easier to understand, models that modularly represent the different physical aspects of system functioning, and (ii) the focusing of reasoning on a selected physical domain. As a consequence, a component that works in more than one physical domain has to be represented by more than one functional primitive. For example, consider a simple circuit composed by a resistor connected to a battery, with the goal of producing heat (Figure 1). The resistor has a function both in the electrical domain (to conduce current), and in the thermal domain (to generate heat). In flow-based approaches, this system is represented by an electrical and a thermal flow-structure, each one including a function associated to the resistor. Since the two functions belong to the same physical component, the modeling approach should also provide a way to represent the relation between them. In general, we call *influence* the relation between two interacting primitives belonging to different flow-structures: the state of one of the two (called the *influencing* one) has the capability to influence the state of the other (called the *influenced* one). In the resistor example, the electrical function of the resistor influences its thermal function: an heat flow is generated by the resistor if and only if the resistor is conducting electrical flow.

MFM represents influences using means-ends relations. A condition relation connects a goal to the influenced function (i.e., the goal must be fulfilled in order for the function to be available). Then, the flow-structure containing the influencing function is connected to the goal by an achieve relation. It is interesting to note that representation of influences in MFM requires to switch to the teleological level of representation, and then return to the functional one. Furthermore, from a practical point of view, the modeler is required to define a specific goal for every interaction he/she needs to model. An MFM model of the resistor circuit is shown in Figure 2(a). The diagnostic use of the condition relation in this example is the following: if the source associated to the resistor is measured to be malfunctioning, goal "keep electrical flow through resistor" is investigated and thus the electrical flow-structure is checked; if the source associated to the resistor is functioning, the goal is not investigated.

Classes represents a component that works in more than one physical domain by assigning it different functional primitives with respect to its inputs and outputs. Influences are implicitly represented in the model. From the Classes point of view (Figure 2(b)), the resistor has an electrical input, and a thermal output: it is a consumer (i.e., it consumes flow) with respect to the electrical input, and a producer (i.e., it produces flow) with respect to the thermal output. The interactions between the two primitives that represent the resistor are not explicitly expressed in the model. During diagnosis, if the resistor becomes suspect in one signal-line, then the other signal-line can be recursively investigated.

In Multimodeling (Chittaro et al. 1993), influences are defined as follows: a role FRi, which refers to a physical equation PEi, influences a role FRj, which refers to a physical equation PEj, if a physical variable of PEi is (or concurs to determine) a parameter of PEj. In the example, the conduit role associated to the resistor in the electrical domain influences the generator role associated to the resistor in the thermal domain. The resulting model is depicted in Figure 2(c), where the influence states that presence of flow in the electrical conduit is required to activate the thermal generator. Although Multimodeling considers influences, FDef does not support them. As a consequence, FDef can only diagnose a flow-structure instantiated in one physical domain.

Introducing influences in FDef

The previous analysis has shown that while FDef exhibits interesting diagnostic capabilities, it imposes an

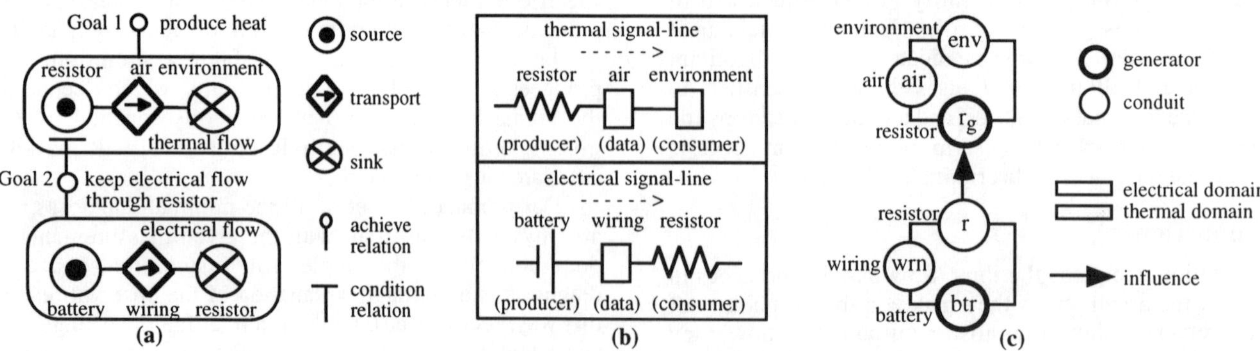

Figure 2. Models of the resistor system.

unacceptable restriction to a single physical domain. In this section, we extend FDef in order to remove that restriction, allowing a scaling up in the complexity of the functional models to be handled.

In addition to what is defined by Multimodeling, we further characterize influences as follows.

With *transduction influences*, the influenced role is a generator, and the state of the influencing role determines if the influenced generator is active. For example, the electrical conduit associated to the resistor causes (if it is traversed by current) the activation of the thermal generator associated to resistor.

With *regulation influences*, the influenced role is not a generator, and the state of the influencing role regulates the state of the influenced one. For example, the mechanical reservoir role associated to the screw of a tap regulates the passage of flow in the tap viewed as an hydraulic conduit.

The relay system case study

In the following, we consider a diagnostic example proposed by (Holtzblatt 1992), where the main component is a single pole, double throw relay. Holtzblatt presents two different cases: in the first, two components (both sensors) are connected to the relay; in the second, sensors are substituted with bulbs. In order to show how we handle both situations, we consider the case in Figure 3, where both a sensor (sns) and a bulb (b) are connected to the relay. The relay can work in two different states: an energized state (V_c is greater than a given threshold) in which current is allowed to flow only between P_{common} and sns, or a de-energized state (V_c is lower than the given threshold), in which current is allowed to flow only between P_{common} and b. Hereinafter, we suppose that three observations are given: (i) Vc>threshold (the relay is thus expected to be in the energized state), (ii) sns is off, and (iii) b is lit.

Figure 4 depicts the functional representation of the relay example, considering the same domains taken into account by (Holtzblatt 1992).

Reasoning with influences

This section presents the extension of FDef, which is structured in three phases: (i) generation of Influence Assigners, (ii) application of influences, and (iii) generation of candidates. First, we characterize influences in more detail. Then, we provide a general treatment of the three

role	normal	abnormal
generator	produces effort and causes flow	does not allow passage of flow and effort, does not produce them
conduit	allows passage of flow and effort	does not allow passage of flow and effort
barrier	does not allow passage of flow and effort	allows passage of flow and effort

Table 1. Normal and abnormal functioning of roles.

role	positively influenced	negatively influenced
generator	unchanged	becomes normal barrier
conduit	unchanged	becomes barrier
barrier	unchanged	becomes conduit

Table 2. Functioning of influenced roles.

phases, also showing the results on the relay example for each of them.

Characterization of influences. For clarity purposes, Table 1 first summarizes what is assumed by FDef as normal and abnormal functioning of roles (e.g., in their normal functioning, conduits allow passage of both flow and effort). FDef also qualitatively characterizes the status of functional roles in this way: a role is *uncrossed* (*crossed*) if the flow associated to it is (is not) zero, a role is *unpushed* (*pushed*) if the effort associated to it is (is not) zero. Hereinafter, an influenced role is said to be *positively influenced* if the influencing role is crossed, or *negatively influenced*, if the influencing role is uncrossed. Table 2 characterizes the functioning of positively influenced and negatively influenced roles.

Generation of Influence Assigners. The diagnosis of systems with influences requires to consider different alternative situations: if the given observations do not allow to derive the status of an influencing role with respect to flow (crossed or uncrossed), the functioning of the influenced role is undetermined. For example, while the three given observations in the relay case study allow to conclude that influencing role b is crossed by electrical flow (because bulb b is lit), they do not allow to conclude anything about neither influencing role sns (the observation that the sensor is off does not mean that current is not flowing through it, because the sensor could be failing in

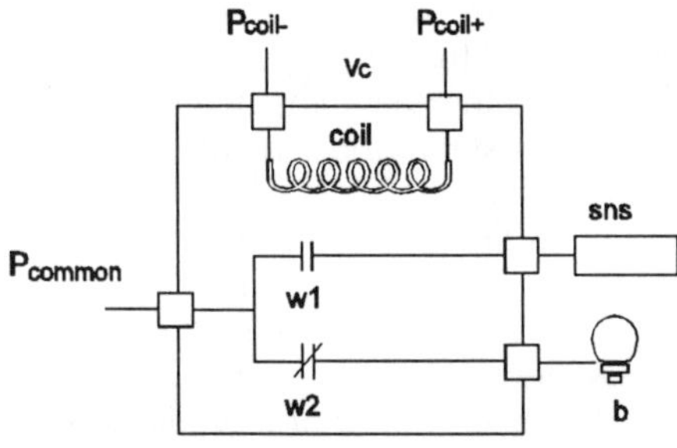

Figure 3. The relay system.

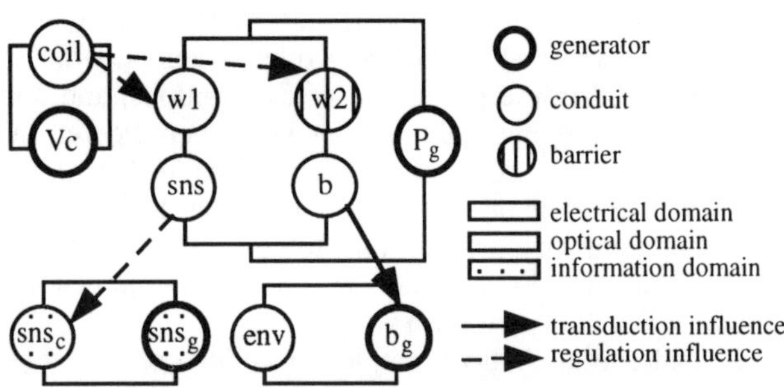

Figure 4. FDef model of the relay system.

communicating information) nor influencing role coil (the observation Vc>threshold does not allow to conclude anything about current through the coil). In order to handle this, we introduce the concept of *Influence Assigner* (IA). An IA is a set of observations from which it is possible to univocally derive the status of every influencing role. When the set of observations currently given on the system is not an IA (i.e., it is not possible to derive the status of at least one influencing role), we need to consider multiple possibilities (the alternative would be to prescribe and take additional measurements until there are no more ambiguities, but this solution would lead to the first problem pointed out in the Comparison section). We thus build a set of IAs, by assuming additional observations concerning some undetermined influencing roles. More specifically, the algorithm that builds the set of IAs is the following (GivenObs denotes the set of observations given on the system, IAS the set of IAs produced by the algorithm, and the predicate obs(role,observation) describes observations on roles):

```
let IAS = ∅;
let SetsOfObs = {GivenObs};
repeat
  foreach set of observations S ∈ SetsOfObs do
    derive all the consequences of the observations in S and
    let UndS be the set of undetermined influencing roles;
    if UndS = ∅ then
      remove S from SetsOfObs;
      add S to IAS;
    endif
  enddo
  if SetsOfObs ≠ ∅ then
    foreach set of observations S ∈ SetsOfObs do
      remove S from SetsOfObs;
      choose r ∈ UndS;
      add the set S ∪ {obs(r,crossed)} to SetsOfObs;
      add the set S ∪ {obs(r,uncrossed)} to SetsOfObs;
    enddo
  endif
until SetsOfObs=∅.
```

Generation of IAs is obviously a possible source of combinatorial explosion, especially when very few measurements are given. However, the propagation activity (carried out both backward and forward before a new observation is assumed) typically allows to determine the status of a number of influencing roles which need not to be considered in the generation of assumptions, and also ensures that only physically feasible IAs are considered and generated. Moreover, inferences are cached and not performed more than once, e.g., when a set S is used (in the second part of the algorithm) to generate two sets that differ just for one assumption, they both inherit the inferences already performed with S.

Considering the relay example, GivenObs contains three elements: obs(Vc, pushed) (voltage is produced by generator Vc), obs(sns_C, uncrossed) (information from the sensor is off), and obs(env, crossed) (light is flowing in the environment around the bulb). As discussed previously, these observations do not allow to determine the status of all the three influencing roles (coil, sns, and b), and thus they are not an IA. Only the status of b can be determined by propagation: since env is crossed, then generator b_g must be positively influenced, i.e., b is crossed. In this case, the following four IAs are generated:

Vc	coil	sns	sns_C	env
pushed	*crossed*	*crossed*	uncrossed	crossed
pushed	*crossed*	*uncrossed*	uncrossed	crossed
pushed	*uncrossed*	*crossed*	uncrossed	crossed
pushed	*uncrossed*	*uncrossed*	uncrossed	crossed

These four IAs are to be considered as different diagnostic situations, and thus handled disjunctively.

Application of influences. For each generated IA, the functional model is transformed according to the definitions of influences in Table 2 (e.g., a negatively influenced conduit is replaced by a barrier, positively influenced roles remain unchanged,...). For example, the application of the fourth generated IA to the model in Figure 4 results in three changes: conduit w1 becomes a barrier, barrier w2 becomes a conduit, and conduit sns_C becomes a barrier.

Generation of candidates. Generation of candidates for an IA and the corresponding model (i.e., the result of the transformation described above) is performed as follows.

First, generation of local minimal candidates is performed for each flow-structure in the model, by locally running the plain FDef engine (as described in (Chittaro 1995)) only on that single flow-structure, feeding it with the observations (contained in the considered IA) concerning roles of that flow-structure. An interesting feature of this procedure is that it focuses diagnostic reasoning only on small sets of components (i.e., those belonging to the currently considered flow-structure). In the case of the fourth generated IA, locally running FDef only on the electrical flow-structure composed by Vc and coil produces the enabling set {Vc} and the disabling set {Vc, coil}. The minimal candidate for this flow-structure is then {coil}, while the local consideration of the other flow-structures does not produce any conflict (and thus no candidates): the coil is faulty, and the remaining part of the relay behaves as expected (the relay is actually in the de-energized state).

Second, global candidates for the currently considered IA are simply obtained by cartesian product of the sets of local candidates generated for the single flow-structures (for the fourth IA, {coil} is thus the only minimal candidate). The generation of consistent global candidates is guaranteed, because the IA and the model transformation ensure that the flow-structures in the model are in a mutually consistent state, and thus the local candidates are also mutually consistent and can be globally combined.

The two activities above are performed for each generated IA, and then the complete set of candidates is obtained as the union of the sets of global minimal candidates obtained with the different IAs. In the relay example, the complete set of minimal candidates generated is {{coil}, {w2, w1}, {w2, sns}, {w2, sns_c}, {w2, sns_g}}.

In order to speed up generation, the results of locally running FDef on a single flow-structure for an IA are saved, avoiding the need of repeating the computation with other IAs that make the same assumptions on that flow-structure.

Our extension of FDef preserves the entropy-based mechanism for test prescription. In the relay example, measuring the flow associated to role coil (or, alternatively, to generator Vc) is the suggested best measurement.

Extending other flow-based approaches

This section provides guidelines to implement the extended FDef reasoning strategy inside the other flow-based approaches. Firstly, enabling sets and disabling sets have to be introduced in the considered approach. FDef uses axioms for the derivation of enabling and disabling sets from observations on flows and efforts (Chittaro 1995; Chittaro, Fabbri & Lopez Cortes 1996). Their adaptation to MFM and Classes is relatively straightforward. For example, reformulating FDef axioms in a more general context, we obtain statements such as: "if in a circuit of functional primitives, we are given at least an observation of presence of flow, and no observations about absence of flow or effort, then that circuit is an enabling set", or "if in a circuit of functional primitives, we are given at least an observation of absence of flow, and no observations about absence of effort, then that circuit is a disabling set". Consider for example the MFM flow-structure in Figure 2(a), representing an electrical circuit made of battery, wiring and a resistor, and suppose to observe current flowing in the resistor. In this case, the first of the two rules mentioned above would conclude that the battery, wiring and resistor allow the passage of flow, i.e., they constitute an enabling set. On the contrary, if absence of current were observed in the resistor, the second rule would conclude that there is at least a component in the circuit that does not allow the passage of flow, i.e., they are a disabling set. The Classes case (Figure 2(b)) is analogous.

The second step is the identification of influences in MFM and Classes. To do this, the following approach can be followed. In MFM, every condition relation can be considered as a transduction influence, that connects two different functions representing the same component in two flow-structures (e.g., the sink and the source associated to the resistor in Figure 2(a)). In Classes, influences can be introduced when a component has ports belonging to different physical domains. For example, in Figure 2(b), the resistor is represented by a consumer class in the electrical signal-line, and a producer class in the thermal signal-line, and thus they can be connected by an influence.

Once the above described adaptations have been carried out, it is straightforward to run the extended FDef engine described in this paper on MFM and Classes models, thus overcoming the shown limitations of these approaches at the expense of some efficiency.

Conclusions

This paper presented (i) an evaluation of the diagnostic power of existing flow-based diagnostic engines, (ii) a relevant and useful extension of the FDef diagnostic engine, and (iii) guidelines to implement the features of extended FDef in the other flow-based approaches.

The techniques presented in this paper are being used on the technical marine system application presented in (Chittaro, Fabbri & Lopez Cortes 1996), where they are allowing us to move from the diagnosis of the considered hydraulic system to the diagnosis of the whole set of subsystems connected to it. The evaluation of the results on this application is pointing out that the approach is good at isolating faults when they result in a loss of functionality. Since some faults in the considered domain are preceded by a slow degradation in performance before turning into a loss of functionality, one of the subjects we are considering is the introduction and exploitation of "too low"/"too high" flow and effort observations in flow-based diagnostic approaches.

References

Chandrasekaran B. 1994. Functional Representation and Causal Processes. *Advances in Computers* 38:73-143.

Chittaro L.; Guida G.; Tasso C. and Toppano E. 1993. Functional and Teleological Knowledge in the Multimodeling Approach for Reasoning About Physical Systems: A Case Study in Diagnosis. *IEEE Transactions on Systems, Man, and Cybernetics* 23(6): 1718-1751.

Chittaro L. 1995. Functional Diagnosis and Prescription of Measurements Using Effort and Flow Variables. *IEE Control Theory and Applications*, 142(5): 420-432.

Chittaro L.; Fabbri R. and Lopez Cortes J. 1996. Functional Diagnosis Goes to the Sea: Applying FDef to the Heavy Fuel Oil Transfer System of a Ship. In *Proceedings of the Ninth Florida AI Research Symposium (FLAIRS)*, Key West, FL.

Hawkins R.; Sticklen J.; McDowell J.K.; Hill T. and Boyer R. 1994. Function-based Modeling and Troubleshooting. *Journal of Applied Artificial Intelligence* 8(2): 285-302.

Holtzblatt, L.J. 1992. Diagnosing Multiple Failures Using Knowledge of Component States. In W. Hamscher, L. Console, J. de Kleer (eds.), *Readings in Model-based Diagnosis*, San Mateo, Calif: Morgan Kaufmann, 165-169.

Hunt J.; Pugh D. and Price C. 1995. Failure Mode Effects Analysis: a Practical Application of Functional Modeling. *Journal of Applied Artificial Intelligence* 9(1): 33-44.

de Kleer J. and Williams B.C. 1987. Diagnosing Multiple Faults. *Artificial Intelligence* 32: 97-130.

Kumar A. N. and Upadhyaya S.J. 1995. Function Based Discrimination during Model-based Diagnosis. *Journal of Applied Artificial Intelligence* 9(1): 65-80.

Larsson J.E. 1996. Diagnosis based on explicit means-end models. *Artificial Intelligence* 80: 29-93.

Paynter H.M. 1961. *Analysis and Design of Engineering Systems*. Cambridge, Mass.: MIT Press.

A Qualitative Model of Physical Fields

Monika Lundell
Artificial Intelligence Laboratory
Computer Science Department
Swiss Federal Institute of Technology
IN–Ecublens, 1015 Lausanne, Switzerland
lundell@lia.di.epfl.ch

Abstract

A qualitative model of the spatio-temporal behaviour of distributed parameter systems based on physical fields is presented. Field-based models differ from the object-based models normally used in qualitative physics by treating parameters as continuous entities instead of as attributes of discrete objects. This is especially suitable for natural physical systems, e.g. in ecology. The model is divided into a static and a dynamic part. The static model describes the distribution of each parameter as a qualitative physical field. Composite fields are constructed from intersection models of pairs of fields. The dynamic model describes processes acting on the fields, and qualitative relationships between parameters. Spatio-temporal behaviour is modelled by interacting temporal processes, influencing single points in space, and spatial processes that gradually spread temporal processes over space. We give an example of a qualitative model of a natural physical system and discuss the ambiguities that arise during simulation.

Introduction

Research in qualitative physics has so far mostly focused on lumped parameter models of man-made physical systems, e.g. refrigerators and electrical circuits. A lumped model describes the temporal but not the spatial variation of the parameters within a system.

This paper focuses on distributed parameter models, describing temporal as well as spatial variation. These models are especially appropriate for natural physical systems that have so far received little attention in qualitative physics, e.g. the atmosphere, the ocean and many other environmental and ecological systems.

Scientists often think of distributed parameter systems in terms of physical fields. A physical field describes the spatial distribution of the values of a parameter. Its properties are functions of space coordinates and of time. This view contrasts with the object-based ontology commonly used in qualitative physics, where models are constructed around a set of interacting objects described by several physical parameters. In a distributed parameter system like the atmosphere, there is usually no obvious object structure to associate the parameters with. Instead, with a field-based view, the parameters of the system are seen as evolving patterns determined by the current spatial configuration of values. The patterns are combined spatially as needed to obtain a more complete view of the system, which evolves due to physical processes acting in regions where patterns intersect.

In this paper, we present a qualitative model of the spatio-temporal behaviour of distributed parameter systems based on physical fields. The model is divided into a static and a dynamic part. The static model describes each parameter as a qualitative physical field by dividing space into contiguous regions according to the quantity space of the parameter. The pattern of a field is described by its regions' boundaries and contiguities. Composite fields are constructed from the region boundaries' coincidence and traversal properties within other fields. The dynamic model describes processes acting on the fields and qualitative relationships between the parameters. Processes are triggered by spatial features in individual or composite fields. Spatio-temporal behaviour is modelled by interacting temporal and spatial processes. Temporal processes directly influence single points in space. Spatial processes have an indirect influence by gradually spreading temporal processes over space.

The purpose of the presented model is to support the qualitative methods used by scientists. In some sciences, e.g. ecology, qualitative methods are a necessity, since many processes lack numerical models. One practical example is landscaping, e.g. envisioning the evolution of a planned garden in order to avoid undesirable events (flooding, spreading of weeds, pests, etc). This involves a number of distributed parameters (land elevation, soil quality, seed distribution, etc), whose interaction is seldom described by precise numerical models. In many cases, exact coordinates are also missing. In other sciences, qualitative methods are used as a complement to existing numerical models. One example is weather forecasting, which is carried out in two phases. The first phase, called the objective analysis, is entirely quantitative. Finite-element simulations of partial differential equations are run on huge amounts of observed data, resulting in a map of predicted data. The second phase, called the subjective analysis, is qualitative. The meteorologist analyzes both the observed and predicted data for each parameter by drawing patterns, e.g. isobars and rain regions, on the maps. This time-consuming analysis is carried out without computer support and builds up an "inner weather picture" (Perby 1988), i.e. an understanding of the current atmospheric processes that enables the meteorologist to produce a final forecast. The working methods of scientists can be characterized as qualitative, model-based and diagrammatic, thus touching on three related fields in artificial intelligence.

In the following, after a brief survey of related work, we present the static and dynamic models and a diagrammatic formalism for visualization of qualitative physical fields. We give an example of a qualitative model of a natural physical system and discuss the ambiguities that arise during simulation. We conclude by outlining further work and discussing the main contributions with respect to other research fields.

Related work

In qualitative physics, this research is related to the early work of FROB (Forbus 1983), in the sense that a qualitative physical field resembles a place vocabulary, i.e. a set of contiguous regions where some important property is constant. However, place vocabularies have not previously been used to model individual and composite parameters of natural physical systems. Instead, most qualitative models of natural physical systems are lumped and adopt the object-based ontology. The process-based ontology and the syntax used in our model have been inspired by Qualitative Process Theory (Forbus 1984).

In spatial information theory, there is extensive work on qualitative spatial reasoning. Most approaches describe relations between points and are not applicable to continuous fields. The topological properties of extended regions have been studied by e.g. (Cui, Cohn, & Randell 1992) and (Egenhofer & Al-Taha 1992). However, these approaches focus on pairs of regions and do not explicitly represent the properties and physics of continuous fields.

Geographical information systems provide methods for storage and analysis of large amounts of spatial data. Although these systems are mainly quantitative, they address many issues relevant to this research. In particular, the representation of individual parameter fields and their subsequent combination corresponds to the traditional cartographic technique of map overlay, where transparent maps of different themes are physically combined in order to produce a complete map. Map overlays can be manipulated using the map algebra of (Tomlin 1991), which, however, is not relevant to our purposes since it requires a predefined discretization of space into a grid.

Static model: structure

The static model describes the structure of a distributed parameter system as a set of qualitative physical fields. It consists of a distribution model for each individual field and an intersection model for each pair of fields that are to be combined in a composite field.

Distribution model: individual fields

Each individual parameter is described as a qualitative physical field by a distribution model. A qualitative physical field represents a double discretization:

First, the value domain of the parameter is discretized into a quantity space, i.e. a finite set of symbols called landmark values, representing qualitatively interesting events in the system, e.g. the critical values. A qualitative value either corresponds to a landmark value or to an interval between two landmark values. Representations of quantity spaces have been discussed in e.g. (Forbus 1984) and (Kuipers 1994). They are totally or partially ordered sets, whose values can only be compared for equality or order.

Second, the space of the physical field is discretized into a pattern of contiguous, non-overlapping regions corresponding to the parameter's qualitative values. The regions are maximal in the sense that no region is adjacent to a region with the same value. We represent the continuous pattern of a qualitative physical field by the boundaries and contiguities of its regions.

The boundary number of a region indicates the number of topological holes. Each region has as many internal boundaries as holes, plus one external boundary. The boundaries, in their turn, represent the contiguities of the region, i.e. its adjacencies to other regions. Each boundary is divided into a number of segments, each indicating an adjacency to another region. For two-dimensional regions, with one-dimensional boundaries, the segments can be ordered in a sequence. In three dimensions, the boundaries are themselves two-dimensional regions with boundaries whose segments can be ordered.

Scientists often use diagrammatic methods to reason about distributed parameter systems. Consequently, we have developed a diagrammatic formalism for visualization of qualitative physical fields. The diagrams are deliberately abstract in order to convey only the qualitative properties represented by the model, i.e. the presence of distinct regions, continuity, boundaries and contiguities. This avoids the problematic issue in diagrammatic reasoning that pictorial representations may be interpreted as containing more information than intended (Wang, Lee, & Zeevat 1995).

Figure 1 shows the distribution models of two different fields. The qualitative information in the left-hand pattern is conveyed by the right-hand diagram, where the regions are represented as circles and circle sectors. Internal boundaries are represented by nesting the circles and contiguities by shared perimeters. The unusual shape of the first diagram reflects the inner regions' contiguity with the outside world.

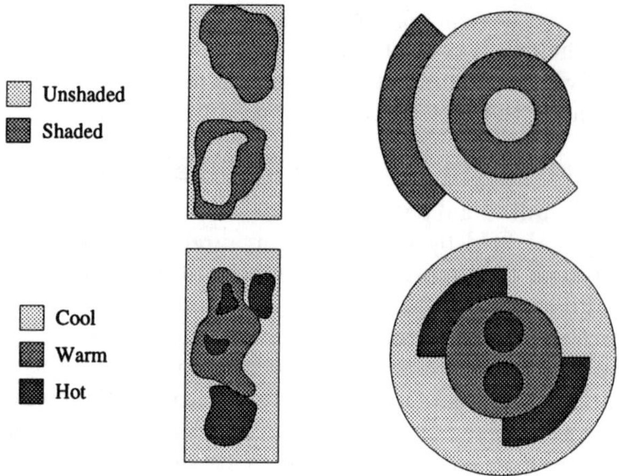

Figure 1: Diagrams of distribution models.

Intersection model: composite fields

A composite field is the spatial combination of two or more fields. It is constructed from intersection models describing the coincidence and traversal properties of the boundaries in each pair of fields to be combined.

For each boundary, the behaviour of its segments within the other field is described. Each segment is divided into an ordered sequence of subsegments representing either coincidence, i.e. a shared path with a subsegment in the other field, or traversal, when the subsegment cuts through a region in the other field.

The intersection model is visualized diagrammatically as indicated in figure 2, corresponding to the physical overlay of the two patterns in figure 1. The subsegments are indicated by small white squares in the diagrams. The mapping between the fields is visualized as a graph. Each subsegment is connected by an edge to either a subsegment (coincidence) or a region (traversal) in the other field. The figure shows a partial mapping. For clarity, the segments in the pattern have been labelled and indicated by arrows.

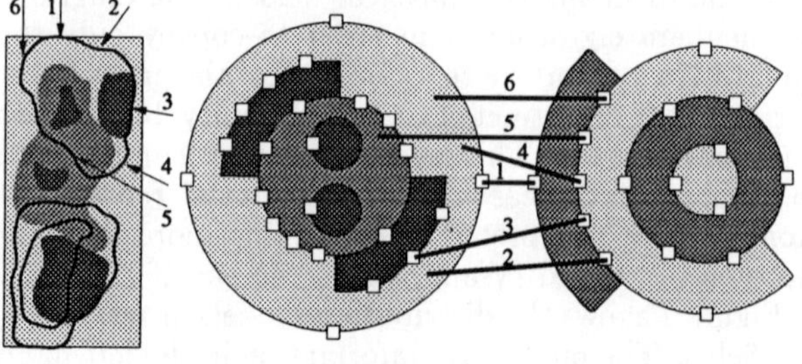

Figure 2: Diagram of intersection model.

Dynamic model: behaviour

The dynamic model describes the behaviour of a distributed parameter system in terms of processes acting on the fields, and qualitative functional relationships between the parameters.

A coherent framework is obtained by letting functional relationships and processes have spatial extent and representing them as physical fields. The regions of applicability are represented by the intersection model of a parameter field and a process or relationship field.

Functional relationships between parameters are described with the vocabulary of Qualitative Process Theory (QPT) (Forbus 1984). We write *(qprop+ parameter1 parameter2)* to indicate the existence of a function that determines the value of *parameter1* and is increasing monotonic in its dependence on *parameter2*. A decreasing monotonic relationship is indicated by *qprop−*.

We follow the ontology of QPT and use processes as the sole mechanism of change. A process is an entity that acts over time to change a parameter. The concept has so far mostly been used in lumped models describing only the temporal progress of the processes. In a distributed model, spatial progress must also be considered. We model spatio-temporal behaviour as an interaction between temporal and spatial processes.

In the following, we discuss the properties of temporal and spatial processes by developing a model of a natural physical system: heat flow in a partially shaded meadow. The system consists of three distributed parameters: irradiaton, shade and temperature. Irradiation indicates the parts of the meadow that could be irradiated by the sun. The irradiation can be considered constant for meadows of normal size, but would have a varying distribution in a model of a larger area, e.g. an entire continent. The shade parameter distinguishes between shaded and unshaded regions, e.g. due to passing clouds or obstructing trees. The dynamic behaviour of the system is modelled by two processes: 1. The temperature will rise in all irradiated regions, but less in shaded regions, 2. A varying temperature distribution will lead to a horizontal flow transporting heat from warmer to cooler regions.

Temporal processes

A temporal process is similar to a QPT process. It selects regions from individual or composite fields and imposes direct influences on their values. A temporal process is represented as a field and acts on each individual point in the selected regions. Since a region is not a fixed object, but can be decomposed with respect to other fields, parts of the region may be influenced by other processes. The process fields are composed in order to determine the net change to the values in the influenced fields and to update the region structures.

We describe temporal processes with a syntax similar to QPT's but adapted to our model as follows:

- The *regions* referred to by the process are specified by pattern templates indicating the following: 1. The name of the region, 2. The individual or composite field to which it belongs, 3. Whether to retrieve an atomic region, which is the default, or a union of contiguous regions, 4. Conditions on values and spatial features. Value conditions compare parameter values, while spatial conditions indicate constraints on boundaries and contiguities. The conditions can refer to other regions by their names. A parameter value is referred to by combining the name of the field and the name of the region.
- The *region-conditions* indicate additional conditions on values and spatial features that could not be expressed earlier. The regions and region-conditions correspond to the individuals, preconditions and quantity-conditions of QPT.
- Names of local *variables*, to be used in the process, are defined.
- The *relations* indicate functional relationships valid during the lifetime of the process. The variables and relations correspond to QPT relations.
- Direct *influences* are specified with QPT syntax. *(I+ parameter variable)* indicates a monotonic increasing influence of the variable on the parameter. *I–* indicates a monotonic decreasing influence.
- The *stop-conditions* indicate conditions on values and spatial features that stop the process.

The following example models the warming of each atomic region in the composite field of irradiation, shade and temperature. The heating-rate is inversely proportional to the amount of shade. The process stops when the irradiation is reduced to zero.

```
temporal-process solar-warming
    :regions          (r :fields        (irradiation shade temp)
                         :atomic        T
                         :conditions (> (irradiation r) zero)
    :variables        heating-rate
    :relations        (qprop– heating-rate (shade r))
    :influences       (I+ (temp r) heating-rate)
    :stop-conditions (<= (irradiation r) zero)
```

Spatial processes

Spatio-temporal behaviour is modelled by interacting spatial and temporal processes.

Spatial processes are different from temporal processes in that they do not act in a single point but gradually spread influences over space, starting from a boundary between two regions. A spatial process is represented as a field with expanding applicability regions, called expansion regions. The segments of the expansion regions correspond to fronts that move at a certain rate. The path of a spatial process can be guided by defining functional relationships between the rates of the fronts and the values of the regions they move through.

A spatial process can change other fields only indirectly by spreading temporal processes. Each expansion region is associated with a temporal process defined as a local variable within the spatial process. These embedded temporal processes do not themselves select a region to act on, but are applied to the points encountered by the fronts of the expansion region. Once applied, a temporal process is activated and decoupled from the spatial process. It obeys its own stop-conditions, which, however, can refer to the local variables of the spatial process.

A spatial process is defined similarly to a temporal process. The main difference lies in the influences. Since parameters are not directly influenced by spatial processes, I+ and I– are not used. Instead, the expansion regions are defined as follows:

```
(E expansion-region from-region to-region
        rate influence stop-conditions)
```

Expansion-region names a local variable for the expansion region. *From-region* and *to-region* define from which boundary and in which direction the region starts expanding at the specified *rate*. *Influence* is the name of an embedded temporal process. The *stop-conditions* for this particular expansion region are indicated. The spatial process can also have global stop-conditions, in analogy with a temporal process, indicating conditions that will stop all expansion regions.

The following example models the second process in our example, horizontal heat flow, which only concerns the temperature field. A spatial process is triggered by adjacent regions of different temperature, *r1* and *r2*. Two local variables, *heating-rate* and *expansion-rate*, are directly proportional to the temperature difference. Two embedded temporal processes are defined, *tp1* and *tp2*, that respectively increase and decrease the temperature at the specified *heating-rate* until the two expansion regions, *ep1* and *ep2*, have equal temperature. The expansion regions are spread into *r1* and *r2* respectively with the specified *expansion-rate*, starting from their common boundary, each applying a temporal process to each passed point. The expansion is defined to stop only when the other region is no longer expanding.

```
spatial-process heat-flow
    :regions    (r1 :fields          temp)
                (r2 :fields          temp
                    :conditions (adjacent? r1 r2)
                                (> (temp r1) (temp r2)))
    :variables heating-rate
               expansion-rate
               (diff (– (temp r1) (temp r2))
               (tp1 (temporal-process heat-flow
                        :influences (I+ temp heating-rate)
                        :stop-conditions (= (temp ep1)
                                            (temp ep2))))
               (tp2 (temporal-process heat-flow
                        :influences (I– temp heating-rate)
                        :stop-conditions (= (temp ep1)
                                            (temp ep2))))
```

```
:relations  (qprop+ expansion-rate diff)
            (qprop+ heating-rate diff)
:influences (E ep1 r1 r2 expansion-rate tp1
                (not (expanding? ep2)))
            (E ep2 r2 r1 expansion-rate tp2
                (not (expanding? ep1)))
```

This example demonstrates a tricky issue with dynamic fields: the identity of a region. The temporal processes must refer to the expansion regions instead of *r1* and *r2*, since the latter cease to exist as distinct regions when the temperature starts changing. The local variable *diff* that is computed from the values of these regions must thus be considered as constant during the lifetime of the process.

This example gives a flavour of the qualitative aspects of natural physical systems that can be modelled. It can be extended with fields describing e.g. the distribution of different kinds of seeds, water availability, soil conditions, etc. Compositions of these parameters indicate varying living conditions, and can be used to model different ecological systems.

Qualitative simulation: ambiguity

The purpose of a qualitative simulation is to describe the evolution of a system as a sequence of qualitatively interesting states. In lumped models, a new state is generated each time a parameter reaches a significant landmark value, called a limit point in QPT.

We use the same technique, but additionally consider spatial limit points that are reached when the structure of the system changes. The change can either concern a distribution model or an intersection model. One example is when a region reaches the same value as one of its neighbours due to an influencing temporal process. Since all regions must be maximal, the two regions will be merged into one, thus changing the distribution model. Another spatial limit point is when an expansion region crosses a boundary in another field, which entails a change to the intersection model of the process field and the parameter field.

Since qualitative models use incomplete information, ambiguities can arise when the next limit point is to be determined. Our model inherits the ambiguities of lumped qualitative models, which can be divided into value ambiguities, e.g. deciding whether the difference of two qualitative values is less or greater than a third value, and temporal ambiguities, e.g. deciding which of two changing parameters will next reach a limit point. Distributed qualitative models additionally have spatial ambiguities, which in our case arise when determining in which order spatial limit points will be encountered by an expansion region.

In lumped qualitative models, a tree of behaviours can be generated when there is a known number of alternatives for each ambiguity. This is not the case for distributed qualitative models lacking shape information. Figure 3 shows an example of two fields whose regions have the same qualitative structure but different shapes. The shaded region is a single expansion region, in a separate spatial process field, that gradually spreads from region A into region B. At the instant indicated in the figure, the expansion region's boundary traverses region C twice in the first field, but only once in the second. The intersection model of the spatial process field and the parameter field thus cannot be unambiguously established within the framework of the qualitatative model, nor is there a known number of alternatives since region C could be of arbitrary shape.

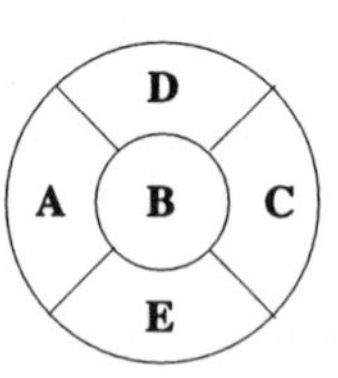

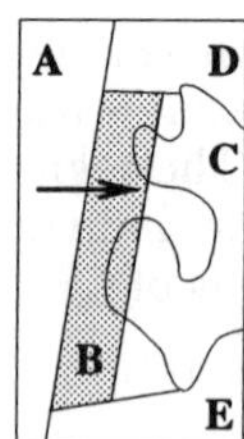

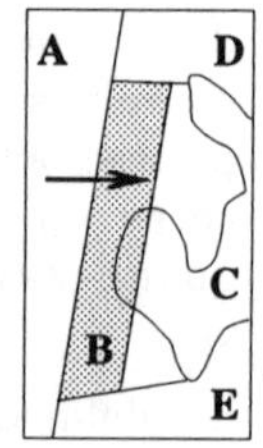

Figure 3: Fields with identical qualitative structure. The grey region is a superimposed single expansion region spreading in the indicated direction.

The existence of spatial ambiguities means that our approach does not provide a general solution to the poverty conjecture of (Forbus, Nielsen, & Faltings 1987) stating that qualitative spatial reasoning requires a metric diagram conveying shape information. However, the poverty conjecture originated in reasoning about objects in small-scale space, e.g. gearwheels, where the coordinates of the metric diagram can be obtained. We argue that qualitative spatial reasoning based on topological and ordinal information is useful for a different kind of situation, where the initial metric data is sparse or incomplete, e.g. in the form of scattered observation points. In these situations, both quantitative and qualitative simulations have to rely on assumptions and simplifications.

In the case of scientists analyzing their data, we hypothesize that intractable ambiguities, like shape, are simplified to a known number of alternatives at a cognitive level, which makes it possible to use the envisioning techniques of qualitative reasoning. We believe this is done by assuming a non-complex spatial configuration, given the known qualitative constraints, as well as a non-complex spatial evolution of the system. Note that this does not mean assuming convex or regular regions, since a continuous field, unless it is a grid, must necessarily contain concave and irregular regions.

Based on this hypothesis, the qualitative simulation algorithm generates an envisionment as a sequence of diagrams differing in as few spatial features as possible. Figure 4 shows a non-complex behaviour of the initial situation in figure 3, generated from a few simple complexity-reducing heuristics. The shaded regions indicate the intersection of the field with a single expansion region as it spreads gradually from region A into region B. In the first diagram, only B is partially covered. The least complex transition to the next state is assuming that the immediate neighbours of B are reached, i.e. D and E. In the next state, B is completely covered and C has been reached. The final least complex transition is to the state where regions B, C, D, and E are entirely covered by the expansion region. The rules governing the simulation algorithm are described in detail in (Lundell 1995).

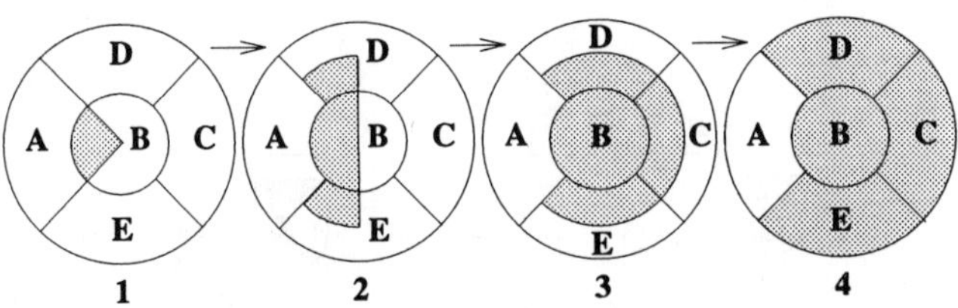

Figure 4: Qualitative simulation as a sequence of diagrams describing one possible non-complex evolution.

Conclusion

The main contributions of the research described in this paper, with respect to related research fields, can be summarized as follows:

- Qualitative physics: We introduce the concept of a qualitative physical field, describing a physical system in terms of parameters instead of objects. A technique for modelling spatio-temporal behaviour and a language for spatial processes are presented.
- Spatial information theory: We do not limit ourselves to pairs of regions, but describe the qualitative properties of continuous fields containing many regions. Spatial features are not only described topologically, but also with ordinal information suitable for qualitative analysis.
- Geographic information systems: We present a qualitative alternative to the quantitative techniques for representation and simulation of spatial data used in current systems. Qualitative methods are advantageous in situations with incomplete spatial data that cannot be satisfactorily represented in a quantitative system.

Distributed parameter systems have several additional features that can be exploited in qualitative reasoning. We are currently working on a number of related issues:

- Extending the qualitative physical fields with regions describing not only point-wise parameters but also amounts, averages and totals. This will also entail extensions to the process language.
- Representation of gradients of regions that are not described by a constant value but by an interval. This requires imposing a direction on the variation of values within a region and developing techniques for compositions of gradient fields.
- Automatic generation of qualitative models from sparse metric data in the form of scattered observation points. Triangulation techniques and Voronoi diagrams combined with heuristics are a possible solution. Preliminary results have been presented in (Lundell 1994).
- Extending the model with ordinal information on the sizes of spatial features. This would make it possible to model processes at different scales, and also to eliminate some of the spatial ambiguities. This technique has been used in a qualitative model of gradient flow presented in (Lundell 1995).

References

Cui, Z.; Cohn, A. G.; and Randell, D. A. 1992. Qualitative simulation based on a logical formalism of space and time. In *AAAI*, 679–684.

Egenhofer, M., and Al-Taha, K. 1992. Reasoning about gradual changes of topological relationships. In *Theories and Methods of Spatio-Temporal Reasoning in Geographic Space*. Springer-Verlag. 196–219.

Forbus, K.; Nielsen, P.; and Faltings, B. 1987. Qualitative kinematics: A framework. In *AAAI*, 430–436.

Forbus, K. 1983. Qualitative reasoning about space and motion. In *Mental Models*. Lawrence Erlbaum. 53–73.

Forbus, K. 1984. Qualitative process theory. *Artificial Intelligence* 24:85–168.

Kuipers, B. 1994. *Qualitative Reasoning: Modelling and Simulation with Incomplete Knowledge*. MIT Press.

Lundell, M. 1994. Qualitative reasoning with spatially distributed parameters. In *Eighth International Workshop on Qualitative Reasoning about Physical Systems*.

Lundell, M. 1995. A qualitative model of gradient flow in a spatially distributed parameter. In *Ninth International Workshop on Qualitative Reasoning about Physical Systems*.

Perby, M.-L. 1988. Computerization and skill in local weather forecasting. In *Knowledge, Skill and Artificial Intelligence*. Springer-Verlag. 39–52.

Tomlin, C. D. 1991. Cartographic modelling. In *Geographical information systems: principles and applications*. Longman. 361–374.

Wang, D.; Lee, J.; and Zeevat, H. 1995. Reasoning with diagrammatic representations. In *Diagrammatic Reasoning, Cognitive and Computational Perspectives*. AAAI Press. 339–401.

Generating Multiple New Designs From a Sketch

Thomas F. Stahovich, Randall Davis, Howard Shrobe*
MIT Artificial Intelligence Laboratory
545 Technology Square
Cambridge, MA 02139
stahov@ai.mit.edu

Abstract

We describe a program called SKETCHIT that transforms a single sketch of a mechanical device into multiple families of new designs. It represents each of these families with a "BEP-Model," a parametric model augmented with constraints that ensure the device produces the desired behavior. The program is based on qualitative configuration space (qc-space), a novel representation that captures mechanical behavior while abstracting away its implementation. The program employs a paradigm of abstraction and resynthesis: it abstracts the initial sketch into qc-space then maps from qc-space to new implementations.

Introduction

SKETCHIT is a computer program capable of taking a single sketch of a mechanical design and generalizing it to produce multiple new designs. The program takes as input a stylized sketch of the original design and a description of the desired behavior and from this generates multiple families of new designs.

It does this by first transforming the sketch into a representation that captures the behavior of the original design while abstracting away its particular implementation. The program then maps from this abstract representation to multiple new families of implementations. This representation, which we call qualitative configuration space, is the key tool allowing SKETCHIT to perform its tasks.

The program represents each of the new families of implementations with what we call a behavior ensuring parametric model ("BEP-Model"): a parametric model augmented with constraints that ensure the geometry produces the desired behavior.[1] Our program takes as input a single sketch of a device and produces as output multiple BEP-Models, each of which will produce the desired behavior.

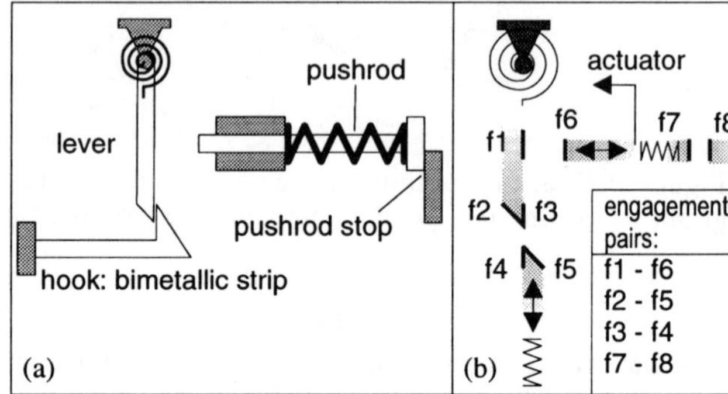

Figure 1: (a) One structure for the circuit breaker. (b) Sketch as actually input to program. Engagement faces are in bold. The actuator represents the reset motion imparted by the user. (Labels for engagement pairs: (f1 f6)=push-pair, (f2 f5)=cam-follower, (f3 f4)=lever-stop, (f7 f8)=pushrod-stop.)

We use the design of a circuit breaker to illustrate the program in operation; one implementation is shown in Figure 1a. In normal use, current flows from the lever to the hook; current overload causes the bimetallic hook to heat and bend, releasing the lever and interrupting the current flow. After the hook cools, pressing and releasing the pushrod resets the device.

The designer describes the circuit breaker to SKETCHIT with the stylized sketch shown in Figure 1b, using line segments for part faces and icons for springs, joints, and actuators. SKETCHIT is concerned only with the *functional geometry*, i.e., the faces where parts meet and through which force and motion are transmitted (lines f1–f8). The designer's task is thus to indicate which pairs of faces are intended to engage each other. Consideration of the connective geometry (the surfaces that connect the functional geometry to make complete solids) is put off until later in the design process.

The designer describes the desired behavior of a device to SKETCHIT using a state transition diagram (Figure 2b). Each node in the diagram is a list of the pairs of faces that are engaged and the springs that are

*Support for this project was provided by the Advanced Research Projects Agency of the Department of Defense under Office of Naval Research contract N00014-91-J-4038.

[1]A parametric model is a geometric model in which the shapes are controlled by a set of parameters.

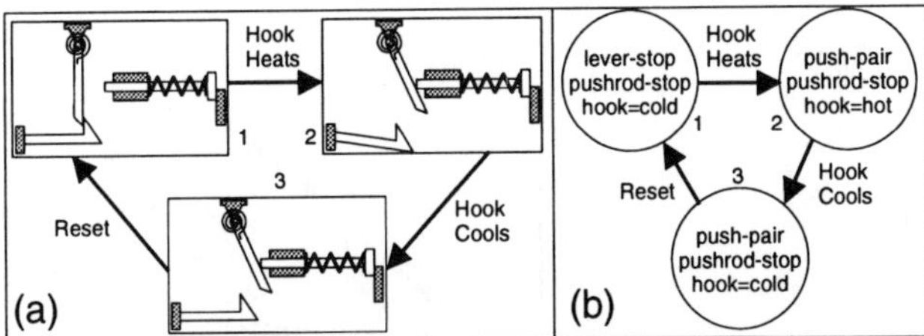

Figure 2: The desired behavior of the circuit breaker. (a) Physical interpretation. (b) State transition diagram. In each of the three states, the hook is either at its hot or cold neutral position.

relaxed. The arcs are the external inputs that drive the device. Figure 2b, for instance, describes how the circuit breaker should behave in the face of heating and cooling the hook and pressing the reset pushrod.

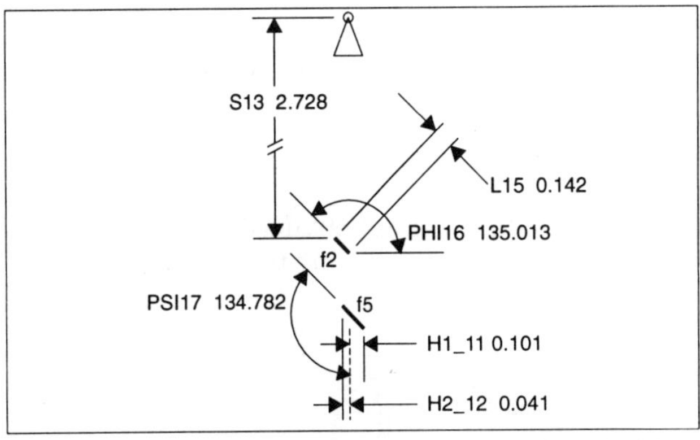


```
H1_11 > 0           H2_12 > 0           S13 > H1_11
L15 > 0             PHI16 > 90          PHI16 < 180
PSI17 > 90          PSI17 < 180
0 > R14/TAN(PSI17) + H2_12/SIN(PSI17)
R14 = SQRT(S13^2 + L15^2 - 2*S13*L15*COS(PHI16))
```

Figure 3: Output from the program (a BEP-Model). Top: the parametric model; the decimal number next to each parameter is the current value of that parameter. Bottom: the constraints on the parameters. For clarity, only the parameters and constraints for faces f2 and f5 are shown.

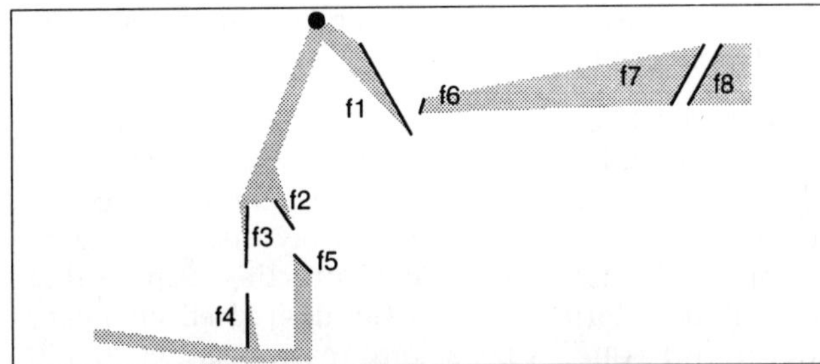

Figure 4: Another solution to the BEP-Model of Figure 3. Shading indicates how the faces might be connected to flesh out the components. This solution shows that neither the pair of faces at the end of the lever nor the pair of faces at the end of the hook need be contiguous.

Figure 3 shows a portion of one of the BEP-models that SKETCHIT derives in this case. The top of the figure shows the parameters that define the sloped face on the lever (f2) and the sloped face on the hook (f5). The bottom shows the constraints that ensure this pair of faces plays its role in achieving the overall desired behavior: i.e., moving the lever clockwise pushes the hook down until the lever moves past the point of the hook, whereupon the hook springs back to its rest position. As one example of how the constraints enforce the desired behavior, the ninth equation, `0 > R14/TAN(PSI17) + H2_12/SIN(PSI17)`, constrains the geometry so that the contact point on face f2 never moves tangent to face f5. This in turn ensures that when the two faces are engaged, clockwise rotation of the lever always increases the deflection of the hook.

The parameter values shown in the top of Figure 3 are solutions to the constraints of the BEP-Model, hence this particular geometry provides the desired behavior. These specific values were computed by a program called DesignView, a commercial parametric modeler based on variational geometry. Using DesignView, we can easily explore the family of designs defined by this BEP-Model. Figure 4, for example, shows another solution to this BEP-Model. Because these parameter values satisfy the BEP-Model, even this rather unusual geometry provides the desired behavior. As this example illustrates, the family of designs defined by a BEP-Model includes a wide range of design solutions, many of which would not be obtained with conventional approaches.

Figures 3 and 4 show members of just one of the families of designs that the program produces for the circuit breaker. SKETCHIT produces other families of designs (i.e., other BEP-Models) by selecting different motion types (rotation or translation) for the components and by selecting different implementations for the pairs of interacting faces. For example, Figure 5 shows a design obtained by selecting a new motion type for the lever: in the original design the lever rotates, here it translates. Figure 6 shows an example of selecting different implementations for the pairs of interacting faces: In the original implementation of the cam-follower engagement pair, the motion of face f2 is roughly perpendicular to the motion of face f5; in the new design of Figure 6, the motions are parallel.

Representation: QC-Space

SKETCHIT's approach to its task is use a representation that captures the behavior of the original design while abstracting away the particular implementation, providing the opportunity to select new implementations.

For the class of devices that SKETCHIT is concerned with, the overall behavior is achieved through a sequence of interactions between pairs of engagement faces. Hence the behavior that our representation must capture is the behavior of interacting faces.

Our search for a representation began with configu-

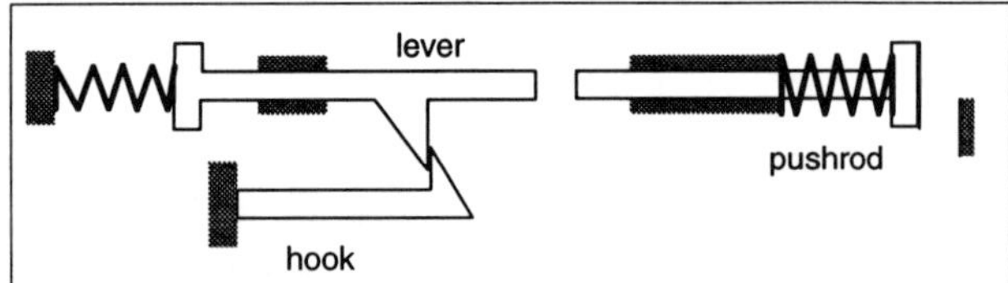

Figure 5: A design variant obtained by replacing the rotating lever with a translating part.

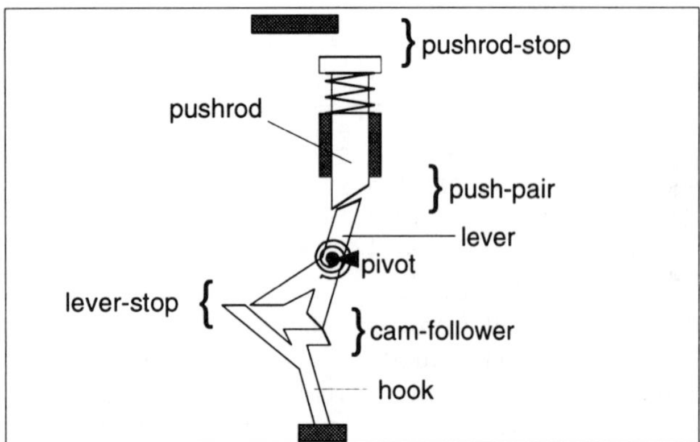

Figure 6: A design variant obtained by using different implementations for the engagement faces. The pushrod is pressed so that the hook is just on the verge of latching the lever.

ration space (c-space), which is commonly used to represent this kind of behavior. Although c-space is capable of representing the behaviors we are interested in, it does not adequately abstract away their implementations. We discovered that abstracting c-space into a qualitative form produces the desired effect; hence we call SKETCHIT's behavioral representation "qualitative configuration space" (qc-space).

This section begins with a brief description of c-space, then describes how we abstract c-space to produce qc-space.

C-Space

Consider the rotor and slider in Figure 7. If the angle of the rotor U_R and the position of the slider U_S are as shown, the faces on the two bodies will touch. These values of U_R and U_S are termed a *configuration* of the bodies in which the faces touch, and can be represented as a point in the plane, called a configuration space plane (cs-plane).

If we determine all of the configurations of the bodies in which the faces touch and plot the corresponding points in the cs-plane (Figure 7), we get a curve, called a configuration space curve (cs-curve). The shaded region "behind" the curve indicates blocked space, configurations in which one body would penetrate the other. The unshaded region "in front" of the curve represents free space, configurations in which the faces do not touch.

The axes of a c-space are the position parameters of the bodies; the dimension of the c-space for a set

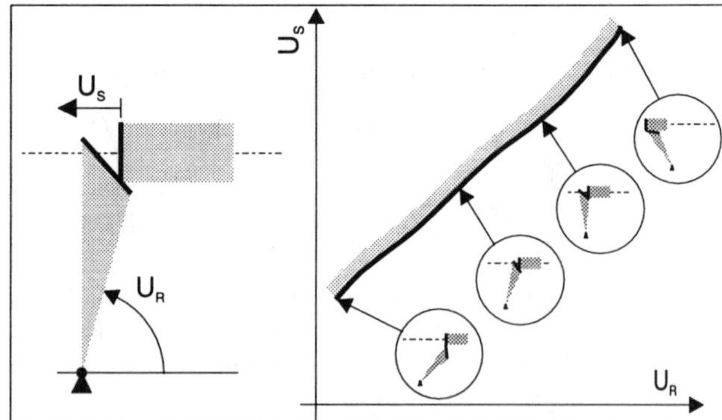

Figure 7: Left: A rotor and slider. The slider translates horizontally. The interacting faces are shown with bold lines. Right: The c-space. The inset figures show the configuration of the rotor and slider for selected points on the cs-curve.

of bodies is the number of degrees of freedom of the set. To simplify geometric reasoning in c-space, we assume that devices are fixed-axis. That is, we assume that each body either translates along a fixed axis or rotates about a fixed axis. Hence in our world the c-space for a pair of bodies will always be a plane (a cs-plane) and the boundary between blocked and free space will always be a curve (a cs-curve).[2] However, even in this world, a device may be composed of many fixed-axis bodies, hence the c-space for the device as a whole can be of dimension greater than two. The individual cs-planes are orthogonal projections of the multi-dimensional c-space of the overall device.

Abstracting to QC-Space

C-space is already an abstraction of the original design. For example, any pair of faces that produces the cs-curve in Figure 7 will produce the same behavior (i.e., the same dynamics), as the original pair of faces. Thus, each cs-curve represents a family of interacting faces that all produce the same behavior.

We can, however, identify a much larger family of faces that produce the same behavior by abstracting the numerical cs-curves to obtain a qualitative c-space. In qualitative c-space (qc-space) we represent cs-curves by their qualitative slopes and the locations of the curves relative to one another. By qualitative slope we mean the obvious notion of labeling monotonic curves as diagonal (with positive or negative slope), vertical, or horizontal; by relative location we mean relative location of the curve end points.[3]

To see how qualitative slope captures something essential about the behavior, we return to the rotor and

[2]The c-space for a pair of fixed-axis bodies will always be 2-dimensional. However, it is possible for the c-space to be a cylinder or torus rather than a plane. See Section "Selecting Motion Type" for details.

[3]We restrict qcs-curves to be monotonic to facilitate qualitative simulation of a qc-space.

slider. The essential behavior of this device is that the slider can push the rotor: positive displacement of the slider causes positive displacement of the rotor, and vice versa. If the motions of the rotor and slider are to be related in this fashion, their cs-curve must be a diagonal curve with positive slope. Conversely, any geometry that maps to a diagonal curve with positive slope will produce the same kind of pushing behavior as the original design.

Their are eight types of qualitative cs-curves, shown in Figure 10. Diagonal curves always correspond to pushing behavior; vertical and horizontal curves correspond to what we call "stop behavior," in which the extent of motion of one part is limited by the position of another.

The key, more general, insight here is that *for monotonic cs-curves, the qualitative slopes and the relative locations completely determine the first order dynamics of the device.* By first order dynamics we mean the dynamic behavior obtained when the motion is assumed to be inertia-free and the collisions are assumed to be inelastic and frictionless.[4] The consequence of this general insight is that qc-space captures *all* of the relevant physics of the overall device, and hence serves as a design space for behavior. It is a particularly convenient design space because it has only two properties: qualitative slope and relative location.

Another important feature of qc-space is that it is constructed from a very small number of building blocks, viz., the different types of qcs-curves in Figure 10. As a consequence we can easily map from qc-space back to implementation using precomputed implementations for each of the building blocks. We show how to do this in Section "Selecting Geometries."

The SKETCHIT System

Figure 8 shows a flow chart of the SKETCHIT system with its two main processes: abstraction and resynthesis.

Abstraction Process

SKETCHIT uses generate and test to abstract the initial design into one or more working qc-spaces, i.e., qc-spaces that provide the behavior specified in the state transition diagram.

The generator produces multiple candidate qc-spaces from the sketch, each of which is a possible interpretation of the sketch. The simulator computes each candidate's overall behavior (i.e., the aggregate behavior of all of the individual interactions), which the tester then compares to the desired behavior.

The generator begins by computing the numerical c-space of the sketch, then abstracts each numerical cs-curve into a qcs-curve, i.e., a curve with qualitative slope and relative location.

As with any abstraction process, moving from specific numerical curves to qualitative curves can introduce ambiguities. For example, in the candidate qc-space in Figure 9 there is ambiguity in the relative location of the abscissa value (E) for the intersection between the push-pair curve and the pushrod-stop curve. This value is not ordered with respect to B and C, the abscissa values of the end points of the lever-stop and cam-follower curves in the hook-lever qcs-plane: E may be less than B, greater than C, or between B and C.[5]

Physically, point E is the configuration in which the lever is against the pushrod and the pushrod is against its stop; the ambiguity is whether in this particular configuration the lever is (a) to the left of the hook (i.e., E < B) (b) contacting the hook (i.e., B < E < C), or (c) to the right of the hook (i.e., C < E). When the generator encounters this kind of ambiguity, it enumerates all possible interpretations, passing each of them to the simulator.

The relative locations of these points are not ambiguous in the original, numerical c-space. Nevertheless, SKETCHIT computes all possible relative locations, rather than taking the actual locations directly from the numerical c-space. One reason for this is that it offers one means of generalizing the design: The original locations may be just one of the possible working designs; the program can find others by enumerating and testing all the possible relative locations.

A second reason the program enumerates and tests all possible relative locations is because this enables it to compensate for flaws in the original sketch. These flaws arise from interactions that are individually correct, but whose global arrangement is incorrect. For example, in Figure 1b the interaction between the lever and hook, the interaction between the pushrod and the lever, and the interaction between the pushrod and its stop may all be individually correct, but the pushrod-stop may be sketched too far to the left, so that the lever always remains to the left of the hook

[4] "Inertia-free" refers to the circumstance in which the inertia terms in the equations of motion are negligible compared to the other terms. One important property of inertia-free motion is that there are no oscillations. This set of physical assumptions is also called quasi-statics.

[5] We do not consider the case where E = B or E = C.

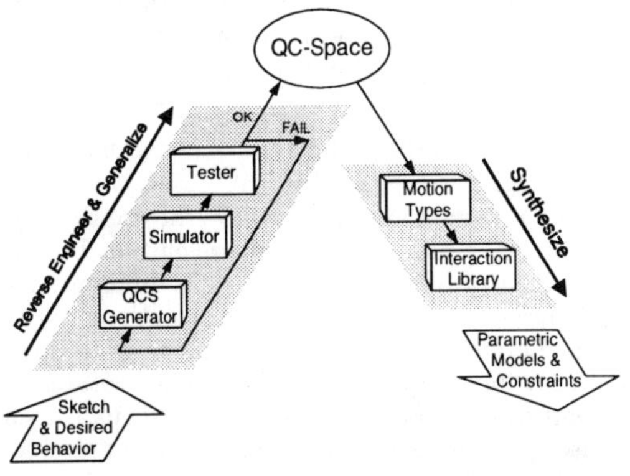

Figure 8: Overview of SKETCHIT system.

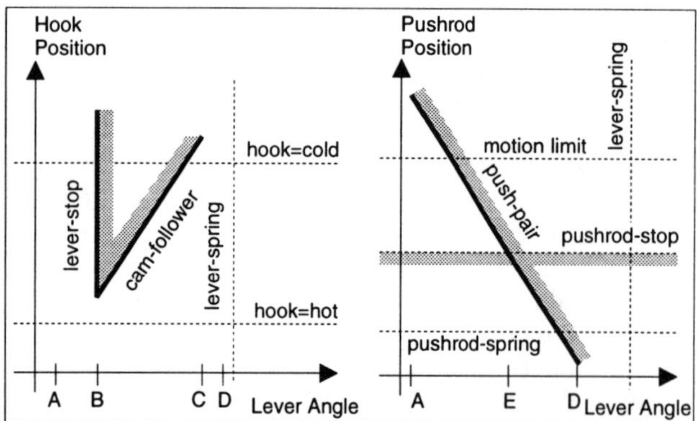

Figure 9: Candidate qc-space for the circuit breaker.

(i.e., the global arrangement of these three interactions prevents the lever from actually interacting with the hook.) By enumerating possible locations for the intersection between the pushrod-stop and push-pair qcs-curves, SKETCHIT will correct this flaw in the original sketch.

Currently, the candidate qc-spaces the generator produces are possible interpretations of ambiguities inherent in the abstraction. The simulator and tester identify which of these interpretations produce the desired behavior. We are also working on repairing more serious flaws in the original sketch, as we describe in the Future Work section.

SKETCHIT employs an innovative qualitative simulator designed to minimize branching of the simulation. See [12] for a detailed presentation of the simulator.

Re-Synthesis

In the resynthesis process, the program turns each of the working qc-spaces into multiple families of new designs. Each family is represented by a BEP-Model.

Qc-space abstracts away both the motion type of each part and the geometry of each pair of interacting faces. Hence there are two steps to the resynthesis process: selecting a motion type for each part and selecting a geometry for each pair of engagement faces.

Selecting Motion Type SKETCHIT is free to select a new motion type for each part because qc-space abstracts away this property. More precisely, qc-space abstracts away the motion type of parts that translate and parts that rotate less than a full revolution.[6]

Changing translating parts to rotating ones, and vice versa, permits SKETCHIT to generate a rich assortment of new designs.

Selecting Geometries The general task of translating from *c-space* to geometry is intractable ([1]). However, *qc-space* is carefully designed to be constructed from a small number of basic building blocks, 40 in all. The origin of 32 of these can be seen by examining Figure 10: there are four choices of qualitative slope; for each qualitative slope there are two choices for blocked space; and the qc-space axes q_1 and q_2 can represent either rotation or translation. The other 8 building blocks represent interactions of rotating or translating bodies with stationary bodies.

Because there are only a small number of basic building blocks, we were able to construct a library of implementations for each building block. To translate a qc-space to geometry, the program selects an entry from the library for each of the qcs-curves.

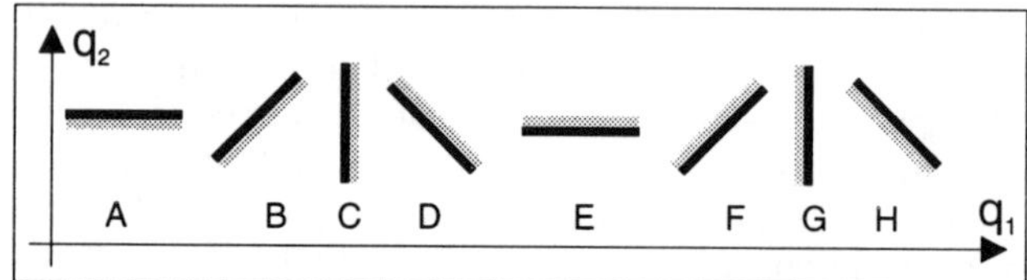

Figure 10: For drawing convenience, qcs-curves are shown as straight line segments; they can have any shape as long as they are monotonic.

Each library entry contains a pair of parameterized faces and a set of constraints that ensure that the faces implement a monotonic cs-curve of the desired slope, with the desired choice of blocked space. Each library entry also contains algebraic expressions for the end point coordinates of the cs-curve.

For example, Figure 11 shows a library entry for qcs-curve F in Figure 10, for the case in which q_1 is rotation and q_2 is translation. For the corresponding qcs-curve to be monotonic, have the correct slope, and have blocked space on the correct side, the following ten constraints must be satisfied:

$$w > 0 \qquad L > 0 \qquad h > 0$$
$$s < h \qquad r > h \qquad \pi/2 < \phi \leq \pi$$
$$\psi > 0 \qquad \psi < \arcsin(h/r) + \pi/2$$
$$\arccos(h/r) + \arccos\left(\frac{L^2+r^2-s^2}{2Lr}\right) < \pi/2$$
$$r = (s^2 + L^2 - 2sL\cos(\phi))^{1/2}$$

The end point coordinates of the cs-curve are:

$$\theta_1 = \arcsin(h/r) \qquad x_1 = -r\cos(\theta_1)$$
$$\theta_2 = \pi - \arcsin(h/r) \qquad x_2 = -r\cos(\theta_2)$$

Figure 12 shows a second way to generate qcs-curve F, using the constraints:

$$h_1 > 0 \qquad h_2 > 0$$
$$s > h_1 \qquad L > 0$$
$$\pi/2 < \phi < \pi \qquad \pi/2 < \psi < \pi$$
$$0 > r/\tan(\psi) + h_2/\sin(\psi) \qquad r = (s^2 + L^2 - 2sL\cos(\phi))^{1/2}$$

The end point coordinates of this cs-curve are:

[6] Qc-space cannot abstract away the motion type of parts that rotate more than a full revolution because the topology of the qc-space for such parts is different: If one of a pair of parts rotates through full revolutions, its motion will be 2π periodic, and what was a plane in qc-space will become a cylinder. (If both of the bodies rotate through full revolutions the qc-space becomes a torus.) Hence, if a pairwise qc-space is a cylinder or torus, the design must employ rotating parts (one for a cylinder, two for a toroid) rather than translating ones.

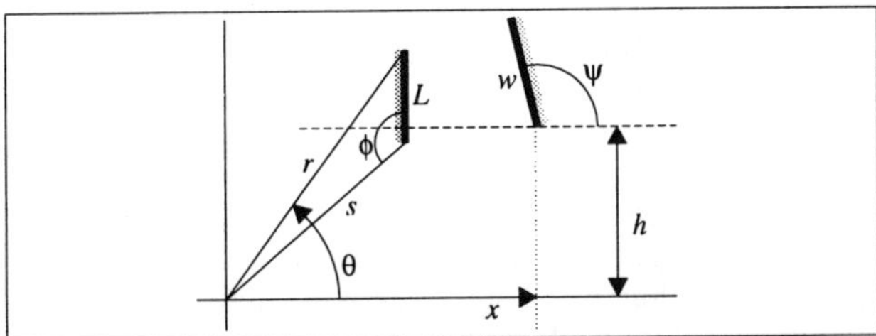

Figure 11: The two faces are shown as thick lines. The rotating face rotates about the origin; the translating face translates horizontally. θ is the angle of the rotor and x, measured positive to the *left*, is the position of the slider.

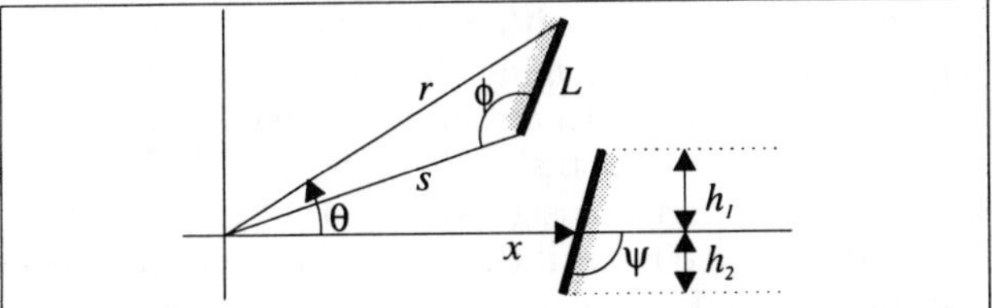

Figure 12: The two faces are shown as thick lines. The rotating face rotates about the origin; the translating face translates horizontally. θ is the angle of the rotor and x, measured positive to the *left*, is the position of the slider.

$$\theta_1 = -\arcsin(h_2/r)$$
$$x_1 = -r\cos(\theta_1) + h_2/\tan(\psi)$$
$$\theta_2 = \arcsin(h_1/s) + \arccos(\frac{s^2+r^2-L^2}{2sr})$$
$$x_2 = -s\cos(\arcsin(h_1/s)) - h_1/\tan(\psi)$$

In the first of these designs the motion of the slider is approximately parallel to the motion of the rotor, while in the second the motion of the slider is approximately perpendicular to the motion of the rotor.[7] The two designs thus represent qualitatively different implementations for the same qcs-curve.

To generate a BEP-Model for the sketch, we select from the library an implementation for each qcs-curve. For each selection we create new instances of the parameters and transform the coordinate systems to match those used by the actual components. The relative locations of the qcs-curves in the qc-space are turned into constraints on the end points of the qcs-curves. We assemble the parametric geometry fragments and constraints of the library selections to produce the parametric model and constraints of the BEP-Model.

Our library contains geometries that use flat faces, although we have begun work on using circular faces.[8] We have at least one library entry for each of the 40 kinds of interactions. We are continuing to generate new entries.

SKETCHIT is able to produce different BEP-Models (i.e., different families of designs) by selecting different library entries for a given qcs-curve. For example, Figure 4 shows a solution to the BEP-Model SKETCHIT generates by selecting the library entry in Figure 12 for the cam-follower qcs-curve. Figure 6 shows a solution to a different BEP-Model SKETCHIT generates by selecting the library entry in Figure 11 for the cam-follower. As these examples illustrate, the program can generate a wide variety of solutions by selecting different library entries.

Refining a Concept

As we have noted, the constraints in each BEP-Model represent the range of values that the geometric parameters can take on, and still provide the behavior originally specified. The constraints thus define an entire family of solutions a designer can explore in order to adapt an initial conceptual design to meet additional design requirements.

We illustrate this with a new example concerning the design of the yoke and rotor device shown in Figure 13a. Continuous counter-clockwise rotation of the rotor causes the yoke to oscillate left and right with a brief dwell between each change in direction.

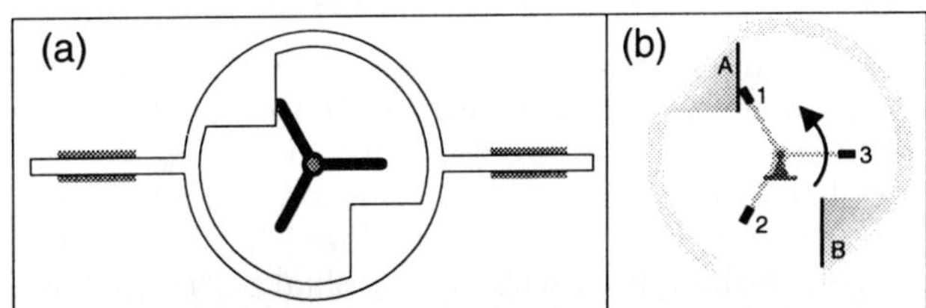

Figure 13: The yoke and rotor device. (a) Structure. (b) Stylized sketch. Each of the rotor faces is intended to engage each of the yoke faces.

We describe the device to SKETCHIT with the stylized sketch in Figure 13b. The desired behavior is to have each of the rotor blades engage each of the yoke faces in turn. From this input SKETCHIT generates the BEP-Model in Figure 14.

The designer now has available the large family of designs specified by the BEP-model and can at this point begin to specify additional design requirements.

Imagine that one requirement is that all strokes have the same length. A simple way to achieve this is to constrain the yoke and rotor to be symmetric. We do this by adding additional constraints to the BEP-Model, such as the following which constrain the rotor blades to be of equal length and have equal spacing: $R1 = R2 = R3$, $AOFF1 - AOFF2 = 120°$, $AOFF3 - AOFF1 = 120°$

Imagine further that all strokes are required to be 1.0cm long. We achieve this by adding the additional constraint:[9] $LM29 - LM27 = 1.0$

[7]The first design is a cam with offset follower, the second is a cam with centered follower.

[8]Circular faces are used when rotors act as stops.

[9]$LM29$ and $LM27$ are variables that SKETCHIT assigns to the extreme positions of the yoke. We obtain the names of these variables by using a graphical browser to inspect SKETCHIT's simulation of the device. Because we have

```
PHI <= 180              PHI > 90                    R > H
H > 0                   L > 0                       W > 0
PSI < 0                 PSI < ASIN(H/R)+90
ACOS(H/R) + ACOS((L^2 + R^2 - S^2)/(2*L*R)) < 90
```

Figure 14: Sample constraints from the yoke and rotor's BEP-Model; For simplicity, new variable names have been substituted for sets of variables constrained to be equal. For example, because all three rotor blades are constrained to have equal length, R replaces $R1$, $R2$, and $R3$.

Finally, imagine that the dwell is required to be 40°, i.e., between each stroke, the rotor turns 40° while the yoke remains stationary. We can achieve this by adding one additional constraint: $LMG - LM8 = 40°$

We can now invoke DesignView to find a solution to this augmented set of constraints; the solution will be guaranteed to produce both the designed behavior and the desired performance characteristics. We have been able to do this design refinement simply by adding additional constraints to the BEP-Model.

RELATED WORK

Our techniques can be viewed as a natural complement to the bond graph techniques of the sort developed in [15]. Our techniques are useful for computing geometry that provides a specified behavior, but because of the inertia-free assumption employed by our simulator, our techniques are effectively blind to energy flow. Bond graph techniques, on the other hand, explicitly represent energy flow but are incapable of representing geometry.

Our techniques focus on the geometry of devices which have time varying engagements (i.e., variable kinematic topology). Therefore, our techniques are complementary to the well know design techniques for fixed topology mechanisms, such as the gear train and linkage design techniques in [3].

There has been a lot of recent interest in automating the design of fixed topology devices. A common task is the synthesis of a device which transforms a specified input motion to a specified output motion ([10], [14] [16]). For the most part, these techniques synthesize a design using an abstract representation of behavior, then use library lookup to map to implementation. However, because our library contains interacting faces, while theirs contain complete components, we can design interacting geometry, while they cannot. Like SKETCHIT, these techniques produce design variants.

To construct new implementations (BEP-Models), we map from qc-space to geometry. [8] and [1] have also explored the problem of mapping between c-space and geometry. They obtain a geometry that maps to a desired c-space by using numerical techniques to directly modify the shapes of parts. However, we map from qc-space to geometry using library lookup.

Our work is similar in spirit to research exploring the mapping from shape to behavior. [9] uses kinematic tolerance space (an extension of c-space) to examine how variations in the shapes of parts affect their kinematic behavior. Their task is to determine how a variation in shape affects behavior, ours is to determine what constraints on shape are sufficient to ensured the desired behavior. [5] examines how much a single geometric parameter can change, all others held constant, without changing the place vocabulary (topology of c-space). Their task is to determine how much a given parameter can change without altering the current behavior, ours is to determine the constraints on all the parameters sufficient to obtain a desired behavior.

More similar to our task is the work in [6]. They describe an interactive design system that modifies user selected parameters until there is a change in the place vocabulary, and hence a change in behavior. Then, just as we do, they use qualitative simulation to determine if the resulting behavior matches the desired behavior. They modify c-space by modifying geometry, we modify qc-space directly. They do a form of generalization by generating constraints capturing how the current geometry implements the place vocabulary; we generalize further by constructing constraints that define new geometries. Finally, our tool is intended to generate design variants while theirs is not.

Our work builds upon the research in qualitative simulation, particularly, the work in [4], [7], and [11]. Our techniques for computing motion are similar to the constraint propagation techniques in [13].

FUTURE WORK

As Section "Abstraction Process" described, the current SKETCHIT system can repair a limited range of flaws in the original sketch. We are continuing to work on techniques for repairing more serious kinds of flaws.

Because there are only two properties in qc-space that matter — the relative locations and the qualitative slopes of the qcs-curves, to repair a sketch, even one with serious flaws, the task is to find the correct relative locations and qualitative slopes for the qcs-curves.

We can do this using the same generate and test paradigm described earlier, but for realistic designs this search space is still far too large. We are exploring several ways to minimize search such as debugging rules that examine *why* a particular qc-space fails to produce the correct behavior, based on its topology. The desired behavior of a mechanical device can be described by a path through its qc-space, hence the topology of the qc-space can have a strong influence on whether the desired path (and the desired behavior) is easy, or even possible. For example, the qc-space may contain a funnel-like topology that "traps" the device,

constrained the yoke and the rotor to be symmetric, all strokes have the same length.

preventing it from traversing the desired path. If we can diagnose these kinds of failures, we may be able to generate a new qc-space by judicious repair of the current one.

We are also working to expand the class of devices that SKETCHIT can handle. Currently, our techniques are restricted to fixed-axis devices. Although this constitutes a significant portion of the variable topology devices used in actual practice (See [11]), we would like extend our techniques to handle particular kinds of non-fixed-axis devices. We are currently working with a commonly occurring class of devices in which a pair of parts has three degrees of freedom (rather than two) but the qc-space is still tractable.

We are beginning to explore how our techniques can be applied to other problem domains. For example, we believe that the BEP-Model will be useful for kinematic tolerance analysis (see [2] for an overview of tolerancing). Here the task is to determine if a given set of variations in the shapes and locations of the parts of a device will compromise the desired behavior.

We have also begun to explore design rationale capture. We believe that the constraints of the BEP-Model will be a useful form of design documentation, serving as a link between the geometry and the desired behavior. The constraints might, for example, be used to prevent subsequent redesign efforts from modifying the geometry in a way that compromises hard won design features in the original design.

CONCLUSION

This work is clearly at an early stage; we have yet to determine how well our techniques will scale to design problems that are more complex than the working examples reported here. Even so, we have successfully used the program on three design problems: the circuit breaker, the yoke and rotor, and the firing mechanism from a single action revolver. We have demonstrated that SKETCHIT can generate multiple families of designs from a single sketch and that it can repair a limited range of flaws in the initial design.

One reason this work is important is that sketches are ubiquitous in design. They are a convenient and efficient way to both capture and communicate design information. By working directly from a sketch, SKETCHIT takes us one step closer to CAD tools that speak the engineer's natural language.

Given the intimate connection between shape and behavior, design of mechanical artifacts is typically conceived of as the modification of shape to achieve behavior. But if changes in shape are attempts to change behavior, and if the mapping between shape and behavior is quite complex [1], then, we suggest, why not manipulate a representation of behavior? Our qualitative c-space is just such a representation. We suggest that it is complete and yet offers a far smaller search space. It is complete because any change in shape will produce a c-space that maps to a new qc-space differing from the original by at most changes in relative locations and qualitative slopes. Qc-space is far smaller precisely because it is qualitative: often many changes to the geometry map to a single change in qc-space. Finally, it is an appropriate level of abstraction because it isolates the differences that matter: changes in the relative locations and qualitative slopes of a qc-space are changes in behavior.

REFERENCES

[1] Caine, M. E., 1993, "The Design of Shape from Motion Constraints," MIT AI Lab. TR 1425, September.

[2] Chase, K. W. and Parkinson, A. R., 1991, "A Survey of Research in the Application of Tolerance Analysis to the Design of Mechanical Assemblies," *Research in Engineering Design*, Vol. 3, pp. 23–37.

[3] Erdman, A. and Sandor, G., 1984, *Mechanism Design: Analysis and Synthesis*, Vol. 1, Prentice-Hall, Inc., NJ.

[4] Faltings, B., 1990, "Qualitative Kinematics in Mechanisms," *JAI*, Vol. 44, pp. 89–119.

[5] Faltings, B., 1992, "A Symbolic Approach to Qualitative Kinematics," *JAI*, Vol. 56, pp. 139–170.

[6] Faltings, B. and Sun, K., 1995, "FAMING: Supporting Innovative Mechanism Shape Design," *CAD*.

[7] Forbus, K., Nielsen, P., and Faltings, B., 1991, "Qualitative Spatial Reasoning: The CLOCK Project," Northwestern Univ., The Institute for the Learning Sciences, TR #9.

[8] Joskowicz, L. and Addanki, S., 1988, "From Kinematics to Shape: An Approach to Innovative Design," *Proceedings AAAI-88*, pp. 347–352.

[9] Joskowicz, L., Sacks, E., and Srinivasan, V., 1995, "Kinematic Tolerance Analysis," *3rd ACM Symposium on Solid Modeling and Applications*, Utah.

[10] Kota, S. and Chiou, S., 1992, "Conceptual Design of Mechanisms Based on Computational Synthesis and Simulation of Kinematic Building Blocks," *Research in Engineering Design*, Vol. 4, #2, pp. 75–88.

[11] Sacks, E. and Joskowicz, L., 1993, "Automated Modeling and Kinematic Simulation of Mechanisms," *CAD*, Vol. 25, #2, Feb., pp. 106–118.

[12] Stahovich, T., 1996, "SKETCHIT: a Sketch Interpretation Tool for Conceptual Mechanical Design," MIT AI Lab. TR 1573, March.

[13] Stallman, R. and Sussman, G., 1976, "Forward Reasoning and Dependency-Directed Backtracking in a System for Computer-Aided Circuit Analysis," MIT AI Lab. TR 380.

[14] Subramanian, D., and Wang, C., 1993, "Kinematic Synthesis with Configuration Spaces," *The 7th International Workshop on Qualitative Reasoning about Physical Systems*, May, pp. 228–239.

[15] Ulrich, K, 1988, "Computation and Preparametric Design," MIT AI Lab. TR-1043.

[16] Welch, R. V. and Dixon, J. R., 1994, "Guiding Conceptual Design Through Behavioral Reasoning," *Research in Engineering Design*, Vol. 6, pp. 169–188.

Natural Language

Tree-bank Grammars

Eugene Charniak
Department of Computer Science, Brown University
Providence RI 02912-1910
ec@cs.brown.edu

Abstract

By a "tree-bank grammar" we mean a context-free grammar created by reading the production rules directly from hand-parsed sentences in a tree bank. Common wisdom has it that such grammars do not perform well, though we know of no published data on the issue. The primary purpose of this paper is to show that the common wisdom is wrong. In particular, we present results on a tree-bank grammar based on the Penn Wall Street Journal tree bank. To the best of our knowledge, this grammar outperforms all other non-word-based statistical parsers/grammars on this corpus. That is, it outperforms parsers that consider the input as a string of tags and ignore the actual words of the corpus.

Introduction

Recent years have seen many natural-language processing (NLP) projects aimed at producing grammars/parsers capable of assigning reasonable syntactic structure to a broad swath of English. Naturally, judging the creations of your parser requires a "gold standard," and NLP researchers have been fortunate to have several corpora of hand-parsed sentences for this purpose, of which the so-called "Penn tree-bank" [7] is perhaps the best known. It is also the corpus used in this study. (In particular, we used the Wall Street Journal portion of the tree bank which consists of about one million words of hand-parsed sentences.)

However, when a convenient standard exists, the research program subtly shifts: the goal is no longer to create any-old parser, but rather to create one that mimics the Penn tree-bank parses. Fortunately, while there is no firm NLP consensus on the exact form a syntactic parse should take, the Penn trees are reasonably standard and disagreements are usually about less common, or more detailed, features. Thus the attempt to find Penn-style trees seems a reasonable one, and this paper is a contribution to this effort.

Of those using tree banks as a starting point, a significant sub-community is interested in using them to support supervised learning schemes so that the grammar/parser can be created with minimal human intervention [1,2,5,6,8]. The benefits of this approach are twofold: learning obviates the need for grammar writers, and such grammars may well have better coverage (assign parses to more sentences) than the hand-tooled variety. At any rate, this is the game we have chosen.

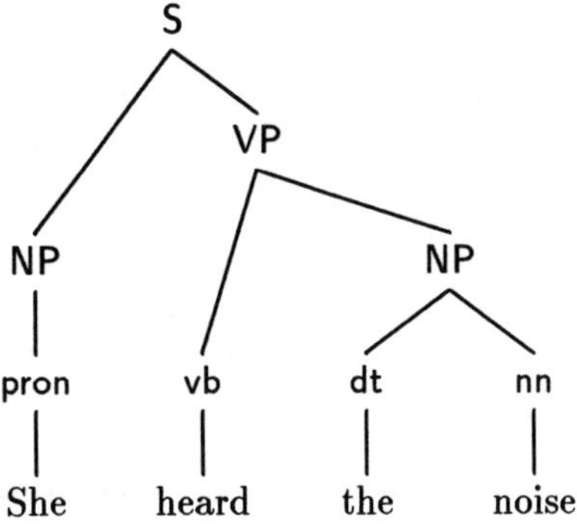

Figure 1: A simple parsed entry in a tree-bank

Now the simplest way to "learn" a context-free grammar from a tree-bank is to read the grammar off the parsed sentences. That is, we can read the following rules off the parsed sentence in Figure 1

$$\begin{array}{lcl} \text{S} & \rightarrow & \text{NP VP} \\ \text{NP} & \rightarrow & \text{pron} \\ \text{VP} & \rightarrow & \text{vb NP} \\ \text{NP} & \rightarrow & \text{dt nn} \end{array}$$

We call grammars obtained in this fashion "tree-bank grammars."

It is common wisdom that tree-bank grammars do not work well. We have heard this from several well-known researchers in the statistical NLP community, and the complete lack of any performance results on such grammars suggests that if they have been researched the results did not warrant publication. The primary purpose of this paper is to refute this common wisdom. The next section does this by presenting some results for a tree-bank grammar. Section 3 compares these results to prior work and addresses why our results differ from the common expectations.

The parser used in our experiments is, for the most

part, a standard chart parser. It does differ from the standard, however, in two ways. One is an efficiency matter — we improved its ability to search for the most probable parse. This is discussed briefly in section 3 as well. The second difference is more unusual. On impressionistic evidence, we have come to believe that standard PCFGs do not match English's preference for right-branching structures. In section 4 we present some ideas on how this might be corrected and show how these ideas contribute to the performance results of section 2.

The Experiment

We used as our tree bank the Penn parsed Wall Street Journal corpus, release 2.[1] We divided the sentences into two separate corpora, about 100,000 words for testing and about 1,000,000 words for training. We ignored all sentences in the testing data of length greater than 40 because of processing-time considerations; at any rate, the actual number of such sentences is quite low, as the overall average sentence length is about 22 words and punctuation. Of the 100,000 words of testing data, half were used for preliminary testing and the other half for "official" testing — the results reported here.

With the exception of the right-bracketing bias discussed later, the training was particularly simple. We obtained a context-free grammar (CFG) by reading the rules off all the sentences in the training data. Trace elements indicated in the parse were ignored. To create a probabilistic CFG, a PCFG, we assigned a probability to each rule by observing how often it was used in the training corpus. Let $|r|$ be the number of times rule r occurred in the parsed training corpus and $\lambda(r)$ be the non-terminal that r expands. Then the probability assigned to r is

$$p(r) = \frac{|r|}{\sum_{r' \in \{r' \mid \lambda(r')=\lambda(r)\}} |r'|} \quad (1)$$

After training we test our parser/grammar on the test data. The input to the tester is the parsed sentence with each word assigned its (presumably) correct part of speech (or *tag*). Naturally the parse is ignored by the parser and only used to judge the parsers output. Also, our grammar does not use lexical information, but only the tags. Thus the actual words of the sentence are irrelevant as far as our parser is concerned; it only notices the tag sequence specified by the tree-bank. For example, the sentence in Figure 1 would be "pron vb dt nn."

We used as our set of non-terminals those specified in the tree-bank documentation, which is roughly the set specified in [7]. It was necessary to add a new start symbol, S1, as all the parses in our version of the tree bank have the following form:

((S (NP The dog) (VP chewed (NP the bone)) .))

Note the topmost unlabeled bracketing with the single S subconstituent, but no label of its own. We handled such cases by labeling this bracket S1.[2]

We use the full set of Penn-tree-bank terminal parts of speech augmented by two new parts of speech, the auxiliary verb categories aux and auxg (an aux in the "ing" form). We introduced these by assigning all occurrences of the most common aux-verbs (e.g., have, had, is, am, are, etc.) to their respective categories.

The grammar obtained had 15953 rules of which only 6785 occurred more than once. We used all the rules, though we give some results in which only a subset are used.

We obtained the most probable parse of each sentence using the standard extension of the HMM Viterbi algorithm to PCFGs. We call this parse the map (maximum a posteriori) parse. We then compared the map parse to the one given in the tree-bank testing data. We measured performance by three observations:

1. precision: the percentage of all non-terminal bracketings appearing in map parses that also appear as a non-terminal bracketing in the corresponding tree-bank parse,
2. recall: the percentage of all non-empty non-terminal bracketings from the tree bank that also appeared as non-terminal bracketings in the map parse, and
3. accuracy: the percentage of all bracketings from the map parses that do not cross over the bracketings in the tree-bank parse.

The results obtained are shown in Figure 2.

Sentence Lengths	Average Length	Precision	Recall	Accuracy
2-12	8.0	91.5	89.1	96.9
2-16	11.5	89.6	87.1	95.0
2-20	13.9	87.3	84.9	92.9
2-25	16.3	85.5	83.3	91.2
2-30	18.8	83.6	81.6	89.7
2-40	22.0	82.0	80.0	88.0

Figure 2: Parsing results for the tree-bank grammar

At about sixteen thousand rules, our grammar is rather large. We also ran some tests using only the

[1] An earlier draft of this paper was based upon a preliminary version of this corpus. As this earlier version was about one-third the size and somewhat less "clean," this version of the paper sports (a) a larger tree-bank grammar (because of more training sentences), and (b) somewhat better results (primarily because of the cleaner test data).

[2] One interesting question is whether this outermost bracketing should be counted when evaluating the precision and recall of the grammar against the tree-bank. We have not counted it in this paper. Note that this bracketing always encompasses the entire sentence, so it is impossible to get wrong. Including it would improve our results by about 1%, i.e., precision would increase from the current 82% to about 83%.

Sentence Lengths	Grammar Size	Precision	Recall	Accuracy
2-16	Full	89.6	87.1	95.0
	Reduced	89.3	87.2	94.9
2-25	Full	85.5	83.3	91.2
	Reduced	85.1	83.3	91.1
2-40	Full	82.0	80.0	88.0
	Reduced	81.6	80.0	87.8

Figure 3: Parsing results for a reduced tree-bank grammar

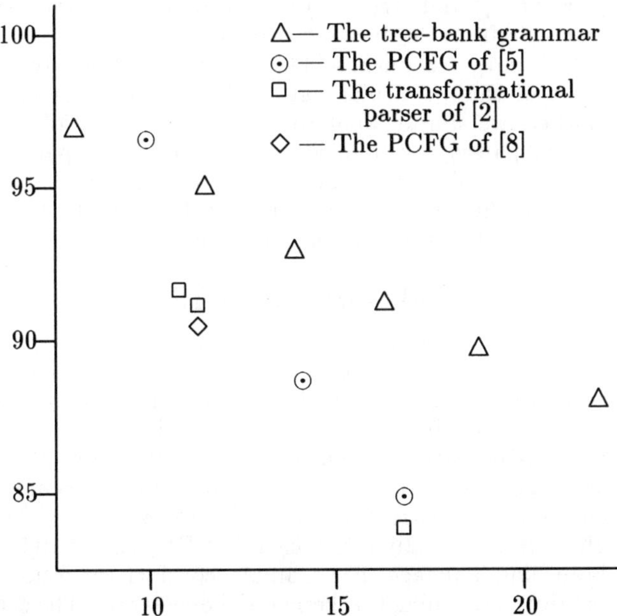

Figure 4: Accuracy vs. average sentence length for several parsers

subset of rules that occurred more than once. As noted earlier, this reduced the number of rules in the grammar to 6785. Interestingly, this reduction had almost no impact on the parsing results. Figure 3 gives first the results for the full grammar followed by the results with the 6785-rule subset; the differences are small.

Discussion

To put the experimental results into perspective it is useful to compare them to previous results on Wall Street Journal data. Figure 4 compares the accuracy figures for our tree-bank grammar with those of three earlier grammars/parsers that also used Wall Street Journal text for testing purposes. We compare only accuracy figures because the earlier work did not give precision and recall figures.

It seems clear that the tree-bank grammar is more accurate than the others, particularly when the average sentence length increases — i.e., when longer sentences are allowed into the testing corpus, The only data point that matches our current results is one for an earlier grammars of ours [5], and that only for very short sentences.

This is not to say, however, that there are no better grammars/parsers. Magerman [6] reports precision and accuracy figures of 86% for WSJ sentences of length 40 and less. The difference is that Magerman's parser uses statistics based upon the actual words of the sentence, while ours and the others shown in Figure 4 use only the tags of the words. We believe this shows the importance of including lexical information, a point to which we return below.

Next we turn to the discrepancy between our results and the prevailing expectations. Roughly speaking, one can identify five reasons why a parser does not identify the "correct" parse for a sentence:

1. the necessary rules are not in the grammar,
2. the rules are there, but the probabilities are incorrect,
3. the probabilities are correct, but the tag sequence by itself does not provide sufficient information to select the correct parse,
4. the information is sufficient, but because the parser could not consider all of the possible parses, it did not find the correct parse,
5. it found the correct parse, but the the tree-bank "gold standard" was wrong (or the correct parse is simply not clear).

Of these, (3) and (5) are important but not relevant to the current discussion. Of the rest, we believe that (1) is a major component of the low expectations for tree-bank grammars. Certainly it was our major concern. Penn-style trees tend to be be rather shallow, and the 40-odd parts of speech allow many possible combinations. For example, consider the NP "the $200 to $400 price range", which has the tag sequence dt $ cd to $ cd nn nn. Our tree-bank grammar does not have the corresponding NP rule (or any reasonable combination of rules as far as we can tell) and thus could not assign a correct parse to a sentence that contained this NP. For this reason we gave some thought to how new rules might be introduced and assigned non-zero probability. Indeed, we started on this work becuase we believed we had a interesting way to do this. In the event, however, no such complications proved necessary. First, our grammar was able to parse all of the test sentences. Second, it is not too hard to show that coverage is not a first-order problem.

In retrospect, our concerns about coverage were not well thought out because of a second property of our tree-bank grammar, its extreme overgeneration. In particular, the following fact is true:

> Let x be the set of the tree-bank parts of speech minus the following parts of speech: forward and

Sentence Lengths	Data Used	Precision	Recall	Accuracy
2-16	Testing	89.6	87.1	95.0
	Training	90.7	88.6	95.4
2-25	Testing	85.5	83.3	91.2
	Training	86.7	84.0	91.6
2-40	Testing	82.0	80.0	88.0
	Training	83.7	81.1	88.6

Figure 5: Parsing results for the tree-bank grammar

> backward single quote mark (neither of which occurred in our corpus), sym (symbol), uh (interjection), • (final punctuation), and). Any string in x* (where "*" is the normal Kleene star operator) is a legitimate prefix to a sentence in the language of our tree-bank-grammar, and furthermore, any non-terminal may start immediately following x*.

In other words, our grammar effectively rules out no strings at all, and every possible part of speech can start at almost any point in the sentence. The proof of this fact is by induction on the length of the string and is straightforward but tedious.[3]

Of course, that our grammar comes up with *some* parse for a sentence does not mean that it is immune to missing rules. However, we can show that possible missing rules are not a first-order problem for our grammar by applying it to sentences from the training corpus. This gives an upper bound on the performance we can expect when we have all of the necessary rules (and the correct probabilities). The results are given in Figure 5. Looking at the data for all sentences of length less than or equal to 40, we see that having all of the necessary rules makes little difference.

We noted earlier that the tree-bank grammar not only overgenerates, but also places almost no constraints on what part of speech may occur at any point in the sentence. This fact suggests a second reason for the bad reputation of such grammars — they can be hard on parsers. We noticed this when, in preliminary testing on the training corpus, a significant number of sentences were not parsed — this despite the fact that our standard parser used a simple best-first mechanism. That is, the parser chooses the next constituent to work on by picking the one with the highest "figure of merit." In our case this is the geometric mean of the inside probability of the constituent.

Fortunately, we have been also working on improved best-first chart parsing and were able to use some new techniques on our tree-bank grammar. We achieved the performance indicated in Figure 2 using the following figure of merit for a constituent $N^i_{j,k}$, that is, a constituent headed by the ith non-terminal, which covers the terms (parts of speech) $t_j \ldots t_{k-1}$

$$p(N^i_{j,k} \mid t_{0,n}) \approx \frac{p(N^i \mid t_{j-1}) p(t_{j,k} \mid N^i) p(t_k \mid N^i)}{p(t_{j,k+1})} \quad (2)$$

Here $p(t_{j,k+1})$ is the probability of the sequence of terms $t_j \ldots t_k$ and is estimated by a tri-tag model, $p(t_{j,k} \mid N^i)$ is the inside probability of $N^i_{j,k}$ and is computed in the normal fashion (see, e.g., [4]), and $p(N^i \mid t_{j-1})$ and $p(t_k \mid N^i)$ are estimated by gathering statistics from the training corpus.

It is not our purpose here to discuss the advantages of this particular figure of merit (but see [3]). Rather, we simply want to note the difficulty of obtaining parses, not to mention high-probability parses, in the face of extreme ambiguity. It is possible that some of the negative "common wisdom" about tree-bank grammars stems from this source.

Right-branching Bias

Earlier we noted that we made one modification to our grammar/parser other than the purely efficiency-related ones discussed in the last section. This modification arose from our long standing belief that our context-free parsers seemed, at least from our non-systematic observations, to tend more toward center-embedding constructions than is warranted in English. It is generally recognized that English is a right-branching language. For example, consider the following right-branching bracketing of the sentence "The cat licked several pans."

((The (cat (licked (several pans)))) .)

While the bracketing starting with "cat" is quite absurd, note how many of the bracketings are correct. This tendency has been exploited by Brill's [2] "transformational parser," which starts with the right-branching analysis of the sentence and then tries to improve on it.

On the other hand, context-free grammars have no preference for right-branching structures. Indeed, those familiar with the theory of computation will recognize that the language $a^n b^n$, the canonical center embedded language, is also the canonical context-free language. It seemed to us that a tree-bank grammar, because of the close connection between the "gold-standard" correct parses and the grammar itself, offered an opportunity to test this hypothesis.

As a starting point in our analysis, note that a right-branching parse of a sentence has all of the closing parentheses just prior to the final punctuation. We call constituents that end just prior to the final punctuation "ending constituents" and the rest "middle constituents." We suspect that our grammar has a smaller

[3] So tedious that after proving this fact for the tree-bank grammar used in the first draft of this paper, we could not muster the enthusiasm necessary to confirm it for the current grammar. However, since the new grammar is larger than that in the earlier draft, the above theorem or a similar one will surely hold.

propensity to create ending constituents than is warranted by correct parses. If this is the case, we want to bias our probabilities to create more ending constituents and fewer middle ones.

The "unbiased" probabilities are those assigned by the normal PCFG rules for assigning probabilities:

$$p(\pi) = \prod_{c \in \pi} p(\text{rule}(c)) \tag{3}$$

Here π is a parse of the tag sequence, c is a nonterminal constituent of this parse, and rule(c) is the grammar rule used to expand this constituent in the parse. Assume that our unbiased parser makes x percent of the constituents ending constituents whereas the correct parses have y percent, and that conversely it makes u percent of the constituents middle constituents whereas the correct parse has v percent.

We hypothesized that $y > x$ and $u > v$. Furthermore it seems reasonable to bias the probabilities to account for the underproduction of ending constituents by dividing out by x to get an "uninfluenced" version and then multiplying by the correct probability y to make the influence match the reality (and similarly for middle constituents). This gives the following equation for the probability of a parse:

$$p(\pi) = \prod_{c \in \pi} p(\text{rule}(c)) \cdot \left\{ \begin{array}{ll} y/x & \text{if } c \text{ is ending} \\ v/u & \text{otherwise} \end{array} \right\} \tag{4}$$

Note that the deviation of this equation from the standard context-free case is heuristic in nature: it derives not from any underlying principles, but rather from our intuition. The best way to understand it is simply to note that if the grammar tends to underestimate the number of ending constituents and overestimate middle constituents, the above equation will multiply the former by y/x, a number greater than one, and the latter by v/u, a number less than one.

Furthermore, if we assume that on the average the total number of constituents is the same in both the map parse and the tree-bank parse (a pretty good assumption), and that y and u (the numbers for the correct parses) are collected from the training data, we need collect only one further number, which we have chosen as the ending factor $\mathcal{E} = y/x$.

To test our theory, we estimated $\mathcal{E}$ from some held-out data. It came out 1.2 (thus confirming, at least for this test sample, our hypothesis that the map parses would underestimate the number of ending constituents). We modified our parse probability equation to correspond to Equation 4. The data we reported earlier is the result. Not using this bias yields the "Unbiased" data shown here:

	Precision	Recall	Accuracy
With bias	82.0	80.0	88.0
Unbiased	79.6	77.3	85.4
Difference	2.4	2.7	2.6

The data is for sentences of lengths 2-40. The differences are not huge, but they are significant — both in the statistical sense and in the sense that they make up a large portion of the improvement over the other grammars in Figure 4. Furthermore, the modification required to the parsing algorithm is trivial (a few lines of code), so the improvement is nearly free.

It is also interesting to speculate whether such a bias would work for grammars other than tree-bank grammars. On the one hand, the arguments that lead one to suspect a problem with context-free grammars are not peculiar to tree-bank grammars. On the other, mechanisms like counting the percentage of ending constituents assume that the parser's grammar and that of the gold standard are quite similar, as otherwise one is comparing incomparables. Some experimentation might be warranted.

Conclusion

We have presented evidence that tree-bank grammars perform much better than one might at first expect and, in fact, seem to outperform other non-word-based grammars/parsers. We then suggested two possible reasons for the mistaken impression of tree-bank grammars' inadequacies. The first of these is the fear that missing grammar rules will prove fatal. Here we observed that our grammar was able to parse all of our test data, and by reparsing the training data have showed that the real limits of the parsers' performance must lie elsewhere (probably in the lack of information provided by the tags alone). The second possible reason behind the mistaken current wisdom is the high level of ambiguity of Penn tree-bank grammars. The ambiguity makes it hard to obtain a parse because the number of possible partial constituents is so high, and similarly makes it hard to find the best parse even should one parse be found. Here we simply pointed to some work we have done on best-first parsing and suggested that this may have tamed this particular problem. Last, we discussed a modification to the probabilities of the parses to encourage more right-branching structures and showed how this led to a small but significant improvement in our results. We also noted that the improvement came at essentially no cost in program complexity.

However, because of the informational poverty of tag sequences, we recognize that context-free parsing based only upon tags is not sufficient for high precision, recall, and accuracy. It seems clear to us that we need to include lexical items in the information mix upon which we base our statistics. Certainly the 86% precision and recall achieved by Magerman [6] supports this contention. On the other hand, [6] abjures grammars altogether, preferring a more complicated (or at least, more unusual) mechanism that, in effect, makes up the rules as it goes along. We would suggest that the present work, with its accuracy and recall of about 81%, indicates that the new grammatical mechanism is not the important thing in those results. That is to say, we estimate that introducing word-based statistics on top of our tree-bank grammar should be able to make up the 5% gap. Showing this is the next step of our research.

Acknowledgements

This research was supported in part by NSF grant IRI-9319516.

References

1. BOD, R. *Using an annotated language corpus as a virtual stochastic grammar.* In *Proceedings of the Eleventh National Conference on Artificial Intelligence.* AAAI Press/MIT Press, Menlo Park, 1993, 778–783.
2. BRILL, E. *Automatic grammar induction and parsing free text: a transformation-based approach.* In *Proceedings of the 31st Annual Meeting of the Association for Computational Linguistics.* 1993, 259–265.
3. CARABALLO, S. AND CHARNIAK, E. Figures of merit for best-first probabilistic chart parsing. Department of Computer Science, Brown University, Technical Report, forthcoming.
4. CHARNIAK, E. *Statistical Language Learning.* MIT Press, Cambridge, 1993.
5. CHARNIAK, E. Parsing with context-free grammars and word statistics. Department of Computer Science, Brown University, Technical Report CS-95-28, 1995.
6. MAGERMAN, D. M. *Statistical decision-tree models for parsing.* In *Proceedings of the 33rd Annual Meeting of the Association for Computational Linguistics.* 1995, 276–283.
7. MARCUS, M. P., SANTORINI, B. AND MARCINKIEWICZ, M. A. Building a large annotated corpus of English: the Penn treebank. *Computational Linguistics 19* (1993), 313–330.
8. PEREIRA, F. AND SCHABES, Y. *Inside-outside reestimation from partially bracketed corpora.* In *27th Annual Meeting of the Association for Computaitonal Linguistics.* ACL, 1992, 128–135.

Left-corner Unification-based Natural Language Processing

Steven L. Lytinen and **Noriko Tomuro**
DePaul University
School of Computer Science, Telecommunications and Information Systems
243 S. Wabash Ave.
Chicago IL 60604
lytinen@cs.depaul.edu

Abstract

In this paper, we present an efficient algorithm for parsing natural language using unification grammars. The algorithm is an extension of *left-corner parsing*, a bottom-up algorithm which utilizes top-down expectations. The extension exploits unification grammar's uniform representation of syntactic, semantic, and domain knowledge, by incorporating all types of grammatical knowledge into parser expectations. In particular, we extend the notion of the *reachability table*, which provides information as to whether or not a top-down expectation can be realized by a potential subconstituent, by including all types of grammatical information in table entries, rather than just phrase structure information. While our algorithm's worst-case computational complexity is no better than that of many other algorithms, we present empirical testing in which average-case linear time performance is achieved. Our testing indicates this to be much improved average-case performance over previous left-corner techniques.

Introduction

A family of *unification-based* grammars has been developed over the last ten years, in which the trend has been to represent syntactic and semantic information more uniformly than in previous grammatical formalisms. In these grammars, many different types of linguistic information, including at least some kinds of syntactic and semantic constraints, are encoded as *feature structures*. In the most extreme versions, such as HPSG (Pollard and Sag, 1994), and our own previous work (Lytinen, 1992), feature structures are used to encode all syntactic and semantic information in a completely uniform fashion.

Standard approaches to unification-based parsing do not reflect this uniformity of knowledge representation. Often a unification-based parser is implemented using an extension of context-free parsing techniques, such as chart parsing or left corner parsing. The context-free (phrase structure) component of the grammar is used to drive the selection of rules to apply, and the additional feature equations of a grammar rule are applied afterward. The result remains a syntax-driven approach, in which in some sense semantic interpretation (and even the application of many syntactic constraints) is performed on the tree generated by the context-free component of the unification grammar.

This standard approach to unification-based parsing is not efficient. Worst-case complexity must be as bad as context-free parsing ($O(n^3)$) and perhaps worse, due to the additional work of performing unifications. Empirical examinations of unification-based parsers have indicated nonlinear average case performance as well (Shann, 1991; Carroll, 1994). Other popular parsing algorithms, such as Tomita's algorithm (Tomita, 1986), also fail to achieve average-case linear performance, even without the inclusion of semantic interpretation.

Our hypothesis is that a uniform approach to processing will result in a more efficient parsing algorithm. To test this hypothesis, we have developed a further extension of left-corner parsing for unification grammars. The extension exploits unification grammar's uniform representation, by incorporating all types of grammatical knowledge into parser expectations. In particular, we have extended the notion of the *reachability table*, which provides information as to whether or not a top-down expectation can be realized by a potential subconstituent, by including all types of grammatical information in table entries, rather than just phrase structure information.[1] We have implemented the extended left-corner parsing algorithm within our unification-based NLP system, called LINK (Lytinen, 1992).

To evaluate the efficiency of our algorithm, we have tested LINK on a corpus of example sentences, taken from the Fifth Message Understanding Competition (MUC-5) (Sundheim, 1993). This corpus consists of a set of newspaper articles describing new developments in the field of microelectronics. Since we competed in MUC-5 using a previous version of LINK, we were able to test our left-corner algorithm using a knowledge base that was developed independent of the algo-

[1]The extended reachability table will be referred to as a *reachability net*, since the additional complexity of table entries requires it to be implemented as a discrimination network.

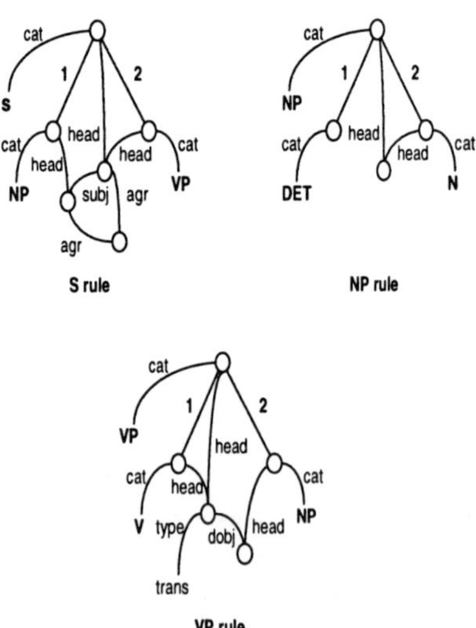

Figure 1: Example LINK grammar rules

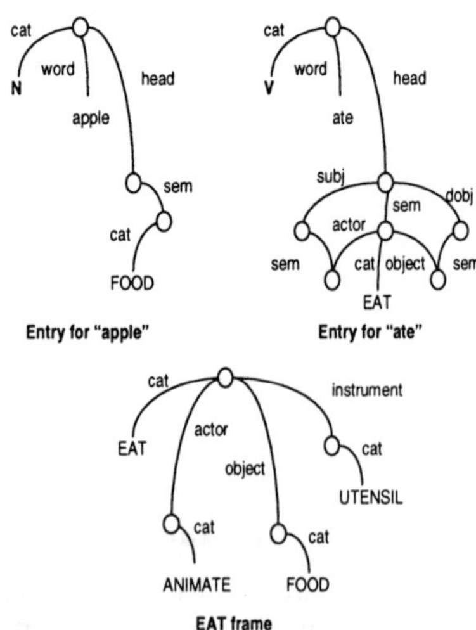

Figure 2: Example LINK lexical entries and frames

rithm, and compare its performance on this corpus directly to the performance of more standard approaches to unification-based parsing. A regression analysis of the data indicates that our algorithm has achieved linear average-case performance on the MUC-5 corpus, a substantial improvement over other unification-based parsing algorithms.

This paper is organized as follows: first we present the uniform knowledge representation used in LINK to represent syntactic, semantic, and domain knowledge. We then discuss LINK's parsing algorithm. Finally, we present results of empirical testing, and discuss its implications.

LINK's Knowledge Representation

All knowledge is encoded in LINK's unification grammar in the form of *feature structures.* A feature consists of a *name* and a *value.* Values may either be atomic or may themselves be feature structures. A feature structure may also have an atomic *label.* Thus, each rule in LINK's knowledge base can be thought of as a directed acyclic graph (DAG), whose edges corresponds to feature names, and whose nodes correspond to feature values.

Figure 1 shows a few simple LINK rules. The **S** rule encodes information about one possible structure of a complete sentence. The **cat** feature of the root indicates that this rule is about the syntactic category **S**. The numbered arcs lead to subconstituents, whose syntactic categories are **NP** and **VP** respectively. Implicit in the numbering of these features is the order in which the subconstituents appear in text. In addition, this rule indicates that the **VP** functions as the **head** of the sentence, that the **NP** is assigned as the **subj** of the sentence, and that the **NP** and **VP** share the same **agr** feature (which encodes the number and person features which must agree between a verb and its subject). Each of the other two rules displayed in figure 1 describes one possible structure for a **NP** and a **VP**, respectively. Other rules exist for the other possible structures of these constituents.

The purpose of the **head** feature is to bundle a group of other features together. This makes it easier for a constituent to inherit a group of features from one of its subconstituents, or vice versa. In this case, the **agr** feature is passed up from the noun and verb to the **NP** and **VP** constituents, to be checked for compatibility in the **S** rule. In the other direction, the **subj** feature is passed down to the verb, where its semantics is checked for compatibility with the semantics of the verb (see figure 2).

Other rules in LINK's knowledge base encode lexical and domain information, such as those in figure 2. Lexical rules typically provide many of the feature values which are checked for compatibility in the grammar rules. For example, the entry for **ate** indicates that this verb is transitive, and thus may be used with the **VP** rule in figure 1. Lexical items also provide semantic information, under the **sem** feature. Thus, "ate" refers to a frame called **EAT**, and "apple" refers to a **FOOD**.

The operation responsible for checking compatibility of features is *unification*, which can be thought of as the combining of information from two DAGs. The result of unifying two DAGs is a DAG with all features from both of the original DAGs. Two DAGs fail to unify if they share a feature with incompatible values.

Domain knowledge is encoded in frame definition rules, such as the **EAT** frame. A node whose **cat** feature has a frame definition must unify with the definition. As a result, semantic type-checking is per-

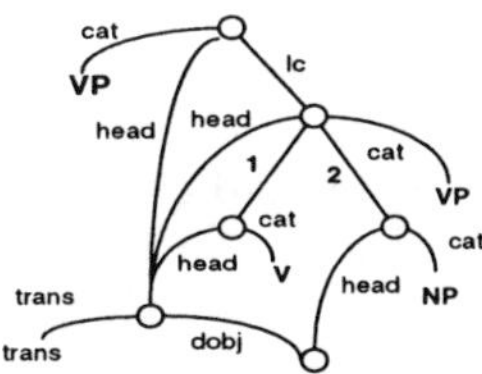

Figure 3: LINK reachability net entry

formed during parsing, resulting in the construction of a semantic interpretation. In these example rules, since the lexical entry for "ate" unifies the **subj** of the verb with the **actor** of its semantic representation, this means the subject of **ate** must be **HUMAN**.

Note that LINK's knowledge base is completely uniform. All rules, including grammar rules, lexical entries, and frame definitions, are represented as DAGs. Moreover, within a DAG there is no structural distinction between syntactic and semantic information. While certain naming conventions are used in the rules for different kinds of features, such as using the **cat** feature for the syntactic category of a constituent and the **sem** feature for its semantic representation, these conventions are only for mnemonic purposes, and play no special role in parsing.

Parsing

The Reachability Net

Context-free left-corner parsers generate top-down expectations in order to filter the possible constituents that are constructed via bottom-up rule application. In order to connect top-down and bottom-up information, a *reachability table* is used to encode what contituents can possibly realize a top-down expectation. The table is constructed by pre-analyzing the grammar in order to enumerate the possible left corner constituents of a particular syntactic category. For example, possible left corners of a NP (noun phrase) might include **DET**, **ADJ**, and **N** (noun), but not **PREP**. In most left-corner unification-based parsers (e.g., see Carroll, 1994), the reachability table is the same: only the syntactic labels of an expectation and a potential subconstituent are used as indices into the table, which then provides information as to which rules may lead to the satisfaction of the expectation.

In LINK, an extended *reachability net* is used, in which entire DAGs, rather than just syntactic labels, serve both as indices and entries. During grammar precompilation in LINK, net entries are constructed by connecting each possible expectation (represented as a DAG) with possible constituents that could be found in a sentence to realize the expectation (also DAGs). A net entry is generated for each possible consituent, which is placed in the **lc** (left corner) arc of the expectation. For example, figure 3 shows the entry for the

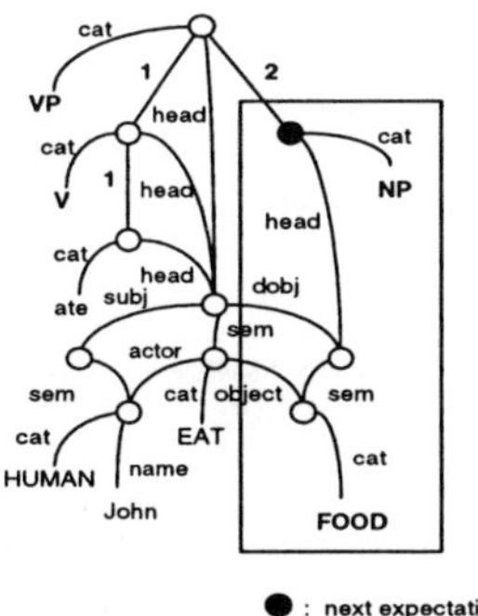

Figure 4: A portion of the parse of the sentence fragment "John ate..."

situation in which a **VP** is expected and a transitive verb is encountered.

The use of the reachability net sometimes enables LINK to prune incorrect parses earlier than they otherwise would be. For example, consider the sentence "John slept." After the word "John," the expectation is for a **VP** to follow. Upon encountering "slept", a standard reachability table would indicate that two possible rules could apply: the **VP** rule for transitive verbs pictured in figure 1, and a similar rule for intransitive verbs. Application of the transitive rule would result in a unification failure, assuming that "slept" is marked as intransitive, while the intransitive rule would succeed. In LINK, because net entries contain more than just syntactic category information, only the intransitive verb rule is retrieved in this situation, because the marking of "slept" as intransitive is part of the DAG which is used as an index into the net. Thus, the unification failure is avoided.

Because all features are utilized in retrieval of net entries, semantics can also come into play in the selection of rules. For example, figure 4 shows the **VP** constituent from the parse of the sentence fragment "John ate ...". At this point, the expectation is for an **NP** which means **FOOD**. This semantic information may be used in lexical disambiguation, in the case of an ambiguous noun. For instance, the word "apple" at this point would be immediately disambiguated to mean **FOOD** (as opposed to **COMPUTER**) by this expectation. Structural ambiguities may also be immediately resolved as a result of the semantic information in expectations. For example, consider the sentence fragment "The course taught...". Upon encountering "taught", a standard left-corner parser would attempt to apply at least two grammar rules: the **VP** rule for transitive verbs (see figure 1), and another rule for reduced relative subclauses. In LINK, assuming the existence of a **TEACH** frame whose **ACTOR** should be a **HUMAN**, the transitive **VP** rule would not be retrieved from the reachability net, since the semantics

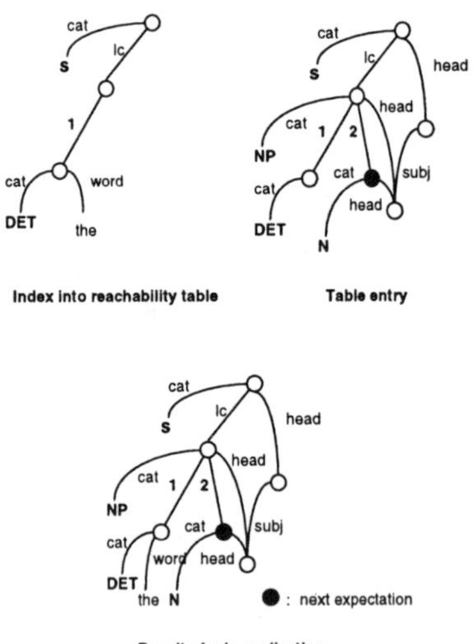

Figure 5: Net entries and DAGs constructed while parsing the word "the"

of "The course taught" do not agree with the **ACTOR** constraint of **TEACH**.

The Parsing Algorithm

At the beginning of the parse of a sentence, LINK constructs an expectation for an **S** (a complete sentence). As the parse proceeds left-to-right, LINK constructs all possible interpretations that are consistent with top-down expectations at each point in the sentence. A rule is applied as soon as its left corner is found in the sentence, assuming the reachability net sanctions the application of that rule given the current expectations. A single-word lookahead is also used to further constrain the application of rules.

LINK's parsing algorithm extends the standard left-corner parsing in the way top-down constraints are propagated down to the lower subconstituents. When a subconstituent is completed (often called a *complete edge* in chart parsing), it is connected to the current expectation through the **lc 1** path. Then, that expectation is used to retrieve the possible rule(s) to apply from the net. If the unification succeeds (creating an active edge with the dot just after the first constituent), the algorithm first checks to see if an expectation for the next word is generated (i.e., there are more constituents to be found after the dot). If there is a new expectation, the iteration stops. Otherwise, the DAG under **lc** arc is complete. That DAG is demoted to **lc 1** path, and the process is repeated. This way, the gap between the expectation and the input word is incrementally filled in a bottom-up fashion, while the top-down constraints are fully intact at each level. Thus, the top-down constraints are applied at the earliest possible time.

Some simple examples will illustrate the key aspects of the algorithm. At the beginning of a sentence, the first DAG in figure 5 is constructed if the word "the" is the first word of a sentence. This DAG is matched against entries in the reachability net, retrieving the entry shown. This entry indicates that the **NP** rule should be applied, resulting in the third DAG shown in figure 5. At this point, the algorithm identifies **N** at the end of **lc 2** path as the expectation for the the next word.

In LINK, a constituent under the **lc** arc is only implicitly connected to the expectation (i.e., the expectation is not completed yet). After all the subconstituents under **lc** arc are found, if the root DAG and the DAG under its **lc** arc unify, it means that the expectation has been fully realized. One possible action at this point is to replace the root with its **lc** arc and continue. This action corresponds to the decision that a constitutent is complete.

Empirical Results

To test the performance of our parsing algorithm, we selected a random set of sentences from the MUC-5 corpus, and parsed them using two different versions of LINK. One version used the extended reachability net as described above; the second version used a standard reachability table, in which only phrase structure information was utilized.

Both versions of LINK were run using a pre-existing knowledge base, developed for the MUC-5 competition. [2] Thus, both versions successfully parsed the same set of 131 sentences from the random sample. These 131 sentences formed the basis of the performance analysis.

Performance was analyzed in terms of several factors. First, a left-corner parser can be thought of as performing several "primitive" actions: rule instantiation and subsequent "dot" advancing, indicating the status of a partially matched grammar rule (i.e., how many of the right-hand side constituents of the rule have matched constituents in the sentence). These two actions involve different operations in the implementation.[3] A rule is instantiated when a constituent in the text (either a lexical item or a completed edge) matches with its left-corner child on the right-hand side. This action involves retrieving the rules from the reachability net and unifying the two constituents. On the other hand, when the dot is advanced, the subconstituent only needs to trace the pointer back to the (partially filled) parent DAG which predicted that constituent at the position right after the dot. Also, since all the expected features were already propagated down when the prediction was made, the subconstituent can be simply replaced into the rule.

[2] In order to improve the coverage of the domain, we added to LINK's original MUC-5 knowledge base for this test.

[3] Both of these actions correspond to the construction of an edge in chart parsing.

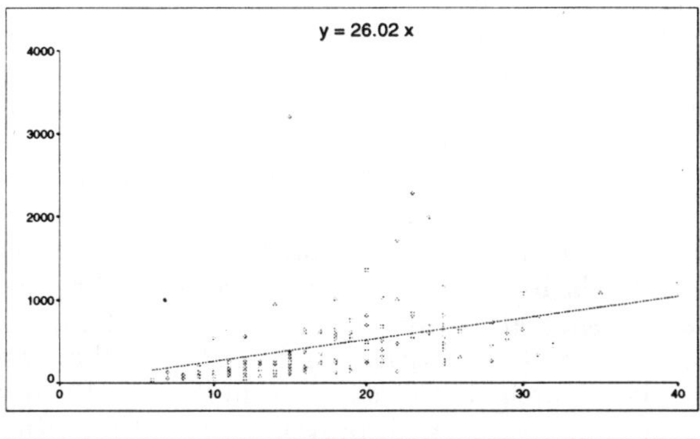

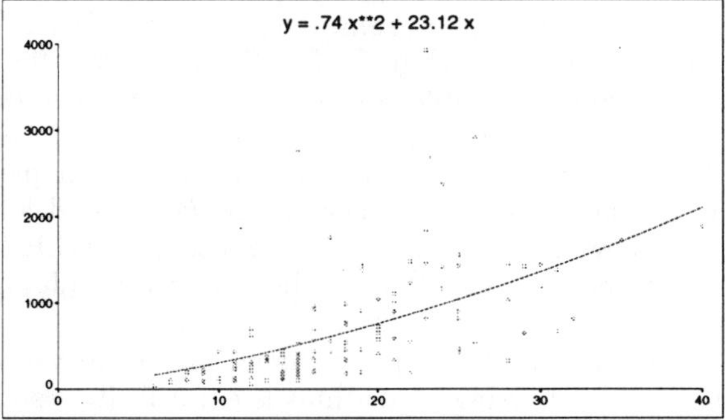

Figure 6: Actions vs. sentence length in LINK using extended and standard reachability tables

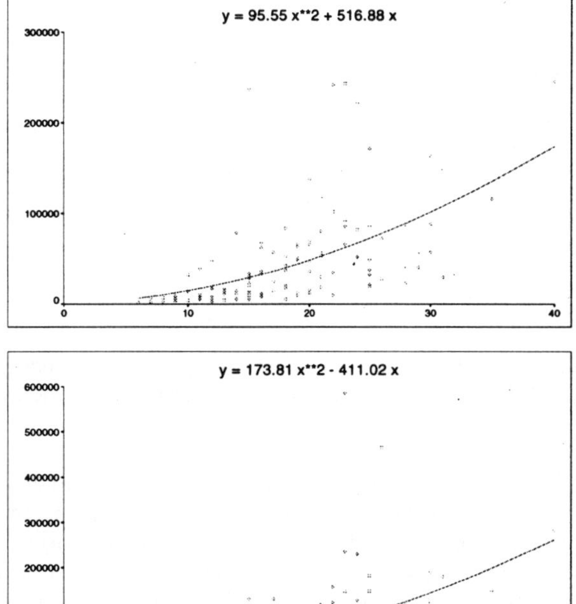

Figure 7: CPU time vs. sentence length in LINK using extended and standard reachability tables

For performance monitoring purpose, those two actions are recorded separately.

Figure 6 shows plots of the number of actions executed during a parse vs. sentence length for LINK using the standard and extended reachability nets. The number of actions also includes failures; i.e., rule instantiations or dot advances which were attempted but in which unification failure occurred (see discussion of rule failures in **Parsing** section). A best regression model analysis[4], using the adjusted R^2 metric, indicates that when using the extended reachability net, LINK achieved linear performance in this respect (R^2 = .599).[5] This is an encouraging result, because parsing time in context-free chart parsing is linearly proportional to the number of edges entered in the chart. When using the standard reachability table, a best regression analysis indicates a small quadratic component to the best-fitting curve (adjusted R^2 = .682 vs. .673 for the best linear model). When comparing best-fit linear models, on average LINK performed 40% more actions using the standard reachability table than when using the extended reachability net.

Figure 7 shows plots of CPU time used vs. sentence length for the two versions of LINK. The best regression model in both cases for this variable is quadratic.[6] Thus, the number of primitive actions taken by the parser is not linearly proportional to processing time, as it would be for a context-free parser. Average CPU time is 20% longer with the standard reachability table than with the extended reachability net. Thus, this analysis indicates that we have achieved a considerable speed-up in performance over the standard left-corner technique.[7]

Further analysis indicated that a potential source of nonlinear performance in our system is the need to copy DAGs when multiple interpretations are produced. If the reachability net indicates that more than one rule can be applied at some point in the parse, it

[4] In all analyses, best-fitting curves were restricted to those with no constant coefficient (i.e., only curves which pass through the origin). Intuitively, this makes sense when analyzing actions vs. sentence length, since parsing a sentence containing 0 words requires no actions.

[5] Although not shown, performance was also analyzed for a no-lookahead version of this algorithm. The action vs. sentence length result was also linear, but with a much steeper slope.

[6] Intuitively, the best model of CPU time vs. sentence length may contain a constant coefficient, since the algorithm may include some constant-time components; however, when allowing for a constant coefficient, the best regression model results in a negative value for the constant. Thus, we did not allow for constant coefficients in the best models.

[7] We speculate that the difference of the reduction ratio between the number of actions and CPU time comes from the processing overhead by other parts of the system, such as the added complexity of looking up entries in the reachability net.

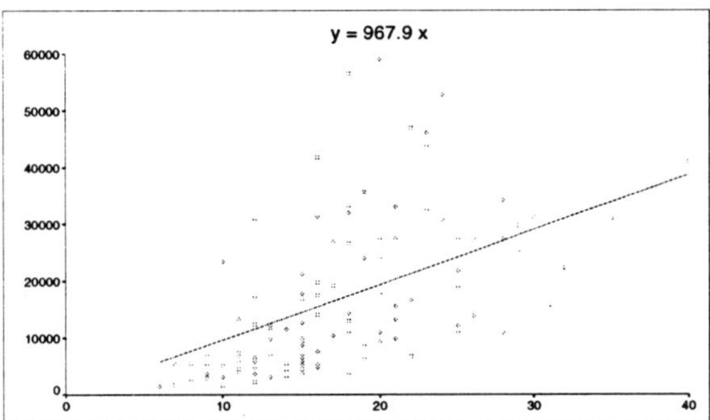

Figure 8: CPU time vs. sentence length in LINK using extended reachability net and improved DAG copying

is necessary to copy the DAG representing the parse so far, so that the alternate interpretations can be constructed without interference from each other. Indeed, a regression analysis of the number of DAGs generated during a parse vs. sentence length using the extended reachability net indicates that a quadratic model is the best for this variable ($R^2 = .637$).

To remedy this problem, we re-implemented the version of LINK using the extended reachability net, this time using a more efficient algorithm for copying DAGs. Our approach is similar to the *lazy unification* algorithm presented in (Godden, 1983). Space constraints prohibit us from describing the copying algorithm in detail. The same set of 131 test sentences was parsed again, and the results were analyzed in a similar fashion. The modified copying algorithm did not affect the number of actions vs. sentence length, since copying had no effect on which rules could or could not be applied. However, it did have a marked effect on the CPU time performance of the system. Figure 8 shows the plot of CPU time vs. sentence length for the lazy version of LINK. On average, the lazy copying algorithm achieved an additional 43% reduction in average CPU time per parse, and an average total speedup of 54% when compared to the version of LINK which used the standard reachability table. In addition, a regression analysis indicates a linear relationship between CPU time and sentence length for the lazy version of LINK (adjusted R^2=.726, vs. an adjusted R^2 of .724 for a quadratic model [8]).

Related Work

Efficient Parsing Algorithms

Many previous efforts have been focused on the construction of efficient parsing algorithms. Some deterministic algorithms such as Marcus' (1980) parser and Register Vector Grammar (Blank, 1989) achieve linear time complexity. However, because linear time is achieved due to the restrictions imposed by determinism, those algorithms consequently limit the generative capacity of the grammar. Our approach, on the other hand, does not limit the generative capacity of our system's unification grammar.

Some nondeterministic algorithms have been developed which utilize efficient encoding techniques. Chart-parsing algorithm uses a *chart* (or table) to record the partial constituents in order to eliminate redundant search. Earley's algorithm (Earley, 1970), a variant of chart-parsing, is proven to run in time $O(n^3)$ for general context-free grammars. Tomita's Generalized LR parsing algorithm (GLR) (Tomita, 1986, 1991) uses a precompiled table, an extension of LR parse table, to guide the search at any given point in the parse. GLR also employs other efficient encoding techniques such as graph-structured stack and *packed* shared forest. However, the worst case complexity of GLR is proven to be no better than Earley's algorithm (Johnson, 1991).

In (Shann, 1991), the performance of several variations of chart-parsing algorithms is empirically tested and compared. In this report, left-corner parsing (LC) with a top-down filtering strategy ranked the highest, and scored even or better in timing than Tomita's GLR. In particular, top-down filtering seemed to make a significant contribution to reducing the parse time. The timing results of this report, however, shows that neither LC nor GLR achieved linear performance in average case.

Parsing Algorithms for Unification Grammars

In (Shieber, 1992), a generalized grammar formalism is developed for the class of unification grammars, and an abstract parsing algorithm is defined. This abstract algorithm involves three components: *prediction*, in which grammar rules are used to predict subsequent constituents that should be found in a sentence; *scanning*, in which predictions are matched against the input text; and *completion*, in which predictions are matched against fully realized subconstituents. Shieber leaves the prediction component intentially vague; depending on the specificity of the predictions generated,[9] the algorithm behaves as a bottom-up parser, a top-down parser, or some combination thereof. On one extreme, if no information is used, the predictor does not propagate any expectations; hence, the algorithm is in essence equivalent to bottom-up parsing. If the predictor limits itself to only the phrase structure information in unification rules, then the algorithm is analogous to traditional (syntax-driven) left-corner parsing. Our algorithm can

[8]While the adjusted R^2 figures for the linear and quadratic models are very close, statistical analysis indicates that the quadratic coefficient in the latter model is not significantly different from 0.

[9]A prediction is created after the filtering function ρ is applied by the predictor.

be characterized as a version of this abstract algorithm in which the most extreme prediction component is used, one in which all possible information is included in the predictions.

Top-down Filtering

Shieber (1985) shows how Earley's algorithm can be extended to unification-based grammars, and the extended algorithm in effect gives a greater power in performing top-down filtering. He proposes *restriction*, a function which selects a set of features by which top-down prediction is propagated. By defining the restriction to select more features (eg. subcategorization, gap or verb form feature) than just phrase structure category, those features are used to prune unsuccessful rule application at the earliest time. Although with a very small example, a substantial effect on parsing efficiency by the use of of restriction is reported.

Another approach taken in (Maxwell and Kaplan, 1994) encodes some (functional) features directly in the context-free symbols (which requires the grammar modification), thereby allowing those features to be propagated down by the *predictor* operation of the Earley's algorithm. Not only does this strategy enable the early detection of parse failure, it can also help exploit the efficiency of the context-free chart-parsing ($O(n^3)$) in unification-based systems. In their report, despite the increased number of rules, the modified grammar showed an improved efficiency.

Early detection of failure is accomplished in LINK in a more pricipled way, by simply including all information in reachability net entries rather than deciding in an *ad hoc* fashion which constraints to encode through subcategorization and which to encode as features.

Conclusion and Future Work

We have presented a unification-based parser which achieves a significant improvement in performance over previous unification-based systems. After incorporating an improved version of DAG copying into the parser, our extended left-corner algorithm achieved average-case linear-time performance on a random sample of sentences from the MUC-5 corpus. This is a significant improvement over standard left-corner parsing techniques used with unification grammars, both in terms of average-case complexity and overall average speed. The improvement is indicated by our own comparative analysis, as well as by comparing our results with empirical testing done by others on standard left-corner parsers and other algorithms such as Tomita's algorithm (e.g., Shann, 1991).

Linear time performance was not achieved without the addition of an improved DAG copying algorithm. Further analysis is required to determine more precisely how much of the improvement in performance is due to the extended reachability net and how much is due to the improved DAG copying. However, our testing indicates that, even without improved copying, the extended reachability net achieves significant improvements in performance as compared to the use of a standard reachability table.

Acknowledgement

The authors would like to thank Joseph Morgan for very useful comments and help on the statistical analysis of the experiment data.

References

Blank, G. (1989). A Finite and Real-Time Processor for Natural Language. *Communications of the ACM, 32*(10) p. 1174-1189.

Carroll, J. (1994). Relating complexity to practical performance in parsing with wide-coverage unification grammars. In *Proceedings of the 32nd Annual Meeting of the Association for Computational Linguistics.*

Earley, J. (1970). An efficient context-free parsing algorithm. *Communications of the ACM*, 13(2).

Godden, K. (1990). Lazy unification. In *Proceedings of the 28th Annual Meeting of the Association for Computational Linguistics*, Pittsburgh PA, pp. 180-187.

Johnson, M. (1991). The computational complexity of GLR parsing. In Tomita, 1991, pp. 35-42.

Lytinen, S. (1992). A unification-based, integrated natural language processing system. *Computers and Mathematics with Applications, 23*(6-9), pp. 403-418.

Marcus, M. (1980). *A theory of syntactic recognition for natural language*, Cambridge, MA: MIT Press.

Maxwell, J. and Kaplan, R. (1994). The interface between phrasal and functional constraints, *Computational Linguistics*, **19** (4).

Pollard, C. and Sag, I. (1994). *Head-driven Phrase Structure Grammar.* Stanford, CA: Center for the Study of Language and Information. The University of Chicago Press.

Shann, P. (1991). Experiments with GLR and chart parsing. In Tomita, 1991, p. 17-34.

Shieber, S. (1985). Using restriction to extend parsing algorithms for complex-feature-based formalisms. In *Proceedings of the 23rd Annual Meeting of the Association for Computational Linguistics*, Chicago, IL, pp. 145-152.

Shieber, S. (1992). *Constraint-based Grammar Formalisms.* Cambridge, MA: MIT Press.

Sundheim, B. (1993). *Proceedings of the Fifth Message Understanding Conference (MUC-5).* San Francisco: Morgan Kaufmann Publishers.

Tomita, M. (1986). *Efficient Parsing for Natural Language.* Boston: Kluwer Academic Publishers.

Tomita, M. (1991). *Generalized LR Parsing.* Boston: Kluwer Academic Publishers.

Automatically Generating Extraction Patterns from Untagged Text

Ellen Riloff
Department of Computer Science
University of Utah
Salt Lake City, UT 84112
riloff@cs.utah.edu

Abstract

Many corpus-based natural language processing systems rely on text corpora that have been manually annotated with syntactic or semantic tags. In particular, all previous dictionary construction systems for information extraction have used an annotated training corpus or some form of annotated input. We have developed a system called AutoSlog-TS that creates dictionaries of extraction patterns using only untagged text. AutoSlog-TS is based on the AutoSlog system, which generated extraction patterns using annotated text and a set of heuristic rules. By adapting AutoSlog and combining it with statistical techniques, we eliminated its dependency on tagged text. In experiments with the MUC-4 terrorism domain, AutoSlog-TS created a dictionary of extraction patterns that performed comparably to a dictionary created by AutoSlog, using only preclassified texts as input.

Motivation

The vast amount of text becoming available on-line offers new possibilities for conquering the knowledge-engineering bottleneck lurking underneath most natural language processing (NLP) systems. Most corpus-based systems rely on a text corpus that has been manually tagged in some way. For example, the Brown corpus (Francis & Kucera 1982) and the Penn Treebank corpus (Marcus, Santorini, & Marcinkiewicz 1993) are widely used because they have been manually annotated with part-of-speech and syntactic bracketing information. Part-of-speech tagging and syntactic bracketing are relatively general in nature, so these corpora can be used by different natural language processing systems and for different domains. But some corpus-based systems rely on a text corpus that has been manually tagged in a domain-specific or task-specific manner. For example, corpus-based approaches to information extraction generally rely on special domain-specific text annotations. Consequently, the manual tagging effort is considerably less cost effective because the annotated corpus is useful for only one type of NLP system and for only one domain.

Corpus-based approaches to information extraction have demonstrated a significant time savings over conventional hand-coding methods (Riloff 1993). But the time required to annotate a training corpus is a non-trivial expense. To further reduce this knowledge-engineering bottleneck, we have developed a system called AutoSlog-TS that generates extraction patterns using untagged text. AutoSlog-TS needs only a *preclassified* corpus of relevant and irrelevant texts. Nothing inside the texts needs to be tagged in any way.

Generating Extraction Patterns from Tagged Text

Related work

In the last few years, several systems have been developed to generate patterns for information extraction automatically. All of the previous systems depend on manually tagged training data of some sort. One of the first dictionary construction systems was AutoSlog (Riloff 1993), which requires tagged noun phrases in the form of annotated text or text with associated answer keys. PALKA (Kim & Moldovan 1993) is similar in spirit to AutoSlog, but requires manually defined frames (including keywords), a semantic hierarchy, and an associated lexicon. Competing hypotheses are resolved by referring to manually encoded answer keys, if available, or by asking a user.

CRYSTAL (Soderland *et al.* 1995) also generates extraction patterns using an annotated training corpus. CRYSTAL relies on both domain-specific annotations plus a semantic hierarchy and associated lexicon. LIEP (Huffman 1996) is another system that learns extraction patterns but relies on predefined keywords, object recognizers (e.g., to identify people and companies), and human interaction to annotate each relevant sentence with an event type. Cardie (Cardie 1993) and Hastings (Hastings & Lytinen 1994) also developed lexical acquisition systems for information extraction, but their systems learned individual word meanings rather than extraction patterns. Both systems used a semantic hierarchy and sentence contexts to learn the meanings of unknown words.

AutoSlog

AutoSlog (Riloff 1996) is a dictionary construction system that creates extraction patterns automatically using heuristic rules. As input, AutoSlog needs answer keys or text in which the noun phrases that should be extracted have been labeled with domain-specific tags. For example, in a terrorism domain, noun phrases that refer to perpetrators, targets, and victims may be tagged. Given a tagged noun phrase and the original source text, AutoSlog first identifies the sentence in which the noun phrase appears. If there is more than one such sentence and the annotation does not indicate which one is appropriate, then AutoSlog chooses the first one. AutoSlog invokes a sentence analyzer called CIRCUS (Lehnert 1991) to identify clause boundaries and syntactic constituents. AutoSlog needs only a flat syntactic analysis that recognizes the subject, verb, direct object, and prepositional phrases of each clause, so almost any parser could be used. AutoSlog determines which clause contains the targeted noun phrase and applies the heuristic rules shown in Figure 1.

PATTERN	EXAMPLE
<subj> passive-verb	<victim> was murdered
<subj> active-verb	<perp> bombed
<subj> verb infin.	<perp> attempted to kill
<subj> aux noun	<victim> was victim
passive-verb <dobj>[1]	killed <victim>
active-verb <dobj>	bombed <target>
infin. <dobj>	to kill <victim>
verb infin. <dobj>	tried to attack <target>
gerund <dobj>	killing <victim>
noun aux <dobj>	fatality was <victim>
noun prep <np>	bomb against <target>
active-verb prep <np>	killed with <instrument>
passive-verb prep <np>	was aimed at <target>

Figure 1: AutoSlog Heuristics

The rules are divided into three categories, based on the syntactic class of the noun phrase. For example, if the targeted noun phrase is the subject of a clause, then the subject rules apply. Each rule generates an expression that likely defines the conceptual role of the noun phrase. In most cases, they assume that the verb determines the role. The rules recognize several verb forms, such as active, passive, and infinitive. An extraction pattern is created by instantiating the rule with the specific words that it matched in the sentence. The rules are ordered so the first one that is satisfied generates an extraction pattern, with the longer patterns being tested before the shorter ones. As an example, consider the following sentence:

```
Ricardo Castellar, the mayor, was kidnapped
yesterday by the FMLN.
```

Suppose that "Ricardo Castellar" was tagged as a relevant victim. AutoSlog passes the sentence to CIRCUS, which identifies Ricardo Castellar as the subject. AutoSlog's subject heuristics are tested and the **<subj> passive-verb** rule fires. This pattern is instantiated with the specific words in the sentence to produce the extraction pattern **<victim> was kidnapped**. In future texts, this pattern will be activated whenever the verb "kidnapped" appears in a passive construction, and its subject will be extracted as a victim.

AutoSlog can produce undesirable patterns for a variety of reasons, including faulty sentence analysis, incorrect pp-attachment, or insufficient context. Therefore a person must manually inspect each extraction pattern and decide which ones should be accepted and which ones should be rejected. This manual filtering process is typically very fast. In experiments with the MUC-4 terrorism domain, it took a user only 5 hours to review 1237 extraction patterns (Riloff 1993). Although this manual filtering process is part of the knowledge-engineering cycle, generating the annotated training corpus is a much more substantial bottleneck.

Generating Extraction Patterns from Untagged Text

To tag or not to tag?

Generating an annotated training corpus is a significant undertaking, both in time and difficulty. Previous experiments with AutoSlog suggested that it took a user about 8 hours to annotate 160 texts (Riloff 1996). Therefore it would take roughly a week to construct a training corpus of 1000 texts. Committing a domain expert to a knowledge-engineering project for a week is prohibitive for most short-term applications.

Furthermore, the annotation task is deceptively complex. For AutoSlog, the user must annotate relevant noun phrases. But what constitutes a relevant noun phrase? Should the user include modifiers or just the head noun? All modifiers or just the relevant modifiers? Determiners? If the noun phrase is part of a conjunction, should the user annotate all conjuncts or just one? Should the user include appositives? How about prepositional phrases? The meaning of simple NPs can change substantially when a prepositional phrase is at-

[1] In principle, passive verbs should not have direct objects. We included this pattern only because CIRCUS occasionally confused active and passive constructions.

tached. For example, "the Bank of Boston" is different from "the Bank of Toronto." Real texts are loaded with complex noun phrases that often include a variety of these constructs in a single reference. There is also the question of which references to tag. Should the user tag all references to a person? If not, which ones? It is difficult to specify a convention that reliably captures the desired information, but not specifying a convention can produce inconsistencies in the data.

To avoid these problems, we have developed a new version of AutoSlog, called AutoSlog-TS, that does not require any text annotations. AutoSlog-TS requires only a preclassified training corpus of relevant and irrelevant texts for the domain.[2] A preclassified corpus is much easier to generate, since the user simply needs to identify relevant and irrelevant sample texts. Furthermore, relevant texts are already available on-line for many applications and could be easily exploited to create a training corpus for AutoSlog-TS.

AutoSlog-TS

AutoSlog-TS is an extension of AutoSlog that operates exhaustively by generating an extraction pattern for every noun phrase in the training corpus. It then evaluates the extraction patterns by processing the corpus a second time and generating relevance statistics for each pattern. The process is illustrated in Figure 2.

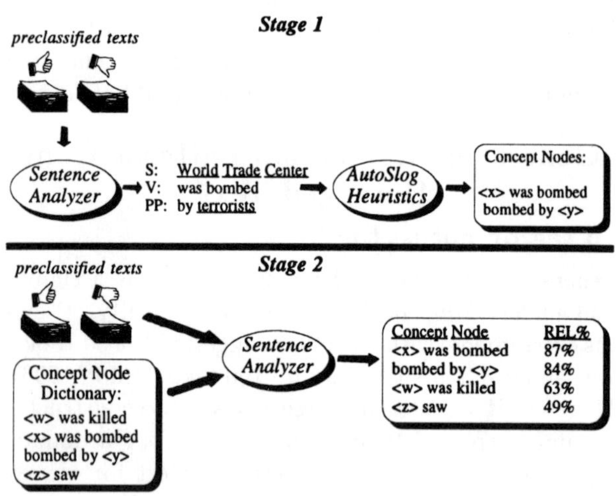

Figure 2: AutoSlog-TS flowchart

In Stage 1, the sentence analyzer produces a syntactic analysis for each sentence and identifies the noun phrases. For each noun phrase, the heuristic rules generate a pattern (called a *concept node* in CIRCUS) to extract the noun phrase. AutoSlog-TS uses a set of 15 heuristic rules: the original 13 rules used by AutoSlog plus two more: **<subj> active-verb dobj** and **infinitive prep <np>**. The two additional rules were created for a business domain from a previous experiment and are probably not very important for the experiments described in this paper.[3] A more significant difference is that AutoSlog-TS allows multiple rules to fire if more than one matches the context. As a result, multiple extraction patterns may be generated in response to a single noun phrase. For example, the sentence "terrorists bombed the U.S. embassy" might produce two patterns to extract the terrorists: **<subj> bombed** and **<subj> bombed embassy**. The statistics will later reveal whether the shorter, more general pattern is good enough or whether the longer pattern is needed to be reliable for the domain. At the end of Stage 1, we have a giant dictionary of extraction patterns that are literally capable of extracting every noun phrase in the corpus.

In Stage 2, we process the training corpus a second time using the new extraction patterns. The sentence analyzer activates all patterns that are applicable in each sentence. We then compute relevance statistics for each pattern. More specifically, we estimate the conditional probability that a text is relevant given that it activates a particular extraction pattern. The formula is:

$$Pr(relevant\ text \mid text\ contains\ pattern_i) = \frac{rel-freq_i}{total-freq_i}$$

where $rel - freq_i$ is the number of instances of $pattern_i$ that were activated in relevant texts, and $total - freq_i$ is the total number of instances of $pattern_i$ that were activated in the training corpus. For the sake of simplicity, we will refer to this probability as a pattern's *relevance rate*. Note that many patterns will be activated in relevant texts even though they are not domain-specific. For example, general phrases such as "was reported" will appear in all sorts of texts. The motivation behind the conditional probability estimate is that domain-specific expressions will appear substantially more often in relevant texts than irrelevant texts.

Next, we rank the patterns in order of importance to the domain. AutoSlog-TS's exhaustive approach to pattern generation can easily produce tens of thousands of extraction patterns and we cannot reasonably expect a human to review them all. Therefore, we use a ranking function to order them so that a person only needs to review the most highly ranked patterns.

We rank the extraction patterns according to the formula: $relevance\ rate * log_2(frequency)$, unless the relevance rate is ≤ 0.5 in which case the function returns zero because the pattern is negatively correlated

[2] Ideally, the irrelevant texts should be "near-miss" texts that are similar to the relevant texts.

[3] See (Riloff 1996) for a more detailed explanation.

with the domain (assuming the corpus is 50% relevant). This formula promotes patterns that have a high relevance rate or a high frequency. It is important for high frequency patterns to be considered even if their relevance rate is only moderate (say 70%) because of expressions like "was killed" which occur frequently in both relevant and irrelevant texts. If only the patterns with the highest relevance rates were promoted, then crucial expressions like this would be buried in the ranked list. We do not claim that this particular ranking function is the best - to the contrary, we will argue later that a better function is needed. But this function worked reasonably well in our experiments.

1. <subj> exploded
2. murder of <np>
3. assassination of <np>
4. <subj> was killed
5. <subj> was kidnapped
6. attack on <np>
7. <subj> was injured
8. exploded in <np>
9. death of <np>
10. <subj> took_place
11. caused <dobj>
12. claimed <dobj>
13. <subj> was wounded
14. <subj> occurred
15. <subj> was located
16. took_place on <np>
17. responsibility for <np>
18. occurred on <np>
19. was wounded in <np>
20. destroyed <dobj>
21. <subj> was murdered
22. one of <np>
23. <subj> kidnapped
24. exploded on <np>
25. <subj> died

Figure 3: The Top 25 Extraction Patterns

Experimental Results

Automated scoring programs were developed to evaluate information extraction (IE) systems for the message understanding conferences, but the credit assignment problem for any individual component is virtually impossible using only the scores produced by these programs. Therefore, we evaluated AutoSlog and AutoSlog-TS by manually inspecting the performance of their dictionaries in the MUC-4 terrorism domain. We used the MUC-4 texts as input and the MUC-4 answer keys as the basis for judging "correct" output (MUC-4 Proceedings 1992).

The AutoSlog dictionary was constructed using the 772 relevant MUC-4 texts and their associated answer keys. AutoSlog produced 1237 extraction patterns, which were manually filtered in about 5 person-hours. The final AutoSlog dictionary contained 450 extraction patterns. The AutoSlog-TS dictionary was constructed using the 1500 MUC-4 development texts, of which about 50% are relevant. AutoSlog-TS generated 32,345 unique extraction patterns. To make the size of the dictionary more manageable, we discarded patterns that were proposed only once under the assumption that they were not likely to be of much value. This reduced the size of the dictionary down to 11,225 extraction patterns. We loaded the dictionary into CIRCUS, reprocessed the corpus, and computed the relevance rate of each pattern. Finally, we ranked all 11,225 patterns using the ranking function. The 25 top-ranked extraction patterns appear in Figure 3. Most of these patterns are clearly associated with terrorism, so the ranking function appears to be doing a good job of pulling the domain-specific patterns up to the top.

The ranked extraction patterns were then presented to a user for manual review.[4] The review process consists of deciding whether a pattern should be accepted or rejected, and labeling the accepted patterns.[5] For example, the second pattern **murder of <np>** was accepted and labeled as a murder pattern that will extract victims. The user reviewed the top 1970 patterns in about 85 minutes and then stopped because few patterns were being accepted at that point. In total, 210 extraction patterns were retained for the final dictionary. The review time was much faster than for AutoSlog, largely because the ranking scheme clustered the best patterns near the top so the retention rate dropped quickly.

Note that some of the patterns in Figure 3 were not accepted for the dictionary even though they are associated with terrorism. Only patterns useful for extracting perpetrators, victims, targets, and weapons were kept. For example, the pattern **exploded in <np>** was rejected because it would extract locations.

To evaluate the two dictionaries, we chose 100 blind texts from the MUC-4 test set. We used 25 relevant texts and 25 irrelevant texts from the TST3 test set, plus 25 relevant texts and 25 irrelevant texts from the TST4 test set. We ran CIRCUS on these 100 texts, first using the AutoSlog dictionary and then using the AutoSlog-TS dictionary. The underlying information extraction system was otherwise identical.

We scored the output by assigning each extracted item to one of four categories: *correct*, *mislabeled*, *duplicate*, or *spurious*. An item was scored as *correct* if it matched against the answer keys. An item was *mislabeled* if it matched against the answer keys but was extracted as the wrong type of object. For example, if "Hector Colindres" was listed as a murder victim but was extracted as a physical target. An item was a *duplicate* if it was coreferent with an item in the answer keys. For example, if "him" was extracted and coreferent with "Hector Colindres." The extraction pattern acted correctly in this case, but the extracted information was not specific enough. Correct items extracted more than once were also scored as duplicates. An item

[4]The author did the manual review for this experiment.

[5]Note that AutoSlog's patterns were labeled automatically by referring to the text annotations.

was *spurious* if it did not refer to any object in the answer keys. All items extracted from irrelevant texts were spurious. Finally, items in the answer keys that were not extracted were counted as *missing*. Therefore *correct* + *missing* should equal the total number of items in the answer keys.[6]

Tables 1 and 2 show the numbers obtained after manually judging the output of the dictionaries. We scored three items: perpetrators, victims, and targets. The performance of the two dictionaries was very similar. The AutoSlog dictionary extracted slightly more correct items, but the AutoSlog-TS dictionary extracted fewer spurious items.[7]

Slot	Corr.	Miss.	Mislab.	Dup.	Spur.
Perp	36	22	1	11	129
Victim	41	24	7	18	113
Target	39	19	8	18	108
Total	116	65	16	47	350

Table 1: AutoSlog Results

Slot	Corr.	Miss.	Mislab.	Dup.	Spur.
Perp	30	27	2	12	97
Victim	40	25	7	19	85
Target	32	23	17	16	58
Total	102	75	26	47	240

Table 2: AutoSlog-TS Results

We applied a well-known statistical technique, the two-sample t test, to determine whether the differences between the dictionaries were statistically significant. We tested four data sets: *correct*, *correct* + *duplicate*, *missing*, and *spurious*. The t values for these sets were 1.1012, 1.1818, 0.1557, and 2.27 respectively. The *correct*, *correct* + *duplicate*, and *missing* data sets were not significantly different even at the $p < 0.20$ significance level. These results suggest that AutoSlog and AutoSlog-TS can extract relevant information with comparable performance. The *spurious* data, however, was significantly different at the $p < 0.05$ significance level. Therefore AutoSlog-TS was significantly more effective at reducing spurious extractions.

We applied three performance metrics to this raw data: **recall**, **precision**, and the **F-measure**. We calculated recall as *correct* / (*correct* + *missing*), and computed precision as (*correct* + *duplicate*) / (*correct* + *duplicate* + *mislabeled* + *spurious*). The F-measure (MUC-4 Proceedings 1992) combines recall and precision into a single value, in our case with equal weight.

As the raw data suggests, Table 3 shows that AutoSlog achieved slightly higher recall and AutoSlog-TS achieved higher precision. The F-measure scores were similar for both systems, but AutoSlog-TS obtained slightly higher F scores for victims and targets. Note that the AutoSlog-TS dictionary contained only 210 patterns, while the AutoSlog dictionary contained 450 patterns, so AutoSlog-TS achieved a comparable level of recall with a dictionary less than half the size.

	AutoSlog			AutoSlog-TS		
Slot	Recall	Prec.	F	Recall	Prec.	F
Perp	.62	.27	.38	.53	.30	.38
Victim	.63	.33	.43	.62	.39	.48
Target	.67	.33	.44	.58	.39	.47
Total	.64	.31	.42	.58	.36	.44

Table 3: Comparative Results

The AutoSlog precision results are substantially lower than those generated by the MUC-4 scoring program (Riloff 1993). There are several reasons for the difference. For one, the current experiments were done with a debilitated version of CIRCUS that did not process conjunctions or semantic features. Although AutoSlog does not use semantic features to create extraction patterns, they can be incorporated as selectional restrictions in the patterns. For example, extracted victims should satisfy a *human* constraint. Semantic features were not used in the current experiments for technical reasons, but undoubtedly would have improved the precision of both dictionaries. Also, the previously reported scores were based on the UMass/MUC-4 system, which included a discourse analyzer that used domain-specific rules to distinguish terrorist incidents from other events. CIRCUS was designed to extract potentially relevant information using only local context, under the assumption that a complete IE system would contain a discourse analyzer to make global decisions about relevance.

Behind the scenes

It is informative to look behind the scenes and try to understand why AutoSlog achieved slightly better recall and why AutoSlog-TS achieved better precision. Most of AutoSlog's additional recall came from low frequency patterns that were buried deep in AutoSlog-TS's ranked list. The main advantage of corpus-tagging is that the annotations provide guidance so the system can more easily hone in on the relevant expressions. Without corpus tagging, we are at the mercy of the ranking function. We believe that the ranking function did a good job of pulling the most impor-

[6] "Optional" items in the answer keys were scored as correct if extracted, but were never scored as missing.

[7] The difference in *mislabeled* items is an artifact of the human review process, not AutoSlog-TS.

tant patterns up to the top, but additional research is needed to recognize good low frequency patterns.

In fact, we have reason to believe that AutoSlog-TS is ultimately capable of producing better recall than AutoSlog because it generated many good patterns that AutoSlog did not. AutoSlog-TS produced 158 patterns with a relevance rate $\geq$ 90% and frequency $\geq$ 5. Only 45 of these patterns were in the original AutoSlog dictionary.

The higher precision demonstrated by AutoSlog-TS is probably a result of the relevance statistics. For example, the AutoSlog dictionary contains an extraction pattern for the expression **<subj> admitted**, but this pattern was found to be negatively correlated with relevance (46%) by AutoSlog-TS. Some of AutoSlog's patterns looked good to the human reviewer, but were not in fact highly correlated with relevance.

In an ideal ranking scheme, the "heavy hitter" extraction patterns should float to the top so that the most important patterns (in terms of recall) are reviewed first. AutoSlog-TS was very successful in this regard. Almost 35% recall was achieved after reviewing only the first 50 extraction patterns! Almost 50% recall was achieved after reviewing about 300 patterns.

Future Directions

The previous results suggest that a core dictionary of extraction patterns can be created after reviewing only a few hundred patterns. The specific number of patterns that need to be reviewed will ultimately depend on the breadth of the domain and the desired performance levels. A potential problem with AutoSlog-TS is that there are undoubtedly many useful patterns buried deep in the ranked list, which cumulatively could have a substantial impact on performance. The current ranking scheme is biased towards encouraging high frequency patterns to float to the top, but a better ranking scheme might be able to balance these two needs more effectively. The precision of the extraction patterns could also be improved by adding semantic constraints and, in the long run, creating more complex extraction patterns.

AutoSlog-TS represents an important step towards making information extraction systems more easily portable across domains. AutoSlog-TS is the first system to generate domain-specific extraction patterns automatically without annotated training data. A user only needs to provide sample texts (relevant and irrelevant), and spend some time filtering and labeling the resulting extraction patterns. Fast dictionary construction also opens the door for IE technology to support other tasks, such as text classification (Riloff & Shoen 1995). Finally, AutoSlog-TS represents a new approach to exploiting on-line text corpora for domain-specific knowledge acquisition by squeezing preclassified texts for all they're worth.

Acknowledgments

This research was funded by NSF grant MIP-9023174 and NSF grant IRI-9509820. Thanks to Kem Mason and Jay Shoen for generating much of the data.

References

Cardie, C. 1993. A Case-Based Approach to Knowledge Acquisition for Domain-Specific Sentence Analysis. In *Proceedings of the Eleventh National Conference on Artificial Intelligence*, 798–803. AAAI Press/The MIT Press.

Francis, W., and Kucera, H. 1982. *Frequency Analysis of English Usage*. Boston, MA: Houghton Mifflin.

Hastings, P., and Lytinen, S. 1994. The Ups and Downs of Lexical Acquisition. In *Proceedings of the Twelfth National Conference on Artificial Intelligence*, 754–759. AAAI Press/The MIT Press.

Huffman, S. 1996. Learning information extraction patterns from examples. In Wermter, S.; Riloff, E.; and Scheler, G., eds., *Connectionist, Statistical, and Symbolic Approaches to Learning for Natural Language Processing*. Springer-Verlag, Berlin.

Kim, J., and Moldovan, D. 1993. Acquisition of Semantic Patterns for Information Extraction from Corpora. In *Proceedings of the Ninth IEEE Conference on Artificial Intelligence for Applications*, 171–176. Los Alamitos, CA: IEEE Computer Society Press.

Lehnert, W. 1991. Symbolic/Subsymbolic Sentence Analysis: Exploiting the Best of Two Worlds. In Barnden, J., and Pollack, J., eds., *Advances in Connectionist and Neural Computation Theory, Vol. 1*. Ablex Publishers, Norwood, NJ. 135–164.

Marcus, M.; Santorini, B.; and Marcinkiewicz, M. 1993. Building a Large Annotated Corpus of English: The Penn Treebank. *Computational Linguistics* 19(2):313–330.

MUC-4 Proceedings. 1992. *Proceedings of the Fourth Message Understanding Conference (MUC-4)*. San Mateo, CA: Morgan Kaufmann.

Riloff, E., and Shoen, J. 1995. Automatically Acquiring Conceptual Patterns Without an Annotated Corpus. In *Proceedings of the Third Workshop on Very Large Corpora*, 148–161.

Riloff, E. 1993. Automatically Constructing a Dictionary for Information Extraction Tasks. In *Proceedings of the Eleventh National Conference on Artificial Intelligence*, 811–816. AAAI Press/The MIT Press.

Riloff, E. 1996. An Empirical Study of Automated Dictionary Construction for Information Extraction in Three Domains. *Artificial Intelligence*. Vol. 85. Forthcoming.

Soderland, S.; Fisher, D.; Aseltine, J.; and Lehnert, W. 1995. CRYSTAL: Inducing a conceptual dictionary. In *Proceedings of the Fourteenth International Joint Conference on Artificial Intelligence*, 1314–1319.

Learning to Parse Database Queries Using Inductive Logic Programming

John M. Zelle
Department of Mathematics and Computer Science
Drake University
Des Moines, IA 50311
jz6011r@acad.drake.edu

Raymond J. Mooney
Department of Computer Sciences
University of Texas
Austin, TX 78712
mooney@cs.utexas.edu

Abstract

This paper presents recent work using the CHILL parser acquisition system to automate the construction of a natural-language interface for database queries. CHILL treats parser acquisition as the learning of search-control rules within a logic program representing a shift-reduce parser and uses techniques from Inductive Logic Programming to learn relational control knowledge. Starting with a general framework for constructing a suitable logical form, CHILL is able to train on a corpus comprising sentences paired with database queries and induce parsers that map subsequent sentences directly into executable queries. Experimental results with a complete database-query application for U.S. geography show that CHILL is able to learn parsers that outperform a pre-existing, hand-crafted counterpart. These results demonstrate the ability of a corpus-based system to produce more than purely syntactic representations. They also provide direct evidence of the utility of an empirical approach at the level of a complete natural language application.

Introduction

Empirical or *corpus-based* methods for constructing natural language systems has been an area of growing research interest in the last several years. The empirical approach replaces hand-generated rules with models obtained automatically by training over language corpora. Recent approaches to constructing robust parsers from corpora primarily use statistical and probabilistic methods such as stochastic grammars (Black, Lafferty, & Roukaos 1992; Periera & Shabes 1992; Charniak & Carroll 1994) or transition networks (Miller *et al.* 1994). Several current methods learn some symbolic structures such as decision trees (Black *et al.* 1993; Magerman 1994; Kuhn & De Mori 1995) and transformations (Brill 1993). Zelle and Mooney (1993, 1994) have proposed a method called CHILL based on the relational learning techniques of Inductive Logic Programming.

To date, these systems have been demonstrated primarily on the problem of syntactic parsing, grouping the words of a sentence into hierarchical constituent structure. Since syntactic analysis is only a small part of the overall problem of understanding, these approaches have been trained on corpora that are "artificially" annotated with syntactic information. Similarly, they are typically evaluated with artificial metrics of parsing accuracy. While such metrics can provide rough comparisons of relative capabilities, it is not clear to what extent these measures reflect differences in performance on real language-processing tasks. The acid test for empirical approaches is whether they allow the construction of better natural language systems, or perhaps allow for the construction of comparable systems with less overall effort. This paper reports on the experience of using CHILL to engineer a natural language front–end for a database–query task.

A database-query task was a natural choice as it represents a significant real-world language-processing problem that has long been a touch-stone in NLP research. It is also a nontrivial problem of tractable size and scope for actually carrying out evaluations of empirical approaches. Finally, and perhaps most importantly, a parser for database queries is easily evaluable. The bottom line is whether the system produces a correct answer for a given question, a determination which is straight-forward for many database domains.

Learning to Parse DB queries

Overview of CHILL

Space does not permit a complete description of the CHILL system here. The relevant details may be found in (Zelle & Mooney 1993; 1994; Zelle 1995). What follows is a brief overview.

The input to CHILL is a set of training instances consisting of sentences paired with the desired parses. The output is a shift-reduce parser that maps sentences into parses. CHILL treats parser induction as a problem of learning rules to control the actions of a shift-reduce parser expressed as a Prolog program. Control-rules are expressed as definite-clause concept definitions. These rules are induced using a general concept learning system employing techniques from Inductive Logic Programming (ILP) a subfield of machine learning that addresses the problem of learning definite-clause logic descriptions from examples (Lavrač & Džeroski 1994; Muggleton 1992).

The central insight in CHILL is that the general operators required for a shift-reduce parser to produce a given set of sentence analyses are directly inferable from the representations themselves. For example, if the target is syntactic analysis, the fact the the parser requires a reduction to combine a determiner and a noun to form an NP follows directly from the existence of such an NP in the training examples. However, just inferring an appropriate set of operators does not produce a correct parser, because more knowledge is required to apply operators accurately during the course of parsing an example.

The current context of a parse is contained in the contents of the stack and the remaining input buffer. CHILL uses parses of the training examples to figure out the contexts in which each of the inferred operators is and is not applicable. These contexts are then given to a general induction algorithm that learns rules to classify the contexts in which each operator should be used. Since the contexts are arbitrarily-complex parser-states involving nested (partial) constituents, CHILL employs an ILP learning algorithm which can deal with structured inputs and produce relational concept descriptions.

Figure 1 shows the basic components of CHILL. During Parser Operator Generation, the training examples are analyzed to formulate an overly-general shift-reduce parser that is capable of producing parses from sentences. The initial parser is overly-general in that it produces a great many spurious analyses for any given input sentence. In Example Analysis, the training examples are parsed using the overly-general parser to extract contexts in which the various parsing operators should and should not be employed. Control-Rule Induction then employs a general ILP algorithm to learn rules that characterize these contexts. Finally, Program Specialization "folds" the learned control-rules back into the overly-general parser to produce the final parser.

Previous experiments have evaluated CHILL's performance in learning parsers to perform case-role parsing (Zelle & Mooney 1993) and syntactic parsers for portions of the ATIS corpus (Zelle & Mooney 1994; 1996). These experiments have demonstrated that CHILL works as well or better than neural-network or statistical approaches on comparable corpora.

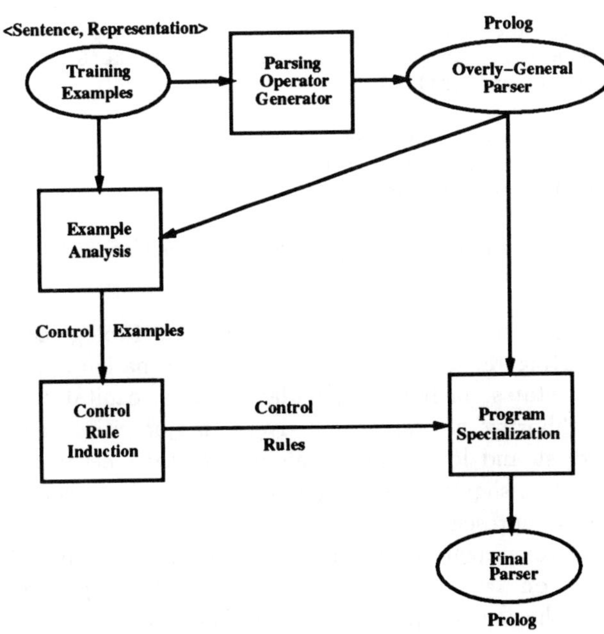

Figure 1: The CHILL Architecture

Parsing DB Queries

Overview of the Problem For the database-query task, the input to CHILL consists of sentences paired with executable database queries. The query language considered here is a logical form similar to the types of meaning representation typically produced by logic grammars (Warren & Pereira 1982; Abramson & Dahl 1989). The semantics of the representation is grounded in a query interpreter that executes queries and retrieves relevant information from the database. The choice of a logical query language rather than the more ubiquitous SQL was made because the former provides a more straight-forward, compositional mapping from natural language utterances—a property that is necessary for the CHILL approach. The process of translating from an unambiguous logical form into other query formats is easily automated.

The domain of the chosen database is United States geography. The choice was motivated by the availability of an existing natural language interface for a simple geography database. This system, called *Geobase* was supplied as an example application with a commercial Prolog available for PCs, specifically Turbo Prolog 2.0 (Borland International 1988). Having such an example provides a database already coded in Prolog for which a front-end can be built; it also serves as a convenient benchmark against which CHILL's performance can be compared.

What is the capital of the state with the largest population?
```
answer(C, (capital(S,C), largest(P, (state(S),
population(S,P))))).
```

What are the major cities in Kansas?
```
answer(C, (major(C), city(C), loc(C,S),
equal(S,stateid(kansas)))).
```

Figure 2: Sample Database Queries

Type	Form	Example
country	`countryid(Name)`	`countryid(usa)`
city	`cityid(Name, State)`	`cityid(austin,tx)`
state	`stateid(Name)`	`stateid(texas)`
river	`riverid(Name)`	`riverid(colorado)`
place	`placeid(Name)`	`placeid(pacific)`

Figure 3: Basic Objects in Geoquery

The Geobase data contains about 800 Prolog facts asserting relational tables for basic information about U.S. states, including: population, area, capital city, neighboring states, major rivers, major cities, and highest and lowest points along with their elevation. Figure 2 shows some sample questions and associated query representations.

Development of the database application required work on two components: a framework for parsing into the logical query representations, and a specific query language for the geography database. The first component is domain-independent and consists of algorithms for parsing operator generation and example analysis to infer the required operators and parse the training examples. The resulting parsing framework is quite general and could be used to generate parsers for a wide range of logic-based representations.

The second component, which is domain specific, is a query language having a vocabulary sufficient for expressing interesting questions about geography. The database application itself comprises a parser produced by CHILL coupled with an interpreter for the query language. The specific query language for these experiments (hereafter referred to as *Geoquery*) was initially developed by considering a sample of 50 sentences. A simple query interpreter was developed concurrently with the query language, thus insuring that the representations were grounded in the database-query task.

The Query Language, Geoquery The query language considered here is basically a first-order logical form augmented with some higher-order predicates or *meta-predicates*, for handling issues such as quantification over implicit sets. This general form of representation is useful for many language processing tasks. The particular constructs of Geoquery, however, were not designed around any notion of appropriateness for representation of natural language in general, but rather as a direct method of compositionally translating English sentences into unambiguous, logic-oriented database queries.

The most basic constructs of the query representation are the terms used to represent the objects referenced in the database and the basic relations between them. The basic forms are listed in Figure 3. The objects of interest are states, cities, rivers and places (either a high-point of low-point of a state). Cities are represented using a two argument term with the second argument containing the abbreviation of the state. This is done to insure uniqueness, since different states may have cities of the same name (e.g. `cityid(columbus,oh)` vs. `cityid(columbus,ga)`). This convention also allows a natural form for expressing partial information; a city known only by name is given an uninstantiated variable for its second term.

Form	Predicate
`capital(C)`	C is a capital (city).
`city(C)`	C is a city.
`major(X)`	X is major.
`place(P)`	P is a place.
`river(R)`	R is a river.
`state(S)`	S is a state.
`capital(C)`	C is a capital (city).
`area(S,A)`	The area of S is A.
`capital(S,C)`	The capital of S is C.
`equal(V,C)`	variable V is ground term C.
`density(S,D)`	The (population) density of S is P
`elevation(P,E)`	The elevation of P is E.
`high_point(S,P)`	The highest point of S is P.
`higher(P1,P2)`	P1's elevation is greater than P2's.
`loc(X,Y)`	X is located in Y.
`low_point(S,P)`	The lowest point of S is P.
`len(R,L)`	The length of R is L.
`next_to(S1,S2)`	S1 is next to S2.
`size(X,Y)`	The size of X is Y.
`traverse(R,S)`	R traverses S.

Figure 4: Basic Predicates in Geoquery

The basic relations are shown in Figure 4. The *equal/2* predicate is used to indicate that a certain variable is bound to a ground term representing an object in the database. For example, a phrase like "the capital of Texas" translates to `(capital(S,C), equal(S, stateid(texas)))` rather than the more traditional `capital(stateid(texas),C)`. The use of `equal` allows objects to be introduced at the point where they are actually named in the sentence.

Although the basic predicates provide most of the expressiveness of Geoquery, meta-predicates are required to form complete queries. A list of the implemented meta-predicates is shown in Figure 5. These predicates

Form	Explanation
`answer(V,Goal)`	V is the variable of interest in Goal.
`largest(V, Goal)`	Goal produces only the solution that maximizes the size of V
`smallest(V,Goal)`	Analogous to `largest`.
`highest(V,Goal)`	Like `largest` (with elevation).
`lowest(V,Goal)`	Analogous to `highest`.
`longest(V,Goal)`	Like `largest` (with length).
`shortest(V,Goal)`	Analogous to `longest`.
`count(D,Goal,C)`	C is count of unique bindings for D that satisfy Goal.
`most(X,D,Goal)`	Goal produces only the X that maximizes the count of D
`fewest(X,D,Goal)`	Analogous to `most`.

Figure 5: Meta-Predicates in Geoquery

are distinguished in that they take completely-formed conjunctive goals as one of their arguments. The most important of the meta-predicates is **answer/2**. This predicate serves as a "wrapper" for query goals indicating the variable whose binding is of interest (i.e. answers the question posed). The other meta-predicates provide for the quantification over and selection of extremal elements from implicit sets.

A Parsing Framework for Queries Although the logical representations of Geoquery look very different from parse-trees or case-structures on which CHILL has been previously demonstrated, they are amenable to the same general parsing scheme as that used for the shallower representations. Adapting CHILL to work with this representation requires only the identification and implementation of suitable operators for the construction of Geoquery-style analyses.

The parser is implemented by translating parsing actions into operator clauses for a shift-reduce parser. The construction of logical queries involves three different types of operators. Initially, a word or phrase at the front of the input buffer suggests that a certain structure should be part of the result. The appropriate structure is pushed onto the stack. For example, the word "capital" might cause the **capital/2** predicate to be pushed on the stack. This type of operation is performed by an **introduce** operator. Initially, such structures are introduced with new (not co-referenced) variables. These variables may be unified with variables appearing in other stack items through a **co-reference** operator. For example, the first argument of the **capital/2** structure may be unified with the argument of a previously introduced **state/1** predicate. Finally, a stack item may be embedded into the argument of another stack item to form conjunctive goals inside of meta-predicates; this is performed by a **conjoin** operation.

For each class of operator, the overly-general operators required to parse any given example may be easily inferred. The necessary **introduce** operators are determined by examining what structures occur in the given query and which words that can introduce those structures appear in the training sentence. **Co-reference** operators are constructed by finding the shared variables in the training queries; each sharing requires an appropriate operator instance. Finally, **conjoin** operations are indicated by the term-embedding exhibited in the training examples. It is important to note that only the operator generation phase of CHILL is modified to work with this representation; the control-rule learning component remains unchanged.

As an example of operator generation, the first query in Figure 2 gives rise to four **introduce** operators: "capital" introduces **capital/2**, "state" introduces **state/1**, "largest" introduces **largest/2** and "population" introduces **population/2**. The initial parser-state has **answer/2** on the stack, so its introduction is not required. The example generates four **co-reference** operators for the variables (e.g., when **capital/2** is on the top of the stack, its second argument may be unified with the first argument of **answer/2**, which is below it). Finally, the example produces four **conjoin** operators. When **largest/2** is on the top of the stack, **state/1** is "lifted" into the second argument position from its position below in the stack. Conversely, when **population/2** is on the top of the stack, it is "dropped" into the second argument of **largest/2** to form the conjunction. Similar operators embed **capital/2** and **largest/2** into the conjunction that is the second argument of **answer/2**.

Experimental Results

Experiments

A corpus of 250 sentences was gathered by submitting a questionnaire to 50 uninformed subjects. For evaluation purposes, the corpus was split into training sets of 225 examples with the remaining 25 held-out for testing. CHILL was run using default values for various parameters.

Testing employed the most stringent standard for accuracy, namely whether the application produced the correct answer to a question. Each test sentence was parsed to produce a query. This query was then executed to extract an answer from the database. The extracted answer was then compared to the answer produced by the correct query associated with the test sentence. Identical answers were scored as a correct parsing, any discrepancy resulted in a failure. Figure 6 shows the average accuracy of CHILL's parsers over 10

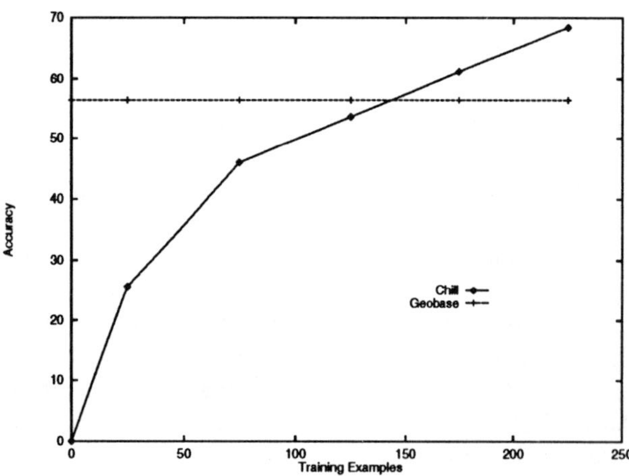

Figure 6: Geoquery: Accuracy

trials using different random splits of training and testing data. The line labeled "Geobase" shows the average accuracy of the Geobase system on these 10 testing sets of 25 sentences. The curves show that CHILL outperforms the existing system when trained on 175 or more examples. In the best trial, CHILL's induced parser comprising 1100 lines of Prolog code achieved 84% accuracy in answering novel queries.

In this application, it is important to distinguish between two modes of failure. The system could either fail to parse a sentence entirely, or it could produce a query which retrieves an incorrect answer. The parsers learned by CHILL for Geoquery produced few spurious parses. At 175 training examples, CHILL produced 3.2% spurious parses, dropping to 2.3% at 200 examples. This compares favorably with the 3.8% rate for Geobase.

Discussion

These results are interesting in two ways. First, they show the ability of CHILL to learn parsers that map sentences into queries without intermediate syntactic parsing or annotation. This is an important consideration for empirical systems that seek to reduce the linguistic expertise needed to construct NLP applications. Annotating corpora with useful *final* representations is a much easier task than providing detailed linguistic annotations. One can even imagine the construction of suitable corpora occurring as a natural side-effect of attempting to automate processes that are currently done manually (e.g. collecting examples of the queries produced by database users in the normal course of their work).

Second, the results demonstrate the utility of an empirical approach at the level of a complete natural-language application. While the Geobase system probably does not represent a state-of-the-art standard for natural language database query systems, neither is it a "straw man." Geobase uses a semantics-based parser which scans for words corresponding to the entities and relationships encoded in the database. Rather than relying on extensive syntactic analysis, the system attempts to match sequences of entities and associations in sentences with an entity-association network describing the schemas present in the database. The result is a relatively robust parser, since many words can simply be ignored. That CHILL performs better after training on a relatively small corpus is an encouraging result.

Related Work

As noted in the introduction, most work on corpus-based parsing has focused on the problem of syntactic analysis rather than semantic interpretation. However, a number of groups participating in the ARPA-sponsored ATIS benchmark for speech understanding have used learned rules to perform some semantic interpretation. The Chronus system from AT&T (Pieraccini *et al.* 1992) used an approach based on stochastic grammars. Another approach employing statistical techniques is the Hidden Understanding Models of Miller, et. al. (1994). Kuhn and De Mori (1995) have investigated an approach utilizing semantic classification trees, a variation on decision trees familiar in machine learning.

These approaches differ from work reported here in that learning was used in only a one component of a larger hand-crafted grammar. The ATIS benchmark is not an ideal setting for the evaluation of empirical components *per se*, as overall performance may be significantly affected by the performance of other components in the system. Additionally, the hand-crafted portions of these systems encompassed elements that were part of the learning task for CHILL. CHILL learns to map from strings of words directly into query representations without any intermediate analysis; thus, it essentially automates construction of virtually the entire linguistic component. We also believe that CHILL's relational learning algorithms make the approach more flexible, as evidenced by the range of representations for which CHILL has successfully learned parsers. Objective comparison of various approaches to empirical NLP is an important area for future research.

Future Work and Conclusions

Clearly, there are many open questions regarding the practicality of using CHILL for the development of NLP systems. Experiments with larger corpora and other domains are indicated. Another interesting avenue of investigation is the extent to which performance can be improved by corpus "manufacturing." Since an initial corpus must be annotated by hand, one method of increasing the regularity in the training corpus (and hence the generality of the resulting parser) would be to allow the annotator to introduce related sentences. Although this approach would require extra effort from the annotator, it would be far easier than annotating an equal number of random sentences and might produce better results.

The development of automated techniques for lexicon construction could also broaden the applicability of CHILL. Currently, the generation of `introduce` operators relies on a hand-built lexicon indicating which words can introduce various predicates. Thompson (1995) has demonstrated an initial approach to corpus-based acquisition of lexical mapping rules suitable for use with CHILL-style parser acquisition systems.

We have described a framework using ILP to learn parsers that map sentences into database queries using a training corpus of sentences paired with queries. This method has been implemented in the CHILL system, which treats parser acquisition as the learning of search-control rules within a logic program representing a shift-reduce parser. Experimental results with a complete application for answering questions about U.S. geography show that CHILL's parsers outperform a pre-existing hand-crafted counterpart. These results demonstrate CHILL's ability to learn semantic mappings and the utility of an empirical approach at the level of a complete natural-language application. We hope these experiments will stimulate further research in corpus-based techniques that employ ILP.

Acknowledgments

Portions of this research were supported by the National Science Foundation under grant IRI-9310819.

References

Abramson, H., and Dahl, V. 1989. *Logic Grammars.* New York: Springer-Verlag.

Black, E.; Jelineck, F.; Lafferty, J.; Magerman, D.; Mercer, R.; and Roukos, S. 1993. Towards history-based grammars: Using richer models for probabilistic parsing. In *Proceedings of the 31st Annual Meeting of the Association for Computational Linguistics*, 31–37.

Black, E.; Lafferty, J.; and Roukaos, S. 1992. Development and evaluation of a broad-coverage probabilistic grammar of English-language computer manuals. In *Proceedings of the 30th Annual Meeting of the Association for Computational Linguistics*, 185–192.

Borland International. 1988. *Turbo Prolog 2.0 Reference Guide.* Scotts Valley, CA: Borland International.

Brill, E. 1993. Automatic grammar induction and parsing free text: A transformation-based approach. In *Proceedings of the 31st Annual Meeting of the Association for Computational Linguistics*, 259–265.

Charniak, E., and Carroll, G. 1994. Context-sensitive statistics for improved grammatical language models. In *Proceedings of the Twelfth National Conference on Artificial Intelligence.*

Kuhn, R., and De Mori, R. 1995. The application of semantic classification trees to natural language understanding. *IEEE Transactions on Pattern Analysis and Machine Intelligence* 17(5):449–460.

Lavrač, N., and Džeroski, S., eds. 1994. *Inductive Logic Programming: Techniques and Applications.* Ellis Horwood.

Magerman, D. M. 1994. *Natrual Lagnuage Parsing as Statistical Pattern Recognition.* Ph.D. Dissertation, Stanford University.

Miller, S.; Bobrow, R.; Ingria, R.; and Schwartz, R. 1994. Hidden understanding models of natural language. In *Proceedings of the 32nd Annual Meeting of the Association for Computational Linguistics*, 25–32.

Muggleton, S. H., ed. 1992. *Inductive Logic Programming.* New York, NY: Academic Press.

Periera, F., and Shabes, Y. 1992. Inside-outside reestimation from partially bracketed corpora. In *Proceedings of the 30th Annual Meeting of the Association for Computational Linguistics*, 128–135.

Pieraccini, R.; Tzoukermann, E.; Z. Gorelov, J. L. G.; Levin, E.; Lee, C. H.; and Wilpon, J. 1992. A speech understanding system based on statistical representation of semantics. In *Proceedings ICASSP 92.* I–193–I–196.

Thompson, C. A. 1995. Acquisition of a lexicon from semantic representations of sentences. In *Proceeding of the 33rd Annual Meeting of the Association for Computational Linguistics*, 335–337.

Warren, D. H. D., and Pereira, F. C. N. 1982. An efficient easily adaptable system for interpreting natural language queries. *American Journal of Computational Linguistics* 8(3-4):110–122.

Zelle, J. M., and Mooney, R. J. 1993. Learning semantic grammars with constructive inductive logic programming. In *Proceedings of the Eleventh National Conference on Artificial Intelligence*, 817–822.

Zelle, J. M., and Mooney, R. J. 1994. Inducing deterministic Prolog parsers from treebanks: A machine learning approach. In *Proceedings of the Twelfth National Conference on Artificial Intelligence*, 748–753.

Zelle, J., and Mooney, R. 1996. Comparative results on using inductive logic programming for corpus-based parser construction. In Wermter, S.; Riloff, E.; and Scheler, G., eds., *Symbolic, Connectionist, and Statistical Approaches to Learning for Natural Language Processing.* Springer Verlag.

Zelle, J. M. 1995. *Using Inductive Logic Programming to Automate the Construction of Natural Language Parsers.* Ph.D. Dissertation, University of Texas, Austin, TX. available via http://cs.utexas.edu/users/ml.

HUNTER-GATHERER: Three Search Techniques Integrated for Natural Language Semantics

Stephen Beale, Sergei Nirenburg and **Kavi Mahesh**
Computing Research Laboratory
Box 30001
New Mexico State University
Las Cruces, New Mexico 88003
sb,sergei,mahesh@crl.nmsu.edu

Abstract

This work[1] integrates three related AI search techniques – constraint satisfaction, branch-and-bound and solution synthesis – and applies the result to semantic processing in natural language (NL). We summarize the approach as "Hunter-Gatherer:"

- branch-and-bound and constraint satisfaction allow us to "hunt down" non-optimal and impossible solutions and prune them from the search space.
- solution synthesis methods then "gather" all optimal solutions avoiding exponential complexity.

Each of the three techniques is briefly described, as well as their extensions and combinations used in our system. We focus on the combination of solution synthesis and branch-and-bound methods which has enabled near-linear-time processing in our applications. Finally, we illustrate how the use of our technique in a large-scale MT project allowed a drastic reduction in search space.

Introduction

The number of possible semantic analyses in an **average**-sized sentence in the Spanish corpus used in the Mikrokosmos MT project is fifty six million, six hundred eighty seven thousand, and forty. Complex sentences have gone past the trillions. Exhaustive search methods applied to real sentences routinely require several minutes to finish, with larger sentences running more than a day. Clearly, techniques must be developed to diffuse this exponential explosion.

Hunters and Gatherers in AI

Search is the most common tool for finding solutions in artificial intelligence. The two paths to higher efficiency in search are

1. Reducing the search space. Looking for sub-optimal or impossible solutions. Removing them. Killing them. "Hunting"
2. Efficiently extracting answer(s) from the search space. Collecting satisfactory answer(s). "Gathering"

Much work has been done with regard to the hunters. Finding and using heuristics to guide search has been a major focus. Heuristics are necessary when other techniques cannot reduce the size of the search space to reasonable proportions. Under such circumstances, "guesses" have to be made to guide the search engine to the area of the search space most likely to contain acceptable answers. "Best-first" search (see, among many others, (Charniak et al. 1987)) is an example of how to **use** heuristics.

The "hunting" techniques applied in this research are most closely related to the field of constraint satisfaction problems (CSP). (Beale 1996) overviews this field and (Tsang 1993) covers it in depth. Further references include (Mackworth 1977), (Mackworth & Freuder 1985) and (Mohr & Henderson 1986).

"Gathering" has been studied much less in AI. Most AI problems are content with a single "acceptable" answer. Heuristic search methods generally are sufficient. Certain classes of problems, however, demand **all** correct answers. "Solution synthesis" addresses this need. Solution synthesis techniques (Freuder 1978; see also Tsang & Foster 1990), iteratively combine (gather) partial answers to arrive at a complete list of all correct answers. Often, this list is then rated according to some separate criteria in order to pick the most suitable answer.

In a "blocks" world, CSP techniques and solution synthesis are powerful mechanisms. Many "real-world" problems, however, have a more complex semantics: constraints are not "yes" or "no" but "maybe" and "sometimes." In NL, certain word-sense combinations might make sense in one context but not in another. This is the central problem with previous attempts at using constraint analysis for NL disambiguation (Nagao 1992; Maruyama 1990).[2] We need a method as powerful as CSP for this more complex environment.

[1]Research reported in this paper was supported in part by Contract MDA904-92-C-5189 from the U.S. Department of Defense.

[2]For instance, Nagao eliminates an **ownership** meaning on the basis that a **file-system** is not a **human** agent. As shown in the next section, metonymy and other figurative

Grupo Roche	**a traves de**	**su**	**compania**	**en**	**espana**	**adquirir**	**Dr. Andreu**
ORGANIZATION	*LOCATION* *INSTRUMENT*	*OWNER*	*CORPORATION* *SOCIAL-EVENT*	*LOCATION* *DURING*	*NATION*	*ACQUIRE* *LEARN*	*HUMAN* *ORGANIZATION*

Figure 1: Example Sentence

Our proposal is to 1) use constraint dependency information to partition problems into appropriate sub-problems, 2) combine (gather) results from these sub-problems using a new solution synthesis technique, and 3) prune (hunt) these results using branch-and-bound techniques. The rest of this paper addresses each of these issues in turn.

Constraint Satisfaction Hunters in NL

NL problems can be almost always viewed as bundles of tightly constrained sub-problems, each of which combine at higher, relatively constraint-free levels to produce a complete solution. Beale (1996) argues that syntactic and semantic constraints effectively partition discourse into clusters of locally interacting networks. Here, we summarize those results and report how solution synthesis and branch-and-bound techniques can improve search efficiency.

Figure 1 illustrates the basic lexical ambiguities in a very simple Spanish sentence from the corpus processed by our semantic analyzer. In the figure the Spanish words and phrases are shown with their readings, expressed as corresponding concepts in the underlying ontology. An exhaustive decision tree for this sentence would include 36 possible combinations of word senses, but, when some fairly obvious "literal" semantic constraints are imposed and propagated using arc consistency, all but one of the paths can be eliminated.

Unfortunately, a literal imposition of constraints does not work in NL. For example, *a traves de*, in *a traves de su compania* could very well be **location**, even though a literal constraint would expect *compania* to be a **place**, because corporation names are often used metonymically to stand for "the place of the corporation:"

I walked to IBM.
I walked to where IBM's building is.

Therefore, the fact that *compania* is not literally a **place** does not rule out the **location** interpretation. In fact, in certain contexts, the **location** interpretation might be preferred. Constraint satisfaction techniques such as arc-consistency, therefore, will be of limited value.

Figure 2 gives a different view of this same NL problem by graphically displaying the constraint dependencies present in Figure 1. These dependencies can be

language often overrides such constraints.

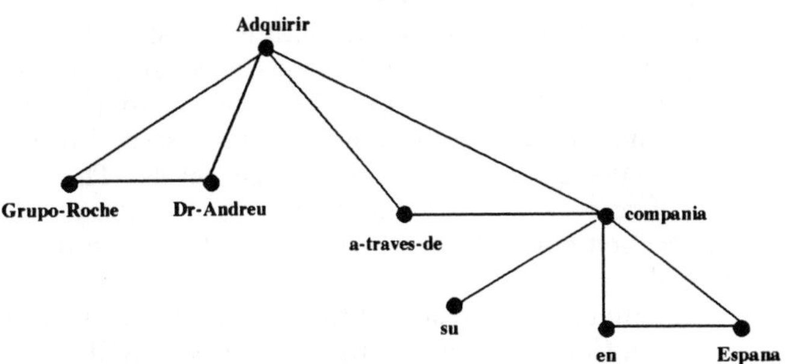

Figure 2: Constraint Dependencies in Sample Sentence

identified simply by iterating through the list of constraints, retrieved from the Mikrokosmos lexicon and ontology (Beale, Nirenburg & Mahesh 1995), and linking any words involved in the same constraint. In Figure 2, three relatively independent sub-parts can be identified. If these sub-parts, or "circles" in our terminology, could be identified, the processing involved in finding a complete solution could be decomposed into three sub-problems. In this paper we assume such a decomposition is possible so that we may concentrate on describing the methods used to combine results from individual circles to form larger and larger solutions, the largest of which will be the solution to the entire problem.

Solution Synthesis Gatherers in NL

Freuder (1978) introduced Solution Synthesis (SS) as a means to "gather up" all solutions for a CSP without resorting to traditional search methods. Freuder's algorithm (SS-FREUDER) created a set of two-variable nodes that contained combinations of **every** two variables. These two-variable nodes were then combined into three-variable nodes, and so on, until a node containing all the variables, i.e. the solution, was synthesized. At each step, constraints were propagated down and then back up the "tree" of synthesized nodes.

Tsang improved on this scheme with the Essex Algorithms (SS-ESSEX). These algorithms assumed that a list of the variables could be made, after which two-variable nodes were created only between adjacent variables in the list. Higher order nodes were then synthesized as usual, starting from the two-variable nodes. Tsang noted that some orderings of the original list would prove more efficient than others, most notably a "Minimal Bandwidth Ordering" (MBO), which seeks to minimize the distance between constrained variables.

The work described here extends and generalizes the concept of MBO. The basic idea of synthesizing solution sets one order higher than their immediate ancestors is discarded. Instead, solution synthesis operates with maximally interacting groupings (circles) of variables of any order and extends to the highest levels of synthesizing. Tsang only creates second order nodes from adjacent variables in a list, with the original list possibly ordered to maximize second order interactions. After that, third and higher order nodes are blindly created from combinations of second order nodes. We extend MBO to the higher levels. The circles of co-constrained variables described in the previous section guide the synthesis process from beginning to end.

The main improvement of this approach comes from a recognition that much of the work in SS-FREUDER and SS-ESSEX was wasted on finding valid combinations of variables which were not related. Even though relatively few words in a sentence are connected through constraints, SS-FREUDER looks for valid combinations of every word pair. Depending on the ordering used, many irrelevant combinations can also be inspected by SS-ESSEX. Furthermore, the ESSEX algorithm tends to carry along unneeded ambiguity. If two related variables are not adjacent in the ESSEX algorithm, their disambiguating power will not be applied until they happen to co-occur in a higher-order synthesis.[3] The current work combines the efficiency of the ESSEX algorithms with the early disambiguation power of the Freuder method.

Our SS-GATHERER algorithm only expends energy on variables directly related by constraints. For instance, for the example in Figure 2, three "base" circles would be formed:

1. `adquirir, grupo roche, dr andreu`
2. `adquirir, a traves de, companía`
3. `compania, en, espana`

The last two are synthesized into a larger circle:

`adq., a traves de, compania, en, espana, su`

This is then synthesized with the first "base" circle above to give the answer to the complete problem.

The bulk of disambiguation occurs in the lower order circles which were chosen to maximize this phenomenon. The correct solution to the example problem was obtained by SS-GATHERER in only five steps. SS-Freuder uses hundreds of extra nodes for this example and SS-ESSEX, 31 extra nodes. Focusing the synthesizer on circles that yield maximum disambiguation power produces huge savings while still guaranteeing the correct solution.

One objection that could be raised to this process is that more work might be needed to create higher-level nodes. For instance, if each variable had three possible values, one needs to test 9 (3^2) combinations for each second-order node, but 27 (3^3) combinations for third order nodes.[4] If two second-order nodes could be created that would form a third-order node, and each second order node could be completely disambiguated to a single solution, then the third order node could be created without any combinatorics, yielding a total of 18 combinations (9 + 9) that were searched in the case of three values for each variable. Directly creating the third-order node requires the 27 combinations to be searched. However, if the second order nodes do **not** disambiguate, nothing is gained from them. For this reason, base circles can be further sub-divided into groups of second-order nodes, **if** those second-order nodes are connected in the constraint graph.

The algorithm below accepts a list of Circles, ordered from smaller to larger. Each circle has the sub-circles from which it is made identified.

```
1 PROCEDURE SS-GATHERER(Circles)
2    FOR each Circle in Circles
3       PROCESS-CIRCLE(Circle)

4 PROCEDURE PROCESS-CIRCLE(Circle)
     ;;Each Circle in form (Vars-in-Circle Sub-Circles)
5    Output-Plans < -- nil
6    Incoming-Non-Circles < -- REMOVE all
       variables in Sub-Circles from Vars-In-Circle
7    Non-Circle-Combos < --
        Get-Combos(Incoming-Non-Circles)
8    Circle-Combos < --
        Combine-Circles(Sub-Circles)
9    FOR each Non-Circle-Combo in Non-Circle-Combos
10      FOR each Circle-Combo in Circle-Combos
           ;; each incoming circle has consistency
           ;; info stored in arrays:
11         AC-Info < -- access arc constraint
              info from input circles
12         Plan < -- add Non-Circle-Combo
             to Circle-Combo
           ;; Plan is a potential solution for this Circle
           ;; with a value assigned to each variable.
13         IF Arc-Consistent(Plan,AC-Info) THEN
14            Output-Plans < -- Output-Plans + Plan
15            ;; update AC-Info for this circle
16   RETURN Output-Plans
```

The Get-Combos procedure (line 7) simply produces all combinations of value assignments for the input variables. This procedure has complexity $O(a^x)$, where x is the number of variables in the input Incoming-Non-Circles, and a is the maximum number of values for a variable. In the worst case, x will be n; this is the case when the initial circle contains all the variables

[3] Freuder's algorithm does not have this disadvantage, because **all** combinations of variables are created, though at great expense.

[4] It should be pointed out that sometimes second order nodes are used in SS-GATHERER, if the dependency structure calls for them. Incidentally, there is nothing special about third-order nodes in SS-GATHERER, although NL constraints seem to produce them the most. It is quite possible that even higher-order nodes could be the starting point.

and no sub-circles. Of course, this is simply an exhaustive search, not Solution Synthesis. In practice, the circles usually contain no more than two variables not involved in input sub-circles, the exceptions almost always pertaining to the base circle, in which case the combine-circles procedure does not add complexity.

The Combine-Circles procedure (line 8) combines all consistent[5] plans already calculated for each input Sub-Circle. In the worst case, where each Sub-Circle contained a single variable, and Sub-Circles contained every variable, then the time complexity would be $O(a^n)$,[6] where a is the maximum size of a variable domain. This is unavoidable, and is the nature of CSPs. However, if the number of circles in Sub-Circles is limited to c, and each circle has at most p possible Plans, then the complexity of this step is $O(p^c)$. This step dominates the time complexity of SS-GATHERER. The next section illustrates how this number can be reduced to a "near" constant value.

The FOR loops in lines 9 and 10 simply combine the possible Plan-Combos from the Incoming-Non-Circles with the Circle-Combos calculated for the Sub-Circles. The worst-case time complexity is no worse than the worst-case time complexity for either Combine-Circles or Get-Var-Combos. If Get-Var-Combos produces a^n combinations, then Combine-Circles will produce none, and vice-versa. In practice, Combine-Circles produces p^c combinations while Plan-Combos produces a constant[7] number of combinations. The total complexity of PROCESS-CIRCLE is therefore $O(p^c)$. Again, this number can be reduced to a "near" constant, as shown below. The complexity of SS-GATHERER, then, is $O(p^c)$ times the number of circles, which is proportional to the number of variables, n. If $O(p^c)$ can be shown to be a "near" constant, then SS-GATHERER has time complexity that is "near" linear with respect to the number of variables.

For each synthesis, arc consistency may be performed (line 13). As discussed above, however, unmodified CSP techniques such as arc-consistency are not usually helpful in problems with non binary-valued constraints. The next section presents a computational substitute that will produce similar efficiency for these kinds of problems.

Using Branch-and-Bound in an Uncertain World

The key observation that enables the application of branch-and-bound to solution synthesis problems is that some variables in a synthesis circle are unaffected by variables outside the circle. For example, in the first circle of Figure 2, (Adquirir, Grupo-Roche, Dr-Andreu), neither Grupo-Roche nor Dr-Andreu is connected (through constraints) to any other variables outside the circle. This will allow us to optimize, or reduce, this circle with respect to these two variables. The reduction process uses branch-and-bound techniques.

Implementing this type of branch-and-bound is quite simple using the apparatus of the previous sections. It is a simple matter to determine if, for a given circle, a variable is connected, through constraints, to variables outside the circle. To implement SS-GATHERER with branch-and-bound, we first need to add to the inputs a list of variables that are affected outside the circle.

All that is needed to complete the upgrade of SS-GATHERER is the addition of one procedure and a modification to SET-UP-CONSTRAINTS, the initialization procedure (not shown) so that it sets up the consistency arrays based not on yes-no constraints but rather on values from the 0 to 1 scale. The best approach is to set a THRESHold below which a constraint score should be considered "not satisfied." This will allow the CSP mechanism to eliminate combinations with low-scoring constraint scores. All other combinations will be allowed to go through.

```
1 PROCEDURE PROCESS-CIRCLE(Circle)
...
16a  REDUCE-PLANS(Output-Plans Constrained-Vars)
16   RETURN Output-Plans

17 PROCEDURE REDUCE-PLANS(Plans Constr-Vars)
18     FOR each Plan in Plans
19         Affected-Assignments < -- all value assgnmnts
               from Plan that involve a Constr-Var
20         IF Affected-Assignments is NIL THEN
               ;;This will only happen for the topmost circle
21             Affected-Assignments < -- TOP
22         This-Score < -- Get-Score(Plan)
23         Best-Score < --
               Best-Score[Affected-Assignments]
24         IF (This-Score > Best-Score) THEN
25             Best-Score[Affected-Assignments] < --
                   This-Score
26             Best-Plan[Affected-Assignments] < -- Plan
27     RETURN the list of all Best-Plans
```

Why does this work? First of all, each previously processed circle has been reduced, so that the input Circle-Combos will only contain reduced plans. In REDUCE-PLANS, then, we want to keep all possible combinations of variables that are affected outside the circle. Line 19 calculates what these affected combinations are for the input plan. The Best-Score and Best-Plan arrays are then indexed by this (consistently ordered) list of combinations. The goal is that, for each possible combination of assignments of variables affected outside the circle, find the Plan that maximizes that combination. Because all of the other, Unconstrained-Vars, are **not** affected outside the circle, we can find the Plan that maximizes each of the

[5] If one circle has a Plan1 with the assignment $< A, X >$ (value X assigned to variable A) and another Circle has a Plan2 with the assignment $< A, Y >$, then Plan1 and Plan2 are not consistent and cannot be combined.

[6] Combining n variables each with a possible values.

[7] a^x, where x is the number of variables in Incoming-Non-Circles, usually 1 or at most 2, except for base circles.

combinations that **are** affected outside the circle.

In the first circle, (Adquirir, Grupo-Roche, Dr-Andreu), only *adquirir* is affected outside the circle. Because there exist other constraints that are not in this circle, we cannot choose a final value for *adquirir*. We will need to retain plans for both possible value assignments: $< adquirir, aquire >$ and $< adquirir, learn >$. On the other hand, *Grupo Roche* and *Dr. Andreu* are not constrained outside the circle. All of the constraints involving them are taken care of within the circle. For this reason, we can find the value assignments of *Grupo Roche* and *Dr. Andreu* that produce the maximum score for the $< adquirir, aquire >$ assignment, and then find the value assignments that produce the maximum score for the $< adquirir, learn >$. All other plans involving non-optimal combinations can be discarded. "Scores" are calculated by comparing constraints, such as a **learn** concept requiring an **animate** agent, with the actual relationships between the value assignments under consideration.

It must be stressed here that discarding the non-optimal plans in no way incurs risk of finding sub-optimal solutions. These are not heuristic decisions being made which might be wrong. Branch-and-bound techniques such as these simply prune off areas of the search space in which optimal solutions can be guaranteed **not** to be found. The only non-certainty present is in the scoring of constraints, which is an inexact science; however, once given a set of scores, these techniques are guaranteed to give the optimal value assignment combinations.

Branch-and-Bound Results To illustrate how Branch-and-Bound dramatically reduces the search space, consider the results of applying it to the sample sentence.

Circle	In-Circles	In-Combos	Reduced-Combos
1	none	2*2*1 = 4	2
2	none	2*2*2 = 8	4
3	none	2*2*1 = 4	2
4	2 and 3	synth only	2
5	1 and 4	synth only	1

The total number of combinations examined is the sum of the input combos; in this case 4+8+4=16. Compare this to an exhaustive search, which would examine (2*1*2*2*2*1*2*1) = 32 combinations. As the input problem size increases, the savings are even more dramatic. This happens because the problem is broken up into manageable sub-parts; the total complexity of the problem is the **sum** of the individual complexities. Without these techniques, the overall complexity is the **product** of the individual complexities. This is the central fact that supports our claim that the number of circles in Sub-Circles is limited to a "near" constant, leading to a "near" linear time complexity for the whole algorithm.

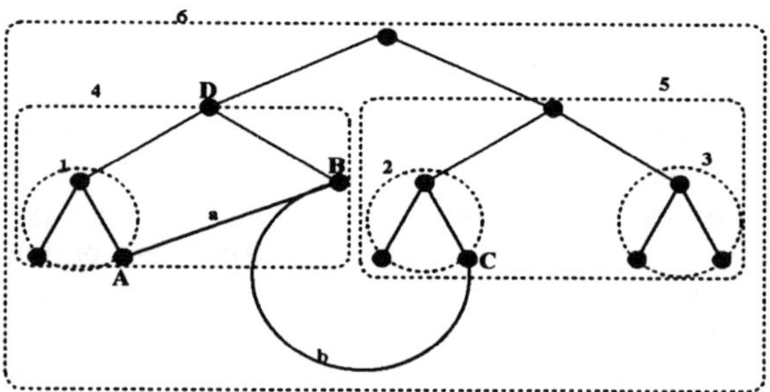

Figure 3: Cross Dependencies

The only way multiplicative growth can occur in SS-GATHERER is when there are constraints across trees, as in Figure 3. In that Figure, several of the circles cannot be fully reduced due to interactions outside the circle. Variable A in Circle 1 cannot be fully reduced[8] because of Arc a. Note, however, that when Circle 4 is synthesized, Variable A **can** be reduced because, at that point, it does not interact outside the larger circle. In Circle 4, Variable B cannot be reduced because it interacts with Variable C. Likewise, Variable C cannot be reduced in Circle 2 because of its interaction with Variable B. In all of these cases, ambiguity must be carried along until no interactions outside the circle exist. For Variables B and C, that does not occur until Circle 6, the entire problem, is processed.

Practically speaking, though, NL problems generally do not allow interactions such as Arc a and Arc b.[9] "Governed" (Haegeman 1991) interactions such as Variable D directly constraining Variable A can occasionally occur, but these only delay reduction to the next higher circle. Thus, some local multiplicative effects can occur, but over the problem as a whole, the complexity is additive.

To illustrate this point, consider what happens as the size of the problem increases. The following table shows actual results of analyses of various size problems. We have tested the SS-GATHERER algorithm extensively on a wide variety of sentences in the context of the Mikrokosmos Machine Translation Project. Over 70 sentences have been analyzed (a relatively large corpus for knowledge-based MT). The claims of near-linear time processing and guaranteed optimal so-

[8] By "fully reduced" we mean all child variables maximized with respect to a single parent, which cannot be reduced because it connects higher up in the tree.

[9] "Long-distance" dependencies do exist, but are relatively rare.

lutions have been verified. These three sentences are representative:

	Sentence A	Sentence B	Sentence C
# plans	79	95	119
exh. combos	7,864,320	56,687,040	235 billion
SS-GATHERER	179	254	327

It is interesting to note that a 20% increase in the number of total plans[10] (79 to 95) results in a 626% increase (7.8M to 56M) in the number of exhaustive combinations possible, but only a 42% increase (179 to 254) in the number of combinations considered by SS-GATHERER. As one moves on to even more complex problems, a 25% increase (95 to 119) in the number of plans catapults the exhaustive complexity by 414,600% (56M to 235B) and yet only increases the SS-GATHERER complexity by 29% (254 to 327). As the problem size increases, the minor effects of "local multiplicative" influences diminish with respect to the size of the problem. We expect, therefore, the behavior of this algorithm to move even closer to linear with larger problems (i.e. discourse). And, again, it is important to note that SS-GATHERER is guaranteed to produce the same results as an exhaustive search.

Although time measurements are often misleading, it is important to state the practical outcome of this type of control advancement. Prior to implementing SS-GATHERER, our analyzer failed to complete processing large sentences. The largest sentence above was analyzed for more than a **day** with no results. Using SS-GATHERER, on the other hand, the same sentence was finished in 17 **seconds**. It must be pointed out as well that this is not an artificially selected example. It is a real sentence occurring in natural text, and not an overly large sentence at that.

Conclusion

We have presented a new control environment for processing Natural Language Semantics. By combining and extending the AI techniques known as constraint satisfaction, solution synthesis and branch-and-bound, we have reduced the search space from billions or more to thousands or less. This paper has concentrated on the combination of branch-and-bound "hunters" with solution synthesis "gatherers."

In the past, the utility of Knowledge-based semantics has been limited, subject to arguments that it only works in "toy" environments. Recent efforts at increasing the size of knowledge bases, however, have created an imbalance with existing control techniques which are unable to handle the explosion of information. We believe that this methodology will enable such work. Furthermore, because this work is a generalization of a control strategy used for simpler binary constraints, we believe that it is applicable to a wide variety of real-life problems. We intend to test this control paradigm on problems outside NLP.

[10]The total number of plans corresponds to the total number of word senses for all the words in the sentence.

References

Beale, S. 1996. Hunter-Gatherer: Applying Constraint Satisfaction, Branch-and-Bound and Solution Synthesis to Natural Language Semantics, Technical Report, MCCS-96-289, Computing Research Lab, New Mexico State Univ.

Beale, S. and Nirenburg, S. 1995. Dependency-Directed Text Planning. In Proceedings of the 1995 International Joint Conference on Artificial Intelligence, Workshop on Multilingual Text Generation, 13-21. Montreal, Quebec.

Beale, S.; Nirenburg, S. and Mahesh, K. 1995. Semantic Analysis in the Mikrokosmos Machine Translation Project. In Proceedings of the 2nd Symposium on Natural Language Processing, 297-307. Bangkok, Thailand.

Charniak, E; Riesbeck, C.K.; McDermott D.V. and Meehan, J.R. 1987. *Artificial Intelligence Programming.* Hillsdale, NJ: Erlbaum.

Freuder, E.C. 1978. Synthesizing Constraint Expressions. *Communications ACM* 21(11): 958-966.

Haegeman, L. 1991. *An Introduction to Government and Binding Theory.* Oxford, U.K.: Blackwell Publishers.

Lawler, E.W. and Wood, D.E. 1966. Branch-and-Bound Methods: a Survey. *Operations Research* 14: 699-719.

Mackworth, A.K. 1977. Consistency in Networks of Relations. *Artificial Intelligence* 8(1): 99-118.

Mackworth, A.K. and Freuder, E.C. 1985. The Complexity of Some Polynomial Consistency Algorithms for Constraint Satisfaction Problems. *Artificial Intelligence* 25: 65-74.

Maruyama, H. 1990. Structural Disambiguation with Constraint Propagation. In Proceedings 28th Conference of the Association for Computational Linguistics, 31-38. Pittsburgh, Pennsylvania.

Mohr, R. and Henderson, T.C. 1986. Arc and Path Consistency Revisited. *Artificial Intelligence* 28: 225-233.

Nagao, K. 1992. A Preferential Constraint Satisfaction Technique for Natural Language Analysis. In Proceedings 10th European Conference on Artificial Intelligence, 523-527. Vienna.

Tsang, E. 1993. *Foundations of Constraint Satisfaction.* London: Academic Press.

Tsang, E. and Foster, N. 1990. Solution Synthesis in the Constraint Satisfaction Problem, Technical Report, CSM-142, Dept. of Computer Science, Univ. of Essex.

Semantic Interpretation of Nominalizations

Richard D. Hull and Fernando Gomez
Department of Computer Science
University of Central Florida
Orlando, FL 32816
hull@cs.ucf.edu

Abstract

A computational approach to the semantic interpretation of nominalizations is described. Interpretation of nominalizations involves three tasks: deciding whether the nominalization is being used in a verbal or non-verbal sense; disambiguating the nominalized verb when a verbal sense is used; and determining the fillers of the thematic roles of the verbal concept or predicate of the nominalization. A verbal sense can be recognized by the presence of modifiers that represent the arguments of the verbal concept. It is these same modifiers which provide the semantic clues to disambiguate the nominalized verb. In the absence of explicit modifiers, heuristics are used to discriminate between verbal and non-verbal senses. A correspondence between verbs and their nominalizations is exploited so that only a small amount of additional knowledge is needed to handle the nominal form. These methods are tested in the domain of encyclopedic texts and the results are shown.

Introduction

Quirk(Quirk *et al.* 1985) defines nominalization as "a [noun phrase] which has a systematic correspondence with a clause structure," where the head nouns of nominalization phrases are related morphologically to either a verb (deverbal noun) or adjective (deadjectival noun). In this paper we focus on deverbal nominalizations, a common linguistic device used as a vehicle for describing specific events, generic actions, and *action concepts* such as evolution. Understanding sentences with nominalizations requires the ability to determine the meaning of the nominalization and to make sense of the nominalization's modifiers, namely, the other words in the noun phrase (NP) containing the nominalization and the prepositional phrases that follow it.

An important problem is distinguishing between the verbal and non-verbal senses of the nominalization, as is necessary for words like "support", "decoration", and "publication". In order to distinguish between verbal and non-verbal senses, we will use the term nominalization to refer to only those *senses* of the noun which are derived from verbs. For example, the noun "decoration" has several senses including a military badge of honor, an ornament, and the nominalization sense, which means the act or process of decorating.

There also is the equally serious problem of what to do when the nominalized verb is polysemous. This problem is quite prevalent, and while there is a large body of work discussing word sense disambiguation using knowledge-based approaches(McRoy 1992; Hirst 1992; Jacobs & Rau 1993; Voorhees 1993; Li, Szpakowicz, & Matwin 1995), a computational approach to this problem has not, to our knowledge, been specifically addressed in the literature. As an illustration of the problem, consider the verb *promote*, which has several different meanings, e.g., to promote a product, to promote a person to a higher position of authority, and to promote a cause. The nominalization, "promotion," therefore, can have different meanings as in *the promotion of Peter* or *the promotion of liberalism.*

The framework of a model of semantic interpretation that can be used to solve these problems is described in detail in (Gomez, Segami, & Hull 1997). While a partial treatment of nominalizations involving the attachment of prepositional phrases to them is presented in that work, its focus is not a complete model of nominalization interpretation and as such does not address the issues of interpreting nominalization NP modifiers and deciding between a nominalization's verbal and non-verbal senses, which will be discussed here.

The remainder of this paper is comprised of five sections. Section describes the essential aspects of the semantic interpreter of which the nominalization algorithms, explained in section , are a part. The testing of these algorithms on a collection of nominalizations is discussed in section . A comparison of this approach to other work in the literature is explained in section . Finally, section presents the authors' conclusions.

Semantic Interpreter

The parser used by our semantic interpreter leaves structural syntactic relations underspecified along the lines of D-Theory (Marcus, Hindle, & Fleck 1983) and minimal commitment parsers (Weinberg 1993). The parser recognizes the following syntactic relations: subject, object1, object2, predicate, and prepositional phrases (PPs). Object1 is built for the first postverbal noun phrases (NPs) of transitive verbs, and object2 for the second postverbal NP of diatransitive verbs. The parser also recognizes temporal adjuncts of the verb; but, as indicated, it does not resolve structural ambiguity. PPs are left unattached in the structure built by the parser until the semantic interpreter finds their meaning and attaches them. As each syntactic relation is identified, it is passed to the semantic interpreter to make semantic sense of it.

All important semantic decisions are delayed until the meaning of the verb is determined. Determining verb meaning is done by rules that use the types of syntactic relations built by the parser and the semantic categories of the nouns in them. For instance, what determines the meaning of "drive" in (1) is the direct object of the verb and the fact that "bus" is a motor-vehicle (here "drive" means *to operate a vehicle*), and that "nail" is a device (here "drive" means *to hammer*).

(1) *Peter drove the bus/the nail.*

In addition to NP complement rules, prepositional phrase rules (PP rules) are also used to determine the meaning of the verb. In (2), the meaning of "left" is identified by two *for*-rules stored in its lexical entry: the meaning of "left" is identified as *transfer of possession* in the first case because the object of the PP is a human and as *depart* in in the second because the object of the PP is a location.

(2) *Jennifer left the orange groves for her son/for home.*

Once the meaning of the verb is established, additional knowledge is needed to interpret subsequent syntactic relations and those which have been parsed but have remained uninterpreted. This knowledge is stored in the representation of the verbal concept or predicate. Below are examples of NP complement rules and preposition rules for the verb "defend":

```
(defend
  ((object
     ((if% is-a obj location)
        (verbal-concept-is defend-physical-thing))
     ((if% is-a obj idea)
        (verbal-concept-is defend-idea)))
   (prep
     (in ((if% equal obj-of-prep court)
           (verbal-concept-is legal-defend))))
   (end-of-clause
     ((if% is-a obj championship)
        (verbal-concept-is defend-championship))
     ( t (verbal-concept-is defend)))))
```

The first set of rules selects the verbal concept based upon the NP complement. If the direct object is a subconcept or an instance of a *location* within a hierarchy of concepts, then the meaning of the verb is *defend-physical-thing*. This rule is designed to handle constructions such as *Carleton defended Quebec*. If the direct object is a subconcept or instance of an *idea* in the concept hierarchy, then the meaning of the verb is represented by the verbal concept *defend-idea*, as in *her defense of the theorem*. If the direct object does not pass either of these two constraints, then the meaning of the verb is left unspecified in hopes that later evidence will disambiguate it. The next rule is a preposition rule for PPs that follow the verb "defend" and begin with the preposition "in". If the object of such a prepositional phrase (the object of the PP is the head of its complement NP) is equal to the word "court", then the meaning of the verb is represented by the verbal concept *legal-defend*. The last set of rules, called end-of-clause rules, is used if the parser reaches the end of a clause and the meaning of the verb is still unknown. If the direct object is a subconcept or instance of a *championship* in the concept hierarchy, then the meaning of the verb is represented by the verbal concept *defend-championship*. Otherwise, the meaning of the verb is the generic *defend*. These five verbal concepts are displayed below.

```
(defend
 (is-a (action-r))
 (subj (agent (actor)))
 (obj (thing (theme))
 (prep (against (thing (against (strong))))
       (from (thing (against (strong))))))

; WordNet sense defend1,4,7
(defend-idea
 (is-a (defend))
 (obj (idea (theme))))

; WordNet sense defend2,5
(defend-physical-thing
 (is-a (defend))
 (obj (physical-thing (theme))))

; WordNet sense defend3
(defend-championship
 (is-a (defend))
 (obj (championship (theme))))

; WordNet sense defend6
(legal-defend
 (is-a (defend))
 (obj (agent (theme)))
 (prep (in (court (at-loc (strong))))))
```

The first entry in the verbal concept *defend*, *(is-a (action-r))*, places *defend* within the hierarchy of action concepts. The next entry is a restriction: if the subject of defense is subsumed by the *agent* concept in the concept hierarchy, then make it fill the *actor* role. The other entries represent restrictions on the object and prepositional phrases. Each of the subconcepts of *defend*; *defend-idea*, *defend-physical-thing*, *defend-championship*, and *legal-defend*, inherits entries from *defend*.

This fine-grained decomposition of "defend" is necessary if one wishes to make specific inferences depending on the type of defense. The structures above embody the knowledge necessary to understand clauses containing the verb "defend" (see (Gomez, Segami, & Hull 1997) for a detailed discussion of VM rules and verbal concepts). This verbal knowledge can be exploited and reused for interpretation of nominalizations, if a small amount of additional information detailing how the nominalization's modifiers relate to the syntactic relations of the VM rules and verbal concepts is constructed. Knowledge indicating whether any thematic roles are "obligatory," that is, necessary for a verbal sense interpretation, is also stored.

The nominalization "defense" is shown below. *Defense* has one obligatory role, *theme*. Because "defense" has both verbal and non-verbal senses, a requirement is made that the *theme* must be present for a verbal sense to be chosen. A nominalization that has only verbal senses does not need an obligatory-role slot. No special mapping rules for genitives or prepositions are present because "defense" behaves like most nominalizations: genitives represent either the actor or theme of the action; and besides the preposition "of" which represents the theme of the transitive verbs and the actor of intransitive verbs, "defense" inherits the meanings of its PP modifiers from its root verb, "defend."

```
(defense (obligatory-role (theme)))
```

For the majority of nominalizations, no information over and above that of the verbal knowledge is necessary. However, there are exceptions. Genitive modifiers of the nominalization "attendance" only make sense as the actors of "attend". In this case, a slot specifying that the genitive should fill the *actor* role is needed. Another situation where additional information is needed is in the handling of certain prepositional phrases. The nominalization "control" takes PPs using the preposition "over" as the verb's object, as in, *his control over the business*, while the verb "control" does not. To handle this, a slot mapping the preposition "over" to the verb's object is added.

In addition to providing the means for disambiguating between nominal and deverbal senses of the nominalization, verbal knowledge can also be used to disambiguate the underlying verb of the nominalization when it exhibits polysemy. It is the prepositional phrase "in court" that selects the meaning *legal-defend* for "defense" in *her defense in court*, and it is the prepositional phrase "of Richmond" that selects the meaning *defend-physical-thing* in *Lee gave up the defense of Richmond.*

Interpretation Algorithms for Nominalizations

The interpretation algorithms attempt to determine the verbal concept of the nominalization and to fill its thematic roles. Determination of the verbal concept requires disambiguation of the meaning of the nominalization's root verb. This ambiguity may be resolved by examining the noun phrase in which the nominalization occurs, or as is true in many cases, disambiguation can only be accomplished by examining postnominal prepositional phrases. Once the verbal concept has been identified, surrounding nouns are then interpreted as verbal concept arguments. There are three separate interpretation algorithms: the nominalization noun phrase algorithm, the prepositional attachment and meaning determination algorithm, and the end-of-clause algorithm. We will discuss the main points and then the details of each algorithm in turn.

Nominalization Noun Phrase Algorithm

The nominalization noun phrase algorithm is triggered when the head noun[1] of some NP is determined to be a potential nominalization. This is accomplished by consulting WordNet(Miller *et al.* 1993) to see if any of the senses of the noun are hypernyms of either actions or events. Conceptually, the algorithm has two objectives:

1. To determine the verbal concept or predicate of the nominalization, and
2. To identify which thematic roles of the verbal concept, if any, each of the remaining nouns and adjectives of the NP fill.

Determining the verbal concept of the nominalization establishes its meaning within the context of the sentence. Occasionally, the nominalization has a single meaning and in those cases we can immediately determine the verbal concept. This trivial disambiguation is attempted first and works for nominalizations like "invasion" and "murder." More often, however, determining the verbal concept requires disambiguating the nominalization because the root verb of the nominalization is polysemous.

In order to disambiguate polysemous nominalizations, the algorithm uses the root verb to select VM rules. In addition, mapping rules and heuristics are needed to handle the fact that nominalizations do not take bare NPs; the verb's syntactic subject and object reappear as genitival, adjectival, or prepositional modifiers. This algorithm addresses genitives, possessive pronouns, single prenominal nouns, i.e., pairs of the form *noun nom*, and adjectives which fill thematic roles. The prepositional attachment and meaning determination algorithm described later handles prepositional modifiers.

Determining the Verbal Concept

The VM rules of the root verb do not include any for handling genitives, pronouns, or noun/adjective modifiers. Therefore, if these rules are to be reused, some way of selecting the appropriate ones is needed. The central problem associated with disambiguation of the nominalization within the NP then becomes *Which VM rules should be fired?* Consider the case where the NP is of the form: (*genitive nominalization*). The genitive may correspond semantically to the verb's subject or object, as is illustrated in the examples below.

(3) *Lincoln's election; The representatives elected Lincoln.*

[1]The algorithm does not currently handle nominalizations in positions other than the head.

(4) *Metternich's resignation; Metternich resigned.*

In (3), the genitive corresponds to the object position, while in (4), it corresponds to the subject position. The verb *resign* is intransitive, except for colloquial expressions such as "resigned his office", and therefore, genitive modifiers of the nominalization *resignation* correspond to the verb's subject. This idea forms the first rule selection heuristic. Passive nominals behave differently; their genitive modifiers correspond to the verbal object. A mapping rule selects the verb's object rules when the nominalization is passive. If the nominalization's verb is neither intransitive nor is the nominalization passive, then the genitive could correspond to either the subject or object. Consequently, the selection of VM rules is postponed, in hopes that following prepositional phrases will disambiguate the nominalization.

If the nominalization is modified by either a noun or adjective, it is not possible to determine exactly which disambiguation rules must be fired. Any ordering of the rules is guaranteed to be wrong in a large percentage of cases. In addition, it would be unproductive to try all of the rules in hopes that only the appropriate one would be triggered. Therefore, disambiguation is postponed until more evidence is available in the form of roles filled by prepositional phrases.

Filling Thematic Roles

Once the verbal concept of the nominalization has been determined, the next step is to determine which of the other constituents of the NP fill thematic roles of the verbal concept and what those roles are. A syntactic relation is said to fill a thematic role if the concept it represents in the concept hierarchy passes the selectional restrictions associated with that role. For example, *humans* elect *humans* to *institutions* as *social-roles*. The hierarchy of concepts is consulted to determine if the argument of the syntactic relation under consideration is subsumed by the subhierarchy of the selectional restriction. If it is, then the restriction is passed.

Even when the verbal concept of the nominalization has been determined, identifying the role that the nominalization's modifier plays is difficult. For this reason it seems appropriate to wait until all of the roles stemming from prepositional phrases have been identified before trying to resolve the nominalization's modifiers in the NP. That way, candidate roles, if already filled, can be weeded out. Thus, only the remaining unfilled roles need to be checked. Below is a detailed description of noun phrase algorithm.

Noun Phrase Algorithm

Let n_0 be the head noun of some noun phrase that is currently under consideration, and one or more of the senses of n_0 represent a nominalized verb. Apply the algorithm below to determine the meaning of n_0:

1. If n_0 has a single sense, set the verbal concept vc_0 to this meaning and continue.
2. If the NP containing n_0 includes a genitive or a possessive pronoun, and there is no modifying "of" PP, attempt to realize the qualifier (or its anaphoric referent) as a thematic role of a verbal concept from the nominalization's root verb as follows:
   (a) If the verbal concept has been determined, then
      i. Fire nominalization mapping rules.
      ii. If no rules are triggered, check the genitive/pronoun against the selectional restrictions of the verbal concept's object and subject entries (subject entries only for intransitive verbs).
      iii. If no meaning was found for the gènitive/pronoun, goto step 4.
   (b) Else, (the verbal concept has not been determined)
      i. Fire nominalization mapping rules.
      ii. Else, if the nominalization is an -ing nominalization, fire the subject rules of the verb.
      iii. If no rules are triggered and the verb is intransitive, fire the subject rules of the verb.
      iv. Else, try both the object and subject rules of the verb. If only one type has a rule that fires, take the triggered verbal concept.
      v. If no rules are triggered, the verbal concept cannot be determined, exit.
3. If the NP containing n_0 includes some other qualifier and the verbal concept is unknown, exit.
4. Else, if the NP containing n_0 includes some other qualifier(s) and the verbal concept is known:
   (a) If the modifier is a noun, attempt to determine which role the noun plays in the verbal concept underlying the nominalization as follows:
      i. Examine the selectional restrictions found in the representation of the verbal concept.
      ii. If the modifier satisfies a single role, make that the interpretation of the modifier.
      iii. Else, procrastinate until more evidence is available.
   (b) Else, if the modifier is an adjective, determine if it can: fill an at-time role, e.g., the 1972 election; is derived from a noun which may fill a role; or is an ordinal adjective, in which case, mark the adjective as a temporal indicator.

Prepositional Attachment and Meaning Algorithm

The prepositional attachment and meaning determination algorithm is activated for each prepositional phrase found within the scope of some nominalization, which is defined to be any postnominal position within the same sentence clause as the nominalization, up to the main verb (for nominalizations before the verb) and to the end of the clause (for nominalizations after the verb). This algorithm has two objectives:

1. To determine if the prepositional phrase attaches to the nominalization, and
2. To determine the meaning of the prepositional phrase attachment within the context of the nominalization.

As each such prepositional phrase is parsed from left to right, the preposition is used to select either VM rules, if the verbal concept has not been established, or to select verbal concept selectional restrictions, if it has been established. If one of these rules fires, indicating that the nominalization takes the preposition, the PP is attached to the nominalization, and its thematic role is noted. The prepositional phrase attachment algorithm, shown below, is part of a general semantic interpretation algorithm that is described in (Gomez, Segami, & Hull 1997).

Prepositional Phrase Attachment Algorithm

Let n_0 be the head noun of some noun phrase where one or more of the senses of n_0 represent a nominalized verb, and let the verbal concept of that verb be vc_0. Let pp_1, pp_2, ..., pp_i be a list of one or more prepositional phrases that follow n_0 in the sentence. Apply the algorithm below to determine whether pp_i attaches to (modifies) n_0 and what the meaning of pp_i is, that is, its thematic role:

1. If the verbal concept, vc_0, underlying the nominalization is not known, then

(a) If the preposition is "of,"
   i. Use the "of" mapping rules of the nominalization, if any exist.
   ii. If no "of" mapping rules exist, attempt to fire the obj rules of the nominalized verb.
(b) Else, (the preposition is not "of")
   i. Use the appropriate mapping rules of the nominalization, if any exist.
   ii. Else, attempt to fire the preposition rules of the nominalized verb for the given preposition.

2. Else, if vc_0 is known,
   (a) If the nominalization has mapping rules for the preposition, use them to select the appropriate verbal concept entry. If the entry's selectional restriction is passed, goto step 3 else goto step 4.
   (b) Else, if the preposition is "of," try the obj entries of vc_0. If the entry's selectional restriction is passed, goto step 3 else goto step 4.
   (c) Else, use the entries of vc_0 indexed under the appropriate preposition. If the entry's selectional restriction is passed, goto step 3 else goto step 4.
3. pp_i attaches to vc_0, therefore, save the attachment to the nominalization, save its meaning, and exit.
4. If vc_0 does not claim pp_i, see if any superconcept of vc_0 has an entry, under the appropriate preposition or using the mapping, that vc_0 inherits, which determines attachment and meaning. Repeat step 2 with the ancestor of vc_0 recursively until either an attachment is found, or the list of superconcepts is exhausted.

Discussion

We examine the progress of the interpreter as the nominalization and its modifying constituents of the sentence below is parsed:

(5) *The king sent another fleet to break the* $\underbrace{\textit{Muslims'}}_{genitive}\ \underbrace{\textit{control}}_{n_0}\ \underbrace{\textit{over spice}}_{pp_1}\ \underbrace{\textit{in that country.}}_{pp_2}$

In (5), the meaning of "control" can not be determined by the noun phrase interpretation algorithm because "Muslims' control" may have several different interpretations. Now the PP algorithm is called with "over spice," and because the verbal concept is unknown, step 1 executes. The nominalization "control" has mapping rules for the preposition "over," which ultimately take the preposition strongly as its *theme*, and determine the verbal concept of "control" to be *control-physical-thing*. The last constituent, pp_2, is handled by step 2c, which attaches it to "control" as the location of the action. PP_2 can also be attached to "spice," but preference is given to the nominalization. The genitive modifier is handled by the end-of-clause algorithm, which is described in the next section.

End-of-Clause Algorithm

The end-of-clause algorithm is activated when the parser reaches the end of a clause containing a nominalization[2]. This algorithm has two objectives:

1. To determine the verbal concept of the nominalization, if it is still unknown, and to determine if the nominalization is being used in a non-verbal sense, and
2. To reevaluate each nominalization modifier to ensure that an interpretation has been found.

If the verbal concept is still undetermined, this algorithm makes one last effort to establish it. First the algorithm fires the end-of-clause rules of the root verb. If none of the rules fires, it may be that the nominalization is part of a collocation. The NP of the nominalization is used to search WordNet's list of collocations. This will provide the verbal concept in cases such as "primary election" and "free trade." If no matching collocation can be found and the nominalization has both verbal and non-verbal senses, a set of heuristics based on work by Grimshaw(Grimshaw 1990) is used to reject any verbal sense. In the absence of any thematic roles, a verbal sense can be rejected if the nominalization is plural or has an indefinite article, e.g., *Maxwell moved the controls* and *Tasha wanted a decoration.* If the verbal sense of the nominalization can be rejected and the nominalization has only one non-verbal sense, then that sense can be selected.

If these heuristics are unsuccessful or a non-verbal sense is selected, a verbal concept will not be found and further processing is abandoned. However, if the verbal concept is already known or is established by the first step of the end-of-clause, each prepositional phrase within the scope of the nominalization and each noun within the nominalization NP is reexamined to verify that it has been interpreted. Reexamination means to reactivate the appropriate algorithm for the nominalization modifier. This is necessary because the determination of the verbal concept might come after several prepositional phrases have been parsed.

End-of-Clause Algorithm

1. If end-of-clause rules do not determine the verbal concept,
   (a) Look up NP (minus articles, quantifiers, etc.) in WordNet's list of collocations.
   (b) If the meaning of the NP is found, save it and goto step 2.
   (c) Else, if the nominalization is plural and there are competing non-verbal senses, assume that this is a non-verbal use of the nominalization and exit.
   (d) Else, if there is only one verbal sense, make it the verbal concept.
2. Reevaluate each nominalization modifier (if verbal concept has been determined)
   (a) See if the modifier has either been assigned a thematic role or has been attached to some other constituent.
   (b) If a modifier that has not been attached is found, fire the appropriate rules (depending on whether the modifier is a prepositional phrase or resides within the nominalization's noun phrase).
   (c) If a rule fires, be sure that the thematic role indicated by the rule has not already been filled.
   (d) If the role has been filled, reject that role and continue firing any other appropriate rules.

Testing

The algorithms were tested to determine how successful they were in disambiguating the nominalization, and in recognizing the underlying verbal concept of the nominalization and filling its thematic roles. The discourse domain was comprised of biographical articles from the World Book Encyclopedia, which are being used in an ongoing research project to acquire historical knowledge from encyclopedic texts(Hull 1994).

[2] Actually, a general end-of-clause algorithm is activated when any clause ends. For the sake of brevity we will describe only those parts of the general end-of-clause algorithm related to the interpretation of nominalizations, and will treat them as a separate algorithm.

Table 1: Algorithm Results

nominal	n	senses	disambig.	gen.	NP	PP
arrest	29	3	100%	100%	33%	91%
birth	78	4	81%	100%	50%	97%
capture	34	5	100%	100%	50%	100%
control	421	11	72%	80%	40%	97%
defense	120	10	97%	96%	38%	97%
execution	25	4	92%	100%	0%	100%
murder	59	1	100%	100%	29%	98%
nomination	212	1	100%	87%	100%	91%
publication	69	3	79%	100%	47%	98%
trade	200	7	94%	89%	57%	97%
total	1247		88%	93%	71%	96%

The algorithms assume the existence of rules for disambiguating the root verb of each of the nominalizations, as well as the mapping rules for those syntactic constructions which are specific to the nominalization. The verb disambiguation rules had already been written as part of our ongoing research, and therefore, the effort needed to handle the nominalizations of these verbs was quite small. Moreover, a list of proper nouns representing proper names was used for recognizing people and locations.

Procedure

The results of the testing are shown in Table 1. Ten nominalizations were selected randomly from a list of nominalizations with at least 20 occurrences in 5000 biography articles from the World Book Encyclopedia. The column *n* shows how many occurrences of the nominalization were found in those articles. The algorithms were applied to each occurrence, and the results of the interpreter were examined to see if the nominalization was correctly disambiguated, if the genitive and the rest of NP was correctly interpreted, and how successfully the algorithms interpreted prepositional phrases modifying the nominalization.

Analysis

The results in Table 1 illustrate the strengths and the one limitation of the algorithms. The correct sense of each nominalization was selected more than 70% of the time, with the worst disambiguation score, 72%, occurring when testing "control," the most ambiguous nominalization with 11 WordNet senses. Failures to disambiguate were most often caused by situations where the verb rules could not be directly applied. For example, in the sentence *Court was noted for her endurance and control*, nothing triggers any of the verb rules. Further, because "control" has both verbal and non-verbal senses, one can't assume that this is an instance of either one. Other disambiguation errors resulted from rules that didn't fire or selected the wrong verbal concept, or that missed a non-verbal sense. On the whole, however, these algorithms provide an effective means of nominalization disambiguation.

The results of determining the thematic roles of deverbal nominalizations are given by the next three columns of Table 1. The thematic roles of genitives were found 93% of the time, showing how regular genitives are. The only statistically relevant problem involved two possessives used together, as in "his party's nomination" or "their country's trade." This problem could be easily handled in a general manner.

Interpreting the other elements of the noun phrase shows a limitation of the algorithms, which shouldn't be surprising considering the difficulty of NP interpretation. The most significant problem was the interpretation of adjectives which do not fill thematic roles but portray a *manner* of the action. Examples include "sole control," "tight control," "profitable trade," "mass murder," and "powerful defense." Related to this problem are other adjectives which are not manners of the action but could not be interpreted as thematic roles, e.g., "foreign trade," "extraordinary breath control," and "important capture."

PPs were correctly attached and their meaning determined over 90% of the time. This shows that the verb's mechanism for handling PPs can be readily used by the nominalization interpretation algorithms. Most failures were due to ambiguous PP heads and cases were the nominalization took prepositions different from the verb, which were unanticipated.

Related Research

Several knowledge-based approaches to interpretation of nominalizations can be found in the current literature. PUNDIT is a system for processing natural language messages, which was used for understanding failure messages generated on Navy ships(Dahl, Palmer, & Passonneau 1987). Nominalizations in PUNDIT are handled syntactically like noun phrases but semantically as clauses, with predicate/argument structure. In fact, PUNDIT uses the same decomposition as the associated verb. Special nominalization mapping rules are used to handle the diverse syntactic realization of constituents of nominalizations. Some components of our approach are similar; nominalizations inherit selectional restrictions and syntactic mappings from their associated verbal concepts and can have their own specialized mappings when appropriate. PUNDIT avoids handling the ambiguity of the nominalization, including the ambiguity between the verbal and non-verbal senses and the polysemy of the nominalized verb. KERNEL(Palmer *et al.* 1993), a successor of PUNDIT, treats nominalizations in much the same way. Voorhees(Voorhees 1993) and Li *et al.*(Li, Szpakowicz, & Matwin 1995) both use WordNet as a source of disambiguation information, but neither addresses interpretation of nominalizations.

Grimshaw(Grimshaw 1990) states that a subclass of nouns, which she refers to as *process* or *event nominals*, have argument structure that is filled by grammatical arguments. Further, these arguments are obligatory to the same extent to which they are obligatory for the nominal's associated verb. Other nouns, which she calls simple events or result nominals, do not have argument structure though they may take either complements or modifiers. Grimshaw explains that the common belief that nouns take arguments optionally (Anderson 1983; Dowty 1989) is really just a case of confusing ambiguous nouns that have both event and simple or result senses, e.g., examination. She then provides a comprehensive list of evidence supporting the notion that nouns take obligatory arguments, including methods for disambiguating these nouns. While knowing that a particular nominalization does or does not have argument structure can help in choosing between its verbal and non-verbal senses, it can not disambiguate the nominalization further. Moreover, the restriction that argument structure is obligatory begs the question of what to do when not all the arguments are present and the nominalization clearly describes an action. This phenomenon, illustrated by the sentences below, occurs quite frequently:

(6) *Some of Johnson's accusers tried to implicate him in Lincoln's* **murder**, *but failed.*

(7) *When the news of Pompey's* **defeat** *at Pharsalus in 48 B.C. reached him, Cato fled to North Africa.*

(8) *He saw that city's* **destruction** *by British and American bombing in 1945.*

Although the nominalizations "murder," " defeat," and "destruction" in the sentences above do not meet Grimshaw's criteria for having argument structure, they do take the arguments "Lincoln," "Pompey," and "city" respectively as their *themes* and they do denote events. Instead of portraying these nouns as passive nominals and calling their arguments *adjuncts*, our approach handles them in the same manner as if they had written as *the murder of Lincoln, the defeat of Pompey,* and *the destruction of that city.*

Conclusions

We have provided knowledge-based algorithms for the semantic interpretation of nominalizations. These algorithms address the problems of differentiating between the nominalization's verbal and non-verbal senses and interpreting the nominalization when it occurs as the head noun of NPs. Interpreting the nominalization involves determining the predicate of the nominalization when it is polysemous, and determining the attachment of the nominalization's PP modifiers and the identification of their thematic roles.

One major limitation of this approach is the need for having hand-crafted representations of VM rules, verbal concepts and a general ontology. We are working on a parallel project that integrates WordNet's lexical knowledge-base into our system. Preliminary results indicate that the task of defining VM rules and verbal concepts can be highly simplified by interfacing our ontology with the WordNet noun ontology and verb hierarchy.

Acknowledgments

This research has been funded by NASA-KSC Contract NAG-10-0120.

References

Anderson, M. 1983. Prenominal genitive nps. *Linguistic Review* 3:1–24.

Dahl, D.; Palmer, M.; and Passonneau, R. 1987. Nominalizations in PUNDIT. In *Proc. of the 25th Annual Meeting of the ACL*, 131–137.

Dowty, D. R. 1989. On the semantic content of the notion 'thematic role'. In Chierchia, G.; Partee, B. H.; and Turner, R., eds., *Properties, Types, and Meaning.* Dordrecht: Kluwer.

Gomez, F.; Segami, C.; and Hull, R. 1997. Determining prepositional attachment, prepositional meaning, verb meaning and thematic roles. *Computational Intelligence* 13(1). To appear.

Grimshaw, J. 1990. *Argument Structure.* Cambridge, Mass.: MIT Press.

Hirst, G. 1992. *Semantic interpretation and the resolution of ambiguity.* New York: Cambridge University Press.

Hull, R. 1994. Acquisition of historical knowledge from encyclopedic texts. Technical report, University of Central Florida, Department of Computer Science. CS-TR-94-05, dissertation proposal.

Jacobs, P., and Rau, L. 1993. Innovations in text interpretation. *Artificial Intelligence* 63:143–191.

Li, X.; Szpakowicz, S.; and Matwin, S. 1995. A wordnet-based algorithm for word sense disambiguation. In *Proc. of IJCAI-95*, 1368–1374.

Marcus, M.; Hindle, D.; and Fleck, M. 1983. D-theory: Talking about talking about trees. In *Proc. of the Annual Meeting of the ACL.*

McRoy, S. 1992. Using multiple sources for word sense discrimination. *Computational Lingusitics* 18:1–30.

Miller, G.; Beckwith, R.; Fellbaum, C.; Gross, D.; and Miller, K. 1993. Introduction to WordNet: An on-line lexical database. Technical report, Princeton. CSL Report 43, revised March 1993.

Palmer, M.; Passonneau, R.; Weir, C.; and Finin, T. 1993. The kernel text understanding system. *Artificial Intelligence* 63:17–68.

Quirk, R.; Greenbaum, S.; Leech, G.; and Svartvik, J. 1985. *A Comprehensive Grammar of the English Language.* New York: Longman Group, Inc.

Voorhees, E. 1993. Using wordnet to disambiguate word senses for text retrieval. In *Proc. of the 16th Annual Int'l ACM SIGIR Conference on Research and Development in Information Retrieval,* 171–180.

Weinberg, A. 1993. Parameters in the theory of sentence processing: Minimal commitment theory goes east. *Journal of Psycholinguistic Research* 22(3):339–364.

Building Up Rhetorical Structure Trees

Daniel Marcu
Department of Computer Science
University of Toronto
Toronto, Ontario
Canada M5S 3G4
marcu@cs.toronto.edu

Abstract

I use the distinction between the nuclei and the satellites that pertain to discourse relations to introduce a compositionality criterion for discourse trees. I provide a first-order formalization of rhetorical structure trees and, on its basis, I derive an algorithm that constructs all the valid rhetorical trees that can be associated with a given discourse.

Motivation

Driven mostly by research in natural language generation, rhetorical structure theory (RST) (Mann & Thompson 1988) has become one of the most widely applied discourse theories. Despite its popularity, RST still lacks both a formal specification that would allow one to distinguish between well- and ill-formed rhetorical structure trees (RS-trees) and algorithms that would enable one to determine all the possible rhetorical analyses of a given discourse. For example, consider the following text (in which each textual unit[1] is labeled for reference):

(1) [No matter how much one wants to stay a non-smoker,^{A_1}] [the truth is that the pressure to smoke in junior high is greater than it will be any other time of one's life.^{B_1}] [We know that 3,000 teens start smoking each day,^{C_1}] [although it is a fact that 90% of them once thought that smoking was something that they'd never do.^{D_1}]

According to Mann and Thompson's definitions (1988), the rhetorical relations given in (2) below hold between the individual text units,[2] because the understanding of both A_1 and D_1 will increase the reader's readiness to accept the writer's right to present B_1; the understanding of C_1 will increase the reader's belief of B_1; the recognition of C_1 as something compatible with the situation presented in D_1 will increase the reader's positive regard for the situation presented in D_1; and the situation presented in D_1 is a restatement of the situation presented in A_1.

$$\textbf{(2)}\quad RR = \left\{ \begin{array}{l} \textit{rhet\_rel}(\text{JUSTIFICATION}, A_1, B_1) \\ \textit{rhet\_rel}(\text{JUSTIFICATION}, D_1, B_1) \\ \textit{rhet\_rel}(\text{EVIDENCE}, C_1, B_1) \\ \textit{rhet\_rel}(\text{CONCESSION}, C_1, D_1) \\ \textit{rhet\_rel}(\text{RESTATEMENT}, D_1, A_1) \end{array} \right.$$

Assume now that one is given the task of building an RS-tree for text (1) and that one produces the candidates in figure 1.[3] Any student in RST would notice from the beginning that the tree in figure 1.d is illegal with respect to the requirements specified by Mann and Thompson (1988) because C_1 belongs to more than one text span, namely A_1–C_1 and C_1–D_1. However, even a specialist in RST will have trouble determining whether the trees in figure 1.a–c represent *all* the possible ways in which a rhetorical structure could be assigned to text (1), and moreover, in determining if these trees are *correct* with respect to the requirements of RST.

In this paper, I provide a formalization of the structure of RS-trees and show how one can use it to find answers to the questions given above. Section 2 reviews the elements of RST that are relevant for this paper, provides an explanation for the ambiguity of RS-trees, and proposes an informal mechanism that would enable one to alleviate the problems that are associated with this ambiguity. Section 3 creates the setting for the full formalization of RS-trees, which is presented in section 4. The last section is dedicated to an algorithmic perspective of the formalization and a discussion of its relevance to discourse processing.

RS-trees: informal intuitions

A critical analysis of RST

I believe that the explanation for the current lack of algorithms capable of automatically building the RS-trees that pertain to a given discourse can be found not only in the ambiguous definition of the rhetorical relations, but also in the incomplete description of RS-trees that is provided in the original theory. A careful analysis of the con-

[1]Throughout this paper, I use interchangeably the terms *textual unit* and *minimal unit* to refer to clauses.

[2]Throughout this paper, I use the convention that rhetorical relations are represented as sorted, first-order predicates having the form *rhet_rel(name, satellite, nucleus)* where *name*, *satellite* and *nucleus* represent the name, satellite, and nucleus of a rhetorical relation, respectively. Multinuclear relations are represented as predicates having the form *rhet_rel(name, nucleus*$_1$*, nucleus*$_2$*)*.

[3]Throughout this paper, I use the graphical representation for RS-trees that is described by Mann and Thompson (1988).

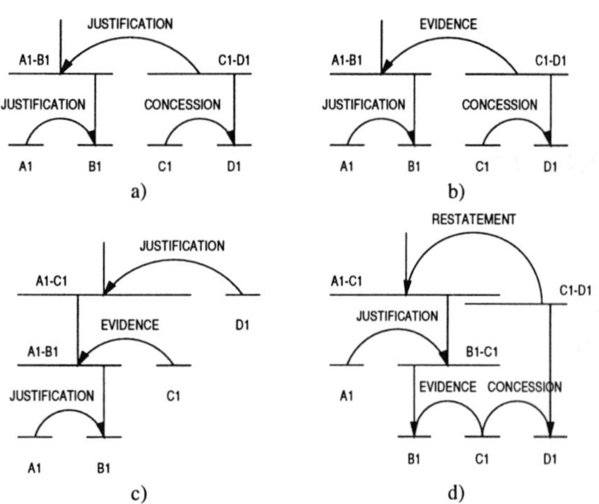

Figure 1: A set of possible rhetorical analyses of text (1).

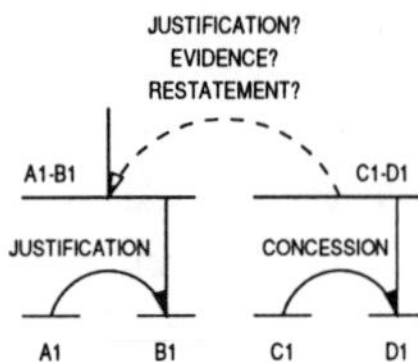

Figure 2: An example of the ambiguity that pertains to the construction of RS-trees.

straints provided by Mann and Thompson (1988, p. 248) shows that their specification for RS-trees is not complete with respect to some compositionality requirements, which would be necessary in order to formulate precisely the conditions that have to be satisfied if two adjacent spans are to be put together. Assume, for example, that an analyst is given text (1) and the set of rhetorical relations that pertain to the minimal units (2), and that that analyst takes the reasonable decision to build the spans A_1–B_1 and C_1–D_1, as shown in figure 2. To complete the construction of the RS-tree, the analyst will have to decide what the best relation is that could span over A_1–B_1 and C_1–D_1. If she considers the elementary relations (2) that hold across the two spans, she has three choices, which correspond to the relations *rhet_rel*(JUSTIFICATION, D_1, B_1), *rhet_rel*(EVIDENCE, C_1, B_1), and *rhet_rel*(RESTATEMENT, D_1, A_1). Which is the correct one to choose?

More generally, suppose that the analyst has already built two partial RS-trees on the top of two adjacent spans that consist of ten and twenty minimal units, respectively. Is it correct to join the two partial RS-trees in order to create a bigger tree just because there is a rhetorical relation that holds between two arbitrary minimal units that belong to those spans? A possible answer is to say that rhetorical relations are defined over spans that are larger than one unit too; therefore, in our case, it is correct to put the two partial RS-trees together if there is a rhetorical relation that holds between the two spans that we have considered. But if this is the case, how can one determine the precise boundaries of the spans over which that relation holds? And how do the rhetorical relations that hold between minimal units relate to the relations that hold between larger text spans? Mann and Thompson (1988) provide no precise answer for these questions.

Nuclearity and RS-trees

Despite the lack of a formal specification of the conditions that must hold in order to join two adjacent text spans, I believe that RST contains an implicit specification, which can be derived from Mann and Thompson's (1988) and Matthiessen and Thompson's (1988) discussion of nuclearity. During the development of RST, these researchers noticed that which is expressed by the nucleus of a rhetorical relation is more essential to the writer's purpose than the satellite; and that the satellite of a rhetorical relation is incomprehensible independent of the nucleus, but not vice-versa. Consequently, deleting the nuclei of the rhetorical relations that hold among all textual units in a text yields an incomprehensible text, while deleting the satellites of the rhetorical relations that hold among all textual units in a text yields a text that is still comprehensible. In fact, as Matthiessen and Thompson put it, "the nucleus-satellite relations are pervasive in texts independently of the grammar of clause combining" (1988, p. 290).

A careful analysis of the RS-trees that Mann, Thompson, and many others built shows that whenever two large text spans are connected through a rhetorical relation, that rhetorical relation holds also between the most important parts of the constituent spans. For example, in figure 1.a, the justification relation that holds between text spans C_1–D_1 and A_1–B_1 holds between their most salient parts as well, i.e., between the nuclei D_1 and B_1.

I propose that this observation can constitute the foundation for a formal treatment of compositionality in RST. More specifically, I will formalize the idea that two adjacent spans can be joined in a larger span by a given rhetorical relation if and only if that relation holds also between the most salient units of those spans. Obviously, such a formalization will also specify the rules for determining the most salient units of the spans.

A precise formulation of the RST problem

Formally, the problem that I want to solve is the following: given a sequence of textual units $U = u_1, u_2, \ldots, u_N$ and a set *RR* of rhetorical relations that hold among these units, find all legal discourse structures (trees) that could be built on the top of the linear sequence $u_1, u_2, \ldots, u_N$. Throughout this paper, I use the predicates *position*(u_i, i) and *rhet_rel*(*name*, *satellite*, *nucleus*) with the following semantics: predicate *position*(u_i, i) is true for a textual unit u_i in sequence U if and only if u_i is the i-th element in the sequence; predicate *rhet_rel*(*name*, u_i, u_j) is true for textual units u_i and u_j with respect to rhetorical relation *name*, if and only if the definition provided by Mann and Thompson (1988) for rhetorical relation *name* applies for textual

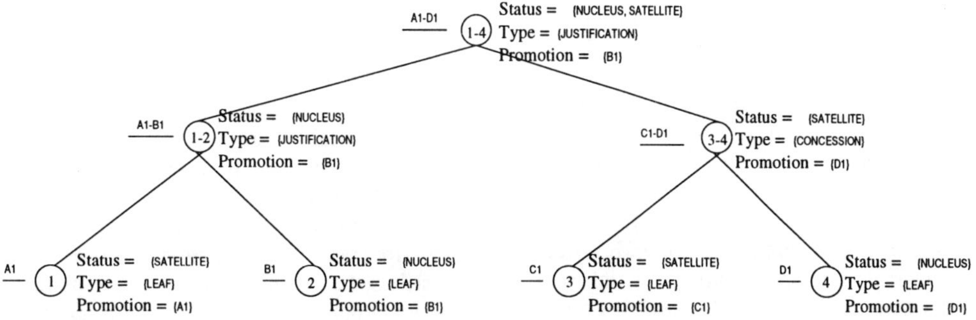

Figure 3: An isomorphic representation of tree in figure 1.a according to the status, type, and promotion features that characterize every node. The numbers associated with each node denote the limits of the text span that that node characterizes. The horizontal segments that pertain to each node underline the limits of the span that that node spans over.

units u_i, in most cases a satellite, and u_j, a nucleus. For example, from a rhetorical perspective, text (1) is completely described at the minimal unit level by the relations given in (2) and the relations given below in (3).

$$(3)\quad \left\{ \begin{array}{l} position(A_1, 1), position(B_1, 2), \\ \qquad position(C_1, 3), position(D_1, 4) \end{array} \right.$$

The formalization that I propose here is built on the following features:

- An RS-tree is a binary tree whose leaves denote elementary textual units.
- Each node has associated a *status* (nucleus or satellite), a *type* (the rhetorical relation that holds between the text spans that that node spans over), and a *salience* or *promotion set* (the set of units that constitute the most "important" part of the text that is spanned by that node). By convention, for each leaf node, the type is LEAF and the promotion set is the textual unit to which it corresponds.

A representation for the tree in figure 1.a, which reflects these characteristics, is given in figure 3. The status, type, and salience unit that are associated with each leaf follow directly from the convention that I have given above. The status and the type of each internal node is a one-to-one mapping of the status and rhetorical relation that are associated with each non-minimal text span from the original representation. The status of the root reflects the fact that text span A_1–D_1 could play either a NUCLEUS or a SATELLITE role in any larger span that contains it.

The most significant differences between the tree in figure 3 and the tree in figure 1.a pertain to the promotion sets that are associated with every internal node. Consider, for example, the JUSTIFICATION relation that holds between units A_1 and B_1: according to the discussion of nuclearity in section 2, the nucleus of the relation, i.e., unit B_1, is the one that expresses what is more essential to the writer's purpose than the satellite A_1. Therefore, it makes sense that if span A_1–B_1 is to be related through other rhetorical relations to another part of the text, then it should do so through its most important or most salient part, i.e., B_1. Similarly, the nucleus D_1 of the rhetorical relation CONCESSION that holds between units C_1 and D_1 is the most salient unit for text span C_1–D_1. The intuition that the tree in figure 3 captures is that spans A_1–B_1 and C_1–D_1 could be assembled in a larger span A_1–D_1, because there is some rhetorical relation, in this case JUSTIFICATION, that holds between their most salient parts, i.e., D_1 and B_1.

The status, type, and promotion set that are associated with each node in an RS-tree provide sufficient information for a full description of an instance of a discourse structure. Given the linear nature of text and the fact that one cannot predict in advance where the boundaries between various text spans will be drawn, I will provide a methodology that permits one to quantify over all possible ways in which a tree could be build on the top of a linear sequence of textual units. The solution that I propose relies on the same intuition that constitutes the foundation of chart parsing: just as a chart parser is capable of quantifying over all possible ways in which different words in a sentence could be clustered into higher-order grammatical units, so my formalization would be capable of quantifying over all the possible ways in which different text spans could be joined into larger spans.

Let $span_{i,j}$, or simply $[i,j]$, denote a text span that includes all the textual units between position i and j. Then, if we consider a sequence of textual units $u_1, u_2, \ldots, u_N$, there are N ways in which spans of length one could be built, $span_{1,1}, span_{2,2}, \ldots, span_{N,N}$; $N - 1$ ways in which spans of length two could be built, $span_{1,2}, span_{2,3}, \ldots, span_{N-1,N}$; $N - 2$ ways in which spans of length three could be built, $span_{1,3}, span_{2,4}, \ldots, span_{N-2,N}; \ldots$; and one way in which a span of length N could be built, $span_{1,N}$. Since it is impossible to determine a priori the text spans that will be used to make up a RS-tree, I will associate with each text span that could possibly become part of an RS-tree a status, a type, and a promotion relation and let the constraints described by Mann and Thompson (1988, p. 248) and the nuclearity constraints that I have described in section 2 generate the correct RS-trees. In fact, my intent is to determine from the set of $N(N + 1)/2 (= N + (N - 1) + (N - 2) + \ldots + 1)$ potential text spans that pertain to a sequence of N textual units, the subset that adheres to the constraints that I have mentioned above. For example, for text 1, there are 10 (= 4+3+2+1) potential spans, i.e., $span_{1,1}, span_{2,2}, span_{3,3}, span_{4,4}, span_{1,2}, span_{2,3}, span_{3,4}, span_{1,3}, span_{2,4}$, and $span_{1,4}$, but only seven of them play an active role in the representation given in figure 3, i.e., $span_{1,1}, span_{2,2}, span_{3,3}, span_{4,4}, span_{1,2}, span_{3,4}$, and $span_{1,4}$.

In formalizing the constraints that pertain to an RS-tree, I assume that each possible text span, $span_{l,h}$,[4] which will or will not eventually become a node in the final discourse tree, is characterized by the following relations:

- $S(l, h, status)$ denotes the status of $span_{l,h}$, i.e., the text span that contains units l to h; *status* can take one of the values NUCLEUS, SATELLITE, or NONE according to the role played by that span in the final RS-tree. For example, for the RS-tree depicted in figure 3, some of the relations that hold are: $S(1,2,\text{NUCLEUS}), S(3,4,\text{SATELLITE}), S(1,3,\text{NONE})$.
- $T(l, h, relation\_name)$ denotes the name of the rhetorical relation that holds between the text spans that are immediate subordinates of $span_{l,h}$ in the RS-tree. If the text span is not used in the construction of the final RS-tree, the type assigned by convention is NONE. For example, for the RS-tree in figure 3, some of the relations that hold are: $T(1,1,\text{LEAF}), T(1,2,\text{JUSTIFICATION}), T(3,4,\text{CONCESSION}), T(1,3,\text{NONE})$.
- $P(l, h, unit\_name)$ denotes the set of units that are salient for $span_{l,h}$ and that can be used to connect this text span with adjacent text spans in the final RS-tree. If $span_{l,h}$ is not used in the final RS-tree, by convention, the set of salient units is NONE. For example, for the RS-tree in figure 3, some of the relations that hold are: $P(1,1,\text{A}_1), P(1,2,\text{B}_1), P(1,3,\text{NONE}), P(3,4,\text{D}_1)$.

A complete formalization of RS-trees

Using the ideas that I have discussed in the previous section, I present now a complete first-order formalization of RS-trees. In this formalization, I assume a universe that consists of the set of natural numbers from 1 to N, where N represents the number of textual units in the text that is considered; the set of names that were defined by Mann and Thompson for each rhetorical relation; the set of unit names that are associated with each textual unit; and four extra constants: NUCLEUS, SATELLITE, NONE, and LEAF. The only function symbols that operate over this domain are the traditional + and − functions that are associated with the set of natural numbers. The formalization uses the traditional predicate symbols that pertain to the set of natural numbers ($<, \leq, >, \geq, =, \neq$) and five other predicate symbols: S, T, and P to account for the status, type, and salient units that are associated with every text span; *rhet_rel* to account for the rhetorical relations that hold between different textual units; and *position* to account for the index of the textual units in the text that one considers.

Throughout the paper, I apply the convention that all unbound variables are universally quantified and that variables are represented in *lower-case letters* while constants in SMALL CAPITALS. I also make use of two extra relations (*relevant_rel* and *relevant_unit*), which I define here as follows: for every text span $span_{l,h}$, $relevant\_rel(l, h, name)$ (4) describes the set of rhetorical relations that are relevant to that text span, i.e., the set of rhetorical relations that span over text spans that have their boundaries within the interval $[l, h]$. For every text span $span_{l,h}$, $relevant\_unit(l, h, u)$ (5) describes the set of textual units that are relevant for that text span, i.e., the units whose positions in the initial sequence are numbers in the interval $[l, h]$:

$$\begin{aligned}(4)\quad & relevant\_rel(l,h,name) \equiv (\exists s,n,sp,np)[\\ & \quad position(s,sp) \wedge position(n,np) \wedge\\ & \quad (l \leq sp \leq h) \wedge (l \leq np \leq h) \wedge\\ & \quad rhet\_rel(name,s,n)]\end{aligned}$$

$$\begin{aligned}(5)\quad & relevant\_unit(l,h,u) \equiv\\ & \quad (\exists x)[position(u,x) \wedge (l \leq x \leq h)]\end{aligned}$$

For example, for text (1), which is described formally in (2) and (3), the following is the set of all *relevant_rel* and *relevant_unit* relations that hold with respect to text segment [1,3]: $\{relevant\_rel(1,3,\text{JUSTIFICATION}), relevant\_rel(1,3,\text{EVIDENCE}), relevant\_unit(1,3,\text{A}_1), relevant\_unit(1,3,\text{B}_1), relevant\_unit(1,3,\text{C}_1)\}$

The constraints that pertain to the structure of an RS-tree can be partitioned into constraints related to the range of objects over which each predicate ranges and constraints related to the structure of the tree. I describe each set of constraints in turn.

Constraints that concern the objects over which the predicates that describe every span $[l, h]$ of an RS-tree range

- **For every span $[l, h]$, the set of objects over which predicate S ranges is the set $\{\text{NUCLEUS}, \text{SATELLITE}, \text{NONE}\}$.** Since every textual unit has to be part of the final RS-tree, the elementary text spans, i.e., those spans for which $l = h$, constitute an exception to this rule, i.e., they could play only a NUCLEUS or SATELLITE role.

$$\begin{aligned}(6)\quad & [(1 \leq h \leq \text{N}) \wedge (1 \leq l \leq h)] \rightarrow\\ & \quad \{[l = h \rightarrow\\ & \qquad (S(l,h,\text{NUCLEUS}) \vee S(l,h,\text{SATELLITE}))] \wedge\\ & \quad [l \neq h \rightarrow\\ & \qquad (S(l,h,\text{NUCLEUS}) \vee S(l,h,\text{SATELLITE}) \vee\\ & \qquad S(l,h,\text{NONE}))]\}\end{aligned}$$

- **The status of any text span is unique**

$$\begin{aligned}(7)\quad & [(1 \leq h \leq \text{N}) \wedge (1 \leq l \leq h)] \rightarrow\\ & \quad [(S(l,h,status_1) \wedge S(l,h,status_2)) \rightarrow\\ & \qquad status_1 = status_2]\end{aligned}$$

[4] In what follows, l and h always denote the left and right boundaries of a text span.

• **For every span $[l,h]$, the set of objects over which predicate T ranges is the set of rhetorical relations that are relevant to that span.** By convention, the rhetorical relation associated with a leaf is LEAF.

$$(8)\quad \begin{array}{l}[(1 \leq h \leq \text{N}) \wedge (1 \leq l \leq h)] \rightarrow \\ \quad \{[l = h \rightarrow T(l,h,\text{LEAF})] \wedge \\ \quad [l \neq h \rightarrow (T(l,h,\text{NONE}) \vee \\ \qquad (T(l,h,name) \rightarrow \\ \qquad\quad relevant\_rel(l,h,name)))]\}\end{array}$$

• **At most one rhetorical relation can connect two adjacent text spans**

$$(9)\quad \begin{array}{l}[(1 \leq h \leq \text{N}) \wedge (1 \leq l < h)] \rightarrow \\ \quad [(T(l,h,name_1) \wedge T(l,h,name_2)) \rightarrow \\ \qquad name_1 = name_2]\end{array}$$

• **For every span $[l,h]$, the set of objects over which predicate P ranges is the set of units that make up that span.**

$$(10)\quad \begin{array}{l}[(1 \leq h \leq \text{N}) \wedge (1 \leq l \leq h)] \rightarrow \\ \quad [P(l,h,\text{NONE}) \vee \\ \quad (P(l,h,u) \rightarrow relevant\_unit(l,h,u))]\end{array}$$

Constraints that concern the structure of the RS-trees

The following constraints are derived from Mann and Thompson's formulation of RS-trees and from the nuclearity constraints that I have described in section 2.

• **Text spans do not overlap**

$$(11)\quad \begin{array}{l}[(1 \leq h_1 \leq \text{N}) \wedge (1 \leq l_1 \leq h_1) \wedge (1 \leq h_2 \leq \text{N}) \wedge \\ \quad (1 \leq l_2 \leq h_2) \wedge (l_1 < l_2) \wedge \\ \quad (h_1 < h_2) \wedge (l_2 \leq h_1)] \\ \quad \rightarrow [\neg S(l_1,h_1,\text{NONE}) \rightarrow S(l_2,h_2,\text{NONE})]\end{array}$$

• **A text span with status NONE does not participate in the tree at all**

$$(12)\quad \begin{array}{l}[(1 \leq h \leq \text{N}) \wedge (1 \leq l < h)] \rightarrow \\ \quad [(S(l,h,\text{NONE}) \wedge P(l,h,\text{NONE}) \wedge \\ \qquad T(l,h,\text{NONE})) \\ \quad \vee (\neg S(l,h,\text{NONE}) \wedge \neg P(l,h,\text{NONE}) \wedge \\ \qquad \neg T(l,h,\text{NONE}))]\end{array}$$

• **There exists a text span, the root, that spans over the entire text**

$$(13)\quad \begin{array}{l}\neg S(1,\text{N},\text{NONE}) \wedge \neg P(1,\text{N},\text{NONE}) \wedge \\ \neg T(1,\text{N},\text{NONE})\end{array}$$

• **The status, type, and promotion set that are associated with a text span reflect the structural and nuclearity constraints that were discussed in section 2**

$$(14)\quad \begin{array}{l}[(1 \leq h \leq \text{N}) \wedge (1 \leq l < h) \wedge \neg S(l,h,\text{NONE})] \rightarrow \\ \quad (\exists name, split\_point, s, n)[(l \leq split\_point \leq h) \\ \qquad \wedge (Nucleus\_first(name, split\_point, s, n) \vee \\ \qquad\quad Satellite\_first(name, split\_point, s, n))]\end{array}$$

Formula (14) specifies that whenever a test span $[l,h]$ denotes an internal node $(l < h)$ in the final RS-tree, i.e., its status is not *none*, the span $[l,h]$ is built on the top of two text spans that meet at index *split_point* and either the formula denoted by *Nucleus_first* or *Satellite_first* holds.

$$(15)\quad \begin{array}{l}Nucleus\_first(name, split\_point, s, n) \equiv \\ \quad rhet\_rel(name, s, n) \wedge T(l,h,name) \wedge \\ \quad position(s, sp) \wedge position(n, np) \wedge \\ \quad l \leq np \leq split\_point \wedge split\_point < sp \leq h \wedge \\ \quad P(l, split\_point, n) \wedge P(split\_point + 1, h, s) \wedge \\ \quad \{(name = \text{CONTRAST} \vee name = \text{JOINT}) \rightarrow \\ \qquad S(l, split\_point, \text{NUCLEUS}) \wedge \\ \qquad S(split\_point + 1, h, \text{NUCLEUS}) \wedge \\ \qquad (\forall p)[P(l,h,p) \rightarrow \\ \qquad\quad (P(l, split\_point, p) \vee \\ \qquad\quad P(split\_point + 1, h, p))]\} \wedge \\ \quad \{name = \text{SEQUENCE} \rightarrow \\ \qquad S(l, split\_point, \text{NUCLEUS}) \wedge \\ \qquad S(split\_point + 1, h, \text{NUCLEUS}) \wedge \\ \qquad (\forall p)(P(l,h,p) \rightarrow P(l, split\_point, p))\} \wedge \\ \quad \{(name \neq \text{SEQUENCE} \wedge name \neq \text{CONTRAST} \wedge \\ \quad\; name \neq \text{JOINT}) \rightarrow \\ \qquad S(l, split\_point, \text{NUCLEUS}) \wedge \\ \qquad S(split\_point + 1, h, \text{SATELLITE}) \wedge \\ \qquad (\forall p)(P(l,h,p) \rightarrow P(l, split\_point, p))\}\end{array}$$

Formula (15) specifies that there is a rhetorical relation with name *name*, from a unit s (in most cases a satellite) that belongs to span $[split\_point + 1, h]$ to a unit n, the nucleus, that belongs to span $[l, split\_point]$; that unit n is salient with respect to text span $[l, split\_point]$ and unit s is salient with respect to text span $[split\_point + 1, h]$; and that the type of span $[l,h]$ is given by the name of the rhetorical relation. If the relation is multinuclear, i.e., CONTRAST or JOINT, the status of the immediate sub-spans is NUCLEUS and the set of salient units for text span $[l,h]$ consists of all the units that make up the set of salient units that are associated with the two sub-spans. If the relation is a SEQUENCE relation, both sub-spans have NUCLEUS status, but the salient units for text span $[l,h]$ are given only by the salient units that are associated with the last member in the sequence, which in this case is realized first. If the relation is not multinuclear, the status of text span $[l, split\_point]$ is NUCLEUS, the status of text span $[split\_point + 1, h]$ is SATELLITE and the set of salient units for text span $[l,h]$ are given by the salient units that are associated with the subordinate nucleus span.

The difference between the formalization of the multinuclear relation of SEQUENCE and the other multinuclear relations stems from the fact that, unlike JOINT or CONTRAST, SEQUENCE is not symmetric. Formula *Satellite_first(name, split_point, s, n)* is a mirror image of (15) and it describes the case when the satellite that pertains to rhetorical relation *rhet_rel(name, s, n)* belongs to text span $[l, split\_point]$, i.e., when the satellite goes before the nucleus. Due to space constraints, I do not reproduce it here.

An algorithmic view of RS-trees

Given the mathematical foundations of RS-trees, i.e., formulas (4)–(14), finding the RS-trees for a discourse described along the lines given in (2) and (3), for example, amounts to finding a model for the first-order theory that consists of formulas (2) to (14).

There are a number of ways in which one can proceed with an implementation: for example, a straightforward choice

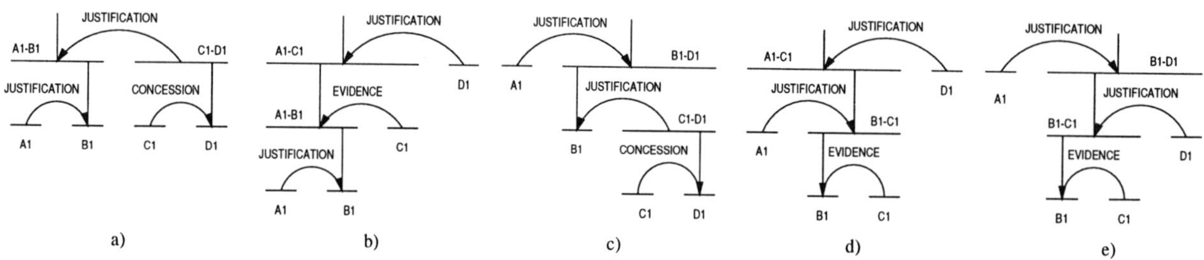

Figure 4: The set of all RS-trees that could be built for text (1).

is one that applies constraint-satisfaction techniques. Given a sequence U of N textual units, one can take advantage of the structure of the domain and associate with each of the $N(N+1)/2$ possible text spans a status, a type, and a salience or promotion variable whose domains consist in the set of objects over which the corresponding predicates S, T, and P range. This gives one a constraint-satisfaction problem with $3N(N+1)/2$ variables, whose domains are defined by formulas (6) to (10). The constraints associated with these variables are a one-to-one mapping of formulas (11) to (14). Finding the set of RS-trees that are associated with a given discourse reduces then to finding all the solutions for this constraint-satisfaction problem.

I have used Lisp and Screamer (Siskind & McAllester 1993), a macro package that provides constraint-satisfaction facilities, to fully implement a system that builds RS-trees. My program takes as input a linear sequence of textual units $U = u_1, u_2, \ldots, u_N$ and the set of rhetorical relations that hold among these units. The algorithm builds automatically the corresponding constraint-satisfaction problem and then uses Screamer to find all the possible solutions for it. A simple procedure prints the RS-trees that pertain to each solution.

For example, for text (1), the program produces five RS-tree configurations (see figure 4). Among the set of trees in figure 4, trees 4.a and 4.b match the trees given in the introductory section in figure 1.a and 1.c. Trees 4.c–e represent trees that are not given in figure 1. Consequently, it follows that five RS-trees could be built on the top of text (1), and that tree 1.b is incorrect. It is easy to see that the reason that makes tree 1.b incorrect with respect to the formalization is that one of the constraints, i.e., the one that pertains to the rhetorical relation of *evidence* that is depicted between spans $[3,4]$ (C_1–D_1) and $[1,2]$ (A_1–B_1), does not hold. More precisely, the rhetorical relation of *concession* between C_1 and D_1 projects D_1 as the salient unit for text span $[3,4]$ (C_1–D_1). The initial set of rhetorical relations (2) depicts an evidence relation only between units C_1 and B_1 and not between D_1 and B_1. Since the nuclearity requirements make it impossible for C_1 to play both a satellite role in the span $[3,4]$ (C_1–D_1), and to be, at the same time, a salient unit for it, it follows that tree 1.b is incorrect.

The formalization and the algorithm that I presented here account for the construction of RS-trees in the cases in which the input specifies rhetorical relations between non-elementary spans as well. For example, if the input is enhanced such that besides the relations given in (2) it also contains the rhetorical relation *rhet_rel*(JUSTIFICATION, A_1, $[B_1$–$D_1]$), only the trees that are consistent with this extra constraint will be valid, i.e., trees 4.c and 4.e.

The formalization presented here distinguishes between correct and incorrect RS-trees only with respect to the original theory (Mann & Thompson 1988). Theme, focus, intention, or other pragmatic factors could rule out some of the trees that are produced by the algorithm; but a discussion of these issues is beyond the scope of this paper.

Conclusion

In this paper I provided a mathematical formulation of rhetorical structure trees that is based on the original Rhetorical Structure Theory (Mann & Thompson 1988) and the nuclearity features that pertain to natural language texts. On the basis of a first-order formulation of valid rhetorical structure trees, I implemented an algorithm that takes as input a sequence of textual units and a set of rhetorical relations that hold between those units, and that builds all the valid rhetorical structure trees that pertain to that sequence.

Acknowledgments. I am especially grateful to Graeme Hirst for long discussions and invaluable comments that helped me polish this work and to Jeff Siskind for bringing to my attention the similarity between charts and rhetorical structure trees, a similarity that catalyzed the emergence of the ideas presented in this paper. I am also grateful to Eduard Hovy, Ray Reiter, Manfred Stede, and Toby Donaldson for their comments on early drafts of the paper.

This reasearch was supported by a grant from the Natural Sciences and Engineering Research Council of Canada.

References

Mann, W., and Thompson, S. 1988. Rhetorical structure theory: Toward a functional theory of text organization. *Text* 8 (3):243–281.

Matthiessen, C., and Thompson, S. 1988. The structure of discourse and 'subordination'. In Haiman, J., and Thompson, S., eds., *Clause combining in grammar and discourse*, volume 18 of *Typological Studies in Language*. John Benjamins Publishing Company. 275–329.

Siskind, J., and McAllester, D. 1993. Nondeterministic Lisp as a substrate for Constraint Logic Programming. In *Proceedings of the Eleventh National Conference on Artificial Intelligence*, AAAI–93, Seattle, 133–138.

Using Plan Reasoning in the Generation of Plan Descriptions *

R. Michael Young
Intelligent Systems Program
University of Pittburgh
Pittsburgh, PA 15260
myoung+@pitt.edu

Abstract

Previous work on the generation of natural language descriptions of complex activities has indicated that the unwieldy amount of text needed to describe complete plans makes for ineffective and unnatural descriptions. We argue here that concise and effective text descriptions of plans can be generated by exploiting a model of the hearer's plan reasoning capabilities. We define a computational model of the hearer's interpretation process that views the interpretation of plan descriptions as refinement search through a space of partial plans. This model takes into account the hearer's plan preferences and the resource limitations on her reasoning capabilities to determine the completed plans she will construct from a given partial description.

Introduction

A number of natural language systems have been developed for the generation of textual descriptions of plans (Mellish & Evans 1989; Vander Linden 1993; Haller 1994). However, systems have been limited in their ability to deal with the large amount of detail found in complex activities: either these systems dealt exclusively with artificial plans of limited size or have generated verbose text describing more realistic plans. The quality of a textual description is strained when that description contains an inappropriate amount of detail. Providing a hearer with too much detail may needlessly cause her to eliminate from consideration compatible alternate plans or may overtax her attentional constraints (Walker 1996). Too little detail, alternatively, may allow the hearer to infer that the speaker is describing a plan that is inconsistent with the speaker's actual plan. Providing too little detail may so underconstrain the interpretation that the hearer's plan reasoning resources are overtaxed. For systems responsible for automatically generating descriptions of plans, understanding the interaction between the quality of the description and the quantity of information it contains is essential

In the approach we describe here, plans are represented by collections of components and the task of describing a plan involves communicating these components. The problem that this research addresses is how to determine an appropriate subset of the components of a plan to communicate as the plan's description. A principal claim we make is that effective description of one plan can be achieved by describing a second *partial* plan that is appropriately related to the first. The partiality of the second plan must be chosen so that the hearer can reconstruct the first from it based on the hearer's knowledge about plans and planning. The hearer must be able to complete the description in much the same way that a planning system completes a partial plan.

Exploiting a Model of Plan Reasoning

This work addresses the communication of plan descriptions in a context we call *plan identification.* In this context, a speaker describes a plan P, called the *source plan*, in order to identify P as a solution to what the speaker believes is a mutually understood planning problem. When identifying a plan, a speaker provides a description of P that is sufficient for the hearer to single out P (or a plan sufficiently close to P) as the indicated plan in the space of possible solutions. The description the speaker provides will contain a description of a subset of the plan components found in P – the speaker constructs this subset by anticipating how the hearer will reconstruct a complete plan from the partial plan defined in the description.

In this paper we will only consider utterances that describe the presence of a component in the source plan.[1] In instructional text, for instance, these types of utterances are often realized as imperatives like "Do action α." The problem we address here is the selection of a subset of the components of a source plan

*Research supported by the Office of Naval Research, Cognitive and Neural Sciences Division, DoD FY92 Augmentation of Awards for Science and Engineering Research Training (ASSERT) Program (Grant Number: N00014-93-I-0812)

[1]This formalism is readily extendable to other types of utterances – see below for a brief discussion.

P sufficient to identify P to the hearer. In our approach, a speaker uses the model of the hearer's plan reasoning capabilities to select a subset with greater or fewer components depending on (at least) two factors. First, the hearer's plan reasoning resources may limit her ability to find completions; the constraints in a description may be so sparse that finding the completions of the constraints is too great a task for the hearer. Candidate subsets that overtax the hearer's abilities can be eliminated from consideration.

The second factor determining the content of a description is the amount of variance the speaker can tolerate between the plan he is describing and the plan the hearer subsequently will form. In general, there may be a number of plans closely related to a source plan which the speaker would be happy for the hearer to identify. The degree to which these closely related plans vary from the actual source plan is dependent upon the measure of *acceptability* that the speaker uses. In the limiting case, acceptability corresponds to identity, although for many domains acceptability may be a much weaker notion. Given the hearer's plan preferences, the particular constraints in a description may guide him to solutions that are unacceptable to the speaker. Subsets that define planning problems where unacceptable plans are likely to be selected can also be eliminated.

We will use a representation of the planning process referred to as *plan-space search* (Kambhampati 1993). Plan-space search provides a flexible representation of partial plans and the types of planning operations hearers may perform when interpreting a partial plan description. In addition, plan-space search characterizes the planning activity of a wide class of current planning systems – developing a text generation system built on plan-space search allows us to apply these techniques to any plan representation that can be characterized in this way. In plan-space search, each node in the search space is defined by a partial plan and denotes a set of plans; this set, called the node's *candidate set*, corresponds to the class of all legal completions of the partial plan at that node. Search through the plan space is performed by refining the partial plan at a given node. Refinements correspond to one of a well-specified set of plan-construction operations (e.g., adding a new step to establish an open precondition). Each refinement of a parent node creates a child node whose candidate set is a subset of the parent's. The plan space forms a graph whose single root node is an empty plan and whose leaf nodes are either inconsistent plans or solutions to the planning problem.

In refinement search, an evaluation function is used to characterize the candidate set of each node encountered in the search, mapping the node to one of three values. When a node evaluates to `FAIL`, there is no plan in the node's candidate set that solves the planning problem. Consequently, the node must be pruned from the search space and the search algorithm must backtrack. When a node evaluates to a complete plan contained in the candidate set, that plan solves the planning problem and the search algorithm can return this plan. When a node evaluates to $\perp$, the evaluation function cannot determine if a solution is contained in the candidate set and further refinement is needed.

In this paper, we will use a partial-order, causal link planner called DPOCL (Young, Pollack, & Moore 1994). This planner extends the UCPOP planner (Penberthy & Weld 1991) by incorporating a hierarchical plan representation. Use of this representation mirrors the hierarchical, incremental development of plans indicated in the manner that people *talk* about planning (Dixon 1987). Because DPOCL is not a system built especially for the generation of task descriptions (i.e., it is a domain-independent planning algorithm), DPOCL plans contain sufficient structure to ensure their executability. Consequently, they serve as strong test cases for the generation of plan descriptions. In addition, DPOCL is readily characterized as a plan-space search algorithm.

A Hearer Model Based on Plan Reasoning

In this section we propose a model to be used for determining an appropriate description of a plan – using this model involves determining specific inferences to be drawn by the hearer from any candidate description. In particular, our model anticipates the plan reasoning that the hearer undertakes to complete the partial description the speaker provides.

Definitions

The computational model we use here is made of a number of components representing the planning algorithms and action representations used by a speaker when modeling the domain of discourse and the hearer's model of the same domain. In our approach, the speaker has a planning model representing his own plan reasoning capabilities and a separate model of the hearer's plan reasoning capabilities. [2]

A planning problem consists of a complete specification of the problem's initial state and the goal state and a complete specification of the domains's action and decompositions operators.

Definition 1 (Planning Problem) *A planning problem $\mathcal{PP}$ is a three-tuple $\prec P_0, \Lambda, \Delta \succ$, where P_0 is a plan specifying only the initial state and the goal state, Λ is the planning problem's set of action operator definitions and Δ is the set of decomposition operator definitions.*

As described above, a plan-space planning algorithm searches a plan space to find a solution to a

[2]We will refer to the speaker's planning model as the *speaker model* and the speaker's model of the hearer's planning model as the *hearer model*.

planning problem. Typical implementations produce a plan graph during this search representing the portion of the plan space searched to that point.

Definition 2 (Plan Graph) *A plan graph* $G_A = \prec n, a \succ$ *for some planning algorithm* $\mathcal{A}$ *is a singly-rooted, strongly connected graph with nodes n and arcs a. Each node* $n_i \in n$ *is a plan defined by algorithm* $\mathcal{A}$ *and an arc* $n_i \rightarrow n_j$ *appears in a precisely when* n_j *is a refinement of* n_i *using algorithm* $\mathcal{A}$.

During the planning process, the hearer model employs a heuristic evaluation function to direct search through the space of plans. This function ranks plans that appear in the fringe of the current plan graph; search proceeds by expanding those fringe nodes that are ranked most promising.

Definition 3 (Plan Ranking Function)
For any plan p and plan graph G_A, $G_A = \prec n, a \succ$ *and* $p \in n$, *a plan ranking function f maps p and* G_A *into a set of plans such that 1) f partitions the plans in n into a totally ordered set of sets of plans, 2) this total order has a single minimal element and 3) each plan in n must be assigned by f into precisely one of these sets.* [3]

For ease of reference, we will identify the total ordering on these sets with the non-negative integers; plans that are assigned a lower number are more preferred than plans assigned a higher ranking.

In order to model the resource limits of a hearer when she is interpreting a description, the hearer's limitations will be represented by a *search limit function* that accepts as input a plan graph representing the space already explored during a plan-space search. The function returns T if the plan graph exceeds the hearer's search limit and returns F if it does not.

Definition 4 (Search Limit Function)
A search limit function d maps a plan graph G onto the set $\{T, F\}$. *For any agent a,* $d_a(G) = T$ *precisely when G exceeds the planning resource limit for a.*

The hearer model's planning system combines a particular planning algorithm, a search limit function and an evaluation function.

Definition 5 (Planning System) *A planning system* $\mathcal{PS}$ *is a three-tuple* $\prec \mathcal{A}, d, f \succ$ *where* $\mathcal{A}$ *is a plan-space search algorithm, d is a search limit function and f is a plan evaluation function.*

Finally, a planning model $\mathcal{PM}$ is a pair consisting of a planning problem and a planning system.

Definition 6 (Planning Model) *A* planning model $\mathcal{PM}$ *consists of a planning problem* $\mathcal{PP}$ *and a planning system* $\mathcal{PS}$.

[3]The system designer is free to rank plans using any criteria and to compute that ranking using any mechanism. See (Elzer, Chu-Carroll, & Carberry 1994).

Complete plans assigned the rank 0 by an evaluation function in a planning model $\mathcal{PM}$ are called the *preferred plans* in $\mathcal{PM}$. In this work we will use as a measure of acceptability the difference between the value of the speaker's evaluation function f applied to a plan and f's value when applied to the speaker's source plan P, We will assume that the speaker has some value δ that serves as a measure of the amount of variance from P that he will tolerate. Let G_s be the plan graph in which P was found by the speaker, and let G_h be some plan graph constructed by the hearer while solving the same planning problem. The set of *acceptable* plans (or simply the *acceptance set*) for a given source plan P contains precisely those plans P' in G_h such that $|f_s(P, G_s) - f_s(P', G_h)| \leq \delta$.

Constraints on the Hearer Model

There are a number of constraints that must be placed on the plans produced by either the speaker or the hearer model. First, as described earlier, we will use DPOCL to model the planning algorithm of the hearer. That is, $\mathcal{A}_h$ = DPOCL. Second, the planning algorithms of both speaker and hearer will be constrained to produce only complete plans that contain no unnecessary steps. We assume that the definition of the planning problem in the speaker and hearer models are identical. That is, the specification of the initial and goal states are the same. Furthermore, the discussion here will not deal with any incompatibility between the speaker and the hearer models' representations of the operators in our domain. [4]

Putting the Hearer Model to Use

This hearer model is put to use during the selection of the contents of a plan description. The constraints in this description create a new planning problem for the hearer, one in which the empty plan P_0 is replaced as the root node by the partial plan characterized by the description. We will refer to this new plan as $\mathcal{P_D}$. $\mathcal{P_D}$ has the same initial and goal states as P_0 but has some amount of plan detail already filled in. As a result, the characteristics of the plan space below this node differ from that of the plan space of the original problem.

By examining the manner in which this new plan space will be searched in the hearer model, the speaker can determine the efficacy of the corresponding description. To be cooperative, a speaker should select a set of plan constraints $\mathcal{P_D}$ such that

- **Acceptability:** the speaker believes that all completions of $\mathcal{P_D}$ of equal or greater preference to the

[4]In general, there may be considerable variance between the planning model used by the speaker and that assumed to be used by the hearer. Our approach does not commit to a particular policy for reconciling differences between speaker and hearer models but instead allows implementors to impose policy as their applications dictate.

source plan in the hearer model also occur in the acceptance set of the speaker, and

- **Resource Adequacy:** the speaker believes that at least one such acceptable completion exists in the plan-space of the hearer model within the bound d_h.

When identifying a plan, the speaker should describe a partial plan whose completions in the hearer model are acceptable with respect to the source plan. One interpretation of Grice's maxim of quantity (Grice 1975) suggests that the speaker must determine a *minimal* set of constraints that meet these requirements. To find a minimal subset of plan constraints to use as a description, the approach defined here uses the planning system of the hearer model to evaluate candidate descriptions. To determine if a collection of plan constraints describe a set of plans that are all acceptable with respect to the source plan, we can initialize the hearer model's planning problem using a subset of the source plan's components and search the space of plans rooted at that node. To find a description that obeys the maxim of quantity, we begin our search with the empty subset and increase the size of the initial component set until we reach the first set defining a plan space where every preferred plan is acceptable.

A Sample Problem

This section examines three descriptions for the same example planning problem. The planning problem we will use involves travel from London to Paris. [5] In this domain, there are three basic ways to travel from London to Paris: by train, by plane and by automobile. Each option involves the specification of some further detail; one can fly to either of the two airports in Paris, take the train to Paris either by ferrying across the English Channel or traveling directly using the Channel Tunnel (on the *Eurostar*) or drive to Paris, again by taking the ferry across the Channel.

The complete plan space for this planning problem is shown in figure 1. Each node in this graph represents a (possibly partial) plan; the graph is rooted at P_0, the null plan that describes only the initial state (being in London) and the goal state (being in Paris). Each arc between two nodes in the graph indicates a refinement of the plan at the first node to form a new plan at the arc's second node. The leaf nodes in this graph are all solutions to the planning problem and are labeled with text giving a rough indication of their structure. Each node is also labeled with an integer indicating the order that the hearer's plan search function f_h will search the space (described further below).

We will define the hearer model as follows. For illustrative purposes, we will assume a limited resource

[5] In these examples, we will use a simplified version of the DPOCL planner and its plan representation to limit the length of the discussion. The techniques we present here, however, are applicable to planning problems of arbitrary complexity.

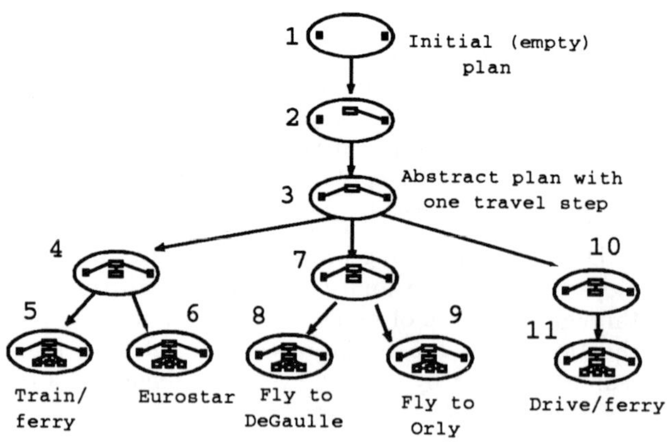

Figure 1: Complete Plan Space for Travel Problem.

bound on the hearer's plan reasoning, bounding the search she can perform to graphs with fewer than 5 nodes. Formally, for any graph $G = \prec n, a \succ$, $d_h(G) = F$ precisely when $|n| < 5$.

The speaker's source plan P is the plan to fly to Paris by taking a plane from Heathrow to De Gaulle (numbered #8 in figure 1). We will assume that the speaker has two simple but strong factors that effect his plan preferences: strong preferences *against* any plan that involves train or ferry travel. The speaker's plan evaluation function f_S and his measure of variance δ will be set such that the only acceptable plans are those numbered #8 and #9 in figure 1.

Providing Too Much Detail Consider the following description:

> **Description 1** `To travel to Paris from London, take the Tube to Heathrow. Next, take a plane to De Gaulle. Then take a bus from De Gaulle to Paris. In order to be in London before taking the Tube, use the effect of starting in London. In order to be at Heathrow before taing the plane to Paris, use the effect of begin at Heathrow after taking the Tube. In order to be at De Gaulle before taking a bus to Paris, use the effect of taking a plane from Heathrow to De Gaulle. In order to be in Paris, use the effect of taking a bus from De Gaulle into Paris.`

This description provides enough detail so that it specifies exactly one completed plan: the source plan P that appears as a leaf node (#8) in the original plan space from figure 1. The new plan space rooted at this node contains just this single plan.

To evaluate this candidate description, the speaker uses the hearer model described above to complete this plan. Because the plan specified by the description is already complete, no search is required; this plan is the only plan in the set of preferred solutions in the hearer model. The plan is acceptable, since it is the source plan.

By including so much detail in the description, the speaker eliminates other acceptable plans – in this case the plan to fly into Paris's De Gaulle airport. Moving the root node of the new plan space farther from the source plan would make for a more concise description while including other acceptable plans in the hearer model's preference set. However, as we show in the next section, this may also result in the inclusion of unacceptable plans in the preference set.

Providing Insufficient Detail Consider the following description:

> **Description 2** `In order to be in Paris, travel to Paris from London.`

This description describes a plan containing only the abstract TRAVEL action with no additional detail. This new plan space is rooted at the node labeled #3 in figure 1 With a search limit function constraining the hearer model's plan graph to contain no more than 5 nodes, the hearer model will only find two solutions to the planning problem: nodes #5 and #6. Both of these nodes are unacceptable given the definition of f_S described earlier. There are, then, no plans in the preferred set of the hearer model that are also acceptable to the speaker, making description 2 unacceptable.

Locating an Appropriate Description

Effective descriptions may make reference to any or all of the components of a plan. Consequently, candidate descriptions lie in the power set of the constraints present in the speaker's source plan. The previous examples use descriptions that lie on either side of an effective, concise description for the source plan. One obvious technique for finding the minimal set of constraints that successfully describes the plan is to use a brute force search algorithm: consider each set in the power set of the constraints of the source plan. This technique would be initialized with the initial, null plan $\mathcal{P}_{\mathcal{D}}$ and would incrementally evaluate sets of constraints, always considering the unexamined sets with smallest cardinality next. The algorithm would halt with it had either found an acceptable plan or exhausted the power set of plan constraints.

Using this technique, it's possible to locate a set of plan constraints corresponding to the following description:

> **Description 3** `In order to be in Paris, travel to Paris from London. Travel to Paris by flying.`

This description describes a plan that contains the TRAVEL step, and a decomposition for that step involving a FLY action. The plan is partial, since it does not specify which airport to fly to. This new plan space is rooted at node labeled #7 in figure 1. The hearer model will search the plan space below this node and find two solutions to the planning problem: nodes #8 and #9. Both of these nodes are acceptable (in fact, they are the only two), making the description acceptable. Any other description of similar or lesser size would either be rooted at one of node #7's siblings or its parents (with spaces that would either lead to unacceptable solutions in the preference set of the hearer model or that would contain no solutions at all) description 3 is minimal as well.

The technique of selecting minimal descriptions using exhaustive search corresponds to Dale and Reiter's full brevity interpretation of Grice's maxims used in the generation of referring expressions (Dale & Reiter 1995). This approach has two weaknesses. First, As Dale and Reiter point out, the approach is computationally expensive, making it unappealing for describing complicated plans or plan spaces. Second, it is not guaranteed to isolate a unique description. For any given planning problem, there may be a number of acceptable descriptions all of minimal size. This simple technique is unable to distinguish between such competing descriptions.

In these cases, the plan constraints themselves may suggest heuristics for choosing between candidate descriptions. For instance, partial plans that are more *referentially coherent* (Long & Golding 1993; Kintsch 1988), that is, whose plan graphs have fewer strong components, may be preferred for explanation over those that are not. Work in the comprehension of narrative texts (Long & Golding 1993; Graesser, Lang, & Roberts 1991; Graesser, Roberston, & Anderson 1981; Trabasso & van den Brock 1985) describes types of inferences drawn from descriptions of actions. It is possible that these cognitive models can given computational definitions in plan identification.

Related Work

Several researchers interested in task-related discourse have employed action representations based on AI plans. The principal work on explaining plans produced by AI planning systems is described by Mellish and Evans (Mellish & Evans 1989). Their system takes a plan produced by the NONLIN planner (Tate 1977) and produces a textual description of the plan. Their system generates clauses describing each component of the input plan and, as Mellish and Evans point out, this often results in unnatural descriptions containing too much detail.

Other projects (Vander Linden 1993; Delin *et al.* 1994) produce more concise texts describing activities, but rely on simplified models of plans whose size and complexity were limited. Dale's dissertation (Dale 1992), focusing on the generation of anaphoric referring expressions in text describing cooking plans, avoided the generation of overly detailed descriptions by a combination of domain-specific techniques (e.g., linguistic information about the verbs associated with actions) and domain-independent ones (e.g., exploiting focus constraints within the text being produced).

Conclusions and Future Work

This paper has defined a computational model of a hearer's plan reasoning capabilities that is useful for selecting between competing candidate descriptions. By viewing the hearer's interpretation of a partial description as the task of searching for a completion in a space of plans, we have been able to provide a formal account for the requirements of this task. The requirements are described in terms of the hearer's planning algorithm, her individual plan preferences and any resource limits placed on her planning capabilities. This model characterizes a number of domain-independent planning algorithms; as a result, the model can potentially be used to generate descriptions of plans produced from a number of automatic planning systems.

Future work will address a number of issues. We will examine the use of additional forms of constraints in text descriptions beyond those discussed here (e.g., negative imperatives) and their role in bounding the search space that the hearer model must deal with. In addition, our future work will explore ways to extend this model to contexts where groups of agents use dialog to coordinate their plan-related beliefs. Finally, we will investigate techniques for reconciling differences between a speaker's model of the hearer and the methods actually employed by the hearer during interpretation of a partial plan description.

Acknowledgements

The author thanks Johanna Moore, Martha Pollack and the reviewers for their helpful comments.

References

Dale, R., and Reiter, E. 1995. Computational interpretations of the Gricean Maxims in the generation of referring expressions. *Applied Artificial Intelligence Journal* 9. to appear.

Dale, R. 1992. *Generating referring expressions: Constructing descriptions in a domain of objects and processes.* Cambridge, Massachusetts: MIT Press.

Delin, J.; Hartley, A.; Paris, C.; Scott, D.; and Vander Linden, K. 1994. Expressing procedural relationships in multilingual instructions. In *Proceedings of the Seventh International Workshop on Natural Language Generation*, 61–70.

Dixon, P. 1987. The structure of mental plans for following directions. *Journal of Experimental Psychology: Learning, Memory and Cognition* 13:18–26.

Elzer, S.; Chu-Carroll, J.; and Carberry, S. 1994. Recognizing and utilizing user preferences in collaborative consultation dialogues. In *Proceedings of the Fourth International Conference on User Modeling*, 19 – 24.

Graesser, A.; Lang, K.; and Roberts, R. 1991. Question answering in the context of stories. *Journal of Experimental Psychology: General* 120:254–277.

Graesser, A.; Roberston, S.; and Anderson, P. 1981. Incorporating inferences in narrative representations: a study of how and why. *Cognitive Psychology* 13:1–26.

Grice, H. P. 1975. Logic and conversation. In Cole, P., and Morgan, J. L., eds., *Syntax and Semantics III: Speech Acts.* New York, NY: Academic Press. 41–58.

Haller, S. 1994. *Interactive Generation of Plan Descriptions and Justifications.* Ph.D. Dissertation, State University of New York at Buffalo.

Kambhampati, S. 1993. Planning as refinement search: A unified framework for comparative analysis of search space size and performance. Technical Report 93-004, Arizona State University, Department of Computer Science and Engineering.

Kintsch, W. 1988. The role of knowledge in discourse comprehension: a construction-integration model. *Psychological Review* 95:163–182.

Long, D. L., and Golding, J. M. 1993. Superordinate goal inferences: Are they automatically generated during comprehension? *Discourse Processes* 16:55–73.

Mellish, C., and Evans, R. 1989. Natural language generation from plans. *Computational Linguistics* 15(4).

Penberthy, J. S., and Weld, D. 1991. UCPOP: A sound, complete partial order planner for ADL. In *Proceedings of the Third International Conference on Knowledge Representation and Reasoning.*

Tate, A. 1977. Generating project networks. In *Proceedings of the International Joint Conference on Artificial Intelligence*, 888 – 893.

Trabasso, T., and van den Brock, P. 1985. Causal thinking and the representation of narrative events. *Journal of Memory and Language* 24:612–630.

Vander Linden, K. 1993. *Speaking of Actions: Choosing Rhetorical Status and Grammatical Form in Instructional Text Generation.* Ph.D. Dissertation, University of Colorado, Department of Computer Science.

Walker, M. 1996. The effect of resource limits and task complexity on collaborative planning in dialog. *Artificial Intelligence.* to appear.

Young, R. M.; Pollack, M. E.; and Moore, J. D. 1994. Decomposition and causality in partial order planning. In *Proceedings of the Second International Conference on AI and Planning Systems*, 188–193.

Perception

Interfacing Sound Stream Segregation to Automatic Speech Recognition — Preliminary Results on Listening to Several Sounds Simultaneously

Hiroshi G. Okuno, Tomohiro Nakatani and **Takeshi Kawabata**

NTT Basic Research Laboratories
Nippon Telegraph and Telephone Corporation
3-1 Morinosato-Wakamiya, Atsugi, Kanagawa 243-01, JAPAN
okuno@nue.org nakatani@horn.brl.ntt.jp kaw@idea.brl.ntt.jp

Abstract

This paper reports the preliminary results of experiments on listening to several sounds at once. Two issues are addressed: segregating speech streams from a mixture of sounds, and interfacing speech stream segregation with automatic speech recognition (*ASR*). Speech stream segregation (*SSS*) is modeled as a process of extracting harmonic fragments, grouping these extracted harmonic fragments, and substituting some sounds for non-harmonic parts of groups. This system is implemented by extending the harmonic-based stream segregation system reported at AAAI-94 and IJCAI-95. The main problem in interfacing SSS with HMM-based ASR is how to improve the recognition performance which is degraded by spectral distortion of segregated sounds caused mainly by the binaural input, grouping, and residue substitution. Our solution is to re-train the parameters of the HMM with training data binauralized for four directions, to group harmonic fragments according to their directions, and to substitute the residue of harmonic fragments for non-harmonic parts of each group. Experiments with 500 mixtures of two women's utterances of a word showed that the cumulative accuracy of word recognition up to the 10th candidate of each woman's utterance is, on average, 75%.

Introduction

Usually, people hear a mixture of sounds, and people with normal hearing can segregate sounds from the mixture and focus on a particular voice or sound in a noisy environment. This capability is known as the *cocktail party effect* (Cherry 1953). Perceptual segregation of sounds, called *auditory scene analysis*, has been studied by psychoacoustic researchers for more than forty years. Although many observations have been analyzed and reported (Bregman 1990), it is only recently that researchers have begun to use computer modeling of auditory scene analysis (Cooke et al. 1993; Green et al. 1995; Nakatani et al. 1994). This emerging research area is called *computational auditory scene analysis (CASA)* and a workshop on CASA was held at IJCAI-95 (Rosenthal & Okuno 1996).

One application of CASA is as a front-end system for *automatic speech recognition* (*ASR*) systems. Hearing impaired people find it difficult to listen to sounds in a noisy environment. Sound segregation is expected to improve the performance of hearing aids by reducing background noises, echoes, and the sounds of competing talkers. Similarly, most current ASR systems do not work well in the presence of competing voices or interfering noises. CASA may provide a robust front-end for ASR systems.

CASA is not simply a hearing aid for ASR systems, though. Computer audition can listen to several things at once by segregating sounds from a mixture of sounds. This capability to listen to several sounds simultaneously has been called the *Prince Shotoku effect* by Okuno (Okuno et al. 1995) after Prince Shotoku (574–622 A.D.) who is said to have been able to listen to ten people's petitions at the same time. Since this is virtually impossible for humans to do, CASA research would make computer audition more powerful than human audition, similar to the relationship of an airplane's flying ability to that of a bird.

At present, one of the hottest topics of ASR research is how to make more robust ASR systems that perform well outside *laboratory conditions* (Hansen et al. 1994). Usually the approaches taken are to reduce noise and use speaker adaptation, and treat sounds other than human voices as noise. CASA takes an opposite approach. First, it deals with the problems of handling general sounds to develop methods and technologies. Then it applies these to develop ASR systems that work in a real world environment.

In this paper, we discuss the issues concerning interfacing of sound segregation systems with ASR systems and report preliminary results on ASR for a mixture of sounds.

Sound Stream Segregation

Sound segregation should be incremental, because CASA is used as a front-end system for ASR systems and other applications that should run in real time. Many representations of a sound have been proposed, for example, auditory maps (Brown 1992) and synchrony strands (Cooke et al. 1993), but most of them are unsuitable for incremental processing. Nakatani and Okuno proposed using a *sound stream* (or simply *stream*) to represent a sound (Nakatani et al. 1994). A sound stream is a group of sound components that have some consistent attributes. By using sound streams, the Prince Shotoku effect can be modeled as shown in Fig. 1. Sound streams are segregated by the sound segregation system, and then speech streams are selected and passed on to the ASR systems.

Sound stream segregation consists of two subprocesses:

1. **Stream fragment extraction** — a fragment of a stream that has the same consistent attributes is extracted from a mixture of sounds.

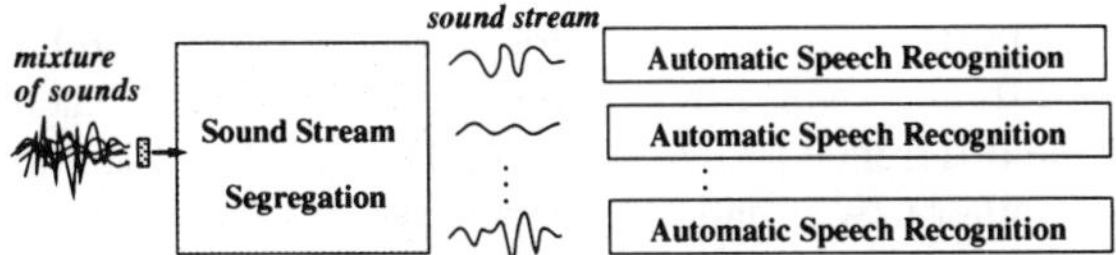

Figure 1: Modeling of the Prince Shotoku Effect or of Listening to Several Sounds Simultaneously

2. **Stream fragment grouping** — stream fragments are grouped into a stream according to some consistent attributes.

Most sound segregation systems developed so far have limitations. Some systems assume the number of sounds, or the characteristics of sounds such as voice or music (e.g., (Ramalingam 1994)). Some run in a batch mode (e.g., (Brown 1992; Cooke et al. 1993)). Since CASA tries to manipulate any kind of sound, it should be able to segregate any kind of sound from a mixture of sounds. For that reason, sound segregation systems should work primarily with the low level characteristics of sound. Once the performance of such systems has been assessed, the use of higher level characteristics of sounds or combining bottom-up and top-down processing should be attempted.

Nakatani et al. used a harmonic structure [1] and the direction of the sound source as consistent attributes for segregation. They developed two systems: the harmonic-based stream segregation (*HBSS*) (Nakatani et al. 1994; Nakatani et al. 1995a), and the binaural harmonic-based stream segregation (*Bi-HBSS*) systems (Nakatani et al. 1996). Both systems were designed and implemented in a multi-agent system with the residue-driven architecture (Nakatani et al. 1995b). We adopted these two systems to extract stream fragments from a mixture of sounds, since they run incrementally by using lower level sound characteristics. This section explains in detail how HBSS and Bi-HBSS work.

Harmonic-based Sound Segregation

The HBSS uses three kinds of agents: an event-detector, a tracer-generator, and tracers (Fig. 2) (Nakatani et al. 1994; Nakatani et al. 1995a). It works as follows:

1. An event-detector subtracts a set of predicted inputs from the actual input and sends the residue to the tracer-generator and tracers.
2. If the residue exceeds a threshold value, the tracer-generator searches for a harmonic structure in the residue. If it finds a harmonic structure and its fundamental stream, it generates a tracer to trace the harmonic structure.
3. Each tracer extracts a harmonic stream fragment by tracing the fundamental frequency of the stream. It also composes a predicted next input by adjusting the segregated stream fragment with the next input and sends this prediction to the event-detector.

[1] A harmonic structure consists of a fundamental frequency and its integer multiples or *overtones*.

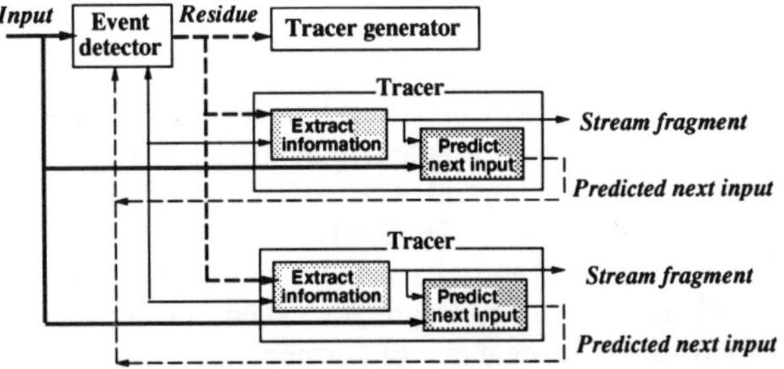

Figure 2: Harmonic-based Stream Segregation (HBSS)

Since tracers are dynamically generated and terminated in response to the input, a HBSS system can manipulate any number of sounds in principle. Of course, the setting of various thresholds determines the segregation performance.

The tracer-generator extracts a fundamental frequency from the residue of each time frame. For that purpose, the *harmonic intensity* $E_t(\omega)$ of the sound wave $x_t(\tau)$ at frame t is defined as

$$E_t(\omega) = \sum_k \| H_{t,k}(\omega) \|^2,$$

$$\text{where} \quad H_{t,k}(\omega) = \sum_\tau x_t(\tau) \cdot \exp(-jk\omega\tau),$$

where τ is time, k is the index of harmonics, $x_t(\tau)$ is the residue, and $H_{t,k}(\omega)$ is the sound component of the kth overtone. Since some components of a harmonic structure are destroyed by other interfering sounds, not all overtones are reliable. Therefore, only a *valid overtone* for a harmonic structure is used. An overtone is defined as *valid* if the intensity of the overtone is larger than a threshold value and the time transition of the intensity can be locally approximated in a linear manner. The *valid harmonic intensity*, $E'_t(\omega)$, is also defined as the sum of the $\| H_{t,k}(\omega) \|$ of valid overtones.

When a (harmonic) tracer is generated, it gets the initial fundamental frequency from the tracer-generator, and at each time frame it extracts the fundamental frequency that maximizes the valid harmonic intensity $E'_t(\omega)$. Then, it calculates the intensity and the phase of each overtone by evaluating the absolute value and that of $H_{t,k}(\omega)$ and extracts a stream fragment of the time frame. It also creates a predicted next input in a waveform by adjusting the phase of its overtones to the phase of the next input frame. If there are no longer valid overtones, or if the valid harmonic intensity drops below a threshold value, it terminates itself.

Binaural Harmonic-based Sound Segregation

When a mixture of sounds has harmonic structures whose fundamental frequencies are very close, HBSS may fail to segregate such sounds. For example, consider two harmonic sounds; one's fundamental frequency is increasing and the other's fundamental frequency is decreasing. When both fundamental frequencies cross, the HBSS cannot know whether two fundamental frequencies are crossing or approaching and departing. To cope with such problems and improve the segregation performance, binaural harmonic-based stream segregation (*Bi-HBSS*), which incorporates direction information into the HBSS, was proposed (Nakatani et al. 1996).

The Bi-HBSS takes a binaural input and extracts the direction of the sound source by calculating the interaural time difference (*ITD*) and interaural intensity difference (*IID*). More precisely, the Bi-HBSS uses two separate HBSS's for the right and left channels of the binaural input to extract harmonic stream fragments. Then, it calculates the ITD and IID by using a pair of harmonic stream fragments segregated. This method of calculating the ITD and IID reduces the computational costs, which is an important advantage since these values are usually calculated over the entire frequency region (Blauert 1983; Bodden 1993; Stadler & Rabinowitz 1993). The Bi-HBSS also utilizes the direction of the sound source to refine the harmonic structure by incorporating the direction into the validity. Thus, Bi-HBSS extracts a harmonic stream fragment and its direction. Internally, direction is represented by ITD (msec) and fundamental frequency is represented by *cent*. The unit, cent, is a logarithmic representation of frequency and 1 octave is equivalent to 1,200 cent.

The Bi-HBSS improves the segregation performance of the HBSS (Nakatani et al. 1995b; Nakatani et al. 1996). In addition, the spectral distortion of segregated sounds became very small when benchmarking was used with various mixtures of two women's utterances of Japanese vowels and interfering sounds (Nakatani et al. 1996).

However, the usage of binaural inputs may cause spectral distortion, because the spectrum of a binaural input is not the same as that of the original sound due to the shape of the human head. Such transformation is called the *head-related transfer function (HRTF)* (Blauert 1983). Due to the HRTF, the power of lower frequencies is usually decreased while that of higher frequencies is increased. Thus, it may make it difficulty to segregate a person's speech. The literature mentioned above did not examine this possibility.

Design of Speech Stream Segregation

Neither HBSS nor Bi-HBSS can segregate a speech stream, because it contains non-harmonic structures (e.g., consonants, especially unvoiced consonants) as well as harmonic structures (e.g., vowels and some voiced consonants). In this paper, we propose a simple method to extract a speech stream. First, the harmonic structures (vowels and some voiced consonants) of each stream are extracted by HBSS or Bi-HBSS and reconstructed by grouping. This process is called **harmonic grouping**. Second, non-harmonic structures (or most consonants) are reconstructed by substituting the residue. This process is called **residue substitution**. These processes also work incrementally, like the stream fragment extraction process. Note that in this scheme, consonants are extracted implicitly.

Harmonic Grouping Suppose that a new harmonic stream fragment ϕ is to be grouped. Let f_ϕ be the fundamental frequency of ϕ. The harmonic part of a stream is reconstructed in one of the following three ways (Nakatani et al. 1996; Rosenthal & Okuno 1996):

1. **F-grouping** — according to the nearness of the fundamental frequencies. Find an existing group, say Ψ, such that the difference $| f_\phi - f_\Psi | < \delta$. The value of δ is 300 cent if other new stream fragments exist at the same time with ϕ, 600 cent otherwise. If more than one existing group is found, ϕ is grouped into the group that is the closest to f_ϕ. If only one existing group is found, ϕ is grouped into Ψ. Otherwise, ϕ forms a new group.
2. **D-grouping** — according to the nearness of the directions of the sound source. The range of nearness in ITD is 0.167 msec, which corresponds roughly to 20°. The algorithm is the same as the F-grouping.
3. **B-grouping** — If a stream fragment, ϕ, satisfies the above two conditions for a group, Ψ, it is grouped into Ψ. However, if ϕ has more than one such group,the group of minimum combined nearness is selected. The combined nearness, K, is defined as follows:

$$K = \alpha \frac{| \Delta f |}{c_f} + (1 - \alpha) \frac{| \Delta d |}{c_d}$$

where $c_f = 300$ cent, and $c_d = 0.167$ msec. The current value of the normalized factor, α, is 0.47.

The grouping is controlled by the gap threshold; if the time gap between two consecutive stream fragments is less than the gap threshold, they are grouped together with information about the missing components. The current value of the gap threshold is 500 msec, which is determined by the maximum duration of the consonants in the utterance database. Note that since HBSS extracts only harmonic structures, only F-grouping is applicable.

Residue substitution The idea behind the residue substitution is based on the observation that human listeners can perceptually restore a missing sound component if it is very brief and replaced by appropriate sounds. This auditory mechanism of phonemic restoration is known as *auditory induction* (Warren 1970). After harmonic grouping, harmonic components are included in a segregated stream or group, while non-harmonic components are left out. Since the missing components are non-harmonic, they cannot be extracted by either HBSS or Bi-HBSS and remain in the residue. Therefore, the missing components of a stream may be restored by substituting the residue produced by HBSS or Bi-HBSS.

The residue substitution, or which part of the residue is substituted for missing components, may be done by one of the following methods:

1. **All-residue substitution** — All the residue is used.
2. **Own-residue substitution** — Only the residue from the direction of the sound source is used.

In this paper, the former method is used, because the latter requires a precise determination of the sound source direction and thus the computational cost of separation is higher. In addition, the recognition performance of the latter is lower than that of the former, as will be shown later.

Issues in Interfacing SSS with ASR

We use an automatic speech recognition system based on a hidden Markov model-based (*HMM*). An HMM usually uses the three characteristics in speech recognition; a spectral envelop, a pitch or a fundamental frequency, and a label or a pair consisting of the onset and offset times of speech. Since the input is a mixture of sounds, these characteristic, in particular the spectral envelop, are critically affected. Therefore, the recognition performance with a mixture of sounds is severely degraded by spectral distortion caused by interfering and competing sounds.

The segregation of the speech streams is intended to reduce the degradation, and is considered effective in recovering spectral distortion from a mixture of sounds. However, it also introduces another kind of spectral distortion to segregated streams, which is caused by extracting the harmonic structure, the head-related transfer function, or a binaural input, and the grouping and residue substitution. In the next section, the degradation of the recognition performance caused by segregation will be assessed and methods of recovery will be proposed.

The pitch error of Bi-HBSS for simple benchmarks is small (Nakatani et al. 1996). However, its evaluation with larger benchmarks is also needed. The onset of a segregated stream is detected only from the harmonic structures in HBSS. Since the beginning and end of speech are usually comprised of non-harmonic structures, the onset and offset times are extended by 40 msec for sounds segregated by HBSS. Since Bi-HBSS can detect whether a leading and/or trailing sound exists according to the directional information, the onset and offset is determined by this.

Influence of SSS on ASR

In this section, we assess the effect of segregation on ASR and propose methods to reduce this effect.

The ASR system used in this paper

The "HMM-LR" developed by ATR Inc. (Kita et al. 1990) is used system in this paper. The HMM-LR is a continuous speech recognition system that uses generalized LR parsing with a single discrete codebook. The size of the codebook is 256 and it was created from a set of standard data. The training and test data used in this paper were also created by ATR Inc. Since the primitive HMM-LR is a gender-dependent speech recognition system, HMM-LRs for male speakers (the *HMM-m*) and for female speakers (the *HMM-f*) were used. The parameters of each system were trained by using 5,240 words from five different sets of 1,048 utterances by each speaker. The recognition performance was evaluated by an open test, and 1,000 testing words were selected randomly from non-training data. The evaluation was based on word recognition. Therefore, the LR grammar for the HMM-m/f consists of only rules that the start symbol derives a terminal symbol directly. The evaluation measure used in this paper is the *cumulative accuracy up to the 10th candidate*, which specifies what percentage of words are recognized up to the 10th candidate by a particular HMM-LR. This measurement is popular for evaluating the actual speech recognition performance in a whole speech understanding system, because the top nth recognition candidates are used in successive language understanding.

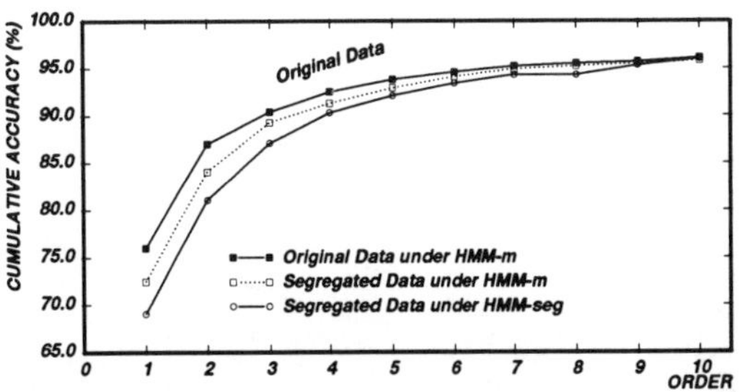

Figure 3: Influence of the Harmonic Structure Extraction (Experiment 1)

Influence of the Harmonic Structure Extraction

To assess the influence of harmonic structure extraction on the word recognition performance, we have defined a new operation called *harmonic structure reconstruction*, which is done as follows:

1. The HBSS extracts harmonic stream fragments from an utterance of a word by a single speaker.
2. All the extracted harmonic stream fragments are grouped into the same stream.
3. All the residue is substituted in the stream for the time frames where no harmonic structure was extracted.

Experiment 1: Harmonic structure reconstruction and word recognition was performed using the HMM-m for over 1,000 utterances of a word by a male speaker. The cumulative accuracy of the recognition is shown in Fig. 3. In Fig. 3, the curve denoted as the *original data* indicates the recognition rate for the same original utterances by the same speaker. The word recognition rate was lower by 3.5% for the first candidate when the HMM-m was used, but was almost equal in cumulative accuracy for the 10th candidate. This demonstrates that the harmonic structure reconstruction has little effect on the word recognition performance.

We tried to improve the recognition rate by re-training the parameters of the HMM-LR by using all the training data provided through harmonic structure reconstruction. The resulting HMM-LR, however, did not improve the recognition rate as shown in Fig. 3. Therefore, we did not adopt any special treatment for harmonic structure reconstruction.

Influence of the Head-related Transfer Function

As we mentioned, a binaural sound is equivalent to its original sound transformed by a head-related transfer function (*HRTF*) with a particular direction.

Experiment 2: To evaluate the influence of the HRTF, all the test data were converted to binaural sounds as follows, and then recognized by the HMM-m.

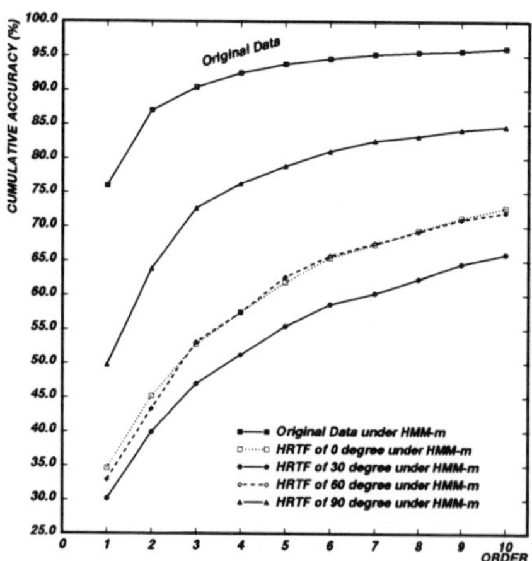

Figure 4: Influence of the Head-related Transfer Function (Experiment 2)

1. HRTFs in four directions (0°, 30°, 60°, and 90°) [2] were applied to each test utterance to generate a binaural sound.
2. For each binaural sound, the monaural sound was extracted from the channel with the larger power, in this case, the left channel.
3. The power level was adjusted so that its average power was equivalent to that of the original sound. This operation is called *power adjustment.*
4. The resulting monaural sounds (the *HRTF'ed* test data) were given to the HMM-m for word recognition.

The cumulative recognition accuracy for the HRTF'ed test data is shown in Fig. 4. The original data is also shown for comparison. The decrease in the cumulative accuracy for the 10th candidate ranged from 11.4% to 30.1%. The degradation depended on the direction of the sound source and was the largest for 30° and the smallest for 90°.

Recovering the Performance Degradation caused by the HRTF

Two methods to recover the decrease in recognition accuracy caused by HRTF have been tried:

1. Re-training the HMM-LR parameters with the HTRF'ed training data, and
2. Correcting the frequency characteristics of the HRTF.

Re-training of the parameters of the HMM-LR We converted the training data for the HMM-LR parameters by applying the HRTF in the four directions to the training data with power adjustment. We refer to the re-trained HMM-LR for male speakers as the *HMM-hrtf-m.*

The cumulative recognition accuracy of the HRTF'ed test data by the HMM-hrtf-m is shown in Fig. 5. The decrease in the cumulative accuracy was significantly reduced and almost vanishes for 90°. However, the degradation still depended on the direction of the sound source.

[2] The angle is calculated counterclockwise from the center, and thus 0°, 90°, and -90° mean the center, the leftmost and the rightmost, respectively.

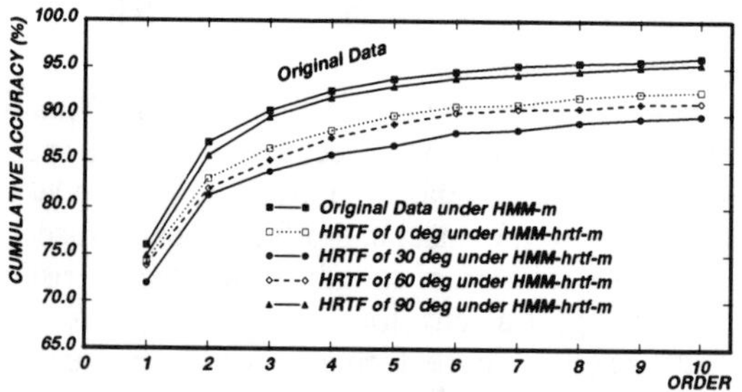

Figure 5: Recovery by Re-trained HMM-LR

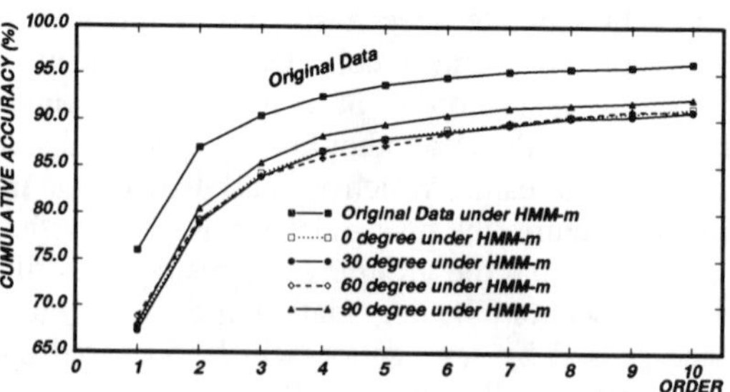

Figure 6: Recovery by Correcting the F-char of HRTF

Frequency Characteristics (F-Char) Correction The effect of the HRTF is to amplify the higher frequency region while attenuating the lower frequency region. For example, the Japanese word "aji" (taste) sounds like "ashi" (foot) if an HRTF of any degree is applied. To recover the spectral distortion caused by the HRTF, we corrected the frequency characteristics (F-Char) of the HRTR'ed test data through power adjustment. After this correction, the test data were recognized by the HMM-m (Fig. 6). The variance in the recognition rate due to different directions was resolved, but the overall improvement was not as great as with the HMM-hrtf-m.

Since the latter method requires a precise determination of the directions, though, it cannot be used when the sound source is moving. In addition, the size of HRTF data for the various directions is very large and its spatial and computational cost is significant. Therefore, we used the HMM-hrtf-m/f to recognize binaural data.

Influence of the Harmonic Grouping and Residue Substitution

Experiment 3: The influence of harmonic grouping by the F-grouping, D-grouping, and B-grouping was evaluated by the following method:

1. The Bi-HBSS extracted harmonic stream fragments from binaural input in four directions (0°, 30°, 60°, and 90°) for a man's utterance.
2. Sound stream fragments were grouped into a stream by one of the three groupings and the non-harmonic components of the stream are filled in through the all-residue substitution.

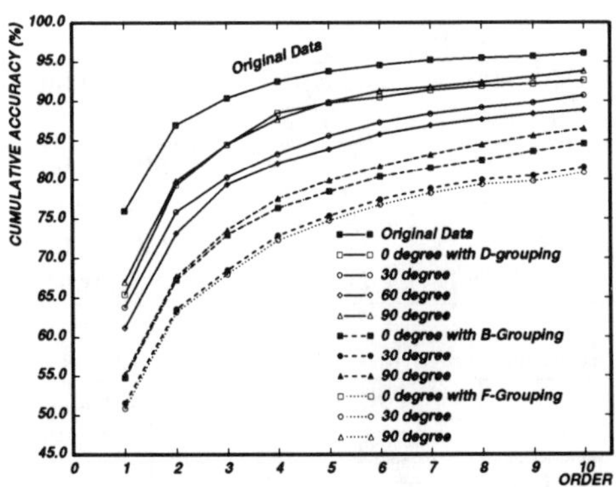

Figure 7: Influence of Harmonic Grouping (Experiment 3)

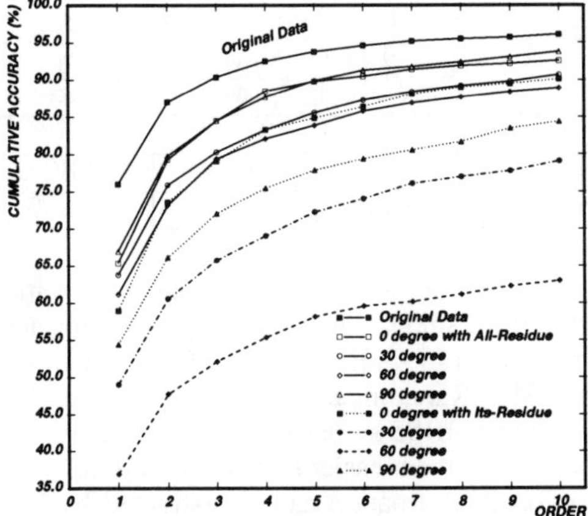

Figure 8: Influence of Residue Substitution (Experiment 4)

3. Power adjustment was applied to the segregated sound streams.
4. The resulting sounds were recognized with the HMM-hrtf-m.

The recognition rate is shown in Fig. 7. The best performance was with the D-grouping, while the worst was with the F-grouping. The recognition with the F-grouping was poor because only the previous state of the fundamental frequency was used to group stream fragments. This also led to poor performance with the B-grouping. Longer temporal characteristics of a fundamental frequency should be exploited, but this remains for future work. Therefore, we adopted the D-grouping for the experiments described in the remainder of this paper.

Experiment 4: We evaluated the effect of residue substitution by either all-residue substitution or own-residue substitution in the same way as Experiment 3. The resulting recognition rates are shown in Fig. 8. The recognition rate was higher with the all-residue substitution than with the own-residue substitution. This is partially because the signals substituted by the own-residue were weaker than those by the all-residue. Therefore, we will use the all-residue substitution throughout the remainder of this paper.

Experiments on Listening to a Sound Mixture

Our assessment of the effect of segregation on ASR suggests that we should use Bi-HBSS with the D-grouping and the all-residue substitution and that segregated speech streams should be recognized by the HMM-hrtf-m/f. We also evaluated monaural segregation by HBSS with the all-residue substitution and the HMM-m/f. The experiments on recognizing a mixture of sounds were done under the following conditions:

1. The first speaker is 30° to the left of the center and utters a word first.
2. The second speaker is 30° to the right of the center and utters a word 150 msec after the first speaker.
3. There were 500 two-word testing combinations.
4. The power adjustment was not applied to any segregated sound, because the system cannot determine the original sound that corresponds to a segregated sound.

The utterance of the second speaker was delayed by 150 msec because the mixture of sounds was to be recognized directly by the HMM-m/f. Note that the actual first utterance is sometimes done by the second speaker.

Listening to Two Sounds at the Same Time

Since the HMM-LR framework we used is gender-dependent, the following three benchmarks were used (see Table 1). The cumulative accuracies of recognition of the original data for Woman 1, Woman 2, Man 1, and Man 2 by the HMM-m/f were 94.19%, 95.10%, 94.99%, and 96.10%, respectively.

The recognition rate was measured without segregation, with segregation by HBSS, and with segregation by Bi-HBSS. The recognition performance in terms of cumulative accuracy up to the 10th candidate is summarized in Tables 2 to 4. The recognition performance of speech segregated by Bi-HBSS was better than when HBSS was used. With Bi-HBSS, the decrease in the recognition rate of the second woman's utterance from that of the original sound was 21.20%. Since these utterances could not be recognized at all without segregation, the error rate was reduced by 75.60% on average by the segregation.

Without segregation, the utterances of the first speaker could be recognized up to 37% if the label (the onset and offset times) was given by some means. In this experiment, the original labels created by human listeners at ATR were used. However, the recognition rate falls to almost zero when another sound is interfering (see the following experiments and Table 6 and 7).

The Bi-HBSS reduces the recognition errors of HBSS by 48.1%, 22.7%, and 23.1% for benchmarks 1, 2, and 3, respectively. The improvement for benchmark 1 is especially large because the frequency region of women's utterances is so narrow that their recognition is prone to recognition errors. Men's utterances, in particular, the second man's utterances of benchmark 3, are not well segregated by HBSS or Bi-HBSS. The fundamental frequency (pitch) of the second man is less than 100 Hz while that of the first man is

Table 1: Benchmark sounds 1–3

Benchmark No.	Speaker 1	Speaker 2
1	Woman 1	Woman 2
2	Man 1	Woman 2
3	Man 1	Man 2

Table 2: Recognition Rate of Benchmark 1

	10th Cumulative Accuracy		
	Average	Speaker 1	Speaker 2
No segregation	—	18.80%	0.60%
HBSS	27.51%	26.31%	28.71%
Bi-HBSS	75.60%	77.31%	73.90%

Table 3: Recognition Rate of Benchmark 2

	10th Cumulative Accuracy		
	average	Speaker 1	Speaker 2
No segregation	—	36.40%	0.40%
HBSS	43.88%	47.19%	40.56%
Bi-HBSS	66.60%	62.25%	71.69%

Table 4: Recognition Rate of Benchmark 3

	10th Cumulative Accuracy		
	average	Speaker 1	Speaker 2
No segregation	—	37.80%	0.40%
HBSS	28.11%	31.73%	24.50%
Bi-HBSS	53.21%	61.24%	45.18%

about 110 Hz. A sound of lower fundamental frequency is in general more difficult to segregate.

Listening to Three Sounds at the Same Time

Our next experiment was to segregate speech streams from a mixture of three sounds. Two benchmarks were composed by adding an intermittent sound to the sounds of benchmark 1 (see Table 5). The intermittent sound was a harmonic sound with a 250 Hz fundamental frequency that was repeated for 1,000 msec at 50 msec intervals. Its direction was 0°, that is, from the center. The signal-to-noise ratio (SNR) of the woman's utterance to the intermittent sound was 1.7 dB and -1.3 dB, respectively, for benchmark 4 and 5. The actual SNR was further reduced, because the other woman's utterance was also an interfering sound.

The recognition performance in terms of 10th cumulative accuracy are summarized in Tables 6 and 7. The degradation with HBSS and Bi-HBSS caused by the intermittent sound of benchmark 4 was 7.9% and 23.3%, respectively. When the power of the intermittent sound was amplified and the SNR of the woman's utterances decreased by 3 dB as in benchmark 5, the additional degradation with HBSS and Bi-HBSS was 1.5% and 5.8%, respectively. Segregation by either HBSS or Bi-HBSS seems rather robust against an increase in the power level of interfering sounds.

Table 5: Benchmark sounds 4–5

No.	1st Speaker (SNR)	2nd Speaker (SNR)	3rd Sound
4	Woman 1 (1.7 dB)	Woman 2 (1.7 dB)	Intermittent Sound
5	Woman 1 (-1.3 dB)	Woman 2 (-1.3 dB)	Intermittent Sound

Table 6: Recognition Rate of Benchmark 4

	10th Cumulative Accuracy		
	average	Speaker 1	Speaker 2
No segregation	—	0.00%	0.40%
HBSS	19.58%	16.87%	22.29%
Bi-HBSS	52.31%	57.63%	46.99%

Table 7: Recognition Rate of Benchmark 5

	10th Cumulative Accuracy		
	average	Speaker 1	Speaker 2
No segregation	—	0.00%	0.20%
HBSS	18.07%	14.26%	21.89%
Bi-HBSS	46.48%	49.09%	43.86%

Discussion and Future work

In this paper, we have described our experiments on the Prince Shotoku effect, or listening to several sounds simultaneously. We would like to make the following observations.

(1) Most of the sound stream segregation systems developed so far (Bodden 1993; Brown 1992; Cooke et al. 1993; Green et al. 1995; Ramalingam 1994) run in batch. However, HBSS and Bi-HBSS systems run incrementally, which is expected to make them easier to run in real time.

(2) Directional information can be extracted by binaural input (Blauert 1983; Bodden 1993) or by microphone arrays (Hansen et al. 1994; Stadler & Rabinowitz 1993). Our results prove the effectiveness of localization by using a binaural input. However, this severely degrades the recognition rate due to spectral distortion; this has not been reported in the literature as far as we know. Therefore, we are currently engaged in designing a sophisticated mechanism to integrate HBSS and Bi-HBSS to overcome the drawbacks caused by a binaural input.

(3) The method to extract a speech with consonants is based on auditory induction, a psychacoustical observation. This method is considered as the first approximation for speech stream segregation, because it does not use any characteristics specific to human voices, e.g., formants. In addition, we should attempt to incorporate a wider set of the segregation and grouping phenomena of psychoacoustics such as common onset, offset, AM and FM modulations, formants, and localization such as elevation and azimuth.

(4) In HMM-based speech recognition systems, the leading part of a sound is very important to focus the search and if the leading part is missing, the recognition fails. Examination of the recognition patterns shows that the latter part of a word or a component of a complex word is often clearly recognized, but this is still treated as failure.

(5) Since a fragment of a word is more accurately segregated than the whole word, top-down processing is expected to play an important role in the recognition. Various methods developed for speech understanding systems should be

incorporated to improve the recognition and understanding.

(6) In this paper, we used standard discrete-type hidden Markov models for an initial assessment. However, HMM technologies have been improved in recent years, especially in terms of their robustness (Hansen et al. 1994; Minami & Furui 1995). The evaluation of our SSS in sophisticated HMM frameworks remains as future work.

(7) Our approach is bottom-up, primarily because one goal of our research is to identify the capability and limitations of the bottom-up approach. However, the top-down approach is also needed for CASA, because a human listener's knowledge and experience plays an essential role in listening and understanding (Handel 1989).

(8) To integrate bottom-up and top-down processes, system architecture is essential. The HBSS and Bi-HBSS systems are modeled on the residue-driven architecture with multi-agent systems. These systems can be extended for such integration by using subsumption architecture (Nakatani et al. 1994). A common system architecture for such integration is the black board architecture (Cooke et al. 1993; Lesser et al. 1993). The modeling of CASA represents an important area for future work.

Conclusions

This paper reported the preliminary results of experiments on listening to several sounds at once. We proposed the segregation of speech streams by extracting and grouping harmonic stream fragments while substituting the residue for non-harmonic components. Since the segregation system uses a binaural input, it can interface with the hidden Markov model-based speech recognition systems by converting the training data to binaural data.

Experiments with 500 mixtures of two women's utterances of a word showed that the 10th cumulative accuracy of speech recognition of each woman's utterance is, on average, 75%. This performance was attained without using any features specific to human voices. Therefore, this result should encourage the AI community to engage more actively in computational auditory scene analysis (CASA) and computer audition. In addition, because audition is more dependent on the listener's knowledge and experience than vision, we believe that more attention should be paid to CASA in the research of Artificial Intelligence.

Acknowledgments

We thank Kunio Kashino, Masataka Goto, Norihiro Hagita and Ken'ichiro Ishii for their valuable discussions.

References

Blauert, J. 1983. *Spatial Hearing: the Psychophysics of Human Sound Localization.* MIT Press.

Bodden, M. 1993. Modeling human sound-source localization and the cocktail-party-effect. *Acta Acustica* 1:43–55.

Bregman, A.S. 1990. *Auditory Scene Analysis – the Perceptual Organization of Sound.* MIT Press.

Brown, G.J. 1992. Computational auditory scene analysis: A representational approach. Ph.D diss., Dept. of Computer Science, University of Sheffield.

Cherry, E.C. 1953. Some experiments on the recognition of speech, with one and with two ears. *Journal of Acoustic Society of America* 25:975–979.

Cooke, M.P.; Brown, G.J.; Crawford, M.; and Green, P. 1993. Computational Auditory Scene Analysis: listening to several things at once. *Endeavour*, 17(4):186–190.

Handel, S. 1989. *Listening – An Introduction to the Perception of Auditory Events.* MIT Press.

Hansen, J.H.L.; Mammone, R.J.; and Young, S. 1994. Editorial for the special issue of the IEEE transactions on speech and audio processing on robust speech processing". *Transactions on Speech and Audio Processing* 2(4):549-550.

Green, P.D.; Cooke, M.P.; and Crawford, M.D. 1995. Auditory Scene Analysis and Hidden Markov Model Recognition of Speech in Noise. In Proceedings of 1995 International Conference on Acoustics, Speech and Signal Processing, Vol.1:401–404, IEEE.

Kita, K.; Kawabata, T.; and Shikano, H. 1990. HMM continuous speech recognition using generalized LR parsing. Transactions of the Information Processing Society of Japan 31(3):472–480.

Lesser, V.; Nawab, S.H.; Gallastegi, I.; and Klassner, F. 1993. IPUS: An Architecture for Integrated Signal Processing and Signal Interpretation in Complex Environments. In Proceedings of the Eleventh National Conference on Artificial Intelligence, 249–255.

Minami, Y, and Furui, S. 1995. A Maximum Likelihood Procedure for A Universal Adaptation Method based on HMM Composition. In Proceedings of 1995 International Conference on Acoustics, Speech and Signal Processing, Vol.1:129–132, IEEE.

Nakatani, T.; Okuno, H.G.; and Kawabata, T. 1994. Auditory Stream Segregation in Auditory Scene Analysis with a Multi-Agent System. In Proceedings of the Twelfth National Conference on Artificial Intelligence, 100–107, AAAI.

Nakatani, T.; Kawabata, T.; and Okuno, H.G. 1995a. A computational model of sound stream segregation with the multi-agent paradigm. In Proceedings of 1995 International Conference on Acoustics, Speech and Signal Processing, Vol.4:2671–2674, IEEE.

Nakatani, T.; Okuno, H.G.; and Kawabata, T. 1995b. Residue-driven architecture for Computational Auditory Scene Analysis. In Proceedings of the th International Joint Conference on Artificial Intelligence, Vol.1:165–172, IJCAI.

Nakatani, T.; Goto, M.; and Okuno, H.G. 1996. Localization by harmonic structure and its application to harmonic sound stream segregation. In Proceedings of 1996 International Conference on Acoustics, Speech and Signal Processing, IEEE. Forthcoming.

Okuno, H.G.; Nakatani, T.; and Kawabata, T. 1995. Cocktail-Party Effect with Computational Auditory Scene Analysis — Preliminary Report —. In *Symbiosis of Human and Artifact — Proceedings of the Sixth International Conference on Human-Computer Interaction*, Vol.2:503–508, Elsevier Science B.V.

Ramalingam, C.S., and Kumaresan, R. 1994. Voiced-speech analysis based on the residual interfering signal canceler (RISC) algorithm. In Proceedings of the International Conference on Acoustics, Speech, and Signal Processing, Vol.I:473–476, IEEE.

Rosenthal, D., and Okuno, H.G. eidtors 1996. *Computational Auditory Scene Analysis*, LEA. Forthcoming.

Stadler, R.W., and Rabinowitz, W.M. 1993. On the potential of fixed arrays for hearing aids. *Journal of Acoustic Society of America* 94(3) Pt.1:1332–1342.

Warren, R.M. 1970. Perceptual restoration of missing speech sounds. *Science*167:392–393.

Motion and Color Analysis for Animat Perception

Tamer F. Rabie and **Demetri Terzopoulos**

Department of Computer Science, University of Toronto
10 King's College Road, Toronto, Ontario, M5S 3G4, Canada
e-mail: {tamer|dt}@cs.toronto.edu

Abstract

We propose novel gaze control algorithms for active perception in mobile autonomous agents with directable, foveated vision sensors. Our agents are realistic artificial animals, or animats, situated in physics-based virtual worlds. Their active perception systems continuously analyze photorealistic retinal image streams to glean information useful for controlling the animat's eyes and body. The vision system computes optical flow and segments moving targets in the low-resolution visual periphery. It then matches segmented targets against mental models of colored objects of interest. The eyes saccade to increase acuity by foveating objects. The resulting sensorimotor control loop supports complex behaviors, such as predation.

Introduction

Animals are active observers of their environment (Gibson 1979). This fact has inspired a trend in the computer vision field popularly known as "active vision" (Bajcsy 1988; Ballard 1991; Swain & Stricker 1993). Unfortunately, efforts to create active vision systems for physical robots have been hampered by hardware and processor limitations. The recently proposed *animat vision* paradigm (Terzopoulos & Rabie 1995) offers an approach to developing biomimetic active vision systems that does not rely on robot hardware. Instead of physical robots, animat vision prescribes the use of virtual robots that take the form of artificial animals, or animats, situated in physics-based virtual worlds. Animats are autonomous virtual agents possessing mobile, muscle-actuated bodies and brains with motor, perception, behavior and learning centers. In the perception center of the animat's brain, computer vision algorithms continually analyze the incoming perceptual information. Based on this analysis, the behavior center dispatches motor commands to the animat's body, thus forming a complete sensorimotor control system. Animat vision, implemented entirely in software, has several important advantages over conventional "hardware vision", at least for research purposes (refer to (Terzopoulos & Rabie 1995; Terzopoulos 1995) for a discussion).

In many biological eyes, the high-acuity fovea covers only a small fraction of a visual field whose resolution decreases monotonically towards the periphery. Spatially nonuniform retinal imaging provides opportunities for increased computational efficiency through economization of photoreceptors and focus of attention, but it forces the visual system to solve problems that do not generally arise with a uniform field of view. A key problem is determining where to redirect the fovea when a target of interest appears in the periphery. In this paper we present a solution to this problem through the exploitation of motion and color information.

Figure 1: Artificial fishes swimming among aquatic plants in a physics-based virtual marine environment.

Motion and color play an important role in animal perception. Birds and insects exploit optical flow for obstacle avoidance and to control their ego-motion (Gibson 1979). Some species of fish are able to recognize the color signatures of other fish and use this information in certain piscene behaviors (Adler 1975). The human visual system is highly sensitive to motion and color. We tend to focus our attention on moving colorful objects. Motionless objects whose colors blend in to the background are not as easily detectable, and several camouflage strategies in the animal kingdom rely on this fact (Cedras & Shah 1995).

Following the animat vision paradigm, the motion and color based gaze control algorithms that we propose in this paper are implemented and evaluated within artificial fishes in a virtual marine world (Fig. 1). The fish animats are the result of research in the domain of artificial life (see (Terzopoulos, Tu, & Grzeszczuk 1994) for the details). In the present work, the fish animat serves as an autonomous mobile robot situated in a photorealistic, dynamic environment.

Our new gaze control algorithms significantly enhance the prototype animat vision system that we implemented in prior work (Terzopoulos & Rabie 1995) and they support more robust vision-guided navigation abilities in the artificial fish. We review the animat vision system in the next section before presenting our new work on integrating motion and color analysis for animat perception in subsequent sections.

A Prototype Animat Vision System

The basic functionality of the animat vision system, which is described in detail in (Terzopoulos & Rabie 1995), starts with binocular perspective projection of the color 3D world onto the animat's 2D retinas. Retinal imaging is accomplished by photorealistic graphics rendering of the world from the animat's point of view. This projection respects occlusion relationships among objects. It forms spatially variant visual fields with high resolution foveas and progressively lower resolution peripheries. Based on an analysis of the incoming color retinal image stream, the visual center of the animat's brain supplies saccade control signals to its eyes to stabilize the visual fields during locomotion, to attend to interesting targets based on color, and to keep moving targets fixated. The artificial fish is thus able to approach and track other artificial fishes visually. Fig. 2 provides a block diagram of the active vision system showing two main modules that control retinal image stabilization and foveation of the eyes.

Eyes and Retinal Imaging

The artificial fish has binocular vision. The movements of each eye are controlled through two gaze angles (θ, ϕ) which specify the horizontal and vertical rotation of the eyeball, respectively. The angles are given with respect to the head coordinate frame, such that the eye is looking straight ahead when $\theta = \phi = 0°$.

Each eye is implemented as four coaxial virtual cameras to approximate the spatially nonuniform, foveal/peripheral imaging capabilities typical of biological eyes. Fig. 3(a) shows an example of the 64×64 images that are rendered by the coaxial cameras in each eye (rendering employs the GL library and graphics pipeline on Silicon Graphics workstations). The level $l = 0$ camera has the widest field of view (about 120°) and the lowest resolution. The resolution increases and the field of view decreases with increasing l. The highest resolution image at level $l = 3$ is the fovea and the other images form the visual periphery. Fig. 3(b) shows the 512×512 binocular retinal images composited from the coaxial images at the top of the figure. To reveal the retinal image structure in the figure, we have placed a white border around each magnified component image. Vision algorithms which process the four 64×64 component images are 16 times more efficient than those that process a uniform 512×512 retinal image.

Foveation by Color Object Detection

The brain of the artificial fish stores a set of color models of objects that are of interest to it. For instance, if the fish is by habit a predator, it would possess models of prey fish.

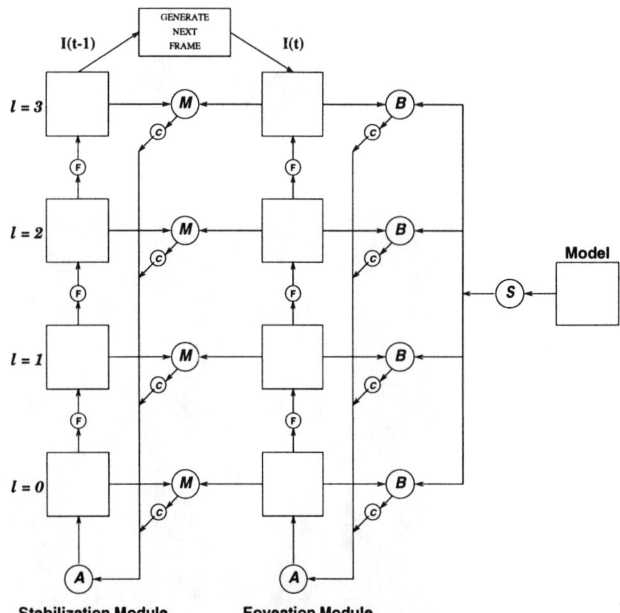

Figure 2: The animat vision system. The flow of the gaze control algorithm is from right to left. A: Update gaze angles (θ, ϕ) and saccade using these angles, B: Search current level for model target and if found localize it, else search lower level, C: Select level to be processed (see text), F: Reduce field of view for next level and render, M: Compute a general translational displacement vector (u, v) between images $I(t-1)$ and $I(t)$, S: Scale the color histogram of the model for use by the current level.

The mental models are stored as a list of 64×64 RGB color images.

To detect and localize any target that may be imaged in the low resolution periphery of its retinas, the animat vision system of the fish employs an improved version of a color indexing algorithm proposed by Swain (Swain & Ballard 1991).[1] Since each model object has a unique color histogram signature, it can be detected in the retinal image by histogram intersection and localized by histogram backprojection.

Saccadic Eye Movements

When a target is detected in the visual periphery, the eyes will saccade to the angular offset of the object to bring it within the fovea. With the object in the high resolution fovea, a more accurate foveation is obtained by a second pass of histogram backprojection. A second saccade typically centers the object accurately in both left and right foveas, thus achieving vergence.

Module A in Fig. 2 performs the saccades by incrementing

[1] Our improvements, which include iterative model histogram scaling and weighted histograms, make the technique much more robust against the large variations in scale that occur in our application. The details of the improved algorithm are presented in (Terzopoulos & Rabie 1995).

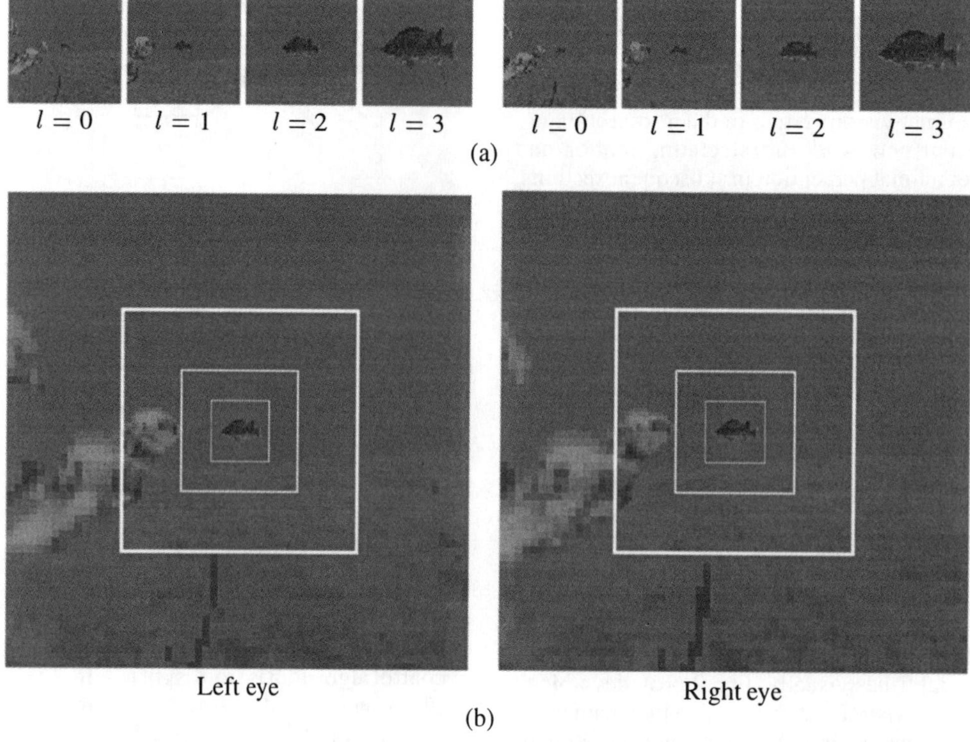

Figure 3: Binocular retinal imaging (monochrome versions of original color images). (a) 4 component images; $l = 0, 1, 2$, are peripheral images; $l = 3$ is foveal image. (b) Composited retinal images (borders of composited component images are shown in white).

the gaze angles (θ, ϕ) in order to rotate the eyes to the required gaze direction.

Visual Field Stabilization using Optical Flow

It is necessary to stabilize the visual field of the artificial fish because its body undulates as it swims. Once a target is verged in both foveas, the stabilization process (Fig. 2) assumes the task of keeping the target foveated during locomotion.

Stabilization is achieved by computing the overall translational displacement (u, v) of intensities between the current foveal image and that from the previous time instant, and updating the gaze angles to compensate. The displacement is computed as a translational offset in the retinotopic coordinate system by a least squares minimization of the optical flow between image frames at times t and $t-1$ (Horn 1986).

The optical flow stabilization method is robust only for small displacements between frames. Consequently, when the displacement of the target between frames is large enough that the method is likely to produce bad estimates, the foveation module is invoked to re-detect and re-foveate the target as described earlier.

Each eye is controlled independently during foveation and stabilization of a target. Hence, the two retinal images must be correlated to keep them verged accurately on the target. Referring to Fig. 4, the vergence angle is $\theta_V = (\theta_R - \theta_L)$ and its magnitude increases as the fish comes closer to the target. Therefore, once the eyes are verged on a target, it is straightforward for the vision system to estimate the range to the target from the gaze angles.

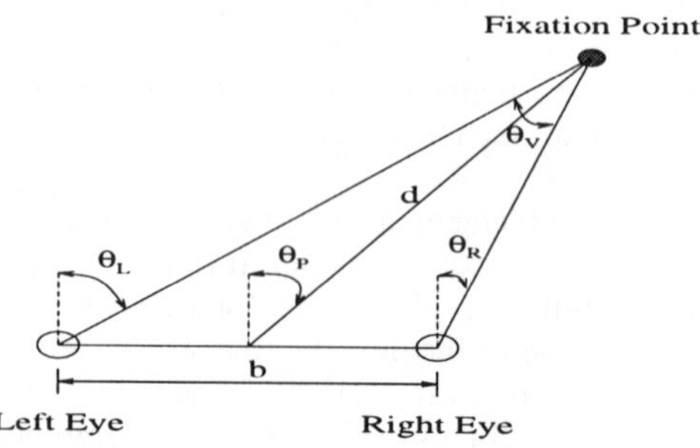

Figure 4: Gaze angles and range to target geometry.

Vision-Guided Navigation

The artificial fish can also employ the gaze direction (i.e., the gaze angles) while the eyes are fixated on a target to navigate towards the target. The θ angles are used to compute the left/right turn angle θ_P shown in Fig. 4, and the ϕ angles are similarly used to compute an up/down turn angle ϕ_P. The fish's turn motor controllers are invoked to execute a left/right turn—right-turn-MC for an above-threshold positive θ_P and left-turn-MC for negative θ_P—with $|\theta_P|$ as parameter. Up/down turn motor commands are issued to the fish's pectoral fins, with an above-threshold positive

ϕ_P interpreted as "up" and negative as "down". The motor controllers are explained in (Terzopoulos, Tu, & Grzeszczuk 1994).

The remainder of the paper presents our new work on integrating color and motion analysis in active vision.

Integrating Motion and Color for Attention

Selective attention is an important mechanism for dealing with the combinatorial aspects of search in vision (Tsotsos *et al.* 1995). Deciding where to redirect the fovea can involve a complex search process (Tsotsos *et al.* 1995; Rimey & Brown 1992; Maver & Bajcsy 1990). In this section we offer an efficient solution which integrates motion and color to increase the robustness of our animat's perceptual functions.

Motion and color have been considered extensively in the literature in a variety of passive vision systems, but rarely have they been integrated for use in dynamic perception systems. The conjunction of color and motion cues has recently been exploited to produce more exact segmentations and for the extraction of object contours from natural scenes (Dubuisson & Jain 1993). Color and motion features of video images have been used for color video image classification and understanding (Gong & Sakauchi 1992).

Integrating motion and color for object recognition can improve the robustness of moving colored object recognition. Motion may be considered a bottom-up *alerting* cue, while color can be used as a top-down cue for model-based recognition (Swain, Kahn, & Ballard 1992). Therefore, integrating motion and color can increase the robustness of the recognition problem by bridging the gap between bottom-up and top-down processes, thus, improving the selective attention of dynamic perceptual systems such as the animat vision system that we are developing.

Where to Look Next

Redirecting gaze when a target of interest appears in the periphery can be a complex problem. One solution would be to section the peripheral image into smaller patches or focal probes (Burt *et al.* 1989) and search of all the probes. The strategy will work well for sufficiently small images, but for dynamic vision systems that must process natural or photorealistic images the approach is not effective.

We choose a simple method based on motion cues to help narrow down the search for a suitable gaze direction (Campani, Giachetti, & Torre 1995). We create a saliency image by initially computing a reduced optical flow field between two stabilized peripheral image frames (an advantage of the multiresolution retina is the small 64×64 peripheral image). Then an affine motion model is fitted to the optical flow using a robust regression method that will be described momentarily. The affine motion parameters are fitted to the dominant background motion. A saliency map is determined by computing an error measure between the affine motion parameters and the estimated optical flow as follows:

$$S(x,y) = \sqrt{[v_x(x,y) - u(x,y)]^2 + [v_y(x,y) - v(x,y)]^2}, \quad (1)$$

where (u, v) is the computed optical flow and

$$\begin{aligned} v_x(x,y) &= a + bx + cy, \\ v_y(x,y) &= d + ex + fy \end{aligned} \quad (2)$$

is the affine flow at retinal image position (x, y). The saliency image S is then convolved with a circular disk of area equal to the expected area of the model object of interest as it appears in the peripheral image.[2]

The blurring of the saliency image emphasizes the model object in the image. The maximum in S is taken as the location of the image probe. The image patches that serve as probes in consecutive peripheral frames form the image sequence that is processed by the motion segmentation module described later. Fig. 5 shows four consecutive peripheral images with the image probes outlined by white boxes. The blurred saliency image is shown at the end of the sequence in Fig. 5. Clearly the maximum (brightness) corresponds to the fast moving blue fish in the lower right portion of the peripheral image.

Robust Optical Flow

A key component of the selective attention algorithm is the use of optical flow. Given a sequence of time-varying images, points on the retina appear to move because of the relative motion between the eye and objects in the scene (Gibson 1979). The vector field of this apparent motion is usually called optical flow (Horn 1986). Optical flow can give important information about the spatial arrangement of objects viewed and the rate of change of this arrangement.

For our specific application, however, we require efficiency, robustness to outliers, and an optical flow estimate at all times. Recent work by Black and Anandan (Black & Anandan 1990; 1993) satisfies our requirements. They propose incremental minimization approaches using robust statistics for the estimation of optical flow which are geared towards dynamic environments. As is noted by Black, the goal is incrementally to integrate motion information from new images with previous optical flow estimates to obtain more accurate information about the motion in the scene over time. A detailed description of this method can be found in (Black 1992). Here we describe our adaptation of the algorithm to the animat vision system.

Ideally optical flow is computed continuously[3] as the animat navigates in its world, but to reduce computational cost and to allow for new scene features to appear when no interesting objects have attracted the attention of the animat, we choose to update the current estimate of the optical flow every four frames. The algorithm is however still "continuous" because it computes the current estimate of the optical flow at time t using image frames at t-3, t-2, t-1, and t in a short-time batch process. Fig. 6 shows this more

[2] Reasonably small areas suffice, since objects in the 64×64 peripheral image are typically small at peripheral resolution. Methods for estimating appropriate areas for the object, such as Jagersand's information theoretic approach (Jagersand 1995), may be applicable.

[3] By continuously, we mean that there is an estimate of the optical flow at every time instant.

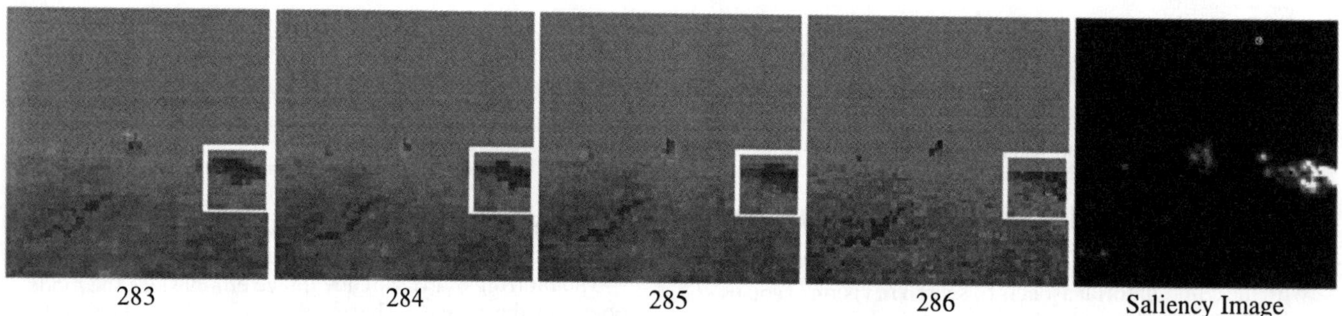

Figure 5: Four consecutive peripheral images with image probes outlined by white squares. Saliency image (right), with bright areas indicating large motions.

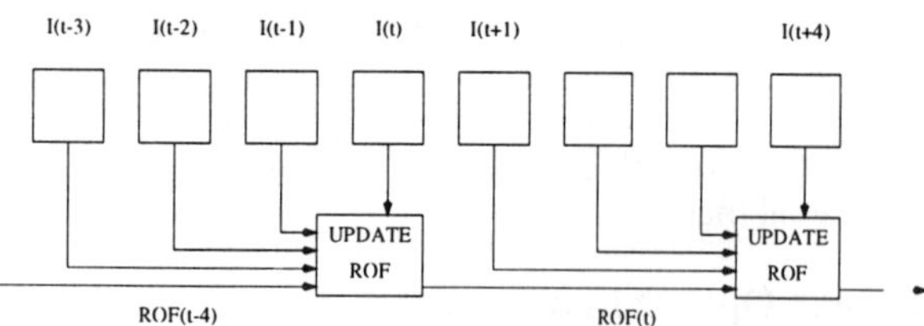

Figure 6: Incremental estimation of robust optical flow over time.

clearly. This arrangement requires storage of the previous three frames for use by the estimation module.

The flow at $t+1$ is initialized with a predicted flow computed by forward warp of the flow estimate at t by itself[4] and then the optical flow at $t+4$ is estimated by spatiotemporal regression over the four frames.

We compute our optical flow estimate by incrementally minimizing the cost function

$$E(u,v) = \lambda_D E_D(u,v) + \lambda_S E_S(u,v) + \lambda_T E_T(u,v), \quad (3)$$

where E_D is the data conservation constraint and is given in terms of the intensity constraint equation as

$$E_D = \rho_{\sigma_D}(uI_x + vI_y + I_t), \quad (4)$$

and E_S is the spatial coherence constraint and is given as

$$E_S = \sum_{m,n \in N} [\rho_{\sigma_S}(u - u(m,n)) + \rho_{\sigma_S}(v - v(m,n))], \quad (5)$$

where N is the 4-connected neighbors of the current pixel position. We formulate our temporal continuity constraint E_T by imposing some coherence between the current flow estimate and its previous and next estimate:

$$E_T = \rho_{\sigma_T}(\mathbf{u} - \mathbf{u}_{BW}) + \rho_{\sigma_T}(\mathbf{u} - \mathbf{u}_{FW}), \quad (6)$$

where $\mathbf{u} = (u,v)$ is the current optical flow estimate at time t, $\mathbf{u}_{BW}$ is the previous estimate at $t-1$ obtained by setting it to the most recent estimate, and $\mathbf{u}_{FW}$ is a prediction of what the optical flow will be at $t+1$ and is computed by forward warp of the current estimate by itself.[5] The λ parameters in (3) control the relative importance of the terms, and the ρ_σ functions in the above equations are taken to be the Lorentzian robust estimator:

$$\rho_\sigma(x) = log\left(1 + \frac{1}{2}\left(\frac{x}{\sigma}\right)^2\right), \quad (7)$$

and its influence function, $\psi_\sigma(x)$, is the first derivative with respect to x. This function characterizes the bias that a particular measurement has on the solution (Hampel 1974; Black & Anandan 1993).

This robust formulation of our cost function E causes it to be non-convex. A local minimum can, however, be obtained using a gradient-based optimization technique. We choose the successive over relaxation minimization technique. The iterative equations for minimizing E are

$$u^{i+1} = u^i - \frac{\mu}{T_u}\frac{\partial E}{\partial u}, \quad (8)$$

where $1 < \mu < 2$ is an overrelaxation parameter that controls convergence. A similar iterative equation for v is obtained by replacing u with v in (8). The terms T_u, T_v are upper bounds on the second partial derivatives of E, and can be given as

$$T_u = \frac{\lambda_D I_x^2}{\sigma_D^2} + \frac{4\lambda_S}{\sigma_S^2} + \frac{2\lambda_T}{\sigma_T^2}, \quad (9)$$

and similarly for T_v by replacing u with v and x with y. The partial derivative in (8) is

$$\frac{\partial E}{\partial u} = \lambda_D I_x \psi_{\sigma_D}(uI_x + vI_y + I_t) + \lambda_S \sum_{m,n \in N} \psi_{\sigma_S}(u - u(m,n)) + \lambda_T[\psi_{\sigma_T}(u - u_{BW}) + \psi_{\sigma_T}(u - u_{FW})], \quad (10)$$

and similarly for $\partial E/\partial v$.

The above minimization will generally converge to a local minimum. A global minimum may be found by constructing an initially convex approximation to the cost function

[4] The flow estimate is being used to warp itself, thus predicting what the motion will be in the future.

[5] Note that $\mathbf{u}_{BW}$ can also be estimated by backward warping of $\mathbf{u}$ by itself.

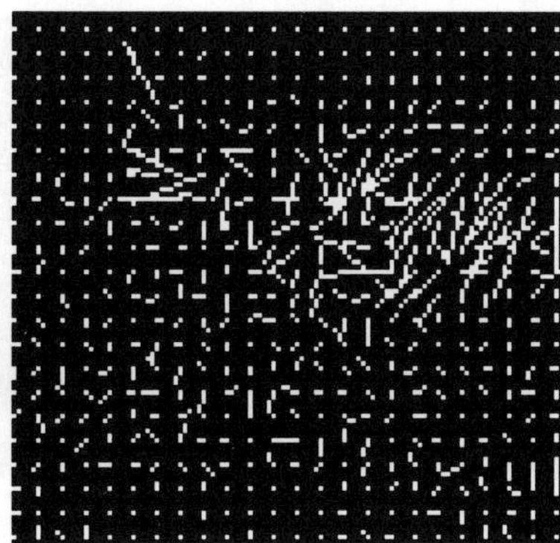

Figure 7: The robust optical flow vectors estimated for the four image probe sequence (Fig. 5). Large vectors indicate large motion of the fish object.

by choosing initial values of the σ parameters to be sufficiently large (equal to the maximum expected outlier in the argument of $\rho_i(\cdot)$), so that the Hessian matrix of E is positive definite at all points in the image. The minimum is then tracked using the graduated non-convexity (GNC) continuation method (Blake & Zisserman 1987) by decreasing the values of the σ parameters from one iteration to the next, which serves to gradually return the cost function to its non-convex shape, thereby introducing discontinuities in the data, spatial, and temporal terms. These discontinuities are, however, dealt with by the robust formulation and are rejected as outliers, thus producing more accurate optical flow estimates. The values of the λ parameters are determined empirically (typically $\lambda_D = 10, \lambda_S = \lambda_T = 1$).

To deal with large motions in the image sequence, we perform the minimization using a coarse-to-fine flow-through strategy. A Gaussian pyramid (Burt & Adelson 1983) is constructed for each image in the sequence, and minimization starts at the coarsest level and flows through to the finest resolution level. Our flow-through technique is based on the assumption that displacements which are less than 1 pixel are estimated accurately at each individual level and thus need not be updated from a coarser level's estimate, while estimates that are greater than 1 pixel are most probably more accurately computed at the coarser level, and are updated by projecting the estimate from the coarser level.

This incremental minimization approach foregoes a large number of relaxation iterations over a 2 frame sequence in favor of a small number of relaxation iterations over a longer sequence. Fig. 7 shows the optical flow estimated for the sequence of four image probes of Fig. 5. The figure clearly shows the complex motion of the target fish. It is a non-trivial task to segment such motions.

Motion Segmentation and Color Recognition

For the animat to recognize objects moving in its periphery it must first detect their presence by means of a saliency map as described earlier. Once it detects something that might be worth looking at, it must then segment its region of support out from the whole peripheral image and then match this segmentation with mental models of important

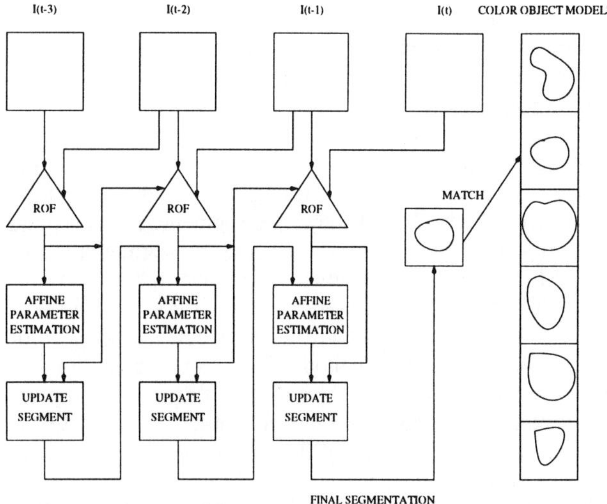

Figure 8: Incremental motion segmentation and object recognition using multi-resolution robust optical flow (ROF) estimation, affine parametric motion segmentation and color object recognition.

objects. Fig. 8 shows the steps involved in an incremental segmentation of the detected object over the duration of the four probe images as explained above.

Segmentation of the optical flow at each time instant is performed by fitting an affine parametric motion model to the robust optical flow (ROF) estimated so far at the current time instant. This is done by incrementally minimizing the cost function given as

$$E(a,b,c,d,e,f) = E_x(a,b,c) + E_y(d,e,f), \quad (11)$$

where (a,b,c,d,e,f) are the affine motion parameters. E_x and E_y are formulated using robust estimation to account for outliers

$$\begin{aligned} E_x &= \sum_{x,y \in R} \rho_\sigma(v_x(x,y) - u(x,y)), \\ E_y &= \sum_{x,y \in R} \rho_\sigma(v_y(x,y) - v(x,y)), \end{aligned} \quad (12)$$

where R is the current region of support of the segmented object (initially equal to the full frame image size). v_x and v_y are horizontal and vertical affine motion flow vectors according to (2). (u,v) is the ROF estimated at the current instant, and $\rho_\sigma(x)$ is taken to be the Lorentzian robust estimator. We use successive over relaxation and GNC to minimize this cost function by using a small number of iterations over a sequence of four image probes and updating the segmentation at every time instant.

The estimated affine motion parameters at the current time instant are then used to update the segmentation by calculating an error norm between the affine flow estimate (v_x, v_y) and the ROF estimate as in (1). This norm is then thresholded by an appropriate threshold taken to be the minimum outlier in the affine fit. The updated segmentation serves as the region of support R for the next frame's affine minimization step.

If more than one moving object is present in the probe sequence, the current segmentation is subtracted from the image, and another affine motion model is fitted to the remaining pixels thus segmenting other moving objects. To clean up the segmentation (in case some pixels where misclassified as outliers) a 9×9 median filter is passed over the segmentation mask to fill in missing pixels and remove misclassified outliers. Fig. 9 shows the segmented background (showing two objects as outliers) and the segmentation of the outlier pixels into the object of interest (a blue fish).

At the end of the motion segmentation stage, the segmented objects are matched to color models using the color histogram intersection method. If a match occurs, the current estimate of the ROF is set to zero thus accounting for the dynamic changes in the system, otherwise the ROF is used to initialize the optical flow at the next time step as shown in Fig. 6.

If the model object matches the peripheral segmented region, the animat localizes the recognized object using color histogram backprojection and foveates it to obtain a high-resolution view. It then engages in appropriate behavioral responses.

Behavioral Response to a Recognized Target

The behavioral center of the brain of the artificial animal assumes control after an object is recognized and fixated. If the object is classified as food the behavioral response would be to pursue the target in the fovea with maximum speed until the animat is close enough to open its mouth and eat the food. If the object is classified as a predator and the animat is a prey fish, then the behavioral response would be to turn in a direction opposite to that of the predator and swim with maximum speed. Alternatively, an object in the scene may serve as a visual frame of reference. When the animat recognizes a reference object (which may be another fish) in its visual periphery, it will fixate on it and track it in smooth pursuit at an intermediate speed. Thus, the fixation point acts as the origin of an object-centered reference frame allowing the animat to stabilize its visual world and explore its surroundings.

Fig. 10 shows a sequence of retinal images taken from the animat's left eye. The eyes are initially fixated on a red reference fish and thus the images are stabilized. In frame 283 to 286 a blue fish swims close by the animat's right side. The animat recognizes this as a reference fish and thus saccades the eyes to foveate the fish. It tracks the fish around, thereby exploring its environment. By foveating different reference objects, the animat can explore different parts of its world.

Fig. 11 shows a plot of the (θ_L, θ_R) gaze angles and turn angle between frames 200 and 400. It is clear from the figure that the animat was first fixated on the red fish which was to the left of the animat (negative gaze angles), and at frame 286 and subsequent frames the animat is foveated on the blue fish which is to its right (positive gaze angles).

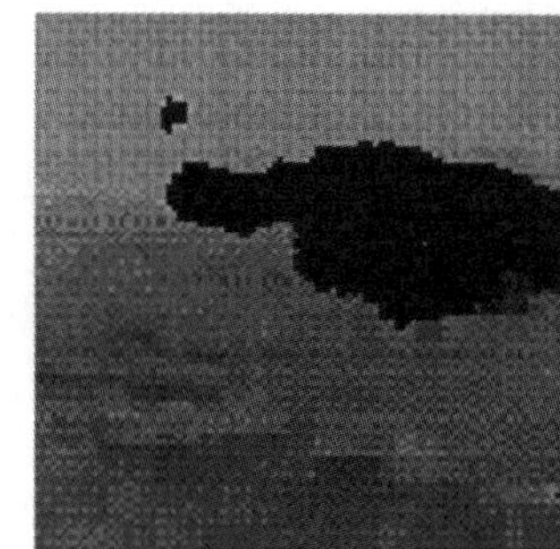

Segmented Background

Segmented Object

Figure 9: Results of incremental motion segmentation module.

Conclusion and Future Work

We have presented computer vision research carried out within an animat vision framework which employs a physics-based, virtual marine world inhabited by lifelike artificial fishes that emulate the appearance, motion, and behavior of real fishes in their natural habitats. We have successfully implemented a set of active vision algorithms for artificial fishes that integrate motion and color analysis to improve focus of attention and enable the animat to better understand and interact with its dynamic virtual environment.

In future work we will endeavor to increase the arsenal of active vision algorithms to support the whole behavioral repertoire of artificial fishes. The animat approach allows us to do this step by step without compromising the complete functionality of the artificial fish. It is our hope that the vision system that we are developing will also provide insights relevant to the design of active vision systems for physical robotics.

Acknowledgements

We thank Xiaoyuan Tu for developing and implementing the artificial fish model, which made this research possible. The research described herein was supported by grants from the Natural Sciences and Engineering Research Council of Canada.

References

Adler, H. E. 1975. *Fish Behavior: Why Fishes do What They Do.* Neptune City, NJ: T.F.H Publications.

Bajcsy, R. 1988. Active perception. *Proceedings of the IEEE* 76(8):996–1005.

Ballard, D. 1991. Animate vision. *Artificial Intelligence* 48:57–86.

Black, M., and Anandan, P. 1990. A model for the detection of motion over time. In *Proc. Inter. Conf. Computer Vision (ICCV'90)*, 33–37.

Black, M., and Anandan, P. 1993. A framework for the robust estimation of optical flow. In *Proc. Inter. Conf. Computer Vision (ICCV'93)*, 231–236.

Black, M. 1992. Robust incremental optical flow. Technical Report YALEU/DCS/RR-923, Yale University, Dept. of Computer Science.

Blake, A., and Zisserman, A., eds. 1987. *Visual Reconstruction.* Cambridge, Massachusetts: The MIT Press.

Burt, P., and Adelson, E. 1983. The laplacian pyramid as a compact image code. *IEEE Trans. on Communications* 31(4):532–540.

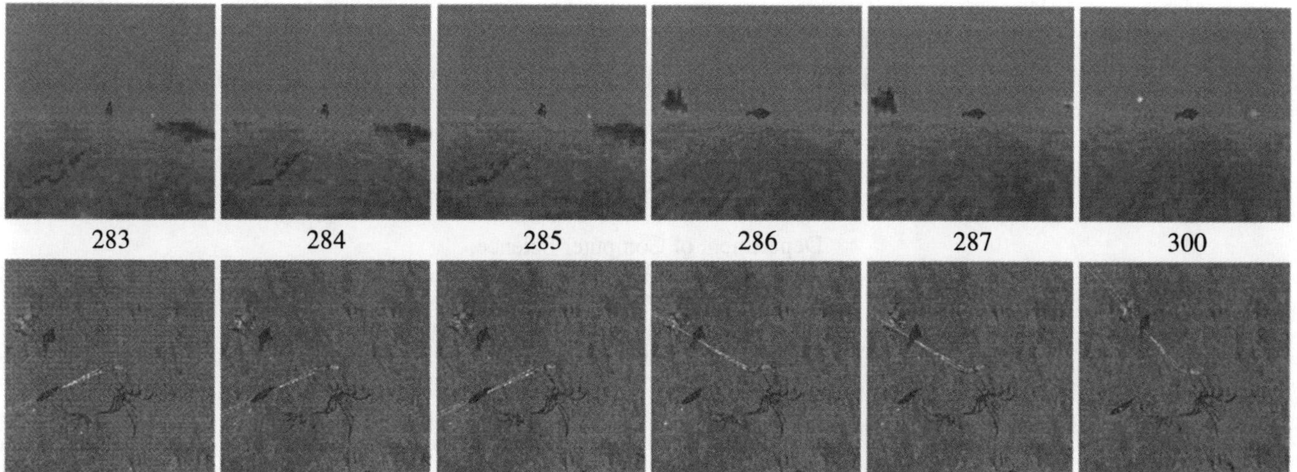

Figure 10: Retinal image sequence from the left eye of the predator (top) and overhead view (bottom) of the predator as it pursues a red reference fish (frames 283–285). A blue reference fish appears in the predator's right periphery and is recognized, fixated, and tracked (frames 286–300). The white lines indicate the gaze direction.

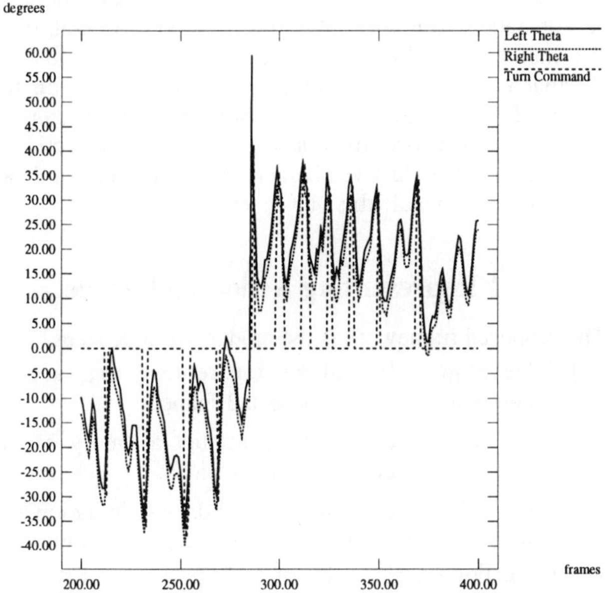

Figure 11: Gaze angles as the animat changes reference points at frame 286 from left (negative angles) to right (positive angles).

Burt, P.; Bergen, J.; Hingorani, R.; Kolczynski, R.; Lee, W.; Leung, A.; Lubin, J.; and Shvaytser, H. 1989. Object tracking with a moving camera: An application of dynamic motion analysis. *Proc. IEEE Workshop Visual Motion* 2 - 12.

Campani, M.; Giachetti, A.; and Torre, V. 1995. Optic flow and autonomous navigation. *Perception* 24:253–267.

Cedras, C., and Shah, M. 1995. Motion-based recognition: A survey. *Image and Vision Computing* 13(2):129–155.

Dubuisson, M., and Jain, A. 1993. Object contour extraction using color and motion. In *Proc. Computer Vision and Pattern Recognition Conf. (CVPR'93)*, 471–476.

Gibson, J. J. 1979. *The Ecological Approach to Visual Perception.* Boston, MA: Houghton Mifflin.

Gong, Y., and Sakauchi, M. 1992. An object-oriented method for color video image classification using the color and motion features of video images. In *2nd. Inter. Conf. on Automation, Robotics and Computer Vision.*

Hampel, F. 1974. The influence curve and its role in robust estimation. *J. Amer. Statistical Association* 69(346):383–393.

Horn, B. K. P. 1986. *Robot Vision.* Cambridge, MA: MIT Press.

Jagersand, M. 1995. Saliency maps and attention selection in scale and spatial coordinates: An information theoretic approach. In *Proc. Inter. Conf. Computer Vision (ICCV'95)*, 195–202.

Maver, J., and Bajcsy, R. 1990. How to decide from from the first view where to look next. In *Proc. DARPA Image Understanding Workshop.*

Rimey, R., and Brown, C. 1992. Where to look next using a bayes net: Incorporating geometric relations. In *Proc. Euro. Conf. Computer Vision (ECCV'92)*, 542–550.

Swain, M., and Ballard, D. 1991. Color indexing. *Inter. J. Computer Vision* 7:11 - 32.

Swain, M., and Stricker, M. 1993. Promising directions in active vision. *Inter. J. Computer Vision* 11(2):109 - 126.

Swain, M.; Kahn, R.; and Ballard, D. 1992. Low resolution cues for guiding saccadic eye movements. In *Proc. Inter. Conf. Computer Vision (ICCV'92)*, 737–740.

Terzopoulos, D., and Rabie, T. 1995. Animat vision: Active vision in artificial animals. In *Proc. Fifth Inter. Conf. Computer Vision (ICCV'95)*, 801 - 808.

Terzopoulos, D.; Tu, X.; and Grzeszczuk, R. 1994. Artificial fishes: Autonomous locomotion, perception, behavior, and learning in a simulated physical world. *Artificial Life* 1(4):327–351.

Terzopoulos, D. 1995. Modeling living systems for computer vision. In *Proc. Int. Joint Conf. Artificial Intelligence (IJCAI'95)*, 1003–1013.

Tsotsos, J.; Culhane, S.; Wai, W.; Lai, Y.; Davis, N.; and Nuflo, F. 1995. Modeling visual attention via selective tuning. *Artificial Intelligence* 78:507–545.

Noise and the Common Sense Informatic Situation for a Mobile Robot

Murray Shanahan

Department of Computer Science,
Queen Mary and Westfield College,
Mile End Road,
London E1 4NS,
England.
mps@dcs.qmw.ac.uk

Abstract

Any model of the world a robot constructs on the basis of its sensor data is necessarily both incomplete, due to the robot's limited window on the world, and uncertain, due to sensor and motor noise. This paper supplies a logical account of sensor data assimilation in which such models are constructed through an abductive process which hypothesises the existence, locations, and shapes of objects. Noise is treated as a kind of non-determinism, and is dealt with by a consistency-based form of abduction.

Introduction

The aim of Cognitive Robotics is to design and build mobile robots based on the idea of logical representation [Lespérance, *et al.*, 1994]. By reinstating the ideals of the Shakey project [Nilsson, 1984], Cognitive Robotics has reinvigorated a research programme that has been largely dormant for the past twenty years.

This has been made possible by recent advances in the field of common sense reasoning: formalisms now exist for reasoning about action which incorporate robust solutions to the frame problem, and which can represent a wide variety of phenomena, including concurrent action, non-deterministic action, and continuous change.

The Cognitive Robotics approach is in marked contrast to that of Brooks and his followers. According to Brooks, work in the style of Shakey is flawed because,

> it [relies] on the assumption that a complete world model [can] be built internally and then manipulated.
>
> [Brooks, 1991a]

A complete model of the world is hard for a robot to construct because, as Brooks points out,

> the data delivered by sensors are not direct descriptions of the world as objects and their relationships [and] commands to actuators have very uncertain effects.
>
> [Brooks, 1991b]

This sort of incompleteness and uncertainty is a feature of what McCarthy [1989] calls the *common sense informatic situation*, and is dealt with extremely well by predicate logic. This paper supplies a logical account of the common sense informatic situation for a small mobile robot with very poor sensors, and thereby defends the Cognitive Robotics approach from arguments along the lines of the one advanced above.

The paper is organised as follows. Section 1 presents a generic formalism for reasoning about action and space. Section 2 applies this formalism to the mobile robot under consideration, and presents an abductive characterisation of sensor data assimilation. A more detailed presentation of the material in these two sections is to be found in [Shanahan, 1996b]. The next two sections focus on the issue of noise. Section 3 shows how noise can be considered as a form of non-determinism, and Section 4 shows how the abductive characterisation of Section 2 can be modified to handle this non-determinism.

1 Representing Action and Space

The proposed framework is the product of three steps.

1. Develop a formalism for representing action, continuous change, space and shape.
2. Using this formalism, construct a theory of the robot's interaction with the world.
3. Consider the process of sensor data assimilation as a form of abduction, following [Shanahan, 1989].

This section concerns the first of these steps. For more details, see [Shanahan, 1996b]. To begin with, we have a formalism for reasoning about action and continuous change, based on the circumscriptive event calculus of [Shanahan, 1995b]. A many sorted language is assumed, with variables for *fluents*, *actions* (events), and *time points*. We have the following axioms, whose conjunction will be denoted CEC. Their main purpose is to constrain the predicate HoldsAt. HoldsAt(f,t) represents that fluent f holds at time t.

$$\text{HoldsAt}(f,t) \leftarrow \text{Initially}(f) \wedge \neg\,\text{Clipped}(0,f,t) \quad \text{(EC1)}$$

$$\text{HoldsAt}(f,t2) \leftarrow \text{Happens}(a,t1) \wedge \text{Initiates}(a,f,t1) \wedge t1 < t2 \wedge \neg\,\text{Clipped}(t1,f,t2) \quad \text{(EC2)}$$

$\neg$ HoldsAt(f,t2) $\leftarrow$ (EC3)
Happens(a,t1) $\wedge$ Terminates(a,f,t1) $\wedge$ t1 < t2 $\wedge$
$\neg$ Declipped(t1,f,t2)

Clipped(t1,f,t2) $\leftrightarrow$ (EC4)
$\exists$ a,t [Happens(a,t) $\wedge$
[Terminates(a,f,t) $\vee$ Releases(a,f,t)] $\wedge$
t1 < t $\wedge$ t < t2]

Declipped(t1,f,t2) $\leftrightarrow$ (EC5)
$\exists$ a,t [Happens(a,t) $\wedge$
[Initiates(a,f,t) $\vee$ Releases(a,f,t)] $\wedge$
t1 < t $\wedge$ t < t2]

HoldsAt(f2,t2) $\leftarrow$ (EC6)
Happens(a,t1) $\wedge$ Initiates(a,f1,t1) $\wedge$ t1 < t2 $\wedge$
t2 = t1 + d $\wedge$ Trajectory(f1,t1,f2,d) $\wedge$
$\neg$ Clipped(t1,f1,t2)

A particular domain is described in terms of Initiates, Terminates, Releases, and Trajectory formulae. Initiates(a,f,t) represents that fluent f starts to hold after action a at time t. Conversely, Terminates(a,f,t) represents that f starts to not hold after action a at t. Releases(a,f,t) represents that fluent f is no longer subject to default persistence after action a at t. The Trajectory predicate is used to capture continuous change. Trajectory(f1,t,f2,d) represents that f2 holds at time t+d if f1 starts to hold at time t.

A particular narrative of events is represented in terms of Happens and Initially formulae. The formula Initially(f) represents that fluent f holds at time 0. Happens(a,t) represents that action a occurs at time t.

In rough terms, if E is a domain description and N is a narrative description, then the frame problem is overcome by considering,

CIRC[N ; Happens] $\wedge$
CIRC[E ; Initiates, Terminates, Releases] $\wedge$ CEC.

However, care must be taken when domain constraints and triggered events are included. The former must be conjoined to CEC, while the latter are conjoined to N. A detailed account of this solution is to be found in [Shanahan, 1996a, Chapter 16].

To construct a theory of the robot's interaction with the world, a means of representing space and shape is required. Space is assumed to be $\mathbb{R}^2$. Objects occupy *regions*, which are open, path-connected subsets of $\mathbb{R}^2$. The following axioms will be required, defining the functions Disc, Distance, Bearing, and Line. The intended meaning of these functions should be obvious.

$p \in \text{Disc}(z) \leftrightarrow \text{Distance}(p,\langle 0,0\rangle) < z$ (Sp1)

$\text{Distance}(\langle x1,y1\rangle,\langle x2,y2\rangle) = \sqrt{(x1-x2)^2 + (y1-y2)^2}$ (Sp2)

Bearing(⟨x1,y1⟩,⟨x2,y2⟩) = r $\leftarrow$ (Sp3)
z = Distance(⟨x1,y1⟩,⟨x2,y2⟩) $\wedge$ z $\neq$ 0 $\wedge$
$\text{Sin}(r) = \frac{x2-x1}{z} \wedge \text{Cos}(r) = \frac{y2-y1}{z}$

p $\in$ Line(p1,p2) $\leftrightarrow$ (Sp4)
Bearing(p1,p) = Bearing(p1,p2) $\wedge$
Distance(p1,p) $\leq$ Distance(p1,p2)

Spatial occupancy is represented by the fluent Occupies. The term Occupies(w,g) represents that region g is the smallest region which covers all the space occupied by object w. Objects cannot overlap, and can only occupy one region at a time.

[HoldsAt(Occupies(w,g1),t) $\wedge$ (Sp5)
HoldsAt(Occupies(w,g2),t)] $\rightarrow$ g1 = g2

HoldsAt(Occupies(w1,g1),t) $\wedge$ (Sp6)
HoldsAt(Occupies(w2,g2),t) $\wedge$ w1 $\neq$ w2 $\rightarrow$
$\neg \exists$ p [p $\in$ g1 $\wedge$ p $\in$ g2]

The Displace function will be used to capture the robot's continuous motion through space. Displace(g,⟨x,y⟩) denotes the region obtained by displacing g by x units east and y units north.

⟨x1,y1⟩ $\in$ Displace(g,⟨x2,y2⟩) $\leftrightarrow$ (Sp7)
⟨x1–x2,y1–y2⟩ $\in$ g

For reasons set out in [Shanahan, 1995a], a means of default reasoning about spatial occupancy is required. This is done by minimising the predicate AbSpace in the presence of the following axiom.

AbSpace(w) $\leftarrow$ Initially(Occupies(w,g)) (Sp8)

Let O denote the conjunction of (Sp1) to (Sp8). As we'll see in the next section, O is included in a separate circumscription describing the initial situation, in which AbSpace is minimised. In the present context, this is a description of the initial locations and shapes of objects, in other words a map.

2 The Robot's Relationship to the World

Shortly, the abductive process whereby maps are constructed out of the robot's sensor data will be defined. First, a theory has to be constructed which captures the robot's relationship to the world: the effects of its actions on the world, and the effect of the world on its sensors. This theory is constructed using the formalism of the previous section.

The robot under consideration is based on the Rug Warrior described by Jones and Flynn [1993]. This is a circular robot with two drive wheels. The three actions it can perform are to rotate by a given number of degrees, to start moving forwards, and to stop. It has two forward bump switches, which can detect collisions.

First we have a pair of uniqueness-of-names axioms for the three fluents Occupies, Facing and Moving, and for the robot-performed actions Rotate, Go and Stop, and the triggered events Bump, Switch1 and Switch2.

UNA[Occupies, Facing, Moving, (B1)
Blocked, Touching]

UNA[Rotate, Go, Stop, Bump, Switch1, Switch2] (B2)

Next we have a Trajectory formula which describes the continuous variation in the Occupies fluent as the robot moves through space, and a collection of domain constraints. The robot moves one unit of distance in one unit of time. Blocked(w1,w2,r) means that object w1 cannot move in direction r because it is obstructed by object w2. Touching(w1,w2,p) means that objects w1 and w2 are touching at point p.

$$\begin{array}{l}\text{Trajectory(Moving,t,Occupies(Robot,g2),d)} \leftarrow \\ \quad \text{HoldsAt(Occupies(Robot,g1),t)} \wedge \\ \quad\quad \text{HoldsAt(Facing(r),t)} \wedge \\ \quad\quad\quad \text{g2} = \text{Displace(g1,}\langle\text{d.Sin(r),d.Cos(r)}\rangle) \end{array} \quad \text{(B3)}$$

$$\begin{array}{l}\text{HoldsAt(Facing(r1),t)} \wedge \\ \quad \text{HoldsAt(Facing(r2),t)} \rightarrow \text{r1=r2} \end{array} \quad \text{(B4)}$$

$$\begin{array}{l}\text{HoldsAt(Blocked(w1,w2,r),t)} \leftrightarrow \\ \quad \exists\ \text{g1,g2 [HoldsAt(Occupies(w1,g1),t)} \wedge \\ \quad\quad \text{HoldsAt(Occupies(w2,g2),t)} \wedge \\ \quad\quad\quad \text{w1} \neq \text{w2} \wedge \exists\ \text{z1 [z1} > 0 \wedge \forall\ \text{z2 [z2} \leq \text{z1} \rightarrow \\ \quad\quad\quad\quad \exists\ \text{p [p} \in \text{g2} \wedge \\ \quad\quad\quad\quad\quad \text{p} \in \text{Displace(g1,}\langle\text{z2.Sin(r),z2.Cos(r)}\rangle)]]]] \end{array} \quad \text{(B5)}$$

$$\begin{array}{l}\text{HoldsAt(Touching(w1,w2,p),t)} \leftrightarrow \\ \quad \text{HoldsAt(Occupies(w1,g1),t)} \wedge \\ \quad\quad \text{HoldsAt(Occupies(w2,g2),t)} \wedge \text{w1} \neq \text{w2} \wedge \\ \quad\quad\quad \exists\ \text{p1, p2 [p} \in \text{Line(p1,p2)} \wedge \text{p} \neq \text{p1} \wedge \text{p} \neq \text{p2} \wedge \\ \quad\quad\quad\quad \forall\ \text{p3 [[p3} \in \text{Line(p1,p)} \wedge \text{p3} \neq \text{p]} \rightarrow \\ \quad\quad\quad\quad\quad \text{p3} \in \text{g1]} \wedge \\ \quad\quad\quad\quad\quad\quad \forall\ \text{p3 [[p3} \in \text{Line(p,p2)} \wedge \text{p3} \neq \text{p]} \rightarrow \\ \quad\quad\quad\quad\quad\quad\quad \text{p3} \in \text{g2]]} \end{array} \quad \text{(B6)}$$

Let B denote the conjunction of CEC with Axioms (B1) to (B6). Next we have a collection of Initiates, Terminates and Releases formulae.

$$\begin{array}{l}\text{Initiates(Rotate(r1),Facing(r1+r2),t)} \leftarrow \\ \quad \text{HoldsAt(Facing(r2),t)} \end{array} \quad \text{(E1)}$$

$$\begin{array}{l}\text{Releases(Rotate(r1),Facing(r2),t)} \leftarrow \\ \quad \text{HoldsAt(Facing(r2),t)} \wedge \text{r1} \neq 0 \end{array} \quad \text{(E2)}$$

$$\text{Initiates(Go,Moving,t)} \quad \text{(E3)}$$

$$\text{Releases(Go,Occupies(Robot,g),t)} \quad \text{(E4)}$$

$$\begin{array}{l}\text{Terminates(a,Moving,t)} \leftarrow \\ \quad \text{a = Stop} \vee \text{a = Bump} \vee \text{a = Rotate(r)} \end{array} \quad \text{(E5)}$$

$$\begin{array}{l}\text{Initiates(a,Occupies(Robot,g),t)} \leftarrow \\ \quad \text{[a = Stop} \vee \text{a = Bump]} \wedge \\ \quad\quad \text{HoldsAt(Occupies(Robot,g),t)} \end{array} \quad \text{(E6)}$$

Let E denote the conjunction of Axioms (E1) to (E6). The final component of the theory describes the conditions under which Bump, Switch1 and Switch2 events are triggered.

$$\begin{array}{l}\text{Happens(Bump,t)} \leftarrow \\ \quad \text{[HoldsAt(Moving,t)} \vee \text{Happens(Go,t)]} \wedge \\ \quad\quad \text{HoldsAt(Facing(r),t)} \wedge \\ \quad\quad\quad \text{HoldsAt(Blocked(Robot,w,r),t)} \end{array} \quad \text{(H1)}$$

$$\begin{array}{l}\text{Happens(Switch1,t)} \leftarrow \\ \quad \text{Happens(Bump,t)} \wedge \text{HoldsAt(Facing(r),t)} \wedge \\ \quad\quad \text{HoldsAt(Occupies(Robot,Displace(Disc(z),p1)),t)} \wedge \\ \quad\quad\quad \text{HoldsAt(Touching(Robot,w,p2),t)} \wedge \\ \quad\quad\quad\quad \text{r}-90 \leq \text{Bearing(p1,p2)} < \text{r}+12 \end{array} \quad \text{(H2)}$$

$$\begin{array}{l}\text{Happens(Switch2,t)} \leftarrow \\ \quad \text{Happens(Bump,t)} \wedge \text{HoldsAt(Facing(r),t)} \wedge \\ \quad\quad \text{HoldsAt(Occupies(Robot,Displace(Disc(z),p1)),t)} \wedge \\ \quad\quad\quad \text{HoldsAt(Touching(Robot,w,p2),t)} \wedge \\ \quad\quad\quad\quad \text{r}-12 \leq \text{Bearing(p1,p2)} < \text{r}+90 \end{array} \quad \text{(H3)}$$

We're now in a position to supply an abductive characterisation of the task of sensor data assimilation, where the robot's sensor data is a stream of Switch1 and Switch2 events. First we have a definition which permits the exclusion of certain anomalous explanations, by ensuring that *only* the sensor data the robot actually receives is abductively explained.

Definition 2.1.

$$\begin{array}{l}\text{COMP}[\Psi] \equiv_{def} \\ \quad \text{[Happens(a,t)} \wedge \text{[a = Switch1} \vee \text{a = Switch2]]} \rightarrow \\ \quad\quad \bigvee_{\langle\alpha,\tau\rangle \in \Gamma} [\text{a} = \alpha \wedge \text{t} = \tau] \end{array}$$

where $\Gamma = \{\langle\alpha,\tau\rangle \mid \text{Happens}(\alpha,\tau) \in \Psi\}$. □

Sensor data assimilation is the task of finding explanations of the sensor data in terms of hypothesised objects. Given an Initially formula M1 describing the initial location of the robot, a collection N2 of Happens formulae describing the robot's actions, and a collection Ψ of Happens formulae describing the sensor data received by the robot, we're interested in finding conjunctions M2 of formulae in which each conjunct has the form,

$$\exists\ \text{g [Initially(Occupies(}\omega\text{,g))} \wedge \forall\ \text{p [p} \in \text{g} \leftrightarrow \Pi]]$$

where ω is an object constant and Π is any formula in which p is free, such that O $\wedge$ M1 $\wedge$ M2 is consistent and,

$$\begin{array}{l}\text{CIRC[O} \wedge \text{M1} \wedge \text{M2 ; AbSpace ; Initially]} \wedge \\ \quad \text{CIRC[N1} \wedge \text{N2 ; Happens]} \wedge \\ \quad\quad \text{CIRC[E ; Initiates, Terminates, Releases]} \wedge \text{B} \vDash \\ \quad\quad\quad \Psi \wedge \text{COMP}[\Psi]. \end{array}$$

This definition is very liberal, and the full paper utilises a *boundary-based* representation of shape to render the space of possible explanations more manageable (see [Davis, 1990, Chapter 6]).

3 Noise as Non-Determinism

The hallmark of the common sense informatic situation for a mobile robot is incomplete and uncertain knowledge of a world of spatio-temporally located objects. Incompleteness is a consequence of the robot's limited window on the world, and uncertainty results from noise in its sensors and actuators. This section deals with noise.

Both noisy sensors and noisy actuators can be captured using non-determinism. (An alternative is to use probability [Bacchus, *et al.*, 1995]). Here we'll only look at the uncertainty in the robot's location that results from its noisy motors. The robot's motors are "noisy" for various reasons. For example, the two wheels might rotate at slightly different speeds when the robot is trying to travel in a straight line, or the robot might be moving on a slope or a slippery surface.

Motor noise of this kind can be captured using a non-deterministic Trajectory formula, such as the following replacement for Axiom (B3).[1] Note that, while objects

[1] The Rotate action could also have been made non-deterministic.

occupy open subsets of $\mathbb{R}^2$, regions of uncertainty are closed.

$$\exists\, p\ [\text{Trajectory(Moving,t,}\ \text{Occupies(Robot,Displace(g,p)),d)} \wedge \text{Distance(p,}\langle \text{d.Sin(r),d.Cos(r)}\rangle) \leq \text{d.}\varepsilon] \leftarrow \text{HoldsAt(Occupies(Robot,g),t)} \wedge \text{HoldsAt(Facing(r),t)} \quad \text{(B7)}$$

In effect, Axiom (B7) constrains the robot's location to be within an ever-expanding *circle of uncertainty* centred on the location it would be in if its motors weren't noisy. The constant ε determines the rate at which this circle grows. Axiom (B8) below ensures that there are no discontinuities in the robot's trajectory. Without this axiom the robot would be able to leap over any obstacle which didn't completely cover the circle of uncertainty for its location. The term Abs(d) denotes the absolute value of d.

$$\text{Trajectory(f,t,Occupies(x,Displace(g,p1)),d1)} \rightarrow \forall\, z\ [z > 0 \rightarrow \exists\, d\ \forall\, d2,p2\ [[d2 > 0 \wedge \text{Abs(d2–d1)} < d \wedge \text{Trajectory(f,t,Occupies(x,Displace(g,p2)),d2)}] \rightarrow \text{Distance(p1,p2)} < z]] \quad \text{(B8)}$$

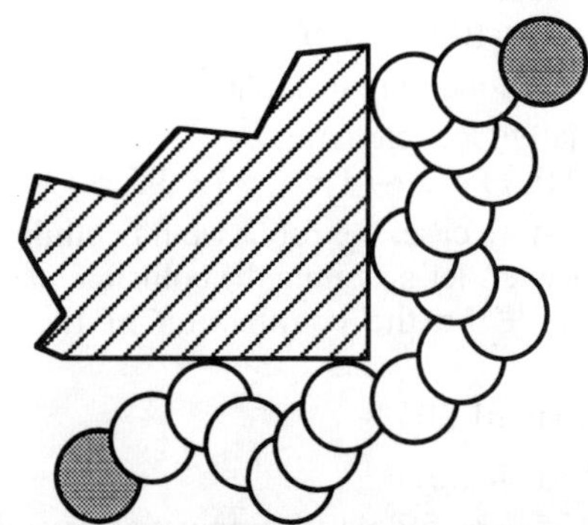

Figure 1: The Robot Explores a Corner

Figure 1 shows the robot exploring the corner of an obstacle. Figure 2 shows the evolution of the corresponding circle of uncertainty, highlighting the points where the robot changes direction.

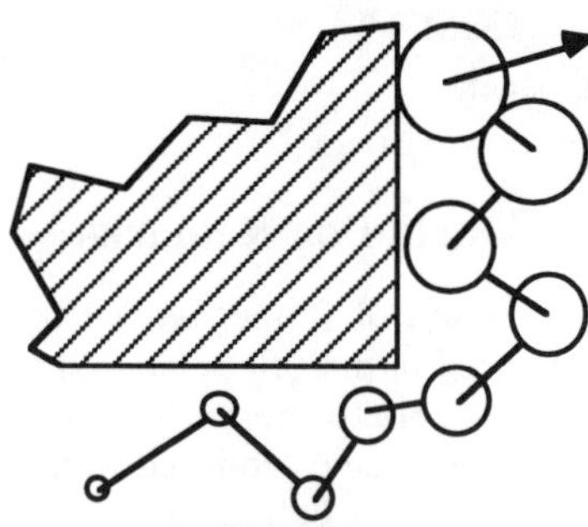

Figure 2:
The Evolution of the Circle of Uncertainty

Figure 2 is somewhat misleading, however. Consider Figure 3. On the left, the evolution of the circle of uncertainty for the robot's location is shown. In the middle, three potential locations are shown for the three changes of direction.

Although these locations all fall within the relevant circles of uncertainty, the robot could never get to the third location from the second. This is because, as depicted on the right of the figure, in any given model the circle of uncertainty for the robot's location at the end of a period of continuous motion can only be defined relative to its actual location at the start of that period. This can be verified by inspecting Axioms (B7) and (B8).

The relative nature of the evolution of the circle of uncertainty means that the robot can acquire a detailed knowledge of some area A1 of its environment, then move to another area A2 which is some distance from A1, and acquire an equally detailed knowledge of A2. The accumulated uncertainty entails only that the robot is uncertain of where A1 is relative to A2. This natural feature of the formalisation conforms with what we would intuitively expect given the robot's informatic situation.

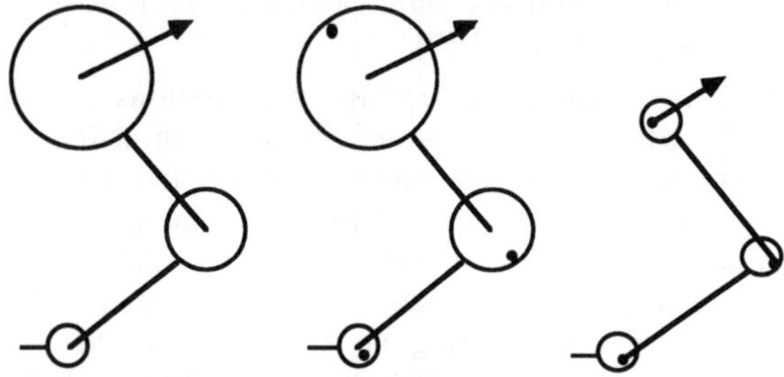

Figure 3: The Circle of Uncertainty Is Relative Not Absolute

In the presence of non-determinism, the abductive account of sensor data assimilation presented in Section 2 will not work. The next section presents a modified characterisation which overcomes the problem.

4 Non-Determinism and Abduction

Non-determinism is a potential source of difficulty for the abductive approach to explanation. Even with a precise and complete description of the initial state of the world, including all its objects and their shapes, a non-deterministic theory incorporating a formula like (B7) will not yield the exact times at which collision events occur. Yet the sensor data to be assimilated has precise times attached to it.

Fortunately we can recast the task of assimilating sensor data as a form of *weak abduction* so that it yields the required results. Intuitively what we want to capture is the fact that without the hypothesised objects, the sensor data could not have been received. This is analogous to the consistency-based approach to diagnosis proposed by Reiter [1987].

Definition 4.1. Given,

- the conjunction B of CEC with Axioms (B1), (B2), and (B4) to (B8),
- the conjunction E of Axioms (E1) to (E6),
- the conjunction O of Axioms (Sp1) to (Sp8),

- a conjunction M1 of Initially formulae describing the initial locations, shapes, and orientations of known objects, including the robot itself,
- the conjunction N1 of Axioms (H1) to (H3),
- a conjunction N2 of Happens formulae describing the robot's actions, and
- a conjunction Ψ of formulae of the form Happens(Switch1,τ) or Happens(Switch2,τ),

an *explanation* of Ψ is a conjunction M2 of formulae in which each conjunct has the form,

$\exists$ g [Initially(Occupies(ω,g)) ∧ ∀ p [p ∈ g ↔ Π]]

where ω is an object constant and Π is any formula in which p is free, such that O ∧ M1 ∧ M2 is consistent, and,

CIRC[O ∧ M1 ∧ M2 ; AbSpace ; Initially] ∧
CIRC[N1 ∧ N2 ; Happens] ∧
CIRC[E ; Initiates, Terminates, Releases] ∧ B ⊭
¬ [Ψ ∧ COMP[Ψ]]. □

There will, naturally, be many explanations for any given Ψ which meet this definition, even using the boundary-based representation of shape adopted in the full version of the paper. A standard way to treat multiple explanations in abductive knowledge assimilation is to adopt their disjunction [Shanahan, 1996a, Chapter 17]. This has the effect of smothering any explanations which are stronger than necessary, such as those which postulate superfluous obstacles. The disjunction of all explanations of Ψ is the *cautious explanation* of Ψ.

A variety of *preference relations* over explanations can also be introduced. For example, it might be reasonable to assume that nearby collision points indicate the presence of a single object. Such preference relations are a topic for further study.

The following theorem establishes that the above definition of an explanation is equivalent to the deterministic specification offered in Section 2 when ε is 0. Let B_{det} be the conjunction of CEC with Axioms (B1) to (B6).

Definition 4.2. A formula M is a *complete spatial description* if the region occupied by each object mentioned in M is the same in every model of,

CIRC[O ∧ M ; AbSpace ; Initially]. □

Theorem 4.3. If ε = 0 and M1 is a complete spatial description, then M2 is an explanation of Ψ if and only if O ∧ M1 ∧ M2 is consistent and,

CIRC[O ∧ M1 ∧ M2 ; AbSpace ; Initially] ∧
CIRC[N1 ∧ N2 ; Happens] ∧
CIRC[E ; Initiates, Terminates, Releases] ∧ B_{det} ⊨
Ψ ∧ COMP[Ψ].

Proof. See full paper. □

To illustrate the new definition, suppose the robot behaves as illustrated in Figure 4. Let N2 be the conjunction of the following formulae, which represent the robot's actions up to and including the time it bumps into obstacle A.

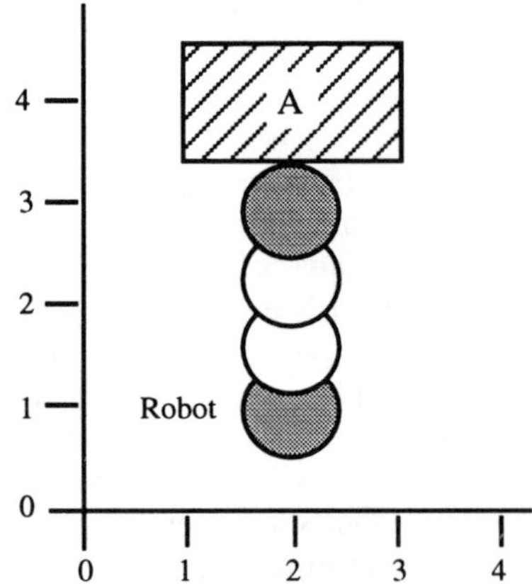

Figure 4: The Robot Collides with an Obstacle

Happens(Go,0) (4.4)

Happens(Stop,2·1) (4.5)

Let M1 be the conjunction of the following formulae.

Initially(Facing(0)) (4.6)

Initially(Occupies(Robot, Displace(Disc(0·5),⟨2,1⟩))) (4.7)

Let M2 be the following formula.

$\exists$ g [Initially(Occupies(A,g)) ∧ ∀ x,y [⟨x,y⟩ ∈ g ↔ 1 < x < 3 ∧ 3·5 < y < 4·5]] (4.8)

In the noise-free case, the robot would collide with A at time 2·0. However, let's assume the collision takes place at time 2·1. Let Ψ be the conjunction of the following formulae.

Happens(Switch1,2·1) (4.9)

Happens(Switch2,2·1) (4.10)

Let ε be 0·25. The following proposition says that M2 is indeed an explanation of Ψ according to the new definition.

Proposition 4.11.

CIRC [O ∧ M1 ∧ M2 ; AbSpace ; Initially] ∧
CIRC[N1 ∧ N2 ; Happens] ∧
CIRC[E ; Initiates, Terminates, Releases] ∧ B ⊭
¬ [Ψ ∧ COMP[Ψ]].

Proof. See full paper. □

Concluding Remarks

A considerable amount of further work has been carried out, which is reported in the full version of the paper, but which it is only possible to present in outline here. Two further theorems have been established which characterise the abductive explanations defined above in terms which appeal more directly to the information available to any map-building algorithm which might be executed on board the robot. These theorems have been used to prove the correctness, with respect to the abductive specification given, of an algorithm for sensor data assimilation which constructs an *occupancy array* [Davis, 1990, Section 6.2.1].

This algorithm forms the core of an implementation in C, which runs on data acquired by the robot in the real world. Some preliminary experiments have been conducted in which the robot, under the control of a behaviour-based architecture [Brooks, 1986], explores an enclosure, and makes a record of its actions and sensor data for subsequent processing using the algorithm.

In the paper accompanying his 1991 Computers and Thought Award Lecture, Brooks remarked that,

> [The field of Knowledge Representation] concentrates much of its energies on anomalies within formal systems which are never used for any practical task.
>
> [Brooks, 1991a]

The work presented in this paper and in [Shanahan, 1996b] should be construed as an answer to Brooks. According to the logical account given in this paper, a robot's incoming sensor data is filtered through an abductive process based on a framework of innate concepts, namely space, time, and causality.[1] The development of a rigorous, formal account of this process bridges the gap between theoretical work in Knowledge Representation and practical work in robotics, and opens up a great many possibilities for further research. The following three issues are particularly pressing.

- The assimilation of sensor data from moving objects, such as humans, animals, or other robots. Movable obstacles should also be on the agenda.
- The assimilation of richer sensor data than that supplied by the Rug Warrior's simple bump switches.
- The control of the robot via the model of the world it acquires through abduction.

Future implementation is expected to adopt a logic programming approach. Existing work in the Cognitive Robotics vein is likely to be influential here [Lespérance, *et al.*, 1994], [Kowalski, 1995], [Poole, 1995].

Acknowledgements

The inspiration for Cognitive Robotics comes from Ray Reiter and his colleagues at the University of Toronto. Thanks to Neelakantan Kartha and Rob Miller. The author is an EPSRC Advanced Research Fellow.

References

[Bacchus, *et al.*, 1995] F.Bacchus, J.Y.Halpren, and H.J.Levesque, Reasoning about Noisy Sensors in the Situation Calculus, *Proceedings IJCAI 95*, pages 1933-1940.

[Brooks, 1986] R.A.Brooks, A Robust Layered Control System for a Mobile Robot, *IEEE Journal of Robotics and Automation*, vol 2, no 1 (1986), pages 14-23.

[Brooks, 1991a] R.A.Brooks, Intelligence Without Reason, *Proceedings IJCAI 91*, pages 569-595.

[Brooks, 1991b] R.A.Brooks, Artificial Life and Real Robots, *Proceedings of the First European Conference on Artificial Life (1991)*, pages 3-10.

[Davis, 1990] E.Davis, *Representations of Commonsense Knowledge*, Morgan Kaufmann (1990).

[Jones & Flynn, 1993] J.L.Jones and A.M.Flynn, *Mobile Robots: Inspiration to Implementation*, A.K.Peters (1993).

[Kowalski, 1995] R.A.Kowalski, Using Meta-Logic to Reconcile Reactive with Rational Agents, in *Meta-Logics and Logic Programming*, ed. K.R.Apt and F.Turini, MIT Press (1995), pages 227-242.

[Lespérance, *et al.*, 1994] Y.Lespérance, H.J.Levesque, F.Lin, D.Marcu, R.Reiter, and R.B.Scherl, A Logical Approach to High-Level Robot Programming: A Progress Report, in *Control of the Physical World by Intelligent Systems: Papers from the 1994 AAAI Fall Symposium*, ed. B.Kuipers, New Orleans (1994), pages 79-85.

[McCarthy, 1989] J.McCarthy, Artificial Intelligence, Logic and Formalizing Common Sense, in *Philosophical Logic and Artificial Intelligence*, ed. R.Thomason, Kluwer Academic (1989), pages 161-190.

[Nilsson, 1984] N.J.Nilsson, ed., *Shakey the Robot*, SRI Technical Note no. 323 (1984), SRI, Menlo Park, California.

[Poole, 1995] D.Poole, Logic Programming for Robot Control, *Proceedings IJCAI 95*, pages 150-157.

[Reiter, 1987] R.Reiter, A Theory of Diagnosis from First Principles, *Artificial Intelligence*, vol 32 (1987), pages 57-95.

[Shanahan, 1989] M.P.Shanahan, Prediction Is Deduction but Explanation Is Abduction, *Proceedings IJCAI 89*, pages 1055-1060.

[Shanahan, 1995a] M.P.Shanahan, Default Reasoning about Spatial Occupancy, *Artificial Intelligence*, vol 74 (1995), pages 147-163.

[Shanahan, 1995b] M.P.Shanahan, A Circumscriptive Calculus of Events, *Artificial Intelligence*, vol 77 (1995), pages 249-284.

[Shanahan, 1996a] M.P.Shanahan, *Solving the Frame Problem: A Mathematical Investigation of the Common Sense Law of Inertia*, MIT Press (1996), to appear.

[Shanahan, 1996b] M.P.Shanahan, Robotics and the Common Sense Informatic Situation, *Proceedings ECAI 96*, to appear.

[Strawson, 1966] P.F.Strawson, *The Bounds of Sense*, Methuen (1966).

[1] This is somewhat reminiscent of Kant, according to whom, "the natural world as we know it . . . is thoroughly conditioned by [certain] features: our experience is essentially experience of a spatio-temporal world of law-governed objects conceived of as distinct from our temporally successive experiences of them" [Strawson, 1966, page 21].

A HYBRID LEARNING APPROACH FOR BETTER RECOGNITION OF VISUAL OBJECTS

Ibrahim F. Imam*

SRA International
4300 Fair Lakes Court
Fairfax, VA 22033
iimam@verdi.iisd.sra.com

Srinivas Gutta

Computer Science Department
George Mason University
Fairfax, VA 22030
sgutta@cs.gmu.edu

Abstract

Real world images often contain similar objects but with different rotations, noise, or other visual alterations. Vision systems should be able to recognize objects regardless of these visual alterations. This paper presents a novel approach for learning optimized structures of classifiers for recognizing visual objects regardless of certain types of visual alterations. The approach consists of two phases. The first phase is concerned with learning classifications of a set of standard and altered objects. The second phase is concerned with discovering an optimized structure of classifiers for recognizing objects from unseen images. This paper presents an application of this approach to a domain of 15 classes of hand gestures. The experimental results show significant improvement in the recognition rate rather than using a single classifier or multiple classifiers with thresholds.

1 Introduction

Recently, there has been a great interest in developing multimedia applications in wide-ranging fields. Communicative applications including audio and video systems require visual information about different objects to be able to recognize these objects, and communicate among each other (Maggioni, 1995; Freeman & Weissman, 1995; Kjeldsen & Kender, 1995). Such applications should be able to recognize objects within any environmental conditions. The reasons for such limitations include learning object classifiers using standard, noise free, and normalized objects; and using a non-adaptive strategy for recognizing new objects.

This paper introduces a new approach for learning optimized structures of classifiers for recognizing visual objects. In this paper, the term "*object*" denotes an image of one of the visual classes (e.g., hand poses). A *structure of classifiers* is a tree where each non-leaf node contains a classifier (e.g., a neural network), branches correspond to different outcomes or quantized intervals of the outcomes of each classifier, and leaves represent different classes of visual objects. The set of classifiers, used for building the decision structures, represents different visual alterations to the standard image of each object.

* Also a Research Affiliate of the MLI Laboratory at GMU.

The main goal of this approach is to recognize a set of visual objects regardless of visual alterations of these objects in the corresponding images. This is done in two phases. The first phase is concerned with generating a set of classifiers (e.g., neural networks), one for each combination of visual alteration of the standard object and parameter settings of the classifiers. Only two alterations were considered, in this paper, by applying a set of geometrical transformations and noise to the original image of each object. The outputs from the alteration processes are called *altered objects*. In the second phase, another set of training images are tested by all classifiers. For each image, the set of values obtained from all classifiers along with the correct recognition are used for discovering an optimized structure of classifiers for recognizing objects in testing (unseen) images. To perform this task, we used a system, called AQDT-2 (Imam & Michalski, 1993), for learning task-oriented decision structures from examples. An *optimal decision structure* is a structure that contains the minimum number of nodes (classifiers), the minimum number of leaves, and correctly classifies the maximum number of testing examples (images of similar and different visual objects).

The methodology was applied on a hand gesture database created by the authors. The hand gesture database contains 15 different gestures. For testing, 9 cycles of two cross-fold testing method were applied to test the recognition rate. *The results obtained in this paper show a significant improvement in the recognition rate when using the proposed approach over using single classifier or ensemble of classifiers.*

2 Related Work

Carpenter *et al.* (1992) proposed a Fuzzy system, called ARTMAP, which achieves a synthesis of the Adaptive Resonance Theory (ART) between neural network and fuzzy logic by exploiting a close formal similarity between the computations of ART category choice and fuzzy membership functions. Greenspan, Goodman, and Chellappa (1994) proposed an architecture for the integration of neural networks and rule-based methods using unsupervised and supervised learning. This approach was used for pattern recognition tasks. Also, Towell and Shavlik (1994) presented a methodology for transferring symbolic knowledge into a neural network and for extracting rules from a trained neural network. The proposed approach defers from the above ones in the fact that it uses an adaptive methodology to combine multiple neural networks with decision tree approach.

An early example of using ensembles of neural networks, called Meta-Pi, was presented by Hamshire and Waibel (1992). The Meta-Pi classifier is a connectionist pattern classifier that consists of a number of source-dependent sub-networks. These sub-networks are integrated by a Time Delay Neural Network (TDNN) superstructure. The TDNN combines the outputs of the modules, trained independently, in order to provide a global classification.

Lincoln and Skrzypek (1990) proposed a clustering multiple back propagation networks to improve the performance and fault tolerance. Following training, a 'cluster' is created by computing the average of the outputs generated by the individual networks. The output of the 'cluster' is used as the desired output during training by feeding it back to the individual networks. The basic idea behind using such a strategy is based on the assumption that while it is possible to 'fool' a single back propagation network all the time one cannot mislead all of them at the same time.

Battiti and Colla (1994) proposed an approach to combine the outputs of different neural network classifiers to improve the rejection-accuracy rates and to make the combined performance better than that obtained from the individual components. Decisions are made based on the majority rule (concept of democracy). The concept of democracy is analogous with the human way of reaching a pondered decision query by consensus.

Several approaches to the problem of recognizing hand gestures have been proposed recently. One can distinguish between methods which assume a physically valid model of the hand (e.g., Quam, 1990; Sturman & Zeltzer, 1994) and those which do not extract or impose these type of 3-D constraints (e.g., Huang & Pavlovic, 1995; Lee & Kunii, 1993; Downton & Drouet, 1991).

3 The Approach

This paper presents a novel approach for learning optimized structures of classifiers for improving image recognition. The proposed approach consists of two phases. In the first phase, all images of visual objects are converted into appropriate format (e.g., digital) and segmented. Then for each image a set of altered objects are generated. An <u>altered object</u> is a transformation of the standard object such that both should be recognized as members of the same class (e.g., same gesture). For each alteration process, a classifier is used for learning classification for all object classes. The second phase is concerned with determining an optimized structure of classifiers for recognizing unseen or new images.

Figure 1 illustrates the proposed approach. All images are segmented and normalized. Then for each image, two identical copies were produced one by adding noise and the other by rotating it. This process is repeated three times using new classifiers with different parameter settings. All nine classifiers were trained using a portion of the training examples (set #1). Then, all classifiers are tested against the remaining portion of the training examples (set #2). The output values from testing the nine classifiers and the correct recognition (i.e., decision class) provided by the user are combined into a data vector, called a <u>record of recognition</u>. All records of recognition are combined together to form a set of examples used later to build the optimized structure of classifiers. Building the optimized structure of classifiers is done by the program AQDT-2 (Imam & Michalski, 1993). This program is selected over other decision tree programs because it can optimize the obtained structures using a variety of cost functions.

3.1 Phase I: Learning Classification of Visual Objects

The first step of capturing an object from an image is to locate the horizontal and vertical boundaries of the object. The method utilized here uses a simple algorithm that operates on the edge image using the Sobel's edge extraction method. All images are passed to the object normalization process. Each object (or an image) is normalized before starting the object recognition phase. This rest of this subsection illustrates the process of

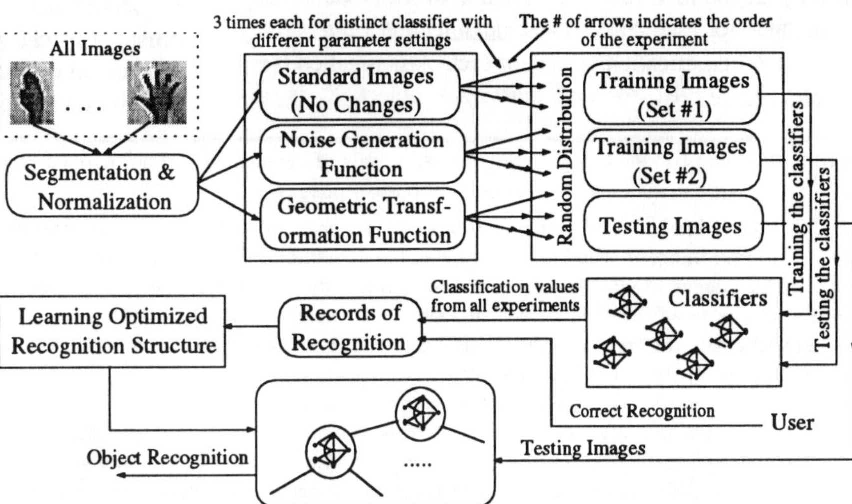

Figure 1: An Illustration of the proposed approach.

building, training and testing a single RBF classifier and an Ensemble of RBF classifiers (ERBF) and using both for object recognition. The ERBF classifiers are used later for acquiring the records of recognition.

Single Classifier: The construction of an RBF network is similar to the construction of any neural network. the number of input nodes in each RBF neural network was always set equal to the number of input images. The number of output nodes was set equal to the number of decision classes. The number of hidden nodes are optimally found, in each single RBF, by varying the number of clusters from fifth to equal number of the input nodes. At each stage of the variation, two additional parameters, the overlap factors and the proportionality constants were changed. These changes are repeated until all training examples (images) were classified correctly by the classifier. The same process is repeated for the cases when training on the original images with Gaussian noise and original images with geometrical transformation. The reason for using RBF network is because of its ability to cluster similar images before classifying them. A new object is assigned to the class with the highest value. To compare the performance of the RBF with the proposed approach, the training set #1 is used for training the classifier and the testing set is used for testing it.

Ensemble of Radial Basis Functions (ERBF): The proposed ERBF model integrates three *RBF components*, C1, C2 and C3, as shown in Figure 2. Each RBF component is further defined in terms of three RBF nodes, each of which specified in terms of the number of clusters and the overlap factors. The three RBF components have been trained on the original images, the original images after adding Gaussian noise, and the original images after geometrically rotating the objects with certain degree Ω, respectively. To recognize a new object, the image is tested by all the nine networks. Each network produces an output value for each class, called *classification value*. The sum of all 9 classification values for each class is called the *recognition rate*, R, for that class. An object X is a member of class C_i, if the recognition rate of this class is greater than the rate of all other classes, equation (1).

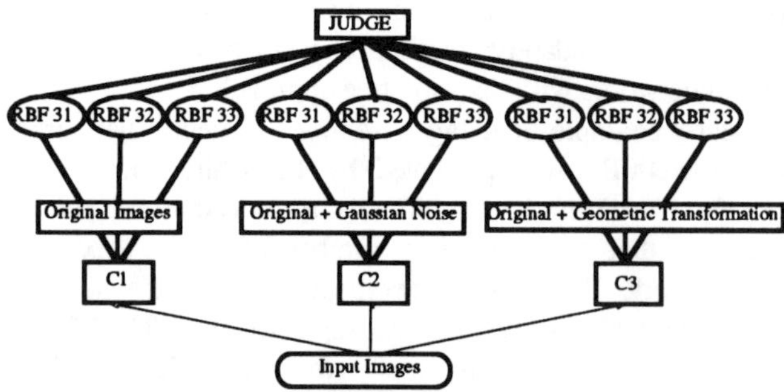

Figure 2: ERBF Architecture.

$$R(X) = \max_{C_j} \sum_{i=1}^{9} \left| O(N_i, C_j) \right| \quad (1)$$

where $O(N_i, C_j)$ is the value assigned by classifier N_i (i= 1, ..., 9) to class C_j (j= 1, ..., m; m is the number of decision classes) when testing the image X.

To generate the records of classification, The classifications provided by different classifiers and the correct recognition are grouped together to form one record. Figure 3 shows a description of the method. Note that the training set #2 is used in this phase as a testing set.

3.2 Phase II: Learning Optimized Structures of Classifiers

The second phase in the proposed approach is concerned with learning an optimized structure of classifiers for recognizing different objects from new images. *The proposed method is based on learning descriptions of situations to determine if the classification should be used for recognition or for selecting the best classifier for recognition*. Figure 4 illustrate the methodology used to determine an optimized structures for object recognition. To obtain such a structure, the AQDT-2 learning system (Imam & Michalski, 1993) is used to learn a task-oriented structure of classifiers that recognizes any new object using the minimum number of classifiers.

Input: Training (set #1.1) and testing (set #2.1) sets of segmented and normalized images.
Output: Classifications of a set of objects in unseen images.

Step 1: For all images (in set #1.1 and set #2.1), generate two identical sets of images (sets #1.2, #1.3, #2.2, and #2.3) .
Step 2: For all image in sets #1.2 and #2.2 add Gaussian noise. For all images in sets #1.3 and #2.3 add geometric transformation.
Note: All images in sets "#1x" are used for training the classifiers, and those in sets "#2x" are used for testing the classifiers.
Step 3: Create three identical copies of each set of images (e.g., #1.1.1, #1.1.2, #1.1.3 for set #1.1). Create a set of 9 RBF networks with different k-mean clustering one for each training set (start with #1).
For each classifier, steps 4 to 5 are repeated:
Step 4: Each classifier is trained using the corresponding set of images.
Step 5: When the training process of each classifier is finished, the corresponding set of testing images is used for testing the network (e.g., testing on set #2.a for training set #1.a. where a is any number or combination of numbers).
Step 6: The classification values obtained from testing each image using the 9 classifiers along with the correct recognition of the object were combined into a data vector.

Figure 3: Learning object classifiers.

Input: A set of training examples (records of recognition) and testing unseen images.
Output: An optimized decision structure that recognizes any new gesture (with or without alterations).
Step 1: Quantize all attribute values in the records of recognition.
Step 2: (Optional) Determine a set of disjoint rules describing the training examples.
Step 3: Specify the learning task for AQDT-2 (in this case, the decision structure should have minimum number of classifiers and minimum number of levels).
Step 4 to Step 6 are repeated until learning task is satisfied.
Step 4: Run AQDT-2 (initially with its default settings) to obtain a decision structure.
Step 5: Compare the information of the obtained decision structure with the optimal one. If the new structure is more optimal, store the values of the cost functions and the optimizing criteria. If the stopping criteria is satisfied, exit.
Step 6: Change the tolerance of the cost functions in AQDT-2 to give high preferences for some attributes. Go to step 4.

Figure 4: The method for learning optimized structure for shape recognition.

The advantages of using AQDT-2 over other decision tree learning programs is that it has adaptive capabilities including forcing partial attribute ranking, restructuring the decision structure according to a set of criteria and cost functions, etc. To select an attribute, AQDT-2 used the disjointness criterion which ranks attributes according to how their values discriminate the decision classes. For the experiments presented in this paper, the learning task was set to minimize the number of neural networks used in the obtained structure, and to maximize the recognition accuracy.

4 The Experiment

This section introduces an application of the proposed approach to a database of hand gestures. These images were taken by a KODAK Quick Take 100 Camera. The database contains 150 images of hand gestures. Images were taken from 5 different persons (2 sets of 15 images per each, Figure 5). The second set of images has been taken after a time gap of 30 minutes. The experiment was performed 3 times. For each time, a set of five different gestures (third, second, then first five gestures respectively) were considered as one decision class. This was done to increase the complexity of the problem.

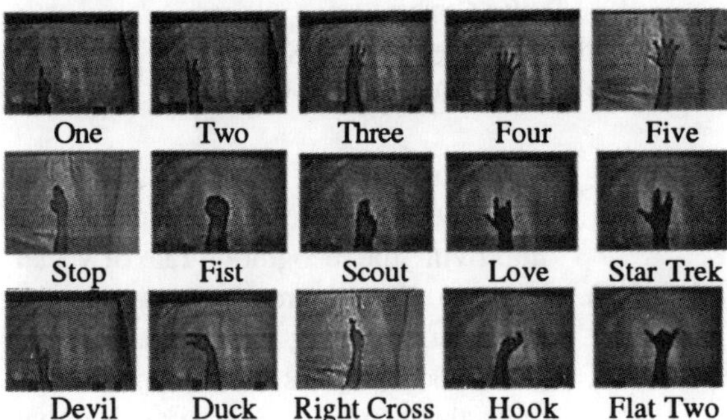

Figure 5: Images of hand gestures used in the experiment.

For each testing combination, a set of 9 testing cycles were performed. A testing cycle uses a two cross-fold method to evaluate each method. This is done by splitting all gestures, first, into two sets. The first set is labeled training set #1. The second set is divided into two subsets with ratio of 1:8. The smaller one is labeled training set #2, and the larger is labeled testing. The sizes of the training sets #1 in the 9 cycles are 7%, 13%, 20%, 27%, 33%, 40%, 47%, 53%, and 60%, respectively.

Original images were of size 240x320. All images were converted from RGB format to gray scale images of intensity varying from 0-255. All 150 hand gesture images were segmented and normalized, then all images were visually verified. Images were normalized to standard size of 64x116 pixels. Two visual alterations are used in this paper: 1) A gaussian noise with 0 mean and a variance of 10 was added to each image to generate new set of images; 2) A geometric transformation of 10^0 was applied to the original images to generate a different set of images.

The Recognition Rate of RBF and ERBF:

To compare the recognition rate of using single RBF classifier and ensemble of classifiers ERBF, the training set #1 is used for training the classifiers and the testing set was used for reporting their performances (Note: training set #2 was not used). Table 1. shows results obtained from testing a single RBF classifier. Each row in this table presents the results obtained from single combination. Table 2 shows results of testing the ERBF. The recognition process is done using equation (1).

Table 1: RBF Results.

Testing Comb.	Accepted (Correct)	False Negative	Rejected (correct)	False Positive
1	56.9%	43.1%	72.8%	27.2%
2	59.6%	40.4%	68.2%	31.8%
3	61.6%	38.4%	77.3%	22.7%

Table 2: ERBF Results.

Testing method	Accepted (Correct)	False Negative	Rejected (correct)	False Positive
1	71.6%	28.4%	81.1%	18.9%
2	69.8%	30.2%	82.2%	17.8%
3	72.4%	27.6%	77.8%	22.2%

Learning an Optimized Structure of Classifiers: To obtain the records of recognition from each experiment, the training set #1 was used for training the classifiers, while the training set #2 was used for testing. All outputs from each classifier were quantized according to a uniform distribution of the length of the interval (e.g., 10 intervals each of length 0.1). A discriminant descriptions of the decision classes of gestures were obtained by the AQ15 learning system (Michalski, et al, 1986). This intermediate process usually improves the overall performance. AQDT-2 used these rules to determine an optimized decision structure to classify any new gesture using the minimum number of networks. The program parameters were set to run 10 iterations with variable costs for all attributes, variable degree of generalizations, and minimizing the number of nodes and levels in the structure.

Each iteration uses random setting for the costs of the nine attributes. Each attribute represents one classifier. The program first learns a decision structure with its default settings. Then it changes the cost of one classifier at a time and re-learns a new structure. If the size of the structure is decreased or changed within a given tolerance, or the number of classifiers is decreased or changed within another tolerance, the system keeps the cost of that attribute and changes another attribute cost. The paper reports the results obtained from the default settings and the best 5 iterations.

Figure 6 shows a decision structure that is learned for one of the cycles of the testing combination #1. This decision structure contains 161 tests (e.g. the sum of number of tests from the root to any leaf node) divided over 56 paths (a path is a connection from the root to a leaf node). *Thus, the average (integer) number of classifiers needed to classify an unseen hand gesture is 3*. The total number of networks needed to classify any gesture belongs to the given group is 6 networks. About 72% of all possible gestures can be classified using only four networks (N4, N5, N7, and N8). For the different testing combinations described above, the AQDT-2 program was very successful in discovering optimized decision structures using subset of the neural networks used in Figure 6. In the second testing combination, only five networks were used to derive a decision (N3 was excluded). The average (integer) number of networks needed to derive a decision was also 3. In the third testing experiment, the same set of networks were used to obtain a decision.

Table 3 shows the error rate when testing the structure obtained by AQDT-2 with its default settings. It also shows the median and mean of error rates of the best five iterations (structures with minimum number of classifiers and have minimum number of average tests). Figure 7 shows a comparison of the error rate of using one RBF network (Baysian classifier), using a combination of nine different classifiers (ERBF) (majority voting), and using the proposed approach for image recognition. The results show a significant improvement in the recognition rate using the combination of the proposed approach.

Table 3: The error rate of using combination of ERBF and AQDT-2 for image recognition.

Testing Combination	Error Rate		
	Default Settings	Best 5 iterations	
		Median	Mean
1	4.3%	3.76%	3.6%
2	5.2%	3.12%	3.15%
3	3.25%	2.41%	2.4%
Average	4.25%	3.1%	3.05%

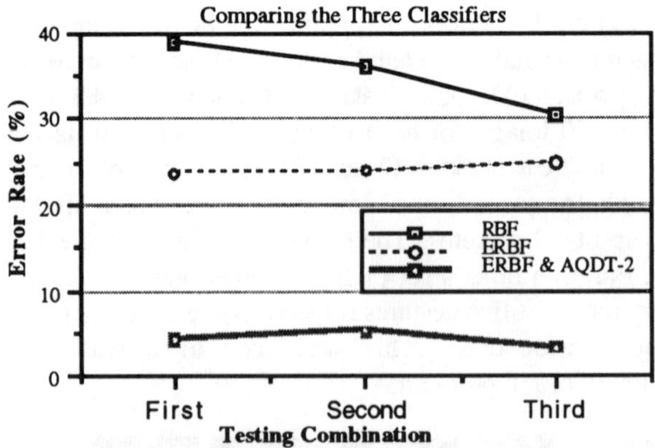

Figure 7: The error rate of using RBF, ERBF, and ERBF+AQDT-2 for gesture recognition.

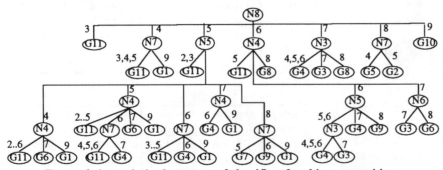

Figure 6: An optimized structure of classifiers for object recognition.

5 Conclusion

The paper introduces a new approach for improving the recognition rate of visual objects. The approach separates the process of learning classifications of a set of visual objects from the process of recognizing new objects. For learning object classifications, the proposed methodology learns classification of all objects from the original images and from different sets of altered images. In this research, only two alterations were considered by either geometric rotating them or adding noise to the original image. For each original or altered set of images, three classifiers with different parameter settings were used to learn classification of different classes of objects. To recognize a new object, a structure of classifiers is obtained by the AQDT-2 learning system. This structure is used as a plan for recognizing objects in unseen images. The maximum classification value obtained by this classifier is used to either assign a class to the object in the image or select another classifier to test the image. The role of AQDT-2 is to determine the minimum set of classifiers needed for recognition and in which order the testing should take place.

The paper presented an application on a database of hand gestures. Three experimental combinations were performed on the data to analyze the performance of the methodology. In each combination, a subset of classes were grouped together as one class to increase the complexity of the problem. The results show a significant improvement in the recognition rate of new objects using the new approach against using a single RBF or ensemble of RBFs for recognition. The method allows more flexibility in recognizing visual objects. More analysis is needed to study the relationship between the number of alterations used and the complexity of obtained structures and the performance of object recognition.

Acknowledgments: The authors thank Zoran Duric, Mark Maloof, and Nirmal Warke for reviewing an earlier draft of this paper. This research was supported partially by the Forensic Lab. at GMU through the US Army Research Lab under Contract DAAL01-93-K-0099; and partially by the MLI Laboratory at GMU through the Advanced Research Projects Agency under grant No. N00014-91-J-1854 administered by the Office of Naval Research, in part by the Advanced Research Projects Agency under grants F49620-92-J-0549 and F49620-95-1-0462 administered by the Air Force Office of Scientific Research.

References

Battiti, R., and Colla, A. M., 1994. Democracy in Neural Nets: Voting Schemes for Classification, *Neural Networks*, Vol. 7, No. 4, pp. 691-707.

Carpenter, G.A., Grossberg, S., Markuzon, N., Reynolds, J.H., and Rosen, D.B., 1992. Fuzzy ARTMAP: A Neural Network Architecture for Incremental Supervised Learning of Analog Multidimensional Maps, *IEEE Trans. on Neural Networks*, Vol. 3, No. 5, pp. 698-713.

Downton, A.C., and Drouet, H., 1991. Image analysis for model-based sign language coding, *In Proceedings of the 6th International Conference on Image Analysis and Processing*, pp. 637-644.

Freeman, W.T., and Weissman, C.D., 1995. Television control by hand gestures, In *Proceedings of the International Workshop on Automatic Face- and Gesture-Recognition (IWAFGR)*, pp. 179-181, Zurich.

Greenspan, H., Goodman, R., and Chellappa, R., 1991.Texture Analysis via Unsupervised and Supervised Learning, In *Proceedings of the International Joint Conference on Neural Networks*, Vol. I, pp. 639-644.

Hampshire, J.B., and Waibel, A., 1992. The Meta-Pi Network: Building Distributed Knowledge Representations for Robust Multisource Pattern Recognition, *IEEE Trans. on Pattern Analysis and Machine Intelligence*, Vol. 14, No. 7, pp. 751-769.

Huang, T.S., and Pavlovic, V.I., 1995. Hand Gesture Modelling, Analysis and Synthesis, In Proceedings of the *International Workshop on Automatic Face- and Gesture-Recognition (IWAFGR)*, pp. 73-79, Zurich.

Imam, I.F. and Michalski, R.S., 1993. Learning Decision Trees from Decision Rules: A method and initial results from a comparative study. The International Journal of Intelligent Information Systems JIIS, Vol. 2, No. 3, pp. 279-304, Kluwer Academic Pub., MA.

Kjeldsen, R., and Kender, J., 1995. Visual Hand Gesture Recognition for Window System Control, *International Workshop on Automatic Face- and Gesture-Recognition (IWAFGR)*, pp. 184-188, Zurich.

Lee, J., and Kunii, T.L., 1993. Constraint-based hand modeling and tracking, *Models and Techniques in Computer Animation*, pp. 110-127, Tokyo, Springer Verlag.

Lincoln, W.P., and Skrzypek, J., 1990. Synergy of Clustering Multiple Back Propagation Networks, *Advances in Neural Information Processing Systems (NIPS)*, Touretzky, D.S., (Ed.), Vol. 2, pp. 650-657, Morgan Kaufmann Publishers, San Francisco, CA.

Maggioni, C., 1995. GestureComputer—New Ways of Operating a Computer, *International Workshop on Automatic Face- and Gesture-Recognition (IWAFGR)*, pp. 166-171, Zurich.

Michalski, R.S., Mozetic, I., Hong, J., and Lavrac, N., 1986. The Multi-Purpose Incremental Learning System AQ15 and its Testing Application to Three Medical Domains, *Proceedings of AAAI-86*, pp. 1041-1045, Philadelphia, PA.

Quam, D.L., 1990. Gesture Recognition with a Dataglove, *Proceedings of the IEEE National Aerospace and Electronics Conference*, Vol. 2.

Sturman, D.J., and Zeltzer, D., 1994. A Survey of glove-based input, *IEEE Computer Graphics and Applications*, Vol. 14, pp. 30-39.

Towell, G.G., and Shavlik, J.W., 1994. Refining Symbolic Knowledge Using Neural Networks, *Machine Learning: A Multistrategy Approach*, Vol. IV, pp. 405-438, Michalski, R.S. and Tecuci, G. (Eds.), Morgan Kaufmann Publishers, San Francisco, CA.

Using Elimination Methods to Compute Thermophysical Algebraic Invariants from Infrared Imagery

J.D. Michel†, N. Nandhakumar†, Tushar Saxena‡, Deepak Kapur‡
† Dept of Electrical Engineering, Univ. of Virginia, Charlottesville, VA 22903
‡ Inst. for Logic and Programming, Dept. of Computer Science, State Univ. of New York, Albany, NY 12222
{michel, nandhu}@virginia.edu,{saxena, kapur}@cs.albany.edu

Abstract

We describe a new approach for computing invariant features in infrared (IR) images. Our approach is unique in the field since it considers not just surface reflection and surface geometry in the specification of invariant features, but it also takes into account internal object composition and thermal state which affect images sensed in the non-visible spectrum. We first establish a non-linear energy balance equation using the principle of conservation of energy at the surface of the imaged object. We then derive features that depend only on material parameters of the object and the sensed radiosity. These features are independent of the scene conditions and the scene-to-scene transformation of the "driving conditions" such as ambient temperature, and wind speed. The algorithm for deriving the invariant features is based on the algebraic elimination of the transformation parameters from the non-linear relationships. The elimination approach is a general method based on the extended Dixon resultant. Results on real IR imagery are shown to illustrate the performance of the features derived in this manner when used for an object recognition system that deals with multiple classes of objects.

Introduction

A very popular and increasingly affordable sensor modality is thermal imaging - where non-visible radiation is sensed in the long-wave infrared (LWIR) spectrum of $8\mu m$ to $14\mu m$. The current generation of LWIR sensors produce images of contrast and resolution that compare favorably with broadcast television quality visible light imagery. However, the images are no longer functions of only surface reflectance. As the wavelength of the sensor transducer passband increases, emissive effects begin to emerge as the dominant mode of electromagnetic energy exitance from object surfaces. The (primarily) emitted radiosity of LWIR energy has a strong dependence on internal composition, properties, and state of the object such as specific heat, density, volume, heat generation rate of internal sources, etc. This dependence may be exploited by specifying image-derived invariants that vary only if these parameters of the physical properties vary.

Here, we describe the use of the principle of conservation of energy at the surface of the imaged object to specify a functional relationship between the object's thermophysical properties (e.g., thermal conductivity, thermal capacitance, emissivity, etc.), scene parameters (e.g., wind temperature, wind speed, solar insolation), and the sensed LWIR image gray level. We use this functional form to derive invariant features that remain constant despite changes in scene parameters/driving conditions. In this formulation the internal thermophysical properties play a role that is analogous to the role of parameters of the conics, lines and/or points that are used for specifying geometric invariants when analyzing visible wavelength imagery. Thus, in addition to the currently available techniques of formulating features that depend only on external shape and surface reflectance discontinuities, the phenomenology of LWIR image generation can be used to establish new features that "uncover" the composition and thermal state of the object, and which do not depend on surface reflectance characteristics.

A general approach is described that enables the specification of invariant features that are satisfactorily justified in a thermophysical sense. The energy balance equation is inherently a non-linear form. We choose the variable labeling such that a polynomial is formed whose variables are the unknowns of the image formation and the coefficients are the object parameters. The choice of labels for the variables determines the form of the transformations from scene to scene. Consideration of the variable inter-dependencies specifies the set of transformation to be a subgroup of the general linear group.

A method based on elimination techniques is used to specify the features. Elimination methods eliminate a subset of variables from a finite set of polynomial equations to give a smaller set of polynomials in the remaining variables while keeping the solution set the same. Invariants can be computed using these methods in three steps – (1) Set up the transformation equa-

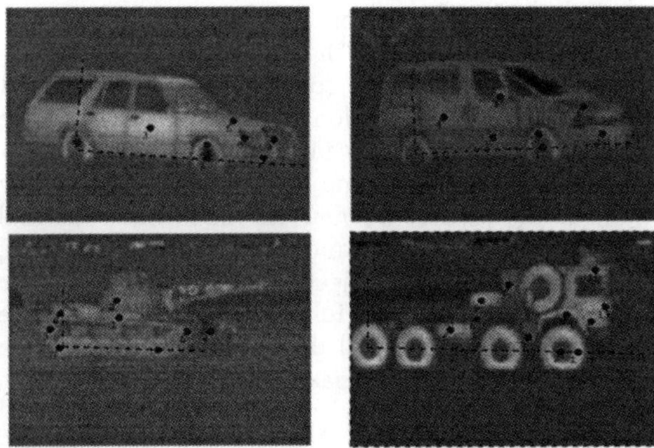

Figure 1: The vehicles used to test the object recognition approach, (from top left clockwise) car, van, truck 1, and tank. The axis superimposed on the image show the object centered reference frames. The numbered points indicate the object surfaces used to form the measurement matrices. These points are selected such that there are a variety of different materials and/or surface normals within the set.

tions relating the generic coefficients of the polynomial form before and after the action of the transformation subgroup, (2) Eliminate the transformation parameters from the transformation equations using any of the elimination methods, and finally, (3) Extract the invariants from the result of elimination from step 2.

Using Elimination Methods for Computing Invariants

Elimination methods are a general class of algorithms designed to eliminate a given set of variables from a finite system of polynomial equations. Some of the most general elimination methods are the Gröbner basis method, characteristic set method, and various resultant methods see (Kapur & Lakshman 1992) for a survey. Such methods find applications in many areas of science and engineering and can be used to solve systems of polynomial equations. They can also be used to automatically compute invariants of a given configuration (or quintic) under various transformation groups see (Kapur, Lakshman, & Saxena 1995).

An *absolute invariant* is a rational function of the configuration parameters whose value remains constant under the action of a transformation group on this configuration. As a consequence, absolute invariants are very useful (Mundy & Zisserman 1992) in recognizing objects from images and building model-based object recognition libraries. Let $\mathbf{p}$ and $\mathbf{q}$ be the object and image parameters. Each absolute invariant f/g generates a *separable invariant relation*, $h(\mathbf{p},\mathbf{q}) = f(\mathbf{p})g(\mathbf{q}) - f(\mathbf{q})g(\mathbf{p})$. In other words, if these separable invariant relations can somehow be derived, then it may be possible to extract absolute invariants (which generate them) from them.

The process of computing invariants using elimination methods can be organized in three phases as follows:

1. **Phase 1:** Set up the *transformation equations* relating the image parameters to the object via the transformation parameters.
2. **Phase 2:** Eliminate transformation parameters from the transformation equations to derive separable invariant relations.
3. **Phase 3:** Extract the *absolute invariants* which generate the separable invariant relations. This is known as the *separability problem.*

In phase 2, elimination methods such as Gröbner basis algorithms, and in certain cases see (Kapur, Lakshman, & Saxena 1995) resultant computations can be used to derive separable invariant relations.

Given a separable invariant relation $h(\mathbf{p},\mathbf{q})$, there exist many (*algebraically dependent*) invariants $\frac{c}{d},\ldots,\frac{f}{g},\ldots,\frac{k}{l}$, which generate them, ie.:

$$\begin{aligned} c(\mathbf{p})d(\mathbf{q}) - c(\mathbf{q})d(\mathbf{p}) &= h(\mathbf{p},\mathbf{q}), \\ &\vdots \\ f(\mathbf{p})g(\mathbf{q}) - f(\mathbf{q})g(\mathbf{p}) &= h(\mathbf{p},\mathbf{q}), \\ &\vdots \\ k(\mathbf{p})l(\mathbf{q}) - k(\mathbf{q})l(\mathbf{p}) &= h(\mathbf{p},\mathbf{q}). \end{aligned}$$

But for a given ordering on the object parameters, there is a **unique** invariant $\mathbf{I} = f/g$ such that the:

1. leading term of g is strictly larger than the leading term of f,
2. leading term of f has zero coefficient in g and
3. leading coefficient of g is 1 (ie. g is monic).

To extract the absolute invariant from separable invariant relations, the algorithm in (Kapur, Lakshman, & Saxena 1995) fixes an ordering on the object and image parameters, and targets this unique invariant as follows. Let $\mathbf{p}^{e_f}$ and $\mathbf{p}^{e_g}$ be the leading terms of $f(\mathbf{p})$ and $g(\mathbf{p})$ respectively, and c_f, the leading coefficient of $f(\mathbf{p})$. Then, using the above properties of this unique invariant, the separable invariant relation can be expressed as

$$\begin{aligned} h(\mathbf{p},\mathbf{q}) &= f(\mathbf{p})g(\mathbf{q}) - g(\mathbf{p})f(\mathbf{q}) \\ &= f(\mathbf{p})\,(\mathbf{q}^{e_g} + \cdots) - g(\mathbf{p})\,(c_f\mathbf{q}^{e_f} + \cdots) \\ &= f(\mathbf{p})\,\mathbf{q}^{e_g} - c_f\,g(\mathbf{p})\,\mathbf{q}^{e_f} + \cdots. \end{aligned}$$

As is evident from the above expansion of the separable invariant relation as a polynomial in $\mathbf{q}$, the numerator $f(\mathbf{p})$ of the absolute invariant is the coefficient of the leading term $\mathbf{q}^{e_g}$. Once $f(\mathbf{p})$ is known, and the denominator $g(\mathbf{p})$ is the coefficient of the term $-c_f\,\mathbf{q}^{e_f}$ and can be easily read off from $h(\mathbf{p},\mathbf{q})$ once it has been sorted according to a predetermined ordering.

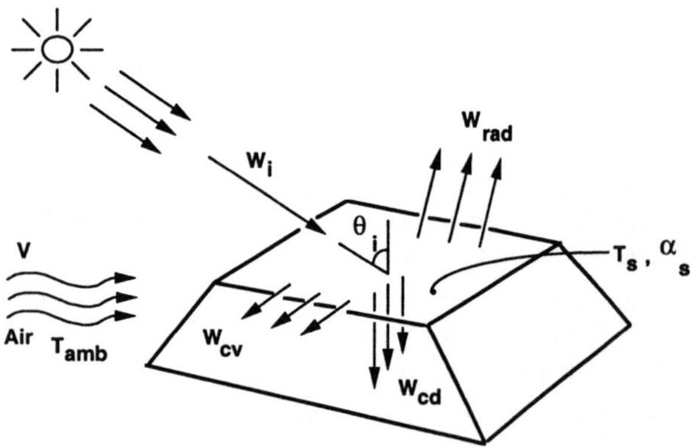

Figure 2: Energy exchange at the surface of the imaged object. Incident energy is primarily in the visible spectrum. Surfaces loses energy by convection to air, via radiation to the atmosphere, and via conduction to the interior of the object. The elemental volume at the surface also stores a portion of the absorbed energy.

A Thermophysical Approach to LWIR Image Analysis

At the surface of the imaged object (figure 2) energy absorbed by the surface equals the energy lost to the environment.

$$W_{abs} = W_{lost} \tag{1}$$

Energy absorbed by the surface is given by

$$W_{abs} \;=\; W_I \; cos\theta_I \; \alpha_s \; , \tag{2}$$

where, W_I is the incident solar irradiation on a horizontal surface, θ_i is the angle between the direction of irradiation and the surface normal, and α_s is the surface absorptivity which is related to the visual reflectance ρ_s by $\alpha_s = 1 - \rho_s$. Note that it is reasonable to use the visual reflectance to estimate the energy absorbed by the surface since approximately 90% of the energy in solar irradiation lies in the visible wavelengths (Incropera & DeWitt 1981).

The energy lost by the surface to the environment was given by

$$W_{lost} \;=\; W_{cv} \;+\; W_{rad} \;+\; W_{cnd} \;+\; W_{st} \tag{3}$$

The energy convected from the surface to the ambient air is given by $W_{cv} \;=\; h(T_s - T_{amb})$ where, T_{amb} is the ambient air temperature, T_s is the surface temperature of the imaged object, and h is the average convected heat transfer coefficient for the imaged surface, which depends on the wind speed, thermophysical properties of the air, and surface geometry (Incropera & DeWitt 1981). We note that surface temperature may be estimated from the thermal image based on an appropriate model of radiation energy exchange between the surface and the infrared camera.

The radiation energy loss is computed from $W_{rad} \;=\; \epsilon \, \sigma \, (T_s^4 - T_{amb}^4)$, where σ denotes the Stefan-Boltzmann constant. The energy conducted to the interior of the object is given by $W_{cnd} \;=\; -k \;dT/dx$, where k is the thermal conductivity of the material, and x is distance below the surface. Here, we assume that lateral energy conduction is insignificant compared to conduction along the direction normal to the surface. The increase in the stored, internal energy of an elemental volume at the surface is given by $W_{st} \;=\; C_T \frac{dT_s}{dt}$, where C_T denotes the lumped thermal capacitance of the object and is given by $C_T = DVc$, D is the density of the object, V is the volume, and c is the specific heat. In the following section we use the energy conservation model described above to derive invariant features using ideas in algebraic elimination theory.

Thermophysical Algebraic Invariants (TAI's)

The balance of energy expression,

$$W_{abs} = W_{rad} + W_{cv} + W_{st} + W_{cnd} \tag{4}$$

is the governing equation in our approach for computing invariant features. Each term in the above equation can be expanded, which results in equation 4 being expressed as a polynomial. The choice of labels for the variables determines both the form of the polynomial and transformation form. Since an absolute invariant feature value is not affected by transformations of the variables, the variables of the form are chosen to be the unknown parameters of the image formation. The coefficients are, then, the known/hypothesized object parameters and sensed measurements.

An Algebraic Invariance Formulation

The balance of energy expression, equation 4, may be written in the non-linear form

$$a_1x_1+a_2x_2+a_3x_3+a_4x_4-a_5x_5+a_6x_1x_6^4+a_7x_4x_6 = 0. \tag{5}$$

where the variables and coefficients are labeled as

$$\begin{array}{ll} a_1 = \sigma T_s^4 & x_1 = \epsilon \\ a_2 = C_T & x_2 = \frac{dT_s}{dt} \\ a_3 = k & x_3 = \frac{dT_s}{dx} \\ a_4 = T\Delta & x_4 = \frac{h}{\Delta} \\ a_5 = -\cos\theta & x_5 = W_I\alpha_s \\ a_6 = -\sigma & x_6 = T_{amb} \\ a_7 = \Delta & \end{array} \tag{6}$$

Thus, the polynomial chosen to represent equation 4 is a quintic form in six variables.

Any pixel in a LWIR image of an object will yield a 7-D measurement vector, **a**. The image measurement (gray value) specifies a_1 and a_4. The values for a_2, a_3, and a_5 are known when the identity and pose of the object are hypothesized. The coefficient a_7, related to the convection term, h, is explained in greater detail in the discussion section. The driving conditions, x_i, $i = \{1 \ldots 6\}$ are the unknown scene parameters that change from scene to scene.

Consider two different LWIR images of a scene obtained under different scene conditions and from different viewpoints. Consider N points on the object that are visible in both views. Assume (for the nonce) that the object pose for each view, and point correspondence between the two views are available (or hypothesized). A point in each view yields a measurement vector $\mathbf{a}$. The ith component of the vector is denoted a_i, where $i = 1, \ldots, 7$ as defined by eqn (6). Let the collection of these vectors be denoted by $a_{i,k}$, $k = 1, \ldots, N$ for the first scene/image and $a'_{i,k}$, $k = 1, \ldots, N$ for the second scene. In the same vein, consider an associated set of driving condition vectors for the first scene. We express the collection as $x_{i,k}$ where $k = 1, \ldots, N$ and $i = 1, \ldots, 6$ as defined in eqn (6). Similarly, the driving condition vector from the second scene is denoted $x'_{i,k}$.

Thermophysical Transformation

Consider a set of $N \leq 6$ points imaged from the surface of an object. This creates a set of N vectors $x_{i,k}$, $k = 1 \ldots N, i = 1, \ldots, 6$ which define the driving conditions on the surface of the object in a scene at time t_n. This forms a variable matrix of dimension $6 \times N$, call it X. These points are transformed from their values at time t_n to their value at time t_{n+1}, $t_{n+1} > t_n$, by a GL transformation, M, $MX = X'$. The transformation matrix M is 6×6.

In order to determine the form of the transformation we view the components of a driving condition vector in terms of the inter-dependencies of the parameters. By doing so, superfluous parameters are eliminated. The dependency of the value of a variable at the current instance on other variables at a previous instance is established by the physical phenomena that cause scene-to-scene change in the different parameter values. The dependencies are shown below (and explanations follow):

variable	dependency
$x'_1 = \epsilon$	$x_1 \quad (\epsilon)$
$x'_2 = \frac{dT_s}{dt}$	$x_2, x_3, x_4, x_5(\frac{dT_s}{dt}, \frac{dT_s}{dx}, \frac{h}{\Delta}, W_I\alpha_s)$
$x'_3 = \frac{dT_s}{dx}$	$x_2, x_3, x_4, x_5(\frac{dT_s}{dt}, \frac{dT_s}{dx}, \frac{h}{\Delta}, W_I\alpha_s)$
$x'_4 = h$	$x_4 \quad (h)$
$x'_5 = W_I\alpha_s$	$x_5 \quad (W_I\alpha_s)$
$x'_6 = T_{amb}$	$x_6 \quad (T_{amb})$

(7)

The change in emissivity is independent of the values of any of the variables. Hence, it is dependent only on itself. The second component, x_2, is the temporal derivative of the surface temperature. Its value at t_{n+1} will be affected by all of the parameters at t_n except emissivity and the ambient temperature. Physically, the temporal derivative is independent of the ambient temperature and the emissivity of the surface; however, it is dependent on (1) its previous value, (2) the spatial derivative of the temperature in the material, (3) the convection coefficient (the surface patches propensity to convect into the air), (4) incident solar irradiation and surface absorptivity. The spatial derivative, x_3, has the same dependencies that x_2 has. The remaining variables, x_4, x_5, and x_6 depend, physically, only on their own previous values.

The variable inter-dependencies determine the thermophysical transformation. Thus the transformation of the variables of equation 5 can be represented by a subgroup of the GL group of the form

$$M = \left\{ \begin{array}{cccccc} m_{11} & 0 & 0 & 0 & 0 & 0 \\ 0 & m_{22} & m_{23} & m_{24} & m_{25} & 0 \\ 0 & m_{32} & m_{33} & m_{34} & m_{35} & 0 \\ 0 & 0 & 0 & m_{44} & 0 & 0 \\ 0 & 0 & 0 & 0 & m_{55} & 0 \\ 0 & 0 & 0 & 0 & 0 & m_{66} \end{array} \right\}. \quad (8)$$

Consider four points to compose X. Further explanation of the thermophysical behavior of these points is included in the discussion section. Each of the four points has seven components. Thus, the transformation induced on the coefficients, a_i, gives 28 constraining equations. Since there are 12 parameters of the transformation, every additional constraining equation that is added to a set of 12 constraining equations gives rise to an invariant relationship. Thus, for a configuration of four points in the thermophysical space and a transformation consisting of 12 parameters, there are 28-12=16 invariant functions; however, a subset of these relations are physically trivial invariant relationships.

Given X, consisting of four copies of the equation 5, the elimination technique described in section 2 was applied to the algebraic configuration. This results in the following non-trivial invariants:

$$I1 = \frac{\begin{vmatrix} a_{2,1} & a_{2,2} & a_{2,3} \\ a_{3,1} & a_{3,2} & a_{3,3} \\ a_{4,1} & a_{4,2} & a_{4,3} \end{vmatrix}}{\begin{vmatrix} a_{2,2} & a_{2,3} & a_{2,4} \\ a_{3,2} & a_{3,3} & a_{3,4} \\ a_{4,2} & a_{4,3} & a_{4,4} \end{vmatrix}} \quad (9)$$

$$I2 = \frac{\begin{vmatrix} a_{2,1} & a_{2,2} & a_{2,3} \\ a_{3,1} & a_{3,2} & a_{3,3} \\ a_{5,1} & a_{5,2} & a_{5,3} \end{vmatrix}}{\begin{vmatrix} a_{2,2} & a_{2,3} & a_{2,4} \\ a_{3,2} & a_{3,3} & a_{3,4} \\ a_{5,2} & a_{5,3} & a_{5,4} \end{vmatrix}} \quad (10)$$

where $a_{i,k}$ is the ith component of the kth point.

Employing TAI's for Object Recognition

The feature computation scheme formulated above is suitable for use in an object recognition system that employs a hypothesize-and-verify strategy. The scheme would consist of the following steps:

1. extract geometric features, e.g., lines and conics.

Figure 3: The truck 2 vehicle used in the recognition tests. The object centered coordinate axis is superimposed on the image. The numbered points correspond to the point sets given in table 1. These points are selected such that there are a variety of different materials and/or surface normals within the set.

2. for image region, r, hypothesize object class, k, and pose using, for example, geometric invariants as proposed by Forsyth, et al (Forsyth *et al.* 1991),
3. use the model of object k and project visible points labeled $i = 1, 2, \ldots$ onto image region r using scaled orthographic projection,
4. for point labeled i in the image region, assign thermophysical properties of point labeled i in the model of object k,
5. use the gray levels at each point and the assigned thermophysical properties, to compute the measurement vectors, $a_{i,k}$, and hence compute the feature I_1 or I_2, and finally,
6. compare feature $f^k(r)$ with model prototype F_k to verify the hypothesis.

Experimental Results

Object Recognition using TAIs

The method of computing thermophysical algebraic invariants discussed above was applied to real LWIR imagery acquired at different times of the day. Five types of vehicles were imaged: a van, two types of trucks, a military tank, and a car (figures 1). Several points were selected (as indicated in the figures) on the surfaces of different materials and/or orientation. The measurement vector given by eqn (6) was computed for each point, for each image/scene.

The features described in section 4 require four points. Given a model of an object that has some Q number of points defined, there is the possibility of forming q different features.

$$q = \binom{Q}{4}\binom{4}{3} \tag{11}$$

Point Set	Mean	STD	Quality
{2 3,4,5}	1.000	0.0026	0.0026
{2,3,4,9}	1.000	0.0061	0.0061
{2,3,4,8}	4.757	0.0352	0.0074
{2,3,4,7}	4.746	0.0280	0.0059
{8,9,3,10}	0.983	0.1951	0.1984
{8,9,10,6}	0.7361	0.1445	0.1963
{8,9,10,2}	0.0795	0.0146	0.1836
{5,6,7,8}	1.057	0.0443	0.0419

Table 1: Intra-class variation over time of the feature, I1, defined by equation 9 applied with the point sets given in column 1 for truck type 2. The features were evaluated at five time instances over two consecutive days, Day 1 - 11am, 12pm, 1pm, Day 2 - 9am, 10am. Column 2 is the mean of the feature over the five time instances and column 3 shows the feature stability in terms of standard deviation. Column 4 shows the quality factor defined as std divided by the mean. The points correspond to the points labeled in figure 3.

The first criterion for finding a useful feature is stable intra-class behavior. Nearly all of the point choices had low variation in intra-class tests; tests where the same object is viewed under different scene conditions. For example, a test was performed on the truck in figure 3. Table 1 shows the results for ten different features evaluated from truck 1. Although the performance of only ten features are shown, the performance is representative of the feature stability over all of the distinct point choices.

As mentioned in section 4, one must consider inter-class behavior as well as intra-class behavior for an object recognition application of the features. To investigate this we adopted the following procedure. Given an image of a vehicle, (1) assume the pose of the vehicle is known, then (2) use the front and rear wheels to establish an object centered reference frame. The center of the rear wheel is used as the origin, and center of the front wheel is used to specify the direction and scaling of the axes. The coordinates of the selected points are expressed in terms of this 2D object-centered frame. For example, when a van vehicle is hypothesized for an image actually obtained of a car or some unknown vehicle, the material properties of the van are used, but image measurements are obtained from the image of the car at locations given by transforming the coordinates of the van points (in the van-centered coordinate frame) to the image frame computed for the unknown vehicle.

Table 2 shows inter-class and intra-class variation when truck 1 is hypothesized. The data are gathered and images obtained at nine times during the daylight hours over a period of two days. The results show good inter-class separation and reasonable intra-class stability. Note that in the cases of wrong hypotheses, the feature values tend to be either indetermined or

Hypothesis: Data From:	Truck 1 Van	Truck 1 Car	Truck 1 Truck 2	Truck 1 Tank
11 am	4.62	1.00	-0.693	0.882
12 pm	1.00	1.00	15.74	-1.00
1 pm	1.00	NaN	1.00	2.846
2 pm	1.00	1.00	2.20	-1.00
3 pm	7.50	-Inf	1.00	1.00
4 pm	1.00	19.0	13.67	1.00
5 pm	2.95	51.0	1.71	4.20
9 am	1.00	1.20	3.00	-1.00
10 am	4.00	1.10	6.33	2.20

Table 2: Mistaken hypothesis feature values shows inter-class variation for feature A-1, consisting of point set $\{1, 2, 3, 7\}$. The model for truck one is hypothesized. The feature value is formed using the model of truck 1 and the data from the respective other vehicles. When this feature is applied to the correctly hypothesized data of truck 1 it has a mean value of 0.0159 and a standard deviation of 0.0022. Thus feature, A-1, shows good separability when compared to the incorrect hypothesis feature value listed in the table.

unitary. This is a result of using the object centered coordinate system where the mistaken points fall on similar material types when dissimilar material types were expected.

Discussion

The approach described above is promising in that it makes available features that are (1) invariant to scene conditions, (2) able to separate different classes of objects, and (3) based on physics based models of the many phenomena that affect LWIR image generation.

Two aspects of the approach require further explanation. First, the factor, a_7, from equation 6 was used in this formulation to expand the number of degrees of freedom in the algebraic expression of the balance of energy equation. Although it is not interpreted directly as a physical parameter, it allows for the creation of a proper form and has no effect on the physical model. The motivation for including a_7 is that it is desirable to label as unknown variables both the convection parameter, h, and the ambient temperature, T_{amb}. These factors appear together in one of the terms of the balance of energy equation. With both factors labeled as variables, the coefficient can then only be unity, $a_7 = 1$. The resulting labeling produces a form that loses important degrees of freedom in the formation of invariant relations. Including $a_7 = \Delta$, implies that there is a scale of the temperature measurement, T_s, in the term $a_4 = T_s\Delta$. The transformation, M, of the variables induces a transformation on the coefficients. For the coefficient in question the induced transformation can be written $a_4' = m_{44}a_4$. Since the features found in section 4 are invariant to transformations of the form 8 it is invariant to an additional scale as in the action of the Δ parameter. Thus the term does not affect the relation of the physical model to the invariant feature. In addition, because a_7 does not appear in the feature there is no need to physically interpret its value.

Next, we consider the thermophysical justification of the transformation defined in the equation

$$X' = MX, \tag{12}$$

where X is a 6×4 collection of thermophysical variable vectors as defined in 6 at a time instance, t_n, and X' is the collection at a later time/scene t_{n+1}. The transformation M is defined in (8). The physical implication of such a transformation is that the four points in the thermophysical configuration are acted upon in the "same manner" by the environment. This is a reasonable assumption for the classes of objects under consideration. Note that if different types of surfaces are chosen (or points on surfaces with different surface orientations) the measurement vectors will, in general, be linearly independent. In other words, it is easy to select points such that the collection of measurement vectors span R^6. Then the existence of a non-singular transformation of the form of, M, for any pair of scenes and for a subset of four such points is guaranteed. Physically, the effect of the convection coefficient, solar irradiation and ambient temperature is consistent for the set of surface points. This fact taken with the fact that the emissivity can be considered relatively constant over time implies that it is reasonable to assume that equation (12) has physical justification.

References

Forsyth, D.; Mundy, J.; Zisserman, A.; Coelho, C.; Heller, A.; and Rothwell, C. 1991. Invariant descriptors for 3d object recognition and pose. *IEEE Transactions on PAMI* 13(12).

Incropera, F., and DeWitt, D. 1981. *Fundamentals of Heat Transfer*. New York, NY: John Wiley and Sons.

Kapur, D., and Lakshman, Y. 1992. Elimination methods: an introduction. In Donald, K., and Mundy., eds., *Symbolic and Numerical Computation for Artificial Intelligence*. Academic Press.

Kapur, D.; Lakshman, Y.; and Saxena, T. 1995. Computing invariants using elimination methods. In *Proc of IEEE International Symposium on Computer Vision*, 97–102. Coral Gables, Florida: IEEE.

Mundy, J., and Zisserman, A. 1992. *Geometric Invariance in Computer Vision*. MIT Press.

Approximate World Models: Incorporating Qualitative and Linguistic Information into Vision Systems

Claudio S. Pinhanez and **Aaron F. Bobick**
Perceptual Computing Group - MIT Media Laboratory
20 Ames St. - Cambridge, MA 02139
pinhanez — bobick@media.mit.edu

Abstract

Approximate world models are coarse descriptions of the elements of a scene, and are intended to be used in the selection and control of vision routines in a vision system. In this paper we present a control architecture in which the approximate models represent the complex relationships among the objects in the world, allowing the vision routines to be situation or context specific. Moreover, because of their reduced accuracy requirements, approximate world models can employ qualitative information such as those provided by linguistic descriptions of the scene. The concept is demonstrated in the development of automatic cameras for a TV studio - *SmartCams*. Results are shown where SmartCams use vision processing of real imagery and information written in the script of a TV show to achieve TV-quality framing.

Introduction

It has been argued — e.g. in (Strat & Fischler 1991) — that in any given situation most visual tasks can be performed by a relatively simple visual routine. For example: finding the ground reduces to finding a large (body-relative) horizontal plane if the observer is vertical and there are no other large horizontal planes. The difficulty in general, of course, is how to know the current state of the world without having to do all the detailed visual tasks first. The numerous possibilities for the fundamental relationships between objects in the scene is as much responsible for the complexity of vision as is the difficulty of the visual routines themselves.

The goal of this paper is to argue that vision systems should separate these two sources of complexity by using coarse models of the objects in the scene called *approximate world models*. This proposal is based on the observation that the real world does not need to be fully and accurately understood to detect many situations where a specific vision method is likely to succeed or fail. For instance, full and precise 3D reconstruction of the human body is not necessary to detect occlusion if the objective of the system is just to recognize faces of people walking through a gate.

A main feature of approximate world models is that their imprecision facilitates the use of incomplete and inaccurate sources of information such as linguistic descriptions of the elements and actions in a scene. In fact, we show in this paper that linguistic information can play a pivotal role in providing the contextual information needed to simplify the vision tasks.

We are employing approximate world models in the development of *SmartCams*, automatic TV cameras able to frame subjects and objects in a studio according to the verbal requests from the TV director. Our SmartCams are tested in the domain of a cooking show. The script of the show is available to SmartCams (in a particular format), and the cameras are shown to be able to produce TV-quality framing of subjects and objects.

Approximate World Models

Approximate world models are coarse descriptions of the main elements of a scene to be used in the selection and control of vision routines. These models are to be incorporated into vision-based systems built from a collection of different, simple, task-specific vision routines whose application is controlled according to the conditions described by the approximate world models.

This proposal comes from the observation that a common reason for the failure of vision routines — especially, view-based methods — is related to the complex geometric relationships among objects in the world. For example, often template-based tracking routines produce wrong results due to partial occlusion. In such situations, a crude 3-D reconstruction of the main objects in the scene can determine if the tracked object is in a configuration where occlusion is probable.

The advantages of using approximate models are at least three-fold. First, coarse reconstruction of the 3-D is arguably within the grasp of current computer vision capabilities. Second, as shown in this paper, control of task-specific vision routines can be based on inaccurate and incomplete information. And third, as we will demonstrate, reducing the accuracy requirements enables the use of qualitative information which might be available to the vision system.

Coarse and/or hierarchical descriptions have been used before in computer vision (Bobick & Bolles 1992; Marr & Nishihara 1978). Particularly, Bobick and Bolles employed a multi-level representational system where different queries were answered by different representations of the same object. Part of the novelty of our work is related to the use of the models in the dynamic selection of appropriate vision methods according to the world situation. And compared to other architectures for context-based vision systems, like Strat and Fischler's *Condor* system, (Strat & Fischler 1991), approximate world models provide a much more clear distinction between the vision component and the 3-D world component.

It is interesting to situate our scheme in the ongoing debate about reconstructionist vs. purposive vision discussed in (Tarr & Black 1994) and in the replies in the same issue. Our proposal falls between the strictly reconstructionist and purely purposive strategies. We are arguing that reconstruction should exist at the approximate level to guide purposive vision routines: by building an approximate model of the scene vision systems can use task-specific, purposive vision routines which work reliably in some but not all situations.

Using Approximate World Models in Vision Systems

To formalize the control exercised by the approximate world models in a vision system, we define *applicability conditions* for each vision routine: the set of assumptions, that, if true in the current situation, warrants faith in the correctness of the results of that routine.

The idea is to have each vision routine encapsulated in an *applicability rule*, which describes pre-conditions (`IF` portion of the rule), application constraints (`THEN` portion), and post-conditions (`TEST IF`), in terms of general properties about the targeted object, other objects in the scene, the camera's point of view, and the result of the vision routine.

As an example, fig. 1 depicts the applicability rule of a vision routine, "`extract-narrowest-movingblob`", and how the rule is applied in a given situation. The routine "`extract-narrowest-moving-blob`" is designed to detect moving regions in a sequence of two consecutive frames using simple frame differencing, and then to divide the result into two areas, of which the narrowest is returned.

To use such a rule, the vision system consults the approximate model of `TARGET` (in the example case, the head of a person) to obtain an estimation of its projection into the image plane of the camera, and also to confirm if `TARGET` is moving. Moreover, the system also looks for other moving objects close to `TARGET`, constructing an *approximate view model* of the camera's view.

If the conditions are satisfied by the approximate view model, the routine is applied on the imagery ac-

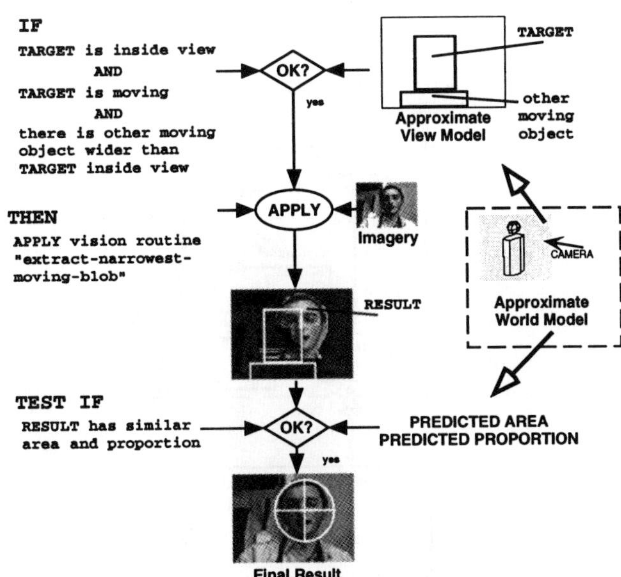

Figure 1: Example of an applicability rule for a vision routine and how the information from the approximate world model is used.

cording to the instructions in the `THEN` portion of the applicability rule which may also include information about routine parameters. The `RESULT` is then checked in the `TEST IF` portion of the rule, reducing the possibility that an incomplete specification of pre-conditions generates incorrect results. For instance, in the case of "`extract-narrowest-moving-blob`", often the lack of actual object movement makes the routine return tiny, incorrectly positioned regions which are filtered out by the post-conditions.

It is important to differentiate the concept of applicability rules from rule-based or expert-system approaches to computer vision (Draper *et al.* 1987; Tsotsos 1985). Although we use the same keywords (`IF`, `THEN`), the implied control structure has no resemblance to a traditional rule-based system: there is no inference or chaining of results. More examples of applicability rules can be found in (Bobick & Pinhanez 1995).

A Working Example: SmartCams

Our approach of using approximate world models is being developed in a system we are constructing for the control of TV cameras. The ultimate objective is to develop a camera for TV that can operate without the cameraman, changing its attitude, zoom, and position to provide specific images upon human request. We call these robot-like cameras *SmartCams*. A "cooking show" is the first domain in which we are experimenting with our SmartCams.

The basic architecture of a SmartCam is shown in fig. 2. Considering the requirements of this application,

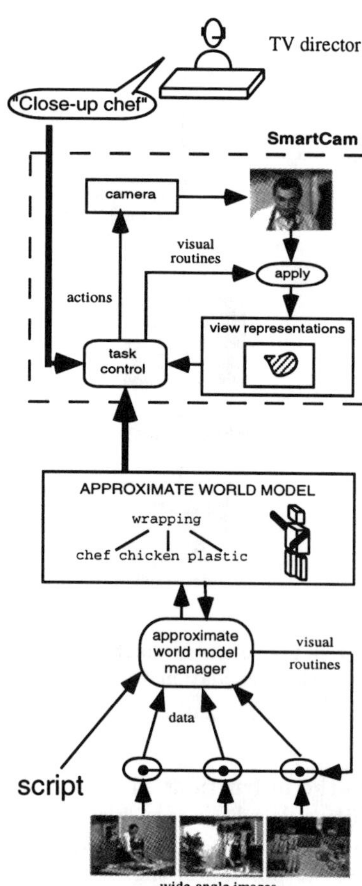

Figure 2: The architecture of a SmartCam. The bottom part of the figure shows the structure of the modules responsible for maintaining the approximate world models.

the approximate world model represents the subjects and objects in the scene as 3-D blocks, cylinders, and ellipsoids, and uses symbolic frame-based representations (slots and keywords). The symbolic description of an object includes information about to which class of objects the object belongs, its potential use, and its roles in the current actions.

The 3-D representations are positioned in a 3-D virtual space corresponding to the TV studio. The cameras' calibration parameters area also approximately known. The precision can be quite low, and in our system the position of an object might be off by an amount comparable to its size.

For example, if there is a bowl present in the studio, its approximate world model is composed by a 3-D geometric model of the bowl and by a frame-like symbolic description. The 3-D geometric model approximates the shape of the bowl, and is positioned in the virtual space according to the available information. The objects in the approximate world model belong to different categories. For example, a bowl is a member of the "**handleable objects**" category. As so, its frame

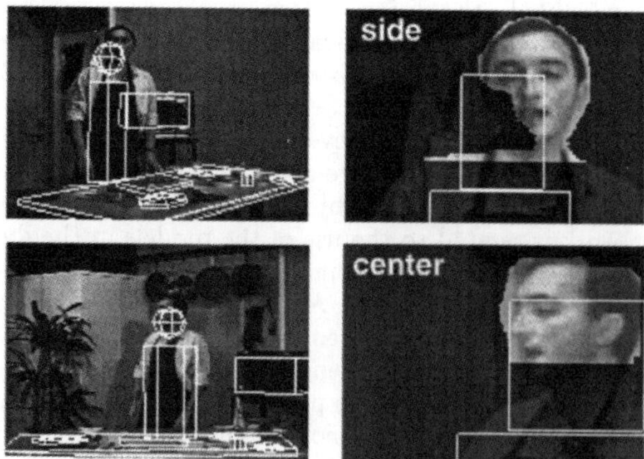

Figure 3: Example of response to the call "**close-up chef**" by two different cameras, **side** and **center**. The left images show the projection of the approximate models on the wide-angle images. The right images display the result of vision routines as highlighted regions, compared to the predicted position according to the approximate model of the head and the trunk, shown as rectangles.

includes slots which describe whether the bowl is being handled by a human, and, if so, there is a slot which explicitly points to him/her.

The system which produced the results shown in this paper does not use real moving cameras, but simulates them using a moving window on wide-angle images of the set. Several performances of a 5-minute scene as viewed by three wide-angle cameras were recorded and digitized. The SmartCam output image is generated by extracting a rectangular window of some size from the wide-angle images.

In fig. 3 we can see a typical result in the SmartCam domain where the inaccuracy of the approximate world models does not affect the final results obtained by the vision routines. Two SmartCams, **side** and **center**, were tasked to provide a close-up of the chef. Although the geometric model corresponding to the chef is quite misaligned, as can be seen by its projection into the wide-angle images of the scene (left side), both SmartCams, using routines similar to "**extract-narrowest-moving-blob**", produce correct results (the highlighted areas on the right of fig.3). Other examples of applicability rules and results can be found in (Bobick & Pinhanez 1995).

Building and Maintaining Approximate World Models

Having shown how the information contained in approximate world models can be exploited by a vision system performing tasks in a dynamic environment, a fundamental issue remains: how does one construct an initial model and then maintain such a model as time progresses and the scene changes.

Contextual and semantic information is rarely employed in model construction because of its inability to provide accurate geometric data. If the geometric accuracy requirements are relaxed, as it is in the case of approximate world models, semantic information can be used to predict possible positions and attitudes of objects.

Furthermore, we view one of the roles of contextual knowledge to be that of providing the basic relationships between objects in a given configuration of the world. For example, while pounding meat the chef remains behind the table, positioned near the cutting board, and the meat mallet is manipulated by the hands. As long as such a context remains in force, these relationships hold, and the job of maintaining the approximate world model reduces to, predominantly, a problem of tracking incremental changes within a known situation.

Occasionally, though, there are major changes in the structure of the world which require a substantial update in the structure of the approximate models. For example, a new activity may have begun, altering most expectations, including, for example, the possible location of objects, which objects are possibly moving, and which objects are likely to be co-located making visual separation unlikely (and, more interestingly, unnecessary). In our view, the intervals between *major contextual changes correspond to the fundamental actions* performed by the subjects in the scene; the contextual shifts themselves reflect the boundaries between actions.

Thus, maintaining approximate world models requires two different methods of updating: one related to the tracking of incremental changes within a fixed context, and the other responsible for performing the substantial changes in the context required at the boundaries between different actions. Of course, it is also necessary to have methods to obtain the initial approximate model. The three required mechanisms are briefly discussed below.

Initializing Approximate World Models

Whenever a vision system is designed using approximate models, it is necessary to face the issue of how the models are initialized when the system is turned on. Current computer vision methods can be employed in the initialization process, if the system is allowed a reasonable amount of time to employ powerful vision algorithms without contextual information.

In our current version of the SmartCams the 3-D models of the subjects and objects are determined and positioned manually in the first frame of the scene. All changes to the model after the first frame are accomplished automatically using vision and processing the linguistic information as described later in this paper.

Tracking Incremental Changes

As proposed, while a particular action is taking place it is presumed that the basic relationships among the subjects and objects do not change. During such periods most of the updating of the approximate models can be accomplished by methods able to detect incremental changes, such as visual tracking algorithms. Though simple, those small updates are vital to maintain the approximate model in an useful state, since approximate position information is normally an essential part of the applicability conditions of the task-specific vision routines.

In the SmartCam domain, the update of the incremental changes in the approximate world model, and especially in its 3-D representations, is accomplished by vision tracking routines able to detect movements of the main components of the scene, as shown in the bottom part of the diagram in fig. 2. The two-dimensional motions of an object detected by each of the wide-angle cameras are integrated to determine the movement of the object in the 3-D world. More details can be found in (Bobick & Pinhanez 1995).

Note that the use of an approximate world model may require additional sensing and computation which might not be performed to directly address current perceptual tasks: e.g. the position of the body of the chef is maintained even though the current task may only involve framing the hands. We believe that this additional cost is compensated by the increase in the competence of the vision routines.

Actions and Structural Changes

Tracking algorithms are likely to fail whenever there is a drastic change in the structure of the scene, as, for example when a subject leaves the scene. If this situation is recognized, the tracking mechanism of that subject should be turned off avoiding false alarms.

It is not the objective of this paper to argue about the different possible meanings of the term *action*. Here, actions refer to major segments of time which people usually describe by single action verbs as discussed by (Newtson, Engquist, & Bois 1977; Thibadeau 1986; Kalita 1991).

A change in the action normally alters substantially the relationships among subjects and objects. For example, we have a situation in the cooking show domain where the chef first talks to the camera, and then he picks up a bowl and starts mixing ingredients. While the action "talking" is happening, there is no need for the system to maintain explicit 3-D models for the arms and the hands of the chef: the important elements involved are the position and direction of the head and body.

When the chef starts mixing ingredients, it is essential that the approximate world model includes his hands, the mixing bowl, and the ingredients. Fortunately, "mixing" also sets up clear expectations about the positions of the hands in relation to the trunk of the chef, to the mixing bowl, to the ingredients' containers, and to table where they are initially on. As this example illustrates, known contextual changes actually improve the robustness of the system since with each such event the system becomes "grounded": there is evidence independent of, and often more reliable than, the visual tracking data about the state of the scene.

Linguistic Sources of Action Information

Without constraints from the domain, determining the actions which might occur can be difficult. However, in many situations the set of actions is severely restricted by the environment or by the task, as, for example, in the case of recognizing vehicle maneuvers in a gas-station as described in (Nagel 1994 5).

The SmartCam domain exemplifies another type of situation, one in which there is available a linguistic description of the sequence of actions to occur. In a TV studio, the set of occurring actions — and, even, the order of the actions — is determined by the script of the show. We find the idea of having vision systems capable of incorporating linguistic descriptions of actions very attractive: linguistic descriptions of actions are the most natural to be generated by human beings. In particular, this form of is suitable in semi-automated vision-based systems.

The use of linguistic descriptions requires their automatic translation into the system's internal representational of actions. This is mostly a Natural Language Processing issue, although the feasibility is certainly dependent on the final representation used by the vision system. In the SmartCam domain the final objective is to employ TV scripts in the format they are normally written (see figure 4).

Cooking-show scenario with a table on which there are bowls, ingredients, and different kitchen utensils. A microwave oven is in the back. Cam1 is a centered camera, cam2 is a left-sided camera, cam3 is a camera mounted in the ceiling. Chef is behind the table, facing cam1.

...

Chef turns back to cam1 and mixes bread-crumbs, parsley, paprika, and basil in a bowl.
"Stir together 3 tablespoons of fine dry bread crumbs, 2 teaspoons snipped parsley, 1/4 teaspoon paprika, and 1/8 teaspoon dried basil, crushed. Set aside."

Chef wraps chicken with a plastic bag.
"Place one piece of chicken, boned side up, between two pieces of clear plastic wrap."

Chef puts the chicken on the chopping-board and shows how to pound the chicken.
"Working from the center to the edges, pound lightly with a meat mallet, forming a rectangle with this thickness. Be gentle, meat become as soft as you treat it."

Chef pounds the chicken with a meat-mallet.

...

Figure 4: The script of a TV cooking show.

Representing Actions

Many formalisms have been developed to represent action, some targeting linguistic concerns (Schank 1975), computer graphics synthesis (Kalita 1991), or computer vision recognition (Siskind 1994 5). Currently we employ a simple representation based on Schank's *conceptualizations* as described in (Schank 1975). In spite of its weaknesses — see (Wilks 1975) — Schank's representation scheme is interesting for us because the reduced number of primitive actions helps the design of both the translation and the inference procedures.

Our representation for actions uses *action frames*, a frame-based representation where each action is represented by a frame whose header is one of Schank's primitive actions — `PROPEL`, `MOVE`, `INGEST`, `GRASP`, `EXPEL`, `PTRANS`, `ATRANS`, `SPEAK`, `ATTEND`, `MTRANS`, `MBUILD` — plus the attribute indexes `HAVE` and `CHANGE`, and an undetermined action `DO`.

Figure 5 contains two examples of action frames. The figure contains the representation for two actions of the script shown in fig. 4, `''chef wraps chicken with a plastic bag''` and `''chef pounds the chicken with a meat-mallet''`. Each action frame begins with a primitive action and contains different slots which supply the essential elements of the action. Undetermined symbols begin with a question mark (?); those symbols are defined only by the relationships they have with other objects. The `actor` slot determines the performer of the action while the `object` slot contains the object of an action or the owner of an attribute. The action frames resulting from an action are specified in the `result` slot, and action frames which are part of the definition of another action frame are contained in `instrument` slots.

In the first example, "wrapping" is translated as some action (unspecified by `DO`) whose result is to make chicken be both contained in and in physical contact with a plastic bag. In the second example, "pounding" is represented as an action where the chef propels a meat mallet from a place which is not in contact with the chicken to a place which is in contact, and whose result is an increase in the flatness of the chicken.

The current version of our SmartCams translates a simplified version of the TV script of fig. 4 into the action frames of fig. 5 using a domain-specific, very simple parser. Building a translator able to handle more generic scripts seems to be clearly a NLP problem, and, as such, it is not a fundamental point in our research.

Part of our current research is focused on designing a better representation for actions than the action frames

```
;; "chef wraps chicken with a plastic bag"
(do
 (actor chef)
 (result
  (change (object chicken)
   (to (and
        (contained plastic-bag)
        (physical-contact plastic-bag))))))

;; "chef pounds the chicken with a meat-mallet"
(propel
 (actor chef)
 (object meat-mallet)
 (from (location ?not-in-contact))
 (to (location ?-in-contact))
 (result
  (change
   (object chicken)
   (from (flatness ?X))
   (to (flatness (greater ?X)))))
 (instrument
  (have (object ?not-in-contact)
   (attribute
        (negation (physical-contact chicken)))))
 (instrument
  (have (object ?in-contact)
   (attribute (physical-contact chicken))))
 (instrument
  (have (object chicken)
   (attribute
        (physical-contact chopping-board)))))
```

Figure 5: Action frames corresponding to two actions from the script shown in fig. 4.

described in this paper. We are still debating the convenience of using Schank's primitives to describe every action. Also, action frames need to be augmented by incorporating at least visual elements, as in (Kalita 1991), and time references, possibly using Allen's interval algebra, (Allen 1984).

Using Action Frames Obtained From a Script

From the examples shown above, it is clear that linguistic descriptions of actions obtained from scripts do not normally include detailed information about the position, attitude, and movement of the persons and objects in the scene. Linguistic accounts of actions normally describe only the essential changes in the scene, but not the implications of those changes.

Therefore, to use information from scripts it is necessary to have an inference mechanism capable of extracting the needed details from the action frames. In particular, to use the action frames generated from the TV script in the SmartCam domain, it was necessary to implement a simple inference system. It is important to make clear that our inference system is extremely simple and designed only to meet the demands of our particular domain. The system was designed to infer position and movement information about human beings' hands, and physical contact and proximity among objects.

The inference system is based on Rieger's inference system for Schank's conceptualizations, (Rieger III 1975). The inferred action frames are sub-actions, or `instrument` actions of the actions from which they are produced. To guarantee termination in a fast time, the inference rules are applied in a pre-determined sequence, in a 1-pass algorithm.

As a typical case, the system uses as its input the action frame corresponding to the sentence `''chef wraps chicken with a plastic bag''` (as shown in fig. 5) and deduces that the chef's hands are close to the chicken. The appendix depicts a more complex example where from the action of pounding the system obtains the fact that the hands are close to the chopping board. From the `PROPEL` action frame shown in fig. 5, the inference system deduces some contact relations between some objects, which imply physical proximity.

The SmartCam's inference system is certainly very simple and works only for some scripts. However, the ability of approximate models to handle inaccurate information helps the system to avoid becoming useless in the case of wrong inferences. For instance, in the "pounding" example, only one of the hands is in fact close to the chopping board: the hand which is grasping the meat mallet is about 1 foot from the board. But, as we have seen above, such errors in positioning are admissible in the approximate world model framework.

Determining the Onset of Actions

In the examples above, the information from the script was represented and augmented by simple inference procedures. However, to use script information it is necessary to "align" the action frames with the ongoing action, that is, the vision-based system need to recognize which action is happening in any given moment in time.

For the work presented here we have relied on manual alignment of the action frames to the events in the scene. All the results shown in this paper use a *timed script*, an extension of the script of fig. 4 which includes information about when each of the action is happening. This is simplified by the fact that the we are using the simulated version of the SmartCams where the visual data is pre-recorded, enabling manual annotation.

The problem of visual recognition of actions is also a current object of our research. The alignment problem mentioned above can be viewed as a sub-problem of the general action recognition problem where the order of the actions is known in advance.

SmartCams in Action

The current version of our SmartCams handles three types of framing (close-ups, medium close shots, medium shots) for a scenario consisting of the chef and about ten objects. All the results obtained so far employ only very simple vision routines similar to "`extract-narrowest-moving-blob`", based on movement detection by frame differencing.

Figure 6 shows typical framing results obtained by the system. The leftmost column of fig. 6 displays some frames generated in response to the call "`close-up chef`". The center column of fig. 6 contains another sequence of frames, showing the images provided by the SmartCam tasked to provide "`close-up hands`".

The rightmost column of fig. 6 is the response to a call for a "`close-up hands`". In this situation, the action `''chef pounds the chicken with a meat-mallet''` is happening. As shown above, this action determines that the hands must be close to the chopping board. This information is used by the system to initialize expectations for the hands in the beginning of the action (both in terms of position and movement), enabling the tracking system to detect the hands' position based solely in movement information.

One 80-second long video sequence is shown in the videotape distributed with these proceedings. It is also available on the WWW-web at:
`http://www-white.media.mit.edu/`
`vismod/demos/smartcams/smartcams.html`
The web-site also contains another performance of the same script where the chef is wearing glasses, and the actions are performed in a faster speed. The sequences were obtained by requesting the SmartCams to perform specific shots (displayed as subtitles); the cuts between cameras were selected manually. Both sequences clearly show that acceptable results can be obtained by our SmartCams in spite of the simplicity of the vision routines employed.

Figure 6: Responses to the calls "`close-up chef`", "`close-up hands`", and "`close-up hands`". Refer to background objects to verify the amount of correction needed to answer those calls appropriately. The grey areas to the right of the last frames of the first "`close-up hands`" sequence correspond to areas outside of the field of view of the wide-angle image sequence used by the simulator.

Conclusion

Approximate world models made the development of SmartCams feasible. Using the information about actions from the script of the show and the control information in the approximate world model, it has been possible to employ simple, fast — sometimes unreliable — vision routines to obtain the information required by TV framing.

One of the major accomplishments of our research is the end-to-end implementation of a system able to deal with multiple levels of information and processing. A SmartCam is able to use contextual information about the world from the text of a TV script, and to represent the information in a suitable format (approximate world models); updating the world model is accomplished through visual tracking, and the approximate world models are used in the selection and control of vision routines, whose outputs control the movement of a simulated robotic camera. The system processes real image sequences with a considerable degree of complexity, runs only one order of magnitude slower than real time, and produces an output of good quality in terms of TV standards.

Appendix

Inferences in the "Pounding" Example

The following is a manually commented printout of the action frames generated by the SmartCam's inference system, using as input the action frame corresponding to the sentence `''chef pounds the chicken with a meat-mallet''`. Only the relevant inferences are shown from about 80 action frames actually generated. The transitive rule used for the inference of proximity is sensitive to the size of the objects, avoiding its use if one of the objects is larger than the others.

```
0 : action frame obtained from the script
(propel
 (actor chef)
 (object meat-mallet)
 (to (location ?in-contact))
 (from (location ?not-in-contact))
 (result
  (change (object chicken)
   (from (flatness ?X))
   (to (flatness (greater ?X)))))
 (instrument
  (have
   (object ?in-contact)
   (attribute (phys-cont chicken))))
 (instrument
  (have
   (object ?not-in-contact)
   (attribute (negation (phys-cont chicken)))))
 (instrument
  (have
   (object chicken)
   (attribute (phys-cont chopping-board)))))
1 : propelling an object (0) requires grasping
(grasp
 (actor chef)
 (object meat-mallet)
 (to hands))
2 : grasping (1) requires physical-contact
(have
 (object hands)
 (attribute (phys-cont meat-mallet)))
3 : physical-contact (0) implies proximity
(have
 (object ?in-contact)
 (attribute (proximity chicken)))
4 : physical-contact (0) implies proximity
(have
 (object chicken)
 (attribute (proximity chopping-board)))
5 : physical-contact (2) implies proximity
(have
 (object hands)
 (attribute (proximity meat-mallet)))
6 : the end of propelling (0) implies proximity
(have
 (object meat-mallet)
 (attribute (proximity ?in-contact)))
7 : transitiveness of proximity, (3) and (6)
(have
 (object chicken)
 (attribute (proximity meat-mallet)))
8 : transitiveness of proximity, (4) and (7)
(have
 (object chopping-board)
 (attribute (proximity meat-mallet)))
9 : transitiveness of proximity, (5) and (8)
(have
 (object chopping-board)
 (attribute (proximity hands)))
```

References

Allen, J. F. 1984. Towards a general theory of action an time. *Artificial Intelligence* 23:123–154.

Bobick, A. F., and Bolles, R. C. 1992. The representation space paradigm of concurrent evolving object descriptions. *IEEE PAMI* 14(2):146–156.

Bobick, A., and Pinhanez, C. 1995. Using approximate models as source of contextual information for vision processing. In *Proc. of the ICCV'95 Workshop on Context-Based Vision*, 13–21.

Draper, B. A.; Collins, R. T.; Brolio, J.; Griffith, J.; Hanson, A. R.; and Riseman, E. M. 1987. Tools and experiments in the knowledge-directed interpretation of road scenes. In *Proc. of the DARPA Image Understanding Workshop*, 178–193.

Kalita, J. K. 1991. *Natural Language Control of Animation of Task Performance in a Physical Domain*. Ph.D. Dissertation, University of Pennsylvania, Philadelphia, Pennsylvania.

Marr, D., and Nishihara, H. K. 1978. Representation and recognition of the spatial organization of three-dimensional shapes. In *Proc. R. Soc. Lond. B*, volume 200, 269–294.

Nagel, H.-H. 1994–5. A vision of 'vision and language' comprises action: An example from road traffic. *Artificial Intelligence Review* 8:189–214.

Newtson, D.; Engquist, G.; and Bois, J. 1977. The objective basis of behavior units. *Journal of Personality and Social Psychology* 35(12):847–862.

Rieger III, C. J. 1975. Conceptual memory and inference. In *Conceptual Information Processing*. North-Holland. chapter 5, 157–288.

Schank, R. C. 1975. Conceptual dependency theory. In *Conceptual Information Processing*. North-Holland. chapter 3, 22–82.

Siskind, J. M. 1994–5. Grounding language in perception. *Artificial Intelligence Review* 8:371–391.

Strat, T. M., and Fischler, M. A. 1991. Context-based vision: Recognizing objects using information from both 2-d and 3-d imagery. *IEEE PAMI* 13(10):1050–1065.

Tarr, M. J., and Black, M. J. 1994. A computational and evolutionary perspective of the role of representation in vision. *CVGIP: Image Understanding* 60(1):65–73.

Thibadeau, R. 1986. Artificial perception of actions. *Cognitive Science* 10:117–149.

Tsotsos, J. K. 1985. Knowledge organization and its role in representation and interpretation of time-varying data: The ALVEN system. *Computational Intelligence* 1:16–32.

Wilks, W. 1975. A preferential, pattern-seeking semantics for natural language inference. *Artificial Intelligence* 6(1):53–74.

Integrating Visual Information Across Camera Movements with a Visual-Motor Calibration Map

Peter N. Prokopowicz
Department of Computer Science
University of Chicago
Chicago, IL 60637
peterp@cs.uchicago.edu

Paul R. Cooper
Department of Computer Science
Northwestern University
Evanston, IL 60201
cooper@ils.nwu.edu

Abstract

Facing the competing demands for wider field of view and higher spatial resolution, computer vision will evolve toward greater use of foveal sensors and frequent camera movements. Integration of visual information across movements becomes a fundamental problem. We show that integration is possible using a biologically-inspired representation we call the visual-motor calibration map. The map is a memory-based model of the relationship between camera movements and corresponding pixel locations before and after any movement. The map constitutes a self-calibration that can compensate for non-uniform sampling, lens distortion, mechanical misalignments, and arbitrary pixel reordering. Integration takes place entirely in a retinotopic frame, using a short-term, predictive visual memory.

Introduction

The competing demands for wider field of view and higher spatial resolution suggest that computer vision systems will inevitably progress towards the trade-off that evolution selected for animal vision systems: foveal (or spatially varying) sampling combined with frequent camera movements. Thus, the integration of visual information across camera movements is a fundamental problem for lifelike computer vision systems. Figure 1 visually evokes the nature of the task.

A variety of possible solutions have been proposed, by researchers from psychology and neurophysiology as well as computer vision. These range from proposals that suggest that integration occurs in "retinotopic" coordinates, through theories that propose that integration occurs in a body- or head-based frame of reference, to theories that suggest integration occurs at a symbolic level of abstraction. Although the problem has received a great deal of attention, no completely convincing model has been developed.

We suggest that visual integration can be achieved through a representation we call the visual-motor calibration map, and that moreover such a map can be developmentally acquired. In this paper, we describe what constitutes a visual-motor calibration map, and how it can be used to solve problems of visual integration, including change detection, perceptual stability across eye movements, and the recognition of forms from multiple foveal observations. In particular, a developmentally-acquired map is sufficient to replicate psychophysical results on a recognition task involving eye movements. We describe the developmental process for the map elsewhere (Prokopowicz 1994).

Figure 1: A series of overlapping views taken by a foveal, or spatially-varying, camera. Slight changes in viewpoint emphasize completely different details. Any visual understanding of the scene demands integration across fixations.

In brief, the visual-motor calibration map is a memory-based "table" representation of the relationship between camera movements and corresponding pixel positions before and after a camera movement. Such a representation is neurobiologically plausible and scales-up to a realistically sized visual integration task. The map provides, in effect, a motor coordinate basis for visual information that allows visual tasks of extent larger than a single view to be computed. The map constitutes an adaptive visual-motor calibration that can compensate for effects including spatially-varying foveal sampling, random pixel reordering, and arbitrary (non-linear) lens distortions, all of which would be extraordinarily difficult to model analytically.

Visual Integration and Memory-based Calibration

It has long been known that our vision is many times more acute in the center of view than outside it, and that, to see, we unconsciously move our eyes two or three times every second, accumulating the details around us (Yarbus 1967). In seeking the mechanisms by which our perception can nevertheless be stable, and relatively uniform, theorists early on appreciated that disrupting the normal relationship between an intended eye movement and the viewpoint that would follow throws off these mechanisms: the world seems jumpy (Stratton 1897). Other experiments showed that, over several weeks, this effect can wear off, sometimes completely, and later rebound when the disruption is removed. These experiments suggest that in normal seeing, we unconsciously account for the expected visual effects of eye movements, and that this is a learned or adaptive ability.

Frames of reference in theories of perceptual integration One theory of perceptual integration holds that the stability and uniformity of perception corresponds to a stable and uniform internal visual representation, formulated in a head or body-centered frame of reference (Feldman 1985). Each succeeding fixation can be viewed as "painting" a different part of a larger inner image, one whose parts persist in memory long enough, perhaps a few seconds, to accumulate a detailed picture of the scene. This representation is invariant with respect to each eye movement, except that the immediate input is directed, or shifted, into the picture according to where the eyes currently point. This stable mental picture, consisting of pixels or some other primitive visual features, constitutes the effective input for the rest of perception, which goes on as if there were no small eye movements at all.

Others suggest that eye movements are not accounted for at this early a stage of perception, but at a much higher level of abstraction, in terms of the geometric relation between concrete objects or components (Pollatsek, Rayner, & Collins 1984). When a nose is perceived, for example, a representation of it is tagged with its visual location, taking into account the current direction of gaze. When the mouth is found, the distance between them can be inferred from the remembered position tags, even though they were perceived from slightly different viewpoints.

Usually, this tagging is thought to go on automatically for each item as it is recognized. A recent and more radical proposition holds that visual features are not compulsively memorized and tagged at any level of abstraction simply on the chance that they might later be usefully integrated with other features (O'Regan & Levy-Schoen 1983). Instead, integration across eye movements occurs only for those features that are part of a working model under construction as part of some specific perceptual task. When some unknown particular of the model is needed to continue with the task at hand, eye movements will be made toward where the information is likely to be found.

Physiologists have something to say about these hypotheses. So far, no invariant visual representations have been found; to the contrary, the visual system responds almost entirely to the retinotopic position of features (van Essen *et al.* 1991). However, it has been observed that in many areas of the visual system, activity shifts itself during an eye movement, as if to predict what the next retinotopic representation will be (Duhamel, Colby, & Goldberg 1992). This predicted activity can persist even without being reinforced with an actual input (Sparks & Porter 1983). In other words, features are envisioned retinotopically in a type of very short term visual memory. Also, it has been shown that subjects can often notice when something moves slightly during a saccade, even when they haven't been looking directly at it. Together, these experiments suggest that there could be a widespread, pre-attentive visual memory for perceptual integration that uses the current retinotopic frame of reference. This is the type of architecture we propose here.

Table-based perceptual motor control Regardless of which frame of reference and level of abstraction underlies integration across eye movements, the process must have access to an accurate quantitative model of the eye/head or camera/mount geometry. Without this, it would be impossible to understand the true geometric relationship between features or objects observed from different viewpoints. Traditional computer vision systems, which, to date, typically have not exploited moving cameras, rely on analytically determined models that are calibrated with reference standards. These models are neither easy to develop nor calibrate, especially considering the trend toward active vision and the potential long-term move towards

Figure 2: Foveal images before and after a camera movement are shown in the left and center columns. Predicted image, generated with an acquired visual-motor calibration map, is at right.

non-uniform sampling. Recently, there has been growing interest in solving visual problems without requiring traditional calibration (Faugeras 1992). Our work takes the approach that the necessary perceptual- motor models can and should be developed by the system itself from natural experience, and tuned continuously as part of every day activity.

As the representational basis for visual-motor calibration information, we propose a memory-based or table-based model of the relationship between camera movements and corresponding pixel locations before and after a movement. This representation is similar in spirit to the Mel's hand-eye kinematic models (Mel 1990) and Atkeson's arm-joint dynamic models (Atkeson 1990). In table-based control, the relationship between two components of a system are directly stored as tuples for every usable configuration of the system. Mel's system used the relationship between the joint angles of an articulated arm, and the retinotopic location of the arm's end-effector as viewed by a fixed camera. Intermediate factors, such as the arm's component lengths, or the camera's focal length, are not explicitly represented. Since it concerns only the direct relationship between relevant variables, such a model doesn't change form when intermediate components are added or replaced; it isn't even necessary to appreciate what these factors are.

The Visual Motor Calibration Map: a new representation for perceptual integration across eye movements

At its lowest level of abstraction, the problem of perceptual integration across eye movements is straightforward to state: *for any particular eye movement, what is the geometric relationship between a point A viewed before the movement and a point B viewed after?* This is the basic metrical information needed to combine or integrate visual information, in any form, from successive viewpoints. This relationship can be

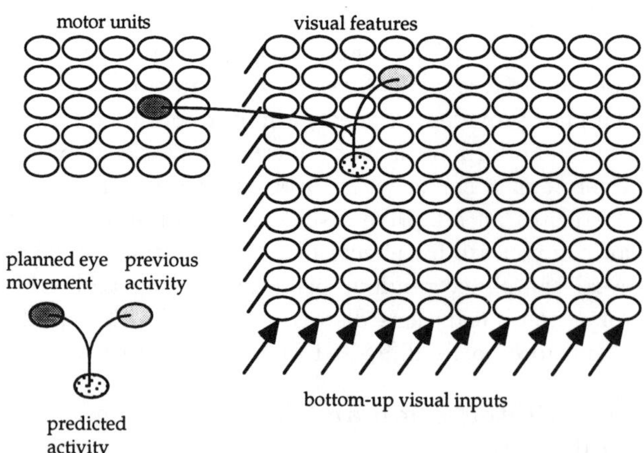

Figure 3: Connectionist architecture for predicting images across saccades. When a particular relative eye movement is about to be made, a motor unit produces a signal. A visual cell then predicts that its value will be that of the visual cell paired with this motor unit. After the movement, the cell receives bottom-up visual input from the sensor array.

described as tuple joining the two lines of sight defined by image points A and B, the visual angle V between the lines, and the eye-movement vector M. It is conceivable that this relation $R(A,B,M,V)$ could be determined and stored. The visual motor calibration map represents a similar relation that defines the image points A and B which correspond to the same line of sight($V = 0$), before and after a movement M.

To find the corresponding post-movement image location, given an eye movement and pre-movement location, the relation can be represented as a two-place look-up table. This has a natural connectionist equivalent (fig. 3) that is similar to other reference frame transformation networks (Feldman 1985). To find the third value of the relation given any other two, a slightly more complex network is needed (Feldman & Ballard 1982).

This relation, $R(A,B,M)$, can be used to predict an image following a particular camera movement M: for each pixel location A, copy that pixel's into location B if and only if $R(A,B,M)$ holds. In the same way, the map makes it possible to envision the post-movement location of any feature or object. We will also see that, if you know the pan and tilt angles of each movement M, the visual motor map completely calibrates the visual-motor system.

A look at the structure of IRV, our robotic visual motor system, will clarify the specific calibration problems that the map faces. The camera is a Panasonic GP-KS102, mounted on a computerized pan-tilt head, the Directed Perception model PTU. We restrict the head to 25 possible relative movements of roughly 2.5 to 5 degrees horizontally and/or vertically. The 400 by 400 digital image, spanning a visual angle of about 30 degrees, is resampled with an artificial foveal pattern (fig. 4) down to 80 by 80 non-uniform pixels, to produce the images like those in fig. 1. Finally, we randomly reorder the resampled pixels (fig. 7 top). An analytic visual model must account for the optical and sampling properties of the camera and artificial fovea, and the relation between the camera and its mount, which is complicated by the optical and mechanical axes not aligning. Arbitrary pixel ordering constitutes a completely general calibration problem, as well as a worst-case model of a developing organism in which the optic nerve and other fiber bundles scramble the topological ordering originally present on the retina.

As mentioned, a table-based model must fit in a reasonable space. We can restrict the visual-motor calibration relation so that for each camera movement, every image location before the movement corresponds to at most one image location after the movement; then, the map can be represented as a table with $N_{movements}N_{pixels}$ entries, 160,000 in IRV's case. A visual system scaled to roughly human levels would have about 1 million image locations, based on the size of the optic nerve, and 100 X 100 possible relative eye movements (Yarbus 1967), requiring a map with 10 billion entries: 10 billion synapses comprise only 0.001% of the brain's total.

Acquiring a visual motor calibration map

The utility of a table-based model as a representation for perceptual-motor coordination depends in large part on whether or not it is actually possible to determine the values that constitute the table. Obviously enough, filling such a table in by hand is intractable. To learn the visual motor calibration map, IRV makes camera movements, systematically or at random, and fills in the table with observed correspondences between pixels before and after a movement. For example, if a particular blue pixel appears at location A before movement M, and then at location B after the movement, the system would add an entry for $R(A, B, M)$.

However, the visual motor calibration map is not amenable to such simple learning by observation and memorization, simply because, for any two views before and after a camera movement, the question of which pixel corresponds to which is ill-posed. This is especially true when the pixels are arbitrarily ordered. Regardless of the criteria used to find corresponding points in the images, many spurious correspondences will occur, and true correspondences will often be missed. The color- matching criteria we used, a 5% difference threshold on the red, green, and blue pixel components, generally produced about 100 false correspondences for every true one, and yet missed true correspondences more than half the time.

Figure 4: The approximate size and location of the sampling regions in a 400x400 input, alternately colored black and white. Each region is actually square, with some overlap.

Despite these difficulties, a successful method for acquiring the visual-motor calibration map has been developed, described in detail elsewhere (Prokopowicz 1994). Very briefly, our solution to this noisy learning problem considers all apparent correspondences as evidence for a possible true correspondence, and accumulates evidence by repeating the movements enough times. A straightforward application of this idea explodes the size of the table by a factor of N_{pixels}, which is not feasible on IRV's or human hardware. A time-space tradeoff is possible that reduces the growth of the table to only a small constant factor while requiring that the movements be repeated a reasonable number of times.

Although it must cope with massive ambiguity and uncertainty, our algorithm is able to identify truly corresponding image locations after only several hundred examples of each movement, in a space only ten times larger than the map size. For IRV, who makes a movement every 4 seconds, the whole process typically takes two days. For a human, whose eyes move about 10 times more frequently, and using a parallel implementation of the algorithm, the process could be complete in roughly 80 days, even though a human can make about 400 times as many different eye movements.

Off-line calibration in motor coordinates

The visual motor map directly supports tasks that demand perceptual integration, by enabling image prediction and short-term envisioning of old features in the current retinotopic frame. This will be clarified and demonstrated shortly. But the map also makes it possible to interpret the scrambled, distorted geometry of a single retinotopic image, which may contain visible and remembered features. Measuring the geometric relationships in an image is crucial in computer vision whether the camera moves or not.

The interpretation process requires that the system know the mount's pan and tilt angles for each relative movement in the table. These angles can be used to define a motor-based coordinate system for measuring the relative visual angle between any two image locations. If the relation $R(A, B, M)$ holds for image locations A and B, and platform movement M, then the image locations describe lines of sight separated by an angle proportional to M. Using A and B to find the movement M for which they correspond, it is possible to uncover the true two-dimensional geometric relationship between any pair of points, provided that those points correspond to the same line of sight before and after some known camera movement.

We have taken another approach, using only a small subset of all the movements needed for complete coverage, and an off-line calibration process which yields another table that directly supports accurate visual-angle judgments using a motor metric. Instead of consulting the visual motor calibration map to find the motor angle between pairs of image locations, we use the map to assign to each scrambled, non-uniform pixel location a canonical coordinate, in a globally consistent way.

Each entry in the visual motor calibration map constrains the coordinates assigned to a pair of points such that they are separated by an angle equal to the movement angle for which they correspond (fig. 5). The local constraints in the map can not normally be satisfied simultaneously, but the total error can be minimized. We use a numerical simulation of a pseudo-physical process that pair-wise forces points into a configuration satisfying their constraints.

The result is a consistent assignment of a motor-based coordinate to each image location. As the table is filled in and refined with more examples, the constraints more accurately reflect the underlying imaging geometry (fig. 6). Fig. 7 (top) shows a foveal image before and after arbitrary pixel reordering. During map development, the off-line calibration process reorders and redistributes the pixels to their original relative positions. This assignment compensates for any optical distortions, sampling geometry, mechanical alignment (fig. 8), and, in the general case, any arbitrary reordering of the pixels.

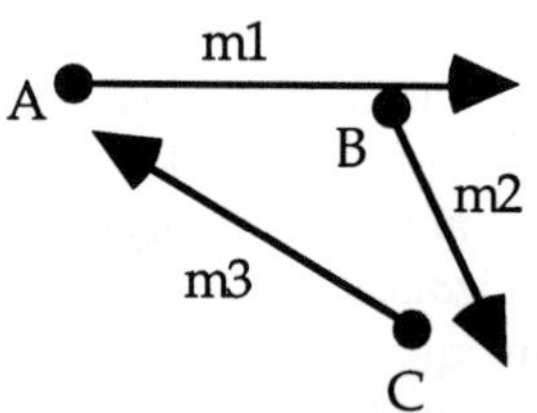

Figure 5: Three mutually corresponding pairs of pixels (A,B) (B,C) and (C,A) whose relative locations are not globally consistent with the movement vectors m1, m2, and m3, over which they have been found to correspond.

Using the visual motor calibration map for perceptual integration across eye movements

The rest of this paper shows how the visual motor calibration map and motor-calibrated image locations can be used for two specific tasks that were designed by psychophysical researchers to measure human capacity for perceptual integration across eye movements: noticing small movements that take place during the saccade itself, and judging large shapes that are presented gradually across a series of fixations.

Stable perception and change detection across saccades A stable world is perceived as stable across saccades under normal conditions, but not when the viewpoint following a movement isn't as expected, nor when something substantially moves during the saccade. These observations motivated the hypothesis that we predict what we will see after a movement and compare it with what we actually get (fig. 9). We tested this feasibility of this hypothesis by using IRV's acquired visual motor calibration map as an image predicting network (fig. 3). During an eye movement, the non-uniform pixels of an image were rearranged, according to the map, to predict the image that would follow the movement (fig. 2). The actual and predicted images were compared pixel by pixel, and those that differed by less than a 20% threshold were considered to match. For a largely stable scene, most of the image is predicted correctly; the scene is perceived as stable. In fig. 9, two small areas are not predicted correctly. These correspond to the area where a mug was displaced slightly on the shelf; IRV noticed this discrepancy and registered its surprise. Humans performed similarly in an experiment that measured the sensitivity to small displacements during a saccade (Bridgeman, Hendry, & Stark 1975). Both humans and IRV

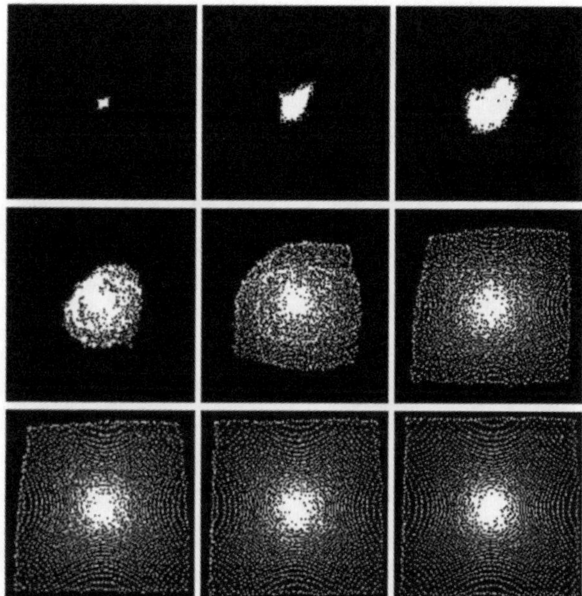

Figure 6: Each pixel of the scrambled, foveated visual representation is assigned a motor coordinate through a pair-wise constraint satisfaction process. Here, the pixels are shown migrating to a pattern that reveals the original sampling distribution (fig. 4). This occurs gradually over approximately 25,000 eye movements, which takes about 24 hours for the robot.

also notice small global scene shifts during a saccade.

Summarizing, through an acquired visual motor calibration map, as embedded in a predictive, retinotopic connectionist architecture, IRV perceives the stability of the external world across camera movements, despite the radically non-uniform changes that result from the movements. Also, IRV can detect small, local scene displacements that occur during eye movements.

Recognition across eye movements Each fixation of a non-uniform sensor gives a highly incomplete view of the world (fig. 1). A crucial component of normal perception under these conditions is recognizing the large-scale relationship among the details acquired from each view. Obviously, this is not the only problem involved in general object recognition, but any theory of recognition that concerns moving, non-uniform sensors must support perceptual integration of large-scale visual geometry across frequent movements.

We propose that when a form is so large that its defining features are not simultaneously visible, a quick series of movements acquires the features foveally, and the features viewed earlier, although no longer recognizable at low resolution, are envisioned in their new retinotopic locations. The basis for visual integration across eye movements is a mental relocation of

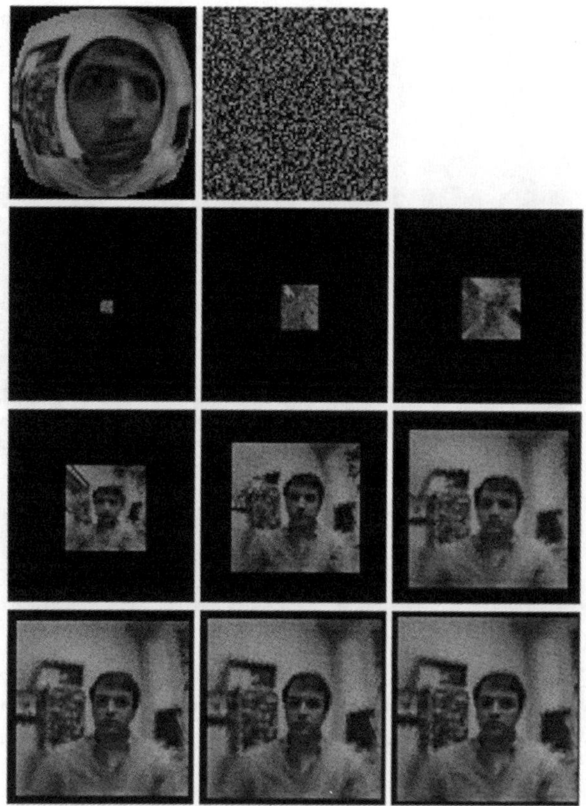

Figure 7: Top row: An example of how IRV's inputs during development are resampled non-uniformly (L) and then reordered (R). Next rows: Each picture shows the same scrambled pixels placed in canonical motor coordinates. As IRV develops an accurate visual-motor calibration map from experience, the assignment of motor-coordinates for distorted and scrambled pixels improves. This sequence represents learning during approximately 25,000 eye movements.

all visual features into a new frame of reference with each eye movement. This process can apply to any retinotopic feature map. These maps preserve the non-uniform distribution of spatial acuity, because it is not possible to represent all visual information at the highest acuity.

The visual motor calibration map provides exactly the geometric information needed to envision the retinotopic location of an object or feature after an eye movement, with the same spatial resolution of the sensor. We have already seen that simple color features (pixels) can be envisioned in their new retinotopic location. The same mechanism is used here to envision the vertices of a triangle as they are presented on successive fixations. Then, the actual geometry of the triangle is judged using the motor-based coordinates

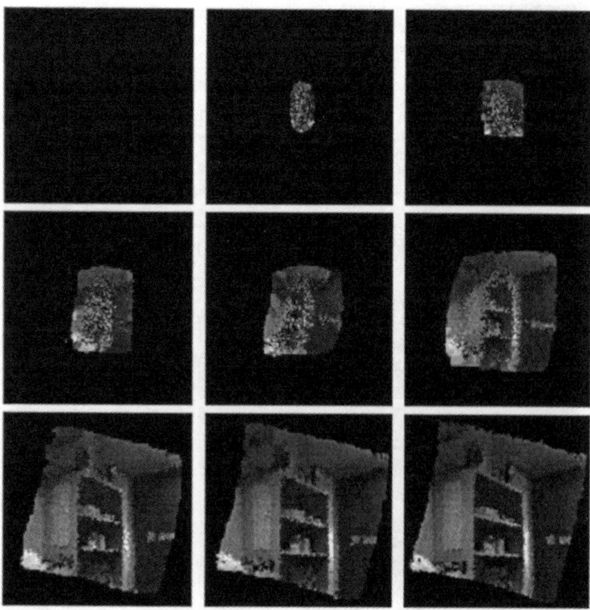

Figure 8: In this sequence, the camera was twisted with respect to the pan and tilt axes. The developing visual motor calibration map gradually uncovers the true imaging and sampling geometry.

Figure 9: Top: Consecutive, foveal views of a scene. A visual robot will want to know if anything in the scene changed from one view to the next. The comparisons needed to do this are one form of perceptual integration across eye movements. Bottom: During the camera movement, an expected image was predicted; most of the scene was confirmed (faded). The two areas not predicted correctly correspond to where a mug was moved during the camera movement (shown analytically unresampled at right).

of the envisioned vertices, based on the off-line image calibration process described earlier.

The perceptual task is a replication of a psychophysical experiment that measures human accuracy of form integration across eye movements (Hayhoe, Lachter, & Feldman 1990). The task is straightforward: judge if the angle formed by three points of light, presented one at a time on successive fixations, is obtuse or acute. An accurate judgment entails knowing the relative positions of the dots with respect to each other, which in turn depend on the size and direction of the intervening eye movements. Since the presentation is entirely empty except for the single point on each fixation, the subject has no visual cue to judge how much the viewpoint changed; only non-visual, or so-called extra-retinal (Matin 1986), eye position information can be used. The subjects judged the angles to within a threshold of six degrees. If a single stable visual cue persisted across the saccades, accuracy roughly doubled, and was equal to the control case in which all three points were presented simultaneously.

In our experiments, three dots, defining a right angle, were presented one at a time, with small, random camera movement between each presentation. During the camera movement, any previously acquired dots were mentally shifted by IRV into a new, predicted retinotopic position. After the third dot was shown, the angle between the dots was determined using the motor-based coordinates of each envisioned point. In ten trials, the average absolute error in perceived angle was 3 degrees.

Conclusions

We have found that the geometric knowledge required for integrating visual information across camera movements can be represented conveniently as a visual-motor calibration map. The map defines image points that correspond to the same sight lines before and after a particular camera movement. It has an equivalent connectionist network that can predictively shift remembered visual information, during a camera movement, into the new retinotopic reference frame. The map and its network constitute the representational basis for an alternative to theories relying on stable, head-centered reference frames hypothesized to exist in our visual systems. Such eye-position invariant visual responses have yet to found, while predictive activity shifts of the sort proposed here are widespread (Duhamel, Colby, & Goldberg 1992).

The experiments described here show that useful processes demanding perceptual integration can be carried out, in a retinocentric frame, by using learned

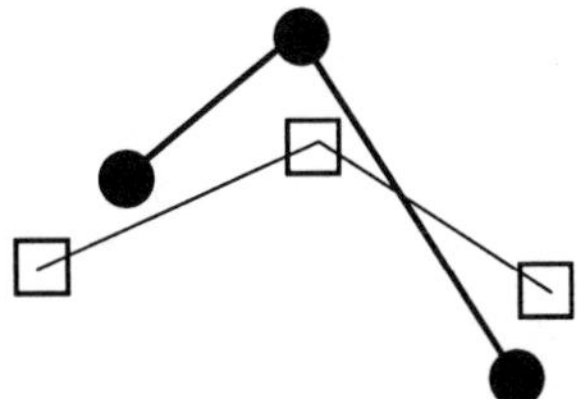

Figure 10: Schematic form-integration problem. Each frame shows the image of one corner of a quadrilateral, relative to the center of view. In order to determine the overall size and shape of the figure, it is necessary to combine information from the four images using knowledge of the intervening eye movements.

visual expectations. Unexpected visual changes that occur during eye movements can be detected by noticing differences between actual and expected pixels; at the same time, confirmed expectations constitute normal stable perception despite frequently shifting inputs. Visual features that are too small and too far apart to resolve simultaneously can be integrated from successive fixations by continually envisioning the retinotopic positions of remembered features, using the same mechanism of learned visual expectations. If the parameters of the eye/camera movements are known, the map can be used to interpret the relative positions of a pair of image points in terms of the movement for which they most closely correspond.

The visual motor calibration map is intrinsically adaptive, since it is acquired from natural, ambiguous visual experience. We have shown how to extrapolate the information in the map to provide a complete calibration of the visual-motor system that accounts for optical parameters and distortions, non-uniform sampling, mechanical misalignments, and arbitrary pixel ordering. In short, the visual motor calibration map can serve as the basis for vision with moving, foveal cameras, providing both a wider field of view and higher spatial resolution.

References

Atkeson, C. G. 1990. Using local models to control movement. In Touretzsky, D. S., ed., *Advances in Neural Information Processing Systems*, 316–323. Morgan Kaufmann.

Bridgeman, B. D.; Hendry, D.; and Stark, L. 1975. Failure to detect displacement of the visual world during saccadic eye movements. *Vision Research* 15.

Duhamel, J. R.; Colby, C. L.; and Goldberg, M. E. 1992. The updating of the representation of visual space in parietal cortex by intended eye movements. *Science* 255(90):90–92.

Faugeras. 1992. What can be seen in three dimesnions with an uncalibrated stereo rig. In Sandini, G., ed., *Proceedings of the 2nd European Conference on Computer Vision.* Springer-Verlag.

Feldman, J. A., and Ballard, D. H. 1982. Connectionist models and their properties. *Cognitive Science* 6.

Feldman, J. A. 1985. Four frames suffice: A provisional model of vision and space. *Behavioral and Brain Sciences* 8(2):265–289.

Hayhoe, M.; Lachter, J.; and Feldman, J. 1990. Integration of form across saccadic eye movements. Technical report, University of Rochester.

Matin, L. 1986. Visual localization and eye movements. In Boff, K. R.; Laufman, L.; and Thomas, J. P., eds., *Handbook of Perception and Human Performance*, volume 1. New York: John Wiley and Sons.

Mel, B. W. 1990. *Connectionist robot motion planning: A neurally-inspired approach to visually-guided reaching*, volume 7 of *Perspectives In Artificial Intelligence.* Academic Press.

O'Regan, J. K., and Levy-Schoen, A. 1983. Integrating visual information from successive fixations: Does trans-saccadic fusion exist? *Vision Research* 23(8):765–768.

Pollatsek, A.; Rayner, K.; and Collins, W. 1984. Integrating pictorial information across eye movements. *Journal of Experimental Psychology: General* 113(3):426–442.

Prokopowicz, P. N. 1994. *The Development of Perceptual Integration Across Eye Movements in Visual Robots.* Ph.D. Dissertation, Institute for the Learning Sciences, Northwestern University.

Sparks, D. L., and Porter, J. D. 1983. The spatial localization of saccade targets. ii. activity of superior colliculus neurons preceding compensatory saccades. *Journal of Neurophysiology* 49:64–74.

Stratton, G. M. 1897. Vision without inversion of the retinal image. *Psychological Review* 4:342–360.

van Essen, D. C.; Felleman, D. J.; DeYoe, E. A.; and Knierim, J. J. 1991. Probing the primate visual cortex: Pathways and perspectives. In Valberg, A., and Lee, B., eds., *Pigments to Perception.* Plenum Press, New York. 227–237.

Yarbus, A. L. 1967. *Eye movements and vision.* Plenum Press.

Planning

A Bias towards Relevance: Recognizing plans where goal minimization fails

Abigail S. Gertner
Learning Research & Development Center
University of Pittsburgh
Pittsburgh PA 15260
gertner+@pitt.edu

Bonnie L. Webber
Department of Computer & Information Science
University of Pennsylvania
Philadelphia PA 19104
bonnie@linc.cis.upenn.edu

Abstract

Domains such as multiple trauma management, in which there are multiple interacting goals that change over time, are ones in which plan recognition's standard inductive bias towards a single explanatory goal is inappropriate. In this paper we define and argue for an alternative bias based on identifying contextually "relevant" goals. We support this claim by showing how a complementary planning system in TraumAID 2.0, a decision-support system for the management of multiple trauma, allows us to define a four-level scale of relevance and therefore, of measurable deviations from relevance. This in turn allows definition of a bias towards relevance in the incremental recognition of physician plans by TraumAID's critiquing interface, TraumaTIQ.

Introduction

Domains such as multiple trauma management, in which there are multiple interacting goals that change over time, are ones in which plan recognition's standard inductive bias towards a single explanatory goal is inappropriate. Yet some kind of bias is nevertheless necessary if plan recognition is to identify a best explanation for observed actions. In this paper, we describe how plans produced by a complementary planning system allow us to define an alternative bias towards contextually relevant goals, along with a four-level scale for relevance, which is used in the incremental recognition and evaluation of physician plans. These functions are carried out by TraumAID's interface, TraumaTIQ, which uses them to produce *critiques* of physician orders in only those cases where it could make a clinically significant difference.

The task of TraumaTIQ's plan recognizer is to build incrementally a model of the physician's plan based on the actions she has ordered. TraumaTIQ then evaluates that plan and compares it to TraumAID's plan in order to determine potential errors to comment on in the critique. The plan evaluation and critique generation components will not be described in this paper. They are discussed in detail in (Gertner 1995).

In the next section, we introduce TraumAID 2.0 and describe the representation of planning knowledge and the process by which it generates plans. We then describe the plan recognition algorithm used by TraumAID's critiquing module, TraumaTIQ, and show how the planning knowledge in TraumAID provides a recognition bias based on relevance. We conclude with a discussion of an evaluation performed on TraumaTIQ's plan recognition algorithm and its implications for further system development.

An Overview of TraumAID 2.0

The TraumAID system is a tool for assisting physicians during the initial definitive management of patients with multiple trauma (Rymon 1993; Webber, Rymon, & Clarke 1992). During this phase of patient care, which often requires urgent action, preliminary diagnoses are pursued and initial treatments are carried out. The current system, TraumAID 2.0, embodies a goal-directed approach to patient management. The system architecture links a rule-based reasoner that derives conclusions and goals from the evidence currently available about the patient, and a planner that constructs a (partially ordered) plan for how best to address the currently relevant goals.

TraumAID 2.0's management plans have been retrospectively validated by a panel of three experienced trauma surgeons in a blinded comparison with actual care. Panel members preferred TraumAID's plans over actual care to a statistically significant extent (Clarke *et al.* 1993; Gertner, Webber, & Clarke 1996). This result suggests that such plans could provide a valid basis for producing critiques of physician plans which could lead to improvements in patient care.

To understand how general knowledge and patient-specific information in TraumAID's planner allow us to define and use an inductive bias towards contextually relevant goals in TraumaTIQ's plan recognition, it is important to understand how TraumAID forms goals and clinically appropriate plans for addressing them.

When a new piece of evidence is entered, TraumAID's reasoner is triggered, forward chaining through its entire set of rules and generating a list of active goals. When rule activity ceases, the planner is invoked to determine how best to satisfy the current combination of management goals and address the competing diagnostic and therapeutic needs arising from multiple injuries.

TraumAID's plans are constructed out of three types of objects: *goals*, *procedures*, and *actions* (see Figure 1).

Part of TraumAID's general knowledge of goals consists of *goal-procedure mappings* – disjunctive lists of procedures for addressing each goal. Procedures in a mapping are ordered preferentially by their cost, effectiveness, invasiveness, etc. For example, the goal NEED ACCESS CHEST CAVITY can be addressed by either PERFORM THORACOTOMY or PERFORM BILATERAL THORACOTOMY WITH TRANSVERSE STERNOTOMY, but the former is preferred.

Given a set of goals, TraumAID's planner selects one procedure for each goal from its goal-procedure mapping. Selection depends on both the *a priori* preference ordering and a more global need to address multiple goals efficiently, since one procedure can sometimes be used to address more than one goal.

A procedure comprises an ordered sequence of actions and/or sub-goals, stored in a *procedure-action mapping*. The use of sub-goals allows TraumAID's planner to *delay* certain decisions about how to address top-level goals. For example, if TraumAID is planning to address the goal TREAT UPPER THORACIC ESOPHAGEAL INJURY by performing PERFORM UPPER ESOPHAGUS REPAIR, it can commit early on to its specific component actions, GIVE ANTIBIOTICS and ESOPHAGUS REPAIR AND DRAIN, while basing its choice of how to address NEED ACCESS CHEST CAVITY on the other currently relevant goals.

Another feature of TraumAID's goal posting and planning is that its reasoner embeds a conservative, *staged* strategy for selecting diagnosis and treatment goals (Rymon 1993): goals whose satisfaction requires expensive and/or risky procedures are not included in a plan until they are justified by less costly tests or observations. These strategies appear in the knowledge base as implicitly related management goals, such as a DIAGNOSE HEMATURIA (blood in the urine), which if present, triggers DIAGNOSE BLADDER INJURY, which in turn can lead to a goal TREAT BLADDER INJURY.

Using context to bias search in plan recognition

Intelligent interaction with another agent often depends on understanding the agent's underlying *mental states* that lead her to act as she does. These mental states include *beliefs* about the world, *desires* for the future state of the world, and *intentions* to act in certain ways. The process of inferring these mental states is generally referred to as plan recognition.

The importance of plan recognition for automated decision support has been recognized by both ourselves and Shahar and Musen (Shahar & Musen 1995). In connection with automated decision support, plan recognition can support several elements of critiquing, including flexible plan evaluation, explanation of critiques, and proposing alternative actions and goals.

Since there are theoretically many possible explanations for any set or sequence of observations, plan recognition requires an inductive *bias*. Previous plan recognition algorithms, most notably (Kautz 1990), incorporated a bias towards minimizing the number of goals used to explain the observed actions. Such a bias is inappropriate in a domain such as multiple trauma management where, as discussed in the preceding section, a range of independent diagnostic and therapeutic goals may be active simultaneously.

Other factors also constrain the kind of bias that can be used: physician orders (which serve the role of observed actions) are not necessarily given and entered in the order in which they are intended to be performed. TraumaTIQ therefore cannot assume that consecutive orders address the same or similar goals. In addition, physicians' plans are not always correct. Since the set of incorrect plans is too large to encode *a priori*, a bias is needed that will still allow interpretation of orders that do not correspond exactly with its knowledge of clinically appropriate plans.

Given these constraints, TraumaTIQ's plan recognizer employs a bias towards *relevance*, attempting to explain physician orders as closely as possible in conformance with the principles of trauma care encoded in TraumAID. TraumAID's current goals and plan then provide a standard of relevance, with ways of interpreting deviations from relevance following from TraumAID's extensive general knowledge base of conclusions, goals, and actions in the domain.

Several researchers have pointed out the advantages of using contextual knowledge and basic domain principles to bias the search for an explanatory plan (Huff & Lesser 1993; Hill & Johnson 1995; London & Clancey 1982). The basic idea is that the plan recognizer can use its knowledge of what actions are appropriate in the current situation to reduce am-

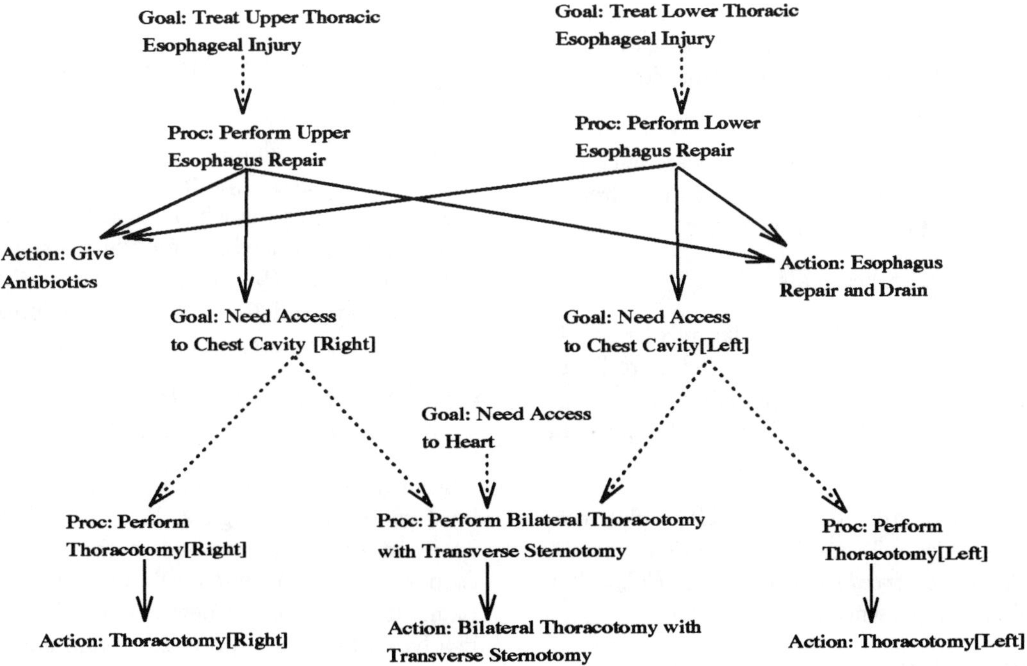

Figure 1: An example plan graph. Dotted arrows indicate disjunctive *goal-procedure mappings*, while solid arrows indicate conjunctive *procedure-action mappings*.

biguities in interpreting observed actions. We believe this is an appropriate bias to use in TraumaTIQ because we can assume:

- The head of the trauma team will have training and experience, and will usually develop plans that are similar to TraumAID's.
- The head of the trauma team is more likely to have appropriate goals but be addressing them in a sub-optimal way, than to be pursuing the wrong goals altogether.
- While TraumAID follows a conservative strategy for pursuing diagnosis and treatment from observations, the head of the trauma team may proceed more rapidly, pursuing a goal for which TraumAID does not yet have enough evidence to conclude its relevance.

The first two assumptions motivate a policy of giving the physician "the benefit of the doubt": if an ordered action can be explained in terms of TraumAID's current goal set, the physician will be assumed to be pursuing the explanatory goal(s). An ordered action can be explained if it appears in TraumAID's plan for addressing a goal in the goal set, *or* if TraumAID has chosen a different action to address this goal.

The third assumption allows the plan recognizer to interpret actions that could be justified by more evidence. Using knowledge about the strategic relationships between goals, TraumaTIQ can identify when the physician's orders may be motivated by a goal that is partially but not yet completely supported by the evidence.

The Plan Recognition algorithm

Informally, our plan recognition algorithm works by first enumerating the set of possible *explanations* for all actions that have been ordered. Each explanation consists of a path in the plan graph from the ordered action to a *procedure* in which the action plays a part, back to a top level *goal*. The path may pass through a series of sub-goals and procedures before reaching a top level goal. Since the same goal may be addressed by more than one procedure, an action may be explained by one goal in the context of two different procedures.

The possible explanations are evaluated in two phases. The first phase considers the top level *goals*. These are sorted according to their *relevance* in the current situation, and the most relevant ones are selected as candidate explanations. The plan recognizer categorizes potential explanatory goals on a 4-level scale:

1. Relevant goals: goals in TraumAID's set of goals to be pursued.
2. Potentially relevant goals: goals that are part of a currently active *diagnostic strategy*, as described ear-

lier. For example, if the goal of diagnosing a fractured rib is currently relevant, then the goal of treating a fractured rib is potentially relevant, depending on the result of the diagnostic test.

3. Previously relevant goals: goals that were once relevant but are no longer so, because either already addressed or ruled out by new evidence.

4. Irrelevant goals: all other goals.

The bias embodied in this phase of plan recognition is that the higher a goal is on this scale, the more likely the physician is considered to be pursuing it.

Formally, phase one of the algorithm can be specified as follows:

1. For each action α ordered, TraumaTIQ's plan recognizer extracts from TraumAID's knowledge base a set of *explanatory procedure-goal chains*, PG_α, that could explain the presence of that action:

   $$PG_\alpha = \{\langle P \ldots G\rangle_1, \ldots, \langle P \ldots G\rangle_n\}$$

   where P is a procedure containing α in its decomposition, and $\langle P \ldots G\rangle_i$ is a backward path through the plan graph ending with the goal G.

2. Now consider the set $\Gamma = \{G_i\}$ where G_i is the top level goal ending $\langle P \ldots G\rangle_i$. In rank order, Γ consists of: Γ_1 the relevant goals, Γ_2 the potentially relevant goals, Γ_3 the previously relevant goals, and Γ_4 all other goals. Let $\Gamma' = \{G_j\}$ be the highest ranking non-empty subset of Γ. If Γ' is the set of irrelevant goals, halt here and add α to the plan with no explanatory procedure-goal chains.

The second phase considers the procedures in the remaining explanations. These are evaluated according to how strongly the physician's other actions/orders provide additional evidence for them. All procedures in the highest non-empty category are accepted as explanations for the action. For simplicity, the procedures are actually sorted according to a four-level scale of evidence:

1. Completed procedures: procedures for which all the actions have been ordered by the physician.

2. Partially completed procedures: procedures for which some of the actions have been ordered.

3. Relevant procedures: procedures that are currently in TraumAID's plan. This means that if an action could address a goal by playing a role in two different procedures, the one in TraumAID's plan is preferred as the explanation for the physician's action.

4. All other procedures.

Formally, phase two of the algorithm can be specified as follows:

3. Let $\mathcal{P} = \{P_j\}$ where P_j is the procedure that is the child of G_j in PG_α. In rank order, $\mathcal{P}$ consists of: $\mathcal{P}_1$, procedures for which all the actions have been ordered, $\mathcal{P}_2$, procedures for which some actions have been ordered, $\mathcal{P}_3$, procedures currently in TraumAID's plan, and $\mathcal{P}_4$, all other procedures. Let $\mathcal{P}'$ be the highest ranking non-empty subset of $\mathcal{P}$.

4. Select the paths $PG' \subseteq PG$ such that PG' contains all paths ending with goals in Γ' with children in $\mathcal{P}'$.

Finally, the explanations with the most relevant top-level goals and the highest level of evidence (i.e., the paths in PG') are ascribed to the physician and incorporated into TraumaTIQ's model of the physician's plan. Incorporating a new explanation into the plan involves adding new procedures and goals if they are not already present, and adding links between items that are not already connected.

Note that there may be more than one explanation for a given action, if the explanatory goals are equally relevant and the procedures equally manifested. For example, TREAT UPPER THORACIC ESOPHAGEAL INJURY and TREAT LOWER THORACIC ESOPHAGEAL INJURY might be accepted as explanatory goals for the action ESOPHAGUS REPAIR AND DRAIN, provided that both goals are in the same category of relevance.

An example of TraumaTIQ's plan recognition process

The use of context to bias the search for explanatory goals means that TraumaTIQ's plan recognizer can distinguish between goals that are otherwise equally good explanations of the observed actions. Continuing the example from Figure 1, suppose that TREAT UPPER THORACIC ESOPHAGEAL INJURY is currently the only goal in TraumAID's relevant goal set, but the physician is erroneously pursuing the goal of treating an *lower* thoracic esophageal injury. If the physician first orders ANTIBIOTICS, TraumaTIQ will infer that they are being given as part of the procedure to treat the upper esophageal injury, even though antibiotics may play a role in a number of other procedures, including treating a lower thoracic esophageal injury.

Next, if the physician orders a BILATERAL THORACOTOMY in order to get access to the left chest, this action will also be inferred as part of TREAT UPPER THORACIC ESOPHAGEAL INJURY. However, since this is the less preferred procedure for addressing that goal, a comment will be produced to the effect that "Doing a right thoracotomy is preferred over doing a bilateral thoracotomy with a transverse sternotomy to get access to the right chest cavity." Note that such a comment leaves it to the physician to determine that the correct sub-goal is getting access to the right half of the chest in order to treat the upper esophagus.

If, on the other hand, the physician orders a LEFT THORACOTOMY, this action is inconsistent with the goal of treating an upper esophageal injury, and so TraumaTIQ infers that it is being done for some reason that TraumAID does not currently consider relevant. This will result in the comment, "Doing a left thoracotomy is not justified at this time. Please reconsider this order or provide justification." Furthermore, since the physician has failed to order a procedure to get access to the right chest cavity, TraumaTIQ will also produce the comment, "Please consider doing a right thoracotomy and repairing and draining the esophagus in order to treat the upper thoracic esophageal injury." Such a comment would make explicit a possible discrepancy in goals between the physician and TraumAID.

Analysis of the plan recognition algorithm

A serious criticism of previous approaches to plan recognition is that they are computationally intractable (Charniak & Goldman 1993; Goodman & Litman 1992). In a time-critical domain like trauma management, it is essential for TraumaTIQ to respond quickly. The complexity of the algorithm is not really a problem in the current implementation of TraumaTIQ because of the limited size and complexity of the plans generated by TraumAID 2.0. To demonstrate how fast the implementation actually is in practice: TraumaTIQ's plan recognizer, implemented in Lucid Common Lisp and compiled on a Sun 4 processed 584 actions in an average of 0.023 cpu seconds per action.

The problem arises when we consider extending the system to cover other areas of the body and/or blunt injury, increasing the number of procedures and goals that might explain an action in the knowledge base. To allow for the growth of the system, it is important that the plan recognition algorithm scale up efficiently.

As Rymon (1993) points out, plan recognition can be formalized as a set-covering problem in which two sets of observations, symptoms and actions, are mapped onto a set of goals which covers both of them: every symptom motivates some goal and every action is motivated by some goal in the covering set (Figure 2). The covering set is optimized according to some cost function, such as set minimization. Since the set covering problem in general is NP-hard, so is this formalization of plan recognition.

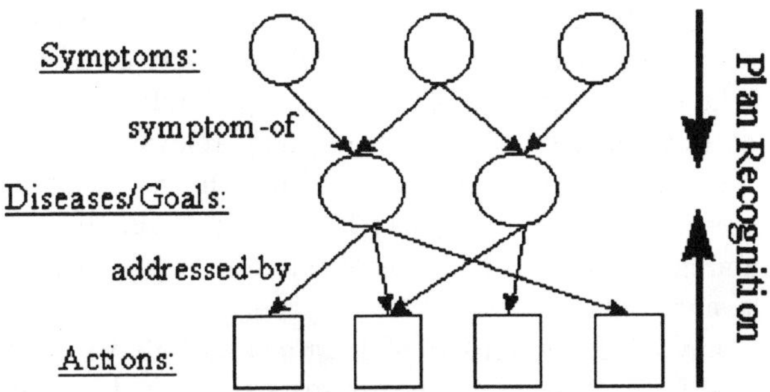

Figure 2: Plan Recognition as a set covering problem

In general, any plan recognition algorithm that considers all possible combinations of explanatory goals for the observed actions is going to grow exponentially with the number of actions. The algorithm we present here avoids the need for an exponential search by grouping the potential explanations according to *relevance* and then greedily accepting all the explanations in the most relevant group. One way to look at this is that rather than trying to optimize the covering goal set according to a cost function, we simply choose to maximize the number of relevant goals in the covering set.

In doing this, for each ordered action α, the algorithm only has to consider $|\Gamma|$ goals, where Γ is the set of possible explanatory goals for α, and $\sum_{|\Gamma'|} |\mathcal{P}_{\Gamma_j}|$ procedures, where Γ' is the most relevant non-empty subset of Γ, and $\mathcal{P}_{\Gamma_j}$ are the procedures linked to each goal Γ_j in Γ'. For each procedure, it has to look at $|\mathcal{A}_{\mathcal{P}}|$ actions in the procedure, and compare them with at most all of the actions that have been ordered. So the total cost of inferring a plan from a set of orders, $\mathcal{A}$, is at most

$$|\mathcal{A}| * (|\Gamma| + (\sum_{|\Gamma'|} |\mathcal{P}_{\Gamma_j}| * |\mathcal{A}_{\mathcal{P}_j}| * |\mathcal{A}|))$$

Thus, this algorithm is polynomial in the number of ordered actions, and linear in the number of possible goals per action, the number of goals in the most relevant goals set, and the number of possible procedures per action.

Evaluation and Discussion

We evaluated the performance of the plan recognition algorithm by applying it to the management plans from the 97 actual trauma cases from the Medical College of Pennsylvania used in the retrospective validation of TraumAID (Clarke *et al.* 1993; Gertner, Webber, & Clarke 1996).

Out of 584 actions, 234 of them were not also part of TraumAID's plan at the time that they were ordered.

Of these 234, 15 of them could be explained by a goal that was currently in TraumAID's relevant goal set. Of the remaining 219, 69 could be explained by a goal that was considered to be potentially relevant, given TraumAID's current knowledge about the state of the patient. The plan recognizer failed to explain the remaining 148 actions in terms of relevant or potentially relevant goals.

Many of the actions that TraumaTIQ fails to infer a goal for are broad diagnostic tests that can be used to look for a number of conditions, and the physician may not actually have a specific goal in mind when ordering them. To understand physicians' plans in such cases it is necessary to have a more complete abstraction hierarchy for goals than is currently available in TraumAID 2.0. Since the knowledge base was implemented in support of plan *generation* rather than plan *recognition*, only goals that could be directly operationalized as actions were included.

Second, some goals that physicians may pursue in these cases are not included in TraumAID's knowledge base because its designers opted not to pursue these goals under any circumstances relevant to the current domain of the system. To have a complete plan recognition system, it will be necessary to include such goals in the knowledge base.

Summary and Conclusion

In this paper we have pointed out the weakness of standard inductive biases, such as goal minimization in domains where agents can have multiple independent goals. We have further argued that the goals and plans that a decision support system would adopt under the circumstances can provide a workable inductive bias. To show this, we have described how TraumAID's planner provides a standard of relevance and of measurable deviations from relevance, providing in turn a context for the incremental recognition of physician plans by TraumaTIQ. The approach to plan recognition presented here is computationally efficient and can be applied in any domain where the user's behavior can be predicted on the basis of contextual information.

Acknowledgments

This work has been supported in part by the National Library of Medicine under grants R01 LM05217-03 and R01 LM05764-01 and the Agency for Health Care Policy and Research under grant RO1 HS06740.

References

Charniak, E., and Goldman, R. P. 1993. A Bayesian model of plan recognition. *Artificial Intelligence* 64:53–79.

Clarke, J. R.; Rymon, R.; Webber, B.; Hayward, C.; Santora, T.; Wagner, D.; and Ruffin, A. 1993. The importance of planning in the provision of medical care. *Medical Decision Making* 13(4):383. abstract.

Gertner, A.; Webber, B.; and Clarke, J. 1996. On-line quality assurance in the initial definitive management of multiple trauma. *submitted to Artificial Intelligence in Medicine.*

Gertner, A. S. 1995. *Critiquing: Effective Decision Support in Time-Critical Domains.* Ph.D. Dissertation, University of Pennsylvania, Philadelphia, Pennsylvania.

Goodman, B. A., and Litman, D. J. 1992. On the interaction between plan recognition and intelligent interfaces. *User Modeling and User-Adapted Interaction* 2(1-2):55–82.

Hill, R. W., and Johnson, W. L. 1995. Situated plan attribution. *Journal of Artificial Intelligence in Education.* to appear.

Huff, K. E., and Lesser, V. R. 1993. Integrating plausible reasoning in an incremental plan recognizer. Technical Report 93-72, University of Massachusetts, Amherst.

Kautz, H. 1990. A circumscriptive theory of plan recognition. In Philip R. Cohen, J. M., and Pollack, M. E., eds., *Intentions in Communication.* Bradford Books.

London, R., and Clancey, W. J. 1982. Plan recognition strategies in student modelling: prediction and description. In *Proceedings of the American Association for Artificial Intelligence*, 335–338.

Rymon, R. 1993. *Diagnostic Reasoning and Planning in Exploratory-Corrective Domains.* Ph.D. Dissertation, Department of Computer & Information Science, University of Pennsylvania. Appears as Technical Report MS-CIS-93-84.

Shahar, Y., and Musen, M. A. 1995. Plan recognition and revision in support of guideline-based care. In *Working notes of the AAAI Spring Symposium on Representing Mental States and Mechanisms*, 118–126.

Webber, B. L.; Rymon, R.; and Clarke, J. R. 1992. Flexible support for trauma management through goal-directed reasoning and planning. *Artificial Intelligence in Medicine* 4(2):145–163.

What is planning in the presence of sensing?*

Hector J. Levesque
Department of Computer Science
University of Toronto
Toronto, ON, M5S 3H5 Canada
hector@cs.toronto.edu

Abstract

Despite the existence of programs that are able to generate so-called conditional plans, there has yet to emerge a clear and general specification of what it is these programs are looking for: what exactly is a plan in this setting, and when is it correct? In this paper, we develop and motivate a specification within the situation calculus of conditional and iterative plans over domains that include binary sensing actions. The account is built on an existing theory of action which includes a solution to the frame problem, and an extension to it that handles sensing actions and the effect they have on the knowledge of a robot. Plans are taken to be programs in a new simple robot program language, and the planning task is to find a program that would be known by the robot at the outset to lead to a final situation where the goal is satisfied. This specification is used to analyze the correctness of a small example plan, as well as variants that have redundant or missing sensing actions. We also investigate whether the proposed robot program language is powerful enough to serve for any intuitively achievable goal.

Much of high-level symbolic AI research has been concerned with planning: specifying the behaviour of intelligent agents by providing goals to be achieved or maintained. In the simplest case, the output of a planner is a sequence of actions to be performed by the agent. However, a number of researchers are investigating the topic of *conditional planning* (see for example, [3, 9, 14, 17]) where the output, for one reason or another, is not expected to be a fixed sequence of actions, but a more general specification involving conditionals and iteration. In this paper, we will be concerned with conditional planning problems where what action to perform next in a plan may depend on the result of an earlier *sensing action*.

Consider the following motivating example:

*Thanks to the members of the University of Toronto Cognitive Robotics group (Yves Lesperance, Fangzhen Lin, Daniel Marcu, Ray Reiter, and Richard Scherl) and to Fahiem Bacchus, for discussion, comments, and suggestions. A special thanks to Yves for helping with the definition in Section 3, and to Fangzhen for asking and helping to answer the question of Section 5. This research was made possible by financial support from the Information Technology Research Center, the Institute for Robotics and Intelligent Systems, and the Natural Science and Engineering Research Council. They also had to pick up the asinine AAAI fee for extra pages.

The Airport Example The local airport has only two boarding gates, Gate A and Gate B. Every plane will be parked at one of the two gates. In the initial state, you are at home. From home, it is possible to go to the airport, and from there you can go directly to either gate. At the airport, it is also possible to check the departures screen, to find out what gate a flight will be using. Once at a gate, the only thing to do is to board the plane that is parked there. The goal is to be on the plane for Flight 123.

There clearly is no sequence of actions that can be shown to achieve the desired goal: which gate to go to depends on the (runtime) result of checking the departure screen.

Surprisingly, despite the existence of planners that are able to solve simple problems like this, there has yet to emerge a clear specification of what it is that these planners are looking for: what is a plan in this setting, and when is it correct? In this paper, we will propose a new definition, show some examples of plans that meet (and fail to meet) the specification, and argue for the utility of this specification independent of plan generation.

What we will *not* do in this paper is propose a new planning procedure. In many cases, existing procedures like the one presented in [3] will be adequate, given various representational restrictions. Moreover, our specification goes beyond what can be handled by existing planning procedures, including problems like the following:

The Omelette Example We begin with a supply of eggs, some of which may be bad, but at least 3 of which are good. We have a bowl and a saucer, which can be emptied at any time. It is possible to break a new egg into the saucer, if it is empty, or into the bowl. By smelling a container, it is possible to tell if it contains a bad egg. Also, the contents of the saucer can be transferred to the bowl. The goal is to get 3 good eggs and no bad ones into the bowl.

While it is far from clear how to automatically generate a plan to solve a problem like this,[1] our account, at least, will make clear what a solution ought to be.

[1]However, see [10] for some ideas on how to generate plans containing loops (when there is no sensing).

Classical planning

There are a number of ways of making the planning task precise, but perhaps the most appealing is to put aside all algorithmic concerns, and come up with a specification in terms of a general theory of action. In the absence of sensing actions, one candidate language for formulating such a theory is the situation calculus [12]. We will not go over the language here except to note the following components: there is a special constant S_0 used to denote the *initial situation*, namely that situation in which no actions have yet occurred; there is a distinguished binary function symbol *do* where $do(a, s)$ denotes the successor situation to s resulting from performing the action a; relations whose truth values vary from situation to situation, are called (relational) *fluents*, and are denoted by predicate symbols taking a situation term as their last argument; finally, there is a special predicate $Poss(a, s)$ used to state that action a is executable in situation s.

Within this language, we can formulate domain theories which describe how the world changes as the result of the available actions. One possibility is a theory of the following form [15]:

- Axioms describing the initial situation, S_0.
- Action precondition axioms, one for each primitive action a, characterizing $Poss(a, s)$.
- Successor state axioms, one for each fluent F, stating under what conditions $F(\vec{x}, do(a, s))$ holds as function of what holds in situation s. These take the place of the so-called effect axioms, but also provide a solution to the frame problem [15].
- Unique names axioms for the primitive actions.
- Some foundational, domain independent axioms.

For any domain theory of this sort, we have a very clean specification of the planning task (in the absence of sensing actions), which dates back to the work of Green [5]:

Classical Planning: Given a domain theory *Axioms* as above, and a goal formula $\phi(s)$ with a single free-variable s, the planning task is to find a sequence of actions[2] $\vec{a}$ such that

$$Axioms \models Legal(\vec{a}, S_0) \wedge \phi(do(\vec{a}, S_0))$$

where $do([a_1, \ldots, a_n], s)$ is an abbreviation for

$$do(a_n, do(a_{n-1}, \ldots, do(a_1, s) \ldots)),$$

and where $Legal([a_1, \ldots, a_n], s)$ stands for

$$Poss(a_1, s) \wedge \ldots \wedge Poss(a_n, do([a_1, \ldots, a_{n-1}], s)).$$

In other words, the task is to find a sequence of actions that is executable (each action is executed in a context where its precondition is satisfied) and that achieves the goal (the goal formula ϕ holds in the final state that results from performing the actions in sequence).[3] A planner is *sound* if any sequence of actions it returns satisfies the entailment; it is *complete* if it is able to find such a sequence when one exists.

Of course in real applications, for efficiency reasons, we may need to move away from the full generality of this specification. In some circumstances, we may settle for a sound but incomplete planner. We may also impose constraints on what what sorts of domain theories or goals are allowed. For example, we might insist that S_0 be described by just a finite set of atomic formulas and a closed world assumption, or that the effect of executable actions not depend on the context of execution, as in most STRIPS-like systems.

However, it is clearly useful to understand these moves in terms of a specification that is unrelated to the limitations of any algorithm or data structure. Note, in particular, that the above account assumes nothing about the form of the preconditions or effects of actions, uses none of the terminology of STRIPS (add or delete lists *etc.*), and none of the terminology of "partial order planning" (threats, protecting links *etc.*). It is neutral but perfectly compatible with a wide range of planners. Indeed the STRIPS representation can be viewed as an *implementation strategy* for a class of planning tasks of this form [6].

Incorporating sensing actions

In classical planning, it is assumed that what conditions hold or do not hold at any point in the plan is logically determined by the background domain theory. However, agents acting in the world may require sensing for a number of reasons:[4]

- There may be incomplete knowledge of the initial state. In the Airport example above, nothing in the background theory specifies where Flight 123 is parked, and the agent needs to check the departure screen at the airport to find out. The Omelette example is similar.
- There may be exogenous actions. The agent may know everything about the initial state of the world, but the world may change as the result of actions performed by other agents or nature. For example, a robot may need to check whether or not a door is open, in case someone has closed it since the last time it checked.
- The effects of actions may be uncertain. For example, a tree-chopping robot may have to check if the tree went down the last time it hit it with the axe.

This then raises an interesting question: is there a specification of the planning task in a domain that includes sensing actions like these which, once again, is neutral with respect to the choice of algorithm and data structure?

Informally, what we expect of a plan in this setting is that it be some sort of *program* that leads to a goal state no matter how the sensing turns out. For the Airport example, an expected solution might be something like

[2]To be precise, what we need here (and similarly below for robot programs) are not actions, but ground terms of the action sort that contain no terms of the situation sort.

[3]This definition is easily augmented to accommodate maintenance goals, conditions that must remain true throughout the execution. For space reasons, we ignore them here.

[4]In this paper, we limit ourselves to the first of these.

go to the airport;
check the departures screen;
if Flight 123 is boarding at Gate A
  then go to Gate A
  else go to Gate B;
board the plane.

Similarly, in the case of the Omelette, we might expect a plan like

/* Assuming the bowl and saucer are empty initially */
until there are 3 eggs in the bowl **do**
  until there is an egg in the saucer **do**
    break an egg into the saucer;
    smell the saucer;
    if the saucer has a bad egg
      then discard its contents
  end until;
  transfer the contents of the saucer to the bowl
end until

Note that in either case, the plan would not be correct without the appropriate sensing action.

The closest candidate that I could find to a formal specification of a plan in this setting is that of Etzioni *et al* in [3]. In addition to a partial-order plan-generation procedure in the style of SNLP [11], they propose a definition of a plan, and what it means for a plan containing sensing actions to be *valid* (achieve a desired goal for a given initial state).

Unfortunately, as a specification, their account has a number of drawbacks. For one thing, it is formulated as a rather complex refinement of the STRIPS account. It deals only with atomic conditions or their negations, assumes that we will be able to "match" the effects of actions with goals to be achieved, and so on. There are also other representational limitations: it does not allow preconditions on sensing actions, and does not handle iteration (and so could not deal with the Omelette example). While limitations like these may be perfectly reasonable and even necessary when it comes to formulating efficient planning procedures, they tend to obscure the logic behind the procedure.

There are other problems as well.[5] In describing plan validity, they insist that every branch of a plan must be valid, where a branch is one of the possible executions paths through any if-then-else in the plan. But this is overly strict in one sense, and not strict enough in another. Imagine a plan like the Airport one above except that it says that if Flight 123 is at Gate A, the agent should jump off the roof of the airport. Suppose however, that the sensing happens to be *redundant* because the agent already knows that the gate for Flight 123 is Gate B. In this context, the plan should be considered to be correct, despite what appears to be a bad branch. Next, imagine a plan like the Airport one above, but without the sensing action. Even though both branches of the if-then-else are handled properly, the plan is now incorrect since an agent executing it would not know the truth value of the condition. This is not to suggest that the *planner* developed by Etzioni *et al* is buggy; they may never end up generating plans like the above. However, as a procedure independent specification, we should be able to evaluate the appropriateness of plans with extra or missing sensing actions.

Instead of building on a STRIPS-like definition of planning, we might again try to formulate a specification of the planning task in terms of a general theory of action, but this time including sensing actions and the effect they have on the knowledge of the agent or robot executing them.

As it turns out a theory of this sort already exists. Building on the work of Moore [13], Scherl and Levesque have provided a theory of sensing actions in the situation calculus [16]. Briefly, what they propose is a new fluent K, whose first argument is also a situation: informally, $K(s', s)$ holds when the agent in situation s, unsure of what situation it is in, thinks it could very well be in situation s'. Since different fluents hold in different situations, the agent is also implicitly thinking about what could be true. Knowledge for the agent, then, is what *must* be true because it holds in all of these so-called accessible situations: $Know(\phi, s)$ is an abbreviation for the formula $\forall s'[K(s', s) \supset \phi(s')]$. Beyond this encoding of traditional modal logic into the situation calculus, Scherl and Levesque provide a successor state axiom for K, that is an axiom which describes for any action (ordinary or sensing) the knowledge of the agent after the action as a function of its knowledge and other conditions before the action.

Assume for simplicity that we have two types of primitive actions: ordinary ones that change the world, and *binary sensing actions*, that is, sensing actions that tell the agent whether or not some condition ϕ_a holds in the current situation.[6] For each sensing action a, we assume the domain theory entails a *sensed fluent axiom* of the form

$$SF(a, s) \equiv \phi_a(s),$$

where *SF* is a distinguished predicate like *Poss*, relating the action to the fluent. For the Airport example, we might have

$$SF(check\_departures, s) \equiv Parked(Flight123, gateA, s)$$

which says that checking the departure screen will tell the agent whether or not Flight 123 is parked at Gate A. Similarly,

$$SF(smell(c), s) \equiv \exists e. Bad\_egg(e, s) \wedge Contains(c, e, s)$$

says that smelling a container c tells the agent whether or not c contains a bad egg e. We also assume that the domain theory entails $[SF(a, s) \equiv \mathbf{True}]$ for every ordinary non-sensing action a. Under these assumptions, we have the following successor state axiom for K:

$$\begin{aligned} Poss(a, s) \supset \{&K(s'', do(a, s)) \equiv \\ &\exists s'.\, s'' = do(a, s') \wedge K(s', s) \wedge Poss(a, s') \wedge \\ &[SF(a, s') \equiv SF(a, s)]\} \end{aligned}$$

Roughly speaking, this says that after doing any action a in situation s, the agent thinks it could be in a situation s'' iff s'' is the result of performing a in some previously accessible

[5] It may be possible to fix their definition to handle these [4].

[6] Later we discuss other types of sensing, especially sensing that involves a sensor reading.

s', provided that action a is possible in s' and s' is identical to s in terms of what is being sensed, if anything. For example, if a is *check_departures*, this would have the effect of ensuring that any such s' would have Flight 123 parked at the same gate as in s. Assuming the successor state axiom for *Parked* is such that where a plane is parked is unaffected by sensing, any accessible s'' would also have Flight 123 parked at the same gate as in s. Thus, the result is that after *check_departures*, the agent will know whether or not Flight 123 is parked at Gate A. More generally, the set of accessible situations after performing any action is completely determined by the action, the state of the world, and the accessible situations before the action. This therefore extends Reiter's solution to the frame problem to the K fluent.

Robot programs

While the above theory provides an account of the relationship between knowledge and action, it does not allow us to use the classical definition of a plan. This is because, in general, there is no *sequence of actions* that can be shown to achieve a desired goal; typically, what actions are required depends on the runtime results of earlier sensing actions.

It is tempting to amend the classical definition of planning to say that the task is now to find a *program* (which may contain conditionals or loops) that achieves the goal, a sequence of actions being merely a special case.

But saying we need a program is not enough. We need a program that does not contain conditions whose truth value (nor terms whose denotations) would be unknown to the agent at the required time: that is, the agent needs to *know how* to execute the program. One possibility is to develop an account of what it means to know how to execute an arbitrary program, for example, as was done by Davis in [2]. While this approach is certainly workable, it does lead to some complications. There may be programs that the agent "knows how" to execute in this sense but that we do not want to consider as plans.[7] Here, we make a much simpler proposal: invent a programming language $\mathcal{R}$ whose programs include both ordinary and sensing actions, and which are all so clearly executable that an agent will trivially know how to do so.

Consider the following simple programming language, defined as the least set of terms satisfying the following:

1. <u>nil</u> and <u>exit</u> are programs;
2. If a is an ordinary action and r is a program, then <u>seq</u>(a, r) is a program;
3. If a is a binary sensing action and r_1 and r_2 are programs, then <u>branch</u>(a, r_1, r_2) is a program;
4. If r_1 and r_2 are programs, then <u>loop</u>(r_1, r_2) is a program.

We will call such terms *robot programs* and the resulting set of terms $\mathcal{R}$, the robot programming language.

Informally, these programs are executed by an agent as follows: to execute <u>nil</u> the agent does nothing; to execute <u>exit</u> it must be executing a <u>loop</u>, in which case see below; to execute <u>seq</u>(a, r), it executes primitive action a, and then r; to execute <u>branch</u>(a, r_1, r_2) it executes a which is supposed to tell it whether or not some condition ϕ_a holds, and so it executes r_1 if it does, and r_2 otherwise; to execute <u>loop</u>(r_1, r_2), it executes the body r_1, and if it ends with <u>nil</u>, it repeats r_1 again, and continues doing so until it ends with <u>exit</u>, in which case it finishes by executing r_2.

The reason a loop-exit construct is used instead of the more "structured" while-loop, is that to ensure that an agent would always know how to execute a robot program, $\mathcal{R}$ does not include any conditions involving fluents. Thus, although we want robot programs to contain branches and loops, we cannot use the traditional if-then-else or while-loop constructs. $\mathcal{R}$ is a minimal language satisfying our criteria, but other designs are certainly possible. Note that it will not be our intent to ever write programs in this language; it should be thought of as an "assembly language" into which planning goals will compile.

Here are two example robot programs. The first, R_{air}, is from the Airport domain:

<u>seq</u>(go(airport),
  <u>branch</u>(check_departures,
    <u>seq</u>(go(gateA),<u>seq</u>(board_plane(Flight123),<u>nil</u>))
    <u>seq</u>(go(gateB),<u>seq</u>(board_plane(Flight123),<u>nil</u>))));

the second, R_{egg}, is from the Omelette domain:

<u>loop</u>(body,
  <u>seq</u>(transfer(saucer,bowl),
    <u>loop</u>(body,
      <u>seq</u>(transfer(saucer,bowl),
        <u>loop</u>(body,
          <u>seq</u>(transfer(saucer,bowl),nil)))))),

where *body* stands for the program

<u>seq</u>(break_new_egg(saucer),
  <u>branch</u>(smell(saucer),
    <u>seq</u>(dump(saucer),<u>nil</u>),
    <u>exit</u>)).

There is an equivalent formulation of robot programs as finite directed graphs. See the regrettably tiny figures squeezed in after the references.

Intuitively at least, the following should be clear:

- An agent can always be assumed to know how to execute a robot program. These programs are completely deterministic, and do not mention any fluents. Assuming the binary sensing actions return a single bit of information to the agent, there is nothing else it should need to know.
- The example robot programs above, when executed, result in final situations where the goals of the above planning problems are satisfied: R_{air} gets the agent on Flight 123, and R_{egg} gets 3 good eggs into the bowl.

In this sense, the programs above constitute a solution to the earlier planning problems.

To be precise about this, we need to first define what situation is the final one resulting from executing a robot program r in an initial situation s. Because a robot program

[7] Consider, for example, the program that says (the equivalent of) "find a plan and then execute it." While this program is easy enough to generate, figuring out how to execute it sensibly is as hard as the original planning problem.

could conceivably loop forever (e.g. $\underline{loop}(\underline{nil},\underline{nil})$), we will use a formula $Rdo(r, s, s')$ to mean that r terminates legally when started in s, and s' is the final situation. Formally, *Rdo* is an abbreviation for the following second-order formula:

$$Rdo(r, s_1, s_2) \stackrel{def}{=} \forall P[\ldots \supset P(r, s_1, s_2, 1)]$$

where the ellipsis is (the conjunction of the universal closure of) the following:

1. Termination, normal case:
   $P(\underline{nil}, s, s, 1)$;
2. Termination, loop body:
   $P(\underline{exit}, s, s, 0)$;
3. Ordinary actions:
   $Poss(a, s) \wedge P(r', do(a, s), s', x) \supset$
   $P(\underline{seq}(a, r'), s, s', x)$;
4. Sensing actions, true case:
   $Poss(a, s) \wedge SF(a, s) \wedge P(r', do(a, s), s', x) \supset$
   $P(\underline{branch}(a, r', r''), s, s', x)$;
5. Sensing actions, false case:
   $Poss(a, s) \wedge \neg SF(a, s) \wedge P(r'', do(a, s), s', x) \supset$
   $P(\underline{branch}(a, r', r''), s, s', x)$;
6. Loops, exit case:
   $P(r', s, s'', 0) \wedge P(r'', s'', s', x) \supset$
   $P(\underline{loop}(r', r''), s, s', x)$;
7. Loops, repeat case:
   $P(r', s, s'', 1) \wedge P(\underline{loop}(r', r''), s'', s', x) \supset$
   $P(\underline{loop}(r', r''), s, s', x)$.

By using second-order quantification in this way, we are defining *Rdo* recursively as the *least* predicate P satisfying the constraints in the ellipsis. Second-order logic is necessary here since there is no way to characterize the transitive closure implicit in unbounded iteration in first-order terms.

Within this definition, the relation $P(r, s, s', 0)$ is intended to hold when executing r starting in s terminates at s' with $\underline{exit}$; $P(r, s, s', 1)$ is the same but terminating with $\underline{nil}$. The difference shows up when executing $\underline{loop}(r, r')$: in the former case, we exit the loop and continue with r'; in the latter, we continue the iteration by repeating $\underline{loop}(r, r')$ once more.

It is not hard to show that these robot programs are *deterministic*, in that there is at most a single s' such that $Rdo(r, s, s')$ holds. Less trivially, we also get:

Theorem 1: *The following formulas are logically valid:*

1. $Rdo(\underline{nil}, s, s') \equiv (s = s')$.
2. $Rdo(\underline{seq}(a, r), s, s') \equiv Poss(a, s) \wedge Rdo(r, do(a, s), s')$.
3. $Rdo(\underline{branch}(a, r, r'), s, s') \equiv Poss(a, s) \wedge$
   $[SF(a, s) \supset Rdo(r, do(a, s), s')] \wedge$
   $[\neg SF(a, s) \supset Rdo(r', do(a, s), s')]$.
4. $Rdo(\underline{loop}(r, r'), s, s') \equiv$
   $Rdo(\mathrm{unwind}(r, r', \underline{loop}(r, r')), s, s')$
   where $\mathrm{unwind}(r, r', r'')$ *is defined recursively by*
   (a) $\mathrm{unwind}(\underline{exit}, r', r'') = r'$
   (b) $\mathrm{unwind}(\underline{nil}, r', r'') = r''$
   (c) $\mathrm{unwind}(\underline{seq}(a, r), r', r'') = \underline{seq}(a, \mathrm{unwind}(r, r', r''))$
   (d) $\mathrm{unwind}(\underline{branch}(a, r_1, r_2), r', r'') =$
   $\underline{branch}(a, \mathrm{unwind}(r_1, r', r''), \mathrm{unwind}(r_2, r', r''))$
   (e) $\mathrm{unwind}(\underline{loop}(r_1, r_2), r', r'') =$
   $\underline{loop}(r_1, \mathrm{unwind}(r_2, r', r''))$

This theorem tells us how to build an interpreter for robot programs. For example, to execute

$$\underline{loop}(\underline{branch}(a, \underline{exit}, \underline{seq}(b, \underline{nil})), r),$$

we can unwind the loop and execute

$$\underline{branch}(a, r, \underline{seq}(b, \underline{loop}(\underline{branch}(a, \underline{exit}, \underline{seq}(b, \underline{nil})), r))).$$

Note that we should not try to define *Rdo* "axiomatically" using axioms like these (as in [13], for example) since they are first-order, and not strong enough to characterize loop termination.

The revised planning task

With the definition of a plan as a robot program, we are now ready to generalize the classical planning task:

> **Revised Planning:** Given a domain theory *Axioms* and a goal formula $\phi(s')$ with a single free-variable s', the planning task is to find a robot program r in the language $\mathcal{R}$ such that:
>
> $$Axioms \models \forall s.K(s, S_0) \supset \exists s'[Rdo(r, s, s') \wedge \phi(s')]$$
>
> where *Axioms* can be similar to what it was, but now covering sensing actions and the K fluent.

To paraphrase: we are looking for a robot program r such that it is known in the initial situation that the program will terminate in a goal state.[8] This reduces to the classical definition when there are no sensing actions, and $K(s, S_0)$ holds iff $(s = S_0)$. In this case, it is sufficient to find an r of the form $\underline{seq}(a_1, \underline{seq}(a_2, \ldots \underline{nil}))$.

Note that we are requiring that the program lead to a goal state s' starting in any s such that $K(s, S_0)$; in different s, r may produce very different sequences of actions.

To show this definition in action, we will formalize a version of the Airport problem and establish the correctness of the above robot program and a few variants.

For our purposes, there are two ordinary actions $go(x)$ and $board\_plane(p)$, one sensing action *check_departures*, and three relational fluents $At(x, s)$, $On\_plane(p, s)$ and $Parked(p, x, s)$, where x is a location, either *home*, *airport*, *gateA*, or *gateB*, and p is a plane. We have the following domain theory:[9]

[8] We are requiring the agent to *know how* to achieve the goal, in that the desired r must be known initially to achieve ϕ. A variant would require an r that achieved ϕ starting in S_0, but perhaps unbeknownst to the agent. A third variant might require not merely ϕ, but that the agent know that ϕ at the end. So many variants; so little space.

[9] We omit here unique name axioms for constants, as well as domain closure axioms, including one saying that Gate A and Gate B are the only gates.

- Precondition axioms:
  $Poss(board\_plane(p), s) \equiv \exists x.Parked(p, x, s) \wedge At(x, s)$
  $Poss(check\_departures) \equiv \neg At(home, s)$
  $Poss(go(x), s) \equiv x = airport \vee At(airport, s)$;
- Successor state axioms: the one above for K and
  $Poss(a, s) \supset \{At(x, do(a, s)) \equiv$
  $a = go(x) \vee (At(x, s) \wedge \neg\exists y.a = go(y))\}$
  $Poss(a, s) \supset \{On\_plane(p, do(a, s) \equiv$
  $a = board\_plane(p) \vee On\_plane(p, s)\}$
  $Poss(a, s) \supset \{Parked(p, x, do(a, s)) \equiv Parked(p, x, s)\}$;
- Sensed fluent axiom:
  $SF(go(x), s) \wedge SF(board\_plane(p), s) \wedge$
  $[SF(check\_departures, s) \equiv$
  $Parked(Flight123, gateA, s)]$.

The goal $\phi(s')$ to be satisfied is $On\_plane(Flight123, s')$. We claim that a solution to this planning problem is the earlier robot program R_{air}. Using the above theorem, the proof is straightforward:[10] We need to show

$$K(s, S_0) \supset \exists s' [Rdo(R_{\text{air}}, s, s') \wedge On\_plane(Flight123, s')].$$

So let us imagine that $K(s, S_0)$ and show that there is an appropriate s'. There are two cases: first suppose that $Parked(Flight123, gateA, s)$.

1. Let $a_1 = go(airport)$ and $s_1 = s$. The program R_{air} is of the form $\underline{seq}(a_1, R_1)$. By a precondition axiom, we have $Poss(a_1, s_1)$. So by the Theorem above, $Rdo(R_{\text{air}}, s, s')$ if $Rdo(R_1, do(a_1, s_1), s')$.
2. Let $a_2 = check\_departures$ and $s_2 = do(a_1, s_1)$. R_1 is of the form $\underline{branch}(a_2, R_{2a}, R_{2b})$. By the successor state axiom for *At*, we have $At(airport, s_2)$, and so by a precondition axiom, we have $Poss(a_2, s_2)$. By the successor state axiom for *Parked*, we have $Parked(Flight123, gateA, s_2)$, and so $SF(check\_departures, s_2)$. So by the Theorem, $Rdo(R_1, s_2, s')$ if $Rdo(R_{2a}, do(a_2, s_2), s')$.
3. Let $a_3 = go(gateA)$ and $s_3 = do(a_2, s_2)$. R_{2a} is of the form $\underline{seq}(a_3, R_3)$. By the successor state axiom for *At*, we have $At(airport, s_3)$, and so by a precondition axiom, we have $Poss(a_3, s_3)$. By the successor state axiom for *Parked*, we have $Parked(Flight123, gateA, s_3)$. So by the Theorem, $Rdo(R_{2a}, s_3, s')$ if $Rdo(R_3, do(a_3, s_3), s')$.
4. Let $a_4 = board\_plane(Flight123)$ and $s_4 = do(a_3, s_3)$. R_3 is the robot program $\underline{seq}(a_4, \underline{nil})$. By the successor state axiom for *At*, we have $At(gateA, s_4)$, and by the successor state axiom for *Parked*, we have $Parked(Flight123, gateA, s_4)$. Thus, by a precondition axiom, we have $Poss(a_4, s_4)$. So by the Theorem, $Rdo(R_3, s_4, s')$ if $s' = do(a_4, s_4)$. Moreover, for this s' we have by the successor state axiom for *On_plane* that $On\_plane(Flight123, s')$.

[10] In the following, for convenience, we will systematically be confusing use with mention: we will be saying that p where p is a logical sentence, meaning that it is true in any interpretation satisfying the above axioms.

Putting all the pieces together, we can see that for any s such that $Parked(Flight123, gateA, s)$, there is an s' such that $Rdo(R_{\text{air}}, s, s')$ and $On\_plane(Flight123, s')$, namely

$$s' = do([go(airport), check\_departures, go(gateA), board\_plane(Flight123)], s).$$

The case where $Parked(Flight123, gateB, s)$ is completely analogous, but leads to

$$s' = do([go(airport), check\_departures, go(gateB), board\_plane(Flight123)], s).$$

Note that in each case there also exists a sequence of actions not containing *check_departures* that puts the agent on Flight 123. However, no robot program without sensing would be able to generate *both* cases.

We can also consider what happens if the agent knows initially where the plane is parked:

- Initial State:
  $\forall s.K(s, S_0) \supset Parked(Flight123, gateB, s)$.

The argument above shows that R_{air} continues to work in this context even with the redundant sensing (there is only one case to consider now). The same argument also shows that if we replace the $\underline{seq}(go(gateA), \ldots)$ part in R_{air} by anything at all, the program still works. Of course, the program with no sensing would work here too.

Observe that the derivation above does not make use of the successor state axiom for K. This is because the agent was not required to know anything in the final state. It is not hard to prove that not only does R_{air} achieve the goal $On\_plane(Flight123, s')$, it also achieves $Know(On\_plane(Flight123), s')$. We can also imagine new primitive actions that depend on knowledge preconditions, such as "going to the gate of a flight," which can only be executed if the agent knows where the plane is parked:

$$Poss(go\_gate(p), s) \equiv At(airport, s) \wedge \exists x.Know(Parked(p, x), s).$$

With a suitable modification to the successor state axiom for *At* to accommodate this new action, an argument like the one above shows that the robot program

$$\underline{seq}(go(airport), \underline{seq}(check\_departures, \underline{seq}(go\_gate(Flight123), \underline{seq}(board\_plane(Flight123), \underline{nil})))),$$

with no conditional branching, achieves the goal. This shows that whether a plan containing sensing needs to be conditional depends on the primitive actions available.

One clear advantage of a specification like ours is that in being independent of any planner, it gives us the freedom to look at plans like these that might never be generated by a planner. This is especially useful if we are using a *plan critic* of some sort to modify an existing plan to reduce cost, or risk, or perhaps just to make sensing actions happen as early as possible. Plan correctness is not tied to any assumptions about how the plan was produced.

Are robot programs enough?

Given the extreme simplicity of the robot program language $\mathcal{R}$, and given that the planning task is defined in terms of the existence of robot programs, one might reasonably wonder if the restriction to $\mathcal{R}$ rules out goals that are intuitively achievable. Consider the following two examples:

The Odd Good Eggs Example The setup is exactly like the Omelette example, except that there is an additional sensing action, which tells you when the supply of eggs is exhausted. The goal is to have a single good egg in the bowl, but only if the supply contains an odd number of good eggs; otherwise, the bowl should remain empty.

The More Good Eggs Example The setup is as above. The goal now is to have a single good egg in the bowl, but only if the supply contains more good eggs than bad; otherwise, the bowl should be empty.

These are unusual goals, admittedly. But they do show that it is possible to encode language-recognition problems (over strings of eggs!) in a robotic setting. Informally, both goals are achievable in that we can imagine physical devices that are able to do so. The formal claim here is this: there is a robot program that achieves the first goal (which we omit for space reasons), but there is provably none that achieves the second. The proof is essentially the proof that a finite automaton cannot recognize the language consisting of binary strings with more 1's than 0's. To do so, you need the equivalent of a counter.

To preserve the simple structure of $\mathcal{R}$, we augment our set of primitive actions to give the robot a *memory*. Thus, we assume that apart from those of the background theory, we have 5 special actions, *left*, *right*, *mark*, *erase*, *read_mark*, and two special fluents *Marked*, *pos*, characterized by the following axioms:

1. Precondition: the 5 actions are always possible
   $Poss(left, s) \wedge Poss(right, s) \wedge Poss(mark, s)$
   $\quad \wedge Poss(erase, s) \wedge Poss(read\_mark, s)$;
2. Successor state: only *erase* and *mark* change *Marked*
   $Poss(a, s) \supset \{Marked(n, do(a, s)) \equiv$
   $\quad a = mark \wedge pos(s) = n \quad \vee$
   $\quad Marked(n, s) \wedge \neg[a = erase \wedge pos(s) = n]\}$;
3. Successor state: only *left* and *right* change the *pos* fluent
   $Poss(a, s) \supset \{pos(do(a, s)) = n \equiv$
   $\quad a = left \wedge pos(s) = n + 1 \quad \vee$
   $\quad a = right \wedge pos(s) = n - 1 \quad \vee$
   $\quad pos(s) = n \wedge a \neq left \wedge a \neq right\}$;
4. Sensed fluent: *read_mark* tells the agent whether the current position is marked
   $SF(left, s) \wedge SF(right, s) \wedge SF(erase, s) \wedge SF(mark, s) \wedge$
   $\quad [SF(read\_mark, s) \equiv Marked(pos(s), s)]$.

These axioms ensure that the 5 special actions provide the robot with what amounts to a Turing machine tape. The idea is that when solving a planning task wrt a background theory Σ, we look for a robot program that works wrt $(\Sigma \cup TM)$, where *TM* is the set of axioms above. We can then prove that the More Good Eggs example is now solvable (again, we omit the program).

We believe that no further extensions to $\mathcal{R}$ will be needed. However, to prove this, we would want to show that any "effectively achievable" goal can be achieved by some robot program. But this requires an independent account of effective achievability, that is, an analogue of computability for robots over a domain-dependent set of actions whose effects are characterized by a set of axioms. To our knowledge, no such account yet exists, so we are developing one.

Conclusion

One limitation of the work presented here is that it offers no suggestions about how to automatically generate plans like those above in a reasonable way. Of course, our specification does provide us with a planning procedure (of sorts):

Planning Procedure (ϕ) {
  repeat with $r \in \mathcal{R}$ {
    if $Axioms \models \forall s. K(s, S_0) \supset$
      $\exists s' [Rdo(r, s, s') \wedge \phi(s')]$
    then return r }}

We can also think of the r as being returned by answer extraction [5] from an attempt to prove the following:

$$Axioms \models \exists r \forall s. K(s, S_0) \supset \exists s' [Rdo(r, s, s') \wedge \phi(s')]$$

Either way, the procedure would be problematic: we are searching blindly through the space of all possible robot programs, and for each one, the constraint to check involves using the K fluent explicitly as well as the (second-order!) *Rdo* formula. However, we do not want to suggest that a specification of the planning task ought to be used this way to generate plans. Indeed, our criticism of earlier accounts was precisely that they were overly tied up with specific planning procedures.

In our own work in Cognitive Robotics, we take a slightly different approach. Instead of planning tasks, we focus on the execution of high-level programs written in the GOLOG programming language [7]. GOLOG programs look like ordinary block-structured imperative programs except that they are nondeterministic, and they use the primitive actions and fluents of a user-supplied domain theory. There is a formula of the situation calculus $Do(\delta, s, s')$, analogous to *Rdo*, which says that s' is one of potentially many terminating situations of GOLOG program δ when started in initial situation s. To execute δ (when there are no sensing actions), a GOLOG processor must first find a legal sequence of primitive actions $\vec{a}$ such that

$$Axioms \models Do(\delta, S_0, do(\vec{a}, S_0)),$$

which it can then pass to a robot for actual execution. This is obviously a special case of planning. Furthermore, when δ contains sensing actions, an argument analogous to the one presented here suggests that instead of $\vec{a}$, the GOLOG processor would need to find a robot program r [8].

With or without sensing, considerable searching may be required to do this type of processing. To illustrate an extreme case, the GOLOG program

while $\neg Goal$ **do** $(\pi\ a)[Appropriate(a)?;\ a]$ **end**, repeatedly selects an appropriate action and performs it until some goal is achieved. Finding a sequence of actions in this case is simply a reformulation of the planning problem. However, the key point here is that at the other extreme, when the GOLOG program is fully deterministic, execution can be extremely efficient since little or no searching is required. The hope is that many useful cases of high-level agent control will lie somewhere between these two extremes.

A major representational limitation of the approach presented here concerns the binary sensing actions and the desire to avoid mentioning fluents in a robot program. Sensing actions that return one of a small set of values (such as reading a digit on a piece of paper, or detecting the colour of an object) can be handled readily by a case-like construct. Even a large or infinite set might be handled, if the values can be ordered in a natural way.

But suppose that sensing involves reading from a noisy sensor, so that instead of returning (say) the distance to the nearest wall, we get a number from a sensor that is only correlated with that distance. An account already exists of how to characterize in the situation calculus such sensing actions, and the effect they have not on knowledge now, but on degrees of belief [1]. However, how robot programs or planning could be defined in terms of this account still remains to be seen.

References

[1] F. Bacchus, J. Halpern, and H. Levesque. Reasoning about noisy sensors in the situation calculus. In *Proc. of IJCAI-95*, pp. 1933–1940, Montréal, August 1995. Morgan Kaufmann Publishing.

[2] E. Davis. Knowledge preconditions for plans. Technical Report 637, Computer Science Department, New York University, 1993.

[3] O. Etzioni, S. Hanks, D. Weld, D. Draper, N. Lesh, and M. Williamson. An approach to planning with incomplete information. In *Principles of Knowledge Representation and Reasoning: Proceedings of the Third International Conference*, pp. 115–125, Cambridge, MA, 1992. Morgan Kaufmann Publishing.

[4] O. Etzioni and S. Hanks. Personal comm., 1995.

[5] Cordell C. Green. Theorem proving by resolution as a basis for question-answering systems. In *Machine Intelligence 4*, pp. 183–205. Edinburgh University Press, 1969.

[6] F. Lin and R. Reiter. How to progress a database II: The STRIPS connection. In *Proceedings of IJCAI-95*, pp. 2001–2007, Montreal, Aug. 20-25, 1995.

[7] H. J. Levesque, R. Reiter, Y. Lespérance, F. Lin, and R. Scherl. GOLOG: A logic programming language for dynamic domains. To appear in the *Journal of Logic Programming*, 1996.

[8] Hector J. Levesque. The execution of high-level robot programs with sensing actions: theory and implementation. In preparation, 1996.

[9] K. Krebsbach, D. Olawsky, and M. Gini. An empirical study of sensing and defaulting in planning. In *Proc. of 1st Conference on AI Planning Systems*, pp. 136–144, San Mateo CA, 1992.

[10] Z. Manna and R. Waldinger. How to clear a block: A theory of plans. *Journal of Automated Reasoning*, 3:343–377, 1987.

[11] D. McAllester and D. Rosenblitt. Systematic nonlinear planning. In *Proc. of AAAI-91*, pp. 634–639, Menlo Park, CA, July 1991.

[12] J. McCarthy and P. J. Hayes. Some philosophical problems from the standpoint of artificial intelligence. In *Machine Intelligence 4*, pp. 463–502. Edinburgh University Press, 1969.

[13] R. C. Moore. A formal theory of knowledge and action. In J. R. Hobbs and R. C. Moore, editors, *Formal theories of the common sense world*, pp. 319–358. Ablex Publishing, Norwood, NJ, 1985.

[14] M. Peot and D. Smith. Conditional nonlinear planning. In *Proc. of 1st Conference on AI Planning Systems*, pp. 189–197, San Mateo CA, 1992.

[15] R. Reiter. The frame problem in the situation calculus: A simple solution (sometimes) and a completeness result for goal regression. In Vladimir Lifschitz, editor, *Artificial Intelligence and Mathematical Theory of Computation: Papers in Honor of John McCarthy*, pp. 359–380. Academic Press, San Diego, CA, 1991.

[16] R. Scherl and H. Levesque. The frame problem and knowledge-producing actions. In *Proc. of AAAI-93*, pp. 689–695, Washington, DC, July 1993. AAAI Press/The MIT Press.

[17] M. Schoppers. Building plans to monitor and exploit open-loop and closed-loop dynamics. In *Proc. of 1st Conference on AI Planning Systems*, pp. 204–213, San Mateo CA, 1992.

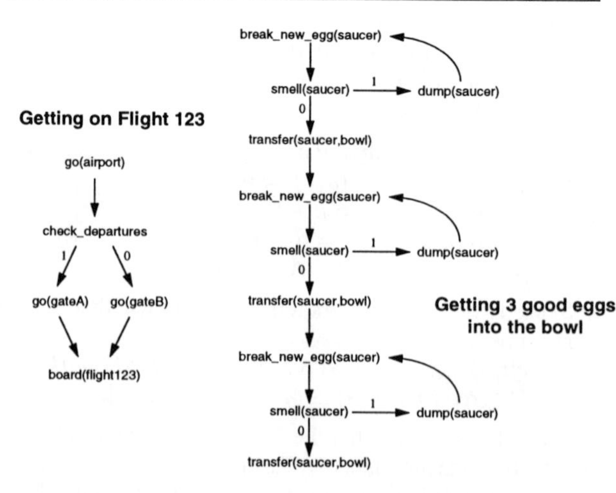

Opportunity recognition in complex environments

Louise Pryor
Department of Artificial Intelligence
University of Edinburgh
80 South Bridge
Edinburgh EH1 1HN
Scotland
louisep@aisb.ed.ac.uk

Abstract

An agent operating in an unpredictable world must be able to take advantage of opportunities but cannot afford to perform a detailed analysis of the effects of every nuance of the current situation on its goals if it is to respond in a timely manner. This paper describes a filtering mechanism that enables the effective recognition of opportunities. The mechanism is based on a characterization of the world in terms of *reference features*, features that are both cheap and functional and that appear to be prevalent in everyday life. Its use enables the plan execution system PARETO to recognize types of opportunities that other systems cannot. Reference features can also play a rôle in the detection of threats, and may be involved in the development of expertise.

Introduction

The world is unpredictable—it is impossible to tell in advance exactly what its state will be at any future time—so plans on their own are not sufficient to govern the behavior of a goal-driven agent. For example, a robot roaming the surface of a strange planet will have to be able to decide for itself where it should take soil samples, what areas to explore and what routes to take. The samples that should be taken may depend *inter alia* on the terrain that is encountered, atmospheric conditions, and the results of tests on earlier samples, none of which can be predicted in detail. Moreover, the number of possibilities is huge: it would be impossible to construct contingency plans for all combinations of circumstances that could be encountered, even if it were possible to predict what they might be.

The traditional approach to AI planning assumes that plans are guaranteed to work and that nothing unexpected can happen during their execution. However, in many real-world domains the inevitability of the unexpected means that any plans that are made in advance will have to be changed during execution (Alterman 1986; Firby 1987; Hammond 1989; Pryor & Collins 1994). Expending a great deal of effort on constructing elaborate and detailed plans by trying to predict exactly what will happen is therefore often unproductive. A more effective approach is to choose simple plans and adapt them when unforeseen circumstances are encountered An agent following this approach must be able to determine when it should change its current plan. This determination is not trivial. Any aspect of the world may in principle affect any of the agent's goals: any change in the world may thus make it desirable to change plans. The agent cannot afford to analyze in detail every circumstance that it encounters if it is to respond appropriately.

This paper presents a filtering mechanism that can be used to decide when a detailed analysis of the agent's circumstances should be performed. The mechanism has been implemented in the plan execution system PARETO.[1] The mechanism used in PARETO is based on the observation that the world, although unpredictable in detail, is in essence very regular. It uses the fact that particular aspects of the world are often associated with the achievement or frustration of certain types of goals. For example, the presence of a sharp object is often implicated in the ability to achieve a goal of cutting something. The *sharp*ness of an object indicates its effect on goals whose achievement is affected if the object cuts something else. There are many concepts such as *sharp* that describe effects on goals: they form the basis of an effective method of opportunity recognition.[2]

The problem

An agent should change its plans when an unpredicted environmental factor affects the achievement of its goals. Goals can be affected in two ways: either opportunities are presented, or threats are posed. This paper concentrates on the recognition of opportunities; the principles involved are much the same for threats.

Opportunity recognition is complex in two ways. First, there is an enormous number of elements in every

[1]Planning and Acting in Realistic Environments by Thinking about Opportunities. The economist, sociologist and philosopher Vilfredo Pareto (1848–1923) is best known for the notion of *Pareto optimality* and for the *Pareto distribution*, neither of which is used in this work.

[2]This work is described in more detail in (Pryor 1994).

situation that no agent can possibly predict (Brand & Birnbaum 1990). None of these elements can be ruled out *a priori* as never being relevant to any goal. Suppose, for example, that you have a goal to open a can of paint. The objects in your garage include your car, the shelves on the wall, engine oil, *etc.* Few of these are relevant to your current goal, but they may be relevant to other goals at other times. Second, there are many subgoals involved in achieving a goal. For instance, to pry the lid off the paint can you must find something that is the right size and shape to act as a lever, a strong rigid surface on which you can rest the can at a convenient height, and so on.

The analysis of each situation element of a complex environment in the light of each of the agent's many goals would involve huge numbers of subgoals and situation elements and would preclude a timely response to unforeseen situations. Moreover, such an analysis would require the determination of each goal's subgoals, thus demanding the existence of a plan to achieve that goal. However, the recognition of an opportunity may trigger a radical change of plan or the construction of a plan for a hitherto unplanned-for goal. PARETO can recognize and take advantage of opportunities in these circumstances.

Related work

Most research on the issues of replanning during plan execution fails to address the issue of opportunism. The need to replan is usually determined by projecting the agent's current plans explicitly (Ferguson 1992; McDermott 1992); as projection may involve arbitrarily complex reasoning, the problem of the timely recognition of opportunities is not addressed.

Hayes-Roth and Hayes-Roth (1979) look at opportunism in plan construction but do not extend the concept to plan execution. Birnbaum and Collins (1984) present a theory of opportunism in plan execution based on the idea that opportunity recognition should be goal-driven rather than environment-driven. They suggest that each goal should be an active *mental agent*, performing the necessary reasoning to recognize opportunities to achieve itself. They do not address the issue of how agents can recognize opportunities with little reasoning: sharing the reasoning among the goals does not necessarily reduce the amount required.

Hammond *et al.* (1993) suggest that each goal should have associated with it the features in the environment that will be involved in achieving it. Such features might include tools and resources, locations at which the goal can be achieved, *etc.* The agent then recognizes an opportunity for the goal when the relevant feature appears in the environment. This approach relies on having specified the plan that will be used in enough detail that the relevant features are already known. It does not allow an agent to recognize opportunities that require a method of achievement other than that in the current plan or for goals that it has not yet decided how to achieve.

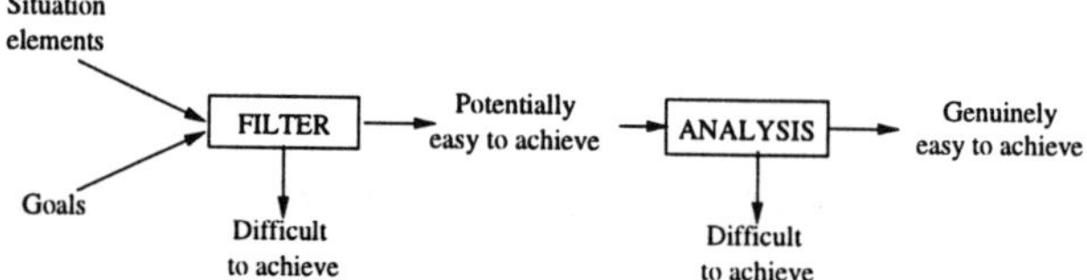

Figure 1: A filter for potential opportunities

The RAPS plan execution system recognizes opportunities only when their possibility has been represented in the plans being executed (Firby 1987; 1989). Reactive systems such as PENGI require the system designer to have encoded potential opportunities into the reaction rules (Agre & Chapman 1987).

PARETO's approach extends the range of opportunism by enabling the speedy recognition of opportunities for goals for which a plan has not yet been chosen and of opportunities whose possibility has not been explicitly foreseen.

A filter for opportunity recognition

PARETO uses a filtering mechanism that indicates those situations in which there are likely to be opportunities and that will therefore repay further analysis (Figure 1). It is based on two key observations: first that there is a large class of opportunities whose presence is indicated by a single critical factor; and second that the causal properties of situation elements, and thus their effects on goals, are in general predictable.

The critical factor hypothesis

Although an opportunity usually arises as the result of a number of factors, in many cases few of these factors by themselves indicate the presence of an opportunity. For example, the presence of a table does not usually constitute an opportunity to open a can of paint. There are many different ways in which the requirement of having somewhere to rest the can could be met, and it happens that the presence of the table is one of them. However, the presence of a screwdriver is more significant; there are comparatively few objects that are suitable for use as a lever. The *critical factor hypothesis* states that the presence of a single factor is often crucial for the existence of an opportunity.

The critical factor hypothesis relies on the observation that many situation elements are stable across many different situations. There is more stability at the functional level than at the purely physical: while there may not always be a table, there is usually something that you can use to support an object. It is thus usually easy to meet most of the preconditions for a given goal and the presence of situation elements that allow you to meet these preconditions does not greatly affect goal achievement. However, there is often one precondition that is more difficult to achieve, such as the availability of a lever that will fit under the lid of the can. The presence of a situation element that enables the achievement of this precondition is then sufficient to indicate the presence of an opportunity.

The critical factor hypothesis appears to hold for a large number of opportunities and forms the basis of an effective filtering mechanism for recognizing opportunities. An agent can take the presence of a factor that is critical for one of its goals as an indication that the goal is worth analyzing in more detail.

Reference features

A filtering process is only effective if it is cheap and adequately predictive.[3] The critical factor hypothesis means that an agent need only recognize the presence of the critical factor for a goal to realize that there may be an opportunity for it. However, the filtering process cannot involve a detailed functional analysis of all the elements of the current situation to determine whether they are critical factors for any of the agent's goals. Instead, we can use the fact that the causal properties of objects tend to be stable across situations: *e.g.*, knives and scissors tend to cut things, tables to support things, and cups to hold liquids.

These functional tendencies can be labeled; for instance, objects that cut other things are labeled as being `sharp`. There are many similar descriptive terms that label functional properties of objects. Words such as `absorbent`, `sturdy` and `fragile` indicate that the object with the property either affects other objects in some way or is itself affected. These properties can be used when planning to achieve goals: something sharp can be used to cut another object, something absorbent to mop up a spill, and something sturdy to support a heavy object. We call these labels *reference features*.

Reference features are cheap to compute To be effective the filtering process must involve minimal reasoning. An important characteristic of reference features is thus the ease of infering them in most situations in which the associated causal effects are present.

Reference features are often associated with perceptual cues: *e.g.*, a `sharp` object has a well-defined edge between two nearly parallel planes. In such cases, the sight of an object is enough to bring the reference feature to mind. There are obvious links to the theory of *affordances* proposed by Gibson (1979): an environment's affordances are the functionalities it offers to an animal in it. There are two main differences between affordances and reference features. First, reference features are not limited to interactions between the agent and its environment: *e.g.*, a surface can have the reference feature `support` even if it could not bear the agent's own weight, as long as its ability to support other objects is useful to the agent. Second, reference features need not be directly linked to perceptual features: *e.g.*, we do not have to feel or even see a rubber band in order to apply the term `elastic` to it.

[3] It is in the nature of heuristic filtering processes such as this that some mistakes will be made.

Surfaces: `smooth`, `sticky`, `slippery`, `rough`, `gritty`, `dull`, `shiny`, `greasy`	Load-bearing: `flimsy`, `sturdy`, `tough`, `heavy`, `light`, `soft`, `hard`, `solid`
Containment: `bulky`, `dense`, `tiny`, `large`, `small`, `big`, `hollow`	Liquids: `impermeable`, `permeable`, `absorbent`, `viscous`
Breaking: `delicate`, `brittle`, `fragile`, `robust`	Deformation: `rigid`, `flexible`, `elastic`
Cutting: `sharp`, `blunt`, `soft`, `hard`	Temperature: `hot`, `cold`, `frozen`
Optics: `transparent`, `translucent`, `opaque`	Use as tools: `lever`, `pointed`, `graspable`
Tasks and plans: `urgent`, `fiddly`, `lengthy`	Stability: `stable`, `precarious`, `balanced`

Table 1: Some reference features in everyday domains

Sloman (1989) proposed compact functional descriptions derived from the possibilities for motion provided by physical descriptions of objects. Reference features are more general, as they are not concerned with motion alone but with any type of relevant functionality. Some reference features from everyday domains are shown in Table 1.

Reference features are highly predictive The filtering process used in PARETO is predictive because it is based on the critical factor hypothesis. A critical factor in the achievement of a goal is characterized in functional terms, *i.e.*, in terms of its causal effects on goals. For example, objects that can cut things are critical factors for the goal of cutting string. Reference features, which label the functional tendencies of objects, can thus be used to recognize critical factors.

It is important to note that reference features do not form a complete functional classification of situation elements. For example, not all objects with the reference feature `sharp` help with the goal of finding something to cut a cake. Reference features are useful only because they form the basis of a heuristic filter that indicates some goals as being potentially easy to achieve. Goals that pass the filter can be analyzed further: although the filtering mechanism must reduce the amount of detailed reasoning required, it need not obviate the need for all reasoning. Reference features form a simplified classification of objects by their functionally interesting properties.

Reference features form the basis of an effective filter for opportunities because they constitute an intermediate level of conceptualizing the world between the physical vocabulary provided by perception and the functional vocabulary required to reason about goals. They are thus both cheap and highly predictive.

Recognizing opportunities

Reference features are attached to the situation elements that tend to cause the effects that they label. They can also be attached to goals by labeling each goal with the reference feature of its critical factor. If there is a situation element that shares a reference feature with one of the agent's goals, that goal is likely to be easily achievable. An agent can then use the following filtering process to spot potential opportunities:

1. Find the reference features in the current situation, indicating the easily achievable effects.
2. Find the reference features of its current goals, indicating the effects needed for goal achievement.
3. Compare the two sets of reference features. The goals whose reference features are found in the current situation are likely to be easily achievable.

The agent then analyzes the indicated goals to see whether they are genuinely easy to achieve.

PARETO

PARETO's world was built using the TRUCKWORLD simulator (Firby & Hanks 1987; Hanks, Pollack, & Cohen 1993). A delivery truck travels between locations, encountering and manipulating objects as it goes. There are three building sites whose workers use the truck to run delivery errands such as "fetch something to carry my tools in." There are over 30 types of object in PARETO's world, of which 20 are used for deliveries. At any moment, there are typically well over 100 different objects at the various locations. PARETO receives delivery orders at random intervals, with a typical run involving between seven and twelve separate deliveries. The world is unpredictable: the truck can sense only those objects at its current location; objects may spontaneously change location; and actions may fail to have the desired results.

How PARETO works

PARETO is based on the RAPS plan execution system (Firby 1987; 1989). When PARETO acquires a new goal, it looks in its library of RAPs (sketchy plans) for one that will achieve the goal. A RAP (Reactive Action Package) specifies all the different *methods* that might be used to achieve a goal. Each method consists of subgoals that must be achieved to execute the plan.

Having chosen a RAP for the goal, PARETO adds a new task to its *task agenda*. A task consists of a goal and a RAP that will achieve it. PARETO's execution cycle consists of choosing a task and processing it:

Either If it has succeeded remove it from the agenda;

Or If it is described by a RAP choose the appropriate method, based on the state of the world at the time that the processing takes place, and add a new task to the task agenda for each new goal;

Or Perform the primitive action specified by the task.

The original task is reprocessed after all its subtasks have succeeded. Their success does not guarantee the success of the original task as some time may pass between their execution and its repeat processing.

At any time during execution the agenda may hold tasks at varying levels of abstraction, ranging from tasks that have not been expanded at all to those consisting of single primitive actions. PARETO can choose any task on the agenda for processing: in general, however, constraints are observed that ensure subgoals are addressed in the correct order and that a parent task is not reprocessed until its subtasks have all succeeded.

PARETO's task selection algorithm, unlike that of the RAPS system, incorporates an opportunity recognition mechanism. Reference features are used to indicate tasks for which there are potential opportunities; they are then analyzed in more detail to determine whether the opportunities are genuine. Finally, PARETO chooses a task from among the set of those for which there are genuine opportunities together with those that are ready for expansion according to the constraints on the task agenda. A set of heuristics is used to ensure that opportunities are pursued when desirable without abandoning the original goal.

Reference features in PARETO

The reference features of situation elements are directly related to the goals they help achieve. PARETO is asked to deliver objects to building sites. Requests are often specified in terms of the type of object required, so every object has its type as a reference feature. Other goals are more loosely specified: *e.g.*, PARETO may be asked to deliver something that can be used to carry tools. Several types of object can be used to carry things; all have the reference feature `carrier`. The functional aspects of objects are relevant only insofar as they affect PARETO's goals; PARETO's reference features may not be those we would attach to the objects' real-world counterparts.

The critical factors for the goals that involve delivering objects are the objects to be delivered; the goals' reference features reflect the objects' properties. A delivery goal that specifies only the class of object to be delivered has the reference features of that class of object. More complex criteria have their own specific reference features: *e.g.*, a task to deliver something with which to carry tools has the reference feature `carrier`. Other tasks include those to travel to the location of a building site or unload an object at a building site, both of which have the reference feature `site`, and the task to refill the fuel tank, which has the reference features `fuel` and `fuel-drum`. There is an inheritance mechanism that ensures that subtasks inherit relevant reference features from their parent tasks.

Opportunity recognition in PARETO

This section gives a detailed example of PARETO's opportunity recognition.[4] PARETO has just received two requests: a `carry-tools` goal for `maple-ave` and a `cut-twine` goal for `sheridan-rd`. Each delivery goal has a `deliver-object` task on the task agenda. The first task PARETO chooses to process

[4]Program output is edited for brevity.

is `<deliver-object carry-tools>` which it expands into several subtasks, one of which is a `find-object` task, which is processed next. Boxes (which are suitable for carrying tools) are generally to be found at the `lumberyard`, so a `<truck-travel-to lumberyard>` subtask is added to the agenda and is then processed.

On the way to the `lumberyard` PARETO arrives at `warehouse-2` and scans its neighborhood as it always does when it arrives at a new place. Most of the objects present are irrelevant to its goals but two of them, a pair of `scissors` and a `bag`, are directly relevant to its `cut-twine` and `carry-tools` goals. The first step of PARETO's filtering process is to find the reference features of the current situation, which include:

```
Reference features for ITEM-20: (BAG CARRIER)
Reference features for ITEM-13: (SCISSORS SHARP)
```

The second step is to find the reference features of its current goals. PARETO attaches reference features directly to tasks on the task agenda: the `carry-tools` tasks have the reference feature `carrier`, while the `cut-twine` task has `sharp`.

The third step is to match the two sets of reference features. The `bag` indicates potential opportunities for several of the subtasks of the `carry-tools` goal:

```
Potential opportunity for
  <DELIVER-OBJECT CARRY-TOOLS MAPLE-AVE>
  ITEM-20 (BAG) has reference feature CARRIER
Potential opportunity for <FIND-OBJECT CARRY-TOOLS>
  ITEM-20 (BAG) has reference feature CARRIER
Potential opportunity for
  <LOAD-PAYLOAD-OBJECT CARRY-TOOLS>
  ITEM-20 (BAG) has reference feature CARRIER
```

The top level `<deliver-object cut-twine>` task has not yet been processed; it is therefore the only task for its goal. It has the reference feature `sharp`, as do the `scissors` that are present at the current location:

```
Potential opportunity for
  <DELIVER-OBJECT CUT-TWINE SHERIDAN-RD>
  ITEM-13 (SCISSORS) has reference feature SHARP
```

Finally, PARETO analyzes the potential opportunities to determine which are genuine. There are two ways in which one of PARETO's task may be easily achievable: if it has already succeeded or if it is ready for processing, *i.e.*, not waiting for any others to be completed (Pryor & Collins 1994). In this case the `<find-object carry-tools>` task has already succeeded. It therefore constitutes a valid opportunity, and PARETO loads the `bag` into its cargo bay.

```
Has already succeeded <FIND-OBJECT CARRY-TOOLS>
Taking unexpected opportunity:
  <FIND-OBJECT CARRY-TOOLS>
```

PARETO also decides that there is an opportunity for the `<deliver-object cut-twine>` task: the presence of the `scissors` prompts it to expand the task.

```
Taking expected opportunity:
  <DELIVER-OBJECT CUT-TWINE SHERIDAN-RD>
Processing task:
  <DELIVER-OBJECT CUT-TWINE SHERIDAN-RD>
```

It then loads the `scissors`. Since there is now no need to go to the `lumberyard`, PARETO now makes its way directly to `maple-ave` where it delivers the `bag` and then to `sheridan-ave` to deliver the `scissors`.

In this example we have seen how PARETO uses reference features to recognize potential opportunities, regardless of whether the goals are being actively pursued. The opportunities that are recognized might involve abandoning an existing plan or choosing a plan for a goal that has not hitherto been addressed.

Discussion

This paper has described a filtering mechanism for opportunity recognition, and its implementation in the plan execution system PARETO.

Reference features and threats

This paper has described how reference features can be used in the recognition of opportunites: they can also be used to recognize threats. Many reference features indicate possible threats to goals. For example, in PARETO's world a `sharp` object, such as a knife, may cut a `soft` object, such as a ball of twine thus rendering it unsuitable for its purpose and making it unacceptable to the worker who has requested it.

A limited form of threat detection through the use of reference features has been implemented in PARETO (Pryor & Collins 1992). PARETO's analysis of potential opportunities is performed in two steps: the goal is first checked to see whether it is easily achievable and then its potential interactions with other goals are examined. A goal with problematic interactions does not constitute an opportunity. Detecting problematic interactions involves the same computational problems as recognizing opportunities: the agent may have many goals, each with a large number of subgoals, and in any case might not have chosen plans for all of them. PARETO uses a filtering process that is very similar to the one used for opportunity recognition. Reference features are used to indicate potentially problematic interactions. The potential interaction is then analyzed in more detail to determine whether it is genuine. The reference features not only indicate that a problematic interaction is possible, they also indicate its probable form thus assisting its avoidance.

Reference features and expertise

The concept *sharp* is useful just because many commonly arising human goals involve structural integrity. If, however, we lived in a world in which structural integrity was unimportant, we might well not even have such a concept, let alone find it useful. The reference features that an agent finds useful depend on the tasks that it habitually performs. Agents performing different tasks in the same world may attach completely different reference features to objects in their environments. Properties that are significant to one agent may be completely meaningless to another.

An important corollary to the task-related functionality of reference features is their rôle in the development of expertise. A domain expert is certainly expected to be able to recognize opportunities, both routine and novel. A domain novice, on the other hand, may not recognize even routine opportunities. The difference between the two is due to their relative familiarities with the domain. An interesting hypothesis is that an expert is one who has a comprehensive set of reference features for the domain: a novice has a limited or nonexistent set. Testing this hypothesis is an important area of future work. A related issue is the question of how reference features are acquired. The development of expertise involves learning about the functional aspects of the domain and learning to associate perceptual cues or other easily inferable features with them. This learning may consist of associating functional tendencies with features that are already available, or of learning to recognize new features.

Reference features appear to provide a bridge between the perceptual cues an agent receives and the functional judgments it must make. However, the question remains as to whether they are a genuine psychological phenomenon or simply the basis of an effective mechanism totally unlike anything actually used by people. Further work is needed to investigate their reality, both by examining their possible use by domain experts and by investigating their use in opportunity recognition, possibly along the lines of the experiments performed by Patalano *et al.* (1993).

Conclusion

The implementation of PARETO has demonstrated that opportunity recognition based on reference features is feasible. To demonstrate its effectiveness the mechanism must be scaled up to a real world domain. This will involve the construction of a set of reference features for that domain. Scaling up will also involve the use of computationally efficient matching algorithms in the filtering stage of the process.

The mechanism described in this paper can recognize only those opportunities indicated by critical factors. PARETO cannot, for example, make a detour while traveling to a specific location. This type of opportunity can be recognized only through detailed analysis and projection of a type that PARETO is not designed to perform. Instead of deciding in advance how the plans for its various goals will be combined, PARETO combines them on the fly through opportunity recognition. This enables robust and reactive behavior because its method of opportunity recognition does not rely on a plan already having been chosen, and allows the recognition of opportunities whose pursuit involves abandoning existing plans.

Acknowledgments. This work was principally performed at the Institute for the Learning Sciences, Northwestern University. Thanks to Gregg Collins for criticism and encouragement, and to Matt Brand, Will Fitzgerald, Eric Jones and Bruce Krulwich for many useful discussions.

References

Agre, P. E., and Chapman, D. 1987. Pengi: An implementation of a theory of activity. In *Proc. 6th Nat. Conf. on Artificial Intelligence.* AAAI.

Alterman, R. 1986. An adaptive planner. In *Proc. 5th Nat. Conf. on Artificial Intelligence*, 65–69. AAAI.

Birnbaum, L., and Collins, G. 1984. Opportunistic planning and freudian slips. In *Proc. 6th Ann. Conf. Cognitive Science Society.* Boulder, CO: LEA.

Brand, M., and Birnbaum, L. 1990. Noticing opportunities in a rich environment. In *Proc. 12th Ann. Conf. Cognitive Science Society.* Cambridge, MA: LEA.

Ferguson, I. A. 1992. TouringMachines: An architecture for dynamic, rational, mobile agents. Technical Report No. 273, Computer Laboratory, University of Cambridge.

Firby, R. J., and Hanks, S. 1987. The simulator manual. Technical Report YALEU/CSD/RR 563, Department of Computer Science, Yale University.

Firby, R. J. 1987. An investigation into reactive planning in complex domains. In *Proc. 6th Nat. Conf. on Artificial Intelligence*, 202–206. Seattle, WA: AAAI.

Firby, R. J. 1989. Adaptive execution in complex dynamic worlds. Technical Report YALEU/CSD/RR 672, Department of Computer Science, Yale University.

Gibson, J. J. 1979. *The ecological approach to visual perception.* Boston, MA: Houghton Mifflin.

Hammond, K.; Converse, T.; Marks, M.; and Seifert, C. 1993. Opportunism and learning. *Machine Learning* 10:279–309.

Hammond, K. 1989. Opportunistic memory. In *Proc. 11th Int. Joint Conf. on Artificial Intelligence*, 504–510.

Hanks, S.; Pollack, M. E.; and Cohen, P. R. 1993. Benchmarks, testbeds, controlled experimentation, and the design of agent architectures. *AI Magazine* 14(4):17–42.

Hayes-Roth, B., and Hayes-Roth, F. 1979. A cognitive model of planning. *Cognitive Science* 3(4):275–310.

McDermott, D. 1992. Transformational planning of reactive behavior. Technical Report YALEU/CSD/RR 941, Yale University, Department of Computer Science.

Patalano, A. L.; Seifert, C. M.; and Hammond, K. J. 1993. Predictive encoding: Planning for opportunities. In *Proc. 15th Ann. Conf. Cognitive Science Society*, 800–805. Boulder, CO: LEA.

Pryor, L., and Collins, G. 1992. Reference features as guides to reasoning about opportunities. In *Proc. 14th Ann. Conf. Cognitive Science Society*, 230–235. Bloomington, IN: LEA.

Pryor, L., and Collins, G. 1994. Opportunities: A unifying framework for planning and execution. In *Proc. 2nd Int. Conf. on Artificial Intelligence Planning Systems*, 329–334. Chicago, IL: AAAI Press.

Pryor, L. 1994. Opportunities and planning in an unpredictable world. Technical Report 53, Institute for the Learning Sciences, Northwestern University.

Sloman, A. 1989. On designing a visual system: Towards a Gibsonian computational theory of vision. *Journal of Experimental and Theoretical Artificial Intelligence* 1(4):189–337.

Generalizing Indexical-Functional Reference

Marcel Schoppers and **Richard Shu**
Robotics Research Harvesting, PO Box 2111, Redwood City, CA 94063

Abstract

The goals of situated agents generally do not specify particular objects: they require only that *some* suitable object should be chosen and manipulated (e.g. any red block). Situated agents engaged in deictic reference grounding, however, may well track a chosen referent object with such fixity of purpose that an unchosen object may be regarded as an obstacle even though it satisfies the agent's goals. In earlier work this problem was bridged by hand-coding. This paper lifts the problem to the symbol level, endowing agents with perceptual referent selection actions and performing those actions as required to allow or disallow opportunistic re-selection of referents. Our work preserves the ability of situated agents to find and track specific objects, adds an ability to automatically exploit the opportunities allowed by nonspecific references, and provides a starting point for studying how much opportunistic perception is appropriate.

Introduction

If an artificial agent is to interact with real objects, associations between references inside the agent and objects outside the agent must be maintained by the agent itself. To solve this basic problem, (Agre 1988) devised PENGI, which showed how to ground and manipulate indexical-functional references (IFR).

Subsequently, (Schoppers&Shu 1990) built the basic IFR capabilities into an execution engine for a symbolic plan representation, and reported that the plan's execution-time behavior was not what they had wished. They gave the agent a goal to stack any red block on any blue block. After waiting for the agent to find red and blue blocks, they then put a different red block on the blue block chosen by the agent. Instead of recognizing this as a serendipitous achievement of its goal, the agent put down its chosen red block, removed the unwanted red block, and then resumed the activity of placing its chosen red block atop the blue block. This behavior was of course appropriate for the agent's construction: the agent was designed to use all variables as vehicles for indexical-functional references, and to ground each such reference in any one suitable object, permanently. Such grounding corresponds to what might be expected if the agent were given an instruction using a definite noun phrase: "Put the (whichever) red block you see first on the (whichever) blue block you see first". But because the references associated with the plan's variables were initially ungrounded, it was easy to want behavior appropriate to a nonspecific indefinite noun phrase ("Put a red block on a blue block").

The foregoing analysis moves the problem into a linguistic realm where there are many varieties of reference, with IFR being only one special case. IFR happens to be basic to the tracking of physical objects, but is relatively rare in statements of things to be accomplished. Usually, any suitable object will do. Even when the language of an instruction identifies a specific object, this often occurs not because that one object must be used, but because the speaker believes one such object to be especially convenient. (Consider the written assembly instruction "With the Phillips screwdriver, ..." when the reader has several but was asked to fetch one in previous instructions.) Thus, the problem is that there remains a large gap to be bridged between implemented reference grounding capabilities (currently for IFR only) and the varieties of object reference available to humans when expressing desired behavior. If we are to produce agents capable of efficiently carrying out human instructions, whether verbal or programmed, we must find ways to make agents more responsive to the variety of object references used by humans. Such responsiveness must be provided both in instruction understanding and in instruction enactment.

It might be argued that PENGI, by using one marker to track the bee believed to be closest to the penguin and a second marker to compare other candidate bees, went beyond enactment of references of the form "that bee" to enact identification of "the nearest bee". While true, this was accomplished by hand-coding a specific defensive behavior, where we wish to devise a mechanism that can be parameterized to allow an automatic choice from a variety of reference types.

The present paper is concerned with augmenting the varieties of reference that can be *enacted* by situated agents; it is not a Natural Language paper. We assume the existence of a Natural Language component capable of maintaining a discourse model, of resolving co-references, and of deciding what kind of reference grounding behavior is implied by received instructions. In the next section, where we are obliged to define a few terms for the sake of describing certain implemented capabilities, it is merely an accident that the terms we find most useful come from the domain of NL research.

In the next section we show that the kind of reference used in a goal restricts the range of situations that satisfy the goal. Then, since nonspecific indefinite reference is common in goals, we describe how we co-opted mechanisms for grounding IFR, to make them produce behavior appropriate to nonspecific indefinite references. As a result, our agent can behave sensibly when given goals combining nonspecific indefinite references with deictic references ("See to it that there's a red block on that blue block.")

Defining the Problem

Varieties of Reference

In English, noun phrases and their reference meanings can be distinguished in many ways, and we list a few distinctions below. Our objective in this and the next subsections is to exhibit some of the most obvious ways in which an artificial agent's behavior *must* be influenced by some basic varieties of reference that can occur in instructions. Our definitions are purposely *ad hoc*, i.e. for the sake of succintly describing what we have implemented we are making some distinctions in slighly different ways than linguists would. See e.g. (Quirk et al 1985) for a more complete classification.

- *Referential* noun phrases (NPs) expect the agent to identify the referent using either contextual or general knowledge. Since we are working on grounding references in physical objects, and since attributions occur at the linguistic level, we consider only referential NPs here.
- In a *specific* reference – and under the restriction to bounded physical objects – the instructor has a particular object "in mind". Only in the specific case can the speaker be expected to answer the question, "Who/what is it?"
- A *deictic* reference depends for its grounding on the instructor's place in space and time, and is used only when the instructor expects the referent to be immediately identifiable in context. Indexicals are deictic ("I", "tomorrow").
- The distinction between *definite and indefinite* NPs is syntactic, based on the use of such determiners as "the" and "a". However, a speaker using a definite NP expects one referent to be uniquely relevant, though perhaps only in some later context, e.g. "Go into the house and pick up the amulet [you will find there]" (Webber 1991).
- *Demonstrative* NPs are indicated syntactically by the presence of the determiners "this", "that", "these", or "those". The associated references are usually specific, definite, and deictic.

Specific reference is especially hard to isolate. For example, the NP "Olaf Palme's assassin" refers (perhaps) to a common knowledge entity, but no-one knows who that person is. Similarly, there is room to debate the specificity of superlatives such as "the biggest apple you can find," of ordinals such as "the first apple you touch," and of collectives such as "the 10,000 men around the castle." Since this paper is concerned with encoding and enacting plans that can identify and manipulate only singular physical objects, we gladly sidestep such complexities. To simplify the rest of this paper we propose that superlative, ordinal, and similar references which are not immediately groundable but may be made so in the future (including some functionals) be considered *nonspecific* references.

The distinctions just elaborated give rise to the following classification of referential, non-generic, non-coreferring, references to singular, physical, bounded, non-collective, objects. We include demonstrative NPs under deictic references.

- nonspecific, indefinite: "Pick up *a red block.*"
- nonspecific, definite, nondeictic: "Identify *the heaviest block* [on the table]" (when the blocks are otherwise indistinguishable). "Olaf Palme's assassin."
- nonspecific, definite, deictic: "Pick up *the block closest to your hand*" (when the instructor can't see it).
- specific, indefinite: "*A red block* just fell off the table" (while the instructor is looking at it).
- specific, definite, nondeictic: "Pick up *the red block on the floor.*"
- specific, definite, deictic: "Pick up *the block I'm pointing at.*" "Pick up *that block.*"

Varieties of Serendipity

Now let us consider what behavior we expect to see from an intelligent embedded agent when it is given instructions specifying goals (desired states) involving the kinds of reference listed above.

First, let us give the agent a goal to "Obtain a state in which a red block is resting on a blue block" (non-specific indefinite reference). This goal is satisfied by any world state in which any red block is on any blue block; the agent need do no more than scan the table.

Next, let us consider the use of what we have decided to call nonspecific definite reference. Strictly speaking, only the object being "identified" will satisfy the request, but by definition, the speaker does not know which object that is and cannot verify that exactly the right one has been found (without executing her own instruction and assuming that the world has not changed)! That being the case, nonspecific definite instructions must be meant either as

1. requests to identify objects (e.g. find Olaf Palme's assassin) to save the instructor some time; or as
2. abstractions (e.g. retrieve the astronaut that just fell off the Shuttle, who it is doesn't matter); or as
3. simplifications that only approximate the instructor's real wishes (e.g. bring the next person in line, assuming no unruly behavior in the queue; or, use the first X you find, instead of "be quick").

In all cases, the definiteness of the reference serves only to communicate the instructor's (possibly false) expectation that one identifiable object is "the right one". Beyond that, it makes no difference to the desired behavior – the agent should find any person who is Olaf Palme's assassin, retrieve any astronaut who fell off the station, and bring whichever person is next in line. Consequently, the distinction between nonspecific indefinite and nonspecific definite instructions is not important to agent implementation.

Next, we find that specific indefinite reference cannot be used for posing goals. Any instruction forces the agent to choose objects to manipulate, but in a specific indefinite instruction the speaker already has specific objects in mind and refuses to say which objects!

Next, let us use specific definite reference (other than a coreference) and give the agent a goal to "Obtain a situation in which that (pointing) red block is resting on that (pointing) blue block." This goal is narrow: exactly the indicated blocks must be made to satisfy the goal condition, no other blocks will do. However, if the two indicated blocks are already in the desired configuration, the agent needs to do no more than look.

Finally, instead of describing a desired situation we can ask the agent to perform an action, such as "Put a red block on a blue block". In this case, no matter how many red blocks are already atop blue blocks, the agent is nevertheless obliged to build another such tower.

The two major kinds of reference (nonspecific and specific) usable in goals, and the distinction between requests for conditions and requests for action, together produce three kinds of behavior that may be distinguished from each other by the kinds of serendipitous circumstances an embedded agent may exploit while performing the requested task. We distinguish the following cases of admissible serendipity:

- *Nonspecific serendipity.* The agent may satisfy the goal using any suitable objects, and is not required to act if suitable objects already satisfy the goal.
- *Specific serendipity.* The agent may satisfy the goal using only the objects specified by the references included as part of the goal, but is not required to act if those specific objects already satisfy the goal.
- *No serendipity.* The agent must not exploit the presence of suitable objects that already satisfy the goal.

Problem Statement

The three kinds of serendipity also allow us to succinctly describe the problem with implementations of indexical-functional reference (IFR), as follows:

- IFR is a form of specific definite reference which naturally delivers only specific serendipity, and which can be made to deliver nonspecific serendipity only with considerable effort.
- Naive attempts to make implementations of IFR deliver nonspecific serendipity result in referential thrashing, i.e. an agent too confused about object selection to get anything done.

Our objective is to use explicit representations, not hand-coding, to specify the behavior of embedded agents, including behavior involving interaction with several indistinguishable objects at the same time. Two problems must be solved to attain our objective.

1. Symbolic plans using IFR must become capable of noticing and exploiting nonspecific serendipity.
2. Symbolic plan representations must become capable of expressing a demand for specific serendipity.

The second problem may be solvable by building on the distinction between rigid and nonrigid designators, as has been done in e.g. (Appelt 1982). In this paper we address the first problem. In particular, we wish to define general, ***domain-independent*** notations and plan execution machinery, such that the execution-time specificity of each of the agent's references can be controlled by domain-specific knowledge (which knowledge may therefore be regarded as a parameter to the agent's re-usable algorithms).

The Experimental Setup

Before we describe our work, the reader must understand some details of the plan encoding we worked with. Our agent consisted of a simulated arm, some simulated sensors, and a repetitively executed decision tree, all operating in a world of simulated blocks. The

```
on(A,B) ?
  T) NO-OP
  F) box(B) ?
       T) clear(B) ?
       .    T) holding(A) ?
       .    .    T) over(B) ?
       .    .    .    T) LOWER
       .    .    .    F) at(top) ?
       .    .    .         T) LATERAL
       .    .    .         F) RAISE
       .    .    F) [subplan to GRASP A]
       .    F) [subplan to CLEAROFF B]
       F) FAIL
```

Figure 1: Decision Tree Schema for Block Stacking.

simulated arm and camera moved horizontally and vertically, in increments that were much smaller than the size of a block. An example decision tree is shown in Figure 1. We refer to each traversal of the decision tree as a *execution cycle.* Blocks had names and colors, and could be indistinguishable. The human observer could move blocks about in the simulated world, thus bringing good or bad luck at will.

Notice that the given decision tree is a *schema* containing unbound variables (in the Prolog convention logical variables begin with an upper case letter). This was important in allowing us to invoke the plan (tree) with whatever parameters we wanted. (The parameters finally became records that contained two position vectors, one for predicted/believed position and one for perceived/known position; lack of information was indicated as a zero vector.)

Following (Schoppers&Shu 1990) we regarded object descriptions as goals. When we wanted a plan to put any red sphere on any blue box, we implemented a plan that achieved **color(X,red)** $\wedge$ **shape(X,sphere)** $\wedge$ **shape(Y,box)** $\wedge$ **on(X,Y)** and we expected the agent to find suitable objects for X and Y to refer to.

This view of descriptions is not as strange as it may seem at first. If we were to augment the agent's capabilities by introducing a painting action, the above goal might induce the agent to paint things, a potentially appropriate behavior. At the same time, one way of satisfying a color goal for a nonspecific indefinite object is to (physically) look for an object that already has the desired color; indeed, that is the only way to achieve a color goal when there is no painting action. Thus we came to regard painting and scanning as alternative ways of achieving color goals.

At the start of the agent's activities, the agent knew nothing at all about the state of the (simulated) world. In particular, when the plan specified that some block should be moved, the agent had first to find a block to move. To solve this problem we implemented a camera movement procedure that systematically scanned the table until the camera viewed a block. This whole scanning procedure was controlled by means of camera positioning coordinates.

As a result, the executing plan could refer to objects by knowing in what direction the camera should be pointed in order to make the object appear in the camera's field of view. That directional knowledge allowed the agent to verify visible properties of objects whenever the property verification could be implemented as a test on the camera image. To test relative positions of blocks, however, or to test the position of the robot arm relative to a block, it was necessary to know both the direction and the range to a block, i.e. the block's position in three dimensions. Thus, "referring to an object" came to mean "truly knowing the object's current 3D position" (versus having a belief or expectation). The required position information was stored (and updated) in records that were passed as parameters to the decision tree. Thus we could define a predicate **known located(X)** to test that variable **X** was bound to a record containing visually verified information about current position. We also defined **believed located(X)** to test that **X**'s record contained an *expectation* of current position. From there we could define actions that achieved **known located(X)** (see next section).

Referent Selection Actions

(Cohen 1981) examined dialogues in which speakers attempted to get hearers to identify specific objects, and argued for extending a plan-based theory of communication with explicit actions representing the hearer's identification of objects. The speaker would adopt a goal of getting the hearer to identify something, and would communicate that goal to the hearer, who would then try to achieve the goal by means of an IDENTIFY action. Our block-stacking agent's decision tree both tests object identification goals and achieves them with IDENTIFY-like actions. However, we have found it useful to endow our agent with many such actions, most of which come down to a visual search that is specialized to exploit known visual features of the object to be identified. Additionally, many of our "referent selection actions" exploit positional expectations.

Candidate referents must be found for each plan (object) variable before any of the conditions mentioning that variable can be tested. The very first thing most plans must do is cause the performance of perceptual searching activities to locate candidate objects. Once candidate objects are found, plan execution can track them and apply perceptual tests to them. But clearly, if objects are selected only once, at the beginning of plan execution, and are tracked thereafter, the resulting behavior can exploit specific serendipity at best. To achieve nonspecific serendipity it must be possible to select new objects for references that already have referents. The cyclic execution paradigm makes this very easy by providing the opportunity to revise all referent selections once per execution cycle, and our definition of **known located(X)** plays the role of having to be constantly reachieved (because a remembered or predicted location is not a known location). The main challenge is to determine a suitable set of referent selection and reselection actions, and to integrate those actions with the existing tracking machinery.

Identifying Efficiently

There are many efficient ways to locate and identify objects. For example, given a goal to put a red block on a blue block, you will first look for either a red or blue block. If the perceptual apparatus can be primed to look for colors, this is already much more efficient than looking for any object at all. Now suppose you have found a blue block. Given that you have been asked to put a red block on top of it, the natural thing to do is: look for a red block on top of the blue block you just found. This behavior is efficient because it tells the perceptual system exactly where to look, and also because finding a red block there would allow you to consider yourself finished with the task.

The preceding paragraph implicitly states the heuristic that, to find referents for nonspecific indefinite references, it is efficient to limit perception by using knowledge of what's wanted, as indicated by current plan goals. This heuristic is the basis of a large body of work on task-directed perception. We are less concerned with the details of perception than with managing perception to support opportunistic task performance.

In our simulated domain we found that there were numerous goals that suggested perceptually efficient referent selection actions. For example:

on(X,Y) To find a referent for X when Y has a referent, look just above the location of Y.

on(X,Y) To find a referent for Y when X has a referent, look just below the location of X.

over(X) To find a referent for X (such that the agent's hand is over it), look at the agent's hand and move the camera in a vertical line downwards.

clear(X) To find a referent for X, start the camera at the left end of the table and follow the "skyline".

holding(X) To find a referent for X, look at the location of the agent's hand, which is always known. Similarly for **around(X)**.

shape(X,box) To find a referent for X, look for any rectangular thing (similarly for other shapes).

color(X,red) To find a referent for X, look for any red thing (similarly for other colors).

For the first few goals above, referents can be found efficiently because the goals are prepositions that identify a direction vector. The more general source of efficiency, as evidenced by the last few goals, is exploitation of capabilities of the perceptual system itself, e.g. the ability to locate only certain colors or shapes. The capability to rapidly look at specified lines or locations is responsible for the usefulness of spatial prepositions in referent selection.

Some Consequences

Because of the association between particular goals and particular actions for finding referents efficiently, we now give referent selection actions postconditions indicating their special suitability. For example, under a standard approach to action representation the action for visually locating red things should have the postconditions **known color(X,red)** $\wedge$ **known located(X)**, where **known located(X)** is as defined in the previous section: perceptually finding a red object also finds the object's position. But these postconditions would represent that the identify-a-red-thing action is also useful for locating nondescript objects, leading to inefficient behavior when the plan wants any nondescript object and all the available objects are blue. Indeed, many color-seeking, shape-seeking, and texture-seeking visual searches might be tried in vain. On the other hand, there are efficient ways to find nondescript objects. Consequently our representation of the identify-a-red-thing action omits the **known located(X)** postcondition. Conversely, even though an identify-anything action can eventually find a red object if there is one, our representation of identify-anything actions has no **known color(X,red)** postcondition. Thus, postconditions now have less to do with actual effects than with the utility of the described action. (We recognize that this is a poor substitute for explicit knowledge about the utility of actions, see the "Future Work" section.)

When a plan variable occurs in several goals, the referent selection actions associated with any of those goals might be used to find a referent. For example, when the plan's goal is a conjunction such as **color(X,red)** $\wedge$ **shape(X,sphere)** $\wedge$ **shape(Y,box)** $\wedge$ **on(X,Y)** there are two referent selection actions that can be used immediately to find a referent for X (using color and shape as guides) after which there are also two referent selection actions for Y (using shape and the location under X).

To ensure that every object variable indexes at least one referent selection action, all goals are enlarged with additional conjuncts **known located(X_i)**, one per object variable X_i appearing in the goal. As a result, most referents can be selected with both goal-specific referent selection actions and a general visual search.[1]

Since the **known located(X_i)** conjuncts need constantly to be reachieved, every execution cycle offers an opportunity to change the object being referred to by X_i. To make the reselection, all of the goals and subgoals in which X_i appeared during the previous execution cycle may provide useful information. For example, **on(X,Y)** is achieved by LOWERING the hand when **holding(X)**, which is therefore a subgoal; this subgoal is achieved by GRASPING when **around(X)**, which is therefore a subsubgoal; this subsubgoal is achieved by **lowering** when **clear(X)**, and so on. To achieve **known located(X)** by possibly choosing a different **X**, it is useful to look at what's already on **Y**, at what's already in the agent's hand, and at the "sky-line" of the current block configuration.

This uniform relevance of everything in the goal stack was especially appreciated in the case of the goal **holding(X)**, whose associated referent selection action caused **X** to refer to "the-thing-I'm-holding" – a reference that is both indexical and functional.

Indeed, when the referential guidance provided by goals is taken seriously, the meaning of a reference comes to depend on which goals apply to the referent. Hence the meanings of our references change dynamically as the agent's goals change, and the semantics of our references is compositional.[2]

Recovering Opportunistic Behavior

Finally we come to the issue of integrating referent (re)selection with deictic tracking. The normal reactive execution cycle is constantly re-achieving **known located(X_i)** for each X_i. The first referent selection action that is relevant and that succeeds in finding a referent for the given X_i will have satisfied the goal, thus preempting the use of other referent selection actions (for the same reference and execution cycle). This means that we have to be careful with the order in which referent selection actions are tried:

- As soon as X_i becomes grounded, deictic tracking can maintain the grounding, but that produces exactly the single-minded tracking we are mitigating. To have any effect, goal-related referent selection actions must be tried before tracking. They can then look for objects in places that will cause the agent to notice nonspecific serendipities. A serendipitous object will ground the reference and preempt deictic tracking; otherwise deictic tracking can continue.
- Similarly, general visual scanning can always find a candidate object for any reference. If it were tried before tracking, then tracking would never be used. Hence, such general backup methods must be tried only after tracking has failed.

Thus we were obliged to try referent selection actions in the specific order **1)** goal-related referent selection actions, **2)** tracking (or, re-perceiving the referent of the preceding execution cycle), and **3)** general, goal-independent visual searching.

Nonspecific indefinite reference, and the corresponding ability to exploit nonspecific serendipity, resulted from trying all the relevant actions in the order just stated, until some action succeeded in finding a referent. Specific definite (deictic) reference could be recovered by disabling the use of (category 1) goal-related referent selection actions. Disabling the use of (2) deictic tracking produced referential thrashing; disabling the use of (3) goal-independent visual searching left the agent unable to find anything.

Summary and Future Work

In this work we have shown that the type of reference used in specifying agent behavior affects the kinds of serendipities the agent may exploit. We have harnassed IFR to provide two additional kinds of situated object reference, namely specific definite reference and nonspecific indefinite reference, as different points on a continuum defined by the presence or absence of three kinds of referent selection actions. The three kinds of referent selection actions are **1)** goal-related, which can detect that goals have been satisfied by objects other than those chosen by the agent; **2)** tracking, which provides referential stability; and **3)** general visual searches, which locate objects when none are known.

Our work raises many performance issues. An agent cannot always afford to re-perceive, in each execution cycle, every object it is already interacting with, let alone looking for serendipitous objects. There is a

[1] It does not matter that the same variable can appear in many **known located(X_i)** conjuncts. For each X_i, the first **known located(X_i)** conjunct encountered in any given execution cycle initiates perceptual activity. This achieves **known located(X_i)** and forestalls re-achievement for the rest of that execution cycle. An equivalent approach could attach a **known located(X_i)** conjunct only to the goal at the root of the subtree containing X_i.

[2] The semantics of (Agre 1988)'s deictic representation was not compositional, i.e. there was no semantic relationship between the notations "the-thing-I'm-holding" and "the-red-thing-I'm-holding".

small body of work discussing when it is worth-while for agents to engage in sensing (Abramson 1993; Chrisman&Simmons 1991; Dean et al 1990; Doyle et al 1989; Draper et al 1994; Hansen 1994). Our own previous work (Schoppers 1995) made sensing intermittent and dependent on environmental dynamics. Our present implementation side-steps these issues by **a)** treating action descriptions as heuristics, and making postconditions encode our subjective judgments about the utility of actions for specific goals[3]; and **b)** restricting our goal-related referent selection actions to look *only* for serendipities involving previously selected objects. Thus, our agent will notice if another block is put down on one of the blocks the agent was using, but will not notice if someone builds a tower that satisfies the agent's goals by using only blocks the agent doesn't care about. In future work we intend to make the agent more conscious of the likelihoods that particular goals will be achieved serendipitously, of the time costs of perceiving those particular serendipities, and of the time costs of achieving the goals deliberately. Performing, in each execution cycle, the perception or action process having the highest probability of goal achievement per unit time cost, will then yield optimally efficient behavior (Simon&Kadane 1975). Since looking above a block already in the field of view is almost free, while looking in a random place for a particular block arrangement is both expensive and probably futile, we expect the resulting behavior to be very similar to what we have now.

Other relevant issues include:

- When the agent must find objects to ground several references, the order in which references are grounded may affect the agent's efficiency.
- There may be useful ways to order the referent selection actions applicable at a given time.
- There are choices to be made between: physically moving lots of things around to find an object that perfectly satisfies a description, versus purely perceptual searching for a perfect object, versus finding an object that is nearly right and then modifying it, versus just building a suitable object.
- Agents could be made very sophisticated about what serendipities they deem likely at any given time, and how much effort to spend on looking for them.

More long-range possibilities include, finding ways to mentally distinguish a selected referent (e.g. you can track one pigeon among a flock by using a distinctive feature); finding ways to *make* an indistinguishable referent distinguishable; how to handle plural references; and how to efficiently spot perceptually complex referents (since the predicate **block(X)** should automatically lead to a search for appropriate features such as lines and angles).

[3]Readers who feel that an effect is an effect no matter how expensive the action is, might yet hesitate to represent an effect having very low probability, and probability is merely the other factor in low utility.

References

Abramson, B. 1993. A decision-theoretic framework for integrating sensors into plans. IEEE Trans SMC 23(2):366–373.

Agre, P. 1988. *The Dynamic Structure of Everyday Life.* Tech rept 1085, AI Lab, MIT.

Appelt, D. 1982. *Planning natural language utterances to satisfy multiple goals.* Tech Note 259, SRI International, Menlo Park, California.

Chrisman, L. & Simmons, R. 1991. Sensible planning: focusing perceptual attention. Proc AAAI Nat'l Conf on AI:756–761.

Cohen, Phil. 1981. The need for identification as a planned action. Proc 7th IJCAI:31–36.

Dean, T. Basye, K. & Lejter, M. 1990. Planning and active perception. Proc DARPA Workshop on Innovative Approaches to Planning, Scheduling and Control:271–276.

Doyle, R. Sellers, S. & Atkinson, D. 1989. A focused, context-sensitive approach to monitoring. Proc 11th IJCAI:1231–1237.

Draper, D. Hanks, S. & Weld, D. 1994. Probabilistic planning with information gathering and contingent execution. Proc Int'l Conf on AI Planning Systems AIPS:31–36.

Hansen, E. 1994. Cost-effective sensing during plan execution. Proc AAAI Nat'l Conf on AI:1029–1035.

Quirk, R. et al. 1985. *A Comprehensive Grammar of the English Language.* Longman Inc., New York.

Schoppers, M. & Shu, R. 1990. An implementation of indexical-functional reference for the embedded execution of symbolic plans. Proc DARPA Workshop on Innovative Approaches to Planning, Scheduling and Control:490–496.

Schoppers, M. 1995. The use of dynamics in an intelligent controller for a space-faring rescue robot. *Artificial Intelligence* 73(1):175–230.

Simon, H. & Kadane, J. 1975. Optimal problem-solving search: all-or-none solutions. *Artificial Intelligence* 6(3):235–247.

Webber, B. 1991. Indexical-functional reference: a natural language perspective. Unpublished extended abstract.

Rewarding Behaviors

Fahiem Bacchus
Dept. Computer Science
University of Waterloo
Waterloo, Ontario
Canada, N2L 3G1
fbacchus@logos.uwaterloo.ca

Craig Boutilier
Dept. Computer Science
University of British Columbia
Vancouver, B.C.
Canada, V6T 1Z4
cebly@cs.ubc.cs

Adam Grove
NEC Research Institute
4 Independence Way
Princeton NJ 08540, USA
grove@research.nj.nec.com

Abstract

Markov decision processes (MDPs) are a very popular tool for decision theoretic planning (DTP), partly because of the well-developed, expressive theory that includes effective solution techniques. But the Markov assumption—that dynamics and rewards depend on the current state only, and not on history—is often inappropriate. This is especially true of rewards: we frequently wish to associate rewards with behaviors that extend over time. Of course, such reward processes can be encoded in an MDP should we have a rich enough state space (where states encode enough history). However it is often difficult to "hand craft" suitable state spaces that encode an appropriate amount of history.

We consider this problem in the case where non-Markovian rewards are encoded by assigning values to formulas of a temporal logic. These formulas characterize the value of temporally extended behaviors. We argue that this allows a natural representation of many commonly encountered non-Markovian rewards. The main result is an algorithm which, given a decision process with non-Markovian rewards expressed in this manner, *automatically* constructs an equivalent MDP (with Markovian reward structure), allowing optimal policy construction using standard techniques.

1 Introduction

Recent years have seen a tremendous interest in extending the classical planning paradigm to deal with domains involving uncertain information, actions with uncertain effects, and problems with competing objectives. Much work in *decision theoretic planning* (DTP), generally aimed at addressing these issues, has adopted the theory of *Markov decision processes* (MDPs) as the underlying conceptual and computational model [DKKN93, TR94, BD94, BDG95]. MDPs allow one to formulate problems in which an agent is involved in an on-going, *process-oriented* interaction with the environment and receives rewards at various system states. This generalizes the classical *goal-oriented* view of planning [BP95]. Instead of classical *plans*, one considers the more flexible concept of a *policy*, namely a mapping from each state to the action that should be executed in that state. Effective optimization methods exist for computing policies such that an agent executing the policy will maximize its accumulated reward over time [Put94].

The fundamental assumption underling the formulation of a planning problem as an MDP is that the system dynamics and rewards are Markovian. That is, the manner in which the system behaves when an action is executed, and the rewards received, depend only on the system's current state, not on states previously visited. For example, if we wish to control a robot it is usually not difficult to find a state space in which the robot's actions can be described as Markovian (stochastic) state transitions. In fact, this is often the most natural way to represent the effects of actions. Assigning natural Markovian rewards can be more problematic.

Although it is sometimes easy to associate rewards with individual states (e.g., in a navigation problem where rewards are associated with locations), often a reward is most naturally assigned to some behavior that occurs over an extended period. In such cases, it can be difficult to encode the reward as a function of state. For instance, we may reward an agent in states where coffee has just been delivered, but *only* if this state was preceded by a state (perhaps within k steps) where a coffee request was issued, withholding reward for spurious delivery. This reward is properly a function of the system *trajectory* or *history*, and not of the state alone. Typical forms of desirable temporally extended behaviors include response to requests, bounded response, lack of response, maintaining safety constraints, and so on. Temporally extended goals of this nature have been examined to some extent in the literature [HH92, Dru89, Kab90, GK91], but not in the context of generating effective policies.

The key difficulty with non-Markovian rewards is that standard optimization techniques, most based on Bellman's [Bel57] dynamic programming principle, cannot be used. One way of dealing with this predicament is to formulate an equivalent decision problem in which the rewards are Markovian. In particular, one can augment the state space of the underlying system by adding variables that keep track of the *history* relevant to the reward function. For instance, Boutilier and Puterman [BP95] suggest straightforward ways of encoding reward functions that involve simple requests. This approach has the advantage that existing optimization methods for MDPs can be used.

Unfortunately, in general, finding a good way to augment the state space requires considerable cleverness—especially if we are concerned with minimizing the size of the resulting augmented space for computational reasons. In this paper, we examine the problem of rewarding temporally extended behaviors. We provide a natural, and quite expressive, means for specifying rewards attached to behaviors extended over time. Furthermore, we solve the problem of computing policies in the face of these non-Markovian rewards by developing an algorithm that *automatically* constructs a Markovian reward process and associated MDP. Our algorithm automates the process of generating an appropriate augmentation of the state space, and, when coupled with traditional policy construction techniques, provides a way of computing policies for a much richer range of reward functions.

In Section 2 we introduce NMRDPs, essentially MDPs with non-Markovian reward. System dynamics are specified as with MDPs, but rewards are associated with formulas in a suitable temporal logic. We define *temporally-extended reward functions* (TERFs) by requiring that the reward associated with a formula be given at any state in which the formula is satisfied. We note that the decision to reward an agent in a given state should depend only on past states, not on future states. For this reason, it will be more natural to encode our reward formulas using a *past* or backward-looking temporal logic rather than the usual future or forward logics like LTL, CTL [Eme90] or MTL [AH90]. In Section 3, we describe a number of interesting and useful classes of target behaviors and show how they can be encoded by TERFs.

In Section 4, we consider the problem of constructing optimal policies for NMRDPs. As mentioned, dynamic programming cannot be used to construct policies in this setting. Nominally, this requires one to resort to optimization over a policy space that maps *histories* (rather than states) into actions, a process that would incur great computational expense. We present a procedure that, instead, expands the original state space by attaching a temporal formula to each state. This formula keeps track of an appropriate amount of relevant history. By constructing a state-based (Markovian) reward function for the extended state space, we convert the NMRDP into an equivalent MDP; in particular, optimal policies for this MDP determine optimal policies for the original NMRDP in a natural way. In this way, we obtain a compact representation of the required history-dependent policy by considering only relevant history, and can produce this policy using computationally-effective MDP algorithms.

2 Non-Markovian Rewards

2.1 Markov Decision Processes

Much recent work in DTP considers planning problems that can be modeled by *completely observable Markov Decision Processes* [How60, Put94]. In this model, we assume that there is a finite set of system states S, a set of actions A, and a reward function R. The effects of actions cannot be predicted with certainty; hence we write $\Pr(s_1, a, s_2) = p$ (or $s_1 \xrightarrow{a,p} s_2$) to denote that s_2 is reached with probability p when action a is performed in state s_1. Complete observability entails that the agent always knows what state it is in. We assume that the state space is characterized by a set of features, or logical propositions. This allows actions to be described compactly using probabilistic STRIPS rules [KHW94, BD94], Bayes nets [DK89, BDG95] or other action representations.

A real-valued *reward function* R reflects the objectives, tasks and goals to be accomplished by the agent, with $R(s)$ denoting the (immediate) utility of being in state s. For our purposes, then, an MDP consists of S, A, R and the set of transition distributions $\{\Pr(\cdot, a, \cdot) : a \in A\}$.

A *stationary Markovian policy* is a mapping $\pi : S \rightarrow A$, where $\pi(s)$ denotes the action an agent should perform whenever it is in state s. One might think of such policies as reactive or universal plans [Sch87]. Given an MDP, an agent ought to adopt a policy that maximizes the expected *value* over its (potentially infinite) trajectory through the state space. The most common value criterion in DTP for infinite-horizon problems is *discounted total reward*: the current value of future rewards is discounted by some factor β $(0 < \beta < 1)$, and we maximize the expected accumulated discounted rewards over an infinite time period. The expected value of a fixed policy π at any given state s can be shown to satisfy [How60]:

$$V_\pi(s) = R(s) + \beta \sum_{t \in S} \Pr(s, \pi(s), t) \cdot V_\pi(t)$$

The value of π at any initial state s can be computed by solving this system of linear equations. A policy π is *optimal* if $V_\pi(s) \geq V_{\pi'}(s)$ for all $s \in S$ and policies π'.

Techniques for constructing optimal policies in the case of discounted rewards have been well-studied, and include algorithms such as *value iteration* [Bel57] and *policy iteration* [How60]. It should be noted that each of these algorithms exploits the Markovian nature of the reward process. We refer to [Put94] for an excellent treatment of MDPs and associated computational methods.

2.2 A Temporal Logic of the Past

To reward agents for (temporally extended) *behaviors*, as opposed to simply reaching certain states, we need a means to specify rewards for specific trajectories through the state space. Generally, we want to associate rewards with *properties* of trajectories rather than rewarding individual trajectories. For example, we might reward an agent whenever condition Q is achieved within k steps of condition P, without regard for the *particular* trajectory the agent is traversing. Therefore, we associate rewards (or penalties) with desirable (or undesirable) *formulas* in a suitable temporal logic that describes such trajectory properties.

The logic we consider is "backward", or past looking. That is, the truth of a temporal formula depends on prior states only, not on what will happen in the future. This accords well with our view of reward processes because, in most contexts, rewards should be earned based on what has actually happened.

We present a past version of LTL [Eme90] called PLTL. We assume an underlying finite set of propositional constants **P**, the usual truth functional connectives, and the following temporal operators: S (since), $\boxminus$ (always in the past), $\Diamond\!\!\!-$ (once, or sometime in the past) and $\ominus$ (previously).[1] The

[1]These are the backward analogs of the LTL operators until,

formulas $\phi_1 \mathsf{S} \phi_2$, $\boxminus\phi_1$, $\diamondminus\phi_1$ and $\ominus\phi_1$ are well-formed when ϕ_1 and ϕ_2 are.[2] We use $\top$ and $\bot$ to denote truth and falsity, respectively. The semantics of PLTL is described with respect to models of the form $T = \langle s_0, \cdots, s_n \rangle$, $n \geq 0$, where each s_i is a *state* or valuation over $\mathbf{P}$ (i.e., $s_i \in 2^{\mathbf{P}}$). Such a T is called a *(finite) trajectory*, or partial history. For any trajectory $T = \langle s_0, \cdots, s_n \rangle$, and any $0 \leq i \leq n$, let $T(i)$ denote the *initial segment* $T(i) = \langle s_0, \cdots, s_i \rangle$.

Intuitively, a temporal formula is true of $T = \langle s_0, \cdots, s_n \rangle$ if it is true at the last (or *current* state) with respect to the history reflected in the trajectory. We define the truth of formulas inductively as follows:

- $T \models P$ iff $P \in s_n$, for $P \in \mathbf{P}$
- $T \models \phi_1 \wedge \phi_2$ iff $T \models \phi_1$ and $T \models \phi_2$
- $T \models \neg\phi$ iff $T \not\models \phi$
- $T \models \phi_1 \mathsf{S} \phi_2$ iff there is some $i \leq n$ s.t. $T(i) \models \phi_2$ and for all $i < j \leq n$, $T(j) \models \phi_1$ (intuitively, ϕ_1 has been true since the last time ϕ_2 held)
- $T \models \boxminus\phi$ iff for all $0 \leq i \leq n, T(i) \models \phi$ (ϕ has been true at each point in the past)
- $T \models \diamondminus\phi$ iff for some $0 \leq i \leq n, T(i) \models \phi$ (ϕ was true at some point in the past)
- $T \models \ominus\phi$ iff $n > 0$ and $T(n-1) \models \phi$ (ϕ was true at the previous state)

One notable consequence of this semantics is the fact that while $\{\ominus\phi, \ominus\neg\phi\}$ is unsatisfiable, $\{\neg\ominus\phi, \neg\ominus\neg\phi\}$ is satisfiable: any model of the form $\langle s \rangle$ satisfies the latter.

It is well-known that the modalities in LTL can be decomposed into present and future components [Eme90]. Similarly, modalities of PLTL can be decomposed into present and past components. For example, $\boxminus\phi$ is equivalent to $\ominus\boxminus\phi \wedge \phi$. That is, $\boxminus\phi$ is true iff ϕ is true of the current state and $\boxminus\phi$ is true of the previous state. Using these equivalences we can determine, for any formula ϕ, what must have been true in the previous state in order that ϕ be true now. We call this the *regression* of ϕ through the current state. Note that if the current component of ϕ is falsified by the current state, then nothing about the previous state can make ϕ true now. In this case the regression of ϕ is $\bot$.

Definition 2.1 *The regression of ϕ through s, denoted* $\text{Regr}(\phi, s)$*, is a formula in PLTL such that, for all trajectories T of length $n > 1$ with final state s, we have*

$$T \models \phi \quad \text{iff} \quad T(n-1) \models \text{Regr}(\phi, s) \qquad \blacksquare$$

$\text{Regr}(\phi, s)$ can be computed recursively:

- If $\phi \in \mathbf{P}$, $\text{Regr}(\phi, s) = \top$ if $s \models \phi$, and $\bot$ otherwise
- $\text{Regr}(\phi_1 \wedge \phi_2, s) = \text{Regr}(\phi_1, s) \wedge \text{Regr}(\phi_2, s)$
- $\text{Regr}(\neg\phi_i, s) = \neg\text{Regr}(\phi_1, s)$
- $\text{Regr}(\ominus\phi, s) = \phi$
- $\text{Regr}(\phi_1 \mathsf{S} \phi_2, s) = \text{Regr}(\phi_2, s) \vee (\text{Regr}(\phi_1, s) \wedge (\phi_1 \mathsf{S} \phi_2))$
- $\text{Regr}(\diamondminus\phi_1, s) = \text{Regr}(\phi_1, s) \vee \diamondminus\phi_1$
- $\text{Regr}(\boxminus\phi_1, s) = \text{Regr}(\phi_1, s) \wedge \boxminus\phi_1$

Finally, we define some useful notation. For an MDP (or NMRDP) with actions A and transition probabilities Pr, a trajectory $\langle s_0, \cdots, s_n \rangle$ is *feasible* iff there are actions $a_1, \cdots, a_n \in A$ such that $\Pr(s_i, a_i, s_{i+1}) > 0$. If ϕ_1 and ϕ_2 are PLTL formulas, ϕ_1 *determines* ϕ_2 iff either $\phi_1 \models \phi_2$ or $\phi_1 \models \neg\phi_2$ hold. Given any PLTL formula ϕ, we define *Subformulas*(ϕ) to be the set of all subformulas of ϕ (including ϕ itself). Note that $|\mathit{Subformulas}(\phi)| \leq \mathit{length}(\phi)$.

2.3 Rewarding Temporally-Extended Behaviors

To reward behaviors, we must adopt a generalization of MDPs that allows the reward given at any stage of the process to depend on past history. A *decision process with non-Markovian reward*, or NMRDP, is similar to an MDP with the exception that the reward function R takes as its domain histories of the form $\langle s_0, \cdots, s_n \rangle$ for all n. Intuitively, the agent receives reward $R(\langle s_0, \cdots, s_n \rangle)$ at stage n if the process has passed through state s_i at stage i for all $i \leq n$. Clearly, the explicit specification of such a reward function is impossible since there are an infinite number of different histories. Instead, we assume that the reward function of an NMRDP can be specified more compactly. In particular, we assume that the reward function is defined by a finite set Φ of *reward formulas* expressed in PLTL, together with a real-valued reward r_i associated with each $\phi_i \in \Phi$ (we sometimes write this $\phi_i : r_i$). The temporally extended reward function (TERF) R is then defined as follows:

$$R(\langle s_0, \cdots, s_n \rangle) = \sum \{r_i : \langle s_0, \cdots, s_n \rangle \models \phi_i\}$$

This formulation gives a reward of r_i at each state that satisfies formula ϕ_i; if ϕ_i has a nontrivial temporal component then the reward is *history-dependent*. Because reward formulas are expressed in PLTL, rewards depend only on past states, and the TERF can be unambiguously evaluated at each stage of the process.[3]

Consideration should not be restricted to Markovian policies when dealing with NMRDPs. The value, and hence the choice, of action at any stage may depend on history. We thus take policies to be mappings from histories to actions. As usual, the value of a given policy π is taken to be the expectation of the discounted accumulated reward:

$$V_\pi(s_0) = E\{\sum_{n=0}^{\infty} \beta^n R(\langle s_0, s_1, \cdots, s_n \rangle) | \pi\}.$$

Since TERFs are finitely specified, we can find good ways of encoding and computing optimal policies (see Section 4). But first we examine the expressive power of TERFs.

always, eventually and next, respectively.

[2]We use the abbreviation $\ominus^k$ for k iterations of the $\ominus$ modality (e.g., $\ominus^3\phi \equiv \ominus\ominus\ominus\phi$), and $\ominus^{\leq k}$ to stand for the disjunction of $\ominus^i$ for $1 \leq i \leq k$, (e.g., $\ominus^{\leq 2}\phi \equiv \ominus\phi \vee \ominus\ominus\phi$).

[3]The r_i are assumed to be additive and independent (this is not restrictive). Any (history *independent*) MDP can be expressed this way by restricting Φ to contain no temporal operators.

3 Encoding Typical Forms of Behavior

To demonstrate that TERFs provide an appropriate and useful language in which to specify rewards for NMRDPs, we examine several common examples to see how they can be encoded in PLTL. We make no claim that all interesting rewards can be encoded in this way, but the evidence suggests that PLTL and TERFs can capture a very large and useful class of reward functions.

Among the common types of behaviors, simple *goal achievement* has retained a special place in classical planning. However, in a process-oriented model, like an MDP or NMRDP, a number of subtleties arise in giving "goal achievement" a precise interpretation. We describe several possibilities. Assume one such goal is the proposition G: we wish the agent to reach a state in which G holds and will reward it with r if it does so. The simplest reward formula for this goal is G. As a TERF, this rewards the agent at every state satisfying G, and hence the agent is more highly rewarded (roughly) the larger fraction of its time it spends in G-states. This provides incentive for the agent to constantly maintain G if r is greater than rewards it may receive for other behaviors.

In many cases, this is not the intended effect of specifying a goal G. If we only care that G is achieved once, there are several different interpretations that can be provided. The strictest offers reward r only to the *first* state at which G holds; that is, $(G \wedge \neg\ominus\diamond G) : r$. A more generous formula, $\diamond G : r$, rewards every state that follows the achievement of G. Finally, we may reward G periodically, but not encourage constant maintenance of G, by rewarding G at most once every k stages: formula $G \wedge \neg(\ominus^{\leq k} G) : r$ will reward G-states that have not occurred within k-stages of a previous G-state. Yet another option rewards any G-state that occurs within k-stages of some $\neg G$-state (allowing up to k consecutive G-rewards), using $G \wedge \ominus^{\leq k} \neg G : r$.

In addition, PLTL allows one to formulate temporally extended goal *sequences*. For instance, if the agent is to be rewarded for achieving G, followed immediately by H and then by I, the reward formula $\ominus^2 G \wedge \ominus H \wedge I$ can be used. Periodic reward of such behavior, or the similar behavior in which other steps are allowed to intervene between G, H, and I, can also be prescribed in a straightforward fashion.

The formulations above assume that there is some goal G that is constantly desirable, a vestige of the classical interpretation of goals. Such behaviors are more suited to background, maintenance goals. In a process-oriented setting, we are likely to want the agent to respond to requests or *commands* to bring about some goal. In these settings, goals are not constant: they arise periodically, can be fulfilled, forgotten, preempted, and might even expire. We model these in PLTL using *response formulas* which specify a relation between a *command* C and rewarded goal achievement G.

The most basic response formula is that of *eventual response*, $G \wedge \diamond C$—the agent is rewarded at any G-state that follows a C-state in which the command is given (or is outstanding). As usual, we may only wish to reward the first state at which G holds following the command, in which case $G \wedge \ominus(\neg G \mathsf{S} C)$ suffices.

Many requests must be achieved in a timely fashion. *Immediate response* formulas have the form $G \wedge \ominus C$, rewarding a goal achieved at the state following a command. More generally, we have *bounded response* formulas of the type $G \wedge \ominus^{\leq k} C$ which reward goal achievement within k steps of a request. This formula does not preclude multiple rewards for a single request, so we might instead prefer $G \wedge \ominus^{\leq k} C \wedge \ominus(\neg G \mathsf{S} C)$, which rewards only the first goal state. Finally, a *graded reward* can be given for faster achievement of G (within limits). For instance, the set

$$\{G \wedge \ominus C : r_1,\ \ G \wedge \ominus^{\leq 2} C : r_2,\ \ G \wedge \ominus^{\leq 3} C : r_3\}$$

rewards goal achievement in one step with reward $r_1 + r_2 + r_3$, in two steps with $r_2 + r_3$, and in three steps with r_3.

In a longer version of this paper, we describe additional types of behaviors, as well as the possibility of using other logics to express different kinds of reward.

4 Modeling NMRDPs with MDPs

As has been pointed out, constructing optimal policies in settings of non-Markovian reward can be computationally prohibitive. In this section, we describe a method of state-space expansion that determines the aspects of history that are *relevant* to an NMRDP (i.e., which must be recorded so that we can verify the truth of the temporal reward formulas), and encodes this history within the state. A straightforward transformation of the reward function, so that rewards are attached to such extended states rather than trajectories, restores the Markovian reward property. Together with an adjustment in action descriptions to deal with the new state space, we then have a (fully-observable) MDP that accurately reflects the NMRDP, that can be solved by standard (relatively efficient) methods. We begin by discussing the basic properties that such a transformation should satisfy, and then specialize to the case of rewards that are given by TERFs.

4.1 Markovian Transformations

To transform an NMRDP into an equivalent MDP requires that we *expand* the state space S of the NMRDP so that each new state in the expanded state space ES carries not just the original state information, but also any additional information required to render reward ascription independent of history.[4] As we shall see, we can think of expanded states as consisting of a base state annotated with a label that summarizes relevant history. If $G_S = (S, A, R)$ is the NMRDP in question, then we wish to produce an MDP $G_{ES} = (ES, A, R_{ES})$ with expanded space ES. The actions A available to the agent remain unchanged (since the aim is to produce a policy suitable for the original NMRDP), but the reward function R_{ES} is now Markovian: it assigns rewards to (expanded) states.

For the new MDP to be useful, we would expect it to bear a strong relationship to the NMRDP from which it was constructed. In particular, we define a strong correspondence between the two as follows:

[4] Here we are concerned only with reward ascription; the system dynamics are already Markovian.

Definition 4.1 *An MDP $G_{ES} = (ES, A, R_{ES})$ is an* expansion *of an NMRDP $G_S = (S, A, R)$ if there are functions $\tau : ES \mapsto S$ and $\sigma : S \mapsto ES$ such that:*

1. *For all $s \in S$, $\tau(\sigma(s)) = s$,*
2. *For all $s, s' \in S$ and $es \in ES$, if $\Pr(s, a, s') = p > 0$ and $\tau(es) = s$, then there is a unique es', $\tau(es') = s'$, such that $\Pr(es, a, es') = p$.*
3. *For any feasible trajectories $\langle s_0, \cdots, s_n \rangle$ in G_S and $\langle es_0, \cdots, es_n \rangle$ in G_{ES}, where $\tau(es_i) = s_i$ and $\sigma(s_0) = es_0$, we have $R(\langle s_0, \cdots, s_n \rangle) = R_{ES}(es_n)$.* ∎

Intuitively, $\tau(es)$ is the *base state* for es, the state in S extended by es. For this reason, we will often speak of extended states being *labeled* or annotated: each extended state can be written $s \circ l$, where $s \in S$ is the base state, and l is a label that distinguishes es from other extensions of s. However, among the extensions of s, we must pick out a unique $\sigma(s) \in ES$ as the "start state" corresponding to s. In other words, $\sigma(s)$ should be thought of as that annotation of s with an "empty" history; i.e., corresponding to an occurrence of s at the very start of a trajectory. We will see below why it is important to distinguish this extension of s from other extensions.

The important parts of this definition are clauses (2) and (3), which assert that G_{ES} and G_S are equivalent (with respect to base states) in both their dynamics and reward structure. In particular, clause (2) ensures, for any trajectory in G_S

$$s_0 \stackrel{a_1,p_1}{\longrightarrow} s_1 \cdots s_{n-1} \stackrel{a_n,p_n}{\longrightarrow} s_n$$

and extended state es_0 with base state s_0, that there is a trajectory in G_{ES} of similar structure

$$es_0 \stackrel{a_1,p_1}{\longrightarrow} es_1 \cdots es_{n-1} \stackrel{a_n,p_n}{\longrightarrow} es_n$$

where $\tau(es_i) = s_i$ for all i. We call $\langle es_0, \cdots, es_n \rangle$ and $\langle s_0, \cdots, s_n \rangle$ *weakly corresponding* trajectories in this case. Clause (3) imposes strong requirements on the reward assigned to the individual states in G_{ES}. In particular, if $\langle es_0, \cdots, es_n \rangle$ and $\langle s_0, \cdots, s_n \rangle$ are weakly corresponding, and $\sigma(s_0) = es_0$ (i.e., es_0 is a start state), we say these trajectories are *strongly corresponding*. It is not hard to see that this relationship is one-to-one: each $\langle s_0, \cdots, s_n \rangle$ has a unique strongly corresponding trajectory, and $\langle es_0, \cdots, es_n \rangle$ has a unique strongly corresponding trajectory iff es_0 is a start state. Clause (3) requires that R_{ES} assign rewards to extended states in such a manner that strongly corresponding trajectories receive the same reward. This need not be the case for weakly corresponding trajectories since, intuitively, different annotations (extensions) of s_0 correspond to different possible histories.

If we can produce an MDP G_{ES} that is an expansion of an NMRDP G_S as specified by Defn. 4.1, then we can find optimal policies for G_S by solving G_{ES} instead.

Definition 4.2 *Let π' be a policy for MDP G_{ES}. The* corresponding *policy π for the NMRDP G_S is defined as $\pi(\langle s_0, \cdots, s_n \rangle) = \pi'(es_n)$, where $\langle es_0, \cdots, es_n \rangle$ is the strongly corresponding trajectory for $\langle s_0, \cdots, s_n \rangle$.* ∎

Proposition 4.3 *For any policy π' for MDP G_{ES}, corresponding policy π for G_S, and $s \in S$, we have $V_\pi(s) = V_{\pi'}(\sigma(s))$.*

Corollary 4.4 *Let π' be an optimal policy for MDP G_{ES}. Then the corresponding policy π is optimal for NMRDP G_S.*

Thus, given a suitable expanded MDP and an optimal policy π', one can produce an optimal policy π for the NMRDP quite easily. In practice, the agent need not construct π explicitly. Instead, it can run π' over the expanded MDP. Once the agent knows what base state it starts in, it determines the corresponding extended state using the function σ. Furthermore, the dynamics of the expanded MDP ensures that it can keep track of the current extended state simply by observing the base state to which each transition is made.

Finally, we should consider the size of the expanded MDP. Often, we can fulfill the requirements of Defn. 4.1 with a trivial MDP, that has states encoding *complete* trajectory information over some finite horizon. But such an expanded space grows exponentially with the horizon. Furthermore, even simple rewards—like $\diamondminus G$, which only require one item of history (a bit indicating if a G state has been passed through)—can require in infinite amount of complete trajectory history using this naive approach. If possible, we want to encode only the *relevant* history, and find an MDP which has a few states as possible (subject to Defn. 4.1). Note that state-space size tends to be the dominant complexity-determining factor in standard MDP solution techniques, especially as applied to planning problems.[5]

4.2 Transformations using TERFs

The problem of finding a small MDP that expands a given NMRDP is made easier if the latter's rewards are given by a TERF. In this case, it is natural to label states with PLTL formulas that summarize history. More precisely, the new state space *ES* consists of *annotated states*, of the form $s \circ f$ where $s \in S$ and f is a formula in PLTL. These annotations will be meaningful and correct assertions about history, in a sense to be made precise below. We give an algorithm that constructs an expansion of the state space by producing labelings of states that are sufficient to determine future reward.

We begin with a simple example to illustrate the essential ideas. Consider a single reward formula $\phi_R = Q \wedge \ominus\ominus P$. Recall that our goal is to encode all relevant history in a state's annotation. Thus, for each state s in which ϕ_R might possibly be true, we need *at least* two distinct labels, one implying the truth of ϕ_R and one its falsity.

Next, imagine that we have an extended state $es = s \circ \psi$, where Q is true in s and $\psi = \ominus\ominus P$. (Thus es implies that ϕ_R is true.) Next, suppose that s is reachable from some other state s^- (i.e., there is some transition in the NMRDP from s^- to s). Since we must ensure that es's label ψ is a correct assertion about its history, in the expanded MDP any transition from an extended version of s^- (es^-, say) to es must satisfy

[5] See [LDK95] on the complexity of solving MDPs. Generally, the state space is problematic in planning problems because it grows exponentially with the number of atomic propositions. Adding history "naively" to the domain exacerbates this problem considerably.

the "historical" constraints imposed by ψ. In this example, if there is a transition from es^- to es it must be the case that es^- satisfies $\ominus P$ (otherwise, es might not satisfy $\ominus\ominus P$). In general, we can use the regression operator to determine what must have been true at earlier states. A reward formula ϕ is true of a trajectory terminating in es iff $\text{Regr}(\phi, s)$ holds at es's predecessor. Thus, the formula $\text{Regr}(\phi, s)$—or a stronger formula implying $\text{Regr}(\phi, s)$—must be part of any label attached to states that reach $es = s \circ \phi$ in one step. This process is, naturally, repeated (states reaching es^- must satisfy P, etc.).

To quickly summarize this example, suppose that every state is reachable from any other, and that P and Q are the only propositions (hence, there are exactly 4 base states). Then 12 extended states are necessary. For each base state where Q is false (i.e., $P \wedge \neg Q$ and $\neg P \wedge \neg Q$) we need one extension labeled with $\neg\ominus P$ and another with $\ominus P$. For each of the two base states in which Q is true, we need 4 extended states, with the labels $\ominus P \wedge \ominus\ominus P$, $\neg\ominus P \wedge \ominus\ominus P$, $\ominus P \wedge \neg\ominus\ominus P$, and $\neg\ominus P \wedge \neg\ominus\ominus P$. Note that every extended state has the property that we can easily tell whether the reward formula $Q \wedge \ominus\ominus P$ is true there. Furthermore, the regression constraints discussed above hold. For example, let $s^- \models P \wedge Q$ and $es^- = s^- \circ (\neg\ominus P \wedge \ominus\ominus P)$, and consider the transition to the base state s where $s \models \neg P \wedge Q$. It is necessary that there be some labeling of s, $es = s \circ \psi$, such that $\text{Regr}(\psi, s)$ is implied by es^-. But this is so, because we can take ψ to be $\ominus P \wedge \neg\ominus\ominus P$. Note that if we had not been able to find such ψ, this would mean that es^-'s label did not encode enough history (because we would be unable to determine the correct subsequent label after a move to s).

Our algorithm constructs the set of extended phases somewhat indirectly, using a two phase approach. Phase I of our algorithm constructs *label sets* for each state, $ls(s)$, containing PLTL formulas that *might* be relevant to future reward. The elements of $ls(s)$ will not necessarily be the labels themselves, but are the ingredients out of which labels are constructed. In a certain sense (to be discussed in Section 4.3) it does not matter if we add "too many" (or too strong) formulas to $ls(s)$, so there are in fact several distinct implementations of Phase I. But as we have just seen, regression should be used to impose constraints on label sets. If $\phi \in ls(s)$, so that ϕ might be (part of) the label of a extension es, then $\text{Regr}(\phi, s)$ must be implied by the annotation of any state es^- from which es is reachable.

Given that Phase I is correct (i.e., it finds all formulas that might be relevant), we can restrict attention to extended states whose labels are combinations of the formulas in $ls(s)$, asserting that some are true and others false. Formally:

Definition 4.5 *If* Ψ *is a set of PLTL formulas, the* atoms *of* Ψ, *denoted* ATOMS(Ψ), *is the set of all conjunctions that can be formed from the members of* Ψ *and their negations. E.g., if* $\Psi = \{q \wedge \ominus p, p\}$, *then* $\text{ATOMS}(\Psi) = \{(q \wedge \ominus p) \wedge p, \neg(q \wedge \ominus p) \wedge p, (q \wedge \ominus p) \wedge \neg p, \neg(q \wedge \ominus p) \wedge \neg p\}$. ∎

Thus, the labels extending s will belong to ATOMS($ls(s)$). In general, however, many of these atoms will be inconsistent, or simply not reachable given the set of feasible trajectories in the original NMRDP. Rather than performing theorem proving to check consistency, we will *generate* the extended states we require in a constructive fashion, by explicitly considering which states are reachable from a start state. This is Phase II of our algorithm.

To illustrate, suppose that we have determined $ls(s_1) = \{Q \wedge \ominus\ominus P, \top \wedge \ominus P, \bot \wedge \ominus P, P\}$, and that $s_1 \models \neg Q \wedge P$. There is only one atom over $ls(s_1)$ that can be true at s_1 in the (length 1) trajectory $\langle s_1 \rangle$, namely:

$$f = \neg(Q \wedge \ominus\ominus P) \wedge \neg(\top \wedge \ominus P) \wedge \neg(\bot \wedge \ominus P) \wedge P.$$

We thus include $s_1 \circ f$ in *ES*. (Note that $s_1 \circ f$ can be logically simplified, to $s_1 \circ \neg\ominus P$.) >From this extended state we consider, for each successor state s_2 of s_1, which atom over s_2's label set is true in the trajectory $\langle s_1, s_2 \rangle$. Again, this will be unique: for instance, if s_1 can succeed itself, we obtain a new extended state $s_1 \circ f'$ where

$$f' = \neg(Q \wedge \ominus\ominus P) \wedge (\top \wedge \ominus P) \wedge \neg(\bot \wedge \ominus P) \wedge P$$

(This also can be simplified, in this case to $s_2 \circ \ominus P$.) For any action a such that $\Pr(s_1, a, s_2) = p > 0$, we assert that $\Pr(s_1 \circ f, a, s_2 \circ f') = p$. By adding extended states to *ES* in this way, we will only add extended states that are reachable and whose history is meaningful. For instance, we see that while $\phi = Q \wedge \ominus\ominus P$ is in $ls(s_1)$, no label that makes ϕ true at s_1 will be reachable (recall s_1 makes Q false). This effectively eliminates ϕ from consideration at s_1.

The algorithm is described in Figure 1. We defer a discussion of Phases I and III until Section 4.3. Note, however, that an easy implementation of Phase I is to set $ls(s)$, for all s, equal to $\bigcup_{\phi_i \in \Phi}$ *Subformulas*(ϕ_i) where Φ is the set of reward formulas. All the results in this section apply to any suitable choice of $ls(\cdot)$, including this one.

The MDP G_{ES} generated by the algorithm is an expansion of G_S. To show this, it is useful to define a more general concept of which G_{ES} is an instance:

Definition 4.6 $G_{ES} = (ES, A, R_{ES})$ *is a* sound annotation *of* $G_S = (S, A, R)$ *if each state* $es \in ES$ *is of the form* $s \circ f$ *for* $s \in S$ *and some PLTL formula* f, *and:*

1. *Fixing* $\tau(s \circ f) = s$, *there exists* $\sigma : S \mapsto ES$ *such that clauses [1] and [2] of Definition 4.1 hold.*
2. *Let* $\langle s_0 \circ f_0, s_1 \circ f_1, \ldots, s_n \circ f_n \rangle$, $n \geq 0$, *be such that* $\sigma(s_0) = s_0 \circ f_0$. *Then:*

$$\langle s_0, s_1, \ldots, s_n \rangle \models f_n$$ ∎

This definition is similar to our definition of expansion (Defn. 4.1), except that we give the extended states a particular form: annotations using PLTL formulas. Furthermore, instead of requiring that annotations summarize enough history for the purposes of determining rewards, we no longer care *why* G_{ES} has the annotations it does; we only insist that whatever history is recorded in these annotations be accurate.

Because of its generality, the notion of sound annotation may have other applications. However, for our purposes we must make one more assumption: that G_{ES}'s labels are informative enough to determine rewards.

Definition 4.7 G_{ES} determines rewards *over a set of reward formulas* Φ *iff, for all* $es = s \circ f \in ES$ *and all* $\phi_i \in \Phi$, f *determines* ϕ_i.

Phase I Find label sets:

Choose any $ls : S \mapsto$ *subsets of* PLTL, such that:

For all $s \in S$, all $f \in$ ATOMS$(ls(s))$, and all formulas ϕ:
If $\phi \in \Phi$, the set of reward formulas for G_S, then:
f determines ϕ
If $\phi \in ls(s')$, where $\Pr(s, a, s') > 0$ for some $a \in A$, then:
f determines $\mathrm{Regr}(\phi, s')$

Note. See text for more discussion of this phase. However, $ls_{\mathrm{sub}}(s) = \cup_{\phi_i \in \Phi}$ *Subformulas*(ϕ_i) is always suitable.

Phase II Generate G_{ES}:

1. For all $s \in S$ do:
(a) Find $f \in$ ATOMS$(ls(s))$ such that $\langle s \rangle \models f$.
Note. Such an atom exists and is unique.
(b) Add $s \circ f$ to *ES*.
Note. This will be the start state corresponding to s.
(c) Mark $s \circ f$ unvisited.
2. While there exists an unvisited state $es \in ES$, $es = s \circ f$ do:
(a) For all s' such that $\Pr(s, a, s') > 0$ for some a do:
i. Find $f' \in$ ATOMS$(ls(s'))$ such that $f \models \mathrm{Regr}(f', s')$.
ii. If $s' \circ f' \notin ES$ then add $s' \circ f'$ to *ES* and mark it unvisited.
iii. Set $\Pr(s \circ f, a, s' \circ f')$ equal to $\Pr(s, a, s')$, for all a.
3. For $es = s \circ f$ in *ES*, set $R_{ES}(es)$ to $\sum_{\phi_i \in \Phi} \{r_i : f \models \phi_i\}$.
4. Set $\Pr(s \circ f, a, s' \circ f') = 0$ for all transition probabilities not previously assigned.

Phase III Minimization: See Section 4.3 for discussion.

Note. This phase is not always necessary.

Figure 1: Algorithm to find Annotated Expansion of G_S

Proposition 4.8 *If $G_{ES} = (ES, A, R_{ES})$ is sound annotation of G_S that determines rewards over Φ, and $R_{ES}(s \circ f) = \sum_{\phi_i \in \Phi} \{r_i : f \models \phi_i\}$, then G_{ES} is an expansion of G_S.*

The key to understanding our algorithm is realizing that it is designed to generate a MDP that satisfies the conditions of this proposition. Thus, by the results of Section 4.1, we have succeeded in our goal of finding an equivalent MDP G_{ES} for any NMRDP G_S whose rewards are given using a TERF. In particular, we have the following key result:

Theorem 4.9 *Let G_S be an NMRDP whose reward function is given by a TERF, over a set of formulas Φ. The Expansion Algorithm of Figure 1 constructs an MDP G_{ES} that is an expansion of G_S.*

Once this expansion G_{ES} is constructed, an optimal policy for the MDP G_{ES} can be computed using standard techniques. The correspondence presented in Section 4.1 shows that an agent executing this policy will behave optimally with respect to the original NMRDP. We note that the labels in G_{ES} determine the history that must be kept track of during policy execution. In particular, suppose we are given a policy π' defined on the extended space to apply to the NMRDP, and the process starts in state s_0. We take the extended state to be s_0's unique start state es_0 and perform $\pi'(es_0) = a$. An observation of the resulting state s_1 is made. The dynamics of the extended MDP ensure that there is a unique es_1 extending s_1 that is reachable from es_0 under action a. Thus, we next execute action $\pi'(es_1)$, and proceed as before. Note that we can keep track of the extended state that we are currently in even though we only get to directly observe base states.

4.3 Other Properties of the Algorithm

In this section, we very briefly discuss some of the other interesting issues raised by the expansion algorithm.

We begin by examining Phase I. As already noted, one possible implementation is $ls(s) = ls_{\mathrm{sub}}(s)$; i.e., the label sets consisting of all subformulas of Φ. An advantage of this choice is that Phase I becomes trivial, with complexity $O(L)$, where $L = \sum_{\phi_i \in \Phi} \mathit{length}(\phi_i)$ is a bound on the number of subformulas we generate. Furthermore, we can bound the size of G_{ES}. Since there are at most 2^L atoms over $ls(s)$, each base state can receive at most this number of distinct labels. Thus G_{ES} can be *at most* this factor larger than G_S (although Phase II does not usually generate all conceivable labels.) The exponential here may seem discouraging, but there are simple, natural examples in which this number of historical distinctions is *required* for implementing an optimal policy. For instance, for the reward formula $\ominus^n P$, we need to keep track of when P was true among the previous n steps, leading to 2^n distinct annotations.

Nevertheless, the main disadvantage of $ls_{\mathrm{sub}}(\cdot)$ is that it can lead to unnecessarily fine distinctions among histories, so that G_{ES} as produced by Phase II is not guaranteed to be minimal (in the sense of having as few states as possible among valid expansions of G_S). If minimality is important, a separate step after Phase II is required. Fortunately, minimizing G_{ES} can be performed using a variant of standard algorithms for minimizing finite state automata [HU79]. We defer discussion to the full paper, but note that the complexity of doing this is only polynomial in the size of G_{ES}. Thus, so long as the intermediate G_{ES} produced by Phase II is of manageable size, minimization is fairly straightforward.[6]

A second implementation of Phase I constructs label sets ls_{w} with "weaker" formulas, subject to the stated requirements. More precisely, we initially set $ls_{\mathrm{w}}(s) = \Phi$, for all s. Then, so long as we can find s, s', such that s' is reachable from s and $\{\mathrm{Regr}(\phi, s') : \phi \in ls_{\mathrm{w}}(s')\} \not\subseteq ls_{\mathrm{w}}(s)$, we add $\{\mathrm{Regr}(\phi, s') : \phi \in ls_{\mathrm{w}}(s')\}$ to $ls_{\mathrm{w}}(s)$. We iterate until this terminates—which it will, so long as we are careful not to add different (but logically equivalent) formulas twice to $ls_{\mathrm{w}}(s)$. This procedure ensures the necessary properties of $ls(\cdot)$. For many natural examples of reward formula, this process terminates quickly, generating small label sets.

The major reason for considering $ls_{\mathrm{w}}(\cdot)$ is that G_{ES}, as constructed subsequently by Phase II, is then guaranteed to have minimal size. But $ls_{\mathrm{w}}(\cdot)$ has a serious drawback as well: Phase I can *potentially* become very complex. The number of iterations until termination can be exponential (in the size of the reward formulas) and the size of the label sets can grow double-exponentially. Perhaps the optimal strategy, then, is to begin to implement Phase I using $ls_{\mathrm{w}}(\cdot)$, but if any reward

[6] If G_{ES} is *much* larger than necessary, Phase II's complexity could cause difficulties.

formula proves troublesome, to then revert to the subformula technique at that point.

We conclude by noting that Phase II is, in comparison, unproblematic. Since each extended state is visited exactly once the complexity is linear in the size of the final answer (i.e., the size of G_{ES}.) Furthermore, none of the operations performed in Phase II are difficult. Steps 1.a and 2.a.i appear to involve theorem-proving, but this is misleading. Step 1.a is actually just *model checking* (over what is, furthermore, a very short trajectory) and in this particular case can be done in time proportional to $\sum_{\phi \in \mathrm{ls}(s)} length(\phi)$. Step 2.a.i can also be performed quickly; the details depend on exactly how Phase I is implemented, but in general (and in particular, for the two proposals discussed above) enough book-keeping information can be recorded during Phase I so that 2.a.i can be performed in time proportional to $|ls(s)|$. Again, space limitations prevent us from providing the details.

In conclusion, the annotation algorithm appears to be quite practical. The potential exists for exponential work (relative to the size of G_S) but this is generally the case exactly when we really do need to store a lot of history (i.e., when G_{ES} is necessarily large).

5 Concluding Remarks

While MDPs provide a useful framework for DTP, some of the necessary assumptions can be quite restrictive (at the very least, requiring that some planning problems be encoded in an unnatural way). We have presented a technique that weakens the impact of one of these assumptions, namely, the requirement of Markovian (or state-based) reward. The main contributions of this work are a methodology for the natural specification of temporally extended rewards, and an algorithm that automatically constructs an equivalent MDP, allowing standard MDP solution techniques to be used to construct optimal policies.

There are a number of interesting directions in which this work can be extended. First, similar techniques can be used to cope with non-Markovian dynamics, and can also be used with partially-observable processes. In addition, other temporal logics (such as more standard forward-looking logics) and process logics can potentially be used in a similar fashion to specify different classes of behaviors.

Another interesting idea is to use compact representations of MDPs to obviate the need for computation involving individual states. For instance, Bayes net representations have been used to specify actions for MDPs in [BDG95], and can be exploited in policy construction. Given an NMRDP specified in this way, we could produce new Bayes net action descriptions involving an expanded set of variables (or propositions) that render the underlying reward process Markovian, rather than expanding states explicitly.

Finally, our technique does not work well if the expanded MDP is large, which may be the case if a lot of history is necessary (note that this is inherent in formulating such a problem as an MDP, whether automatically constructed or not). The complexity of policy construction is typically dominated by the size of the state space. An important direction for future work is to combine policy construction with state space expansion. The hope is that one can avoid generating many expanded states using dominance arguments particular to the reward structure of the given NMRDP.

Acknowledgements

The work of Fahiem Bacchus and Craig Boutilier was supported by the Canadian government through their NSERC and IRIS programs.

We thank the anonymous referees for their thoughtful reviews. It is unfortunate that space limitations prevented us from responding to several of their valuable suggestions.

References

[AH90] R. Alur and T. Henzinger. Real-time logics: complexity and expressiveness. *LICS-90*, Philadelphia, 1990.

[BD94] C. Boutilier and R. Dearden. Using abstractions for decision-theoretic planning with time constraints. *AAAI-94*, pp.1016–1022, Seattle, 1994.

[BDG95] C. Boutilier, R. Dearden, and M. Goldszmidt. Exploiting structure in policy construction. *IJCAI-95*, pp.1104–1111, Montreal, 1995.

[Bel57] R. E. Bellman. *Dynamic Programming*. Princeton University Press, Princeton, 1957.

[BP95] C. Boutilier and M. L. Puterman. Process-oriented planning and average-reward optimality. *IJCAI-95*, pp.1096–1103, Montreal, 1995.

[DK89] T. Dean and K. Kanazawa. A model for reasoning about persistence and causation. *Comp. Intel.*, 5:142–150, 1989.

[DKKN93] T. Dean, L. P. Kaelbling, J. Kirman, and A. Nicholson. Planning with deadlines in stochastic domains. *AAAI-93*, pp.574–579, Washington, D.C., 1993.

[Dru89] M. Drummond. Situated control rules. *KR-89*, pp.103–113, Toronto, 1989.

[Eme90] E. A. Emerson. Temporal and modal logic. In J. van Leeuwen, ed., *Handbook Theor. Comp. Sci., Vol.B*, pp.997–1072, 1990.

[GK91] P. Godefroid and F. Kabanza. An efficient reactive planner for synthesizing reactive plans. *AAAI-91*, pp.640–645, 1991.

[HH92] P. Haddawy and S. Hanks. Representations for decision-theoretic planning: Utility functions for deadline goals. *KR-92*, pp.71–82, Cambridge, 1992.

[How60] R. A. Howard. *Dynamic Programming and Markov Processes*. MIT Press, Cambridge, 1960.

[HU79] J. E. Hopcroft and J. D. Ullman. *Introduction to Automata Theory, Languages and Computation*. Addison-Wesley, 1979.

[Kab90] F. Kabanza. Synthesis of reactive plans for multi-path environments. *AAAI-90*, pp.164–169, 1990.

[KHW94] N. Kushmerick, S. Hanks and D. Weld. An algorithm for probabilistic least-commitment planning. *AAAI-94*, pp.1073–1078, Seattle, 1994.

[LDK95] M. Littman, T. L. Dean and L. P. Kaelbling. On the complexity of solving Markov decision problems. *UAI-95*, pp.394–402, Montreal, 1995.

[Put94] M. L. Puterman. *Markov Decision Processes: Discrete Stochastic Dynamic Programming*. Wiley, New York, 1994.

[Sch87] M. J. Schoppers. Universal plans for reactive robots in unpredictable environments. *IJCAI-87*, 1039–1046, Milan, 1987.

[TR94] J. Tash and S. Russell. Control strategies for a stochastic planner. *AAAI-94*, 1079–1085, Seattle, 1994.

Computing Optimal Policies for Partially Observable Decision Processes using Compact Representations

Craig Boutilier and David Poole
Department of Computer Science
University of British Columbia
Vancouver, BC V6T 1Z4, CANADA
cebly@cs.ubc.ca, poole@cs.ubc.ca

Abstract

Partially-observable Markov decision processes provide a general model for decision theoretic planning problems, allowing trade-offs between various courses of actions to be determined under conditions of uncertainty, and incorporating partial observations made by an agent. Dynamic programming algorithms based on the *belief state* of an agent can be used to construct optimal policies without explicit consideration of past history, but at high computational cost. In this paper, we discuss how structured representations of system dynamics can be incorporated in classic POMDP solution algorithms. We use Bayesian networks with structured conditional probability matrices to represent POMDPs, and use this model to structure the belief space for POMDP algorithms, allowing irrelevant distinctions to be ignored. Apart from speeding up optimal policy construction, we suggest that such representations can be exploited in the development of useful approximation methods.

1 Introduction

Recent interest in *decision-theoretic planning* (DTP) has been spurred by the need to extend planning algorithms to deal with quantified uncertainty regarding an agent's knowledge of the world and action effects, as well as competing objectives [9, 7, 4, 16] (see [2] for a brief survey). A useful underlying semantic model for such DTP problems is that of *partially observable Markov decision processes* (POMDPs) [6]. This model, used in operations research [17, 12] and stochastic control, accounts for the tradeoffs between competing objectives, action costs, uncertainty of action effects and observations that provide incomplete information about the world. However, while the model is very general, these problems are typically specified in terms of state transitions and observations associated with individual states—even specifying a problem in these terms is problematic given that the state space grows exponentially with the number of variables used to describe the problem.

Influence diagrams (IDs) and Bayesian networks (BNs) [10, 14] provide a much more natural way of specifying the dynamics of a system, including the effects of actions and observation probabilities, by exploiting problem structure and independencies among random variables. As such, problems can be specified much more compactly and naturally [8, 4, 16]. In addition, algorithms for solving IDs can exploit such regularities for computational gain in decision-making. Classic solution methods for POMDPs within the OR community, in contrast, have been developed primarily using explicit state-based representations which adds a sometimes unwanted computational burden. However, unlike ID algorithms, for which policies grow exponentially with the time horizon, POMDP algorithms offer concepts (in particular, that of *belief state*) that sometimes alleviate this difficulty.

In this paper we propose a method for optimal policy construction, based on standard POMDP algorithms, that exploits BN representations of actions and reward, as well as tree [4] or rule [16] representations within the BN itself. In this way, our technique exploits the advantages of classic POMDP and ID representations and provides leverage for approximation methods.

In Section 2, we define POMDPs and associated notions, at the same time showing how structured representations, based on BNs (augmented with *tree-structured conditional probability tables*), can be used to specify POMDPs. In Section 3, we describe a particular POMDP algorithm due to Monahan [12], based on the work of Sondik [17]. In Section 4, we describe how we can incorporate the structure captured by our representations to reduce the effective state space of the Monahan algorithm at any point in its computation. Our algorithm exploits ideas from the SPI algorithm of [4] for fully observable processes. In Section 5 we suggest that our method may enable good approximation schemes for POMDPs.

2 POMDPs and Structured Representations

In this section we build upon the classic presentation of POMDPs adopted in much of the OR community. We refer to [17, 11, 6] for further details and [12, 5] for a survey. We describe the main components of POMDPs and related concepts. However, by assuming that problems are specified in terms or propositional (or other random) variables, we are able to describe how structured representations, in particular, decision trees or if-then rules, can be used to describe these components compactly. We begin with a (running) example.

Example Imagine a robot that can check whether a user wants coffee and can get it by going to the shop across the

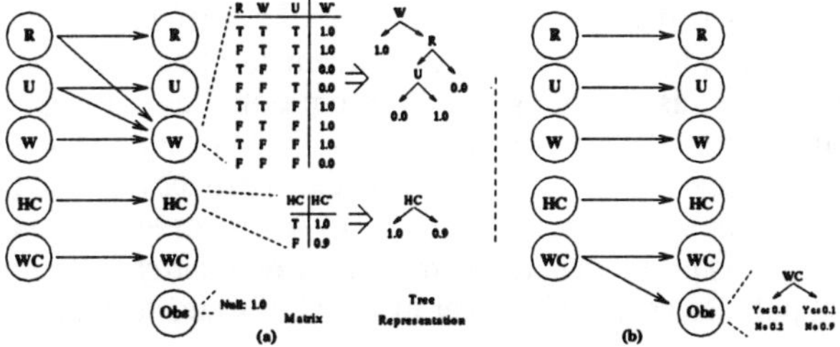

Figure 1: Action Networks for (a) GetC and (b) TestC

street. The robot is rewarded if the user wants coffee *WC* and has coffee *HC*, but is penalized if *HC* is false when *WC* is true. The robot will also get wet *W* if it is raining *R* when it goes for coffee, unless it has its umbrella *U*. We can imagine a number of other tasks here as well. Although the robot can check on the weather, grab its umbrella, etc., we focus on two actions: getting coffee *GetC* and checking whether the user wants coffee by means of a quick inspection *TestC*.

2.1 System Dynamics

We assume a finite set of propositions $\mathcal{P}$ that describe all relevant aspects of the system we wish to control. This induces a finite state space $\mathcal{S} = \mathbf{2}^{\mathcal{P}}$ consisting of all possible assignments of truth values to $\mathcal{P}$. There is a finite set of actions $\mathcal{A}$ available to the agent or controller, with each action causing a state transition. We assume the system can be modeled as a POMDP with a stationary dynamics (i.e., the effects of actions do not depend on the stage of the process). For simplicity we assume all actions can be taken (or attempted) at all states. While an action takes an agent from one state to another, the effects of actions cannot be predicted with certainty; hence (slightly abusing notation) we write $Pr(s_2|s_1, a)$ to denote the probability that s_2 is reached given that action a is performed in state s_1. This formulation assumes the Markov property for the system in question.

One can represent the transition probabilities associated with action a explicitly using a $|\mathcal{S}| \times |\mathcal{S}|$ probability matrix. However, the fact that $|\mathcal{S}|$ increases exponentially with the number of problem characteristics $|\mathcal{P}|$ generally requires more compact representation; thus we represent an action's effects using a "two-slice" (temporal) Bayes net [8]: we have one set of nodes representing the state prior to the action (one node for each variable P), another set representing the state after the action has been performed, and directed arcs representing causal influences between these sets (see Figure 1). We require that the induced graph be acyclic. For simplicity we assume also that arcs are directed only from pre-action to post-action nodes.[1] See [8, 4] for details.

The post-action nodes have the usual conditional probability tables (CPTs) describing the probability of their values given the values of their parents, under action a. We assume that these CPTs are represented using a decision tree, as in [4] (or if-then rules as in [15]). These are essentially compact function representations that exploit regularities in the CPTs. We will exploit the compactness and structure of such representations when producing optimal policies. We denote the tree for variable P under action a by *Tree*$(P'|a)$.[2]

Example Figure 1(a) illustrates the network for action *GetC*. The network structure shows, for instance, that the truth of W', whether the robot is wet after performing *GetC*, depends on the values of R, U and W prior to the action. The matrix for W' quantifies this dependence; and *Tree*$(W'|GetC)$ illustrates the more compact representation (the leaf nodes indicate the probability of W' after *GetC* given the conditions labeling its branch: left arcs denote true and right arcs false). We elaborate on the *Obs* variable below.

2.2 Observations

Since the system is partially observable, the planning agent may not be able to observe its exact state, introducing another source of uncertainty into action selection. However, we assume a set of possible *observations* $\mathcal{O}$ that provide evidence for the true nature of (various aspects of) the state. In general, the observation at any stage will depend stochastically on the state, the action performed and its outcome.

We assume a family of distributions over observations, For each s_i, s_j, a_k such that $Pr(s_j|s_i, a_k) > 0$, let $Pr(o_l|s_i, a_k, s_j)$ denote the probability of observing o_l when action a_k is executed at state s_i and results in state s_j. (As a special case, a fully observable system can be modeled by assuming $\mathcal{O} = \mathcal{S}$ and $Pr(o_l|s_i, a_k, s_j) = 1$ iff $o_l = s_j$.) We assume for simplicity that the observation probability depends only on the action and starting state, not the resulting state; that is, $Pr(o_l|s_i, a_k, s_h) = Pr(o_l|s_j, a_k, s_h)$ for each s_i, s_j.[3]

To represent observation probabilities compactly, we add a distinguished variable *Obs* to each action network that represents the observations possible after performing that action. We use *Obs*(a) to denote the set of possible observations given a.[4] The variables that influence the observation are indicated by directed arcs, and this effect is described, as above, using a decision tree. We note that complex observations may also be factored into distinct observation variables (e.g., should the agent get information pertaining to propositions P and Q by performing one action, two distinct variables Obs_1 and Obs_2 might be used); we ignore this possibility here.

[1] We often denote post-action variables by P' instead of P to prevent confusion. Causal influences between post-action variables should be viewed as *ramifications* and will complicate our algorithm slightly, but only in minor detail.

[2] The network structure is not strictly necessary: the parent of a post-action node can be determined from its CPT or decision tree (see, e.g., Poole's [15] rule-based representation of Bayes nets).

[3] This is a natural assumption for information-gathering actions, but others are possible; e.g., Sondik's [17] original presentation of POMDPs assumes the observation depends only on the resulting state. This assumption makes our algorithm somewhat simpler to describe; but it can generalized (see Section 4).

[4] These are similar to observation variables in influence diagrams [10]; however, there are no emanating information arcs.

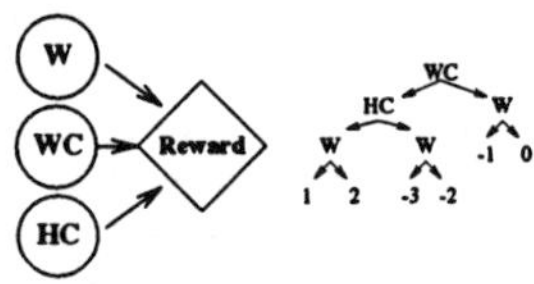

Figure 2: Reward Function Network

Example The variable *Obs* in Figure 1(a) takes on a single value (*Null*), obtained with certainty when *GetC* is executed (i.e., the action provides no feedback). More interesting is the action *TestC* shown in Figure 1(b). Although it has no effect on the state variables (we assume persistence), it is useful as an *information gathering action*: the value of the variable *Obs* (*Yes* or *No*) is strongly dependent on whether the user wants coffee. Should the value *Yes* be observed, our robot may be quite confident the user does, in fact, want coffee (see below).

2.3 Rewards

The final component needed to describe a POMDP is a real-valued *reward function* R that associates rewards or penalties with various states: $R(s)$ denotes the relative goodness of being in state s. We also assume a *cost function* $C(a, s)$ denoting the cost of taking action a in state s. The reward (cost) function can be represented in a structured fashion using a value node and decision tree describing the influence of various combinations of variables on rewards (as with tree-structured CPTs). Leaves of the tree represent the reward associated with the states consistent with the labeling of the corresponding branch.

Example Figure 2 shows the reward function for our problem, indicating that the reward for a particular state is influenced only by the truth of the propositions W, *WC* and *HC*. A similar representation for action cost can be used. In this example action costs are constant: a cost of 1.0 for *GetC* and 0.5 for *TestC* is assumed.

The sets of actions, states and observations, the associated transition and observation probabilities, and the reward and cost functions, make up a POMDP. We now turn our attention to the various concepts used in decision-making.

2.4 Policies

We focus on *finite-horizon problems* here: given a horizon of size n an agent executes n actions at stages 0 through $n-1$ of the process, ending up in a terminal state at stage n. The agent receives reward $R(s)$ for each state s passed through at stages 0 through n (its trajectory). A plan or *policy* is a function that determines the choice of action at any stage of the system's evolution. The *value* of a policy is the expected sum of rewards accumulated (incorporating both action costs and state rewards and penalties). A policy is optimal if no other policy has larger value.

In choosing the action to perform at stage k of the process, the agent can rely only on its knowledge of the initial state s_0 (whether it knows the state exactly, or had an initial distribution over states), and the history of actions it performed and observations it received prior to stage k. Different action-observation histories can lead an agent to choose different actions. Thus, a policy can be represented as a mapping from any initial state estimate, and k-stage history, to the action for stage $k+1$. This is roughly the approach adopted by solution techniques for IDs [10]. However, an elegant way to treat this problem is to maintain a current *belief state*, and treat policies as mapping over from belief states to actions.

2.5 Belief States

A *belief state* $\pi \in \Delta(S)$ is a probability distribution over states. The probability π_i assigned to state s_i by π is the degree of belief that the true (current) state of the system is s_i.

Given some state of belief π^k estimating the system state at stage k of the decision process, we can update our belief state based on the action a^k taken and observation o^k made at stage k to form a new belief state π^{k+1} characterizing the state of the system at stage $k+1$. Once we have π^{k+1} in hand, the fact that a^k, o^k and π^k gave rise to it can be forgotten. We use $T(\pi, a, o)$ to denote the *transformation* of the belief state π given that action a is performed and observation o is made: it is defined as

$$T(\pi, a, o)_i = \frac{\sum_{s_j \in S} Pr(o|s_j, a, s_i) Pr(s_i|s_j, a)\pi_j}{\sum_{s_j, s_k \in S} Pr(o|s_j, a, s_k) Pr(s_k|s_j, a)\pi_j}$$

$T(\pi, a, o)_i$ denotes the probability that the system is in state i once a, o are made, given prior belief state π.

The new belief state $T(\pi, a, o)$ summarizes all information necessary for subsequent decisions, accounting for all past observations, actions and their influence on the agent's estimate of the system state. This is the essential assumption behind classical POMDP techniques: at any stage of the decision process, assuming π^k accurately summarizes past actions and observations, the optimal decision can be based solely on π^k — history (now summarized) can be ignored [17]. Intuitively, we can think of this as converting a partially observable MDP over the original state space S into a *fully observable* MDP over the *belief space* B (the set of belief states π).

A belief state may be represented using a vector of $|S|$ probabilities; but structured representations are possible. We do not pursue these here, since most POMDP solution algorithms do not use a belief state to construct a policy.

2.6 Value Functions

State Value Functions: A *state value function* $VS : S \rightarrow \mathbb{R}$ associates a value $VS(s)$ with each state s. This reflects the expected sum of future rewards the agent will receive, assuming some fixed policy or sequence of actions in the future. In addition, a *state Q-function* $Q : S \times \mathcal{A} \rightarrow \mathbb{R}$ denotes the value $Q(s, a)$ of performing an action a in state s, assuming future value is dictated by a fixed course of action [18]. In particular, let VS^k and Q^k be the *k-stage-to-go* value and Q-functions. If the function VS^{k-1} is known, then Bellman's [1] optimality equation ensures that

$$Q^k(s_i, a) = C(a, s_i) + R(s_i) + \sum_{s_j \in S} Pr(s_j|s_i, a) VS^{k-1}(s_j) \quad (1)$$

$$VS^k(s_i) = \max_{a \in \mathcal{A}}\{Q^k(s_i, a)\} \quad (2)$$

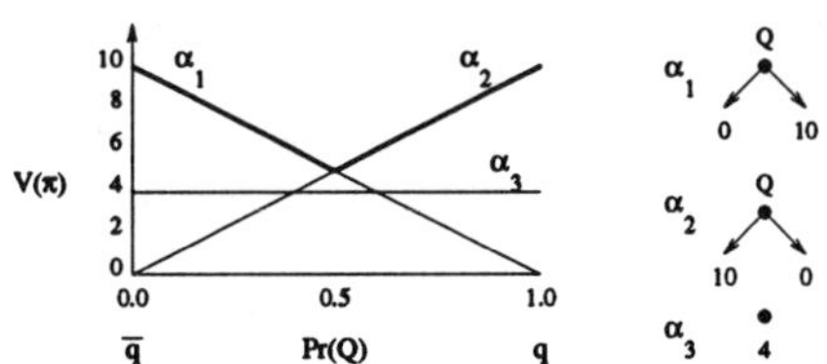

Figure 3: Piecewise Linear, Convex Value Function

Intuitively, once the agent has determined a course of action for the last $k-1$ stages of the process (giving rise to VS^{k-1}), Equation 1 determines the value of executing action a at any state. In the case of fully observable MDPs, this forms the basis of a dynamic programming algorithm that can be used to optimize the choice of action according to Equation 2.

We can represent value and Q-functions using decision trees in precisely the same manner as reward functions (e.g., Figure 2). Figure 5 illustrates just such value and Q-trees. In fact, as we will see below, we can apply these equations directly to such structured representations.

Belief State Value Functions: Unfortunately, in the case of POMDPs, determining the best action for individual states is not often helpful, for the agent will typically not know the exact state. However, the assignment of value to states via value and Q-functions can also be viewed as an assignment of value to belief states. In particular, any state value function VS induces a value function over belief states:

$$\alpha(\pi) = \pi \cdot VS = \sum_{s_i \in S} \pi_i VS(s_i)$$

Following Monahan [12] we call these *α-functions*. The value of a belief state is the weighted sum of the individual state values; thus, such α-functions our linear functions over belief states. Q-functions can be applied similarly to belief states. Finally, we note that a value tree or Q-tree can be used to represent a linear value function over belief states; when interpreted this way, we call these α-trees. In the sequel, we assume that α-functions are represented by α-trees.

In determining optimal policies for POMDPs, we need to represent the optimal (k-stage-to-go) value functions $V : \Delta(S) \rightarrow \mathbb{R}$ for belief states. Clearly, α-functions, being linear, are quite restrictive in expressiveness. However, a key observation of Sondik [17] is that optimal value functions are *piecewise linear and convex (p.l.c.)* over the belief space. In other words, we can represent the optimal (k-stage-to-go) value function for any POMDP as a set $\aleph$ of α-functions, with

$$V(\pi) = \max\{\alpha(\pi) : \alpha \in \aleph\}$$

(We will see exactly why this is so in the next section.)

As a graphical illustration of this p.l.c. representation, consider Figure 3. Assume a single proposition Q (two states q and $\overline{q}$) and the three α-functions $\alpha_1, \alpha_2, \alpha_3$, all represented as trees. Each α-tree determines a linear value function for any belief state (e.g., α_1 takes its highest value at belief state $\pi(q) = 0; \pi(\overline{q}) = 1$). The set $\{\alpha_1, \alpha_2, \alpha_3\}$ corresponds to the p.l.c. value function indicated by the thick line.

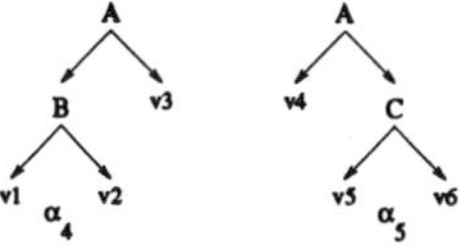

Figure 4: Structured Domination Testing

Dominated α-functions: Finally, we note that certain elements of a set $\aleph$ of α-functions may contribute nothing to the induced p.l.c. value function, namely, those elements that are *stochastically dominated.* For instance, α_3 in Figure 3 is dominated by one of α_1 or α_2 at all points in the belief space. Monahan [12] suggests that such dominated elements be detected by means of a simple linear program and eliminated from $\aleph$ (see also [5]). Once again, the use of α-trees can in many cases considerably reduce the size of these LPs, which normally involve variables for each state. For example, to consider whether the tree α_4 dominates α_5, as shown in Figure 4, the required LP need only have variables corresponding to the propositions AB, $A\overline{B}$, $\overline{A}C$ and $\overline{AC}$, rather than $|S|$ variables.

3 Computation of Optimal Policies

We now describe how to use the ideas above to to determine optimal policies for POMDPs. We begin by presenting the intuitions underlying Monahan's [12] variant of Sondik's [17] algorithm, and how the p.l.c. nature of value functions is exploited. We describe how our compact tree representations can be exploited in the next section.

Given a POMDP, we want to determine a policy that selects, for any belief state π, and $k > 0$ within the problem horizon, the optimal action to be performed. Intuitively, $Pol(\pi, k) \in \mathcal{A}$ is the best action available to the agent assuming its state of belief is π and there are k stages of the process remaining. Unfortunately, representing such a function can be problematic, since the set of belief states $\mathcal{B}$ is a $|S|$-dimensional continuous space. However, Sondik's key observation that k-stage-to-go value functions are p.l.c., and thus finitely representable, also provides a means to finitely represent policies (albeit indirectly). Intuitively, the determination of the "pieces" of the the k-stage-to-go value function will attach actions to each of these pieces. To determine the best action to be performed for a given belief state π, the action associated with the "maximal piece" of the value function for π will be the best action. Thus, actions are associated with various *regions* of the belief space, regions determined by the value function itself.

To see this, we first note that with zero stages-to-go the agent has no action choice to make, and the expected value of being in any belief state is given by the α-function determined by immediate reward R; that is, $V^0(\pi) = \pi \cdot R$. Thus, V^0 is a linear function of π. We call this single α-function α^0.

The computation of V^1 depends only on V^0 and illustrates why the value functions remain p.l.c. The value of performing any action a in a given *state* s is given by $Q(a, s)$, as defined in Equation 1, using R (or V^0) as the terminal value.

Since the agent has no choice of action at stage 0, any observations it makes subsequent to performing this action can have no influence on its behavior or the expected value of the action. Hence, this Q-function can be interpreted as an α-function (say α_a^1) over belief states in the obvious way. The *value* of π with one stage remaining requires that we choose an action a that has maximal Q-value; in other words,

$$V^1(\pi) = \max\{\alpha_a^1(\pi) : a \in \mathcal{A}\}$$

However, since each of the α_a^1 is linear, V^1 is p.l.c. and has a finite representation — the set of α^1-functions themselves. We dub this set $\aleph^1$.

It is worth noting that the optimal action choice given π with one stage-to-go, while not represented explicitly, is easily determined from $\aleph^1$: if α_a^1 is the member of $\aleph^1$ that maximizes $\alpha_a^1(\pi)$, then a is the best action choice. For any $\alpha_a^k \in \aleph^k$, we say a is the *action associated with* α_a^k. In this algorithm, a policy is represented implicitly in this way.

Determining V^2 requires that we take observations into account. To begin, we note that to determine the value of action a with 2 stages-to-go, we allow for the fact that the action b chosen with 1 stage-to-go (and therefore the function α_b^1 representing future value) can depend on the observation o made after a. This dependence is accounted for using *observational strategies*: the action chosen with k-stages-to-go can depend on the observation made following the execution of action a with $k+1$ stages-to-go. Specifically, given a set $\aleph^k$ of α-functions denoting possible future value, an *observational strategy* is a function $OS : \mathcal{A} \times Obs \rightarrow \aleph^k$. For any $o \in Obs(a)$, we use $\alpha_{a,o}^k$ to denote $OS(a,o)$. We write OS_a to denote the restriction of OS to a particular action a.

For a given action a, the value of performing a with $k+1$ stages-to-go, given an observational strategy OS_a, is given by

$$\begin{aligned} & Q_{OS}(a, s_i) \\ = \;& C(a,s_i) + R(s_i) + \sum_{o \in Obs(a)} \sum_{s_j \in S} Pr(s_j|o, s_i, a)\alpha_{a,o}^k(s_j) \\ = \;& \sum_{o \in Obs(a)} Pr(o|s_i, a) Q_{\alpha_{a,o}^k}(a, s_i) \qquad (3) \end{aligned}$$

where $Q_{\alpha_{a,o}^k}$ is the Q-function given by Equation 1, using $\alpha_{a,o}^k$ as the terminal value function. Each Q_{OS} also determines an α-function over belief states. From this we derive the true Q-function, by maximizing over observational strategies:

$$Q(a,s) = \max_{OS_a}\{Q_{OS_a}(a,s)\}$$

The state value function is determined using the Q-functions by Equation 2, leaving us with a definition of the $k+1$ stage value function over belief states:

$$V^{k+1}(\pi) = \pi \cdot V = \sum_{s_i} \pi_i \cdot \max_a \max_{OS_a}\{Q_{OS_a}(a,s)\}$$

Thus, V^{k+1} is p.l.c. and can be represented by the set of α-functions $\{Q_{OS_a} : a \in \mathcal{A}\}$. We let $\aleph^{k+1}$ be this set of α-functions, defined in terms of $\aleph_k$ (since each OS_a maps an observation into an element of $\aleph_k$).

This gives the basic intuitions underlying Monahan's variant of Sondik's algorithm. To determine the set of k-stage-to-go value functions V^k for $k \leq n$, where n is some finite horizon, we simply iterate the following algorithm for n steps:

1. Let $\aleph^0 = \{R\}$
2. For $0 \leq k < n$, compute $\aleph^{k+1} = \{Q_{OS_a} : a \in \mathcal{A}\}$

As mentioned above, the optimal action choice at stage k for any π is determined by the computing the $\alpha_a^k \in \aleph_k$ that maximizes value of π and adopting the the action associated with α^k. We emphasize that the policy is not explicitly represented.

Generally, many of the generated α-functions in $\aleph_k$ will be irrelevant: they never influence the optimal policy because they are dominated by other elements of $\aleph_k$. Monahan's algorithm includes a pruning phase at each iteration that removes dominated components from $\aleph_k$ (see Section 2.6).

4 Structured Computation of α-Functions

We now turn our attention to using the structured representations described in Section 2 in Monahan's algorithm. The aim is to obviate the need to compute and represent the values of each state—each coefficient in the α-functions—individually. Beginning with a tree representation of the reward and cost functions, we use the tree-structured representation of CPTs in our action and observation descriptions to ensure that as much structure as possible is preserved in the generation of the elements of $\aleph_{k+1}$ from $\aleph_k$. Thus, we treat each $\aleph_k$ as a collection of α-*trees*, and show in two steps how to generate a the set of trees $\aleph_{k+1}$ from the set $\aleph_k$.

4.1 Generation of a Single α-tree for an action

The generation of an α-tree in $\aleph_{k+1}$, using a particular action a and strategy OS_a, requires we compute the function Q_{OS_a}, given by Equation 3, in structured form. We note that this computation naturally breaks into two parts: first, we compute the function $Q_{\alpha_{a,o}^k}$ for the individual observations $o \in Obs(a)$; and then we piece them together, taking the sum of the $Q_{\alpha_{a,o}^k}$-functions, weighted by the probability of observing o. We focus on the construction of $Q_{\alpha_{a,o}^k}$ first.

The function $Q_{\alpha_{a,o}^k}$ describes the value of performing a fixed action a at a state s, assuming the value of subsequent states is given by $\alpha_{a,o}$. For clarity, we let α denote the α-tree for $\alpha_{a,o}$ and Q_a denote the tree-structured function $Q_{\alpha_{a,o}^k}$ we wish to construct (i.e., a and o are fixed). Our method for generating the new Q-tree exploits the ideas described in [4], and is closely related to [15] (we refer to [4] for further details). Roughly, given a structured value function α, the conditions under which two states can have different expected future value given by α (under action a) can be easily determined by appeal to the action network for a. In particular, although an action may have different effects at two states, if the differences pertain only to variables (or variable assignments) that are *not relevant to the value function* α,

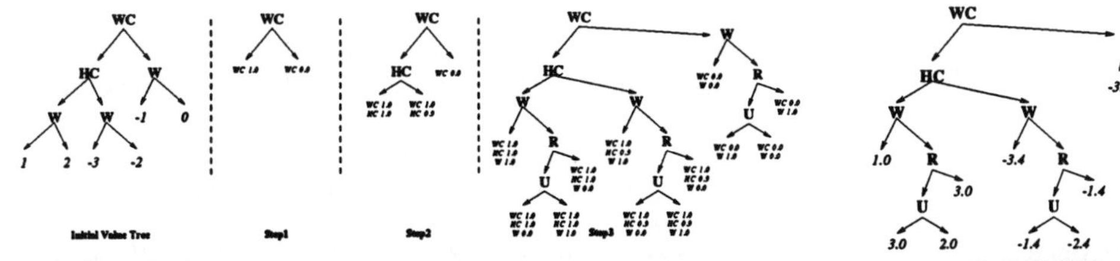

Figure 5: Generating Explanation of Future Value

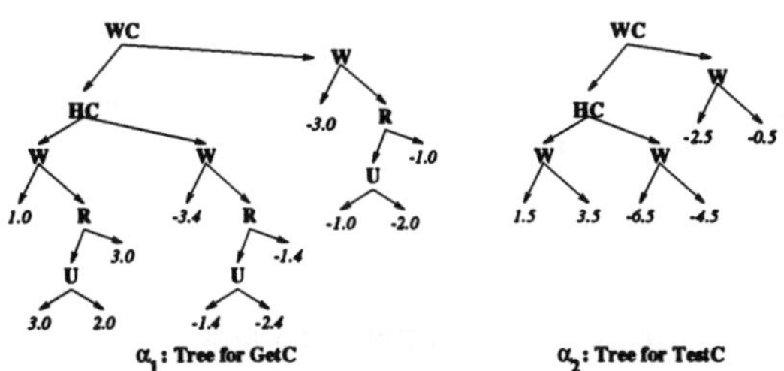

Figure 6: α-trees with 1 Stage-to-go

then those states have identical expected future value and need not be distinguished in the function Q_a. We construct the tree α^k so that only these relevant distinctions are made.

Construction of Q_a proceeds abductively: given the tree α, we want to generate the conditions that, *prior to the performance* of action a, could cause the outcome probabilities (with respect to the partitions induced by α) to vary. We proceed in a stepwise fashion, "explaining" each of the interior nodes of α in turn, beginning with the root node and proceeding recursively with its children. It is important to remember that all of the propositions in α refer to the state at stage k, and that each of the propositions in Q_a refer to stage $k+1$. These propositions are related to each other via the state-transition trees for action a. Space precludes a full exposition of the method—we refer to [4] for details of this method (applied to fully observable MDPs)—so we present a simple example.

Example To illustrate this process, consider the following example, illustrated in Figure 5. We take the immediate reward function (see Figure 2) to be a tree α^0 (the initial value tree), and we wish to generate the expected future value tree for stage 1 assuming action *GetC* is taken and that α^0 determines value at stage 0. We begin by explaining the conditions that influence the probability of *WC'* under *GetC* (Step 1 of Figure 5). This causes *Tree*(*WC'*|*GetC*) to be inserted into the tree α: as indicated by Figure 1, *WC'* is not affected by the action *GetC*, and thus remains true or false with certainty. The leaves of this partial tree denote the probability of *WC'* being true *after* the action given its value (*WC*) *before* the action. We then explain *HC'* (Step 2). Since the initial value tree asserts that *HC* is only relevant when *WC* is true, the new subtree *Tree*(*HC'*|*GetC*) is added only to the left branch of the existing tree, since *WC'* has probability zero on the right.

Again, the probabilities labeling the leaves describe the probability of the variable in question *after the action*, while the labels on interior nodes of the branches relate the conditions *before the action* under which these probabilities are valid. This becomes clear in Step 3, where we consider the conditions (prior to *GetC*) that affect the occurrence of W' (wet) after *GetC*: the relation (*Tree*(W'|*GetC*)) is complex, depending on whether the robot had an umbrella and whether it was raining. This final tree has all the information needed to compute expected *future* value at each leaf—the probabilities at each leaf uniquely determine the probability of landing in any partition of initial value tree under *GetC*.

Finally, we note that to get the true expected value (not just future value), we must add to each of these trees both the current state value $R(s)$ and the action cost $C(a,s)$. This will generally require the simple addition of cost/reward to the values labeling the leaves of the current tree, though occasionally a small number of additional distinctions may be required. Figure 6 shows the expected (total) value tree for *GetC* obtained by adding $R(s)$ and $C(a,s)$ to the future value tree of Figure 5. Figure 6 also shows the tree for *TestC*.

4.2 Incorporating Observations

To account for observations, every element of $\aleph^k$ must correspond to a given action choice a and an observation strategy that assigns a vector in $\aleph^{k-1}$ to each $o \in Obs(a)$. We now consider the problem of generating the actual α-tree corresponding to action a and the strategy assigning $\alpha_j \in \aleph^{k-1}$ to the observation o_j.

Since the conditions that influence the probability of a given observation affect expected future value (since they affect the subsequent choice of α-vector with $k-1$ stages-to-go), the new tree α must contain these distinctions. Thus α is partially specified by $Tree(Obs|a)$, the observation tree corresponding to action a. Recall that the branches of this tree correspond to the conditions relevant to observation probability, and the leaves are labeled with the probability of making any observation o_j. To the leaves of $Tree(Obs|a)$ we add the *weighted sum of the explanation trees* (see also [16]). More specifically, at each leaf of $Tree(Obs|a)$ we have a set of possible (nonzero probability) observations; for exposition, assume for some leaf these are o_i and o_j. Under the conditions corresponding to that leaf, we expect to observe o_i and o_j with the given probabilities $Pr(o_i)$ and $Pr(o_j)$, respectively. We thus expect to receive the value associated with the explanation tree for α_i with probability $Pr(o_i)$, and that for α_j with probability $Pr(o_j)$. We thus take the weighted sum of these trees and add the resulting merged tree to the appropriate leaf node in $Tree(Obs|a)$.[5]

[5] Computing the weighted sum of these trees is relatively straightforward. We first multiply the value of each leaf node in a given tree by its corresponding probability. To add these weighted trees together involves constructing a *smallest* single tree that forms a partition of the state space that subsumes each of the explanation trees. This can be implemented using a simple tree merging opera-

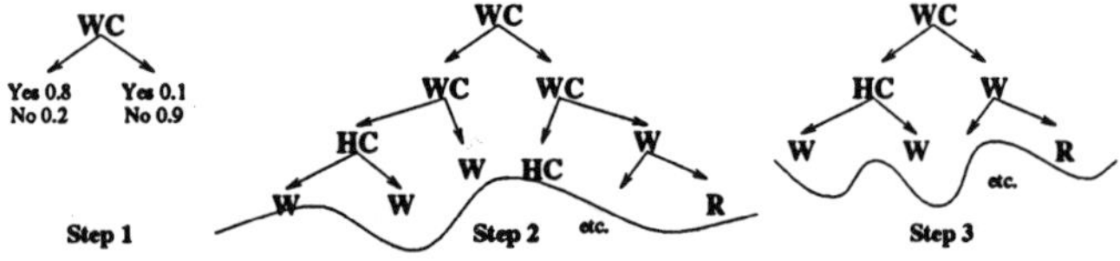

Figure 7: New α-tree for Stage $n-2$

Example Consider the following example illustrated in Figure 7. We assume that trees α_1 and α_2, the trees for *GetC* and *TestC* in Figure 6, are elements of $\aleph^1$. We consider generating the new tree α to be placed in $\aleph^2$ that corresponds to the action *TestC* and invokes the strategy that associates α_1 with the observation *Yes* and α_2 with the observation *No*. We begin by using the observation tree for *TestC*: the observation probability depends only on WC (see Step 1 of Figure 7). We then consider the weighted combination of the trees α_1 and α_2 at each leaf: to the leaf WC we add the tree $0.8\alpha_1 + 0.2\alpha_2$ and to $\overline{WC}$ we add $0.1\alpha_1 + 0.9\alpha_2$. This gives the "redundant" tree in the middle of Figure 7. We can prune away the inconsistent branches and collapse the redundant nodes to obtain the final tree α, shown to the right.

We note that this simple combination of trees is due in part to the dependence of observations on only the pre-action state (as is the "separation" in Equation 3). This allows the direct use of $Tree(Obs|a)$ in assessing the influence of observations on the values of pre-action states. However, should observations depend instead on the post-action state as is usual in the POMDP literature [17, 6], our algorithm is complicated only in slight detail. In this case, $Tree(Obs|a)$ refers to variables in the state following the action, (recall we are interested in the values of states prior to the action). Generating the probability of the observations based on pre-action variables is, however, a simple matter: we simply generate an explanation for the observation in a manner similar to that described in Section 4.1 (though, in fact, much less complicated). The standard explanation trees are then merged together within this slightly more complicated tree instead of $Tree(Obs|a)$.

4.3 Generation of $\aleph_k$ and Pruning

The algorithm for construction of the structured value function proceeds exactly as Monahan's algorithm in the previous section. The substantial difference is that we start with a tree-structured initial reward function as the sole α-tree at stage 0, and generate collections $\aleph^k$ of α-trees rather than simple (e.g., vector-represented) α-functions. The process described above involves some overhead in the construction of explanation trees and piecing them together with observation probabilities. We note, however, that we need not generate the trees for $Q_{\alpha^k_{a,o}}$ for each observation strategy individually. This tree depends only on a and $\alpha^k_{a,o}$, not on o. Thus, we need only construct $|\mathcal{A}||\aleph^k|$ such trees; the $|\mathcal{A}||\mathcal{O}||\aleph^k|$ different trees in $\aleph^{k+1}$ are simply different weighted combinations of these (corresponding to different observational strategies). Further savings are possible in piecing together certain strategies (e.g., if OS_a associates the same vector with each observation, the explanation tree for a can be used directly).

One can prune away dominated α-trees from $\aleph^k$, as suggested by Monahan. As described in Section 2.6, this too exploits the structured nature of the α-trees.

Finally we note that most POMDP algorithms are more clever about generating the set of possible α-vectors. For example, Sondik's algorithm does not enumerate all possible combinations of observational strategies and then eliminate useless vectors. We focus here on Monahan's approach because it is conceptually simple and allows us to illustrate the exact nature of structured vector representations and how they can be exploited computationally. We are currently investigating how algorithms that use more direct vector generation can be adapted to our representation. The Witness algorithm [6] appears to be a promising candidate in this respect, for the LPs used to generate "promising" α-vectors are amenable to the representations described here.

4.4 Executing Policies

Given $\aleph^k$ and a belief state π, we can determine the optimal action with k stages-to-go by choosing an $\alpha \in \aleph^k$ such that $\pi \cdot \alpha$ is maximal, and carrying out the action associated with α. We can then make our observations, and use Bayes rule to update our belief state. We are then ready to repeat and choose an action for the next stage.

The structured representation of value functions, which will generally be compact, can aid policy execution as well. This will be especially true if the belief state is itself represented in a structured way. The expected value of belief state π is the sum of the values at the leaves of the α-tree multiplied by the probabilities of the leaves. The probability at each leaf is the probability of the conjunction of propositions that lead to it (which can be derived from the belief state). Moreover, this also specifies which probabilities are *required* as part of the belief state (and which may be ignored). For instance, if it is discovered in the generation of the value function that certain variables are never relevant to value, these distinctions need not be made in the belief state of the agent.

5 Approximation Methods

While the standard vector representation of α-functions requires vectors of exponential size (in the number of propositions), computing with decision trees allows one to keep the size of the representation relatively small (with potentially exponential reduction in representation size). However, our example illustrates the natural tendency for these trees to become more "fine-grained" as the horizon increases. Depending on the problem, the number of leaves can approach (or reach) the size of the state space. In such cases, the overhead involved in constructing trees may outweigh the marginal decrease in effective state-space size.

tion (for example, see [4] where similar tree merging is used for a different purpose). In terms of rules [16], this effect is obtained by explaining the conjunction of the roots of the trees.

However, an additional advantage of tree (or related) representations is the ease with which one can impose approximation schemes. If the α-tree makes certain distinctions of marginal value, the tree can be pruned by deleting interior nodes corresponding to these distinctions. Replacing the subtrees rooted at U in tree α_1 of Figure 6 by a midpoint value introduces a (maximum) error of 0.5 in the resulting approximate value function. This may be acceptable given the shrinkage in the representation size it provides. This contraction has the effect of reducing the size of new trees generated for subsequent stages, as well. In addition, the error introduced can be tightly controlled, bounded and traded against computation time.[6] In this sense, tree-based representations provide an attractive basis for approximation in large discrete problems.

A major difficulty with Monahan's algorithm is the fact that the number of (unpruned) α-functions grows exponentially with the horizon: $\aleph^k$ contains $(|\mathcal{A}||\mathcal{O}|)^k$ pieces. Of course, pruning dominated α-functions can help, but does not reduce worst-case complexity. The methods above address the size of α-trees, but not (apart from pruning) their number.

A second advantage of the tree-based representation, and approximation schemes based upon it, is the possibility of greatly reducing the number of α-trees needed at each stage. By blurring or ignoring certain distinctions, the number of dominated vectors (hence the amount of pruning) may be increased. In addition, "approximate domination" testing can be aided: for example, if one tree has strictly worse values than another except for slightly better values in one small region of the state space, it could be pruned away. Again, the compactness of the α-trees can be exploited in such tests, as in Section 2.6. Indeed, this complements certain work that reduces the number of α-functions, such as [13].[7] These suggestions are, admittedly, not developed completely at this point. However, a firm grasp of optimal decision making with structured representations provides a sound basis for further investigation of structured approximation methods.

6 Concluding Remarks

We have sketched an algorithm for constructing optimal policies for POMDPs that exploits problem structure (as exhibited by rules or decision trees) to reduce the effective state space at various points in computation. The crucial aspect of this approach is the ability to construct the conditions relevant at a certain stage of the process given the relevant distinctions at the following stage. This merging of planning and optimization techniques (and related approaches) should provide significant improvements in policy construction algorithms.

Of great interest are extensions of this work to algorithms that enumerate "vectors" (in our case, trees) in a more direct fashion (rather than by exhaustive enumeration and elimination), as well as empirical evaluation of the overhead of tree construction. In addition, the development of approximation methods such as those alluded to above is an important step.

Acknowledgements: Thanks to Tony Cassandra, Leslie Kaelbling, Michael Littman and Ron Parr for their helpful discussion and comments. This research supported by NSERC Grants OGP0121843 and OGPO044121.

References

[1] R. E. Bellman. *Dynamic Programming*. Princeton, 1957.

[2] C. Boutilier, T. Dean, and S. Hanks. Planning under uncertainty: Structural assumptions and computational leverage. *3rd Eur. Workshop on Planning*, Assisi, 1995.

[3] C. Boutilier and R. Dearden. Approximating value trees in structured dynamic programming. *ML-96*, to appear, 1996.

[4] C. Boutilier, R. Dearden, and M. Goldszmidt. Exploiting structure in policy construction. *IJCAI-95*, pp.1104–1111, Montreal, 1995.

[5] A. R. Cassandra. Optimal policies for partially observable Markov decision processes. TR CS-94-14, Brown Univ., Providence, 1994.

[6] A. R. Cassandra, L. P. Kaelbling, and M. L. Littman. Acting optimally in partially observable stochastic domains. *AAAI-94*, pp.1023–1028, Seattle, 1994.

[7] T. Dean, L. P. Kaelbling, J. Kirman, and A. Nicholson. Planning with deadlines in stochastic domains. *AAAI-93*, pp.574–579, Washington, D.C., 1993.

[8] T. Dean and K. Kanazawa. A model for reasoning about persistence and causation. *Comp. Intel.*, 5(3):142–150, 1989.

[9] T. Dean and M. Wellman. *Planning and Control*. Morgan Kaufmann, 1991.

[10] R. A. Howard and J. E. Matheson. Influence diagrams. R. A. Howard and J. Matheson, eds., *The Principles and Applications of Decision Analysis*, pp.720–762, 1981.

[11] W. S. Lovejoy. Computationally feasible bounds for partially observed Markov processes. *Op. Res.*, 39:162-175, 1991.

[12] G. E. Monahan. A survey of partially observable Markov decision processes: Theory, models and algorithms. *Mgmt. Sci.*, 28:1–16, 1982.

[13] R. Parr and S. Russell. Approximating optimal policies for partially observable stochastic domains. *IJCAI-95*, pp.1088–1094, Montreal, 1995.

[14] J. Pearl. *Probabilistic Reasoning in Intelligent Systems: Networks of Plausible Inference*. Morgan Kaufmann, 1988.

[15] D. Poole. Probabilistic Horn abduction and Bayesian networks. *Art. Intel.*, 64(1):81–129, 1993.

[16] D. Poole. Exploiting the rule structure for decision making within the independent choice logic. *UAI-95*, pp.454–463, Montreal, 1995.

[17] R. D. Smallwood and E. J. Sondik. The optimal control of partially observable Markov processes over a finite horizon. *Op. Res.*, 21:1071–1088, 1973.

[18] C. J. C. H. Watkins and P. Dayan. Q-Learning. *Mach. Learning*, 8:279–292, 1992.

[6] See [3] on this type of pruning.

[7] In [13], a continuous approximation of the value function is adjusted via gradient descent on the Bellman error; but there is one adjustable parameter per state. A (dynamic) tree-based representation of the value function may be exploited here.

A Qualitative Model for Temporal Reasoning with Incomplete Information

Hector Geffner*
Departamento de Computación
Universidad Simón Bolívar
Aptdo 89000, Caracas 1080-A, Venezuela

Abstract

We develop a qualitative framework for temporal reasoning with incomplete information that features a modeling language based on rules and a semantics based on infinitesimal probabilities. The framework relates logical and probabilistical models, and accommodates in a natural way features that have been found problematic in other models like non-determinism, action qualifications, parallel actions, and abduction to actions and fluents.

Introduction

Logic, probabilities and dynamic systems are standard frameworks for reasoning with time but are not always good modeling languages. This has led in recent years to the development of alternative languages, more suitable for modeling, that can be thought of as one of two types. *Translation languages,* on the one hand, aim to provide ways for specifying logical, probabilistic and deterministic dynamic systems by means of shorter and more intuitive descriptions (e.g., (Pednault 1989; Dean & Kanazawa 1989; Gelfond & Lifschitz 1993)). *Default languages,* on the other, aim to extend classical logic with the ability to express the *expected* effects of actions and the *expected* evolution of fluents (e.g. (McCarthy 1986)).

In this paper we develop a model for temporal reasoning that is hybrid in the sense that it features a language based on defaults and a semantics based on 'approximate' Markov Processes. More precisely, the user describes the dynamics of the domain of interest in terms of default rules, and the defaults get mapped into a Markov Process with probabilities replaced by order-of-magnitude approximations. This results in a framework that relates logical and probabilistic models and accommodates in a natural way features that have been found problematic in other models like non-determinism, action qualifications, parallel actions, and abduction to both fluents and actions.

*Mailing address from US and Europe: Hector Geffner, Bamco CCS 144-00, P.O.BOX 02-5322, Miami Florida 33102-5322, USA. E-mail: hector@usb.ve.

Dynamic Systems

Dynamic systems can often modeled by means of a transition function f that maps states s_i and inputs u_i into unique successor states $s_{i+1} = f(s_i, u_i)$ (Padulo & Arbib 1974; Dean & Wellman 1991).[1] The language for actions developed by Gelfond and Lifschitz (1993) is a language for specifying systems of this sort by means of rules of the form:

$$A \textbf{ causes } B \textbf{ if } C \tag{1}$$

Rules such as these are understood as constraints over the function f that must map states s_i where B holds into states s_{i+1} where C holds when the input u_i is A. Under the assumption that B and C are conjunctions of literals, and that all atoms (except actions) *persist by default,* these rules determine the function f completely.

The semantics of Gelfond's and Lifschitz's language is given in terms of such functions. Roughly, a literal L_i follows from a sequence of actions $a_0, a_1, \ldots$ and observations $o_1, o_2, \ldots$ when L_i is true in all the state-space trajectories $s_0, s_1, \ldots,$ that are compatible with the rules (i.e., $s_{i+1} = f(s_i, a_i)$) and the observations (s_i satisfies o_i).

Gelfond and Lifschitz model is not affected by the difficulties reported by Hanks and McDermott (1986) because the transition function f provides the right semantic structure for interpreting defaults in this context. Persistence defaults — which are present in the model even if they are not encoded explicitly by means of rules — are regarded constraints on the possible transitions from one state to the immediate successor states, *independent of both future and past, and the actual observations.* Other models based on a similar idea are Baker's (1991) and Sandewall's (1991).

Markov Processes

The model above assumes that the dynamics of the system is *deterministic* in the sense that knowledge of the state and the inputs is sufficient to predict the

[1]This is for systems that are discrete-time, time-invariant and deterministic; see (Padulo & Arbib 1974).

future with complete certainty. For the cases where this assumption is not good a different class of models has been developed in which the state and the inputs predict the future behavior of the system with some known probability (Howard 1971).

Formally, a state s_i and an input u_i determine now a set of possible successor states s_{i+1} with probabilities $P(s_{i+1}|s_i, u_i)$. Then, under the assumptions that future inputs do not affect past states (the causality principle) and that the future is independent of the past given the present (Markovian assumption), the probability of each state *trajectory* $s_0, s_1, \ldots, s_N$ given a sequence of inputs $u_0, u_1, \ldots, u_{N-1}$ is given by the equation:

$$P(s_0, \ldots, s_N | u_0, \ldots, u_{N-1}) = P(s_0) \cdot \prod_{i=0}^{N-1} P(s_{i+1}|s_i, u_i) \tag{2}$$

When a set of observations O is obtained, this probability is multiplied by a normalizing constant if the trajectory satisfies the observations, and by zero otherwise. The probability of a proposition is simply the sum of the probabilities of the *trajectories* that make the proposition true.

Models of this type, known as Markov Processes, are significantly more expressive than deterministic models in which transition probabilities can only be zero or one. This generality comes at the price of *specifying* and *computing* with such models. For this reason, attempts to use probabilistic dynamic models in AI have focused on the development of languages that trade off some of the expressive power of probabilistic models for the benefit of simple rule-based specifications (Dean & Kanazawa 1989; Hanks & McDermott 1994).

In this paper we develop a different type of probabilistic temporal model based on rules that may be adequate when exact probabilities are not needed and the distinction between likely and unlike consequences suffices. The key concepts are two: an abstraction of Markov Processes in which probabilities are replaced by their *order-of-magnitude approximations* and a way to specify systems of that sort by means of *partial and incomplete sets of rules.* We consider each idea in turn.

Qualitative Markov Processes

The order-of-magnitude of a probability measure p relative to a small parameter ϵ can be defined as the smallest *integer* $\kappa(p)$ such that $p \leq \epsilon^{\kappa(p)}$. For example, if $\epsilon = 0.2$, the order-of-magnitude of $p_1 = 0.5$ and $p_2 = 0.01$ are $\kappa(p_1) = 0$ and $\kappa(p_2) = 2$ respectively. Interestingly, as shown by Spohn (1988), as the parameter ϵ is made smaller and smaller, in the limit, the order-of-magnitude measures κ obey a calculus given by the axioms:[2]

$$\kappa(p) = \min_{w \models p} \kappa(w),\ \kappa(p \vee \neg p) = 0,\ \kappa(p|q) = \kappa(p \wedge q) - \kappa(q) \tag{3}$$

which is structurally similar to the calculus of probabilities, with products replaced by sums, sums by minimizations, etc.

Spohn refers to the κ measures as degrees of surprise or disbelief as lower κ measures stand for higher probabilities and higher κ measures stand for lower probabilities. In particular, a proposition p is deemed *plausible* if $\kappa(p) = 0$ and *implausible* or *disbelieved* if $\kappa(p) > 0$. Since the axioms rule out two complementary propositions from being disbelieved at the same time, p is *accepted* or *believed* when its negation is disbelieved, i.e., if $\kappa(\neg p) > 0$.

The appeal of Spohn's κ-calculus is that it combines the basic intuitions underlying probability theory (context dependence, conditionalization, etc.) with the notion of plain belief. The beliefs sanctioned by κ functions are *plain* and *revisable* in the sense that p can be believed given q, and yet $\neg p$ can believed given q and something else. Indeed, the function κ expresses a preference relations on worlds in which a world w is preferred to w' if $\kappa(w) < \kappa(w')$. From this point of view, the criterion $\kappa(\neg p|q) > 0$ for *accepting* p given q is nothing else but an abbreviation of the standard condition in non-monotonic logics that require p to be true in all maximally preferred worlds that satisfy q (e.g., (Lehmann & Magidor 1988)).

Goldszmidt and Pearl (1992) were the first to exploit the dual connection of the κ-calculus to probabilities and non-monotonic reasoning, showing how some problems in causal default reasoning could be solved by using κ functions that satisfy a *stratification* condition analogous to the condition that defines Probabilistic Bayesian Networks (Pearl 1988). They refer to κ measures as qualitative probabilities, and to stratified κ functions as Qualitative Bayesian Networks (Goldszmidt & Darwiche 1994)

In the same perspective, we consider in this paper *Qualitative Markov Processes,* defined as the κ functions for which the plausibility of trajectories $s_0, \ldots, s_N$ given the inputs $u_0, \ldots, u_{N-1}$ is given by the qualitative version of (2):

$$\kappa(s_0, \ldots, s_N | u_0, \ldots, u_{N-1}) = \kappa(s_0) + \sum_{i=0}^{N-1} \kappa(s_{i+1}|s_i, u_i) \tag{4}$$

The model for temporal reasoning below is a language for specifying systems of this sort by means of partial and incomplete sets of rules.

[2] We also assume $\kappa(p) = \infty$ and $\kappa(q|p) = 0$ when p is unsatisfiable.

The Proposed Model

Language

We deal with temporal models or *theories* specified by means of three type of constructs: *temporal rules*, *observations*, and what we call *completion functions*. The first two are familiar and their precise syntax will be given below. The third one is less familiar and will be introduced in the next section. Intuitively, rules will be restrictions on the possible state transitions, observations will be restrictions on the actual trajectories, and completion functions will be functions that fill out missing information to determine the plausibility of state transitions uniquely.

The syntax of temporal rules and observations presumes a finite set P of time-dependent primitive propositions (atoms) $p, q, r, \ldots$, and a time set T given by the non-negative integers $0, 1, \ldots$. We will refer to the language comprised of the propositions in P closed under the standard propositional connectives as $\mathcal{L}$, and use the symbols A, B, etc. to denote arbitrary formulas in $\mathcal{L}$. We will also use the symbol L to refer to literals in $\mathcal{L}$ (atoms or their negations) and $\sim L$ to refer to their complements.

The temporal *rules* are *default* rules of the form $A \rightarrow L$ saying that if A is true at time i, then by default L will be true at time $i+1$ for any $i \in T$. Each rule has a *priority* which is represented by a non-negative integer: the higher the number, the higher the priority. The idea is that when two rules say different things about the same literal, the higher priority rule prevails.

Non-deterministic rules (Sandewal 1991) are accommodated by expressions of the form $A \rightarrow p|\neg p$ and are understood as a *shorthand* for the pair of rules $A \rightarrow p$ and $A \rightarrow \neg p$. Non-deterministic rules express that A sometimes makes p true and sometimes makes p false (e.g., dropped-cup $\rightarrow$ *breaks*$|\neg$*breaks*). Unless otherwise specified, the priority of rules is assumed to be zero (lowest priority).

Finally, the *observations* are formulas that have been observed to be true at some specific time points. We use the notation $p(i)$ to express that the primitive proposition p is true at time i and call such expressions *temporal propositions*. We refer to the language that results from closing such temporal propositions under the standard propositional connectives as $\mathcal{L}_T$. $\mathcal{L}_T$ will thus be the language of the observations and the conclusions that we may want to draw from them. We will call the formulas in $\mathcal{L}_T$ the *temporal formulas*. Thus, if a, b and c are primitive propositions $a(2) \vee a(3) \supset c(4) \vee \neg b(1)$ will be a valid temporal formula and hence a possible conclusion or observation.

Semantics

A set of temporal rules augmented with a *completion function* will determine one specific Qualitative Markov Process represented by a particular κ function. A conclusion C will then follow from a set of observations O if $\kappa(\neg C|O) > 0$. We make this precise by defining the states, trajectories, and the form of the κ function.

The *states* are truth assignments to the primitive propositions that determine the truth value of all formulas in $\mathcal{L}$. The notation s_i, s_j, etc. will be used to denote states at times i, j, etc., while state-space *trajectories* will be denoted as $s_0, s_1, \ldots, s_i, \ldots$. We will say that a trajectory *satisfies* a temporal proposition $p(i)$ if the state s_i in the trajectory satisfies the primitive proposition p. Following the standard interpretation of the propositional connectives, trajectories represent logical interpretations over the temporal language $\mathcal{L}_T$ assigning a truth-value to all temporal formulas, and hence, to all observations.

For example, a trajectory $s_0, s_1, \ldots$ with a state s_1 that satisfies p and q, and a state s_2 that satisfies only p, will satisfy the *temporal* formulas $p(1) \supset p(2)$ and $\neg q(2)$, but not $p(1) \supset q(2)$ or $\neg q(1) \vee \neg p(1)$.

Our dynamic systems will have *no inputs*. Actions, which in other frameworks are represented as inputs, will be represented here in the *state*. Thus to express that a switch was toggled at time $i = 5$, we will simply say that *toggle*(5) was observed. With no inputs, the transition plausibilities that characterize our Markov Processes will simplify from $\kappa(s_{i+1}|s_i, u_i)$ to $\kappa(s_{i+1}|s_i)$. Later on we will show that by representing inputs as observations we are not giving up the 'causality property' by which actions should not affect past states (Padulo & Arbib 1974). Instead we will gain the ability to deal naturally with parallel actions, action qualifications and abduction to actions.

Transition Plausibilities. We are left to determine the prior and transition plausibilities $\kappa(s_i)$ and $\kappa(s_{i+1}|s_i)$ from the information provided by the user. Let us say that a state s makes a rule $A \rightarrow L$ *active* in the theory when s satisfies A but s does not satisfy B for any conflicting rule $B \rightarrow \sim L$ with higher priority. Let us also use the notation L_i to stand for temporal literals like $p(i)$ or $\neg p(i)$ and say that L_{i+1} is *supported* by a state s_i when a rule $A \rightarrow L$ is active in s_i. Then the proposed mapping from rules to transition plausibilities $\kappa(s_{i+1}|s_i)$ can be understood in terms of the following assumptions:

1. Literals L_{i+1} and L'_{i+1} that are logically independent are conditionally *independent* given the past s_i.[3]
2. L_{i+1} is *not disbelieved* when s_i supports L_{i+1}
3. L_{i+1} is *completely disbelieved* when s_i supports $\sim L_{i+1}$ but not L_{i+1}
4. The plausibilities of two complementary literals L_{i+1} and $\sim L_{i+1}$ that are not supported by s_i are *independent* of s_i

[3]Two literals are logically independent if the truth of one does not constraint the truth of the other.

Assumption 1 excludes the possibility of *ramifications* and translates into the identity:

$$\kappa(s_{i+i}|s_i) = \sum_{L \in s_{i+1}} \kappa(L_{i+1}|s_i) \quad (5)$$

where L ranges over the literals that are true in s_{i+1}. Assumptions 2 and 3 are consequences of the default reading of the rules.[4] The last assumption is the most important and follows from assuming that *the past influences the future only through the active rules;* i.e., *same active rules mean same transition plausibilities.*

These assumptions impose restrictions on the type of Qualitative Markov Processes that can be expressed, yet with the exception of Assumption 1, we have found them reasonable in domains where predictions can be explained qualitatively in terms of rules and prior judgements. Later on we will show that received models for temporal reasoning that do not deal with ramifications embed these and other assumptions.

The assumptions determine the following mapping from rules to plausibilities:

$$\kappa(L_{i+1}|s_i) = \begin{cases} 0 & \text{when } s_i \text{ supports } L_i \\ \infty & \text{when } s_i \text{ supports } \sim L_i \text{ but not } L_i \\ \pi(L) & \text{when } s_i \text{ supports neither} \end{cases} \quad (6)$$

We call this model of interaction the *Noisy-Rule model* in analogy to the Noisy-OR model used in Bayesian Networks (Pearl 1988) In this model, the parameters $\pi(L)$ and $\pi(\sim L)$ determine the plausibilities of the literals L and $\sim L$ *in the absence of reasons to believe in either one of them* (see (Geffner 1996) for a different application of this model). The function π is what we call the *completion function* and must be such that for each literal L, $\pi(L)$ must be a non-negative integer and either $\pi(L)$ or $\pi(\sim L)$ must be zero (i.e., π is a plausibility function over L and $\sim L$). For literals L_{i+1} and $\sim L_{i+1}$ that are not supported by *any* state s_i, e.g., the literals L_0 referring to the initial state, $\pi(L_{i+1})$ and $\pi(\sim L_{i+1})$ encode the *prior plausibilities* $\kappa(L_{i+1})$ and $\kappa(\sim L_{i+1})$ respectively.[5]

Two completion functions that we will find useful are the *grounded* and *uniform* functions. The first makes $\pi(\neg p) = 0$ and $\pi(p) = 1$ for each primitive proposition p, expressing that in the absence of reasons for or against p, $\neg p$ is assumed more plausible (like in the Closed World Assumption). The second makes $\pi(p) = \pi(\neg p) = 0$, expressing that in the absence of reasons for or against p, the literals p and $\neg p$ are assumed equally plausible. Later on we will show that some familiar systems embed assumptions that fit naturally with these functions.

[4] We could make Assumption 3 less extreme by replacing 'complete disbelief' (infinite κ) by 'partial disbelief' (non-zero κ). Yet this weaker condition would make the specification of the resulting models more complex.

[5] This is because in that case $\kappa(L_{i+1}) = \min_{s_i} \kappa(L_{i+1}|s_i)$ and $\kappa(L_{i+1}|s_i) = \pi(L)$.

As an illustration, given the rules $q \rightarrow p$ and $r \rightarrow p$, the grounded completion function produces a Noisy-OR type of model in which p is certain given q or r and $\neg p$ is more likely than p when q and r are false (below s_i^+ and s_i^- stand for the states that make $q \vee r$ true or false respectively).

$$\kappa(p_{i+1}|s_i^+) = 0 \quad \kappa(\neg p_{i+1}|s_i^+) = \infty$$
$$\kappa(p_{i+1}|s_i^-) = 1 \quad \kappa(\neg p_{i+1}|s_i^+) = 0$$

Summary

The proposed model works as follows. The user provides the rules and the completion function and from (6) we get the plausibilities $\kappa(L_0)$ and $\kappa(L_{i+1}|s_i)$ for all literals and states. These plausibilities are combined by means of (5) to yield the prior and transition plausibilities $\kappa(s_0)$ and $\kappa(s_{i+1}|s_i)$, which plugged into (4) give us the plausibility of any trajectory, and hence, of any formula (3). To determine whether a temporal formula C follows from the observations O we check then whether $\kappa(\neg C|O) > 0$, where $\kappa(\neg C|O)$ is the difference between the plausibilities of the most plausibility trajectories that satisfy $\neg C \wedge O$ and O respectively (3).

Example. Consider the expressions 'if a block is pushed it moves', 'if a block is pushed and is held, it may not move', and 'if a very heavy block is pushed, it does not move', represented by the rules:

$$a \rightarrow p \; ; \; a \wedge b \rightarrow p|\neg p \; ; \; a \wedge q \rightarrow \neg p$$

in increasing order of priority. We also consider a rule $q \rightarrow q$ capturing the persistence of the property 'heavy', and a grounded completion function π where for every positive literal q, $\pi(\neg q) = 0$ and $\pi(q) = 1$ (i.e., atoms are assumed false by default).

We want to determine whether $p(1)$ follows from $a(0)$; i.e., whether a block will move if pushed. We will use the fact that for the completion function above $\kappa(s_{i+1}|s_i)$, when finite, is equal to the number of atoms x true in s_{i+1} that are not supported by s_i. This also applies to the initial states s_0 where no atom is supported and hence where $\kappa(s_0)$ is equal to the number of atoms true in s_0.

Consider now the trajectory $t = s_0, s_1, \ldots$ that only makes two atoms true: $a(0)$ and $p(1)$. We want to show that t is the single most plausible trajectory compatible with $a(0)$. From the considerations above, $\kappa(s_0) = 1$, and since s_0 supports $p(1)$ but no other atom, $\kappa(s_1|s_0) = 0$. This means that $\kappa(t) = 1$, as all states $s_1, s_2, \ldots$ support no atoms and hence $\kappa(s_{i+1}|s_i) = 0$ for all $i > 1$.

We need to show that for any other trajectory $t' = s'_0, s'_1, \ldots$ satisfying $a(0)$, $\kappa(t') > 1$. This is actually straightforward as any state s'_0 compatible with $a(0)$ but different than s_0 will have a plausibility $\kappa(s'_0) > 1$, and similarly, any state s'_{i+1} different than s_{i+1} will have a plausibility $\kappa(s'_{i+1}|s_i) > 0$. Thus, t is the *single* most plausible trajectory compatible with $a(0)$, and hence, $a(0)$ implies $p(1)$.

This scenario provides an example of a projection. Examples of parallel actions, non-determinism, action qualifications and abduction can all be obtained by using similar arguments in slightly different settings. For instance, if both $a(0)$ and $b(0)$ are observed (i.e., the block is pushed while held), neither $p(1)$ nor $\neg p(1)$ will be predicted (as both literals are supported by the states s_0 that make $a(0) \wedge b(0)$ true and $q(0)$ false). Similarly, if the observation $q(5)$ is added (the block is very heavy), $\neg p(1)$ will be predicted. Finally, if the rule $\neg a \rightarrow \neg p$ is added, $a(0)$ will follow from $p(1)$ ('the blocked moved, therefore it was pushed').

Action Theories

In this section we will specialize the framework laid out above by introducing some common assumptions about actions and fluents that facilitate the specification and processing of temporal theories. These assumptions are: 1) every primitive proposition represents either an action or a fluent, 2) fluents persist by default, 3) actions are exogenous, 4) actions occur with low probability, and 5) changes occur only in the presence of actions (that are not necessarily known).

Formally, this means that 1) every rule will be a persistence rule or an action rule, 2) persistence rules will be of the form $p \rightarrow p$ and $\neg p \rightarrow \neg p$ (actually we assume one such pair of rules for every fluent p), 3) action symbols a do not occur in the head of the rules, 4) actions are unlikely, i.e., $\pi(a) > 0$, and 5) action rules have priority over persistence rules, and actions symbols are not negated in the body of such rules. We will also assume that all observations are *literals*.

Theories of this type are similar to some of the theories considered in the literature (e.g., Gelfond's and Lifschitz's) yet they allow for non-determinism, arbitrary plausibility function over fluents, abduction to actions and fluents, action qualifications, and parallel actions. We will call such theories, *action theories*.

We mention briefly three main properties of action theories. First, in spite of representing actions as part of the state, actions remain independent of past states in compliance with the so-called *causality principle* (Padulo & Arbib 1974)):[6]

Proposition 1 *In action theories, actions are independent of past states, i.e., if a_i denotes the occurrence of a number of actions at time i,* $\kappa(s_i|s_{i-1}, a_{i-1}, a_i, a_{i+1}, \ldots) = \kappa(s_i|s_{i-1}, a_{i-1})$.

Second, all uncertainty in action theories is summarized by the prior plausibility of actions and the prior plausibility of fluents:

Proposition 2 *In action theories, the plausibility measure of a trajectory $t = s_0, s_1, \ldots,$ when finite, is given by the sum of the prior plausibilities of the actions that occur in t and the prior plausibilities of the literal fluents that occur in s_0:*[7]

$$\kappa(t) = \sum_{L \in s_0} \pi(L) + \sum_i \sum_{a \in s_i} \pi(a)$$

The last property we mention is that only the *relative* prior plausibilities of actions and fluents matter when the theories are *predictive* (i.e., when there are no surprises). For such theories, any two completion functions π and π' that order complementary literals in the same way, i.e., $\pi(L) < \pi(\sim L)$ iff $\pi'(L) < \pi'(\sim L)$, will yield the same behavior.

Definition 1 *An action theory is* predictive *given a set of observations O and a completion function π, if $\kappa(O|O_A, O_0) = 0$, where $O_A \subseteq O$ refers to the observed actions and $O_0 \subseteq O$ refers the observed fluents at time $i = 0$.*

Proposition 3 *The conclusions sanctioned by a predictive action theory are not affected by changes in the completion function that preserve the plausibility ordering of complementary literals.*

This means that in these theories the exact value of $\pi(L)$ is irrelevant as long as $\pi(L) > 0$, because in such case $\pi(\sim L) < \pi(L)$. For this reason, in such cases it is sufficient to determine whether each positive literal is true by default, false by default, or undecided. The grounded and uniform completion functions, for example, make the second and third choices respectively.

Related Models

The *semantics* of the model draws from approaches in the literature that exploit the double connection of Spohn's κ functions to non-monotonic reasoning and probabilities (Goldszmidt & Pearl 1992; Goldszmidt & Darwiche 1994). The latter work in particular deals with temporal reasoning and is based on structures similar to Bayesian Networks (Pearl 1988) in which conditional probabilities $P(\cdot|\cdot)$ are replaced by conditional plausibilities $\kappa(\cdot|\cdot)$ provided by the user.

The *language* of this model, on the other hand, draws from temporal logics like Gelfond's and Lifschitz's (1993) that do not handle uncertainty. We want to show in this section that the proposed model provides a natural generalization of such logics by representing uncertainty explicitly in the form of completion functions. We focus here on Gelfond's and Lifschitz's logic only; equivalent formalizations are discussed in (Kartha 1993).

For simplicity, and without any loss of generality, we consider domain descriptions with actions rules 'A **causes** B **if** C' and initial conditions '**initially** L'

[6] Actually, since actions are part of the state, actions affect the present state yet they do not affect the present state of *fluents*.

[7] This is because fluent literals in s_0 and actions anywhere are not supported and hence for them $\kappa(x) = \pi(x)$, while for all other fluent literals $\kappa(L_{i+1}|s_i) = 0$ or $\kappa(L_{i+1}|s_i) = \infty$.

only. Given a domain description D, we define T_D as the action theory with rules $A \wedge B \rightarrow C$ and observations L_0 (all action rules have the same priority, and persistence rules for fluents are implicit as in any action theory). The relation between D and T_D is then as follows:

Proposition 4 *Let D be a consistent domain description.*[8] *Then a* value proposition *'L* ***after*** *$A_0, \ldots A_n$' is entailed by D according to Gelfond and Lifschitz iff the literal L_{n+1} follows from T_D and the actions $A_i(i)$, $i = 0, \ldots, n$, under the* uniform *completion function.*

In other words, Gelfond's and Lifschitz's model can be understood in this framework in terms of two assumptions: that complementary fluents are equally plausible, and all actions are implausible a priori. The advantage of the model proposed is that these assumptions are explicit and can be modified by a change in the completion function π (e.g., a grounded completion functions for fluents, for example, leads to the behavior characteristic of negation as failure). This actually explains why we can accommodate action qualifications and represent actions in the state. If we only had the uniform completion function we would get a behavior *monotonic* in the set of actions, very much like Gelfond's and Lifschitz's model yields a monotonic behavior in the observations.

Summary

We have developed a qualitative model for temporal reasoning that relates logical and probabilistic approaches, and handles non-determinism, actions qualifications, parallel actions and abduction in a natural way. The model is limited in other ways such as in its inability to deal with ramifications. We hope to address this limitation in the future by making the mapping from rules to transition plausibilities sensitive to the domain constraints. We have also developed inference procedures that we plan to include in the full version of this paper.

Acknowledgments. Many of these ideas originated in conversations with Yoav Shoham. I also want to thank Blai Bonet, Nir Friedman, Joe Halpern for useful discussions, and the anonymous AAAI reviewers for useful comments.

References

Baker, A. 1991. Nonmonotonic reasoning in the framework of the situation calculus. *AIJ* 49:5–23.

Dean, T., and Kanazawa, K. 1989. A model for reasoning about persistence and causation. *Computational Intelligence* 5:142–150.

Dean, T., and Wellman, M. 1991. *Planning and Control.* Morgan Kaufmann.

[8] D is consistent if no pair of rules associated with the same action have antecedents that are jointly satisfiable and consequents that are jointly unsatisfiable.

Geffner, H. 1996. A formal framework for causal modeling and argumentation. In *Proceedings FAPR'96.* Bonn. Springer Verlag.

Gelfond, M., and Lifschitz, V. 1993. Representing action and change by logic programs. *J. of Logic Programming* 17:301–322.

Goldszmidt, M., and Darwiche, A. 1994. Action networks. In *Proceedings Spring AAAI Symposium on Decision-Theoretic Planning.*

Goldszmidt, M., and Pearl, J. 1992. Rank-based systems. In *Proceedings KR-92*, 661–672. Morgan Kaufmann.

Hanks, S., and McDermott, D. 1986. Default reasoning, non-monotonic logics, and the frame problem. In *Proceedings AAAI-86*, 328–333.

Hanks, S., and McDermott, D. 1994. Modeling a dynamic and uncertain world I: symbolic and probabilistic reasoning about change. *AIJ* 66(1):1–55.

Howard, R. 1971. *Dynamic Probabilistic Systems–Volume I: Markov Models.* New York: Wiley.

Kartha, G. 1993. Soundness and completeness results for three formalizations of action. In *Proceedings IJCAI-93*, 724–729.

Lehmann, D., and Magidor, M. 1988. Rational logics and their models. Dept. of Computer Science, Hebrew University, Israel.

McCarthy, J. 1986. Applications of circumscription to formalizing commonsense knowledge. *Artificial Intelligence* 28:89–116.

Padulo, L., and Arbib, M. 1974. *System Theory.* Hemisphere Publishing Co.

Pearl, J. 1988. *Probabilistic Reasoning in Intelligent Systems.* Los Altos, CA.: Morgan Kaufmann.

Pednault, E. 1989. ADL: Exploring the middle ground between Strips and the situation calculus. In *Proceedings KR-89*, 324–332.

Sandewal, E. 1991. Features and fluents. Technical Report R-91-29, CS Department, Linkoping University, Linkoping, Sweden.

Spohn, W. 1988. A general non-probabilistic theory of inductive reasoning. In *Proceedings 4th Workshop on Uncertainty*, 315–322.

On the Size of Reactive Plans

Peter Jonsson and Christer Bäckström
Department of Computer and Information Science
Linköping University, S-581 83 Linköping, Sweden
{petej,cba}@ida.liu.se

Abstract

One of the most widespread approaches to reactive planning is Schoppers' universal plans. We propose a stricter definition of universal plans which guarantees a weak notion of soundness not present in the original definition. Furthermore, we isolate three different types of completeness which capture different behaviours exhibited by universal plans. We show that universal plans which run in polynomial time and are of polynomial size cannot satisfy even the weakest type of completeness unless the polynomial hierarchy collapses. However, by relaxing either the polynomial time or the polynomial space requirement, the construction of universal plans satisfying the strongest type of completeness becomes trivial.

Introduction

In recent years reactive planning has been proposed as an alternative to classical planning, especially in rapidly changing, dynamic domains. Although this term has been used for a number of more or less related approaches, these have one thing in common: There is usually very little or no planning ahead. Rather the idea is centered around the stimulus-response principle—prompt reaction to the input. One of the most well-known methods for reactive planning is the *universal plans* by Schoppers (1987). A universal plan is a function from the set of states into the set of operators. Hence, a universal plan does not generate a sequence of operators leading from the current state to the goal state as a classical planner; it decides after each step what to do next based on the current state.

Universal plans have been much discussed in the literature. In a famous debate (Ginsberg 1989b; Schoppers 1989; Ginsberg 1989a; Schoppers 1994), Ginsberg criticised the approach while Schoppers defended it[1]. Based on a counting argument, Ginsberg claims that almost all (interesting) universal plans takes an infeasibly large amount of space. Schopper's defence has, to a large extent, built on the observation that planning problems are structured. According to Schoppers, this structure can be exploited in order to create small, effective universal plans. We refrain from going into the details of this debate and merely note that both authors have shown great ingenuity in their argumentation. However, from the standpoint of formal rigour, these papers do not settle the question. One of the few papers that treats universal plans from a formal, complexity-theoretic point of view is the paper by Selman (1994). He shows that the existence of small (polynomially-sized) universal plans with the ability to generate *minimal* plans implies a collapse of the polynomial hierarchy. Since a collapse of the polynomial hierarchy is widely conjectured to be false in the literature (Johnson 1990; Papadimitriou 1994), the existence of such universal plans seems highly unlikely. It should be noted that this result holds even for severely restricted problems such as the blocks-world.

In our opinion, one of the problems with universal plans is the over-generality of the definition. This generality makes formal analysis hard or even impossible. Therefore, we begin this paper by giving a stricter definition of universal plans, a definition that embodies the notion of *soundness*. In addition, we supply three different types of *completeness*. These notions of completeness capture different desirable properties of universal plans. For example, A-completeness states that if the problem has a solution, then the universal plan will find a solution in a finite number of steps. The main result of this paper is that universal plans which run in polynomial time and are of polynomial size cannot satisfy even this weakest type of completeness[2]. However, by relaxing either the polynomial time requirement or the polynomial space requirement, it becomes trivial to construct universal plans that satisfy the strongest type of completeness. Also in this case, the result holds for severely restricted problems.

The organisation of the paper is as follows: We begin by defining the basic STRIPS formalism and formally

[1]This list is not exhaustive. Other authors, such as Chapman (1989), have joined the discussion. However, it seems that the main combatants have been Schoppers and Ginsberg.

[2]Under the assumption that the polynomial hierarchy does not collapse.

define universal plans and various restrictions on them. We continue by showing that small, fast universal plans cannot be complete even in a very weak sense. The paper is concluded with a brief discussion of the results.

Basic Formalism

We base our work in this paper on the propositional STRIPS formalism with negative goals (Bylander 1994), which is equivalent to most other variants of propositional STRIPS (Bäckström 1995).

Definition 1 An instance of the *PSN planning problem* is a quadruple $\Pi = \langle \mathcal{P}, \mathcal{O}, \mathcal{I}, \mathcal{G} \rangle$ where

- $\mathcal{P}$ is a finite set of *atoms*;
- $\mathcal{O}$ is a finite set of *operators* where $o \in \mathcal{O}$ has the form $Pre \Rightarrow Post$ where
  - *Pre* is a satisfiable conjunction of positive and negative atoms in $\mathcal{P}$, respectively called the *positive preconditions* ($pre^+(o)$) and the *negative preconditions* ($pre^-(o)$);
  - *Post* is a satisfiable conjunction of positive and negative atoms in $\mathcal{P}$, respectively called the *positive postconditions* ($add(o)$) and the *negative postconditions* ($del(o)$);
- $\mathcal{I} \subseteq \mathcal{P}$ denotes the *initial state*;
- and $\mathcal{G} = \langle \mathcal{G}^+, \mathcal{G}^- \rangle$ denote the *positive* and *negative goal*, respectively, satisfying $\mathcal{G}^+, \mathcal{G}^- \subseteq \mathcal{P}$ and $\mathcal{G}^+ \cap \mathcal{G}^- = \varnothing$.

A *PSN structure* is a tuple $\Phi = \langle \mathcal{P}, \mathcal{O} \rangle$ where $\mathcal{P}$ is a set of atoms and $\mathcal{O}$ is a set of operators over $\mathcal{P}$.

We denote the negation of an atom by overlining it. As an example, the operator o defined as $\overline{p} \Rightarrow q, \overline{r}$ satisfies $pre^+(o) = \varnothing$, $pre^-(o) = \{p\}$, $add(o) = \{q\}$ and $del(o) = \{r\}$.

Definition 2 Given a set of operators $\mathcal{O}$, we define the set of all operator sequences over $\mathcal{O}$ as $Seqs(\mathcal{O}) = \{\langle\rangle\} \cup \{\langle o \rangle; \omega | o \in \mathcal{O} \text{ and } \omega \in Seqs(\mathcal{O})\}$, where ; is the sequence concatenation operator.

A sequence $\langle o_1, \ldots, o_n \rangle \in Seqs(\mathcal{O})$ of operators is called a *PSN plan* (or simply plan) over Π. We can now define when a plan solves a planning instance.

Definition 3 The ternary relation $Valid \subseteq Seqs(\mathcal{O}) \times 2^{\mathcal{P}} \times (2^{\mathcal{P}} \times 2^{\mathcal{P}})$ is defined s.t. for arbitrary $\langle o_1, \ldots, o_n \rangle \in Seqs(\mathcal{O})$ and $S, T^+, T^- \subseteq \mathcal{P}$, $Valid(\langle o_1, \ldots, o_n \rangle, S, \langle T^+, T^- \rangle)$ iff either

1. $n = 0$, $T^+ \subseteq S$ and $T^- \cap S = \varnothing$ or
2. $n > 0$, $pre^+(o_1) \subseteq S$, $pre^-(o_1) \cap S = \varnothing$ and $Valid(\langle o_2, \ldots, o_n \rangle, (S - del(o_1)) \cup add(o_1), \langle T^+, T^- \rangle)$.

A plan $\langle o_1, \ldots, o_n \rangle \in Seqs(\mathcal{O})$ is a *solution* to Π iff $Valid(\langle o_1, \ldots, o_n \rangle, \mathcal{I}, \langle \mathcal{G}^+, \mathcal{G}^- \rangle)$.

We define the planning problems that we will consider as follows.

Definition 4 Let $\Pi = \langle \mathcal{P}, \mathcal{O}, \mathcal{I}, \langle \mathcal{G}^+, \mathcal{G}^- \rangle \rangle$ be a given PSN instance. The *plan generation problem* (**PG**) is to find some $\omega \in Seqs(\mathcal{O})$ s.t. ω is a solution to Π or answer that no such ω exists. The *bounded plan generation problem* (**BPG**) takes an integer $K \geq 0$ as additional parameter and the object is to find some $\omega \in Seqs(\mathcal{O})$ s.t. ω is a solution to Π of length $\leq K$ or answer that no such ω exists.

Universal Plans

Universal plans are defined as follows in the literature (Ginsberg 1989b).

> A universal plan is an arbitrary function from the set of possible situations S into the set of primitive actions A.

Using the terminology we have adopted in this paper results in the following equivalent definition.

Definition 5 Given a PSN structure $\Phi = \langle \mathcal{P}, \mathcal{O} \rangle$, a universal plan is a function from the set of states $2^{\mathcal{P}}$ into the set of operators $\mathcal{O}$.

This very general notion of universal plans is difficult to use as a basis for formal analyses. We would like, for example, to discuss the issuses of correctness and resource consumption. In the sequel, we will try to classify universal plans in greater detail. For a given PSN structure $\Phi = \langle \mathcal{P}, \mathcal{O} \rangle$ let $\mathcal{S} = 2^{\mathcal{P}}$, $\mathcal{S}_\perp = 2^{\mathcal{P}} \cup \{\perp\}$ and $\mathcal{O}^+ = \mathcal{O} \cup \{o_\perp, o_\top\}$. Here $\perp$ is a new state denoting undefinedness and $o_\perp, o_\top$ are two "special" operators. These operators are not to be considered as operators in the sense of Definition 1 but rather as two completely new symbols without internal structure. The special operators will be used by the universal plans for "communication with the environment". The following definition is needed for defining soundness of universal plans.

Definition 6 Let $\Phi = \langle \mathcal{P}, \mathcal{O} \rangle$ be a PSN structure. The *update* operator $\oplus : \mathcal{S}_\perp \times \mathcal{O}^+ \to \mathcal{S}_\perp$ is defined as follows: $\perp \oplus o = \perp$ for all $o \in \mathcal{O}^+$. Let $S \in \mathcal{S}$. If o is a standard operator then $S \oplus o = (S - del(o)) \cup add(o)$ iff $pre^+(o) \subseteq S \wedge pre^-(o) \cap S = \varnothing$. Otherwise, $S \oplus o = \perp$. If o is not a standard operator then $S \oplus o_\perp = \perp$ and $S \oplus o_\top = S$. An operator $o \in \mathcal{O}^+$ is *admissible* in a state $S \in \mathcal{S}_\perp$ iff $S \oplus o \neq \perp$.

We can now refine our notion of universal plans.

Definition 7 Let $\Phi = \langle \mathcal{P}, \mathcal{O} \rangle$ be a PSN structure and let $\mathcal{G}$ be a goal over $\mathcal{P}$. A *sound universal plan* $U_{\mathcal{G}}$ for the goal $\mathcal{G}$ is a function that maps $\mathcal{S}_\perp$ to $\mathcal{O}^+$ such that

1. for every $S \in \mathcal{S}_\perp$, if $U_{\mathcal{G}}(S) = o \in \mathcal{O}$ then o is admissible in S;
2. for every $S \in \mathcal{S}_\perp$, $U_{\mathcal{G}}(S) = o_\top$ iff S satisfies $\mathcal{G}$;

The first point in the definition says that if the universal plan generates an operator, then this operator is executable in the current state. This restriction seems to have been tacitly assumed in the literature. The second point tells us that the special operator $o_\top$ is generated if and only if the universal plan is applied to a state satisfying the goal state. Thus, $o_\top$ is used by $U_\mathcal{G}$ to report success. The reason for introducing the operator $o_\top$ is to avoid the generation of new operators when the current state satisfies the goal state. The special operator $o_\bot$, on the other hand, indicates that the universal plan cannot handle the current state. This can, for instance, be due to the fact that the goal state is not reachable from the current state. Observe that no operator is admissible in $\bot$ so $U_\mathcal{G}$ must generate $o_\bot$ whenever applied to $\bot$. Henceforth, we will use the term universal plan as an abbreviation for sound universal plan.

We continue by defining four properties of universal plans. For a universal plan $U_\mathcal{G}$ we use the notation $U_\mathcal{G}^K(S)$ to denote the operator $U_\mathcal{G}(S_K)$ where $S_1 = S$ and $S_{K+1} = S_K \oplus U_\mathcal{G}(S_K)$.

Definition 8 A universal plan $U_\mathcal{G}$ for a PSN structure $\Phi = \langle \mathcal{P}, \mathcal{O} \rangle$ is

P$_T$ *poly-time* iff $U_\mathcal{G}$ can be implemented as a deterministic algorithm that runs in polynomial time in the size of Φ;

P$_S$ *poly-space* iff $U_\mathcal{G}$ can be implemented as a deterministic algorithm A satisfying

1. the size of A is polynomially bounded by the size Φ and
2. the size of the space used by A is polynomially bounded by the size of Φ;

A *acceptance-complete* iff for every $S \in \mathcal{S}$ such that $\langle \mathcal{P}, \mathcal{O}, S, \mathcal{G} \rangle$ is solvable there exists an integer K such that $U_\mathcal{G}^K(S) = o_\top$;

R *rejection-complete* iff for every $S \in \mathcal{S}$ such that $\langle \mathcal{P}, \mathcal{O}, S, \mathcal{G} \rangle$ is not solvable there exists an integer K such that $U_\mathcal{G}^K(S) = o_\bot$.

Universal plans satisfying some subset of the restrictions P$_T$, P$_S$, A and R are named by combining the corresponding letters. For example, a P$_T$AR universal plan is poly-time, acceptance-complete and rejection-complete. The definition of poly-time should be quite clear while the definition of poly-space may need further explanation. The first part of the definition ensures that $U_\mathcal{G}$ can be stored in a polynomially-bounded memory. The second part guarantees that any computation will use only a polynomially-bounded amount of auxiliary memory. Hence, we can both store and run the algorithm in a memory whose size is bounded by a polynomial in the size of Φ. This restriction excludes algorithms using extremely large fixed data structures as well as algorithms building such structures during run-time.

For the sake of brevity, we use the terms A- and R-completeness for acceptance- and rejection-completeness, respectively. A minimal requirement on universal plans is that they are A-complete so we are guaranteed to find a solution within a finite number of steps if there is one. Observe that if an A-complete universal plan is not R-complete then $U_\mathcal{G}^K(S)$ can differ from $o_\bot$ for all K if $\mathcal{G}$ is not reachable from S. R-completeness is, thus, desirable but not always necessary. In domains such as the blocks-world, where we know that a solution exists in advance, R-completeness is of minor interest. To have R-completeness without A-completeness is useless since we can trivially construct universal plans satisfying P$_{T,S}$R for all problems. Simply let $U_\mathcal{G}(S) = o_\bot$ for all $S \in \mathcal{S}_\bot$. This R-complete universal plan can trivially be implemented as a poly-time and poly-space deterministic algorithm.

In certain applications, we need a stronger form of R-completeness.

Definition 9 A universal plan $U_\mathcal{G}$ for a PSN structure $\langle \mathcal{P}, \mathcal{O} \rangle$ is *strongly rejection-complete* (R^+) iff for every $S \in \mathcal{S}$ such that $\langle \mathcal{P}, \mathcal{O}, S, \mathcal{G} \rangle$ is not solvable, $U_\mathcal{G}(S) = o_\bot$.

The motivation for introducing strong R-completeness is simple. If the universal plan outputs operators, we cannot know whether they will lead to a solution or not. Executing such operators is not advisable, since we may wish to try planning for some alternative goal if there is no solution for the first one. However, executing the "invalid" operators may prevent us from reaching the alternative goal.

From a complexity-theoretic point of view, it can be argued that universal plans have to be both poly-time and poly-space to be feasible in practice. This is a hard restriction since by dropping any of the polynomiality requirements, constructing universal plans become easy.

Theorem 10 For every PSN structure $\Phi = \langle \mathcal{P}, \mathcal{O} \rangle$ and goal state $\mathcal{G}$ over $\mathcal{P}$ there exist universal plans $U_\mathcal{G}$ and $U'_\mathcal{G}$ satisfying P$_T$AR$^+$ and P$_S$AR$^+$, respectively.

Proof: *Construction of $U_\mathcal{G}$*: We define a function $f : \mathcal{S}_\bot \rightarrow \mathcal{O}^+$ as follows. For each $K \geq 1$ and $S \in \mathcal{S}$ such that $\langle \mathcal{P}, \mathcal{O}, S, \mathcal{G} \rangle$ has a shortest solution of length K, choose an $o \in \mathcal{O}$ such that $\langle \mathcal{P}, \mathcal{O}, S \oplus o, \mathcal{G} \rangle$ has a shortest solution of length $K-1$. Denote this operator o_S and let

$$f(S) = \begin{cases} o_\bot & \text{if } \langle \mathcal{P}, \mathcal{O}, S, \mathcal{G} \rangle \text{ is not solvable} \\ o_\top & S \text{ satisfies } \mathcal{G} \\ o_S & \text{otherwise} \end{cases}$$

Clearly, for every $S \in \mathcal{S}$ there exists an integer K such that if $\langle \mathcal{P}, \mathcal{O}, S, \mathcal{G} \rangle$ is solvable then $U_\mathcal{G}^K(S) = o_\top$. Otherwise, $U_\mathcal{G}(S) = o_\bot$. Consequently, f is both A-complete and strongly R-complete. The proposed construction of the function f is obviously of exponential size. However, it can be arranged as a balanced decision tree of depth $|\mathcal{P}|$ and, hence, be accessed in polynomial time. Consequently, we have constructed $U_\mathcal{G}$.

Construction of $U'_\mathcal{G}$: Consider a forward-chaining PSN planning algorithm P that is sound, complete and generates shortest plans. We modify the algorithm to output only the first operator of the plan that leads from S to $\mathcal{G}$. Since a plan might be of exponential size this cannot necessarily be implemented in polynomial space. However, we can guess the plan one operator at a time and compute the resulting state after each action, using only polynomial space. Hence, this modified planner can be represented by a non-deterministic algorithm using polynomial space. Thus, by Savitch's theorem (Savitch 1970), it can also be represented by a deterministic algorithm that uses polynomial space. This modified planner can be the same for all problems simply by giving the PSN structure Φ and the goal state $\mathcal{G}$ as additional inputs. Hence, it is of constant size, *i.e* its size does not depend on the size of the given PSN structure. Consequently, we can disregard the size of the planner and we have constructed a poly-space universal plan. (Observe that the soundness of P implies soundness of $U'_{\mathcal{G}}$ if we modify $U'_{\mathcal{G}}$ to generate $o_{\top}$ whenever the current state satisfies the goal state.)

The planner P is complete and generates minimal plans. Hence, if the shortest plan from the current state S to the goal state $\mathcal{G}$ is of length L, the length of the shortest plan from $S \oplus U'_{\mathcal{G}}(S)$ to $\mathcal{G}$ is $L-1$. By this observation and the fact that P is complete, A-completeness of $U'_{\mathcal{G}}$ follows.

Finally, if there is no plan from the current state to the goal state, the planner will fail to generate even the first operator. In this case we simply output $o_{\perp}$ and strong R-completeness follows. □

It is crucial that the planner used in the previous theorem generates shortest plans. Otherwise, we cannot guarantee A-completeness. We illustrate this with a small, contrived example.

Example 11 Consider the following PSN structure $\Phi = \langle \mathcal{P}, \mathcal{O} \rangle = \langle \{p,q\}, \{p^+, q^+, q^-\} \rangle$ where the operators are defined as follows: $p^+ = (\overline{p} \Rightarrow p)$, $q^- = (q \Rightarrow \overline{q})$ and $q^+ = (\overline{q} \Rightarrow q)$.

Let $\mathcal{I}_1 = \{q\}$, $\mathcal{I}_2 = \varnothing$, $\mathcal{G} = \langle \{p\}, \varnothing \rangle$, $\Pi_1 = \langle \mathcal{P}, \mathcal{O}, \mathcal{I}_1, \mathcal{G} \rangle$ and $\Pi_2 = \langle \mathcal{P}, \mathcal{O}, \mathcal{I}_2, \mathcal{G} \rangle$. The shortest plan for both Π_1 and Π_2 is $\langle p^+ \rangle$. Assume a planning algorithm A that generates the plan $\omega_1 = \langle q^-, p^+ \rangle$ for Π_1 and $\omega_2 = \langle q^+, p^+ \rangle$ for Π_2. A universal plan $U_{\mathcal{G}}$ based on A would then satisfy $U_{\mathcal{G}}(\mathcal{I}_1) = q^+$ and $U_{\mathcal{G}}(\mathcal{I}_2) = q^-$. Consequently, $U_{\mathcal{G}}^K(\mathcal{I}_1) = q^+$ for odd K and $U_{\mathcal{G}}(\mathcal{I}_1) = q^-$ for even K. In other words, the universal plan will toggle q forever. Hence, $U_{\mathcal{G}}$ is not A-complete.

For planning problems such that **BPG**[3] can be solved in polynomial-time, we can construct universal plans satisfying $\mathrm{P}_{T,S}\mathrm{AR}^+$ by Theorem 10. For planning problems such that **PG** is polynomial but **BPG** is not, the theorem does not apply. This method for constructing universal plans is pointed out by Selman (1994) but he does not explicitly state that generating the shortest plan is necessary. The question whether we can construct $\mathrm{P}_{T,S}\mathrm{AR}^+$ universal plans for problems where **PG** is polynomial but **BPG** is not remains open.

[3] Recall that **BPG** and **PG** denote the bounded and unbounded plan generation problem respectively.

Non-Existence of $\mathrm{P}_{T,S}\mathrm{A}$ Universal Plans

In order to show that $\mathrm{P}_{T,S}\mathrm{A}$ universal plans do not exist for all PSN planning problems, we will use *advice-taking* Turing machines (Johnson 1990). Advice-taking TMs are an alternative way of describing non-uniform circuits, which is the approach adopted by Selman (1994).

Definition 12 An *advice-taking* Turing machine is a TM T that has associated with it a special "advice oracle" A, which is a (not necessarily computable) function. Let x be an arbitrary input string and let $|x|$ denote the size of x. When T is applied to x, a special "advice tape" is automatically loaded with $A(|x|)$ and from then on the computation proceeds as normal, based on the two inputs, x and $A(|x|)$. An advice-taking Turing machine uses *polynomial advice* iff its advice oracle satisfies $|A(n)| \leq p(n)$ for some fixed polynomial p and all nonnegative integers n. The class P/poly is the set of languages defined by polynomial-time advice-taking TMs with polynomial advice.

Advice-taking TMs are very powerful. They can, for instance, compute certain undecidable functions. Despite their apparent power, it is highly unlikely that all problems in NP can be solved by P/poly TMs.

Theorem 13 (Karp & Lipton 1982) If NP $\subseteq$ P/poly then the polynomial hierarchy collapses into Σ_2^p.

Σ_2^p is a complexity class in the second level of the polynomial hierarchy (Johnson 1990). Collapse of the polynomial hierarchy is widely conjectured to be false in the literature (Johnson 1990; Papadimitriou 1994). Our proofs rely on the following construction.

Lemma 14 Let $\mathcal{F}_n$ be the set of all 3SAT (Garey & Johnson 1979) instances with n variables. For every n, there is a PSN structure $\Theta_n = \langle \mathcal{P}, \mathcal{O} \rangle$ and a goal state $\mathcal{G}_n$ such that for every $F \in \mathcal{F}_n$, there exists an $\mathcal{I}_F$ with the following property: $\Pi_F = \langle \mathcal{P}, \mathcal{O}, \mathcal{I}_F, \mathcal{G}_n \rangle$ is a planning instance which is solvable iff F is satisfiable. Furthermore, any solution to Π_F must have a length less than or equal to $8n^3 + 2n$.

Proof: Let $U = \{u_1, \ldots, u_n\}$ be the set of variables used by the formulae in $\mathcal{F}_n$. Observe that there can only be $(2n)^3$ different clauses in any formula in $\mathcal{F}_n$. Let $\mathcal{C} = \{C_1, \ldots, C_{8n^3}\}$ be an enumeration of the possible clauses over the variable set U. Let $\mathcal{P} = \{T(i), F(i), C(j) | 1 \leq i \leq n,\ 1 \leq j \leq 8n^3\}$. The atoms will have the following meanings: $T(i)$ is true iff the variable u_i is true, $F(i)$ is true iff the variable u_i is false and $C(j)$ is true iff the clause C_j is satisfied. For each variable u_i, two operators are needed:

- $\overline{T(i)}, \overline{F(i)} \Rightarrow T(i)$,

- $\overline{T(i)}, \overline{F(i)} \Rightarrow F(i)$.

That is, $T(i)$ can be made true iff $F(i)$ is false and vice versa. In this fashion, only one of $T(i)$ and $F(i)$ can be true. For each case where a clause $C(j) \in \mathcal{C}$ contains a variable u_i, the first operator below is needed: for a negated variable $\neg u_i$, the second operator is needed:

- $T(i), \overline{C(j)} \Rightarrow C(j)$,
- $F(i), \overline{C(j)} \Rightarrow C(j)$.

We specify the goal such that $\mathcal{G}_n = \langle \mathcal{G}_n^+, \mathcal{G}_n^- \rangle = \langle \{C_1, \ldots, C_{8n^3}\}, \varnothing \rangle$. Let $F \in \mathcal{F}$. We want to construct an initial state $\mathcal{I}_F$ such that $\Pi = \langle \mathcal{P}, \mathcal{O}, \mathcal{I}_F, \mathcal{G}_n \rangle$ is solvable iff F is satisfiable. Let $\mathcal{I}_F = \{C(j) | C(j) \notin F\}$. Clearly, every $C(j)$ can be made true iff a satisfying assignment for F can be found. Finally, it is easy to see that any solution to Π_F must be of length $\leq 8n^3 + 2n$ since we have exactly $8n^3 + 2n$ atoms and each atom can be made true at most once. □

Lemma 15 If, for every integer $n \geq 1$, there exists a polynomial advice function that allows us to solve Π_F for all $F \in \mathcal{F}_n$ in polynomial time, then the polynomial hierarchy collapses into Σ_2^p.

Proof: Suppose Π_F is solvable iff F has a satisfying truth assignment, then NP $\subseteq$ P/poly so, by Theorem 13, the polynomial hierarchy collapses into Σ_2^p. □

We can now prove our main theorem.

Theorem 16 If there exists a universal plan $U_{\mathcal{G}_n}$ satisfying $\mathrm{P}_{T,S}\mathrm{A}$ for Θ_n, $n \geq 1$, then the polynomial hierarchy collapses into Σ_2^p.

Proof: Assume $U_{\mathcal{G}_n}$ to be a $\mathrm{P}_{T,S}\mathrm{A}$ universal plan for Θ_n. Consider the algorithm A in Figure 1. $U_{\mathcal{G}_n}$ is sound so it must generate an operator that is admissible in the given state or generate one of the special operators $o_\perp, o_\top$. Hence, by Lemma 14, the **repeat** loop can iterate at most $8n^3 + 2n$ times before o equals either $o_\perp$ or $o_\top$. We have assumed that $U_{\mathcal{G}_n}$ is a polynomial-time algorithm so algorithm A runs in polynomial time. We show that algorithm A accepts iff F has a satisfying truth assignment. The if-part is trivial by noting that if F has a satisfying truth assignment then the algorithm accepts by A-completeness. For the only-if part, assume that the algorithm accepts. Then $U_{\mathcal{G}_n}$ has returned the operator $o_\top$ when applied to some state S. By Definition 7, $U_{\mathcal{G}_n}(S) = o_\top$ iff S satisfies $\mathcal{G}_n$. Consequently, F is satisfiable by Lemma 14. Hence, the algorithm accepts iff F is satisfiable and rejects iff F is not satisfiable. Furthermore, $U_{\mathcal{G}_n}$ is a polynomial advice function since we have restricted $U_{\mathcal{G}_n}$ to be of polynomial size and the theorem follows by Lemma 15. □ The generality of this theorem has to be emphasized. Recall that an advice is an *arbitrary* function from the size of the input. This function does not even have to be computable. Hence, there does not exist any mechanism whatsoever that is of polynomial size and can be accessed in polynomial time with the ability to solve

```
Algorithm A.
Input: A 3SAT formula F with n variables.
S ← I_F
 repeat
   o ← U_Gn(S)
   S ← S ⊕ o
until o ∈ {o⊥, o⊤}
if o = o⊤ then accept
else reject
```

Figure 1: The algorithm used in the proof of Theorem 16.

problems like those exhibited in the previous theorem. Methods that have been proposed to reduce the size of universal plans, such as the *variables* introduced by Schoppers (1994), cannot change this fact.

Moreover, observe that Theorem 16 applies even to a class of severely restricted PSN structures. The restrictions are, among others, that all delete-lists are empty and each operator has at most two preconditions. Since the delete-lists are empty, this restricted class is in NP (Bylander 1994). Consequently, it is a class with considerably less expressive power than the general PSN planning problem which is PSPACE-complete (under the plausible assumption that NP$\neq$PSPACE). Yet, $\mathrm{P}_{T,S}\mathrm{A}$ universal plans do not exist for this class of planning problems. Note that this is not caused by the existence of exponentially-size minimal plans since all minimal plans in this class are polynomially bounded.

Finally, we would like to compare Theorem 16 with a negative result by Selman (1994).

Theorem 17 Unless NP$\subseteq$P/poly, there exists a blocks-world planning goal for which there is no $\mathrm{P}_{T,S}\mathrm{A}$ universal plan for generating the minimal sequence of operators leading to the goal.

It is important to note the difference between this theorem and Theorem 16. Where Selman shows that $\mathrm{P}_{T,S}\mathrm{A}$ universal plans cannot generate minimal plans under certain conditions, we show that there are cases when they cannot generate any plans at all.

Discussion

The results in this paper should not be interpreted too negatively. What they tell us is that naïve approaches to universal planning will not work. In particular, we cannot hope for efficient universal plans solving arbitrary planning problems. However, we question only the efficiency of universal plans. We do not claim universal plans to be inferior to classical planners in all aspects. It is, for instance, highly probable that universal planning can offer great advantages over classical planning in rapidly changing, dynamic domains. Thus, one of the challenges for the future is to characterize which planning problems can be efficiently solved by universal plans. We have seen that if a problem can be solved optimally in polynomial time, then there is an efficient universal plan solving it. Almost certainly, there are other interesting classes of planning problems that can be solved by small, fast universal plans.

Another question to be answered in the future is how to make universal planning more powerful. Several approaches are conceivable. One would be to give universal plans access to random sources—thus making universal planning probabilistic. Recent research has shown that probabilistic algorithms can be surprisingly efficient for certain types of problems. To mention one example, the probabilistic GSAT algorithm (Selman, Levesque, & Mitchell 1992) for satisfiability testing of propositional formulae has shown good performance in empirical studies. Another extension would be to allow universal plans to have an internal state; that is, the output of the universal plan is not only dependent on the current state, but also on previous states. Universal plans with internal states have been studied briefly by Selman (1994). The results are unfortunately not encouraging.

Universal planning should also be compared with *incremental planning* (Ambros-Ingerson & Steel 1988; Jonsson & Bäckström 1995). The idea behind incremental planning is to have a planner that can output valid prefixes of the final plan before it has finished planning. It has been argued that this method could considerably bring down the time lost in planning, especially in dynamic domains, where replanning has to occur frequently. This motivation is almost exactly the same as the motivation for introducing universal plans (or reactive planning in general). Here we have a spectrum of different approaches to planning ranging from classical planning which first computes the complete plan and then executes it, via incremental planning, where chunks of the plan are generated and executed in an interleaved fashion, to universal planning, where just one operator at a time is generated and immediately executed.

Conclusions

We have proposed a stricter definition of universal plans which guarantees a weak notion of soundness not present in the original definition. In addition, we have identified three different types of completeness which capture different behaviours exhibited by universal plans. A-completeness guarantees that if there exists a plan from the current state to the goal state, then the universal plan will find a solution in a finite number of steps. R-completeness is the converse of A-completeness, *i.e.* if there does not exist a plan from the current state to the goal state, then the universal plan will report this after a finite number of applications. R^+-completeness is a stronger version of R-completeness, stating that if there does not exist a plan from the current state to the goal state, then the universal plan will report this after one application. We show that universal plans which run in polynomial time and are of polynomial size cannot be A-complete unless the polynomial hierarchy collapses. However, by dropping either the polynomial time or the polynomial space requirement, the construction of A- and R^+-complete universal plans becomes trivial.

References

Ambros-Ingerson, J. A., and Steel, S. 1988. Integrating planning, execution and monitoring. In *Proc. 7th (US) Nat'l Conf. on Artif. Intell. (AAAI-88)*, 83–88.

Bäckström, C. 1995. Expressive equivalence of planning formalisms. *Artif. Intell.* 76(1–2):17–34.

Bylander, T. 1994. The computational complexity of propositional STRIPS planning. *Artif. Intell.* 69:165–204.

Chapman, D. 1989. Penguins can make cake. *AI Mag.* 45–50.

Garey, M., and Johnson, D. 1979. *Computers and Intractability: A Guide to the Theory of NP-Completeness.* New York: Freeman.

Ginsberg, M. L. 1989a. Ginsberg replies to Chapman and Schoppers. *AI Mag.* 61–62.

Ginsberg, M. L. 1989b. Universal planning: An (almost) universally bad idea. *AI Mag.* 40–44.

Johnson, D. S. 1990. A catalog of complexity classes. In van Leeuwen, J., ed., *Handbook of Theoretical Computer Science: Algorithms and Complexity*, volume A. Amsterdam: Elsevier. chapter 2, 67–161.

Jonsson, P., and Bäckström, C. 1995. Incremental planning. In Ghallab, M., and Milani, A., eds., *New Trends in AI Planning: Proc. 3rd Eur. WS. Planning (EWSP'95).* Assisi, Italy: IOS Press.

Karp, R. M., and Lipton, R. 1982. Turing machines that take advice. *Enseign. Math* 28:191–209.

Papadimitriou, C. H. 1994. *Computational Complexity.* Reading, MA: Addison Wesley.

Savitch, W. J. 1970. Relationships between nondeterministic and deterministic tape complexities. *Journal of Computer and System Sciences* 4(2):177–192.

Schoppers, M. J. 1987. Universal plans for reactive robots in unpredictable environments. In *Proc. 10th Int'l Joint Conf. on Artif. Intell. (IJCAI-87)*, 1039–1046.

Schoppers, M. J. 1989. In defense of reaction plans as caches. *AI Mag.* 51–62.

Schoppers, M. 1994. Estimating reaction plan size. In *Proc. 12th (US) Nat'l Conf. on Artif. Intell. (AAAI-94)*, 1238–1244.

Selman, B.; Levesque, H.; and Mitchell, D. 1992. A new method for solving hard satisfiability problems. In *Proc. 10th (US) Nat'l Conf. on Artif Intell. (AAAI-92)*, 440–446.

Selman, B. 1994. Near-optimal plans, tractability, and reactivity. In *Proc. 4th Int'l Conf. on Principles of Knowledge Repr. and Reasoning (KR-94)*, 521–529.

Is "early commitment" in plan generation ever a good idea?

David Joslin
Computational Intelligence Research Laboratory
1269 University of Oregon
Eugene, OR 97403
joslin@cirl.uoregon.edu

Martha E. Pollack
Department of Computer Science
and Intelligent Systems Program
University of Pittsburgh
Pittsburgh, PA 15260
pollack@cs.pitt.edu

Abstract

Partial-Order Causal Link planners typically take a "least-commitment" approach to some decisions (notably, step ordering), postponing those decisions until constraints force them to be made. However, these planners rely to some degree on early commitments in making other types of decisions, including threat resolution and operator choice. We show why existing planners cannot support full least-commitment decision-making, and present an alternative approach that can. The approach has been implemented in the *Descartes* system, which we describe. We also provide experimental results that demonstrate that a least-commitment approach to planning can be profitably extended beyond what is done in POCL and similar planners, but that taking a least-commitment approach to every planning decision can be inefficient: early commitment in plan generation is sometimes a good idea.

Introduction

The "least-commitment" approach to plan generation has, by and large, been successful where it has been tried. Partial-Order Causal Link (POCL) planners, for example, typically take a least-commitment approach to decisions about step ordering, postponing those decisions until constraints force them to be made. However, these planners rely to some degree on early commitments for other decisions, including threat resolution and choice of an operator to satisfy open conditions. An obvious question is whether the least-commitment approach should be applied to *every* planning decision; in other words, is early commitment ever a good idea?

An obstacle to addressing this question experimentally arises from the way in which POCL (and similar) planners manage decision-making. They take what we call a *passive postponement* approach, choosing one decision at a time to focus on, and keeping all the other, postponed decisions on an "agenda." Items on the agenda play no role in planning until they are selected for consideration, despite the fact that they may impose constraints on the planning process.

In this paper, we present experimental evidence of the efficiency penalty that can be incurred with passive postponement. We also present an alternative approach, *active postponement*, which has been implemented in the Descartes system. In Descartes, planning problems are transformed into Constraint Satisfaction Problems (CSPs), and then solved by applying both planning and CSP techniques. We present experimental results indicating that a least-commitment approach to planning can be profitably extended beyond what is done in most planners. We also demonstrate that taking a least-commitment approach to every planning decision can be inefficient: early commitment in plan generation is sometimes a good idea.

Passive postponement

POCL algorithms use *refinement search* (Kambhampati, Knoblock, & Yang 1995). A node N (a partial plan) is selected for refinement, and a flaw F (a threat or open condition) from N is selected for repair. Successor nodes are generated for each of the possible repairs of F. All other (unselected) flaws from the parent node are inherited by these successor nodes. Each flaw represents a decision to be made about how to achieve a goal or resolve a threat; thus, each unselected flaw represents a postponed decision. We term this approach to postponing decisions *passive postponement.* Decisions that are postponed in this manner play no role in planning until they are actually selected.

Passive postponement of planning decisions can incur severe performance penalties. It is easiest to see this in the case of a node that has an unrepairable flaw. Such a node is a dead end, but the node may not be *recognized* as a dead end if some other, repairable flaw is selected instead: one or more successor nodes will be generated, each inheriting the unrepairable flaw, and each, therefore, also a dead end. In this manner, a single node with a fatal flaw may generate a large number of successor nodes, all dead ends.

The propagation of dead-end nodes is an instance of a more general problem. Similar penalties are paid when a flaw that can be repaired in only one way—a "forced" repair—is delayed; in that case, the forced repair may have to be repeated in multiple successor nodes. Passive postponement also means that interactions among the constraints imposed by postponed decisions are not recognized until all the relevant decisions have been selected for repair.

The propagation of dead-end nodes is not just a theoretical problem; it can be shown experimentally to cause serious efficiency problems. We ran UCPOP (Penberthy & Weld 1992) on the same test set of 49 problems from 15 domains previously used in (Joslin & Pollack 1994), with the default search heuristics provided by UCPOP. As in the earlier experiments, 32 of these problems were solved by UCPOP, and 17 were not, within a search limit of 8000 nodes generated. We counted the number of nodes examined, and the number of those nodes that were immediate successors of dead-end nodes, i.e., nodes that would never have been generated if fatal flaws were always selected immediately. For some problems, as many as 98% of the nodes examined were successors of dead-end nodes. The average for successful problems was 24%, and for unsuccessful problems, 48%. See (Joslin 1996) for details.

One response to this problem is to continue passive postponement, but to be smarter about which decisions are postponed. This is one way to think about the Least-Cost Flaw Repair (LCFR) flaw selection strategy we presented in (Joslin & Pollack 1994). Indeed, LCFR is a step in the direction of least-commitment planning, because it prefers decisions that are forced to ones that are not. However, even with an LCFR-style strategy, postponed decisions do not play a role in reasoning about the plan until they are selected. Because of this, LCFR can only recognize forced decisions (including dead-ends) that involve just a single flaw on the agenda, considered in isolation. When a decision is forced as a result of flaw interactions, LCFR will not recognize it as forced, and thus may be unable to take a least-commitment approach.

Overview of active postponement

The *active postponement* approach to planning recognizes that flaws represent decisions that will eventually have to be made, and that these postponed decisions impose constraints on the plan being developed. It represents these decisions with constrained variables whose domains represent the available options, and posts constraints that represent correctness criteria on those still-to-be-made decisions. A general-purpose constraint engine can then be used to enforce the constraints throughout the planning process.

To illustrate active postponement for threat resolution, consider a situation in which there is a causal link from some step A to another step B. Assume a third step C, just added to the plan, threatens the causal link from A to B. A constrained variable, D_t, is introduced, representing a decision between promotion and demotion, i.e., $D_t \in \{p, d\}$, and the following constraints will be posted:

$$(D_t = p) \rightarrow \mathit{after}(C, B)$$
$$(D_t = d) \rightarrow \mathit{before}(C, A)$$

The decision about how to resolve the threat can then be postponed, and made at any time by binding D_t.

Suppose that at some later point it becomes impossible to satisfy $\mathit{after}(C, B)$. The constraint engine can deduce that $D_t \neq p$, and thus $D_t = d$, and thus C must occur before A. Similarly, if the threat becomes unresolvable, the constraint engine can deduce that $D_t \in \{p, d\}$ cannot be satisfied, and thus that the node is a dead end. This reasoning occurs automatically, by constraint propagation, without the need to "select" the flaw that D_t represents.

When a threat arises, all of the options for resolving that threat are known; other changes to the plan may eliminate options, but cannot introduce new options. Active postponement for goal achievement is more complex, because the repair options may not all be known at the time the goal arises: steps added later to the plan may introduce new options for achieving a goal. To handle this, we allow the decision variables for goal achievement (termed *causal variables*) to have *dynamic domains* to which new values can be added. We notate dynamic domains using ellipses, e.g., $D_g \in \{\ldots\}$ represents the decision about how to achieve some goal g, for which there are not yet any candidate establishers. An empty dynamic domain does not indicate a dead end, because new options may be added later; it does, however, mean that the problem cannot be solved unless some new option is introduced. Suppose that at a later stage in planning, some new step F is introduced, with g as an effect. An active postponement planner will expand the domain so that $D_g \in \{F, \ldots\}$. Constraints will be posted to represent the conditions, such as parameter bindings, that must be satisfied for F to achieve g.

Least-commitment planning

The active-postponement approach just sketched has been implemented in the Descartes planning system. Descartes provides a framework within which a wide variety of planning strategies can be realized (Joslin 1996). In this section, we provide the details of the algorithm used by Descartes to perform fully "least-commitment" planning: LC-Descartes.

LC-Descartes (Figure 1) can be viewed as performing plan generation *within a single node* that contains both a partial plan Π and a corresponding CSP, C. Π contains a set of steps, some of which have been only tentatively introduced. C contains a set of variables and constraints on those variables. Variables in C represent planning decisions in Π. For example, each precondition p of a step in Π will correspond to a causal variable in C representing the decision of how to achieve p. Parameters of steps in Π will correspond to variables in C representing the binding options.

LC-Descartes($N = \langle \Pi, C \rangle$, Λ)

1. If some variable $v \in C$ has an empty static domain, then fail.
2. Else, if some variable $v \in C$ has an empty dynamic domain, then
   (a) Let p be the precondition corresponding to v.
   (b) **Restricted expansion.** For each operator $o \in \Lambda$ with an effect e that can achieve p, call *Expand(N,o)* to *tentatively* add o to Π, and the corresponding constraints and variables to C.
   (c) Convert v to have a static domain (i.e., commit to using one of the new steps to achieve p.)
   (d) Recursion: Return *LC-Descartes(N, Λ)*
3. Else, call *Solve(C)*; if it finds a solution to the CSP, then return that solution.
4. Else,
   (a) **Unrestricted expansion.** For each $o \in \Lambda$, call *Expand(N,o)* to tentatively add a new step.
   (b) Recursion: Return *LC-Descartes(N, Λ)*.

Figure 1: LC-Descartes algorithm

Expand($N = \langle \Pi, C \rangle$, σ)

1. For each threat that arises between the new step, σ, and steps already in the plan, Π, expand the CSP, C, to represent the possible ways of resolving the threat.
2. For each precondition, p, of step σ, add a new causal variable to C whose dynamic domain includes all the existing steps in Π that might achieve p. Add constraints for the required bindings and temporal ordering.
3. For each precondition, p, in Π that might be achieved by σ, if the causal variable for p has a dynamic domain, add σ to that domain, and add constraints for the required bindings and temporal ordering.
4. For any step α in Π, add the constraint that if σ and α are actually in the plan, they occur at different times.
5. Add step σ to Π.
6. Apply constraint reduction techniques (Tsang 1993) to prune impossible values from domains.

Figure 2: Expand algorithm

Initially, LC-Descartes is called with a node to which only pseudo-steps for the initial and goal state, S_i and S_g, have been added. Following the standard planning technique, S_i's effects are the initial conditions, and S_g's preconditions are the goal conditions. The third argument to LC-Descartes is the operator library, Λ.

LC-Descartes first checks whether any variable has an empty static domain, indicating failure of the planning process. If failure has not occurred, it checks whether any causal variable v has an empty *dynamic* domain, indicating a forced decision to add some step to achieve the goal corresponding to v. In this case, it invokes the *Expand* function (see Figure 2), to add a tentative step for each possible way of achieving the goal, postponing the decision about which might be used in the final plan. As *Expand* adds each new, tentative step to the plan, it also expands the CSP (1) to resolve threats involving the new step, (2) to allow any step already in the plan to achieve preconditions of the new step, (3) to allow the new step to achieve preconditions of steps already in the plan, and (4) to prevent the new step from occurring at the same time as any step already in the plan. This approach to goal achievement generalizes multi-contributor causal structures (Kambhampati 1994).

If no variable has an empty domain, LC-Descartes invokes *Solve*, which applies standard CSP search techniques to try to solve the CSP. At any point, the CSP has a solution if and only the current set of plan steps can be used to solve the planning problem. A solution of the CSP must, of course, bind all of the variables, satisfying all of the constraints. Binding all of the variables means that all planning decisions have been made—the ordering of plan steps, parameter bindings, etc. Satisfying all of the constraints means that these decisions have been made correctly.

In *Solve*, dynamic domains may be treated as static since what we want to know is whether the current set of plan steps are sufficient to solve the planning problem; for this reason, *Solve* uses standard CSP solution techniques. We will assume that *Solve* performs an exhaustive search, but this is not required in practice.

If *Solve* is unsuccessful, then LC-Descartes performs an *unrestricted expansion*, described in the example below. The algorithm continues in this fashion until failure is detected or a solution is found.

A short example. Consider the Sussman Anomaly Blocks World problem, in which the goal is to achieve *on(A,B)*, designated *g1*, and *on(B,C)*, designated *g2*, from an initial state in which *on(C,A)*, *on(A,Table)*, and *on(B,Table)*. The initial CSP is formed by calling *Expand* to add the pseudo-actions for the initial and goal states. At this point, the only dynamic variables will be the causal variables for *g1* and *g2*; call these D_{g1} and D_{g2}. Since neither goal can be satisfied by any step currently in the plan (i.e., they aren't satisfied in the initial state), both of these variables have empty domains.

There are no empty static domains, but both D_{g1} and D_{g2} have empty dynamic domains. LC-Descartes selects one of them; assume it selects D_{g1}. It performs a *restricted expansion* to add one instance of each action type that might achieve this goal. For this example, suppose we have only one action type, *puton(?x,?y,?z)*, that takes block ?x off of ?z and puts ?x on ?y. The new *puton* step will be restricted so that it must achieve *on(A,B)*, which here means that the new step is *puton(A,B,?z1)*; call this step *S1*. Adding this step means that $D_{g1} = S1$. (The domain of D_{g1} is no longer dynamic because a commitment is made to use the new step; this also causes *S1* to be actually in the plan, not just tentatively.) New variables and constraints will also be added to the CSP for any threats that are introduced by this new step.

The resulting CSP again has a variable with an empty dynamic domain, D_{g2}, corresponding to the goal *on(B,C)*. A restricted expansion adds the step *puton(B,C,?z2)*, and adds this step (*S2*) to the domain of D_{g2}. Threat resolution constraints and variables are again added. Some of the preconditions of *S1* are potentially satisfiable by *S2*, and vice versa, and the corresponding variables will have their dynamic domains expanded appropriately.

At this point, the CSP turns out to have no variables with empty domains. This indicates that *as far as can be determined by CSP reduction alone*, it is possible that the problem can be solved with just the current set of plan steps. *Solve* is called, but fails to find find a solution; this indicates that, in fact, the current plan steps are not sufficient.

The least-commitment approach demands that we do only what we are forced to do. The failure to find a solution told us that we are forced to expand the plan, adding at least one new step. Unlike the restricted expansions, however, we have no information about which precondition(s) cannot be satisfied, and therefore, do not know which action(s) might be required. That is, there are no empty dynamic domains, so every condition has at least one potential establisher, but conflicts among the constraints prevent establishers being selected for all of them.

Under these conditions, the least-commitment approach requires that we add new steps that can achieve any precondition currently in the plan. In LC-Descartes, this is an *unrestricted expansion*, and is accomplished by adding one step of each type in the operator library. In the current example, this is simplified by the fact that there is only one action type.

The new step, *S3*, will be *puton(?x3,?y3,?z3)*, and as before, variables and constraint will be added to allow *S3* to achieve any goal it is capable of achieving, and to resolve any threats that were introduced by the addition of *S3*. The CSP still has no variables with empty domains, so *Solve* is again called. This time the standard solution to the Sussman anomaly is found.

As promised by its name, LC-Descartes will only commit to decisions that are forced by constraints. However, this least-commitment behavior requires unrestricted expansions, which are are potentially very inefficient. They introduce steps that can be used for *any* goal; note that unlike the first two steps, which were constrained to achieve specific goals, step *S3* above has no bound parameters. Even worse, a new step of each action type must be introduced. In addition, detecting

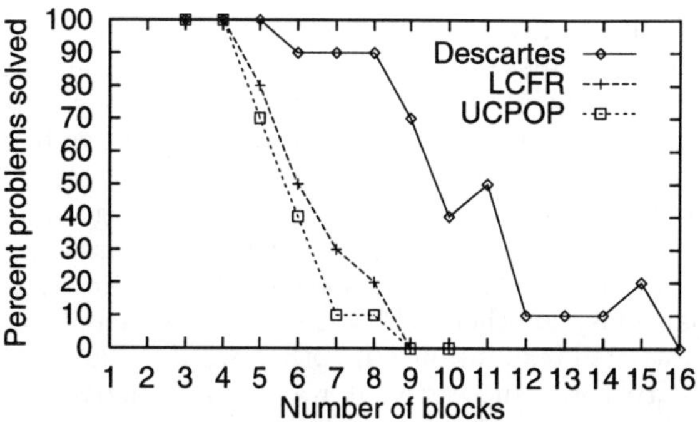

Figure 3: Blocks World, random problems

the need for an unrestricted expansion is much more laborious than checking for variables with empty domains, since it requires that the *Solve* function fail an exhaustive search for a solution.

Experimental results

We begin with a special type of domain, one that has only a single action type. Although unlikely to be of practical interest, such domains allow us to test the limits of LC-Descartes. If unrestricted expansions are a problem even in single-action domains, we know that they will be prohibitive in more realistic domains.

Figure 3 shows experimental results on randomly generated Blocks World problems, using the single-action encoding given in the previous section. Problems were generated using the problem generator provided in the UCPOP 2.0 distribution. The number of blocks was varied from 3 to 16, with 10 problems at each level, for a total of 140 problems. UCPOP, LCFR and LC-Descartes were run on the test problems, with a search limit of 300 CPU seconds on a SPARCstation 20. We report the percentage of problems solved within the CPU limit, and not the number of nodes generated, because LC-Descartes does all its planning within a single node.

UCPOP solved all of the 4-block problems, but its performance fell off rapidly after that point. It dropped below 50 percent at six blocks, and solved no problems of more than eight blocks. LCFR's performance followed a similar pattern. LC-Descartes started to fail on some problems at seven blocks, and dropped below 50 percent at ten blocks. It solves problems of up to fifteen blocks, and fails to solve any problems larger than that. Roughly speaking, on a given set of problems LC-Descartes performed about as well as UCPOP or LCFR performed on problems with half as many blocks. (Doubling the CPU limit did not change the results appreciably.) In interpreting this result, note that the difficulty of blocks world problems increases exponentially with the number of blocks. Also note that because it takes a fully least-commitment approach, in a single-action domain LC-Descartes will always generate minimal-length plans, something not guaranteed by either UCPOP or LCFR.

We investigated what LC-Descartes is doing on the larger problems (see (Joslin 1996) for details), and saw that virtually all of its work is in the form of restricted expansions. Of the 58 successful plans for five-block problems and larger, the average number of steps in each plan was 7.3; of these, only an average of 1.1 steps were added via unrestricted expansions. 31% of these 58 problems were solved with only restricted expansions, another 39% were solved with only one unrestricted expansion. In other words, where LC-Descartes was successful, it was because active postponement allowed it to exploit the structure of the problem enough to either reach a solution directly, or at least get very close to a solution. Success depended on avoiding unrestricted expansions.

EC-Descartes. These results led us to conjecture that the least-commitment approach should be taken at all points *except* those at which LC-Descartes performs unrestricted expansions. We explored this idea by modifying Descartes to make some early commitments: EC-Descartes. EC-Descartes still differs significantly from other planning algorithms, which make early commitments at many points. In POCL planners, for example, threat resolution generates separate successor nodes for promotion and demotion; each node represents a commitment to one step ordering. If both promotion and demotion are viable options, however, then a commitment to either is an early commitment. EC-Descartes avoids this kind of early commitment by posting a disjunctive constraint representing all of the possible options, and postponing the decision about which will be used to resolve the threat.

EC-Descartes and LC-Descartes behave identically except at the point at which LC-Descartes would perform an unrestricted expansion. There, EC-Descartes instead generates more than one successor node. Its objective is to exchange one node that has become under-constrained, and so difficult to solve, for a larger number of nodes that all have at least one variable with an empty domain, static or dynamic. In each of these branches, EC-Descartes then returns to the least-commitment approach, until a solution is found or the problem again becomes under-constrained.

We implemented two versions of EC-Descartes that achieve this objective. The first, EC(1), adopts the simple strategy of selecting the dynamic domain variable with the smallest domain; because only causal variables have dynamic domains, these will be early commitments about action selection. EC(1) generates two successor nodes. In one, all values are removed from the selected variable's domain, forcing a restricted expansion in that node. In the other successor node, the domain is made static. These early commitments are complete; the latter commits to using some step currently in the node, and the former commits to using some step that will be added later. (If EC(1) fails to find a variable with a dynamic domain, it uses EC(2)'s strategy instead.)

Problem	LC	EC(1)	EC(2)
1	* (2)	7.2	6.7
2	* (2)	31.5	142.4
3	* (2)	94.7	*
4	8.7 (1)	4.8	5.1
5	38.0 (1)	5.2	9.8
6	* (2)	155.2	*
7	9.0 (1)	7.4	6.2
8	4.0 (0)	3.6	3.6
9	5.8 (1)	5.7	*

CPU times are in seconds; * = exceeded time limit

Figure 4: Early- and least-commitment

The second version of EC-Descartes performs early commitments in a manner analogous to the "divide and conquer" technique sometimes used with CSPs. EC(2) performs early commitment at the same time as EC(1), but it selects a *static* variable with minimal domain size, and then generates two successor nodes, each inheriting half of the domain of the selected variable. In that both EC(1) and EC(2) select decisions with minimum domain size (within their respective classes of variables), both bear some resemblance to LCFR.

Figure 4 shows CPU times for LC-Descartes and both versions of EC-Descartes on a set of nine problems from the DIPART transportation planning domain (Pollack *et al.* 1994); it also shows in parentheses the number of unrestricted expansions performed by LC-Descartes. EC(1) solved all of the problems, while EC(2) failed on three problems, and LC-Descartes failed to solve four, hitting a search limit of 600 CPU seconds. On all but the "easiest" problem (# 8), LC-Descartes needs to resort to at least one unrestricted expansion, and it failed on all the problems on which it performed a second unrestricted expansion. Although this domain only has three action types, the added overhead of carrying unneeded (tentative) steps, and all of the associated constraints, is considerable. Not surprisingly (at least in retrospect) the fully least-commitment approach loses its effectiveness rapidly after the transition to unrestricted expansions occurs. The relative advantage of EC(1) over EC(2) suggests that early commitments on action selection are particularly effective.

Related work

Work related to LCFR includes DUnf and DMin (Peot & Smith 1993), branch-1/branch-n (Currie & Tate 1991), and ZLIFO (Schubert & Gerevini 1995). DMin, which enforces ordering consistency for postponed threats, could be viewed as a "weakly active" approach. To a lesser extent, even LCFR and ZLIFO could be thought of as using "weakly active" postponement, since enough reasoning is done about postponed decisions to detect flaws that become dead ends.

Virtually all modern planners do *some* of their work by posting constraints, including codesignation constraints on possible bindings, and causal links and temporal constraints on step ordering. Allen and Koomen (Allen & Koomen 1990) and Kambhampati (Kambhampati 1994) generalize the notions of temporal and causal constraints, respectively.

Planners that make more extensive use of constraints include Zeno (Penberthy & Weld 1994) and O-Plan (Tate, Drabble, & Dalton 1994). Zeno uses constraints and temporal intervals to reason about goals with deadlines and continuous change. O-Plan makes it possible for a number of specialized "constraint managers" to work on a plan, all sharing a constraint representation that allows them to interact. Both Zeno and O-Plan maintain an agenda; Descartes differs from them in its use of active postponement.

Previous work that has used constraints in a more active sense during plan generation includes (Stefik 1981; Kautz & Selman 1992; Yang 1992). MOLGEN (Stefik 1981) posts constraints on variables that represent certain kinds of goal interactions in a partial plan. These constraints then guide the planning process, ruling out choices that would conflict with the constraint. Descartes can be seen as taking a similar constraint-posting approach, but extending it to apply to all decisions, not just variable binding, and placing it within a more uniform framework. Kautz and Selman have shown how to represent a planning problem as a CSP, given an initial user-selected set of plan steps; if a solution cannot be found using some or all of those steps, an expansion would be required, much like an unrestricted expansion in LC-Descartes. WATPLAN (Yang 1992) uses a CSP mechanism to resolve conflict among possible variable bindings or step orderings; its input is a possibly incorrect plan, which it transforms to a correct one if possible. WATPLAN will not extend the CSP if the input plan is incomplete.

Conclusions

The Descartes algorithm transforms planning problems into dynamic CSPs, and makes it possible to take a fully least-commitment approach to plan generation. This research shows that the least-commitment approach can be profitably extended much further than is currently done in POCL (and similar) planners.

There are, however, some fundamental limits to the effectiveness of the least-commitment approach; early commitments are sometimes necessary. In particular, one can recognize that constraints have ceased to be effective in guiding the search for a plan, and at that point shift to making early commitments. These early commitments can be viewed as trading one node whose refinement has become difficult for some larger number of nodes in which constraints force restricted expansions to occur, i.e., trading one "hard" node for several "easy" nodes. One direction for future research will be to look for more effective techniques for making this kind of early commitment.

Acknowledgements. This research has been supported by the Air Force Office of Scientific Research (F49620-91-C-0005), Rome Labs (RL)/ARPA (F30602-93-C-0038 and F30602-95-1-0023), an NSF Young Investigator's Award (IRI-9258392), an NSF CISE Postdoctoral Research award (CDA-9625755) and a Mellon pre-doctoral fellowship.

References

Allen, J., and Koomen, J. 1990. Planning using a temporal world model. In *Readings in Planning*. Morgan Kaufmann Publishers. 559–565.

Currie, K., and Tate, A. 1991. O-plan: The open planning architecture. *Art. Int.* 52:49–86.

Joslin, D., and Pollack, M. E. 1994. Least-cost flaw repair: A plan refinement strategy for partial-order planning. In *Proc. AAAI-94*, 1004–1009.

Joslin, D. 1996. Passive and active decision postponement in plan generation. Ph.D. dissertation, Intelligent Systems Program, University of Pittsburgh.

Kambhampati, S.; Knoblock, C. A.; and Yang, Q. 1995. Planning as refinement search: A unified framework for evaluating design tradeoffs in partial-order planning. *Art. Int.* 76(1-2):167–238.

Kambhampati, S. 1994. Multi-contributor causal structures for planning: a formalization and evaluation. *Art. Int.* 69(1-2):235–278.

Kautz, H. and Selman, B. 1992. Planning as Satisfiability. *Proc. ECAI-92* Vienna, Austria, 1992, 359-363.

Penberthy, J. S., and Weld, D. 1992. UCPOP: A sound, complete, partial order planner for ADL. In *Proc. 3rd Int. Conf. on KR and Reasoning*, 103–114.

Penberthy, J. S., and Weld, D. 1994. Temporal planning with continuous change. In *Proc. AAAI-94*, 1010–1015.

Peot, M., and Smith, D. E. 1993. Threat-removal strategies for partial-order planning. In *Proc. AAAI-93*, 492–499.

Pollack, M. E.; Znati, T.; Ephrati, E.; Joslin, D.; Lauzac, S.; Nunes, A.; Onder, N.; Ronen, Y.; and Ur, S. 1994. The DIPART project: A status report. In *Proceedings of the Annual ARPI Meeting*.

Schubert, L., and Gerevini, A. 1995. Accelerating partial order planners by improving plan and goal choices. Tech. Rpt. 96-607, Univ. of Rochester Dept. of Computer Science.

Stefik, M. 1981. Planning with constraints. *Art. Int.* 16:111–140.

Tate, A.; Drabble, B.; and Dalton, J. 1994. Reasoning with constraints within O-Plan2. Tech. Rpt. ARPA-RL/O-Plan2/TP/6 V. 1, AIAI, Edinburgh.

Tsang, E. 1993. *Foundations of Constraint Satisfaction.* Academic Press.

Yang, Q. 1992. A theory of conflict resolution in planning. *Art. Int.* 58(1-3):361–392.

Pushing the Envelope: Planning, Propositional Logic, and Stochastic Search

Henry Kautz and **Bart Selman**
AT&T Laboratories
600 Mountain Avenue
Murray Hill, NJ 07974
{kautz, selman}@research.att.com
http://www.research.att.com/~{kautz, selman}

Abstract

Planning is a notoriously hard combinatorial search problem. In many interesting domains, current planning algorithms fail to scale up gracefully. By combining a general, stochastic search algorithm and appropriate problem encodings based on propositional logic, we are able to solve hard planning problems many times faster than the best current planning systems. Although stochastic methods have been shown to be very effective on a wide range of scheduling problems, this is the first demonstration of its power on truly challenging classical planning instances. This work also provides a new perspective on representational issues in planning.

Introduction

There is a widespread belief in the AI community that planning is not amenable to general theorem-proving techniques. The origin of this belief can be traced to the early 1970's, when work on plan generation using first-order, resolution theorem-proving (Green 1969) failed to scale up to realistically-sized problems. The relative success of the STRIPS system (Fikes and Nilsson 1971) established the basic paradigm for practically all subsequent work in planning. Planning is viewed as a systematic search through either a state-space or through a space of partial plans. Different representations are used for actions and for states or fluents. Control strategies are not discussed in terms of general rules of inference, but rather in terms of rules for establishing and protecting goals, detecting conflicts between actions, and so forth.

The results described in this paper challenge this belief. We have applied general reasoning systems to the task of plan synthesis, and obtained results that are competitive with, and in many cases superior to, the best specialized planning systems. Why was this possible? We believe that the lesson of the 1970's should not have been that planning required specialized algorithms, but simply that *first-order deductive* theorem-proving does not scale well. By contrast, the past few years have seen dramatic progress in the size of problems that can be handled by *propositional satisfiability* testing programs (Trick and Johnson 1993, Selman 1995). In particular, new algorithms based on randomized local search (Selman *et al.* 1992) can solve certain classes of hard problems that are an order of magnitude larger than those that can be solved by older approaches. Therefore, our formalization of planning is based on propositional satisfiability, rather than first-order refutation.

We ran experiments with both one of the best systematic satisfiability algorithms ("tableau", by Crawford and Auton (1993)) and one of the best stochastic algorithms ("Walksat", by Selman *et al.* (1994; 1996)). All task-specific information was given a uniform clausal representation: the inference engines had no explicit indication as to what stood for a goal or what stood for an operator. This meant that the solvers were not constrained to perform a strict backward or forward chaining search, as would be done by most planning systems. Far from being a disadvantage, this greatly adds to the power of approach, by allowing constraints to propagate more freely and thus more quickly reduce the search space. (The idea of viewing planning as general constraint satisfaction rather than directional search has also been explored by other authors; see, for example, Joslin and Pollack (1995).)

The notion of formalizing planning as *propositional* reasoning immediately raises certain questions. Planning is a notoriously hard problem. In fact, the general plan-existence problem for STRIPS-style operators is PSPACE-complete (Bylander 1991, Erol *et al.* 1992, Backstrom 1992). How, then, is it possible to formulate planning as only an NP-complete problem? This difficulty disappears when we realize that the PSPACE-hardness result only holds when the potential solutions can be of exponential length. If we are only interested in polynomial-length plans, then planning is indeed NP-complete.

Many other planning systems can be viewed as specialized propositional reasoning engines. A surprisingly efficient recent planning system is Graphplan, developed by Blum and Furst (1995). Graphplan works in two phases: in the first, a problem stated using STRIPS notation is converted to a data structure called a "planning graph". In the second, the graph is systematically searched for a solution. The planning graph is in fact a propositional representation. In some of our experiments, we directly converted planning graphs into sets of clauses, and then applied Walksat or tableau. For other experiments we developed by hand even more compact and efficient clausal encodings of the problems. As we will see, it was often the case that Walksat dramatically outperformed both the general and specialized systematic search engines.

The success of stochastic local search for planning may come as a surprise. Although local search has been successfully applied to *scheduling* problems (Adorf and Johnston 1990, Minton *et al.* 1990, 1992), it has seen little use for planning. Some authors (Kautz and Selman (1992), Crawford and Baker (1994)) have suggested that planning (finding a partially-ordered set of operators that achieve a goal) and scheduling (assigning times and resources to a given, fixed set of operators) require different control mechanisms, and that planning is inherently a systematic process. Our present success can be mainly attributed to two factors: first, the greater speed and power of Walksat over earlier local search satisfiability algorithms (*e.g.*, GSAT (Selman *et al.* 1992)); and second, our use of better problem encodings – including "compiling away" plan operators, and extending a technique from Blum and Furst for encoding partially-ordered plans with parallel actions. Our results appear to be the first convincing evidence that stochastic local search is indeed a powerful technique for planning.

We will discuss techniques for encoding planning problems as propositional SAT in some detail below. Our experience has been that the search for domain axiomatizations with better computational properties has led us to valuable insights at the representational level. For example, we will describe one encoding we used that "compiles away" any explicit propositions that stand for actions, leaving only fluents. While this encoding was initially motivated by a concern for reducing the number of different propositions in the final formula, it turned out to also enable a particularly simple and elegant solution to the frame problem with parallel actions. It is important to note that we are emphatically *not* suggesting that control knowledge should be "mixed-in" with declarative information, as occurs in logic programming. Instead, we are suggesting that it can be advantageous to try to optimize the *gross statistical properties* of an axiomatization when developing or choosing between declarative representations.

This paper is organized as follows. After a short preview of the results, we discuss general approaches to planning as satisfiability, and particular encoding techniques. We then present experimental results drawn from several domains, including logistics problems, the "rocket" domain, and the blocks world. We compare the performance of both systematic and stochastic algorithms on different kinds of SAT encodings to the performance of Graphplan, and cite comparisons of Graphplan with the well-known Prodigy (Carbonell *et al.* 1992, Stone *et al.* 1994) and UCPOP (Penberthy and Weld 1992) systems.

Preview of Results

Before we describe our approach in detail, we will first highlight some of our main experimental results. In order to evaluate our method, we considered planning domains that lead to serious computational difficulties in traditional planners. Barrett and Weld (1994) discuss various characteristics of such domains. In general, the hardest planning domains contain intricate interactions between planning operators, and various types of goal and subgoal interactions. These interactions complicate the order in which the goals and subgoals should be established, and make it difficult to select the right operator for establishing a goal. Real-world domains often contain both sources of computational difficulties.

In our experiments, we focussed on two natural domains: the "rocket" domain (Blum and Furst 1995) and the "logistics" domain (Veloso 1992). Blum and Furst showed that Graphplan outperforms Prodigy and UCPOP on the rocket problems. We extended this problem somewhat to make it more challenging for Graphplan. The logistics domain can be viewed as yet a further extension of the rocket domain, making it even harder. We also considered several relatively large blocks world problems, because even *small* blocks world instances are often already surprisingly hard for traditional planners.

Table 1 gives the results on some of the hardest instances we considered.[1] From the last column, it is clear that using a stochastic method (Walksat) and a direct SAT encoding, we can solve these instances two or more orders of magnitude faster than Graphplan. Walksat actually found the optimal (*i.e.*, shortest possible plans) for these problems. Thus, for example, it found an optimal 36 step plan to the blocks world problem "bw_large.d". This instance contains 19 blocks and has multiple stacks in both the initial and goal state. We not aware of any other planning algorithm that can solve instances this size without incorporating domain-specific search control knowledge.

The table also contains our results of running on the SAT encodings *derived* from Graphplan's planning graphs. The first two instances are again solved significantly faster than by using Graphplan itself. The SAT encodings for the last two instances became too large for our SAT procedures. Our SAT encoding is more compact than the original Graphplan representation, but Graphplan can handle larger internal data structures than can our SAT procedures. The planning graph for "bw_large.b" contains 18,069 nodes and has over one million exclusion relations. This is just within Graphplan's reach, taking over 7 hours; on our state-base encoding, Walksat takes only 22 seconds. Walksat's solution was proved optimal using the systematic algorithm tableau. Interestingly, although tableau is able to show that there is no shorter solution, it cannot actually find the solution itself! This show how stochastic and the systematic methods can complement one another.

Planning as Satisfiability

While planning has traditionally been formulated as deduction in first-order logic (Green 1969, McCarthy and Hayes 1969, Pednault 1988, Allen 1991), Kautz

[1]Walksat and Graphplan are implemented in C and ran on an SGI Challenge with a 150 MHz MIPS R4400 processor. We thank Avrim Blum for providing us with his code. Tableau ran on a SPARC-10 processor. We thank Jimi Crawford for making a sparc executable of the latest version of his tableau program available to us. The tableau code is optimized for the sparc architecture. Based on previous code comparisons, we estimate the tableau code would run approximately 20% faster on our SGI processor. Our experimental data and code is available from the authors.

problem	time / actions	Graphplan	SAT from planning graph		Direct SAT encoding
			systematic	stochastic	stochastic
rocket_ext.a	7/34	520	4.4	4.7	0.1
logistics.c	13/65	—	23,040	240	1.9
bw_large.b	9/18	27,115	—	—	22
bw_large.d	18/36	—	—	—	937

Table 1: Preview of experimental results. Times in seconds. A long dash (—) indicates that the experiment was terminated after 10 hrs with no solution found.

and Selman (1992) formalized planning in terms of propositional satisfiability. In this framework, a plan corresponds to any model (*i.e.*, truth-assignment) that satisfies a set of logical constraints that represent the initial state, the goal state, and domain axioms. Time consists of a fixed, discrete number of instances. A proposition corresponds either to a time-varying condition (a *fluent*) holding at a particular instant (*e.g.*, `on(A,B,3)`), or to an action that begins to occur at the specified instance and ends at the following instance (*e.g.*, `pickup(A,3)`). General constraints over facts and actions are written as axiom schemas, which are then instantiated for the objects and number of time instances used by a particular problem. The maximal length of a plan is thus fixed at instantiation time; if this quantity is not known in advance, it is straightforward to perform a binary search on instantiations of various sizes, to find the smallest for which a solution is found. (For example, if the optimal plan length is 7, the search would proceed through plans of length 2, 4, 8 (plan found), 6 (no plan found), and finally 7.)

The satisfiability approach can be directly implemented using SAT algorithms, that in general have much better scaling properties than deductive FOL theorem provers. Another advantage is its expressive power. It is easy to represent arbitrary constraints over intermediate states (not just the initial and goal states), and over the structure of the plan itself. For example, to assert that every `pickup` is immediately followed by a `stack`, one could write a schema like

$$\texttt{pickup(x,i)} \supset \exists \texttt{y.stack(x,y,i+1)} .$$

It is quite hard to represent these kinds of constraints in STRIPS. Finally, because it a "real logic" as opposed to STRIPS, the relationships between predicates can be stated explicitly, and it is unnecessary to distinguish "primitive" from "derived" predicates. For example, most STRIPS-style operators for planning handle the predicates `clear` and `on` separately, whereas in our framework one can simply assert

$$\texttt{clear(x,i)} \equiv \neg\exists \texttt{y.on(y,x,i)}$$

The domain axioms for the satisfiability approach are in general stronger than those used by the deductive framework, because it is necessary to rule out all "unintended" models. We will describe several ways this can be done: *(i)* encodings derived from the planning graphs of Graphplan (Blum and Furst 1995); *(ii)* the linear encodings of Kautz and Selman (1992); and *(iii)* general state-based encodings, which incorporate the best features of the previous two. We refer to the both the linear and state-based encodings as "direct" encodings.

Graphplan-based Encodings

As mentioned above, the Graphplan system (Blum and Furst 1995) works by converting a STRIPS-style specification into a planning graph. This is an ordered graph, where alternating layers of nodes correspond to grounds facts (indexed by the time step for that layer) and fully-instantiated operators (again indexed by the time step). Arcs lead from each fact to the operators that contain it as a precondition in the next layer, and similarly from each operator to its effects in the next layer. For every operator layer and every fact there is also a no-op "maintain" operator that simply has that fact as both a precondition and "add" effect.

A solution is a subgraph of the planning graph that contains all the facts in the initial and goal layers, and contains no two operators in the same layer that conflict (*i.e.*, one operator deletes a precondition or an effect of the other). Thus, a solution corresponds to a partially-ordered plan, which may contain several operators occuring at the same time step, with the semantics that those operators may occur in any order (or even in parallel). For planning problems that can take advantage of this kind of parallelism, the planning graph can have many fewer layers than the number of steps in a linear solution — and therefore be much smaller.

A planning graph is quite similar to a propositional formula, and in fact, we were able to automatically convert planning graphs into CNF notation. The translation begins at goal-layer of the graph, and works backward. Using the "rocket" problem in Blum and Furst (1995, Fig. 2) as an example (where "`load(A,R,L,i)`" means "load `A` into `R` at location `L` at time `i`", and "`move(R,L,P,i)`" means "move `R` from `L` to `P` at time `i`"), the translation is:

- the initial state holds at layer 1, and the goals hold at the highest layer;
- each fact at level i implies the disjunction of all the operators at level $i-1$ that have it as an add-effect; *e.g.*,

  $$\texttt{in(A,R,3)} \supset (\texttt{load(A,R,L,2)} \lor \texttt{load(A,R,P,2)} \lor \texttt{maintain(in(A,R),2)})$$
- operators imply their preconditions, *e.g.*,

  $$\texttt{load(A,R,L,2)} \supset (\texttt{at(A,L,1)} \land \texttt{at(R,L,1)})$$
- conflicting actions are mutually exclusive; *e.g.*,

  $$\neg\texttt{load(A,R,L,2)} \lor \neg\texttt{move(R,L,P,2)}$$

Graphplan uses a set of rules to propagate the effects of mutually exclusive actions, leading to additional exclusiveness constraints. In our logical formulation, these additional constraints are logically implied by the original formulation.

Linear Encodings

Kautz and Selman (1992) described a set of sufficient conditions for ensuring that all models of the domain axioms, initial, and goal states correspond to valid plans. These were:

- an action implies *both* its preconditions and effects;
- exactly one action occurs at each time instant;
- the initial state is completely specified;
- classical frame conditions for all actions (*i.e.*, if an action does not change the truth condition of fact, then the fact remains true or remains false when the action occurs).

Intuitively, the first condition makes sure that actions only occur when their preconditions hold, and the "single action" and frame axioms force any state that follows a legal state to also be a legal state. Models under this encoding correspond to linear plans; as the number of operators in a plan increases, these encodings become very large. Kautz and Selman observed that the number of propositional variables can be significantly reduced by replacing certain predicates that take two or more arguments (plus a time-index argument) with ones that take a single argument (plus a time-index). For example, instead of the predicate `move(x,y,z,i)` (meaning "move block `x` from `y` to `z` at time `i`"), they used three predicates, `object`, `source`, and `destination`, with the correspondence

$$\texttt{move(x,y,z,i)} \equiv (\texttt{object(x,i)} \wedge \texttt{source(y,i)} \wedge \texttt{destination(z,i)})$$

When instantiated, this yields $O(3n^2)$ propositions rather than $O(n^4)$ propositions. This technique can also be viewed as a kind of "lifting." The blocks world problems described below use these kind of linear encodings.

State-Based Encodings

The ability to express partially-ordered plans by a single model gives Graphplan a powerful performance advantage. On the other hand, we have seen that the STRIPS-style input notation has many expressive limitations. We have developed a methodology that we call "general state-based encodings", which enjoys the advantages of the two previous approaches, as well as incorporating further representational refinements.

We use the term "state-based" because it emphasizes the use of axioms that assert what it means for each individual state to be valid, and gives a secondary role to the axioms describing operators. For example, in the blocks world, the state axioms assert that only one block can be on another, every block is on something, a block cannot both be clear and have something on it, *etc.* In the logistics domain, state axioms include assertions that each transportable object can only be in a single truck, and that a truck is only at a single location.

Given that the state axioms force each state to be internally consistent, it turns out that only a relatively small number of axioms are needed to describe state transitions, where each transition can be the result of the application of any number of mutually non-conflicting actions. These axioms describe what it means for a fact to change its truth value between states.

One way to do this is to write axioms about the possible actions that could account for each change. For example, in the logistics domain, if an instance of `in` goes from false to true, then the object must have been loaded:

$$(\neg\texttt{in(x,y,i)} \wedge \texttt{in(x,y,i+1)}) \supset \exists \texttt{z.load(x,y,z,i)}$$

This style of axiom can be seen as an instance of the "domain specific" frame axioms described by Haas (1987) and Schubert (1989). Note that classical frame axioms of the type used above for linear encodings are *not* included — in fact, they are inconsistent with parallel actions. These axioms are also similar to the "backward-chaining" axioms used in the Graphplan encodings above. The Graphplan example axiom can be rewritten as

$$(\neg\texttt{maintain(in(A,R),2)} \wedge \texttt{in(A,R,3)}) \supset (\texttt{load(A,R,L,2)} \vee \texttt{load(A,R,P,2)}).$$

This formula can be identified as an instance of the general schema, once the dummy `maintain` proposition is replaced by its precondition, `in(A,R,2)`. Finally, axioms are added that assert that actions entail both their preconditions and effects, and that conflicting actions are mutually exclusive.

As described thus far, this approach has greater expressive power than the Graphplan encodings, but is no more compact. However, the number of propositional variables in this form of encoding can be significantly decreased by using the trick of reducing the arity of predicates, as described in the previous section. Furthermore, many of the axioms relating actions to their preconditions and effects can be safely eliminated, because the strong state consistency axioms propagate the consequences of the remaining assertions. This process of eliminating propositions and simplifying axioms can be carried to the extreme of *completely eliminating propositions that refer to actions!* Only fluents are used, and the axioms directly relate fluents betweens adjacent state. We have done this for the logistics domain, a relatively complex domain that involves moving packages between various locations using trucks and airplanes. The STRIPS-style formalization requires operators such as `load-truck`, `unload-truck`, `drive-truck`, `load-airplane`, *etc.* On the other hand, instead of using explicit `load` axioms, we use a single schema that relates the predicates `at` and `in`:

$$\begin{array}{l}\texttt{at(obj,loc,i)} \supset \\ \quad \texttt{at(obj,loc,i+1)} \vee \\ \quad \exists \texttt{x} \in \texttt{truck} \cup \texttt{airplane}. \\ \quad\quad \texttt{in(obj,x,i+1)} \wedge \\ \quad\quad \texttt{at(x,loc,i)} \wedge \\ \quad\quad \texttt{at(x,loc,i+1)}\end{array}$$

In English, this simply asserts that if an object is at a location, it either remains at that location or goes into some truck or plane that is parked at that location. Another schema accounts for the state-transitions associated with unloading, by asserting that an object in a vehicle either stays in the vehicle, or becomes `at` the location where the vehicle is parked. Interestingly, no additional transition axioms at all are needed for the vehicle movement operators, `drive-truck` and `fly-airplane`, in this domain. The state validity axioms alone ensure that each vehicle is always at a single location.

A solution to a state-based encoding of a planning problem yields a sequence of states. The "missing" actions are easily derived from this sequence, because each pair of adjacent states corresponds to the (easy) problem of finding a unordered plan of length 1. (In the most general case, even finding unordered plans of length 1 is NP-hard; however, in domains we have examined so far, including the logistics and blocks world domains, there is a linear-time algorithm for finding such plans.) The initial motivation for developing this purely state-based representation was pragmatic: we wished to find very compact logical encodings, of a size that could be handled by our SAT algorithms. We achieved this goal: for example, we can use our stochastic algorithm to solve state-based encodings of logistic problems that cannot be solved by *any* other domain-independent planner of which we are aware. (For an example of high-performance planning using domain-*dependent* control heuristics for the blocks world, see Bacchus and Kabanza (1995).) Beyond these computational concerns, the encodings are interesting from a purely representational standpoint. There are no explicit frame axioms, or axioms about preconditions and effects, or axioms about conflicts between actions; everything is subsumed by simple, uniform relationships between fluents. These axiomatizations appear at least as "natural" as situation-calculus or STRIPS formalizations, and avoid many of the traditional problems those approaches encounter.

The experiments reported in this paper do not involve an automatic way of deriving state-based encodings from a STRIPS-style problem specification. The encodings we used in our experiments were created by hand, based on our understanding of the semantics of the various benchmark domains (which were, indeed, described by STRIPS operators). A separate paper (Kautz *et al.* 1996) describes our initial results on automating the process of *compiling away* the operators for a given domain. However, one could equally well take a state-based description of a domain as *primary*, and then add actions to the axioms through meaning postulates.

Experiments: Systematic versus Stochastic Search

In this section, we will discuss our experimental results. We first compare the various encoding schemes with respect to the cost of finding a plan. We then show that the solutions we obtained are optimal, by showing that no shorter plans exist.

To solve our SAT encodings, we consider both a systematic and a stochastic method. Tableau, the systematic procedure, is based on the Davis-Putnam procedure, and was developed by Crawford and Auton (1993). It's one of the fastest current complete SAT procedures (Trick and Johnson 1993; Dubois *et al.* 1996). Walksat, the stochastic procedure, is a descendant of GSAT, a randomized greedy local search method for satisfiability testing (Selman *et al.* 1992, Selman *et al.* 1994, 1996). Such stochastic local search methods have been shown to outperform the more traditional systematic methods on various classes of hard Boolean satisfiability problems. Note, however, that these procedures are inherently incomplete: they cannot *prove* that a formula is unsatisfiable.

Walksat operates as follows. It first picks a random truth assignment, and randomly selects one of the clauses in the SAT instance that is not satisfied by the assignment. It then flips the truth assignment of one of the variables in that clause, thereby satisfying the clause. However, in the process, one or more other clauses may become unsatisfied. Therefore, in deciding which variable to flip from the clause, Walksat uses a greedy bias that tends to increase the total number of satisfied clauses. Specifically, the bias picks the variable that minimizes the number of clauses that are satisfied by the current assignment, but which would become unsatisfied if the variable were flipped. Because the bias can lead the algorithm into local minima, performance is enhanced if the bias is not always applied. The best rule appears to be to always apply the bias if there is a choice that would make no other clauses become unsatisfied; otherwise, randomly apply it half the time. The procedure keeps flipping truth values until a satisfying assignment is found or until some predefined maximum number of flips is reached. In Selman *et al.* (1994, 1996), it was shown that this method significantly outperforms basic GSAT, and other local search methods such as such as simulated annealing (Kirkpatrick *et al.* 1983).

Finding Plans

Table 2 gives the computational cost of solving several hard planning problems. We consider two SAT encodings for each instance, one Graphplan-based and the other direct (linear or state-based). For our SAT encodings, we give both the timings for the systematic tableau method and for the stochastic Walksat procedure. We compare our results to those of the Graphplan system.

As mentioned in the preview of results, we considered hard instances from the rocket and the logistics domains (Blum and Furst 1995, Veloso 1992), as well as the blocks world. We noted that Graphplan has been shown to outperform Prodigy and UCPOP on the rocket problems. The logistics domain is a strictly richer environment than the rocket domain.[2] In the column marked with "time/actions", we give the length of the plan found in terms of the number of time steps. Since we allow for parallel (independent) actions, we also give the total number of actions that will lead us from the initial state to the goal. We created a state-based encoding for rocket and logistics problems, and for the blocks world used the original

[2]Preliminary data indicate that Graphplan, and thus our algorithms, outperform UCPOP on the logistics domain, as expected (Friedman 1996). However, it is important to note that UCPOP is a regression planner, and certain state-based notions are inaccessible or obscure to it. UCPOP may well prove superior on other domains, in which reasoning is more causal, and less related to topological notions.

				SAT Encoding					
	time /	Graphplan		Graphplan-Based			Direct		
problem	actions	nodes	time	vars	syst.	stoch.	vars	syst.	stoch.
rocket_ext.a	7/34	1,625	520	1,103	4.4	4.7	331	0.8	0.1
rocket_ext.b	7/30	1,701	2,337	1,179	2.8	21	351	2.5	0.2
logistics.a	11/54	2,891	6,743	1,782	6.9	29	828	—	2.7
logistics.b	13/47	3,382	2,893	2,069	6.4	47	843	—	1.6
logistics.c	13/65	4,326	—	2,809	23,061	262	1,141	—	1.9
bw_large.a	6/12	5,779	11.5	5,772	—	—	459	0.5	0.3
bw_large.b	9/18	18,069	27,115		—	—	1,087	1.5	22
bw_large.c	14/28		—		—	—	3,016	564	670
bw_large.d	18/36		—		—	—	6,764	—	937

Table 2: The computational cost of finding plans for several hard planning problems. For each instance, the optimal (minimal length) plan was found. Times in seconds. A long dash (—) indicates that the experiment was terminated after 10 hrs with no solution found, or, when we do not give the number of variables or the number of nodes, it means that the problem instance was too large to fit into main memory. The rocket and logistic direct encodings are state-based, and the bw (blocks world) direct encodings are linear.

linear encodings from Kautz and Selman (1992). Before applying the solvers, all of the SAT instances were first simplified by a linear-time algorithm for unit propagation, subsumption, and deletion of unit clauses. Table 2 gives the number of variables in each instance *after* simplification.

The results for "rocket_ext.a" show the general trend. The direct encodings are the most compact, and can be solved many times faster than the Graphplan-based SAT encodings, which is in turn are more efficient than extracting the plans directly from the planning graphs, using the Graphplan system.[3]

We also see that stochastic search (Walksat; see column marked "stoch.") often outperforms systematic search (tableau; see column marked "syst.") by an order of magnitude. Especially striking is the performance of Walksat on the state-based encodings (last column). These results strongly suggest that stochastic methods combined with efficient encoding techniques are a promising method for solving challenging classical planning problems.

As the instances become harder, the difference in performance between Walksat on the direct encodings and the other approaches becomes more dramatic. For example, see "logistic.c" and "bw_large.d." As we will discuss in the next section, all problems were solved to optimality. Thus, for the blocks world instance, bw_large.d, we found the minimal length plan of 36 operations (pickup/putdown/stack/unstack) from the initial state to the goal state. Only Walksat on the linear encoding could synthesize this plan. The problem involves 19 blocks, with 4 stacks in the initial and 3 stacks in the goal state. Note that we did not encode *any* special search control knowledge (such as, "move a block directly to a goal position, if possible"). To get a better feel for the computational difficulty of this problem, let us briefly consider some of the formal computational properties of the blocks world domain.

Optimal blocks world planning was shown to be NP-complete in 1991, but a plan within a factor two of optimal can be obtained in polynomial time (Gupta and Nau 1991, 1992, Chenoweth 1991). Gupta and Nau (1992) give an algorithm for finding such approximate solutions. The basic idea is to first move blocks to the table and then build up the goal stacks. Gupta and Nau's approximation algorithm would generate a plan with 58 operations for our instance, requiring 12 via-the-table moves. (Some blocks don't have to be moved to the table. Note that a via-the-table move generally involves an unstack, a putdown, a pickup, and a stack operation.) Selman (1994) shows that it's unlikely that we can find a better polytime approximation algorithm: All the difficulty lies in deciding how one can avoid via-the-table moves by making direct stack-to-stack moves. To do so, one has to determine which stack-to-stack moves to make and in what order. Walksat manages to eliminate 11 of the 12 via-the-table moves — leaving an optimal plan of 36 steps with only a single, unavoidable via-the-table move! We do not know of any other planning system that can optimally solve unrestricted blocks world problems of this size without using any kind of domain-specific control knowledge. Despite the fact that the blocks world domain is somewhat artificial, we are encouraged by our results because we believe that the rich interactions between operator and sub-goal sequencing, which makes the domain relatively hard, is also quite likely to be found in more practical domains, such as, for example, the softbot planning domain (Etzioni and Weld 1994). (Indeed, in the next phase of this project, we hope to apply our methods to the softbot domain.)

Finally, from the columns that give the number of nodes and number of variables, we see that direct encodings (and in particular, the state-based encodings) result in a significant reduction of the number of variables in the problem instances. Our Graphplan-based SAT encodings also have fewer variables than the number of nodes in the corresponding planning graph, because of the unit-propagation simplification described above.

Although our results are quite promising for stochastic methods, we do not mean to suggest that these methods will always outperform systematic ones. In fact, we have done some preliminary experiments on one of the artificial domains (D^1S^1) studied in Barrett and Weld (1994) and in Blum and Furst (1994). We considered the Graphplan-based encoding, and found

[3]Our timings do not include the time needed for generating the planning graph or for constructing the SAT encodings. On the harder instances, those times are just a fraction of what it takes to solve the planning graph or the SAT problems.

that the Graphplan system itself scales better than our SAT approach using either Walksat or tableau. The special structure of the domain, which is specifically designed to check the sequencing of operators, appears to steer Walksat repeatedly in the wrong direction. Tableau performs poorly because it performs a depth-first search, and the domain appears to require a breadth-first approach.[4] State-based encodings may again give better results on this domain. We also obtained some promising results on these instances using SAT encodings based on McAllester and Rosenblitt's (1991) "causal" planning formulation. In general, we expect that systematic and stochastic methods will complement each other — each having different relative strengths depending on the domain. In the next section, we'll discuss another way in which these methods complement each other.

Proving Optimality

To show that the plans we found in our previous experiments are optimal, we now show that no shorter plan exists. Table 3 gives our results. This time we can only use methods that systematically explore the space of all possible plans up to a certain size, because we have to demonstrate that shorter plans do not exist.

From the table, we see that in this case using tableau on the Graphplan-based SAT encoding is not very effective (except for "logistics.a"). Neither the Graphplan system nor tableau with direct SAT encodings strictly dominate one another; the former is superior on the logistics problems, and the latter on the blocks world problems.

None of the methods could show the inconsistency of "logistics.c" when using at most 12 time steps. Therefore, to show the optimality of a 13 step solution to "logistics.c", we constructed "logistics.b" as a strictly smaller subproblem. Graphplan was able to show that this problem does not have 12 step solution. It follows that "logistics.c" does have a 12 step solution either.

In general, our results suggests that it's harder to show the non-existence of a plan up to a certain length than it is to find such a plan if it exists. This kind of asymmetry has also been observed in several other problem domains (Selman 1995). The issue is closely related to the practical difference between solving NP and co-NP complete problems.

Tableau can show the infeasibility of a 17 time slot (34 stack/unstack) solution for "bw_large.d", while Walksat can find a 18 time slot (36 stack/unstack) plan (Table 2). No systematic approach could find the feasible solution. This demonstrates how stochastic and systematic methods are complementary: one can be used for plan synthesis and the other to determine lower-bounds on the plan length.

Conclusions

We have shown that for solving hard planning problems from several challenging domains, our approach of using linear or state-based axiomatizations and a general, stochastic satisfiability algorithm (Walksat) outperforms some of the best specialized planning algorithms by orders of magnitude. Furthermore, Walksat is often superior to good general (tableau) and specialized (Graphplan) systematic search engines on SAT encodings derived from STRIPS-style operators. These results challenge the common assumptions in AI that planning requires specialized search techniques, and that planning is an inherently systematic process. Of course, we are not ruling out the possibility that in other domains some of the specialized planning systems could prove superior. This is an important issue for further research.

We have also shown that systematic and local search algorithms complement each other well in the planning as satisfiability framework. Systematic algorithms can be used to provide a lower-bound on the length of solution plans, and then stochastic algorithms can be used to find the actual solutions. It is interesting to observe that in certain cases systematic algorithms are better at proving infeasibility than at finding solutions to problems instances of comparable size.

Finally, our experiments with different SAT encodings of planning problems indicates that much progress can be made by considering novel kinds of axiomatizations. In particular, our experience suggests that axiomatizations that concentrate on states and fluents can be more compact and easier to solve than approaches that directly encode STRIPS-style state-changing operators. Furthermore, these state-based encodings are interesting from a representational standpoint, and appear to provide clean and elegant ways to handle parallel actions and frame conditions.

[4] For a discussion of issue of depth-first version breadth-first search in variations of the Davis-Putnam procedure, see Dechter and Rish (1994).

References

Adorf, H.M., Johnston, M.D. (1990). A discrete stochastic neural network algorithm for constraint satisfaction problems. *Proc. of the Int. Joint Conf. on Neural Networks*, San Diego, CA, 1990.

Allen, J. (1991). Planning as temporal reasoning. *Proc. KR-89*, Cambridge, MA, 1991.

Bacchus, F. and Kabanza, F. (1995). Using temporal logic to control search in a forward chaining planner. *Proc. EWSP-95*, 157–169.

Backstrom, C. (1992). *Computational complexity of reasoning about plans*, Ph.D. thesis, Linkoping University, Linkoping, Sweden.

Barrett, A. and Weld, D. (1994). Partial-order planning: evaluating possible efficiency gains. *Artificial Intelligence*, 67:71-112, 1994.

Blum, A. and Furst, M.L. (1995). Fast planning through planning graph analysis. *Proc. IJCAI-95*, Montreal, Canada.

Bylander, T. (1991). Complexity results for planning. *Proc. IJCAI-91*, Sidney, Australia, 274-279.

Carbonell, J. , Blythe J., Etzioni, O., Gil, Y., Joseph, R., Kahn, D., Knoblock, C., Minton, S., Perez, A., Reilly, S., Veloso, M., Wang, X (1992). Prodigy 4.0: the manual and tutorial. CMU, CS Tech. Report CMU-CS-92-150.

Chenoweth, S.V. (1991). On the NP-hardness of the blocks world. *Proc. AAAI-91*, Anaheim, CA, 623–628.

Crawford, J.M. and Auton, L.D. (1993) Experimental Results on the Cross-Over Point in Satisfiability Problems. *Proc. AAAI-93*, Washington, DC, 21–27.

Crawford, J. and Baker, A.B. (1994). Experimental results on the application of satisfiability algorithms to

problem	time	Graphplan nodes	Graphplan time	SAT Encoding Graphplan-Based vars	SAT Encoding Graphplan-Based syst.	SAT Encoding State-Based vars	SAT Encoding State-Based syst.
rocket_ext.a	6	1,295	60.3	773	4.5	263	2.5
rocket_ext.b	6	1,372	68.6	849	3.5	283	7.2
logistics.a	10	2,469	1,273	1,415	80.1	728	—
logistics.b	12	3,002	2,946	1,729	—	757	—
logistics.c	12	3,826	—	2,353	—	1,027	—
bw_large.a	5/10	4,946	8.8	4,939	—	415	0.6
bw_large.b	8/16	16,590	—		—	920	1.2
bw_large.c	13/26		—		—	4,405	250
bw_large.d	17/34		—		—	5,886	25,289

Table 3: Showing the infeasibility of shorter plans. Times in seconds.

scheduling problems. *Proc. AAAI-94*, Seattle, WA.

Dechter, R. and Rish, I. (1994). Directional resolution: the Davis-Putnam procedure, revisited. *Proc. KR-94*, Bonn, Germany.

Dubois, O. , Andre, P., Boufkhad, Y., and Carlier, J. (1996). A-SAT and C-SAT. *Dimacs Series in Discrete Mathematics and Theoretical Computer Science.* (to appear)

Erol, K., Nau, D.S., and Subrahmanian, V.S. (1992). On the complexity of domain-independent planning. *Proc. AAAI-92*, 381–386.

Etzioni, O. and Weld, D. S. (1994). A softbot-based interface to the internet. *Comm. ACM*, July 1994.

Fikes, R.E. and Nilsson, N.J. (1971). STRIPS: A new approach to the application of theorem proving to problem solving. *Artificial Intelligence*, 2(3/4), 189–208.

Friedman, M. (1996). Personal communication.

Green, C. (1969). Application of Theorem Proving to Problem Solving. In *Proc. IJCAI-69*, Washington, D.C., 1969, 219–239.

Gupta and Nau (1991). Complexity results for blocks-world planning. *Proc. AAAI-91*, Anaheim, CA, 629–633.

Gupta and Nau (1992). On the complexity of blocks-world planning. *Artificial Intelligence*, **56**, 139–403.

Haas, A. (1987). The case for domain-specific frame axioms. In *The Frame Problem in Artificial Intelligence, Proceedings of the 1987 Workshop*, F.M. Brown, ed., Lawrence, KS, 1987. Morgan Kaufmann Publishers, Los Altos, CA.

Joslin, D. and Pollack, M. (1995). Passive and Active Decision Postponement in Plan Generation. In the *European Workshop on Planning (EWSP)*, Assisi, Italy, Sept. 1995.

Kautz, H. and Selman, B. (1992) Planning as Satisfiability. *Proc. ECAI-92*, Vienna, Austria, 1992, 359–363.

Kautz, H., McAllester, D., and Selman, B. (1996). Encoding Plans in Propositional Logic. In preparation.

Kirkpatrick, S., Gelatt, C.D., and Vecchi, M.P. (1983). Optimization by simulated annealing. *Science*, 220 (1983) 671–680.

McCarthy, J. and Hayes, P. (1969). Some philosophical problems from the standpoint of artificial intelligence. In *Machine Intelligence 4*, D. Michie, ed., Ellis Horwood, Chichester, England, 1969, page 463ff.

McAllester, D. and Rosenblitt, D. (1991). Systematic non-linear planning. *Proc. AAAI-91*, Anaheim, CA.

Minton, S., Johnston, M.D., Philips, A.B., and Laird, P. (1990) Solving large-scale constraint satisfaction an scheduling problems using a heuristic repair method. *Proc. AAAI-90*, 1990, 17–24.

Minton, S., Johnston, M.D., Philips, A.B., and Laird, P. (1992) Minimizing conflicts: a heuristic repair method for constraint satisfaction and scheduling problems. *Artificial Intelligence,* (58)1–3, 1992, 161–205.

Pednault, E. (1988). Synthesizing plans that contain actions with context-dependent effects. *Computational Intelligence*, 4(4):356–372, 1988.

Penberthy, J. and Weld, D. (1992). UCPOP: A sound, complete, partial order planner for ADL. In the *Proc. KR-92*, Boston, MA, 103–114.

Davis, M., Logemann, G., and Loveland, D. (1962). A machine program for theorem proving. *Comm. ACM*, 5, 1962, 394–397.

Schubert, L. (1989). Monotonic Solution of the Frame Problem in the Situation Calculus: an Efficient Method for Worlds with Fully Specified Actions. In *Knowledge Representation and Defeasible Reasoning*, H. Kyburg, R. Loui, and G. Carlson, eds.

Selman, B. (1994). Near-Optimal Plans, Tractability, and Reactivity. *Proc. KR-94*, Bonn, Germany, 1994, 521–529.

Selman, B. (1995). Stochastic Search and Phase Transitions: AI Meets Physics. *Proc. IJCAI-95*, Montreal, Canada, 1995.

Selman, B. , Kautz, H., and Cohen, B. (1994). Noise Strategies for Local Search. *Proc. AAAI-94*, Seattle, WA, 1994, 337–343.

Selman, B., Kautz, H., and Cohen, B. (1996) Local Search Strategies for Satisfiability Testing. *Dimacs Series in Discrete Mathematics and Theoretical Computer Science.* (to appear)

Selman, B., Levesque, H., and Mitchell, D. (1992). A New Method For Solving Hard Satisfiability Problems. *Proc. AAAI-92*, San Jose, CA, 1992, 440-446.

Stone, P., Veloso, V., and Blythe, J. (1994). The need for different domain-independent heuristics. In *AIPS94*, pages 164-169, Chicago, 1994.

Trick, M. and Johnson, D. (Eds.) (1993) *Proc. DIMACS Challenge on Satisfiability Testing.* Piscataway, NJ, 1993. (DIMACS Series on Discr. Math.)

Veloso, M. (1992). Learning by analogical reasoning in general problem solving. Ph.D. Thesis, CMU, CS Techn. Report CMU-CS-92-174.

Finding Optimal Solutions to the Twenty-Four Puzzle

Richard E. Korf and **Larry A. Taylor**
Computer Science Department
University of California, Los Angeles
Los Angeles, Ca. 90024
korf@cs.ucla.edu, ltaylor@cs.ucla.edu

Abstract

We have found the first optimal solutions to random instances of the Twenty-Four Puzzle, the 5×5 version of the well-known sliding-tile puzzles. Our new contribution to this problem is a more powerful admissible heuristic function. We present a general theory for the automatic discovery of such heuristics, which is based on considering multiple subgoals simultaneously. In addition, we apply a technique for pruning duplicate nodes in depth-first search using a finite-state machine. Finally, we observe that as heuristic search problems are scaled up, more powerful heuristic functions become both necessary and cost-effective.

Introduction

The sliding-tile puzzles, such as the Eight and Fifteen Puzzle, have long served as testbeds for heuristic search in AI. A square frame is filled with numbered tiles, leaving one position empty, called the blank. Any tile that is horizontally or vertically adjacent to the blank can be slid into the blank position. The task is to rearrange the tiles from some random initial configuration into a particular goal configuration, ideally or optimally in a minimum number of moves. The state space for the Eight Puzzle contains over 10^5 nodes, the Fifteen Puzzle space contains about 10^{13} nodes, and the Twenty-Four Puzzle contains almost 10^{25} nodes.

Due to its small search space, optimal solutions to the Eight Puzzle can be found with breadth-first search. We first found optimal solutions to the Fifteen Puzzle using Iterative-Deepening-A* (IDA*) and the Manhattan distance heuristic function (Korf 1985). IDA* is a variant of the well-known A* algorithm (Hart, Nilsson, and Rafael 1968), which runs in space that is linear in the maximum search depth, rather than exponential. IDA* proceeds in a series of depth-first search iterations, starting from the initial state. Each path is explored until a node n is reached where the number of moves from the initial state, $g(n)$, plus the heuristic estimate of the number of moves necessary to reach the goal state, $h(n)$, exceeds a threshold for that iteration. The threshold for the first iteration is the heuristic estimate for the initial state, and the threshold for each succeeding iteration is the minimum total cost, $f(n) = g(n) + h(n)$, of all nodes on the frontier of the previous iteration. The algorithm continues until a goal node is chosen for expansion.

	1	2	3	4
5	6	7	8	9
10	11	12	13	14
15	16	17	18	19
20	21	22	23	24

Figure 1: The Twenty-Four Puzzle in its goal state

The Manhattan distance heuristic is computed by taking each tile, counting the number of grid units to its goal location, and then summing these values for all tiles. Since only one tile can move at a time, Manhattan distance never overestimates the number of moves needed to solve a given problem. Given such an *admissible* heuristic function, IDA* is guaranteed to return an optimal solution, if one exists.

IDA* with the Manhattan distance heuristic can solve random instances of the Fifteen Puzzle (Korf 1985). In spite of considerable work on this problem in the last decade, however, nobody has solved a significantly larger version of the puzzle. Note that the state space of the Twenty-Four Puzzle is almost a trillion times larger than that of the Fifteen Puzzle.

We present the first random Twenty-Four Puzzle instances for which optimal solutions have been found. Ten random solvable instances were generated, and so far we have found optimal solutions to all but one.

Three factors have contributed to this limited success. The first is simply faster computers. The Sun Ultra Sparc workstation that these experiments were run on is about 70 times faster than the DEC 2060 that the Fifteen Puzzle was originally solved on. The second is a technique we developed for pruning duplicate nodes in depth-first search (Taylor and Korf 1993). Finally, we have discovered more powerful heuristic functions for this problem. The most important contribution of this paper, however, is a new theory that allows these heuristics to be automatically learned and applied. All examples in this paper refer to the Twenty-Four Puzzle, where positions are labelled by the tiles that occupy them in the goal state shown in Figure 1.

Improved Admissible Heuristics

Linear Conflict Heuristic

The first significant improvement to Manhattan distance was the linear-conflict heuristic (Hansson, Mayer, and Yung 1992). It applies when two tiles are in their goal row or column, but are reversed relative to their goal positions. For example, if the top row of the puzzle contains the tiles (2 1) in that order, to reverse them, one of the tiles must move down out of the top row, to allow the other to pass by, and then back up. Since these two moves are not counted in the Manhattan distance of either tile, two moves can be added to Manhattan distance without violating admissibility.

As another example, if the top row contains the tiles (3 2 1) in that order, four more moves can be added to the Manhattan distance, since every pair of tiles is reversed, and two tiles must move out of the row temporarily. Furthermore, a tile in its goal position may be in both a row and a column conflict. Since the extra moves required to resolve a row conflict are vertical moves, and those required by a column conflict are horizontal, both sets of moves can be added to the Manhattan distance, and still preserve admissibility.

This addition to the Manhattan distance heuristic reduces the number of nodes generated by IDA* on the Fifteen Puzzle by roughly an order of magnitude. The additional complexity of computing the linear conflicts slows down node generation by about a factor of two, however, for a net improvement of a factor of five. Efficiently computing this heuristic involves precomputing and storing all possible permutations of tiles in a row or column, and incrementally computing the heuristic value of a child from that of its parent.

Last Moves Heuristic

The next enhancement to the heuristic is based on the last moves of a solution, which must return the blank to its goal position, the upper-left corner in this case. Thus, the last move must either move the 1 tile right, or the 5 tile down. Therefore, immediately before the last move, either the 1 or 5 tile must be in the upper-left corner. Since the Manhattan distance of these tiles is computed to their goal positions, unless the 1 tile is in the left-most column, its Manhattan distance will not accommodate a path through the upper-left corner. Similarly, unless the 5 tile is in the top row, its Manhattan distance will not accommodate a path through the upper-left corner. Thus, if the 1 tile is not in the left-most column, and the 5 tile is not in the top row, we can add two moves to the Manhattan distance, and still preserve admissibility.

While two moves may seem like a small improvement, it can be added to about 64% of random Twenty-Four Puzzle states. The effect of two additional moves is to save an entire iteration of IDA*. Since each iteration of IDA* on the Twenty-Four Puzzle can generate up to ten times as many nodes as the previous iteration, saving an iteration can result in an order of magnitude savings in nodes generated.

We can extend the same idea to the last two moves. If the last move is made by the 1 tile, the next-to-last move must either move the 2 tile right, or the 6 tile down. Similarly, if the last move is made by the 5 tile, the next-to-last move must either move the 6 tile right, or the 10 tile down. Considering the last two moves can add up to four moves to the Manhattan distance. Extending this idea to the last three moves was not cost effective on the Twenty-Four Puzzle.

To benefit from both the linear conflict and last moves enhancements, and maintain admissibility, we must consider their interactions. For example, assume that the 1 tile is not in the left-most column, and the 5 tile is not in the top row. If the 1 tile is in its goal column, and in a column conflict with another tile, then the two additional moves added by the linear conflict could be used to move the 1 tile left, allowing it to pass through the upper-left corner. Similarly, if the 5 tile is in its goal row, and in a row conflict, the two additional linear conflict moves could be used to move it up and hence through the upper-left corner. Thus, if either of these conditions occur, we can't add two more moves for the last move, since that may count twice moves already added by the linear conflict heuristic. Similarly, any additional moves added for the last two moves must also be checked against linear conflicts involving the 2, 6, and 10 tiles. In general, whenever more than one heuristic is being used, we must compute their interactions to maintain admissibility.

Relation to Bidirectional Search The reader may notice that a heuristic based on the last moves in the solution is related to bi-directional search. The most effective form of bidirectional heuristic search is called perimeter search (Dillenburg and Nelson 1994) (Manzini 1995). A limited breadth-first search backward from the goal state is performed, and the nodes on the perimeter of this search are stored. IDA* is then run from the initial state, with heuristic calculations made to determine the minimum distance to any state on the perimeter. This heuristic value is then added to the distance from the initial state to the given node, plus the distance from the perimeter to the goal state, for a more accurate admissible heuristic.

In a unidirectional search, the heuristic function is always computed to a single goal state. As a result, the heuristic calculation can be optimized to take advantage of this. With any form of bidirectional search, however, the heuristic must be calculated between arbitrary pairs of states, reducing the opportunities for optimization. While (Manzini 1995) reports speedups of up to a factor of eight on the Fifteen Puzzle using his improved perimeter search, he uses only the Manhattan distance heuristic function. It's not clear if similar results could be achieved with a more complex heuristic such as linear conflict.

Corner-Tiles Heuristic

The next enhancement to our heuristic focuses on the corners of the puzzle. For example, if the 3 tile is in its goal position, but some tile other than the 4 is in the 4 position, the 3 tile will have to move temporarily to correctly position the 4 tile. This requires two moves of the 3 tile, one to move it out of position, and another to move it back. If the 3 tile is involved in a row conflict, then two moves will already be counted for it, and no more can be added. It can't be involved in a column conflict if it's in its goal position.

The same rule applies to the 9 tile, unless the 9 is involved in a column conflict. In fact, if both the 3 and 9 tiles are correctly positioned, and the 4 tile is not, then four moves can be added, since both the 3 and 9 tiles will have to move to correctly position the 4.

This rule also applies to the 15, 19, 21, and 23 tiles. It applies to the 1 and 5 tiles as well, but the interaction of this heuristic with the last moves heuristic is so complex that to avoid the overhead of this calculation, we exclude the 1 and 5 tiles from the corner heuristic.

The corner-tile heuristic can potentially add up to twelve additional moves to the Manhattan distance, two for each of the six tiles adjacent to three of the corners. These extra moves require that at least one of these six tiles be in its goal position, a situation that only occurs in about 22% of random states. A search for the goal, however, does not generate a random sample of states, but is biased toward states that are close to the goal, or at least appear to the heuristic to be close. In other words, the search is trying to correctly position the tiles, and hence this heuristic adds extra moves much more often than would be expected from a random sample of states.

In summary, we have considered three enhancements to the Manhattan distance heuristic, based on linear conflicts, the last moves, and the corner tiles. The last two are introduced here for the first time.

A New Theory of Admissible Heuristics

While these enhancements result in a much more powerful heuristic, they appear to be a collection of domain-specific hacks. Furthermore, integrating the enhancements together into an admissible heuristic seems to require even more domain-specific reasoning. However, all these heuristics can be derived from a general theory that is largely domain-independent, and the heuristics can be automatically learned and applied. While we would like to be able to claim that these heuristics were discovered from the general theory, in reality the theory was discovered after the fact.

The classic theory of admissible heuristic functions is that they are the costs of optimal solutions to simplified problems, derived by removing constraints from the original problem (Pearl 1984). For example, if we remove the condition that a tile can only be moved into the blank position, the resulting problem allows any tile to move to any adjacent position at any time, and allows multiple tiles to occupy the same position. The number of moves to optimally solve this simplified problem is the Manhattan distance from the initial state to the goal state. While this theory accounts for many heuristics for many problems, it doesn't explain any of the above enhancements to Manhattan distance.

Automatically Learning the Heuristics

An alternative derivation of Manhattan distance is based on the original problem, but focuses on only one tile at a time. For each possible location of each individual tile, we perform a search to correctly position that tile, ignoring all other tiles, and only counting moves of the tile in question. In this search, a state is uniquely determined by the position of the tile of interest and the position of the blank, since all other tiles are equivalent. Since the operators of the sliding-tile puzzle are invertible, we can perform a single search for each tile, starting from its goal position, and record how many moves of the tile are required to move it to every other position. Doing this for all tiles results in a table which gives, for each possible position of each tile, its Manhattan distance from its goal position. Then, noticing that each move only moves one tile, for a given state we add up the Manhattan distances of each tile to get an admissible heuristic for the state. Of course, we don't really need to do the search in this case, since we can easily determine the values from the problem, but we presented it in this way to eliminate as much domain-specific reasoning as possible, and replace it with domain-independent search.

The value of this reconstruction of Manhattan distance is that it suggests a further generalization. The above formulation considers each tile in isolation, and the inaccuracy of the resulting heuristic stems from ignoring the interactions between the tiles. The obvious next step is to repeat the above process on all possible pairs of tiles. In other words, for each pair of tiles, and each combination of positions they could occupy, perform a search to their goal positions, and count only moves of the two tiles of interest. We call this value the *pairwise distance* of the two tiles from their goal locations. A state of this search consists of the positions of the two tiles and the position of the blank, since all other tiles are equivalent. Again for efficiency, for each pair of tiles we can perform a single search starting from their goal positions, with the blank also in its goal position, and store the pairwise distances to all other positions. The goal of this search is to find the shortest path from the goal state to all possible positions of the two tiles, where only moves of the two tiles of interest are counted. We can do this with a best-first search, counting only these moves.

Since states of these searches are only distinguishable by the positions of the two tiles and the blank, the size of these search spaces is $O(n^3)$, where n is the number of tiles. There are $O(n^2)$ such searches to perform, one for each pair of tiles, for a time complexity of $O(n^5)$. The size of the resulting table is $O(n^4)$, for each pair of tiles in each combination of positions.

For almost all pairs of tiles and positions, their pairwise distances equal the sum of their Manhattan distances from their goal positions. However, there are three types of cases where the pairwise distance exceeds the combined Manhattan distance. The first is when the two tiles are in a linear conflict. The second is when the two tiles are 1) a tile in its goal position adjacent to a corner, and 2) the tile that either belongs in, or that happens to be in, the corresponding corner. The third case is tiles 1 and 5, which are adjacent to the blank position in the goal state. The reason their pairwise distance may exceed their combined Manhattan distances is that the backwards pairwise search starts from the goal state, and hence the first move is to move the 1 or the 5 tile into the corner. Thus, computing all the pairwise distances by a simple search "discovers" Manhattan distance along with all three of the heuristic enhancements described above, with very little domain-specific reasoning. No other enhancements are discovered by the pairwise searches.

Applying the Heuristics

The next question is how to automatically handle the interactions between these heuristics to compute an admissible heuristic estimate for a particular state. Assume that we have precomputed all the pairwise tile distances and stored them in a table. Given a particular state, we look up all the pairwise distances for the current positions of the tiles. To compute the overall heuristic, we then partition the tiles into groups of two, and sum the corresponding pairwise distances, in a way that maximizes the resulting heuristic value.

To see this problem more clearly, represent a state as a graph with a node for each tile, and an edge between each pair of tiles, labelled with their pairwise distance. We need to select a set of edges from this graph, so that no two edges are connected to a common node, and the sum of the labels of the selected edges is maximized. This problem is called the maximum weighted matching problem, and can be solved in $O(n^3)$ time, where n is the number of nodes (Papadimitriou and Steiglitz 1982). Thus, this approach to heuristic generation can be automated, and runs in polynomial time.

Higher-Order Heuristics

Unfortunately, the pairwise distances do not account for the full power of the heuristic enhancements described above. For example, consider the linear conflicts represented by the tiles (3 2 1), in that order in the top row. The linear conflict heuristic would add four moves to the Manhattan distance of these tiles, since all pairs are reversed, and two of the tiles must move out of the row. The pairwise distance of each pair of these tiles is two moves plus their Manhattan distances. The graph representation of this situation is a triangle of tiles, with each edge of the triangle having weight two, ignoring the Manhattan distances. The maximum matching on this graph only contains one edge, with a total weight of two, since any two edges have a node in common. Thus, the pairwise distances capture only part of the linear conflict heuristic.

As another example, consider the corner-tile heuristic, and a state in which the 3 and 9 tiles are correctly positioned, but the 4 tile is not. The corner heuristic would add four moves to the Manhattan distance of the 4 tile, since both the 3 and 9 tiles must move to correctly place the 4 tile. The graphical representation of this situation consists of an edge between the 3 and 4 tiles, and an edge between the 9 and 4 tiles, each with a label of two, if we ignore the Manhattan distance. Since both these edges include the 4 tile, we can only select one of them, for an addition of only two moves.

Finally, while the pairwise distances capture the enhancement due to the last move of the solution, it doesn't capture the last two moves, since these involve the 2, 6, and 10 tiles, in addition to the 1 and 5 tiles.

In order to capture the full power of these heuristics, we extend the idea of pairwise distances to include triples of tiles, quadruples, etc. The linear conflict example of (3 2 1) requires us to consider all three tiles together to get four additional moves. If we consider each corner tile together with both adjacent tiles, we get the full power of the corner-tile heuristic. Finally, the last-two-moves enhancement requires considering all five tiles that may be involved. The corresponding matching problem is hypergraph matching, where a single edge "connects" three or more nodes, and unfortunately is NP-Complete. Thus, we may have to rely on a greedy approach to the higher-dimensional matching problem, and a lower heuristic value. As we consider higher-order heuristics, the complexity of the learning search, the size of the lookup table, and the complexity of the matching all increase, in return for more accurate heuristic values.

We believe this is a general theory for the discovery and implementation of admissible heuristic functions. All combinatorial problems involve solving multiple subgoals. Many admissible heuristics are constructed by considering the solution to each individual subproblem in isolation, and ignoring the interactions with other subproblems. We are proposing heuristics based on the simultaneous consideration of two, three, or more subgoals. As another example, consider a job-shop scheduling problem. There are a set of jobs to be performed, and a collection of machines with which to accomplish them. Each machine can only process a single job at a time. One way to derive a lower bound on the optimal solution is to consider the resources required by each job individually, and sum this over all jobs, ignoring resource conflicts between the jobs. Following our approach, one would consider all pairs of jobs, compute the resources required for each pair, and then compute the total resources by summing these values for a pairwise partition of the jobs.

Pruning Duplicate Nodes

While the main concern of this paper is the heuristic functions, we also used another orthogonal technique to significantly speed up the experiments.

Any depth-first search, such as IDA*, will generate the same node multiple times on a graph with cycles. For example, consider a square grid problem space, with the moves Up, Down, Left, and Right, each moving one unit in the indicated direction. Since there are four moves from every state, the asymptotic complexity of a depth-first search to depth d is $O(4^d)$. However, there are only $O(d^2)$ distinct states at depth d in a grid, and a breadth-first search, which stores all nodes generated and checks for duplicates, will run in $O(d^2)$ time. The difference in complexity between the breadth-first and depth-first search in this example illustrates the magnitude of this problem.

In the grid example, the operator pairs Left-Right and Up-Down are inverses of each other. Any good depth-first search implementation will remember the last operator applied, and never immediately apply its inverse. This can be done by encoding the last operator applied as the state of a finite-state machine. The machine has five states, an initial transient state and four recurrent states, one for each last move. Each arc of the machine represents an operator, except that the inverse of the last move is excluded. This reduces the complexity of the depth-first search from $O(4^d)$ to $O(3^d)$, a significant reduction, but still far from the $O(d^2)$ complexity of the breadth-first search.

This idea can be carried further, and is described in detail in (Taylor and Korf 1993). Ideally, we would like to allow only one path to each node in the grid. This can be done by first making all Left or Right moves, if any, followed by a single turn, and then all Up moves or all Down moves, if any. These rules can also be enforced by a five-state finite-state machine. The initial state allows all four operators, and each resulting state encodes the last move applied. If the last move was to the Right, all moves are allowed except a move to the Left. Similarly, if the last move was to the Left, all moves are allowed except a move to the Right. If the last move was Up, however, the only allowable move is another Up move. Similarly, if the last move was Down, the only allowable move is another Down move. This finite-state machine can only generate a single path to each point of the grid, and hence a depth-first search controlled by this machine runs in time $O(d^2)$, which is the same as a breadth-first search.

These finite-state machines can be automatically learned, from a small breadth-first search to discover duplicate operator strings. In this case, a breadth-first search to depth two is sufficient to learn all the duplicate strings to construct the above machine. Once the machine is constructed, there is almost no overhead to using it to control the depth-first search.

This technique can be applied to other problems, such as the sliding tile-puzzles. After rejecting inverse operators, the next shortest cycle in the sliding-tile puzzles is twelve moves long, corresponding to rotating the tiles in a 2×2 square. Using a breadth-first search, a finite-state machine for the Twenty-Four Puzzle was constructed with over 619,000 states. This machine is then used to control a depth-first search, rejecting operators that lead to duplicate nodes. The effect of this duplicate pruning is to reduce the asymptotic complexity of a depth-first search from $O(2.368^d)$ to $O(2.235^d)$. While this may seem like a small improvement, in the two easiest problems reported below, duplicate pruning decreased the running time of IDA* by factors of 2.4 and 3.6, with the larger improvement coming on the harder problem.

Experimental Results

We implemented IDA*, taking full advantage of the Manhattan distance, linear conflict, last-two-moves, and corner-tile heuristics, as well as the finite-state machine pruning. Since we were concerned with efficiency, our implementation was specialized to these heuristics and their interactions, rather than using a general table lookup and matching algorithm.

As a first test of our program, we ran it on 100 randomly generated solvable instances of the Nineteen Puzzle. The Nineteen Puzzle is the 4×5 sliding-tile puzzle, and its state space contains about 10^{18} states. All the puzzle instances were solved optimally, and the average solution length was 71.5 moves, as compared to an average solution length of 52.6 moves for the Fifteen Puzzle. The average number of node generations per problem instance was almost a billion, which is comparable to those generated by IDA* on the Fifteen Puzzle using just the Manhattan distance heuristic. To our knowledge, these are the first random Nineteen Puzzle problem instances to be solved optimally.

We then turned our attention to the Twenty-Four Puzzle. Ten random solvable instances were generated. Since there is enormous variation in the time to solve these problems, different iterations of IDA* were interleaved on different problem instances, in order find and solve the easier ones first. To date, nine of these prob-

No.	Initial State	Nodes Generated	Optimal Sol.
1	17 1 20 9 16 2 22 19 14 5 15 21 0 3 24 23 18 13 12 7 10 8 6 4 11	8,110,532,608	100
2	14 5 9 2 18 8 23 19 12 17 15 0 10 20 4 6 11 21 1 7 24 3 16 22 13	18,771,430,922	95
3	7 13 11 22 12 20 1 18 21 5 0 8 14 24 19 9 4 17 16 10 23 15 3 2 6	82,203,971,683	108
4	18 14 0 9 8 3 7 19 2 15 5 12 1 13 24 23 4 21 10 20 16 22 11 6 17	83,573,198,724	98
5	2 0 10 19 1 4 16 3 15 20 22 9 6 18 5 13 12 21 8 17 23 11 24 7 14	221,769,436,018	101
6	16 5 1 12 6 24 17 9 2 22 4 10 13 18 19 20 0 23 7 21 15 11 8 3 14	523,772,060,498	96
7	21 22 15 9 24 12 16 23 2 8 5 18 17 7 10 14 13 4 0 6 20 11 3 1 19	792,795,062,385	104
8	6 0 24 14 8 5 21 19 9 17 16 20 10 13 2 15 11 22 1 3 7 23 4 18 12	1,415,436,865,760	97
9	3 2 17 0 14 18 22 19 15 20 9 7 10 21 16 6 24 23 8 5 1 4 11 12 13	3,033,449,077,924	113
10	23 14 0 24 17 9 20 21 2 18 10 13 22 1 3 11 4 16 6 5 7 12 8 15 19	$> 3,000,000,000,000$	≥ 112

Table 1: Twenty-four puzzle problem instances, nodes generated, and optimal solution lengths

lems have been solved optimally, with a lower bound established for the remaining one. Table 1 shows all ten problem instances, sorted by difficulty. For the solved problems, we give the number of nodes generated and the optimal solution length, and for the unsolved one we give lower bounds on these values. The tiles are listed from left to right and top to bottom, with 0 representing the blank. In this notation, the tiles of the goal state in Figure 1 would be listed in numerical order. The average optimal solution length for these ten problems is at least 102.4 moves. The code was written in C, runs on a Sun Ultra Sparc workstation, and generates about a million nodes per second. The easiest problem took about two hours and 15 minutes to solve, and the most difficult solved problem took over a month. To date, the remaining unsolved problem has run for over a month. These are the first random Twenty-Four Puzzle instances to be solved optimally.

Conclusions

We have found the first optimal solutions to random instances of the Twenty-Four Puzzle, a problem with almost 10^{25} states. The branching factor is 2.368, and the optimal solutions average over 100 moves long. We implemented IDA* on a state-of-the-art workstation, with a more powerful admissible heuristic function, and a method for pruning duplicate nodes in depth-first search. The most important contribution of this paper is a new general theory for the automatic discovery and application of admissible heuristics. Instead of considering individual subgoals in isolation, our approach considers two or more subgoals simultaneously. This theory allows one to automatically discover Manhattan distance, along with the linear conflict, last moves, and corner-tile enhancements to it, with nothing more than small searches of the problem space. By considering three or more subgoals at a time, even more powerful heuristics can be derived.

A more powerful heuristic function increases the time per node generation by a polynomial amount. On the other hand, it generally decreases the effective branching factor by a small amount, yielding an asymptotic improvement. For small problems, more powerful heuristics may not be cost effective, since one doesn't search deep enough to overcome the polynomial overhead. As machines get faster and larger problems are addressed, however, seeming small improvements in a heuristic function eventually become cost effective. Thus, as problem size increases, it becomes both necessary and cost-effective to encode more knowledge of the problem in the form of improved heuristics. We have developed an approach to doing this automatically.

Acknowledgements

This work was supported by NSF Grant IRI-9119825, and a grant from Rockwell International.

References

Dillenburg, J.F., and P.C. Nelson, Perimeter search, *Artificial Intelligence*, Vol. 65, No. 1, Jan. 1994, pp. 165-178.

Hansson, O., A. Mayer, and M. Yung, Criticizing solutions to relaxed models yields powerful admissible heuristics, *Information Sciences*, Vol. 63, No. 3, 1992, pp. 207-227.

Hart, P.E., N.J. Nilsson, and B. Raphael, A formal basis for the heuristic determination of minimum cost paths, *IEEE Transactions on Systems Science and Cybernetics*, Vol. 4, No. 2, 1968, pp. 100-107.

Korf, R.E., Depth-first iterative-deepening: An optimal admissible tree search, *Artificial Intelligence*, Vol. 27, No. 1, 1985, pp. 97-109.

Manzini, G., BIDA*: An improved perimeter search algorithm, *Artificial Intelligence*, Vol. 75, No. 2, June 1995, pp. 347-360.

Papadimitriou, C.H., and K. Steiglitz, *Combinatorial Optimization: Algorithms and Complexity*, Prentice-Hall, Englewood Cliffs, N.J., 1982.

Pearl, J. *Heuristics*, Addison-Wesley, Reading, MA, 1984.

Taylor, L., and R.E. Korf, Pruning duplicate nodes in depth-first search, *Proceedings of the National Conference on Artificial Intelligence (AAAI-93)*, Washington D.C., July 1993, pp. 756-761.

Linear Time Near-Optimal Planning in the Blocks World

John Slaney
Automated Reasoning Project
Australian National University
Canberra, ACT 0200, Australia
John.Slaney@anu.edu.au

Sylvie Thiébaux
IRISA
Campus de Beaulieu
35042 Rennes Cedex, France
Sylvie.Thiebaux@irisa.fr

Abstract

This paper reports an analysis of near-optimal Blocks World planning. Various methods are clarified, and their time complexity is shown to be linear in the number of blocks, which improves their known complexity bounds. The speed of the implemented programs (ten thousand blocks are handled in a second) enables us to make empirical observations on large problems. These suggest that the above methods have very close average performance ratios, and yield a rough upper bound on those ratios well below the worst case of 2. Further, they lead to the conjecture that in the limit the simplest linear time algorithm could be just as good on average as the optimal one.

Motivation

The Blocks World (BW) is an artificial planning domain, of little practical interest. Nonetheless, we see at least two reasons for examining it in more detail.

In the first place, for good or ill, BW is by far the most extensively used example in the planning literature. It often serves for demonstrating the merit of domain-independent techniques, paradigms and planners. See (Bacchus & Kabanza 1995; Kautz & Selman 1992; 1996; Schoppers 1994) for recent examples. In order to assess the benefits of these approaches and the significance of the claims formulated in the literature, it is therefore necessary to know certain basic facts about BW, such as what makes optimal[1] BW planning hard (Gupta & Nau 1992), how it may best be approximated and what BW-specific information our systems must be able to represent and use in order to cope with it. In the cited papers, for example, Bacchus and Kabanza show how specific methods for near-optimal BW planning can be encoded in a general system, while Kautz and Selman exhibit domain-independent techniques that dramatically improve performance for BW. These facts should not be misinterpreted as showing that such systems are really effective for problems like BW unless they match the best domain-specific ones, both in time complexity and in solution quality. We do not suppose that the cited authors are themselves confused on this point, but as long as little is known about the behavior of BW-specific methods, such misinterpretation of their claims is dangerously easy.

The second motivation for studying BW arises from research on identifying tractable classes of planning problems. We note that within some restricted classes of domain-independent formalisms, such as SAS$^+$-US or the restriction of STRIPS to ground literals and operators with positive preconditions and one postcondition, planning is tractable while optimal planning and even near-optimal planning are not (Bäckström & Nebel 1995; Bylander 1994; Selman 1994).[2] However, near-optimal planning is tractable for certain domains that are too sophisticated to be encoded within such classes. BW is one such domain. This suggests that there is more to learn by focusing first on tractable near-optimal planning in the domain-dependent setting, where the specific features responsible for intractability are more easily identified and coped with. Indeed, the identification of tractable subclasses of SAS$^+$ originated from the careful examination of a simple problem in sequential control. BW appears then as a good candidate for identifying in a similar way a class of planning problems for which near-optimal planning is tractable. Again, this requires that we first acquire detailed knowledge of near-optimal BW planning, keeping in mind that it has many properties that are not necessarily shared by other applications.

Although we hope that our investigations will help towards this second goal, our direct concern in this paper is with the first one, i.e. improving the current knowledge of BW to be used for assessment purposes. We shall focus on the performance in time complexity and average solution quality of polynomial time near-optimal algorithms for BW planning. Various methods for near-optimal BW planning within a factor of 2 exist, for which we shall take (Gupta & Nau 1991; 1992) as sources. However, we find that these methods are

[1]In the following, optimal planning denotes the problem of finding a plan of minimal length, and near-optimal planning the problem of finding a plan of length at most k times the minimal, for some constant factor k.

[2]The intractability of near-optimal planning for SAS$^+$-US follows directly from the corresponding intractability result for the mentioned subclass of STRIPS (Selman 1994) and from the inclusion of this latter subclass in SAS$^+$-US.

nowhere clearly formulated and that little is known about their performance.

The paper makes the following contributions. The first part formulates those methods and shows that they can all be implemented to run in time linear in the number of blocks. This improves the cubic upper bound given in (Gupta & Nau 1992). The speed of the implemented programs (10000 blocks in under a second) also makes it possible to look at the plans produced by the algorithms on *large* problems.

The second part then, is devoted to experimental results. We first introduce a technique for producing truly random BW problems, which is a nontrivial task. Experiments on these random problems give us a rough upper bound of around 1.2 on the average performance ratios of the near-optimal algorithms, and suggest that when the number of blocks is large, it makes little difference which of these algorithms (more sophisticated or trivial) is used, because all produce plans of length close to twice the number of blocks on average. Further, though optimal BW planning is NP-equivalent (Gupta & Nau 1992) and though there is a hard lower bound on *absolute* performance ratios tractably achievable (Selman 1994), the experiments lead to the conjecture that on average and in the limit, linear time algorithms could be just as good as the optimal one.

Definitions

Before presenting the algorithms, we shall enter some definitions. We assume a finite set $\mathcal{B}$ of blocks, with TABLE as a special member of $\mathcal{B}$ which is not on anything. Noting that the relation ON is really a function, we write it as a unary S (for 'support'), where $S(x)$ picks out, for block x, the block which x is on. Thus S is a partial function from $\mathcal{B}\backslash\{\text{TABLE}\}$ to $\mathcal{B}$, injective except possibly at TABLE and such that its transitive closure is irreflexive. We refer to the pair $\langle\mathcal{B}, S\rangle$ as a *part-state*, and identify a *state* of BW with such a part-state in which S is a total function.

For a part-state $\sigma = \langle\mathcal{B}, S\rangle$ and for any a and b in $\mathcal{B}$, we define: $\text{ON}_\sigma(a,b)$ iff $S(a) = b$, $\text{CLEAR}_\sigma(a)$ iff either $a = \text{TABLE}$ or $\neg\exists b(\text{ON}_\sigma(b,a))$, ABOVE_σ as the transitive closure of ON_σ, and $\text{POSITION}_\sigma(a)$ as the sequence $\langle a :: \text{POSITION}_\sigma(S(a))\rangle$ if $S(a)$ exists and $\langle a\rangle$ otherwise. That is, the position of a block is the sequence of blocks at or below it. We refer to the position of a clear block as a *tower*. A tower is *grounded* iff it ends with the table. Note that in a state (as opposed to a mere part-state) every tower is grounded.

A BW planning *problem* over $\mathcal{B}$ is a pair of states $\langle\langle\mathcal{B}, S_1\rangle, \langle\mathcal{B}, S_2\rangle\rangle$. In problem $\langle I, G\rangle$, I is the *initial* state and G is the *goal* state. Here we consider only problems with completely specified goal states.

A *move* in state $\sigma = \langle\mathcal{B}, S\rangle$ is a pair $m = \langle a, b\rangle$ with $a \in \mathcal{B}\backslash\{\text{TABLE}\}$ and $b \in \mathcal{B}$, such that $\text{CLEAR}_\sigma(a)$, $\text{CLEAR}_\sigma(b)$ and $\neg\text{ON}_\sigma(a,b)$. The result of m in σ is the state $\text{RES}(m, \sigma) = \langle\mathcal{B}, S'\rangle$ where $S'(a) = b$ and $S'(x) = S(x)$ for $x \in \mathcal{B}\backslash\{\text{TABLE}, a\}$.

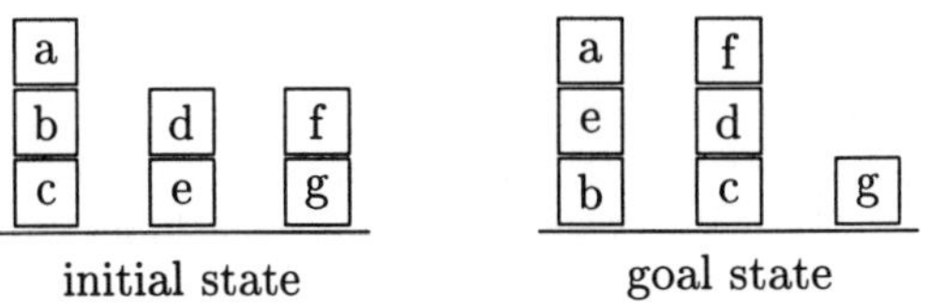

Figure 1: BW Planning Problem

A *plan* for BW problem $\langle I, G\rangle$ is a finite sequence $\langle m_1, \ldots, m_p\rangle$ of moves such that either $I = G$ and $p = 0$ or else m_1 is a move in I and $\langle m_2, \ldots, m_p\rangle$ is a plan for $\langle \text{RES}(m_1, I), G\rangle$ in virtue of this definition.

We say that a block whose position in I is different from its position in G is *misplaced* in $\langle I, G\rangle$, and that one which is not misplaced is *in position*. Next, we say that a move $\langle a, b\rangle$ is *constructive* in $\langle I, G\rangle$ iff a is in position in $\langle\text{RES}(\langle a,b\rangle, I), G\rangle$. That is, iff a is put into position by being moved to b. Once a block has been moved constructively it need never be moved again in the course of solving the problem. If no constructive move is possible in a given problem, we say that the problem is *deadlocked*.[3] In that case, for any misplaced block b_1 there is some block b_2 which must be moved before a constructive move with b_1 is possible. Since the number of blocks is finite the sequence $\langle b_1, b_2 \ldots\rangle$ must eventually loop. The concept of a deadlock, adapted from that given in (Gupta & Nau 1992), makes this idea precise. A deadlock for BW problem $\langle I, G\rangle$ over $\mathcal{B}$ is a nonempty subset of $\mathcal{B}$ that can be ordered $\langle d_1, \ldots, d_k\rangle$ in such a way that:

$$\begin{cases} \text{for all } i,\ 1 \leq i < k,\ B_{\langle I,G\rangle}(d_i, d_{i+1}) \\ B_{\langle I,G\rangle}(d_k, d_1) \end{cases}$$

where

$$\begin{aligned} B_{\langle I,G\rangle}(a,b) \equiv\ & \text{POSITION}_I(a) \neq \text{POSITION}_G(a)\ \wedge \\ & \text{POSITION}_I(b) \neq \text{POSITION}_G(b)\ \wedge \\ & \exists x \neq \text{TABLE}\ (\text{ABOVE}_I(b,x) \wedge \text{ABOVE}_G(a,x)) \end{aligned}$$

E.g., the problem in Figure 1 is deadlocked, the deadlocks being $\{\text{a}\}$ and $\{\text{a}, \text{d}\}$.[4] It is easy to see that if $B_{\langle I,G\rangle}(a,b)$ then in any plan for $\langle I, G\rangle$, the first time b is moved must precede the last time a is moved. A deadlock being a loop of the $B_{\langle I,G\rangle}$ relation, at least one block in each deadlock must be moved twice. The first move of this block may as well always be to the table, so as to break deadlocks without introducing new ones. What makes optimal BW planning hard is to choose those deadlock-breaking moves so that it pays in the long term (Gupta & Nau 1992).

[3] By slight abuse of notation, we allow ourselves to speak of moves as constructive in a state, rather than in a problem, of a state rather than a problem as deadlocked and so forth, leaving mention of the goal to be understood.

[4] To see this, note that $B_{\langle I,G\rangle}(\text{a}, \text{d})$ taking the third block in the definition to be $x = \text{e}$, that $B_{\langle I,G\rangle}(\text{d}, \text{a})$ taking $x = \text{c}$, and that $B_{\langle I,G\rangle}(\text{a}, \text{a})$ taking $x = \text{b}$.

Near-Optimal BW Planning

There is a nondeterministic algorithm which solves BW problems optimally in polynomial time (Gupta & Nau 1991; 1992). It consists basically of a loop, executed until broken by entering case 1:

1. If all blocks are in position, stop.
2. Else if a constructive move $\langle a, b\rangle$ exists, move a to b.
3. Else nondeterministically choose a misplaced clear block not yet on the table and move it to the table.

In the course of their discussion, Gupta and Nau also note three deterministic polynomial time algorithms which approximate optimality within a factor of 2.

US The first and simplest is one we have dubbed US (Unstack-Stack). It amounts to putting all misplaced blocks on the table (the 'unstack' phase) and then building the goal state by constructive moves (the 'stack' phase). No block is moved by US unless it is misplaced, and no block is moved more than twice. Every misplaced block must be moved at least once even in an optimal plan. Hence the total number of moves in a US plan is at worst twice the optimal.

GN1 Another algorithm which is usually better in terms of plan length than US (and never worse) is the simple deterministic version of the above optimal one given on pages 229–230 of (Gupta & Nau 1992). It differs from the nondeterministic version just in choosing *arbitrarily* some move of a misplaced clear block to the table whenever no constructive move is available. We call it GN1 for Gupta and Nau.

GN2 Yet another algorithm is suggested (Gupta & Nau 1991) though with no details of how it may be achieved. This one uses the concept of a deadlock. We call it GN2 and it is the same as GN1 except that the misplaced clear block to be moved to the table is chosen not completely arbitrarily but in such a way as to break at least one deadlock. That is:

3. Else arbitrarily choose a clear block which is in a deadlock and move it to the table.

Gupta and Nau (1992, p. 229, step 7 of their algorithm) say that in a deadlocked state every misplaced clear block is in at least one deadlock. If this were true, GN1 and GN2 would be identical. It is false, however, as may be seen from the example in Figure 1. Block f is not in any deadlock, and so can be chosen for a move to the table by GN1 but not by GN2. It is possible for GN1 to produce a shorter plan than GN2 (indeed to produce an optimal plan) in any given case, though on average GN2 performs better because it never completely wastes a non-constructive move by failing to break a deadlock.

In order for GN2 to be complete, in every deadlocked state there must be at least one clear block which is in a deadlock. In fact, we can prove the stronger result that in every deadlocked state there exists a deadlock consisting entirely of clear blocks. We now sketch the proof, since it makes use of the notion of a Δ sequence which will be needed in implementing GN2.

Let $\sigma = \langle \mathcal{B}, S\rangle$ be a state that occurs during the attempt to solve a problem with goal state $G = \langle \mathcal{B}, S_G\rangle$ and suppose the problem $\pi = \langle \sigma, G\rangle$ is deadlocked. Let b be misplaced and clear in σ. Consider $\text{POSITION}_G(\text{b})$, the sequence of blocks which in G will lead from b down to the table. Let c be the first (highest) block in this sequence which is already in position in σ (c may be the table, or $S_G(b)$, or somewhere in between). In the goal state, either b or some block below b will be on c. Let us call this block d. What we need to do, in order to advance towards a constructive move with b, is to put d on c. This is not immediately possible because there is no constructive move in σ, so either c is not clear or else d is not clear. If c is not clear, we must move the blocks above it, starting with the one at the top of the tower which contains c in σ. If c is clear, we should next move the clear block above d in σ. This is how the function δ_π is defined: $\delta_\pi(b) = x$ such that

$$\text{CLEAR}_\sigma(x) \text{ and } \begin{cases} \text{ABOVE}_\sigma(x, d) & \text{if } \text{CLEAR}_\sigma(c) \\ \text{ABOVE}_\sigma(x, c) & \text{if } \neg\text{CLEAR}_\sigma(c) \end{cases}$$

If b is in position or not clear or if $S_G(b)$ is in position and clear, let $\delta_\pi(b)$ be undefined. Now let $\Delta_\pi(b)$ be the sequence of blocks obtained from b by chasing the function δ_π:

$$\Delta_\pi(b) = \begin{cases} \langle b :: \Delta_\pi(\delta_\pi(b))\rangle & \text{if } \delta_\pi(b) \text{ exists} \\ \langle b\rangle & \text{otherwise} \end{cases}$$

The point of the construction is that if $\delta_\pi(b)$ exists, then $\text{CLEAR}_\sigma(\delta_\pi(b))$ and $B_\pi(b, \delta_\pi(b))$. To see why the latter holds, note that either c or d is below $\delta_\pi(b)$ in σ and below b in the goal. Now for any misplaced clear b, if $\Delta_\pi(b)$ is finite then there is a constructive move in σ using the last block in $\Delta_\pi(b)$, while if it is infinite then it loops and the loop is a deadlock consisting of clear blocks. This loop need not contain b of course: again Figure 1 shows an example, where $\Delta_\pi(\text{d})$ is $\langle \text{d}, \text{a}, \text{a}, \ldots\rangle$.

Our suggestion for a way of implementing GN2, therefore, is to replace the original clause 3 with:

3. Else arbitrarily choose a misplaced clear block not on the table; compute its Δ sequence until this loops; detect the loop when for some x in Δ_π, $\delta_\pi(x)$ occurs earlier in Δ_π; move x to the table.

Linear time algorithms

We now show how to implement all of US, GN1 and GN2 to run in time linear in the number n of blocks. This improves on the known complexity of these algorithms. The original (Gupta & Nau 1992) did not mention any bound better than $O(n^3)$ for near optimal BW planning, though $O(n^2)$ implementations have been described by other authors (Chenoweth 1991; Bacchus & Kabanza 1995).

```
function INPOS (b : block) : boolean
   if b = TABLE then
      return true
   if not Examined_b then
      Examined_b ← true
      if Si_b ≠ Sg_b then
         InPosition_b ← false
      else InPosition_b ← INPOS(Si_b)
   return InPosition_b

procedure US ()
   INIT()
   for each b ∈ B\{TABLE} do
      if Clear_b then
         UNSTACK(b)
   for each b ∈ B\{TABLE} do
      STACK(b)

procedure INIT ()
   Plan ← ⟨ ⟩
   for each b ∈ B\{TABLE} do
      Clear_b ← true
      Examined_b ← false
   for each b ∈ B\{TABLE} do
      INPOS(b)
      if Si_b ≠ TABLE then
         Clear_{Si_b} ← false

procedure UNSTACK (b : block)
   if (not InPosition_b) and
      (Si_b ≠ TABLE) then
      (local) c ← Si_b
      MOVE(⟨b, TABLE⟩)
      UNSTACK(c)

procedure MOVE (⟨a, b⟩ : move)
   Plan ← ⟨⟨a, b⟩ :: Plan⟩
   if Si_a ≠ TABLE then
      Clear_{Si_a} ← true
   if b ≠ TABLE then
      Clear_b ← false
      InPosition_a ← (Sg_a = b) and
                     InPosition_b
   else InPosition_a ← (Sg_a = TABLE)
   Si_a ← b

procedure STACK (b : block)
   if not InPosition_b then
      STACK(Sg_b)
      MOVE(⟨b, Sg_b⟩)
```

Figure 2: The US Algorithm

How to make US linear

The key to making US a linear time algorithm is to find a way to compute which blocks are in position in $\mathcal{O}(n)$, and to execute this computation only once in the course of the problem solution. We do this by means of a combination of recursion and iteration, as shown in Figure 2. The algorithm makes use of several variables associated with each block b:

Clear_b	True iff b is clear in the current state.
$\mathsf{InPosition}_b$	True iff b is already in position.
$\mathsf{Examined}_b$	True iff $\mathsf{InPosition}_b$ has been determined.
Si_b	Block currently below b.
Sg_b	Block below b in the goal.

During initialization, INPOS can be called at most twice with any particular block b as parameter: once as part of the iteration through the blocks and at most once recursively from a call with the block above b. Hence the number of calls to INPOS is bounded above by $2n$. Similar considerations apply to the recursive STACK and UNSTACK procedures. The stored information is updated in constant time by MOVE.

How to make GN1 linear

For GN1, we add organizational structure to the problem representation. At any given time, each block has a status. It may be:

1. ready to move constructively. That is, it is misplaced but clear and its target is in position and clear.
2. stuck on a tower. That is, it is misplaced, clear and not on the table, but cannot move constructively because its target is either misplaced or not clear.
3. neither of the above.

More variables are now associated with each block. One records the status of this block, while others denote the blocks (if any) which are on this one currently and in the goal. Initialising and updating these does not upset the $O(n)$ running time. To make it possible to select moves in constant time, the blocks of status 1 and 2 are organized into doubly linked lists, one such list containing the blocks of each status. Inserting a block in a list and deleting it from a list are constant time operations as is familiar. The next block to move is that at the head of the 'ready' list unless that list is empty, in which case it is the block at the head of the 'stuck' list. If both lists are empty, the goal is reached.

When a block a moves, it changes its status as well as its position. At most three other blocks may also change status as a result of the move: the block currently below a (if any), the block that will be on a in the goal (if any), and the block which in the goal will be on the block currently below a (if any). Hence the number of delete-insert list operations is at worst linear in the number of moves in the plan, and so in the number of blocks. Nothing else stands in the way of a linear time implementation of GN1.

How to make GN2 linear

GN2, however, is a different matter. To implement GN2 via Δ sequences, it is necessary to compute $\delta_\pi(b)$ for various blocks b, and to achieve linear time there must be both a way to do this in constant time and a way to limit the number of δ calculations to a constant number per block. On the face of it, neither of these is easy. To find $\delta_\pi(b)$ it is necessary to know which is the highest block in position in the goal tower of b and to know which is the clear block above a given one. These items of information change as moves are made, and each time such an item changes for one block it changes for all the $O(n)$ blocks in a tower, so how can those changes be propagated in constant time? Moreover, when a deadlock is to be broken, a new Δ sequence has to be computed, as many blocks may have moved since the last one was computed, thus changing δ. Computing a Δ sequence appears to be irreducibly an $O(n)$ problem, and since $O(n)$ such sequences may be needed, this appears to require GN2 to be of $O(n^2)$ even if $\delta_\pi(b)$ can somehow be found in constant time.

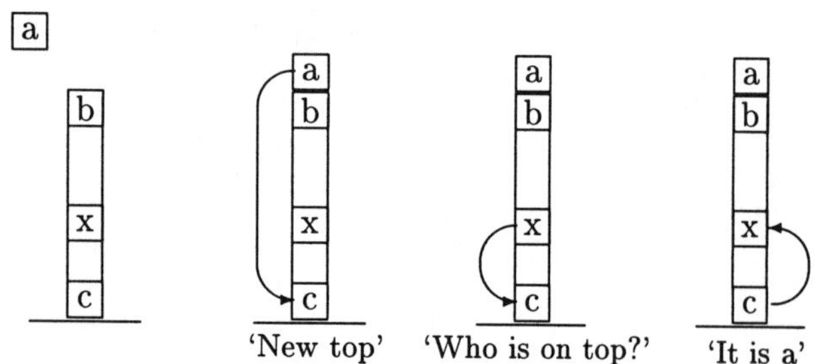

Figure 3: 'Who lives at the top of the tower?'

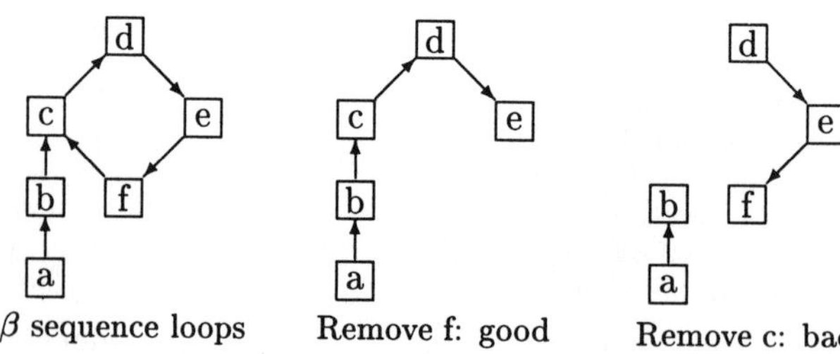

Figure 4: How [not] to break a deadlock

The first trick that begins to address these difficulties is to note that whatever changes in a tower of blocks, one thing does not change: the block on the table at the bottom of the tower. We call the bottom block in a tower the *concierge* for that tower. Now if we want to know who lives at the top of the tower, we can ask the concierge. When a block comes or goes at the top of the tower, only the concierge need be informed (in constant time) and then since every block knows which is its concierge, there is a constant time route from any given block to the information as to which block above it is clear (see Figure 3). Not only the towers in the initial (or current) state have concierges, but so do the towers in the goal state. These keep track of which block in their tower is the highest already in position. Additional variables associated with each block b denote its initial and goal concierges. In case b is a concierge, there are more variables denoting the clear block above it, and the highest block already in position in its goal tower. Through the concierges, there is a a constant time route from b to the c and d required to define $\delta_\pi(b)$. The procedure for initialising the additional variables is closely analogous to that for determining which blocks are in position and can be executed in linear time for the same reason. Updating them when a move is made takes constant time.

Next, the key to managing the Δ sequences is that although δ may change the B_π relation is indestructible except by moving the blocks involved. That is, if $B_{\langle\sigma,G\rangle}(x,y)$ then that relationship persists in the sense that in all future states θ, $B_{\langle\theta,G\rangle}(x,y)$ unless x or y has moved in getting from σ to θ. Moreover, if $B_\pi(x,y)$ then x cannot move constructively until y has moved at least once. Now, let $\beta = \langle b_1,\ldots,b_k\rangle$ be a non-looping sequence of clear blocks which are stuck on towers, each except the last linked to its successor by the relation B_π. At some point, b_k may cease to be stuck and become ready to move, but no other block in β can change its status until b_k actually moves. Thus the β sequence may dwindle, and even become null, as moves are made, but it always remains a single sequence—it never falls into two pieces as would happen if a block from the middle of it changed status—and because B_π is indestructible β remains linked by B_π. For the algorithm, then, we maintain such a sequence β, constructed from parts of Δ sequences as follows. Initially, β is null. If the problem becomes deadlocked, first if β is null then it is set to consist just of the block at the head of the 'stuck' list, and then it is extended by adding $\delta_\pi(b_k)$ to the end of it. This is done repeatedly until the sequence threatens to loop because δ_π of the last block b_m is already in β. At that point b_m is chosen to break the deadlock. It is important not to choose $\delta_\pi(b_m)$ for this purpose, since that could result in breaking β into two pieces (see Figure 4). Each addition to β takes only constant time, and any given block can be added to the sequence at most once. Therefore maintenance of the β sequence requires only linear time.

Pseudo-code for our implementations of both GN1 and GN2 is given in the technical report (Slaney & Thiébaux 1995).

Generating Random BW-Problems

In designing the experiments to be presented in the next section, we needed a supply of uniformly distributed random BW problems (pairs of BW states). Every state of the chosen size must have the same probability of being generated, otherwise the sample will be skewed and experiments on the average case may be biased. Note that, contrary to what might have been expected, generating such random BW states is not entirely trivial. Naïvely incorporating a random number generator into an algorithm for producing the states does not work: typically, it makes some states more probable than others by a factor exponential in the number of blocks. The unconvinced reader is invited to try by hand the case n=2 with a view to generating the three possible states each with a probability of 1/3 (most methods give probabilities 1/2, 1/4 and 1/4).

To build a BW state of size n, we start with the part-state containing n ungrounded towers each consisting of a single block, and extend this part-state progressively by selecting at each step an arbitrary ungrounded tower and placing it on top of another tower (already grounded or not) or putting it on the table. The difficulty is that the probabilities of these placements are not all the same.

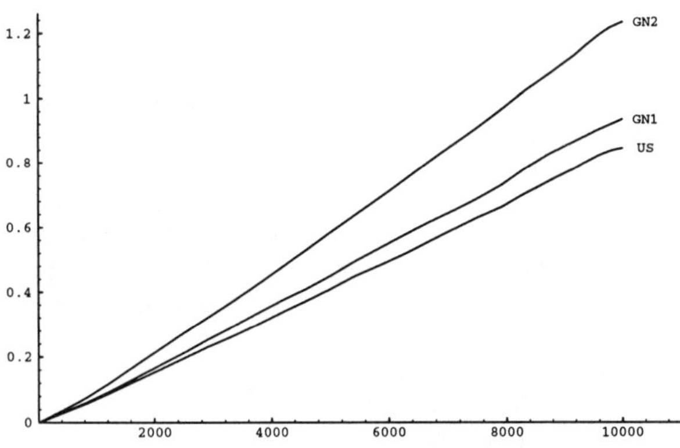

Figure 5: Average CPU time (in seconds)

The solution is to count the states that extend a part-state in which there are τ grounded towers and $\phi + 1$ ungrounded ones. Let this be $g(\phi + 1, \tau)$.[5] At the next step in the construction process, there will be ϕ ungrounded towers, since one ungrounded tower will have been placed on something. The probability that the selected tower will be on the table in an arbitrary reachable state is $g(\phi, \tau + 1)/g(\phi + 1, \tau)$ while each of the other possible placements has probability $g(\phi, \tau)/g(\phi + 1, \tau)$.

The recursive definition of g is quite simple. First $g(0, \tau) = 1$ for all τ, since if $\phi = 0$ then every tower is already grounded. Now consider $g(\phi + 1, \tau)$. In any reachable state, the first ungrounded tower is either on the table or on one of the $\phi + \tau$ other towers. If it goes on the table, that gives a part-state with ϕ ungrounded towers and with $\tau + 1$ grounded ones. If it goes on another tower, that leaves ϕ ungrounded towers and τ grounded ones. In sum:

$$g(\phi + 1, \tau) = g(\phi, \tau)(\phi + \tau) + g(\phi, \tau + 1)$$

An equivalent iterative definition is:

$$g(\phi, \tau) = \sum_{i=0}^{\phi} \binom{\phi}{i} \frac{(\phi + \tau - 1)!}{(i + \tau - 1)!} \qquad (\text{for } \phi + \tau > 0)$$

In fact, for present purposes it is hard to work with g directly, as the numbers rapidly become too large. For example, $g(100, 0) \simeq 2.4\ 10^{164}$. It is better to work with the ratio $\mathcal{R}(\phi, \tau) = g(\phi, \tau + 1) \,/\, g(\phi, \tau)$ since this is always a fairly small real number lying roughly in the range $1 \ldots \sqrt{\phi}$.[6] Elementary calculation shows that $\mathcal{R}(0, \tau) = 1$ for all τ and that

$$\mathcal{R}(\phi + 1, \tau) = \frac{\mathcal{R}(\phi, \tau)(\phi + \tau + 1 + \mathcal{R}(\phi, \tau + 1))}{\phi + \tau + \mathcal{R}(\phi, \tau)}$$

[5]As a special case, note that $g(n, 0)$ is the number of BW states of size n.

[6]In the limit, as ϕ becomes much larger than τ it converges to $\sqrt{\phi}$. On the other hand, where τ is much larger than ϕ the limiting value is 1 (Slaney & Thiébaux 1995). A corollary of these results is that the average number of towers in a state of n blocks converges to $\sqrt{n}$.

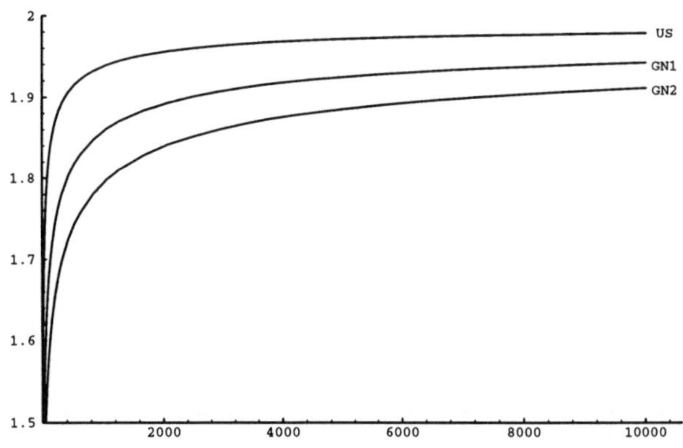

Figure 6: Average plan length: $\frac{\text{number of moves}}{\text{number of blocks}}$

Experimental Results

With a random BW states generator using $\mathcal{R}$ to calculate the relevant probabilities,[7] we generated between 1000 and 10000 random BW problems for each of the 160 sizes we considered, up to $n = 10000$ blocks. With this test set of some 735000 problems, we observed the average performance of US, GN1 and GN2. The graphs in this section are continuous lines passing through all data points.

Average Run Times

Figure 5 shows the average runtimes of the near-optimal algorithms as a function of n. As will be clear from the next experiment, there is no significant difference betweeen the average and worst cases runtimes. Times were obtained on a Sun 670 MP under Solaris 2.3. Naturally, since nobody really wants to convert one BW state into another, the program speeds are not important in themselves. The point of this experiment was just to confirm empirically the theoretical claims that linear execution time may be attained.

Average Plan Length

The length of the plan produced by all near-optimal algorithms, as well as the optimal plan length, is $2n - 2$ in the worst case. Figure 6 shows that the average case approaches this worst case quite closely. As expected, US gives the longest plans on average and GN2 the shortest, but for large numbers of blocks it makes little difference which algorithm is used. In particular, it is evident from the graphs that the algorithms will give very close (and maybe identical) average plan lengths in the limit.

The immediate questions raised by the present results are whether all of the algorithms converge to the same average plan length and if so whether this limiting figure is $2n$. For what our opinion is worth, we conjecture positive answers to both questions.

[7]The generator is made available by the first author at `http://arp.anu.edu.au/arp/jks/bwstates.html`.

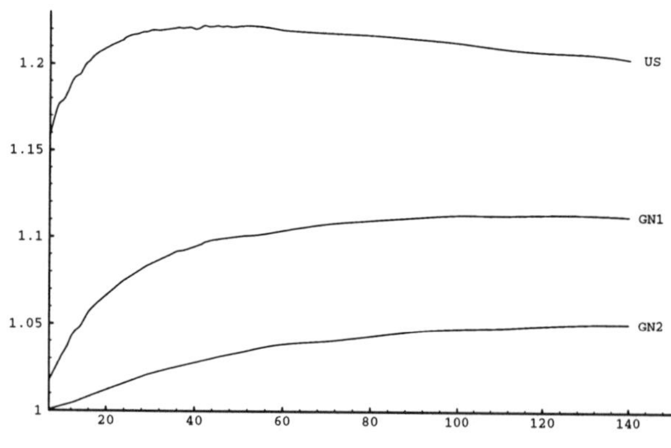

Figure 7: Average perf. ratio: $\frac{\text{plan length}}{\text{optimal plan length}}$

Average Performance Ratio

The *absolute* performance ratio of the near-optimal algorithms is 2 in the limit (for a description of the worst-case instances, see (Slaney & Thiébaux 1995)). Figure 7 shows the *average* performance ratios. The optimal plan lengths were determined by running an optimal BW planner (Slaney & Thiébaux 1995).

This graph contains a real surprise: the average performance of US does not degrade monotonically but turns around at about $n = 50$ and begins to improve thereafter. The explanation seems to be that the plan lengths for US quickly approach the ceiling of $2n$, at which point the optimal plan lengths are increasing more quickly than the US ones because the latter are nearly as bad as they can get. We expect that the other near-optimal algorithms would exhibit similar curves if it were possible to observe the length of optimal plans for high enough values of n.

One result readily available from the graphs is an upper bound around 1.23 for average performance ratios. However, Figures 6 and 7 together suggest that the limiting value will be well below this rough upper bound. Our open question following this experiment is whether the optimal plans tend to a length of $2n$ in the limit. If they do, then not only the near-optimal algorithms, but even the 'baby' algorithm of unstacking *all* blocks to the table before building the goal, are optimal on average in the limit. A positive answer would be implied if the number of singleton deadlocks tended to n, but on investigating this figure experimentally we found that it appears to be only around $0.4n$.

Conclusion and Future Work

By presenting linear time algorithms for near-optimal BW planning within a factor of 2, this paper has closed the question of its time complexity. We hope that both this result and the algorithms we have presented will contribute to clarification and thus to the understanding of BW planning needed for assessment purposes, and that the present paper will not be seen merely as a report on how to stack blocks fast.

While the time complexity questions have been closed, a number of open questions remain concerning the average solution quality of these algorithms. We do not believe that further experimentation alone will answer those questions, because this would require generating optimal BW plans for very large problems, which is impossible on complexity grounds. On the other hand, the theoretical investigation does not appear easy either. Indeed, even to prove (Slaney & Thiébaux 1995) that the average length of the plans produced by the 'baby' algorithm converges to $2(n - \sqrt{n})$ we needed nontrivial mathematics involving complex analysis and the theory of Laguerre polynomials.

Therefore, we consider that we have stopped at a convenient point. It appears likely that extensions of the present investigations will belong less directly to planning and increasingly to pure number theory. The most important future direction is to address the second goal mentioned in the introduction of this paper: to exploit our investigations in identifying a class of problems for which near-optimal planning is tractable, and to generalize them to related phenomena in planning domains of greater practical interest.

References

Bacchus, F., and Kabanza, F. 1995. Using temporal logic to control search in a forward chaining planner. In *Proc. EWSP-95*, 157–169.

Bäckström, C., and Nebel, B. 1995. Complexity results for SAS$^+$ planning. *Computational Intelligence* 11(4).

Bylander, T. 1994. The computational complexity of propositional STRIPS planning. *Artificial Intelligence* 69:165–204.

Chenoweth, S. 1991. On the NP-hardness of blocks world. In *Proc. AAAI-91*, 623–628.

Gupta, N., and Nau, D. 1991. Complexity results for blocks world planning. In *Proc. AAAI-91*, 629–633.

Gupta, N., and Nau, D. 1992. On the complexity of blocks world planning. *Artificial Intelligence* 56:223–254.

Kautz, H., and Selman, B. 1992. Planning as satisfiability. In *Proc. ECAI-92*, 359–363.

Kautz, H., and Selman, B. 1996. Pushing the envelope: Planning, propositional logic, and stochastic search. In *Proc. AAAI-96*. In this issue.

Schoppers, M. 1994. Estimating reaction plan size. In *Proc. AAAI-94*, 1238–1244.

Selman, B. 1994. Near-optimal plans, tractability, and reactivity. In *Proc. KR-94*, 521–529.

Slaney, J., and Thiébaux, S. 1995. Blocks world tamed: Ten thousand blocks in under a second. Technical Report TR-ARP-17-95, Automated Reasoning Project, Australian National University. `ftp://arp.anu.edu.au/pub/techreports`.

Planning for Temporally Extended Goals*

Fahiem Bacchus
Dept. of Computer Science
University of Waterloo
Waterloo, Ontario
Canada, N2L 3G1

Froduald Kabanza
Dept. de Math et Informatique
Universite de Sherbrooke
Sherbrooke, Quebec
Canada, J1K 2R1

Abstract

In planning, goals have traditionally been viewed as specifying a set of desirable final states. Any plan that transforms the current state to one of these desirable states is viewed to be correct. Goals of this form are limited as they do not allow us to constrain the manner in which the plan achieves its objectives.

We propose viewing goals as specifying desirable sequences of states, and a plan to be correct if its execution yields one of these desirable sequences. We present a logical language, a temporal logic, for specifying goals with this semantics. Our language is rich and allows the representation of a range of temporally extended goals, including classical goals, goals with temporal deadlines, quantified goals (with both universal and existential quantification), safety goals, and maintenance goals. Our formalism is simple and yet extends previous approaches in this area.

We also present a planning algorithm that can generate correct plans for these goals. This algorithm has been implemented, and we provide some examples of the formalism at work. The end result is a planning system which can generate plans that satisfy a novel and useful set of conditions.

Introduction

One of the features that distinguishes *intelligent* agents is their flexibility: generally they have the ability to accomplish a task in a variety of ways. Such flexibility is necessary if the agent is to be able to accomplish a variety of tasks under a range of conditions. Yet this flexibility also poses a problem: how do we communicate to such an agent the task we want accomplished in a sufficiently precise manner so that it does what we *really* want.

In the area of planning, methods and algorithms are studied by which, given information about the current situation, an intelligent agent can compose its primitive abilities so as to accomplish a desired task or goal. The afore mentioned problem then becomes the problem of designing sufficiently expressive and precise ways of specifying goals.

Much of the work in planning has dealt with goals specified as conditions on a final state. For example, we might specify a goal as a list of literals. The intent of such goals is that the agent should find a plan that will transform the current situation to a configuration that satisfies all of the literals in the goal. Any plan that achieves such a satisfying final state is deemed to be correct. However, there are many important constraints we might wish to place on the agent's behavior that simply cannot be expressed using these semantics for goals. The importance of specifying such constraints on the agent's plans has been recognized. For example, Weld and Etzioni [WE94] present strong arguments for looking beyond the simple achievement of a final state, and suggest two additional constraints on plans, a notion of *don't-disturb* and *restore*.

In this paper we present a richer formalism for specifying goals that borrows from work in verification [MP92], and develop a planning algorithm for generating plans to achieve such goals. Our formalism suggests a different way of viewing goals in planning. Instead of viewing goals as characterizing some set of acceptable final states and a plan as being correct if it achieves one of these states, we will view a goal as specifying a set of acceptable *sequences* of states and a plan as being correct if its execution results in one of these sequences. As we will show our formalism for goals subsumes the suggestions of Weld and Etzioni, except that instead of viewing *don't-disturb* and *restore* as constraints on plans, we view them as simply being *additional goals*.

Our formalism allows us to specify a wide range of *temporally extended goals*. This range includes classical goals of achieving some final state; goals with temporal deadlines; safety and maintenance goals like those discussed by Weld and Etzioni and others [HH93]; and quantified goals (both universally and existentially quantified). Furthermore, our formalism is a logical language that carries with it a precise, and quite intuitive, semantics. This latter is important, as without a precise semantics for our goals we will not be able to analyze and verify exactly what it is our agents will be accomplishing.

Temporally extended goals have previously been examined in the literature. Haddawy and Hanks [HH93] have provided utility models for some types of temporally extended goals. Kabanza et al. [Kab90, GK91, BKSD95] have developed methods for generating reactive plans that achieve temporally extended goals, as has Drummond [Dru89]. Plan-

* This work was supported by the by the Canadian government through their NSERC and IRIS programs. Fahiem Bacchus also wishes to thank the University of Toronto for hosting his sabbatical leave during which much of this work was accomplished.

ning systems and theories specifically designed to deal with temporal constraints (and sometimes other metric resources) have also been developed [Ver83, Wil88, AKRT91, CT91, Lan93, PW94].

The main difference between these previous works and what we present here, lies in our use of a temporal logic that supports a unique approach to computing plans, an approach based on formula progression. The method of formula progression lends itself naturally to the specification and utilization of domain dependent search control knowledge. As shown in our previous work [BK95], the approach of domain dependent search control offers considerable promise, and has motivated our approach to dealing with temporally extended goals. The other works that have constructed temporal planners have utilized complex constraint management techniques to deal with temporal information.

In [Kab90, GK91, BKSD95] similar temporal logics and similar notions of formula progression have been utilized. In this case the main difference is that here we address classical plans, i.e., finite sequences of actions, while these works have concentrated on generating reactive plans, i.e., mappings from states to actions (sometimes called universal plans). Reactive plans have to specify an on-going interaction between an agent and its environment, and thus pose a quite distinct set of problems.

To generate plans that achieve the goals expressed in our formalism we present a planning algorithm that uses the logical mechanism of formula progression. This notion was previously utilized in our TLPLAN system [BK95]. In fact we have implemented the planning algorithm by extending the TLPLAN system. TLPLAN is planning system whose key feature is that it is able to utilize domain dependent search control information.. This control is expressed in a temporal logic that is a limited form of the logic presented here, and it is utilized by the planner via the mechanism of formula progression.

The planning algorithm we develop is sound and complete and as we will demonstrate it is able to generate a range of interesting plans. Further work is required, however, to evaluate the planner's performance on realistic planning problems.

In the rest of the paper we will first provide the details of the logic we propose for expressing goals. This logic is a temporal logic that is based on previous work by Alur et al. [AFH91]. We then present our approach to planning, provide examples to demonstrate the range of goals that our system can cope with, and discuss the heuristic adequacy of our approach to planning. Finally, we close with some conclusions and discussion of future work.

Expressing goals in MITL

We use a logical language for expressing goals. The logic is based on Metric Interval Temporal Logic developed by Alur et al. [AFH91], but we have extended it to allow first-order quantification.

Syntax

We start with a collection of n-ary predicate (including equality and the predicate constants TRUE and FALSE) function and constant symbols, variables, and the connectives $\neg$ (not) and $\wedge$ (and). We add the quantifiers $\forall$ and $\exists$ and the modal operators $\bigcirc$ (next) and U (until). From this collection of symbols we generate MITL, the language we use to express goals. MITL is defined by the traditional rules for generating terms, atomic formulas, and Boolean combinations, taken from ordinary first-order logic. In addition to those formula formation rules we add: (1) if ϕ is a formula then so is $\bigcirc\phi$; (2) if ϕ_1 and ϕ_2 are formulas and I is an interval then so is $\phi_1 \mathsf{U}_I \phi_2$ (the syntax of intervals is defined below); and (3) if $\alpha(x)$ is an *atomic* formula in which the variable x is free, and ϕ is a formula then so are $\forall[x{:}\alpha(x)]\,\phi$, and $\exists[x{:}\alpha(x)]\,\phi$.

Notice that in our language we use *bounded* quantification. The atomic formula α is used to specify the range over which the quantified variable ranges. The precise semantics are given below.

The syntax of intervals is as one would expect. The allowed intervals are all intervals over the non-negative real line, and we specify an interval by giving its two endpoints, both of which are required to be non-negative numbers. To allow for unbounded intervals we allow the right endpoint to be ∞. For example, $[0,\infty)$ specifies the interval of numbers x such that $0 \leq x$, $(5.1, 6.1]$ specifies the interval $5.1 < x \leq 6.1$, and $[5,5]$ specifies the interval $5 \leq x \leq 5$ (i.e., the point $x = 5$).

Although non-negative intervals are the only ones allowed in the formulas of MITL, in the semantics and algorithms we will need to utilize shifted intervals and to test for negative intervals. For any interval I, let $I + r$ be the set of numbers x such that $x - r \in I$, $I - r$ be the set of numbers x such that $x + r \in I$, and $I < 0$ be true iff all numbers in I are less than 0. For example, $(5,\infty) + 2.5$ is the new interval $(7.5,\infty)$, $(0,2) - 2.5$ is the new interval $(-2.5,-0.5)$, and $(-2.5,-0.5) < 0$ is true.

Finally, we introduce $\Rightarrow$ (implication), and $\vee$ (disjunction) as standard abbreviations. We also introduce the temporal modalities eventually $\Diamond$ and always $\Box$ as abbreviations with $\Diamond_I\phi \equiv \text{TRUE}\ \mathsf{U}_I\ \phi$, and $\Box_I\phi \equiv \neg\Diamond_I\neg\phi$. We will also abbreviate intervals of the form (r,∞) and $[0,r)$, e.g., $\Diamond_{(r,\infty)}$ will be written as $\Diamond_{>r}$ and $\Box_{[0,4]}$ as $\Box_{\leq 4}$. Finally, we will often omit writing the interval $[0,\infty]$, e.g., we will write $\phi_1 \mathsf{U}_{[0,\infty]} \phi_2$ as $\phi_1 \mathsf{U}\, \phi_2$.[1]

Semantics

We intend that goals be expressed as sentences of the language MITL. As hinted in the introduction such formulas are intended to specify sets of sequences of states. Hence, it should not be surprising that the underlying semantics we assign to the formulas of MITL be in terms of state sequences.

[1]The temporal modalities with the interval $[0,\infty]$ correspond precisely to the traditional untimed modalities of Linear Temporal Logic [Eme90].

A model for MITL is a *timed sequence of states*, $M = \langle s_0, \ldots, s_n, \ldots \rangle$. In particular, a model is an infinite sequence of states, and each state is a first-order model over a fixed domain D. That is, each state s_i assigns a denotation for each predicate and function symbol over the domain D. Furthermore, there is a timing function $\mathcal{T}$ that maps each state s_i in M to a point on the non-negative real line such that for all i, $\mathcal{T}(s_i) \leq \mathcal{T}(s_{i+1})$ and for all real numbers r there exists an i such that $\mathcal{T}(s_i) > r$. This means that time is only required to be non-decreasing, not strictly increasing. Time can stall at a single point for any finite number of states. Eventually, however, time must increase without bound.

Let V be a variable assignment, i.e., a mapping from the variables to elements of D; ϕ, ϕ_1, and ϕ_2 be formulas of MITL; and M be an MITL model. The semantics of MITL are then defined by the following clauses.

- $\langle M, s_i, V\rangle \models \phi$, when ϕ is atemporal (i.e., contains no temporal modalities) and quantifier free, iff $\langle s_i, V\rangle \models \phi$.[2]
- $\langle M, s_i, V\rangle \models \bigcirc\phi$ iff $\langle M, s_{i+1}, V\rangle \models \phi$.
- $\langle M, s_i, V\rangle \models \phi_1 \, \mathsf{U}_I \, \phi_2$ iff there exists s_j with $\mathcal{T}(s_j) \in I + \mathcal{T}(s_i)$ such that $\langle M, s_j, V\rangle \models \phi_2$ and for all s_k with $i \leq k < j$ we have $\langle M, s_k, V\rangle \models \phi_1$.
- $\langle M, s_i, V\rangle \models \forall[x{:}\alpha(x)]\,\phi$ iff for all $d \in D$ such that $\langle s_i, V(x/d)\rangle \models \alpha(x)$ we have $\langle M, s_i, V(x/d)\rangle \models \phi$.
- $\langle M, s_i, V\rangle \models \exists[x{:}\alpha(x)]\,\phi$ iff there exists $d \in D$ such that $\langle s_i, V(x/d)\rangle \models \alpha(x)$ and $\langle M, s_i, V(x/d)\rangle \models \phi$.

It is not difficult to show that any formula of MITL that has no free variables, called a sentence of MITL, has a truth value that is independent of the variable assignment V. Given a sentence ϕ of MITL we say it is true in a model M, $M \models \phi$, iff $\langle M, s_0\rangle \models \phi$.

Since sentences of MITL are either true or false on any individual timed sequence of states, we can associate with every sentence a set of sequences: those sequences on which it is true. We express goals as sentences of MITL, hence we obtain our desired semantics for goals: a set of acceptable sequences.

Discussion

Intuitively, the temporal modalities can be explained as follows. The next modality $\bigcirc$ simply specifies that something must be true in the next state. Its semantics do not depend on the time of the states. It is important to realize, however, that what it requires to be true in the next state may itself be a formula containing temporal modalities. MITL gets its expressive power from its ability to nest temporal modalities.

The until modality is more subtle. The formula $\phi_1 \, \mathsf{U}_{[5,7]} \, \phi_2$, for example, requires that ϕ_2 be true in some state whose time is between 5 and 7 units into the future, and that ϕ_1 be true in all states until we reach a state where ϕ_2 is true. The eventually modality thus takes on the semantics that $\Diamond_I\phi$ requires that ϕ be true in some state whose time lies in the interval I, and $\Box_I\phi$ requires that ϕ be true in all states whose time lies in I.

Turning to the clauses for the bounded quantifiers we see that the range of the quantifier is being restricted to the set of domain elements that satisfy α. If α is true of all domain individuals, then the bounded quantifiers become equivalent to ordinary quantification. Similarly, we could express bounded quantification with ordinary quantifiers using the syntactic equivalences $\forall[x{:}\alpha(x)]\,\phi \equiv \forall x.\alpha(x) \Rightarrow \phi$ and $\exists[x{:}\alpha(x)]\,\phi \equiv \exists x.\alpha(x) \wedge \phi$. We have defined MITL to use bounded quantification because we will need to place finiteness restrictions on quantification when we do planning.

[2]Note that s_i is a first-order model, so the relationship "$\langle s_i, V\rangle \models \phi$" is defined according to the standard rules for first-order semantics.

Planning

Planning Assumptions and Restrictions

Now we turn to the problem of generating plans for goals expressed in the language MITL. First we specify the assumptions we are making. (1) We have as input a complete description of the initial state. (2) Actions preserve this completeness. That is, if an action is applied to a completely described state, then the resulting state will also be completely described. (3) Actions are deterministic; that is, in any world they must produce a unique successor world. (4) Plans are finite sequences of actions. (5) Only the agent who is executing the plan changes the world. That is, there are no other agents nor any exogenous events. (6) All quantifier bounds, i.e., the atomic formulas $\alpha(x)$ used in the definition of quantified formulas, range over a *finite* subset of the domain.

These assumptions allow us to focus on a particular extension of planning technology. They are essentially the same assumptions as made in classical planning. For example, the assumption that actions preserve completeness is implied by the standard STRIPS assumption.

It is possible to weaken our assumptions of completeness. Incomplete state descriptions will suffice as long as they are complete enough to (1) determine the truth of the preconditions of every action and (2) determine the truth of all atemporal subformulas of the goal formula. The price that is paid however is efficiency, instead of a database lookup, theorem proving may be required to determine the truth of these two items. However, more conservative notions of incompleteness like locally closed worlds [EGW94] could be utilized in our framework without imposing a large computational burden.

Also, it should be made clear that restricting ourselves to deterministic actions does not mean actions cannot have conditional effects. In fact, the planner we implemented handles full ADL conditional actions [Ped89] including actions with disjunctive and existentially quantified preconditions.

Plan Correctness

Given a goal g expressed as a sentence of MITL we want to develop a method for generating plans that satisfy g. Sentences of MITL are satisfied by the timed state sequences described above. Hence, to determine whether or not a plan satisfies g we must provide a semantics for plans in terms of the models of MITL.

Inputs: A state s_i, with formula label ϕ, and a time duration Δ to the successor state.
Output: A new formula ϕ^+ representing the formula label of the successor state.
Algorithm *Progress*(ϕ,s_i,Δ)
Case

1. ϕ contains no temporal modalities:
   if $s_i \models \phi$ $\quad \phi^+ :=$ TRUE
   else $\quad \phi^+ :=$ FALSE
2. $\phi = \phi_1 \wedge \phi_2$: $\quad \phi^+ := \mathit{Progress}(\phi_1, s_i, \Delta) \wedge \mathit{Progress}(\phi_2, s_i, \Delta)$
3. $\phi = \neg\phi_1$: $\quad \phi^+ := \neg\mathit{Progress}(\phi_1, s_i, \Delta)$
4. $\phi = \bigcirc\phi_1$: $\quad \phi^+ := \phi_1$
5. $\phi = \phi_1 \,\mathsf{U}_I\, \phi_2$:
   if $I < 0$ $\quad \phi^+ :=$ FALSE
   else if $0 \in I$ $\quad \phi^+ := \mathit{Progress}(\phi_2, s_i, \Delta) \vee (\mathit{Progress}(\phi_1, s_i, \Delta) \wedge \phi_1 \,\mathsf{U}_{I-\Delta}\, \phi_2)$
   else $\quad \mathit{Progress}(\phi_1, s_i, \Delta) \wedge \phi_1 \,\mathsf{U}_{I-\Delta}\, \phi_2$
6. $\phi = \forall[x{:}\alpha]\,\phi_1$: $\quad \phi^+ := \bigwedge_{\{c:s_i \models \alpha(c)\}} \mathit{Progress}(\phi_1(x/c), s_i, \Delta)$
7. $\phi = \exists[x{:}\alpha]\,\phi_1$: $\quad \phi^+ := \bigvee_{\{c:s_i \models \alpha(c)\}} \mathit{Progress}(\phi_1(x/c), s_i, \Delta)$

Table 1: The progression algorithm.

Since actions map states to new states, any finite sequence of actions will generate a finite sequence of states: the states that would arise as the plan is executed. Furthermore, we will assume that part of an action's specification is a specification of its duration, which is constrained to be greater than or equal to 0. This means that if we consider s_0 to commence at time 0, then every state that is visited by the plan can be given a time stamp. Hence, a plan gives rise to a finite timed sequence of states—almost a suitable model for MITL.

The only difficulty is that models of MITL are infinite sequences. Intuitively, we intend to control the agent for some finite time, up until the time the agent completes the execution of its plan. Since we are assuming that the agent is the only source of change, once it has completed the plan the final state of the plan *idles*, i.e., it remains unchanged. Formally, we define the MITL model corresponding to a plan as follows:

Definition 1 Let plan P be the finite sequence of actions $\langle a_1, \ldots, a_n \rangle$. Let $S = \langle s_0, \ldots, s_n \rangle$ be the sequence of states such that $s_i = a_i(s_{i-1})$, and s_0 is the initial state. S is the sequence of states visited by the plan. Then the MITL *model corresponding to* P *and* s_0 is defined to be $\langle s_0, \ldots, s_n, s_n, \ldots \rangle$, i.e., S with the final state s_n idled, where $\mathcal{T}(s_i) = \mathcal{T}(s_{i-1}) + \mathit{duration}(a_i)$, $0 < i \leq n$, $\mathcal{T}(s_0) = 0$, and the time of the copies of s_n increases without bound.

Therefore, every finite sequence of actions we generate corresponds to a *unique* model in which the final state is idling. Given a goal expressed as a sentence of MITL we can determine, using the semantics defined above, whether or not the plan satisfies the goal.

Definition 2 Let P be a plan, g be a goal expressed as a formula of MITL, s_0 be the initial state, and M be the model corresponding to P and s_0. P is a *correct plan* for g given s_0 iff $M \models g$.

Generating Plans

We will generate plans by adopting the methodology of our previous work [BK95]. In particular, we have constructed a forward-chaining planning engine that generates linear sequences of actions, and thus linear sequences of states. As these linear sequences of states are generated we *incrementally* check them against the goal. Whenever we can show that achieving the goal is impossible along a particular sequence we can prune that sequence and all of its possible extensions from the search space. And we can stop when we find a sequence that satisfies the goal. The incremental checking mechanism is accomplished by the logical progression of the goal formula.

Formula Progression The technique of formula progression works by labeling the initial state with the sentence representing the goal, call it g. For each successor of the initial state, generated by forward chaining, a new formula label is generated by *progressing* the initial state's label using the algorithm given in Table 1. This new formula is used to label the successor states. This process continues. Every time a state is expanded during planning search each of its successors is given a new label generated by progression.

Intuitively a state's label specifies a condition that we are looking for. That is, we want to find a sequence of states starting from this state that satisfies the label. The purpose of the progression algorithm is to update this label as we extend the state sequence. It takes as input the current state and the duration of the action that yields the successor state.

The logical relationship between the input formula and output formula of the algorithm is characterized by the following proposition:

Proposition 3 *Let* $M = \langle s_0, s_1, \ldots \rangle$ *be any MITL model. Then, we have for any formula* ϕ *of MITL,* $\langle M, s_i \rangle \models \phi$ *if and only if* $\langle M, s_{i+1} \rangle \models \mathit{Progress}(\phi, s_i, \mathcal{T}(s_{i+1}) - \mathcal{T}(s_i))$.

This proposition can easily be proved by utilizing the definition of MITL semantics.

Say that we label the start state, s_0, with the formula ϕ, and we generate new labels using the progression algorithm. Furthermore, say we find a sequence of states, $S = \langle s, s^1, s^2, \ldots \rangle$, starting at state s that satisfies s's label. Then a simple induction using Proposition 3 shows that the sequence leading from s_0 to s followed by the sequence S, i.e., $\langle s_0, \ldots, s, s^1, s^2, \ldots \rangle$, satisfies ϕ. The progression algorithm keeps the labels up to date: they specify what we are looking for given that we have arrived where we are.

From this insight we can identify two important features of the formula progression mechanism. First, if we find any state whose idling satisfies its label, we have found a correct plan.

Proposition 4 *Let* $\langle s_0, s_1, \ldots, s_n \rangle$ *be a sequence of states generated by forward chaining from the initial state* s_0 *to* s_n. *For each state* s_i *let its label be* $\ell(s_i)$. *Let the labels of the states be computed via progression, i.e., for each state* s_i *in the sequence*

$$\ell(s_{i+1}) = \mathit{Progress}(\ell(s_i), s_i, \mathcal{T}(s_{i+1}) - \mathcal{T}(s_i)).$$

Inputs: A state s, and a formula ϕ.
Output: True if the state sequence $\langle s, s, \ldots \rangle$, where time increases without bound, satisfies ϕ. False otherwise.
Algorithm *Idle*(ϕ,s)
Case
1. ϕ contains no temporal modalities:
   if $s \models \phi$ **return** TRUE
   else **return** FALSE
2. $\phi = \phi_1 \wedge \phi_2$: **return** $\mathit{Idle}(\phi_1, s) \wedge \mathit{Idle}(\phi_2, s)$
3. $\phi = \neg\phi_1$: **return** $\neg\mathit{Idle}(\phi_1, s)$
4. $\phi = \circ\phi_1$: **return** $\mathit{Idle}(\phi_1, s)$
5. $\phi = \phi_1 \mathsf{U}_I \phi_2$:
   if $I < 0$ **return** FALSE
   else if $0 \in I$ **return** $\mathit{Idle}(\phi_2, s)$
   else **return** $\mathit{Idle}(\phi_1, s) \wedge \mathit{Idle}(\phi_2, s)$
6. $\phi = \forall[x{:}\alpha]\phi_1$: **return** $\bigwedge_{\{c: s \models \alpha(c)\}} \mathit{Idle}(\phi_1(x/c), s)$
7. $\phi = \exists[x{:}\alpha]\phi_1$: **return** $\bigvee_{\{c: s \models \alpha(c)\}} \mathit{Idle}(\phi_1(x/c), s)$

Table 2: The idling algorithm.

Then $M = \langle s_0, , \ldots, s_n, s_n, \ldots \rangle \models \ell(s_0)$ *iff* $\langle s_n, s_n, \ldots \rangle \models \ell(s_n)$.

The proof of this proposition follows directly from Proposition 3.

Since $\ell(s_0)$ is a formula specifying the goal, this proposition shows that the plan leading to s_n satisfies the goal. Hence, if we have a method for testing for any state s and any formula $\phi \in$ MITL whether or not $\langle s, s, \ldots \rangle \models \phi$, we have a termination test for the planning algorithm that guarantees soundness of the algorithm. We will describe an appropriate method below.

Furthermore, as long as the search procedure used by the algorithm eventually examines all finite sequences of states the planning algorithm will also be complete.

The second feature of formula progression is that it allows us to prune the search space without losing completeness. As we compute the progressed label we simplify it by processing all TRUE and FALSE subformulas. For example, if the label $\phi \wedge$ TRUE is generated we simplify this to ϕ. If any state receives the label FALSE we can prune it from the search space, thus avoiding searching any of its successors. From Proposition 3 we know that this label specifies a requirement on the sequences that start at this state. No sequence can satisfy the requirement FALSE, hence no sequences starting from this state can satisfy the goal and this state and its successors can be safely pruned from the search space.

Termination As indicated above, we can detect when a plan satisfies the goal if we can detect when an idling state satisfies its label. This computation is accomplished by the algorithm given in Table 2.

Proposition 5 *Idle*(ϕ, s) *returns* TRUE *if and only if* $\langle s, s, \ldots \rangle \models \phi$. *That is, Idle detects if an idling state satisfies a formula.*

The Planning Algorithm Given the pieces developed in the previous sections we specify the planning algorithm presented in Table 3. The algorithm labels the initial state with the goal and searches among the space of state-formula pairs. We test for termination by running the *Idle* algorithm on the state's formula. To expand a state-formula pair we apply all applicable actions to its state component, returning all pairs containing a successor state and the action that produced that state (this is accomplished by Expand(s)). We then compute the new labels for those successor states using the *Progress* algorithm.

Inputs: An initial state s_0, and a sentence $g \in$ MITL specifying the goal.
Returns: A plan P consisting of finite sequence of actions.
Algorithm *Plan*(g,s)
1. Open $\leftarrow \{(g, s_0)\}$.
2. **While** Open is not empty.
   2.1 $(\phi, s) \leftarrow$ Remove an element of Open.
   2.2 **if** $\mathit{Idle}(\phi, s)$ **Return** $((\phi, s))$.
   2.3 Successors $\leftarrow$ Expand(s).
   2.4 **For** all $(s^+, a) \in$ Successors
      2.4.1 $\phi^+ \leftarrow \mathit{Progress}(\phi, s, \mathit{duration}(a))$.
      2.4.2 **if** $\phi^+ \neq$ FALSE
         2.4.2.1 Parent$((\phi^+, s^+)) \leftarrow (\phi, s)$.
         2.4.2.2 Open $\leftarrow$ Open $\cup \{(s^+, \phi^+)\}$.

Table 3: The planning algorithm.

It should be noted that we cannot treat action sequences that visit the same state as being cyclic. If we are only looking for a path to a final state, as in classical planning, we could eliminate such cycles. Goals in MITL, however, can easily require visiting the same state many times. Nevertheless, we can view visiting the same state-formula pair as a cycle, and optimize those cycles using the standard techniques.[3] Intuitively, when we visit the same state-formula node we have arrived at a point in the search were we are searching for the same set of extensions to the same state.

Proposition 6 *The planning algorithm is sound and complete. That is, it produces a plan that is correct for g given* s_0 *(Definition 2), and so long as nodes are selected from Open in such a manner that every node is eventually selected, it will find a correct plan if one exists.*

This proposition follows from the soundness of our termination test (Proposition 4).

We have implemented the planning algorithm as an extension of the TLPLAN system [Bac95]. This allowed us to utilize many of the features already built into the TLPLAN system, including full support of the ADL formalism [Ped89] for specifying actions.

Example and Empirical Results

Types of Goals

The domain we used is a variant of the classical STRIPS robot rooms domain [FN71]. The configuration of the rooms is illustrated in Figure 1. In this domain there are objects and a robot, which can be located at any of the 2 locations in the corridor, $C1$ or $C4$, or any of the 4 rooms $R1, \ldots, R4$. The robot can move between connected locations, it can

[3] For example, we can eliminate that node or search from it again if the new path we have found to it is better than the old path. These considerations will determine how we decide to set Parent$((\phi^+, s^+))$ in step 2.4.2.1

Operator	Precondition	Adds	Deletes
open($?d$)	$at(robot, ?x)$ $connects(?d, ?x, ?y)$ $closed(?d)$ $door(?d)$	$opened(?d)$	$closed(?d)$
close($?d$)	$at(robot, ?x)$ $connects(?d, ?x, ?y)$ $opened(?d)$ $door(?d)$	$closed(?d)$	$opened(?d)$
grasp($?o$)	$at(robot, ?x)$ $at(?o, ?x)$ $handempty$ $object(?o)$	$holding(?o)$	$handempty(?d)$
release($?o$)	$holding(?o)$	$handempty$	$holding(?o)$
move($?x, ?y$)	$at(robot, ?x)$ $connects(?d, ?x, ?y)$ $opened(?d)$	$at(robot, ?y)$ $holding(?o) \Rightarrow at(?o, ?y)$	$at(robot, ?x)$ $holding(?o) \Rightarrow at(?o, ?x)$

Table 4: Operators for Robot Room domain.

open and close doors (indicated as gaps in the walls), and it can grasp and carry one object at a time. The operators that characterize its capabilities are shown in Table 4. In this table variables are preceded by a question mark "?". Also, the *move* operator is an ADL operator with conditional effects. For all objects that the robot is holding it updates their position. This is indicated in Table 4 by the notation $f_1 \Rightarrow \ell$ in the add and delete columns: the literal ℓ is added or deleted if f_1 holds. The duration of most of the actions is set to 1. Our implementation allows us to set the duration of an action to be dependent on the instantiation of its parameters. In particular, we set the duration of $move(x, y)$ to be 1, except for $move(C1, C4)$ which has duration 3.

Any initial state for this domain must specify the location of the robot and the existence and location of any objects in the domain. It must also specify whether each door is opened or closed. The doors connect the rooms to each other and to the corridor locations, and a set of *connects* relations must be specified, e.g., $connects(D1, C1, R1)$. Door $D1$ connects the corridor location $C1$ and $R1$, door $D4$ connects $C4$ and $R4$, and the doors Dij connect rooms Ri and Rj ($i, j \in \{1, 2, 3\}$).

Finally, the two corridor locations are connected by a "*corridor*" which is always "open". So literals of the form $connects(corridor, C1, C4)$, and $opened(corridor)$, must also be present in the initial state description.

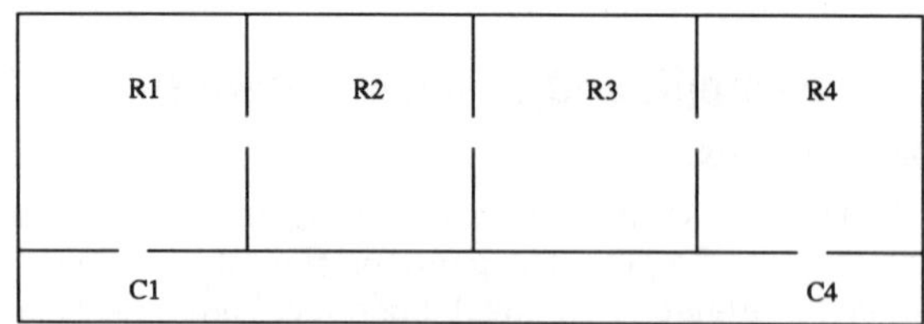

Figure 1: Robot Room domain

Classical Goals: Classical goals can easily be encoded as untimed eventualities that hold forever. For example, the classical goal $\{at(robot, C1), at(objl, R4)\}$ expressed as a set of literals, can be encoded as the MITL formula $\Diamond\Box(at(robot, C1) \wedge at(objl, R4))$. Any classical goal can be encoded in this manner. Given the semantics of plans as idling their final state, this formula will be satisfied by a plan only if the final state satisfies the goal.

More generally we can specify a classical "achieve a final state" goal by enclosing any atemporal formula of our language in an eventuality. We can specify disjunctive goals, negated conditions, quantified goals, etc. The formula $\Diamond(\exists[x{:}object(x)]\, at(x, R4) \vee at(robot, R4))$, for example, specifies the goal state where some object or the robot is in room $R4$.

Safety and Maintenance Goals: In [WE94] Weld and Etzioni discuss the need for safety conditions in plans. Such conditions have also been studied in the verification literature [MP92]. MITL can express a wide range of such conditions. Maintenance goals (e.g., [HH93]) which involve keeping some condition intact, are very similar.

Weld and Etzioni propose two specific constructions, *don't-disturb* and *restore*, as a start towards the general goal of expressing safety conditions. Both of these constructions are easily encoded as goals in MITL.

Don't-disturb specifies a condition $\phi(x)$. A plan is defined to satisfy a *don't-disturb* condition if during its execution no instantiation of $\phi(x)$ changes truth value. Such conditions are easily specified by conjoining the formula $\forall x.\phi(x) \Rightarrow \Box\phi(x)$ to the original goal.[4] For example, the goal $\Diamond\Box(at(robot, C1) \wedge at(objl, R4)) \wedge \forall[x{:}opened(x)]\, \Box opened(x)$, can only be satisfied by a plan that does not disturb any open doors.

Restore also specifies a condition $\phi(x)$. A plan satisfies a *restore* condition if it tidies up after it has finished. That is, at the end of its plan it must append a new plan to restore the truth of all instantiations of $\phi(x)$ that held in the initial state.

We can specify *restore* goals in MITL by conjoining the formula $\forall x.\phi(x) \Rightarrow \Diamond\Box\phi(x)$, which specifies that the final state of the plan must satisfy all instantiations of ϕ that held

[4]We must appropriately rewrite $\forall x.\phi(x)$ in terms of bounded quantification. Also it is not difficult to see that multiple variables in ϕ can be handled by additional quantifiers. Similar remarks hold for encoding *restore*.

in the initial state.[5] Notice that the semantic distinction between *restore* and *don't-disturb* goals is made clear by our formalism. *Restore* goals use $\Diamond\Box$ while *don't-disturb* goals use $\Box$. That is, *restore* goals allow the violation of ϕ during the plan, as long as these conditions are eventually restored in the final state.

Both of these conditions are limited special cases. MITL can express much more than this. For example, say that we want to constrain the robot to close doors that it opens. We cannot place a *don't-disturb* condition $closed(x)$, as this would prohibit the robot from moving into rooms where the doors are closed. If we specify this as a *restore* condition, the robot might leave a door opened for a very long time until it has finished the rest of its plan. In MITL, however we can use the formula

$$\begin{aligned}&\Box(\forall[x, y, z{:}connects(z, x, y)] \qquad (1)\\ &\quad at(robot, x) \wedge closed(z) \wedge \bigcirc open(z)\\ &\quad \Rightarrow \bigcirc\bigcirc at(robot, y) \wedge \bigcirc\bigcirc\bigcirc closed(z))\end{aligned}$$

This formula specifies that if the robot opens a closed door ($closed(z) \wedge \bigcirc(open(z))$), then it must go through the door ($\bigcirc\bigcirc at(robot, y)$) and then it must close the door ($\bigcirc\bigcirc\bigcirc closed(z)$). Hence, the robot is forced to be tidy with respect to doors: it only opens doors for the purpose of moving through them, and it closes the doors it opens behind it.

Timing Deadlines: MITL is also capable of expressing goals with timing conditions. For example $\Box_{\geq 10}\phi$ requires the condition ϕ be achieved within ten time units.

Empirical Results

We have tested different goals from each of the categories mentioned above. Most of the plans were generated from the initial state in which $at(objl, R1)$, $at(obj2, R2)$, $at(robot, C1)$, *handempty*, $object(objl)$, $object(obj2)$, and all of the doors are opened.

G1: From this initial state we set the goal to be $\Diamond\Box(at(robot, C1) \wedge at(objl, R2))$. This corresponds to the classical goal $\{at(robot, C1), at(objl, R2)\}$. The planner generates the plan: $move(C1, R1)$, $grasp(objl)$, $move(R1, R2)$, $release(objl)$, $move(R2, R1)$, $move(R1, C1)$. It took the planner 22 sec., expanding 636 worlds to find this plan.[6]

G2: From the same initial state we set the goal to be $\Diamond\Box(\exists[x{:}object(x)]\, at(x, R3) \wedge handempty)$. Now the planner generates the plan: $move(C1, R1)$, $move(R1, R2)$, $grasp(O2)$, $move(R2, R3)$, $release(O2)$. In this case it has generated a plan for a quantified goal. This plan takes the planner 3 sec., expanding 126 worlds to find the plan.

[5] When we add this formula as a conjunct to the original goal we force the planner to find a plan that satisfies the restore. If we want to give *restore* conditions lower priority, as discussed in [WE94], we could resort to the techniques of replanning suggested there.

[6] Timings are taken on a SPARC station 20, and a breadth first strategy was used so as to find the shortest plans.

G3: Now we change the initial state so all of the doors are closed. We set the goal to be $\Diamond\Box(at(robot, C1) \wedge at(objl, R2))$ conjoined with Formula 1. This is simply a classical goal with an additional constraint on the robot to ensure it closes doors behind it. For this goal the planner generates the plan $open(D1)$, $move(C1, R1)$, $close(D1)$, $grasp(O1)$, $open(D12)$, $move(R1, R2)$, $close(D12)$, $release(O1)$, $open(D12)$, $move(R2, R1)$, $close(D12)$, $open(D1)$, $move(R1, C1)$, $close(D1)$. This plan took the planner 77 sec., expanding 1571 worlds, to find.

G4: We reset the initial state to one where all of the doors are open and set the goal to be $\Box_{\geq 20} at(objl, R4) \wedge \Box_{\geq 5} at(obj2, R3) \wedge \forall[x{:}opened(x)]\, \Box opened(x)$. This is a goal with a tight deadline. The robot must move directly to $R2$ and move *obj2* to $R3$. If it stops to grasp *objl* along the way it will fail to get *obj2* into $R3$ on time. Also we conjoin a subgoal of not closing any open doors. As we will discuss below this safety constraint acts as a form of search control, it stops the planner pursing useless (for this goal) *close* actions. The planner generates the plan: $move(C1, R1)$, $move(R1, R2)$, $grasp(O2)$, $move(R2, R3)$, $release(O2)$, $move(R3, R2)$, $move(R2, R1)$, $grasp(O1)$, $move(R1, R2)$, $move(R2, R3)$, $move(R3, R4)$. This plan took the planner 8 sec., expanding 284 worlds, to find.

G5: If we change the time deadlines in the previous goal and set the goal it to be $\Box_{\geq 9} at(objl, R4) \wedge \Box_{\geq 20} at(obj2, R3) \wedge \forall[x{:}opened(x)]\, \Box opened(x)$ The planner generates the plan: $move(C1, R1)$, $grasp(O1)$, $move(R1, R2)$, $move(R2, R3)$, $move(R3, R4)$, $release(O1)$, $move(R4, R3)$, $move(R3, R2)$, $grasp(O2)$, $move(R2, R3)$. It took the planner 120 sec. to find this plan, expanding 1907 worlds on the way.

Search Control

Although our planner can generate an interesting range of plans, by itself it is not efficient enough for practical problems. For example, when it is only given the goal of achieving some final state, it has to resort to blind search to find a plan. Similarly, it has no special mechanisms for planning for quantified goals, it simply searches until it finds a state satisfying the goal. Safety goals offer better performance, as such goals prune the search space of sequences that falsify them. This is why we included safety conditions on open doors in the fourth and fifth tests above: they allow the planner to find a plan faster. Again for goals with complex timing constraints, the planner does not utilize any special temporal reasoning.

The major advantage of our approach lies in the ability of the planner to utilize domain dependent search control information. Such information can be expressed as formulas of MITL and conjoined with the goal. We have explored this approach to search control in [BK95] where we demonstrate that is often possible to construct *polynomial time* planners using quite simple search control knowledge. We know of no other approach to increasing the efficiency of planners that has been able to produce polynomial time behavior in these domains.

As a simple illustration of the power of this using search control consider the following trivial search control formula:

$$\Box\Big(\forall[x{:}at(robot,x)]\ \neg(\bigcirc\neg at(robot,x) \land \bigcirc\bigcirc at(robot,x)) \land \forall[z{:}object(z)]\ \neg(\neg holding(z) \land \bigcirc holding(z) \land \bigcirc\bigcirc\neg holding(z))\Big)$$

If we conjoin this formula with any other goal, the planner will prune sequences in which (1) the robot grasps an object and then immediately releases it, and (2) the robot moves away from a location and then immediately moves back. For this domain these sequences serve no purpose even in plans where the robot must visit the same state more than once.[7]

Conjoining this formula with the example goals given above we obtain the following speedups.

Example	Time	World	New-Time	New-Worlds
1	22	636	12	405
2	3	126	2	93
3	77	1571	18	304
4	8	284	1	38
5	120	1907	7.75	199

The columns give the planning time and the number of worlds expanded, before and after we add the search control formula. Note in particular, the speedups obtained on the harder problems. Furthermore, it should be noted that this is only the simplest and most obvious of control formulas for this domain.

References

[AFH91] Rajeev Alur, Tomas Feder, and Thomas Henzinger. The benefits of relaxing punctuality. In *Tenth Annual ACM Symposium on Principles of Distributed Computing (PODC 1991)*, pages 139–152, 1991.

[AKRT91] J. Allen, H. Kautz, Pelavin R., and J. Tenenberg. *Reasoning about Plans*. Morgan Kaufmann, San Mateo, CA, 1991.

[Bac95] Fahiem Bacchus. Tlplan (version 2.0) user's manual. Available via the URL ftp://logos.uwaterloo.ca:/pub/bacchus/tlplan-manual.ps.Z, 1995.

[BK95] Fahiem Bacchus and Froduald Kabanza. Using temporal logic to control search in a forward chaining planner. In *Proceedings of the 3rd European Workshop on Planning*, 1995. Available via the URL ftp://logos.uwaterloo.ca:/pub/tlplan/tlplan.ps.Z.

[BKSD95] M. Barbeau, F. Kabanza, and R. St-Denis. Synthesizing plant controllers using real-time goals. In *Proc. Thirteenth International Joint Conference on Artificial Intelligence (IJCAI '95)*, pages 791–798, 1995.

[CT91] K. Currie and A. Tate. O-plan: the open planning architecture. *Artificial Intelligence*, 52:49–86, 1991.

[7] In general, in order to achieve some timed goals we may need to allow the robot to wait. But, in that case it is more effective to introduce a specific wait action and still outlaw pointless cycles.

[Dru89] M. Drummond. Situated control rules. In *Proc. First International Conference on Principles of Knowledge Representation and Reasoning (KR '89)*, pages 103–113. Morgan Kaufmann, 1989.

[EGW94] O. Etzioni, K. Golden, and D. Weld. Tractable closed world reasoning with updates. In *Principles of Knowledge Representation and Reasoning: Proc. Forth International Conference (KR '94)*, pages 178–189, 1994.

[Eme90] E. A. Emerson. Temporal and modal logic. In J. van Leeuwen, editor, *Handbook of Theoretical Computer Science, Volume B*, chapter 16, pages 997–1072. MIT, 1990.

[FN71] Richard Fikes and Nils Nilsson. Strips: A new approach to the application of theorem proving to problem solving. *Artificial Intelligence*, 2:189–208, 1971.

[GK91] P. Godefroid and F. Kabanza. An efficient reactive planner for synthesizing reactive plans. In *Proc. National Conference on Artificial Intelligence (AAAI '91)*, pages 640–645, 1991.

[HH93] P. Haddawy and S. Hanks. Utility models for goal-directed decision-theoretic planners. Technical Report 93–06–04, University of Washington, 1993. Technical Report.

[Kab90] F. Kabanza. Synthesis of reactive plans for multi-path environments. In *Proc. National Conference on Artificial Intelligence (AAAI '90)*, pages 164–169, 1990.

[Lan93] A. Lansky. Localized planning with diversified plan construction methods. Technical Report T.R. FIA-93-17, NASA Ames Research Center, 1993. Technical Report.

[MP92] Zohar Manna and Amir Pnueli. *The temporal logic of reactive and concurrent systems: Specication*. Springer-Verlag, New York, 1992.

[Ped89] E. Pednault. ADL: Exploring the middle ground between STRIPS and the situation calculus. In *Proc. First International Conference on Principles of Knowledge Representation and Reasoning (KR '89)*, pages 324–332, 1989.

[PW94] J. Scott Penberthy and Daniel Weld. Temporal planning with continuous change. In *Proc. National Conference on Artificial Intelligence (AAAI '94)*, pages 1010–1015. Morgan Kaufmann, 1994.

[Sch87] M. J. Schoppers. Universal plans for reactive robots in unpredictable environments. In *Proc. Tenth International Joint Conference on Artificial Intelligence (IJCAI '87)*, pages 1039–1046, 1987.

[Ver83] S. Vere. Planning in time: Windows and durations for activities and goals. *IEEE Trans. on Pattern Analysis and Machine Intelligence*, 5, 1983.

[WE94] Daniel Weld and Oren Etzioni. The first law of robotics (a call to arms). In *Proc. National Conference on Artificial Intelligence (AAAI '94)*, pages 1042–1047, 1994.

[Wil88] D. Wilkins. *Practical Planning*. Morgan Kaufmann, San Mateo, CA, 1988.

A Cost-Directed Planner: Preliminary Report

Eithan Ephrati
AgentSoft Ltd. and
Department of Mathematics
and Computer Science
Bar Ilan University
Ramat Gan 52900, ISRAEL
tantush@sunlight.cs.biu.ac.il

Martha E. Pollack
Computer Science Department
and Intelligent Systems Program
University of Pittsburgh
Pittsburgh, PA 15260, USA
pollack@cs.pitt.edu

Marina Milshtein
Computer Science Department
University of Pittsburgh
Pittsburgh, PA 15260, USA
marisha@cs.pitt.edu

Abstract

We present a cost-directed heuristic planning algorithm, which uses an A^* strategy for node selection. The heuristic evaluation function is computed by a deep lookahead that calculates the cost of complete plans for a set of pre-defined top-level subgoals, under the (generally false) assumption that they do not interact. This approach leads to finding low-cost plans, and in many circumstances it also leads to a significant decrease in total planning time. This is due in part to the fact that generating plans for subgoals individually is often much less costly than generating a complete plan taking interactions into account, and in part to the fact that the heuristic can effectively focus the search. We provide both analytic and experimental results.

Introduction

Most of the work on search control for planning has been based on the assumption that all plans for a given goal are equal, and so has focused on improving planning efficiency. Of course, as has been recognized in the literature on decision-theoretic planning (Williamson & Hanks 1994; Haddawy & Suwandi 1994), the solutions to a given planning problem are not necessarily equal: some plans have lower execution cost, some are more likely to succeed, and so on.

In this paper, we present a cost-directed heuristic planner, which is capable of finding low-cost plans in domains in which actions have different costs associated with them. Our algorithm performs partial-order causal-link (POCL) planning, using an A^* strategy. The heuristic evaluation function is computed by a deep lookahead that calculates the cost of complete plans for a set of pre-defined top-level subgoals, under the (generally false) assumption that those subgoals do not interact. The essential idea is to treat a set of top-level subgoals as if they were independent, in the sense of (Korf 1987). For each of these subgoals, we independently find a subplan that is consistent with the current global plan, i.e., the partial plan in the current node. The sum of the costs of these subplans is then used as the heuristic component, h', of the A^* algorithm. The overall estimate f' $(= g + h'$, where g is the cost of the actions in the global partial plan) is used to determine which node to work on next. This contrasts with most POCL planners, which perform node selection using a shallow heuristic, typically a function of the number of steps and flaws in each node.

Our approach leads to finding low-cost plans, and in many circumstances it also leads to a significant decrease in total planning time. This is due in part to the fact that generating plans for subgoals individually is often much less costly than generating a complete plan, taking interactions into account(Korf 1987; Yang, Nau, & Hendler 1992). Moreover, while focusing on lower-cost plans, the heuristic function effectively prunes the search space. The use of the deep evaluation in node selection can outweigh the marginal additional complexity.

The Algorithm

We model plans and actions similarly to other POCL systems, except that we assume that each action has an associated cost. We also assume that the cost of a plan is equal to the sum of the costs of its consituent actions. At the beginning of the planning process, the global goal is partitioned into n exhaustive and mutually disjoint subgoal sets, which should be roughly equivalent in complexity. For simplicity in this paper we assume that each subgoal set is a singleton, and just speak about top-level subgoals, sg_i, for $1 \leq i \leq n$; we call the set of all these top-level subgoals SG . At a high level, our algorithm is simply the following:

Until a solution has been found do:

1. Select [1] a node p representing a partial global plan with minimal f' value.
2. Select a flaw in p to refine. For each successor node p_i generated:
   - Set the actual cost function $g(p_i)$ to be the actual cost of p plus the cost of any new action added

[1]The choose operator denotes non-deterministic choice, and hence, a possible backtrack point; the select operator denotes a heuristic choice at a point at which back-tracking is not needed.

in the refinement. (If the refinement is a threat resolution, then $g(p_i) = g(p)$).

- Independently generate a complete plan to achieve each of the *original* subgoals sg_i. Each such subplan must be consistent with the partial global plan that p_i represents, i.e., it must be possible to incorporate it into p_i without violating any ordering or binding constraints. Set $h'(p_i)$ to the sum of the costs of the complete subplans generated.

A formal definition of the algorithm is given in Figure 1. It relies on the following definitions, which are similar to those of other POCL algorithms, except for the inclusion of cost information for actions, and g and h' values, and subgoal partitions, for plans:

Definition 1 (Operator Schemata) *An* operator schema *is a tuple* $\prec T, V, P, E, B, c \succ$ *where* T *is an action type,* V *is the list of free variables,* P *is the set of preconditions for the action,* E *is the set of effects for the action,* B *is the set of binding constraints on the variables in* V*, and* c *is the cost.*[2] *A copy of some action* a *with fresh variables will be denoted by* $Fresh(a)$*. Given some action instance,* s*, we will refer to its components by* $T(s)$*,* $V(s)$*,* $P(s)$*,* $E(s)$*,* $B(s)$*, and* $c(s)$*.*

Definition 2 (Plan) *A* plan *is a tuple* $\prec \mathcal{S}, \mathcal{L}, \mathcal{O}, \mathcal{B}, \mathcal{A}, \mathcal{T}, SG, g, h' \succ$*, where* $\mathcal{S}$ *is a set of the plan steps,* $\mathcal{L}$ *is a set of causal links on* $\mathcal{S}$*,* $\mathcal{O}$ *is a set of ordering constraints on* $\mathcal{S}$*,* $\mathcal{B}$ *is a set of bindings of variables in* $\mathcal{S}$*,* $\mathcal{A}$ *is the set of open conditions,* $\mathcal{T}$ *is the set of unresolved threats,* SG *is the partition of* $\mathcal{A}$ *induced by the initial partition of top-level subgoals,* g *is the accumulated cost of the plan so far, and* h' *is the heuristic estimate of the remaining cost.*

The initial input to the planner is: $\{\prec \{s_0, s_\infty\}, \emptyset, \{s_0 < s_\infty\}, \emptyset, G, \emptyset, SG, 0, 0 \succ\}$, where s_0 is the dummy initial step, s_∞ is the dummy final step, G is the initial set of goals, and SG is a partition of G. The algorithm also accesses an operator library Λ.

As described above, the algorithm iteratively refines nodes in the plan space until a complete plan has been generated. Its main difference from other POCL planners is its computation of heuristic estimates of nodes. (See the boxed parts of the algorithm.) The algorithm maintains a queue of partial plans, sorted by f'; on each iteration, it selects a node with minimal f'. During refinement of that node, both the g and h' compnents must be updated. Updating g is straightforward: whenever a new step is added to the plan, its cost is added to the existing g value (Step 2(a)ii). Updating h' occurs in Step 4, in which subplans are generated for each of the top-level subgoals.

CostDirectedPlanSearch (Q)

While $Q \neq \emptyset$ **Select** the first plan, $p = \prec \mathcal{S}, \mathcal{L}, \mathcal{O}, \mathcal{B}, \mathcal{A}, \mathcal{T}, SG, g, h' \succ$, in Q

1. `[Termination]` If $\mathcal{A} = \mathcal{T} = \emptyset$ return p.
2. `[Generate Successors]` Let $o' = l' = b' = s' = \emptyset$, and **Select** either:
   (a) An open condition $\langle d, s_d \rangle$ (in $\mathcal{A}$ of p), and **Choose** an establisher:
      i. `[An Existing Global Step]` $s' \in \mathcal{S}$ and b', s.t. $e \in E(s')$, $(e \equiv_{\mathcal{B} \cup b'} d)$, and $(s' < s_d)$ is consistent with $\mathcal{O}$, or
      ii. `[A New Step]` $s' = Fresh(a)$ such that $a \in \Lambda$ and b', s.t. $e \in E(a)$, $(e \equiv_{\mathcal{B} \cup b'} d)$. Let $g = g + c(s')$.
      Let $o' = (s' < s_d), l' = \{\langle s', d, s_d \rangle\}$.
   (b) An unresolved threat $\langle s_t, s_e, d, s_d \rangle \in \mathcal{T}$ of p, and Choose either:
      i. `[Demotion]` If $(s_t < s_e)$ is consistent with $\mathcal{O}$, let $o' = \{(s_t < s_e)\}$, or
      ii. `[Promotion]` If $(s_t > s_d)$ is consistent with $\mathcal{O}$, let $o' = \{(s_t > s_d)\}$.
   If there is no possible establisher or no way to resolve a threat, then fail.
3. `[Update Plan]` Let $\mathcal{S}' = \mathcal{S} \cup s'$, $\mathcal{L}' = \mathcal{L} \cup l'$, $\mathcal{O}' = \mathcal{O} \cup o'$, $\mathcal{B}' = \mathcal{B} \cup b'$, $\mathcal{A}' = (\mathcal{A} \setminus d) \cup P(s')$. Update $\mathcal{T}$ to include new threats.
4. `[Update Heuristic Value]`
   $h' = \sum_{sg_i^* \in SG} \mathsf{SubPlan}(\prec \mathcal{S}', \mathcal{L}', \mathcal{O}', \mathcal{B}', \emptyset, sg_i^*, 0 \succ)$.
5. `[Update Queue]` Merge the plan $\prec \mathcal{S}', \mathcal{L}', \mathcal{O}', \mathcal{B}', \mathcal{A}', SG, g, h' \succ$ back into Q sorted by its $g + h'$ value.

Figure 1: The Search for a Global Plan

There are two alternatives for subplanning. In this paper, we assume that subplanning is done by a fairly standard POCL algorithm, performing best first search. The subplanning process is invoked from the main program (in Step 4) with its steps, links, and ordering and binding constraints initialized to their equivalents in the global plan. The set of open conditions is initialized to sg_i^*, which consists of the open conditions associated with the ith original subgoal: any conditions from the original partition that remain open, plus any open conditions along paths to members of sg_i.[3] Essentially, when subplanning begins, it is as if it were already in the midst of planning, and had found the global partial plan; it then forms a plan for the set of open conditions associated with a top-level subgoal. As a result, the plan for the subgoal will be consistent with global plan. If a consistent subplan cannot be found, then the global plan is due to fail. Subplanning can thus detect dead-end paths.

[2]To maintain an evaluation function that tends to underestimate, the cost of a step with uninstantiated variables is heuristically taken to be equivalent to the cost of its minimal-cost grounded instance.

[3]The main algorithm tags each establisher chosen in step 2a with the top-level goal(s) that it supports. We have omitted this detail from the Figure 1 to help improve readibility.

The subplanning process keeps track of the actual cost of the complete subplan found, and returns that value to the main algorithm.

An alternative method for subplanning would be to recursively call the global planning algorithm in Figure 1. This would be likely to further reduce the amount of time spent on each node, because it would amount to assuming independence not only among top-level goals, but also among their subgoals, and their subgoals' subgoals, and so on. On the other hand, it would lead to a less accurate heuristic estimate, and thus might reduce the amount of pruning. We are conducting further experiments, not reported in this paper, to analyze this trade-off.

Complexity

We next analyze the complexity of the cost-directed planning algorithm. Let b be the maximum branching factor (number of possible refinements for each node), and let d be the depth of search (number of refinements performed to generate a complete plan). Then, as is well known, the worst-case complexity of planning search is $O(b^d)$. During each iteration of the cost-directed algorithm, the most promising partial plan is refined, and, for each possible refinement, a complete subplan for each of the n elements of the original subgoal set (SG) is generated. Let b_i and d_i denote the breadth and depth of subplanning for the subgoal sg_i, and let $\hat{b}_i = \max_i b_i$, and let $\hat{d}_i = \max_i d_i$ $(1 < i < n)$. Then the complexity of each subplanning step in the algorithm (Step 4) is $O(n \times (\hat{b}_i)^{\hat{d}_i})$. So in the worst case, if there is no pruning, the overall complexity of the search is $O(b^d \times n \times (\hat{b}_i)^{\hat{d}_i})$. Because $\hat{b}_i \leq b$, and $\hat{d}_i \leq d$, the absolute worst case complexity is $O(n \times b^{2d})$.

However, for many planning domains, $\hat{b}_i$ and $\hat{d}_i$ are likely to be smaller than b and d. As noted by Korf (Korf 1987, p.68), and by Yang *et al.* (Yang, Nau, & Hendler 1992), planning separately for n subgoals will tend to reduce both b and d by a factor of n, i.e., $b_i \approx \frac{b}{n}$ and $d_i \approx \frac{d}{n}$. Note that reduction in search depth is due to the fact that, if there were no interactions among the subgoals, an overall plan would have length equal to the sum of the lengths of the plans for the subgoals. Of course, positive interactions will decrease the length of the overall plan, while negative interactions will increase it. We assume that the effects of negative interactions will be at least as great as the effects of positive interactions, which appears to be the case in many domains.

To obtain the maximum benefits of planning for individual subgoals separately, the subgoals must be of roughly equal "complexity" to one another. If virtually all of the work of the top-level planning problem is associated with a single subgoal, then planning separately for that subgoal will be almost as costly as planning for the entire set of subgoals. We therefore also assume planning domains in which it is possible to partition subgoals into sets of equal complexity. For domains for which this does not hold, it may still be possible to use the cost-directed planning algorithm, but it would require invoking it recursively for subplanning, as described earlier.

We next consider the effect of pruning. The heuristic function in the A^* search reduces the complexity of the search from $O(b^d)$ to $O(h^d)$ where h is the heuristic branching factor (Korf 1987). Thus, for planning problems with the properties mentioned above (balanced positive and negative interactions; capable of being paritioned into subgoals with roughly equal complexity) the overall complexity of the cost-directed algorithm is $O(h^d \times n \times (\frac{b}{n})^{\frac{d}{n}})$. Cost-directed search for these problems will thus consume less time than a full breadth-first planner as long as the following inequality holds:[4]

$$n/(n-1)\log h \leq \log b - \log n$$

Of course, no POCL planning algorithms actually use breadth-first node selection; this inequality simply provides a baseline for theoretical comparison. Later, we provide experimental comparison of our algorithm with best-first and branch-and-bound control strategies.

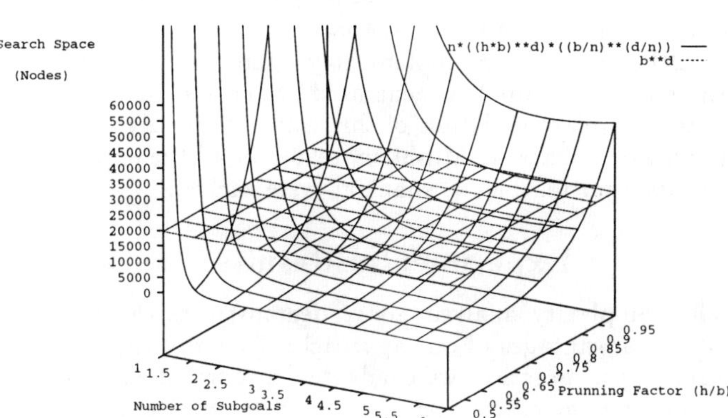

Figure 2: Typical Search Space Complexity

Figure 2 illustrates the inequality, comparing the complexity of cost-directed search with a breadth-first search (the level plane) as a function of the number of subgoals (n) and the pruning effect (h/b). We use a planning problem with a branching factor of 3 and a depth of 9 as an example. As the figure demonstrates, there exists a region in which the cost-directed planner performs better, namely the area in which the values of the curve fall below the level plane. In general, the effectiveness of the cost-directed planner increases with the pruning effect and the number of subgoals being used.

Note that this analysis assumes that the pruning factor is independent of the number of subgoal partitions.

[4]The complete derivation is given in (Ephrati, Pollack, & Milshtein 1996).

In reality, the pruning factor is inversely related to the number of subgoals—the higher the number of subgoals that are being used, the less accurate the heuristic evaluation will tend to become. Thus, for a specific problem, there exists some domain-dependent decomposition into subgoals which will optimize the performance of cost-directed search.

Caching Subplans

In the algorithm as so far presented, all subplans are recomputed on each iteration. Often, however, previously generated subplans may remain compatible with the current global partial plan, and it may thus make sense to cache subplans, and to check whether they are still consistent before attempting to regenerate them. An added advantage of caching the subplans is that the top-level planner can then attempt to re-use subplan steps; this helps maintain the accuracy of the heuristic evaluation function.

We therefore modify the original algorithm by attaching to each global plan a set of subplans ($\mathcal{P} = \{P_1, \ldots, P_n\}$) instead of just a partition of subgoals. Then, following each refinement of the global plan, the set of subplans is checked for consistency (with the newly refined global plan) and only the subplans that are incompatible are regenerated.

Although caching subplans may significantly reduce the number of subplans generated, it can also increase space complexity; details of this trade-off are given in (Ephrati, Pollack, & Milshtein 1996). In all the experiments reported below, subplans were cached.

Experimental Results

The complexity analysis above demonstrates the potential advantages of our approach. To verify the advantages in practice, we conducted a series of experiments comparing the cost-directed search with caching against the standard UCPOP algorithm with the built-in default search control, and againt UCPOP with a control mechanism that finds the minimal cost plan using branch-and-bound over action costs (henceforth called B&B).

Effects of Subgoal Independence

In the first experiment, our aim was to study the performance of the algorithms in domains in which the top-level subgoals had different levels of dependence. We therefore constructed three synthetic operator sets in the style of (Barrett & Weld 1994):

- Independent Subgoals: Barrett and Weld's $\theta_j D^0 S^n$ (p. 86). S^n means that it takes n steps to achieve each top-level subgoal. D^0 means that the delete set of each operators is empty, so all the top-level subgoals are independent. θ_j means that there are j different operators to achieve each precondition.
- Heavily Dependent Subgoals: Barrett and Weld's $\theta_j D^m S^n *$ (p. 93). As above, there are j different operators to achieve each precondition, and each top-level subgoal requires an n-step plan. $D^m *$ refers to a pattern of interaction among the operators. There is a single operator that must end up in the middle of the plan, because it deletes all the preconditions of the operators in stages 1 through k for some k, as well as all the effects of the operators in stages $k+1$ through n. In addition, for each stage, the operators for the ith subgoal delete all the preconditions of the same-stage operators for subgoals $j < i$. Consequently, there is only a single valid linearization of the overall plan; the dependency among top-level subgoals is heavy.
- Moderately Dependent Subplans: A variant of Barrett and Weld's $\theta_j D^m S^n$ (p. 91). Here again there are j different operators to achieve each precondition, and each top-level subgoal requires an n-step plan. In addition, the union of delete lists of the $k+1$st stage operators for each subgoal sg_i delete *all* of the preconditions for the kth stage operators for all other $sg_j, j \neq i$. Because these preconditions are partitioned among the alternative kth stage operators, there are multiple valid linearizations of the overall plan. Although the top-level subgoals interact, the dependency isn't as tight, given the multiple possible solutions.

One thing to note is that the individual subplanning tasks in our experiments are relatively easy: the interactions occur among the subplans for *different* subgoals. Of course, this means that planning for UCPOP and B&B is comparatively easy as well. Further experiments are being conducted using operator sets with interactions within each subplan.

For the first experiment, we used problems with 4 top-level subgoals, and built the operator sets so that each top-level subgoal required a plan of length 3 (i.e., we used the S^3 version of each of the operator sets). The actions were randomly assigned costs between 1 and 10. Finally, we varied the number of operators achieving each goal (the j in θ_j) to achieve actual branching factors, as measured by UCPOP, of about 3 for the case of independent subgoals, about 2 for medium dependent subgoals, and about 1.5 for heavily dependent subgoals. The results are shown in Table 1, which lists

- the number of nodes generated and the number of nodes visited (these numbers are separated by an arrow in the tables);
- the CPU time spent in planning.[5]

[5]For certain problems that required a great deal of memory, the garbage collection process caused Lisp to crash, reporting an internal error. Schubert and Gerevini (Schubert & Gerevini 1995) encountered the same problem in their UCPOP-based experiments, with problems that required a

• the cost of the plans generated (sum of action costs).

As can be seen in the table, COST performed best in all cases, not only examining significantly fewer nodes, but taking an order of magnitude less time to find a solution than B&B. Not surprisingly, COST's advantage increases with the degree of independence among the subgoals: the greater the degree of independence among the subplans, the more accurate is COST's heuristic function, and thus the more effective its pruning. However, even in the case of heavy dependence among top-level subgoals, COST performs quite well.

Dependency	Planner	Nodes	Time	Cost
Independent	UCPOP	failure	39927.89	-
	B&B	35806 → 12900	2183.21	37
	COST	60 → 22	126.13	37
Medium	UCPOP	failure	40348.54	-
	B&B	2/4 failures 14827 → 5198 (succ. only)	9185.691	-
	COST	309 → 146	613.54	37
Heavy	UCPOP	failure	*	-
	B&B	2/4 failures 42978 → 17567 (succ. only)	12727.83	-
	COST	780 → 444	3834.517	37

Table 1: Varying dependency (4 medium uniform subgoals, 3 Steps each, $b \approx 3$ for independent, $b \approx 2$ for medium, $b \approx 1.5$ for heavy)

Effects of Uniformity

The next thing we varied was the uniformity of action cost: see Tables 2 and 3. For this experiment, we used the independent subgoal operator set described above, with 3 steps to achieve each subgoal, and an actual branching factor of approximately 3. The experiment in Table 2 involved 6 top-level subgoals, while the experiment in Table 3 involved 4. In both experiments, we varied the distribution of action costs: in the highly uniform environment, all actions were assigned a cost of 1; in the medium uniform environment, they were randomly assigned a cost between 1 and 10; in the the low uniform environments, they were randomly assigned a cost between 1 and 100.

Both UCPOP and B&B failed to find a solution for problems with 6, and even with 4 independent subgoals within the 150,000 nodes-generated limit. In highly uniform domains, i.e., those in which all actions had the same cost, our cost-directed algorithm fared no better: it also failed, although by exceeding memory limits. This is not surprising: if all actions have the same costs, then no pruning will result from a strategy based on cost comparison, and the space taken by caching subplans will be enormous.

lot of memory. We do not report results for these problems, but instead put an asterisk (*) in the time column. Also, in some cases, B&B succeeded on some operator sets, and failed on others. For those cases, we report the average time taken on *all* runs (which will be an underestimate, as the failed run were terminated after 150,000 generated nodes). We report the number of nodes only for the successful cases. Finally, we do not report the costs found in these cases, because the high-cost plans are typically the cases that fail. In no case did B&B find a lower-cost plan than COST.

Degree	Planner	Nodes	Time	Cost
Low	UCPOP	failure	28980.45	-
	B&B	failure	26165.37	-
	COST	70 → 26	210.44	2167
Medium	UCPOP	failure	36519.96	-
	B&B	failure	26952.57	-
	COST	134 → 44	407.84	54
High	UCPOP	failure	14986.58	-
	B&B	failure	27304.23	-
	COST	failure	*	-

Table 2: Varying Uniformity (6 independent subgoals, 3 Steps each, $b \approx 3$)

Degree	Planner	Nodes	Time	Cost
Low	UCPOP	failure	14617.54	-
	B&B	65000 → 23158	12708.66	1761
	COST	50 → 18	98.22	1761
Medium	UCPOP	failure	39927.89	-
	B&B	35806 → 12900	2183.21	37
	COST	60 → 22	126.13	37
High	UCPOP	failure	14528.38	-
	B&B	failure	26988.26	-
	COST	failure	*	-

Table 3: Varying Uniformity (4 independent subgoals, 3 Steps each, $b \approx 3$)

However, when the environments become less uniform, we see the payoff in the cost-directed approach. For low uniform environments and a planning problem with 6 subgoals (Table 2), the cost-directed planner finds plans by generating less than 70 nodes, taking about 3.5 minutes—while UCPOP and B&B failed, after generating 150,000 nodes, and taking over 7 hours. Even with medium uniformity, cost-directed planning succeeds quickly, while the other two approaches fail. Similar results are observed for the smaller (4 subgoal) problem (Table 3).

Note again that these are very easy problems, given the independence of the top-level subgoals. Indeed, the optimal strategy would have been to plan completely separately for each subgoal, and then simply concatenate the resulting plans. However, one may not know, in general, whether a set of subgoals is independent, prior to performing planning. The cost-directed search performs very well, while maintaining a general, POCL strategy that is applicable to interacting, as well as independent, goals.

Other Factors Effecting Planning

Several other key factors that are known to effect the efficiency of planning are the average branching factor, the length of the plan, and the number of top-level subgoals. We have conducted, and are continuing to conduct, experiments that vary each of these factors; so far, our results demonstrate that in a wide range of environments, the COST algorithm performs very well, finding low-cost plans in less time than either UCPOP or B&B (Ephrati, Pollack, & Milshtein 1996).

Related Research

Prior work on plan merging (Fousler, Li, & Yang 1992; Yang, Nau, & Hendler 1992) has studied the problem of forming plans for subgoals independently and then merging them back together. Although similarly motivated by the speed-up one gets from attending to subgoals individually, our work differs in performing complete planning using a POCL-style algorithm, as opposed to using separate plan merging procedures.

The idea of using information about plan quality during plan generation dates back to (Feldman & Sproull 1977); more recent work on this topic has involved the introduction of decision-theoretic notions (Haddawy & Suwandi 1994). Pérez studied the problem of enabling a system to learn ways to improve the quality of the plans it generates (Pérez 1995). Particularly relevant is Williamson's work on the PYRRHUS system (Williamson & Hanks 1994), which uses plan quality information to find an optimal plan. It performs standard POCL planning, but does not terminate with the first complete plan. Instead, it computes the plans's utility, prunes from the seach space any partial plans that are guaranteed to have lower utility, and then resumes execution. The process terminates when no partial plans remain, at which point PYRRHUS is guaranteed to have found an optimal plan. What is interesting about PYRRHUS from the perspective of the current paper is that, although one might expect that PYRRHUS would take significantly longer to find an optimal plan than to find an arbitrary plan, in fact, in many circumstances it does not. The information provided by the utility model results in enough pruning of the search space to outweigh the additional costs of seeking an optimal solution. This result, although obtained in a different framework from our own, bears a strong similarity to our main conclusion, which is that the pruning that results from attending to plan quality can outweigh the cost of computing plan quality.

Conclusions

We have presented an efficient cost-directed planning algorithm. The key idea underlying it is to replace a shallow, syntactic heuristic for node selection in POCL planning with an approximate, full-depth lookahead that computes complete subplans for a set of top-level subgoals, under the assumption that these subgoals are independent. Our analytical and experimental results demonstrate that in addition to finding low-cost plans, the algorithm can significantly improve planning time in many circumstances. The performance of the algorithm is dependent upon the possibility of decomposing the global goal into subgoal sets that are relatively (though not necessarily completely) independent, and that are roughly equivalent in complexity to one another.

The experiments we presented in this paper support the main hypothesis, but are by no means complete. We are continuing our experimentation, in particular, studying domains that involve a greater degree of interaction within each subplan. In addition, we are investigating the trade-off between using a complete POCL planner for subplanning, as in the experiments reported here, and recursively calling the main algorithm for subplanning. Finally, we are developing techniques to make the cost-directed search admissible.

Acknowledgments This work has been supported by the Rome Laboratory of the Air Force Material Command and the Advanced Research Projects Agency (Contract F30602-93-C-0038), by the Office of Naval Research (Contract N00014-95-1-1161) and by an NSF Young Investigator's Award (IRI-9258392).

References

Barrett, A., and Weld, D. 1994. Partial-order planning: Evaluating possible efficiency gains. *Artificial Intelligence* 67(1):71–112.

Ephrati, E.; Pollack, M. E.; and Milshtein, M. 1996. A cost-directed planner. Technical Report, Dept. of Computer Science, Univ. of Pittsburgh, in preparation.

Feldman, J. A., and Sproull, R. F. 1977. Decision theory and artificial intelligence II: The hungry monkey. *Cognitive Science* 1:158–192.

Fousler, D.; Li, M.; and Yang, Q. 1992. Theory and algorithms for plan merging. *Artificial Intelligence* 57:143–181.

Haddawy, P., and Suwandi, M. 1994. Decision-theoretic refinement planning using inheritance abstraction. In *Proceedings of the Second International Conference on AI Planning Systems*, 266–271.

Korf, R. E. 1987. Planning as search: A quantitative approach. *Artificial Intelligence* 33:65–88.

Pérez, M. A. 1995. Improving search control knoweldge to improve plan quality. Technical Report CMU-CS-95-175, Dept. of Computer Science, Carnegie Mellon University. Ph.D. Dissertation.

Schubert, L., and Gerevini, A. 1996. Accelerating partial order planners by improving plan and goal choices. Technical Report 96-607, Univ. of Rochester Dept. of Computer Science.

Williamson, M., and Hanks, S. 1994. Optimal planning with a goal-directed utility model. In *Proceedings of the Second International Conference on Artificial Intelligence Planning Systems*, 176–181.

Yang, Q.; Nau, D. S.; and Hendler, J. 1992. Merging separately generated plans with restricted interactions. *Computational Intelligence* 8(2):648–676.

Monitoring the Progress of Anytime Problem-Solving

Eric A. Hansen and Shlomo Zilberstein
Computer Science Department
University of Massachusetts
Amherst, MA 01003
{hansen,shlomo}@cs.umass.edu

Abstract

Anytime algorithms offer a tradeoff between solution quality and computation time that has proved useful in applying artificial intelligence techniques to time-critical problems. To exploit this tradeoff, a system must be able to determine the best time to stop deliberation and act on the currently available solution. When the rate of improvement of solution quality is uncertain, monitoring the progress of the algorithm can improve the utility of the system. This paper introduces a technique for run-time monitoring of anytime algorithms that is sensitive to the variance of the algorithm's performance, the time-dependent utility of a solution, the ability of the run-time monitor to estimate the quality of the currently available solution, and the cost of monitoring. The paper examines the conditions under which the technique is optimal and demonstrates its applicability.

Introduction

Anytime algorithms are being used increasingly for time-critical problem-solving in domains such as planning and scheduling (Boddy & Dean 1994; Zilberstein 1996), belief network evaluation (Horvitz, Suermondt, & Cooper 1989; Wellman & Liu 1994), database query processing (Shekhar & Dutta 1989; Smith & Liu 1989), and others. The defining property of an anytime algorithm is that it can be stopped at any time to provide a solution, such that the quality of the solution increases with computation time. This property allows a tradeoff between computation time and solution quality, making it possible to compute approximate solutions to complex problems under time constraints. It also introduces a problem of meta-level control: making an optimal time/quality tradeoff requires determining how long to run the algorithm, and when to stop and act on the currently available solution.

Meta-level control of an anytime algorithm can be approached in two different ways. One approach is to allocate the algorithm's running time before it starts and to let the algorithm run for the predetermined length of time no matter what (Boddy & Dean 1994). If there is little or no uncertainty about the rate of improvement of solution quality, or about how the urgency for a solution might change after the start of the algorithm, then this approach can determine an optimal stopping time. Very often, however, there is uncertainty about one or both. For AI problem-solving in particular, variance in solution quality is common (Paul et al. 1991). Because the best stopping time will vary with fluctuations in the algorithm's performance, a second approach to meta-level control is to monitor the progress of the algorithm and to determine at run-time when to stop deliberation and act on the currently available solution (Breese & Horvitz 1991; Horvitz 1990; Zilberstein & Russell 1995).

Monitoring the progress of anytime problem-solving involves assessing the quality of the currently available solution, making revised predictions of the likelihood of further improvement, and engaging in metareasoning about whether to continue deliberation. Previous schemes for run-time monitoring of anytime algorithms have assumed continuous monitoring, but the computational overhead this incurs can take resources away from problem-solving itself. This paper introduces a framework in which the run-time overhead for monitoring can be included in the problem of optimizing the stopping time of anytime problem-solving. It describes a framework for determining not only when to stop an anytime algorithm, but at what intervals to monitor its progress and re-assess whether to continue or stop. This framework makes it possible to answer such questions as:

- How much variance in the performance of an anytime algorithm justifies adopting a run-time monitoring strategy rather than determining a fixed running time ahead of time?
- How should the variance of an algorithm's performance affect the frequency of monitoring?
- Is it better to monitor periodically or to monitor more frequently toward the algorithm's expected stopping time?

For a large class of problems, the rate of improvement of solution quality is the only source of uncertainty about how long to continue deliberation. Examples include optimizing a database query (Shekhar & Dutta 1989), reformulating a belief net before solving it (Breese & Horvitz 1991), and planning the next move in a chess game (Russell & Wefald 1991). For other problems, the utility of a solution may also depend on the state of a dynamic environment that can change unpredictably after the start of the algorithm. Examples include real-time planning and diagnosis (Boddy & Dean 1994; Horvitz 1990). For such problems, meta-level control can be further improved by monitoring the state of the environment as well as the progress of problem-solving. We focus in this paper on uncertainty about improvement in solution quality. However, the framework can be extended in a reasonably straightforward way to deal with uncertainty about the state of a dynamic environment.

We begin by describing a framework for constructing an optimal policy for monitoring the progress of anytime problem-solving, assuming the quality of the currently available solution can be measured accurately at run-time. Because this assumption is often unrealistic, we then describe how to modify this framework when a run-time monitor can only estimate solution quality. A simple example is described to illustrate these results. The paper concludes with a brief discussion of the significance of this work and possible extensions.

Formal Framework

Meta-level control of an anytime algorithm – deciding how long to run the algorithm and when to stop and act on the currently available solution – requires a model of how the quality of a solution produced by the algorithm increases with computation time, as well as a model of the time-dependent utility of a solution. The first model is given by a *performance profile* of the algorithm. A conventional performance profile predicts solution quality as a function of the algorithm's overall running time. This is suitable for making a one-time decision about how long to run an algorithm, before the algorithm starts. To take advantage of information gathered by monitoring its progress, however, a more informative performance profile is needed that makes it possible to predict solution quality as a function of both time allocation and the quality of the currently available solution.

Definition 1 *A* ***dynamic performance profile*** *of an anytime algorithm, $Pr(q_j|q_i, \Delta t)$, denotes the probability of getting a solution of quality q_j by resuming the algorithm for time interval Δt when the currently available solution has quality q_i.*

We call this conditional probability distribution a dynamic performance profile to distinguish it from a performance profile that predicts solution quality as a function of running time only. The conditional probabilities are determined by statistical analysis of the behavior of the algorithm. For simplicity, we rely on discrete probability distributions. Time is discretized into a finite number of time steps, $t_0 \ldots t_n$, where t_0 represents the starting time of the algorithm and t_n its maximum running time. Similarly, solution quality is discretized into a finite number of levels, $q_0 \ldots q_m$, where q_0 is the lowest quality level and q_m is the highest quality level. Let q_{start} denote the starting state of the algorithm before any result has been computed. By discretizing time and quality, the dynamic performance profile can be stored as a three-dimensional table; the degree of discretization controls a tradeoff between the precision of the performance profile and the size of the table needed to store it. A dynamic performance profile can also be represented by a compact parameterized function.

Meta-level control requires a model of the time-dependent utility of a solution as well as a performance profile. We assume that this information is provided to the monitor in the form of a time-dependent utility function.

Definition 2 *A* ***time-dependent utility function****, $U(q_i, t_k)$, represents the utility of a solution of quality q_i at time t_k.*

In this paper, we assume that utility is a function of time and not of an external state of the environment. This assumption makes it possible to set to one side the problem of modeling uncertainty about the environment in order to focus on the specific problem of uncertainty about improvement in solution quality.

Finally, we assume that monitoring the quality of the currently available solution and deciding whether to continue or stop incurs a cost, C. Because it may not be cost-effective to monitor problem-solving continuously, an optimal policy must specify when to monitor as well as when to stop and act on the currently available solution. For each time step t_k and quality level q_i, the following two decisions must be specified:

1. how much additional time to run the algorithm; and
2. whether to monitor at the end of this time allocation and re-assess whether to continue, or to stop without monitoring.

Definition 3 *A* ***monitoring policy****, $\pi(q_i, t_k)$, is a mapping from time step t_k and quality level q_i into a monitoring decision $(\Delta t, m)$ such that Δt represents the additional amount of time to allocate to the anytime algorithm, and m is a binary variable that represents whether to monitor at the end of this time allocation or to stop without monitoring.*

An initial decision, $\pi(q_{start}, t_0)$, specifies how much time to allocate to the algorithm before monitoring for the first time or else stopping without monitoring. Note that the variable Δt makes it possible to control the time interval between one monitoring action and the next; its value can range from 0 to $t_n - t_i$, where t_n is the maximum running time of the algorithm and t_i is how long it has already run. The binary variable m makes it possible to allocate time to the algorithm without necessarily monitoring at the end of the time interval; its value is either *stop* or *monitor*.

An *optimal monitoring policy* is a monitoring policy that maximizes the expected utility of an anytime algorithm.

Given this formalization, it is possible to use dynamic programming to compute a combined policy for monitoring and stopping. Dynamic programming is often used to solve optimal stopping problems; the novel aspect of this solution is that dynamic programming is also used to determine when to monitor. A monitoring policy is found by optimizing the following value function:

$$V(q_i, t_k) = \max_{\Delta t, m} \begin{bmatrix} \sum_j Pr(q_j|q_i, \Delta t)U(q_j, t_k + \Delta t) \\ \text{if } m = \text{stop}, \\ \sum_j Pr(q_j|q_i, \Delta t)V(q_j, t_k + \Delta t) - C \\ \text{if } m = \text{monitor} \end{bmatrix}$$

Theorem 1 *A monitoring policy that maximizes the above value function is optimal when quality improvement satisfies the Markov property.*

This is an immediate outcome of the application of dynamic programming under the Markov assumption (Bertsekas 1987). The assumption requires that the probability distribution of future quality depends only on the current "state" of the anytime algorithm, which is taken to be the quality of the currently available solution. The validity of this assumption depends on both the algorithm and how solution quality is defined, and so must be evaluated on a case-by-case basis. But we believe it is at least a useful approximation in many cases.

Uncertain measurement of quality

We have described a framework for computing a policy for monitoring an anytime algorithm, given a cost for monitoring. Besides the assumption that quality improvement satisfies the Markov property, the optimality of the policy depends on the assumption that the quality of the currently available solution can be measured accurately by a run-time monitor. How reasonable is this second assumption likely to be in practice?

We suggest that for certain types of problems, calculating the precise quality of a solution at run-time is not feasible. One class of problems for which anytime algorithms are widely used are optimization problems in which a solution is iteratively improved over time by minimizing or maximizing the value of an objective function. For such problems, the quality of an approximate solution is usually measured by how close the approximation comes to an optimal solution. For cost-minimization problems, this can be defined as

$$\frac{Cost(\text{Approximate Solution})}{Cost(\text{Optimal Solution})}$$

The lower this *approximation ratio*, the higher the quality of the solution, and when it is equal to one the solution is optimal.

The problem with using this measure of solution quality for run-time monitoring is that it requires knowing the optimal solution at run-time. This is no obstacle to using it to construct a performance profile for an anytime algorithm, because the performance profile can be constructed off-line and the quality of approximate solutions measured in terms of the quality of the eventual optimal solution. But a run-time monitor needs to make a decision based on the approximate solution currently available, without knowing what the optimal solution will eventually be. As a result, it cannot know with certainty the actual quality of the approximate solution. In some cases, it will be possible to bound the degree of approximation, but a run-time monitor can only estimate where the optimal solution falls within this bound.

A similar observation can be made about other classes of problems besides optimization problems. For problems that involve estimating a point value, the difference between the estimated point value and the true point value can't be known until the algorithm has converged to an exact value (Horvitz, Suermondt, & Cooper 1989). For anytime problem-solvers that rely on abstraction to create approximate solutions, solution quality may be difficult to assess for other reasons. For example, it may be difficult for a run-time monitor to predict the extent of planning needed to fill in the details of an abstract plan (Zilberstein 1996). We conclude that for many problems, the best a run-time monitor can do is estimate the quality of an anytime solution with some degree of probability.

Monitoring based on estimated quality

When the quality of approximate solutions cannot be accurately measured at run-time, the success of run-time monitoring requires solving two new problems. First, some reliable method must be found for estimating solution quality at run-time. It is impossible to specify a universal method for this – how solution quality is estimated will vary from algorithm to algorithm. We sketch a general approach and, in the section that follows, describe an illustrative example. The second problem is that a monitoring policy must be conditioned on the estimate of solution quality rather than solution quality itself.

To solve these problems, we condition a run-time estimate of solution quality on some feature f_r of the currently available solution that is correlated with solution quality. When a feature is imperfectly correlated with solution quality, we have also found it useful to condition the estimate on the running time of the algorithm, t_k. Conditioning an estimate of solution quality on the algorithm's running time as well as some feature observed by a run-time monitor provides an important guarantee; it ensures that the estimate will be at least as good as if it were based on running time alone.

As a general notation, let $Pr(q_i|f_r, t_k)$ denote the probability that the currently available solution has quality q_i when the run-time monitor observes feature f_r after running time t_k. In addition, let $Pr(f_r|q_i, t_k)$ denote the probability that the run-time monitor will observe feature f_r if the currently available solution has quality q_i after running time t_k. Again, these probabilities can be determined from statistical analysis of the behavior of the algorithm. These "partial observability" functions, together with the dynamic performance profile defined earlier, can be used to calculate the following probabilities for use in predicting the improvement of solution quality after additional time allocation Δt when the quality of the currently available solution can only be estimated.

$$Pr(q_j|f_r, t_k, \Delta t) = \sum_i Pr(q_i|f_r, t_k) Pr(q_j|q_i, \Delta t)$$
$$Pr(f_s|f_r, t_k, \Delta t) = \sum_i Pr(q_i|f_r, t_k) \sum_j Pr(q_j|q_i, \Delta t) Pr(f_s|q_j, t_k+\Delta t) - C$$

These probabilities can also be determined directly from statistical analysis of the behavior of the algorithm, without the intermediate calculations. In either case, these probabilities make it possible to find a monitoring policy by optimizing the following value function using dynamic programming.

$$V(f_r, t_k) = \max_{\Delta t, m} \begin{cases} \sum_j Pr(q_j|f_r, t_k, \Delta t) U(q_j, t_k+\Delta t) \\ \text{if } m = \text{stop}, \\ \sum_s Pr(f_s|f_r, t_k, \Delta t) V(f_s, t_k+\Delta t) - C \\ \text{if } m = \text{monitor} \end{cases}$$

The resulting policy may not be optimal in the sense that it may not take advantage of all possible run-time evidence about solution quality, for example, the trajectory of observed improvement. Finding an optimal policy may require formalizing the problem as a partially observable Markov decision process and using computationally intensive algorithms developed for such problems (Cassandra, Littman, & Kaelbling 1994). The approach we have described is simple and efficient, however, and it provides an important guarantee: it only recommends monitoring if it results in a higher expected value than allocating a fixed running time without monitoring. This makes it possible to distinguish cases in which monitoring is cost-effective from cases in which it is not. Whether monitoring is cost-effective will depend on the variance of the performance profile, the time-dependent utility of the solution, how well the quality of the currently available solution can be estimated by the run-time monitor, and the cost of monitoring – all factors weighed in computing the monitoring policy.

Example

As an example of how this technique can be used to determine a combined policy for monitoring and stopping, we apply it to a tour improvement algorithm for the traveling salesman problem developed by Lin and Kernighan (1973).

quality	$\frac{Length(Current\ tour)}{Length(Optimal\ tour)}$
5	$1.05 \rightarrow 1.00$
4	$1.10 \rightarrow 1.05$
3	$1.20 \rightarrow 1.10$
2	$1.35 \rightarrow 1.20$
1	$1.50 \rightarrow 1.35$
0	$\infty \rightarrow 1.50$

Table 1: Discretization of solution quality.

feature	$\frac{Length(Current\ tour)}{Length(Lower\ bound)}$
6	$1.3 \rightarrow 1.0$
5	$1.4 \rightarrow 1.3$
4	$1.5 \rightarrow 1.4$
3	$1.6 \rightarrow 1.5$
2	$1.7 \rightarrow 1.6$
1	$2.0 \rightarrow 1.7$
0	$\infty \rightarrow 2.0$

Table 2: Discretization of feature correlated with solution quality.

This local optimization algorithm begins with an initial tour, then repeatedly tries to improve the tour by swapping random paths between cities. The example is representative of anytime algorithms that have variance in solution quality as a function of time.

We defined solution quality as the approximation ratio of a tour,

$$\frac{Length(\text{Current tour})}{Length(\text{Optimal tour})}$$

and discretized this metric using Table 1. The maximum running time of the algorithm was discretized into twelve time-steps, with one time-step corresponding to approximately 0.005 CPU seconds. A dynamic performance profile was compiled by generating and solving a thousand random twelve-city traveling salesman problems. The time-dependent utility of a solution of quality q_i at time t_k was arbitrarily defined by the function

$$U(q_i, t_k) = 100q_i - 20t_k.$$

Note that the first term of the utility function can be regarded as the *intrinsic value* of a solution and the second term as the *time cost*, as defined by Russell and Wefald (1991).

Without monitoring, the optimal running time of the algorithm is eight time-steps, with an expected value of 269.2. Assuming solution quality can be measured accurately by the run-time monitor (an unrealistic assumption in this case) and assuming a monitoring cost of 1, the dynamic programming algorithm described earlier computes the monitoring policy shown in Table 3. The number in each cell of Table 3 represents how much additional time to allocate to the

						time-step						
quality	start	1	2	3	4	5	6	7	8	9	10	11
5		0	0	0	0	0	0	0	0	0	0	0
4		1M	1M	1M	1M	1M	1M	1M	1M	1M	1	0
3		1M	1M	1M	1M	1M	1M	1M	1M	1M	1	0
2		3M	3M	3M	3M	3M	3M	3M	3M	2	1	0
1		4M	4M	4M	4M	4M	5	4	3	2	1	0
0	5M	5M	5M	5M	5M	6	5	4	3	2	1	0

Table 3: Optimal policy based on actual solution quality.

						time-step						
feature	start	1	2	3	4	5	6	7	8	9	10	11
6				0	0	0	0	0	0	0	0	0
5			1	1	1	1	0	0	0	0	0	0
4			2M	2M	1M	1M	1M	1M	1	0	0	0
3		4M	3M	2M	1M	1M	1M	1M	1M	1	0	0
2		4M	3M	2M	2M	2M	2M	1M	3	2	1	0
1		4M	3M	3M	3M	3M	3M	2M	2M	1M	1	
0	5M	4M	3M	3M	3M	3M	3M					

Table 4: Policy when solution quality is estimated.

algorithm based on the observed quality of the solution and the current time. The letter M next to a number indicates a decision to monitor at the end of this time allocation, and possibly allocate additional running time; if no M is present, the decision is to stop at the end of this time allocation without monitoring. The policy has an expected value of **303.3**, better than the expected value of allocating a fixed running time despite the added cost of monitoring. Its improved performance is due to the fact that the run-time monitor can stop the algorithm after anywhere from 5 to 11 time steps, depending on how quickly the algorithm finds a good result. (If there is no cost for monitoring, a policy that monitors every time step has an expected value of 309.4.)

The policy shown in Table 3 was constructed by assuming the actual quality of an approximate solution could be measured by the run-time monitor, an unrealistic assumption because measuring the quality of the current tour requires knowing the length of an optimal tour. The average length of an optimal tour can provide a very rough estimate of the optimal tour length in a particular case, and this can be used to estimate the quality of the current tour. For a traveling salesman problem that satisfies the triangle inequality, however, much better estimates can be made by using one of a number of algorithms for computing a lower bound on the optimal tour length (Reinelt 1994). Computing a lower bound involves solving a relaxation of the problem; it is analogous to an admissable heuristic function in search. For a traveling salesman problem that satisfies the triangle inequality, there exist polynomial-time algorithms that can compute a lower bound that is on average within two or three percent of the optimal tour length. For our test, however, we used Prim's minimal spanning tree algorithm that very quickly computes a bound that is less tight, but still correlated with the optimal tour length. The feature

$$\frac{\mathit{Length}(\text{Current tour})}{\mathit{Length}(\text{Lower bound})}$$

was discretized using Table 2. The cost overhead of monitoring consists of computing the lower bound at the beginning of the algorithm and monitoring the current tour length at intervals thereafter.

Table 4 shows the monitoring policy given a monitoring cost of 1, when an estimate of solution quality is conditioned on both this feature and the running time of the algorithm. The expected value of the policy is **282.3**, higher than for allocating a fixed running time without monitoring but lower than if the run-time monitor could determine the actual quality of an approximate solution. As this demonstrates, the less accurately a run-time monitor can measure the quality of an approximate solution, the less valuable it is to monitor.

When an estimate of solution quality is based only on this feature, and not also on running time, the expected value of monitoring is **277.0**. This is still an improvement over not monitoring, but the performance is not as good as when an estimate is conditioned on running time as well. Because conditioning a dynamic performance profile on running time significantly increases its size, however, this tradeoff may be acceptable in cases when the feature used to estimate quality is very reliable. For all of these results, the improved performance predicted by dynamic programming was confirmed by simulation experiments.

For the tour improvement algorithm, variance in solution quality over time is minor and the improved performance with run-time monitoring correspondingly small. We plan to apply this technique to other problems for which variance in solution quality is larger and the payoff for run-time monitoring promises to be more significant. However, the fact that this technique improves performance even when variance is small, solution quality is difficult to estimate at run-time, and monitoring incurs a cost, supports its validity and potential value.

Conclusion

The framework developed in this paper extends previous work on meta-level control of anytime algorithms. One contribution is the use of dynamic programming to compute a non-myopic stopping rule. Previous schemes for run-time monitoring have relied on myopic computation of the expected value of continued deliberation to determine a stopping time (Breese & Horvitz 1991; Horvitz 1990), although Horvitz has also recommended various degrees of lookahead search to overcome the limitations of a myopic approach. Because dynamic programming is particularly well-suited for off-line computation of a stopping rule, it is also an example of what Horvitz calls compilation of metareasoning.

Another contribution of this framework is that it makes it possible to find an intermediate strategy between continuous monitoring and not monitoring at all. It can recognize whether or not monitoring is cost-effective, and when it is, it can adjust the frequency of monitoring to optimize utility. An interesting property of the monitoring policies found is that they recommend monitoring more frequently near the expected stopping time of an algorithm, an intuitive strategy.

Perhaps the most significant aspect of this framework is that it makes it possible to evaluate tradeoffs between various factors that influence the utility of monitoring. For example, the dynamic programming technique is sensitive to both the cost of monitoring and to how well the quality of the currently available solution can be estimated by the run-time monitor. This makes it possible to evaluate a tradeoff between these two factors. Most likely, there will be more than one method for estimating a solution's quality and the estimate that takes longer to compute will be more accurate. Is the greater accuracy worth the added time cost? The framework developed in this paper can be used to answer this question by computing a monitoring policy for each method and comparing their expected values to select the best one.

Acknowledgments

Support for this work was provided in part by the National Science Foundation under grant IRI-9409827 and in part by Rome Laboratory, USAF, under grant F30602-95-1-0012.

References

Bertsekas, D.P. 1987. *Dynamic Programming: Deterministic and Stochastic Models.* Englewood Cliffs, N.J.: Prentice-Hall.

Boddy, M., and Dean., T. 1994. Deliberation scheduling for problem solving in time-constrained environments. *Artificial Intelligence* 67:245-285.

Breese, J.S., and Horvitz, E.J. 1991. Ideal reformulation of belief networks. Proceedings of the Sixth Conference on Uncertainty in Artificial Intelligence, 129-143.

Cassandra, A.R.; Littman, M.L.; and Kaelbling, L.P. 1994. Acting optimally in partially observable stochastic domains. Proceedings of the Twelth National Conference on Artificial Intelligence, 1023-1028.

Horvitz, E.J.; Suermondt, H.J.; and Cooper, G.F. 1989. Bounded conditioning: Flexible inference for decisions under scarce resources. Proceedings of the Fifth Workshop on Uncertainty in Artificial Intelligence.

Horvitz, E.J. 1990. Computation and Action under Bounded Resources. PhD Thesis, Stanford University.

Lin, S., and Kernighan, B.W. 1973. An effective heuristic algorithm for the Traveling Salesman problem. *Operations Research* 21:498-516.

Paul, C.J.; Acharya, A.; Black, B.; and Strosnider, J.K. 1991. Reducing problem-solving variance to improve predictability. *CACM* 34(8):80-93.

Reinelt, G. 1994. *The Traveling Salesman: Computational Solutions for TSP Applications.* Springer-Verlag.

Russell, S., and Wefald, E. 1991. *Do the Right Thing: Studies in Limited Rationality.* The MIT Press.

Shekhar, S., and Dutta, S. 1989. Minimizing response times in real time planning and search. Proceedings of the Eleventh IJCAI, 238-242.

Smith, K.P., and Liu, J.W.S. 1989. Monotonically improving approximate answers to relational algebra queries. *COMPSAC-89*, Orlando, Florida.

Wellman, M.P., and Liu, C.-L. 1994. State-space abstraction for anytime evaluation of probabilistic networks. Proceedings of the Tenth Conference on Uncertainty in Artificial Intelligence, 567-574.

Zilberstein, S. 1993. Operational Rationality through Compilation of Anytime Algorithms. Ph.D. dissertation, Computer Science Division, University of California at Berkeley.

Zilberstein, S. 1996. Resource-bounded sensing and planning in autonomous systems. To appear in *Autonomous Robots.*

Zilberstein S., and Russell S. 1995. Approximate reasoning using anytime algorithms. In S. Natarajan (Ed.), *Imprecise and Approximate Computation*, Kluwer Academic Publishers.

A Linear-Programming Approach to Temporal Reasoning

Peter Jonsson and Christer Bäckström
Department of Computer and Information Science
Linköping University, S-581 83 Linköping, Sweden
{petej,cba}@ida.liu.se

Abstract

We present a new formalism, Horn Disjunctive Linear Relations (Horn DLRs), for reasoning about temporal constraints. We prove that deciding satisfiability of sets of Horn DLRs is polynomial by exhibiting an algorithm based upon linear programming. Furthermore, we prove that most other approaches to tractable temporal constraint reasoning can be encoded as Horn DLRs, including the ORD-Horn algebra and most methods for purely quantitative reasoning.

Introduction

Reasoning about temporal constraints is an important task in many areas of AI and elsewehere, such as planning, natural language processing, diagnosis, time serialization in archeology *etc.* In most applications, knowledge of temporal constraints is expressed in terms of collections of relations between time intervals or time points. Typical reasoning tasks include determining the satisfiability of such collections and deducing new relations from those that are known. The research has largely concentrated on two kinds of formalisms; systems of inequalities on time points (Dechter, Meiri, & Pearl 1991; Meiri 1991; Koubarakis 1992) to encode quantitative information, and systems of constraints in Allen's algebra (Allen 1983) to encode qualitative relations between time intervals. Some attempts have been made to integrate quantitative and qualitative reasoning into unified frameworks (Kautz & Ladkin 1991; Meiri 1991). Since the satisfiability problem is NP-complete for Allen's algebra the qualitative and unified approaches have suffered from computational difficulties.

In response to the computational hardness of the full Allen algebra, several polynomial subalgebras have been proposed in the literature (van Beek & Cohen 1990; Golumbic & Shamir 1993; Nebel & Bürckert 1995). Some of these algebras have later been extended with mechanisms for handling quantitative information. For example the TimeGraph II system (Gerevini, Schubert, & Schaeffer 1993) extends the *pointisable algebra* (van Beek & Cohen 1990) with a limited type of quantitative information. Of special interest is the ORD-Horn algebra (Nebel & Bürckert 1995) which, under certain conditions, is the *unique* maximal tractable subclass of Allen's algebra. Hence, it would be especially interesting to extend this algebra with quantitative information since the maximality result would carry over to the new algebra, at least with respect to its qualitative expressiveness. To our knowledge, no such attempt have been made.

Now, to make the topic of reasoning about temporal constraint more concrete, consider the following fictious crime scenario. Professor Jones has been found shot on the beach near her house. Rumours tell that she was almost sure of having a proof that P≠NP, but had not yet shown it to any of her colleagues. The graduate student Hill is soon to defend his thesis on his newly invented complexity class, $\mathrm{NRQP}_{\Sigma}(\mathfrak{d})^{\maltese}$, which would unfortunately be of no value were it to be known for certain that P≠NP. Needless to say, Hill is thus one of the prime suspects and inspector Smith is faced with the following facts and observations:

- Professor Jones died between 6 pm and 11 pm, according to the post-mortem.
- Mr Green, who lives close to the beach, is certain that he heard a gunshot sometime in the evening, but certainly after the TV news.
- The TV news is from 7.30 pm to 8.00 pm.
- A reliable neighbour of Hill claims Hill arrived at home sometime between 9.15 pm and 9.30 pm.
- It takes between 10 and 20 mins. to walk or run from the place of the crime to the closest parking lot.
- It takes between 45 and 60 mins. to drive from this parking lot to Hill's home.

The first thing to do is verifying that these facts and observations are consistent, which is obviously the case here. We can also draw some further conclusions, like narrowing the time of death to the interval between 8.00 pm and 11 pm, assuming the gunshot heard by mr Green actually was the killing shot.

Now, suppose inspector Smith adds the hypothesis that Hill was at the place of the murder at the time of the gunshot, which is only known to occur somewhere in the interval from 8.00 pm to 11.00 pm. If the set of facts and observations together with this hypothesis becomes inconsistent, then inspector Smith can rule out Hill as the murderer[1].

This problem can easily be cast in terms of a temporal-constraint-reasoning problem, involving both quantitative and qualitative relations over time points, intervals and durations. Unfortunately, it seems like this simple example cannot be solved by any of the computationally tractable methods reported in the literature. It can, however, be solved in polynomial time by the method proposed in this paper.

We introduce *Horn Disjunctive Linear Relations* (Horn DLRs for short) which is a temporal constraint formalism that allows for polynomial-time satisfiability checking. Horn DLRs subsumes the ORD-Horn algebra *and* most of the formalisms for encoding quantitative information proposed in the literature. The approach is rather different from the commonly used constraint network or graph-theoretic approaches. We base our method upon linear programming which proves to be a convenient tool for managing temporal information. Since most of the low-level handling of time points is thus abstracted away, the resulting algorithm is surprisingly simple. We strongly believe that Horn DLRs are useful in other areas of computer science than temporal reasoning. For instance, the proposal for constraint query languages in deductive databases by Kanellakis *et al.* (1995) has some resemblance with Horn DLRs.

The paper is structured as follows. We begin by giving basic terminology and definitions used in the rest of the paper together with a brief introduction to complexity issues in linear programming. We continue by presenting the polynomial-time algorithm for deciding satisfiability of Horn DLRs. The paper concludes with a short discussion of the results.

Disjunctive Linear Relations

We begin by defining different types of linear relations.

Definition 1 Let $X = \{x_1, \ldots, x_n\}$ be a set of real-valued variables. Let α, β be linear polynomials (*i.e.* polynomials of degree one) over X. A *linear disequation* over X is an expression of the form $\alpha \neq \beta$. A *linear equality* over X is an expression of the form $\alpha = \beta$. A *linear relation* over X is an expression of the form $\alpha r \beta$ where $r \in \{<, \leq, =, \neq, \geq, >\}$. A *convex linear relation* over X is an expression of the form $\alpha r_c \beta$ where $r_c \in \{<, \leq, =, \geq, >\}$. A *disequational linear relation* over X is an expression of the form $\alpha \neq \beta$. A *disjunctive linear relation* (DLR) is a disjunction of one or more linear relations.

Example 2 A typical DLR over $\{x_1, x_2, x_3\}$ is $(1.2x_1 + x_2 \leq x_3 + 5) \vee (12x_3 \neq 7.5x_2) \vee (x_2 = 5)$.

[1]Unfortunately, it seems like Hill will be in need of juridicial assistance.

Throughout this paper, we assume all sets of DLRs to be finite. The definition of satisfiability for DLRs is straightforward.

Definition 3 Let $X = \{x_1, \ldots, x_n\}$ be a set of real-valued variables and let $R = \{R_1, \ldots, R_k\}$ be a set of DLRs over X. We say that R is *satisfiable* iff there exists an assignment of real values to the variables in X that makes at least one member of each R_i, $1 \leq i \leq k$, true.

It is important to note that we only consider assignments of *real* values, thus assuming that time is linear, dense and unbounded. (We will see that it is sufficient to consider assignments of rational values further on.) We continue by classifying different types of DLRs.

Definition 4 Let γ be a DLR. $\mathcal{C}(\gamma)$ denotes the convex relations in γ and $\mathcal{NC}(\gamma)$ the disequational relations in γ. We say that γ is *convex* iff $|\mathcal{NC}(\gamma)| = 0$ and that γ is *disequational* iff $|\mathcal{C}(\gamma)| = 0$. If γ is convex or disequational we say that γ is *homogenous* and otherwise *heterogenous*. Furthermore, if $|\mathcal{C}(\gamma)| \leq 1$ then γ is *Horn*. We extend these definitions to sets of relations in the obvious way. For example, if Γ is a set of DLRs and all $\gamma \in \Gamma$ are Horn, then Γ is Horn.

This classification provides the basis for the forthcoming proofs. One detail to note is that if a Horn DLR is convex then it is a unit clause, *i.e.* a disjunction with only one member.

For Horn DLRs, we restrict ourselves only to use $\leq$ and $\neq$ in the relations. This is no loss of generality since we can express all the other relations in terms of these two. For example, a DLR of the form $x < y \vee D$ can be replaced by the disjunctions $\{x \leq y \vee D, x \neq y \vee D\}$. Observe that the resulting set of disjunctions can contain at most twice as many disjunctions as the original one. Hence, this is a polynomial time transformation. (Note, however, that this does not hold for general DLRs.)

Definition 5 Let A be a satisfiable set of DLRs and let γ be a DLR. We say that γ *blocks* A iff for every $d \in \mathcal{NC}(\gamma)$, $A \cup \{d\}$ is not satisfiable.

Observe that if $A \cup \{\gamma\}$ is satisfiable and γ blocks A then there must exist a relation $\delta \in \mathcal{C}(\gamma)$ such that $A \cup \{\delta\}$ is satisfiable. This observation will be of great importance in forthcoming sections.

Linear Programming

Our method for deciding satisfiability of Horn DLRs will be based on linear programming techniques and we will provide the basic facts needed in this section. The linear programming problem is defined as follows.

Definition 6 Let A be an arbitrary $m \times n$ matrix of rationals in finite precision and let $x = (x_1, \ldots, x_n)$ be an n-vector of variables over the real numbers. Then an instance of the *linear programming* (LP) problem is defined by: $\{\min c^{\mathrm{T}} x \text{ subject to } Ax \leq b\}$ where b is an m-vector of rationals and c an n-vector of rationals. The computational problem is as follows:

1. Find an assignment to the variables $x_1, \ldots, x_n$ such that the condition $Ax \leq b$ holds and $c^T x$ is minimial subject to these conditions, or
2. Report that there is no such assignment, or
3. Report that there is no lower bound for $c^T x$ under the conditions.

Analogously, we can define an LP problem where the objective is to maximize $c^T x$ under the condition $Ax \leq b$. We have the following important theorem.

Theorem 7 The linear programming problem is solvable in polynomial time.

Observe that the restriction to finite precision is not a restriction in practice since computers are (almost without exception) using finite precision arithmetics. Several polynomial algorithms have been developed for solving LPs. Well-known examples are the algorithms by Khachiyan (1979) and Karmarkar (1984). Despite their theoretical value, it is not at all clear that they out-perform the simplex algorithm which is exponential in the worst case (Klee & Minty 1972). In fact, recent theoretical analyses lend support to its favourable average-case performance. (See for example (Smale 1983).) In the following, we assume all coeffecients to be rationals represented in finite precision.

Satisfiability of Horn DLRs

In this section we present a polynomial algorithm for deciding satisfiability of Horn DLRs. The algorithm can be found in Figure 1. The problem of deciding satisfiability for a set of Horn DLRs is denoted HORNDLRSAT. We begin by exhibiting a simple method for deciding whether a set of convex linear relations augmented with one disequation is satisfiable or not. There may be more efficient methods for checking this than the one we propose. However, throughout this paper we will stress simplicity instead of tuning efficiency.

Lemma 8 Let A be an arbitrary $m \times n$ matrix, b be an m-vector and $x = (x_1, \ldots, x_n)$ be an n-vector of variables over the real numbers. Let α, β be linear polynomial over $x_1, \ldots, x_n$. Deciding whether the system $S = \{Ax \leq b, \alpha \neq \beta\}$ is satisfiable or not is polynomial.

Proof: Let $\alpha' = \alpha - c$ and $\beta' = \beta - d$ where c and d are the constant terms in α and β, respectively. Consider the following instances of LP:

LP1= $\{\min \alpha' - \beta' \text{ subject to } Ax \leq b\}$

LP2= $\{\max \alpha' - \beta' \text{ subject to } Ax \leq b\}$

If LP1 and LP2 have no solutions then S is not satisfiable. If both LP1 and LP2 yield the same optimal value $d - c$ then S is not satisfiable since every solution to LP1 and LP2 forces α to equal β. Otherwise S is obviously satisfiable. Since we can solve the LP problem in polynomial time by Theorem 7, the lemma follows. □

Before proceeding, we recapitulate some standard mathematical concepts.

Definition 9 Given two points $x, y \in R^n$, a *convex combination* of them is any point of the form $z = \lambda x + (1-\lambda)y$ where $0 \leq \lambda \leq 1$. A set $S \subseteq R^n$ is *convex* iff it contains all convex combinations of all pairs of points $x, y \in S$.

Definition 10 A *hyperplane* H in R^n is a non-empty set defined as $\{x \in R^n \mid a_1x_1 + \ldots + a_nx_n = b\}$ for some $a_1, \ldots, a_n, b \in R$.

Definition 11 Let A be an arbitrary $m \times n$ matrix and b be an m-vector. The *polyhedron* defined by A and b is the set $\{x \in R^n | Ax \leq b\}$.

The connection between polyhedrons and convex sets is expressed in the following well-known fact.

Fact 12 Every non-empty polyhedron is convex.

Consequently, the convex relations in a set of Horn DLRs defines a convex set in R^n. Furthermore, we can identify the disequations with hyperplanes in R^n. These observations motivate the next lemma.

Lemma 13 Let $S \subseteq R^n$ be a convex set and let $H_1, \ldots, H_k \subseteq R^n$ be distinct hyperplanes. If $S \subseteq \bigcup_{i=1}^k H_i$ then there exists a j, $1 \leq j \leq k$ such that $S \subseteq H_j$.

Proof: If it is possible to drop one or more hyperplanes from H and still have a union containing S then do so. Let $H' = \{H'_1, \ldots, H'_m\}$, $m \leq k$, be the resulting minimal set of hyperplanes. Every $H'_i \in H'$ contains some point x_i of S not in any other $H'_j \in H'$. We want to prove that there is only one hyperplane in H'.

If this is not the case, consider the line segment L adjoining x_1 and x_2. (The choice of x_1 and x_2 is not important. Every choice of x_i and x_j, $1 \leq i, j \leq m$ and $i \neq j$, would do equally well.) By convexity, $L \subseteq S$. Each $H'_i \in H'$ either contains L or meets it in at most one point. But no $H'_i \in H'$ can contain L, since then it would contain both x_1 and x_2. Thus each H'_i has at most one point in common with L, and the rest of L would not be a subset of $\bigcup_{i=1}^m H'_i$ which contradicts that $L \subseteq S \subseteq \bigcup_{i=1}^m H'_i$. □

We can now tie together the results and end up with a sufficient condition for satisfiability of Horn DLRs.

Lemma 14 Let Γ be a set of arbitrary Horn DLRs. Let $C \subseteq \Gamma$ be the set of convex DLRs in Γ and let $D = \{D_1, \ldots, D_k\} \subseteq \Gamma$ be the set of DLRs that are not convex. Under the condition that C is satisfiable, Γ is satisfiable if D_i does not block C for any $1 \leq i \leq k$.

Proof: Pick one disequation d_i out of every D_i such that $\{C, d_i\}$ is satisfiable. This is possible since no D_i blocks C. We show that $\Gamma' = \{C, d_1, \ldots, d_k\}$ is

1 **algorithm** SAT(Γ)
2 $A \leftarrow \bigcup\{\mathcal{C}(\gamma) | \gamma \in \Gamma \text{ is convex}\}$
3 **if** A not satisfiable **then reject**
4 **if** $\exists \gamma \in \Gamma$ that blocks A and is disequational **then reject**
5 **if** $\exists \gamma \in \Gamma$ that blocks A and is heterogenous **then** SAT$((\Gamma - \{\gamma\}) \cup \mathcal{C}(\gamma))$
6 **accept**

Figure 1: Algorithm for deciding satisfiability of Horn DLRs.

satisfiable and, hence, Γ is satisfiable. Assume that $d_i = (\alpha_i \neq \beta_i)$. Define the hyperplanes $H_1, \ldots, H_k$ such that $H_i = \{x \in R^n \mid \alpha_i(x) = \beta_i(x)\}$. Since every $\{C, d_i\}$ is satisfiable, the polyhedron P defined by C (which is non-empty and hence convex by Fact 12) is not a subset of any H_i. Suppose Γ' is not satisfiable. Then $P - \bigcup_{i=1}^{k} H_i = \varnothing$ which is equivalent with $P \subseteq \bigcup_{i=1}^{k} H_i$. By Lemma 13, there exists a H_j, $1 \leq j \leq k$ such that $S \subseteq H_j$. Clearly, this contradicts our initial assumptions. □

It is important to note that the previous lemma does not give a necessary condition for satisfiability of Horn DLRs. We claim that the algorithm in Figure 1 correctly solves HORNDLRSAT in polynomial time. To show this, we need an auxiliary lemma which is a formal version of an observation made in the second section of this paper.

Lemma 15 Let Γ be a set of Horn DLRs and let $C \subseteq \Gamma$ be the set of convex DLRs in Γ. If there exists a heterogenous DLR $\gamma \in \Gamma$ such that γ blocks C, then Γ is satisfiable iff $(\Gamma - \{\gamma\}) \cup \mathcal{C}(\gamma)$ is satisfiable.

Proof: *if:* Trivial.
only-if: If Γ is satisfiable, then γ has to be satisfiable. Since γ blocks C, $\mathcal{C}(\gamma)$ must be satisfied in any solution of Γ. □

We can now prove the soundness and completeness of SAT.

Lemma 16 Let Γ be a set of Horn DLRs. If SAT(Γ) accepts then Γ is satisfiable.

Proof: Induction over n, the number of heterogenous DLRs in Γ.
Basis step: If $n = 0$ and SAT(Γ) accepts then the formulae in A are satisfiable and there does not exist any $\gamma \in \Gamma$ that blocks A. Consequently, Γ is satisfiable by Lemma 14.
Induction hypothesis: Assume the claim holds for $n = k$, $k \geq 0$.
Induction step: Γ contains $k+1$ heterogenous DLRs. If SAT accepts in line 5 then $(\Gamma - \{\gamma\}) \cup \mathcal{C}(\gamma)$, which contains k heterogenous DLRs, is satisfiable by the induction hypothesis. By Lemma 15, this is equivalent with Γ being satisfiable. If SAT accepts in line 6 then there does not exist any disequational or heterogenous $\gamma \in \Gamma$ which blocks A. By Lemma 14, this means that Γ is satisfiable. □

Before proving the completeness of SAT we need the following lemma.

Lemma 17 Let Γ be a set of Horn DLRs. Let $C \subseteq \Gamma$ be the set of convex DLRs in Γ. If there exists a disequational DLR $\gamma \in \Gamma$ that blocks C then Γ is not satisfiable.

Proof: In any solution to Γ, the relations in $C \cup \{\gamma\}$ must be satisfied. Since γ is disequational and blocks C this is not possible and the lemma follows. □

Lemma 18 Let Γ be a set of Horn DLRs. If SAT(Γ) rejects then Γ is not satisfiable.

Proof: Induction over n, the number of heterogenous DLRs in Γ.
Basis step: If $n = 0$ then SAT can reject in lines 3 and 4. If SAT rejects in line 3 then, trivially, Γ is not satisfiable. If SAT rejects in line 4 then there exists a disequational $\gamma \in \Gamma$ that blocks A. Hence, Γ is not satisfiable by Lemma 17.
Induction hypothesis: Assume the claim holds for $n = k$, $k \geq 0$.
Induction step: Γ contains $k+1$ heterogenous DLRs. If SAT rejects in line 3 then Γ is not satisfiable. If SAT rejects in line 4 then Γ is not satisfiable by Lemma 17. If SAT rejects in line 5 then $(\Gamma - \{\gamma\}) \cup \mathcal{C}(\gamma)$, which contains k heterogenous DLRs, is not satisfiable by the induction hypothesis. By Lemma 15, this is equivalent with Γ not being satisfiable. □

Finally, we can show that SAT is a polynomial-time algorithm and, thus, show that HORNDLRSAT is polynomial.

Theorem 19 HORNDLRSAT is polynomial.

Proof: By Lemmata 16 and 18, it is sufficient to show that SAT is polynomial. The number of recursive calls is bounded by the number of heterogenous DLRs in the given input. By Lemma 8, we can in polynomial time decide whether a linear inequality system with one disequation is satisfiable. Since we need only check a polynomial number of such systems in each recursion, the theorem follows. □

We conclude this section with a discussion about whether HORNDLRSAT can be effeciently solved on parallel computers. The complexity class NC consists of the problems that can be solved with a polynomial number of processors in polylogarithmic time and it is often argued that NC captures our intuitive notion of problems satisfactorily solved by parallel computers. Recall that the satisfiability problem for propositional Horn clauses (HORNSAT) is P-complete under log-space reductions (Greenlaw, Hoover, & Russo 1993).

Clearly, it is trivial to reduce HORNSAT to HORNDLR-SAT in log-space. Since HORNDLRSAT is polynomial, it follows that it is P-complete as well. This implies that HORNDLRSAT is not in NC and, hence, there does not exist parallel algorithms for HORNDLRSAT that is substantially faster than ordinary sequential algorithms. (Unless NC=P which is considered very unlikely.)

Comparison

In this section, we show that Horn DLRs subsumes several other methods for temporal constraint reasoning. Let x, y be real-valued variables, c, d constants and $\mathcal{A}$ Allen's algebra (Allen 1983) in the definitions below.

Definition 20 (Nebel & Bürckert 1995) An *ORD clause* is a disjunction of relations of the form xry where $r \in \{\leq, =, \neq\}$. The *ORD-Horn* subclass $\mathcal{H}$ is the relations in $\mathcal{A}$ that can be written as ORD clauses containing only disjunctions with at most one relation of the form $x = y$ or $x \leq y$ and an arbitrary number of relations of the form $x \neq y$.

Note that the ORD-Horn class subsumes both the continuous endpoint algebra (Vilain, Kautz, & van Beek 1989) and the pointisable endpoint algebra (van Beek & Cohen 1990).

Definition 21 (Koubarakis 1992) Let $r \in \{\leq, \geq, \neq\}$. A *Koubarakis formula* is a formula on one of the following forms (1) $(x - y)rc$, (2) xrc or (3) a disjunction of formulae of the form $(x - y) \neq c$ or $x \neq c$.

Definition 22 (Dechter, Meiri, & Pearl 1991) A *simple temporal constraint* is a formula on the form $c \leq (x - y) \leq d$.

Simple temporal constraints are equivalent with the *simple metric constraints* (Kautz & Ladkin 1991).

Definition 23 (Meiri 1991) A *CPA/single interval* formula is a formula on one of the following forms: (1) $c\, r_1\, (x - y)\, r_2\, d$; or (2) $x\, r\, y$ where $r \in \{<, \leq, =, \neq, \geq, >\}$ and $r_1, r_2 \in \{<, \leq\}$.

Definition 24 (Gerevini, Schubert, & Schaeffer 1993) A *TG-II* formula is a formula on one of the following forms: (1) $c \leq x \leq d$, (2) $c \leq x - y \leq d$ or (3) $x\, r\, y$ where $r \in \{<, \leq, =, \neq, \geq, >\}$.

We can now state the main theorem of this section.

Theorem 25 The formalisms defined in Definitions 20 to 24 can trivially be expressed as Horn DLRs.

Note that Meiri (1991) considers two further tractable classes that cannot (in any obvious way) be transformed into Horn DLRs. The finding that the ORD-Horn algebra can be expressed as Horn DLRs is especially important in the light of the following theorem.

Theorem 26 (Nebel & Bürckert 1995) Let $\mathcal{S}$ be any subclass of $\mathcal{A}$ that contains all basic relations. Then either

1. $\mathcal{S} \subseteq \mathcal{H}$ and the satisfiability problem for $\mathcal{S}$ is polynomial, or
2. Satisfiability for $\mathcal{S}$ is NP-complete.

By the previous theorem, we cannot expect to find tractable classes that are able to handle all basic relations in $\mathcal{A}$ and, at the same time, are able to handle any single relation that cannot be expressed as a Horn DLR. In other words, the qualitative fragment of HORNDLRSAT inherits the maximality of the ORD-Horn algebra.

Discussion

Several researchers in the field of temporal constraint reasoning have expressed a feeling that their proposed methods should be extended so they can express relations between more than two time points. As a first example, in (Dechter, Meiri, & Pearl 1991) one can read "The natural extension of this work is to explore TCSPs with higher-order expressions (e.g. "John drives to work at least 30 minutes more than Fred does"; $X_2 - X_1 + 30 \leq X_4 - X_3$)..." Even though they do not define the exact meaning of "higher-order expressions" we can notice that their example is a simple Horn DLR. Something similar can be found in (Koubarakis 1992) who wants to express "the duration of interval I exceeds the duration of interval J". Once again, this can easily be expressed as a Horn DLR. These claims seem to indicate that the use of Horn DLRs is a significant contribution to temporal reasoning.

We have shown that the satisfiability problem for Horn DLRs can be carried out in polynomial time. However, the method builds on solving linear programs and it is well-known that such calculations can be computationally heavy. It is important to remember the reasons for introducing Horn DLRs. The main reason was not to provide an extremely efficient method, but to find a method unifying most of the other tractable classes reported. It is fairly obvious that the proposed method cannot outperform highly specialized algorithms for severely restricted classes. It should be likewise obvious that the specialized methods cannot compete with Horn DLRs in terms of expressivity. We are, as always in tractable reasoning, facing the tradeoff between expressivity and computational complexity. We believe, though, that the complexity of deciding satisfiability can be drastically improved by devising better algorithms than SAT. The algorithm SAT is constructed in a way that facilitates its correctness proofs and it is not optimized with respect to execution time in any way. The question whether improved versions can compete with algorithms such as TIME-GRAPH II or not remains open.

Throughout this paper we have assumed that time is linear, dense and unbounded but this may not be the case in real applications. For example, in a sampled system we cannot assume time to be dense. One question to answer in the future is what the effects of changing the assumptions of time are. Switching to discrete time will probably make reasoning computationally harder. There are some positive results concerning discrete time, however. Meiri (1991) presents a class of temporal constraint reasoning problems where integer time satisfiability is polynomial.

Conclusion

We have introduced the Horn DLR as a means for temporal constraint reasoning. We have proven that deciding satisfiability of sets of Horn DLRs is polynomial by exhibiting an algorithm based upon linear programming. Furthermore, we have shown that several other approaches to tractable temporal constraint reasoning can be encoded as Horn DLRs, including the ORD-Horn algebra and most methods for purely quantitative reasoning.

Acknowledgements

We would like to thank Marcus Bjäreland and Thomas Drakengren for discussions and comments. We are also indebted to William C. Waterhouse who improved our original proof of Lemma 13.

References

American Association for Artificial Intelligence. 1991. *Proceedings of the 9th (US) National Conference on Artificial Intelligence (AAAI-91)*, Anaheim, CA, USA: AAAI Press/MIT Press.

Allen, J. F. 1983. Maintaining knowledge about temporal intervals. *Communications of the ACM* 26(11):832–843.

Dechter, R.; Meiri, I.; and Pearl, J. 1991. Temporal constraint networks. *Artificial Intelligence* 49:61–95.

Gerevini, A.; Schubert, L.; and Schaeffer, S. 1993. Temporal reasoning in Timegraph I–II. *SIGART Bulletin* 4(3):21–25.

Golumbic, M. C., and Shamir, R. 1993. Complexity and algorithms for reasoning about time: A graph-theoretic approach. *Journal of the ACM* 40(5):1108–1133.

Greenlaw, R.; Hoover, H. J.; and Russo, W. L. 1993. *A Compendium of Problems Complete for P*. Oxford: Oxford University Press.

Kanellakis, P. C.; Kuper, G. M.; and Revesz, P. Z. 1995. Constraint query languages. *Journal of Computer and System Sciences* 51(1):26–52.

Karmarkar, N. 1984. A new polynomial time algorithm for linear programming. *Combinatorica* 4:373–395.

Kautz, H., and Ladkin, P. 1991. Integrating metric and temporal qualitatvie temporal reasoning. In AAAI-91 (1991), 241–246.

Khachiyan, L. G. 1979. A polynomial algorithm in linear programming. *Soviet Mathematics Doklady* 20:191–194.

Klee, V., and Minty, G. J. 1972. How good is the simplex algorithm? In Shisha, O., ed., *Inequalities III*, 159–175.

Koubarakis, M. 1992. Dense time and temporal constraints with $\neq$. In Swartout, B., and Nebel, B., eds., *Proceedings of the 3rd International Conference on Principles on Knowledge Representation and Reasoning (KR-92)*, 24–35. Cambridge, MA, USA: Morgan Kaufmann.

Meiri, I. 1991. Combining qualitative and quantitative constraints in temporal reasoning. In AAAI-91 (1991), 260–267.

Nebel, B., and Bürckert, H.-J. 1995. Reasoning about temporal relations: A maximal tractable subclass of Allen's interval algebra. *Journal of the ACM* 42(1):43–66.

Smale, S. 1983. On the average speed of the simplex method of linear programming. *Mathematical Programming* 27:241–262.

van Beek, P., and Cohen, R. 1990. Exact and approximate reasoning about temporal relations. *Computational Intelligence* 6(3):132–144.

Vilain, M. B.; Kautz, H. A.; and van Beek, P. G. 1989. Constraint propagation algorithms for temporal reasoning: A revised report. In Weld, D. S., and de Kleer, J., eds., *Readings in Qualitative Reasoning about Physical Systems.* San Mateo, Ca: Morgan Kaufmann. 373–381.

Rule-Based Reasoning & Connectionism

Production Systems Need Negation As Failure

Phan Minh Dung
Computer Science Program, Asian Institute of Technology
PO Box 2754, Bangkok 10501, Thailand
dung@cs.ait.ac.th

Paolo Mancarella
Dipartimento di Informatica, University of Pisa
Corso Italia 40, 56125 Pisa, Italy
paolo@di.unipi.it

Abstract

We study action rule based systems with two forms of negation, namely classical negation and "negation as failure to find a course of actions". We show by several examples that adding negation as failure to such systems increase their expressiveness, in the sense that real life problems can be represented in a natural and simple way. Then, we address the problem of providing a formal declarative semantics to these extended systems, by adopting an argumentation based approach, which has been shown to be a simple unifying framework for understanding the declarative semantics of various nonmonotonic formalisms. In this way, we naturally define the grounded (well-founded), stable and preferred semantics for production systems with negation as failure. Next, we characterize the class of stratified production systems, which enjoy the properties that the above mentioned semantics coincide and that negation as failure can be computed by a simple bottom-up operator.

Introduction and Motivations

In this section we first give examples to motivate the extension of the production systems paradigm (Hayes-Roth 1985) by the introduction of negation as failure (to find a course of actions). We then discuss its role as a specification mechanism for reactive systems.

On the need for negation as failure in production systems

Example 1 Imagine the situation of a person doing his household work. Clothes have to be washed and the person has two options, either hand washing or machine washing. If there is machine powder in house, then machine washing can take place. This is represented by the production rule

r_1 : **if** Powder **then** machine-wash.

If no machine powder is in house, then it can be acquired by either buying it in the shop (provided the shops are open) or by borrowing it from the neighbor (if he is in). The rules for acquiring powder can be represented by the following two classical production rules

r_2 : **if** $\neg$ Powder, Shop-Open **then** buy

r_3 : **if** $\neg$ Powder, Neighbor-In **then** borrow.

Of course, hand washing is undesirable and will be taken up if *there is no way to acquire machine powder*. The naive representation of this rule using classical negation

if $\neg$ Powder **then** hand-wash

is clearly not correct, since the meaning of such a rule is that if there is no machine powder in house at the current state, then the clothes should be hand washed, while the intuitive meaning of "there is no way to acquire machine powder" is that there is no *course of actions* starting from the current state leading to acquiring machine powder. Hence in a state where there is no machine powder in house and the neighbor is in, the above naive representation would allow hand washing though there is a way to acquire machine powder by borrowing it from the neighbor. Hence it fails to capture the intuitive understanding of the problem.

Here we need to use a different kind of negation, called negation as failure (to find a course of actions) and denoted by the operator *not*. The previous naive representation is now replaced by

r_4 : **if** *not* Powder **then** hand-wash.

It is not difficult to find other real life situations governed by rules with negation as failure.

Example 2 Consider the rules for reviewing the work of faculties at the end of each academic year in a university. The first rule specifies the conditions for offering tenure to assistant professors. It states that assistant professors with good publications and with a working experience of at least five years should be offered tenure. This rule could be formalized by:

if Assistant-Prof(X), Good-Pub(X),
Work-at-least-5-years(X) **then** offer-tenure(X).

The second rule states that *if an assistant professor has no prospect of getting a tenure then fire him.* Though the intuitive meaning of this rule is clear, it is not possible to represent it as a classical production rule since the premises of a classical production rule represent conditions which must be satisfied in the current state of the world while the premises of the second rule represent a projection into the future. It says that if there is no possibility for an assistant professor to get a tenure in the future then sack him now. In other words, the rule says that if an assistant will fail in all possible course of actions in the future to get a tenure then fire him. To represent this rule, we use again negation as failure to find a course of actions. The second rule can then be represented as follows:

if Assistant-Prof(X), *not* Getting-Tenure(X)
then fire(X)

In real life, we often find ourselves in situations where we have to deal with risky or undesirable actions. For example, a doctor may have to take the decision of cutting the foot of his patient due to some severe frostbite. This is a very risky, undesirable decision and the commonsense rule specifying the conditions for taking this action is that the doctor is allowed to cut if *there is no other way* to save the foot of the patient. This can be represented, using negation as failure, as follows:

if *not* Save **then** cut.

Finally, we can expect that in real life, intelligent systems could be employed to satisfy multiple goals. These goals can have different priorities, and negation as failure (to find a course of actions) can be used to represent these priorities as in the following example.

Example 3 Consider a robot fire fighter that should be sent into a fire to save lives and properties. The priority here is certainly saving lives first. Imagine now that the robot is standing before a valuable artifact. Should it take it and get out of the fire? The answer should be yes *only if* the robot is certain that there is nothing it can do to save any life. The rule can be represented as follows

if Artifact(X), In-Danger(X), *not* Human-Found
then save(X)

Note that the *not* Human-Found here means that no human being could be found in the current and all other possible states of the world reachable by firing a sequence of actions the robot is enabled to perform.

Negation as failure as a specification mechanism for reactive systems

Let us consider again the example 1. Checking whether the conditions of the rule

r_4 : **if** *not* Powder **then** hand-wash

are satisfied in the current state involves checking whether there is any way to acquire machine powder from the current state, a process which could be time consuming and expensive. In a concrete application, as in our example where there are only two ways to get powder: buying it in the shop or borrowing it from the neighbor, negation as failure can be "compiled" into classical negation to produce a more efficient rule:

if ¬ Powder, ¬ Shop-Open, ¬ Neighbor-In
then hand-wash.

However, the environment in which a production system with the above rule is applied can change. For example, you may get a new neighbor who may not have any interest for good relations to other peoples, and so you will not be able to borrow anything from him. Hence the rule for borrowing must be dropped. Consequently the above production rule must be revised to

if ¬ Powder, ¬ Shop-Open **then** hand-wash

It is clear that the rule r_4 with negation as failure is still correct and serves as a specification for checking the correctness of the new rule.

The point we want to make here is that in many cases, though negation as failure is not employed directly, it could be used as a specification mechanism for a classical production system. This situation can be encountered quite often in many real life situations. Imagine the work of a physician in an emergency case dealing with a patient who is severely injured in a road accident. In such cases, where time is crucial, what a doctor would do is to follow certain treatments he has been taught to apply in such situations. He more or less simply *react* depending on the physical conditions of the patient. The treatment may even suggest a fateful decision to operate the patient to cut some of his organs. Now it is clear that such treatment changes according to the progress of the medical science. One treatment which was correct yesterday may be wrong today. So what decides the correctness of such treatments? We can think of such treatments in a simplified way as a set of production rules telling the doctors what to do in a concrete state of a patient. The correctness of such rules are determined by such *commonsense principles* like: *Operate and cut an organ only if there is no other way to save the patient.* And such a principle can be expressed using negation as failure.

Aim of this work

We have seen in the examples that using negation as failure in production systems allows one to naturally and correctly represent many real life problems. The main aim of this paper is to provide a declarative semantics to production systems where two kinds of negation are used, classical negation and negation as failure (to find a course of actions). In this respect, we show that the argumentation based approach (Dung 1995), which has been successfully adopted to understand logic programming with negation as failure as well as many other nonmonotonic formalisms, can also be adopted to provide a natural and simple declarative semantics to production systems with two kind of negations. The basic idea is that negation as failure literals, such as "*not* Powder" in example 1, represent *assumptions* underlying potential computations of a production system. The intuitive meaning of such an assumption is that the computation goes on by assuming that there is no course of actions (i.e. computation) from the current state of the world leading to a state which defeats the assumption itself. Referring back to example 1, assuming *not* Powder corresponds to assuming that from the current state there is no course of actions leading to a state where machine powder is in house. A computation which is supported by a sequence of assumptions is plausible (acceptable) if its underlying assumptions cannot be defeated by actually find a course of actions which defeats them.

These informal, intuitive notions can be formalized by viewing a production system as an argumentation system along the lines of (Dung 1995). This provides us with many natural semantics, such as the grounded (well-founded), the preferred and the stable semantics (Dung 1995). These semantics are arguably the most popular and widely accepted semantics for nonmonotonic and commonsense reasoning in the literature (Gelfond & Lifschitz 1988; Bondarenko *et al.* 1995; McDermott & Doyle 1980; Van Gelder, Ross, & Schlipf 1988).

Moreover, we address the problem of actually computing negation as failure. In this respect, we introduce the class of *stratified* production systems, where negation as failure can be computed using a simple bottom-up operator. As for the case of general stratified argumentation systems, stratified production systems enjoy the property that all the previously mentioned semantics (grounded, preferred and stable) coincide.

Classical production systems

We introduce here the notations and basic terminologies we are going to use in the following. The production system language we use is similar to classical ones (see, e.g. (Forgy 1981)). We assume a first order language $\mathcal{L}$ representing the ontology used to describe the domain of interest. A *state* of the world is interpreted as a snapshot of this world, hence is represented as a Herbrand interpretation of $\mathcal{L}$, i.e. as a set of ground atoms of $\mathcal{L}$. The set of states is denoted by *Stat*. Further we assume that a set of *primitive actions* $\mathcal{A}$ is given. The semantics (effect) of actions is described by the function

$$effect : \mathcal{A} \times Stat \rightarrow Stat.$$

A *production rule* is a rule of the form

if $l_1, \ldots, l_n$ **then** a

where $l_1, \ldots, l_n$ are ground literals of $\mathcal{L}$ and a is an action in $\mathcal{A}$. The conditions (resp. action) of a rule r will be referred to by $cond(r)$ (resp. $action(r)$). A *production system* P is a set of production rules.

A production rule **if** $l_1, \ldots, l_n$ **then** a is said to be *applicable* in a state S iff the conditions $l_1, \ldots, l_n$ are true in S, i.e. $S \models l_1 \wedge \ldots \wedge l_n$.

Definition 4 A *partial computation* C of a production system P is a sequence

$$S_0 \xrightarrow{r_1} S_1 \ldots \xrightarrow{r_n} S_n$$

$n \geq 0$, such that S_i's are states, r_i's are production rules in P and for each $i \geq 1$, r_i is applicable in S_{i-1}, and $S_i = effect(action(r_i), S_{i-1})$. S_0 will be referred to as $initial(C)$ and S_n as $final(C)$.

A partial computation C

$$S_0 \xrightarrow{r_1} S_1 \ldots \xrightarrow{r_n} S_n$$

is called a *complete computation* if no production rule in P is applicable in S_n. ◇

Note that, if $n = 0$, then the partial computation is an empty computation.

The behavior of a production system P can be defined as the set of pairs of states (S, S') such that S (resp. S') is the initial (resp. final) state of some complete computation of P. This is formalized in the next definition.

Definition 5 For a production system P, the input-output semantics of P is defined by

$$\mathcal{IO}(P) = \{(initial(C), final(C)) \mid C \text{ is a complete computation of } P\}.$$ ◇

Production rules with NAF

We introduce a new form of negation into the language $\mathcal{L}$, denoted by *not*. A general literal is now either a (classical) literal l or a *naf*-literal *not* l, where l is a classical literal. For each classical literal l, the intuition of *not* l is that *it is not possible to find a course of actions to achieve* l.

Definition 6 A *general* production rule has the form

if $l_1, \ldots, l_n$ **then** a_i

where each l_i is a ground general literal. ◇

Given a general production rule

if $l_1, \ldots, l_n$ **then** a_i

the set of classical literals in r will be referred to as $cl\text{-}cond(r)$, and the set of naf-literals will be referred to as $hyp(r)$.

A *general* production system (GPS) P is a set of general production rules. A general production rule is said to be *possibly applicable* in a state S if $S \models cl\text{-}cond(r)$. Notice that a rule satisfying the condition that $S \models cl\text{-}cond(r)$ in a state S is not necessarily applicable in S since it is not clear whether its naf-conditions are satisfied in S.

Definition 7 Given a GPS P, a *possible partial computation* in P is a sequence

$$S_0 \xrightarrow{r_1} S_1 \ldots \xrightarrow{r_n} S_n.$$

where S_i's are states, r_i's are general production rules in P, for each $i \geq 1$, r_i is possibly applicable in S_{i-1} and $S_i = effect(action(r_i), S_{i-1})$.

Given a GPS P, the set of all possible partial computations of P is denoted by $\mathcal{C}(P)$. ◇

When a possible partial computation is acceptable: a motivating discussion

The basic idea in understanding the meaning of naf-conditions *not* l's in general production rules is to view them as hypotheses which can be assumed if there is no possible course of actions to achieve l. So, intuitively we can say that a rule is applicable in a state S if it is possibly applicable and each of its hypotheses could be assumed. A partial (pre)computation is then an acceptable partial computation if each of its rules is applicable. The whole problem here is to understand formally what does it mean that there is no possible course of actions starting from a state S to achieve some result l. Let us consider again the example 1.

Example 8 Let us consider again the washing example. The effects of the actions are specified below:

$effect(\text{hand-wash}, S) = S \cup \{\text{Clean}, \text{Tired}\}$

$effect(\text{machine-wash}, S) = (S \backslash \{\text{Powder}\}) \cup \{\text{Clean}\}$ if Powder $\in S$

$effect(\text{machine-wash}, S) = S$ if Powder $\notin S$

$effect(\text{buy}, S) = S \cup \{\text{Powder}, \text{Less-Money}\}$

$effect(\text{borrow}, S) = S \cup \{\text{Powder}\}$

Assume that in the initial state we have no powder, shops are closed and the neighbor is in. This state is represented by the interpretation $S_0 = \{$Neighbor-In$\}$. From this state there are three possible nonempty partial computations starting from S_0, namely

$C_1 : S_0 \xrightarrow{r_4} \{\text{Neighbor-In, Clean, Tired}\}$

$C_2 : S_0 \xrightarrow{r_3} \{\text{Neighbor-In, Powder}\} \xrightarrow{r_1} \{\text{Neighbor-In, Clean}\}.$

$C_3 : S_0 \xrightarrow{r_3} \{\text{Neighbor-In, Powder}\}$

First, notice that both C_2 and C_3 are not based on any assumption. Our commonsense dictate that C_2 and C_3 represent acceptable course of actions from the initial state which lead to the commonsense result that clothes are machine washed. Hence they both must be accepted as possible courses of actions. On the other hand C_1 is based on the assumption "*not* Powder", meaning that C_1 assumes that there is no possible way to acquire the machine powder. However, C_3 represents just one such possible way. Hence, C_3 represents an *attack* against the assumption "*not* Powder". So C_3 can also be viewed as an attack against the acceptability of C_1 as a legitimate computation. On the other hand, both C_2 and C_3 are not based on any assumption, hence there is no way they can be attacked.

This example points out that the semantics of GPS's is a form of argumentation reasoning, where arguments are represented by possible partial computations. In the following, we first recall the general notion of argumentation systems from (Dung 1995) and then we show that the natural semantics of GPS can be defined using the theory of argumentation.

Argumentation systems We review here the basic notions and definitions of argumentation systems (the reader can refer to (Dung 1995) for more details and for a discussion of the role of argumentation systems in many fields of Artificial Intelligence).

An *argumentation system* is a pair $\langle AR, attacks \rangle$ where AR is the set of all possible *arguments* and $attacks \subseteq AR \times AR$, representing the attack relationship between arguments. If the pair $(A, B) \in attacks$, then we say that A attacks B or B is attacked by A. Moreover, A attacks a set of arguments H if A attacks an argument $B \in H$. We also say that H attacks A if an argument $B \in H$ attacks A.

A set H of arguments is *conflict-free* if no argument in H attacks H.

An argument A is defended by a set of arguments H if H attacks any attack against A, i.e. for each argument $B \in AR$, if B attacks A then H attacks B. We also say that H defends A if A is defended by H.

The basic notion which underlies all the semantics for argumentation systems that we are going to review in the rest of this section, is the following, intuitive notion of acceptability of a set of arguments. A set H of arguments is ***acceptable*** if it is conflict-free and it can defend each argument in it.

Let H be a set of arguments and let $Def(H)$ be the set of all arguments which are defended by H. It is not difficult to see that H is acceptable iff $H \subseteq Def(H)$ and H is conflict-free. Further it is easy to see that $Def : \mathcal{P}(AR) \rightarrow \mathcal{P}(AR)$ is monotonic. Hence the equation $H = Def(H)$ has a least solution which is also acceptable (following from the fact that $Def(\emptyset)$ is acceptable and if H is acceptable then also $H \cup Def(H)$ is also acceptable).

The various semantics for argumentation systems are basically solutions of the above equation $H = Def(H)$. In particular, the ***grounded*** (well-founded) semantics of an argumentation system is the least solution of the equation $H = Def(H)$.

Another semantics for argumentation systems, called the ***preferred semantics***, is defined by the maximal acceptable sets of arguments. It is not difficult to see that these sets are the conflict-free maximal solutions of the equation $H = Def(H)$. In general, preferred sets contain the grounded semantics, but do not coincide with it. In the next section, we will give an example for this.

Finally, a popular semantics of nonmonotonic reasoning and argumentation systems is the stable semantics, defined as follows. A conflict-free set of arguments H is said to be ***stable*** if it attacks each argument not belonging to it. It is not difficult to see that each stable set of arguments is acceptable. Furthermore, it is also easy to see that each stable set is preferred, hence it is a maximal, conflict-free solution of the equation $H = Def(H)$, but not vice versa.

It has been shown that argumentation systems provide a simple and unifying semantical framework for commonsense reasoning. For example, logic programming and different logics for nonmonotonic reasoning and n-person games are showed to be different representations of the argumentation systems presented above (see (Dung 1995) for further details) where for instance, the grounded semantics of argumentation corresponds to the well-founded semantics in logic programming (Van Gelder, Ross, & Schlipf 1988) and stable semantics of argumentation correspond to stable semantics of logic programming (Gelfond & Lifschitz 1988) and other prominent nonmonotonic logics like Reiter's default logic (Reiter 1980) or Moore's autoepistemic logic (Moore 1985).

In the following we show that general production systems with two kinds of negation are also a form of argumentation systems.

Computations as arguments The semantics of a GPS P is defined by viewing it as an argumentation framework $\langle AR(P), attacks \rangle$, where $AR(P)$ is the set of all possible partial computations of P and the relation *attacks* is defined as follows.

Definition 9 Let C be a possible partial computation
$$S_0 \xrightarrow{r_1} S_1 \longrightarrow \ldots \longrightarrow S_i \xrightarrow{r_{i+1}} S_{i+1} \longrightarrow \ldots \xrightarrow{r_n} S_n.$$
An *attack* against C is a possible partial computation C' such that $initial(C') = S_i$, for some i, and there exists an underlying assumption *not* l in $hyp(r_{i+1})$ such that l holds in $final(C')$. ◇

Remark: Empty computations cannot be attacked. Hence, empty computations are contained in any semantics.

Notice that, in the above definition, the initial state of the attack C', which defeats the assumption *not* l underlying C, has to be the actual state S_i in which such an assumption was made. In other words, whether an assumption *not* l can be defeated or not, depends on the state in which this assumption is made and on whether or not this state can be lead by a computation to a state in which l holds.

The view of a GPS as an argumentation system, allows us to provide it with three different semantics: grounded (well-founded), preferred and stable semantics.

It is easy to see that the following proposition hold.

Proposition 10
(*i*) If a computation C attacks a computation C' and C' is a prefix of C'', then C also attacks C''.
(*ii*) Let H be a set of computations which is either the grounded, or a preferred, or a stable set. For any $C \in H$, any prefix of C also belongs to H. ◇

We can now define the set of complete acceptable computations, with respect to a selected semantics.

Definition 11 Let P be a GPS and $\mathcal{R}$ be a selected semantics of P, i.e. $\mathcal{R}$ is either the grounded, or a preferred, or a stable, set of possible partial computations. A partial computation $C \in \mathcal{R}$ is called an *$\mathcal{R}$-complete* computation if there exists no other partial computation $C' \in \mathcal{R}$ such that C is a prefix of C'. ◇

If all the semantics of a GPS coincide, we simply talk about *complete* computations instead of $\mathcal{R}$-complete computations. Referring back to the example 8, the only complete computation starting from S_0 is C_2.

The input-output semantics of classical production systems can be extended to general production systems with respect to a selected (grounded, preferred, stable) semantics.

Definition 12 Let P be a GPS.
(*i*) The grounded input-output semantics of P is defined by
$$\mathcal{IO}_G(P) = \{(initial(C), final(C)) \mid C \text{ is a grounded complete computation}\}.$$
(*ii*) Let $\mathcal{R}$ be a set of arguments which is preferred or stable. Then
$$\mathcal{IO}_{\mathcal{R}}(P) = \{(initial(C), final(C)) \mid C \text{ is an } \mathcal{R}\text{-complete computation of } P\}.$$ ◇

Stratified Production Systems

In this section we consider only special kinds of GPS, where the actions are of two types, **assert**(p) and **retract**(p), where p is an atom. The effect of **assert**(p) (resp. **retract**(p)) on a state S is adding (resp. removing) p to S (resp. from S). Moreover, the rules have the following structure:
$$\neg p, l_1, \ldots, l_k, not\ l_{k+1}, \ldots, not\ l_n \rightarrow \mathbf{assert}(p)$$
$$p, l_1, \ldots, l_k, not\ l_{k+1}, \ldots, not\ l_n \rightarrow \mathbf{retract}(p)$$
where l_i's are classical literals. Rules of the first kind are called *assert* rules, and rules of the second kind are called *retract* rules. If it is not important to distinguish between assert and retract rules, we will simply write a rule as
$$l, l_1, \ldots, l_k, not\ l_{k+1}, \ldots, not\ l_n \rightarrow a.$$
Taking inspiration from the notion of stratification in logic programming (Apt, Blair, & Walker 1988), we define *stratified* GPS's in such a way that negation as failure can be computed bottom-up. In the following, given a classical literal l, we refer to *the atom of* l as l if it is a positive atom, and as p if l is $\neg p$.

Definition 13 A GPS P is *stratified* if there exists a partition $P_0 \cup \ldots \cup P_n$ of its rules such that the following conditions are satisfied. Let
$$l, l_1, \ldots, l_k, not\ l_{k+1}, \ldots, not\ l_h \rightarrow a$$
be a rule in P_j. Then
(*i*) for each l_i, $i = 1, \ldots, k$, each rule containing the atom of l_i in the head must belong to $\bigcup_{m \leq j} P_m$
(*ii*) for each l_i, $i = k+1, \ldots, h$, each rule containing the atom of l_i in the head must belong to $\bigcup_{m < j} P_m$. ◇

For stratified GPS's, the grounded, preferred and stable semantics coincide (see theorem 15). Moreover, this semantics can be computed in a bottom-up way, by a simple operator $\mathcal{S}$, that we define next.

Let C be a possible partial computation
$$S_0 \xrightarrow{r_1} S_1 \ldots \xrightarrow{r_n} S_n.$$
Then for any h, k such that $0 \leq h < k \leq n$, the sequence
$$S_h \xrightarrow{r_{h+1}} S_{h+1} \ldots \xrightarrow{r_k} S_k$$
is called a subcomputation of C.

Definition 14 Let $P = P_0 \cup \ldots \cup P_n$ be a stratified GPS. Let $\mathcal{S}$ be the operator defined as follows.
$\mathcal{S}(P_0) = \mathcal{C}(P_0)$
$\mathcal{S}(P_0 \cup \ldots \cup P_{i+1}) = \{C \in \mathcal{C}(P_0 \cup \ldots \cup P_{i+1}) \mid$

- $*$ for each subcomputation C' of C if $C' \in \mathcal{C}(P_0 \cup \ldots \cup P_i)$ then $C' \in \mathcal{S}(P_0 \cup \ldots \cup P_i)$
- $*$ for each subcomputation of C of the form $S_{j-1} \xrightarrow{r_j} S_j$ such that $r_j \in P_{i+1}$ then for each *not* $l \in hyp(r_j)$, there is no computation

$C' \in \mathcal{S}(P_0 \cup \ldots \cup P_i)$ such that $initial(C') = S_{j-1}$ and $final(C') \models l\}$ ◇

Roughly speaking, the operator $\mathcal{S}$ formalizes the intuition that the acceptability of a possible partial computation using rules in $P_0 \cup \ldots \cup P_{i+1}$ depends only on computations in $P_0 \cup \ldots \cup P_i$. Thus, the semantics of a stratified GPS P can be computed bottom-up by iterating the operator $\mathcal{S}$ on the strata of P.

Theorem 15 Let P be a stratified GPS. Then:
(*i*) $\mathcal{S}(P)$ is grounded
(*ii*) $\mathcal{S}(P)$ is the unique preferred set of computations
(*iii*) $\mathcal{S}(P)$ is the unique stable set of computations ◇

Conclusions and future work

Production systems with negation as failure to find a course of actions are a natural extension of classical production systems, which increases their expressiveness in the sense that they allow a natural and simple representation (specification) of many real life problems. This extension can be given a simple semantics based on an argumentation theoretic framework. There are still several issues which deserve a deeper study and understanding.

We have seen that our semantics reflects the inherent nondeterminism of production systems. In fact, in our semantics different complete computations starting from the same initial state can yield different final states, even for stratified GPS's. This contrasts with many efforts in the literature aiming at finding a method to select one of the complete computations as the expected semantics (Froidevaux 1992; Raschid 1994). Even though we believe that in many cases these efforts contrast with the inherent nondeterministic nature of the problems represented by the production rules, there are situations in which selecting only one out of (possibly) many complete computations may not harm at all. In these cases, it is worth studying computational strategies which basically provide us with a deterministic operational semantics for production systems. Still, the declarative semantics serves as a basis for reasoning about the correctness of these methods.

We are investigating the application of our approach in the active databases area. Active databases (Ceri, Dayal, & Widom 1995) is an important research topic in the database community due to the fact that they find many applications in practice. Typical active database rule is an event-condition-action form. We are currently extending our argumentation based approach to active rules which also contain negation as failure in the condition part of the rules.

Finally, a few words about the relationship between "negation as failure to find a course of actions" presented in this paper and "negation as failure to prove" in logic programming. In (Dung 1995), it has been showed that every argumentation framework can be represented by a simple logic program using negation as failure to prove. This means that negation as failure to find a course of actions can be represented using naf to prove. In a following paper we have also showed that naf to prove is a special kind of negation as failure to find a course of actions. Hence the conclusion is that the two kinds of naf have the same expressive power. Which one should be used in a concrete application depends on which one allows a more natural specification of the problem at hand.

Acknowledgments This research was supported in part by EEC Keep in Touch Activity KIT011-LPKRR.

References

Apt, K.; Blair, H.; and Walker, A. 1988. Towards a theory of declarative knowledge. In Minker, J., ed., *Foundations of Deductive Databases and Logic Programming*. Morgan Kaufmann.

Bondarenko, A.; Dung, P.; Kowalski, R.; and Toni, F. 1995. An abstract, argumentation-based theoretic approach to default reasoning. Technical report, Dept. of Computing, Imperial College of Science, Technology and Medicine, London.

Ceri, S.; Dayal, U.; and Widom, J. 1995. *Active Database Systems*. Morgan-Kauffman.

Dung, P. 1995. The acceptability of arguments and its fundamental role in logic programming, nonmonotonic reasoning and n-person games. *Artificial Intelligence* 77(2).

Forgy, C. 1981. OPS5 user's manual. Technical Report CMU-CS-81-135, Carnegie Mellon University.

Froidevaux, C. 1992. Default logic for action rule-based systems. In Neumann, B., ed., *Proc. 10th European Conference on Artificial Intelligence (ECAI 92)*, 413–417. John Wiley & Sons.

Gelfond, M., and Lifschitz, V. 1988. The stable model semantics for logic programming. In Kowalski, R., and Bowen, K., eds., *Proceedings of the Fifth International Conference on Logic Programming*, 1070–1080. The MIT Press.

Hayes-Roth, F. 1985. Rule based systems. *Communications of the ACM* 28(9).

McDermott, D., and Doyle, J. 1980. Non-Monotonic Logic I. *Artificial Intelligence* 13(1-2):41–72.

Moore, R. 1985. Semantical considerations on non-monotonic logics. *Artificial Intelligence* 25(1):75–94.

Raschid, L. 1994. A semantics for a class of stratified production system programs. *Journal of Logic programming*.

Reiter, R. 1980. A logic for default reasoning. *Artificial Intelligence* 13:81–132.

Van Gelder, A.; Ross, K.; and Schlipf, J. 1988. Unfounded sets and well-founded semantics for general logic programs. In *Proceedings of the Seventh Symposium on Principles of Database Systems, ACM-SIGACT-SIGCOM*, 221–230. The MIT Press.

Using Constraints to Model Disjunctions in Rule-Based Reasoning

Bing Liu and Joxan Jaffar

Department of Information Systems and Computer Science
National University of Singapore
Lower Kent Ridge Road, Singapore 119260, Republic of Singapore
{liub, joxan}@iscs.nus.sg

Abstract

Rule-based systems have long been widely used for building expert systems to perform practical knowledge intensive tasks. One important issue that has not been addressed satisfactorily is the disjunction, and this significantly limits their problem solving power. In this paper, we show that some important types of disjunction can be modeled with Constraint Satisfaction Problem (CSP) techniques, employing their simple representation schemes and efficient algorithms. A key idea is that disjunctions are represented as constraint variables, relations among disjunctions are represented as constraints, and rule chaining is integrated with constraint solving. In this integration, a constraint variable or a constraint is regarded as a special fact, and rules can be written with constraints and information about constraints. Chaining of rules may trigger constraint propagation, and constraint propagation may cause firing of rules. A prototype system (called CFR) based on this idea has been implemented.

1. Introduction

Rule-based systems are one of the great successes of AI (e.g., Newell 1973; Lucas & Van Der Gaag). They are widely used to build knowledge-based systems to perform tasks that normally require human knowledge and intelligence. However, there are still some important issues that have not been addressed satisfactorily in the current rules-based systems. One of them is the disjunction. This limits their problem solving power.

In the Constraint Satisfaction Problem (CSP) research, many efficient constraint propagation algorithms have been produced (Mackworth 1977; Hentenryck *et al* 1992). A number of languages or systems based on the model have also been developed and used for solving real-life problems (Jaffar & Maher 1994; Ilog Solver 1992).

In this paper, we show that some types of important disjunctions can be modeled with CSP. Thus, it is possible to use the simple representation scheme and efficient problem solving methods in CSP to handle these types of disjunctions. Specifically, the disjunctions can be represented as constraint variables and their domains. The relations among disjunctions can be represented as constraints. In this paradigm, constraint propagation and rule chaining are integrated. A constraint can be added as a special fact, and rules can be written with constraints and information about constraints. Chaining of rules may trigger constraint propagation, and constraint propagation may cause firing of rules. With the incorporation of CSP techniques, the power and the expressiveness of rule-based systems will be greatly increased. Based on this idea, a prototype system, called CFR, has also been implemented.

The idea of incorporating CSP into a logic-based system is not new. Constraint solving has long been integrated with logic programming languages such as Prolog. This integration has resulted in a number of Constraint Logic Programming (CLP) languages (Jaffar & Maher 1994), such as CLP(*R*) (Jaffar & Lassez, 1987) and Chip (Hentenryck 1989). These languages are primarily used for modeling and solving real-life optimization problems, such as scheduling and resource allocations. However, this work is different from that in CLP in a number of ways. The main difference is that CLP languages are all based on Horn clauses and backward chaining, while the proposed integration is based on forward chaining, which is suitable for solving a different class of reasoning problems. Integration of constraint solving and forward chaining has some specific problems that do not exist in CLP languages. The proposed integration is also mainly for improving reasoning capability of existing rule-based systems rather than for solving combinatorial search problems. Thus the types of constraints and their representations in the proposed approach are quite different from those in CLP languages.

We regard this work as the first step to a full integration of the CSP model with forward chaining rule-based systems. The current integration presented in this paper is still restrictive in the sense that it is mainly to help model and handle the problems with some disjunctions. A full integration could potentially change the way that people use rule-based systems and change the way that people solve practical reasoning problems, which are the main applications of the rule-based systems today. It may be just like the way that CLP languages have changed the way that people model and solve practical combinatorial search problems.

2. Rule-Based Systems and Constraint Satisfaction Problems

This section reviews rule-based systems and CSP. The coverage is by no means complete; rather the focus is on highlighting the problems with disjunctions in current rule-based systems.

2.1. Rule-Based Systems

A rule-based system consists of three main components.

1. A working memory (WM): a set of facts representing the current state of the system.
2. A rule memory (RM): a set of *IF-THEN* rules to test and to alter the WM.
3. A rule interpreter (RI): it applies the rules to the WM.

The rule interpreter repeatedly looks for rules whose conditions match facts in the WM. On each cycle, it picks a rule, and performs its actions. A rule is of the form:

IF <conditions> THEN <actions>

There are three common connectives in a rule-based system, i.e., *and, or* and *not*. We will only discuss *or* here as we are mainly interested in disjunctions. *or* in logic can be defined as *inclusive* ($\vee$) or *exclusive* ($\oplus$). Let us first look at the inclusive *or*. For example, "if something is a block or a pyramid, then it is a pointy_object" (adapted from (Charniak *et al* 1987)) can be expressed as follows:

IF *isa(?x, block)* $\vee$ *isa(?x, pyramid)*
THEN *add(isa(?x, pointy_object))*

where *?x* is a variable, and *add* adds a fact to the WM. This rule, however, cannot be used in a typical rule-based system. Instead, it is usually replaced by two rules:

IF *isa(?x, block)*
THEN *add(isa(?x, pointy_object))*, and
IF *isa(?x, pyramid)*
THEN *add(isa(?x, pointy_object))*.

However, this does not say exactly the same thing as the $\vee$ version does, since there might be situations where we know that either *?x* is a *block* or *?x* is a *pyramid*, but do not know which. In this case, neither of these rules applies, but the original one that uses $\vee$ does.

Now, let us look at the exclusive *or*. For example, the following formula says that "either *NYC* or *albany* is the capital of *NY*, but not both".

capital(NY, NYC) $\oplus$ *capital(NY, albany)*

This can be rephrased as two rules: "*NYC* is the capital of *NY*, if *albany* is not", and "*albany* is the capital of *NY*, if NYC is not"

IF *not(capital(NY, albany))*
THEN *add(capital(NY, NYC))*, and
IF *not(capital(NY, NYC))*
THEN *add(capital(NY, albany))*.

Unfortunately, *not* used in current rule-based systems is different from $\neg$ in logic. In a typical rule-based system, *not(P)* is satisfied if there is no fact in WM matching *P*.

In general, disjunctions are difficult to handle in reasoning. In Section 3, we will show that CSP provides a convenient model to represent these situations.

2.2. Constraint Satisfaction Problem

A Constraint Satisfaction Problem (CSP) is characterized as finding values for variables subject to a set of constraints. The standard CSP has three components:

- Variables: A finite set $V = \{v_1, v_2, ..., v_n\}$ of n variables v_i, which are also referred to as constraint variables.
- Values: Each variable v_i is associated with a finite domain D_i, which contains all the possible alternative values for v_i.
- Constraints: A set $C = \{C_1, C_2, ..., C_p\}$ of p constraints or relations on the variables.

The main approach used for solving CSPs is to embed constraint propagation (also known as consistency check) techniques in a backtrack search environment, where backtrack search performs the search for a solution and consistency check techniques prune the search space.

Consistency techniques are characterized by using constraints to remove inconsistent values from the domains of variables. Past research has produced many techniques for such a purpose. The main methods used in practice are arc consistency techniques, e.g., AC-3 (Mackworth 1977), AC-5 (Hentenryck *et al*, 1992), and AC-7 (Bessiere *et al* 1995), and their generalizations and specializations (Hentenryck 1989; Hentenryck *et al* 1992; Liu 1996). For a complete treatment of these methods, please refer to (Mackworth 1977; Mohr & Henderson 1986; Hentenryck 1989; Hentenryck *et al* 1992; Bessiere *et al* 1995; Liu 1995; Liu 1996).

3. Modeling Disjunctions with CSP

This section shows how CSP can be used to model certain types of disjunction in a rule-based system. In this new paradigm with rules and constraints, the underlying techniques for reasoning are forward rule-chaining, constraint propagation and backtrack search.

3.1. The New Paradigm

In the new paradigm, constraints are integrated into rule-based reasoning. It is described by:

1. A working memory (WM): a set of facts representing the current state of the system. There are three types of facts:
   - Simple facts: these are the traditional facts used in the existing rule-based systems.
   - *csp*-disjunctions (inclusive and exclusive): these are special types of disjunctions (defined below) represented by the CSP model.
   - Constraints: these are relations on the *csp*-disjunctions.
2. A rule memory: a set of *IF-THEN* rules.

3. A rule interpreter: this applies the rules to WM by using the traditional forward rule-chaining mechanism, and it is integrated with the constraint solver below.
4. A constraint solver: this uses consistency check and backtrack search for constraint satisfaction. It is integrated with the rule interpreter above.

Thus, the key advance of this new paradigm lies in its use of the CSP model and a constraint solver, resulting in an integration of forward chaining and constraint solving.

3.2. Using Constraint Variables and Domains to Represent Disjunctions

This sub-section describes how constraint variables and their domains can be used to represent disjunctions. We assume the basic definitions of *term* and *atom*, which are *ground* when they contain no variables.

We now define the two kinds of disjunctions that we will handle, the inclusive *csp*-disjunctions and exclusive *csp*-disjunctions. In what follows, we shall, for simplicity with respect to our examples later, restrict the terms in disjunctions to differ only in the last argument.

Definition 1: An exclusive *csp*-disjunction has the following form

$\oplus(P(t_1, ..., t_{n-1}, t_{n1}), P(t_1, ..., t_{n-1}, t_{n2}), ..., P(t_1, ..., t_{n-1}, t_{nm}))$

where $P(t_1, ..., t_{n-1}, t_{ni})$ is a ground atom, $n \geq 1$, t_{ni} is a constant, and $i \neq j$ implies $t_{ni} \neq t_{nj}$. The expression is TRUE *iff* exactly one of the m ground atoms is TRUE.

Note that for all the atoms, the predicate symbols are the same, i.e., P, and so are the first n -1 ground terms. Note also that t_{ni} may appear in any position as long as they are at the same position in each atom. We arbitrarily choose to put them at the end.

This exclusive *csp*-disjunction can be represented by an expression $\oplus P(t_1, ..., t_{n-1}, D)$, where D is a set with the initial value $\{t_{n1}, t_{n2}, ..., t_{nm}\}$. During the reasoning process, some of the atoms (e.g., $P(t_1, ..., t_{n-1}, t_{nk})$) may be proven to be FALSE, then D will be modified to reflect the effect. Thus D changes during the reasoning process, but it is always a subset of $\{t_{n1}, t_{n2}, ..., t_{nm}\}$. When $|D| = 1$, we say D (= $\{t_{ni}\}$) is *decided*, which means that $P(t_1, ..., t_{n-1}, t_{ni})$ is TRUE. When $D = \varnothing$, it means that the exclusive *csp*-disjunction is proven to be FALSE.

An important point is that $\oplus P(t_1, ..., t_{n-1}, D)$ can be represented by a constraint variable, written as $\oplus P(t_1, ..., t_{n-1}, \_)$, whose initial domain is D.

For example,

$\oplus$*Isa(john, {soldier, teacher})*

can represent the fact that *John* is a *soldier* or a *teacher*, and that *John* is only in one of the professions. The corresponding constraint variable $\oplus$*Isa(john, _)* can be used in constraints which hopefully eventually determine *John*'s real profession.

The second type of *csp*-disjunction is defined below.

Definition 2: An inclusive *csp*-disjunction

$\vee(P(t_1,...,t_{n-1}, t_{n1}), P(t_1, ..., t_{n-1}, t_{n2}), ..., P(t_1, ..., t_{n-1}, t_{nm}))$

is like an exclusive *csp*-disjunction, except that this formula is TRUE *iff* $\exists P(t_1, ..., t_{n-1}, t_{ni})$ is TRUE.

This inclusive *csp*-disjunction can be represented by an expression $\vee P(t_1, ..., t_{n-1}, S)$, where the initial value of S is the power set of $\{t_{n1}, t_{n2}, ..., t_{nm}\}$ excluding the empty set. It is convenient to think of S in two parts (R, Q):

- A set of required elements R: the elements that have been proven to be true, i.e., whose associated atoms have been proven to be TRUE.
- A set of possible elements Q: the elements that belong to at least one possible value of S.

Then, R and Q satisfy these conditions: $R \cap Q = \varnothing$ and $R \cup Q \subseteq \{t_{n1}, t_{n2}, ..., t_{nm}\}$. The initial value of S may be $(\{\}, \{t_{n1}, t_{n2}, ..., t_{nm}\})$, and R will grow and Q will shrink in the reasoning process. When $Q = \varnothing$ and $|R| = 0$, we say the inclusive *csp*-disjunction is FALSE. When $Q = \varnothing$ and $|R| \neq 0$, we say S is *decided*, which means the following atoms are all TRUE:

$P(t_1, ..., t_{n-1}, r_1), P(t_1, ..., t_{n-1}, r_2), ...,$ and $P(t_1, ..., t_{n-1}, r_k)$

where $R = \{r_1, r_2, ..., r_k\} \subseteq \{t_{n1}, t_{n2}, ..., t_{nm}\}$. We can see that $\vee P(t_1, ..., t_{n-1}, (R, Q))$ (or $\vee P(t_1, ..., t_{n-1}, S)$) can be represented by a constraint variable $\vee P(t_1, ..., t_{n-1}, \_)$ whose initial domain is the pair (R, Q). Note that we now have constraint variables with a set as a domain, and with a pair of sets as a domain. Call the latter *set* constraint variables.

For example,

$\vee$*IsFdOf(mike, ({}, {john, james, mary}))*

can represent the fact that *john* or *james* or *mary* is a friend of *mike* (*or* is inclusive) with $R = \{\}$ and $Q = \{john, james, mary\}$. The corresponding constraint variable $\vee$*IsFdOf(mike, _)* can be used in constraints which hopefully eventually determine who are really *mike*'s friends. If it is decided that *john* is definitely a friend of *mike*, then $R = \{john\}$ and $Q = \{james, mary\}$.

3.3. Using Constraints to Represent Relations among Disjunctions

After introducing the two types of constraint variables to represent the two types of disjunctions, we now in the position to describe some of the constraints that can be used for representing relations among the disjunctions.

Constraint:

$cst\_eq(\oplus P_1(t_{11}, ..., t_{1(n-1)}, \_), \oplus P_2(t_{21}, ..., t_{2(m-1)}, \_))$

where $t_{11}, ..., t_{1(n-1)}, t_{21}, ...,$ and $t_{2(m-1)}$ are ground terms.

Let D_1 and D_2 be the domains of the constraint variables $\oplus P_1(t_{11}, ..., t_{1(n-1)}, \_)$ and $\oplus P_2(t_{21}, ..., t_{2(m-1)}, \_))$ respectively. This constraint ensures that the sets D_1 and D_2 are equal at all time. Its operational semantics is the following (which is an abstraction of the real algorithm implemented):

- $D = D_1 \cap D_2$; **if** $D \neq \varnothing$ **then**
  if $D = \{v\}$ **then**
  add $P_1(t_{11}, ..., t_{1(n-1)}, v)$ to WM;
  add $P_2(t_{21}, ..., t_{2(m-1)}, v)$ to WM
  endif
  $D_1 = D$; $D_2 = D$;
  return(TRUE);
  else return(FALSE)

For example, we have
⊕Isa(john, {soldier, teacher, professor, doctor}), and
⊕Isa(james, {teacher, doctor, student}).
If we know that *john* and *james* have the same profession, we can express this with the constraint
cst_eq(⊕Isa(john, _), ⊕Isa(james, _)).

The system will automatically propagate the constraint by using the built-in consistency algorithms to reduce both sets so that the following are obtained:
⊕Isa(john, {teacher, doctor}), and
⊕Isa(james, {teacher, doctor})
If due to some other constraint (or information) it is decided that *john* is a *teacher*, then the following two elements will be added to WM:
Isa(john, teacher), and *Isa(james, teacher)*
If we have the following rule in the rule memory:
IF *Isa(?x, teacher)*
THEN *add(has(?x, many_students))*
This rule will be fired to obtain two more facts:
has(john, many_students), and
has(james, many_students)
This example shows that constraint propagation and rule chaining are integrated.

Constraint:
cst_not_eq$(\oplus P_1(t_{11}, ..., t_{1(n-1)}, \_), \oplus P_2(t_{21}, ..., t_{2(m-1)}, \_))$
where $t_{11}, ..., t_{1(n-1)}, t_{21}, ...,$ and $t_{2(m-1)}$ are ground terms.

Let D_1 and D_2 be the domains of $\oplus P_1(t_{11}, ..., t_{1(n-1)}, \_)$ and $\oplus P_2(t_{21}, ..., t_{2(m-1)}, \_)$ respectively. Then the constraint's operational semantics is given by:

- **if** $|D_1| = 1$ **and** $|D_2| > 1$ **then**
  $D_2 = D_2 - D_1$;
  if $D_2 = \{v\}$ **then** add $P_2(t_{21},..., t_{2(m-1)}, v)$ to WM
  endif
  return(TRUE);
  elseif $|D_2| = 1$ and $|D_1| > 1$ **then**
  this case is similar to the above one;
  elseif $|D_1| = 1$ and $|D_2| = 1$ **then**
  if $D_1 \neq D_2$ **then** return(TRUE) **else** return(FALSE)
  endif
  else return(TRUE)

For example, we have
⊕Isa(john, {soldier, teacher, professor, doctor}),
and *⊕Isa(james, {teacher, doctor, student})*.
The following constraint says that *john* and *james* have different professions:
cst_not_eq(⊕Isa(john, _), ⊕Isa(james, _))

Constraint:
cst_not_in$(v, \oplus P(t_1, ..., t_{n-1}, \_))$
where t_1, ..., and t_{n-1} are ground terms, and v is a constant.

Let D be the domain of $\oplus P(t_1, ..., t_{n-1}, \_)$. This constraint constrains that v is not a possible element in D, which also means that $P(t_1, ..., t_{(n-1)}, v)$ is FALSE. We have:

- $D = D - \{v\}$; **if** $D = \varnothing$ **then** return(FALSE)
  else if $D = \{u\}$ (or $|D| = 1$) **then**
  add $P(t_1,..., t_{n-1}, u)$ to WM;
  endif
  return(TRUE)
  endif

Constraint:
cst_set_eq$(\vee P_1(t_{11}, ..., t_{1(n-1)}, \_), \vee P_2(t_{21}, ..., t_{2(m-1)}, \_))$
where $t_{11}, ..., t_{1(n-1)}, t_{21}, ...,$ and $t_{2(m-1)}$ are ground terms.

Let (R_1, Q_1) and (R_2, Q_2) be the domains of $\vee P_1(t_{11}, ..., t_{1(n-1)}, \_)$ and $\vee P_2(t_{21}, ..., t_{2(m-1)}, \_)$ respectively. Then this constraint is handled by:

- $R = R_1 \cup R_2$; $Q = \{r \mid r \in Q_1 \cap Q_2, r \notin R\}$;
  if $R \subseteq R_1 \cup Q_1$ and $R \subseteq R_2 \cup Q_2$ and ($R \neq \varnothing$ or $Q \neq \varnothing$)
  then $R_1 = R$; $R_2 = R$; $Q_1 = Q$; $Q_2 = Q$;
  for each $r \in R$ and $r \notin R_1$ **do**
  add $P_1(t_{11}, ..., t_{1(n-1)}, r)$ to WM;
  for each $r \in R$ and $r \notin R_2$ **do**
  add $P_2(t_{21}, ..., t_{2(m-1)}, r)$ to WM;
  return(TRUE);
  else return(FALSE)

For example, we have
∨IsFdOf(mike, ({john}, {james, steve, david})), and
∨IsFdOf(andrew, ({steve}, {john, kate, david}))
If we set the constraint
cst_set_eq(∨IsFdOf(mike, _), ∨IsFdOf(andrew, _)),
which says that *mike* and *andrew* have the same set of friends, we will obtain:
∨IsFdOf(mike, ({john, steve}, {david})), and
∨IsFdOf(andrew, ({john, steve}, {david})).
Two more facts will be added in WM, i.e.,
IsFdOf(mike, steve), and *IsFdOf(andrew, john)*.

Constraint:
cst_set_not_in$(v, \vee P(t_1, ..., t_{n-1}, _))$
where t_1, ..., and t_{n-1} are all ground terms.

Let (R, Q) be the domain of $\vee P(t_1, ..., t_{n-1}, \_)$, this constraint constrains that v is not a possible element in Q, which means that $P(t_1, ..., t_{n-1}, v)$ cannot be TRUE. Its operational semantics is obvious, and omitted.

3.4. Introducing Choice Making and Backtracking

The consistency techniques used above for constraint solving are all based on arc consistency (Hentenryck *et al* 1992; Liu 1995). Arc consistency alone may not be sufficient to solve a CSP because arc consistency does not guarantee global consistency (Mackworth 1977). Then, a combination of backtrack search and consistency check is required. This approach can be described as an iterative procedure of two steps: consistency check and choice making. If a choice is proved to be wrong (when the consistency check returns FALSE), backtracking will be initiated. In the process, the previous state is restored, and an alternative is selected (Hentenryck 1989).

Let us define some choice making functions. Each of them sets up a choice point for later backtracking. The choice functions are also constraints because each value selection will trigger consistency check.

Choice function: *cst_select*($\oplus P(t_1, \ldots, t_{n-1}, \_)$, *func*)

where t_1, ..., and t_{n-1} are all ground terms, and *func* is a user defined procedure.

Let D be the domain of $\oplus P(t_1, \ldots, t_{n-1}, \_)$, this function selects a value v from D using the procedure *func*. *func* allows the user to control the selection process in order to find the solution quickly. This choice function behaves as follows:

- **if** there is no more value to be selected in D **then**
  return(FALSE)
  else v is selected from D using *func*;
  $D = \{v\}$;
  add $P(t_1, \ldots, t_{n-1}, v)$ in WM;
  return(TRUE)
  endif

For example, we have:

⊕Capital(NY, {NYC, albany}),

which says that the capital of *New York* (*NY*) is either *NYC* or *albany*, but not both. We can apply the selection by using

cst_select(⊕Capital(NY, _), func).

Suppose that *func* chooses the first possible value first, i.e., *NYC*. After it is selected, *Capital(NY, NYC)* will be automatically added in WM, and then constraint propagation will be carried out, etc. When backtracking occurs, the second value will be tried and so on.

Choice function: *cst_set_select*($\vee P(t_1, \ldots, t_{n-1}, \_)$, *func*)

where t_1, ..., and t_{n-1} are all ground terms, and *func* is a user defined procedure.

Let (R, Q) be the domain of $\vee P(t_1, \ldots, t_{n-1}, \_)$. This function selects a value V (a set) from Q ($V \subseteq Q$) using the procedure *func*. It behaves as follows:

- **if** there is no more value to be selected from Q **then**
  return(FALSE)
  else A set V is selected from Q using *func*;
  $Q = \emptyset$; $R = R \cup V$;
  for each $r \in V$ **do** add $P(t_1, \ldots, t_{n-1}, r)$ to WM;
  return(TRUE)
  endif

For instance, we have

∨IsFdOf(mike, ({john}, {james, mary, steve}))

and we know that *mike* has only two friends. We can try the following:

cst_set_select(∨IsFdOf(mike, _), func)

Suppose that *func* chooses the first possible value first, i.e., *james*, which effectively rules out the other values. Then, *mike*'s friends are *john* and *james*. We obtain

∨IsFdOf(mike, ({john, james}, {})).

After that, other necessary operations are performed, e.g., adding *IsFdOf(mike, james)* to WM and constraint propagation, etc. When a selection is proved to be wrong, backtracking will be performed. The second element, the third element, etc., will be tried and so on.

3.5. Some Test Functions on Constraint Variables

Here, we present some test functions on constraint variables. They are used to exploit the partial information provided by disjunctions for various purposes.

Test function: *test_in*(T, $\oplus P(t_1, \ldots, t_{n-1}, \_)$)

where t_1, ..., and t_{n-1} are all ground terms, and T is a set of constants.

Let D be the domain of $\oplus P(t_1, \ldots, t_{n-1}, \_)$. This test function behaves as follows:

- **if** $D \subseteq T$ **then** return(TRUE) **else** return(FALSE)

For example, we have *⊕Capital(NY, {NYC, albany})*, which says that the capital of *New York* (*NY*) is either *NYC* or *albany*, but not both, and the following rule:

IF *include(?tour, capitalOf(NY))* and
test_in({NYC, albany}, ⊕Capital(NY, _))
THEN *add(join(I, ?tour)))*

This rule allows the system to act on the partial information, i.e., *test_in* does not have to find the fact *Capital(NY, NYC)* or *Capital(NY, albany)* in WM before firing. Instead, it only needs to check whether any one of these two cities or both are the only possible values for the capital of *NY*. It does not matter which.

If WM has the following two facts:

include(tour16, capitalOf(NY)), and
⊕Capital(NY, {NYC, albany})

the rule will fire to add *join(I, tour16))* to WM.

Test function: *test_set_in*(T, $\vee P(t_1, \ldots, t_{n-1}, \_)$)

where t_1, ..., and t_{n-1} are all ground terms, and T is a set of constants.

Let (R, Q) be the domain of $\vee P(t_1, \ldots, t_{n-1}, \_)$, This test function behaves as follows:

- **if** $(T \cap R) \neq \emptyset$ or ($R = \emptyset$ and $Q \subseteq T$) **then**
  return(TRUE)
  else return(FALSE)

For example, we wish to express that "if something is a block or a pyramid, then it is a pointy_object" (*or* is inclusive). We can write:

IF *test_set_in({block, pyramid}, isa(?x, _))*
THEN *add(isa(?x, pointy_object))*

3.6. Complications With the Integration of Choice Making and Rule Chaining

Combining backtrack search and forward chaining creates some complications. The problem lies in the handling of inconsistency. For our discussion, we classify two types of inconsistency. The first type is the normal inconsistency in logic (IL), e.g., both A and $\neg A$ are deduced, and the other is the inconsistency of constraints (IC). IC is easy to detect and to handle because when the domain of a constraint variable is empty, it is known that there is a inconsistency, and backtracking can be used to deal with it. However, IL is hard to detect as most rule-based systems are informal systems that have no mechanism for this purpose. This has some implications for our proposed integration.

- If a rule-based system is unable to detect IL, then (1) constraints cannot be conditions in a rule, (2) choice making and backtracking should not be allowed.

The reason is that both (1) and (2) could introduce IL. Due to space limitation, we are unable to discuss this further. Interested readers, refer to (Liu & Jaffar 1996).

In general, if a rule-based system is unable to detect IL, (1) and (2) should not be allowed. Then, constraints can only appear as consequents of rules, and there will be no backtrack search but only consistency check.

However, if an inconsistency checker is implemented for detecting IL, then both (1) and (2) can be allowed, and both IC and IL will trigger backtracking.

Apart from the above two situations, a third one is also reasonable. We assume that only ICs may occur in an application, then we can also allow both (1) and (2) because IC is easily detected. Our prototype system makes this assumption. This assumption is realistic because that is the case in most existing rule-based systems. They do not have mechanisms for detecting IL. It is the user's responsibility not to introduce any or to check it.

4. An Implementation

We have implemented a prototype system (called CFR) in Common Lisp. Below are some implementation issues.

- Apart from WM and rule memory in a rule-based system, a constraint variable memory is introduced to store constraint variables.
- For consistency check of constraints involving normal constraint variables, we used those algorithms in (Hentenryck *et al* 1992; Liu 1995) as they are the most efficient algorithms. For set constraints, we designed our own algorithms as there is little reported work on this type of constraints. Consistency check of *cst_eq*, *cst_not_eq*, and *cst_set_eq* can all be done in linear time to the size of the domain D or $|R \cup Q|$. *cst_not_in* and *cst_set_not_in* can be done in constant time.
- A choice stack is used to keep track of the choices that have been made and to remember the information necessary for restoring state upon backtracking. This is similar to CLP languages such as CHIP (Hentenryck 1989). The difference is that each choice here has to remember the facts that have been added to WM after a choice is made. When backtracking comes to the choice, these facts must be removed.
- Finally, the pattern matching algorithm for rule-chaining needs to be modified to accommodate the constraint satisfaction facility. Due to the space limitation, we are unable to discuss this and many other issues.

Below, we briefly describe the syntax of rules, constraint variables, and constraints in CFR.

***IF-THEN* rules**: A rule is defined using the construct:

(define-rule <name> <conditions> -> <actions>)

For example, the rule:

```
(define-rule is_food
    (edible ?x)
        -> (add `(is_food ,x)))
```

says that if there is a fact in WM that matches *(edible ?x)*, this rule will fire and add the evaluation result `*(is_food ,x)* to WM. `*(is_food ,x)* is in Lisp syntax ("`", "'", and "," are used according to their meanings in Lisp), and x here will be substituted to whatever value $?x$ has after matching with the fact in WM.

Constraint variable declarations:

1). $\oplus P(t_1, ..., t_{n-1}, D)$ => (corresponding to)
(cst_in '(P t_1 ... t_{n-1} D))
e.g., $\oplus capital(NY, \{NYC, albany\})$ =>
(cst_in '(capital NY (NYC albany)))

2). $\vee P(t_1, ..., t_{n-1}, (R, Q))$ =>
(cst_set_in '(P t_1 ... t_{n-1} (R Q)))
e.g., $\vee IsFdOf(joe, (\{steve\}, \{john, kate\}))$ =>
(cst_set_in '(IsFdOf joe ((steve) (john kate))))

Constraints:

1). *cst_eq*($\oplus P_1(t_{11}, ..., t_{1(n-1)}, \_)$, $\oplus P_2(t_{21}, ..., t_{2(m-1)}, \_)$)
=> (cst_eq '(P_1 t_{11} ... $t_{1(n-1)}$ _) '(P_2 t_{21} ... $t_{2(m-1)}$ _))
e.g., *cst_eq*($\oplus Isa(john, \_)$, $\oplus Isa(james, \_)$) =>
(cst_eq '(Isa john _) '(Isa james _))

2). *cst_not_eq*($\oplus P_1(t_{11},...,t_{1(n-1)},\_)$,$\oplus P_2(t_{21}, ..., t_{2(m-1)}, \_)$)
=> (cst_not_eq '(P_1 t_{11} ... $t_{1(n-1)}$ _) '(P_2 t_{21} ... $t_{2(m-1)}$ _))
e.g., *cst_not_eq*($\oplus Isa(john, \_)$, $\oplus Isa(james, \_)$) =>
(cst_not_eq '(Isa john _) '(Isa james _))

3). *cst_set_eq*($\vee P_1(t_{11},...,t_{1(n-1)}, \_)$, $\vee P_2(t_{21}, ..., t_{2(m-1)}, \_)$)
=> (cst_set_eq '(P_1 t_{11} ... $t_{1(n-1)}$ _) '(P_2 t_{21} ... $t_{2(m-1)}$ _))
e.g., *cst_set_eq*($\vee IsFdOf(mike, \_)$,$\vee IsFdOf(joe, \_)$)
=> (cst_set_eq '(IsFdOf mike _) '(IsFdOf joe _))

Due to lack of space, we will not describe the corresponding constructs in CFR for the other constraints and choice and test functions. They are quite similar to the ones above.

5. An Example

We now present a simple example to illustrate how rules and constraints interact with each other in the reasoning process. The rule definitions here are self-explanatory.

```
(define-rule professor
  (isa ?x science_professor)
   -> (add `(works_in_a ,x university))
      (cst_in `(teaches ,x (computer math physics
      chemistry biology))))
(define-rule computer
  (isa ?x science_professor)
  (has_no ?x computer)
  -> (cst_not_in 'computer `(,x teaches _)))
(define-rule math
  (is_good_in ?x math)
  (isa ?x science_professor)
   -> (cst_in `(teaches ,x (computer math physics))))
(define-rule csp-test
  (test_in (physics math) (teaches ?x _))
   -> (add `(gives_lecture_in ,x science_building)))
(define-rule lab
  (does_not_do ?x lab_work)
   -> (cst_not_in 'chemistry `(teaches ,x _))
      (cst_not_in 'biology `(teaches ,x _)))
(define-rule degree
  (teaches ?x ?y)
  -> (add `(likes ,x ,y))
     (cst_set_in `(has ,x `(((PhD in ,y)) `((MSc in ,y))))))
```

Let us run the system with the following facts:

```
(add '(isa fred science_professor))
(add '(has_no fred computer))
(add '(isa john science_professor))
(add '(does_not_do john lab_work))
(cst_eq '(teaches john _) '(teaches fred _))
```

After all the rule chaining and constraint propagation, the working memory becomes:

```
1:  (isa fred science_professor)
2:  (works_in_a fred university)
3:  (cst_fact (teaches fred _) (math physics))
4:  (has_no fred computer)
5:  (isa john science_professor)
6:  (works_in_a john university)
7:  (cst_fact (teaches john _) (math physics))
8:  (does_not_do john lab_work)
9:  (gives_lecture_in john science_building)
10: (gives_lecture_in fred science_building)
```

Fact 3 and 7 are special facts representing two constraint variables and their remaining domains. From them, we know that both *fred* and *john* teach either *math* or *physics*, but we still do not know which.

Let us say that we are not satisfied with the result. We would like to make a guess about what they teach. We can use the following selection function:

```
(cst_select '(teaches fred _) #'car)
```

This selects *math* as the subject that *fred* teaches. After constraint propagation and rule chaining, we obtain the fact that *john* also teaches *math*. The following facts are deduced:

```
11: (teaches fred math)
12: (teaches john math)
13: (likes fred math)
14: (likes john math)
15: (has fred (PhD in math))
16: (has john (PhD in math))
17: (cst_set_fact (has fred _) ((PhD in math))
                                ((MSc in math)))
18: (cst_set_fact (has john _) ((PhD in math))
                                ((MSc in math)))
```

The last two facts (17 and 18) say that *fred* and *john* have a *PhD* in *math* and may or may not have a *MSc* in *math*.

If later we have some more information saying that *fred* does not have a *PhD* degree in *math*, this can be expressed like this:

```
(cst_set_not_in '(PhD in math) '(has fred _))
```

It immediately causes a conflict with fact 17 because fact 17 says that *fred* has a *PhD* in *math*. Then, backtracking is performed. The facts from 11 to 18 are removed to restore the previous state. *physics* is selected this time as the subject that *fred* teaches, which in turn causes a number of facts to be produced:

```
11: (teaches fred physics)
12: (teaches john physics)
13: (likes fred physics)
14: (likes john physics)
15: (has fred (PhD in physics))
16: (has john (PhD in physics))
17: (cst_set_fact (has fred _) ((PhD in physics))
                                ((MSc in physics)))
18: (cst_set_fact (has john _) ((PhD in physics))
                                ((MSc in physics)))
```

Since *math* is eliminated as the possible course that *fred* and *john* teach. Fact 3 and 7 in WM become:

```
3: (cst_fact (teaches fred _) (physics))
7: (cst_fact (teaches john _) (physics))
```

The kind of reasoning illustrated here cannot be carried out in an existing rule-based system.

6. Related Work

The most closely related work to our research is constraint logic programming (CLP) (Jaffar & Maher 1994) where a considerable amount of research has been done to integrate constraint satisfaction with logic programming. A number of systems have been built, and many successful applications have also been reported (Jaffar & Maher 1994). Two representative CLP languages are CLP(*R*) (Jaffar & Lassez 1987) and CHIP (Hentenryck 1989). These languages are based on Horn clauses and backward chaining. Our work is different from CLP in a number of ways. The main differences are as follows.

1. Our proposed technique is based on forward chaining rather than backward chaining as in CLP languages. Forward chaining and backward chaining reason from different directions and are suitable for solving different types of problems. Forward chaining are mainly used for building expert systems for solving real-life knowledge intensive tasks. Since the CLP languages based on backward chaining have been very successful in practice for solving practical combinatorial search problems, it is only natural that forward chaining should also be integrated with constraint solving to provide a more powerful reasoning technique for solving practical reasoning problems.
2. In CLP languages, backtracking and choice making are provided by the host language Prolog. While in forward chaining, backtracking and choice making facilities have to be added, which creates some complications as discussed in Section 3.6.

To the best our knowledge, limited work has been done on combining constraint solving with forward chaining rule-based system. BABYLON (Christaller *et al* 1992) is one of the hybrid environments for developing expert systems that has attempted to include constraint solving in its rule-based system. BABYLON provides representation formalisms of objects, rules, Prolog and constraints. CONSAT is the constraint system of BABYLON, which is separated from others and cannot access rules. Although in the condition part of the rules, it is possible to verify whether a constraint is satisfied, the action part of a rule cannot access constraints. This is quite different from our system, within which constraint solving and rule-chaining are integrated. Rules can post and test constraints, and constraint satisfaction can also trigger chaining of rules.

7. Conclusion

This paper shows how CSP can be used to model two types of important disjunctions in rule-based reasoning. These disjunctions have not been handled satisfactorily in the current rule-based systems. In the proposed scheme, the simple representation and efficient algorithms in CSP are used to deal with these types of disjunction. This results in the integration of two important types of reasoning techniques, i.e., constraint solving and (forward) rule-chaining. Hence. the power of rule-based systems is increased.

The current integration of CSP with rule-based reasoning is still restricted, i.e., mainly for modeling the two types of disjunction. Our next step is to deal with general constraints in a forward chaining framework.

Acknowledgments: Bing Liu thanks Peter Lucas from Utrecht University for his advice on some expert system issues. We thank Roland Yap for his help. Finally, we are grateful to the AAAI reviewers for their insightful comments.

References

Bessiere, C., Freuder, E. C. and Regin, J-C. 1995. "Using inference to reduce arc consistency computation," *IJCAI-95*, 592-598.

Charniak, E., Riesbeck, C., McDermott, D. and Meehan, J. 1987. *Artificial Intelligence Programming*, Lawrence Erlbaum Associates Inc.

Christaller, T., di Primio, F., Schnepf, U. and Voss, A. 1992. *The AI Workbench BABYLON*. Academic Press.

Hentenryck, P.V. 1989. *Constraint Satisfaction in Logic Programming*, MIT Press.

Hentenryck, P.V., Deville, Y. and Teng, C-M. 1992. "A generic arc consistency algorithm and its specializations," *Artificial Intelligence* 27, 291-322.

Ilog Solver. 1992. *Reference Manual*, ILOG, France.

Jaffar, J. and Lassez, J. 1987. "Constraint logic programming," *Proceedings of the Fourteenth Annual ACM Symposium on Principle of Programming Language*.

Jaffar, J. and Maher, M. 1994. "Constraint logic programming: a survey." *J. Logic Programming* 19, 503-581.

Liu, B. 1995. "Increasing functional constraints need to be checked only once," *IJCAI-95*, 586-591.

Liu, B. and Jaffar, J. 1996. *Using Constraints to Model Disjunction in Rule-Based Reasoning*. DISCS Technical Report.

Liu, B. 1996. "An improved generic arc consistency algorithm and its specializations." To Appear in *Proceedings of Fourth Pacific Rim International Conference On Artificial Intelligence (PRICAI-96)*.

Lucas, P. and Van Der Gaag, L. 1991. *Principles of Expert Systems*, Addison-Wesley.

Mackworth, A.K. 1977. "Consistency in networks of relations," *Artificial Intelligence* 8, 99-118.

Mackworth, A.K. 1992. "The logic of constraint satisfaction," *Artificial Intelligence* 58, 3-20.

Mohr, R. and Henderson, T. 1986. "Arc and path consistency revisited," *Artificial Intelligence* 28, 225-233.

Newell, A. 1973. "Production systems: models for control structure," In *Visual Information Processing*, W.G. Chase (Eds), Academic Press, 1973.

A Connectionist Framework for Reasoning: Reasoning with Examples

Dan Roth*

Dept. of Appl. Math. & CS,
Weizmann Institute of Science,
Israel
danr@wisdom.weizmann.ac.il

Abstract

We present a connectionist architecture that supports almost instantaneous deductive and abductive reasoning. The deduction algorithm responds in few steps for single rule queries and in general, takes time that is linear with the number of rules in the query. The abduction algorithm produces an explanation in few steps and the best explanation in time linear with the size of the assumption set. The size of the network is polynomially related to the size of other representations of the domain, and may even be smaller.

We base our connectionist model on Valiant's Neuroidal model (Val94) and thus make minimal assumptions about the computing elements, which are assumed to be classical threshold elements with states. Within this model we develop a reasoning framework that utilizes a model-based approach to reasoning (KKS93; KR94b). In particular, we suggest to interpret the connectionist architecture as encoding *examples* of the domain we reason about and show how to perform various reasoning tasks with this interpretation. We then show that the representations used can be acquired efficiently from interactions with the environment and discuss how this learning process influences the reasoning performance of the network.

Introduction

Any theory aiming at understanding *commonsense* reasoning, the process that humans use to cope with the mundane but complex aspects of the world in evaluating everyday situations, should account for the flexibility, adaptability and speed of commonsense reasoning.

Consider, for example, the task of language understanding, which humans perform effortlessly and effectively. It depends upon our ability to disambiguate word meanings, recognize speaker's plans, perform predictions and generate explanations. These, and other "high level" cognitive tasks such as high level vision and planning have been widely interpreted as *inference* tasks and collectively comprise what we call commonsense reasoning.

*Research supported by the Feldman Foundation and a Grant from the Israeli Ministry of Science and the Arts.

Deductive and abductive reasoning are the basic inference tasks considered in the context of high level cognitive tasks. In this paper we suggest an alternative to the current connectionist account of these tasks.

Connectionist networks have been argued to be better suited than traditional knowledge representations for studying everyday common sense reasoning. Some of the arguments used are that these models have the ability to simultaneously satisfy multiple constraints, dynamically adapt to changes, achieve robustness and provide a useful way to cope with conflicting and uncertain information (Sun95; Pin95; Der90). This should be contrasted with the view that connectionist model are incapable of performing high level cognitive tasks because of their difficulties with representing and applying general knowledge rules (FP88).

The latter opinion, we believe, may reflect on the fact that a lot of the research on understanding high level cognition using connectionist models is actually *trying* to represent and apply general knowledge rules.

Indeed, a lot of the research in this direction is influenced by a research program launched in the fifties, the "*knowledge-base+inference engine*" approach (McC58), which is still the generally accepted framework for reasoning in intelligent systems. The idea is to store the knowledge, expressed in some *representation language* with a well defined meaning assigned to its sentences, in a Knowledge Base (KB). The KB is combined with a reasoning mechanism ("inference engine") that is used to determine what can be inferred from the sentences in the KB. The effort to develop a *logical inference engine* within a connectionist architecture is represented by works such as (BH93; HK91; SA90; SA93; Sun95; LD91; Pin95; Der90).

Given the intractability of the general purpose knowledge base+inference engine approach to reasoning, a significant amount of recent work in reasoning concentrates on (1) identifying classes of limited expressiveness, with which one can still perform reasoning efficiently or (2) resorting to an approximate inference engine. These directions have been pursued both in the knowledge representation and reasoning ($KR\&R$) community and in the connectionism community. The former line of research is represented in *KR&R* by many works such as (BL84; Lev92; Rot93; SK90; Cad95) and in the connectionism community by (SA90; BH93; HK91). The latter usually builds on using Hopfield's networks (HT82) or Boltzmann machines (HS86), in an effort to solve optimization problems that are relaxations of propositional satisfiability. This approach is used, for example, in (Pin95; Der90) and is related to approaches suggested in the *KR&R* community (SLM92; MJP90).

None of these works, however, meets the strong tractability requirements required for common-sense reasoning as argued e.g., in (Sha93). Moreover, many of these works have carried out the "knowledge base+inference engine" research program also by neglecting to consider the question of how this knowledge might be acquired[1] and by measuring performance of the reasoning process in absolute terms rather than with respect to the preceding learning process.

We utilize a model-based approach to reasoning (KKS93; KR94b) to yield a network that is not a "logical inference engine" but, under some (formally phrased) restrictions, behaves "logically" with respect to a world it interacts with. Our model-based algorithms support instantaneous deduction and abduction, in cases that are intractable using other knowledge representations. The interpretation of the connectionist architecture as encoding *examples* acquired via interaction with the environment, allows for the integration of the inference and learning processes (KR94a) and yields reasoning performance that naturally depends on the process of learning the network.

We develop the reasoning framework within Valiant's Neuroidal paradigm (Val94), a computational model that is intended to be consistent with the gross biological constraints we currently understand. In particular, this is a programmable model which makes minimal assumptions about the computing elements, assumed to be classical threshold elements with states.

In this abstract we focus on presenting the reasoning framework: the architecture, its interpretation as a set of examples and the reasoning algorithms. The learning issues are discussed only briefly.

The Reasoning Framework

This paper considers two inference tasks, Deduction[2] and Abduction. *Deduction*, the basic inference task considered in the context of high level cognitive tasks is usually modeled as follows: given a Boolean function W, represented as a conjunction of rules and assumed to capture our knowledge of the world, and a Boolean function α, a query that is supposed to capture the situation at hand, decide whether W logically implies α (denoted $W \models \alpha$). *Abduction* is a term coined by Peirce (Pei55) to describe the inference rule that concludes A from an observation B and the rule $A \rightarrow B$, given that there is no "better" rule explaining B. The importance of studying abduction became clear in the past few years when some general approaches to Natural Language interpretation have been advanced within the abduction framework (HSME93).

We adopt an alternative, model-based approach to the study of commonsense reasoning, in which the knowledge base is represented as a set of models (satisfying assignments) of the domain of interest (the "world") rather than a logical formula describing it. It is not hard to motivate a model-based approach to reasoning from a cognitive point of view and indeed, most of the proponents of this approach to reasoning have been cognitive psychologists (JL83; JLB91; Kos83), who have alluded to the notion of "reasoning from examples" on a qualitative basis. Building on the work of (KKS93; KR94b) we show that model-based reasoning can be implemented in a connectionist network to yield an efficient reasoning network.

In our framework, when reasoning with respect to the "world" W, information about the W is stored in a network N and is interpreted as a collections of examples observed in W.[3] We present both deduction and the abductive task of *verifying* that an explanation is consistent as a series of forward evaluation tasks. Each takes 5 computational steps. The task of *producing* an explanation utilizes the backwards connections in the networks, and is also instantaneous. In both cases, if the content of the network is a good representation of W, in a well defined sense, for a wide class of queries the network response is provably correct. Interaction with the network for queries presentation and learning the representation is done in a unified manner, via *observations* and the performance of the reasoning is shown to depend naturally on this interaction.

Reasoning Tasks

We briefly present the reasoning tasks and some relevant results. See (KR94b; KR94a) for details. We consider reasoning over a propositional domain. The reasoning queries are with respect to a "world" (domain of interest) that is modeled as a Boolean function (a propositional expression) $f : \{0,1\}^n \rightarrow \{0,1\}$. Let $X = \{x_1, \ldots, x_n\}$ be a set of *variables*, each of which is associated with a world's attribute and can take the value 1 or 0 to indicate whether the associated attribute is true or false in the world. (n is our complexity parameter.) An assignment $x \in \{0,1\}^n$ satisfies f if $f(x) = 1$. (x is also called a *model* of f.) By "f entails (implies) g", denoted $f \models g$, we mean that every model of f is also a model of g.

[1] (Pin95) is an exception.

[2] We emphasize that these terms are used only to give semantics to the network's behavior. The network is not a "logical inference engine" but, under some restrictions on the queries presented, behaves "logically" with respect to a world it had interactions with.

[3] We restrict our discussion to this fragment of the network; in general, this will be part of a larger network and will overlap with network representations of other "worlds".

In deduction (entailment), given Boolean functions f (assumed to capture our knowledge of the world) and α (a query that is supposed to capture the situation at hand) we need to decide whether f implies α (denoted $f \models \alpha$). For abduction, we refer here to one of the propositional formalisms in which abduction is defined as the task of finding a *minimal* explanation, given a knowledge base f (the *background theory*), a set of propositional letters A (the *assumption set*), and a query letter q. An *explanation* of q is a minimal subset $\mathcal{E} \subseteq A$ such that (1) $f \wedge (\wedge_{x \in \mathcal{E}} x) \models q$ and (2) $f \wedge (\wedge_{x \in \mathcal{E}} x) \neq \emptyset$. Thus, abduction involves tests for entailment (1) and consistency (2), but also a search for a minimal[4] explanation that passes both tests.

Reasoning with Models

The model based strategy for the deduction problem $f \models \alpha$ is to try and verify the implication relation using model evaluation. In doing so, the knowledge base consists of a set Γ of models of f rather than a Boolean function. When presented with a query α the algorithm evaluates α on all the models in Γ. If a counterexample x such that $\alpha(x) = 0$ is found, then the algorithm returns "No". Otherwise it returns "Yes".

Clearly, the model based approach solves the inference problem if Γ is the set of *all* models of f. However, the set of all models might be too large, making this procedure infeasible computationally. A model-based approach becomes useful if one can show that it is possible to use a fairly small set of models as the test set Γ, and still perform reasonably good inference.

Exact Reasoning using models is based on a theory developed in a series of papers (KKS93; KR94b; KR94a; KR95) where a characterization of when a model based approach to reasoning is feasible is developed. An important feature of the theory is that the correctness of reasoning depends on the type of *queries* presented and not so much on the world we reason about (provided that the reasoner holds a "good" description of the world). The class of queries which allows efficient model-based reasoning is called the class of *common queries* ($\mathcal{Q}_c$). It contains a rich class of theories and, in particular, all Horn and all $\log n$CNF functions. Proving the feasibility of model-based reasoning involves showing that for the purpose of reasoning with respect to $\mathcal{Q}_c$, a Boolean function f can be represented using a polynomial size set of models, Γ_f.

Theorem 1 ((KR94b)) *For any knowledge base f there exists a set Γ_f of models whose size is polynomially[5] related to the DNF size of f. Deduction (with respect to $\mathcal{Q}_c$) and Abduction (given a query q and assumption set A) can be performed correctly in polynomial time, using Γ_f.*

Approximate Reasoning is related to the notion of pac learning (Val84) and was developed in (KR94a). We assume that the occurrences of observations in the world is governed by a fixed but arbitrary and unknown probability distribution D defined on $\{0,1\}^n$.

A query α is called *(f,ϵ)-fair* if either $f \subseteq \alpha$ or $Prob_D[f \setminus \alpha] > \epsilon$. An algorithm for approximate deduction will is to err on non-fair queries. (Intuitively, it is allowed to err in case $f \not\models \alpha$, but the weight (under D) of f outside α is very small.) Along with the *accuracy* parameter ϵ, we use a *confidence* parameter δ which stands for the small probability that the reasoning algorithm errs on fair queries.

Theorem 2 *Let $\mathcal{Q}$ be a class of queries of interest, and let $0 < \delta, \epsilon$ be given confidence and accuracy parameters. Suppose that we select $m = \frac{1}{\epsilon}(\ln|\mathcal{Q}| + \ln\frac{1}{\delta})$ independent examples according to D and store in Γ all those samples that satisfy f. Then the probability that the model-based deduction procedure errs on an (f,ϵ)-fair query in $\mathcal{Q}$ is less than δ.*

Since the queries in $\mathcal{Q}$ are Boolean functions of polynomial size, the number m of samples required is polynomial. Moreover, given a set of possible explanations as input, this approach efficiently supports the entailment and consistency stages of abductive reasoning.

The Connectionist Framework

The architecture investigated is based on Valiant's Neuroidal model (see (Val94) for details). We present just the few aspects we need to describe the knowledge representation that supports the reasoning tasks.

Valiant's Neuroidal model is a programmable model which makes minimal assumptions on the computing elements, assumed to be classical threshold elements with states. We make a few minor abstractions for methodological purposes. Most importantly, we abstract away the important notion that in the localist representation assumed, every item is represented as a "cloud" of nodes rather than a single node.

A 5-tuple $(G(G,E), W, M, \delta, \lambda)$ defines a network N. Here $G = G(G,E)$ is a *directed graph* describing the topology of the network, W is the set of possible *weights* on edges of G, M is the set of *modes* a node can be in at any instant, δ is the *update function of the mode* and λ is the *update function of the weights*.

We view the nodes of the net as a set G of propositions. The set E is a set of directed edges between the nodes. The set of weights W is a set of numbers. e_{ij} denotes the edge directed from i to j, and its weight is w_{ij}. Sometimes both $e_{ij}, e_{ji} \in E$. The *mode*, (s,T), of the node describes every aspect of its instantaneous condition other than the weights on its incoming edges. $s \in S$ is a finite set of states and T is a threshold. In particular, S consists of two kinds of states F and Q,

[4] Here minimal means that no subset of it is a valid explanation. In general this is not, by itself, adequate for choosing among explanations and more general schema can be discussed in our framework.

[5] Thus, Γ_f is in general exponentially smaller than the number of satisfying assignments of f, and sometimes even exponentially smaller than the DNF representation.

which stand for *firing* (that is, the node is active at this time), and *quiescent* (a non-active state).

The *mode transition function* δ specifies the updates that occur to the mode of the node from time t to $t+1$. δ depends on the current state of the node and the sum of weights $w_i = \sum_k \{w_{ki} | e_{ki} \in E, k \in F\}$, of its active parents. Similarly, the *weight transition function* λ defines for each weight w_{ij} at time t the weight to which it will transit at time $t+1$. The new value may depend on the values of the weights on the edges between node i and its parents, their firing state and the mode of i, all at time t. Two default transitions are assumed. First, a *threshold transition* by default occurs whenever $w_i > T_i$ at the ith node, provided that no explicit condition that overrides the default is stated. The second default assumed is that a node in a firing state ceases firing at the end of the time unit.

To further specify a network we need to define the *initial conditions* IC, (i.e., initial weights and modes of the nodes) and *input sequence* IS. The interaction of the network with the outside world is modeled by assuming the existence of *peripherals*. They have the power to cause various sets of nodes in the network to fire simultaneously at various times. Every interaction like that we call here an *observation*. It specifies the set of nodes that the peripherals activate at an instant, i.e., the set of propositions that are observed to be active in the environment. The actual choices of the sets and the times in which the observations are presented to the network determine the input sequences IS.

Timing is crucially important to the model. After the peripherals prompt the network and cause some subset of nodes to fire simultaneously, a cascade of computation follows, and the algorithm has to ensure that it terminates in a stable situation, before the time unit has elapsed. Typically, the peripherals will prompt low level nodes and the algorithm being executed may need to modify nodes representing higher level concepts, that are separated in the network from the prompted ones by several intermediate nodes.

Knowledge Representation

To emphasize the correspondence between the network and propositional reasoning, we consider a subset of the nodes in N which are controlled by the peripherals and view it as a set $X = \{x_1, \ldots, x_n\}$ of propositions. For simplicity, in order to describe both the presence and the absence of an attribute x_i, it is duplicated in the representation: one node describes x_i and another describes $\overline{x_i}$. We represent each interaction with the network as an observation $v = (x_{i_1} = v_{i_1}, x_{i_2} = v_{i_2}, \ldots, x_{i_d} = v_{i_d})$, with $d \leq n, v_i \in \{0,1\}$, and this is translated to a corresponding node activation by the peripherals. For example, when the observation is $(x_1 = 1, x_2 = 1, x_3 = 0)$, the peripherals activate nodes corresponding to x_1, x_2 and $\overline{x_3}$. An observation v can be interpreted also as a *query* presented to the network in the reasoning stage. The presentation of v is interpreted as the Boolean query $\alpha = l_{i_1} \wedge \ldots \wedge l_{i_d}$, where $l_j = x_j$ if $v_j = 1$, $l_i = \overline{x_i}$ if $v_j = 0$.

Definition 1 *Let y be a node in N, $E_y = \{z | e_{zy} \in E\}$ its set of parents. A node $z \in E_y$ is called a* model *of y and $e_z = \{i \in E_z | w_{iz} = 1\}$ its set of* components. *The* model-based representation *of y, $M_y = \{(z, e_z) | z \in E_y\}$, is the set of models and their components.*

We assume also that the positive and negative literals of each proposition are connected via a *relay node*. Figure 1 depicts a model-based representation of y. The edges are assumed to be bidirectional (i.e., each line represents two edges) and all the weights on the edges drawn are assumed to be 1. Every model is connected to all $2n$ literals, and the n not drawn are assumed to have weight 0. Initially, all the thresholds in the representation are set to a high value, denoted by ∞. The algorithms also assume a specific set of initial modes of the nodes in the representation.

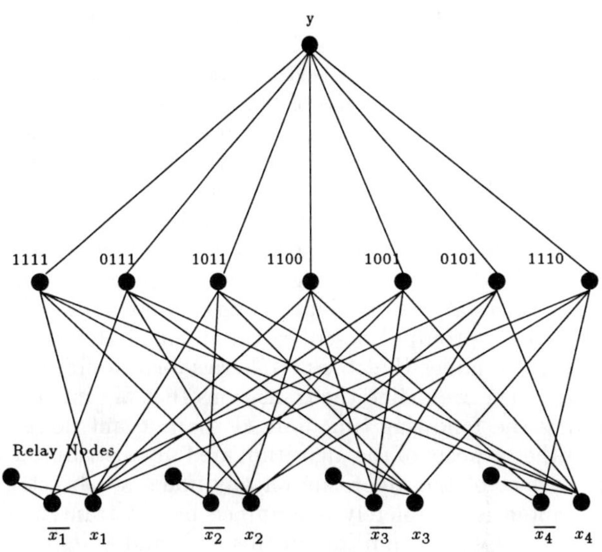

Figure 1: A Connectionist Model-Based Representation

A model z can be represented as a Boolean vector. If $e_z = (l_1, l_2, \ldots l_n)$ is a representation of z as a set of its components ($l_i \in \{x_i, \overline{x_i}\}$), than $e_z = [b_1, b_2, \ldots b_n]$ is its Boolean representation, where $b_i \in \{0,1\}$ is defined by: $b_i = 1$ if $l_i = x_i$, $b_i = 0$ if $l_i = \overline{x_i}$. It can be verified that the model-based representation presented in Figure 1 is the representation of the function $f = \{\overline{x_1} \wedge \overline{x_2} \rightarrow x_3, \ \overline{x_1} \wedge \overline{x_4} \rightarrow x_2, \ x_1 \wedge x_2 \wedge x_4 \rightarrow x_3\}$ with respect to all Horn queries. (See (KR94b).)

In general, a network N will be a collection of such model-based representations. These can share nodes and any input to the network may influence many of them. Thus, although we discuss "logical" behavior, no global consistency is required. Note that while n is our complexity parameter, it is not related to the size of the whole network, but only to the number of propositions "related" to y in its local network.

Reasoning in the Network

We briefly describe the reasoning algorithms, for lack of space. A complete description appears in (Rot96a).

We note that within this framework, there are quite a few other ways to achieve the same goal. In particular, we could define other modes and use other ways to evaluate the queries on the models stored in the model-based representation. We emphasize two design decisions that we view as important to the approach. First, queries are presented to the network as conjunctions. Thus, consistently with the natural interface considered when learning the network, queries are viewed as *observations* – a list of propositions that are active (or non-active) in the environment. Second, in our algorithms, the top node, where the decision is being made, need not know the size of its input domain (the number of propositional letters). This is essential also to the extension to reasoning with incomplete information.

Let N be a network which contains a model-based representation for f. That is, there exists a network structure as in Definition 1 and Figure 1. We imply nothing on the models stored in the network (i.e., which are the components of the models). We also assume that various nodes are in suitable initial states.

Algorithms are described in the format of a sequence of steps (following (Val94)). First, we describe the initial (pre-)conditions assumed in the network. The input ("prompt") is orchestrated by the peripherals, which also "collect" the algorithm's response, represented as a pattern of firings of one or more nodes. At each step, "prompt" describes the input at this stage - the set of nodes that the peripherals force to fire this time. Then, we define the transitions that are invoked during the following time unit at the relevant nodes. All other aspects of the algorithm are fully distributed. The effect of the algorithm on any node not directly prompted is completely determined by the transition rules and by the conditions at this node and at its parents. The overall algorithm can be invoked at any time, by having the preconditions of the first step satisfied as a result of an appropriate prompt.

Deduction Consider the deduction problem $f \models \alpha$. Queries are presented to the network as conjunctions of rules, $\alpha = C_1 \wedge \ldots \wedge C_k$. Every rule has the form $C = A \rightarrow B$, where A and B are conjunctions of literals. Since $f \models C_1 \wedge \ldots \wedge C_k$ iff $f \models C_i \; \forall i \in (1,k)$, it is sufficient to consider the single[6] rule case.

We respond to $f \models (A \rightarrow B)$ using the following version of the reasoning with models algorithm. Given the set Γ of models, filter out the models that do not satisfy A. Respond *no* (y inactive) iff one of the remaining models (which satisfied A) does not satisfy B.

[6]It is easy to extend the algorithm to handle sequentially the presented rules, timed by the peripherals, and respond only after seeing the last rule. The thing to note is that it takes constant time to respond to a single rule, and the total time is linear in the number of rules.

Only the top node y and the example nodes take part in the deduction algorithm *AlgD*. It takes five steps: in the first two steps, the A part of the query is presented by the peripherals and is evaluated on all the models; in the next two steps, the B part of the query is presented by the peripherals and is evaluated on all the models that satisfied the A part; finally, the top node fires if all the models that satisfied A satisfy also B.

In the first step, an example node that receives activity wakes up and stores the total incoming weight for later comparison. A weight flip is used to evaluate the query presented to the network on the examples stored in it. In the second step, the same propositional nodes are prompted. This time, due to the weight flip, an example satisfies the observation (query) presented iff the input it sees doubles. In this case it fires and changes its mode to wait for the second part of the query. The same mechanisms works for the second part of the query, but applies only to examples which satisfied A. Therefore, it is sufficient for the top node to record (by setting its threshold) the *number* of these examples and make sure they all satisfy B also. Finally, the peripherals also prompt the target node y and this is used for the case where no model satisfies A, in which the response should also be "yes". The algorithm also makes sure that all the nodes return to their original states. Depending on the content of the representation we can prove:

Theorem 3 *Let y be a node in the network N, and let M_y be its model-based representation. (1) If M_y consists of the set of models $\Gamma_f^{\mathcal{Q}_c}$ then AlgD performs correct deduction whenever presented with a common query. (2) If M_y consists of a set of models of f acquired by sampling the environment according to distribution D then, with high probability, AlgD performs correct deduction whenever presented with an (f,ϵ)-fair query with respect to D.*

Abduction The algorithms for abductive reasoning, are not presented here. They perform the following tasks: (i) Given a candidate explanation $\mathcal{E}$ and a query, verify that $\mathcal{E}$ is a valid explanation. (ii) Provided that candidate explanations are represented as dedicated nodes in the network, given a query, the algorithm fires a valid explanation $\mathcal{E}$. All these tasks can be performed in constant time. In addition, the peripherals can use (i) to greedily present (subsets of) the collected output of (ii), in search for a minimal explanation.

The algorithm is similar to the deduction algorithm with the main distinction being that in this case we utilize the relay nodes and the backwards connections in order to communicate information down the network.

Learning to Reason

An essential part of the developed framework is that reasoning is performed by a network that has been learned from interaction with the environment (KR94a). For this purpose we have defined the interaction with the network via queries that are represented as *observations*. This allows for combining the interfaces to the world used by known learning models with the reasoning task. For example, the main avenue of interaction with the world used in the formal study of learning is an *Example Oracle*. When accessed, this oracle returns $v \in \{0,1\}^n$, drawn at random according to a distribution D; v can be viewed as an *observations* $v = (v_{i_1}, \ldots, v_{i_d})$ and interpreted also as a query. Examples presented in this way can be "memorized" into our network (Val94), and in combination with *AlgD* this provides a Learning to Reason algorithm that interacts with the environment, learns a model-based representation and supports correct entailment. Furthermore, using (2) of Theorem 3, the dependence of the reasoning performance on the learning process can be stated qualitatively. This type of interaction is supported also by the *on-line* L2R models (KR94a; Rot95) and can be shown to support other reasoning tasks, when augmented with membership and reasoning queries.

Conclusion

This paper develops a new approach to reasoning in connectionist networks. We suggest to interpret the connectionist architecture as encoding *examples* and show how to perform various reasoning tasks with this interpretation. Assuming the network encodes a (reasonably small) set of *representative* examples of a "world", we proved that our algorithms perform correct deduction and abduction, tasks that were considered intractable under other knowledge representations. Moreover, our framework naturally supports Learning to Reason and the representations used can be efficiently acquired by interaction with the world.

We believe that these results make this model suitable for studying *reflexive* reasoning (Sha93; Val94).

This work is part of a project in which we are trying to understand how networks of simple and slow neuron-like elements can encode a large body of knowledge and perform a wide range of interesting inferences almost instantaneously. It provides the theoretical framework for a system that learns knowledge representations for natural language understanding tasks.

References

A. Beringer and S. Holldobler. On the adequateness of the connection method. In *AAAI-93*, pages 9–14.

R. Brachman and H. Levesque. The tractability of subsumption in framebased description languages. *AAAI-84*.

M. Cadoli. *Tractable Reasoning in Artificial Intelligence.* Springer-verlag, 1995. Lec. notes in AI, vol 941.

M Dertthick. Mundane reasoning by settling on a plausible model. *Artificial Intelligence*, 46:107–157, 1990.

J. A. Fodor and Z. W. Pyilshyn. Connectionism and cognitive architecture: a critical analysis. *Cognition*, 28, 1988.

S. Holldobler and F. Kurfeb. CHCL *Parallelization in Inference Systems.* Springer-Verlag, 1991.

G. E. Hinton and T. J. Sejnowski. Learning and relearning in Botzmann machines. *PDP (Volume I: Foundations)*, pages 282–317. MIT Press, 1986.

R. Hobbs, J, M. Stickel, P. Martin, and D. Edwards. Interpretation as abduction. *Art. Intell.*, 63:69–142, 1993.

J. J. Hopfield and D. W. Tank. Neural computation of decisions in optimization problems. *Biol. Cyber.*, 1982.

P. N. Johnson-Laird. *Mental Models.* Harvard Press, 1983.

P. N. Johnson-Laird and R. M. J. Byrne. *Deduction.* Lawrence Erlbaum Associates, 1991.

H. Kautz, M. Kearns, and B. Selman. Reasoning with characteristic models. In *AAAI-93*, pages 34–39.

S. M. Kosslyn. *Image and Mind.* Harvard Press, 1983.

R. Khardon and D. Roth. Learning to reason. In *AAAI-94*, pages 682–687.

R. Khardon and D. Roth. Reasoning with models. In *AAAI-94*, pages 1148–1153.

R. Khardon and D. Roth. Default-reasoning with models. In *IJCAI-95*, pages 319–325.

T. E. Lange and M. G. Dyer. High-level inferencing in a connectionist network. *Connection Science*, 1991.

H. Levesque. Is reasoning too hard ? In *Proceeding of the 3rd NEC research Symposium.* 1992.

J. McCarthy. Programs with common sense. In R. Brachman and H. Levesque, *Readings in KR, 1985.*

S. Minton, M. D. Johnson, and A. B. Phillips. Solving large scale constraint satisfaction and scheduling problems using a heuristic repair method. In *AAAI-90.*

C. S. Peirce. *Abduction and Induction.* Dover, NY, 1955.

G. Pinkas. Reasoning, nonmonotonicity and learning in connectionist network that capture propositional knowledge. *Artificial Intelligence*, 77:203–247, 1995.

D. Roth. On the hardness of approximate reasoning. In *IJCAI-93*, pages 613–618.

D. Roth. Learning to reason: The non-monotonic case. In *IJCAI-95*, pages 1178–1184.

D. Roth. A connectionist framework for reasoning: Reasoning with examples. Tech. report, Dept. of App. Math. and CS, Weizmann Inst. of Science, 1996.

L. Shastri and V. Ajjanagadde. An optimally efficient limited inference system. In *AAAI-90*, pages 563–570.

L. Shastri and V. Ajjanagadde. From simple associations to systematic reasoning: A connectionist representation of rules, variables and dynamic binding using temporal synchrony. *Behavioral and Brain Sciences*, 1993.

L. Shastri. A computational model of tractable reasoning - taking inspiration from cognition. In *IJCAI-93.*

B. Selman and H. Kautz. Model-preference default theories. *Artificial Intelligence*, 45:287–322, 1990.

B. Selman, H. Levesque, and D. Mitchell. A new method for solving hard satisfiability problems. In *AAAI-92.*

R. Sun. Robust reasoning: Integrating rule-based similarity-based reasoning. *Artificial Intelligence*, 1995.

L. G. Valiant. A theory of the learnable. *Communications of the ACM*, 27(11):1134–1142, November 1984.

L. G. Valiant. *Circuits of the Mind.* Oxford University Press, November 1994.

Uncertainty

Goal Oriented Symbolic Propagation in Bayesian Networks

Enrique Castillo*, José Manuel Gutiérrez* and Ali S. Hadi**
* Department of Applied Mathematics and Computational Sciences,
University of Cantabria, SPAIN
Castie@ccaix3.unican.es and Gutierjm@ccaix3.unican.es
** Department of Social Statistics, Cornell University, USA
Ali-hadi@cornell.edu

Abstract

The paper presents an efficient goal oriented algorithm for symbolic propagation in Bayesian networks. The proposed algorithm performs symbolic propagation using numerical methods. It first takes advantage of the independence relationships among the variables and produce a reduced graph which contains only the relevant nodes and parameters required to compute the desired propagation. Then, the symbolic expression of the solution is obtained by performing numerical propagations associated with specific values of the symbolic parameters. These specific values are called the canonical components. Substantial savings are obtained with this new algorithm. Furthermore, the canonical components allow us to obtain lower and upper bounds for the symbolic expressions resulting from the propagation. An example is used to illustrate the proposed methodology.

Introduction

Bayesian networks are powerful tools both for graphically representing the relationships among a set of variables and for dealing with uncertainties in expert systems. A key problem in Bayesian networks is evidence propagation, that is, obtaining the posterior distributions of the variables when some evidence is observed. Several efficient exact and approximate methods for propagation of evidence in Bayesian networks have been proposed in recent years (see, for example, Pearl 1988, Lauritzen and Spiegelhalter 1988, Henrion 1988, Shachter and Peot 1990, Fung and Chang 1990, Poole 1993, Bouckaert, Castillo and Gutiérrez 1995). However, these methods require that the joint probabilities of the nodes be specified numerically, that is, all the parameters must be assigned numeric values. In practice, when exact numeric specification of these parameters may not be available, or when sensitivity analysis is desired, there is a need for symbolic methods which are able to deal with the parameters themselves, without assigning them numeric values. Symbolic propagation leads to solutions which are expressed as functions of the parameters in symbolic form.

Recently, two main approaches have been proposed for symbolic inference in Bayesian networks. The symbolic probabilistic inference algorithm (SPI) (Shachter, D'Ambrosio and DelFabero 1990 and Li and D'Ambrosio 1994) is a goal oriented method which performs only those calculations that are required to respond to queries. Symbolic expressions can be obtained by postponing evaluation of expressions, maintaining them in symbolic form. On the other hand, Castillo, Gutiérrez and Hadi 1995, 1996a, 1996b, exploit the polynomial structure of the marginal and conditional probabilities in Bayesian networks to efficiently perform symbolic propagation by calculating the associated numerical coefficients using standard numeric network inference algorithms (such as those in Lauritzen and Spiegelhalter). As opposed to the SPI algorithm, this method is not goal oriented, but allows us to obtain symbolic expressions for all the nodes in the network. In this paper we show that this algorithm is also suitable for goal oriented problems. In this case, the performance of the method can be improved by taking advantage of the independence relationships among the variables and produce a reduced graph which contains only the nodes relevant to the desired propagation. Thus, only those operations required to obtain the desired computations are performed.

We start by introducing the necessary notation. Then, an algorithm for efficient computation of the desired conditional probabilities is presented and illustrated by an example. Finally, we show how to obtain lower and upper bounds for the symbolic expressions solution of the given problem.

Notation

Let $X = \{X_1, X_2, \ldots, X_n\}$ be a set of n discrete variables, each can take values in the set $\{0, 1, \ldots, r_i\}$, the possible states of the variable X_i. A Bayesian network over X is a pair (D, P), where the graph D is a directed acyclic graph (DAG) with one node for each variable in X and $P = \{p_1(x_1|\pi_1), \ldots, p_n(x_n|\pi_n)\}$ is a set of n conditional probabilities, one for each variable, where Π_i is the set of parents of node X_i. Using the chain rule, the joint probability distribution of X can be written as:

$$p(x_1, x_2, \ldots, x_n) = \prod_{i=1}^{n} p_i(x_i|\pi_i). \quad (1)$$

Some of the conditional probability distributions (CDP) in (1) can be specified numerically and others symbolically, that is, $p_i(x_i|\pi_i)$ can be a parametric family. When $p_i(x_i|\pi_i)$ is a parametric family, we refer to the node X_i as a symbolic node. A convenient notation for the parameters in this case is given by

$$\theta_{ij\pi} = p_i(X_i = j|\Pi_i = \pi), \; j \in \{0, \ldots, r_i\}, \quad (2)$$

where π is any possible instantiation of the parents of X_i. Thus, the first subscript in $\theta_{ij\pi}$ refers to the node number, the second subscript refers to the state of the node, and the remaining subscripts refer to the parents' instantiations. Since $\sum_{j=0}^{r_i} \theta_{ij\pi} = 1$, for all i and π, any one of the parameters can be written as one minus the sum of all others. For example, $\theta_{ir_i\pi}$ is

$$\theta_{ir_i\pi} = 1 - \sum_{j=0}^{r_i-1} \theta_{ij\pi}. \quad (3)$$

If X_i has no parents, we use θ_{ij} to denote $p_i(X_i = j)$, $j \in \{0, \ldots, r_i\}$, for simplicity.

Goal Oriented Algorithm

Suppose that we are interested in a given goal node X_i, and that we want to obtain the CDP $p(X_i = j|E = e)$, where E is a set of evidential nodes with known values $E = e$. Using the algebraic characterization of the probabilities given by Castillo, Gutiérrez and Hadi 1995, the unnormalized probabilities $\hat{P}(X_i = j|E = e)$ are polynomials of the form:

$$\hat{P}(X_i = j|E = e) = \sum_{m_r \in M_j} c_{jr} m_r = p_j(\Theta), \quad (4)$$

where m_j are monomials in the symbolic parameters, Θ, contained in the probability distribution of the Bayesian network. For example, suppose we have a discrete Bayesian network consisting of five binary variables $\{X_1, \ldots, X_5\}$, with values in the set $\{0, 1\}$. The associated DAG is given in Figure 1. Table 1 gives the corresponding parameters, some in numeric and others in symbolic form. Node X_4 is numeric because it contains only numeric parameters and the other four nodes are symbolic because some of their parameters are specified only symbolically.

For illustrative purposes, suppose that the target node is X_3 and that we have the evidence $X_2 = 1$. We wish to compute the conditional probabilities $p(X_3 = j|X_2 = 1), j = 0, 1$. We shall show that

$$p(X_3 = 0|X_2 = 1) = \frac{0.4\theta_{10}\theta_{210} + 0.3\theta_{301} - 0.3\theta_{10}\theta_{301}}{0.3 - 0.3\theta_{10} + \theta_{10}\theta_{210}}, \quad (5)$$

Node		Parameters
X_i	Π_i	$X_i = 0$
X_1	None	$\theta_{10} = p(X_1 = 0)$
X_2	X_1	$\theta_{200} = p(X_2 = 0\|X_1 = 0)$
		$\theta_{201} = p(X_2 = 0\|X_1 = 1) = 0.7$
X_3	X_1	$\theta_{300} = p(X_3 = 0\|X_1 = 0) = 0.4$
		$\theta_{301} = p(X_3 = 0\|X_1 = 1)$
X_4	X_2, X_3	$\theta_{4000} = p(X_4 = 0\|X_2 = 0, X_3 = 0) = 0.2$
		$\theta_{4001} = p(X_4 = 0\|X_2 = 0, X_3 = 1) = 0.4$
		$\theta_{4010} = p(X_4 = 0\|X_2 = 1, X_3 = 0) = 0.7$
		$\theta_{4011} = p(X_4 = 0\|X_2 = 1, X_3 = 1) = 0.8$
X_5	X_3	$\theta_{500} = p(X_5 = 0\|X_3 = 0)$
		$\theta_{501} = p(X_5 = 0\|X_3 = 1)$

Node		Parameters
X_i	Π_i	$X_i = 1$
X_1	None	$\theta_{11} = p(X_1 = 1)$
X_2	X_1	$\theta_{210} = p(X_2 = 1\|X_1 = 0)$
		$\theta_{211} = p(X_2 = 1\|X_1 = 1) = 0.3$
X_3	X_1	$\theta_{310} = p(X_3 = 1\|X_1 = 0) = 0.6$
		$\theta_{311} = p(X_3 = 1\|X_1 = 1)$
X_4	X_2, X_3	$\theta_{4100} = p(X_4 = 1\|X_2 = 0, X_3 = 0) = 0.8$
		$\theta_{4101} = p(X_4 = 1\|X_2 = 0, X_3 = 1) = 0.6$
		$\theta_{4110} = p(X_4 = 1\|X_2 = 1, X_3 = 0) = 0.3$
		$\theta_{4111} = p(X_4 = 1\|X_2 = 1, X_3 = 1) = 0.2$
X_5	X_3	$\theta_{510} = p(X_5 = 1\|X_3 = 0)$
		$\theta_{511} = p(X_5 = 1\|X_3 = 1)$

Table 1: Numeric and symbolic conditional probabilities.

and

$$p(X_3 = 1|X_2 = 1) = \frac{0.3 - 0.3\theta_{10} + 0.6\theta_{10}\theta_{210} - 0.3\theta_{301} + 0.3\theta_{10}\theta_{301}}{0.3 - 0.3\theta_{10} + \theta_{10}\theta_{210}}, \quad (6)$$

where the denominator in (5) and (6) is a normalizing constant.

Algorithm 1 gives the solution for this goal oriented problem by calculating the coefficients c_{jr} in (4) of these polynomials. It is organized in four main parts:

- **PART I : Identify all Relevant Nodes.**
  The CDP $p(X_i = j|E = e)$ does not necessarily

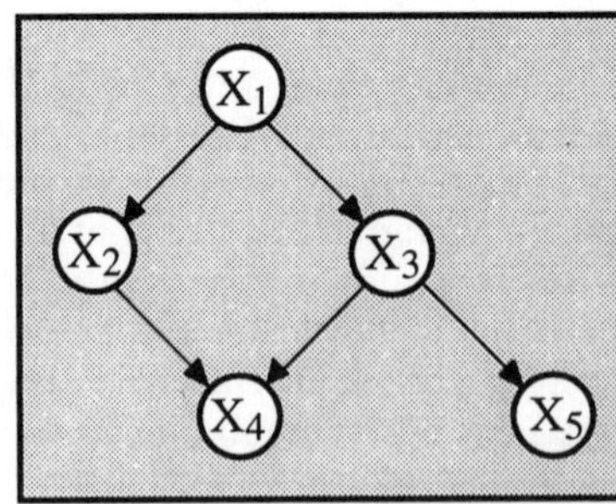

Figure 1: An example of a five-node Bayesian Network.

involve parameters associated with all nodes. Thus, we identify the set of nodes which are relevant to the calculation of $p(X_i = j|E = e)$, using either one of the two algorithms given in Geiger, Verma, and Pearl 1990 and Shachter 1990. Once this has been done we can remove the remaining nodes from the graph and identify the associated set of relevant parameters Θ.

- **PART II : Identify Sufficient Parameters.** By considering the values of the evidence variables, the set of parameters Θ can be further reduced by identifying and eliminating the set of parameters which are in contradiction with the evidence. These parameters are eliminated using the following two rules:
  - **Rule 1:** Eliminate the parameters $\theta_{jk\pi}$ if $x_j \neq k$ for every $X_j \in E$.
  - **Rule 2:** Eliminate the parameters $\theta_{jk\pi}$ if parents' instantiations π are incompatible with the evidence.
- **PART III : Identify Feasible Monomials.** Once the minimal sufficient subsets of parameters have been identified, they are combined in monomials by taking the Cartesian product of the minimal sufficient subsets of parameters and eliminating the set of all infeasible combinations of the parameters using:
  - **Rule 3:** Parameters associated with contradictory conditioning instantiations cannot appear in the same monomial.
- **PART IV : Calculate Coefficients of all Polynomials.** This part calculates the coefficients applying numeric network inference methods to the reduced graph obtained in Part I. If the parameters Θ are assigned numerical values, say θ, then $p_j(\theta)$ can be obtained using any numeric network inference method to compute $p(X_i = j|E = e, \Theta = \theta)$. Similarly, the monomials m_r take a numerical value, the product of the parameters involved in m_r. Thus, we have

$$\hat{P}(X_i = j|E = e, \Theta = \theta) = \sum_{m_r \in M_j} c_{jr} m_r = p_j(\theta). \tag{7}$$

  Note that in (7) all the monomials m_r, and the unnormalized probability $p_j(\theta)$ are known numbers, and the only unknowns are the coefficients c_{jr}. To compute these coefficients, we need to construct a set of independent equations each of the form in (7). These equations can be obtained using sets of distinct instantiations Θ.

To illustrate the algorithm we use, in parallel, the previous example.

Algorithm 1 Computes $p(X_i = j|E = e)$.

Input: A Bayesian network (D, P), a target node X_i and an evidential set E (possibly empty) with evidential values $E = e$.

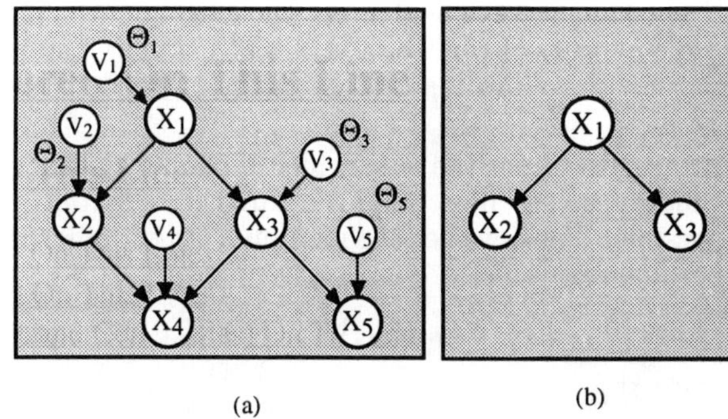

Figure 2: (a) Augmented graph D^* after adding a dummy node V_i for every symbolic node X_i, and (b) the reduced graph D' sufficient to compute $p(X_i = j|E = e)$.

Output: The CPD $p(X_i = j|E = e)$.

PART I:

- **Step 1:** Construct a DAG D^* by augmenting D with a dummy node V_j and adding a link $V_j \to X_j$ for every node X_j in D. The node V_j represents the parameters, Θ_j, of node X_j.
- **Example:** We add to the initial graph in Figure 1, the nodes V_1, V_2, V_3, V_4, and V_5 The resulting graph in shown in Figure 2(a).
- **Step 2:** Identify the set V of dummy nodes in D^* not d-separated from the goal node X_i by E. Obtain a new graph D' by removing from D those nodes whose corresponding dummy nodes are not contained in V with the exception of the target and evidential nodes. Let Θ be the set of all the parameters associated with the symbolic nodes included in the new graph and V.
- **Example:** The set V of dummy nodes not d-separated from the goal node X_3 by the evidence node $E = \{X_2\}$ is found to be $V = \{V_1, V_2, V_3\}$. Therefore, we remove X_4 and X_5 from the graph obtaining the graph shown in Figure 2(b). Thus, the set of all the parameters associated with symbolic nodes of the new graph is

$$\Theta = \{\Theta_1, \Theta_2, \Theta_3\} = \{\{\theta_{10}, \theta_{11}\}; \{\theta_{200}, \theta_{210}, \theta_{201}, \theta_{211}\}; \{\theta_{300}, \theta_{310}, \theta_{301}, \theta_{311}\}\}.$$

PART II:

- **Step 3:** If there is evidence, remove from Θ the parameters $\theta_{jk\pi}$ if $x_j \neq k$ for $X_j \in E$ (Rule 1).
- **Example:** The set Θ contains the symbolic parameters θ_{200} and θ_{201} that do not match the evidence $X_2 = 1$. Then, applying Rule 1 we eliminate these parameters from Θ.

- **Step 4:** If there is evidence, remove from Θ the parameters $\theta_{jk\pi}$ if the set of values of parents' instantiations π are incompatible with the evidence (Rule 2).
- **Example:** Since the only evidential node X_2 has no children in the new graph, no further reduction is possible. Thus, we get the minimum set of sufficient parameters:

$$\Theta = \{\{\theta_{10}, \theta_{11}\}; \{\theta_{210}, \theta_{211}\}; \{\theta_{300}, \theta_{310}, \theta_{301}, \theta_{311}\}\}.$$

PART III:

- **Step 5:** Obtain the set of monomials M by taking the Cartesian product of the subsets of parameters in Θ.
- **Example:** The initial set of candidate monomials is given by taking the Cartesian product of the minimal sufficient subsets, that is,

$$M = \{\theta_{10}, \theta_{11}\} \times \{\theta_{210}, \theta_{211}\} \times \{\theta_{300}, \theta_{310}, \theta_{301}, \theta_{311}\}.$$

Thus, we obtain 16 different candidate monomials.

- **Step 6:** Using Rule 3, remove from M those monomials which contain a set of incompatible parameters.
- **Example:** Some of the monomials in M contain parameters with contradictory instantiations of the parents. For example, the monomial $\theta_{10}\theta_{210}\theta_{301}$ contains contradictory instantiations of the parents because θ_{10} indicates that $X_1 = 0$ whereas θ_{301} indicates that $X_1 = 1$. Thus, applying Rule 3, we get the following set of feasible monomials $M = \{\theta_{10}\theta_{210}\theta_{300}, \theta_{10}\theta_{210}\theta_{310}, \theta_{11}\theta_{211}\theta_{301}, \theta_{11}\theta_{211}\theta_{311}\}$.
- **Step 7:** If some of the parameters associated with the symbolic nodes are specified numerically, then remove these parameters from the resulting feasible monomials because they are part of the numerical coefficients.
- **Example:** Some symbolic nodes involve both numeric and symbolic parameters. Then, we remove from the monomials in M the numerical parameters $\theta_{300}, \theta_{310}$ and θ_{211} obtaining the set of feasible monomials $M = \{\theta_{10}\theta_{210}, \theta_{11}\theta_{301}, \theta_{11}\theta_{311}\}$. Note that, when removing these numeric parameters from Θ, the monomials $\theta_{10}\theta_{210}\theta_{300}$ and $\theta_{10}\theta_{210}\theta_{310}$ become $\theta_{10}\theta_{210}$. Thus, finally, we only have three different monomials associated with the probabilities $p(X_3 = j|X_2 = 1), j = 0, 1$.

PART IV:

- **Step 8:** For each possible state j of node X_i, $j = 0, \ldots, r_i$, build the subset M_j by considering those monomials in M which do not contain any parameter of the form $\theta_{iq\pi}$, with $q \neq j$.
- **Example:** The sets of monomials needed to calculate $p(X_3 = 0|X_2 = 1)$ and $p(X_3 = 1|X_2 = 1)$ are $M_0 = \{\theta_{10}\theta_{210}, \theta_{11}\theta_{301}\}$ and $M_1 = \{\theta_{10}\theta_{210}, \theta_{11}\theta_{311}\}$, respectively. Then, using (4), we have:

$$\begin{aligned} p_0(\Theta) &= \hat{P}(X_3 = 0|X_2 = 1) \\ &= c_{01}m_{01} + c_{02}m_{02} \\ &= c_{01}\theta_{10}\theta_{210} + c_{02}\theta_{11}\theta_{301}. \end{aligned} \quad (8)$$

$$\begin{aligned} p_1(\Theta) &= \hat{P}(X_3 = 1|X_2 = 1) \\ &= c_{11}m_{11} + c_{12}m_{12} \\ &= c_{11}\theta_{10}\theta_{210} + c_{12}\theta_{11}\theta_{311}. \end{aligned} \quad (9)$$

- **Step 9:** For each possible state j of node X_i, calculate the coefficients c_{jr} of the conditional probabilities in (4), $r = 0, \ldots, n_j$, as follows:
  1. Calculate n_j different instantiations of Θ, $C = \{\theta_1, \ldots, \theta_{n_j}\}$ such that the canonical $n_j \times n_j$ matrix $\mathbf{T}_j$, whose rs-th element is the value of the monomial m_r obtained by replacing Θ by θ_s, is a non-singular matrix.
  2. Use any numeric network inference method to compute the vector of numerical probabilities $\mathbf{p}_j = (p_j(\theta_1), \ldots, p_j(\theta_{n_j}))$ by propagating the evidence $E = e$ in the reduced graph D' obtained in Step 2.
  3. Calculate the vector of coefficients $\mathbf{c}_j = (c_{j1}, \ldots, c_{jn_j})$ by solving the system of equations

$$\mathbf{T}_j\mathbf{c}_j = \mathbf{p}_j, \quad (10)$$

which implies

$$\mathbf{c}_j = \mathbf{T}_j^{-1}\mathbf{p}_j. \quad (11)$$

- **Example:** Thus, taking appropriate combinations of extreme values for the symbolic parameters (canonical components), we can obtain the numeric coefficients by propagating the evidence not in the original graph D (Castillo, Gutiérrez and Hadi 1996), but in the reduced graph D', saving a lot of computation time. We have the symbolic parameters $\Theta = (\theta_{10}, \theta_{11}, \theta_{200}, \theta_{210}, \theta_{301}, \theta_{311})$ contained in D', We take the canonical components $\theta_1 = (1, 0, 1, 0, 1, 0)$ and $\theta_2 = (0, 1, 0, 1, 1, 0)$ and using any (exact or approximate) numeric network inference methods to calculate the coefficients of $p_0(\Theta)$. We obtain, $p_0(\theta_1) = 0.4$ and $p_0(\theta_2) = 0.3$. Note that, in the above equation, the vector $(p_0(\theta_1), p_0(\theta_2))$ can be calculated using any of the standard exact or approximate numeric network inference methods, because all the symbolic parameters have been assigned a numerical value:

$$\begin{aligned} p_0(\theta_1) &= p(X_3 = 0|X_2 = 1, \Theta = \theta_1) \\ p_0(\theta_2) &= p(X_3 = 0|X_2 = 1, \Theta = \theta_2). \end{aligned}$$

Then, no symbolic operations are performed to obtain the symbolic solution. Thus, (11) becomes

$$\begin{pmatrix} c_{01} \\ c_{02} \end{pmatrix} = \begin{pmatrix} 1 & 0 \\ 0 & 1 \end{pmatrix}^{-1} \begin{pmatrix} p_0(\theta_1) \\ p_0(\theta_2) \end{pmatrix} = \begin{pmatrix} 0.4 \\ 0.3 \end{pmatrix}. \quad (12)$$

Similarly, taking the canonical components $\theta_1 = (1,0,1,0,1,0)$ and $\theta_2 = (0,1,0,1,0,1)$, for the probability $p_1(\Theta)$ we obtain

$$\begin{pmatrix} c_{11} \\ c_{12} \end{pmatrix} = \begin{pmatrix} 0.6 \\ 0.3 \end{pmatrix}. \quad (13)$$

Then, by substituting in (8) and (9), we obtain the unnormalized probabilities:

$$\hat{P}(X_3 = 0|X_2 = 1) = 0.4\theta_{10}\theta_{210} + 0.3\theta_{11}\theta_{301}, \quad (14)$$
$$\hat{P}(X_3 = 1|X_2 = 1) = 0.6\theta_{10}\theta_{210} + 0.3\theta_{11}\theta_{311}. \quad (15)$$

- **Step 10:** Calculate the unnormalized probabilities $p_j(\Theta), j = 0, \ldots, r_i$ and the conditional probabilities $p(X_i = j|E = e) = p_j(\Theta)/N$, where

$$N = \sum_{j=0}^{r_i} p_j(\Theta)$$

is the normalizing constant.

- **Example:** Finally, normalizing (14) and (15) we get the final polynomial expressions:

$$p(X_3 = 0|X_2 = 1) = \frac{0.4\theta_{10}\theta_{210} + 0.3\theta_{11}\theta_{301}}{\theta_{10}\theta_{210} + 0.3\theta_{11}\theta_{301} + 0.3\theta_{11}\theta_{311}} \quad (16)$$

and

$$p(X_3 = 1|X_1 = 1) = \frac{0.6\theta_{10}\theta_{210} + 0.3\theta_{11}\theta_{311}}{\theta_{10}\theta_{210} + 0.3\theta_{11}\theta_{301} + 0.3\theta_{11}\theta_{311}}. \quad (17)$$

- **Step 11:** Use (3) to eliminate dependent parameters and obtain the final expression for the conditional probabilities.

- **Example:** Now, we apply the relationships among the parameters in (3) to simplify the above expressions. In this case, we have: $\theta_{311} = 1 - \theta_{301}$ and $\theta_{11} = 1 - \theta_{10}$. Thus, we get Expressions (5) and (6). Equations (5) and (6) give the posterior distribution of the goal node X_3 given the evidence $X_2 = 1$ in symbolic form. Thus, $p(X_3 = j|X_2 = 1), j = 0, 1$ can be evaluated directly by plugging in (5) and (6) any specific combination of values for the symbolic parameters without the need to redo the propagation from scratch for every given combination of values.

Remark: In some cases, it is possible to obtain a set of canonical instantiations for the above algorithm that leads to an identity matrix $\mathbf{T}_j$. In those cases, the coefficients of the symbolic expressions are directly obtained from numeric network inferences, without the extra effort of solving a system of linear equations.

θ_k			$p(X_3 = j\|X_2 = 1, \theta_k)$	
θ_{10}	θ_{210}	θ_{301}	$j = 0$	$j = 1$
0	0	0	0.0	1.0
0	0	1	1.0	0.0
0	1	0	0.0	1.0
0	1	1	1.0	0.0
1	0	0	0.4	0.6
1	0	1	0.4	0.6
1	1	0	0.4	0.6
1	1	1	0.4	0.6

Table 2: Conditional probabilities for the canonical cases associated with $\theta_{10}, \theta_{210}$, and θ_{301}.

Sensitivity Analysis

The lower and upper bound of the resulting symbolic expressions are a useful information for performing sensitivity analysis (Castillo, Gutiérrez and Hadi 1996a). In this section we show how to obtain an interval, $(l, u) \subset [0, 1]$, that contains all the solutions of the given problem, for any combination of numerical values for the symbolic parameters. The bounds of the obtained ratios of polynomials as, for example (5) and (6), are attained at one of the canonical components (vertices of the feasible convex parameter set). We use the following theorem given by Martos 1964.

Theorem 1 If the linear fractional functional of u,

$$\frac{\mathbf{c} * \mathbf{u} - c_0}{\mathbf{d} * \mathbf{u} - d_0}, \quad (18)$$

where u is a vector, $\mathbf{c}$ and $\mathbf{d}$ are vector coefficients and c_0 and d_0 are real constants, is defined in the convex polyhedron $\mathbf{Au} \leq a_0, \mathbf{u} \geq 0$, where $\mathbf{A}$ is a constant matrix and a_0 is a constant vector, and the denominator in (18) does not vanish in the polyhedron, then the functional reaches the maximum at least in one of the vertices of the polyhedron. ∎

In our case, $\mathbf{u}$ is the set of symbolic parameters and the fractional functions (18) are the symbolic expressions associated with the probabilities, (5) and (6). In this case, the convex polyhedron is defined by $\mathbf{u} \leq 1, \mathbf{u} \geq 0$, that is, $\mathbf{A}$ is the identity matrix. Then, using Theorem 1, the lower and upper bounds of the symbolic expressions associated with the probabilities are attained at the vertices of this polyhedron. In our case, the vertices of the polyhedron are given by all possible combinations of values 0 or 1 of the symbolic parameters, that is, by the complete set of canonical components associated with the set of free symbolic parameters appearing in the final symbolic expressions.

As an example, Table 2 shows the canonical probabilities associated with the symbolic expressions (5) and (6) obtained for the CDP $p(X_3 = j|X_2 = 1)$. The minimum and maximum of these probabilities are 0 and 1, respectively. Therefore, the lower and upper bounds are trivial bounds in this case. The same

θ_k		$p(X_3 = j\|X_2 = 1, \theta_k)$	
θ_{10}	θ_{210}	$j = 0$	$j = 1$
0	0	0.5	0.5
0	1	0.5	0.5
1	0	0.4	0.6
1	1	0.4	0.6

Table 3: Conditional probabilities for the canonical cases associated with θ_{10} and θ_{210} for $\theta_{301} = 0.5$.

bounds are obtained when fixing the symbolic parameters θ_{10} or θ_{210} to a given numeric value.

However, if we consider a numeric value for the symbolic parameter θ_{301}, for example $\theta_{301} = 0.5$, we obtain the canonical probabilities shown in Table 3. Therefore, the lower and upper bounds for the probability $p(X_3 = 0|X_2 = 1)$ become $(0.4, 0.5)$, and for $p(X_3 = 1|X_2 = 1)$ are $(0.5, 0.6)$, i.e., a range of 0.1.

If we instantiate another symbolic parameter, for example $\theta_{10} = 0.1$, the new range decreases. We obtain the lower and upper bounds (0.473, 0.5) for $p(X_3 = 0|X_2 = 1)$, and $(0.5, 0.537)$ for $p(X_3 = 1|X_2 = 1)$.

Conclusions and Recommendations

The paper presents an efficient goal oriented algorithm for symbolic propagation in Bayesian networks, which allows dealing with symbolic or mixed cases of symbolic-numeric parameters. The main advantage of this algorithm is that uses numeric network inference methods, which make it superior than pure symbolic methods. First, the initial graph is reduced to produce a new graph which contains only the relevant nodes and parameters required to compute the desired propagation. Next, the relevant monomials in the symbolic parameters appearing in the target probabilities are identified. Then, the symbolic expression of the solution is obtained by performing numerical propagations associated with specific numerical values of the symbolic parameters. An additional advantage is that the canonical components allow us to obtain lower and upper bounds for the symbolic marginal or conditional probabilities.

Acknowledgments

We thank the Dirección General de Investigación Científica y Técnica (DGICYT) (project PB94-1056), Iberdrola and NATO Research Office for partial support of this work.

References

Bouckaert, R. R., Castillo, E. and Gutiérrez, J. M. 1995. A Modified Simulation Scheme for Inference in Bayesian Networks. *International Journal of Approximate Reasoning*, 14:55–80.

Castillo, E., Gutiérrez, J. M., and Hadi, A. S. 1995. Parametric Structure of Probabilities in Bayesian Networks. *Lectures Notes in Artificial Intelligence*, Springer–Verlag, 946:89–98.

Castillo, E., Gutiérrez, J. M., and Hadi, A. S. 1996a. A New Method for Efficient Symbolic Propagation in Discrete Bayesian Networks. *Networks*. To appear.

Castillo, E., Gutiérrez, J. M., and Hadi, A. S. 1996b. *Expert Systems and Probabilistic Network Models*. Springer–Verlag, New York.

Fung, R. and Chang, K. C. 1990. Weighing and Integrating Evidence for Stochastic Simulation in Bayesian Networks, in *Uncertainty in Artificial Intelligence 5*, Machine Intelligence and Pattern Recognition Series, 10, (Henrion et al. Eds.), North Holland, Amsterdam, 209–219.

Geiger, D., Verma, T., and Pearl, J. 1990. Identifying Independence in Bayesian Networks. *Networks*, 20:507–534.

Henrion, M. 1988. Propagating Uncertainty in Bayesian Networks by Probabilistic Logic Sampling, in *Uncertainty in Artificial Intelligence*, (J.F. Lemmer and L. N. Kanal, Eds.), North Holland, Amsterdam, 2:317–324.

Lauritzen, S. L. and Spiegelhalter, D. J. 1988. Local Computations with Probabilities on Graphical Structures and Their Application to Expert Systems. *Journal of the Royal Statistical Society (B)*, 50:157–224.

Li, Z., and D'Ambrosio, B. 1994. Efficient Inference in Bayes Nets as a Combinatorial Optimization Problem. *International Journal of Approximate Reasoning*, 11(1):55–81.

Martos, B. 1964. Hyperbolic Programming. *Naval Research Logistic Quarterly*, 32:135–156.

Pearl, J. 1988. *Probabilistic Reasoning in Intelligent Systems: Networks of Plausible Inference.* Morgan Kaufmann, San Mateo, CA.

Poole, D. 1993. Average-case Analysis of a Search Algorithm for Estimating Prior and Posterior Probabilities in Bayesian Networks with Extreme Probabilities, in *Proceedings of the 13th International Joint Conference on Artificial Intelligence*, 13(1):606–612.

Shachter, R. D. 1990. An Ordered Examination of Influence Diagrams. *Networks*, 20:535–563.

Shachter, R. D., D'Ambrosio, B., and DelFabero, B. 1990. Symbolic Probabilistic Inference in Belief Networks, in *Proceedings Eighth National Conference on AI*, 126–131.

Shachter, R. D. and Peot, M. A. 1990. Simulation Approaches to General Probabilistic Inference on Belief Networks, in *Uncertainty in Artificial Intelligence*, Machine Intelligence and Pattern Recognition Series, 10 (Henrion et al. Eds.), North Holland, Amsterdam, 5:221–231.

A Clinician's Tool for Analyzing Non-compliance

David Maxwell Chickering and Judea Pearl

Cognitive Systems Laboratory
Computer Science Department
University of California, Los Angeles, CA 90024
dmax@cs.ucla.edu
judea@cs.ucla.edu

Abstract

We describe a computer program to assist a clinician with assessing the efficacy of treatments in experimental studies for which treatment assignment is random but subject compliance is imperfect. The major difficulty in such studies is that treatment efficacy is not "identifiable", that is, it cannot be estimated from the data, even when the number of subjects is infinite, unless additional knowledge is provided. Our system combines Bayesian learning with Gibbs sampling using two inputs: (1) the investigator's prior probabilities of the relative sizes of subpopulations and (2) the observed data from the experiment. The system outputs a histogram depicting the posterior distribution of the average treatment effect, that is, the probability that the average outcome (e.g., survival) would attain a given level, had the treatment been taken uniformly by the entire population. This paper describes the theoretical basis for the proposed approach and presents experimental results on both simulated and real data, showing agreement with the theoretical asymptotic bounds.

Introduction

Standard clinical studies in the biological and medical sciences invariably invoke the instrument of randomized control, that is, subjects are assigned at random to various groups (or treatments or programs) and the mean differences between participants in different groups are regarded as measures of the efficacies of the associated programs. For example, to determine if a new drug is useful for treating some disease, subjects will be divided (at random) into a control group and a treatment group. The members of the control group are given a placebo and the members of the treatment group are given the drug in question. For each group, the clinician records the fraction of subjects that recover from the disease. By comparing these fractions the clinician can derive a quantitative measure of effectiveness of the drug for treating the disease. In particular, if f_c and f_t are the fractions of subjects that recovered from the control group and treatment group respectively, then the difference $E = f_c - f_t$ is an indication of the effectiveness of the drug.

The major source of difficulty in managing and analyzing such experiments has been subject noncompliance. For example, a subject in the treatment group may experience negative side effects and will stop taking the drug. Alternatively, if the experiment is testing a drug for a terminal disease, a subject suspecting that he is in the control group may obtain the drug from other sources. Imperfect compliance poses a problem because simply comparing the fractions as above may provide a misleading estimate for how effective the drug would be if applied uniformly to the population. For example, if those subjects who refused to take the drug are precisely those who would have responded adversely, the experiment might conclude that the drug is more effective than it actually is. It can be shown, in fact, that treatment effectiveness in such studies is *non-identifiable.* That is, in the absence of additional modeling assumptions, treatment effectiveness cannot be estimated from the data without bias, even as the number of subjects in the experiment approaches infinity, and even when a record is available of the action and response of each subject (Pearl 1995a).

In a popular compromising approach to the problem of imperfect compliance, researchers perform an *intent-to-treat* analysis, in which the control and treatment group are compared without regard to whether the treatment was actually received[1]. The result of such an analysis is a measure of how well the treatment *assignment* effects the disease, as opposed to the desired measure of how well the treatment itself effects the disease. Estimates based on intent-to-treat analysis are valid only as long as the experimental conditions perfectly mimic the conditions prevailing in the eventual usage of the treatment. In particular, the experiment should mimic subjects' incentives for receiving each treatment. In situations where field incentives are more compelling than experimental incentives, as is usually the case when drugs receive the approval of a government agency, treatment effectiveness may vary significantly from assignment effectiveness. For example, imagine a study in which (a) the drug has an

[1]This approach is currently used by the FDA to approve new drugs.

adverse effect on a large segment of the population and (b) only those members of the segment who drop from the treatment arm recover. The intent-to-treat analysis will attribute these cases of recovery to the drug since they are part of the intent-to-treat arm, while in reality these cases have recovered by avoiding the treatment (Pearl 1995b).

Another approach to the problem is to use a correction factor based on an "instrumental variables" formula (Angrist, Imbens, & Rubin 1993), according to which the intent-to-treat measure should be divided by the fraction of subjects who comply with the treatment assigned to them. Angrist et al. (1993) have shown that, under certain conditions, the corrected formula is valid for the subpopulation of "responsive" subjects, that is, subjects who would have changed treatment status if given a different assignment. Unfortunately, this subpopulation cannot be identified and, more seriously, it cannot serve as a basis for policies involving the entire population because it is instrument dependent—individuals who are responsive in the study may not remain responsive in the field, where the incentives for obtaining treatment differ from those used in the study.

Using a graphical model with latent variables, Balke and Pearl (1994) derive bounds, rather than point estimates, for the treatment effect, while making no assumptions about the relationship between subjects' compliance and subjects' physical response to treatment. However, the derived bounds are "asymptotic", i.e., they ignore sampling variations by assuming that the proportions measured in the experiment are representative of the population as a whole, a condition which is valid only when the number of subjects is large. This large-sample assumption may be problematic when the study includes a relatively small number of subjects.

In this paper we describe a system that provides an assessment of the actual treatment effect and is not limited to studies with large samples. The system uses the graphical model of Balke and Pearl (1994) to learn the treatment effect using Bayesian updating combined with Gibbs sampling. The system takes as input (1) the investigator's prior knowledge about subject compliance and response behaviors and (2) the observed data from the experiment, and outputs the posterior distribution of the treatment effect. The use of graphical models and Gibbs' methods for deriving posterior distributions in such models are both well known. The main contribution of this paper is a description of how these techniques can be applied to the causal analysis of clinical trials, and a presentation of experimental results of a practical system applied to various simulated and real data. While the basic idea of estimating causal effects using Bayesian analysis goes back to Rubin (1978), and was further used by Imbens and Rubin (1994) to estimate the correctional formula advocated by Angrist et al. (1993), we believe that this is the first time an assumption-free assessment of the *average treatment effect* is made available to the clinical research community.

The paper is organized as follows. First, we introduce a graphical, causal model that represents a prototypical clinical trial with partial compliance, and define *treatment effect* in terms of the model. Next, we describe an equivalent graphical model, using potential-response variables (Balke & Pearl 1994), that allows the compliance and response behavior to be represented more efficiently. Next, we describe the general Bayesian-learning and Gibbs-sampling methods that were used to derive the posterior parameter densities in the graphical model. Finally, we describe experimental results obtained when our system is applied to various simulated and real data sets. We include results obtained when the system is modified to answer counterfactual queries about specific individuals, e.g., "what if Joe (who died with no treatment) were to have taken the treatment?"

The Graphical Model

Graphical models are convenient tools for representing causal and statistical assumptions about variables in a domain (Pearl 1995a). In this section, we describe the graphical model of Figure 1, which is used to represent a prototypical clinical trial with partial compliance. We use Z, D and Y to denote observed binary variables from the experiment, where Z represents the treatment assignment, D represents the treatment received, and Y represents the observed outcome. To facilitate the notation, we let z, d, and y represent, respectively, the values taken by the variables Z, D, and Y, with the following interpretation: $z \in \{z_0, z_1\}$, z_1 asserts that the treatment has been assigned (z_0 its negation); $d \in \{d_0, d_1\}$, d_1 asserts that the treatment has been administered (d_0 its negation); and $y \in \{y_0, y_1\}$, y_1 asserts a positive observed response (y_0 its negation). We use U to denote all characteristics, both observed and unobserved, that influence the value of D and Y for the subjects. The domain of U is left unspecified, and in general will combine the spaces of several random variables, both discrete and continuous.

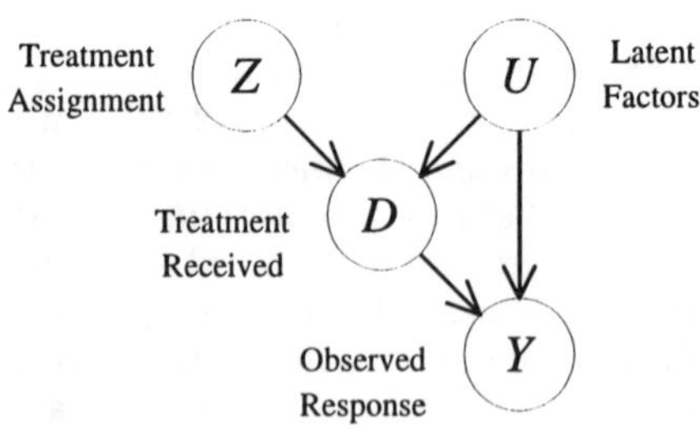

Figure 1: Graphical model for a prototypical clinical trial with partial compliance

Let ν_e denote the *physical probability* of the event $E = e$, or equivalently, the fraction of subjects in the population for which $E = e$. The graphical model explicitly represents two independence assumptions about the joint physical probability distribution $\nu_{z,d,y,u}$. First, the model asserts that the treatment assignment Z can influence: Y only through the actual treatment D. That is, Z and Y are conditionally independent given D and U. Second, the model asserts that Z and U are marginally independent. This second independence is ensured through the randomization of Z, which rules out both (1) the existence of a common cause for both Z and U, and (2) the possibility that U has causal influence on Z. The two independence assumptions together induce the following decomposition of the joint distribution:

$$\nu_{z,d,y,u} = \nu_z \nu_u \nu_{d|z,u} \nu_{y|d,u}$$

In addition to the independence assumptions, the graphical model also encodes causal assumptions (e.g., that Z does not effect Y directly) which permit one to predict how the joint probability will change in light of *exogenous* local interventions (Pearl 1995a). In particular, the absence of any direct link (or any spurious path) from Z to Y implies that $\nu_{y|d,u}$ is the same regardless if d is measured in an observational study, or dictated by some (exogenous) public policy. Consequently, if we wish to predict the distribution $\nu^*_{y|d}$ of Y, under a new condition where the treatment $D = d$ is applied uniformly to the population, we should calculate

$$\nu^*_{y|d} = E_u[\nu_{y|d,u}]$$

where E_u denotes the expectation with respect to ν_u. Likewise, if we are interested in the average *change* in Y due to treatment, we use the *average causal effect*, denoted ACE$(D \to Y)$, as defined by Holland (1988):

$$\text{ACE}(D \to Y) = E_u[\nu_{y_1|d_1,u} - \nu_{y_1|d_0,u}] \quad (1)$$

Let $\mathcal{D}$ denote the observed collection of triples $\{z, d, y\}$, one for each subject, that we obtain from the experiment. Given $\mathcal{D}$, the objective of our system is to derive the posterior Bayesian probability distribution $p(\text{ACE}(D \to Y) \mid \mathcal{D})$.

The Potential-Response Model

The graphical model presented in the previous section is attractive for representing the assumptions that underlie a given experimental design, but may not be convenient for computation. For example, the graph of Figure 1 represents explicitly the assumptions that Z is randomized and that Z does not affect Y directly, while making no assumption about the relationship between compliance and the way subjects would respond to the treatment. However, leaving the domain of the unobserved variable U unspecified makes it difficult to derive the distribution of interest, namely, $p(\text{ACE}(D \to Y) \mid \mathcal{D})$.

As is done by Balke and Pearl (1994), we exploit the observation of Pearl (1994) that U can always be replaced by a single discrete and finite variable such that the resulting model is equivalent with respect to all observations and manipulations of Z, D, and Y. In particular, because Z, D, and Y are all binary variables, the state space of U divides into 16 equivalence classes: each equivalence class dictates two functional mappings; one from Z to D, and the other from D to Y. To describe these equivalence classes, it is convenient to regard each of them as a point in the joint space of two four-valued variables C and R. The variable C determines the compliance behavior of a subject through the mapping:

$$d = F_D(z, c) = \begin{cases} d_0 & \text{if} \quad c = c_0 \\ \\ d_0 & \text{if} \quad c = c_1 \quad \text{and} \quad z = z_0 \\ d_1 & \text{if} \quad c = c_1 \quad \text{and} \quad z = z_1 \\ \\ d_1 & \text{if} \quad c = c_2 \quad \text{and} \quad z = z_0 \\ d_0 & \text{if} \quad c = c_2 \quad \text{and} \quad z = z_1 \\ \\ d_1 & \text{if} \quad c = c_3 \end{cases} \quad (2)$$

Imbens and Rubin (1994) call a subject with compliance behavior c_0, c_1, c_2 and c_3, respectively, a *never-taker*, a *complier*, a *defier* and an *always-taker*. Similarly, the variable R determines the response behavior of a subject through the mapping:

$$y = F_Y(d, r) = \begin{cases} y_0 & \text{if} \quad r = r_0 \\ \\ y_0 & \text{if} \quad r = r_1 \quad \text{and} \quad d = d_0 \\ y_1 & \text{if} \quad r = r_1 \quad \text{and} \quad d = d_1 \\ \\ y_1 & \text{if} \quad r = r_2 \quad \text{and} \quad d = d_0 \\ y_0 & \text{if} \quad r = r_2 \quad \text{and} \quad d = d_1 \\ \\ y_1 & \text{if} \quad r = r_3 \end{cases} \quad (3)$$

Following Heckerman and Shachter (1995), we call the response behavior r_0, r_1, r_2 and r_3, respectively, *never-recover*, *helped*, *hurt* and *always-recover*.

Let CR denote the variable whose state space is the cross-product of the states of C and R. We use cr_{ij}, with $0 \le i, j \le 3$ to denote the state of CR corresponding to compliance behavior c_i and response behavior r_j. Figure 2 shows the graphical model that results from replacing U from Figure 1 by the 16-state variable CR. A state-minimal variable like CR is called a *response variable* by Balke and Pearl (1994) and a *mapping variable* by Heckerman and Shachter (1995), and its states correspond to the *potential response* vectors in Rubin's model (Rubin 1978).

Applying the definition of ACE$(D \to Y)$ given in Equation 1, it follows that using the model of Figure 2 we have:

$$\text{ACE}(D \to Y) = \left[\sum_i \nu_{cr_{i1}} \right] - \left[\sum_i \nu_{cr_{i2}} \right] \quad (4)$$

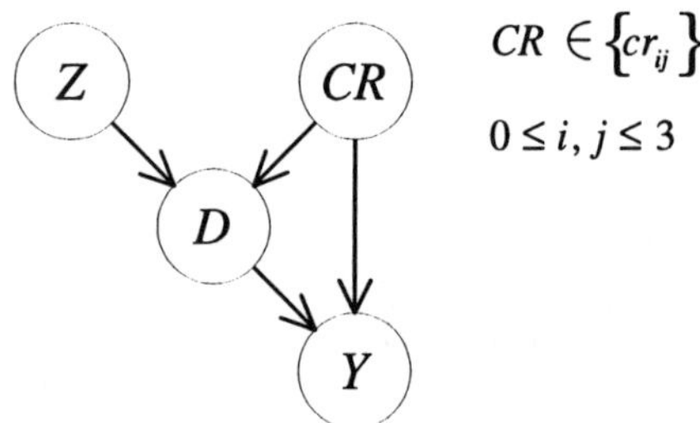

Figure 2: Potential-response model invoking a 16 state variable CR

Equivalently, ACE($D \to Y$) is the difference between the fraction of subjects who are helped by the treatment ($R = r_1$) and the fraction of subjects who are hurt by the treatment ($R = r_2$).

Learning the Causal Effect

Given the observed data $\mathcal{D}$ from the experiment, as well as a prior distribution over the unknown fractions ν_{CR}, our system uses the potential-response model defined in the previous section to derive the posterior distribution for ACE($D \to Y$) . In this section, we describe how this computation can be done. To simplify discussion, we introduce the following notation. Assume there are m subjects in the experiment. We use z^i, d^i and y^i to denote the observed value of Z, D and Y, respectively, for subject i. Similarly, we use cr^i to denote the (unobserved) compliance and response behavior for subject i. We use $\mathcal{D}^i$ to denote the triple $\{z^i, d^i, y^i\}$.

The posterior distribution of the causal effect can be derived using the graphical model shown in Figure 3, which explicitly represents the independences that hold in the joint (Bayesian) probability distribution defined over the variables $\{\mathcal{D}, \nu_{CR}, \text{ACE}(D \to Y)\}$. The model can be understood as m realizations of the potential-response model, one for each triple in $\mathcal{D}$, connected together using the node representing the unknown fractions ν_{CR}. The model explicitly represents the assumption that, given the fractions ν_{CR}, the probability of a subject belonging to any of the compliance-response subpopulations does not depend on the compliance and response behavior of the other subjects in the experiment. From Equation 4, ACE($D \to Y$) is a deterministic function of ν_{CR} and consequently ACE($D \to Y$) is independent of all other variables in the domain once these fractions are known.

Determining the posterior probability for a node using a graphical model is known as performing *inference* in that model. In many cases, the independences of the model can be exploited to make the process of inference efficient. Unfortunately, because the cr^i are never observed, deriving the posterior distribution for ACE($D \to Y$) is not tractable even with the given in-

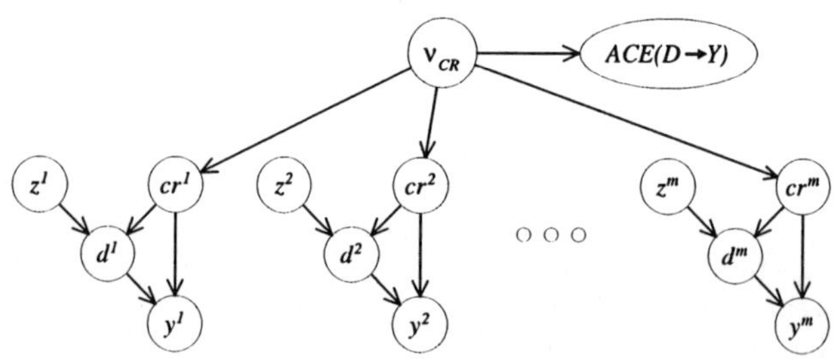

Figure 3: Model used to represent the independences in $p(\{\mathcal{D}\} \cup \{\nu_{CR}\} \cup \{\text{ACE}(D \to Y)\})$

dependences. To obtain the posterior distribution, our system applies an approximation technique known as Gibbs sampling, which we describe in the following section.

Gibbs Sampling

Gibbs sampling is a well-known Markov chain sampling method that can be used to approximate the expected value of a function. The method can easily be applied to approximate the posterior density of ACE($D \to Y$) by exploiting the independences in the model from Figure 3.

Suppose we are interested in the expected value of some function $f(X)$ with respect to the distribution $p(X|Y)$:

$$E_{X|Y}[f] = \int_X f(X)p(X|Y)dX$$

In many cases, it may not be easy to solve the above integral analytically. However, we can approximate $E_{X|Y}[f]$ by repeatedly sampling values for X from the distribution $p(X|Y)$, and then taking an average. Assuming that N samples are taken and letting X^i denote the value for X on the *ith* sample we have:

$$E_{X|Y}[f] \approx \frac{1}{N} \sum_{i=1}^{N} f(X^i) \tag{5}$$

In practice, sampling points directly from $p(X|Y)$ may be difficult. The Gibbs sampling method draws points from the distribution by repeatedly sampling from the *conditional* distributions $p(X_i|X \setminus X_i, Y)$, which are often very easy to derive in closed from. After initially instantiating all the values of X, the algorithm repeatedly uninstantiates a single component X_i, and re-samples that component according to the conditional distribution $p(X_i|X \setminus X_i, Y)$. It can be shown that as the number of iterations of the Gibbs sampler grows large, the sampled values for X are distributed as $p(X|Y)^2$.

[2]The resulting Markov chain must be ergodic for this result to hold, a property that can be easily established for our application.

We can use a Gibbs sampler to approximate the posterior distribution of ACE$(D \rightarrow Y)$ as follows. Let $f_{a,b}(\nu_{CR})$ denote the indicator function that is 1 if $a \leq$ ACE$(D \rightarrow Y) \leq b$ and 0 otherwise. Then we have:

$$\begin{aligned} & p(a \leq \text{ACE}(D \rightarrow Y) \leq b|\mathcal{D}) \\ = \; & E_{\nu_{CR}|\mathcal{D}}[f_{a,b}(\nu_{CR})] \\ = \; & \int f_{a,b}(\nu_{CR}) \cdot p(\nu_{CR}|\mathcal{D}) \cdot d\nu_{CR} \end{aligned}$$

After expanding the integral to include the unobserved compliance and response behavior for each of the subjects we have:

$$\begin{aligned} & p(a \leq \text{ACE}(D \rightarrow Y) \leq b|\mathcal{D}) \\ = \; & \int f_{a,b}(\nu_{CR}) \cdot p(\nu_{CR}, cr^1, \ldots, cr^m|\mathcal{D}) \\ & \cdot d\nu_{CR} \cdot dcr^1 \cdot \ldots \cdot dcr^m \end{aligned}$$

Thus we can use the approximation of Equation 5 in conjunction with the Gibbs sampler to estimate the probability that ACE$(D \rightarrow Y)$ falls within any interval $[a, b]$. The conditional distributions from which we sample are easily derived in light of the independences depicted in Figure 3. In particular, letting $X = \{\nu_{CR}, cr^1, \ldots, cr^m\}$, we have:

$$p(cr^i|X \setminus cr^i, \mathcal{D}) \;=\; \alpha \cdot p(d^i, y^i|z^i, cr^i) \cdot \nu_{cr^i}$$

where α is the normalization constant. $p(d^i, y^i|z^i, cr^i)$ is either one or zero, depending on whether the observed values of z^i, d^i and y^i agree with the given compliance and response behavior. Note that we have used the fact that if the fractions ν_{CR} are known, then the probability of cr^i is simply ν_{cr^i}.

To update ν_{CR} we sample from the posterior distribution:

$$p(\nu_{CR}|X \setminus \nu_{CR}, \mathcal{D}) \;=\; \beta \prod_{i=0}^{3} \prod_{j=0}^{3} \nu_{cr_{ij}}{}^{N_{cr_{ij}}} \cdot p(\nu_{CR})$$

where β is the normalization constant and $N_{cr_{ij}}$ is the number of times cr_{ij} occurs in X.

One choice of the functional form for $p(\nu_{CR})$ is particularly convenient for our application. In particular, if the prior $p(\nu_{CR})$ is a *Dirichlet* distribution, then both efficiently computing the posterior distribution in closed form and sampling from that distribution are easy. Assuming that the prior distribution for ν_{CR} is Dirichlet implies there exists exponents $N'_{cr_{00}}, \ldots, N'_{cr_{33}}$ such that

$$p(\nu_{CR}) = \gamma \prod_{i=0}^{3} \prod_{j=0}^{3} \nu_{cr_{ij}}{}^{N'_{cr_{ij}}-1}$$

where γ is the normalization constant. Let $N'_{CR} = \sum_{i=0}^{3} \sum_{j=0}^{3} N'_{cr_{ij}}$. Having the given Dirichlet prior can be thought of as at some point being ignorant about the fractions ν_{CR}, and then observing the compliance and response behavior of N'_{CR} subjects, $N'_{cr_{ij}}$ of which have behavior cr_{ij}. Using this simplifying assumption, we update ν_{CR} by sampling from the following Dirichlet distribution:

$$p(\nu_{CR}|cr^1, \ldots, cr^n) = \gamma\beta \prod_{i=0}^{3} \prod_{j=0}^{3} \nu_{cr_{ij}}{}^{N_{cr_{ij}}+N'_{cr_{ij}}-1}$$

For accurate results, the Gibbs sampler is typically run in two distinct phases. In the first phase, enough samples are drawn until it is reasonable to assume that the resulting Markov chain has converged to the correct distribution. These initial samples are commonly referred to as the *burn-in* samples, and the corresponding values of the function being estimated are ignored. In the second phase, the values of the function are recorded and are used in the approximation of Equation 5. There are countless techniques for determining when a series has converged, and no single method has become universally accepted among researchers. Another complication of the Gibbs sampler is that successive samples in the second phase are inherently dependent, yet we use these samples to approximate independent samples from the distribution. As a consequence of the many different methods to address these problems, tuning a Gibbs sampler for the best results tends to be more of an art than a science.

The approach we took for the results presented in the next section can be explained as follows. We ran the Gibbs sampler for enough iterations to ensure a relatively smooth estimate of the distribution, always discarding a large number of the initial points sampled. We then repeated the same schedule, starting with a different random seed, and compared the resulting outputs. If the distributions were reasonably distinct, we repeated the process using more samples. We emphasize that the any one of the many methods of data analysis can readily be applied to the output of our system.

Experimental Results

We have applied the Gibbs sampling algorithm to the model of Figure 3 for various real and simulated data sets. Our system takes as input (1) the observed data $\mathcal{D}$, expressed as the number of cases observed for each of the 8 possible instantiations of $\{z, d, y\}$, and (2) a Dirichlet prior over the unknown fractions ν_{CR}, expressed as the 16 exponents N'_{CR}. The system outputs the posterior distribution of ACE$(D \rightarrow Y)$, expressed in a histogram.

To investigate the effect of the prior distribution on the output, we have run all our experiments using two different priors as input. The first is a flat (uniform) distribution over the 16-vector ν_{CR}, and is commonly used to express ignorance about the domain. The second prior is skewed to represent a dependency between the compliance and response be-

Table 1: Population fractions resulting in an identifiable ACE($D \to Y$)

z	d	y	$\nu_{z,d,y}$
0	0	0	0.275
0	0	1	0.0
0	1	0	0.225
0	1	1	0.0
1	0	0	0.225
1	0	1	0.0
1	1	0	0.0
1	1	1	0.275

havior of the subjects. Figure 4 shows the distribution of ACE($D \to Y$) induced by these two prior distributions. Note that the skewed prior of Figure 4b assigns almost all the weight to negative values of ACE($D \to Y$) .

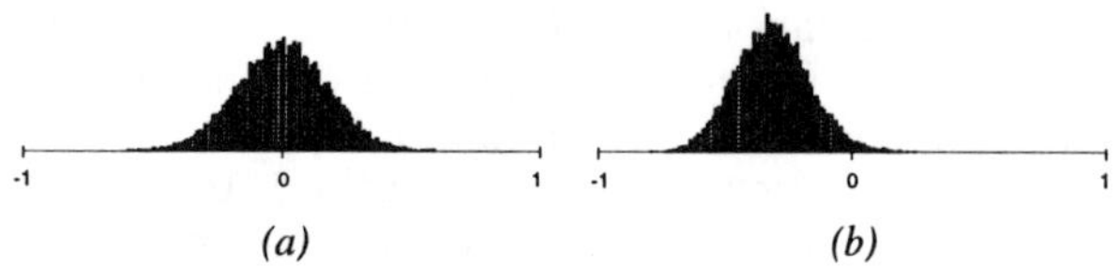

Figure 4:
(a) The prior distribution of ACE($D \to Y$) induced by flat priors over the parameters ν_{CR}, and (b) the distribution for ACE($D \to Y$) induced by skewed priors over the parameters.

In the following sections, we present the output of our system using (1) a simulated data set for which the causal effect is identifiable, (2) a real data set from an experiment designed to determine the effect of cholestyramine on reduced cholesterol level, and (3) a real data set from a study to determine the effect of vitamin A supplementation on childhood mortality.

Simulated Data Example: Identifiable Causal Effect

As we noted in the introduction, Balke and Pearl (1994) have derived the tightest bounds for ACE($D \to Y$) under the large-sample assumption. They show that for some distributions of Z, D and Y, the resulting upper and lower bounds collapse to a single point. We say that ACE($D \to Y$) is *identifiable* in this case. In this section, we show the output of our system when run on data sets derived from a distribution for which ACE($D \to Y$) is identifiable. One such distribution is shown in Table 1, yielding ACE($D \to Y$) $= 0.55$.

Figure 5 shows the the output of our system when applied to data sets of various sizes drawn from the distribution shown in Table 1, using both the flat and the skewed prior. As expected, as the number of cases increases, the posterior distributions become increasingly concentrated near the value 0.55. In general, because the skewed prior for ACE($D \to Y$) is concentrated further from 0.55 than the uniform prior, more cases are needed before the posterior distribution converges to the value 0.55.

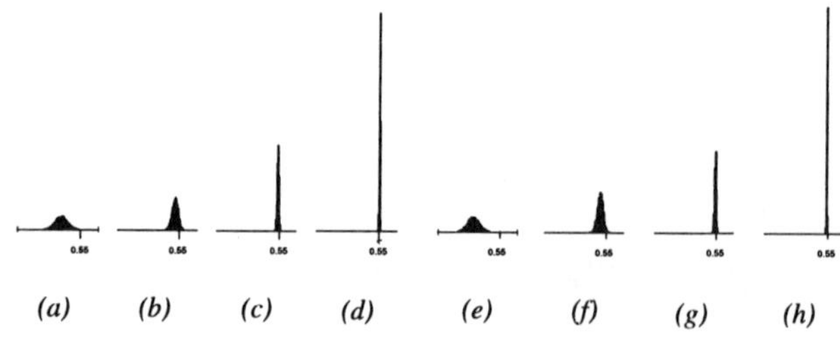

Figure 5: Output histograms for identifiable treatment effect using two priors. (a), (b), (c) and (d) show the posteriors for ACE($D \to Y$) using the flat prior and a data set consisting of 10, 100, 1000 and 10000 subjects, respectively. (e), (f), (g) and (h) show the posteriors for ACE($D \to Y$) using the skewed prior with the same respective data sets.

Real Data Example: Effect of Cholestyramine on Reduced Cholesterol

Consider the Lipid Research Clinics Coronary Primary Prevention data described in . A portion of this data consisting of 337 subjects was analyzed by Efron and Feldman (1991) using a model that incorporates subject compliance as an explanatory variable; this same data set is the focus of this section.

A population of subjects was assembled and two preliminary cholesterol measurements were obtained: one prior to a suggested low-cholesterol diet and one following the diet period. The initial cholesterol level was taken as a weighted average of these two measures. The subjects were randomized into two groups: in the first group all subjects were prescribed cholestyramine (z_1), while the subjects in the other group were prescribed a placebo (z_0). During several years of treatment, each subject's cholesterol level was measured multiple times, and the average of these measurements was used as the post-treatment cholesterol level. The compliance of each subject was determined by tracking the quantity of prescribed dosage consumed.

We transformed the (continuous) data from the Lipid study to the binary variables D and Y using the same method as Balke and Pearl (1994). The resulting data set is shown in Table 2. Using the large-sample assumption, Balke and Pearl (1994) use the given data to derive the bounds $0.39 \leq$ ACE($D \to Y$) ≤ 0.78.

Figure 6 shows posterior densities for ACE($D \to Y$) given the data. The density of Figure 6a corresponds to flat priors (over the

Table 2: Observed data for the Lipid study and the Vitamin A study

z	d	y	Lipid Study Observations	Vitamin A Study Observations
0	0	0	158	11514
0	0	1	14	74
0	1	0	0	0
0	1	1	0	0
1	0	0	52	2385
1	0	1	12	34
1	1	0	23	9663
1	1	1	78	12

parameters) and the density of Figure 6b corresponds to skewed priors. Rather remarkably, even with only 337 cases in the data, both posterior distributions are highly concentrated within the large-sample bounds.

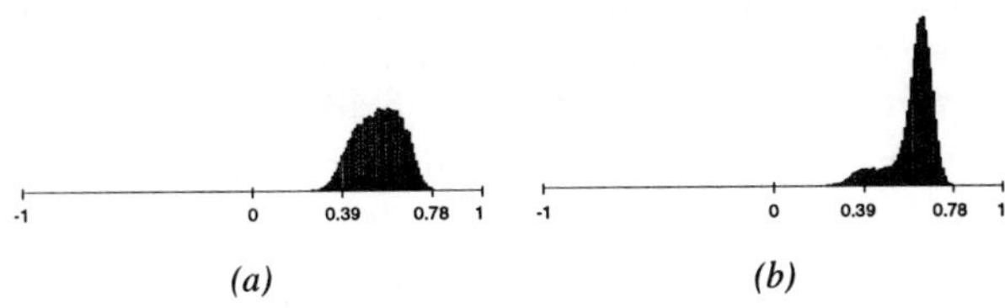

Figure 6: Output histograms for the Lipid data. (a) Using flat priors and (b) using skewed priors.

Real Data Example: Effect of Vitamin A Supplements on Child Mortality

In this section, we consider an experiment described by Sommer et al. (1986) designed to determine the impact of vitamin A supplementation on childhood mortality. In the study, 450 villages in northern Sumatra were randomly assigned to participate in a vitamin A supplementation scheme or serve as a control group for one year. Children in the treatment group received two large doses of vitamin A (d_1), while those in the control group received no treatment (d_0). After the year had expired, the number of deaths y_0 were counted for both groups. The results of the study are shown in Table 2.

Under the large-sample assumption, the method of Balke and Pearl (1994) yields the bounds: $-0.01 \leq \text{ACE}(D \rightarrow Y) \leq 0.19$. Figure 7 shows posterior densities for $\text{ACE}(D \rightarrow Y)$ given the data. The density of Figure 7a corresponds to flat priors over the parameters and the density of Figure 7b corresponds to skewed priors over the parameters.

It is interesting to note that for this study, the choice of the prior distribution has a significant effect on the posterior. This suggests that if the clinician is not very confident in the prior, a sensitivity analysis should be performed.

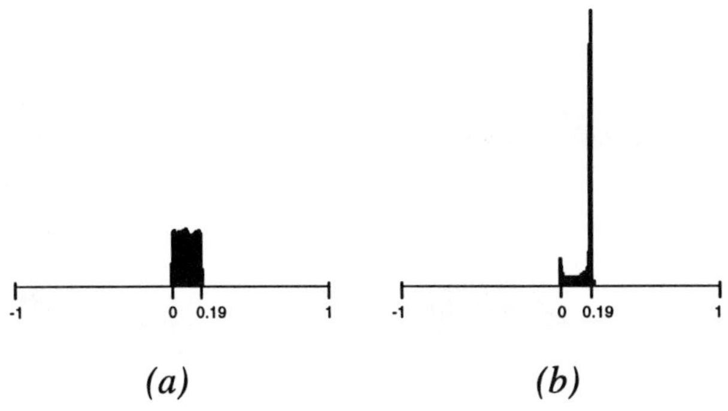

Figure 7: Output histograms for the Vitamin A Supplementation data. (a) Using flat priors and (b) using skewed priors.

A Counterfactual Query

In addition to assessing the average treatment effect, the system is also capable (with only minor modification) of answering a variety of counterfactual queries concerning individuals with specific characteristics. In this section, we show the result of our system when modified to answer the following query: What is the probability that Joe would have had an improved cholesterol reading had he taken cholestyramine, given that (1) Joe was in the control group of the Lipid study, (2) Joe took the placebo as prescribed, and (3) Joe's cholesterol level did not improve.

We can answer the above query by running the Gibbs' sampler on a model identical to that shown in Figure 3, except that the function $\text{ACE}(D \rightarrow Y)$ (Equation 4) is replaced by another function of ν_{CR}, one that represents our query. If Joe was in the control group and took the placebo, that means that he is either a complier or a never-taker. Furthermore, because Joe's cholesterol level did not improve, Joe's response behavior is either never-recover or helped. Consequently, Joe must be a member of one of the following four compliance-response populations: $\{cr_{01}, cr_{02}, cr_{11}, cr_{12}\}$. Joe would have improved had he taken cholestyramine if his response behavior is either helped (r_1) or always-recover (r_3). It follows that the query of interest is captured by the function

$$f(\nu_{CR}) = \frac{\nu_{cr_{01}} + \nu_{cr_{11}}}{\nu_{cr_{01}} + \nu_{cr_{02}} + \nu_{cr_{11}} + \nu_{cr_{12}}}$$

Figure 8a and Figure 8b show the prior distribution over $f(\nu_{CR})$ that follows from the flat prior and the skewed prior, respectively. Figure 8c and Figure 8d show the posterior distribution $p(f(\nu_{CR}|\mathcal{D}))$ obtained by our system when run on the Lipid data, using the flat prior and the skewed prior, respectively. From the bounds of Balke and Pearl (1994), it follows that under the large-sample assumption, $0.51 \leq f(\nu_{CR}|\mathcal{D}) \leq 0.86$.

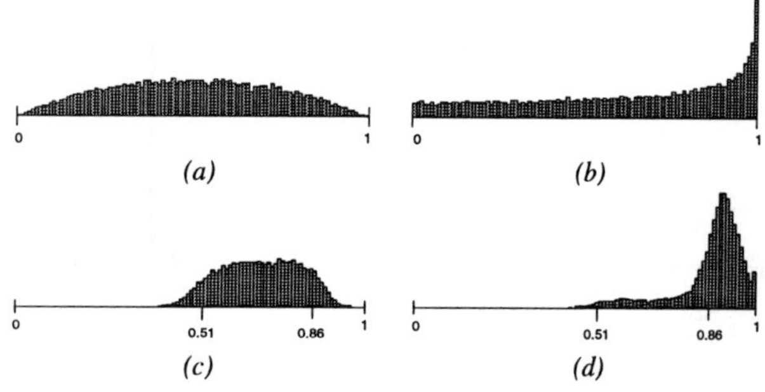

Figure 8: Prior (a, b) and posterior (c,d) distributions for a subpopulation $f(\nu_{CR}|\mathcal{D})$ specified by the counterfactual query "Would Joe have improved had he taken the drug, given that he did not improve without it". (a) corresponds to the flat prior, (b) to the skewed prior.

Thus, despite 39% non-compliance in the treatment group, and despite having just 337 subjects, the study strongly supports the conclusion that, given Joe's specific history, he would have been better off taking the drug. Moreover, the conclusion holds for both priors.

Conclusion

This paper identifies and demonstrates a new application area for network-based inference techniques – the management of causal analysis in clinical experimentation. These techniques, which were originally developed for medical diagnosis, are shown capable of circumventing one of the major problems in clinical experiments – the assessment of treatment efficacy in the face of imperfect compliance. While standard diagnosis involves purely probabilistic inference in fully specified networks, causal analysis involves partially specified networks in which the links are given causal interpretation and where the domain of some variables are unknown.

The system presented in this paper provides the clinical research community, we believe for the first time, an assumption-free[3], unbiased assessment of the average treatment effect. We offer this system as a practical tool to be used whenever full compliance cannot be enforced and, more broadly, whenever the data available is insufficient for answering the queries of interest to the clinical investigator.

Acknowledgements. The research of D. Chickering was supported by NSF grant #IRI-9119825 and a grant from Rockwell International. The research of J. Pearl was suppported by gifts from Microsoft Corporation and Hewlett-Packard Company.

[3] "Assumption-transparent" may be a better term, since the two basic assumptions in our analysis (i.e., randomized assignment and no-side-effects) are vividly displayed in the graph (e.g., Figure 1), and the impact of the prior distribution is shown by histograms such as those of Figure 4.

References

Angrist, J.; Imbens, G.; and Rubin, D. 1993. Identification of causal effects using instrumental variables. Technical Report 136, Department of Economics, Harvard University, Cambridge, MA. Forthcoming, Journal of American Statistical Association, 1996.

Balke, A., and Pearl, J. 1994. Counterfactual probabilities: Computational methods, bounds and applications. In *Proceedings of Tenth Conference on Uncertainty in Artificial Intelligence,* Seattle, WA, 46–54. Morgan Kaufman.

Efron, B., and Feldman, D. 1991. Compliance as an explanatory variable in clinical trials. *Journal of the American Statistical Association* 86(413):9–26.

Heckerman, D., and Shachter, R. 1995. Decision-theoretic foundations for causal reasoning. *Journal of Artificial Intelligence Research* 3:405–430.

Holland, P. W. 1988. Causal inference, path analysis, and recursive structural equations models. In Clogg, C., ed., *Sociological Methodology.* Wachington, DC: American Socialogical Association. chapter 13, 449–484.

Imbens, G., and Rubin, D. 1994. Bayesian inference for causal effects in randomized experiments with noncompliance. Technical report, Harvard University.

Lipid Research Clinic Program. 1984. The lipid research clinics coronary primary prevention trial results, parts I and II. *Journal of the American Medical Association* 251(3):351–374. January.

Pearl, J. 1994. From Bayesian networks to causal network. In *Proceedings of the UNICOM Seminar on Adaptive Computing and Information Processing,* Brunel University, London, 165–194. Also in A. Gammerman (Ed.), Bayesian Networks and Probabilistic Reasoning, Alfred Walter Ltd., London, 1-31, 1995.

Pearl, J. 1995a. Causal diagrams for experimental research. *Biometrika* 82(4):669–710.

Pearl, J. 1995b. Causal inference from indirect experiments. *Artificial Intelligence in Medicine Journal* 7(6):561–582.

Rubin, D. 1978. Bayesian inference for causal effects: The role of randomization. *Annals of Statistics* 7:34–58.

Sommer, A.; Tarwotjo, I.; Djunaedi, E.; West, K. P.; Loeden, A. A.; Tilden, R.; and Mele, L. 1986. Impact of vitamin A supplementation on childhood mortality: A randomized controlled community trial. *The Lancet* i:1169–1173.

Building Classifiers using Bayesian Networks

Nir Friedman
Stanford University
Dept. of Computer Science
Gates Building 1A
Stanford, CA 94305-9010
nir@cs.stanford.edu

Moises Goldszmidt*
Rockwell Science Center
444 High St., Suite 400
Palo Alto, CA 94301
moises@rpal.rockwell.com

Abstract

Recent work in supervised learning has shown that a surprisingly simple Bayesian classifier with strong assumptions of independence among features, called *naive Bayes*, is competitive with state of the art classifiers such as C4.5. This fact raises the question of whether a classifier with less restrictive assumptions can perform even better. In this paper we examine and evaluate approaches for inducing classifiers from data, based on recent results in the theory of learning *Bayesian networks*. Bayesian networks are factored representations of probability distributions that generalize the naive Bayes classifier and explicitly represent statements about independence. Among these approaches we single out a method we call *Tree Augmented Naive Bayes* (*TAN*), which outperforms naive Bayes, yet at the same time maintains the computational simplicity (no search involved) and robustness which are characteristic of naive Bayes. We experimentally tested these approaches using benchmark problems from the U. C. Irvine repository, and compared them against C4.5, naive Bayes, and wrapper-based feature selection methods.

1 Introduction

A somewhat simplified statement of the problem of supervised learning is as follows. Given a *training set* of labeled instances of the form $\langle a_1, \ldots, a_n \rangle, c$, construct a *classifier* f capable of predicting the value of c, given instances $\langle a'_1, \ldots, a'_n \rangle$ as input. The variables $A_1, \ldots, A_n$ are called *features* or *attributes*, and the variable C is usually referred to as the *class variable* or *label*. This is a basic problem in many applications of machine learning, and there are numerous approaches to solve it based on various functional representations such as decision trees, decision lists, neural networks, decision-graphs, rules, and many others. One of the most effective classifiers, in the sense that its predictive performance is competitive with state of the art classifiers such as C4.5 (Quinlan 1993), is the so-called *naive Bayesian* classifier (or simply *naive Bayes*) (Langley, Iba, & Thompson 1992). This classifier learns the conditional probability of each attribute A_i given the label C in the training data. Classification is then done by applying Bayes rule to compute the probability of C given the particular instantiation of $A_1, \ldots, A_n$. This computation is rendered feasible by making a strong independence assumption: all the attributes A_i are conditionally independent given the value of the label C.[1] The performance of naive Bayes is somewhat surprising given that this is clearly an unrealistic assumption. Consider for example a classifier for assessing the risk in loan applications. It would be erroneous to ignore the correlations between age, education level, and income.

This fact naturally begs the question of whether we can improve the performance of Bayesian classifiers by avoiding unrealistic assumptions about independence. In order to effectively tackle this problem we need an appropriate language and effective machinery to represent and manipulate independences. *Bayesian networks* (Pearl 1988) provide both. Bayesian networks are directed acyclic graphs that allow for efficient and effective representation of the joint probability distributions over a set of random variables. Each vertex in the graph represents a random variable, and edges represent direct correlations between the variables. More precisely, the network encodes the following statements about each random variable: each variable is independent of its non-descendants in the graph given the state of its parents. Other independences follow from these ones. These can be efficiently read from the network structure by means of a simple graph-theoretic criteria. Independences are then exploited to reduce the number of parameters needed to characterize a probability distribution, and to efficiently compute posterior probabilities given evidence. Probabilistic parameters are encoded in a set of tables, one for each variable, in the form of local conditional distributions of a variable given its parents. Given the independences encoded in the network, the joint distribution can be reconstructed by simply multiplying these tables.

When represented as a Bayesian network, a naive Bayesian classifier has the simple structure depicted in Figure 1. This network captures the main assumption behind the naive Bayes classifier, namely that every attribute (every leaf in the network) is independent from the rest of the attributes given the state of the class variable (the root in the network). Now that we have the means to represent and

*Current address: SRI International, 333 Ravenswood Way, Menlo Park, CA 94025, moises@erg.sri.com

[1] By independence we mean probabilistic independence, that is A is independent of B given C whenever $\Pr(A|B,C) = \Pr(A|C)$ for all possible values of A, B and C.

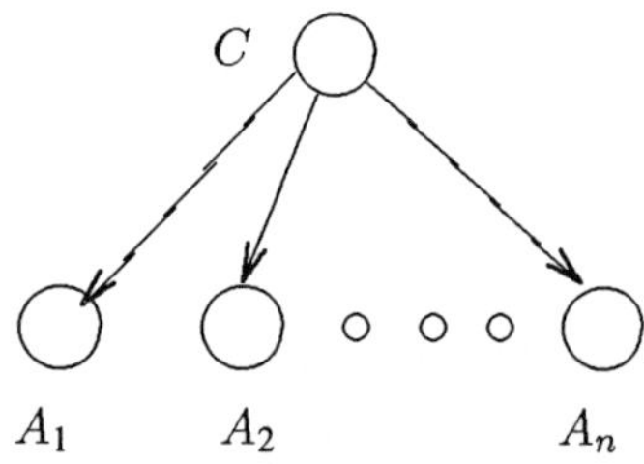

Figure 1: The structure of the naive Bayes network.

manipulate independences, the obvious question follows: can we learn an unrestricted Bayesian network from the data that when used as a classifier maximizes the prediction rate?

Learning Bayesian networks from data is a rapidly growing field of research that has seen a great deal of activity in recent years, see for example (Heckerman 1995; Heckerman, Geiger, & Chickering 1995; Lam & Bacchus 1994). This is a form *unsupervised* learning in the sense that the learner is not guided by a set of informative examples. The objective is to induce a network (or a set of networks) that "best describes" the probability distribution over the training data. This optimization process is implemented in practice using heuristic search techniques to find the best candidate over the space of possible networks. The search process relies on a scoring metric that asses the merits of each candidate network.

We start by examining a straightforward application of current Bayesian networks techniques. We learn networks using the *MDL* metric (Lam & Bacchus 1994) and use them for classification. The results, which are analyzed in Section 3, are mixed: although the learned networks perform significantly better than naive Bayes on some datasets, they perform worse on others. We trace the reasons for these results to the definition of the MDL scoring metric. Roughly speaking, the problem is that the MDL scoring metric measures the "error" of the learned Bayesian network over all the variables in the domain. Minimizing this error, however, does not necessarily minimize the local "error" in predicting the class variable given the attributes. We argue that similar problems will occur with other scoring metrics in the literature.

In light of these results we limit our attention to a class of network structures that are based on the structure of naive Bayes, requiring that the class variable be a parent of every attribute. This ensures that in the learned network, the probability $\Pr(C|A_1, \ldots, A_n)$ will take every attribute into account. Unlike the naive Bayes structure, however, we allow additional edges between attributes. These additional edges capture correlations among the attributes. Note that the process of adding these edges may involve an heuristic search on a subnetwork. However, there is a restricted sub-class of these structures, for which we can find the best candidate in polynomial time. This result, shown by Geiger (1992), is a consequence of a well-known result by Chow and Liu (1968) (see also (Pearl 1988)). This approach, which we call *Tree Augmented Naive Bayes* (*TAN*), approximates the interactions between attributes using a tree-structure imposed on the naive Bayes structure. We note that while this method has been proposed in the literature, it has never been rigorously tested in practice. We show that *TAN* maintains the robustness and computational complexity (the search process is bounded) of naive Bayes, and at the same time displays better performance in our experiments. We compare this approach with C4.5, naive Bayes, and *selective naive Bayes*, a wrapper-based feature subset selection method combined with naive Bayes, on a set of benchmark problems from the U. C. Irvine repository (see Section 4). This experiments show that *TAN* leads to significant improvement over all of these three approaches.

2 Learning Bayesian Networks

Consider a finite set $\mathbf{U} = \{X_1, \ldots, X_n\}$ of discrete random variables where each variable X_i may take on values from a finite domain. We use capital letters, such as X, Y, Z, for variable names and lowercase letters x, y, z to denote specific values taken by those variables. The set of values X can attain is denoted as $Val(X)$, the cardinality of this set is denoted as $||X|| = |Val(X)|$. Sets of variables are denoted by boldface capital letters $\mathbf{X}, \mathbf{Y}, \mathbf{Z}$, and assignments of values to the variables in these sets will be denoted by boldface lowercase letters $\mathbf{x}, \mathbf{y}, \mathbf{z}$ (we use $Val(\mathbf{X})$ and $||\mathbf{X}||$ in the obvious way). Finally, let P be a joint probability distribution over the variables in $\mathbf{U}$, and let $\mathbf{X}, \mathbf{Y}, \mathbf{Z}$ be subsets of $\mathbf{U}$. $\mathbf{X}$ and $\mathbf{Y}$ are *conditionally independent* given $\mathbf{Z}$ if for all $\mathbf{x} \in Val(\mathbf{X}), \mathbf{y} \in Val(\mathbf{Y}), \mathbf{z} \in Val(\mathbf{Z})$, $P(\mathbf{x} \mid \mathbf{z}, \mathbf{y}) = P(\mathbf{x} \mid \mathbf{z})$ whenever $P(\mathbf{y}, \mathbf{z}) > 0$.

A *Bayesian network* is an annotated directed acyclic graph that encodes a joint probability distribution of a domain composed of a set of random variables. Formally, a Bayesian network for $\mathbf{U}$ is the pair $B = \langle G, \Theta \rangle$. G is a directed acyclic graph whose nodes correspond to the random variables $X_1, \ldots, X_n$, and whose edges represent direct dependencies between the variables. The graph structure G encodes the following set of independence assumptions: each node X_i is independent of its non-descendants given its parents in G (Pearl 1988).[2] The second component of the pair, namely Θ, represents the set of parameters that quantifies the network. It contains a parameter $\theta_{x_i|\Pi_{x_i}} = P(x_i|\Pi_{x_i})$ for each possible value x_i of X_i, and Π_{x_i} of Π_{X_i} (the set of parents of X_i in G). B defines a unique joint probability distribution over $\mathbf{U}$ given by:

$$P_B(X_1, \ldots, X_n) = \prod_{i=1}^{n} P_B(X_i|\Pi_{X_i}) = \prod_{i=1}^{n} \theta_{X_i|\Pi_{X_i}} \quad (1)$$

Example 2.1: Let $\mathbf{U}^* = \{A_1, \ldots, A_n, C\}$, where the variables $A_1, \ldots, A_n$ are the *attributes* and C is the *class* variable. In the *naive Bayes* structure the class variable

[2]Formally there is a notion of minimality associated with this definition, but we will ignore it in this paper (see (Pearl 1988)).

is the root, i.e., $\Pi_C = \emptyset$, and the only parent for each attribute is the class variable, i.e., $\Pi_{A_i} = \{C\}$, for all $1 \leq i \leq n$. Using (1) we have that $\Pr(A_1, \ldots, A_n, C) = \Pr(C) \cdot \prod_{i=1}^{n} \Pr(A_i|C)$. From the definition of conditional probability we get that $\Pr(C|A_1, \ldots, A_n) = \alpha \cdot \Pr(C) \cdot \prod_{i=1}^{n} \Pr(A_i|C)$, where α is a normalization constant. This is the definition of naive Bayes commonly found in the literature (Langley, Iba, & Thompson 1992). ∎

The problem of learning a Bayesian network can be stated as follows. Given a *training set* $D = \{\mathbf{u}_1, \ldots, \mathbf{u}_N\}$ of instances of $\mathbf{U}$, find a network B that *best matches* D. The common approach to this problem is to introduce a scoring function that evaluates each network with respect to the training data, and then to search for the best network. In general, this optimization problem is intractable, yet for certain restricted classes of networks there are efficient algorithms requiring polynomial time (in the number of variables in the network). We will indeed take advantage of these efficient algorithms in Section 4 where we propose a particular extension to naive Bayes. We start by examining the components of the scoring function that we will use throughout the paper.

Let $B = \langle G, \Theta \rangle$ be a Bayesian network, and let $D = \{\mathbf{u}_1, \ldots, \mathbf{u}_N\}$ (where each $\mathbf{u}_i$ assigns values to all the variables in $\mathbf{U}$) be a training set. The *log-likelihood* of B given D is defined as

$$LL(B|D) = \sum_{i=1}^{N} \log(\Pr_B(\mathbf{u}_i)). \quad (2)$$

This term measures the likelihood that the data D was generated from the model B (namely the candidate Bayesian network) when we assume that the instances were independently sampled. The higher this value is, the closer B is to modeling the probability distribution in the data D. Let $\hat{P}_D(\cdot)$ be the measure defined by frequencies of events in D. Using (1) we can decompose the the log-likelihood according to the structure of the network. After some algebraic manipulations we can easily derive:

$$LL(B|D) = N \sum_i \sum_{x_i, \Pi_{x_i}} \hat{P}_D(x_i, \Pi_{x_i}) \log(\theta_{x_i|\Pi_{x_i}}) \quad (3)$$

Now assume that the structure of the network is fixed. Standard arguments show that $LL(B|D)$ is maximized when $\theta_{x_i|\Pi_{x_i}} = \hat{P}_D(x_i|\Pi_{x_i})$.

Lemma 2.2: *Let $B = \langle G, \Theta \rangle$ and $B' = \langle G, \Theta' \rangle$ such that $\theta'_{x_i|\Pi_{x_i}} = \hat{P}_D(x_i|\Pi_{x_i})$. Then $LL(B'|D) \geq LL(B|D)$.*

Thus, we have a closed form solution for the parameters that maximize the log-likelihood for a given network structure. This is crucial since instead of searching in the space of Bayesian networks, we only need to search in the smaller space of network structures, and then fill in the parameters by computing the appropriate frequencies from the data.

The log-likelihood score, while very simple, is not suitable for learning the structure of the network, since it tends to favor complete graph structures (in which every variable is connected to every other variable). This is highly undesirable since such networks do not provide any useful representation of the independences in the learned distributions. Moreover, the number of parameters in the complete model is exponential. Most of these parameters will have extremely high variance and will lead to poor predictions. This phenomena is called *overfitting*, since the learned parameters match the training data, but have poor performance on test data.

The two main scoring functions commonly used to learn Bayesian networks complement the log-likelihood score with additional terms to address this problem. These are the *Bayesian scoring* function (Heckerman, Geiger, & Chickering 1995), and the one based on *minimal description length* (MDL) (Lam & Bacchus 1994). In this paper we concentrate on MDL deferring the discussion on the Bayesian scoring function for the full paper.[3]

The motivation underlying the MDL method is to find a compact encoding of the training set D. We do not reproduce the derivation of the the MDL scoring function here, but merely state it. The interested reader should consult (Friedman & Goldszmidt 1996; Lam & Bacchus 1994). The MDL score of a network B given D, written *MDL*$(B|D)$ is

$$MDL(B|D) = \frac{1}{2} \log N |B| - LL(B|D) \quad (4)$$

where $|B|$ is the number of parameters in the network. The first term simply counts how many bits we need to encode the specific network B, where we store $1/2 \cdot \log N$ bits for each parameter in Θ. The second term measures how many bits are needed for the encoded representation of D. Minimizing the MDL score involves tradeoffs between these two factors. Thus, the MDL score of a larger network might be worse (larger) than that of a smaller network, even though the former might match the data better. In practice, the MDL score regulates the number of parameters learned and helps avoid overfitting of the training data. Note that the first term does not depend on the actual parameters in B, but only on the graph structure. Thus, for a fixed the network structure, we minimize the MDL score by maximizing the LL score using Lemma 2.2.

It is important to note that learning based on the MDL score is asymptotically correct: with probability 1 the learned distribution converges to the underlying distribution as the number of samples increases (Heckerman 1995).

Regarding the search process, in this paper we will rely on a greedy strategy for the obvious computational reasons. This procedure starts with the empty network and successively applies local operations that maximally improve the score and until a local minima is found. The operations applied by the search procedure are: arc addition, arc deletion and arc reversal. In the full paper we describe results using other search methods (although the methods we examined so far did not lead to significant improvements.)

3 Bayesian Networks as Classifiers

[3]There are some well-known connections between these two proposals (Heckerman 1995).

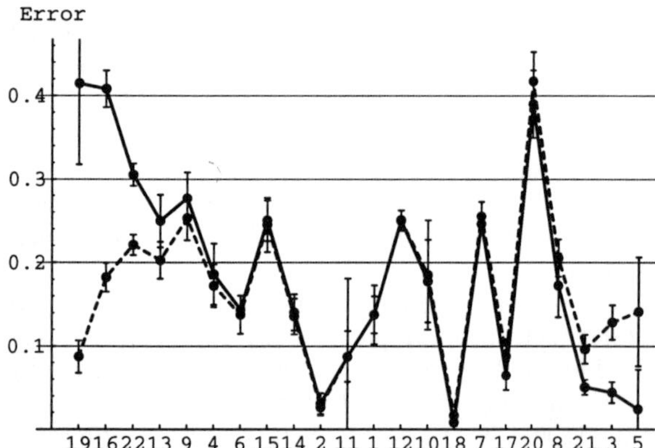

Figure 2: Error curves comparing unsupervised Bayesian networks (solid line) to naive Bayes (dashed line). The horizontal axis lists the datasets, which are sorted so that the curves cross only once. The vertical axis measures fraction of test instances that were misclassified (i.e., prediction errors). Thus, the smaller the value, the better the accuracy. Each data point is annotated by a 90% confidence interval.

Using the methods just described we can induce a Bayesian network from the data and then use the resulting model as a classifier. The learned network represents an approximation to the probability distribution governing the domain (given the assumption that the instances are independently sampled form a single distribution). Given enough samples, this will be a close approximation Thus, we can use this network to compute the probability of C given the values of the attributes. The predicted class c, given a set of attributes $a_1, \ldots, a_n$ is simply the class that attains the maximum posterior $P_B(c|a_1, \ldots, a_n)$, where P_B is the probability distribution represented by the Bayesian network B.

It is important to note that this procedure is *unsupervised* in the sense that the learning procedure does not distinguish the class variable from other attributes. Thus, we do not inform the procedure that the evaluation of the learned network will be done by measuring the predictive accuracy with respect to the class variable.

From the outset there is an obvious problem. Learning unrestricted Bayesian networks is an intractable problem. Even though in practice we resort to greedy heuristic search, this procedure is often expensive. In particular, it is more expensive than learning the naive Bayesian classifier which can be done in linear time.

Still, we may be willing to invest the extra effort required in learning a (unrestricted) Bayesian network if the prediction accuracy of the resulting classifier outperforms that of the naive Bayesian classifier. As our first experiment shows, Figure 2, this is not always the case. In this experiment we compared the predictive accuracy of classification using Bayesian networks learned in an unsupervised fashion, versus that of the naive Bayesian classifier. We run this experiment on 22 datasets, 20 of which are from the U. C. Irvine repository (Murphy & Aha 1995). Appendix A describes in detail the experimental setup, evaluation methods, and results (Table 1).

As can be seen from Figure 2 the classifier based on unsupervised networks performed significantly better than naive Bayes on 6 datasets, and performed significantly worse on 6 datasets. A quick examination of the datasets revels that all the datasets where unsupervised networks performed poorly contain more than 15 attributes.

It is interesting to examine the two datasets where the unsupervised networks performed worst (compared to naive Bayes): "soybean-large" (with 35 attributes) and "satimage" (with 36 attributes). For both these datasets, the size of the class' *Markov blanket* in the networks is rather small—less than 5 attributes. The relevance of this is that prediction using a Bayesian network examines only the values of attributes in the class variable's Markov blanket.[4] The fact that for both these datasets the Markov blanket of the class variable is so small indicates that for the MDL metric, the "cost" (in terms of additional parameters) of enlarging the Markov blanket is not worth the tradeoff in overall accuracy. Moreover, we note that in all of these experiments the networks found by the unsupervised learning routine had better MDL score than the naive Bayes network. This suggest that the root of the problem is the scoring metric—a network with a better score is not necessarily a better classifier.

To understand this problem in detail we re-examine the MDL score. Recall that the likelihood term in (4) is the one that measures the quality of the learned model. Also recall that $D = \{\mathbf{u}_1, \ldots, \mathbf{u}_N\}$ is the training set. In a classification task each $\mathbf{u}_i$ is a tuple of the form $\langle a_1^i, \ldots, a_n^i, c^i \rangle$ that assigns values to the attributes $A_1, \ldots, A_n$ and to the class variable C. Using the chain rule we can rewrite the log-likelihood function (2) as:

$$LL(B|D) = \sum_{i=1}^{N} \log P_B(c^i|a_1^i, \ldots, a_n^i) + \sum_{i=1}^{N} \log P_B(a_1^i, \ldots, a_n^i) \quad (5)$$

The first term in this equation measures how well B estimates the probability of the class given the attributes. The second term measures how well B estimates the joint distribution of the attributes. Since the classification is determined by $P_B(C|A_1, \ldots, A_n)$ only the first term is related to the score of the network as a classifier (i.e., its prediction accuracy). Unfortunately, this term is dominated by the second term when there are many attributes. As n grows larger, the probability of each particular assignment to $A_1, \ldots, A_n$ becomes smaller, since the number of possible assignments grows exponentially in n. Thus, we expect the terms of the form $P_B(A_1, \ldots, A_n)$ to yield smaller values which in turn will increase the value of the log function. However,

[4]More precisely, for a fixed network structure the Markov blanket of a variable X (Pearl 1988) consists of X's parents, X's children, and parents of X's children in G. This set has the property that conditioned on X's Markov blanket, X is independent of all other variables in the network.

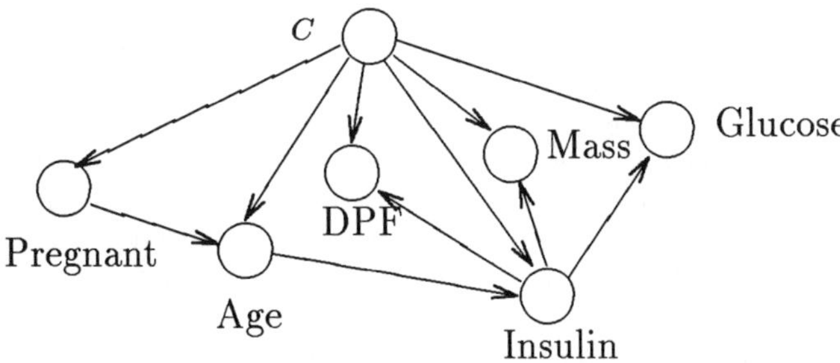

Figure 3: A TAN model learned for the dataset "pima".

at the same time, the conditional probability of the class will remain more of less the same. This implies that a relatively big error in the first term will not reflect in the MDL score. Thus, as indicated by our experimental results, using a non-specialized scoring metric for learning an unrestricted Bayesian network may result in a poor classifier when there are many attributes.[5]

A straightforward approach to dealing with this problem would be to specialize the scoring metric (MDL in this case) for the classification task. We can easily do so by restricting the log-likelihood to the first term of (5). Formally, let the *conditional log-likelihood* of a Bayesian network B given dataset D be $CLL(B|D) = \sum_{i=1}^{N} \log P_B(C^i|A_1^i, \ldots, A_n^i)$. A similar modification to Bayesian scoring metric in (Heckerman, Geiger, & Chickering 1995) is equally easy to define. The problem with applying these conditional scoring metrics in practice is that they do not decompose over the structure of the network, i.e., we do not have an analogue of (3). As a consequence it is no longer true that setting the parameters $\theta_{x_i|\Pi_{x_i}} = \hat{P}_D(x_i|\Pi_{x_i})$ maximizes the score for a fixed network structure.[6] We do not know, at this stage, whether there is a computational effective procedure to find the parameter values that maximize this type of conditional score. In fact, as reported by Geiger (1992), previous attempts to defining such conditional scores resulted in unrealistic and sometimes contradictory assumptions.

4 Learning Restricted Networks for Classifiers

In light of this discussion we examine a different approach. We limit our attention to a class of network structures that are based on the naive Bayes structure. As in naive Bayes, we require that the class variable be a parent of every attribute. This ensures that, in the learned network, the probability $P(C|A_1, \ldots, A_n)$ will take every attribute into account, rather than a shallow set of neighboring nodes.

[5]In the full paper we show that the same problem occur in the Bayesian scoring metric.

[6]We remark that decomposition still holds for a restricted class of structures—essentially these where C does not have any children. However, these structures are usually not useful for classification.

In order to improve the performance of a classifier based on naive Bayes we propose to augment the naive Bayes structure with "correlation" edges among the attributes. We call these structures *augmented naive Bayes*.

In an the augmented structure an edge from A_i to A_j implies that the two attributes are no longer independent given the class variable. In this case the influence of A_i on the assessment of class variable also depends on the value of A_j. Thus, in Figure 3, the influence of the attribute "Glucose" on the class C depends on the value of "Insulin", while in naive Bayes the influence of each on the class variable is independent of other's. Thus, a value of "Glucose" that is surprising (i.e., $P(g|c)$ is low), may be unsurprising if the value of its correlated attribute, "Insulin," is also unlikely (i.e., $P(g|c,i)$ is high). In this situation, the naive Bayesian classifier will over-penalize the probability of the class variable (by considering two unlikely observations), while the network in Figure 3 will not.

Adding the best augment naive Bayes structure is an intractable problem. To see this, note this essentially involves learning a network structure over the attribute set. However, by imposing restrictions on the form of the allowed interactions, we can learn the correlations quite efficiently.

A *tree-augmented naive Bayes* (*TAN*) model, is a Bayesian network where $\Pi_C = \emptyset$, and Π_{A_i} contains C and at most one other attribute. Thus, each attribute can have one correlation edge pointing to it. As we now show, we can exploit this restriction on the number of correlation edges to learn *TAN* models efficiently. This class of models was previously proposed by Geiger (1992), using a well-known method by Chow and Liu (1968), for learning tree-like Bayesian networks (see also (Pearl 1988, pp. 387–390)).[7]

We start by reviewing Chow and Liu's result on learning trees. A directed acyclic graph is a *tree* if Π_{X_i} contains exactly one parent for all X_i, except for one variable that has no parents (this variable is referred to as the *root*). Chow and Liu show that there is a simple procedure that constructs the maximal log-probability tree. Let n be the number of random variables and N be the number of training instances. Then

Theorem 4.1: (Chow & Lui 1968) *There is a procedure of time complexity $O(n^2 \cdot N)$, that constructs the tree structure B_T that maximizes $LL(B_T|D)$.*

The procedure of Chow and Liu can be summarized as follows.

1. Compute the *mutual information* $I(X_i; X_j) = \sum_{x_i, x_j} \hat{P}_D(x_i, x_j) \log \frac{\hat{P}_D(x_i, x_j)}{\hat{P}_D(x_i)\hat{P}_D(x_j)}$ between each pair of variables, $i \neq j$.
2. Build a complete undirected graph in which the vertices are the variables in $\mathbf{U}$. Annotate the weight of an edge connecting X_i to X_j by $I(X_i; X_j)$.
3. Build a *maximum weighted spanning tree* of this graph (Cormen, Leiserson, & Rivest 1990).

[7]These structures are called "Bayesian conditional trees" by Geiger.

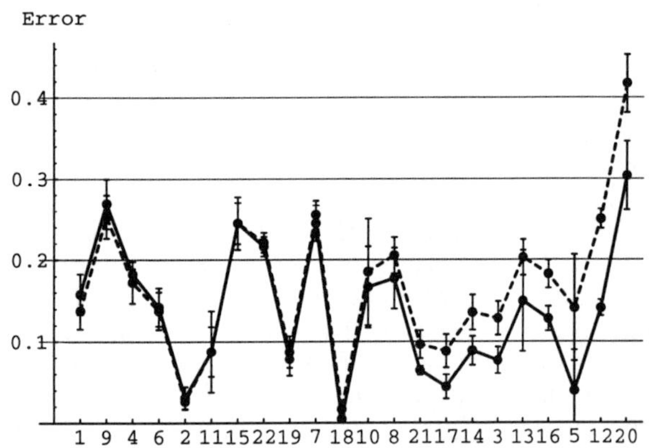

Figure 4: Error curves comparing smoothed *TAN* (solid line) to naive Bayes (dashed line).

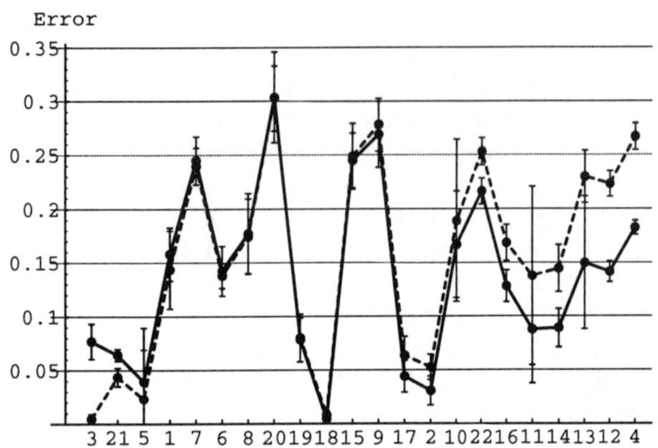

Figure 5: Error curves comparing smoothed *TAN* (solid line) to C4.5 (dashed line).

4. Transform the resulting undirected tree to a directed one by choosing a root variable and setting the direction of all edges to be outward from it. (The choice of root variable does not change the log-likelihood of the network.)

The first step has complexity of $O(n^2 \cdot N)$ and the third step has complexity of $O(n^2 \log n)$. Since we usually have that $N > \log n$, we get the resulting complexity.

This result can be adapted to learn the maximum likelihood *TAN* structure.

Theorem 4.2: (Geiger 1992) *There is a procedure of time complexity $O(n^2 \cdot N)$ that constructs the TAN structure B_T that maximize $LL(B_T|D)$.*

The procedure is very similar to the procedure described above when applied to the attributes $A_1, \ldots, A_n$. The only change is in the choice of weights. Instead of taking $I(A_i; A_j)$, we take the *conditional mutual information* given C, $I(A_i; A_j|C) = \sum_{a_i,a_j,c} \hat{P}_D(a_i, a_j, c) \log \frac{\hat{P}_D(a_i,a_j|c)}{\hat{P}_D(a_i|c)\hat{P}_D(a_j|c)}$. Roughly speaking, this measures the gain in log-likelihood of adding A_i as a parent of A_j when C is already a parent.

There is one more consideration. To learn the parameters in the network we estimate conditional frequencies of the form $\hat{P}_D(X|\Pi_X)$. This is done by partitioning the training data according to the possible values of Π_X and then computing the frequency of X in each partition. A problem surfaces when some of these partitions contain very few instances. In these small partitions our estimate of the conditional probability is unreliable. This problem is not serious for the naive Bayes classifier since it partitions the data according to the class variable, and usually all values of the class variables are adequately represented in the training data. In *TAN* models however, for each attribute we asses the conditional probability given the class variable and another attribute. This means that the number of partitions is at least twice as large. Thus, it is not surprising to encounter unreliable estimates, especially in small datasets.

To deal with this problem we introduce a smoothing operation on the parameters learned in *TAN* models. This operation takes every estimated parameter $\theta_{x|\Pi_x}$ and biases it toward the observed marginal frequency of X, $\hat{P}_D(x)$. Formally, we let the new parameter $\theta^s(x|\Pi_x) = \alpha \cdot \hat{P}_D(x|\Pi_x) + (1-\alpha)\hat{P}_D(x)$, taking $\alpha = \frac{N \cdot \hat{P}_D(\Pi_x)}{N \cdot \hat{P}_D(\Pi_x)+s}$, where s is the *smoothing parameter*, which is usually quite small (in all the experiments we choose $s = 5$).[8] It is easy to see that this operation biases the learned parameters in a manner that depends on our confidence level as expressed by s: the more instances we have in the partition from which we compute the parameter, the less bias is applied. If the number of instances that with a particular parents' value assignment is significant, than the bias essentially disappears. On the other hand, if the number of instances with the a particular parents' value assignment is small, then the bias dominates. We note that this operation is performed after the structure of the *TAN* model are determined. Thus, the smoothed model has exactly the same qualitative structure as the original model, but with different numerical parameters. In our experiments comparing the prediction error of smoothed *TAN* to that of unsmoothed *TAN*, we observed that smoothed *TAN* performs at least as well as *TAN* and occasionally significantly outperforms *TAN* (see for example the results for "soybean-large", "segment", and "lymphography" in Table 1). From now on we will assume that the version of *TAN* uses the smoothing operator unless noted otherwise.

Figure 4 compares the prediction error of the *TAN* classifier to that of naive Bayes. As can be seen, the performance of the *TAN* classifier dominates that of naive Bayes.[9] This result supports our hypothesis that by relaxing the strong independence assumptions made by naive Bayes we can indeed learn better classifiers.

[8] In statistical terms, we are essentially applying a *Dirichlet prior* on $\theta_{X|\Pi_X}$ with mean expected value $\hat{P}_D(X)$ and equivalent sample size s. We note that this use of Dirichlet priors is related to the class of Dirichlet priors described in (Heckerman, Geiger, & Chickering 1995).

[9] In our experiments we also tried smoothed version of naive Bayes. This did not lead to significant improvement over the unsmoothed naive Bayes.

Finally, we also compared *TAN* to C4.5 (Quinlan 1993), a state of the art decision-tree learning system, and to the *selective naive Bayesian* classifier (Langley & Sage 1994; John, Kohavi, & Pfleger 1995). The later approach searches for the subset of attributes over which naive Bayes has the best performance. The results displayed in Figure 5 and Table 1, show that *TAN* is quite competitive with both approaches and can lead to big improvements in many cases.

5 Concluding Remarks

This paper makes two important contributions. The first one is the analysis of unsupervised learning of Bayesian networks for classification tasks. We show that the scoring metrics used in learning unsupervised Bayesian networks do not necessarily optimize the performance of the learned networks in classification. Our analysis suggests a possible class of scoring metrics that are suited for this task. These metrics appear to be computationally intractable. We plan to explore effective approaches to learning with approximations of these scores. The second contribution is the experimental validation of tree augmented naive Bayesian classifiers, *TAN*. This approach was introduced by Geiger (1992), yet was not extensively tested and as a consequence has received little recognition in the machine learning community. This classification method has attractive computational properties, while at the same time, as our experimental results show, it performs competitively with reported state of the art classifiers.

In spite of these advantages, it is clear that in some situations, it would be useful to model correlations among attributes that cannot be captured by a tree structure. This will be significant when there is a sufficient number of training instances to robustly estimate higher-order conditional probabilities. Thus, it is interesting to examine the problem of learning (unrestricted) augmented naive Bayes networks. In an initial experiment we attempted to learn such networks using the MDL score, where we restricted the search procedure to examine only networks that contained the naive Bayes backbone. The results were somewhat disappointing, since the MDL score was reluctant to add more than a few correlation arcs to the naive Bayes backbone. This is, again, a consequence of the fact that the scoring metric is not geared for classification. An alternative approach might use a cross-validation scheme to evaluate each candidate while searching for the best correlation edges. Such a procedure, however, is computationally expensive.

We are certainly not the first to try and improve naive Bayes by adding correlations among attributes. For example, Pazzani (1995) suggests a procedure that replaces, in a greedy manner, pairs of attributes A_i, A_j, with a new attribute that represents the cross-product of A_i and A_j. This processes ensures that paired attributes influence the class variable in a correlated manner. It is easy to see that the resulting classifier is equivalent to an augmented naive Bayes network where the attributes in each "cluster" are fully interconnected. Note that including many attributes in a single cluster may result in overfitting problems. On the other hand, attributes in different clusters remain (conditionally) independent of each other. This shortcoming does not occur in *TAN* classifiers. Another example is the work by Provan and Singh (1995), in which a wrapper-based feature subset selection is applied to an unsupervised Bayesian network learning routine. This procedure is computationally intensive (it involves repeated calls to a Bayesian network learning procedure) and the reported results indicate only a slight improvement over the selective naive Bayesian classifier.

The attractiveness of the tree-augmented naive Bayesian classifier is that it embodies a good tradeoff between the quality of the approximation of correlations among attributes, and the computational complexity in the learning stage. Moreover, the learning procedure is guaranteed to find the optimal *TAN* structure. As our experimental results show this procedure performs well in practice. Therefore we propose *TAN* as a worthwhile tool for the machine learning community.

Acknowledgements

The authors are grateful to Denise Draper, Ken Fertig, Dan Geiger, Joe Halpern, Ronny Kohavi, Pat Langley and Judea Pearl for comments on a previous draft of this paper and useful discussions relating to this work. We thank Ronny Kohavi for technical help with the MLC++ library. Parts of this work were done while the first author was at Rockwell Science Center. The first author was also supported in part by an IBM Graduate fellowship and NSF Grant IRI-95-03109.

A Experimental Methodology and Results

We run our experiments on the 22 datasets listed in Table 1. All of the datasets are from the U. C. Irvine repository (Murphy & Aha 1995), with the exception of "mofn-3-7-10" and "corral". These two artificial datasets were used for the evaluation of feature subset selection methods by (John, Kohavi, & Pfleger 1995). All these datasets are accessible at the MLC++ ftp site.

The accuracy of each classifier is based on the percentage of successful predictions on the test sets of each dataset. We estimate the prediction accuracy for each classifier as well as the variance of this accuracy using the MLC++ system (Kohavi *et al.* 1994). Accuracy was evaluated using the holdout method for the larger datasets, and using 5-fold *cross validation* (using the methods described in (Kohavi 1995)) for the smaller ones. Since we do not deal, at the current time, with missing data we had removed instances with missing values from the datasets. Currently we also do not handle continuous attributes. Instead, in each invocation of the learning routine, the dataset was pre-discretized using a variant of the method of (Fayyad & Irani 1993) using only the training data, in the manner described in (Dougherty, Kohavi, & Sahami 1995). These preprocessing stages where carried out by the MLC++ system. We note that experiments with the various learning procedures were carried out on exactly the same training sets and evaluated on the same test sets. In particular, the cross-validation folds where the same for all the experiments on each dataset.

Table 1: Experimental results

	Dataset	# Attributes	# Instances		Accuracy					
			Train	Testl	NBC	Unsup	TAN	TAN^s	C4.5	SNBC
1	australian	14	690	CV-5	86.23+-1.10	86.23+-1.76	81.30+-1.06	84.20+-1.24	85.65+-1.82	**86.67+-1.81**
2	breast	10	683	CV-5	**97.36+-0.50**	96.92+-0.63	95.75+-1.25	96.92+-0.67	94.73+-0.59	96.19+-0.63
3	chess	36	2130	1066	87.15+-1.03	95.59+-0.63	92.40+-0.81	92.31+-0.82	**99.53+-0.21**	94.28+-0.71
4	cleve	13	296	CV-5	**82.76+-1.27**	81.39+-1.82	79.06+-0.65	81.76+-0.33	73.31+-0.63	78.06+-2.41
5	corral	6	128	CV-5	85.88+-3.25	97.60+-2.40	95.32+-2.26	96.06+-2.51	**97.69+-2.31**	83.57+-3.15
6	crx	15	653	CV-5	**86.22+-1.14**	85.60+-0.17	83.77+-1.34	85.76+-1.16	**86.22+-0.58**	85.92+-1.08
7	diabetes	8	768	CV-5	74.48+-0.89	75.39+-0.29	75.13+-0.98	75.52+-1.11	**76.04+-0.85**	**76.04+-0.83**
8	flare	10	1066	CV-5	79.46+-1.11	82.74+-1.90	82.74+-1.60	82.27+-1.86	82.55+-1.75	**83.40+-1.67**
9	german	20	1000	CV-5	**74.70+-1.33**	72.30+-1.57	72.20+-1.54	73.10+-1.54	72.20+-1.23	73.70+-2.02
10	heart	13	270	CV-5	81.48+-3.26	82.22+-2.46	82.96+-2.51	**83.33+-2.48**	81.11+-3.77	81.85+-2.83
11	hepatitis	19	80	CV-5	**91.25+-1.53**	**91.25+-4.68**	85.00+-2.50	**91.25+-2.50**	86.25+-4.15	90.00+-4.24
12	letter	16	15000	5000	74.96+-0.61	75.02+-0.61	83.44+-0.53	**85.86+-0.49**	77.70+-0.59	75.36+-0.61
13	lymphography	18	148	CV-5	79.72+-1.10	75.03+-1.58	66.87+-3.37	**85.03+-3.09**	77.03+-1.21	77.72+-2.46
14	mofn-3-7-10	10	300	1024	86.43+-1.07	85.94+-1.09	**91.70+-0.86**	91.11+-0.89	85.55+-1.10	87.50+-1.03
15	pima	8	768	CV-5	**75.51+-1.63**	75.00+-1.22	75.13+-1.36	**75.52+-1.27**	75.13+-1.52	74.86+-2.61
16	satimage	36	4435	2000	81.75+-0.86	59.20+-1.10	77.55+-0.93	**87.20+-0.75**	83.15+-0.84	82.05+-0.86
17	segment	19	1540	770	91.17+-1.02	93.51+-0.89	85.32+-1.28	**95.58+-0.74**	93.64+-0.88	93.25+-0.90
18	shuttle-small	9	3866	1934	98.34+-0.29	99.17+-0.21	98.86+-0.24	**99.53+-0.15**	99.17+-0.21	99.28+-0.19
19	soybean-large	35	562	CV-5	91.29+-0.98	58.54+-4.84	58.17+-1.43	92.17+-1.02	92.00+-1.11	**92.89+-1.01**
20	vehicle	18	846	CV-5	58.28+-1.79	61.00+-2.02	67.86+-2.92	69.63+-2.11	**69.74+-1.52**	61.36+-2.33
21	vote	16	435	CV-5	90.34+-0.86	94.94+-0.46	89.20+-1.61	93.56+-0.28	**95.63+-0.43**	94.71+-0.59
22	waveform-21	21	300	4700	77.89+-0.61	69.45+-0.67	75.38+-0.63	**78.38+-0.60**	74.70+-0.63	76.53+-0.62

Finally, in Table 1 we summarize the accuracies of the six learning procedures we discussed in this paper: **NBC**–the naive Bayesian classifier; **Unsup**–unsupervised Bayesian networks learned using the MDL score; **TAN**—*TAN* networks learned according to Theorem 4.2; **TAN**^{s}—smoothed *TAN* networks; **C4.5**–the decision-tree classifier of (Quinlan 1993); **SNBC**—the selective naive Bayesian classifier, a wrapper-based feature selection applied to naive Bayes, using the implementation of (John, Kohavi, & Pfleger 1995).

References

Chow, C. K., and Lui, C. N. 1968. Approximating discrete probability distributions with dependence trees. *IEEE Trans. on Info. Theory* 14:462–467.

Cormen, T. H.; Leiserson, C. E.; and Rivest, R. L. 1990. *Introduction to Algorithms*. MIT Press.

Dougherty, J.; Kohavi, R.; and Sahami, M. 1995. Supervised and unsupervised discretization of continuous features. In *ML '95*.

Fayyad, U. M., and Irani, K. B. 1993. Multi-interval discretization of continuous-valued attributes for classification learning. In *IJCAI '93*, 1022–1027.

Friedman, N., and Goldszmidt, M. 1996. Discretization of continuous attributes while learning Bayesian networks. In *ML '96*.

Geiger, D. 1992. An entropy-based learning algorithm of Bayesian conditional trees. In *UAI '92*. 92–97.

Heckerman, D.; Geiger, D.; and Chickering, D. M. 1995. Learning Bayesian networks: The combination of knowlege and statistical data. *Machine Learning* 20:197–243.

Heckerman, D. 1995. A tutorial on learning Bayesian networks. Technical Report MSR-TR-95-06, Microsoft Research.

John, G.; Kohavi, R.; and Pfleger, K. 1995. Irrelevant features and the subset selection problem. In *ML '94*. 121–129.

Kohavi, R.; John, G.; Long, R.; Manley, D.; and Pfleger, K. 1994. MLC++: A machine learning library in C++. In *Tools with Artificial Intelligence*. 740–743.

Kohavi, R. 1995. A study of cross-validation and bootstrap for accuracy estimation and model selection. In *IJCAI '95*. 1137–1143.

Lam, W., and Bacchus, F. 1994. Learning Bayesian belief networks. An approach based on the MDL principle. *Computational Intelligence* 10:269–293.

Langley, P., and Sage, S. 1994. Induction of selective Bayesian classifiers. In *UAI '94*. 399–406.

Langley, P.; Iba, W.; and Thompson, K. 1992. An analysis of bayesian classifiers. In *AAAI '90*. 223–228.

Murphy, P. M., and Aha, D. W. 1995. UCI repository of machine learning databases. `http://www.ics.uci.edu/~mlearn/MLRepository.html`.

Pazzani, M. J. 1995. Searching for dependencies in Bayesian classifiers. In *Proc. of the 5'th Int. Workshop on Artificial Intelligence and Statistics*.

Pearl, J. 1988. *Probabilistic Reasoning in Intelligent Systems*. Morgan Kaufmann.

Quinlan, J. R. 1993. *C4.5: Programs for Machine Learning*. Morgan Kaufmann.

Singh, M., and Provan, G. M. 1995. A comparison of induction algorithms for selective and non-selective bayesian classifiers. In *ML '95*.

Generalized Queries on Probabilistic Context-Free Grammars

David V. Pynadath and **Michael P. Wellman**
Artificial Intelligence Laboratory
University of Michigan
1101 Beal Avenue
Ann Arbor, MI 48109 USA
{pynadath,wellman}@umich.edu

Abstract

Probabilistic context-free grammars (PCFGs) provide a simple way to represent a particular class of distributions over sentences in a context-free language. Efficient parsing algorithms for answering particular queries about a PCFG (i.e., calculating the probability of a given sentence, or finding the most likely parse) have been applied to a variety of pattern-recognition problems. We extend the class of queries that can be answered in several ways: (1) allowing missing tokens in a sentence or sentence fragment, (2) supporting queries about intermediate structure, such as the presence of particular nonterminals, and (3) flexible conditioning on a variety of types of evidence. Our method works by constructing a Bayesian network to represent the distribution of parse trees induced by a given PCFG. The network structure mirrors that of the chart in a standard parser, and is generated using a similar dynamic-programming approach. We present an algorithm for constructing Bayesian networks from PCFGs, and show how queries or patterns of queries on the network correspond to interesting queries on PCFGs.

Introduction

Most pattern-recognition problems start from observations generated by some structured stochastic process. Probabilistic context-free grammars (PCFGs) (Gonzalez & Thomason 1978; Charniak 1993) have provided a useful method for modeling uncertainty in a wide range of structures, including programming languages (Wetherell 1980), images (Chou 1989), speech signals (Ney 1992), and RNA sequences (Sakakibara *et al.* 1995). Domains like plan recognition, where non-probabilistic grammars have provided useful models (Vilain 1990), may also benefit from an explicit stochastic model.

Once we have created a PCFG model of a process, we can apply existing PCFG parsing algorithms to answer a variety of queries. However, these techniques are limited in the types of evidence they can exploit and the types of queries they can answer. In particular, the standard techniques generally require specification of a complete observation sequence. In many contexts, we may have only a partial sequence available, or other kinds of contextual evidence. In addition, we may be interested in computing the probabilities of types of events that the extant techniques do not directly support. Finally, the PCFG model itself imposes restrictions on the probabilistic dependence structure, which we may wish to relax.

To extend the forms of evidence, queries, and distributions supported, we need a flexible and expressive representation for the distribution of structures generated by the grammar. We adopt Bayesian networks for this purpose, and define an algorithm to generate a network representing the distribution of possible parse trees corresponding to a given PCFG. We then present algorithms for extending the class of queries to include the conditional probability of a symbol appearing anywhere within any region of the parse tree, conditioned on any evidence about symbols appearing in the parse tree. The Bayesian network also provides a flexible structure for future extensions to context-sensitive probabilities, similar to the probabilistic parse tables of (Briscoe & Carroll 1993).

Probabilistic Context-Free Grammars

A probabilistic context-free grammar is a tuple $\langle H_T, H_N, E^1, P\rangle$, where H_T is the set of terminal symbols, H_N the set of nonterminal symbols, $E^1 \in H_N$ the start symbol, and P the set of productions. Productions take the form $E \rightarrow \xi\ (p)$, with $E \in H_N, \xi \in (H_T \cup H_N)^+$, and $p = \Pr(E \rightarrow \xi)$, the probability that E will be expanded into the string ξ. The probability of applying a particular production to an intermediate string is conditionally independent of what productions were previously applied to obtain the current string, or what productions will be applied to the other symbols in the current string, given the presence of the left-hand symbol. Therefore, the probability of a given derivation is simply the product of the probabilities of the individual productions involved. The probability of a string in the language is the sum taken over all possible derivations. In the grammar (from (Charniak 1993)) shown in Figure 1, the start symbol is s.

s	→	np vp	(0.8)	pp	→	p np	(1.0)
s	→	vp	(0.2)	p	→	like	(1.0)
np	→	n	(0.4)	v	→	swat	(0.2)
np	→	n pp	(0.4)	v	→	flies	(0.4)
np	→	n np	(0.2)	v	→	like	(0.4)
vp	→	v	(0.3)	n	→	swat	(0.05)
vp	→	v np	(0.3)	n	→	flies	(0.45)
vp	→	v pp	(0.2)	n	→	ants	(0.5)
vp	→	v np pp	(0.2)				

Figure 1: A probabilistic context-free grammar.

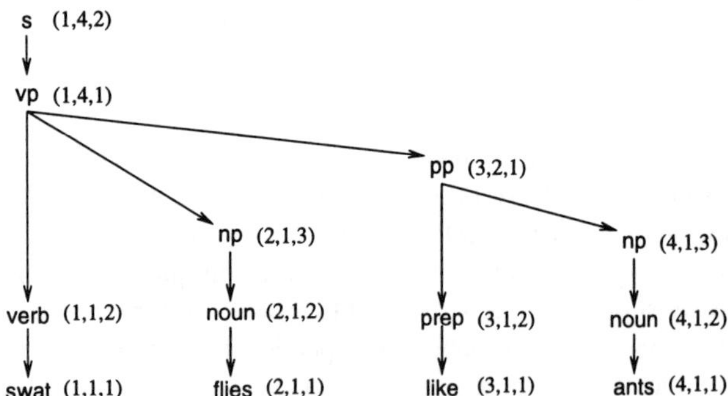

Figure 2: Parse tree for Swat flies like ants, with (i, j, k) indices labeled.

Indexing Parse Trees

Calculating the probability of a particular parse tree can sometimes be useful, but we may also wish to derive the probability of some more abstract feature of a parse tree. To pose such queries, we require a scheme to specify events as the appearance of symbols at designated points in the parse tree. We use three indices to identify a node in a parse in terms of the structure of the subtree rooted at that node. Two indices delimit the leaf nodes of the subtree, defining a substring of the entire terminal sequence. The index i refers to the position of the substring within the entire terminal string, with $i = 1$ indicating the start of the string. The index j refers to the length of the substring. For example, the pp node in the parse tree of Figure 2 is the root of the subtree whose leaf nodes are like and ants, so $i = 3$ and $j = 2$. These i and j indices are commonly used in PCFG algorithms.

However, we cannot always uniquely specify a node with these two indices alone. In the branch of the parse tree passing through np, n, and flies, all three nodes have $i = 2$ and $j = 1$. To differentiate them, we introduce the k index, defined recursively. If a node has no child with the same i and j indices, then it has $k = 1$. Otherwise, its k index is one more than the k index of its child. Thus, the flies node has $k = 1$, the n node above it has a $k = 2$, and its parent np has $k = 3$. We have labeled each node in the parse tree of Figure 2 with its (i, j, k) indices.

We can think of the k index of a node as its level of abstraction, with higher values indicating more abstract symbols. For instance, the flies symbol is a specialization of the n concept, which, in turn, is a specialization of the np concept. Each possible specialization corresponds to an *abstraction production* of the form $E \rightarrow E'$. In a parse tree involving such a production, the nodes for E and E' will have identical i and j values, but the k value for E will be one more than that of E'. We denote the set of abstraction productions as $P_A \subseteq P$.

All other productions are *decomposition productions*, in the set $P_D = P \setminus P_A$, and have two or more symbols on the right-hand side. If a node E is expanded by a decomposition production, the sum of the j values for its children will equal its own j value, since the length of the original substring derived from E must equal the total lengths of the substrings of its children. In addition, since each child must derive a string of nonzero length, no child has the same j index as E, which must then have a k value of 1. Therefore, abstraction productions connect nodes whose indices match in the i and j components, while decomposition productions connect nodes whose indices differ.

Dynamic Programming Algorithm

We can compute the probability of a string by summing probabilities over the set of its possible parse trees, which grows exponentially with the string's length. Fortunately, parse trees often share common subtrees, a fact exploited by the standard dynamic programming approach for both probabilistic and non-probabilistic CFGs (Jelinek, Lafferty, & Mercer 1992). The central structure is a table, or *chart*, storing previous results for each substring in the input sentence. Each entry in the chart corresponds to a substring $x_i \cdots x_{i+j-1}$ (ignoring abstraction level, k) of the observation string $x_1 \cdots x_L$. For each symbol E, an entry contains the probability that the corresponding substring is derived from that symbol, $\Pr(x_i \cdots x_{i+j-1} | E)$.

At the bottom of the table are the results for substrings of length one, and the top entry holds the result for the entire string, $\Pr(x_1 \cdots x_L | E^1)$, which is exactly the probability of the observed string. We can compute these probabilities bottom-up, since we know that $\Pr(x_i | E) = 1$ if E is the observed symbol x_i, and 0 otherwise. We can define all other probabilities recursively as the sum, over all productions $E \rightarrow \xi$ (p), of the product of p and the probability $\Pr(x_i \cdots x_{i+j-1} | \xi)$. Here, we can make use of the PCFG independence assumptions, and compute this probability as the product of the probabilities of the individual symbols, where we have to consider all possible substring lengths for these symbols. A slight alteration to this procedure also allows us to obtain the most probable parse tree for the observed string.

To compute the probability of the sentence Swat flies like ants, we would use the algorithm to generate the table shown in Figure 3, after eliminating any intermediate entries

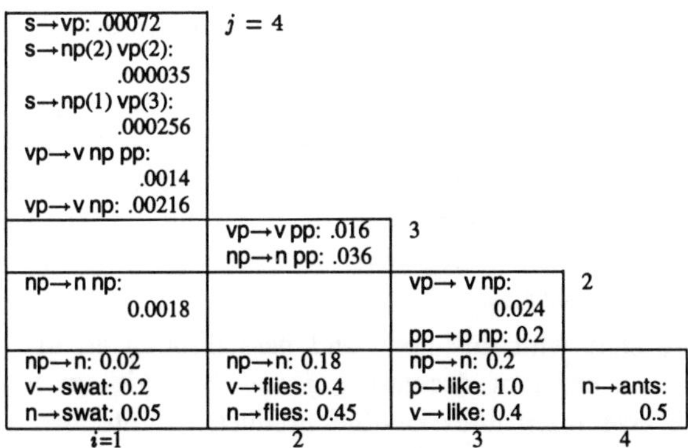

Figure 3: Chart for Swat flies like ants.

that were not referenced by higher-level entries. There are also separate entries for each production, though this is not necessary if we are only interested in the final sentence probability. In the top entry, there are two listings for the production s→np vp, with different substring lengths for the right-hand side symbols. The sum of all probabilities for productions with s on the right-hand side in this entry yields the total sentence probability of 0.001011.

This algorithm is capable of computing any "inside" probability, the probability of a particular terminal string appearing inside the subtree rooted by a particular nonterminal. We can work top-down in an analogous manner to compute any "outside" probability (Charniak 1993), the probability of a subtree rooted by a particular nonterminal appearing amid a particular terminal string. Given these probabilities we can compute the probability of any particular nonterminal symbol appearing in the parse tree as the root of a subtree covering some substring. For example, in the sentence Swat flies like ants, we can compute the probability that like ants is a prepositional phrase, using a combination of inside and outside probabilities. The Left-to-Right Inside (LRI) algorithm (Jelinek, Lafferty, & Mercer 1992) specifies how we can manipulate certain probability matrices and combine the results with the inside probabilities to obtain the probability of a given initial substring, such as the probability of a sentence (of any length) beginning with the words Swat flies. Furthermore, we can use such initial substring probabilities to compute the conditional probability of the next observation given all previous observations.

However, there are still many types of queries not covered by existing algorithms. For example, given observations of arbitrary partial observation strings, it is unclear how to exploit the standard chart directly. Similarly, we are unaware of methods to handle observation of nonterminals only (e.g., the last two words form a prepositional phrase). We seek, therefore, a mechanism that would admit observational evidence of any form as part of a query about a PCFG, without requiring us to enumerate all consistent parse trees.

Bayesian Networks for PCFGs

Bayesian networks (Pearl 1987) provide an expressive and efficient representation for probability distributions. They are expressive in that they can represent any joint distribution over a finite set of discrete-valued random variables. They are efficient in that they exploit an important class of conditional independence relationships among the random variables. Moreover, Bayesian networks are convenient computational devices, supporting the calculation of arbitrary conditional probability expressions involving their random variables. Therefore, if we can create a Bayesian network representing the distribution of parse trees for a given probabilistic grammar, then we can incorporate partial observations of a sentence as well as other forms of evidence, and determine the resulting probabilities of various features of the parse trees.

We base our Bayesian-network encoding of PCFGs on the parse tree indexing scheme presented in the previous section. The random variable N_{ijk} denotes the symbol in the parse tree at the position indicated by the (i, j, k) indices. Index combinations not appearing in the tree correspond to N variables taking on the null value nil. To simplify the dependency structure, we also introduce random variables P_{ijk} to represent the productions that expand the corresponding symbols N_{ijk}. However, the identity of the production is not quite sufficient to render the corresponding children in the parse tree conditionally independent, so we dictate that the P variable take on different values for each breakdown of the right-hand symbols' substring lengths. This increases the state space of the variables, but simplifies the dependency structure.

Dynamic Programming Phase

To complete the specification of the network, we identify the symbols and productions making up the domains of our random variables, as well as the conditional probability tables representing their dependencies. The PCFG specifies the relative probabilities of different productions for each nonterminal, but to specify the probabilities of alternate parse trees in terms of the N_{ijk} variables we need the probabilities of the length breakdowns. We can calculate these with a modified version of the standard dynamic programming algorithm sketched in the previous section.

This modified algorithm constructs a chart based on the set of all possible terminal strings, up to a bounded length n. Our resulting chart defines a function $\beta(E, j, k)$ (analogous to the inside probability in the standard parsing algorithm), specifying the probability that symbol E is the root node of a subtree, at abstraction level k, with a terminal substring of length j. Because this probability is not relative to a particular observation string, we can ignore the i index.

As in the previous dynamic programming algorithms, we can define this function recursively, initializing the entries to

k	E	$\beta(E,4,k)$	k	E	$\beta(E,3,k)$	k	E	$\beta(E,1,k)$
2	s	0.02016	2	s	0.0208	4	s	0.06
1	s	0.0832	1	s	0.0576	3	np	0.4
	np	0.0672		np	0.176		vp	0.3
	vp	0.1008		vp	0.104	2	p	1.0
	pp	0.176		pp	0.08		v	1.0
			k	E	$\beta(E,2,k)$		n	1.0
			2	s	0.024	1	like	1.0
			1	s	0.096		swat	1.0
				np	0.08		flies	1.0
				vp	0.12		ants	1.0
				pp	0.4			

Figure 4: Final table for sample grammar.

0. Again, we start at $j = 1$ and work upward to $j = n$. For each terminal symbol x, $\beta(x, 1, 1) = 1$. For $k > 1$, only abstraction productions are possible, because, as discussed before, decomposition productions are applicable only when $k = 1$. For each abstraction production $E \to E'$ (p), we increment $\beta(E, j, k)$ by $p \cdot \beta(E', j, k-1)$. If $k = 1$, only decomposition productions are applicable, so for each decomposition production $E \to E_1 E_2 \cdots E_m$ (p), each substring length breakdown $j_1, \ldots, j_m$ (such that the $\sum_t j_t = j$), and each abstraction level k_t legal for each j_t, we increment $\beta(E, j, k)$ by $p \cdot \prod_{t=1}^{m} \beta(E_t, j_t, k_t)$. The table of Figure 4 lists the nonzero β values for our grammar over strings of maximum length 4.

For analysis of the complexity of this algorithm, it is useful to define d as the maximum abstraction level, and m as the maximum number of symbols on a production's right-hand side. For a maximum string length of n, the table requires space $O(n^2 d |H_N|)$, exploiting the fact that β for terminal symbols is one in the bottom row and zero elsewhere. For a specific value of j, there are $O(d)$ possible k values greater than 1, each requiring time $O(|P_A|)$. For $k = 1$, the algorithm requires time $O(|P_D| j^{m-1} d^m)$, for the evaluation of all decomposition productions, as well as all possible combinations of substring lengths and levels of abstractions for each symbol on the right-hand side. Therefore, the whole algorithm would take time $O(n[d|P_A| + |P_D| n^{m-1} d^m]) = O(|P| n^m d^m)$.

As an alternative, we can modify the standard chart parsing algorithm (Younger 1967; Earley 1970) to compute the required values for β by recording the k values and probabilities associated with each edge. We would also ignore any distinctions among terminal symbols, since we are computing values over all possible terminal strings. Therefore, the time required for computing β is equivalent to that required for parsing a terminal string of length n, which is $O(n^3)$ ignoring the parameters of the grammar.

Network Generation Phase

Upon completion of the dynamic programming phase, we can use the table entries to compute the domains of random variables N_{ijk} and P_{ijk} and the required conditional probabilities. We begin at the top of the abstraction hierarchy for strings of the maximum length n starting at position 1. The corresponding symbol variable can be either E^1 or the special null symbol nil*, indicating that the parse tree begins at some other point below. The prior probability of the start symbol is proportional to $\beta(E^1, n, k)$, while that of nil* is proportional to the sum of all other β values for the start symbol E^1. The exact probabilities are normalized so that the sum equals one.

We start with this node and pass through all of the nodes in order of decreasing j and k. With each N node, we insert the possible productions into the domain of its corresponding P node. For a production rule r that maps E to $E_1 \cdots E_m$ with probability p and a breakdown of substring lengths and abstraction levels $(j_1, k_1), \ldots, (j_m, k_m)$, the conditional probability $\Pr(P_{ijk} = r \langle (j_1, k_1), \ldots, (j_m, k_m) \rangle | N_{ijk} = E) \propto p \cdot \prod \beta(E_t, j_t, k_t)$. The exact probability is normalized so that the sum over all rules r and breakdowns $\langle (j_t, k_t) \rangle$ for a particular left-hand symbol E is 1. For any symbol $E' \neq E$ in the domain of N_{ijk}, we can set the conditional probability $\Pr(P_{ijk} = r \langle (j_1, k_1), \ldots, (j_m, k_m) \rangle | N_{ijk} = E') = 0$.

A symbol variable which takes on the value nil has no children, so its production variable will also take on a null value (i.e., $\Pr(P_{ijk} = \text{nil} | N_{ijk} = \text{nil}) = 1$). For the special symbol nil*, there are two possibilities, either the parse tree starts at the next level below, or it starts further down the tree. In the first case, the production is nil* $\to E^1$, and has a conditional probability proportional to the β value of E^1 at the j and k value immediately below the current position, given that $N_{ijk} =$ nil*. In the second case, the production is nil* $\to$ nil*, and has a conditional probability proportional to the sum of the β values of E^1 at all j and k more than one level below, given that $N_{ijk} =$ nil*.

When all possible values for a production variable are added, we add a link from the corresponding node to the variables corresponding to each symbol on the right-hand side and insert these symbols into the domains of these child variables. A child nodes takes on the appropriate right-hand side symbol with probability 1 if the parent node has taken on the value of the given production. A child node takes on the value nil with probability 1 if none of its parent nodes assign it a symbol value.

Figure 5 illustrates the network structure resulting from applying this algorithm to the table of Figure 4 with a length bound of 4. In general, the resulting network has $O(n^2 d)$ nodes. The n N_{i11} variables have $O(|H_T|)$ states each, while the $O(n^2 d)$ other N variables have $O(|H_N|)$ possible states. The P_{ijk} variables for $k > 1$ (of which there are $O(n^2 d)$) have a domain of $O(|P_A|)$ states. For P_{ij1} variables, there are states for each possible decomposition production, for each possible combination of substring lengths, and for each possible level of abstraction of the symbols on the right-hand side. Therefore, the P_{ij1} variables (of which

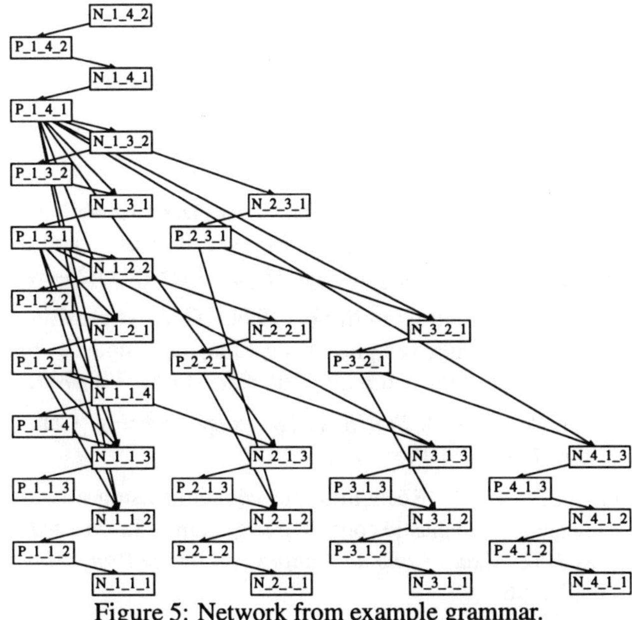

Figure 5: Network from example grammar.

there are $O(n^2)$) have a domain of $O(|P_D|j^{m-1}d^m)$ states.

Unfortunately, even though each particular P variable has only the corresponding N variable as its parent, a given N_{ijk} variable could have potentially $O(i \cdot (n - i - j))$ P variables as parents, and the size of a node's conditional probability table is exponential in the number of its parents. If we define T to be the maximum number of entries of any conditional probability table in the network, then the total time complexity of the algorithm is then $O(n^2 d|P_A|T + n^2|P_D|n^{m-1}d^m T^m + ndT + n^2 dT) = O(|P|n^{m+1}d^m T^m)$, which dwarfs the complexity of the dynamic programming algorithm for the β function. However, this network is created only once for a particular grammar and length bound.

Inference

The Bayesian network can answer any of the queries addressed by the usual parsing algorithm. To find the probability of a particular terminal string $x_1 \cdots x_L$, we can instantiate the variables N_{i11} to be x_i, for $i \leq L$, and nil, for $i > L$. Then, we can use any of the standard Bayesian network propagation algorithms to compute the probability of this evidence. The result is the conditional probability of the sentence, given that the string is bounded in length by n. We can easily acquire the unconditional probability, since the probability of a string having length no more than n is the sum of the β values for E^1 over all lengths of n and under. To find the most probable parse tree, we would use the standard network algorithms for finding the most probable configuration of the network.

The network represents a distribution over strings of bounded length, so we cannot obtain the same probability of an initial substring $x_1 x_2 \cdots x_L$ as (Jelinek, Lafferty, & Mercer 1992), which considered all completion lengths. However, we can find initial substring probabilities over completions of length bounded by $n - L$. The algorithm is identical to that for the probability of the entire sentence, except that we do not instantiate the N_{i11} variables beyond $i = L$ to be nil.

The procedure for finding the probability that a particular symbol derives a particular substring is complicated by the fact that there are multiple levels of abstraction possible for a particular substring. Therefore, after we instantiate the evidence, we must query all of the N variables for the particular i and j values of interest. We can start with the a particular k value and find the posterior probability of N_{ijk} being the symbol of interest. Having "counted" this event, we set the likelihood of N_{ijk} being that symbol to be zero, and proceed to a different k. We maintain a running total as we proceed, with the final probability being the result when all of the nodes have been counted.

In general, we can answer any query about an event that can be expressed in terms of the basic N and P random variables. Obviously, if we are interested in whether a symbol appeared at a particular i, j, k location in the parse tree, we only need to examine the marginal probability distribution of the corresponding N variable. Alternatively, we can find the probability of a particular symbol deriving *any part* of a particular substring (specified by i and j indices) by performing a similar procedure to that for an exact substring described above. However, in this case, we would continue computing posterior probabilities over *all* i and j variables within the bounds.

As another example, consider the case of possible four-word sentences beginning with the phrase Swat flies. In the network of Figure 5, we instantiate N_{111} to be swat and N_{211} to be flies and then propagate this evidence. We then need only to examine the joint distributions of N_{311} and N_{411} to find that like flies is the most likely completion. This is similar to the Left-to-Right Inside algorithm of (Jelinek, Lafferty, & Mercer 1992), except that we can find the most probable joint configuration over multiple time steps, instead of over only the one immediately subsequent.

A greater advantage is in the utilization of evidence. Any of the queries mentioned previously can be conditioned on any event that can be expressed in terms of N and P variables. If we only have a partial observation of the string, we simply instantiate the N_{i11} variables corresponding to the positions of whatever observations we have, and then propagate to find whatever posterior probability we require. In addition, we can exploit additional evidence about nonterminals within the parse tree. For instance, we may want to find the probability of the sentence Swat flies like ants with the additional stipulation that like ants is a prepositional phrase. In this case, we instantiate the N_{i11} variables as usual, but we also instantiate N_{321} to be pp.

Conclusion

The algorithms presented here automatically generate a Bayesian network representing the distribution over all parses of strings (bounded in length by some parameter) in the language of a PCFG. The first stage uses a dynamic programming approach similar to that of standard parsing algorithms, while the second stage generates the network, using the results of the first stage to specify the probabilities. This network is generated only once for a particular PCFG and length bound. Once created, we can use this network to answer a variety of queries about possible strings and parse trees. In general, we can use the standard inference algorithms to compute the conditional probability or most probable configuration of any collection of our basic random variables, given any other event which can be expressed in terms of these variables.

These algorithms have been implemented and tested on a number of grammars, with the results verified against those of existing dynamic programming algorithms when applicable, and against enumeration algorithms when given nonstandard queries. When answering standard queries, the time requirements for network inference were comparable to those for the dynamic programming techniques. Our network inference methods achieved similar response times for some other types of queries, providing a vast improvement over the much slower brute force algorithms.

The network representation of the probability distribution also allows possible relaxations of the independence assumptions of the PCFG framework. We could extend the context-sensitivity of these probabilities within our network formalism by adjusting the probability tables associated with our production nodes. For instance, we may make the conditional probabilities a function of the (i, j, k) index values. Alternatively, we may introduce additional dependencies on other nodes in the network, or perhaps on features beyond the parse tree itself. The context-sensitivity of (Charniak & Carroll 1994), which conditions the production probabilities on the parent of the left-hand side symbol, would require only an additional link from N nodes to their potential children P nodes. Other external influences could include explicit context representation in natural language problems or influences of the current world state in planning, as required by many plan recognition problems (Pynadath & Wellman 1995).

Therefore, even though the evidence propagation is exponential in the worst case, our method incurs this cost in the service of greatly increased generality. Our hope is that the enhanced scope will make PCFGs a useful model for plan recognition and other domains that require more flexibility in query forms and in probabilistic structure. In addition, these algorithms may extend the usefulness of PCFGs in natural language processing and other pattern recognition domains where they have already been successful.

Acknowledgments We are grateful to the anonymous reviewers for careful reading and helpful suggestions. This work was supported in part by Grant F49620-94-1-0027 from the Air Force Office of Scientific Research.

References

Briscoe, T., and Carroll, J. 1993. Generalized probabilistic LR parsing of natural language (corpora) with unification-based grammars. *Computational Linguistics* 19(1):25–59.

Charniak, E., and Carroll, G. 1994. Context-sensitive statistics for improved grammatical language models. In *Proceedings of the National Conference on AI*, 728–733.

Charniak, E. 1993. *Statistical Language Learning*. Cambridge, MA: MIT Press.

Chou, P. 1989. Recognition of equations using a two-dimensional stochastic context-free grammar. In *Proceedings SPIE, Visual Communications and Image Processing IV*, 852–863.

Earley, J. 1970. An efficient context-free parsing algorithm. *Communications of the Association for Computing Machinery* 13(2):94–102.

Gonzalez, R. C., and Thomason, M. S. 1978. *Syntactic pattern recognition: An introduction*. Reading, MA: Addison-Wesley Publishing Company. 177–215.

Jelinek, F.; Lafferty, J. D.; and Mercer, R. 1992. Basic methods of probabilistic context free grammars. In Laface, P., and DeMori, R., eds., *Speech Recognition and Understanding*. Berlin: Springer. 345–360.

Ney, H. 1992. Stochastic grammars and pattern recognition. In Laface, P., and DeMori, R., eds., *Speech Recognition and Understanding*. Berlin: Springer. 319–344.

Pearl, J. 1987. *Probabilistic Reasoning in Intelligent Systems: Networks of Plausible Inference*. San Mateo, CA: Morgan Kaufmann.

Pynadath, D. V., and Wellman, M. P. 1995. Accounting for context in plan recognition, with application to traffic monitoring. In *Proceedings of the Conference on Uncertainty in AI*, 472–481.

Sakakibara, Y.; Brown, M.; Underwood, R. C.; Mian, I. S.; and Haussler, D. 1995. Stochastic context-free grammars for modeling RNA. In *Proceedings of the 27th Hawaii International Conference on System Sciences*, 284–293.

Vilain, M. 1990. Getting serious about parsing plans: A grammatical analysis of plan recognition. In *Proceedings of the National Conference on AI*, 190–197.

Wetherell, C. S. 1980. Probabilistic languages: a review and some open questions. *Comp. Surveys* 12(4):361–379.

Younger, D. 1967. Recognition and parsing of context-free languages in time n^3. *Info. and Control* 10(2):189–208.

On the Foundations of Qualitative Decision Theory

Ronen I. Brafman
Computer Science Department
University of British Columbia
Vancouver, B.C., Canada V6T 1Z4
brafman@cs.ubc.ca

Moshe Tennenholtz
Faculty of Industrial Engineering and Mgmt.
Technion – Israel Institute of Technology
Haifa 32000, Israel
moshet@ie.technion.ac.il

Abstract

This paper investigates the foundation of *maximin*, one of the central qualitative decision criteria, using the approach taken by Savage (Savage 1972) to investigate the foundation and rationality of classical decision theory. This approach asks "which behaviors could result from the use of a particular decision procedure?" The answer to this question provides two important insights: (1) under what conditions can we employ a particular agent model, and (2) how rational is a particular decision procedure. Our main result is a constructive representation theorem in the spirit of Savage's result for expected utility maximization, which uses two choice axioms to characterize the *maximin* criterion. These axioms characterize agent behaviors that can be modeled compactly using the *maximin* model, and, with some reservations, indicate that *maximin* is a reasonable decision criterion.

Introduction

Decision theory plays an important role in fields such as statistics, economics, game-theory, and industrial engineering. More recently, the realization that decision making is a central task of artificial agents has led to much interest in this area within the artificial intelligence research community. Some of the more recent work on decision theory in AI concentrates on qualitative decision making tools. For example, Boutilier (Boutilier 1994) and Tan and Pearl (Tan & Pearl 1994) examine semantics and specification tools for qualitative decision makers, while Darwiche and Goldszmidt (Darwiche & Goldszmidt 1994) experiment with qualitative probabilistic reasoning in diagnostics.

There are two major reasons for this interest in qualitative tools. One reason is computational efficiency: one hopes that qualitative tools, because of their simplicity, will lead to faster algorithms. Another reason is a simpler knowledge acquisition process: often, qualitative information is easier to obtain from experts and layman. However, while there is abundant work on the foundations of quantitative approaches to decision making, usually based on the principle of expected utility maximization (e.g.,(Savage 1972; Anscombe & Aumann 1963; Blum, Brandenburger, & Dekel 1991; Kreps 1988; Hart, Modica, & Schmeidler 1994)), we are aware of very little work on the foundations of qualitative methods.[1]

Work on the foundations of decision theory is motivated by two major applications: agent modeling and decision making. Agent modeling is often the main concern of economists and game-theorists; they ask: under what assumptions can we model an agent as if it were using a particular decision procedure? In artificial intelligence, we share this concern in various areas, most notably in multi-agent systems, where agents must represent and reason about other agents. Decision making is often the main concern of statisticians, decision analysts, and engineers. They ask: how should we model our state of information? And how should we choose our actions? The relevance of this question to AI researchers is obvious. The foundational approach helps answer these questions by describing the basic principles that underlie various decision procedures.

One of the most important foundational results in the area of classical decision theory is Savage's theorem (Savage 1972), described by Kreps (Kreps 1988) as the "crowning achievement" of choice theory. Savage provides a number of conditions on an agent's preference among actions. Under these conditions, the agent's choices can be described as stemming from the use of probabilities to describe her state of information, utilities to describe her preferences over action outcomes, and the use of expected utility maximization to choose her actions. For example, one of Savage's postulates, the *sure-thing principle*, roughly states that: if

[1] An interesting related work is the axiomatic approach taken by Dubois and Prade (Dubois & Prade 1995), which proves the existence of a utility function representing a preference ordering among possibility distributions. Many axiom systems that are weaker than Savage's appear in (Fishburn 1988), but we are not aware of any that resemble ours.

an agent prefers action a over b given that the possible worlds are s_1 and s_2, and she prefers a over b when the possible worlds are s_3 and s_4, then she should still prefer a over b when the possible worlds are s_1, s_2, s_3 and s_4. Economists use Savage's results to understand the assumptions under which they can use probabilities and utilities as the basis for agent models; decision theorists rely on the intuitiveness of Savage's postulates to justify the use of the expected utility maximization principle.

Our aim in this paper is to initiate similar work on the foundations of qualitative decision making. Given that we have compelling practical reasons to investigate such tools, we would like to have as sound an understanding of the adequacy of qualitative decision tools as we do of the classical, quantitative tools; both for the purpose of decision making and agent modeling. Our main contribution is a representation theorem for the *maximin* decision criterion.[2] Using a setting similar to that of Savage, we provide two conditions on an agent's choice over actions under which it can be represented as a qualitative decision maker that uses *maximin* to make its choices. One of these conditions is similar to Savage's sure thing principle. It says that if an agent prefers action a over b when the possible worlds are s_1 and s_2 and she prefers a over b when her possible worlds are s_2 and s_3, then she still prefers a over b when the possible worlds are s_1, s_2 and s_3. The other condition is more technical, and we defer its presentation to Section 4.

Beyond qualitative decision theory, the results presented in this paper have another interesting interpretation: There are different ways in which we can encode an agent's behavior (or program). One simple manner is as an explicit mapping from the agent's local state to actions. This is often highly inefficient in terms of space. Alternative, implicit, representations are often used if we desire to cut down on program storage or transmission costs. Probabilities and utilities and their qualitative counterparts can be used to obtain a compact, albeit implicit, representation of programs. Our (constructive) results characterize a class of agent programs that can be represented in $O(n \log n)$ space, where n is the number of states of the world. This is to be contrasted with a possibly exponential explicit representation.

In Section 2 we define a model of a situated agent and two alternative representations for its program or behavior. One is a simple policy that maps an agent's state of information to actions, while the other represents the agent's program (or behavior) implicitly using the *maximin* decision criterion. Our aim is to present conditions under which policies can be represented implicitly using the *maximin* criterion. This will be carried out in two steps: In Section 3 we discuss the case of an agent which has to decide among two actions in various states, while in Section 4 we consider the case where the agent has any finite number of actions to choose from. Proofs of these results, which are constructive, are omitted due to space constraints. Section 5 concludes with a discussion of some issues raised by our results and a short summary.

[2](Hart, Modica, & Schmeidler 1994) presents an axiomatization for maximin in the context of 2-person zero-sum games. However, their axiomatization is probabilistic, and does not fit the framework of qualitative decision theory.

The Basic Model

In this section, we define a fairly standard agent model and the concept of a policy, which describes the agent's behavior. Then, we suggest one manner for implicitly representing (some) policies using the concept of utility and the decision criterion *maximin*.

Definition 1 *States is a finite set of possible states of the world. An* agent *is a pair of sets, (LocalStates, Actions), which are called, respectively, the agent's set of* local states *and* actions.

PW : LocalStates $\rightarrow 2^{States} \setminus \emptyset$ *is the function describing the set of world states consistent with every local state. PW satisfies the following conditions: (1)* $PW(l) = PW(l')$ *iff* $l = l'$, *and (2) For each subset S of States, there exists some* $l \in$ *LocalStates such that* $PW(l) = S$.

Each state in the set *States* describes one possible state of the world, or the agent's environment. This description does not tell us about the internal state of the agent (e.g., the content of its registers). These internal states are described by elements of the set of local states. Intuitively, local states correspond to the agent's possible states of information, or its *knowledge* (see (Fagin *et al.* 1995; Rosenschein 1985)). In addition to a set of possible local states, the agent has a set *Actions* of actions. One can view these actions as the basic control signals the agent can send to its actuators.

With every local state $l \in$ *LocalStates* we associate a subset $PW(l)$ of *States*, understood as the possible states of the world consistent with the agent's information at l. That is, $s \in PW(l)$ iff the agent can be in local state l when the current state of the world is s. In fact, in this paper we identify l with $PW(l)$ and use both interchangeably. Hence, we require that $l = l'$ iff $PW(l) = PW(l')$ and that for every $S \subseteq States$ there exists some $l \in$ *LocalStates* such that $PW(l) = S$.

Like other popular models of decision making (e.g., (Savage 1972; Anscombe & Aumann 1963)), our model considers one-shot decision making. The agent starts at some initial state of information and chooses one of its possible actions based on its current state of information (i.e., its local state); this function is called the agent's *policy* (see also *protocol* (Fagin *et al.* 1995) and *strategy* (Luce & Raiffa 1957)). This policy maps each state of information of the agent into an action.

Definition 2 *A* policy *for agent* $(LocalStates, Actions)$ *is a function* $\mathcal{P} : LocalStates \rightarrow Actions$.

A naive description of the policy as an explicit mapping between local states and actions is exponentially large in the number of possible worlds because $|LocalStates| = 2^{|States|}$. Requiring a designer to supply this mapping explicitly is unrealistic. Hence, a method for implicitly specifying policies is desirable. In particular, we would like a specification method that helps us judge the quality of a policy. Classical decision theory provides one such manner: the policy is implicitly specified using a probability assignment pr over the set $States$ and a real valued utility function u over a set O of action outcomes. The action to be performed at local state l is obtained using the principle of expected utility maximization:

$$argmax_{a\in Actions}\{\sum_{s\in PW(l)} pr(s)\cdot u(a(s))\}$$

where $a(s)$ is the outcome of action a when the state of the world is s. We wish to present a different, more qualitative representation. We will not use a probability function, and our utility function $u(\cdot,\cdot)$ takes both the state of the world and the action as its arguments and returns some value in a totally pre-ordered set. (Notice the use of qualitative, rather than quantitative representation of utilities.) For convenience, we will use integers to denote the relative positions of elements within this set. In our representation, the agent's action in a local state l is defined as:

$$argmax_{a\in Actions}\{\min_{s\in PW(l)}(u(a,s))\}.$$

That is, the agent takes the action whose worst-case utility is maximal. *Maximin* is a qualitative decision criterion that seems well-tailored to risk-averse agents.

Definition 3 *A policy* $\mathcal{P}$ *has a* maximin representation *if there exists a utility function on States × Actions such that for every* $l \in LocalStates$

$$\mathcal{P}(l) = argmax_{a\in Actions}\{\min_{s\in PW(l)}(u(a,s))\}.$$

That is, $\mathcal{P}$ has a *maximin* representation if for every local state l, an agent with this utility function that makes her decision by applying *maximin* to the utilities of actions in $PW(l)$, would choose the action $\mathcal{P}(l)$.

Given an arbitrary agent and a policy $\mathcal{P}$ adopted by the agent, it is unclear whether this policy has a *maximin* representation. It is the goal of this paper to characterize the class of policies that have this representation. From this result, we can learn about the conditions under which we can use the *maximin* representation to model agents and understand the rationality of using *maximin* as a decision criterion. Unlike the exponential naive representation of policies, the *maximin* representation requires only $O(logM \cdot |States| \cdot |Actions|)$ space, where $M = \max_{a,a'\in Actions;s,s'\in States}|u(a,s) - u(a',s')|$.

Representing Binary Decisions

This section presents two representation theorems for *maximin* for agents with two possible actions. We start by describing a basic property of *maximin* representable policies.

Definition 4 *We say that a policy* $\mathcal{P}$ *is* closed under union *if* $\mathcal{P}(U) = \mathcal{P}(W)$ *implies* $\mathcal{P}(U \cup W) = \mathcal{P}(U)$, *where* $U, W \subseteq States$.

That is, suppose that the agent would take the same action a when its local state is l or l', and let $\hat{l}$ be the local state in which the agent considers possible all worlds that are possible in l and in l'. That is $PW(\hat{l}) = PW(l) \cup PW(l')$. If the agent's policy is closed under unions, it would choose the action a at $\hat{l}$.

For example, suppose that our agent is instructed to bring coffee when it knows that the weather is cold or warm and when it knows that the weather is warm or hot. If all the agent knows is that the weather is cold, warm, or hot, it should still bring coffee if its policy is closed under unions. This sounds perfectly reasonable. Consider another example: Alex likes Swiss chocolate, but dislikes all other chocolates. He finds an unmarked chocolate bar and must decide whether or not he should eat it. His policy is such that, if he knows that this chocolate is Swiss or American, he will eat it; if he knows that this bar is Swiss or French, he will eat it as well. If Alex's policy is closed under unions, he will eat this bar even if he knows it must be Swiss, French, or American.

Our first representation theorem for *maximin* shows that policies containing two possible actions that are closed under unions are representable using a utility function defined on *Actions* and *States*.

Theorem 1 *Let* $\mathcal{P}$ *be a policy assigning only one of two possible actions at each local state, and assume that* $\mathcal{P}$ *is closed under union. Then,* $\mathcal{P}$ *is maximin representable.*

Notice that this corresponds to a completeness claim, while soundness, which implies that the above conditions hold for *maximin*, is easily verified.

The following example illustrates our result.

Example 1 *Consider the following policy (or precondition for wearing a sweater) in which Y stands for "wear a sweater" and N stands for "do not wear a sweater".*

{cold}	{ok}	{hot}	{c,o}	{c,h}	{o,h}	{c,o,h}
Y	N	N	Y	N	N	N

It is easy to verify that this policy is closed under unions. For example, the sweater is not worn when the weather is ok or when the weather is either hot or cold, hence it is not worn when there is no information at all, i.e., the weather is either cold, ok, or hot.

Using the proof of Theorem 1 we construct the following utility function representing the policy above:

	cold	*ok*	*hot*
Y	*3*	*2*	*0*
N	*1*	*3*	*3*

A slight generalization of this theorem allows for policies in which the agent is indifferent between the two available choices. In the two action case discussed here, we capture such indifference by assigning both actions at a local state, e.g., $\mathcal{P}(l) = \{a, a'\}$. Hence we treat the policy as assigning sets of actions rather than actions. We refer to such policies as set-valued policies, or *s*-policies. Closure under union is defined in this context as follows:

Definition 5 *An s-policy $\mathcal{P}$ is* closed under unions *if for every pair of local states $U, W \subseteq States$, $\mathcal{P}(U \cup W)$ is either $\mathcal{P}(W), \mathcal{P}(U)$, or $\mathcal{P}(U) \cup \mathcal{P}(W)$.*

We require a number of additional definitions before we can proceed with the representation theorem for *s*-policies. First, we define two binary relationships on subsets of *States*:

Definition 6 *$U >_{\mathcal{P}} W$, where $U, W \subseteq States$, if $\mathcal{P}(U \cup W) = \mathcal{P}(U)$ and $\mathcal{P}(U) \neq \mathcal{P}(W)$. $U =_{\mathcal{P}} W$, where $U, W \subseteq States$, if $\mathcal{P}(U), \mathcal{P}(W)$ and $\mathcal{P}(U \cup W)$ are all different.*

That is $U >_{\mathcal{P}} W$ tells us that the preferred action in U is preferred in $U \cup W$. $U =_{\mathcal{P}} W$ is basically equivalent to $U \not>_{\mathcal{P}} W$ and $W \not>_{\mathcal{P}} U$. Next, we define a condition on these relations which closely resembles transitivity.

Definition 7 *We say that $>_{\mathcal{P}}$ is* transitive-like *if whenever $U_1 *_1 \cdots *_{k-1} U_k$, where $*_j \in \{>_{\mathcal{P}}, =_{\mathcal{P}}\}$, and $\mathcal{P}(U_1) \neq \mathcal{P}(U_k)$, we have that $U_1 * U_k$. Here, $*$ is $>_{\mathcal{P}}$ if any of the $*_i$ are $>_{\mathcal{P}}$, and it is $=_{\mathcal{P}}$ otherwise.*

Finally, we say that $\mathcal{P}$ respects domination if the action assigned to the union of a number of sets does not depend on those sets that are dominated by other sets w.r.t. $>_{\mathcal{P}}$.

Definition 8 *We say that $\mathcal{P}$* respects domination *if for all $W, U, V \subseteq States$ we have that $W >_{\mathcal{P}} U$ implies that $\mathcal{P}(W \cup U \cup V) = \mathcal{P}(W \cup V)$.*

We have the following representation theorem for *s*-policies:

Theorem 2 *Let $\mathcal{P}$ be an s-policy for an agent (LocalStates, Actions) such that (1) $|Actions| = \{a, a'\}$, (2) $\mathcal{P}$ is closed under unions, (2) $\mathcal{P}$ respects domination, (4) $>_{\mathcal{P}}$ is transitive-like. Then, $\mathcal{P}$ is maximin representable.*

A General Existence Theorem

In the previous section we provided representation theorems for a class of policies in which the agent chooses between two actions. We would like to generalize these results to represent choice among an arbitrary set of actions. We will assume that, rather than a single most preferred action, the agent has a total order over the set of actions associated with each local state. This total order can be understood as telling us what the agent would do should its first choice became unavailable. The corresponding representation using *maximin* will tell us not only which action is most preferred, but also, which action is preferred to which.

Definition 9 *A* generalized policy *for an agent (LocalStates, Actions) is a function $\mathcal{P}$: LocalStates $\rightarrow$ TO(Actions), where TO(Actions) is the set of total orders on Actions.*

Generalized policy $\mathcal{P}$ is maximin representable *if there exists a utility function $u(\cdot,\cdot)$ on States $\times$ Actions such that a is preferred to a' in local state l according to $\mathcal{P}(l)$ iff*

$$\min_{s \in PW(l)} (u(a, s)) > \min_{s \in PW(l)} (u(a', s))$$

for every pair of actions $a, a' \in Actions$ and for every local state $l \in LocalStates$.

The generalization of closure under unions to generalized policies is not a sufficient condition on policies for obtaining a *maximin* representation. The following definition introduces an additional property needed:

Definition 10 *Let $\{\succ_W \mid W \subseteq S\}$, be a set of total orders over Actions. Given $s, s' \in States$ and $a, a' \in Actions$, we write $(s, a) < (s', a')$ if (1) $a' \succ_s a$, $a \succ_{s'} a'$, and $a' \succ_{\{s,s'\}} a$; or (2) $s = s'$ and $a' \succ_s a$. We say that $<$ is* transitive-like *if whenever $(s_1, a_1) < (s_2, a_2) < \cdots < (s_k, a_k)$ and either (1)*

s	s'	$s \cup s'$
a'	a	a'
a	a'	a

	s	s'
a	1	3
a'	3	2

Figure 1: $(s, a) < (s', a')$

$a_k \succ_{s_1} a_1$ *and* $a_1 \succ_{s_k} a_k$ *or (2)* $s_1 = s_k$, *then* $(s_1, a_1) < (s_k, a_k)$.

The left table in Figure 1 helps us clarify this definition. In it, we depict the conditions under which $(s, a) < (s', a')$ holds. There are three columns in this table, each showing the agent's preference relation over actions in different local states. The possible worlds in these local states are s, s', and $\{s, s'\}$. In s the agent prefers a' over a, in s' it prefers a over a', but when all the agent knows is that the world is either in state s or s', it prefers a' over a. Roughly, we can say that $(s, a) < (s', a')$ if the agent dislikes taking action a in state s more than it dislikes taking action a' in state s'.

The following example illustrates the transitivity-like condition.

Example 2 *Suppose that there are three possible states of the world: snowing and cold, raining and cold, neither and warm. I prefer skiing to walking when it is snowing, but prefer walking to skiing when it is raining. However, when I am uncertain about whether it will rain or snow, I'd choose to walk. In this case* $(ski, rain) < (walk, snow)$. *I prefer skiing to jogging when it is warm, and I prefer jogging to skiing when it is raining. However, I really dislike jogging when it is not cold, so I prefer skiing to jogging if I am uncertain whether it is warm or snowing. Hence* $(jog, warm) < (ski, rain)$. *Suppose that, in addition, I prefer walking to jogging when it is warm, and I prefer jogging to walking when it snows. The transitivity-like condition implies that* $(jog, warm) < (walk, snow)$, *and hence I'd prefer walking to jogging if I am uncertain whether it will be warm or it will snow. This seems quite plausible.*

Theorem 3 *Let Actions be an arbitrary set of actions, and let* $\succ_W$, *for every* $W \subseteq S$, *be a total order over Actions such that*

1. *if* $a \succ_W a'$ *and* $a \succ_V a'$ *then* $a \succ_{W \cup V} a'$, *and*
2. $<$ *is transitive-like.*

Then, $\{\succ_W \mid W \subseteq S\}$ *is maximin representable.*

Again, it is easy to see that a preference relation based on *maximin* will have the properties described in this theorem, and this result can be viewed as a sound and complete characterization of the *maximin* criterion for total orders. In addition, this theorem characterizes a class of policies that can be represented using $O(n \cdot log(n))$ space in contrast with the exponentially large naive representation.

Discussion

Decision theory is clearly relevant to AI, and there is little doubt about the need for decision making techniques that are more designer friendly and have nice computational properties. Qualitative decision procedures could offer such an alternative, but the question is: how rational are they? One method of addressing this question is experimentation, as in (Darwiche & Goldszmidt 1994). However, the prominent approach for understanding and justifying the rationality of decision criteria has been the axiomatic approach. This approach characterizes the properties of a decision criterion in a general, domain independent manner. Given a particular domain of application, we can assess the rationality of employing a particular decision criterion using its characteristic properties. Our work provides one of a few results within the axiomatic approach that deals with qualitative decision criteria and helps us understand the inherent properties of *maximin*, assess the rationality of using *maximin*, and understand the conditions under which an arbitrary agent can be modeled *as if* it were a qualitative decision maker.

In classical decision theory, the agent has both a utility function and a probability function. In our representation theorems, the emphasis has been on utilities rather than beliefs. The agent's state of information is modeled by means of the set of worlds consistent with its current local state, $PW(l)$. Most authors (e.g., (Fagin *et al.* 1995)) regard this set as representing the agent's knowledge, rather than belief. However, the concept of belief can be incorporated into this model by imposing additional structure on the set *States* in the form of a ranking function. This model has been suggested by e.g., (Brafman & Tennenholtz 1994; Friedman & Halpern 1994; Lamarre & Shoham 1994). Given a ranking function $r : States \to N$, we define the agent's beliefs at local state l as:

$$B(l) = \{s \in PW(l) \mid s' \in PW(l) \text{ implies } r(s) \leq r(s')\}.$$

$B(l)$ are often called the agent's *plausible* states at the local state l. We can modify *maximin* by applying it to the plausible states, instead of the possible states (see, e.g.,(Brafman & Tennenholtz 1994)). That is, at state l the agent chooses

$$argmax_{a \in Actions}\{\min_{s \in B(l)} u(a, s)\}.$$

A similar approach is taken in (Boutilier 1994; Tan & Pearl 1994)).

Clearly, any behavior that is *maximin* representable can be represented using the ranked *maximin* representation suggested above. (We would use a ranking function that maps all states to the same integer). We can show that the converse is true as well. That is, if an agent can be represented as using ranked *maximin* it can also be represented as using the standard *maximin* approach discussed in this paper; a formal proof is deferred to the full paper. Therefore, the ranked *maximin* representation is no more expressive than our standard maximin representation, i.e., it can capture the same set of behaviors. Hence, ranked *maximin* is not, *a priori*, a more rational decision criterion.

Our work differs from most other foundational work in decision theory in its definition of the utility function. We define utilities as a function of both the agent's action and the state of the world. Savage, and many others, define the notion of an *outcome*, i.e., a description of the state of the world following the performance of an action. In these works, utilities are a function of outcomes. Savage defines actions as mappings between states and outcomes, and it is possible to obtain the same outcome when two different actions are performed in two different states of the world. Our approach is motivated by the fact that, in practice, an agent chooses an action, not an outcome. That is, the only physically observable aspect of the agent's behavior is its choice of action, e.g., the control signal it sends to its actuators. The outcome of these actions is not directly chosen by the agent. Our representation is identical to the standard representation if it is assumed that the outcomes of different actions on different states are different. Moreover, using utility functions that depend on both the state and the action makes practical sense in our qualitative context: it is reasonable when the manner in which the outcome was received is important, e.g., the cost of an action, and it allows us to use the utility function to encode both the desirability of the action's outcomes and the likelihood of the state in which it is obtained. Nevertheless, obtaining representation theorems for *maximin* in the more standard framework is an interesting challenge.

Acknowledgments: Comments from Joe Halpern, Daniel Lehmann, and the anonymous referees provided much help in improving the content and presentation of this paper. We thank Ehud Kalai, Dov Monderer, and Ariel Rubinstein for useful comments and pointers to related work in other disciplines.

References

Anscombe, F. J., and Aumann, R. J. 1963. A definition of subjective probability. *Annals of Mathematical Statistics* 34:199–205.

Blum, L.; Brandenburger, A.; and Dekel, E. 1991. Lexicographic probabilities and equilibrium refinements. *Econometrica* 59:61–79.

Boutilier, C. 1994. Toward a Logic for Qualitative Decision Theory. In *Proc. of the 4th Int. Conf. on Prin. of Knowledge Rep. and Reas.*, 75–86.

Brafman, R. I., and Tennenholtz, M. 1994. Belief ascription and mental-level modelling. In *Proc. of the 4th Int. Conf.. on Princ. of Knowledge Rep. and Reas.*, 87–98.

Darwiche, A., and Goldszmidt, M. 1994. On the relation between kappa calculus and probabilistic reasoning. In *Proc. 10th Conf. on Uncertainty in AI*, 145–153.

Dubois, D., and Prade, H. 1995. Possibility Theory as a Basis for Qualitative Decision Theory. In *Proc. 14th International Joint Conference on Artificial Intelligence*, 1924–1930.

Fagin, R.; Halpern, J. Y.; Moses, Y.; and Vardi, M. Y. 1995. *Reasoning about Knowledge.* MIT Press.

Fishburn, P. C. 1988. *Nonlinear Preference and Utility Theory.* Johns Hopkins University Press.

Friedman, N., and Halpern, J. Y. 1994. A knowledge-based framework for belief change. Part I: Foundations. In *Proc. of the 5th Conf. on Theoretical Aspects of Reas. About Knowledge.*

Hart, S.; Modica, S.; and Schmeidler, D. 1994. A neo bayesian foundation of the maxmin value for two-parson zero-sum games. *International Journal of Game Theory* 23:347–358.

Kreps, D. M. 1988. *Notes on the Theory of Choice.* Boulder: Westview Press.

Lamarre, P., and Shoham, Y. 1994. Knowledge, certainty, belief and conditionalization. In *Proc. of 4th Intl. Conf. on Principles of Knowledge Rep. and Reas.*

Luce, R. D., and Raiffa, H. 1957. *Games and Decisions.* New York: John Wiley & Sons.

Rosenschein, S. J. 1985. Formal Theories of Knowledge in AI and Robotics. *New Generation Computing* 3(3):345–357.

Savage, L. J. 1972. *The Foundations of Statistics.* New York: Dover Publications.

Tan, S., and Pearl, J. 1994. Specification and Evaluation of Preferences under Uncertainty. In *Proc. of the 4th Int. Conf. on Principles of Knowledge Rep. and Reas.*, 530–539.

Plausibility Measures and Default Reasoning

Nir Friedman
Stanford University
Gates Building 1A
Stanford, CA 94305-9010
nir@cs.stanford.edu

Joseph Y. Halpern
IBM Almaden Research Center
650 Harry Road
San Jose, CA 95120–6099
halpern@almaden.ibm.com

Abstract

In recent years, a number of different semantics for defaults have been proposed, such as preferential structures, ϵ-semantics, possibilistic structures, and κ-rankings, that have been shown to be characterized by the same set of axioms, known as the KLM properties (for Kraus, Lehmann, and Magidor). While this was viewed as a surprise, we show here that it is almost inevitable. We do this by giving yet another semantics for defaults that uses *plausibility measures*, a new approach to modeling uncertainty that generalize other approaches, such as probability measures, belief functions, and possibility measures. We show that all the earlier approaches to default reasoning can be embedded in the framework of plausibility. We then provide a necessary and sufficient condition on plausibilities for the KLM properties to be sound, and an additional condition necessary and sufficient for the KLM properties to be complete. These conditions are easily seen to hold for all the earlier approaches, thus explaining why they are characterized by the KLM properties.

1 Introduction

There have been many approaches to default reasoning proposed in the literature (see (Ginsberg 1987; Gabbay, Hogger, & Robinson 1993) for overviews). The recent literature has been guided by a collection of axioms that have been called the *KLM properties* (since they were discussed in (Kraus, Lehmann, & Magidor 1990)), and many of the recent approaches to default reasoning, including preferential structures (Kraus, Lehmann, & Magidor 1990; Shoham 1987), ϵ-semantics (Adams 1975; Geffner 1992b; Pearl 1989), possibilistic structures (Dubois & Prade 1991), and κ-rankings (Goldszmidt & Pearl 1992; Spohn 1987), have been shown to be characterized by these properties. This has been viewed as somewhat surprising, since these approaches seem to capture quite different intuitions. As Pearl (1989) said of the equivalence between ϵ-semantics and preferential structures, "It is remarkable that two totally different interpretations of defaults yield identical sets of conclusions and identical sets of reasoning machinery."

The goal of this paper is to explain why all these approaches are characterized by the KLM properties. Our key tool is the use of yet another approach for giving semantics to defaults, that makes use of *plausibility measures* (Friedman & Halpern 1995a). A plausibility measure associates with a set a *plausibility*, which is just an element in a partially ordered space. The only property that we require is that the plausibility of a set is at least as great as the plausibility of any of its subsets. Probability distributions, Dempster-Shafer belief functions (Shafer 1976), and possibility measures (Dubois & Prade 1990) are all easily seen to be special cases of plausibility measures. Of more interest to us here is that all the approaches that have been used to give semantics to defaults that can be characterized by the KLM properties can be embedded into the plausibility framework.

In fact, we show much more. All of these approaches can be understood as giving semantics to defaults by considering a class $\mathcal{P}$ of structures (preferential structures, possibilistic structures, etc.). A default d is then said to follow from a knowledge base Δ of defaults if all structures in $\mathcal{P}$ that satisfy Δ also satisfy d. We define a notion of *qualitative plausibility measure*, and show that the KLM properties are sound in a plausibility structure if and only if it is qualitative. Moreover, as long as a class $\mathcal{P}$ of plausibility structures satisfies a minimal richness condition, we show that the KLM properties will completely characterize default reasoning in $\mathcal{P}$. We then show that when we map preferential structures (or possibilistic structures or any of the other structures considered in the literature on defaults) into plausibility structures, we get a class of qualitative structures that is easily seen to satisfy the richness conditioning. This explains why the KLM axioms characterize default reasoning in all these frameworks. Far from being surprising that the KLM axioms are complete in all these cases, it is almost inevitable.

The KLM properties have been viewed as the "conservative core" of default reasoning (Pearl 1989), and much recent effort has been devoted to finding principled methods of going beyond KLM. Our result shows that any approach that gives semantics to defaults with respect to a collection $\mathcal{P}$ of structures will almost certainly not go beyond KLM. This result thus provides added insight into and justification for approaches such as those of (Bacchus *et al.* 1993; Geffner 1992a; Goldszmidt & Pearl 1992; Goldszmidt, Morris, & Pearl 1993; Lehmann & Magidor 1992; Pearl 1990) that, roughly speaking, say d follows from Δ if d is true in a particular structure $P_\Delta \in \mathcal{P}$ that satisfies Δ

(not necessarily all structures in $\mathcal{P}$ that satisfy Δ).

This paper is organized as follows. In Section 2, we review the relevant material from (Friedman & Halpern 1995a) on plausibility measures. In Section 3, we review the KLM properties and various approaches to default reasoning that are characterized by these properties. In Section 4, we show how the various notions of default reasoning considered in the literature can all be viewed as instances of plausibility measures. In Section 5, we define qualitative plausibility structures, show that the KLM properties are sound in a structure if and only if it is qualitative, and provide a weak richness condition that is necessary and sufficient for them to be complete. In Section 6, we discuss how plausibility measures can be used to give semantics to a full logic of conditionals, and compare this with the more traditional approach (Lewis 1973). In the full paper (Friedman & Halpern 1995b) we also consider the relationship between our approach to plausibility and *epistemic entrenchment* (Gärdenfors & Makinson 1988). We conclude in Section 7 with a discussion of other potential applications of plausibility measures.

2 Plausibility Measures

A probability space is a tuple $(W, \mathcal{F}, \mu)$, where W is a set of worlds, $\mathcal{F}$ is an algebra of *measurable* subsets of W (that is, a set of subsets closed under union and complementation to which we assign probability) and μ is a *probability measure*, that is, a function mapping each set in $\mathcal{F}$ to a number in $[0, 1]$ satisfying the well-known Kolmogorov axioms ($\mu(\emptyset) = 0$, $\mu(W) = 1$, and $\mu(A \cup B) = \mu(A) + \mu(B)$ if A and B are disjoint).

A plausibility space is a direct generalization of a probability space. We simply replace the probability measure μ by a *plausibility measure* Pl, which, rather than mapping sets in $\mathcal{F}$ to numbers in $[0, 1]$, maps them to elements in some arbitrary partially ordered set. We read $\mathrm{Pl}(A)$ as "the plausibility of set A". If $\mathrm{Pl}(A) \leq \mathrm{Pl}(B)$, then B is at least as plausible as A. Formally, a *plausibility space* is a tuple $S = (W, \mathcal{F}, \mathrm{Pl})$, where W is a set of worlds, $\mathcal{F}$ is an algebra of subsets of W, and Pl maps the sets in $\mathcal{F}$ to some set D, partially ordered by a relation $\leq_D$ (so that $\leq_D$ is reflexive, transitive, and anti-symmetric). We assume that D is *pointed*: that is, it contains two special elements $\top_D$ and $\bot_D$ such that $\bot_D \leq_D d \leq_D \top_D$ for all $d \in D$; we further assume that $\mathrm{Pl}(W) = \top_D$ and $\mathrm{Pl}(\emptyset) = \bot_D$. The only other assumption we make is

A1. If $A \subseteq B$, then $\mathrm{Pl}(A) \leq_D \mathrm{Pl}(B)$.

Thus, a set must be at least as plausible as any of its subsets.

Some brief remarks on the definition: We have deliberately suppressed the domain D from the tuple S, since the choice of D is not significant in this paper. All that matters is the ordering induced by $\leq_D$ on the subsets in $\mathcal{F}$. The algebra $\mathcal{F}$ also does not play a significant role in this paper; for our purposes, it suffices to take $\mathcal{F} = 2^W$. We have chosen to allow the generality of having an algebra of measurable sets to make it clear that plausibility spaces generalize probability spaces. For ease of exposition, we omit the $\mathcal{F}$ from here on in, always taking it to be 2^W, and just denote a plausibility space as a pair (W, Pl). As usual, we define the ordering $<_D$ by taking $d_1 <_D d_2$ if $d_1 \leq_D d_2$ and $d_1 \neq d_2$. We omit the subscript S from $\leq_D$, $<_D$, $\top_D$ and $\bot_D$ whenever it is clear from context.

Clearly plausibility spaces generalize probability spaces. We now briefly discuss a few other notions of uncertainty that they generalize:

- A *belief function Bel* on W is a function $Bel : 2^W \rightarrow [0, 1]$ satisfying certain axioms (Shafer 1976). These axioms certainly imply property A1, so a belief function is a plausibility measure.
- A *fuzzy measure* (or a *Sugeno measure*) f on W (Wang & Klir 1992) is a function $f : 2^W \mapsto [0, 1]$, that satisfies A1 and some continuity constraints. A *possibility measure* (Dubois & Prade 1990) Poss is a fuzzy measure such that $\mathrm{Poss}(W) = 1$, $\mathrm{Poss}(\emptyset) = 0$, and $\mathrm{Poss}(A) = \sup_{w \in A}(\mathrm{Poss}(\{w\})$.
- An *ordinal ranking* (or *κ-ranking*) κ on W (as defined by (Goldszmidt & Pearl 1992), based on ideas that go back to (Spohn 1987)) is a function mapping subsets of W to $\mathbb{N}^* = \mathbb{N} \cup \{\infty\}$ such that $\kappa(W) = 0$, $\kappa(\emptyset) = \infty$, and $\kappa(A) = \min_{w \in A}(\kappa(\{w\}))$. Intuitively, an ordinal ranking assigns a degree of surprise to each subset of worlds in W, where 0 means unsurprising and higher numbers denote greater surprise. It is easy to see that if κ is a ranking on W, then (W, κ) is a plausibility space, where $x \leq_{\mathbb{N}^*} y$ if and only if $y \leq x$ under the usual ordering on the ordinals.
- A *preference ordering* on W is a partial order $\prec$ over W (Kraus, Lehmann, & Magidor 1990; Shoham 1987). Intuitively, $w \prec w'$ holds if w is *preferred* to w'.[1] Preference orders have been used to provide semantics for *default* (i.e., conditional) statements. In Section 4 we show how to map preference orders on W to plausibility measures on W in a way that preserves the ordering of events of the form $\{w\}$ as well as the truth values of defaults.
- A *parametrized probability distribution* (PPD) on W is a sequence $\{\mathrm{Pr}_i : i \geq 0\}$ of probability measures over W. Such structures provide semantics for defaults in *ϵ-semantics* (Pearl 1989; Goldszmidt, Morris, & Pearl 1993). In Section 4 we show how to map PPDs into plausibility structures in a way that preserves the truth-values of conditionals.

Plausibility structures are motivated by much the same concerns as two other recent symbolic generalizations of probability by Darwiche (1992) and Weydert (1994). Their approaches have a great deal more structure though. They start with a domain D and several algebraic operations that have properties similar to the usual arithmetic operations (e.g., addition and multiplication) over $[0, 1]$. The result

[1] We follow the standard notation for preference here (Lewis 1973; Kraus, Lehmann, & Magidor 1990), which uses the (perhaps confusing) convention of placing the more likely world on the left of the $\prec$ operator.

is an algebraic structure over the domain D that satisfies various properties. Their structures are also general enough to capture all of the examples above except preferential orderings. These orderings cannot be captured precisely because of the additional structure. Moreover, as we shall see, by starting with very little structure and adding just what we need, we can sometimes bring to light issues that may be obscured in richer frameworks. We refer the interested reader to (Friedman & Halpern 1995a) for a more detailed comparison to (Darwiche 1992; Weydert 1994).

3 Approaches to Default Reasoning: A Review

Defaults are statements of the form "if φ then typically/likely/by default ψ", which we denote $\varphi \rightarrow \psi$. For example, the default "birds typically fly" is represented $Bird \rightarrow Fly$. There has been a great deal of discussion in the literature as to what the appropriate semantics of defaults should be, and what new defaults should by entailed by a knowledge base of defaults. For the most part, we do not get into these issues here. While there has been little consensus on what the "right" semantics for defaults should be, there has been some consensus on a reasonable "core" of inference rules for default reasoning. This core, known as the KLM properties, was suggested by (Kraus, Lehmann, & Magidor 1990), and consists of the following axiom and rules of inference (where we use $\Rightarrow$ to denote material implication):

LLE. From $\varphi \Leftrightarrow \varphi'$ and $\varphi \rightarrow \psi$ infer $\varphi' \rightarrow \psi$ (left logical equivalence)

RW. From $\psi \Rightarrow \psi'$ and $\varphi \rightarrow \psi$ infer $\varphi \rightarrow \psi'$ (right weakening)

REF. $\varphi \rightarrow \varphi$ (reflexivity)

AND. From $\varphi \rightarrow \psi_1$ and $\varphi \rightarrow \psi_2$ infer $\varphi \rightarrow \psi_1 \wedge \psi_2$

OR. From $\varphi_1 \rightarrow \psi$ and $\varphi_2 \rightarrow \psi$ infer $\varphi_1 \vee \varphi_2 \rightarrow \psi$

CM. From $\varphi \rightarrow \psi_1$ and $\varphi \rightarrow \psi_2$ infer $\varphi \wedge \psi_1 \rightarrow \psi_2$ (cautious monotonicity)

LLE states that the syntactic form of the antecedent is irrelevant. Thus, if φ_1 and φ_2 are equivalent, we can deduce $\varphi_2 \rightarrow \psi$ from $\varphi_1 \rightarrow \psi$. RW describes a similar property of the consequent: If ψ (logically) entails ψ', then we can deduce $\varphi \rightarrow \psi'$ from $\varphi \rightarrow \psi$. This allows us to can combine default and logical reasoning. REF states that φ is always a default conclusion of φ. AND states that we can combine two default conclusions: If we can conclude by default both ψ_1 and ψ_2 from φ, we can also conclude $\psi_1 \wedge \psi_2$ from φ. OR states that we are allowed to reason by cases: If the same default conclusion follows from each of two antecedents, then it also follows from their disjunction. CM states that if ψ_1 and ψ_2 are two default conclusions of φ, then discovering that ψ_1 holds when φ holds (as would be expected, given the default) should not cause us to retract the default conclusion ψ_2.

This system of rules is called system **P** in (Kraus, Lehmann, & Magidor 1990). The notation $\Delta \vdash_{\mathbf{P}} \varphi \rightarrow \psi$ denotes that $\varphi \rightarrow \psi$ can be deduced from Δ using these inference rules.

There are a number of well-known semantics for defaults that are characterized by these rules. We sketch a few of them here, referring the reader to the original references for further details and motivation. All of these semantics involve structures of the form (W, X, π), where W is a set of possible worlds, $\pi(w)$ is a truth assignment to primitive propositions, and X is some "measure" on W such as a preference ordering, a κ-ranking, or a possibility measure. We define a little notation that will simplify the discussion below. Given a structure (W, X, π), we take $[\![\varphi]\!] \subseteq W$ to be the set of of worlds satisfying φ, i.e., $[\![\varphi]\!] = \{w \in W : \pi(w)(\varphi) = \mathbf{true}\}$.

The first semantic proposal was provided by Kraus, Lehmann and Magidor (1990), using ideas that go back to (Lewis 1973; Shoham 1987). Recall that a preference ordering on W is partial order (i.e., irreflexive and transitive relation) $\prec$ over W. A *preferential structure* is a tuple $(W, \prec, \pi)$, where $\prec$ is a partial order on W.[2] The intuition (Shoham 1987) is that a preferential structure satisfies a conditional $\varphi \rightarrow \psi$ if all the the most preferred worlds (i.e., the minimal worlds according to $\prec$) in $[\![\varphi]\!]$ satisfy ψ. However, there may be no minimal worlds in $[\![\varphi]\!]$. This can happen if $[\![\varphi]\!]$ contains an infinite descending sequence $\ldots \prec w_2 \prec w_1$. What do we do in these structures? There are a number of options: the first is to assume that, for each formula φ, there are minimal worlds in $[\![\varphi]\!]$; this is the assumption actually made in (Kraus, Lehmann, & Magidor 1990), where it is called the *smoothness* assumption. A yet more general definition—one that works even if $\prec$ is not smooth—is given in (Lewis 1973; Boutilier 1994). Roughly speaking, $\varphi \rightarrow \psi$ is true if, from a certain point on, whenever φ is true, so is ψ. More formally,

> $(W, \prec, \pi)$ satisfies $\varphi \rightarrow \psi$, if for every world $w_1 \in [\![\varphi]\!]$, there is a world w_2 such that (a) $w_2 \preceq w_1$ (so that w_2 is at least as normal as w_1), (b) $w_2 \in [\![\varphi \wedge \psi]\!]$, and (c) for all worlds $w_3 \prec w_2$, we have $w_3 \in [\![\varphi \Rightarrow \psi]\!]$ (so any world more normal than w_2 that satisfies φ also satisfies ψ).

It is easy to verify that this definition is equivalent to the earlier one if $\prec$ is smooth. A knowledge-base Δ *preferentially entails* $\varphi \rightarrow \psi$, denoted $\Delta \models_{\mathrm{P}} \varphi \rightarrow \psi$, if every preferential structure that satisfies (all the defaults in) Δ also satisfies $\varphi \rightarrow \psi$.

Lehmann and Magidor show that preferential entailment is characterized by system **P**.

[2] We note that the formal definition of preferential structures in (Kraus, Lehmann, & Magidor 1990; Lehmann & Magidor 1992) is slightly more complex. Kraus, Lehmann, and Magidor distinguish between *states* and *worlds*. In their definition, a preferential structure is an ordering over states together with a labeling function that maps states to worlds. They take worlds to be truth assignments to primitive propositions. Our worlds thus correspond to states in their terminology, since we allow two worlds $w \neq w'$ such that $\pi(w) = \pi(w')$. Despite these minor differences, all the results that we prove for our version of preferential structures hold (with almost no change in proof) for theirs.

Theorem 3.1: (Lehmann & Magidor 1992; Boutilier 1994) $\Delta \models_p \varphi \rightarrow \psi$ *if and only if* $\Delta \vdash_{\mathbf{P}} \varphi \rightarrow \psi$.

Thus, reasoning with preferential structures corresponds in a precise sense to reasoning with the core properties of default reasoning.

As we mentioned earlier, we usually want to add additional inferences to those sanctioned by the core. Lehmann and Magidor (1992) hoped to do so by limiting attention to a special class of preferential structures. A preferential structure $(W, \prec, \pi)$ is *rational* if $\prec$ is a *modular* order, so that for all worlds $u, v, w \in W$, if $w \prec v$, then either $u \prec v$ or $w \prec u$. It is not hard to show that modularity implies that possible worlds are clustered into equivalence classes, each class consisting of worlds that are incomparable to one another, with these classes being totally ordered. Thus, rational structures form a "well-behaved" subset of preferential structures. Unfortunately, Lehmann and Magidor showed that restricting to rational structures gives no additional properties (at least, as far as the limited language of defaults is concerned). We say that a knowledge base Δ *rationally entails* $\varphi \rightarrow \psi$, denoted $\Delta \models_r \varphi \rightarrow \psi$, if every rational structure that satisfies Δ also satisfies $\varphi \rightarrow \psi$.[3]

Theorem 3.2: (Lehmann & Magidor 1992) $\Delta \models_r \varphi \rightarrow \psi$ *if and only if* $\Delta \vdash_{\mathbf{P}} \varphi \rightarrow \psi$.

Thus, we do not gain any new patterns of default inference when we restrict our attention to rational structures.

Pearl (1989) considers a semantics for defaults grounded in probability, using an approach due to Adams (1975). In this approach, a default $\varphi \rightarrow \psi$ denotes that $\Pr(\psi \mid \varphi)$ is extremely high, i.e., almost 1. Roughly speaking, a collection Δ of defaults implies a default $\varphi \rightarrow \psi$ if we can ensure that $\Pr(\varphi|\psi)$ is arbitrarily close to 1, by taking the probabilities of the defaults in Δ to be sufficiently high.

The formal definition needs a bit of machinery.[4] Recall that a PPD on W is a sequence $\{\Pr_i : i \geq 0\}$ of probability measures over W. A *PPD structure* is a tuple $(W, \{\Pr_i : i \geq 0\}, \pi)$, where $\{\Pr_i\}$ is PPD on W. Intuitively, it satisfies a conditional $\varphi \rightarrow \psi$ if the conditional probability ψ given φ goes to 1 in the limit. Formally, $\varphi \rightarrow \psi$ is satisfied if $\lim_{i \rightarrow \infty} \Pr_i([\![\psi]\!] | [\![\psi]\!]) = 1$ (Goldszmidt, Morris, & Pearl 1993) (where $\Pr_i([\![\psi]\!] | [\![\varphi]\!])$ is taken to be 1 if $\Pr_i([\![\varphi]\!]) = 0$). Δ *ϵ-entails* $\varphi \rightarrow \psi$, denoted $\Delta \models_\epsilon \varphi \rightarrow \psi$, if every PPD structure that satisfies all the defaults in Δ also satisfies $\varphi \rightarrow \psi$. Surprisingly, Geffner shows that ϵ-entailment is equivalent to preferential entailment.

Theorem 3.3: (Geffner 1992b) $\Delta \models_\epsilon \varphi \rightarrow \psi$ *if and only if* $\Delta \vdash_{\mathbf{P}} \varphi \rightarrow \varphi$.[5]

Possibility measures and ordinal rankings provide two more semantics for defaults. A *possibility structure* is a tuple $PS = (W, \text{Poss}, \pi)$ such that Poss is a possibility measure on W. We say $PS \models_{Poss} \varphi \rightarrow \psi$ if either $\text{Poss}([\![\varphi]\!]) = 0$ or $\text{Poss}([\![\varphi \wedge \psi]\!]) > \text{Poss}([\![\varphi \wedge \neg\psi]\!])$. Intuitively, $\varphi \rightarrow \psi$ holds vacuously if φ is impossible; otherwise, it holds if $\varphi \wedge \psi$ is more "possible" than $\varphi \wedge \neg\psi$. For example, *Bird*$\rightarrow$*Fly* is satisfied when *Bird* $\wedge$ *Fly* is more possible than *Bird* $\wedge \neg$*Fly*. Similarly, an *ordinal ranking structure* is a tuple $R = (W, \kappa, \pi)$ if κ is a an ordinal ranking on W. We say that $R \models_\kappa \varphi \rightarrow \psi$ if either $\kappa([\![\varphi]\!]) = \infty$ or $\kappa([\![\varphi \wedge \psi]\!]) < \kappa([\![\varphi \wedge \neg\psi]\!])$. We say that Δ *possibilistically entails* $\varphi \rightarrow \psi$, denoted $\Delta \models_{Poss} \varphi \rightarrow \psi$ (resp., Δ *κ-entails* $\varphi \rightarrow \psi$, denoted $\Delta \models_\kappa \varphi \rightarrow \psi$) if all possibility structures (resp., all ordinal ranking structures) that satisfy Δ also satisfy $\varphi \rightarrow \psi$.

These two approaches are again characterized by the KLM properties.

Theorem 3.4: (Geffner 1992b; Dubois & Prade 1991) $\Delta \models_{Poss} \varphi \rightarrow \psi$ *if and only if* $\Delta \models_\kappa \varphi \rightarrow \psi$ *if and only if* $\Delta \vdash_{\mathbf{P}} \varphi \rightarrow \psi$.

Why do we always seem to end up with the KLM properties? As we are about to show, thinking in terms of plausibility measures provides the key to understanding this issue.

4 Default Reasoning Using Plausibility

We can give semantics to defaults using plausibility measures much as we did using possibility measures. A *plausibility structure* is a tuple $PL = (W, \text{Pl}, \pi)$, where (W, Pl) is a plausibility space and π maps each possible world to a truth assignment. We define $PL \models_{PL} \varphi \rightarrow \psi$ if either $\text{Pl}([\![\varphi]\!]) = \perp$ or $\text{Pl}([\![\varphi \wedge \psi]\!]) > \text{Pl}([\![\varphi \wedge \neg\psi]\!])$.

Notice that if Pl is a probability function Pr, then $\varphi \rightarrow \psi$ holds exactly if either $\Pr([\![\varphi]\!]) = 0$ or $\Pr([\![\psi]\!] | [\![\varphi]\!]) > 1/2$. How does this semantics for defaults compare to others that have been given in the literature? It is immediate from the definitions that the semantics we give to defaults in possibility structures is the same as that given to them if we view these possibility structures as plausibility structures (using the obvious mapping described above, and similarly for ordinal ranking structures. What about preferential structures and PPD structures? Can we map them into plausibility structures while still preserving the semantics of defaults? As we now show, we can.

Theorem 4.1: **(a)** *Let $\prec$ be a preference ordering on W. There is a plausibility measure $\text{Pl}_\prec$ on W such that $(W, \prec, \pi) \models_p \varphi \rightarrow \psi$ iff $(W, \text{Pl}_\prec, \pi) \models_{PL} \varphi \rightarrow \psi$.*

(b) *Let $PP = \{\Pr_i\}$ be a PPD on W. There is a plausibility measure Pl_{PP} on W such that $(W, \{\Pr_i\}, \pi) \models_\epsilon \varphi \rightarrow \psi$ iff $(W, \text{Pl}_{PP}, \pi) \models_{PL} \varphi \rightarrow \psi$.*

Proof: We first sketch the proof of part (a). Let $\prec$ be a preference order on W. We define a plausibility measure $\text{Pl}_\prec$ on W as follows. Let D_0 be the domain of plausibility values consisting of one element d_w for every element $w \in W$. We use $\prec$ to determine the order of these elements: $d_v < d_w$ if $w \prec v$. (Recall that $w \prec w'$ denotes that w is preferred to w'.) We then take D to be the smallest set containing D_0 closed under least upper bounds (so that

[3]Rational entailment should not be confused with the notion of *rational closure*, also defined by Lehmann and Magidor.

[4]We adopt the presentation used in (Goldszmidt, Morris, & Pearl 1993).

[5]Geffner's result is stated in terms of the original formulation of ϵ-entailment, as described in (Pearl 1989). However, results of (Goldszmidt, Morris, & Pearl 1993) show that the formulation we describe here is equivalent to the original one.

every set of elements in D has a least upper bound in D). In the full paper, we show that this construction results in the following ordering over subsets of W:

$\mathrm{Pl}_{\prec}(A) \leq \mathrm{Pl}_{\prec}(B)$ if and only if for all $w \in A - B$, there is a world $w' \in B$ such that $w' \prec w$ and there is no $w'' \in A - B$ such that $w'' \prec w'$.

It is not hard to show that $\mathrm{Pl}_{\prec}$ satisfies the requirements of the theorem.

We next sketch the proof of part (b). Let $PP = \{\Pr_1, \Pr_2, \ldots,\}$ be a PPD on W. We define Pl_{PP} so that $\mathrm{Pl}_{PP}(A) \leq \mathrm{Pl}_{PP}(B)$ iff $\lim_{i\to\infty} \Pr_i(B|A \cup B) = 1$. It is easy to see that this definition uniquely determines the effect of Pl_{PP}. It is also easy to show that Pl_{PP} satisfies the requirements of the theorem. ∎

Thus, each of the semantic approaches to default reasoning that were described above can be mapped into plausibility structures in a way that preserves the semantics of defaults.

5 Default Entailment in Plausibility Structures

In this section we characterize default entailment in plausibility structures. To do so, it is useful to have a somewhat more general definition of entailment in plausibility structures.

Definition 5.1: If $\mathcal{P}$ is a class of plausibility structures, then a knowledge base Δ entails $\varphi \rightarrow \psi$ with respect to $\mathcal{P}$, denoted $\Delta \models_{\mathcal{P}} \varphi \rightarrow \psi$, if every $PL \in \mathcal{P}$ that satisfies Δ also satisfies $\varphi \rightarrow \psi$. ∎

The classes of structures we are interested in include $\mathcal{P}^{PL}$, the class of all plausibility structures, and $\mathcal{P}^{Poss}$, $\mathcal{P}^{\kappa}$, $\mathcal{P}^{p}$, $\mathcal{P}^{r}$, and $\mathcal{P}^{\epsilon}$, the classes that arise from mapping possibility structures, ordinal ranking structures, preferential structures, rational structures, and PPDs, respectively, into plausibility structures. (In the case of possibility structures and ordinal ranking structures, the mapping is the obvious one discussed in Section 2; in the case of preferential and rational structures and PPDs, the mapping is the one described in Theorem 4.1.) Recall that all these mappings preserve the semantics of defaults.

It is easy to check that our semantics for defaults does *not* guarantee that the axioms of system **P** hold in all structures in $\mathcal{P}^{PL}$. In particular, they do not hold in probability structures. It is easy to construct a plausibility structure PL where Pl is actually a probability measure Pr such that $\Pr([\![p \wedge q]\!]) > 0$, $\Pr([\![q]\!]|[\![p]\!]) > .5$, $\Pr([\![r]\!]|[\![p]\!]) > .5$, but $\Pr([\![q \wedge r]\!]|[\![p]\!]) < .5$ and $\Pr([\![r]\!]|[\![p \wedge q]\!]) < .5$. Recall that if $\Pr(\varphi) > 0$ then $\varphi \rightarrow \psi$ holds if and only if $\Pr(\psi|\varphi) > .5$. Thus, $PL \models_{PL} (true \rightarrow p) \wedge (true \rightarrow q)$, but $PL \not\models_{PL} true \rightarrow p \wedge q$ and $PL \not\models_{PL} (true \wedge p \rightarrow q)$. This gives us a violation of both AND and CM. We can similarly construct a counterexample to OR. On the other hand, as the following result shows, plausibility structures do satisfy the other three axioms of system **P**. Let system **P′** be the system consisting of LLE, RW, and REF.

Theorem 5.2: *If $\Delta \vdash_{\mathbf{P}'} \varphi \rightarrow \psi$, then $\Delta \models_{\mathcal{P}^{PL}} \varphi \rightarrow \psi$.*

What extra conditions do we have to place on plausibility structures to ensure that AND, OR, and CM are satisfied? We focus first on the AND rule. We want an axiom that cuts out probability functions, but leaves more qualitative notions. Working at a semantic level, taking $[\![\varphi]\!] = A$, $[\![\psi_1]\!] = B_1$, and $[\![\psi_2]\!] = B_2$, and using $\overline{X}$ to denote the complement of X, the AND rule translates to:

A2′. For all sets A, B_1, and B_2, if $\mathrm{Pl}(A \cap B_1) > \mathrm{Pl}(A \cap \overline{B_1})$ and $\mathrm{Pl}(A \cap B_2) > \mathrm{Pl}(A \cap \overline{B_2})$, then $\mathrm{Pl}(A \cap B_1 \cap B_2) > \mathrm{Pl}(A \cap \overline{(B_1 \cap B_2)})$.

It turns out that in the presence of A1, the following somewhat simpler axiom is equivalent to A2′:

A2. If A, B, and C are pairwise disjoint sets, $\mathrm{Pl}(A \cup B) > \mathrm{Pl}(C)$, and $\mathrm{Pl}(A \cup C) > \mathrm{Pl}(B)$, then $\mathrm{Pl}(A) > \mathrm{Pl}(B \cup C)$.

Proposition 5.3: *A plausibility measure satisfies A2 if and only if it satisfies A2′.*

A2 can be viewed as a generalization of a natural requirement of qualitative plausibility: if A, B, and C are pairwise disjoint, $\mathrm{Pl}(A) > \mathrm{Pl}(B)$, and $\mathrm{Pl}(A) > \mathrm{Pl}(C)$, then $\mathrm{Pl}(A) > \mathrm{Pl}(B \cup C)$. Moreover, since A2 is equivalent to A2′, and A2′ is a direct translation of the AND rule into conditions on plausibility measures, any plausibility structure whose plausibility measure satisfies A2 satisfies the AND rule. Somewhat surprisingly, a plausibility measure Pl that satisfies A2 satisfies CM. Moreover, Pl satisfies the non-vacuous case of the OR rule. That is, if $\mathrm{Pl}([\![\varphi_1]\!]) > \perp$, then from $\varphi_1 \rightarrow \psi$ and $\varphi_2 \rightarrow \psi$ we can conclude $(\varphi_1 \vee \varphi_2) \rightarrow \psi$.[6] To handle the vacuous case of OR we need an additional axiom:

A3. If $\mathrm{Pl}(A) = \mathrm{Pl}(B) = \perp$, then $\mathrm{Pl}(A \cup B) = \perp$.

Thus, A2 and A3 capture the essence of the KLM properties. To make this precise, define a plausibility space (W, Pl) to be *qualitative* if it satisfies A2 and A3. We say $PL = (W, \mathrm{Pl}, \pi)$ is a *qualitative plausibility structure* if (W, Pl) is a qualitative plausibility space. Let $\mathcal{P}^{QPL}$ consist of all qualitative plausibility structures.

Theorem 5.4: *If $\mathcal{P} \subseteq \mathcal{P}^{QPL}$, then for all Δ, φ and ψ, if $\Delta \vdash_{\mathbf{P}} \varphi \rightarrow \psi$, then $\Delta \models_{\mathcal{P}} \varphi \rightarrow \psi$.*

Thus, the KLM axioms are sound for qualitative plausibility structures. We remark that Theorem 5.4 provides, in a precise sense, not only a sufficient but a necessary condition for a set of preferential structures to satisfy the KLM properties. As we show in the full paper, if the KLM axioms are sound with respect to $\mathcal{P}$, then even if there is a structure

[6] We remark that if we dropped requirement A1, then we can define properties of plausibilities measures that correspond precisely to CM and OR. The point is that in the presence of A1, A2—which essentially corresponds to AND—implies CM and the non-vacuous case of OR. Despite appearances, A1 does *not* correspond to RW. Semantically, RW says that if A and B are disjoint sets such that $\mathrm{Pl}(A) > \mathrm{Pl}(B)$, and $A \subseteq A'$, $B' \subseteq B$, and A' and B' are disjoint, then $\mathrm{Pl}(A') > \mathrm{Pl}(B')$. While this follows from A1, it is much weaker than A1.

$P = (W, \mathrm{Pl}, \pi) \in \mathcal{P}$ that is not qualitative, P is "essentially qualitative" for all practical purposes. More precisely, we can show that Pl', the restriction of Pl to sets of the form $[\![\varphi]\!]$ is qualitative.

This, of course, leads to the question of which plausibility structures are qualitative. All the ones we have been focusing on are.

Theorem 5.5: *Each of $\mathcal{P}^{Poss}$, $\mathcal{P}^{\kappa}$, $\mathcal{P}^{\epsilon}$, $\mathcal{P}^{p}$, and $\mathcal{P}^{r}$ is a subset of $\mathcal{P}^{QPL}$.*

It follows from Theorems 5.4 and 5.5 that the KLM properties hold in all the approaches to defaults considered in Section 3. While this fact was already known, this result gives us a deeper understanding as to *why* the KLM properties should hold. In a precise sense, it is because A2 and A3 holds for all these approaches. In the full paper we also show that each of the classes considered in Theorem 5.5 is, in a nontrivial sense, a subset of $\mathcal{P}^{QPL}$; this remains true even if we restrict to totally ordered plausibility measures in the case of $\mathcal{P}^{Poss}$ and $\mathcal{P}^{\kappa}$.[7]

We now turn to the problem of completeness. To get soundness we had to ensure that $\mathcal{P}$ did not contain too many structures, in particular, no structures that are not qualitative. To get completeness we have to ensure that $\mathcal{P}$ contains "enough" structures. In particular, if $\Delta \not\vdash_{\mathbf{P}} \varphi \rightarrow \psi$, we want to ensure that there is a plausibility structure $PL \in \mathcal{P}$ such that $PL \models_{PL} \Delta$ and $PL \not\models_{PL} \varphi \rightarrow \psi$. The following weak condition on $\mathcal{P}$ does this.

Definition 5.6: We say that $\mathcal{P}$ is *rich* if for every collection $\varphi_1, \ldots, \varphi_n$ of mutually exclusive formulas, there is a plausibility structure $PL = (W, \mathrm{Pl}, \pi) \in \mathcal{P}$ such that:

$$\bot = \mathrm{Pl}([\![\varphi_1]\!]) < \mathrm{Pl}([\![\varphi_2]\!]) < \cdots < \mathrm{Pl}([\![\varphi_n]\!]). \blacksquare$$

The requirement of richness is quite mild. It says that we do not have *a priori* constraints on the relative plausibilities of a collection of disjoint sets. Certainly every collection of plausibility measures we have considered thus far can be easily shown to satisfy this richness condition.

Theorem 5.7: *Each of $\mathcal{P}^{Poss}$, $\mathcal{P}^{\kappa}$, $\mathcal{P}^{p}$, $\mathcal{P}^{r}$, $\mathcal{P}^{\epsilon}$, and $\mathcal{P}^{QPL}$ is rich.*

More importantly, richness is a necessary and sufficient condition to ensure that the KLM properties are complete.

Theorem 5.8: *A set $\mathcal{P}$ of qualitative plausibility structures is rich if and only if for all Δ and defaults $\varphi \rightarrow \psi$, we have that $\Delta \models_{\mathcal{P}} \varphi \rightarrow \psi$ implies $\Delta \vdash_{\mathbf{P}} \varphi \rightarrow \psi$.*

Putting together Theorems 5.4, 5.5, and 5.8, we get

Corollary 5.9: *For $\mathcal{P} \in \{\mathcal{P}^{Poss}, \mathcal{P}^{\kappa}, \mathcal{P}^{p}, \mathcal{P}^{r}, \mathcal{P}^{\epsilon}, \mathcal{P}^{QPL}\}$, and all Δ, φ, and ψ, we have $\Delta \vdash_{\mathbf{P}} \varphi \rightarrow \psi$ if and only if $\Delta \models_{\mathcal{P}} \varphi \rightarrow \psi$.*

Not only does this result gives us a straightforward and uniform proof that the KLM properties characterize default reasoning in each of the systems considered in Section 3, it gives us a general technique for proving completeness of the KLM properties for other semantics as well. All we have to do is to provide a mapping of the intended semantics into plausibility structures, which is usually straightforward, and then show that the resulting set of structures is qualitative and rich.

Theorem 5.8 also has important implications for attempts to go beyond the KLM properties (as was the goal in introducing rational structures). It says that any semantics for defaults that proceeds by considering a class $\mathcal{P}$ of structures satisfying the richness constraint, and defining $\Delta \models_{\mathcal{P}} \varphi \rightarrow \psi$ to hold if $\varphi \rightarrow \psi$ is true in every structure in $\mathcal{P}$ that satisfies Δ cannot lead to new properties for entailment.

Thus, to go beyond KLM, we either need to consider interesting non-rich classes of structures, or to define a notion of entailment that does not amount to considering what holds in all the structures of a given class. It is possible to construct classes of structures that are arguably interesting and violate the richness constraint. One way is to impose independence constraints. For example, suppose we consider all structures where p is independent of q in the sense that $true \rightarrow q$ holds if and only if $p \rightarrow q$ holds if and only if $\neg p \rightarrow q$ holds, so that discovering either p or $\neg p$ does not affect whether or not q is believed.[8] Restricting to such structures clearly gives us extra properties. For example, from $true \rightarrow q$ we can infer $p \rightarrow q$, which certainly does not follow from the KLM properties. Such structures do not satisfy the richness constraint, since we cannot have, for example, $\mathrm{Pl}([\![p \wedge q]\!]) > \mathrm{Pl}([\![p \wedge \neg q]\!]) > \mathrm{Pl}([\![\neg p \wedge \neg q]\!]) > \mathrm{Pl}([\![\neg p \wedge q]\!])$. Much of the recent work in default reasoning (Bacchus *et al.* 1993; Geffner 1992a; Goldszmidt & Pearl 1992; Goldszmidt, Morris, & Pearl 1993; Lehmann & Magidor 1992; Pearl 1990) has taken the second approach, of not looking at entailment with respect to a class of structures. Roughly speaking, these approaches can be viewed as taking the basic idea of preferential semantics—placing a preference ordering on worlds—one step further: They try to get from a knowledge base one preferred *structure* (where the structure itself puts a preference ordering on worlds)—for example, in (Goldszmidt, Morris, & Pearl 1993), the PPD of maximum entropy is considered—and carry out all reasoning in that preferred structure. We believe that plausibility measures will provide insight into techniques for choosing such preferred structures, particularly through the use of independence, but the discussion of this issue is beyond the scope of this paper.

6 A Logic of Defaults

Up to now, we have just focused on whether a set of defaults implies another default. We have not considered a full logic of defaults, with negated defaults, nested defaults, and dis-

[7] Since, for example, the range of a possibility measure is [0,1], there are totally ordered plausibility measures that are not possibility measures, although they may put the same ordering on sets. However, for example, we can have a qualitative plausibility measure on $\{1,2\}$ such that $\mathrm{Pl}(\{1\}) = \mathrm{Pl}(\{2\}) < \mathrm{Pl}(\{1,2\})$. This cannot correspond to a possibility measure, since $\mathrm{Poss}(\{1\}) = \mathrm{Poss}(\{2\})$ would imply that $\mathrm{Poss}(\{1\}) = \mathrm{Poss}(\{1,2\})$.

[8] We remark that if we define independence appropriately in plausibility structures, this property does indeed hold; see (Friedman & Halpern 1995a).

junctions of defaults. It is easy to extend all the approaches we have defined so far to deal with such a logic. *Conditional logic* is a logic that treats $\rightarrow$ as a modal operator. The syntax of the logic is simple: let $\mathcal{L}^C$ be the language defined by starting with primitive propositions, and close off under $\wedge$, $\neg$, and $\rightarrow$. Formulas can describe logical combination of defaults (e.g., $(p \rightarrow q) \vee (p \rightarrow \neg q)$) as well as nested defaults (e.g., $(p \rightarrow q) \rightarrow r$).

The semantics of conditional logic is similar to the semantics of defaults.[9] The usual definition (Lewis 1973) associates with each world a preferential order over worlds. We now give a similar definition based on plausibility measures. Given a preferential structure $PL = (W, \mathrm{Pl}, \pi)$, we define what it means for a formula φ to be true at a world w in PL. The definition for the propositional connectives is standard, and for $\rightarrow$, we use the definition already given:

- $(PL, w) \models p$ if $\pi(w) \models p$ for a primitive proposition p
- $(PL, w) \models \neg\varphi$ if $(PL, w) \not\models \varphi$
- $(PL, w) \models \varphi \wedge \psi$ if $(PL, w) \models \varphi$ and $(PL, w) \models \psi$
- $(PL, w) \models \varphi \rightarrow \psi$ if either $\mathrm{Pl}([\![\varphi]\!]_{PL}) = \perp$ or $\mathrm{Pl}([\![\varphi \wedge \psi]\!]_{PL}) > \mathrm{Pl}([\![\varphi \wedge \neg\psi]\!]_{PL})$, where we define $[\![\varphi]\!]_{PL} = \{w \in W : (\mathrm{Pl}, w) \models \varphi\}$.[10]

We now want to axiomatize default reasoning in this framework. Clearly we need axioms and inference rules that generalize those of system **P**. Let $N\varphi$ be an abbreviation for $\neg\varphi \rightarrow$*false*. (This operator is called the *outer modality* in (Lewis 1973).) Expanding the definition of $\rightarrow$, we get that $N\varphi$ holds at w if and only if $\mathrm{Pl}([\![\neg\varphi]\!]) = \perp$. Thus, $N\varphi$ holds if $\neg\varphi$ is considered completely implausible. Thus, it implies that φ is true "almost everywhere". Let system **C** be the system consisting of LLE, RW, and the following axioms and inference rules:

C0. All the propositional tautologies

C1. $\varphi \rightarrow \varphi$

C2. $((\varphi \rightarrow \psi_1) \wedge (\varphi \rightarrow \psi_2)) \Rightarrow (\varphi \rightarrow (\psi_1 \wedge \psi_2))$

C3. $((\varphi_1 \rightarrow \psi) \wedge (\varphi_2 \rightarrow \psi)) \Rightarrow ((\varphi_1 \vee \varphi_2) \rightarrow \psi)$

C4. $((\varphi_1 \rightarrow \varphi_2) \wedge (\varphi_1 \rightarrow \psi)) \Rightarrow ((\varphi_1 \wedge \varphi_2) \rightarrow \psi)$

C5. $[(\varphi \rightarrow \psi) \Rightarrow N(\varphi \rightarrow \psi)] \wedge [\neg(\varphi \rightarrow \psi) \Rightarrow N\neg(\varphi \rightarrow \psi)]$

MP. From φ and $\varphi \Rightarrow \psi$ infer ψ.

It is easy to see that system **C** is very similar to system **P**. The richer language lets us replace a rule like AND by the axiom C2. Similarly, C1 to REF, C3 to OR and C4 to CM. We need C0 and MP to deal with propositional reasoning. Finally, C5 captures the fact that the plausibility function Pl is independent of the world. Thus, if a default is true (false) at some world, it is true (false) at all of them. If we had enriched plausibility structures to allow a different plausibility function Pl_w for each world w (as is done in the general definition of conditional logic (Lewis 1973)) then we would not need this axiom. There is no KLM property analogous to C5 since a formula such as $N(\varphi \rightarrow \psi)$ involves nested $\rightarrow$'s.

It is well known (Lewis 1973; Burgess 1981; Friedman & Halpern 1994) that system **C** captures reasoning in preferential structures.

Theorem 6.1: (Burgess 1981; Friedman & Halpern 1994) *System* **C** *is a sound and complete axiomatization of* $\mathcal{L}^C$ *with respect to* $\mathcal{P}^p$.

Since the axioms of system **C** are clearly valid in all the structures in $\mathcal{P}^{QPL}$ and $\mathcal{P}^p \subseteq \mathcal{P}^{QPL}$, we immediately get

Corollary 6.2: *System* **C** *is a sound and complete axiomatization of* $\mathcal{L}^C$ *with respect to* $\mathcal{P}^{QPL}$.

This result shows that, at least as far as the language $\mathcal{L}^C$ goes, plausibility structures are no more expressive than preferential structures. We return to this issue in Section 7.

The language $\mathcal{L}^C$ allows us to make distinctions that we could not make using just implication between defaults, as in Section 4. For example, consider the following axiom:

C6. $\varphi \rightarrow \psi \wedge \neg(\varphi \wedge \xi \rightarrow \psi) \Rightarrow \varphi \rightarrow \neg\xi$

Axiom C6 corresponds to the rule of *rational monotonicity* discussed in (Kraus, Lehmann, & Magidor 1990; Lehmann & Magidor 1992). It is not hard to show that C6 is valid in systems where the plausibility ordering is modular. In particular, it is valid in each of $\mathcal{P}^r$, $\mathcal{P}^{Poss}$, and $\mathcal{P}^\kappa$, although it is not valid in $\mathcal{P}^p$. In fact, it is well-known that system **C**+C6 is a sound and complete axiomatization of $\mathcal{L}^C$ with respect to $\mathcal{P}^r$ (Burgess 1981).[11]

7 Conclusions

We feel that this paper unifies earlier results regarding the KLM properties, and explains why they arise so frequently. It also points out the advantage of using plausibility measures as a semantics for defaults.

Do we really need plausibility measures? If all we are interested in is propositional default reasoning and the KLM properties, then the results of Section 6 show that preferential structures provide us all the expressive power we need. Roughly speaking, this is so because when doing propositional reasoning, we can safely restrict to finite structures. (Technically, this is because we have a *finite model property*: if a formula in $\mathcal{L}^C$ is satisfiable, it is satisfiable in a finite plausibility structure (Friedman & Halpern 1994).) As we show in companion paper (Friedman, Halpern, & Koller 1996), preferential structures and plausibility structures are no longer equally expressive once we move to a first-order logic, precisely because infinite structures now play a more important role. The extra expressive power of plausibility structures makes them more appropriate than

[9]The connections between default reasoning and conditional logics are well-known; see (Boutilier 1994; Kraus, Lehmann, & Magidor 1990; Katsuno & Satoh 1991).

[10]We redefine $[\![\varphi]\!]_{PL}$ since φ can involve conditional statements. Note that if φ does not contain occurrences of $\rightarrow$ then this definition is equivalent to the one we gave earlier. Again, we omit the subscript when it is clear from the context.

[11]To capture $\mathcal{P}^\kappa$ and $\mathcal{P}^{poss}$, we need the additional axiom $\neg$(*true*$\rightarrow$*false*). This axiom together with system **C** also provides a complete axiomatization for $\mathcal{P}^\epsilon$. These results are based on well-known results in conditional logic (Burgess 1981; Friedman & Halpern 1994) and are proved in the full paper.

preferential structures for providing semantics for first-order default reasoning.

Beyond their role in default reasoning, we expect that plausibility measures will prove useful whenever we want to express uncertainty and do not want to (or cannot) do so using probability. For example, we can easily define a plausibilistic analogue of conditioning (Friedman & Halpern 1995a). While this can also be done in many of the other approaches we have considered, we believe that the generality of plausibility structures will allow us to again see what properties of independence we need for various tasks. In particular, in (Friedman & Halpern 1996), we use plausibilistic independence to define a plausibilistic analogue of Markov chains. We plan to further explore the properties and applications of plausibility structures in future work.

Acknowledgements

The authors are grateful to Ronen Brafman, Adnan Darwiche, Moises Goldszmidt, Adam Grove, and Daphne Koller for useful discussions relating to this work. The authors were supported in part by the Air Force Office of Scientific Research (AFSC), under Contract F49620-91-C-0080 and by NSF grant IRI-95-03109. The first author was also supported in part by Rockwell Science Center.

References

Adams, E. 1975. *The Logic of Conditionals*. Reidel.

Bacchus, F.; Grove, A. J.; Halpern, J. Y.; and Koller, D. 1993. Statistical foundations for default reasoning. In *IJCAI '93*, 563–569. Available at http://logos.uwaterloo.ca.

Boutilier, C. 1994. Conditional logics of normality: a modal approach. *Artificial Intelligence* 68:87–154.

Burgess, J. 1981. Quick completeness proofs for some logics of conditionals. *Notre Dame J. of Formal Logic* 22:76–84.

Darwiche, A. 1992. *A Symbolic Generalization of Probability Theory*. Ph.D. Dissertation, Stanford University.

Dubois, D., and Prade, H. 1990. An introduction to possibilistic and fuzzy logics. In Shafer, G., and Pearl, J., eds., *Readings in Uncertain Reasoning*. Morgan Kaufmann.

Dubois, D., and Prade, H. 1991. Possibilistic logic, preferential models, non-monotonicity and related issues. In *IJCAI '91*, 419–424.

Friedman, N., and Halpern, J. Y. 1994. On the complexity of conditional logics. In *KR '94*, 202–213.

Friedman, N., and Halpern, J. Y. 1995a. Plausibility measures: a user's manual. In *UAI '95*, 175–184.

Friedman, N., and Halpern, J. Y. 1995b. Plausibility measures and default reasoning. Technical Report RJ 9959, IBM. Available at `http://robotics.stanford.edu/users/nir`.

Friedman, N., and Halpern, J. Y. 1996. A qualitative Markov assumption and its implications for belief change. Submitted to UAI '96.

Friedman, N.; Halpern, J. Y.; and Koller, D. 1996. Conditional first-order logic revisited. In *AAAI '96*.

Gabbay, D. M.; Hogger, C. J.; and Robinson, J. A., eds. 1993. *Nonmonotonic Reasoning and Uncertain Reasoning*, volume 3 of *Handbook of Logic in Artificial Intelligence and Logic Programming*. Oxford University Press.

Gärdenfors, P., and Makinson, D. 1988. Revisions of knowledge systems using epistemic entrenchment. In *Proc. 2nd Conf. on Theoretical Aspects of Reasoning about Knowledge*. 83–95.

Geffner, H. 1992a. *Default Reasoning*. MIT Press.

Geffner, H. 1992b. High probabilities, model preference and default arguments. *Mind and Machines* 2:51–70.

Ginsberg, M. L., ed. 1987. *Readings in Nonmonotonic Reasoning*. Morgan Kaufmann.

Goldszmidt, M., and Pearl, J. 1992. Rank-based systems: A simple approach to belief revision, belief update and reasoning about evidence and actions. In *KR '92*, 661–672.

Goldszmidt, M.; Morris, P.; and Pearl, J. 1993. A maximum entropy approach to nonmonotonic reasoning. *IEEE Trans. of Pattern Analysis and Machine Intelligence* 15(3):220–232.

Katsuno, H., and Satoh, K. 1991. A unified view of consequence relation, belief revision and conditional logic. In *IJCAI '91*, 406–412.

Kraus, S.; Lehmann, D.; and Magidor, M. 1990. Nonmonotonic reasoning, preferential models and cumulative logics. *Artificial Intelligence* 44:167–207.

Lehmann, D., and Magidor, M. 1992. What does a conditional knowledge base entail? *Artificial Intelligence* 55:1–60.

Lewis, D. K. 1973. *Counterfactuals*. Harvard University Press.

Pearl, J. 1989. Probabilistic semantics for nonmonotonic reasoning: a survey. In *KR '89*, 505–516.

Pearl, J. 1990. System Z: A natural ordering of defaults with tractable applications to nonmonotonic reasoning. In *Theoretical Aspects of Reasoning about Knowledge: Proc. 3rd Conference*, 121–135.

Shafer, G. 1976. *A Mathematical Theory of Evidence*. Princeton University Press.

Shoham, Y. 1987. A semantical approach to nonmonotonic logics. In *Proc. 2nd IEEE Symp. on Logic in Computer Science*, 275–279.

Spohn, W. 1987. Ordinal conditional functions: a dynamic theory of epistemic states. In Harper, W., and Skyrms, B., eds., *Causation in Decision, Belief Change and Statistics*, volume 2. Reidel. 105–134.

Wang, Z., and Klir, G. J. 1992. *Fuzzy Measure Theory*. Plenum.

Weydert, E. 1994. General belief measures. In *UAI '94*, 575–582.

First-Order Conditional Logic Revisited

Nir Friedman
Dept. of Computer Science
Stanford University
Gates Building 1A
Stanford, CA 94305-9010
nir@cs.stanford.edu

Joseph Y. Halpern
IBM Almaden Research Center
650 Harry Road
San Jose, CA 95120–6099
halpern@almaden.ibm.com

Daphne Koller
Dept. of Computer Science
Stanford University
Gates Building 1A
Stanford, CA 94305-9010
koller@cs.stanford.edu

Abstract

Conditional logics play an important role in recent attempts to investigate default reasoning. This paper investigates first-order conditional logic. We show that, as for first-order probabilistic logic, it is important not to confound *statistical* conditionals over the domain (such as "most birds fly"), and *subjective* conditionals over possible worlds (such as "I believe that Tweety is unlikely to fly"). We then address the issue of ascribing semantics to first-order conditional logic. As in the propositional case, there are many possible semantics. To study the problem in a coherent way, we use *plausibility structures*. These provide us with a general framework in which many of the standard approaches can be embedded. We show that while these standard approaches are all the same at the propositional level, they are significantly different in the context of a first-order language. We show that plausibilities provide the most natural extension of conditional logic to the first-order case: We provide a sound and complete axiomatization that contains only the KLM properties and standard axioms of first-order modal logic. We show that most of the other approaches have additional properties, which result in an inappropriate treatment of an infinitary version of the *lottery paradox*.

1 Introduction

In recent years, conditional logic has come to play a major role as an underlying foundation for default reasoning. Two of the more successful default reasoning systems (Geffner 1992; Goldszmidt, Morris, & Pearl 1993) are based on conditional logic. Unfortunately, while it has long been recognized that first-order expressive power is necessary for a default reasoning system, most of the work on conditional logic has been restricted to the propositional case. In this paper, we investigate the syntax and semantics of *first-order conditional logic*, with the ultimate goal of providing a first-order default reasoning system.

Many seemingly different approaches have been proposed for giving semantics to conditional logic, including preferential structures (Lewis 1973; Boutilier 1994; Kraus, Lehmann, & Magidor 1990), ϵ-semantics (Adams 1975; Pearl 1989), *possibility theory* (Benferhat, Dubois, & Prade 1992), and κ-*rankings* (Spohn 1987; Goldszmidt & Pearl 1992). In preferential structures, for example, a model consists of a set of possible worlds, ordered by a preference ordering $\prec$. If $w \prec w'$, then the world w is strictly more preferred/more normal than w'. The formula *Bird*$\rightarrow$*Fly* holds if in the most preferred worlds in which *Bird* holds, *Fly* also holds. (See Section 2 for more details about this and the other approaches.)

The extension of these approaches to the first-order case seems deceptively easy. After all, we can simply have a preferential ordering on first-order, rather than propositional, worlds. However, there is a subtlety here. As in the case of first-order *probabilistic* logic (Bacchus 1990; Halpern 1990), there are two distinct ways to define conditionals in the first-order case. In the probabilistic case, the first corresponds to (objective) statistical statements, such as "90% of birds fly". The second corresponds to subjective degree of belief statements, such as "the probability that Tweety (a particular bird) flies is 0.9". The first is captured by putting a probability distribution over the domain (so that the probability of the set of flying birds is 0.9 that of the set of birds), while the second is captured by putting a probability on the set of possible worlds (so that the probability of the set of worlds where Tweety flies is 0.9 that of the set of worlds where Tweety is a bird). The same phenomenon occurs in the case of first-order conditional logic. Here, we can have a measure (e.g., a preferential ranking) over the domain, or a measure over the set of possible worlds. The first would allow us to capture qualitative statistical statements such as "most birds fly", while the second would allow us to capture subjective beliefs such as "I believe that the bird Tweety is likely to fly". It is important to have a language that allows us to distinguish between these two very different statements. Having distinguished between these two types of conditionals, we can ascribe semantics to each of them using any one of the standard approaches.

There have been previous attempts to formalize first-order conditional logic; some are the natural extension of some propositional formalism (Delgrande 1987; Brafman 1991), while others use alternative approaches (Lehmann & Magidor 1990; Schlechta 1995). (We defer a detailed discussion of these approaches to the full paper; see also Section 5.) How do we make sense of this plethora of alternatives? Rather than investigating them separately, we use a single common framework that generalizes almost all of them. This framework uses a notion of uncertainty called a *plausibility measure*, introduced by Friedman and Halpern (1995). A plausibility measure associates with set of worlds its *plausibility*, which is just an element in a partially ordered space. Probability measures are a subclass of plausibility measures, in which the plausibilities lie in [0, 1], with the standard ordering. In (Friedman & Halpern 1996), it is shown that the different standard approaches to conditional logic can all be mapped to plausibility measures, if we interpret $Bird \rightarrow Fly$ as "the set of worlds where $Bird \wedge Fly$ holds has greater plausibility than that of the set of worlds where $Bird \wedge \neg Fly$ holds".

The existence of a single unifying framework has already proved to be very useful in the case of propositional conditional logic. In particular, it allowed Friedman and Halpern (1996) to explain the intriguing "coincidence" that all of the different approaches to conditional logic result in an identical reasoning system, characterized by the *KLM axioms* (Kraus, Lehmann, & Magidor 1990). In this paper, we show that plausibility spaces can also be used to clarify the semantics of first-order conditional logic. However, we show that, unlike the propositional case, the different approaches lead to different properties in the first-order case. Intuitively, these are infinitary properties that require quantifiers and therefore cannot be expressed in a propositional language. We show that, in some sense, plausibilities provide the most natural extension of conditional logic to the first-order case. We provide a sound and complete axiomatization for the subjective fragment of conditional logic that contains only the KLM properties and the standard axioms of first-order modal logic.[1] (We provide a similar axiomatization for the statistical fragment of the language in the full paper.) Essentially the same axiomatization is shown to be sound and complete for the first-order version of ϵ-semantics, but the other approaches are shown to satisfy additional properties.

One might think that it is not so bad for a conditional logic to satisfy additional properties. After all, there are some properties—such as indifference to irrelevant information—that we would *like* to be able to get. Unfortunately, the additional properties that we get from using these approaches are not the ones we want. The properties we get are related to the treatment of *exceptional individuals*. This issue is perhaps best illustrated by the *lottery paradox* (Kyburg 1961).[2] Suppose we believe about a lottery that any particular individual typically does not win the lottery. Thus we get

$$\forall x(true \rightarrow \neg Winner(x)). \tag{1}$$

However, we believe that typically someone does win the lottery, that is

$$true \rightarrow \exists x\, Winner(x). \tag{2}$$

Unfortunately, in many of the standard approaches, such as Delgrande's (1987) version of first-order preferential structures, from (1) we can conclude

$$true \rightarrow \forall x(\neg Winner(x)). \tag{3}$$

Intuitively, from (1) it follows that in the most preferred worlds, each individual d does not win the lottery. Therefore, in the most preferred worlds, no individual wins. This is exactly what (3) says. Since (2) says that in the most preferred worlds, some individual wins, it follows that there are no most preferred worlds, i.e., we have $true \rightarrow false$. While this may be consistent (as it is in Delgrande's logic), it implies that all defaults hold, which is surely not what we want. Of all the approaches, only ϵ-semantics and plausibility structures, both of which are fully axiomatized by the first-order extension of the KLM axioms, do not suffer from this problem.

It may seem that this problem is perhaps not so serious. After all, how often do we reason about lotteries? But, in fact, this problem arises in many situations which are clearly of the type with which we would like to deal. Assume, for example, that we express the default "birds typically fly" as Delgrande does, using the statement

$$\forall x(Bird(x) \rightarrow Fly(x)). \tag{4}$$

If we also believe that Tweety is a bird that does not fly, so that our knowledge base contains the statement $true \rightarrow Bird(Tweety) \wedge \neg Fly(Tweety)$, we could similarly conclude $true \rightarrow false$. Again, this is surely not what we want.

Our framework allows us to deal with these problems. Using plausibilities, (1) and (2) do not imply $true \rightarrow false$, since (3) does not follow from (1). That is, the lottery paradox simply does not exist if we use plausibilities. The flying bird example is somewhat more subtle. If we take Tweety to be a *nonrigid designator* (so that it might denote different individuals in different worlds), the two statements are consistent, and the problem disappears. If, however, Tweety is a rigid designator, the pair is inconsistent, as we would expect.

This inconsistency suggests that we might not always want to use (4) to represent "birds typically fly". After all, the former is a statement about a property believed to hold of each individual bird, while the latter is a statement about the class of birds. As argued in (Bacchus *et al.* 1994), defaults often arise from statistical facts about the domain. That is, the default "birds typically fly" is often a consequence of the empirical observation that "almost all birds fly". By defining a logic which allows us to express statistical conditional statements, we provide the user an alternative way of representing such defaults. We would, of course, like such statements to impact our beliefs about individual birds. In (Bacchus *et al.* 1994), the same issue was addressed in the probabilistic context, by presenting an approach for going from statistical knowledge bases to subjective degrees of belief. We leave the problem of providing a similar mechanism for conditional logic to future work.

The rest of this paper is organized as follows. In Section 2, we review the various approaches to conditional

[1]By way of contrast, there is no (recursively enumerable) axiomatization of first-order probabilistic logic (Halpern 1990).

[2]We are referring to Kyburg's original version of the lottery paradox (Kyburg 1961), and not to the finitary version discussed by Poole (1991). As Poole showed, any logic of defaults that satisfies certain minimal properties—properties which are satisfied by all the logics we consider—is bound to suffer from his version of the lottery paradox.

logic in the propositional case; we also review the definition of plausibility measures from (Friedman & Halpern 1996) and show how they provide a common framework for these different approaches. In Section 3, we discuss the two ways in which we can extend propositional conditional logic to first-order—statistical conditionals and subjective conditionals—and ascribe semantics to both using plausibilities. In Section 4, we provide a sound and complete axiomatization for first-order subjective conditional assertions. In Section 5, we discuss the generalization of the other propositional approaches to the first-order case, by investigating their behavior with respect to the lottery paradox. We also provide a brief comparison to some of the other approaches suggested in the literature, deferring detailed discussion to the full paper. We conclude in Section 6 with discussion and some directions for further work.

2 Propositional conditional logic

The syntax of propositional conditional logic is simple. We start with a set Φ of propositions and close off under the usual propositional connectives ($\neg$, $\vee$, $\wedge$, and $\Rightarrow$) and the conditional connective $\rightarrow$. That is, if φ and ψ are formulas in the language, so is $\varphi \rightarrow \psi$.

Many semantics have been proposed in the literature for conditionals. Most of them involve structures of the form (W, X, π), where W is a set of possible worlds, $\pi(w)$ is a truth assignment to primitive propositions, and X is some "measure" on W such as a preference ordering (Lewis 1973; Kraus, Lehmann, & Magidor 1990).[3] We now describe some of the proposals in the literature, and then show how they can be generalized. Given a structure (W, X, π), let $[\![\varphi]\!] \subseteq W$ be the set of worlds satisfying φ.

- A *possibility measure* (Dubois & Prade 1990) Poss is a function Poss : $2^W \mapsto [0, 1]$ such that $\text{Poss}(W) = 1$, $\text{Poss}(\emptyset) = 0$, and $\text{Poss}(A) = \sup_{w \in A}(\text{Poss}(\{w\}))$. A *possibility structure* is a tuple (W, Poss, π), where Poss is a possibility measure on W. It satisfies a conditional $\varphi \rightarrow \psi$ if either $\text{Poss}([\![\varphi]\!]) = 0$ or $\text{Poss}([\![\varphi \wedge \psi]\!]) > \text{Poss}([\![\varphi \wedge \neg\psi]\!])$ (Dubois & Prade 1991). That is, either φ is impossible, in which case the conditional holds vacuously, or $\varphi \wedge \psi$ is more possible than $\varphi \wedge \neg\psi$.
- A *κ-ranking* (or *ordinal ranking*) on W (as defined by (Goldszmidt & Pearl 1992), based on ideas that go back to (Spohn 1987)) is a function $\kappa : 2^W \rightarrow \mathbb{N}^*$, where $\mathbb{N}^* = \mathbb{N} \cup \{\infty\}$, such that $\kappa(W) = 0$, $\kappa(\emptyset) = \infty$, and $\kappa(A) = \min_{w \in A}(\kappa(\{w\}))$. Intuitively, an ordinal ranking assigns a degree of surprise to each subset of worlds in W, where 0 means unsurprising and higher numbers denote greater surprise. A *κ-structure* is a tuple (W, κ, π), where κ is an ordinal ranking on W. It satisfies a conditional $\varphi \rightarrow \psi$ if either $\kappa([\![\varphi]\!]) = \infty$ or $\kappa([\![\varphi \wedge \psi]\!]) < \kappa([\![\varphi \wedge \neg\psi]\!])$.
- A *preference ordering* on W is a partial order $\prec$ over W (Kraus, Lehmann, & Magidor 1990; Shoham 1987). Intuitively, $w \prec w'$ holds if w is *preferred* to w'. A *preferential structure* is a tuple $(W, \prec, \pi)$, where $\prec$ is a partial order on W. The intuition (Shoham 1987) is that a preferential structure satisfies a conditional $\varphi \rightarrow \psi$ if all the most preferred worlds (i.e., the minimal worlds according to $\prec$) in $[\![\varphi]\!]$ satisfy ψ. However, there may be no minimal worlds in $[\![\varphi]\!]$. This can happen if $[\![\varphi]\!]$ contains an infinite descending sequence $\ldots \prec w_2 \prec w_1$. The simplest way to avoid this is to assume that $\prec$ is *well-founded*; we do so here for simplicity. A yet more general definition—one that works even if $\prec$ is not well-founded—is given in (Lewis 1973; Boutilier 1994). We discuss that in the full paper.
- A *parameterized probability distribution* (PPD) on W is a sequence $\{\Pr_i : i \geq 0\}$ of probability measures over W. A *PPD structure* is a tuple $(W, \{\Pr_i : i \geq 0\}, \pi)$, where $\{\Pr_i\}$ is PPD over W. Intuitively, it satisfies a conditional $\varphi \rightarrow \psi$ if the conditional probability ψ given φ goes to 1 in the limit. Formally, $\varphi \rightarrow \psi$ is satisfied if $\lim_{i \rightarrow \infty} \Pr_i([\![\psi]\!] | [\![\psi]\!]) = 1$ (where $\Pr_i([\![\psi]\!] | [\![\varphi]\!])$ is taken to be 1 if $\Pr_i([\![\varphi]\!]) = 0$). PPD structures were introduced in (Goldszmidt, Morris, & Pearl 1993) as a reformulation of Pearl's *ϵ-semantics* (Pearl 1989).

These variants are quite different from each other. However, as shown in (Friedman & Halpern 1996), we can provide a uniform framework for all of them using the notion of plausibility measures. In fact, plausibility measures generalize other types of measures, including probability measures (see (Friedman & Halpern 1995)).

A *plausibility measure* Pl on W is a function that maps subsets of W to elements in some arbitrary partially ordered set. We read $\text{Pl}(A)$ as "the plausibility of set A". If $\text{Pl}(A) \leq \text{Pl}(B)$, then B is at least as plausible as A. Formally, a *plausibility space* is a tuple $S = (W, \text{Pl})$, where W is a set of worlds and Pl maps subsets of W to some set D, partially ordered by a relation $\leq$ (so that $\leq$ is reflexive, transitive, and anti-symmetric). As usual, we define the ordering $<$ by taking $d_1 < d_2$ if $d_1 \leq d_2$ and $d_1 \neq d_2$. We assume that D is *pointed*: that is, it contains two special elements $\top$ and $\bot$ such that $\bot \leq d \leq \top$ for all $d \in D$; we further assume that $\text{Pl}(W) = \top$ and $\text{Pl}(\emptyset) = \bot$. Since we want a set to be at least as plausible as any of its subsets, we require:

A1. If $A \subseteq B$, then $\text{Pl}(A) \leq \text{Pl}(B)$.

Clearly, plausibility spaces generalize probability spaces. Other approaches to dealing with uncertainty, such as possibility measures, κ-rankings, and *belief functions* (Shafer 1976), are also easily seen to be plausibility measures.

We can give semantics to conditionals using plausibility in much the same way as it is done using possibility. A *plausibility structure* is a tuple $PL = (W, \text{Pl}, \pi)$, where Pl is a plausibility measure on W. We then define:

- $PL \models \varphi \rightarrow \psi$ if either $\text{Pl}([\![\varphi]\!]) = \bot$ or $\text{Pl}([\![\varphi \wedge \psi]\!]) > \text{Pl}([\![\varphi \wedge \neg\psi]\!])$.

Intuitively, $\varphi \rightarrow \psi$ holds vacuously if φ is impossible; otherwise, it holds if $\varphi \wedge \psi$ is more plausible than $\varphi \wedge \neg\psi$. It is

[3] We could also consider a more general definition, in which one associates a different "measure" with each world, as done by Lewis, for example (Lewis 1973). It is straightforward to extend our definitions to handle this. Since this issue is orthogonal to the main point of the paper, we do not discuss it further here.

easy to see that this semantics for conditionals generalizes the semantics of conditionals in possibility structures and κ-structures. As shown in (Friedman & Halpern 1996), it also generalizes the semantics of conditionals in preferential structures and PPD structures. More precisely, a mapping is given from preferential structures to plausibility structures such that $(W, \prec, \pi) \models \varphi$ if and only if $(W, \mathrm{Pl}_{\prec}, \pi) \models \varphi$, where $\mathrm{Pl}_{\prec}$ is the plausibility measure that corresponds to $\prec$. A similar mapping is also provided for PPD structures.

These results show that our semantics for conditionals in plausibility structures generalizes the various approaches examined in the literature. Does it capture our intuitions about conditionals? In the AI literature, there has been discussion of the right properties of default statements (which are essentially conditionals). While there has been little consensus on what the "right" properties for defaults should be, there has been some consensus on a reasonable "core" of inference rules for default reasoning. This core, is known as the KLM properties (Kraus, Lehmann, & Magidor 1990).[4]

Do conditionals in plausibility structures satisfy these properties? In general, they do not. To satisfy the KLM properties we must limit our attention to plausibility structures that satisfy the following conditions:

A2. If A, B, and C are pairwise disjoint sets, $\mathrm{Pl}(A \cup B) > \mathrm{Pl}(C)$, and $\mathrm{Pl}(A \cup C) > \mathrm{Pl}(B)$, then $\mathrm{Pl}(A) > \mathrm{Pl}(B \cup C)$.

A3. If $\mathrm{Pl}(A) = \mathrm{Pl}(B) = \perp$, then $\mathrm{Pl}(A \cup B) = \perp$.

A plausibility space (W, Pl) is *qualitative* if it satisfies A2 and A3. A plausibility structure (W, Pl, π) is qualitative if (W, Pl) is a qualitative plausibility space. In (Friedman & Halpern 1996) it is shown that, in a very general sense, qualitative plausibility structures capture default reasoning. More precisely, the KLM properties are sound with respect to a class of plausibility structures if and only if the class consists of qualitative plausibility structures. Furthermore, a very weak condition is necessary and sufficient in order for the KLM properties to be a complete axiomatization of conditional logic. As a consequence, once we consider a class of structures where the KLM axioms are sound, it is almost inevitable that they will also be complete with respect to that class. This explains the somewhat surprising fact that KLM properties characterize default entailment not just in preferential structures, but also in ϵ-semantics, possibility measures, and κ-rankings. Each one of these approaches corresponds, in a precise sense, to a class of qualitative plausibility structures. These results show that plausibility structures provide a unifying framework for the characterization of default entailment in these different logics.

3 First-order conditional logic

We now want to generalize conditional logic to the first-order case. As mentioned above, there are two distinct notions of conditionals in first-order logic, one involving statistical conditionals and one involving subjective conditionals. For each of these, we use a different syntax, analogous to the syntax used in (Halpern 1990) for the probabilistic case.

The syntax for statistical conditionals is fairly straightforward. Let Φ be a first-order vocabulary, consisting of predicate and function symbols. (As usual, constant symbols are viewed as 0-ary function symbols.) Starting with atomic formulas of first-order logic, we form more complicated formulas by closing off under truth-functional connectives (i.e., $\wedge, \vee, \neg$, and $\Rightarrow$), first-order quantification, and the family of modal operators $\varphi \leadsto_{\vec{x}} \psi$, where $\vec{x}$ is a sequence of distinct variables. We denote the resulting language $\mathcal{L}^{stat}$. The intuitive reading of $\varphi \leadsto_{\vec{x}} \psi$ is that almost all of the $\vec{x}$'s that satisfy φ also satisfy ψ. Thus, the $\leadsto_{\vec{x}}$ modality binds the variables $\vec{x}$ in φ and ψ. A typical formula in this language is $\exists y(P(x, y) \leadsto_x Q(x, y))$, which can be read "there is some y such that most x's satisfying $P(x, y)$ also satisfy $Q(x, y)$".[5] Note that we allow arbitrary nesting of first-order and modal operators.

The syntax for subjective plausibilities is even simpler than that for statistical plausibilities. Starting with a first-order vocabulary Φ, we now close off under truth-functional connectives, first-order quantification, and the single modal operator $\rightarrow$. Thus, a typical formula is $\forall x(P(x) \rightarrow \exists y Q(x, y))$. Let $\mathcal{L}^{subj}$ be the resulting language (the "subj" stands for "subjective", since the conditionals are viewed as expressing subjective degrees of belief).

We can ascribe semantics to both types of conditionals using any one of the approaches described in the previous section. (In fact, we do not even have to use the same approach for both.) However, since we can embed all of the approaches within the class of plausibility structures, we use these as the basic semantics. As in the propositional case, we can then analyze the behavior of the other approaches simply by restricting attention to the appropriate subclass of plausibility structures.

To give semantics to $\mathcal{L}^{stat}$, we use *(first-order) statistical plausibility structures*, which generalize the semantics of statistical probabilistic structures (Halpern 1990) and statistical preferential structures (Brafman 1991). Statistical plausibility structures are tuples of the form $PL = (Dom, \pi, \mathcal{P})$, where *Dom* is a domain, π is an interpretation assigning each predicate symbol and function symbol in Φ a predicate or function of the right arity over *Dom*, and $\mathcal{P}$ associates with each number n a plausibility measure Pl_n on Dom^n. As usual, a *valuation* maps each variable to an element of *Dom*. Given a structure PL and a valuation v, we can associate with every formula φ a truth value in a straightforward way. The only nontrivial case is $\varphi \leadsto_{\vec{x}} \psi$. We define $I_{(PL,v,\vec{x})}(\varphi) = \{\vec{d} : (PL, v[\vec{x}/\vec{d}]) \models \varphi\}$, where $v[\vec{x}/\vec{d}]$ is a valuation that maps each x in $\vec{x}$ to the corresponding element in $\vec{d}$ and agrees with v elsewhere.

- $(PL, v) \models \varphi \leadsto_{\vec{x}} \psi$ if either $\mathrm{Pl}_n(I_{(PL,v,\vec{x})}(\varphi)) = \perp$ or $\mathrm{Pl}_n(I_{(PL,v,\vec{x})}(\varphi \wedge \psi)) > \mathrm{Pl}_n(I_{(PL,v,\vec{x})}(\varphi \wedge \neg\psi))$, where n is the length of $\vec{x}$.

[4]Due to space limitations we do not review the KLM properties here; see (Friedman & Halpern 1996) in this proceedings.

[5]This syntax is borrowed from Brafman (1991), which in turn is based on that of (Bacchus 1990; Halpern 1990).

We remark that we need the sequence of plausibility measures to deal with tuples of different arity. The analogous sequence of probability measures was not needed in (Halpern 1990), since, given a probability measure on *Dom*, we can consider the product measure on Dom^n. In the full paper, we place some requirements on Pl_n to force it to have the key properties we expect of product measures. We omit further discussion of statistical plausibilities here, and focus instead on subjective plausibilities.

To give semantics to $\mathcal{L}^{subj}$, we use *(first-order) subjective plausibility structures*. These are tuples of the form $PL = (Dom, W, \mathrm{Pl}, \pi)$, where *Dom* is a domain, (W, Pl) is a plausibility space and $\pi(w)$ is an interpretation assigning to each predicate symbol and function symbol in Φ a predicate or function of the right arity over *Dom*. We define the set of worlds that satisfy φ given the valuation v to be $[\![\varphi]\!]_{(PL,v)} = \{w : (PL, w, v) \models \varphi\}$. (We omit the subscript whenever it is clear from context.) For subjective conditionals, we have

- $(PL, w, v) \models \varphi{\rightarrow}\psi$ if $\mathrm{Pl}([\![\varphi]\!]_{(PL,v)}) = \perp$ or $\mathrm{Pl}([\![\varphi \wedge \psi]\!]_{(PL,v)}) > \mathrm{Pl}([\![\varphi \wedge \neg\psi]\!]_{(PL,v)})$.

We do not treat terms as *rigid designators* here. That is, in different worlds, a term can denote different individuals. For example, if $\pi(w)(c) \neq \pi(w')(c)$, the constant c denotes different individuals in w and w'. Because terms are not rigid designators, we cannot substitute terms for universally quantified variables. (A similar phenomenon holds in other modal logics where terms are not rigid (Garson 1977).) For example, let $\Box\varphi$ be an abbreviation for $\neg\varphi{\rightarrow}$*false*. Notice that $(PL, w) \models \Box\varphi$ if $\mathrm{Pl}([\![\neg\varphi]\!]) = \perp$; i.e., $\Box\varphi$ asserts that the plausibility of $\neg\varphi$ is the same as that of the empty set, so that φ is true "almost everywhere". We define $\Diamond\varphi$ as $\neg\Box\neg\varphi$; this says that φ is true in some non-negligible set of worlds. Suppose c is a constant that does not appear in the formula φ. As we show in the full paper, $\forall x \Diamond\varphi(x) \Rightarrow \Diamond\varphi(c)$ is not valid in our framework; that is, we cannot substitute constants for universally quantified variables. We could substitute if c were rigid. We can get the effect of rigidity by assuming that $\exists x(\Box(x = c))$ holds. Thus, we do not lose expressive power by not assuming rigidity.

4 Axiomatizing default reasoning in plausibility structures

We now want to show that plausibility structures provide an appropriate semantics for a first-order logic of defaults. As in the propositional case, this is true only if we restrict attention to qualitative plausibility structures, i.e., those satisfying conditions A2 and A3 above. Let $\mathcal{P}_{subj}^{QPL}$ be the class of all subjective qualitative plausibility structures. We provide a sound and complete axiom system for $\mathcal{P}_{subj}^{QPL}$, and show that it is the natural extension of the KLM properties to the first-order case.

The axiomatization $\mathbf{C}^{subj}$, specified in Figure 1, consists of three parts. The first set of axioms (C0–C5 together with the rules MP, LLE, and RW) is simply the standard axiomatization of propositional conditional logic (Hughes & Cresswell 1968); the second set (axioms F1–F5) consists of the standard axioms of first-order logic (Enderton 1972); the final set (F6–F8) contains the standard axioms relating the two (Hughes & Cresswell 1968). F6 is known as the *Barcan formula*; it describes the relationship between $\Box$ and $\forall$ in structures where all the worlds have the same domain (as is the case here). F7 and F8 describe the interaction between $\Box$ and equality, and hold because we are essentially treating variables as rigid designators.

C0. All instances of propositional tautologies
C1. $\varphi{\rightarrow}\varphi$
C2. $((\varphi{\rightarrow}\psi_1) \wedge (\varphi{\rightarrow}\psi_2)) \Rightarrow (\varphi{\rightarrow}(\psi_1 \wedge \psi_2))$
C3. $((\varphi_1{\rightarrow}\psi) \wedge (\varphi_2{\rightarrow}\psi)) \Rightarrow ((\varphi_1 \vee \varphi_2){\rightarrow}\psi)$
C4. $((\varphi_1{\rightarrow}\varphi_2) \wedge (\varphi_1{\rightarrow}\psi)) \Rightarrow ((\varphi_1 \wedge \varphi_2){\rightarrow}\psi)$
C5. $[(\varphi{\rightarrow}\psi) \Rightarrow \Box(\varphi{\rightarrow}\psi)] \wedge [\neg(\varphi{\rightarrow}\psi) \Rightarrow \Box\neg(\varphi{\rightarrow}\psi)]$
F1. $\forall x\varphi \Rightarrow \varphi[x/t]$, where t is *substitutable* for x in the sense discussed below
F2. $\forall x(\varphi \Rightarrow \psi) \Rightarrow (\forall x\varphi \Rightarrow \forall x\psi)$
F3. $\varphi \Rightarrow \forall x\varphi$ if x does not occur free in φ
F4. $x = x$
F5. $x = y \Rightarrow (\varphi \Rightarrow \varphi')$, where φ is a quantifier-free and $\rightarrow$-free formula and φ' is obtained from φ by replacing zero or more occurrences of x in φ by y
F6. $\Box\forall x\varphi \Leftrightarrow \forall x\Box\varphi$
F7. $x = y \Rightarrow \Box(x = y)$
F8. $x \neq y \Rightarrow \Box(x \neq y)$
MP. From φ and $\varphi \Rightarrow \psi$ infer ψ
LLE. From $\varphi_1 \Leftrightarrow \varphi_2$ infer $\varphi_1{\rightarrow}\psi \Leftrightarrow \varphi_2{\rightarrow}\psi$
RW. From $\psi_1 \Rightarrow \psi_2$ infer $\varphi{\rightarrow}\psi_1 \Rightarrow \varphi{\rightarrow}\psi_2$.

Figure 1: The system $\mathbf{C}^{subj}$ consists of all generalizations of the following axioms (where φ is a *generalization* of ψ if φ is of the form $\forall x_1 \ldots \forall x_n \psi$) and rules; x and y denote variables, while t denotes an arbitrary term.

It remains to explain the notion of "substitutable" in F1. Clearly we cannot substitute a term t for x with free variables that might be captured by some quantifiers in φ; for example, while $\forall x \exists y(x \neq y)$ is true as long as the domain has at least two elements, if we substitute y for x, we get $\exists y(y \neq y)$, which is surely false. In the case of first-order logic, it suffices to define "substitutable" so as to make sure this does not happen (see (Enderton 1972) for details). However, in modal logics such as this one, we have to be a little more careful. As we observed in Section 3, we cannot substitute terms for universally quantified variables in a modal context, since terms are not in general rigid. Thus, we require that if φ is a formula that has occurrences of $\rightarrow$, then the only terms that are substitutable for x in φ are other variables.

Theorem 4.1: $\mathbf{C}^{subj}$ *is a sound and complete axiomatization of* $\mathcal{L}^{subj}$ *with respect to* $\mathcal{P}_{subj}^{QPL}$.

We claim that $\mathbf{C}^{subj}$ is the weakest "natural" first-order extension of the KLM properties. The bulk of the propositional fragment of this axiom system (axioms C1–C4, LLE, and RW) corresponds precisely to the KLM properties. The remaining axiom (C5) captures the fact that the plausibility function Pl is independent of the world. This property does not appear in (Kraus, Lehmann, & Magidor 1990) since they do not allow nesting of conditionals. As discussed above, the remaining axioms are standard properties of first-order modal logic.

5 Alternative Approaches

In the previous section we showed that $\mathbf{C}^{subj}$ is sound and complete with respect to $\mathcal{P}^{QPL}_{subj}$. What happens if we use one of the approaches described in Section 2 to give semantics to conditionals? As noted above, we can associate with each of these approach a subset of qualitative plausibility structures. Let $\mathcal{P}^{p,w}_{subj}$, $\mathcal{P}^{p}_{subj}$, $\mathcal{P}^{\kappa}_{subj}$, $\mathcal{P}^{poss}_{subj}$, and $\mathcal{P}^{\epsilon}_{subj}$ be the subsets of $\mathcal{P}^{QPL}_{subj}$ that correspond to well-founded preferential orderings, preferential orderings, κ-rankings, possibility measures, and PPDs, respectively. From Theorem 4.1, we immediately get

Theorem 5.1: $\mathbf{C}^{subj}$ *is sound in* $\mathcal{P}^{p,w}_{subj}$, $\mathcal{P}^{p,s}_{subj}$, $\mathcal{P}^{p}_{subj}$, $\mathcal{P}^{\kappa}_{subj}$, $\mathcal{P}^{poss}_{subj}$, *and* $\mathcal{P}^{\epsilon}_{subj}$.

Is $\mathbf{C}^{subj}$ complete with respect to these approaches? Even at the propositional level, it is well known that because κ rankings and possibility measures induce plausibility measures that are total (rather than partial) orders, they satisfy the following additional property:

C6. $\varphi \rightarrow \psi \wedge \neg(\varphi \rightarrow \neg\xi) \Rightarrow (\varphi \wedge \xi \rightarrow \psi)$.

In addition, the plausibility measures induced by κ rankings, possibility measures, and ϵ semantics are easily seen to have the property that $\top > \bot$. This leads to the following axiom:

C7. $\neg(\mathit{true} \rightarrow \mathit{false})$.

In the propositional setting, these additional axioms and the basic propositional conditional system (i.e., C0–C5, MP, LLE, and RW) lead to sound and complete axiomatization of the corresponding (propositional) structures.

Does the same phenomenon occur in the first-order case? For ϵ-semantics, it does.

Theorem 5.2: $\mathbf{C}^{subj}$+C7 *is a sound and complete axiomatization of* $\mathcal{L}^{subj}$ *w.r.t.* $\mathcal{P}^{\epsilon}_{subj}$.

But, unlike the propositional case, the remaining approaches all satisfy properties beyond $\mathbf{C}^{subj}$, C6, and C7. And these additional properties are ones that we would argue are undesirable, since they cause the lottery paradox. Recall that the lottery paradox can be represented with two formulas: (1) $\forall x(\mathit{true} \rightarrow \neg \mathit{Winner}(x))$ states that every individual is unlikely to win the lottery, while (2) $\mathit{true} \rightarrow \exists x \mathit{Winner}(x)$ states that is is likely that some individual does win the lottery. We start by showing that (1) and (2) are consistent in $\mathcal{P}^{QPL}_{subj}$. We define a first-order subjective plausibility structure $PL_{lot} = (Dom_{lot}, W_{lot}, \mathrm{Pl}_{lot}, \pi_{lot})$ as follows: Dom_{lot} is a countable domain consisting of the individuals $1, 2, 3, \ldots$; W_{lot} consists of a countable number of worlds $w_1, w_2, w_3, \ldots$; Pl_{lot} gives the empty set plausibility 0, each non-empty finite set plausibility 1/2, and each infinite set plausibility 1; finally, the denotation of *Winner* in world w_i according to π_{lot} is the singleton set $\{d_i\}$ (that is, in world w_i the lottery winner is individual d_i). It is easy to check that $[\![\neg \mathit{Winner}(d_i)]\!] = W - \{w_i\}$, so $\mathrm{Pl}_{lot}([\![\neg \mathit{Winner}(d_i)]\!]) = 1 > 1/2 = \mathrm{Pl}([\![\mathit{Winner}(d_i)]\!])$; hence, PL_{lot} satisfies (1). On the other hand, $[\![\exists x \mathit{Winner}(x)]\!] = W$, so $\mathrm{Pl}_{lot}([\![\exists x \mathit{Winner}(x)]\!]) > \mathrm{Pl}_{lot}([\![\neg\exists x \mathit{Winner}(x)]\!])$; hence PL_{lot} satisfies (2). It is also easy to verify that Pl_{lot} is a qualitative measure, i.e., satisfies A2 and A3. A similar construction allows us to capture a situation where birds typically fly but we know that Tweety does not fly.

What happens to the lottery paradox in the other approaches? First consider well-founded preferential structures, i.e., $\mathcal{P}^{p,w}_{subj}$. In these structures, $\varphi \rightarrow \psi$ holds if ψ holds in all the preferred worlds that satisfy φ. Thus, (1) implies that for any domain element d, d is not a winner in the most preferred worlds. On the other hand, (2) implies that in the most preferred worlds, some domain element wins. Together both imply that there are no preferred worlds. When, in general, does an argument of this type go through? As we now show, it is a consequence of

A2*. If $\{A_i : i \in I\}$ are pairwise disjoint sets, $A = \cup_{i \in I} A_i$, $0 \in I$, and for all $i \in I - \{0\}$, $\mathrm{Pl}(A - A_i) > \mathrm{Pl}(A_i)$, then $\mathrm{Pl}(A_0) > \mathrm{Pl}(A - A_0)$.

Recall that A2 states that if A_0, A_1, and A_2 are disjoint, $\mathrm{Pl}(A_0 \cup A_1) > \mathrm{Pl}(A_2)$, and $\mathrm{Pl}(A_0 \cup A_2) > \mathrm{Pl}(A_1)$, then $\mathrm{Pl}(A_0) > \mathrm{Pl}(A_1 \cup A_2)$. It is easy to check that for any finite number of sets, a similar property follows from A1 and A2 by induction. A2* asserts that a condition of this type holds even for an infinite collection of sets. This is not implied by A1 and A2. To see this, consider the plausibility model PL_{lot} that we used to capture the infinite lottery: Take A_0 to be empty and take A_i, $i > 1$, to be the singleton consisting of the world w_i. Then $\mathrm{Pl}_{lot}(A - A_i) = 1 > 1/2 = \mathrm{Pl}_{lot}(A_i)$, but $\mathrm{Pl}_{lot}(A_0) = 0 < 1 = \mathrm{Pl}(\cup_{i>0} A_i)$. Hence, A2* does not hold for plausibility structures in general. It does, however, hold for certain subclasses:

Proposition 5.3: *A2* holds in every plausibility structure in* $\mathcal{P}^{p,w}_{subj}$ *and* $\mathcal{P}^{\kappa}_{subj}$.

In the full paper we show that A2* is characterized by the axiom called $\forall$3 by Delgrande:

$\forall$3. $\forall x(\varphi \rightarrow \psi) \Rightarrow (\varphi \rightarrow \forall x \psi)$ if x does not occur free in φ.

This axiom can be viewed as an infinitary version of axiom C2 (which is essentially KLM's And Rule). Since A2* holds in $\mathcal{P}^{p,w}_{subj}$ and $\mathcal{P}^{\kappa}_{subj}$, it follows that $\forall$3 does as well. It is easy to see that the axiom $\forall$3 leads to the lottery paradox: From $\forall x(\mathit{true} \rightarrow \neg \mathit{Winner}(x))$, $\forall$3 would imply that $\mathit{true} \rightarrow \forall x(\neg \mathit{Winner}(x))$.

As we show in the full paper, A2* does not hold in $\mathcal{P}^{poss}_{subj}$ and $\mathcal{P}^{p}_{subj}$. In fact, the infinite lottery is consistent in these classes, although a somewhat unnatural model is required to express it. For example, we can represent the lottery via a possibility structure $(Dom_{lot}, W_{lot}, \mathrm{Poss}, \pi_{lot})$, where all the components besides Poss are just as in the plausibility structure PL_{lot} that represents the lottery scenario, and $\mathrm{Poss}(w_i) = i/(i+1)$. This means that if $i > j$, then it is more possible that individual i wins than individual j. Moreover, this possibility approaches 1 as i increases. It is not hard to show that this possibility structure satisfies formulas (1) and (2).

We can block this type of behavior by considering a *crooked lottery*, where there is one individual who is more likely to win than the rest, but is still unlikely to win. To formalize this in the language, we add the following formula that we call *Crooked*:

$$\neg\exists x(\mathit{Winner}(x)\rightarrow\mathit{false}) \wedge \exists y\forall x(x \neq y \Rightarrow ((\mathit{Winner}(x) \vee \mathit{Winner}(y))\rightarrow \mathit{Winner}(y)))$$

The first part of this formula states that each individual has some plausibility of winning; in the language of plausibility, this means that $\mathrm{Pl}(d) > \perp$ for each domain element d. The second part states that there is an individual who is more likely to win than the rest. To see this, recall that $(\varphi \vee \psi)\rightarrow\psi$ implies that either $\mathrm{Pl}([\![\varphi \vee \psi]\!]) = \perp$ (which cannot happen here because of the first clause of *Crooked*) or $\mathrm{Pl}([\![\varphi]\!]) < \mathrm{Pl}([\![\psi]\!])$. We take the crooked lottery to be formalized by the formula $\forall x(\mathit{true}\rightarrow\neg\mathit{Winner}(x)) \wedge (\mathit{true}\rightarrow\exists x\mathit{Winner}(x)) \wedge$ *Crooked*. Note, that $\forall x(\mathit{true}\rightarrow\neg\mathit{Winner}(x))$ implies that every individual is unlikely to win.

It is easy to model the crooked lottery using plausibility. Consider the structure $PL'_{lot} = (Dom_{lot}, W_{lot}, \mathrm{Pl}'_{lot}, \pi_{lot})$, which is identical to PL_{lot} except for the plausibility measure Pl'_{lot}. We define $\mathrm{Pl}'_{lot}(w_1) = 3/4$; $\mathrm{Pl}'_{lot}(w_i) = 1/2$ for $i > 1$; $\mathrm{Pl}'_{lot}(A)$ of a finite set A is $3/4$ if $w_1 \in A$, and $1/2$ if $w_1 \notin A$; and $\mathrm{Pl}_{lot}(A) = 1$ for infinite A. It is easy to verify that PL'_{lot} satisfies *Crooked*, taking d_1 to be the special individual who is most likely to win (since $\mathrm{Pl}([\![\mathit{Winner}(d_1)]\!]) = 3/4 > 1/2 = \mathrm{Pl}([\![\mathit{Winner}(d_i)]\!])$ for $i > 1$). It is also easy to verify that $PL'_{lot} \models \forall x(\mathit{true}\rightarrow\neg\mathit{Winner}(x)) \wedge (\mathit{true}\rightarrow\exists x\mathit{Winner}(x))$.

As we show in the full paper, the crooked lottery cannot be captured in $\mathcal{P}^{poss}_{subj}$ and $\mathcal{P}^{p}_{subj}$. This shows that, once we move to first-order logic, possibility structures and preferential structures satisfy extra properties over and above those characterized by $\mathbf{C}^{subj}$.

Although our focus thus far has been on subjective conditionals, the situation for statistical conditionals is similar. We have already remarked that we can construct "statistical" first-order analogues of all the approaches considered in the propositional case. As in the subjective case, all of them suffer From problems except for the one based on ϵ-semantics. We illustrate this using by considering the extension of well-founded preferential structures to first-order conditionals over the domain, as defined by Brafman (1991). Consider the statement

$$\forall y(\mathit{true} \leadsto_x \neg\mathit{Married}(x,y)) \qquad (5)$$

This states that for any individual y, most individuals are not married to y. This seems reasonable since each y is married to at most one individual, which clearly constitutes a small fraction of the population. The analogue of $\forall3$ holds in Brafman's logic, for the same reason that it does in $\mathcal{P}^{p,w}_{subj}$. As a consequence, (5) implies

$$\mathit{true} \leadsto_x \forall y\neg\mathit{Married}(x,y).$$

That is, most people are not married! This certainly does not seem to be a reasonable conclusion. It is straightforward to construct similar examples for the statistical variants of the other approaches, again, with the exception of plausibility structures and ϵ-semantics. We note that these problems occur for precisely the same reasons they occur in the subjective case. In particular, property A2*, when stated for the plausibility over domain elements, is the necessary property for the statistical analogue of $\forall3$.

We observe that problems similar to the lottery paradox occur in the approach of Lehmann and Magidor (1990), which can be viewed as a hybrid of subjective and statistical conditionals based on on preferential structures. Finally, we observe that the approach of (Schlechta 1995), which is based on a novel representation of "large" subsets, is in the spirit of our notion of statistical defaults (although his language is somewhat less expressive than ours). We defer a detailed discussion of these approaches to the full paper.

6 Discussion

We have shown how to ascribe semantics to a first-order logic of conditionals in a number of ways. Our analysis shows that, once we move to the first-order case, significant differences arise between approaches that were shown to be equivalent in the propositional case. This vindicates the intuition that there are significant differences between these approaches, which the propositional language is simply too weak to capture. Our analysis also supports our choice of plausibility structures as the semantics for first-order defaults: it shows that, with the exception of ϵ-semantics, all the previous approaches have significant shortcomings, which manifest themselves in lottery-paradox type situations.

What does all this say about default reasoning? As we have argued, statements like "birds typically fly" should perhaps be thought of as statistical statements, and should thus be represented as $\mathit{Bird}(x) \leadsto_x \mathit{Fly}(x)$. Such a representation gives us a logic of defaults, in which statements such as "birds typically fly" and "birds typically do not fly" are inconsistent, as we would expect.

Of course, what we really want to do with such typicality statements is to draw default conclusions about individuals. Suppose we believe such a typicality statement. What other beliefs should follow? In general, $\forall x(\mathit{Bird}(x)\rightarrow\mathit{Fly}(x))$ does not follow; we should not necessarily believe that *all* birds are likely to fly. We may well know that Tacky the penguin does not fly. As long as Tacky is a rigid designator, this is simply inconsistent with believing that all birds are likely to fly. In the absence of information about any particularly bird, $\forall x(\mathit{Bird}(x)\rightarrow\mathit{Fly}(x))$ may well be a reasonable belief to hold. Moreover, no matter what we know about exceptional birds, it seems reasonable to believe $\mathit{true} \leadsto_x (\mathit{Bird}(x)\rightarrow\mathit{Fly}(x))$: almost all birds are likely to fly (assuming we have a logic that allows the obvious combination of statistical and subjective plausibility).

Unfortunately, we do not have a general approach that will let us go from believing that birds typically fly to believing that almost all birds are likely to fly. Nor do we have an approach that allows us to conclude that Tweety is likely to fly given that birds typically fly and Tweety is a bird (and that we know nothing else about Tweety). These issues were addressed in the first-order setting by both Lehmann and Magidor (1990) and Delgrande (1988). The key feature of their approaches, as well as other propositional approaches rests upon getting a suitable notion of irrelevance. While we also do not have a general solution to the problem of irrelevance, we believe that plausibility structures give us the tools to study it in an abstract setting. We suspect that many of the intuitions behind probabilistic approaches that allow us to cope with irrelevance (Bacchus *et al.* 1994) can also be brought to bear here. We hope to return to this issue in future work.

Acknowledgements

We would like to thank Ronen Brafman, Ron Fagin, and Adam Grove for their comments on an earlier version of the paper. Some of this work was done while all three authors were at the IBM Almaden Research Center, supported by the Air Force Office of Scientific Research (AFSC) under Contract F49620-91-C-0080. Some was done while Daphne Koller was at U.C. Berkeley, supported by a University of California President's Postdoctoral Fellowship. This work is also partially supported by NSF grant IRI-95-03109.

References

Adams, E. 1975. *The Logic of Conditionals.* Reidel.

Bacchus, F.; Grove, A. J.; Halpern, J. Y.; and Koller, D. 1994. From statistical knowledge bases to degrees of belief. Technical Report RJ 9855, IBM. Available at `http://robotics.stanford.edu/users/koller`. A preliminary version of this work appeared in *IJCAI '93*, 1993, pp. 563–569.

Bacchus, F. 1990. *Representing and Reasoning with Probabilistic Knowledge.* MIT Press.

Benferhat, S.; Dubois, D.; and Prade, H. 1992. Representing default rules in possibilistic logic. In *KR '92.* pp. 673–684.

Boutilier, C. 1994. Conditional logics of normality: a modal approach. *Artificial Intelligence* 68:87–154.

Brafman, R. I. 1991. A logic of normality: Predicate calculus incorporating assertions. Master's thesis, Hebrew University, Jesrusalem.

Delgrande, J. P. 1987. A first-order conditional logic for prototypical properties. *Artificial Intelligence* 33:105–130.

Delgrande, J. P. 1988. An approach to default reasoning based on a first-order conditional logic: revised report. *Artificial Intelligence* 36:63–90.

Dubois, D., and Prade, H. 1990. An introduction to possibilistic and fuzzy logics. In Shafer, G., and Pearl, J., eds., *Readings in Uncertain Reasoning.* Morgan Kaufmann.

Dubois, D., and Prade, H. 1991. Possibilistic logic, preferential models, non-monotonicity and related issues. In *IJCAI '91.* pp. 419–424.

Enderton, H. B. 1972. *A Mathematical Introduction to Logic.* Academic Press.

Friedman, N., and Halpern, J. Y. 1995. Plausibility measures: a user's manual. In *UAI '95.* pp. 175–184.

Friedman, N., and Halpern, J. Y. 1996. Plausibility measures and default reasoning. In *AAAI '96.* An extended version appeared as IBM Research Report RJ 9959, available at `http://robotics.stanford.edu/users/nir`.

Garson, J. W. 1977. Quantification in modal logic. In Gabbay, D., and Guenthner, F., eds., *Handbook of Philosophical Logic, Vol. II.* Reidel. pp. 249–307.

Geffner, H. 1992. *Default reasoning: causal and conditional theories.* MIT Press.

Goldszmidt, M., and Pearl, J. 1992. Rank-based systems: A simple approach to belief revision, belief update and reasoning about evidence and actions. In *KR '92.* pp. 661–672.

Goldszmidt, M.; Morris, P.; and Pearl, J. 1993. A maximum entropy approach to nonmonotonic reasoning. *IEEE Trans. of Pattern Analysis and Machine Intelligence* 15(3):220–232.

Halpern, J. Y. 1990. An analysis of first-order logics of probability. *Artificial Intelligence* 46:311–350.

Hughes, G. E., and Cresswell, M. J. 1968. *An Introduction to Modal Logic.* Methuen.

Kraus, S.; Lehmann, D.; and Magidor, M. 1990. Nonmonotonic reasoning, preferential models and cumulative logics. *Artificial Intelligence* 44:167–207.

Kyburg, Jr., H. E. 1961. *Probability and the Logic of Rational Belief.* Wesleyan University Press.

Lehmann, D., and Magidor, M. 1990. Preferential logics: the predicate calculus case. In *Theoretical Aspects of Reasoning about Knowledge: Proc. 3rd Conf.*. pp. 57–72.

Lewis, D. K. 1973. *Counterfactuals.* Harvard University Press.

Pearl, J. 1989. Probabilistic semantics for nonmonotonic reasoning: a survey. In *KR '89*, pp. 505–516.

Poole, D. 1991. The effect of knowledge on belief: conditioning, specificity and the lottery paradox in default reasoning. *Artificial Intelligence* 49(1–3):282–307.

Schlechta, K. 1995. Defaults as generalized quantifiers. *J. Logic and Computation* 5(4):473–494.

Shafer, G. 1976. *A Mathematical Theory of Evidence.* Princeton University Press.

Shoham, Y. 1987. A semantical approach to nonmonotonic logics. In *Proc. 2nd IEEE Symp. on Logic in Computer Science*, pp. 275–279.

Spohn, W. 1987. Ordinal conditional functions: a dynamic theory of epistemic states. In Harper, W., and Skyrms, B., eds., *Causation in Decision, Belief Change and Statistics*, volume 2. Reidel. pp. 105–134.

A Counterexample to Theorems of Cox and Fine

Joseph Y. Halpern
IBM Research Division
Almaden Research Center, Dept. K53-B2
650 Harry Road
San Jose, CA 95120–6099
halpern@almaden.ibm.com

Abstract

Cox's well-known theorem justifying the use of probability is shown not to hold in finite domains. The counterexample also suggests that Cox's assumptions are insufficient to prove the result even in infinite domains. The same counterexample is used to disprove a result of Fine on comparative conditional probability.

1 Introduction

One of the best-known and seemingly most compelling arguments in favor of the use of probability is given by Cox (1946). Suppose we have a function Bel that associates a real number with each pair (U, V) of subsets of a domain W such that $U \neq \emptyset$. We write $\mathrm{Bel}(V|U)$ rather than $\mathrm{Bel}(U, V)$, since we think of $\mathrm{Bel}(V|U)$ as the credibility or likelihood of V given U.[1] Cox further assumes that $\mathrm{Bel}(\overline{V}|U)$ is a function of $\mathrm{Bel}(V|U)$ (where $\overline{V}$ denotes the complement of V in W), that is, there is a function S such that

A1. $\mathrm{Bel}(\overline{V}|U) = S(\mathrm{Bel}(V|U))$ if $U \neq \emptyset$,

and that $\mathrm{Bel}(V \cap V'|U)$ is a function of $\mathrm{Bel}(V'|V \cap U)$ and $\mathrm{Bel}(V|U)$, that is, there is a function F such that

A2. $\mathrm{Bel}(V \cap V'|U) = F(\mathrm{Bel}(V'|V \cap U), \mathrm{Bel}(V|U))$ if $V \cap U \neq \emptyset$.

Notice that if Bel is a probability function, then we can take $S(x) = 1 - x$ and $F(x, y) = xy$. Cox makes much weaker assumptions: he assumes that F is twice differentiable, with a continuous second derivative, and that S is twice differentiable. Under these assumptions, he shows that Bel is isomorphic to a probability distribution in the sense that there is a continuous one-to-one onto function $g : I\!R \rightarrow I\!R$ such that $g \circ \mathrm{Bel}$ is a probability distribution on W, and

$$g(\mathrm{Bel}(V|U)) \times g(\mathrm{Bel}(U)) = g(\mathrm{Bel}(V \cap U)) \text{ if } U \neq \emptyset, \quad (1)$$

where $\mathrm{Bel}(U)$ is an abbreviation for $\mathrm{Bel}(U|W)$.

Not surprisingly, Cox's result has attracted a great deal of interest in the AI literature. For example

- Cheeseman (1988) has called it the "strongest argument for use of standard (Bayesian) probability theory".
- Horvitz, Heckerman, and Langlotz (1986) used it as a basis for comparison of probability and other nonprobabilistic approaches to reasoning about uncertainty.
- Heckerman (1988) uses it as a basis for providing an axiomatization for belief update.

The main contribution of this paper is to show (by means of an explicit counterexample), that Cox's result does not hold in finite domains, even under strong assumptions on S and F (stronger than those made by Cox and those made in all papers proving variants of Cox's results). Since finite domains are arguably those of most interest in AI applications, this suggests that arguments for using probability based on Cox's result—and other justifications similar in spirit—must be taken with a grain of salt, and their proofs carefully reviewed. Moreover, the counterexample suggests that Cox's assumptions are insufficient to prove the result even in infinite domains.

It is known that some assumptions regarding F and S must be made to prove Cox's result. Dubois and Prade (1990) give an example of a function Bel, defined on a finite domain, that is not isomorphic to a probability distribution. For this choice of Bel, we can take $F(x, y) = \min(x, y)$ and $S(x) = 1 - x$. Since min is not twice differentiable, Cox's assumptions block the Dubois-Prade example.

Aczél (1966, Section 7 (Theorem 1)) does not make any assumptions about F, but he does make two other assumptions, each of which block the Dubois-Prade example. The first is that the $\mathrm{Bel}(V|U)$ takes on every value in some range $[e, E]$, with $e < E$. In the Dubois-Prade example, the domain is finite, so this certainly cannot hold. The second is that if V and V' are disjoint, then there is a continuous function $G : I\!R^2 \rightarrow I\!R$, strictly increasing in each argument, such that

A3. $\mathrm{Bel}(V \cup V'|U) = G(\mathrm{Bel}(V|U), \mathrm{Bel}(V'|U))$.

Dubois and Prade point out that, in their example, there is no function G satisfying A3 (even if we drop the requirement that G be continuous and strictly increasing in each argument).[2] With these assumptions, he gives a proof much

[1] Cox writes $V|U$ rather than $\mathrm{Bel}(V|U)$, and takes U and V to be propositions in some language rather than events, i.e., subsets of a given set. This difference is minor—there are well-known mappings from propositions to events, and vice versa. I use events here since they are more standard in the probability literature.

[2] In fact, Aczél allows there to be a different function G_U for each set U on the right-hand side of the conditional. However, the

in the spirit of that of Cox to show that Bel is essentially a probability distribution.

Reichenbach (1949) earlier proved a result similar to Aczél's, under somewhat stronger assumptions. In particular, he assumed A3, with G being $+$.

Other variants of Cox's result have also been considered in the literature. For example, Heckerman (1988) and Horvitz, Heckerman, and Langlotz (1986) assume that F is continuous and strictly increasing in each argument and S is continuous and strictly decreasing. Since min is not strictly continuous in each argument, it fails this restriction too.[3] Aleliunas (1988) gives yet another collection of assumptions and claims that they suffice to guarantee that Bel is essentially a probability distribution.

The first to observe potential problems with Cox's result is Paris (1994). As he puts it, "Cox's proof is not, perhaps, as rigorous as some pedants might prefer and when an attempt is made to fill in all the details some of the attractiveness of the original is lost." Paris provides a rigorous proof of the result, assuming that the range of Bel is contained in $[0, 1]$ and using assumptions similar to those of Horvitz, Heckerman, and Langlotz. In particular, he assumes that F is continuous and strictly increasing in $(0, 1]^2$ and that S is decreasing. However, he makes use of one additional assumption that, as he himself says, is not very appealing:

A4. For any $0 \leq \alpha, \beta, \gamma \leq 1$ and $\epsilon > 0$, there are sets U_1, U_2, U_3, and U_4 such that $U_3 \cap U_2 \cap U_1 \neq \emptyset$, and each of $|\mathrm{Bel}(U_4|U_3 \cap U_2 \cap U_1) - \alpha|$, $|\mathrm{Bel}(U_3|U_2 \cap U_1) - \beta|$, and $|\mathrm{Bel}(U_2|U_1) - \gamma|$ is less than ϵ.

Notice that this assumption forces the range of Bel to be dense in $[0, 1]$. This means that, in particular, the domain W on which Bel is defined cannot be finite.

Is this assumption really necessary? Paris suggests that Aczél needs something like it. (This issue is discussed in further detail below.) The counterexample of this paper gives further evidence. It shows that Cox's result fails in finite domains, even if we assume that the range of Bel is in $[0, 1]$, $S(x) = 1 - x$ (so that, in particular, S is twice differentiable and monotonically decreasing), $G(x, y) = x + y$, and F is infinitely differentiable and strictly increasing on $(0, 1]^2$. We can further assume that F is commutative, $F(0, x) = F(x, 0) = 0$, and that $F(x, 1) = F(1, x) = x$. The example emphasizes the point that the applicability of Cox's result is far narrower than was previously believed. It remains an open question as to whether there is an appropriate strengthening of the assumptions that does give us Cox's result in finite settings.

In fact, the example shows even more. In the course of his proof, Cox claims to show that F must be an associative function, that is, that $F(x, F(y, z)) = F(F(x, y), z)$. For the Bel of the counterexample, there can be no associative function F satisfying A2. It is this observation that is the key to showing that there is no probability distribution isomorphic to Bel.

What is going on here? Actually, Cox's proof just shows that $F(x, F(y, z)) = F(F(x, y), z)$ only for those triples (x, y, z) such that, for some sets U_1, U_2, U_3, and U_4, we have $x = \mathrm{Bel}(U_4|U_3 \cap U_2 \cap U_1)$, $y = \mathrm{Bel}(U_3|U_2 \cap U_1)$, and $z = \mathrm{Bel}(U_2|U_1)$. If the set of such triples (x, y, z) is dense in $[0, 1]^3$, then we conclude by continuity that F is associative. The content of A4 is precisely that the set of such triples is dense in $[0, 1]^3$. Of course, if W is finite, we cannot have density. As my counterexample shows, we do not in general have associativity in finite domains. Moreover, this lack of associativity can result in the failure of Cox's theorem.

A similar problem seems to exist in Aczél's proof (as already observed by Paris (1994)). While Aczél's proof does not involve showing that F is associative, it does involve showing that G is associative. Again, it is not hard to show that G is associative for appropriate triples, just as is the case for F. But it seems that Aczél also needs an assumption that guarantees that the appropriate set of triples is dense, and it is not clear that his assumptions do in fact guarantee this.[4] As shown in Section 2, the problem also arises in Reichenbach's proof.

This observation also shows that another well-known result in the literature is not completely correct. In his seminal book on probability and qualitative probability (1973), Fine considers a non-numeric notion of *comparative (conditional) probability*, which allows us to say "U given V is at least as probable as U' given V'", denoted $U|V \succeq U'|V'$. Conditions on $\succeq$ are given that are claimed to force the existence of (among other things) a function Bel such that $U|V \succeq U'|V'$ iff $\mathrm{Bel}(U|V) \geq \mathrm{Bel}(U'|V')$ and an associative function F satisfying A2. (This is Theorem 8 of Chapter II in (Fine 1973).) However, the Bel defined in my counterexample to Cox's theorem can be used to give a counterexample to this result as well.

The remainder of this paper is organized as follows. In the next section there is a more detailed discussion of the problem in Cox's proof. The counterexample to Cox's theorem is given in Section 3. The following section shows that it is also a counterexample to Fine's theorem. Section 5 concludes with some discussion.

2 The Problem With Cox's Proof

To understand the problems with Cox's proof, I actually consider Reichenbach's proof, which is similar in spirit Cox's proof (it is actually even close to Aczél's proof), but uses some additional assumptions, which makes it easier to explain in detail. Aczél, Cox, and Reichenbach all make critical use of functional equations in their proof, and they make the same (seemingly unjustified) leap at corresponding points in their proofs.

Dubois-Prade example does not even satisfy this weaker condition.

[3] Actually, the restriction that F be strictly increasing in each argument is a little too strong. If $e = \mathrm{Bel}(\emptyset)$, then it can be shown that $F(e, x) = F(x, e) = e$ for all x, so that F is not strictly increasing if one of its arguments is e.

[4] I should stress that my counterexample is not a counterexample to Aczél's theorem, since he explicitly assumes that the range of Bel is infinite. However, it does point out potential problems with his proof, and certainly shows that his argument does not apply to finite domains.

In the notation of this paper, Reichenbach (1949, pp. 65–67) assumes (1) that the range of $\mathrm{Bel}(\cdot|\cdot)$ is a subset of $[0,1]$, (2) $\mathrm{Bel}(V|U) = 1$ if $U \subseteq V$, (3) that if V and V' are disjoint, then $\mathrm{Bel}(V \cup V'|U) = \mathrm{Bel}(V|U) + \mathrm{Bel}(V'|U)$ (thus, he assumes that A3 holds, with G being $+$), and (4) that A2 holds with a function F that is differentiable. (He remarks that the result holds even without assumption (4), although the proof is more complicated; Aczél in fact does not make an assumption like (4).)

Reichenbach's proof proceeds as follows: Replacing V' in A2 by $V_1 \cup V_2$, where V_1 and V_2 are disjoint, we get that

$$\mathrm{Bel}(V \cap (V_1 \cup V_2)|U) = F(\mathrm{Bel}(V_1 \cup V_2|V \cap U), \mathrm{Bel}(V|U)). \tag{2}$$

Using the fact that G is $+$, we immediately get

$$\mathrm{Bel}(V \cap (V_1 \cup V_2)|U) = \mathrm{Bel}(V \cap V_1|U) + \mathrm{Bel}(V \cap V_2|U) \tag{3}$$

and

$$\begin{aligned} &F(\mathrm{Bel}(V_1 \cup V_2|V \cap U), \mathrm{Bel}(V|U)) \\ &= F(\mathrm{Bel}(V_1|V \cap U) + \mathrm{Bel}(V_2|V \cap U), \mathrm{Bel}(V|U)) \end{aligned} \tag{4}$$

Moreover, by A2, we also have, for $i = 1, 2$,

$$\mathrm{Bel}(V \cap V_i|U) = F(\mathrm{Bel}(V \cap V_i|V \cap U), \mathrm{Bel}(V|U)). \tag{5}$$

Putting together (2), (3), (4), and (5), we get that

$$\begin{aligned} &F(\mathrm{Bel}(V \cap V_1|V \cap U), \mathrm{Bel}(V|U)) + \\ &\quad F(\mathrm{Bel}(V \cap V_2|V \cap U), \mathrm{Bel}(V|U)) \\ &= F(\mathrm{Bel}(V \cap V_1|V \cap U) + \mathrm{Bel}(V \cap V_2|V \cap U, \mathrm{Bel}(V|U)). \end{aligned} \tag{6}$$

Taking $x = \mathrm{Bel}(V \cap V_1|V \cap U)$, $y = \mathrm{Bel}(V \cap V_2|V \cap U)$, and $z = \mathrm{Bel}(V|U)$ in (6), we get the functional equation

$$F(x, z) + F(y, z) = F(x + y, z). \tag{7}$$

Suppose we assume (as Reichenbach implicitly does) that this functional equation holds for all $(x, y, z) \in P = \{(x, y, z) \in [0,1]^3 : x + y \leq 1\}$. The rest of the proof now follows easily. First, taking $x = 0$ in (7), it follows that

$$F(0, z) + F(y, z) = F(y, z),$$

from which we get that

$$F(0, z) = 0.$$

Next, fix z and let $g_z(x) = F(x, z)$. Since F is, by assumption, differentiable, from (7) we have that

$$g'_z(x) = \lim_{y \to 0}(F(x + y, z) - F(x, z)/y) = \lim_{y \to 0} F(y, z)/y.$$

It thus follows that $g'_z(x)$ is a constant, independent of x. Since the constant may depend on z, there is some function h such that $g'_z(x) = h(z)$. Using the fact that $F(0, z) = 0$, elementary calculus tells us that

$$g_z(x) = F(x, z) = h(z)x.$$

Using the assumption that for all U, V, we have $\mathrm{Bel}(V|U) = 1$ if $U \subseteq V$, we get that

$$\begin{aligned} &\mathrm{Bel}(V|U) = \mathrm{Bel}(V \cap V|U) \\ &= F(\mathrm{Bel}(V|V \cap U), \mathrm{Bel}(V|U)) = F(1, \mathrm{Bel}(V|U)). \end{aligned}$$

Thus, we have that

$$F(1, z) = h(z) = z.$$

We conclude that $F(x, z) = xz$.

Note, however, that this conclusion depends in a crucial way on the assumption that the functional equation (7) holds for all $(x, y, z) \in P$.[5] In fact, all that we can conclude from (6) is that it holds for all (x, y, z) such that there exist U, V, V_1, and V_2, with V_1 and V_2 disjoint, such that $x = \mathrm{Bel}(V \cap V_1|V \cap U)$, $y = \mathrm{Bel}(V \cap V_2|V \cap U)$, and $z = \mathrm{Bel}(V|U)$.

Let us say that a triple that satisfies this condition is *acceptable*. As I mentioned earlier, Aczél also assumes that $\mathrm{Bel}(V|U)$ takes on all values in $[e, E]$, where $e = \mathrm{Bel}(\emptyset|U)$ and $E = \mathrm{Bel}(U|U)$. (In Reichenbach's formulation, $e = 0$ and $E = 1$.) There are two ways to interpret this assumption. The weak interpretation is that for each $x \in [0,1]$, there exist U, V such that $\mathrm{Bel}(V|U) = x$. The strong interpretation is that for each U and x, there exists V such that $\mathrm{Bel}(V|U) = x$. It is not clear which interpretation is intended by Aczél. Neither one obviously suffices to prove that every triple in P is acceptable, although it does seem plausible that it might follow from the second assumption.

In any case, both Aczél and Reichenbach (as well as Cox, in his analogous functional equation) see no need to check that Equation (7) holds throughout P. However, it turns out to be quite necessary to do this. Moreover, it is clear that if W is finite, there are only finitely tuples in P which are acceptable, and it is not the case that all of P is. As we shall see in the next section, this observation has serious consequences as far as all these proofs are concerned.

3 The Counterexample to Cox's Theorem

The goal of this section is to prove

Theorem 3.1: *There is a function Bel_0, a finite domain W, and functions S, F, and G satisfying A1, A2, and A3 respectively such that*

- *$Bel_0(V|U) \in [0,1]$ for $U \neq \emptyset$,*
- *$S(x) = 1 - x$ (so that S is strictly decreasing and infinitely differentiable),*
- *$G(x, y) = x + y$ (so that G is strictly increasing in each argument and is infinitely differentiable),*
- *F is infinitely differentiable, nondecreasing in each argument in $[0,1]^2$, and strictly increasing in each argument in $(0,1]^2$. Moreover, F is commutative, $F(x, 0) = F(0, x) = 0$, and $F(x, 1) = F(1, x) = x$.*

However, there is no one-to-one onto function $g : [0,1] \to [0,1]$ satisfying (1).

Note that the hypotheses on Bel_0, S, G, and F are at least as strong as those made in all the other variants of Cox's result, while the assumptions on g are weaker than those made in the variants. For example, there is no requirement that g be continuous or increasing nor that $g \circ \mathrm{Bel}_0$ is a probability distribution (although Paris and Aczél both prove that,

[5]Actually, using the continuity of F, it suffices that the functional equation holds for a set of triples which is dense in P.

under their assumptions, g can be taken to satisfy all these requirements). This serves to make the counterexample quite a strong one.

Proof: Consider a domain W with 12 points: $w_1, ..., w_{12}$. We associate with each point $w \in W$ a weight $f(w)$, as follows.

$$\begin{array}{ll} f(w_1) = 3 & f(w_4) = 5 \times 10^4 \\ f(w_2) = 2 & f(w_5) = 6 \times 10^4 \\ f(w_3) = 6 & f(w_6) = 8 \times 10^4 \end{array}$$

$$\begin{array}{ll} f(w_7) = 3 \times 10^8 & f(w_{10}) = 3 \times 10^{18} \\ f(w_8) = 8 \times 10^8 & f(w_{11}) = 2 \times 10^{18} \\ f(w_9) = 8 \times 10^8 & f(w_{12}) = 14 \times 10^{18} \end{array}$$

For a subset U of W, we define $f(U) = \sum_{w \in U} f(w)$. Thus, we can define a probability distribution Pr on W by taking $\Pr(U) = f(U)/f(W)$.

Let f' be identical to f, except that $f'(w_{10}) = (3 - \delta) \times 10^{18}$ and $f'(w_{11}) = (2 + \delta) \times 10^{18}$, where δ is defined below. Again, we extend f' to subsets of W by defining $f'(U) = \sum_{w \in U} f'(w)$. Let $W' = \{w_{10}, w_{11}, w_{12}\}$. If $U \neq \emptyset$, define

$$\mathrm{Bel}_0(V|U) = \begin{cases} f'(V \cap U)/f(U) & \text{if } W' \subseteq U \\ f(V \cap U)/f(U) & \text{otherwise.} \end{cases}$$

Bel_0 is clearly very close to Pr. If $U \neq \emptyset$, then it is easy to see that $|\mathrm{Bel}_0(V|U) - \Pr(V|U)| = |f'(V \cap U) - f(V \cap U)|/f(U) \leq \delta$. We choose $\delta > 0$ so that

$$\text{if } \Pr(V|U) > \Pr(V'|U'), \text{ then } \mathrm{Bel}_0(V|U) > \mathrm{Bel}_0(V'|U'). \quad (8)$$

Since the range of Pr is finite, all sufficiently small δ satisfy (8).

The exact choice of weights above is not particularly important. One thing that is important though is the following collection of equalities:

$$\begin{array}{l} \Pr(w_1|\{w_1, w_2\}) = \Pr(w_{10}|\{w_{10}, w_{11}\}) = 3/5 \\ \Pr(\{w_1, w_2\}|\{w_1, w_2, w_3\}) = \Pr(w_4|\{w_4, w_5\}) = 5/11 \\ \Pr(\{w_4, w_5\}|\{w_4, w_5, w_6\}) = \\ \quad \Pr(\{w_7, w_8\}|\{w_7, w_8, w_9\}) = 11/19 \\ \Pr(w_4|\{w_4, w_5, w_6\}) = \\ \quad \Pr(\{w_{10}, w_{11}\}|\{w_{10}, w_{11}, w_{12}\}) = 5/19 \\ \Pr(w_1|\{w_1, w_2, w_3\}) = \Pr(w_7|\{w_7, w_8\}) = 3/11. \end{array} \quad (9)$$

It is easy to check that exactly the same equalities hold if we replace Pr by Bel_0.

Although, as is shown below, the function F satisfying A2 can be taken to be infinitely differentiable and increasing in each argument, the equalities in (9) suffice to guarantee that it cannot be taken to be associative, that is, we do not in general have

$$F(x, F(y, z)) = F(F(x, y), z).$$

Indeed, there is no associative function F satisfying A2, even if we drop the requirements that F be differentiable or increasing.

Lemma 3.2: *For Bel_0 as defined above, there is no associative function F satisfying A2.*

Proof: Suppose there were such a function F. From (9), we must have that

$$\begin{array}{ll} & F(5/11, 11/19) \\ = & F(\mathrm{Bel}_0(w_4|\{w_4, w_5\}), \mathrm{Bel}_0(\{w_4, w_5\}|\{w_4, w_5, w_6\})) \\ = & \mathrm{Bel}_0(w_4|\{w_4, w_5, w_6\}) = 5/19 \end{array}$$

and that

$$\begin{array}{ll} & F(3/5, 5/11) \\ = & F(\mathrm{Bel}_0(w_1|\{w_1, w_2\}), \mathrm{Bel}_0(\{w_1, w_2\}|\{w_1, w_2, w_3\})) \\ = & \mathrm{Bel}_0(w_1|\{w_1, w_2, w_3\}) = 3/11. \end{array}$$

It follows that

$$F(3/5, F(5/11, 11/19)) = F(3/5, 5/19)$$

and that

$$F(F(3/5, 5/11), 11/19) = F(3/11, 11/19).$$

Thus, if F were associative, we would have

$$F(3/5, 5/19) = F(3/11, 11/19).$$

On the other hand, from (9) again, we see that

$$\begin{array}{ll} & F(3/5, 5/19) \\ = & F(\mathrm{Bel}_0(w_{10}|\{w_{10}, w_{11}\}), \mathrm{Bel}_0(\{w_{10}, w_{11}\}|\{w_{10}, w_{11}, w_{12}\})) \\ = & \mathrm{Bel}_0(w_{10}|\{w_{10}, w_{11}, w_{12}\}) = (3 - \delta)/19, \end{array}$$

while

$$\begin{array}{ll} & F(3/11, 11/19) \\ = & F(\mathrm{Bel}_0(w_7|\{w_7, w_8\}), \mathrm{Bel}_0(\{w_7, w_8\}|\{w_7, w_8, w_9\})) \\ = & \mathrm{Bel}_0(w_7|\{w_7, w_8, w_9\}) = 3/19. \end{array}$$

It follows that F cannot be associative. ∎

The next lemma shows that Bel_0 cannot be isomorphic to a probability function.

Lemma 3.3: *For Bel_0 as defined above, there is no one-to-one onto function $g : [0, 1] \to [0, 1]$ satisfying (1).*

Proof: Suppose there were such a function g. First note that $g(\mathrm{Bel}_0(U)) \neq 0$ if $U \neq \emptyset$. For if $g(\mathrm{Bel}_0(U)) = 0$, then it follows from (1) that for all $V \subseteq U$, we have

$$g(\mathrm{Bel}_0(V)) = g(\mathrm{Bel}_0(V|U)) \times g(\mathrm{Bel}_0(U)) = g(\mathrm{Bel}_0(V|U)) \times 0 =$$

Thus, $g(\mathrm{Bel}_0(V)) = g(\mathrm{Bel}_0(U))$ for all subsets V of U. Since the definition of Bel_0 guarantees that $\mathrm{Bel}_0(V) \neq \mathrm{Bel}_0(U)$ if V is a strict subset of U, this contradicts the assumption that g is one-to-one. Thus, $g(\mathrm{Bel}_0(U)) \neq 0$ if $U \neq \emptyset$. It now follows from (1) that if $U \neq \emptyset$, then

$$g(\mathrm{Bel}_0(V|U)) = g(\mathrm{Bel}_0(V \cap U))/g(\mathrm{Bel}_0(U)). \quad (10)$$

Now define $F(x, y) = g^{-1}(g(x) \times g(y))$. Notice that, by applying the observation above repeatedly, if $V \cap U \neq \emptyset$, we get

$$\begin{array}{ll} & F(\mathrm{Bel}_0(V'|V \cap U), \mathrm{Bel}_0(V|U)) \\ = & g^{-1}((g(\mathrm{Bel}_0(V'|V \cap U)) \times g(\mathrm{Bel}_0(V|U)) \\ = & g^{-1}(g(\mathrm{Bel}_0(V' \cap V \cap U))/g(\mathrm{Bel}_0(U))) \\ = & g^{-1}(g(\mathrm{Bel}_0(V' \cap V|U))) \\ = & \mathrm{Bel}_0(V' \cap V|U). \end{array}$$

Thus, F satisfies A2. Moreover, notice that F is associative, since

$$\begin{aligned} F(F(x,y),z) &= g^{-1}(g(g^{-1}(g(x)\times g(y)))\times g(z)) \\ &= g^{-1}(g(x)\times g(y)\times g(z)) \\ &= g^{-1}(g(x)\times g(g^{-1}(g(y)\times g(z)))) \\ &= F(x,F(y,z)). \end{aligned}$$

But this contradicts Lemma 3.2. ∎

Despite the fact that Bel_0 is not isomorphic to a probability function, functions S, F, and G can be defined that satisfy A1, A2, and A3, respectively, and all the other requirements stated in Theorem 3.1. The argument for S and G is easy; all the work goes into proving that an appropriate F exists.

Lemma 3.4 : *There exists an infinitely differentiable, strictly decreasing function* $S : [0,1] \to [0,1]$ *such that* $Bel_0(\overline{V}|U) = S(Bel_0(V|U))$ *for all sets* $U, V \subseteq W$ *with* $U \neq \emptyset$. *In fact, we can take* $S(x) = 1 - x$.

Proof: This is immediate from the observation that $\text{Bel}_0(\overline{V}|U) = 1 - \text{Bel}_0(V|U)$ for $U, V \subseteq W$. ∎

Lemma 3.5: *There exists an infinitely differentiable function* $G : [0,1]^2 \to [0,1]$, *increasing in each argument, such that if* $U, V, V' \subseteq W$, $V \cap V' = \emptyset$, *and* $U \neq \emptyset$, *then* $Bel_0(V \cup V'|U) = G(Bel_0(V|U), Bel_0(V', U))$. *In fact, we can take* $G(x, y) = x + y$.

Proof: This is immediate from the definition of Bel_0. ∎

Thus, all that remains is to show that an appropriate F exists. The key step is provided by the following lemma, which essentially shows that there is a well defined F that is increasing.

Lemma 3.6: *If* $U_2 \cap U_1 \neq \emptyset$ *and* $V_2 \cap V_1 \neq \emptyset$, *then*

(a) *if* $Bel_0(V_3|V_2 \cap V_1) \leq Bel_0(U_3|U_2 \cap U_1)$ *and* $Bel_0(V_2|V_1) \leq Bel_0(U_2|U_1)$, *then* $Bel_0(V_3 \cap V_2|V_1) \leq Bel_0(U_3 \cap U_2|U_1)$,

(b) *if* $Bel_0(V_3|V_2 \cap V_1) < Bel_0(U_3|U_2 \cap U_1)$, $Bel_0(V_2|V_1) \leq Bel_0(U_2|U_1)$, $Bel_0(U_3|U_2 \cap U_1) > 0$, *and* $Bel_0(U_2|U_1) > 0$, *then* $Bel_0(V_3 \cap V_2|V_1) < Bel_0(U_3 \cap U_2|U_1)$,

(c) *if* $Bel_0(V_3|V_2 \cap V_1) \leq Bel_0(U_3|U_2 \cap U_1)$, $Bel_0(V_2|V_1) < Bel_0(U_2|U_1)$, $Bel_0(U_3|U_2 \cap U_1) > 0$, *and* $Bel_0(U_2|U_1) > 0$, *then* $Bel_0(V_3 \cap V_2|V_1) < Bel_0(U_3 \cap U_2|U_1)$,

Proof: First observe that if $\text{Bel}_0(V_3|V_2 \cap V_1) \leq \text{Bel}_0(U_3|U_2 \cap U_1)$ and $\text{Bel}_0(V_2|V_1) \leq \text{Bel}_0(U_2|U_1)$, then from (8), it follows that $\Pr(V_3|V_2 \cap V_1) \leq \Pr(U_3|U_2 \cap U_1)$ and $\Pr(V_2|V_1) \leq \Pr(U_2|U_1)$. If we have either $\Pr(V_3|V_2 \cap V_1) < \Pr(U_3|U_2 \cap U_1)$ or $\Pr(V_2|V_1) < \Pr(U_2|U_1)$, then we have either $\Pr(V_3 \cap V_2|V_1) < \Pr(U_3 \cap U_2|U_1)$ or $\Pr(U_3|U_2 \cap U_1) = 0$ or $\Pr(U_2|U_1) = 0$. It follows that either $\text{Bel}_0(V_3 \cap V_2|V_1) < \text{Bel}_0(U_3 \cap U_2|U_1)$ (this uses (8) again) or that $\text{Bel}_0(V_3 \cap V_2|V_1) = \text{Bel}_0(U_3 \cap U_2|U_1) = 0$. In either case, the lemma holds.

Thus, it remains to deal with the case that $\Pr(V_3|V_2 \cap V_1) = \Pr(U_3|U_2 \cap U_1)$ and $\Pr(V_2|V_1) = \Pr(U_2|U_1)$, and hence $\Pr(V_3 \cap V_2|V_1) = \Pr(U_3 \cap U_2|U_1)$. The details of this analysis are left to the full paper. ∎

Lemma 3.7: *There exists a function* $F : [0,1]^2 \to [0,1]$ *satisfying all the assumptions of the theorem.*

Proof: Define a partial function F' on $[0,1]^2$ whose domain consists of all pairs (x, y) such that for some subsets U, V, V' of W, we have $x = \text{Bel}_0(V'|V \cap U)$ and $y = \text{Bel}_0(V|U)$. For such (x, y), we define $F'(x, y) = \text{Bel}_0(V' \cap V|U)$. *A priori*, it is possible that there exist sets $U_1, U_2, U_3, V_1, V_2, V_3$ such that $x = \text{Bel}_0(U_3|U_2 \cap U_1) = \text{Bel}_0(V_3|V_2 \cap V_1)$ and $y = \text{Bel}_0(U_2|U_1) = \text{Bel}_0(V_2|V_1)$, yet $\text{Bel}_0(U_3 \cap U_2|U_1) \neq \text{Bel}_0(V_3 \cap V_2|V_1)$. If this were the case, then $F'(x, y)$ would not be well defined. However, Lemma 3.6 says that this cannot happen. Moreover, the lemma assures us that F' is increasing on its domain, and strictly increasing as long as one of its arguments is not 0. Notice that if $\text{Bel}_0(V|U) = x \neq 0$ for some V, U, then $(0, x)$, $(x, 1)$ and $(1, x)$ are in the domain of F', and $F'(x, 1) = F'(1, x) = x$, while $F'(0, x) = 0$. It is easy to see that there are no pairs $(x, 0)$ in the domain of F'. Finally, there are no pairs (x, y) and (y, x) that are both in the domain of F' unless one of x or y is 1.

The domain of F' is finite. It is straightforward to extend F' to a commutative, infinitely differentiable, and increasing function F defined on all of $[0,1]^2$, which is strictly increasing on $(0,1]^2$, and satisfies $F(x, 1) = F(1, x) = x$ and $F(x, 0) = F(0, x) = 0$. (Note that to make F commutative, we first define it on pairs (x, y) such that $x \geq y$, and then if $x < y$, we define $F((x, y) = F(y, x)$. Since F' is commutative on its domain of definition, this approach does not run into problems.) Clearly F satisfies A2, since (by construction) F' does, and A2 puts constraints only on the domain of F'. ∎

Theorem 3.1 now follows from Lemmas 3.3, 3.4, 3.5, and 3.7. ∎

4 The Counterexample to Fine's Theorem

Fine is interested in what he calls *comparative conditional probability*. Thus, rather than associating a real number with each "conditional object" $V|U$, he puts an ordering $\succeq$ on such objects. As usual, $V|U \succ V'|U'$ is taken to be an abbreviation for $V|U \succeq V'|U'$ and not$(V'|U' \succeq V|U)$.

Fine is interested in when such an ordering is induced by a real-valued belief function with reasonable properties. He says that a real-valued function P on such objects *agrees with* $\succeq$ if $P(V|U) \geq P(V'|U')$ iff $V|U \succeq V'|U'$. Fine then considers a number of axioms that $\succeq$ might satisfy. For our purposes, the most relevant are the ones Fine denotes QCC1, QCC2, QCC5, and QCC7.

QCC1 just says that $\succeq$ is a linear order:

QCC1. $V|U \succeq V'|U'$ or $V'|U' \succeq V|U$.

QCC2 says that $\succeq$ is transitive:

QCC2. If $V_1|U_1 \succeq V_2|U_2$ and $V_2|U_2 \succeq V_3|U_3$, then $V_1|U_1 \succeq V_3|U_3$.

QCC5 is a technical condition involving notions of order topology. The relevant definitions are omitted here (see (Fine 1973) for details), since QCC5, as Fine observes, holds vacuously in finite domains (the only ones of interest here).

QCC5. The set $\{V|U\}$ has a countable basis in the order topology induced by $\succ$.

Finally, QCC7 essentially says that $\succeq$ is increasing, in the sense of Lemma 3.6.

QCC7.

(a) If $V_3|V_2 \cap V_1 \succeq U_3|U_2 \cap U_1$ and $V_2|V_1 \succeq U_2|U_1$ then $V_3 \cap V_2|V_1 \succeq U_3 \cap U_2|U_1$.

(b) If $V_3|V_2 \cap V_1 \succeq U_2|U_1$ and $V_2|V_1 \succeq U_3|U_2 \cap U_1$ then $V_3 \cap V_2|V_1 \succeq U_3 \cap U_2|U_1$.

(c) If $V_3|V_2 \cap V_1 \succ U_3|U_2 \cap U_1$, $V_2|V_1 \succeq U_2|U_1$, and $V_2|V_1 \succ \emptyset|W$, then $V_3 \cap V_2|V_1 \succ U_3 \cap U_2|U_1$.

Fine then claims the following theorem:

Fine's Theorem: (Fine 1973, Chapter II, Theorem 8) *If $\succeq$ satisfies QCC1, QCC2, QCC5, then there exists some agreeing function P. There exists a function F of two variables such that*

1. $P(V \cap V'|U) = F(P(V'|V \cap U), P(V|U))$,[6]
2. $F(x, y) = F(y, x)$,
3. $F(x, y)$ *is increasing in* x *for* $y > P(\emptyset|W)$,
4. $F(x, F(y, z)) = F(F(x, y), z)$,
5. $F(P(W|U), y) = y$,
6. $F(P(\emptyset|U), y) = P(\emptyset|U)$.

iff $\succeq$ also satisfies QCC7.

The only relevant clauses for our purposes are Clause (1), which is just A2, and Clause (4), which says that F is associative. As Lemma 3.2 shows, there is no associative function satisfying A2 for Bel_0. As I now show, this means that Fine's theorem does not quite hold either.

Before doing so, let me briefly touch on a subtle issue regarding the domain of $\succeq$. In the counterexample of the previous section, $\text{Bel}_0(V|U)$ is defined as long as $U \neq \emptyset$. Fine does not assume that the $\succeq$ relation is necessarily defined on all objects $V|U$ such that $U, V \subseteq W$ and $U \neq \emptyset$. He assumes that there is an algebra $\mathcal{F}$ of subsets of W (that is, a set of subsets closed under finite intersections and complementation) and a subset $\mathcal{F}'$ of $\mathcal{F}$ closed under finite intersections and not containing the empty set such that $\succeq$ is defined on conditional objects $V|U$ such that $V \in \mathcal{F}$ and $U \in \mathcal{F}'$. Since $\mathcal{F}'$ is closed under intersection and does not contain the empty set, $\mathcal{F}'$ cannot contain disjoint sets. If W is finite, then the only way a collection $\mathcal{F}'$ can meet Fine's restriction is if there is some nonempty set U_0 such that all elements in $\mathcal{F}'$ contain U_0. This restriction is clearly too strong to the extent that comparative conditional probability is intended to generalize probability. If Pr is a probability function, then it certainly makes sense to compare $\Pr(V|U)$ and $\Pr(V'|U')$ even if U and U' are disjoint sets. Fine [private communication, 1995] suggested that it might be better to constrain QCC7 so that we do not condition on events U that are equivalent to $\emptyset$ (where U is equivalent to $\emptyset$ if $\emptyset \succeq U$ and $U \succeq \emptyset$). Since the only event equivalent to $\emptyset$ in the counterexample of the previous section is $\emptyset$ itself, this means that the counterexample can be used without change. This is what is done in the proof below. In the full paper, I indicate how to modify the counterexample so that it satisfies Fine's original restrictions.

Theorem 4.1: *There exists an ordering $\succeq$ satisfying QCC1, QCC2, QCC5, and QCC7, such that for every function P agreeing with $\succeq$, there is no associative function F of two variables such that $P(V \cap V')|U) = F(P(V'|V \cap U), P(V|U))$.*

Proof: Let W and Bel_0 be as in the counterexample in the previous section. Define $\succeq$ so that Bel_0 agrees with $\succeq$. Thus, $V|U \succeq V'|U'$ iff $\text{Bel}_0(V|U) \geq \text{Bel}_0(V'|U')$. Clearly $\succeq$ satisfies QCC1 and QCC2. As was mentioned earlier, since W is finite, $\succeq$ vacuously satisfies QCC5. Lemma 3.6 shows that $\succeq$ satisfies parts (a) and (c) of QCC7. To show that $\succeq$ also satisfies part (b) of QCC7, we must prove that if $\text{Bel}_0(V_3|V_2 \cap V_1) \geq \text{Bel}_0(U_2|U_1)$ and $\text{Bel}_0(V_2|V_1) \geq \text{Bel}_0(U_3|U_2 \cap U_1)$, then $\text{Bel}_0(V_3 \cap V_2|V_1) \geq \text{Bel}_0(U_3 \cap U_2|U_1)$. The proof of this is almost identical to that of Lemma 3.6; we simply exchange the roles of $\Pr(V_2|V_1)$ and $\Pr(V_3|V_2 \cap V_1)$ in that proof. I leave the details to the reader. Lemma 3.2 shows that there is no associative function F satisfying A2 for Bel_0. All that was used in the proof was the fact that Bel_0 satisfied the inequalities of (9). But these equalities must hold for any function agreeing with $\succeq$. Thus, exactly the same proof shows that if P is any function agreeing with $\succeq$, then there is no associative function F satisfying $P(V \cap V'|U) = F(P(V'|V \cap U), P(V|U))$. ∎

5 Discussion

Let me summarize the status of various results in the light of the counterexample of this paper:

- Cox's theorem as originally stated does not hold in finite domains. Moreover, even in infinite domains, the counterexample and the discussion in Section 2 suggest that more assumptions are required for its correctness. In particular, the claim in his proof that F is associative does not follow.
- Although the counterexample given here is not a counterexample to Aczél's theorem, his assumptions do not seem strong enough to guarantee that the function G is associative, as he claims it is.
- The variants of Cox's theorem stated by Heckerman (1988), Horvitz, Heckerman, and Langlotz (1986), and Aleliunas (1988) all succumb to the counterexample.
- The claim that the function F must be associative in Fine's theorem is incorrect. Fine has an analogous result (Fine 1973, Chapter II, Theorem 4) for unconditional comparative probability involving a function G as in Aczél's theorem. This function too is claimed to be associative, and again, this does not seem to follow (although my counterexample does not apply to that theorem).

[6] Fine assumes that $P(V \cap V'|U) = F(P(V|U), P(V'|V \cap U))$. I have reordered the arguments here for consistency with Cox's theorem.

Of course, the interesting question now is what it would take to recover Cox's theorem. Paris's assumption A4 suffices. As we have observed, A4 forces the domain of Bel to be infinite, as does the assumption that the range of Bel is all of $[0, 1]$. We can always extend a domain to an infinite—indeed, uncountable—domain by assuming that we have an infinite collection of independent fair coins, and that we can talk about outcomes of coin tosses as well as the original events in the domain. (This type of "extendibility" assumption is fairly standard; for example, it is made by Savage (1954) in quite a different context.) In such an extended domain, it seems reasonable to also assume that Bel varies uniformly between 0 (certain falsehood) and 1 (certain truth). If we also assume A4 (or something like it), we can then recover Cox's theorem. Notice, however, that this viewpoint disallows a notion of belief that takes on only finitely many or even countably many gradations.

Suppose we really are interested in a particular finite domain, and we do not want to extend it. What assumptions do we then need to get Cox's theorem? The counterexample given here could be circumvented by requiring that F be associative on all tuples (rather than just on the tuples (x, y, z) that arise as $x = \text{Bel}_0(U_4|U_3 \cap U_2 \cap U_1)$, $y = \text{Bel}_0(U_3|U_2 \cap U_1)$, and $z = \text{Bel}_0(U_2|U_1)$). However, if we really are interested in a single domain, the motivation for making requirements on the behavior of F on belief values that do not arise is not so clear. Moreover, it is far from clear that assuming that F is associative suffices to prove the theorem. For example, Cox's proof makes use of various functional equations involving F and S, analogous to the equation (7) that appears in Section 2. These functional equations are easily seen to hold for certain tuples. However, as we saw in Section 2, the proof really requires that they hold for *all* tuples. Just assuming that F is associative does not appear to suffice to guarantee that the functional equations involving S hold for all tuples. Futher assumptions appear necessary.

One condition (suggested by Nir Friedman) that does seem to suffice (although I have not checked details) is that of assuming that essentially all beliefs are distinct. More precisely, we could assume

- if $\emptyset \subset U \subset V$, $\emptyset \subset U' \subset V'$, and $(U, V) \neq (U', V')$, then $\text{Bel}(U|V) \neq \text{Bel}(U'|V')$.

Even if this condition suffices, note that it precludes, for example, a uniform probability distribution, and thus again seems unduly restrictive.

So what does all this say regarding the use of probability? Not much. Although I have tried to argue here that Cox's justification of probability is not quite as strong as previously believed, and the assumptions underlying the variants of it need clarification, I am not trying to suggest that probability should be abandoned. There are many other justifications for its use.

Acknowledgments

I'd like to thank Peter Cheeseman, Terry Fine, Ron Fagin, Nir Friedman, David Heckerman, Eric Horvitz, Jeff Paris, and an anonymous referee for useful comments on an earlier draft of the paper. I'd also like to thank Judea Pearl for pointing out Reichenbach's work to me. This work was supported in part by NSF grant IRI-95-03109.

References

Aczél, J. 1966. *Lectures on Functional Equations and Their Applications*. New York: Academic Press.

Aleliunas, R. 1988. A summary of a new normative theory of probabilistic logic. In *Proceedings of the Fourth Workshop on Uncertainty in Artificial Intelligence,* Minneapolis, MN, 8–14. Also in R. Shachter, T. Levitt, L. Kanal, and J. Lemmer, editors, *Uncertainty in Artificial Intelligence 4,* pages 199–206. North-Holland, New York, 1990.

Cheeseman, P. 1988. An inquiry into computer understanding. *Computational Intelligence* 4(1):58–66.

Cox, R. 1946. Probability, frequency, and reasonable expectation. *American Journal of Physics* 14(1):1–13.

Dubois, D., and Prade, H. 1990. The logical view of conditioning and its application to possibility and evidence theories. *International Journal of Approximate Reasoning* 4(1):23–46.

Fine, T. L. 1973. *Theories of Probability*. New York: Academic Press.

Heckerman, D. 1988. An aximoatic framework for belief updates. In Lemmer, J. F., and Kanal, L. N., eds., *Uncertainty in Artificial Intelligence 2*. Amsterdam: North-Holland. 11–22.

Horvitz, E. J.; Heckerman, D.; and Langlotz, C. P. 1986. A framework for comparing alternative formalisms for plausible reasoning. In *Proc. National Conference on Artificial Intelligence (AAAI '86)*, 210–214.

Paris, J. B. 1994. *The Uncertain Reasoner's Companion*. Cambridge, U.K.: Cambridge University Press.

Reichenbach, H. 1949. *The Theory of Probability*. University of California Press, Berkeley. This is a translation and revision of the German edition, published as *Wahrscheinlichkeitslehre*, in 1935.

Savage, L. J. 1954. *Foundations of Statistics*. John Wiley & Sons.

Invited Talks

Robots With AI: A Retrospective on the AAAI Robot Competitions and Exhibitions

Pete Bonasso* and Tom Dean**

*Metrica, Inc., Johnson Space Center, NASA
Houston, TX 77059
bonasso@aio.jsc,nasa.gov
**Department of Computer Science, Brown University,
Providence, RI 02912
tld@cs.brown.edu

There have been five years of robot competitions and exhibitions since the inception of this annual event in 1992. Since that first show we have seen 30 different teams compete and almost that many more exhibit their robots. These teams ranged from universities to industry and government research labs to one or two inventors working out of garages. Their composition ranged from seasoned AI researchers to eager undergraduates, and they hailed from the United States, Canada, Europe and the Far East. Despite the concerns of some about the relevance and even the appropriateness of such an event, the robots have become a key attraction of the national and international conferences. In this talk, we look back on the form and function of the five years of exhibitions and competitions and attempt to draw some lessons in retrospect as well as future implications for the AI community and our society at large.

A cornerstone of this event has always been the emphasis on fully autonomous robots, and hence the apparent need for AI. We will survey the role that the hallmarks of AI -- planning, learning, machine vision and spoken language understanding -- have played in the competitions, particularly with those teams ranked high in the standings. We will touch on the use of single and multiple agents, reactive and deliberative control schemes, use of active perception, and the basic problem-solving approaches brought to bear each year by the teams in the competition.

The past five years have also seen an increase in the need for and even the use of autonomous mobile robots in the service industries -- those industries requiring the use of robots in natural environments among humans. We are beginning to see the almost routine use of autonomous robots vacuuming large warehouse and hotel areas, ferrying x-rays and medicines in hospitals, and even filling pharmaceutical prescriptions. We will sample from the competition results and some of the exhibitions to suggest which AI technologies can or cannot be made relevant for service industry needs.

Finally, we want to convey some of the atmosphere of the competitions both in front of and behind the scenes: the camaraderie, the sleepless nights, the sharing of ideas, the last minute requisitions for hardware and the up to the minute software hacks. There is every much a thrill of victory and an agony of defeat in these events as there are in sports contests in other settings. Through the liberal use of video tape and anecdotes, we hope we can make these aspects of the competition realizable so that listeners can glimpse the intangible benefits of this important coming together of people and ideas to produce intelligent -- and useful -- robots.

Moving Up the Information Food Chain: Deploying Softbots on the World Wide Web

Oren Etzioni
Department of Computer Science and Engineering
University of Washington
Seattle, WA 98195
`http://www.cs.washington.edu/homes/etzioni`

Abstract

I view the World Wide Web as an *information food chain* (figure 1). The maze of pages and hyperlinks that comprise the Web are at the very bottom of the chain. The WebCrawlers and Alta Vistas of the world are *information herbivores*; they graze on Web pages and regurgitate them as searchable indices. Today, most Web users feed near the bottom of the information food chain, but the time is ripe to move up. Since 1991, we have been building *information carnivores*, which intelligently hunt and feast on herbivores in Unix (Etzioni, Lesh, & Segal 1993), on the Internet (Etzioni & Weld 1994), and on the Web (Doorenbos, Etzioni, & Weld 1996; Selberg & Etzioni 1995; Shakes, Langheinrich, & Etzioni 1996).

Motivation

Today's Web is populated by a panoply of primitive but popular information services. Consider, for example, an information cow such as Alta Vista. Alta Vista requires massive memory resources (to store an index of the Web) and tremendous network bandwidth (to create and continually refresh the index). The cost of these resources is amortized over millions of queries per day. As a result, the CPU cycles devoted to satisfying each individual query are sharply curtailed. There is no *time* for intelligence. Furthermore, each query is independent of the previous one. No attempt is made to customize Alta Vista's responses to a particular individual. The result is homogenized, least-common-denominator service.

In contrast, visionaries such as Alan Kay and Nicholas Negroponte have been advocating agents — personal assistants that act on your behalf in cyberspace. While the notion of agents has been popular for more than a decade, we have yet to build agents that are both widely used *and* intelligent. The Web presents a golden opportunity and an implicit challenge for the AI community. As the old adage goes "If not us, then who? And if not now, when?"

The challenge of deploying web agents will help revitalize AI and forge closer links with other areas of computer science. But be warned, the Web community is hungry, impatient, and skeptical. They expect:

- **Robustness:** a working system, accessible seven days a week, twenty-four hours a day.
- **Speed:** virtually all widely-used Web resources begin transmitting useful (or at least entertaining) information within seconds.
- **Added Value:** any increase in sophistication had better yield a tangible benefit to users.

Is the Web challenge a distraction from our long-term goal of understanding intelligence and building intelligent agents? I believe that the field benefits from a mixture of long-term and short-term goals and from both empirical and theoretical work. Work toward the goal of deploying intelligent agents on the Web is a valuable addition to the current mix for two reasons. First, the Web suggests new problems and new constraints on existing techniques. Second, intelligent Web agents will provide tangible evidence of the power and utility of AI techniques. Next time you encounter AI bashing, wouldn't it be satisfying to counter with a few well-chosen URLs? Personally, I find the Web irresistible. To borrow Herb Simon's phrase, it is today's "Main Chance." Simon describes his move from the "academic backwater" of public administration to AI and cognitive psychology as "gravitating toward the sun" (Simon 1991, pages 113-114). While AI is not an academic backwater, the Web *is* today's sun. Turning towards the sun and responding to the Web challenge, my collaborators and have begun to deploy a species of information carnivores (called *softbots*) on the Web.

Softbots

Softbots (software robots) are intelligent agents that use software tools and services on a person's behalf (see figure 2 for a softbot family tree). Tool use is one of the hallmarks of intelligence. In many cases, softbots rely on the same tools and utilities available to human computer users — tools for sending mail, printing files, and so on. Mobile robots have yet to achieve the physical analog — using vacuum cleaners,

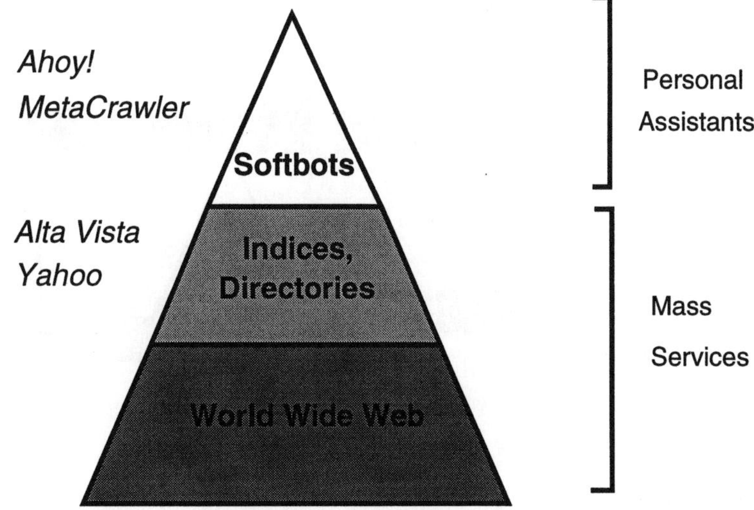

Figure 1: The Information Food Chain

lawn mowers, etc.[1]

Much of our work has focused on the Internet softbot (also known as Rodney) (Etzioni & Weld 1994). Rodney enables a person to state *what* he or she wants accomplished. Rodney disambiguates the request and dynamically determines *how* and *where* to satisfy it, utilizing a wide range of Internet services and Unix commands. Rodney relies on a declarative representation of the different software tools at its disposal, enabling it to chain together multiple tools in response to a user's request. Rodney uses automatic planning technology to dynamically generate the appropriate action sequence. The Internet softbots project has led to a steady stream of technical results (*e.g.*, (Etzioni *et al.* 1992; Etzioni, Golden, & Weld 1994; Golden, Etzioni, & Weld 1994; Kwok & Weld 1996; Perkowitz & Etzioni 1995)). Closely related projects include (Kirk *et al.* 1995; Arens *et al.* 1993).

Unfortunately, we have yet to produce a planner-based softbot that meets the stringent demands of the Web community. While continuing our ambitious long-term project to develop planner-based softbots, we have embraced a new strategy for the creation of intelligent agents which I call "useful first." Instead of starting with grand ideas about intelligence and issuing a promissory note that they will eventually yield useful intelligent agents, we take the opposite tack; we begin with useful softbots deployed on the Web, and issue a promissory note that they will evolve into more intelligent agents. We are still committed to the goal of producing agents that are *both* intelligent and useful. However, I submit that we are more likely to achieve this conjunctive goal if we reverse the traditional subgoal ordering and focus on building useful systems first.

The argument for "useful first" is analogous to the argument made by Rod Brooks (Brooks 1991) and others (Etzioni 1993; Mitchell *et al.* 1990) for building complete agents and testing them in a real world. As Brooks put it, "with a simplified world...it is very easy to accidentally build a submodule of the systems which happens to rely on some of those simplified properties... the disease spreads and the complete system depends in a subtle way on the simplified world." This argument applies equally well to user demands and real-time constraints on Web agents.

There is a huge gulf between an AI prototype and an agent ready for deployment on the Web. One might argue that this gulf is of no interest to AI researchers. However, the demands of the Web community constrain the AI techniques we use, and lead us to new AI problems. We need to recognize that intelligent agents are ninety-nine percent computer science and one percent AI. The AI is critical but we cannot ignore the context into which it is embedded. Patrick Winston has called this the "raisin bread" model of AI. If we want to bake raisin bread, we cannot focus exclusively on the raisins.[2]

Operating on a shoestring budget, we have been able

[1]softbots are an attractive substrate for intelligent-agent research for the following reasons (Etzioni 1993; 1994). First, the cost, effort, and expertise necessary to develop and systematically experiment with software artifacts are relatively low. Second, software environments circumvent many of the thorny but peripheral problems that are inescapable in physical environments. Finally, in contrast to simulated physical worlds, software environments are readily available (sophisticated simulations can take years to perfect), intrinsically interesting, and *real.* However, Softbots are *not* intended to replace robots; Robots and softbots are complimentary.

[2]See (Brachman 1992) for an account of the massive re-engineering necessary to transform an "intelligent first" knowledge representation system into a usable one.

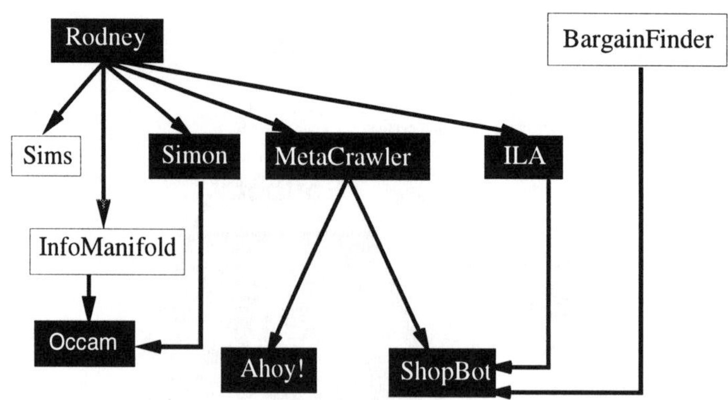

Figure 2: The Softbot Family Tree. The black boxes represent softbots developed at the University of Washington. MetaCrawler, Ahoy!, and ShopBot have been deployed on the Web.

to deploy several softbots on the Web within one year. I review our fielded softbots and then consider both the benefits and pitfalls of the "useful first" approach.

MetaCrawler

The MetaCrawler softbot[3] provides a single, unified interface for Web document searching (Selberg & Etzioni 1995). MetaCrawler supports an expressive query language that allows searching for documents that contain certain phrases and excluding documents containing other phrases. MetaCrawler queries nine of the most popular information herbivores in parallel. Thus, MetaCrawler eliminates the need for users to try and retry queries across different herbivores. Furthermore, users need not remember the address, interface and capabilities of each one. Consider searching for documents containing the phrase "four score and seven years ago." Some herbivores support phrase searching whereas others do not. MetaCrawler frees the user from having to remember such details. If a herbivore supports phrase searching, MetaCrawler automatically invokes this feature. If a herbivore does not support phrase searching, MetaCrawler automatically downloads the pages returned by that herbivore and performs its own phrase search locally.

In a recent article, Forbes Magazine asked Lycos's Michael Maudlin "why aren't the other spiders as smart as MetaCrawler?" Maudlin replied "with our volume I have to turn down the smarts...MetaCrawler will too if it gets much bigger." Maudlin's reply misses an important point: because MetaCrawler relies on information herbivores to do the resource-intensive grazing of the Web, it is sufficiently lightweight to run on an average PC and serve as a personal assistant. Indeed, MetaCrawler-inspired PC applications are now on the market.

MetaCrawler demonstrates that Web services and their interfaces may be de-coupled. MetaCrawler is a *meta-interface* with three main benefits. First, the same interface can be used to access *multiple* services simultaneously. Second, since the meta-interface has relatively modest resource requirements it can reside on an individual user's machine, which facilitates customization to that individual. Finally, if a meta-interface resides on the user's machine, there is no need to "turn down the smarts." In a Web-mediated client/server architecture, where intelligence resides in the client, "volume" is no longer a limiting factor on the "smarts" of the overall system.

While MetaCrawler does not currently use AI techniques, it is evolving rapidly. For example, we are investigating the use of document clustering to enable users to rapidly focus on relevant subsets of the references returned by MetaCrawler. In addition, we are investigating mixed-initiative dialog to help users focus their search. Most important, MetaCrawler is an enabling technology for softbots that are perched above it in the information food chain.

Ahoy! The Home Page Finder

The Ahoy! softbot[4] specializes in locating people's home pages on the Web by filtering MetaCrawler output (Shakes, Langheinrich, & Etzioni 1996). Ahoy! takes as input a person's name and affiliation, and attempts to find the person's home page. Ahoy! queries MetaCrawler and uses knowledge of Web geography (*e.g.*, the URLs of home pages at the University of Washington end with `washington.edu`) and home page appearance (a home page title is likely to contain a person's last name) to filter MetaCrawler's output. Typically, Ahoy! is able to cut the number of references returned by a factor of forty but still maintain

[3] `http://www.cs.washington.edu/research/metacrawler`

[4] `http://www.cs.washington.edu/research/ahoy`

very high accuracy.

Since Ahoy!'s filtering algorithm is heuristic, it asks its users to label its answers as correct or not. Ahoy! uses the feedback it receives from its users to continually improve its performance. It rapidly collects a set of home pages and near misses (labeled as such by users) to use as training data for an algorithm that attempts to learn the conventions underlying home page placement. For example, home pages at the University of Washington's Computer Science Department typically have the form `http://www.cs.washington.edu/homes/<lastname>`. After learning, Ahoy! is able to locate home pages of individuals even *before* they are indexed by MetaCrawler's herd of information herbivores.

In the context of Ahoy!, the "useful first" constraint led us to tackle an important impediment to the use of machine learning on the Web. Data is abundant on the Web, but it is unlabeled. Most concept learning techniques require training data labeled as positive (or negative) examples of some concept. Techniques such as uncertainty sampling (Lewis & Gale 1994) reduce the amount of labeled data needed, but do not eliminate the problem. Instead, Ahoy! attempts to harness the Web's interactive nature to solve the labeling problem. Ahoy! relies on its initial power to draw numerous users to it and to solicit their feedback; it then uses this feedback to solve the labeling problem, make generalizations about the Web, and improve its performance. Note that by relying on feedback from *multiple* users, Ahoy! rapidly collects the data it needs to learn; systems that are focused on learning an individual users taste do not have this luxury. Ahoy!'s boot-strapping architecture is not restricted to learning about home pages; user feedback may be harnessed to learn in a variety of Web domains.

ShopBot

ShopBot[5] is a softbot that carries out comparison shopping at Web vendors on a person's behalf (Doorenbos, Etzioni, & Weld 1996). Whereas virtually all previous Web agents rely on hard-coded interfaces to the Web sites they access, ShopBot autonomously *learns* to extract product information from Web vendors given their URL and general information about their product domain (*e.g.*, software). Specifically, ShopBot learns how to query a store's searchable product catalog, learns the format in which product descriptions are presented, and learns to extract product attributes such as price from these descriptions.

ShopBot's learning algorithm is based in part on that of the Internet Learning Agent (ILA) (Perkowitz & Etzioni 1995). ILA learns to extract information from unfamiliar sites by querying with familiar objects and analyzing the relationship of output tokens to the query object. ShopBot borrows this idea from ILA; ShopBot learns by querying stores for information on popular products, and analyzing the stores' responses. However, ShopBot tackles a more ambitious learning problem than ILA because Web vendors are far more complex and varied than the Internet directories that ILA was tested on.

In the software shopping domain, ShopBot has been given the home pages for 12 on-line software vendors. After its learning is complete, ShopBot is able to speedily visit the vendors, extract product information such as availability and price, and summarize the results for the user. In a preliminary user study, ShopBot users were able to shop four times faster (and find better prices!) than users relying only on a Web browser (Doorenbos, Etzioni, & Weld 1996).

Discussion

Every methodology has both benefits and pitfalls; the softbot paradigm is no exception. Perhaps the most important benefit has been the discovery of new research challenges, the imposition of tractability constraints on AI algorithms, and the resulting innovations. In recent years, planner-based softbots have led us to the challenge of incorporating information goals, sensory actions, and closed world reasoning into planners in a tractable manner. Our focus on tractability led us to formulate UWL (Etzioni *et al.* 1992) and Local Closed World Reasoning (Etzioni, Golden, & Weld 1994; 1995). We expect "useful first" to be equally productive over the next few years. For example, MetaCrawler has led us to investigate on-line, real-time document clustering. Previous approaches to document clustering typically assume that the entire document collection is available ahead of time, which permits analysis of the collection and extensive preprocessing. In the context of MetaCrawler, document snippets arrive in batches and the delay due to document clustering has to be minimal. As a result, clustering must take place as the snippets are rolling in.

I acknowledge that our approach has numerous pitfalls. Here are a couple, phrased as questions: will we fail to incorporate substantial intelligence into our softbots? Does the cost of deploying softbots on the Web outweigh the benefit? Our preliminary success in incorporating AI techniques into our deployed softbots makes me optimistic, but time will tell.

Conclusion

Each of the softbots described above uses multiple Web tools or services on a person's behalf. Each softbot enforces a powerful abstraction: a person is able to state *what* they want, the softbot is responsible for deciding *which* Web services to invoke in response and *how* to do so. Each softbot has been deployed on the Web, meeting the requirements of robustness, speed, and added value. Currently, MetaCrawler receives close to 100,000 hits a day. Ahoy! and ShopBot have yet to be announced publicly. However, shortly after its

[5] `http://www.cs.washington.edu/research/shopbot`

release on the Web, Ahoy! was discovered by Yahoo and mentioned in its directory. Immediately, it began receiving hundreds of queries per day.

Having satisfied the "useful first" constraint, our challenge is to make our current softbots more intelligent, inventing new AI techniques and extending familiar ones. We are committed to doing so while keeping our softbots both usable and useful. If we succeed, we will help to rid AI of the stereotype "if it works, it ain't AI." To check on our progress, visit the URLs mentioned earlier. Softbots are standing by...

Acknowledgments

I would like to thank Dan Weld, my close collaborator on many of the softbots described above, for his numerous contributions to the softbots project and its vision; he cannot be held responsible for the polemic tone and subversive methodological ideas of this piece. I would also like to thank my co-softbotists David Christianson, Bob Doorenbos, Marc Friedman, Keith Golden, Nick Kushmerick, Cody Kwok, Neal Lesh, Mark Langheinrich, Sujay Parekh, Mike Perkowitz, Richard Segal, and Jonathan Shakes for making softbots real. Thanks are due to Steve Hanks and other members of the UW AI group for helpful discussions and collaboration. I am indebted to Ema Nemes for her assistance in writing this paper and creating its figures. This research was funded in part by Office of Naval Research grant 92-J-1946, by ARPA / Rome Labs grant F30602-95-1-0024, by a gift from Rockwell International Palo Alto Research, and by National Science Foundation grant IRI-9357772.

References

Arens, Y.; Chee, C. Y.; Hsu, C.-N.; and Knoblock, C. A. 1993. Retrieving and integrating data from multiple information sources. *International Journal on Intelligent and Cooperative Information Systems* 2(2):127–158.

Brachman, R. 1992. "Reducing" CLASSIC to Practice: Knowledge Representation Theory Meets Reality. In *Proc. 3rd Int. Conf. on Principles of Knowledge Representation and Reasoning.*

Brooks, R. 1991. Intelligence without representation. *Artificial Intelligence* 47:139–159.

Doorenbos, B.; Etzioni, O.; and Weld, D. 1996. A scalable comparison-shopping agent for the world-wide web. Technical Report 96-01-03, University of Washington, Department of Computer Science and Engineering. Available via FTP from `pub/ai/` at `ftp.cs.washington.edu`.

Etzioni, O., and Weld, D. 1994. A Softbot-Based Interface to the Internet. *CACM* 37(7):72–76. See `http://www.cs.washington.edu/research/softbots`.

Etzioni, O.; Hanks, S.; Weld, D.; Draper, D.; Lesh, N.; and Williamson, M. 1992. An Approach to Planning with Incomplete Information. In *Proc. 3rd Int. Conf. on Principles of Knowledge Representation and Reasoning.* San Francisco, CA: Morgan Kaufmann. Available via FTP from `pub/ai/` at `ftp.cs.washington.edu`.

Etzioni, O.; Golden, K.; and Weld, D. 1994. Tractable closed-world reasoning with updates. In *Proc. 4th Int. Conf. on Principles of Knowledge Representation and Reasoning*, 178–189. San Francisco, CA: Morgan Kaufmann.

Etzioni, O.; Golden, K.; and Weld, D. 1995. Sound and efficient closed-world reasoning for planning. Technical Report 95-02-02, University of Washington. Available via FTP from `pub/ai/` at `ftp.cs.washington.edu`.

Etzioni, O.; Lesh, N.; and Segal, R. 1993. Building softbots for UNIX (preliminary report). Technical Report 93-09-01, University of Washington. Available via anonymous FTP from `pub/etzioni/softbots/` at `cs.washington.edu`.

Etzioni, O. 1993. Intelligence without robots (a reply to brooks). *AI Magazine* 14(4). Available via anonymous FTP from `pub/etzioni/softbots/` at `cs.washington.edu`.

Etzioni, O. 1994. Etzioni Responds. *AI Magazine.* Response to commentary on "Intelligence without Robots (A Reply to Brooks)".

Golden, K.; Etzioni, O.; and Weld, D. 1994. Omnipotence without omniscience: Sensor management in planning. In *Proc. 12th Nat. Conf. on A.I.*, 1048–1054. Menlo Park, CA: AAAI Press.

Kirk, T.; Levy, A. Y.; Sagiv, Y.; and Srivastava, D. 1995. The information manifold. In *Working Notes of the AAAI Spring Symposium: Information Gathering from Heterogeneous, Distributed Environments*, 85–91. Stanford University: AAAI Press. To order a copy, contact sss@aaai.org.

Kwok, C., and Weld, D. 1996. Planning to gather information. Technical Report 96-01-04, University of Washington, Department of Computer Science and Engineering. Available via FTP from `pub/ai/` at `ftp.cs.washington.edu`.

Lewis, D., and Gale, W. 1994. Training text classifiers by uncertainty sampling. In *17th Annual Int'l ACM SIGIR Conference on Research and Development in Information Retrieval.*

Mitchell, T. M.; Allen, J.; Chalasani, P.; Cheng, J.; Etzioni, O.; Ringuette, M.; and Schlimmer, J. C. 1990. Theo: A framework for self-improving systems. In VanLehn, K., ed., *Architectures for Intelligence.* Hillsdale, NJ.: Erlbaum.

Perkowitz, M., and Etzioni, O. 1995. Category translation: Learning to understand information on the internet. In *Proc. 15th Int. Joint Conf. on A.I.*

Selberg, E., and Etzioni, O. 1995. Multi-Service Search and Comparison Using the MetaCrawler. In *Proc. 4th World Wide Web Conf.*, 195–208. See `http://www.cs.washington.edu/research/metacrawler`.

Shakes, J.; Langheinrich, M.; and Etzioni, O. 1996. Ahoy! the home page finder. Technical report, University of Washington. To appear, see `http://www.cs.washington.edu/research/ahoy`.

Simon, H. 1991. *Models of My Life.* Basic Books.

Brain dynamics in the genesis of trust as the basis for communication by representations.

Walter J Freeman

Department of Molecular & Cell Biology, LSA 129
University of California at Berkeley CA 94720

wfreeman@garnet.berkeley.edu http://sulcus.berkeley.edu

Abstract

A theory of brain dynamics is proposed according to which brains construct external representations by actions into the world for communication. The prior brain patterns constitute meanings, not representations of meanings. The representations have no meaning in themselves. They are shaped in accordance with meaning inside transmitting brains, and they can elicit the construction of meaning inside receiving brains, provided that trust has been established between the transmitters and the receivers through appropriate neurochemical changes.

The Nature of Minds

There are three classes of theory about the nature of minds, each with its remarkable successes, and also its intractable problems.

A. Material, Empirical - minds are "nothing but ..." the activity of neurons according to most neurobiologists; hierarchies of reflexes for behaviorists; a chemical stew for geneticists, clinicians, and pharmacologists; or quantum coherences for physicists. These approaches have given powerful tools for investigating and treating disorders of both brain and behavior, but have conceived minds either as epiphenomena or as mysteries, leaving unexplained how the meaningless firing of neurons can lead to meaningful subjective experiences (Searle, 1995).

B. Cognitive, Idealist - minds are sets of representations, such as thoughts and ideas that are processed according to rules discovered by psychologists, or images and symbols that are manipulated according to syntactical rules. The intractable problems are those of introducing motivations, drives and instincts, and of devising rules on how to attach meanings and values to signs. If robots are built in conformance to look-up tables and difference equations, can they ever be conscious, or have free will?

C. Intentional, Existential - minds are actions into the world, from John Dewey (1914) ("mind is action into the stimulus") and Merleau-Ponty (1945) ("La Structure du Comportement"). Though discussed *in extenso* by pragmatists, Gestaltists including JJ Gibson (1963), Piagetians and others, the intractable problems have been how to account for the inner construction of intentional behavior and perception through self-organizing brain dynamics, and for the genesis of knowledge in the face of the problem of solipsism (Freeman, 1995).

A biological approach to the brain-mind problem is to study the evolution of minds and brains, on the premiss that animals have minds and brains that are prototypic of our own, and that their brains and behaviors can tell us much about our own minds.

Observations of the EEG

Experimental observations of the brain activity that follows sensory stimulation of animals show that sensory cortices engage in construction of activity patterns in response to stimuli. The operation is not that of filter, storage, retrieval, addressing or correlation mechanisms. It is a state transition by which a cortex switches abruptly from one basin of attraction to another, thereby to change one spatial pattern to another like frames in a cinema (Freeman, 1975, 1992). The transitions in the primary sensory cortices are shaped by interactions with the limbic system, which formulate the intentional nature of percepts. They result from goal-directed actions in time and space. Each transition involves learning, so that cumulatively a trajectory is formed by each brain over its lifetime. Each spatial pattern as it occurs reflects the entire content of individual experience. It is a meaning and not the representation of a meaning. It is the basis for consciousness.

Inferences made from EEG studies about the nature of meaning are as follows. Brains are open with respect to energy and information, but closed systems with respect to meaning. Brains create their own frames of reference, and can have no direct communication, such as by ESP. Each consciousness is isolated from all others. Brains have no direct access to the physical world. All perceptions are constructs from raw sensory input. Intentionality is texture and context in the dynamical structure of space-time memory. It is based in a neural net by neurochemical modulations of synapses and trigger zones. Meanings are places in this structure.

A Theory of Representation

Four findings led to these conclusions and the demise of a theory of representations in the experiments designed to test (Freeman, 1983; Skarda and Freeman, 1987):

1. The EEG spatial amplitude patterns observed during training lacked invariance with respect to the conditioned stimuli over time and learning.

2. The EEG spatial patterns in the control periods reflected the null hypothesis and not the specific expectations that had been established by training.

3. The EEG phase patterns did not show a requisite convergence to synchrony ("binding") with arrival of expected stimuli.

4. The EEG phase patterns did manifest the repeated nonlinear state transitions that enable the sensory cortices to construct the spatial patterns of amplitude appropriate for the conditioned stimuli and conditioned responses.

A Theory of Trust

It follows that each brain creates its own frames of reference, which are not directly accessible by any other brain. How, then, can two or more brains be shaped by learning, so as to form cooperative pairs for reproduction and groups for survival? Evolution has provided a biological mechanism that first came under scientific scrutiny in the form of Pavlovian 'brain washing'. Under now well known conditions of stress in the internal and external environments, a global transition takes place, following which brains sustain a remarkable period of malleability (Freeman, 1995). I believe that Pavlov manipulated a mammalian mechanism of pair bonding, for the nurture of altricial young through sexual orgasm and lactation, mediated by oxytocin, and that our remote ancestors evolved to adapt this mechanism for tribal bonding through dance, chanting, rituals, and evangelical conversions (Sargant 1957). These dimensions of human experience can be encompassed by a neurodynamical theory of intentionality, but not by theories of representation and symbol manipulation.

References

Dewey J (1914) Psychological doctrine in philosophical teaching. Journal of Philosophy 11: 505-512.

Freeman WJ (1975) Mass Action in the Nervous System. New York: Academic.

Freeman WJ (1983) The physiology of mental images. Biological Psychiatry 18:1107-1125.

Freeman WJ (1992) Tutorial in Neurobiology. International Journal of Bifurcation and Chaos 2: 451-482.

Gibson JJ (1979) The Ecological Approach to Visual Perception. Boston: Houghton Mifflin.

Freeman WJ (1995) Societies of Brains. Hillsdale NJ, Lawrence Erlbaum.

Merleau-Ponty M (1942/1963) The Structure of Behavior (AL Fischer, Trans.). Boston: Beacon Press.

Sargant W (1957) Battle for the Mind. Westport CT, Greenwood Press.

Searle JR (1995) The Mystery of Consciousness. New York Rev 2-18 Nov.

Skarda CA and Freeman WJ (1987) How brains make chaos in order to make sense of the world. Behav. & Brain Sci. 10: 161-195.

Using Multi-Agent Systems to Represent Uncertainty

Joseph Y. Halpern
IBM Almaden Research Center
San Jose, CA 95120
email: halpern@almaden.ibm.com

Abstract

I consider a logical framework for modeling uncertainty, based on the use of possible worlds, that incorporates knowledge, probability, and time. This turns out to be a powerful approach for modeling many problems of interest. I show how it can be used to give insights into (among other things) several well-known puzzles.

Introduction

Uncertainty is a fundamental—and unavoidable—feature of daily life. In order to deal with uncertainty intelligently, we need to be able to represent it and reason about it. This invited talk describes one systematic approach for doing so.

Reasoning about uncertainty can be subtle. Consider the following well-known puzzles. (These puzzles are presented under the assumption that the uncertainty is quantified in terms of probability, but the issues that they bring out arise whatever method we use to represent uncertainty.)

The second-ace puzzle (Bar-Hillel & Falk 1982; Freund 1965; Shafer 1985): Suppose we have a deck with four cards: the ace and deuce of hearts, and the ace and deuce of spades. After a fair shuffle of the deck, two cards are dealt to Alice. It is easy to see that, at this point, there is a probability of 1/6 that Alice has both aces, probability 5/6 that Alice has at least one ace, probability 1/2 that Alice has the ace of spades, and probability 1/2 that Alice has the ace of hearts: Out of the six possible deals of two cards out of four, Alice has both aces in one of them, at least one ace in five of them, the ace of hearts in three of them, and the ace of spades in three of them.

Alice then says "I have an ace". Conditioning on this information, Bob computes the probability that Alice holds both aces to be 1/5. This seems reasonable: The probability of Alice having two aces goes up if we find out she has an ace. Next, Alice says "I have the ace of spades". Conditioning on this new information, Bob now computes the probability that Alice holds both aces to be 1/3. Of the three deals in which Alice holds the ace of spades, she holds both aces in one of them. As a result of learning not only that Alice holds at least one ace, but that the ace is actually the ace of spades, the conditional probability that Alice holds both aces goes up from 1/5 to 1/3. Similarly, if Alice had said "I have the ace of hearts", the conditional probability that Alice holds both aces would be 1/3.

But is this reasonable? When Bob learns that Alice has an ace, he knows that she must have either the ace of hearts or the ace of spades. Why should finding out which particular ace it is raise the conditional probability of Alice having two aces?

The Monty Hall Puzzle (Savant 1990/91; Morgan *et al.* 1991): Suppose you're on a game show and given a choice of three doors. Behind one is a car; behind the others are goats. You pick door 1. Before opening door 1, Monty Hall, the host (who knows what is behind each door), opens door 2, which has a goat. He then asks you if you still want to take what's behind door 1, or to take what's behind door 3 instead. Should you switch?

There is certainly far more to representing uncertainty than dealing with puzzles such as these. Nevertheless, the analysis of these puzzles will give us deeper insight into the process of reasoning under uncertainty and the problems involved with getting a good representation.

So how do we represent and reason about uncertainty? I shall use the *possible-worlds* framework. This is the standard approach for giving semantics to modal logic. The intuition is that besides the true state of affairs, there are a number of other possible states of affairs or "worlds", that an agent considers possible. We can view the set of worlds that an agent considers possible as a qualitative way to measure her uncertainty. The more worlds she considers possible, the more uncertain she has as to the true state of affairs, and the less she knows. This is not quite enough for dealing with the puzzles above. We need to add two more features to the picture: time and probability. To add time, we need to have possible worlds describing not only the current state of affairs, but the state of affairs at each time point of interest. As we shall see, it is also useful to assume that these states have some internal structure. This gives us the *multi-agent systems* framework of (Fagin *et al.* 1995). To add probability, we need to associate with each possible world a probability distribution over other possible worlds; this issue is discussed in detail in (Fagin & Halpern 1994; Halpern & Tuttle 1993).

The resulting multi-agent systems provide a powerful framework in which we can represent, in a natural way, time, knowledge, and probability. But where does the system come from? Typically, it is generated by a *protocol.* An important theme in the talk is the importance of specifying clearly the protocol generating the system. In particular (as already pointed out by Shafer 1985), this is the key to understanding puzzles such as the second-ace puzzle.

The material in this talk is largely covered in (Halpern 1995).

References

Bar-Hillel, M., and Falk, R. 1982. Some teasers concerning conditional probabilities. *Cognition* 11:109–122.

Fagin, R., and Halpern, J. Y. 1994. Reasoning about knowledge and probability. *Journal of the ACM* 41(2):340–367.

Fagin, R.; Halpern, J. Y.; Moses, Y.; and Vardi, M. Y. 1995. *Reasoning about Knowledge.* Cambridge, Mass.: MIT Press.

Freund, J. E. 1965. Puzzle or paradox? *American Statistician* 19(4):29–44.

Halpern, J. Y., and Tuttle, M. R. 1993. Knowledge, probability, and adversaries. *Journal of the ACM* 40(4):917–962.

Halpern, J. Y. 1995. A logical approach for reasoning about uncertainty. Research Report RJ 9972, IBM.

Morgan, J. P.; Chaganty, N. R.; Dahiya, R. C.; and Doviak, M. J. 1991. Let's make a deal: the player's dilemma (with commentary). *The American Statistician* 45(4):284–289.

vos Savant, M. 1990/91. Ask Marilyn. *Parade Magazine* (Sept. 9, 1990; Dec. 2, 1990; Feb. 17, 1991).

Shafer, G. 1985. Conditional probability. *International Statistical Review* 53(3):261–277.

Refinement Planning: Status and Prospectus

Subbarao Kambhampati*
Department of Computer Science and Engineering
Arizona State University, Tempe, AZ 85287, rao@asu.edu

Abstract

Most current-day AI planning systems operate by iteratively refining a partial plan until it meets the goal requirements. In the past five years, significant progress has been made in our understanding of the spectrum and capabilities of such refinement planners. In this talk, I will summarize this understanding in terms of a unified framework for refinement planning and discuss several current research directions.

Introduction

Developing automated methods for generating and reasoning about plans and schedules, whether in aid of autonomous or human agents, has been part and parcel of AI research from the beginning. The need for planning arises naturally when an agent is interested in controlling the evolution of its environment. Algorithmically, a planning problem has as input a set of possible courses of actions, a predictive model for the underlying dynamics, and a performance measure for evaluating the courses of action. The output or solution is one or more courses of action that satisfy the specified requirements for performance. A planning problem thus involves deciding "what" actions to do, and "when" to do them. The "when" part of the problem has traditionally been called the "scheduling" problem [20].

The simplest case of the planning problem, where the environment is static and deterministic, and the planner has complete information about the current state of the world, has come to be known as the **classical planning problem**. My talk is concerned with algorithms for synthesizing plans in classical planning. Generating plans for classical planners has received significant attention over the past twenty years. Most of the plan generation algorithms that have been developed are informally called "refinement planners", in that they iteratively refine a partial plan until it meets the specified goals. In this talk, I will attempt to provide a coherent semantic picture of refinement planning, and describe the various existing approaches in terms of this framework. I will also consider the tradeoffs inherent in refinement planning, and possible directions for developing more efficient refinement planners.

*This research is supported in part by NSF research initiation award (RIA) IRI-9210997, NSF young investigator award (NYI) IRI-9457634 and ARPA/Rome Laboratory planning initiative grants F30602-93-C-0039 and F30602-95-C-0247. Special thanks to Biplav Srivastava, Gopi Bulusu, Suresh Katukam, and Laurie Ihrig for the many hours of discussions, David McAllester for his patient correspondence regarding SNLP and refinement search, and Dan Weld for his encouragement. Portions of this paper are borrowed from a recent overview of planning approaches, which I co-authored with Tom Dean.

Preliminaries of Modeling Change: Before proceeding further, let me briefly review how classical planning problems are modeled. In most classical planning approaches, a state is described in terms of a set of boolean state variables. Suppose that we have three boolean state variables: P, Q, and R. We represent the particular state s in which P and Q are true and R is false by the *state-variable assignment*, $s = \{P = \text{true}, Q = \text{true}, R = \text{false}\}$, or, somewhat more compactly, by $s = \{P, Q, \neg R\}$.

An action is represented as a *state-space operator* α defined in terms of *preconditions* (Pre(α)) and *postconditions* (also called effects) (Post(α)). If an operator (action) is applied (executed) in a state in which the preconditions are satisfied, then the variables mentioned in the postconditions are assigned their respective values in the resulting state. If the preconditions are not satisfied, then there is no change in state.

Several syntactic extensions can be added on top of this basic operator representation, facilitating conditional effects and effects quantified over finite universes. Pednault [17] shows that this action representation is semantically equivalent to the largest subset of situation calculus for which we can get by without writing frame axioms explicitly.

Goals are represented as state-variable assignments that assign values to subsets of the set of all state variables. By assigning values to one or more state variables, we designate a set of states as the goal. We say that a state s *satisfies* a goal ϕ, notated $s \models \phi$, just in case the assignment ϕ is a subset of the assignment s. Given an initial state s_0, a goal ϕ, and a library of operators, the *objective* of the planning problem is to find a sequence of state-space operators $\langle \alpha_1, \ldots, \alpha_n \rangle$ such that $f(s_0, \langle \alpha_1, \ldots, \alpha_n \rangle) \models \phi$.

Semantic picture of Refinement Planning

Refinement planners [8] attempt to solve a planning problem by navigating the space of *sets of potential solutions (action sequences)*. The potential solution sets are represented and manipulated in the form of "partial plans." Syntactically, a partial plan π can be seen as a set of constraints (see below). Semantically, a partial plan is a shorthand notation for the set of action sequences that are consistent with its constraints. The set of such action sequences is called the set of candidates (or candidate set) of the partial plan.

We define a generic refinement planning procedure, Refine(π), as follows [8].

1. If an action sequence $\langle \alpha_1, \alpha_2, \ldots, \alpha_n \rangle$ is a candidate of π and also solves the planning problem, terminate and return the action sequence.
2. If the constraints in π are inconsistent, then eliminate π from future consideration.
3. Select a refinement strategy, and apply the strategy to π and add the resulting refinements to the set of plans under consideration.
4. Nondeterministically select a plan π' from those under consideration and call Refine(π').

The first step of the search process is the "solution construction" process, where the planner attempts to extract a solution from the current partial plan's candidate set. We shall see later that the solution constructor function checks only on the minimal candidates of the plan, since the candidate set of a partial plan can be infinitely large [8]. The second step is closely related to the first, and attempts to prune the plan from further refinement if it can be shown not to contain any solutions. The last two steps involve applying a refinement operator to the partial plan to generate new partial plans, and recursing on one of those refinements. Refinements can be understood as operations that split the candidate set of the partial plan to which they are applied. Specifically, a refinement strategy converts a partial plan π into a set of new plans $\{\pi_1, \ldots, \pi_n\}$ such that the candidate set of each π_i is a subset of the candidate set of π. A refinement operator is said to be *complete* if every solution belonging to the candidate set of the plan will be in the candidate sets of at least on of the plans generated by the refinement operator. A refinement operator is said to be *systematic* if the candidate sets of the refinements are disjoint. It is easy to see that the selection of refinement strategy does not have to backtracked over, as long as the refinement operators are complete.

The specifics of a refinement planning algorithm will differ depending on the representation of the partial plans used (i.e., what specific constraints are employed) and the type of refinements employed on that representation. We already pointed out that syntactically, a partial plan is a set of constraints. The semantic status of a plan constraint is clarified by specifying when a given action sequence is said to satisfy the constraint. Within these broad guidelines, a large variety of syntactic representations can be developed. Once a representation for a partial plan is given, a refinement operator can be specified in terms of the types of constraints that it adds to a partial plan. If the constraint sets added by refinements are mutually exclusive and exhaustive, then the refinement operators will be systematic and complete.

Representing Partial Plans

To focus our discussion, we will start by looking at a specific partial plan representation that is useful for modeling most existing planners (later, we will consider alternative representations that are promising). In this representation, *partial plan* consists of a set of *steps*, a set of *ordering constraints* that restrict the order in which steps are to be executed, and a set of *auxiliary constraints* that restrict the value of state variables over particular intervals of time. Each step is associated

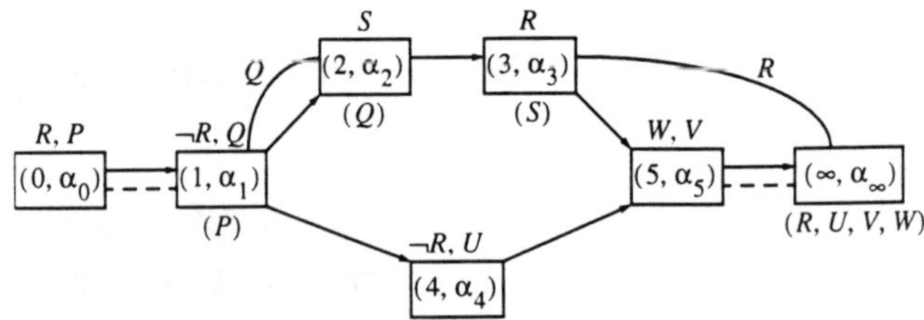

Figure 1: This figure depicts the partial plan π_{eg}. The postconditions (effects) of the steps are shown above the steps, while the preconditions are shown below the steps in parentheses. The ordering constraints between steps are shown by arrows. The interval preservation constraints are shown by arcs, while the contiguity constraints are shown by dotted lines.

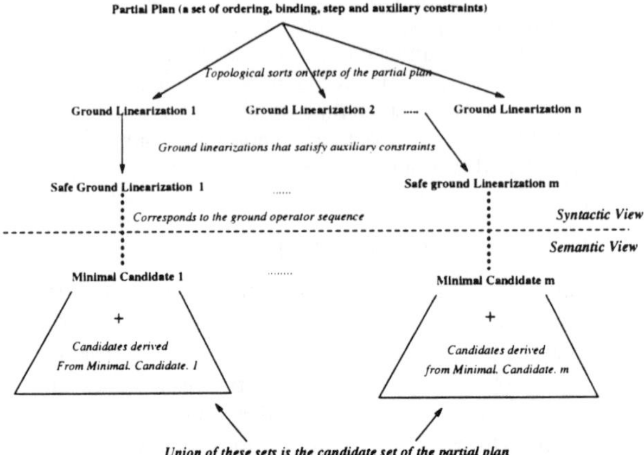

Figure 2: A schematic illustration of the relation between a partial plan and its candidate set. T

with a state-space operator. To distinguish between multiple instances of the same operator appearing in a plan, we assign to each step a unique integer i and represent the ith step as the pair (i, α_i) where α_i is the operator associated with the ith step. Figure 1 shows a partial plan π_{eg} consisting of seven steps. The plan π_{eg} is represented as follows.

$$\langle \; \{(0,\alpha_0),(1,\alpha_1),(2,\alpha_2),(3,\alpha_3),(4,\alpha_4),(5,\alpha_5),(\infty,\alpha_\infty\},$$
$$\{(0 \bar{\prec} 1),(1 \prec 2),(1 \prec 4),(2 \prec 3),(3 \prec 5),(4 \prec 5),(5 \bar{\prec} \infty)\},$$
$$\{(1 \overset{Q}{-} 2),(3 \overset{R}{-} \infty)\} \; \rangle$$

An ordering constraint of the form $(i \prec j)$ indicates that Step i precedes Step j. An ordering constraint of the form $(i \bar{\prec} j)$ indicates that Step i is contiguous with Step j, that is Step i precedes Step j and no other steps intervene. The steps are *partially ordered* in that Step 2 can occur either before or after Step 4. An auxiliary constraint of the form $(i \overset{P}{-} j)$ is called an *interval preservation constraint* and indicates that P is to be preserved in the range between Steps i and j (and therefore no operator with postcondition $\neg P$ should occur between Steps i and j). In particular, according to the constraint $(3 \overset{R}{-} \infty)$, Step 4 should not occur between Steps 3 and ∞.

Figure 2 shows the schematic relations between a partial plan in such a representation and its candidate set, and we will illustrate it with respect to the example plan in Figure 1. Each partial plan corresponds to a set of topological sorts (e.g. $\langle 1,2,3,4,5\rangle$ and $\langle 1,2,4,3,5\rangle$). The subset of these that satisfy the auxiliary constraints of the plan (e.g. $\langle 1,2,4,3,5\rangle$) are said to be the safe-ground linearizations of the plan. Each safe ground linearization of the plan corresponds to an action sequence which is a minimal candidate of the partial plan (e.g. $\langle \alpha_1, \alpha_2, \alpha_4, \alpha_3, \alpha_5\rangle$). An infinite number of additional candidates can be derived from each minimal candidate of the plan by augmenting (padding) it with additional actions without violating the auxiliary constraints (e.g. $\langle \alpha_1, \alpha_2, \alpha_2, \alpha_4, \alpha_3, \alpha_5\rangle$). Thus, the candidate set of a partial plan is infinite, but the set of its minimal candidates is finite. The solution constructor functions search the minimal candidates of the plan to see if any of them are solutions to the planning problem. Refinement process can be understood as incrementally increasing the size of these minimal candidates so that action sequences of increasing lengths are examined to see if they are solutions to the problem. The search starts with the null plan $\langle\{(0,\alpha_0),(\infty,\alpha_\infty)\},\{(0\prec\infty)\},\{\}\rangle$, where α_0 is a dummy operator with no preconditions and postconditions corresponding to the initial state, and α_∞ is a dummy operator with no postconditions and preconditions corresponding the goal.

Refining Partial Plans

There are several possible ways of refining partial plans, corresponding intuitively to different ways of splitting the set of potential solutions represented by the plan. In the following sections, I outline several popular refinement strategies employed in the planning literature.

State-Space Refinements

The most straightforward way of refining partial plans involves using progression to convert the initial state into a state satisfying the goal conditions, or using regression to convert a set of goal conditions into a set of conditions that are satisfied in the initial state. From the point of view of partial plans, this corresponds to growing prefix or the suffix of the plan. The refinements are called state-space refinements since given either the prefix or the suffix of a plan, we can uniquely determine the nature of the world state following the prefix and preceding the suffix.

The set of steps $\{\sigma_1,\sigma_2,\ldots,\sigma_n\}$ with contiguity constraints $\{(\sigma_0 \,\bar{\prec}\, \sigma_1),(\sigma_1 \,\bar{\prec}\, \sigma_2),\ldots,(\sigma_{n-1} \,\bar{\prec}\, \sigma_n)\}$ is called the *header* of the plan π. The last element of the header, σ_n, is called the *head step*. The state defined by $f(s_0,\langle\alpha_{\sigma_1},\ldots,\alpha_{\sigma_n}\rangle)$, where α_{σ_i} is the operator associated with σ_i is called the *head state*. In a similar manner, we can define the *tail*, *tail step*, and *tail state*. As an example, the partial plan π_{eg} shown in Figure 1 has the Steps 0 and 1 in its header, with Step 1 being the head step. The head state (which is the state resulting from applying α_1 to the initial state) is $\{P,Q\}$. Similarly, the tail consists of Steps 5 and ∞, with Step 5 being the tail step. The tail state (which is the result of regressing the goal conditions through the operator α_5) is $\{R,U\}$.

Progression (or forward state-space) refinement involves advancing the head state by adding a step σ, such that the preconditions of α_σ are satisfied in the current head state, to the header of the plan. The step σ may be newly added to the plan or currently present in the plan. In either case, it is made contiguous to the current head step and becomes the new head step.

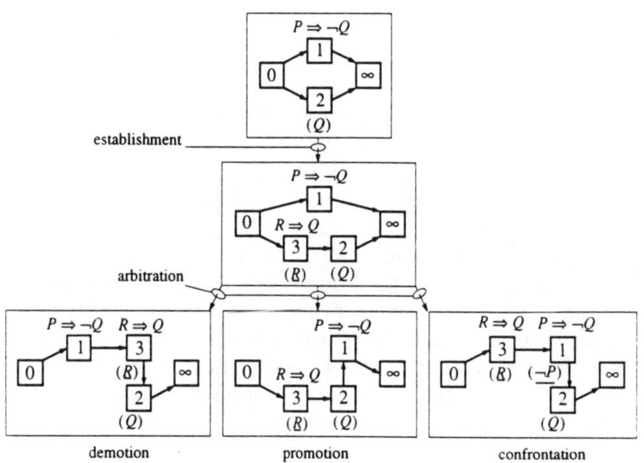

Figure 3: Example of plan-space refinement

As an example, one way of refining the plan π_{eg} in Figure 1 using progression refinement would be to apply an instance of the operator α_2 (either the instance that is currently in the plan $(2,\alpha_2)$ or a new instance) to the head state (recall that it is $\{P,Q\}$). This is accomplished by putting a contiguity constraint between $(2,\alpha_2)$ and the current head step $(1,\alpha_1)$ (thereby making the former the new head step).

In realistic problems, many operators may be applicable in the head state and very few of them may be relevant to the top level goals. To improve efficiency, some planners use **means-ends analysis** to focus on relevant operators. The general idea is the following: Suppose we have an operator α whose postconditions match a goal of the problem. Clearly, α is a relevant operator. If the preconditions of α are satisfied in the head state of the current partial plan, we can apply it directly. Suppose they are not all satisfied. In such a case, we can consider the preconditions of α as subgoals, look for an operator α' whose postconditions match one of these subgoals, and check if it is applicable to the head state. This type of recursive analysis can be continued to find the set of relevant operators, and focus progression refinement [14].

We can also define a refinement strategy based on regression, which involves regressing the tail state of a plan through an operator. For example, the operator α_3 is applicable (in the backward direction) through this tail state (which is $\{R,U\}$), while the operator α_4 is not (since its postconditions are inconsistent with the tail state). Thus, one way of refining π_{eg} using regression refinement would be to apply an instance of the operator α_3 (either the existing instance in Step 3 or a new one) to the tail state in the backward direction. This is accomplished by putting a contiguity constraint between $(3,\alpha_3)$ and the current tail step.

In both progression and regression, solution constructor function can be simplified as follows: check to see if head state is a super set of the tail state, and if so, return the header concatenated with tail.

Plan-Space Refinements

State-space refinements have to guess correct answers to two questions up front: (a) whether a specific action is relevant to the goals of the planning problem and (b) where exactly in the final plan does the action take place. Often, it is easier to see whether or not a given action is relevant to a plan, but much harder to guess the precise position at which a step must occur in the final plan. The latter question more naturally falls in the purview of "scheduling" and cannot be answered well until all of the steps have been added. To avoid this premature forced commitment, we would like to introduce the new action into the plan, without committing to its position in the final solution. This is the intuition behind plan-space refinements. The refinement is named "plan-space" because when we allow an action to be part of a plan without constraining it to be either in the prefix or the suffix, the partial plan does not represent a unique world state. Thus, the search cannot be recast in terms of the space of world states.

The main idea in plan-space refinement is to shift the attention from advancing or regressing the world state to establishing goals in the partial plan. A precondition P of a step (i, α_i) in a plan is said to be *established* if there is some step (j, α_j) in the plan that precedes i and causes P to be true, and no step that can possibly intervene between j and i has postconditions that are inconsistent with P. It is easy to see that if every precondition of every step in the plan is established, then that plan will be a solution plan. Plan-space refinement involves picking a precondition P of a step (i, α_i) in the partial plan, and adding enough additional step, ordering, and auxiliary constraints to ensure the establishment of P. One problem with this precondition-by-precondition establishment approach is that the steps added in establishing a precondition might unwittingly violate a previously established precondition. Although this does not affect the completeness of the refinement search, it can lead to wasted planning effort, and necessitate repeated establishments of the same precondition within the same search branch. Many variants of plan-space refinements avoid this inefficiency by *protecting* their establishments using IPCs. When the planner uses plan-space refinements exclusively, its refinement process can terminate as soon as any of the safe ground linearization of the plan correspond to solutions.

Let me illustrate the main ideas in precondition establishment through an example. Consider the partial plan at the top in Figure 3. Step 2 in this plan requires a precondition Q. To establish this precondition, we need a step which has Q as its postcondition. None of the existing steps have such a postcondition. Suppose an operator α_3 in the library has a postcondition $R \Rightarrow Q$. We introduce an instance of α_3 as Step 3 into the plan. Step 3 is ordered to come before Step 2 (and after Step 0). Since α_3 makes Q true only when R is true before it, to make sure that Q will be true following Step 3, we need to ensure that R is true before it. This can be done by posting R as a precondition of Step 3. Since R is not a normal precondition of α_3, and is being posted only to guarantee one of its conditional effects, it is called a *secondary precondition* [17]. Finally, we can protect the establishment of precondition Q by adding the constraint $3 \overset{Q}{-} 2$. If we also want to ensure that 3 remains the sole establisher of Q in the final solution, we can add another auxiliary constraint $3 \overset{\neg Q}{-} 2$. In [13], McAllester shows that adding these two auxiliary constraints ensures systematicity of plan-space refinement.

Tractability Refinements: Since the position of the steps in the plan is not uniquely determined after a plan space refinement, there is uncertainty regarding (a) the state of the world preceding or following a step, (b) the relative order of steps in the plan and (c) the truth of IPC constraints in the plan. A variety of refinement strategies exist that attempt to make the reasoning with partial plans tractable by pushing the complexity into the search space. These refinements, called *tractability refinements*, fall into three broad classes: *pre-positioning, pre-ordering and pre-satisfaction* refinements. The first pick a pair of steps α_1 and α_2 in the plan and generate two refinements one in which $\alpha_1 \bar{\prec} \alpha_2$, and the other in which $\alpha_1 \bar{\not\prec} \alpha_2$. The pre-ordering refinements do the same thing except they enforce ordering rather than contiguity constraints between the chosen steps. Finally, the pre-satisfaction refinements pick an IPC in the plan, and enforce constraints such that every ground linearization of the plan satisfies the IPC (see below).

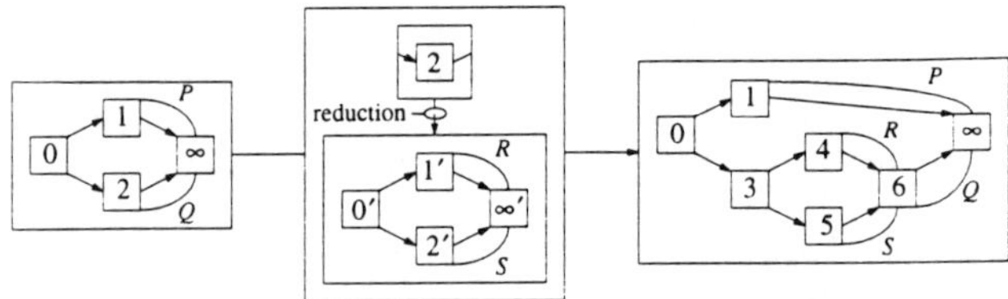

Figure 4: Step 2 in the partial plan shown on the left is reduced to obtain a new partial plan shown on the right. In the new plan, Step 2 is replaced with the (renamed) steps and constraints specified in the reduction shown in the center box.

We can illustrate the pre-satisfaction refinements through the example in Figure 3, after we have introduced Step 3 and ensured that it produces Q as a postcondition, we need to make sure that Q is not violated by any steps possibly intervening between Steps 3 and 2. In our example, Step 1, which can possibly intervene between Steps 3 and 2, has a postcondition $P \Rightarrow \neg Q$, that is potentially inconsistent with Q. To avert this inconsistency, we can either order Step 1 to come before Step 3 (demotion), or order Step 1 to come after Step 2 (promotion), or ensure that the offending conditional effect will not occur. This last option, called confrontation, can be carried out by posting $\neg P$ as a (secondary) precondition of Step 1.

Depending on whether protection strategies are used, and what tractability refinements are used, we can get a very large spectrum of plan-space refinements [8]. The effectiveness of plan space refinement in controlling the search is determined by a variety of factors, including (a) the order in which the various preconditions are selected for establishment (b) the manner in which tractability refinements are applied during search. See [8] for a discussion of some of the trade-offs.

Task-Reduction Refinements

In both the state-space and plan-space refinements, the only knowledge that is assumed to be available about the planning task is in terms of primitive actions (that can be executed by the underlying hardware), and their preconditions and postconditions. Often, one has more structured planning knowledge available in a domain. For example, in a travel planning domain, we might have the knowledge that one can reach a destination by either "taking a flight" or by "taking a train". We may also know that "taking a flight" in turn involves making a reservation, buying a ticket, taking a cab to the airport, getting on the plane etc. In such a situation, we can consider "taking a flight" as an abstract task (which cannot be directly executed by the hardware). This abstract task can then be reduced to a plan fragment consisting of other abstract or primitive tasks (in this case "making a reservation", "buying a ticket", "going to the airport", "getting on the plane"). This way, if there are some high-level problems with the "taking flight" action and other goals, (e.g. there is not going to be enough money to take a flight as well paying the rent), we can resolve them *before* we work on low level details such as getting to the airport. The resolution is can be carried out by the generalized versions of tractability refinements used in plan-space refinement.

This idea forms the basis for task reduction refinement. Specifically, we assume that in addition to the knowledge about primitive actions, we also have some abstract actions, and a set of schemas (plan fragments) that can replace any given abstract action. Task reduction refinement takes a partial plan π containing abstract and primitive tasks, picks an abstract task σ, and for each reduction schema (plan fragment) that can be used to reduce σ, a refinement of π is generated with σ replaced by the reduction schema (plan fragment). As an example, consider the partial plan on the left in Figure 4. Suppose the operator α_2 is an abstract operator. The central box in Figure 4 shows a reduction schema for Step 2, and the partial plan shown on the right of the figure shows the result of refining the original plan with this reduction schema. At this point any interactions between the newly introduced plan fragment and the previously existing plan steps can be resolved using techniques such as promotion, demotion and confrontation discussed in the context of plan-space refinement. This type of reduction is carried out until all the tasks are primitive.

Notice that the partial plans used in task reduction planning contain one additional type of constraint -- the non-primitive tasks. Informally, when a plan contains a non-primitive task t, then every candidate of the plan must have the actions comprising at least one concretization of t (where a concretization of a non-primitive task is the set of primitive partial plans that can be generated by reducing it using task reduction schemas).

Tradeoffs in Refinement Planning

Now that we looked at a variety of approaches to refinement planning, it is worth looking at the broad tradeoffs in refinement planning. There are two classes of tradeoffs -- the first arising from algorithmic modifications to the generic refinement search, and the second arising from the match between refinements and the characteristics of the planning domain.

An example of the first class of tradeoffs is that between the cost of solution constructor vs. size of the search space. We can reduce the search space size by considering partial plans that can compactly represent a larger number of minimal candidates. From a planning view point, this leads to *least commitment* on the part of the planners. However, as the number of candidates represented by a partial plan grow, the cost of the picking a solution from the partial plan increases.

This tradeoff is well represented in the refinements that we have looked at. Plans produced by state-space refinements will have single minimal candidates, while those produced by plan space refinements can have multiple minimal candidates (corresponding roughly to the many topological sorts of the plan). Finally, partial plans produced using task reduction refinements may have even larger number of minimal candidates since the presence of a non-primitive tasks essentially allows any action sequence that contains any concretization of the non-primitive task as a minimal candidate.

There are also certain tradeoffs that arise from the match between the plan representations and refinements used, and the characteristics of the planning domain and problem. For example, it is known that the plan-space refinements can be more efficient compared to state-space refinements in domains where the ordering of steps cannot be guessed with reasonable accuracy *a priori* [1; 16]. The plan-space refinements also allow separation of action selection and establishment phases from the "scheduling" phase of the planning, thus facilitating easier adaptation of the plan to more situations [7], and to more closely integrate the planning and scheduling phases [4]. On the other hand, state-space refinements provide a good sense of the state of the world corresponding to the partial plan, and can thus be useful to agents who need to do non-trivial reasoning about the world state to focus their planning and execution efforts [2; 14]. Finally, task-reduction refinements facilitate user control of planner's access to the primitive actions, and are thus the method of choice in any domain where the user has preferences among the solution plans [9].

Prospectus

Although early refinement planning systems tended to subscribe exclusively to a single refinement strategy, our unifying treatment of refinement planning demonstrates that it is possible to use multiple refinement strategies. As an example, the partial plan π_{eg} shown in Figure 1 can be refined with progression refinement (*e.g.,* by putting a contiguity constraint between Step 1 and Step 2), with regression refinement (*e.g.,* by putting a contiguity constraint between Step 3 and Step 5), or plan-space refinement (*e.g.,* by establishing the precondition S of Step 3 with the help of the effect Step 2). Finally, if the operator α_4 is a non-primitive operator, we can also use task reduction refinement to replace α_4 with its reduction schema. There is some evidence that planners using multiple refinement strategies intelligently can outperform those using single refinement strategies [10]. However, the question as to which refinement strategy should be preferred when is still largely open.

We can be even more ambitious however. Most existing refinement planners have trouble scaling up to larger problems, because of the very large search spaces they generate. While application of machine learning techniques to planning [15] hold a significant promise, we can also do better by improving the planning algorithms. One way of controlling the search space blow-up is to introduce appropriate forms of disjunction into the partial plan representation. By doing this, we can allow a single partial plan to stand for a larger number of minimal candidates. The conventional wisdom in refinement planning has been to keep the solution construction function tractable by pushing the complexity into the search space [8]. Some recent work by Blum and Furst [3] shows that partial plan representations that push all the complexity into the solution construction function may actu-

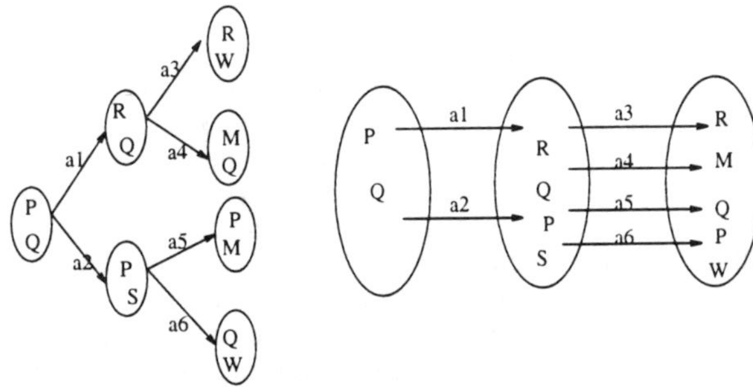

Figure 5: To the left is the search space generated by a refinement planner using progression refinement. To the right is the partial plan representation, called plan graph, used in Graphplan [3]. Each candidate plan of the plan graph must have some subset of the actions in i^{th} level coming immediately before some subset of actions in the $i+1^{th}$ level (for all i). The minimal candidates corresponding to all plans generated by the progression planner are compactly represented by a single partial plan (plan graph) in Graphplan.

ally perform much better in practice. They describe a system called Graphplan in which the partial plan representation, called plan graph, corresponds to a disjunctive representation of the search space of a progression planner (see Figure 5) [11]. The Graphplan refinement process (i.e., the process of growing the plan-graph) does not introduce any branching into the search space. Thus, all the complexity is transferred to the solution construction process which has to search the plan graph structure for minimal candidates that are solutions. Empirical results demonstrate this apparently extreme solution to the refinement and solution construction tradeoff in fact leads to significant improvements in performance.

The success of Graphplan shows that there is a lot to be gained by considering other disjunctive partial plan representations. An important issue in handling disjunctive partial plans is how to avoid losing all the search space savings in increased plan handling costs. One of the tricks in increasing least commitment without worsening the overall performance significantly seems to be to use constraint propagation techniques to enforce local consistency among the partial plan constraints. In CSP problems [18], refinement is used hand-in-hand with local consistency enforcement through constraint propagation to improve search performance. Although most refinement planning systems ignored the use of constraint propagation in planning, the situation is changing slowly. In addition to Graphplan [3], which uses the constraint propagation process in both the partial plan construction, and solution construction phase, there are also systems such as Descartes [6], which attempt to incorporate constraint propagation techniques directly into existing refinement planners. Solution construction process can also be represented as an instance of propositional satisfiability problem, and there is some recent evidence [12] that nonsystematic search techniques such as GSAT can give very good performance on such SAT instances.

Summary

In this talk, I described the current state of refinement planning algorithms using a unified framework for refinement planning. The framework explicates the tradeoffs offered by plan representation and refinement strategies. I have concluded by outlining several directions in which refinement planning algorithms can be made more efficient. These involve using disjunctive partial plan representations, and the using of CSP techniques for handling partial plans.

References

[1] A. Barrett and D. Weld. Partial Order Planning: Evaluating Possible Efficiency Gains. *Artificial Intelligence*, Vol. 67, No. 1, 1994.

[2] F. Bachus and F. Kabanza. Using Temporal Logic to Control Search in a forward chaining planner. In *Proc European Planning Workshop*, 1995.

[3] A. Blum and M. Furst. Fast planning throug planning graph analysis. In *Proc. IJCAI-95*, 1995.

[4] K. Currie and A. Tate. O-Plan: The open planning architecture. *Artificial Intelligence*, 51(1):49--86, 1991.

[5] R. Fikes and N. Nilsson. Strips: A new approach to the application of theorem proving to problem solving. *Artificial Intelligence*, 2:189--208, 1971.

[6] D. Joslin and M. Pollack. Passive and active decision postponement in plan generation. In *Proc. 3rd European Workshop on Planning*, 1995.

[7] L. Ihrig and S. Kambhampati. Derivational replay for partial order planning. In *Proc. AAAI-94*.

[8] S. Kambhampati, C. Knoblock, and Q. Yang. Refinement search as a unifying framework for evaluating design tradeoffs in partial order planning. *Artificial Intelligence*, 76(1-2), 1995.

[9] S. Kambhampati. A comparative analysis of partial-order planning and task-reduction planning. *ACM SIGART Bulletin*, 6(1), 1995.

[10] S. Kambhampati and B. Srivastava. Universal Classical Planner: An algorithm for unifying state space and plan space approaches. In *Proc European Planning Workshop*, 1995.

[11] S. Kambhampati. Planning Methods in AI (Notes from ASU Planning Seminar). ASU CSE TR 96-004. *http://rakaposhi.eas.asu.edu:8001/yochan.html*

[12] H. Kautz and B. Selman. Pushing the Envelope: Planning, Propositional Logic, and Stochastic Search In *Proc. AAAI-96*.

[13] D. McAllester and D. Rosenblitt. Systematic Nonlinear Planning. In *Proc. 9th AAAI*, 1991.

[14] D. McDermott. A heuristic estimator for means-ends analysis in planning. In *Proc. AIPS-96*, 1996.

[15] Steve Minton, editor. *Machine Learning Methods for Planning and Scheduling*. Morgan Kaufmann, 1992.

[16] S. Minton, J. Bresina and M. Drummond. Total Order and Partial Order Planning: a comparative analysis. Journal of Artificial Intelligence Research 2 (1994) 227-262.

[17] E.P.D. Pednault. Synthesizing plans that contain actions with context-dependent effects. *Computational Intelligence*, 4(4):356--372, 1988.

[18] E. Tsang. *Foundations of Constraint Satisfaction*. Academic Press, San Diego, California, 1993.

[19] D.E. Wilkins. *Practical Planning: Extending the Classical AI Planning Paradigm*. Morgan Kaufmann, 1988.

[20] M. Zweben and M.S. Fox, editors. *Intelligent Scheduling*. Morgan Kaufmann, San Francisco, California, 1994.

Boosting Theory Towards Practice: Recent Developments in Decision Tree Induction and the Weak Learning Framework

Michael Kearns
AT&T Research
mkearns@research.att.com

Difficulties in Comparing Machine Learning Heuristics

One of the original goals of computational learning theory was that of formulating models that permit meaningful comparisons between the different machine learning heuristics that are used in practice [Kearns *et al.*, 1987]. Despite the other successes of computational learning theory, this goal has proven elusive. Empirically successful machine learning algorithms such as **C4.5** and the backpropagation algorithm for neural networks have not met the criteria of the well-known Probably Approximately Correct (PAC) model [Valiant, 1984] and its variants, and thus such models are of little use in drawing distinctions among the heuristics used in applications. Conversely, the algorithms suggested by computational learning theory are usually too limited in various ways to find wide application.

The Theoretical Status of Decision Tree Learning

As an illustration, let us review what has been discovered about decision tree learning algorithms in the computational learning theory literature. Consider the simple framework in which a learning algorithm receives random examples, uniformly drawn from the hypercube $\{0,1\}^n$, that are assigned binary labels according to some decision tree T that has at most s nodes. A natural goal would be to find an algorithm that can infer a good approximation to T in time and sample complexity that is bounded by a polynomial in n and s. [1]

The existence of such an algorithm remains an apparently challenging open problem, so even with the various favorable and unrealistic assumptions (uniform input distribution, no noise or missing attributes in the data, the existence of a small "target" tree, and so on), computational learning theory has so far not provided vast advances in algorithm design for decision tree induction from random examples. On the other hand, in the framework under consideration, the heuristics for decision tree learning that are in wide experimental use do not fare much better. It is rather easy to show that **CART** and **C4.5** will fail to meet the stated criteria, and for the usual reasons: if the target decision tree computes the parity of just two out of the n variables, top-down heuristics like **CART** and **C4.5** may simply build a complete binary tree of depth n before achieving non-trivial error. Of course, this particular construction does not rule out the possibility that slight *modifications* of the standard heuristics might succeed — but a recent result [Blum *et al.*, 1994] demonstrated that small decision trees can not be learned by *any* algorithm that works solely by "estimating conditional probabilities" [Kearns, 1993]. The precise definition of this notion is slightly technical, but suffice to say that **CART** and **C4.5** — which operate primarily by estimating the probabilities of reaching certain nodes in a decision tree, or the conditional distribution of the label given that a node is reached — are canonical examples of the notion. Thus, although computational learning theory has yet to suggest powerful algorithms for decision tree learning from random examples, we can assert that if such algorithms exist, they will look nothing like the standard heuristics. Perhaps the more likely outcome is that the problem is simply intractable. This would mean that the assumption that a small decision tree is labeling the data is not especially helpful when examining decision tree learning algorithms, and we must seek alternative assumptions if we wish to account for the empirical success of **CART** and **C4.5**.

Provably efficient algorithms become available if we are willing to assume that the learning algorithm is provided with black-box access to the unknown target decision tree (that is, *membership queries*, which let the learner actively choose the instances to be labeled). A number of rather simple and elegant learning algorithms have recently been proposed in this setting [Bshouty, 1993; Kushilevitz and Mansour, 1991] that will infer the unknown tree in polynomial time,

[1] Here we are in the PAC model, where there is no noise in the sample data, with the additional restriction that the input distribution is uniform.

in strong contrast to the case where only random examples are available. However, because of the requirement for a source of information rarely available in real applications, these algorithms seem unlikely to replace the top-down heuristics, and their analysis sheds no light on why such heuristics succeed.

Viewing Top-Down Decision Tree Heuristics as Boosting Algorithms

The preceding summary indicates that some of the models of computational learning theory are unable to provide nontrivial insights into the behavior of **CART** and **C4.5**. One might be tempted to attribute this state of affairs to an inevitable chasm between theory and practice — that is, to claim that the standard heuristics succeed in practice due to some favorable structure possessed by real problems that simply cannot be captured by theory as we currently know it. Fortunately, some recent developments seem to demonstrate that such a defeatist position is not necessary.

The *weak learning* or *boosting* model is a descendant of the PAC model in which, rather than directly assuming that the target function can be represented in a particular fashion, we instead assume that there is always a "simple" function that is at least weakly correlated with the target function. We refer the reader to the literature for the precise technical definition, but for our informal purposes here, it suffices to assume that on any input distribution, there is an attribute whose value is correlated with the label.

In this setting, nontrivial performance bounds have recently been proven for both **CART** and **C4.5** [Kearns and Mansour, 1996]. More precisely, if we assume that there is always an attribute whose value correctly predicts the binary label with probability $1/2 + \gamma$ (thus, the attribute provides an advantage γ over random guessing), then for **CART** it suffices to grow a tree of size

$$\left(\frac{1}{\epsilon}\right)^{c/(\gamma^2\epsilon^2\log(1/\epsilon))} \quad (1)$$

in order to achieve error less than ϵ (where $c > 0$ is a constant), and for **C4.5**, a tree of size

$$\left(\frac{1}{\epsilon}\right)^{c\log(1/\epsilon)/\gamma^2} \quad (2)$$

suffices (see [Kearns and Mansour, 1996] for detailed statements and proofs). These bounds imply, among other things, that if we assume that the advantage γ is a fixed constant, then both algorithms will drive the error below any fixed ϵ in a constant number of splits. Until the result of [Schapire, 1990], the existence of *any* algorithm — much less a standard heuristic — possessing this "boosting" behavior was not known. The results given by Equations (1) and (2) provide nontrivial peformance guarantees for **CART** and **C4.5** in an independently motivated theoretical model.

A Framework for Comparisons

The theoretical results for **CART** and **C4.5** in the weak learning model do more than simply reassure us that these empirically successful algorithms can in fact be *proven* successful in a reasonable model. As one might have hoped, these results also provide a technical language in which one can attempt to make detailed comparisons between algorithms. Developing this language further has been the focus of our recent experimental efforts [Dietterich *et al.*, 1996], which we now summarize.

First of all, notice that the bounds of Equations (1) and (2) predict that the performance of **C4.5** should be superior to that of **CART**. In the analysis of [Kearns and Mansour, 1996], there are good technical reasons for this difference that are beyond our current scope, but that have to do with the differing concavity of the information gain splitting criterion used by **C4.5** and the Gini splitting criterion used by **CART**. Furthermore, again based on concavity arguments, they also suggest a new splitting criterion that enjoys an even better bound of

$$\left(\frac{1}{\epsilon}\right)^{c/\gamma^2} \quad (3)$$

on the tree size required to achieve error ϵ. In [Dietterich *et al.*, 1996] we demonstrate experimentally that this new splitting criterion results in small but statistically significant improvements in accuracy and tree size over **C4.5**, so the weak learning analysis seems to have pointed us to some modest improvements to the standard algorithms.

Another intriguing issue raised by the theoretical results emerges if one compares any of Equations (1), (2) and (3) to the bounds enjoyed by the recently introduced **Adaboost** algorithm due to [Freund and Schapire, 1995], which requires only

$$\frac{1}{2\gamma^2}\ln\frac{1}{\epsilon} \quad (4)$$

"rounds" (where each round is roughly analogous to a single split made by a top-down decision tree algorithm) to achieve error ϵ. The naive interpretation of this bound, which is only the logarithm of the best bound achieved by a top-down decision tree algorithm given by Equation (3), would lead us to predict that **Adaboost** should vastly outperform, for instance, **C4.5**. In practice, the two algorithms are in fact rather comparable [Freund and Schapire, 1996; Dietterich *et al.*, 1996]. In the latter citation, we provide extensive experimental evidence that this discrepancy between the disparate theoretical bounds and the parity of the algorithms on real problems can be explained by our interpretation of the advantage parameter γ. Briefly, while theoretical boosting results often assume for convenience that there is a simple function with a predictive advantage of γ over random guessing on *any* input distribution, in reality this advantage varies from distribution to distribution (possibly degrading to the trivial value of zero on "hard" distributions). Since **Adaboost** and **C4.5** explore very different spaces of input distributions as they grow their hypotheses, and since the theoretical bounds are valid only for the smallest advantage γ that holds on the distributions actually explored by the algorithm in question, γ has different meaning for the two algorithms. In [Dietterich *et al.*, 1996], we plot the advantages for each algorithm and demonstrate that while the theoretical bounds for a fixed advantage γ may be *worse* for **C4.5** than for **Adaboost**, the value of γ achieved on real problems is *better*. This empirical fact largely reconciles the theoretical statements with the observed behavior.

Thus, although the weak learning model provides what seems to be the right parameter to study (namely, the advantage γ), experimental examination of this parameter was required for real understanding of what the theory was saying and not saying. This kind of interaction — where the theory suggests improvements to the popular algorithms, and experimentation with these algorithms modifies our interpretation of the theory — seems like a good first step towards the goal mentioned at the outset. There is of course still much work to be done to further close the gap between theory and practice; but at least in the case of decision tree learning, the weak learning framework seems to have provided some footholds that were missing in previous models.

In the bibliography, we provide some additional references on the topics discussed here.

References

Aslam, J. A. and Decatur, S. E. 1993. General bounds on statistical query learning and PAC learning with noise via hypothesis boosting. In *Proceedings of the 35th IEEE Symposium on the Foundations of Computer Science.* IEEE Computer Society Press, Los Alamitos, CA. 282–291.

Blum, A.; Furst, M.; Jackson, J.; Kearns, M.; Mansour, Y.; and Rudich, S. 1994. Weakly learning DNF and characterizing statistical query learning using Fourier analysis. In *Proceedings of the 26th ACM Symposium on the Theory of Computing.* ACM Press, New York, NY.

Breiman, L.; Friedman, J. H.; Olshen, R. A.; and Stone, C. J. 1984. *Classification and Regression Trees.* Wadsworth International Group.

Bshouty, N. and Mansour, Y. 1995. Simple learning algorithms for decision trees and multivariate polynomials. In *Proceedings of the 36th IEEE Symposium on the Foundations of Computer Science.* IEEE Computer Society Press, Los Alamitos, CA. 304–311.

Bshouty, N. H. 1993. Exact learning via the monotone theory. In *Proceedings of the 34th IEEE Symposium on the Foundations of Computer Science.* IEEE Computer Society Press, Los Alamitos, CA. 302–311.

Dietterich, Tom; Kearns, Michael; and Mansour, Yishay 1996. Applying the weak learning framework to understand and improve C4.5. In *Machine Learning: Proceedings of the Thirteenth International Conference.* Morgan Kaufmann.

Drucker, H.; Schapire, R.; and Simard, P. 1992. Improving performance in neural networks using a boosting algorithm. In Hanson, S.J.; Cowan, J.D.; and Giles, C.L., editors 1992, *Advances in Neural Information Processing Systems.* Morgan Kaufmann, San Mateo, CA. 42–49.

Freund, Yoav and Schapire, Robert E. 1995. A decision-theoretic generalization of on-line learning and an application to boosting. In *Second European Conference on Computational Learning Theory.* Springer-Verlag. 23–37.

Freund, Y. and Schapire, R. 1996. Some experiments with a new boosting algorithm. In *Machine Learning: Proceedings of the Thirteenth International Conference.* Morgan Kaufmann.

Freund, Yoav 1995. Boosting a weak learning algorithm by majority. *Information and Computation* 121(2):256–285.

Jackson, J. 1994. An efficient membership query algorithm for learning DNF with respect to the uniform distribution. In *Proceedings of the 35th IEEE Symposium on the Foundations of Computer Science.* IEEE Computer Society Press, Los Alamitos, CA.

Kearns, M. and Mansour, Y. 1996. On the boosting ability of top-down decision tree learning algorithms. In *Proceedings of the 28th ACM Symposium on the Theory of Computing.* ACM Press, New York, NY.

Kearns, Michael J. and Vazirani, Umesh V. 1994. *An Introduction to Computational Learning Theory.* The MIT Press.

Kearns, M.; Li, M.; Pitt, L.; and Valiant, L. 1987. Recent results on boolean concept learning. In Langley, Pat, editor 1987, *Proceedings of the Fourth International Workshop on Machine Learning.* Morgan Kaufmann, San Mateo, CA. 337–352.

Kearns, M. 1993. Efficient noise-tolerant learning from statistical queries. In *Proceedings of the 25th ACM Symposium on the Theory of Computing.* ACM Press, New York, NY. 392–401.

Kushilevitz, E. and Mansour, Y. 1991. Learning decision trees using the Fourier spectrum. In *Proc. of the 23rd Symposium on Theory of Computing.* ACM Press, New York, NY. 455–464.

Quinlan, J.R. 1993. *C4.5: Programs for Machine Learning.* Morgan Kaufmann.

Schapire, R. E. 1990. The strength of weak learnability. *Machine Learning* 5(2):197–227.

Valiant, L. G. 1984. A theory of the learnable. *Communications of the ACM* 27(11):1134–1142.

Challenge Problems for Artificial Intelligence

(panel statement)

Bart Selman
(moderator)
AT&T

Rodney A. Brooks
MIT

Thomas Dean
Brown University

Eric Horvitz
Microsoft

Tom M. Mitchell
CMU

Nils J. Nilsson
Stanford University

Introduction: Bart Selman

AI textbooks and papers often discuss the big questions, such as "how to reason with uncertainty", "how to reason efficiently", or "how to improve performance through learning." It is more difficult, however, to find descriptions of concrete problems or challenges that are still ambitious and interesting, yet not so open-ended.

The goal of this panel is to formulate a set of such challenge problems for the field. Each panelist was asked to formulate one or more challenges. The emphasis is on problems for which there is a good chance that they will be resolved within the next five to ten years.

A good example of the potential benefit of a concrete AI challenge problem is the recent success of Deep Blue. Deep Blue is the result of a research effort focused on a single problem: develop a program to defeat the world chess champion. Although Deep Blue has not yet quite achieved this goal, it played a remarkably strong game against Kasparov in the recent ACM Chess Challenge Match.

A key lesson we learn from Deep Blue's strength is that efficient brute-force search can be much more effective than sophisticated, heuristically guided search. In fact, brute-force was so successful that it led Kasparov to exclaim "I could feel — I could smell — a new kind of intelligence across the table." (Kasparov 1996)

The experience with Deep Blue shows that a good challenge problem can focus research, lead to concrete progress, and bring us important new insights. Many AI researchers may not like the particular lesson about the value of brute-force over more "intelligent" forms of search, but, nevertheless, it is a very tangible result. In fact, the issue of general purpose ultra-fast search procedures versus heuristically guided domain-dependent methods is currently being revisited in the search and reasoning community.

Finally, as a meta-issue, we will consider how to measure progress in the field. Determining whether a particular piece of work in AI actually brings us any closer to the ultimate goals of AI has proven to be quite difficult. By introducing a set of well-defined challenge problems, we hope that this panel will help provide some benchmarks against which we can measure research progress.

Eight Challenges for Artificial Intelligence: Rodney Brooks

There are two very different sorts of challenges that I see for Artificial Intelligence — first, our systems are pathetic compared to biological systems, along many dimensions, and secondly, moderately good performance from some approaches has sociologically led to winner-take-all trends in research where other promising lines of research have been snuffed out too soon.

If we compare either software systems, or robotic systems to biological systems, we find that our creations are incredibly fragile by comparison. Below I pose some challenges that are aimed at narrowing this distance. The challenges themselves are general in nature — they do not solve particular problems, but the acts of meeting these challenges will force the creation of new general purpose techniques and tools which will allow us to solve more particular problems.

Challenge 1. Biological systems can adapt to new environments — not perfectly, they die in some environments, but often they can adapt. Currently our programs are very brittle, and certainly a program compiled for one architecture cannot run on another architecture. Can we build a program which can install itself and run itself on an unknown architecture? This sounds very difficult. How about a program which can probe an unknown architecture from a known machine and reconfigure a version of itself to run on the unknown machine? Still rather difficult, so perhaps we have to work up to this by making some "blocks worlds" artificial architectures where we can do this. This might lead to some considerations of how future architectures might be designed so that software is self-configurable, and then even perhaps self-optimizing.

Challenge 2. Minsky (1967) was foundational in establishing the theory of computation, but after Hartmanis (1971) there has been a fixation with asymptotic complexity. In reality lots of problems we face in building real AI systems do not get out of hand in terms of the size of problems for individual modules — in particular with behavior-based systems most of the submodules need only deal with bounded size problems. There are other ways theory could have gone. For instance one might try to come up with a theory of computation based on how much divergence there might be in programs given a one bit error in either the program or data representation. If theory were based on this fundamental concern we might start to understand how to make programs more robust.

Challenge 3. Recent work with evolutionary system has produced some tantalizing spectacular results, e.g., Sims (1994). But it is hard to know how to take things from successes and apply them to new problems. We do not have the equivalent of the Perceptron book (Minsky and Papert 1969) for evolutionary systems.[1] We need such a new book of mathematics so that we understand the strengths and weaknesses of this exciting new approach.

Challenge 4. We have been living with the basic formalizations made by McCulloch and Pitts (1943) for over fifty years now. Their formalization included that the activity of the neuron is an "all-or-none" process, that a certain fixed number of synapses must be excited within the period of latent addition in order to excite a neuron at any time, and this number is independent of the synapses' previous activity and position on the neuron, that the only significant delay within the nervous system is synaptic delay, that the activity of any inhibitory synapse absolutely prevents excitation of the neuron at that time, and that the structure of the net does not change with time. With the addition of changing synaptic weights by Hebb (1949) we pretty much have the modern computational model of neurons used by most researchers. With 50 years of additional neuroscience, we now know that there is much more to real neurons. Can newer models provide us with new computational tools, and will they lead to new insights to challenge the learning capabilities that we see in biological learning?

Over time we become trapped in our shared visions of appropriate ways to tackle problems, and even more trapped by our funding sources where we must constantly justify ourselves by making incremental progress. Sometimes it is worthwhile stepping back and taking an entirely new (or perhaps very old) look at some problems and to think about solving them in new ways. This takes courage as we may be leading ourselves into different sorts of solutions that will for many years have poorer performance than existing solutions. With years of perseverance we may be able to overcome initial problems with the new approaches and eventually leapfrog to better performance. Or we may turn out to be totally wrong. That is where the courage comes in.

Challenge 5. Despite some early misgivings (Selfridge 1956) back when chess playing programs had search trees only two deep (Newell et al. 1958), our modern chess programs completely rely on deep search trees and play chess not at all like humans. Can we build a program that plays chess in the way that a human plays? If we could, then perhaps we could prove how good it was by getting it to play GO—tree search just cannot cut it with GO.

Challenge 6. All of the competitive speech understanding systems today use hidden Markov models. While trainable, these systems have some unfortunate properties. They have much higher error rates than we might desire, they require some restriction in domain, and they are often inordinately sensitive to the choice of microphone. It seems doubtful that people use HMM's internally (even if one doesn't believe that generative grammars are the right approach either). Can we build a speech understanding system that is based on very different principles?

[1] Note that these evolutionary systems are much more that straight genetic algorithms as there is both a variable length genotype and a morphogenesis phase that produces a distinctly different phenotype.

Challenge 7. We live in an environment where we make extensive use of non-speech sound cues. There has been very little work on noise understanding. Can we build interesting noise understanding systems?

Challenge 8. Can we build a system by evolution that is better at a non-trivial task than anything that has been built by hand?

Integrating Theory and Practice in Planning: Thomas Dean

I issue a challenge to theorists, experimentalists, and practitioners alike to raise the level of expectation for collaborative scientific research in planning. Niels Bohr was first and foremost a theoretical physicist. Ernest Rutherford was first and foremost an experimentalist. It can be argued that neither Bohr nor Rutherford would have made as significant contributions to nuclear physics without an appreciation and understanding of one another's results. By analogy, I believe that a deeper understanding of planning problems is possible only through the concerted efforts of theorists, experimentalists, and practitioners. The current interplay between these groups (perhaps factions is the appropriate word) is minimal.

The pendulum of popular opinion swings back and forth between theory and practice. At different times, experimentalist have had to pepper their papers with equations and theorists have had to build systems and run experiments in order to get published. With the exception of the rare person gifted as mathematician and hacker, the requirement of both theory and practice in every result is a difficult one to satisfy; difficult and, I believe, unnecessary. This requirement implies that every publishable result must put forth a theoretical argument and then verify it both analytically and experimentally. The requirement tends to downplay the need for a community effort to weave together a rich tapestry of ideas and results.

A scientific field can nurture those who lean heavily toward theory or practice as long as the individuals direct their research to contribute to problems of common interest. Of course, the field must identify the problems that it considers worthy of emphasis and marshal its forces accordingly. I suggest planning as such a problem and the study of propositional STRIPS planning a good starting point. By analogy to physics in the 1930's, I recommend continued study of the STRIPS planning (the hydrogen atom of planning) and its stochastic counterparts (Markov decision problems) in parallel with investigations into a wide range of more expressive languages for specifying planning problems (the whole of the periodic table).

In terms of concrete proposals, I mention approaches from theoretical computer science that provide alternatives to the standard measures of performance, specifically asymptotic worst-case analysis. As an alternative to worst-case analysis relying on all-powerful, all-knowing adversaries, I discuss the average-case performance measures and the properties of distributions governing the generation of problem instances. Regarding asymptotic arguments, I consider sharp-threshold functions, the relevance of phase-transition phenomena, and the statistical properties of graphs of small order. The resulting perspective emphasizes particular problem instances and specific algorithms rather than problem classes and complexity results that pertain to all algorithms of a given order of growth. I also point out the embarrassing lack of 'real' planning problems, posit the reason for such a deficit, and suggest how recent progress in learning theory might provide a rich source of planning problems.[2]

Decisions, Uncertainty and Intelligence: Eric Horvitz

To be successful in realistic environments, reasoning systems must identify and implement effective actions in the face of inescapable incompleteness in their knowledge about the world. AI investigators have long realized the crucial role that methods for handling incompleteness and uncertainty must play in intelligence. Although we have made significant gains in learning and decision making under uncertainty, difficult challenges remain to be tackled.

Challenge: Creating Situated Autonomous Decision Systems

A key challenge for AI investigators is the development of comprehensive autonomous decision-making systems that are *situated* in dynamic environments over extended periods of time, and that are entrusted with handling varied, complex tasks. Such robust decision systems need the ability to process streams of events over time, and to continue, over their lifetimes, to pursue actions with the greatest expected utility.

Mounting a response to this broad challenge immediately highlights several difficult subproblems, each of which may be viewed as a critical challenge in itself. Pursuing solutions to these subproblems will bring us closer to being able to field a spectrum of application-specific challenges such as developing robotic systems that are given the run of our homes, tractable medical decision making associates that span broad areas of medicine, automated apprentices for helping people with scientific exploration, ideal resource management

[2] Additional details can be found in ftp://www.cs.brown.edu/u/tld/postscript/DeanetalAAAI-96.ps.

in multimedia systems, and intelligent user interfaces that employ rich models of user intentions and can engage in effective dialogue with people.

To address the broad challenge, we need to consider key phases of automated decision making, including the steps of perceiving states of the world, framing decisions, performing inference to compute beliefs about the world, making observations, and, most importantly, identifying a best set of actions. Under limited resources, we also need to carefully guide the allocation of resources to the different phases of analysis, and to extend decision making to the realm of monitoring and control of the entire decision-making process. I will dive into several problems associated with these components of decision making.

Subproblem: Automated Framing of Decision Problems

Faced with a challenge, a decision-making system must rely on some rules or, more generally, a model that expresses relationships among observations, states of the world, and system actions. Several methods have been studied for dynamically building representations of the world that are custom-tailored to perceived challenges. *Framing* a decision problem refers to identifying a set of relevant distinctions and relationships, at the appropriate level of detail, and weaving together a decision model. Framing a decision problem has resisted formalization. Nevertheless, strides have been made on model-construction techniques, typically relying on the use of logical or decision-theoretic procedures to piece together or prune away distinctions, as a function of the state of the world, yielding manageable focused models. We have a long way to go in our understanding of principles for tractably determining what distinctions and dependencies will be relevant given a situation.

Subproblem: Handling Time, Synchronicity, and Streams of Events

Autonomous systems must make decisions in an evolving environment that may change dramatically over time, partly in response to actions that a system has or will take. Most research on action under uncertainty has focused on models and inference procedures that are fundamentally atemporal, or that encode temporal distinctions as static variables. We must endow systems with the ability to represent and reason about the time-dependent dynamics of belief and action, including such critical notions as the persistence and dynamics of world states. We also need to develop better means of synchronizing an agent's perceptions, inference, and actions with important events in the world.

Subproblem: Modeling Preferences and Utility

The axioms of utility give us the fundamental *principle of maximum expected utility*: an agent should take actions that maximizes its expected (or average) measure of reward. Although it is easy to state the principle, we are forced in practice to wrestle with several difficult problems. Where does information about the utility of states come from? Whose utility is being maximized? How can we derive utilities associated with solving subproblems from assertions about high-level goals (e.g., "survive for as long as possible!") or from utilities on goal states? What is the most reasonable utility model for evaluating a finite sequence of actions an agent might take over time (e.g., should we assume an infinite number of future actions and discount value of future rewards, or assume a finite set of steps and compute average reward?, etc.). Different assumptions about the specific structure of the utility model lead to different notions of the "best" behaviors and to different computational efficiencies with evaluating sequences of plans.

Subproblem: Mastery of Attention and Architecture

Perceiving, reasoning, and acting all require costly resources. Controlling the allocation of computational resources can be a critical issue in maximizing the value of a situated system's behavior. What aspects of a problem and problem-solving strategy should a system attend to and when? We need to develop richer models of attention. There is promise in continuing work that turns the analytic machinery of decision-theoretic inference onto problem solving itself, and using such measures as the expected value of computation (EVC) to make design-time and run-time decisions about the ideal quantities of computation and memory to allocate to alternative phases of reasoning — including to the control processes themselves. More generally, there is great opportunity in applying these methods in offline and on-line settings to optimize the overall nature and configuration of a system's architecture, including decisions about the compilation of results.

Subproblem: Learning about Self and Environment

Continual learning about the environment and about the efficacy of problem solving is critical for systems situated in complex, dynamic environments, especially when systems may wander into one of several specialized environmental niches. We need to better understand how we can endow our systems with awareness of having adequate or inadequate knowledge about specific types of problems so that they can allocate appropriate resources for exploration and active learning. There has been research on methods for computing the confidence in results given a model and problem instance. This work highlights opportunities for developing methods that an agent could use to probe for critical gaps in its knowledge about the world.

Continuing this research will be valuable for building decision-making systems that can perform active, directed learning.

Subproblem: Living Life Fully—Harnessing Every Second

To date, most of our reasoning systems have no choice but to idle away the precious time between their active problem-solving sessions. Systems immersed in complex environments should always have something to do with their time. We need to develop techniques that allow an agent to continuously partition its time not only among several phases of a pressing analysis but also among a variety of tasks that will help the agent to maximize the expected utility of its behavior over its entire lifetime. Tasks that can benefit from ongoing attention include planning for future challenges, probing and refining a utility model, prefetching information that is likely to be important, compilation of portions of expected forthcoming analyses, experimenting (playing?) with its reasoning and motion control systems, and learning about critical aspects of the external world.

Think Big — AI Needs More Than Incremental Progress: Tom Mitchell

1. Let's build programs that turn the WWWeb into the world's largest knowledge-base. Doug Lenat had a good idea that we should have a large AI knowledge base covering much of human knowledge. One problem with building it is that it might take millions of people. And then we'd have to maintain it afterwards. The web is built and growing already, and it's online, and people are already maintaining it. Unfortunately, it's in text and images and sounds, not logic. So the challenge is to build programs that can "read" the web and turn it into, say, a frame-based symbolic representation that mirrors the content of the web. It's hard, but there is no evidence that it's impossible. And, even partial solutions will be of incredible value.

2. Apply Machine Learning to learn to understand Natural Language. Natural language has always been considered to be too difficult to do for real. But things have changed over the past three years in an interesting way — for the first time in history we have hundreds of millions of supervised training examples indicating the meaning of sentences and phrases: those hyperlinks in all those web pages. Now agreed, they're not quite the kind of supervised training data we'd ask for if we were to choose training data to learn natural language. But when it comes to training data you take what you can get, especially if it numbers in the millions (when there are less than 100,000 words to begin with). So each hyperlink like `my recent publications` has a meaning that is revealed by the web page you get if you click on it. How can we learn something useful about natural language understanding from this kind of data? (We probably need to use more than just this kind of data to learn language, but once we have some basic ontology defined, this kind of data should be of great use in learning the details.)

3. Let's build agents that exhibit *life-long* machine learning, rather than machine learning algorithms that learn one thing and then get rebooted. Consider people and consider current ML approaches such as decision tree or neural network learning. People *mature*, they learn things, then use these things they know to make it easier to learn new things. They use the things they know to choose what to learn next. ML has made good progress on approximating isolated functions from examples of their input/output. But this is just a *subroutine* for learning, and it's more of less a solved problem at this point. The next question is how can we build agents that exhibit long-term learning that is cumulative in a way more like people learn.

Toward Flexible and Robust Robots: Nils J. Nilsson

I start with the premise that it would be desirable to have mobile, AI-style robots that have *continuous existence* — ones that endure and perform useful work for long periods of time rather than ones that merely hold together long enough for a quick demo and video-taping session. Of course, some limited-capability robots — such as those currently used in automobile assembly and hospital-item delivery — do stay on the job for long periods of time. But all of these robots are far from being as robust and flexible as we want robots to be.

My challenge problem is to produce a robot factotum and errand-runner for a typical office building — an office building that is not specially equipped to accommodate robots. The kinds of tasks that such a robot will be able to perform will depend, of course, on its effectors and sensors as well as on its software. There are plenty of important challenge problems concerned with sensors and effectors, but I leave it to others to pose those. Instead, my challenge is to AI people to develop the software for a robot with more-or-less state-of-the art range-finding and vision sensors and locomotion and manipulation effectors. Let's assume that our robot can travel anywhere in the building — down hallways, into open offices, and up and down elevators (but perhaps not escalators). Assume that it can pick up, carry, and put down small parcels, such as books and packages. For communication with humans, suppose it has a speech synthesizer and word or phrase recognizer and a small keyboard/display console. Any such set of sensors and effectors would be sufficient for an extensive list of tasks *if* only we had the software to perform them.

Here is the specific challenge: The robot must be able to perform (or learn to perform with instruction and training — but without explicit post-factory computer programming) *any task* that a human might "reasonably" expect it to be able to perform given its effector/sensor suite. Of course, some tasks will be impossible — it cannot climb ladders, and it doesn't do windows. And, I don't mean the challenge to be one of developing a "Cyc-like" commonsense knowledge base and reasoning system. Our factotum will be allowed some lapses in commonsense so long as it can learn from its mistakes and benefit from instruction. It is not my purpose to set high standards for speech understanding and generation. The human task-givers should be tolerant of and adapt to the current limited abilities of systems to process natural language.

The second part of the challenge is that the robot must stay on-the-job and functioning for a year without being sent back to the factory for re-programming.

What will be required to meet this challenge? First, of course, a major project involving the application and extension of several robotic and AI technologies and architectures for integrating them. I do not think that it will be feasible for the robot's builders to send it to its office building with a suite of programs that anticipate *all* of the tasks that could be given. I think the robot will need to be able to *plan* and to *learn* how to perform some tasks that the building occupants (who know only about its sensors and effectors) might expect it to be able to perform but that its programmers did not happen to anticipate. To plan and to learn efficiently, I think it will need to be able to construct for itself hierarchies of useful action routines and the appropriate associated perceptual processing routines for guiding these actions. Perhaps something like the "twin-tower" architecture of James Albus (1991) would be appropriate for overall control. But the towers will have to grow with instruction and experience. The computational models of developmental learning proposed by Gary Drescher (1991) seem to me to be a good place to start for the tower-building aspect of the problem.

Work on this challenge problem would be good for AI. It would encourage progress on extending and integrating the many disparate components of intelligent systems: reacting, planning, learning, perception, and reasoning. It might also connect the bottom-up and top-down AI approaches — to the benefit of both. (It could also produce a useful factotum.) Good luck!

References

J.S. Albus. Outline for a Theory of Intelligence. *IEEE Systems, Man, and Cybernetics*, Vol 21, No. 3, pp. 473-509, May/June 1991.

G. Drescher. *Made Up Minds: A Constructivist Approach to Artificial Intelligence*, Cambridge, MA: MIT Press, 1991.

E.A. Feigenbaum, and J. Feldman. *Computers and Thought*, New York, NY: McGraw-Hill, 1963.

M. L. Ginsberg. Do computers need common sense? Techn. report, CIRL, Univerity of Oregon, 1996.

J. Hartmanis. Computational complexity of random access stored program machines. *Mathematical Systems Theory*, 5:232–245, 1971.

D.O. Hebb. *The Organization of Behavior*. John Wiley and Sons, New York, New York, 1949.

G. Kasparov. The day that I sensed a new kind of intelligence. *Time*, March 25, 1996, p. 55.

W.S. McCulloch and W. Pitts. A logical calculus of the ideas immanent in nervous activity. *Bull. of Math. Biophysics*, 5:115–137, 1943.

Marvin Minsky. *Computation: finite and infinite machines*. Prentice-Hall, 1967.

Marvin Minsky and Seymour Papert. *Perceptrons*. MIT Press, Cambridge, Massachusetts, 1969.

Allen Newell, J.C. Shaw, and Herbert Simon. Chess playing programs and the problem of complexity. *Journal of Research and Development*, 2:320–335, 1958. Also appeared in (Feigenbaum and Feldman 1963).

Oliver G. Selfridge. Pattern recognition and learning. In Colin Cherry, editor, *Proceedings of the Third London Symposium on Information Theory*, New York, New York, 1956. Academic Press.

Karl Sims. Evolving 3d morphology and behavior by competition. In Rodney A. Brooks and Pattie Maes, editors, *Artificial Life IV: Proceedings of the Fourth International Workshop on the Synthesis and Simulation of Living Systems*, pages 28–39. MIT Press, Cambridge, Massachusetts, 1994.

The Database Approach to Knowledge Representation

Jeffrey D. Ullman

Department of Computer Science
Stanford University
Stanford CA 94305
ullman@cs.stanford.edu
http://db.stanford.edu/~ullman

Abstract

The database theory community, centered around the PODS (Principles of Database Systems) conference has had a long-term interest in logic as a way to represent "data," "information," and "knowledge" (take your pick on the term — it boils down to facts or atoms and rules, usually Horn clauses). The approach of this community has been "slow and steady," preferring to build up carefully from simple special cases to more general ideas, always paying attention to how efficiently we can process queries and perform other operations on the facts and rules. A powerful theory has developed, and it is beginning to have some impact on applications, especially information-integration engines.

Datalog

The term *Datalog* has been coined to refer to Prolog-like rules without function symbols, treated as a logic program. Unlike Prolog, however, the conventional least-fixed-point semantics of the rules is used whenever possible.

Example 1: The rules for ancestors can be written as the following Datalog program.

```
anc(X,Y) :- par(X,Y)
anc(X,Y) :- anc(X,Z), anc(Z,Y)
```

That is, Y is an ancestor of X if Y is a parent of X or if there is some Z that is an ancestor of X and a descendant of Y. Because of the least-fixed-point semantics, there is no question of this program entering a loop, as the corresponding Prolog program would. □

Generally, we divide predicates into two classes. EDB (*extensional database*) predicates are stored as relations, while IDB (*intensional database*) predicates are defined by the *heads* (left sides) of rules only. Either EDB or IDB predicates can appear in subgoals of the *bodies* (right sides) of rules.

Sometimes, Datalog is extended to allow negated subgoals. That extension causes the least-fixed-point semantics to become problematic when the rules are recursive, and several approaches such as stratified negation and well-founded semantics have been developed to define suitable meanings for such Datalog programs. A survey of this subject, analogous to "nonmonotonic reasoning," can be found in Ullman [1994], and we shall not address this set of issues further here.

Example 2: A Datalog rule for ancestors that were not parents could be expressed as

```
oldAnc(X,Y) :- anc(X,Y), NOT par(X,Y)
```

□

Conjunctive Queries

A single Datalog rule in which an IDB predicate is defined in terms of one or more IDB and EDB predicates other than itself is called a *conjunctive query* (CQ). For instance, the rule of Example 2 is a CQ.

Containment and Equivalence

We say one CQ or Datalog program is *contained* in another if whatever the values of the EDB predicates (the "database") is, the set of facts provable from the first is a subset of those provable from the second. CQ's or Datalog programs are *equivalent* if the sets of provable facts are always the same for any database, i.e., the containment goes both ways.

Example 3: Consider

Q_1: `p(X) :- arc(X,Y), arc(Y,X)`
Q_2: `p(X) :- arc(X,X)`

We say that $Q_2 \subseteq Q_1$. Intuitively, Q_1 defines the set of nodes of a directed graph that are on any cycle of two nodes or loop of one node, while Q_2 defines only the set of nodes that have loops. It is also easy to check that Q_1 is not contained in Q_2; that is, there are graphs with cycles of two nodes but no loops. Thus, $Q_1 \neq Q_2$. □

Chandra and Merlin [1977] first studied conjunctive queries and showed that there is a simple test for containment, and thus for equivalence. The question of whether one CQ is contained in another is NP-complete, but all the complexity is caused by "repeated predicates," that is, predicates appearing three or more times in the body. In the very common case that no predicate appears more than twice in any one query, containment can be tested in linear time (Saraiya [1991]). Moreover, CQ's tend to be short, so in practice containment testing is not likely to be too inefficient.

Also, in exponential time at most we can test whether a CQ is contained in a Datalog program (Ramakrishnan et al. [1989]). The opposite containment, of a Datalog program in a CQ is harder, but still decidable (Chaudhuri and Vardi [1992]).

When we extend rules by allowing negated subgoals and/or by allowing arithmetic comparisons in the subgoals, things rapidly become undecidable. However, if we restrict ourselves to CQ's, not Datalog programs, then the problem is exponential at worst. Levy and Sagiv [1993] give a containment test for CQ's with negation, while the most efficient known algorithm for CQ's with arithmetic comparisons (but no negation) is found in Zhang and Ozsoyoglu [1993].

Application to Information Integration

A system for integrating heterogeneous information sources can be described logically by *views* that tell us what queries the various sources can answer. These views might be CQ's or Datalog programs, for example. The "database" of EDB predicates over which these views are defined is not a concrete database but rather a collection of "global" predicates whose actual values are determined by the sources, via the views.

Given a query Q, typically a CQ, one can ask whether it is possible to answer Q by using the various views in some combination. For example, *Information Manifold* at Bell Labs (Levy, Rajaraman, and Ordille [1996]) searches for all combinations of views that answer a query, while *Tsimmis* at Stanford (Garcia et al. [1995]) tries to find one such solution.

Example 4: The following example is contrived but will illustrate the ideas. Suppose we have a global parent relation $par(X, Y)$, meaning that Y is a parent of X. Suppose also that one source is capable only of providing a grandparent view. That is, it gives us the view:

```
gp(X,Y) :- par(X,Z), par(Z,Y)
```

A second source gives us a great-grandparent view:

```
ggp(X,Y) :- par(X,A), par(A,B), par(B,Y)
```

Our query Q is "find the first cousins once removed of individual a. That is, we must go up two generations from a, then down three generations. Formally, in terms of the global "database":

```
fcor(X) :- par(a,A), par(A,B),
    par(C,B), par(D,C), par(X,D)
```

We can answer Q in terms of the given views by:

```
fcor(X) :- gp(a,B), ggp(X,B)
```

□

Solving Queries in Terms of Views

The fundamental work on how to find an expression for a given query in terms of views is Levy, Mendelzon, Sagiv, and Srivastava [1994]. This paper handles the case where both the views and the query are CQ's.

Rajaraman, Sagiv, and Ullman [1994] extends the latter to the case where the views have "binding patterns"; that is, the source can only answer a query in which one or more arguments are bound. An example of this situation is a bibliographic source that can find a book given an author or an author given a book, but cannot answer the query "tell be about all books and their authors." In Example 4, there is a solution only if the source of view *gp* can handle a query with the first argument bound, and the source of *ggp* can handle a query with the second argument bound.

There has also been some progress allowing the views to be described by Datalog programs rather than CQ's. Specifically, each Datalog program can be expanded into a (possibly infinite) set of CQ's, and we may suppose that a source will answer any one of these CQ's. That model covers the case where the source is an SQL database, for instance.

In Papakonstantinou et al. [1995], the test for containment of a CQ in a Datalog program is exploited to find an expansion of the Datalog program that contains a given query. Levy, Rajaraman, and Ullman [1996] show how to decide equivalence of a query to some expression built from (a finite subset of) the infinite set of views that are the expansions of a Datalog program. This result extends Levy, Mendelzon et al. [1995] to the situation where sources support infinite sets of views that are described by a Datalog program.

Acknowledgements

This work was supported by NSF grant IRI–92–23405, ARO grant DAAH04–95–1–0192, and USAF contract F33615–93–1–1339.

References

Chandra, A. K. and P. M. Merlin [1977]. "Optimal implementation of conjunctive queries in relational databases," *Proc. Ninth Annual ACM Symposium on the Theory of Computing*, pp. 77–90.

Chaudhuri, S. and M. Y. Vardi [1992]. "On the equivalence of datalog programs," *Proc. Eleventh ACM Symposium on Principles of Database Systems*, pp. 55–66.

Garcia-Molina, H., Y. Papakonstantinou, D. Quass, A. Rajaraman, Y. Sagiv, J. Ullman, and J. Widom [1995]. "The TSIMMIS approach to mediation: data models and languages," Second Workshop on Next-Generation Information Technologies and Systems, Naharia, Israel, June, 1995.

Levy, A., A. Mendelzon, Y. Sagiv, and D. Srivastava [1995]. "Answering queries using views," *Proc. Fourteenth ACM Symposium on Principles of Database Systems*, pp. 113–124.

Levy, A. Y., A. Rajaraman, and J. J. Ordille [1996]. "Querying heterogeneous information sources using source descriptions," ATT Technical Memorandum, submitted for publication.

Levy, A. Y., A. Rajaraman, and J. D. Ullman [1996]. "Answering queries using limited external processors," to appear in *PODS* 1996.

Levy, A. Y. and Y. Sagiv [1993]. "Queries independent of update," *Proc. International Conference on Very Large Data Bases*, pp. 171–181.

Papakonstantinou, Y., A. Gupta, H. Garcia-Molina, and J. D. Ullman [1995]. "A query translation scheme for rapid implementation of wrappers," Fourth *DOOD*, Singapore, Dec., 1995.

Rajaraman, A., Y. Sagiv, and J. D. Ullman [1995]. "Query optimization using templates with binding patterns," *Proc. Fourteenth ACM Symposium on Principles of Database Systems*, pp. 105–112.

Ramakrishnan, R., Y. Sagiv, J. D. Ullman, and M. Y. Vardi [1989]. "Proof tree transformation theorems and their applications," *Proc. Eighth ACM Symposium on Principles of Database Systems*, pp. 172–181.

Saraiya, Y. [1991]. "Subtree elimination algorithms in deductive databases," Doctoral Thesis, Dept. of CS, Stanford Univ., Jan., 1991.

Ullman, J. D. [1994]. "Assigning an appropriate meaning to database logic with negation," in *Computers as Our Better Partners* (H. Yamada, Y. Kambayashi, and S. Ohta, eds.), pp. 216–225, World Scientific Press.

Zhang, X. and M. Z. Ozsoyoglu [1993]. "On efficient reasoning with implication constraints," *Proc. Third DOOD Conference*, pp. 236–252.

Robot Competition & Exhibition Abstracts

A reactive mobile robot based on a formal theory of action

C. Baral[*], L. Floriano, A. Gabaldon, D. Morales, T. Son and R. Watson
Department of Computer Science University of Texas at El Paso
El Paso, Texas 79968, U.S.A.
chitta@cs.utep.edu

One of the agenda behind research in reasoning about actions is to develop autonomous agents (robots) that can act in a dynamic world. The early attempts to use theories of reasoning about actions and planning to formulate a robot control architecture were not successful for several reasons:

- The early theories based on STRIPS and its extensions allowed only observations about the initial state. A robot control architecture using these theories was usually of the form: (i) make observations (ii) Use the action theory to construct a plan to achieve the goal, and (iii) execute the plan.

  For such an architecture to work the world must be static so that it does not change during the execution of the plans. This assumption is not valid for a dynamic world where other agents may change the world and/or the robot may not have all the information about the environment when it makes the plan.

- Moreover, planning is a time consuming activity and it is not usually wise for the robot to spend a lot of time creating a plan, especially when it is supposed to interact with the environment in real time.

This led to the development of several robot control architectures that were reactive in nature and usually were based on the paradigm of 'situated activity' which emphasized ongoing physical interaction with the environment as the main aspect in designing autonomous agents. These approaches were quite successful, especially in the domain of mobile robots. But most of them distanced themselves from the traditional approach based on theories of actions.

Our intention in the AAAI 96 robot contest is to use reactive rules. But, we will show that the reactive rules we use are *correct* w.r.t. a formal theory of action called $\mathcal{L}$[1]. Unlike STRIPS, the language $\mathcal{L}$ allows specification of dynamic worlds. But it makes assumptions such as: we know the effect of actions, the observations (sensor data) are correct, the robot has perfect control, etc.

The last two assumptions are not consistent with the real world. Nevertheless, as we explain in the succeeding paragraphs, our approach based on this language is appropriate.

Consider a reactive rule of the form

if $f_1, \ldots, f_n$ **then** a,

where, f_i's are fluents (that depend on the sensor readings) and a is an action. A simple reactive control module may consist of a set of such rules such that at any time the 'if' part of only one of the rules is satisfied.

A robot equipped with this control after sensing finds a rule in the module whose 'if' part is satisfied and performs the corresponding action. *We say a reactive rule is correct w.r.t. an action theory and a goal if for any situation that is consistent with the 'if' part of the rule, the action in the 'then' part is the first action in a minimal plan that will take the robot from the current situation to a situation where the goal is satisfied.*

The fact that we only have the first action of the minimal plan in the reactive rule is important. Having a complete minimal plan will not work because of the dynamic nature of the world. By having only the first action of the minimal plan we can take into account the possibility of incorrect sensors, world unpredictability and imperfect control.

After the robot executes an action based on its sensing and the reactive rules, it does not rely on a model of the world, rather it senses again. Hence the assumptions in $\mathcal{L}$ only mean that the minimal plan works if everything is perfect for a reasonable amount of time.

Based on these ideas we are currently developing reactive control programs for the AAAI 96 robot contest on a B-14 mobile robot from RWI. A detailed report on our approach can be found through http://cs.utep.edu/chitta/chitta.html.

[*]Support was provided by the National Science Foundation under grant Nr. IRI-9211662 and IRI-9501577.

[1]Please see the paper by Baral, Gabaldon and Provetti in this volume and the proceedings of the AAAI 96 workshop on 'Reasoning about actions, planning and control: Bridging the gap'.

CoMRoS: Cooperative Mobile Robots Stuttgart

Thomas Bräunl, Martin Kalbacher, Paul Levi, Günter Mamier

Universität Stuttgart, IPVR
Applied Computer Science – Computer Vision, Prof. Levi
Breitwiesenstr. 20-22, D-70565 Stuttgart, Germany
http://www.informatik.uni-stuttgart.de/ipvr/bv/comros

Project CoMRoS has the goal to develop intelligent cooperating mobile robots. Several different vehicles are to solve a single task autonomously by exchanging plans without a central control (Levi, Bräunl, Muscholl, Rausch. 1994).

We use "Robuter II" vehicles from Robosoft France, adapted to our needs. The standard vehicle has very little local intelligence (VME bus system) and is controlled remotely by wireless Ethernet for sending steering commands and receiving sonar sensor data. A wireless video link is used to transmit camera images. Data exchange between vehicles is then performed among the corresponding workstations. The remote control is basically used to simplify testing and debugging of robot programs. However, each vehicle can also be driven completely autonomous by using a laptop PC. (Bayer, Bräunl, Rausch, Sommerau, Levi 1995).

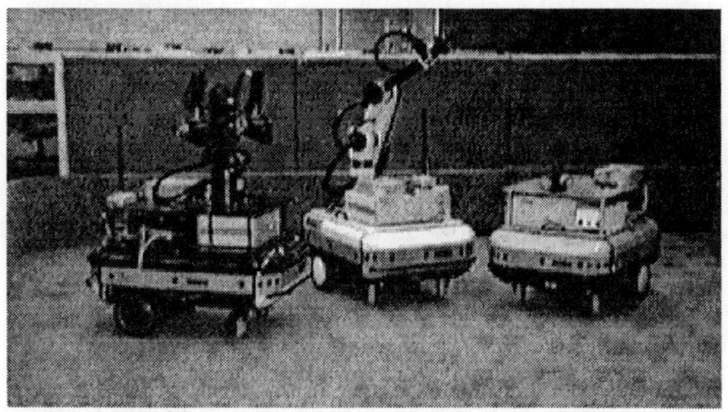

Figure: The three CoMRoS "musketeers"

On the PC, we are using the Linux version of Unix as operating system, while the robot itself has a real-time operating system (Albatros or D'nia Oberon). Quite a number of libraries for Ethernet connection, polling sonar sensor data, and digitizing video frames have been implemented by members of our group for various tasks on various machines, including our massively parallel MasPar MP-1216 system. We also implemented a physically-based simulation and animation system for our vehicles (Stolz, Bräunl, Levi 1995).

For the robot competition tasks, we configured one of our robots completely autonomous. For event 1, "call a meeting", we will almost exclusively rely on a belt of 24 sonar sensors around the robot, to detect walls, doors, hallways, and obstacles. However, it is planned to use a simple vision difference algorithm to determine whether a conference room is empty by asking any people inside the room to wave their hands. An alternative being investigated is implementing voice input. The Floyd algorithm is used to determine shortest driving paths. Using standard sound tools, the robot will tell the audience about its actions and plans.

For event 2, "clean up the tennis court", we first intended to use a robot with an on-board manipulator. However, this approach required a lot of time consuming image processing and manipulator control. Then, we took on an approach similar to a harvester machine. We developed a rotating cylinder to be mounted in front of the vehicle, in order to pick up any balls in the drive path of the robot. With this device, the ball collecting task is reduced to an area filling algorithm. Collected balls are being unloaded by reversing the rotation direction of the harvester. Only in a subsequent step will image processing be used to look for balls missed (e.g. the "squiggle ball"). The vehicle will then drive directly towards remaining balls and pick them up.

Acknowledgments

The authors would like to thank all assistants and students participating in the CoMRoS project, especially Alexander Rausch, Norbert Oswald, Michael Vogt, Marco Sommerau, Niels Mache, Hans-Georg Filipp, Ralf Taugerbeck, Frank Doberenz, Wolfgang Hersmann, and Normann Ness.

References

Levi, Bräunl, Muscholl, Rausch. Architektur der Kooperativen Mobilen Robotersysteme Stuttgart. In Levi, Bräunl (Eds.) 10. AMS, Stuttgart, Oct. 1994, pp. 262–273 (12)

Bayer, Bräunl, Rausch, Sommerau, Levi. Autonomous Vehicle Control by Remote Computer Systems. In Proceedings of the 4th Intl. Conf. on Intelligent Autonomous Systems, IAS–4, Karlsruhe, March 1995, pp. 158–165 (8)

Stolz, Bräunl, Levi. A Mobile Robot Simulation System. In Proc. ISATA Intl. Symposium on Automotive Technology & Automation, Böblingen, Sep. 1995, pp. 377–382 (6)

McMaster University's Artificial Computing System

Andrew Dawes, Mark Bentley

McMaster University
Department of Engineering Physics
1280 Main St. W
Hamilton, Ontario, Canada L8S 4L7
u9312519@muss.cis.mcmaster.ca

Introduction

This will be McMaster University's first entry into the AAAI Mobile Robotics competition. As such, this year will serve as a testing ground for future developments. It is the goal of the designers to experiment with new techniques and approaches based on their engineering background.

Project Objectives

The developers of this robot intend to simplify the complex task of making a robot intelligent by classifying the types of problems faced by the robot. In that way, the robot can determine the best course of action depending upon the task required. Obviously, a lot of time will be spent determining the key factors necessary to identify each type of problem.

To simplify the task of classifying the problems faced by the robot, we intend to use our engineering physics background to develop an approach. By understanding the key underlying physical factors specific to a situation, and using these to develop a solution, the amount of processing required of the system will be greatly reduced. Only essential data will be collected, with the actual system determining what data and how much data is needed to solve the problem.

In keeping a general approach to problem solving, the robot will need to identify situations that have been previously encountered. The key to identifying similar problems is collecting the proper data to determine the robot's situation. For example, finding four solid objects enclosing the robot could be interpreted as a room. What to do in this room would then be the new problem faced by the robot. The initial task of finding the four walls would be simplified by first getting the correct data to identify the objects as walls and not obstacles to be avoided. We hope to avoid relying on properties specific only to one goal to keep the algorithms general. Complex tasks would then be accomplished by separating them into components that can be dealt with. Only then will specific properties of the task be used to allow the system to make assumptions in determining solutions to certain situations.

System Components

In keeping with the theme of dividing the programming task into manageable pieces, the hardware will follow the same design philosophy. Specific computations will be carried out in certain areas of the system. The main processor, where the decision making is carried out, will communicate with the sub-processors to request and receive data. The central intelligence of the system will run on a standard desktop computer, on board the robot platform. Other tasks such as data collection and motion control will be accomplished through use of embedded controllers. Existing technology will be used for the sensors of the system. Specific components used for data collection will include ultrasonic ranging for quick obstacle avoidance. As well, laser ranging and scanning will be used for acquiring positional data and information about surroundings. The intelligence of the robot will be distributed throughout the system to minimize the load on each processor. The sub-processors will then notify the main system that important information is available. In this way only when new information is ready will the main processor look for the data. This is done to mimic the brain, or the main processor collecting information from the senses, or sub-processors.

Acknowledgements

This project is being supported by the Engineering Physics Department at McMaster University. It is through the support and dedication of its professors and staff that this project will be a success.

Doing tasks with multiple mini-robots

John Fischer and **Paul Rybski** and **Dirk Edmonds** and **Maria Gini**
Department of Computer Science, University of Minnesota
200 Union St SE, Minneapolis, MN 55455
{jfischer, rybski, dedmonds, gini}@cs.umn.edu

We are interested in building robots that are simple and have limited computing power yet are capable of surviving in an unstructured environment while achieving their assigned task. We have shown that even with limited computing small robots can learn how to achieve their task (Hougen *et al.* 1996), provided that the task is not extremely difficult and the learning algorithm is capable of fast learning.

One of our mini-robots, named Walleye, was built to pick up cups and cans for the Mobile Robot Competition that took place at IJCAI in August 1995 (Fischer & Gini 1996). Walleye, shown in Figure 1, is built out of a radio controlled car with the original electronics replaced by specially designed boards. All boards are built around the 68hc11 microcontroller, and have 16k of ROM and 32k of RAM. The vision system uses a CCD chip with digital output, a wide-angle lens, and a frame grabber board on which the vision processing is done. Two 7.2 volt rechargeable batteries are used, one for the motors, one for the computer boards. All software is written in C, with some routines in assembly. Walleye is built with off-the-shelf components at a cost of approximately $500.

The limited computing power has forced us to look for creative solutions that are simple and fast. This is particularly important considering that we do image processing on a 68hc11 with limited memory. Our image processing algorithms are specialized to the task at hand and so extremely fast. In nature specialization is often the key to survival.

One way of overcoming the limitations of a mini-robot is to construct a team of mini-robots. Unfortunately, there are a number of problems that come from having multiple robots. At the minimum, we have to ensure that the robots do not damage each other, do not interfere with each other, and can handle the presence of other moving robots in the same environment. Partitioning the task is not always easy, and a poor partitioning of the task might make the task unsolvable in the case a robot breaks down.

Figure 1: Walleye, the trash collecting mini-robot

The approach we are taking is to partition tasks in such a way that robots are independent of each other as much as possible and so have almost no need for communication. Take, for instance, a trash collecting task. Multiple independent robots are likely to work faster than a single robot, even though not as efficiently as robots that partition the space each has to cover. However, when each robot operates independently the overall system is more robust and less likely to fail catastrophically. We expect to demostrate multiple mini-robots at the 1996 competition.

Acknowledgements

We wish to thank all the people who have helped building our mini-robots, Elena Beltran, Abraham Nemitz, Luis Ortiz, Chris Smith, Erik Steinmetz, Maxim Tsvetovatyy, and Paul Zobitz, We would like to acknowledge the support of NSF under grant NSF/DUE-9351513, the UROP project at the University of Minnesota, and the AT&T Foundation.

References

Fischer, J., and Gini, M. 1996. Vision-based mini-robots. *Robotics Practitioner.* (to appear).

Hougen, D.; Fischer, J.; Gini, M.; and Slagle, J. 1996. Fast connectionist learning for trailer backing using a real robot. In *Proc. IEEE International Conference on Robotics and Automation.*

Lola, the mobile robot from NC State

Ricardo Gutierrez-Osuna, Daniel S. Schudel, Jason A. Janet and Ren C. Luo
Center for Robotics and Intelligent Machines
North Carolina State University
Raleigh, NC 27695-7911
rgutier, dsschude, jajanet, luo [@eos.ncsu.edu]

Introduction

The North Carolina State University team intends to participate in the 1996 Mobile Robot Competition and Exhibition with Lola, a Nomad 200. This year marks our third entry in this competition.

Robot description

Lola is a Nomad 200 with a standard 16-transducer sonar ring and tactile bumper sensors. We have taken advantage of the Nomad's modularity and moved 3 of the rear sonars to the front just above the bumper. This provides Lola with the ability to sense chairs and other potential obstacles that might otherwise be unseen.

Lola's main processor is a 486DX2-66 running Linux (Unix). The combination of Linux and wireless Ethernet makes code development on Lola a real joy. That is, from any workstation on the network (including the Internet) we can telnet to Lola and export the display for developing, debugging and executing code while monitoring Lola's status during operation, which beats having to wheel around a terminal and extension cord. The idea is to do all development without leaving your chair.

The vision hardware consists of an on-board image processor and a single RGB camera mounted on a pan/tilt unit. Lola's image processor was purchased from Traquair Data Systems and is blessed with two 'C40 DSP's running in parallel. Performing all computation on-board has several advantages: the video data is not corrupted by radio transmission noise, commands are not lost, and there is no communication lag that may result in Lola crashing into things. These findings are consistent with those of previous competitors. On the downside, the on-board image processor contributes significantly to the battery drain, which is partly due to its intended desktop use. Still, we are able to get about 2 hours of operation per charge.

Software

We intend to extend the software we used in the 1995 Mobile Robot Competition. As of this writing not all the modules have been implemented. The basic approach for each event has been determined and is summarized in the following sections.

Navigation architecture for Event I

The navigation architecture consists of the following modules:

- **High-level planning:** We perform path planning on the topological map of the arena. The map is searched for an optimal path to the goal location.
- **Navigation:** We use a Partially Observable Markov Decision Process to estimate the location of the robot in the topological map from dead-reckoning and sonar information.
- **Feature detection:** We use a Certainty Grid to extract topological features from the sonar information and find the robot's orientation with respect to the walls.
- **Low-level control:** Low-level control is based on "artificial forces", where the robot is attracted by a desirable state (i.e., follow a direction) and repulsed by sensed obstacles.

Perception/Manipulation for Event II

For this event we will use the following approach:

- **Perception:** The vision system on the robot and a color-histogramming technique are used to recognize and track tennis balls and the squiggle ball.
- **Manipulation:** We intend to design and build a 5-degree-of-freedom arm to retrieve the balls.
- **Neural networks:** It is expected that we will use a Region and Feature Based neural network for object detection/recognition and control of the arm.

Team members

Ricardo Gutierrez-Osuna, Daniel S. Schudel and Jason A. Janet are graduate students at NCSU's Electrical and Computer Engineering Department. Dr. Ren C. Luo is Professor and Director of the Center for Robotics and Intelligent Machines at NCSU.

Clementine: Colorado School of Mines

Undergraduate Interdisciplinary Robotics Team
Robin R. Murphy, Associate Director and Advisor
Center for Robotics and Intelligent Systems
Colorado School of Mines
Golden, CO 80401-1887
phone: (303) 273-3874 fax: (303) 273-3975
rmurphy@mines.edu

The 1996 Entry

The Colorado School of Mines (CSM) is fielding a team comprised of undergraduates in Computer Science or Engineering who are enrolled in the Robotics and AI Minor. The intent is to provide a forum for the students to a) transfer what they have learned in the classroom to a more realistic setting, b) meet with top researchers in the field, c) have an undergraduate research experience, and d) have fun. The students work with the team advisor and graduate students at CSM to integrate and modify code developed for NSF, ARPA, and NASA funded research projects. This will be the fourth year CSM has participated in the competition.

The team's platform is *Clementine*, a Denning-Branch MRV-4 research robot. She has a ring of 24 ultrasonics, a laser navigation system, and supports two cameras. All processing is done onboard by a 75MHz Pentium processor. A SoundBlaster board and speakers provides feedback on the robot's activities. *Clementine* is used for research in indoor task domains such as the surveillance and maintenance of stockpiles of hazardous materials, site assessment of dangerous environments such as a burning building or a collapsed mine, or security. A custom robot, *C2*, is used for outdoor environments.

Objectives

This year's team is concentrating on Event 1. There are two primary pedagogical objectives. *1. Gain familiarity with hybrid deliberative/reactive architectures by applying it to a well defined problem.* This objective is being met by having the students use a subset of the CSM hybrid architecture. The deliberative layer handles all activities which require knowledge about the robot's task. The *task manager* receives the the topological map, starting node, and goal node for the event via a human interface. It then activates the *cartographer* which produces a list of nodes, called the path plan, representing the best path between the start and goal. The task manager selects the behavior(s) for traveling between the current node and the next node on the path plan. The *reactive*, or behavioral, layer is responsible for executing the constituent behaviors encapsulated by the abstract navigation behavior.

2. Gain practical experience in using multiple sensing modalities. As mobile robots are developed for more demanding applications, it will become necessary to use multiple sensing modalities (e.g., vision, sonar, range finders, inclinometers, GPS, etc.). Accordingly, the students are required to use ultrasonics (sonar) for obstacle avoidance and basic navigation, and computer vision for identification of rooms.

Research Innovations

The students are incorporating two novel concepts from ongoing research at CSM: *scripts* for the coordination and control of concurrent and sequential activities in the reactive layer, and the partitioning of behaviors into *strategic* and *tactical* categories. Scripts, originally developed as a representation for Natural Language Processing, serve as a template for coordinating and controlling a collection of behaviors needed to perform a highly stereotyped task over time. The navigational activities needed for Event 1 have been collected into two abstract behaviors: **NavigateHall** and **NavigateDoor**.

Another novel aspect of the CSM hybrid architecture is its organization of behaviors in the reactive layer into strategic and tactical activities. Strategic behaviors, such as **NavigateHall**, generate strategic directions or navigational goals for the robot based on large scale concerns. Tactical behaviors such as **avoid-obstacle** and **fuzzy speed-control**, interpret the robot's strategic intent (e.g., go straight) in terms of the immediate situation (e.g., there's an obstacle directly ahead) and actually produce the action for the robot to take.

Acknowledgments

The Undergraduate Interdisciplinary Robotics Team entry is supported in part by Denning-Branch International Robotics, Pittsburgh, PA.

Mobile Robot Navigation and Control: A Case Study

Nicholas Roy, Gregory Dudek, Michael Daum
Research Centre for Intelligent Machines
McGill University
Montreal, Quebec, Canada

1 Introduction

Robotic systems (and in particular mobile autonomous agents) embody a complex interaction of computational processes, mechanical systems, sensors, and communications hardware. System integration can present significant difficulties to the construction of a real system, because the hardware is often built around convenience of design rather than convenience of system integration. Nonetheless, in order for robots to perform real-world tasks such as navigation, localization and exploration, the different subsystems of motion, sensing and computation must be merged into a single, realisable unit.

Our group is investigating particular problems in the domain of computational perception, in the context of mobile robotics. In particular, we are concerned with environment exploration, position estimation, and map construction. We have several mobile platforms integrating different sensing modalities, which we are able to control simultaneously from a single source.

2 Methodology

To support this work, we have developed a layered software architecture, that facilitates a modular approach to problems, in addition to building an abstraction of a robotic system [1]. Our architecture involves three software layers: on-board real-time subsystems, off-board hardware-specific systems that abstract away hardware dependencies, and top-level "client" processes. This abstraction allows external software to interact with either a simulated robot and environment or a real robot complete with sensors. The implementation is distributed across a network, and allows software to run on remote hardware, thus taking advantage of specialized hardware available on the network.

In appreciation of the necessity of simulation in addition to real-robot control, we have developed a graphical environment for the development of algorithms and software for mobile robotics. The environment was produced as a result of the recognition that progress in mobile robotics entails a progression from basic implementation of simple routines, through to the development of efficiently-implemented algorithms. With these considerations in mind, we have constructed a control and development interface for mobile robotics experiments that permits a single robot to be controlled and/or simulated using any combination of manual experimentation, simple automation and high-level algorithms.

*The support of NSERC and the Federal Centres of Excellence program is gratefully acknowledged.

3 Implementation

In the context of the AAAI competition, we are tapping this infrastructure by rapidly constructing a set of client processes which embody task specific objectives for the meeting scheduling problem. The client processes group simple sonar measurements into clusters used to classify regions of the map according to a simple labelling hierarchy. By recognizing and following corridors in the environment, the system travels between open spaces, or corridors using a set of simple control heuristics.

Our software tool allows us to transparently control and simulate several different types of mobile robots. In addition, our work entails the use of a variety of sensing modalities, for example, sonar, laser-range, tactile sensing [5] and video images. Furthermore, we have developed a customized video and range-sensing platform called Quadris. The Quadris sensor can be used to further refine the labelling hypotheses generated from sonar data.

4 Long-term Development

Our long term objectives involve using these tools to examine questions of spatial representation and exploration. In particular, we have performed image-based positioning [2], model-based localisation and exploration [3], and topological map representation and exploration. We are also working on extending this work to collaborative multi-robot exploration, with several agents performing independent exploration and fusion of spatial information [4].

References

[1] Gregory Dudek and Michael Jenkin. A multi-layer distributed development environment for mobile robotics. In *Proceedings of the Conference on Intelligent Autonomous Systems (IAS-3)*, pages 542–550, Pittsburgh, PA, February 1993. IOS Press.

[2] Gregory Dudek and Chi Zhang. Vision-based robot localization without explicit object models. In *Proc. International Conference of Robotics and Automation*, Minneapolis, MN, 1996. IEEE Press.

[3] Paul MacKenzie and Gregory Dudek. Precise positioning using model-based maps. In *Proceedings of the International Conference on Robotics and Automation*, San Diego, CA, 1994. IEEE Press.

[4] Nicholas Roy and Gregory Dudek. What to do when you're lost at the zoo: Multi-robot rendezvous in unknown environments. CIM-96-900-1, McGill University, June 1996.

[5] Nicholas Roy, Gregory Dudek, and Paul Freedman. Surface sensing and classification for efficient mobile robot navigation. In *Proc. IEEE International Conference on Robotics and Automation*, Minneapolis, MN, April 1996. IEEE Press.

YODA: The Young Observant Discovery Agent

Wei-Min Shen, Jafar Adibi, Bonghan Cho, Gal Kaminka,
Jihie Kim, Behnam Salemi, Sheila Tejada
Information Sciences Institute
University of Southern California
Email: shen@isi.edu

The YODA project at USC/ISI consists of a group of young researchers who share a passion for autonomous systems that can bootstrap their knowledge of real environments by exploration, experimentation, learning, and discovery. Our goal is to create a mobile agent that can autonomously learn from its environment based on its own actions, percepts, and missions [1].

The current YODA system has a Denning MRV-3 mobile robot and an on-board portable personal computer. The robot is a three-wheel cylindrical system with separate motors for motion and steering. It is equipped with 24 long range sonar sensors, three cameras for stereo vision, a speaker for sound emission, and a voice recognition system. The communication between the robot and the control computer is accomplished through an RS232 serial port using a remote programming interface [2]. The robot is controlled by a set of commands and the sensor readings include sonar ranges, motor status, and position vectors (vision is not used in this competition). As with any real sensing device, the sensor readings from the robot are not always reliable and this poses challenges for building a robust system.

YODA's software is implemented in MCL3.0 on a Macintosh Powerbook computer. The control architecture is designed to integrate reactive behaviors with deliberate planning. It also has facilities to accommodate learning and discovery in the future. Currently, the architecture is divided into two layers: the lower layer contains modules for navigation and reactive behaviors; and the higher layer contains modules for mission (re)planning.

The lower layer is a combination of production rules and behavior-based systems [3] with each behavior represented as a set of rules. These rules are different from traditional productions in that they have associated probabilities and make predictions. We believe the probabilities are important for robust behaviors in a real environment, and the predictions (i.e., the expected consequences of the robot's actions) are the key for self-organized learning and discovery. Given a set of goals delivered from the higher layer, the behavior rules will compete with each other based on the current sensor readings. Actions associated with the winning rules are then executed (these actions are in some sense collaborating with each other). This cycle of perception, decision, and action repeats itself until the goals are accomplished. In the case where the goals are impossible to reach, the lower layer will pass that failure to the higher layer for replanning.

To deal with imprecision in sensor readings, the system fuses information from different sensors and treat them as a whole. Decisions are never made based on any single sensor but on "patterns" of sensed information. This gives the system the ability to incorporate the idea of "signatures" for recognizing locations and features in the environment. For example, YODA has four basic built-in signatures based the 24 sonar sensors for this competition: corridor, corner, at-a-door, and at-a-foyer. These signatures, combined with the map and the (imprecise) position vector, greatly increase the reliability of determining the current location of the robot. To detect whether a room is occupied or not, the system will enter the room and ask verbally if any person in the room would like come closer to the robot. If this results some changes in the sonar readings, we conclude the room is occupied. Otherwise, after several trials of asking, we conclude the room is empty.

The movement control system of YODA is designed to bypass any obstacle during its movement towards a goal. However, if an obstacle is so large that the passage to a goal position is completely blocked, the robot will stop and wait until the obstacle moves away. Currently, we are implementing and testing the system on a real floor in the ISI office building, with furniture and people traffic present.

The higher layer in the architecture contains a planner that controls the mission-oriented and long-term behaviors. This planner uses a given map and determines a sequence of goals that must be accomplished by the robot. It can also replan based on information gathered by the lower layer (such as that a corridor is blocked or a door is closed). There are two alternate criteria for finding the best solutions: the "risky" one for finding a shortest path based on the current information, and the "conservative" one for taking into account any dynamic information that might be collected during a plan execution. We are currently investigating the trade-off between the two.

Finally, we would like to thank Dr. Ramakant Nevatia for providing us with the Denning Robot. Special thanks also to the various projects and people in ISI's Intelligent Systems Division for their moral support and their tolerance for sharing space (and occasionally "forces") with YODA.

References

[1] W.M. Shen. *Autonomous Learning from the Environment.* W.H. Freeman, Computer Science Press, 1994.

[2] Denning Robot Manual. *Denning MRV-3 Product Maunal.* Denning Mobile Robotics Inc. 1989.

[3] Ronald C. Arkin. Motor Schema-Based Mobile Robot Navigation. *International Journal of Robotics Research.* 1987.

Amelia

Reid Simmons Sebastian Thrun Greg Armstrong Richard Goodwin
Karen Haigh Sven Koenig Shyjan Mahamud Daniel Nikovski Joseph O'Sullivan

School of Computer Science
Carnegie Mellon University
Pittsburgh, PA 15213-3891
mahamud@cs.cmu.edu

Amelia was built by Real World Interface (RWI) using Xavier—a mobile robot platform developed at CMU on a B24 base from RWI—as a prototype. Amelia has substantial engineering improvements over Xavier. Amelia is built on a B21 base. It has a top speed of 32 inches per second, while improved integral dead-reckoning insures extremely accurate drive and position controls.

The battery life is six hours, and are hot-swappable. Two Pentium-100s are the main CPU's on board with special shock-mounted hard drives. A 75Mhz 486 laptop acts as onboard console. All these are interconnected by an internal 10M Ethernet, and to the world via a 2MBs Wavelan wireless system. Sonar and infrared sensor arrays ring the robot, mounted on Smart Panels for quick and easy access to internal components. These Smart Panels also contain bump sensors. A Sony color camera is mounted on a Directed Perception pan/tilt head for visual sensing. Finally, an arm can extend for 4-degree of freedom manipulation of Amelia's world.

Like Xavier, Amelia has a distributed, concurrent software system, which runs under the Linux operating system. All programming is done in C, and processes communicate and are sequenced and synchronized via the TASK CONTROL ARCHITECTURE (TCA) (Simmons 1995).

Communication with Amelia is graphical (via the laptop), remote (via zephyr), and speech-driven. An off-board Next computer runs the SPHINX real-time, speaker-independent speech recognition system and a text-to-speech board provides speech generation. Thus, we can give verbal commands to the robot and the robot can respond verbally to indicate its status. In addition, a graphical user interface is available for giving commands and monitoring the robot's status.

Amelia plans to participate in the "Call a meeting" event. She will use the ROGUE system (Haigh & Veloso 1996) for high-level task planning through PRODIGY, a planning and learning system (Veloso et al. 1995). ROGUE is able to create a branching plan based on the observations of the real world, select appropriate orderings of goal locations, and monitor the robot's progress towards those goals. Planning actions are defined at the granularity of "goto-location" and "observe-room", requiring more detailed schema for execution.

Navigation is accomplished using a Partially Observable Markov Decision Process (POMDP) model of the environment (Simmons and Koenig 1995). POMDP models allow the robot to account for actuator and sensor uncertainty and to integrate topological map information with approximate metric information. They also allow the robot to recover gracefully if they are uncertain about their current location.

Amelia will use vision for detecting doorways as well as for detecting faces. Doorways are detected without the help of markers. Detection is accomplished with a combination of region-growing, appearance-based matching and sonar range readings. Faces are detected in two stages. The first stage uses a fast color histogram technique to identify candidate regions that have appropriate sizes and shapes. The second stage consists of a computationally costlier step that verifies whether the chosen regions are face-like or not.

References

Simmons, R., and Koenig, S. 1995. Probabilistic Robot Navigation in Partially Observable Environments. In Proceedings of the IJCAI, 1080–1087.

Veloso, M.; Carbonell, J. C.; Perez, A.; Borrajo, D.; Fink, E.; and Blythe, J. 1995. Integrating Planning and Learning: The PRODIGY Architecture. *Journal of Theoretical and Experimental Artificial Intelligence* 7(1).

Haigh, K. Z., and Veloso, M. 1996. Interleaving Planning and Robot Execution for Asynchronous User Requests. In the Proceedings of the AAAI-96 Spring symposium on Planning with Incomplete Information for Robot Problems.

Simmons, R. 1995. Towards Reliable Autonomous Agents. In AAAI Spring symposium on Software Architectures.

SIGART / AAAI Doctoral Consortium Abstracts

Selection of Passages for Information Reduction *

Jody J. Daniels
Department of Computer Science
University of Massachusetts
Amherst, MA 01003 USA
Email: daniels@cs.umass.edu

There currently exists a bottleneck in extracting information from pre-existing texts to generate a symbolic representation of the text that can be used by a case-based reasoning (CBR) system. Symbolic case representations are used in legal and medical domains among others. Finding similar cases in the legal domain is crucial because of the importance precedents play when arguing a case. Further, by examining the features and decisions of previous cases, an advocate or judge can decide how to handle a current problem. In the medical domain, remembering or finding cases similar to the current patient's may be key to making a correct diagnosis: they may provide insight as to how an illness should be treated or which treatments may prove to be the most effective.

This thesis demonstrates methods of locating, automatically and quickly, those textual passages that relate to predefined important features contained in previously unseen texts. The important features are those defined for use by a CBR system as slots and fillers and constitute the frame-based representation of a text or case. Broadly, we use a set of textual "annotations" associated with each slot to generate an information retrieval (IR) query. Each query is aimed at locating the set of passages most likely to contain information about the slot under consideration.

Currently, a user must read through many pages of text in order to find fillers for all the slots in a case-frame. This is a huge manual undertaking, particularly when there are fifty or more texts. Unfortunately, full-text understanding is not yet feasible as an alternative and information extract techniques themselves rely on large numbers of training texts with manually encoded answer keys. By locating and presenting relevant passages to the user, we will have significantly reduced the time and effort expenditure. Alternatively, we could save an automated information extraction system from processing an entire text by focusing the system on those portions of the text most likely to contain the desired information.

This work integrates a case-based reasoner with an IR engine to reduce the information bottleneck. SPIRE [Selection of Passages for Information REduction] works as follows: the CBR system evaluates its case-base relative to a current problem situation. It passes along to the IR engine the identifiers of the documents that describe fact situations the most similar to the current problem. The IR engine treats these documents as though they were hand-marked as relevant and uses them to generate a query against a larger corpus of texts (Daniels and Rissland 1995).

After retrieving additional relevant texts, we might wish to add them to the CBR system's knowledge base. However, the documents must be converted from their original text into a frame-based representation, a time-consuming and error-prone activity. To assist the knowledge engineer, we save a set of "annotations", which we derive when creating the original case-base. An annotation contains the words and phrases that describe the value of a particular slot filler and the annotation is associated with its respective slot. An annotation may be a segment of a sentence, an entire sentence, or several sentences. For example, for the slot that contains the value of someone's *monthly-income*, sample annotations from SPIRE's case-base are: "net disposable monthly income for 1979 averaged $1,624.82" and "His current gross income is $24,000 per year."

SPIRE passes the case-base of annotations for each slot to the IR system. Using these annotations, the IR component generates a new query aimed at retrieving small relevant passages from the documents just retrieved. By combining into a query those descriptive terms and phrases used to identify the slot fillers within the current case-base, we can locate relevant passages within novel texts.

By retrieving passages for display to the user, we have winnowed a text down to several sets of sentences. This process is repeated for each slot in the case-based reasoner's representation of the problem. By locating and displaying these important passages to a user, we have reduced reading an entire document to examining several sets of sentences, resulting in a tremendous savings in time and effort.

References

Jody J. Daniels and Edwina L. Rissland. A Case-Based Approach to Intelligent Information Retrieval. In *Proceedings of the 18th Annual International ACM/SIGIR Conference*, pages 238–245, Seattle, WA, July 1995. ACM.

*This research was supported by NSF Grant no. EEC-9209623, State/Industry/University Cooperative Research on Intelligent Information Retrieval, Digital Equipment Corporation and the National Center for Automated Information Research.

Towards a Unified Approach to Concept Learning

Pedro Domingos*

Department of Information and Computer Science
University of California, Irvine
Irvine, California 92717, U.S.A.
pedrod@ics.uci.edu
http://www.ics.uci.edu/~pedrod

Rule induction (either directly or by means of decision trees) and case-based learning (forms of which are also known as instance-based, memory-based and nearest-neighbor learning) arguably constitute the two leading symbolic approaches to concept and classification learning. Rule-based methods discard the individual training examples, and remember only abstractions formed from them. At performance time, rules are applied by logical match (i.e., only rules whose preconditions are satisfied by an example are applied to it). Case-based methods explicitly memorize some or all of the examples; they avoid forming abstractions, and instead invest more effort at performance time in finding the most similar cases to the target one.

There has been much debate over which of these two approaches is preferable. While each one can be extended to fit the results originally presented as evidence for the other, it typically does so at the cost of a more complex, less parsimonious model. In classification applications, each approach has been observed to outperform the other in some, but not all, domains.

In recent years, multistrategy learning has become a major focus of research within machine learning. Its main insight is that a combination of learning paradigms is often preferable to any single one. However, a multistrategy learning system typically operates by calling the individual approaches as subprocedures from a control module of variable sophistication, and again this is not completely satisfactory from the point of view of parsimony.

In my thesis work I argue that rule induction and case-based learning have much more in common than a superficial examination reveals, and can be unified into a single, simple and coherent model of symbolic learning. The proposed unification rests on two key observations. One is that a case can be regarded as a maximally specific rule (i.e., a rule whose preconditions are satisfied by exactly one case). Therefore, no syntactic distinction need be made between the two. The second observation is that rules can be matched approximately, as cases are in a case-based classifier (i.e., a rule can match an example if it is the closest one to it according to some similarity-computing procedure, even if the example does not logically satisfy all of the rule's preconditions). A rule's extension, like a case's, then becomes the set of examples that it is the most similar rule to, and thus there is also no necessary semantic distinction between a rule and a case.

The RISE algorithm is a practical, computationally efficient realization of this idea. RISE starts with a rule base that is simply the case base itself, and gradually generalizes each rule to cover neighboring cases, as long as this does not increase the rule base's error rate on the known cases. If no generalizations are performed, RISE acts as a pure case-based learner. If all cases are generalized and the resulting set of rules covers all regions of the instance space that have nonzero probability, it acts as a pure rule inducer. More generally, it will produce rules along a wide spectrum of generality; sometimes a rule that is logically satisfied by the target case will be applied, and in other cases an approximate match will be used. This unified model is more elegant and parsimonious than a subprocedure-style combination. Experiments with a large number of benchmark classification problems have also shown it to consistently outperform either of the component approaches alone, and lesion studies and experiments on artificial domains have confirmed that its power derives from its ability to simultaneously harness the strengths of both components (Domingos 1996).

The remaining proposed thesis work will focus on further elucidating what the bias of RISE is compared to that of its parent paradigms (and thus determining when it will be the more appropriate algorithm to use), on applying the ideas contained in RISE to problems like context dependency, feature selection, fragmentation avoidance, and data mining, and on bringing the use of domain knowledge into the RISE framework.

References

Domingos, P. 1996. Unifying Instance-Based and Rule-Based Induction. *Machine Learning*. Forthcoming.

*Partly supported by a PRAXIS XXI scholarship.

A Computational Theory of Turn-taking

Toby Donaldson
University of Waterloo
Department of Computer Science
Waterloo, Ontario, Canada
tjdonald@neumann.uwaterloo.ca

A Turn-taking Framework

My research is concerned with the problem of turn-taking in discourse, especially as applied to intelligent interfaces, such as advice-giving systems or software help systems. A limitation of many discourse systems is their need for explicit turn-ending signals (e.g. pressing a return key). In such systems, mid-turn interruptions are impossible, although there are practical examples of where mid-turn interruptions are highly desirable. For example, an interface agent should promptly inform the user of important pieces of information, such as a lack of disk space or the loss of a network connection, especially if the user is enaged in some activity that relies on that information.

Interruptions are a particularly useful instance of turn-taking, and we have outlined a general three-part goal-oriented model of turn-taking:

Motivation An agent must first have some motivating reason to take a turn. Motivations include, for example, recognition of an inconsistency in the beliefs of the speaker, or a desire for plan clarification;

Goal Adoption It is often inappropriate to take a turn the moment you have something to say — you should wait until the other person has finished speaking. Thus, motivations trigger the adoption of turn-taking goals;

Turn Execution Conversants typically coordinate turn-taking by giving and receiving various vocal and semantic signals. For example, decreased speaking volume can indicate that a speaker is willing to give up the floor (Oreström 1983).

Time-bounded Persistent Goals

We have designed a goal-based framework for controlling an agent's actions based on the idea of *time-bounded persistent goals*, a time-sensitive variation of Cohen and Levesque's *persistent goals* (Allen 1983; Cohen & Levesque 1990). In their most general form, time-bounded persistent goals looks like this:

Bounded-persistent-goal(ϕ,T)
While: $\textit{simple-goal}(\phi)$
Adopt-when: $B(\textit{holds}(B\neg\phi, \textit{some-head-of}(T)))$
Drop-when: $B(\textit{holds}(B\phi, \textit{some-tail-of}(T)))$
$B(\textit{holds}(B\neg\phi, \textit{some-tail-of}(T)))$
$B(\textit{after}(T, \textit{now}))$

A bounded persistent goal to make ϕ hold over T is adopted when the agent has a simple goal to achieve ϕ, and the agent believes ϕ does not already hold at the start of T. The goal is dropped when the agent believes ϕ holds over some interval that ends T, or that $\neg\phi$ holds over some interval that ends T, or T is in the past. By defining different kinds of simple goals, the bounded persistent goals can be used to help a rational agent decide how to manage its turn-taking activities.

We have considered applying bounded-persistent goals to the problem of the initiation of clarification dialogs in advice-giving settings (for cases of misconceptions and plan ambiguity). While it is typically assumed that, for example, a possible misconception should be dealt with immediately, time-bounded persistent goals allow certain turns to be put aside, and not actually executed until absolutely necessary. Such "lazy" turn-taking thus allows for the possibility that perceived problems may actually be corrected by the speaker, and thus no clarification dialog need be entered into at all.

References

Allen, J. 1983. Maintaining knowledge about temporal intervals. *Communications of the ACM* 26(11):832–843.

Cohen, P., and Levesque, H. 1990. Intention is choice with commitment. *Artificial Intelligence* 42:213–261.

Oreström, B. 1983. *Turn-taking In English Conversation.* CWK Gleerup.

Learning in multi-agent systems

Claudia V. Goldman *
Institute of Computer Science
The Hebrew University
Givat Ram, Jerusalem, Israel
clag@cs.huji.ac.il

Learning agents acting in a multi agent environment can improve their performance. These agents might decide upon their course of action by learning about other agents with whom they interact. The learning agents can learn about the others' information and rules of behavior. The agents will not need to plan their actions beforehand, each time they are asked to solve the same problem they have already solved or when dealing with similar problems.

Our research focusses in finding learning algorithms for multi agent environments. In particular, we want to develop agents that learn how to cooperate with other agents and learn how to become experts. I am studying these themes in several domains to achieve a more broader understanding of how learning is influenced by different multi-agent domains and thus how learning algorithms can be developed. The research aims at answering the following questions:

1. How do agents learn how to act? I am looking at a teacher-learner model in which the teacher might also play the role of the learner, and the learner might also behave as a teacher. I am investigating two main directions. One direction regards a 2-phase model and we investigate how agents can be trained by other agents and then how they generalize the knowledge they acquired (Goldman & Rosenschein 1995). The second direction focusses on a dynamic learning model in which the agents learn from the others incrementally and also act based on the current knowledge they have.

   I am also investigating the behavior of learning agents that are implemented as automata (determinisitic and probabilistic). We investigated (Mor, Goldman, & Rosenschein 1995) how one learning agent can decide which action to play while he learns his opponent's strategy. Currently, we are focussing on mutual learning

   In both cases, I am looking at reinforcement learning, where the feedback is given to the agents by the other agents, in contrast to most methods used in reinforcement learning in which the agents receive their feedbacks from the world in which they perform their actions.

2. How do agents learn about information (i.e. understand, share and compose new information)? Currently, I am working on three projects: Musag (Goldman, Langer, & Rosenschein 1996): a system based on four software agents, that learns about concepts by "reading" html documents in the Web. I am currently working on expanding the system to include a group of such systems that will interact in order to learn more about the concepts they are learning, by sharing information they have, with the others.

   Courtz (Goldman, Mor, & Rosenschein 1996): a software agent dedicated to looking for information about a topic given by a user in a fuzzy way, i.e. the information is not well defined and might have ambiguous meanings.

   NetNeg (Goldman, Gang, & Rosenschein 1995): a hybrid system built on a neural network module and an agents based module. This agents deal with multi-media information.

*This research is supervised by Dr. Jeffrey S. Rosenschein and supported by the Eshkol Fellowship, Israeli Ministry of Science

References

Goldman, C. V., and Rosenschein, J. S. 1995. Mutually supervised learning in multiagent systems. In *Workshop on Adaptation and Learning in MAS at IJCAI*.

Goldman, C. V.; Gang, D.; and Rosenschein, J. S. 1995. Netneg: A hybrid system architecture for composing polyphonic music. In *Workshop on AI and Music at IJCAI*.

Goldman, C. V.; Langer, A.; and Rosenschein, J. S. 1996. Musag: an agent that learns what you mean. In *PAAM96*.

Goldman, C. V.; Mor, Y.; and Rosenschein, J. S. 1996. Courtz: an agent that pleases you. In *PAAM96*.

Mor, Y.; Goldman, C. V.; and Rosenschein, J. S. 1995. Learn your opponent's strategy (in polynomial time)! In *Workshop on Adaptation and Learning in MAS at IJCAI*.

Bounding the Cost of Learned Rules: A Transformational Approach

Jihie Kim
Information Sciences Institute and Computer Science Department
University of Southern California
4676 Admiralty Way, Marina del Rey, CA 90292, U.S.A.
jihie@isi.edu

My dissertation research centers on application of machine learning techniques to speed up problem solving. In fact, many speed-up learning systems suffer from the *utility problem*; time after learning is greater than time before learning. Discovering how to assure that learned knowledge will in fact speed up system performance has been a focus of research in explanation-based learning (EBL). One way of finding a solution which can guarantee that *cost after learning is bounded by cost of problem solving* is to analyze all the sources of cost increase in the learning process and then eliminate these sources. I began on this task by decomposing the learning process into a sequence of transformations that go from a problem solving episode, through a sequence of intermediate problem solving/rule hybrids, to a learned rule. This transformational analysis itself is important to understand the characteristics of the learning system, including cost changes through learning.

Such an analysis has been performed for Soar/EBL(Kim & Rosenbloom 1995). The learning process has been decomposed into a sequence of transformations from the problem solving to learned rule. By analyzing these transformations, I have identified three sources which can make the output rule expensive.

First, ignoring search-control rules which constrained the problem solving can increase the cost. For example, PRODIGY/EBL (Minton 1993) and Soar ignore a large part of the search-control rules in learning to increase the generality of the learned rules. The consequence of this omission is that the learned rules are not constrained by the path actually taken in the problem space, and thus can perform an exponential amount of search even when the original problem-space search was highly directed (by the control rules). By incorporating search control in the explanation structure, this problem can be avoided (Kim & Rosenbloom 1993).

Second, when the structure of the problem solving differs from the structure of the match process for the learned rules, time after learning can be greater than time before learning. During problem solving, the rules that fire tend to form a hierarchical structure in which the early rules provide information upon which the firing of later rules depends. This hierarchical structure is reflected in EBL most obviously in the structure of the explanation (and the more general explanation structure). However, if this hierarchical structure is then flattened into a linear sequence of conditions for use in matching the rule that is learned, the time after learning can be greater than the time before learning. If instead, the learning mechanism is made sensitive to the problem-solving structure, this source of expensiveness can be avoided (Kim & Rosenbloom 1996).

Third and finally, ignoring the optimization employed in the problem solving can increase the cost. In Soar, working memory is a set. Whenever two different instantiations create the equivalent working memory elements, they are merged into one. Eliminating this process in learning, and keeping equivalent set of partial instantiations separately can increase the cost. By preprocessing the partial instantiations, and merging the equivalent instantiations into one, this cost increase can be avoided.

The results on a set of known expensive-rule-learning tasks have shown that such modifications can effectively eliminate the identified set of sources of expensiveness. My future work would be extending the experimental results to a wider range of tasks, both traditional expensive-rule tasks and non-expensive-rule tasks. Also, experiments on a practical domain rather than a toy domain would allow a more realistic analysis of the approach. In addition to the sources of expensiveness which have found so far, I am working toward identifying other potential sources of expensiveness, should they exist. By finding the complete set of sources of expensiveness and avoiding those sources, the cost of using the learned rules should always be bounded by the cost of the problem solving episode from which they were learned.

References

Kim, J., and Rosenbloom, P. S. 1993. Constraining learning with search control. In *Proc. 10th Int'l Conf. on Machine Learning*, 174–181.

Kim, J., and Rosenbloom, P. S. 1995. Transformation analyses of learning in Soar. Technical Report ISI/RR-95-4221, USC-ISI.

Kim, J., and Rosenbloom, P. S. 1996. Learning efficient rules by maintaining the explanation structure. In *Proc. 13th Nat'l Conf. on Artificial Intelligence (to appear)*.

Minton, S. 1993. Personal communication.

Agent-Centered Search: Situated Search with Small Look-Ahead

Sven Koenig
School of Computer Science
Carnegie Mellon University
Pittsburgh, PA 15213-3891
skoenig@cs.cmu.edu

Situated search is the process of achieving a goal in the world. Traditional single-agent search algorithms (such as the A* algorithm) usually assume completely known, stationary domains with deterministic actions. These assumptions favor search approaches that first determine open-loop plans (sequences of actions) that can then be executed blindly in the world. Consequently, single-agent search in AI is often performed in a mental model of the world (state space): states are represented as memory images and search is a process inside the computer (search-in-memory).

Situated search can interleave or overlap search-in-memory with action execution. This approach has advantages over traditional approaches in non-deterministic, non-stationary, or only partially known domains. It allows one, for example, to gather information by executing actions. This information can be used to resolve uncertainty caused by missing knowledge of the domain, inaccurate world models, or actions with non-deterministic effects. For instance, one does not need to plan for every contingency in non-deterministic domains; planning is necessary only for those situations that actually result from the execution of actions.

My research focuses on the design and analysis of agent-centered search methods. Agent-centered search methods are situated search methods that restrict the search-in-memory to a small part of the state space that is centered around the current state of the agent before committing to the execution of the next action. Since agent-centered search methods perform a small amount of search-in-memory around the current state of the agent, they can be characterized as "situated search with small look-ahead." Examples of agent-centered search methods include real-time heuristic search methods (they search forward from the current state of the agent), many on-line reinforcement learning algorithms, and exploration approaches.

A major difference between search-in-memory and agent-centered search is that search-in-memory methods can "jump around in the state space." If, after they have expanded a state, a state in a different part of the state space looks promising, they can expand this state next. In contrast, in situated search, if an agent wanted to explore a state, it would have to execute actions that get it there. The further the state is from the current state of the agent, the more expensive it is to get to that state. Furthermore, backtracking to a previous state might not be easy: it can be very expensive in state spaces with asymmetric costs and the agent might not even have learned how to "undo" an action execution. Thus, one can expect situated (agent-centered) search methods to have different properties than search-in-memory methods.

To date, agent-centered search methods have mostly been studied in the context of specific applications. The few existing results are mostly of empirical nature and no systematic or comparative studies have yet been conducted. It is therefore unclear when (and why) agent-centered search algorithms perform well. My research explores, both theoretically and experimentally, how agent-centered search methods behave. This includes an analysis of the factors that influence their performance. Such an analysis is helpful, for example, for predicting their performance in non-deterministic domains, for distinguishing easy from hard search problems, for representing situated search problems in a way that allows them to be solved efficiently, and for developing more adequate testbeds for agent-centered search methods than sliding tile puzzles, blocks worlds, and grid worlds. The second step then is to use these results to extend the functionality of agent-centered search algorithms to better fit typically encountered situated search situations. This includes probabilistic domains with non-linear reward structures, which can be caused, for instance, by the presence of dead-lines or risk attitudes. For more details and references to the literature, see (Koenig & Simmons 1996).

References

Koenig, S., and Simmons, R. 1996. Easy and hard testbeds for real-time search algorithms. In *Proceedings of the National Conference on Artificial Intelligence (AAAI)*, this volume.

Recurrent Expert Networks

Cathie LeBlanc
Dept of Computer Science
Florida State Univ
Tallahassee, FL 32306-4019
leblanc@cs.fsu.edu

Research has shown that computational techniques such as neural networks often provide classification abilities that are more accurate than methods which rely on explicit knowledge acquisition alone (Ben-David & Mandel 1995). On the other hand, because no "reason" for a particular classification can be given when a computational technique has been used, human experts tend to be skeptical of such systems. As a result, many researchers have developed tools, called hybrid systems, which combine the pattern recognition capabilities and parallel processing of neural systems while retaining the domain knowledge encoded in expert systems (Medsker 1994).

Because the widely known "knowledge acquisition bottleneck" makes explicit knowledge acquisition tools (such as expert systems) expensive to create, Kuncicky, Hruska and Lacher (Kuncicky, Hruska, & Lacher 1992) have developed expert networks, which eliminate the need for the expert to associate a certainty factor with each rule. Instead, the expert system rules, acquired from the human expert, are translated into the topology of a computational network, called an expert network. The individual nodes in an expert network are not all identical but instead have functionalities that match the part of the knowledge base which they encode. For example, a node which encodes an AND between two pieces of knowledge in the knowledge base might take the minimum of its inputs and if that minimum is above a certain threshold, outputs that minimum (Lacher & Nguyen 1994). The certainty factors correspond to the trainable weights between the nodes. Example data are presented to the network and the weights are learned via a backpropagation-like algorithm (Lacher, Hruska, & Kuncicky 1992). The topologies and learning algorithms developed for expert networks thus far have been strictly feed-forward.

Some classification tasks, however, will be difficult to complete using a strictly feed-forward architecture. In particular, the solution to many problems requires that "state" information be maintained. State information is the context in which the problem is currently being solved. The context of a problem solution will change as the solution proceeds. Certain sets of rules need only be considered in certain contexts. For example, if the problem is to read email, the state must include information about whether the computer is on or off. The rules to turn on the computer will only be considered if the state tells us that the computer is off.

Such state information will be difficult to manage using feed-forward architectures. In fact, in standard artificial neural networks, such state information is handled by the addition of recurrent connections in the topology of the network (Hertz, Krogh, & Palmer 1991). The recurrent connections allow the context information to be input to the network at succeeding steps. Therefore, I will extend the notion of expert networks so that they will be able to maintain state information via recurrent connections while at the same time encoding previously discovered expert knowledge.

The problem domain to which I will apply this technology is the protein folding problem. In this problem, state information about secondary structure predictions for amino acids earlier in the protein's primary sequence will play an important role in the secondary structure prediction for the current amino acid.

References

Ben-David, A., and Mandel, J. 1995. Classification accuracy: Machine learning vs. explicit knowledge acquisition. *Machine Learning* 18:109–114.

Hertz, J.; Krogh, A.; and Palmer, R. G. 1991. *Introduction to the theory of neural computation.* Redwood City, California: Addison-Wesley Publishing Company.

Kuncicky, D.; Hruska, S.; and Lacher, R. 1992. Hybrid systems: the equivalence of expert system and neural network inference. *International Journal of Expert Systems* 4:281–297.

Lacher, R., and Nguyen, K. 1994. Hierarchical architectures for reasoning. In Sun, R., and Bookman, L., eds., *Computational Architectures for Integrating Neural and Symbolic Processes*, 117–150. Boston: Kluwer Academic Publishers.

Lacher, R.; Hruska, S.; and Kuncicky, D. 1992. Backpropagation learning in expert networks. *IEEE Transactions on Neural Networks* 3:62–72.

Medsker, L. R. 1994. *Hybrid Neural Network and Expert Systems.* Boston: Kluwer Academic Publishers.

Semi-Deterministic Reasoning

Chengjiang Mao

Department of Computer and Information Sciences
University of Delaware
Newark, DE 19716
mao@cis.udel.edu

In typical AI systems, we employ so-called nondeterministic reasoning (NDR), which resorts to some systematic search with backtracking in the search spaces defined by knowledge bases (KBs). An eminent property of NDR is that it facilitates programming, especially programming for those difficult AI problems such as natural language processing for which it is difficult to find algorithms to tell computers what to do at every step. However, poor efficiency of NDR is still an open problem. Our work aims at overcoming this efficiency problem.

There exists a lot of work done for this problem. For example, separation of domain knowledge from control knowledge to facilitate pruning search spaces has been employed in many knowledge based systems such as blackboard systems. However, the improvement is restricted by the fact that it is difficult for programmers to acquire precise control knowledge by analyzing search spaces with only the help of their intuition.

Meanwhile, researches in machine learning, such as chunking and explanation-based learning, provide some means of automatic construction of control knowledge to prune search spaces. Unfortunately, improvement of efficiency is limited by a so-called utility problem.

The common strategy underlying these various existing techniques is that they prune search spaces at every step of search by matching control knowledge against the current working memory (i.e., the current state in a search space). This "on-line" pruning of search spaces does not change the static organization of search spaces, and it keeps the NDR behavior throughout.

Different from the above techniques, our work introduces a way of "off-line" pruning of search spaces. It computationally analyzes the search space defined by a KB by learning NDR implementation results based on the KB, and then reorganizes the search space into a new organization which supports semi-deterministic reasoning (SDR) as defined in the following. For any problem instance to be solved, SDR first deterministically chooses a sub-search space and then does nondeterministic search in the chosen sub-search space until the end of the whole process of search.

Reorganization of a search space defined by a KB can be realized by reorganizing the KB into independent sub-knowledge bases (SKBs). Two SKBs are independent *iff* throughout the problem solving process for any problem instance, at most one of the two SKBs is activated. The KB organization with independent SKBs is called a solution-oriented KB organization (SOK) (Mao, 1992). Based on the SOK, SDR first deterministically chooses an SKB, and then does NDR based on the chosen SKB. The determinism of SDR indicates that for any problem instance, at most one SKB can be activated. If an activated SKB fails to deduce a solution, then, without checking any other SKBs, SDR will claim that there is no solution for the problem instance.

In our work, we choose Prolog as an NDR inference engine. To transform a typically unorganized first-order logic based Prolog KB (i.e., a Prolog program) into an SOK organized KB, an integrated learning system THOUGHT-PROLOG (Mao & Chester, 1996) first calls a Prolog interpreter to do NDR and records the inference paths, and then classifies these inference paths into disjoint groups which form SKBs, and finally generates control knowledge to describe what problem instances can be solved in each SKB. A small scale experiment on a Prolog program with 22 rules and 33 facts shows that the average activated rules are reduced by 41.3% by THOUGHT-PROLOG.

Our work can also be viewed as learning for knowledge base organization. It recognizes knowledge base organization as the meta-meta knowledge which defines the ways for control knowledge (meta-knowledge) to guide the use of domain knowledge.

References

Mao, C. (1992). THOUGHT: An Integrated Learning System for Acquiring Knowledge Structure. In Proceedings of the Ninth International Machine Learning Conference. 300-309. Aberdeen, Scotland.

Mao, C. and Chester, D. (1996). Transformation of Non-Deterministic Problem Solvers into Semi-Deterministic Problem Solvers. Technical Report, NLP-HCI-AI-96-01. Dept. of Computer and Information Sciences, Univ. of Delaware.

A Connectionist Model Of Instructed Learning

David C. Noelle
Computer Science & Engineering
University of California, San Diego
La Jolla, California 92093-0114
dnoelle@cs.ucsd.edu

The focus of this research is on how people blend knowledge gained through explicit instruction with knowledge gained through experience. The product of this work will be a cognitively plausible computational learning model which integrates instructed learning with inductive generalization from examples. The success of this model will require the attainment of both a technical and a scientific goal.

The technical goal is the design of a computational mechanism in which induction and instruction are smoothly integrated. The design of such a multistrategy learner might be implemented within a symbolic rule-based framework (Huffman, Miller, & Laird 1993), within a framework strong in inductive generalization, such as connectionism (Noelle & Cottrell 1995), or within a hybrid architecture (Maclin & Shavlik 1994). This work pursues the second of these three general approaches. Following an intuition concerning the primacy of induction (which precedes linguistic rule following both phylogenetically and ontogenetically) and with an eye on future reduction to neurological explanations, the model proposed here is built within a wholly connectionist framework.

The scientific goal of this research is to account for certain interaction effects between instruction and induction that have been observed in humans, including:

- the performance improvements brought by experience following direct instruction.
- the apparent superiority of providing direct instruction *prior* to the presentation of examples.
- the relative insensitivity to contingencies exhibited by subjects when following a simple rule.
- the intrusion of similarity into instructed category learning, resulting in a failure to follow instructions.

If successful, our computational model will exhibit all of these phenomena, and it will produce testable hypotheses concerning the accuracy and time course of human learning in various contexts.

Typical connectionist models learn via the modification of connection weights in response to an external error signal. Such methods, however, are essentially too slow to account for the rapid effects of "learning by being told". Instead, our approach captures the effects of direct instruction in the dynamic activation state of a recurrent network. The combinatoric space of valid instruction sequences is represented by the space of *articulated attractors* in the network's dynamics. Each fixed-point attractor in this structured activation space encodes a unique collection of instructed knowledge. Linguistic advice is viewed as input activity which *pushes* the network into an appropriate basin of attraction, allowing the network to settle to a representation of the received knowledge. By modeling explicit instruction in this way, connection weight modification is left in the capable hands of standard inductive learning techniques. This allows induction and instruction to operate in tandem, and it opens the door to complex interactions between them.

We have already demonstrated the ability of our networks to learn a simple instructional language in the service of a task and to thereafter exhibit rapid instruction following behavior. We have also begun applying our model to experimental results from the category learning and implicit/explicit learning literature. A detailed comparison of our model with some symbolic models of instructed learning, such as Instructo-SOAR (Huffman, Miller, & Laird 1993), will also be conducted.

References

Huffman, S. B.; Miller, C. S.; and Laird, J. E. 1993. Learning from instruction: A knowledge-level capability within a unified theory of cognition. In *Proceedings of the 15th Annual Conference of the Cognitive Science Society*, 114–119. Boulder: Lawrence Erlbaum.

Maclin, R., and Shavlik, J. W. 1994. Incorporating advice into agents that learn from reinforcements. In *Proceedings of the 12th National Conference on Artificial Intelligence*, 694–699. Seattle: AAAI Press.

Noelle, D. C., and Cottrell, G. W. 1995. A connectionist model of instruction following. In Moore, J. D., and Lehman, J. F., eds., *Proceedings of the 17th Annual Conference of the Cognitive Science Society*, 369–374. Pittsburgh: Lawrence Erlbaum.

Symptom Management for Schizophrenic Agents

Phoebe Sengers
Department of Computer Science and Program in Literary and Cultural Theory
Carnegie Mellon University
5000 Forbes Ave.
Pittsburgh, PA 15213-3891
phoebe@cs.cmu.edu

Behavior-based paradigms are a promising avenue towards creating full-blown integrated autonomous agents. However, until now they have had a major stumbling block: programmers can create robust, subtle, and expressive behaviors, but the agent's overall behavior gradually falls apart as these behaviors are combined. For small numbers of behaviors, this disintegration can be managed by the programmer, but as more behaviors are combined their interactions become so complex that they become at least time-consuming and at worst impossible to manage.

One of the characteristic modes of breakdown that occurs in such an agent is that it engages in stereotyped behavior with abrupt switching between relatively homogeneous modes of behavior. I term this symptom, inspired by cultural theory, *schizophrenia*, and identify its cause in a methodology of *atomization*. Atomization is the reduction of a complex and not necessarily well-defined phenomenon to a set of relatively simple parts with limited interaction; it is what makes behavior switching so abrupt. Unfortunately, the implementation of agents depends on this reduction, since complicated, wholistic agents are nearly impossible to design, build, and debug. While this may mean that we must build atomistic agents, it does not necessarily consign us to the schizophrenic scrapheap—provided we take a fresh perspective.

Cultural theory suggests that when agents appear schizophrenic, it may be because their social and cultural environment is ignored. While alternative AI (including Artificial Life, situated action, and behavior-based AI) insists that agents must be thought of in terms of their environment, this environment is usually thought of only in terms of the physical objects the agent encounters, leaving out the designer and audience of the agent. The problem with ignoring part of the agent's environment is that it obscures the origin of various technical problems, thereby making them harder to solve. I propose an AI methodology that does not ignore the social situation of the agent, but instead uses it to help design the agent.

In particular, "socially situated AI" may help solve schizophrenia. In schizophrenia, behaviors are too atomized, causing agents to switch abruptly between behaviors. From a social perspective, schizophrenia means the user can see the way the designer has broken the agent up. Therefore, schizophrenia may go away *if we make the breaks somewhere the user is unlikely to look.*

To be more specific, behavior-based agents are typically broken up into visible behaviors. But if users are meant to recognize these behaviors, abrupt switching between them will be obvious. Instead, internal switching should occur without changing the visible behavior of the agent. These internal switches may be less obvious, since the user sees the agent doing the same thing before and after the switch.

I am building an architecture in which "atoms" of agents are not just behaviors but also *behavior transitions*, special behaviors that change from an old high-level activity to a new one. Switches among such activities are now implemented smoothly as behaviors, instead of occuring abruptly between them. Behavior transitions need to allow programmers to manage the complexity of combining many activities while making the agent's behavior look more smooth and natural.

Potential technical problems with behavior transitions include quadratic explosion of code; large amounts of state to communicate between behaviors and the transitions taking over for them; and complicated, inter-related, undebugable code. I am developing solutions to these problems based on a socially situated approach, which integrates, not the agent's *behavior*, but the *effect* of the behavior on the user. The designer is given the capability to manage the agent's *effect*, instead of just the agent's behavior. I hope to show that a behavior-transition architecture based on these principles will allow designers to use the benefits of atomization (modularization; clean code; understandability) without the drawback of schizophrenia, thereby creating larger, more coordinated agents.

Acknowledgments

This work was supported by the Office of Naval Research under grant N00014-92-J-1298. Many thanks to my advisors, Joseph Bates and Camilla Griggers.

Adaptive Shared Control for an Intelligent Power Wheelchair

Richard C. Simpson, M.S. and Simon P. Levine, Ph.D.

University of Michigan Rehabilitation Engineering Program
1C335 University of Michigan Hospital
Ann Arbor, Michigan 48109-0032
{rsimpson, silevine}@umich.edu

The NavChair Assistive Navigation System (Levine, Koren, & Borenstein 1990) is being developed to increase the mobility of severely handicapped individuals by providing navigation assistance for a power wheelchair. While designing the NavChair it became clear that obtaining the full range of desired functionality required several different "operating modes," each of which was appropriate in different contexts. This also necessarily created a need for a method of choosing between these modes. One solution is for the user to manage the task of mode determination, which may place unacceptable performance burdens on NavChair users with severe disabilities. Instead, a means for the NavChair to automatically choose the proper operating mode is being sought.

Research to develop such an adaptation method impacts a general class of human-machine systems that change their behavior based on fluctuations in the needs, goals, or capabilities of their human operator. Automatic adaptation is important for the NavChair because it allows both the operator and system to achieve levels of performance neither could reach alone.

Researchers have produced a variety of methods to perform automatic adaptation. Often, even though several sources of information relevant to the adaptation process may exist for a given man-machine system, very little effort is made to combine multiple information sources together within one system. An adaptation method that can make use of more information should make better adaptation decisions than one that is limited in the information it can consider. This research will examine one promising approach called Bayesian networks, which provide a method of probabilistically modeling a situation in which causality is important, but our knowledge of what is actually going on is not complete (Charniak 1991).

Experiments employing the NavChair are proposed to evaluate the performance of Bayesian networks in adaptation tasks through the following specific aims:

1. Test the hypothesis that combining multiple information sources improves adaptation in a man-machine system.
2. Determine whether reasoning about adaptation degrades the NavChair's performance in situations where no mode change (adaptation) is required.

This research will implement an adaptation system within the NavChair that makes use of Bayesian networks. The information available to the network will include the identities of objects in the NavChair's environment and an internal map of the larger environment in which the NavChair is moving.

This work represents a preliminary effort in the development of adaptation methods that are applicable to a wide variety of man-machine systems. The immediate impact on the NavChair will be an improved ability to make adaptation decisions and an increased ability to meet the needs of people with disabilities. Beyond the scope of this research, Bayesian networks could be used to drive adaptation in applications in fields such as intelligent vehicle control, aviation, factory automation and human-computer interaction. For example, an adaptive control system similar to the NavChair's could provide assistance to automobile drivers to improve driving safety and traffic flow on the highways.

Several of the pieces needed for the proposed research have been completed. Mechanisms for automatically steering the NavChair through doorways and along walls have been developed, and integrated into a method for recognizing environmental cues and automatically adapting the NavChair's behavior in response to them. Finally, a mapping mechanism for use in location-based adaptation has been completed.

References

[1] Levine, S.; Koren, Y.; and Borenstein, J. 1990. NavChair Control System for Automatic Assistive Wheelchair Navigation. In Proceedings of the 13th Annual RESNA International Conference, 193-194. Washington, D.C.: RESNA.

[2] Charniak, E. 1991. Bayesian Networks Without Tears. *AI Magazine* 12(4): 50-63.

Induction of Selective Bayesian Networks from Data

Moninder Singh*

Department of Computer and Information Science
University of Pennsylvania, Philadelphia, PA 19104-6389
msingh@gradient.cis.upenn.edu

Bayesian networks (Pearl 1988), which provide a compact graphical way to express complex probabilistic relationships among several random variables, are rapidly becoming the tool of choice for dealing with uncertainty in knowledge based systems. Amongst the many advantages offered by Bayesian networks over other representations such as decision trees and neural networks are the ease of comprehensibility to humans, effectiveness as complex decision making models and elicitability of informative prior distributions.

However, approaches based on Bayesian networks have often been dismissed as unfit for many real-world applications because they are difficult to construct and probabilistic inference is intractable for most problems of realistic size. Given the increasing availability of large amounts of data in most domains, learning of Bayesian networks from data can circumvent the first problem. This research deals primarily with the second problem. We address this issue by learning **selective** Bayesian networks — a variant of the Bayesian network that uses only a subset of the given attributes to model a domain. Our aim is to learn networks that are smaller, and hence computationally simpler to evaluate, but display accuracy comparable to that of networks induced using all attributes.

We have developed two methods for inducing selective Bayesian networks from data. The first method, K2-AS (Singh & Provan 1995), selects a subset of attributes that maximizes predictive accuracy prior to the network learning phase.The idea behind this approach is that attributes which have little or no influence on the accuracy of learned networks can be discarded without significantly affecting their performance. The second method we have developed, Info-AS (Singh & Provan 1996), uses information-theoretic metrics to efficiently select a subset of attributes from which to learn the classifier. The aim is to discard those attributes which can give us little or no information about the class variable, given the other attributes in the network. We have showed that relative to networks learned using all attributes, networks learned by both K2-AS and Info-AS are significantly smaller and computationally simpler to evaluate but display comparable predictive accuracy. Moreover, they display faster learning rates, hence requiring smaller datasets to achieve their asymptotic accuracy. We have also shown that both methods significantly outperform the *naive* Bayesian classifier, one of the most widely-studied Bayesian methods within the machine learning community.

These results have several important ramifications. First, they give us a way of applying Bayesian networks to problems where it was not possible to do so previously, due to computational intractability. Second, they show that decreasing the size of the networks does not significantly reduce the classification accuracy which may be very important in some applications (e.g. medicine). Third, in real world applications, features may have an associated cost (e.g. a feature representing an expensive test). The learning algorithms proposed can be modified to prefer removal of such high-cost tests.

Since databases from most real life domains, especially medicine, are replete with missing data, we are also working on extending our learning algorithms to deal with such data.Previous work in this area basically deals with learning the conditional probability tables assuming that the Bayesian network structure is known. We are trying to extend this work to learn both network structure as well as the probability tables from data that has missing values/variables and incorporate it with the feature selection approaches presented in this paper. Moreover, we would like to test our methods of learning selective Bayesian networks on two real-world databases in the domain of acute abdominal pain. This domain is relatively hard, yielding about 65% accuracy with other learning methods. Thus, it offers a good test bed for our ideas.

References

Pearl, J. 1988. *Probabilistic Reasoning in Intelligent Systems.* San Mateo, CA: Morgan Kaufmann.

Singh, M., and Provan, G. M. 1995. A comparison of induction algorithms for selective and non-selective Bayesian classifiers. In *Proc. 12th Intl. Conference on Machine Learning*, 497–505.

Singh, M., and Provan, G. M. 1996. Efficient learning of selective Bayesian network classifiers. To appear in *Proc. 13th Intl. Conference on Machine Learning.*

*This work is funded by an IBM Cooperative fellowship.

Why Dissect a Frog When You Can Simulate a Lion?

Brian K. Smith

School of Education and Social Policy & The Institute for the Learning Sciences
Northwestern University
Evanston, IL 60208
bsmith@ils.nwu.edu

We are concerned with creating computer-based learning environments which provide students with opportunities to develop causal explanations of complex phenomena through experimentation and observation. We combine video and simulation to facilitate such exploration in high school biology classrooms. Specifically, we focus on issues in behavioral ecology and the predation behaviors of the Serengeti lion.

The question explored by students concerns the effectiveness of the lion's hunting strategies. Although popularized as a skilled predator, only 15-30% of the hunts attempted by lions result in the successful capture of prey (Schaller 1972). Explaining the causal factors underlying this statistic requires an understanding of cooperative behavior, optimality, resource competition, and variation. The conjecture is that active explanation will result in a greater understanding of these concepts than passive lecture/textbook teaching approaches.

Students first watch a collection of video clips showing lions employing various hunting strategies. Their task is to create narratives by explaining and comparing features of the videos. Video is useful for detecting dynamic features such as speed or use of cover, but factors that are "implicit" (*e.g.*, time of day), invisible (*e.g.*, wind direction), or obscured (*e.g.*, spatial positioning of predator/prey) in the film can be difficult to isolate and understand.

To highlight such salient events, we are building a simulation of the lion hunt called the *Animal Landlord*. Animals are behavioral agents possessing perceptual, motor, and action selection routines. Students observe an aerial view of the creatures and can manipulate parameters influencing their behaviors (*e.g.*, number of predators, vegetation density). Thus, the simulation provides a setting in which further data can be collected to investigate questions raised during the video exercise.

Students require assistance in open-ended experimentation tasks, so unlike similar systems (*e.g.*, Resnick 1994), we provide domain-specific guidance. We monitor the progress of agents to structure a debriefing episode (Johnson 1994) upon completion of a hunt. The rule system and logic-based truth maintenance system described in (Everett & Forbus 1996) records logical dependencies between aspects of the environment, creatures and their actions, and justifications for these actions.

Agents can be queried about all actions taken during the hunt through a multimedia interface. The dependencies are traced to provide justifications of these actions, justifications that might otherwise go unnoticed by students (*e.g.*, "Warthog-11 became alert when it heard a noise due north of it."). In addition, the dependencies are used as indices into a library of investigation prompts, suggestions about possible exploration paths based on ecological assumptions and methodological strategies. For a stalking lion, the system would suggest considering the significance of the average stalk distance and comparing conditions between stalking hunts and ambushes. Investigation prompts are retrieved using probes combining local dependency information and global properties of the world. By using this context information to present appropriate guidance, we hope to assist students in generating and exploring hypotheses.

We have piloted the video portion of the learning environment with a small group of students, and further testing begins in classrooms in the spring of 1996. The focus of these evaluations is to determine the types of guidance required in the simulation to assist student investigations. We are also refining and evaluating our agent models in accordance with ecological literature on the lions and their prey.

This work is being advised by Brian J. Reiser and has benefited from discussions with Aggelici Agganis, John Everett, Ken Forbus, Hans Landel, and David Scheel.

References

Everett, J. O., and Forbus, K. D. 1996. Scaling Up Logic-Based Truth Maintenance Systems via Fact Garbage Collection. In Proceedings of the Thirteenth National Conference on Artificial Intelligence. Menlo Park, CA: AAAI Press.

Johnson, W. L. 1994. Agents That Learn How to Explain Themselves. In Proceedings of the Twelfth National Conference on Artificial Intelligence, 1257-1263. Menlo Park, CA: AAAI Press.

Resnick, M. 1994. *Turtles, Termites, and Traffic Jams: Explorations in Massively Parallel Microworlds*. Cambridge, MA: The MIT Press.

Schaller, G. B. 1972. *The Serengeti Lion: A Study of Predator-Prey Relations*. Chicago, IL: University of Chicago Press.

Algorithm Evolution for Signal Understanding

Astro Teller
Computer Science Department
Carnegie Mellon University
Pittsburgh, PA 15213
astro@cs.cmu.edu http://www.cs.cmu.edu/ astro

Automated program evolution has existed in some form for over thirty years. Signal understanding (e.g., signal classification) has been a scientific concern for even longer than that. Interest in generating, through machine learning techniques, a general signal understanding system is a newer topic, but has recently attracted considerable attention. First, I have proposed to define and create a machine learning mechanism for generating signal understanding systems independent of the signal's type and size. Second, I have proposed to do this through an evolutionary strategy that is an extension of genetic programming. Third, I have proposed to introduce a suite of sub-mechanisms that not only contribute to the power of the thesis mechanism, but are also contributions to the understanding of the learning technique developed.

Existing machine learning techniques have some advantages and disadvantages with respect to finding solutions to the general signal-to-symbol problem. Concretely, the goal of this thesis work is to overcome some of these disadvantages without losing any of the important advantages of existing systems.

Two particularly prominent disadvantages of existing machine learning techniques for signal understanding are that the input must almost always be preprocessed and that domain knowledge must be input in the form of preprocessing or technical details that are not obvious to a signal expert. These two disadvantages can be avoided by the evolution of programs that use *parameterized signal primitives.*

Three prominent advantages of existing machine learning techniques for signal understanding are: that "real-world" signals can be handled; that, even when learning must be done off line, the learned function can be run in real time; and that the technique mechanisms are well understood, thereby generating faith in the method. One of the thesis goals is to transfer these advantages to the evolution of algorithms.

My thesis work involves iteratively improving the representation, evolutionary environment, and coordination of programs. These evolved programs are each expected to learn to discriminate one signal type from all others in a set of signal training examples. Then multiple, highly fit programs from each "discrimination pool" are orchestrated in a signal understanding system. I have called this paradigm PADO: Parallel Algorithm Discovery and Orchestration. My preliminary work developing the PADO approach and system can be seen in papers such as (Teller & Veloso 1995b; 1995c; 1995a; Teller 1996).

My work concentrates on these learning mechanism innovations and in real world signal domains where the signals are typically large and/or poorly understood. This thesis work is unique in three aspects: No system currently exists that can learn to classify signals with no space or size penalties for the signal's size or type. No genetic programming system currently exists that purposefully generates and orchestrates a variety of experts along problem specific lines. There is currently no analytically sound mechanism for explaining and reinforcing specific parts of an evolved program.

The main question that this thesis will answer is:

Can the algorithm evolution paradigm be extended (and how far) to apply successfully as a machine learning technique to the general signal-to-symbol problem?

Acknowledgements

This research is supported through the generosity of the Fannie and John Hertz foundation.

References

Teller, A., and Veloso, M. 1995a. Algorithm evolution for face recognition: What makes a picture difficult. In *Proceedings of the International Conference on Evolutionary Computation.* IEEE Press.

Teller, A., and Veloso, M. 1995b. PADO: A new learning architecture for object recognition. In Ikeuchi, K., and Veloso, M., eds., *Symbolic Visual Learning.* Oxford University Press. 81–116.

Teller, A., and Veloso, M. 1995c. Program evolution for data mining. In Louis, S., ed., *The International Journal of Expert Systems. Third Quarter. Special Issue on Genetic Algorithms and Knowledge Bases.* JAI Press.

Teller, A. 1996. Evolving programmers: The co-evolution of intelligent recombination operators. In Kinnear, K., and Angeline, P., eds., *Advances in Genetic Programming II.* MIT Press.

The Use of Knowledge-Based Systems Techniques for Risk Assessment

Botond Virginas

University of Portsmouth, Department of Information Science
Locksway Road, Southsea
PO4 8JF Hampshire, United Kingdom
botond@sis.port.ac.uk

Introduction

Several accidents during the last decade have emphasized the need to properly analyse and manage the low probability high consequence risks associated with plant operations in the nuclear, chemical and other industries. Formal risk assessment methods are vital tools for this task, and include a number of qualitative and quantitative techniques.

The increasing need to perform risk analyses induces a growing interest in standardised analysis procedures and corresponding computerised supporting tools. The amount and type of information handled in risk assessment calls for the application of knowledge-based systems.

The research investigates how knowledge-based systems techniques can be used in conjunction with conventional risk assessment methods in order to develop a **K**n**o**wledge-**B**ased **R**isk **A**ssessor (**KoBRA**) supporting the various phases of risk assessment. The **KoBRA** environment takes the form of a toolkit containing a variety of tools performing the different tasks involved in risk assessment. The following research area problems have been identified:

- A safety oriented process model needs to be developed for a given type of process within a certain application domain. Different knowledge representation formalisms have to be investigated.
- Different reasoning strategies have to be explored for the construction of different logic models. A mixed programming language approach will be examined.
- A platform concept will be analysed.

The research concentrates mainly on:

- Review of the risk assessment field
- Evaluation of the existing computer support for risk assessment
- Design of a risk assessment framework within an overall risk management strategy
- Design of an integrated set of computer aided risk assessment tools
- Implementation and testing of **KoBRA**

Review of the work completed

A general review of the risk assessment field has been completed. In parallel, computerised tools supporting various phases of the risk assessment process have been explored. It has been decided that an application domain from the chemical process industry will be chosen and the toolkit will be tested on several particular processes within that domain.

The design of the risk assessment framework has been completed. A substantial part of **KoBRA** has been implemented on a **Sun SPARC** workstation. The different risk assessment tools are being developed and tested incrementally. A mixed language programming environment (**POPLOG**) is used for the implementation.

As the development of the different tools from **KoBRA** continues, so a safety oriented process model is being built incrementally. This model takes the form of an object oriented database with functional and structural links between the objects. Generic objects describe what is known in general about a particular type of system or component. The user builds his process description with process specific instantiations of these objects. The objects are represented with a hybrid formalism using rules and frames. The different tools in the toolkit perform the various risk assessment tasks on this model.

A platform concept will be used for testing **KoBRA** . A pilot system will be built for one chosen process maintaining a distinction between process-specific and process-independent (but still domain-specific) knowledge. The process-specific knowledge will then be removed from the pilot system leaving the knowledge that will form the basis of the platform. The platform will then be used to build a subsequent pilot system for another process.

References

1. Center for Chemical Process Safety 1989. *Guidelines for Chemical Process Quantitative Risk Analysis*. New York, N.Y.: American Institute of Chemical Engineers.

2. Apostolakis, G.E. ed. 1990. The Role and Use of Personal Computers in Probabilistic Safety Assessment and Decision Making. *Reliability Engineering & System Safety 30*. Elsevier Applied Science.

3. Poucet, A. 1992. Knowledge Based Systems for Risk Assessment and Monitoring. In Computer Applications in Ergonomics, Occupational Safety and Health, 29-36. Elsevier Science Publishers B.V.

4. Barett, R.; Ramsay, A.; and Sloman, A. 1986. *Pop11: A Practical Language for Artificial Intelligence*. Chichester, England: Ellis Horwood Limited.

Student Abstracts

Efficient Planning by Graph Rewriting

José Luis Ambite and **Craig A. Knoblock**
Information Sciences Institute and Department of Computer Science
University of Southern California
4676 Admiralty Way, Marina del Rey, CA 90292
{ambite, knoblock}@isi.edu

Planning involves the generation of a network of actions that achieves a desired goal given an initial state of the world. There has been significant progress in the analysis of planning algorithms, particularly in partial-order and in hierarchical task network (HTN) planning (Kambhampati 95; Erol et al. 94). In this abstract we propose a more general framework in which planning is seen as a graph rewriting process. This approach subsumes previous work and offers new opportunities for efficient planning.

As motivation, we will look at two domains: query processing in a distributed environment and manufacturing operation planning. Distributed query processing involves generating an efficient plan to satisfy a user query. This plan is composed of data retrieval actions at diverse information sources and operations on this data (such as join, selection, etc). Some systems use a general-purpose planner to solve this problem (Knoblock 95). We have observed that, in this domain, it is relatively easy to construct an initial plan, and then transform it using a hill-climbing search to reduce its cost. The plan transformations exploit the commutative and associative properties of the (relational algebra) operators, and the fact that when a group of operators can be executed together at a remote information source it is generally more efficient to do so. Some sample rules are: join-swap, $get(q1, db1) \bowtie (get(q2, db2) \bowtie get(q3, db3)) \Leftrightarrow get(q2, db2) \bowtie (get(q1, db1) \bowtie get(q3, db3))$; and remote-eval, $get(R, db) \bowtie get(S, db) \Leftrightarrow get(R \bowtie S, db)$. In centralized databases, some domain-specific planners exploited a similar idea (Graefe and DeWitt 87).

In manufacturing, the problem is to find an economical plan of machining operations that implement the desired features of a design. In a feature-based approach (Nau et al. 95), it is possible to enumerate the possible actions involved in building a piece by analyzing its CAD model. It is more difficult to find an ordering of the operations and the setups that optimize the machining cost. However, similar to query planning, it is possible to incrementally transform a (possibly inefficient) initial plan. Often, the order of actions does not affect the design goal, only the quality of the plan, thus actions can commute. Also, it is important to minimize the number of setups because fixing a piece on the machine is rather time consuming. Such grouping of machining operations on a setup is analogous to evaluating a subquery at a remote information source.

A (partial) plan is a labelled graph whose nodes are actions and whose edges express constraints (ordering, causal links, etc). In planning by graph rewriting we allow the substitution of an arbitrary partial plan by another partial plan. This subsumes the main transformations present in partial-order planners (adding a new node or linking to a previous one for goal establishment, adding ordering edges for threat resolution), and in HTN planners (substituting a non-primitive action by a partial plan). We have seen several planning domains that benefit from expressive plan transformations (as the query evaluation rules above). We expect that hill-climbing from a (possibly suboptimal but easily constructed) initial plan using such transformations will be efficient for many domains, similarly to (Minton et al. 92). Moreover, this more expressive planning language should give users more control over the kind of solutions they prefer (Kambhampati 95).

References

S. Kambhampati. 1995. A Comparative Analysis of Partial-Order Planning and Task Reduction Planning. SIGART 6(1).

K. Erol, D. Nau, and J. Hendler. 1994. UMCP: A Sound and Complete Planning Procedure for Hierarchical Task-Network Planning. AIPS'94.

C. A. Knoblock. 1995. Planning, Executing, Sensing, and Replanning for Information Gathering. IJCAI'95.

G. Graefe and D. J. DeWitt. 1987. The EXODUS Optimizer Generator. SIGMOD'87.

D. S. Nau, S. K. Gupta, and W. C. Regli. 1995. AI Planning versus Manufacturing-Operation Planning: A Case Study. IJCAI'95.

S. Minton, M. D. Johnston, A. B. Philips & P. Laird. 1992. Minimizing Conflicts: A Heuristic Repair Method for Constraint-Satisfaction and Scheduling Problems. Artificial Intelligence, 58(1–3).

Expecting the Unexpected: Detecting and Reacting to Unplanned-for World States

Ella M. Atkins **Edmund H. Durfee** **Kang G. Shin**

University of Michigan
AI Lab, EECS Department, 1101 Beal Ave.
Ann Arbor, MI 48109
{marbles, durfee, kgshin}@umich.edu

Developing autonomous systems is challenging because complete and correct models do not exist for complex domains such as aircraft flight. Realistic systems bound the state set expanded during planning and compensate for unexpected situations with reactive mechanisms. This abstract describes a method by which a system can determine if it is unprepared for the current world state and a means to successfully respond to such an unhandled state.

We first identify subclasses of unhandled states, then investigate how system performance improves when detecting them. The Cooperative Intelligent Real-time Control Architecture (CIRCA) (Musliner, Durfee, & Shin 1995) combines a planner, scheduler, and real-time plan executor to provide guaranteed performance for controlling complex systems. Domain knowledge includes action (ac) and temporal transitions (tt) that model how the world state changes over time. We have implemented and tested algorithms to detect and respond to unhandled states in CIRCA.

Figure 1 shows the relationship between subclasses of possible world states. Modeled states have distinguishing features/values represented in the planner knowledge base; we have not considered methods (e.g., discovery) to handle unmodeled states. The planned-for set are states from which failure is avoided. Handled states are on a path to a goal, while deadend are not. The planner can model other states, including those that are reachable but "removed" due to resource limitations, and "imminent-failure" that are not considered reachable but, if reached, are modeled as leading to failure. As shown in Figure 1, states actually reached may include any subclass.

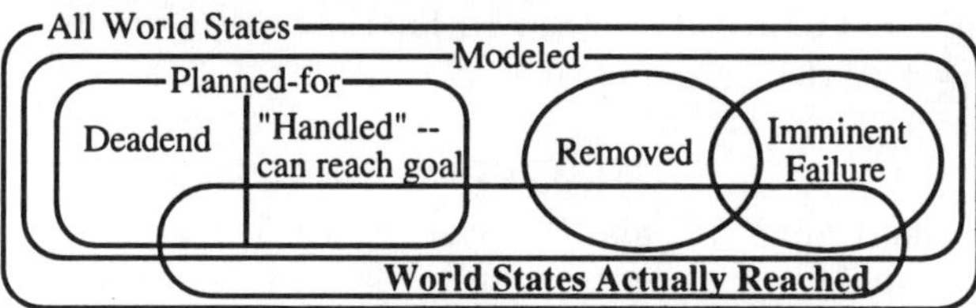

Figure 1. World State Classification.

Because they are either more probable or more critical, we have targeted deadend (D), removed (R), and imminent-failure (IF) states for detection. Figure 2a shows a deadend state. The planner expands states until finding a goal path, but state D remains either because no action can reach the goal (G) or because the planner minimized resources by not selecting such actions. After completing a plan, CIRCA builds a deadend state list then uses ID3 (Quinlan 1986), with deadend states as positive examples and all other reachable states as negative examples, to build a minimal test condition set for detecting deadend states.

CIRCA's planner backtracks when a proposed plan cannot be scheduled for guaranteed real-time execution. We have modified CIRCA's planner to remove improbable states after backtracking, but detect such states using ID3 as described above. Figure 2b illustrates this concept -- a low probability tt leads from state I to a state (R) removed after backtracking. Without R, downstream actions to avoid failure (F) are not required so scheduling becomes easier. The shaded region encloses the removed state set.

Figure 2c shows an imminent-failure state (IF). The planner considers IF unreachable because no modeled transition set connects I to IF, thus it plans no action to avoid F. However, if IF is reached, the system will fail unless it reacts. We modified CIRCA to list all unreachable states that lead via a single temporal transition to failure (ttf), then use ID3 to build tests for detecting these IF states.

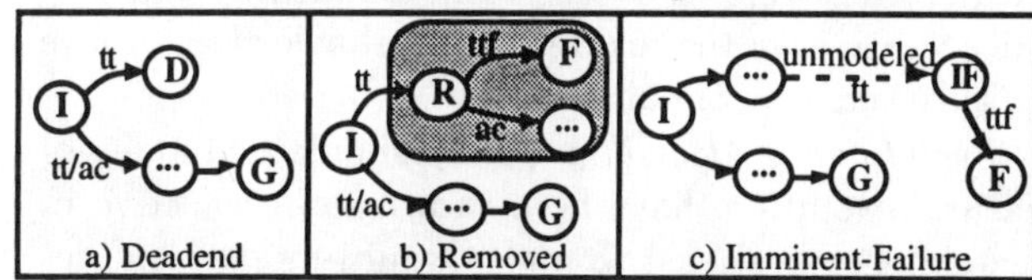

Figure 2. Unhandled State Illustrations.

Upon detecting an unhandled state (D, R, or IF), CIRCA reacts by replanning based on the current state. We have performed tests using an aircraft simulator. After CIRCA successfully flew normal "flight around an airport pattern", we modeled an unhandled "gear fails on final approach to landing" emergency. By differing CIRCA's aircraft gear model, we produced each type of unhandled state. CIRCA was able to detect and respond (e.g., execute "go-around" and "gear-down" action) to each D, R, or IF state, whereas without detecting that unhandled state it would consistently fail (i.e., plane would crash). We continue tests with more complex flight examples, and are studying associated research issues such as imposing time bounds on CIRCA's planner to guarantee timely responses to unhandled states.

Acknowledgment: Supported by NSF Grant IRI-9209031.

References

Musliner, D. J.; Durfee, E. H.; and Shin, K.G. 1995. World Modeling for the Dynamic Construction of Real-Time Control Plans. *Artificial Intelligence* 74:83-127.

Quinlan, J. R. 1986. Induction of Decision Trees. *Machine Learning* 1:81-106.

Experiments in Evolutionary Synthesis of Robotic Neurocontrollers

Karthik Balakrishnan and Vasant Honavar
Artificial Intelligence Research Group
Department of Computer Science
Iowa State University, Ames, IA - 50011.
balakris@cs.iastate.edu, honavar@cs.iastate.edu

Artificial neural networks offer an attractive paradigm for the design of behavior and control systems in robots and autonomous agents for a variety of reasons, including: ability to adapt and learn, potential for resistance to noise, faults and component failures, potential for real-time performance in dynamic environments (through massive parallelism and suitable hardware realization) etc.

However, designing a good neurocontroller for a given robotic application is an instance of a difficult multi-criterion optimization problem, requiring complicated trade-offs among different, often competing measures of the network, like performance, cost, complexity etc., which is further compounded by competing objectives in the realization of behavior (e.g., move quickly versus avoid obstacles).

Evolutionary Algorithms (EAs), simulated models of natural evolution, have been shown to be effective in searching several vast, complex, multi-modal, and deceptive search spaces. They are therefore viable candidates to employ in the design of neurocontrollers (Balakrishnan & Honavar 1995).

Although this synergy of approaches is not new (see (Balakrishnan & Honavar 1995) for a bibliography), this field still offers many exciting avenues of research. Our recent work has been based on a simulation task that requires a robot to clear an arena by pushing boxes to the enclosing walls. The number of boxes that the robot pushes to the walls, within an allocated time, is taken to be a measure of its fitness. We use *Genetic Algorithms* (GAs) to evolve high-fitness neurocontrollers for this robot.

Our simulation results indicate that *recurrent* networks achieve much higher fitnesses on this task compared to their *feedforward* counterparts. By analysing the evolved networks we have been able to determine that a large, negative, *self-loop* at the output unit that decides the action (move forward or turn), is what gives these networks such an advantage. This recurrent link biases the robot to frequently switch actions (interleave moves and turns), thereby guarding it from getting into permanently stuck states (e.g., fruitlessly trying to move into the wall), which is a real possibility in this environment (where there is no feedback and the robot does not bounce off walls). With networks that are *initially feedforward* (but capable of evolving recurrent links through mutation), evolution produces high fitness neurocontrollers with 30% (and sometimes even 70%) fewer recurrent links compared to networks fully recurrent from the start (Balakrishnan & Honavar 1996). This suggests a potentially useful approach to the design of networks with near-minimal recurrence.

Through our experiments on *sensor evolution*, we have shown the utility of designing the sensory systems of robots in addition to the usual practice of designing just the neurocontroller. Since real world domains are often noisy and faulty, we are also exploring the evolution of noise and fault-tolerant neurocontrollers. Preliminary results look extremely promising.

Our ongoing research aims to examine the intricate interplay between the environment and the evolutionary processes in determining the structure and function of the resulting neurocontrollers. Our results are suggestive of the possibility that as the contraints are changed, evolution can potentially discover behaviors that are tailored for success within the constraints imposed by the environment.

References

Balakrishnan, K., and Honavar, V. 1995. Evolutionary design of neural architectures — a preliminary taxonomy and guide to literature. Technical Report CS TR 95-01, Department of Computer Science, Iowa State University, Ames, IA - 50011.

Balakrishnan, K., and Honavar, V. 1996. Analysis of neurocontrollers designed by simulated evolution. In *Proceedings of IEEE International Conference on Neural Networks ICNN'96*. To appear.

A Reinforcement Learning Framework for Combinatorial Optimization

Justin A. Boyan
Computer Science Department
Carnegie Mellon University
Pittsburgh, PA 15213
email: jab@cs.cmu.edu

The combination of reinforcement learning methods with neural networks has found success on a growing number of large-scale applications, including backgammon move selection (Tesauro 1992), elevator control (Crites & Barto 1996), and job-shop scheduling (Zhang & Dietterich 1995). In this work, we modify and generalize the scheduling paradigm used by Zhang and Dietterich to produce a general reinforcement-learning-based framework for combinatorial optimization.

The problem of combinatorial optimization is simply stated: given a finite state space X and an *objective function* $f : X \rightarrow \Re$, find an optimal state $x^* = \text{argmax}_{x \in X} f(x)$. Typically, X is huge, and finding an optimal x^* is intractable. However, there are many effective heuristic algorithms that attempt to exploit f's structure to locate good optima. One important class of such algorithms is based on hillclimbing (HC). HC makes use of a neighborhood structure on X. In its simplest form, HC works by starting at a random state $x = x_0$, then repeatedly considering transitions from x to a random neighbor x'. When $f(x') \geq f(x)$, the transition is accepted, and x is set to x'. HC terminates upon reaching a local maximum.

HC corresponds exactly to following a greedy trajectory through a generalized Markov Decision Process (MDP). This MDP may be defined as follows: state space = X; uniform stochastic transitions defined by the neighborhood structure; action space = {Accept, Reject}; and Reward$(x \rightarrow x') = f(x') - f(x)$. In this context, simulated annealing and other popular approaches to improving HC can be seen as poor approximations to the correct, principled approach: solving the MDP by learning its *optimal value function* V^*. V^* maps each state x to the discounted return expected when optimal Accept/Reject decisions are made: $V^*(x) = \max \mathrm{E}\left[\sum_{t=0}^{\infty} \gamma^t \mathrm{Reward}(x_t \rightarrow x_{t+1}) | x_0 = x\right]$ (We set γ slightly less than 1.) Once learned, V^* can be used in hillclimbing or simulated annealing as a plug-in replacement for the objective function $f(x)$. Unlike $f(x)$, however, V^* "sees past" local optima: greedy actions taken with respect to V^* maximize $f(x)$ *globally*.

The value function V^* gives a principled way to choose actions in an optimization domain. Our belief is that in practical large-scale domains, V^* will have significant underlying structure, allowing a useful approximation to be learned. There are several reasons for optimism:

- All relevant features of state x can be given as input to the function approximator. (By contrast, standard hillclimbing and simulated-annealing techniques cannot incorporate structural information about the state space.)
- During learning, extrapolation by the function approximator can be used to help guide exploration of the space, focusing successive searches on regions identified as promising during previous runs.
- Even a poor approximation to V^* may aid optimization. In this framework, $V^*_{\text{approx}} \equiv 0$ produces regular hillclimbing; any deviation from 0 which correlates with long-term reward should improve optimization performance.

We are using two algorithms to approximate V^*: Tesauro's variant of TD(λ) for control (Tesauro 1992), and an original algorithm called ROUT (Boyan & Moore 1996). We are also exploring several alternative MDP formulations to the one sketched above. Our poster will contrast our frameworks with that of Zhang and Dietterich; discuss the types of problem that this approach should benefit; and present results on several large-scale optimization problems, including VLSI channel routing and an information retrieval task.

Acknowledgments: Thanks to Andrew Moore, Michael Littman, Wei Zhang and the anonymous reviewers.

References

Boyan, J. A., and Moore, A. W. 1996. Learning evaluation functions for large acyclic domains. In Saitta, L., ed., *ICML-13*. Morgan Kaufmann.

Crites, R., and Barto, A. 1996. Improving elevator performance using reinforcement learning. In Touretzky, D.; Mozer, M.; and Hasselno, M., eds., *NIPS-8*.

Tesauro, G. 1992. Practical issues in temporal difference learning. *Machine Learning* 8(3/4).

Zhang, W., and Dietterich, T. G. 1995. A reinforcement learning approach to job-shop scheduling. In *IJCAI-95*.

Learning Topological Maps: An alternative Approach

Arno Bücken

University of Bonn
Römerstr. 164, 53117 Bonn
buecken@informatik.uni-bonn.de

Sebastian Thrun

University of Bonn
Römerstr. 164, 53117 Bonn
thrun@informatik.uni-bonn.de

Abstract

Our goal is autonomous real-time control of a mobile robot. In this paper we want to show a possibility to learn topological maps of a large-scale indoor environment autonomously. In the literature there are two paradigms how to store information on the environment of a robot: as a grid-based (geometric) or as a topological map. While grid-based maps are considerably easy to learn and maintain, topological maps are quite compact and facilitate fast motion-planning.

We integrated both kinds of maps to gain the best of both worlds. This paper describes an approach to convert grid-based maps into topological maps. It differs from previous approaches because it integrates grid-based maps. Therefore it is automatically consistent, not dependent on disambiguous landmarks and all geometric information is available. It scales better to large-scale environments. Previous approaches constructed topological maps from the scratch.

This algorithm builds on our software for building grid-based maps. For every point in these maps the probability is given wether it is occupied or not.
The algorithm could be divided into the following parts:

- Tresholding: Divides the map into "free" and "occupied" space
- Voronoi: Generates the Voronoi-diagram [Lat1] V of the grid-based map (fig. (a) black line). Let the nearest occupied point be called basis-point and the line(s) between the basis-points of $v \in V$ basis-line(s).
- Critical points: A point $v \in V$ is a critical point, if its clearance [Lat1] is a local, linear-oriented minimum. In other words: v is a critical point, if (a) it is part of the voronoi diagram and (b) on the perpendicular to its basis-line is no point v' with smaller clearance within an ε-surrounding. Each basis line of a critical point is called critical line. (fig. (b))
- Region-segmentation: The entirety of the critical lines divides the map into regions. (fig. (c)) These regions can be connected by a graph (from center to center), which is a topological map for the given grid-based map.

- Optionally pruning is possible: Let each region, that has a maximum of two neighbor-regions, be pruned with each neighbor-region, that has a maximum of two neighbor-regions, too. The result is a map that is close to human communication because the regions come nearly rooms or part of rooms (entry part of room x) (fig. (d)). It is possible to label the regions by room-names.

Results: The algorithm is integrated into the current RHINO software, that is already capable of building grid-based maps. It works in nearly real-time (<10 sec.) and accelerates motion-planning by 10^3 to 10^6. Tests have shown that the detour caused by topological map based planning is only about two percent (detour if it is possible to reach the destination-point faster than first driving to nearest point of the destination-region), but this is equalized by the smaller time for calculating the motion-path.
Another advantage of this representation of the environment is the possibility to count narrow passages easily (critical lines). These narrow passages are most likely to be blocked by obstacles. So an "optimal" path should be as short as possible and includes as little as possible critical lines or should cross as little as possible regions.

References:

[Lat1] J. C. Latombe: Robot Motion Planning, Kluwer

Computing Default Logic Extensions: An Implementation

A.P. Courtney and **N.Y. Foo**

Basser Department of Computer Science
University of Sydney, NSW 2006, Australia
allenc | norman@cs.usyd.edu.au

G. Antoniou

Computing & Information Technology
Griffith University, QLD 4111, Australia
ga@cit.gu.edu.au

Default logic [3] is a useful formalism for reasoning with incomplete information, its intuitive characteristics making it particularly suited for applications. *Exten* is a system currently capable of computing first-order Reiter, Justified and Constrained default extensions. It is part of a project to create a full default logic workbench, with future work involving query evaluation, further support for default variants and integration with belief revision. As such, it has been implemented in an object-oriented manner, and is designed to facilitate experimentation. The interface is based around a small language, giving the user flexibility in editing default theories and changing various parameters (such as compute next n extensions or carry out 'success' checks every m steps).

Default reasoning is known to be computationally hard. One efficiency increasing technique used in *Exten* is stratification [1] which, if applicable, allows the computation of extensions in a modular way. *Exten* uses a forward-chaining approach and applies additional pruning techniques, some of which are outlined below.

```
PROCEDURE Compute-Ext( Π, Drest, Dout)
NotClosed := false;
M := { δ ∈ Drest | pre(δ) ∈ In(Π) } = { δ_1,...,δ_n };
FOR i := 1 TO n DO
   Drest := Drest - { δ_i };
   IF ∀ψ ∈ just(δ_i) are consistent with In(Π) THEN
      Compute-Ext(Π ∘ δ_i, Drest, Dout);
      NotClosed := true;
   Dout := Dout ∪ { δ_i };
IF NotClosed = false THEN
   IF ∀δ ∈ Dout are blocked by In(Π) THEN
      ext := ext ∪ { In(Π) };
```

(failure checking not shown, $In(\Pi)$ refers to the knowledge state where Π is the current default chain)

When a default δ_i has its prerequisite met at a node in the process tree (the map of default application chains used), all extensions containing δ_i can be found underneath this node. Thus δ_i can be safely removed from the set of available defaults *Drest*, resulting in smaller subtrees for remaining extensions and effective use of common tree branches. The justifications of defaults in *Dout* are checked when testing for closure of a process - if all are blocked we can conclude that a *new* extension has been found. This means that *Compute-Ext* will not produce multiple copies of the same extension.

Theorem 1. *Let $\pi = \pi_1 \circ \pi_2$ be a successful path of the process tree, closed under the defaults currently available (Drest). Further suppose that no default was added to Dout during the construction of π_2. Then no new extensions can be found by expanding the process tree under π_1.*

In many cases this will substantially reduce the search tree size. The method has a *local* effect to the search tree, ie. beneath π_1. In contrast, a more general method with a *global* effect is as follows.

Theorem 2. *Let π be a maximally successful path of the process tree $T = (W,D)$. Let M be the set of defaults in D (including those in Dout) that are blocked or failed along this path. Then every new extension computed after π must contain at least one default from M. M is called a goal.*

Instead of trying every available default at a given node, theorem 2 shows us that if a goal is applicable we only need to expand those subtrees starting with defaults in M. Different goals may be used at nodes along a path, with *Exten* using a heuristic prefering shorter goals.

A final comment is that all pruning methods described are general purpose in the sense that they apply to arbitrary default theories. We have already found they integrate well with stratification, and it seems plausible that other techniques could be added to offer further reductions in specific cases (*Exten already incorporates some optimizations for theories with normal defaults*). Proofs for the given theorems and algorithm can be found in [2].

References

[1] Cholewinski, P. Stratified Default Theories. *Proc. Computer Science Logic 1994*, Springer LNCS 993

[2] Courtney, A.P. Towards a Default Logic Workbench: Computing Extensions. Hons Thesis, Basser Dep. of Computer Science, University of Sydney, 1995.

[3] Reiter, R. A Logic for Default Reasoning. *Artificial Intelligence* 13(1980): 81-132

Characterizing temporal repetition[o]

Diana Cukierman and James Delgrande
School of Computing Science
Simon Fraser University
Burnaby, BC, Canada V5A 1S6
{diana,jim}@cs.sfu.ca

We are investigating the representation and reasoning about schedulable, repeated activities, specified using calendars. Examples of such activities include meeting every Tuesday and Thursday during a semester and attending a seminar every first day of a month. This research provides for a valuable framework for scheduling systems, financial systems and, in general, date-based systems. Very recently work has been done related to reasoning about repetition in the Artificial Intelligence community and others. A partial reference list is provided here (Cukierman & Delgrande 1995; Leban, McDonald, & Forster 1986). However, to our knowledge no extensive taxonomy of repetition has been proposed in the literature. We believe that reasoning about repeated activities calls for a study and precise definition of the topological characteristics in a repetitive series. In this abstract we summarize a proposal to classify types of repetition according to parameters. The combination of all possible values of these parameters provides a complete taxonomy of repetitive classes with respect to the proposed parameters. Several notions of repetition are considered, some are extremely general, some are very specific.

Time intervals and time points during which a repeated event, activity or property of interest occur are referred to as *temporal objects*. *Gaps* are also conceived as temporal objects, representing the separation between successive repeats in a *series*. A *temporal series* $\mathcal{T}$ of $n \in N$ *repeats* is a sequence of $2n$ elements: $\mathcal{T} =< r_1, g_1, r_2, g_2, \ldots, r_n, g_n >$, where r_i and g_i are temporal objects, the ith *repeat* and the ith *gap* respectively; $i \in N, 1 \leq i \leq n$. The *interval of reference* is the interval that starts when the first repeat starts and finishes when the nth gap finishes. Durations are expressed with *time units*. See (Cukierman & Delgrande 1995) for a formal definition of time units, examples of time units include *year*, *week*, etc. An *interval series* is a temporal series whose repeats are intervals. The beginning point of a subsequent repeat can be equal or after the beginning point of the previous one. Therefore two contiguous intervals relate with the relations in the set {before, meets, overlaps, finished-by, contains, starts, started-by, equals} or a disjunction of the previous. These relations are part of the basic 13 interval relations (Allen 1983). Series are organized in a taxonomy according to possible combinations of "values" each parameter or classification axis takes. We distinguish five parameters: *Interval series qualitative structure*, *Duration of repeats pattern*, *Distance between repeats pattern*, *Frequency of repeats per period of time*, and additionally, we distinguish repetitions which stem from the *application domain* and not the temporal domain and we analyze how the *reference frame* can be specified. For example, the *duration of repeats* pattern can be *constant durations* as in "series of experiments of 10 min each". Another possible value is *(time unit) based constant durations*, where the constancy is apparent because of the time unit. Other values that we consider are *bounded durations*, *probabilistic durations*, *cyclical equal durations*, *cyclical functionally related durations*, *known a-priori durations* and *unspecified repetition pattern of durations*.

The combination of all the possible values of the parameters defined generates a taxonomy of repetitive series. Arguably not all the values generate a realistic repetition pattern, and several combinations may result in the same class. The analysis of all possible combinations of the parameter values is under study. We believe this characterization already provides for a simple and complete classification or scheme of classification of repetitive series.

References

Allen, J. F. 1983. Maintaining knowledge about temporal intervals. *Communications of the ACM* 26(11):832–843.

Cukierman, D., and Delgrande, J. 1996. Expressing time intervals and repetition within a formalization of calendars. Accepted in the Computational Intelligence journal subject to revisions.

Leban, B.; McDonald, D. D.; and Forster, D. R. 1986. A representation for collections of temporal intervals. In *Proc. of the AAAI-86*, 367–371.

[o]This is an extended abstract of our paper in the TIME'96 workshop.

Achieving Agent Coordination via Distributed Preferences

Joseph G. D'Ambrosio & William P. Birmingham

The University of Michigan
Artificial Intelligence Lab, EECS Department,
Ann Arbor, MI 48109
jdambros@eecs.umich.edu

Agent-based systems provide hope for solving a wide variety of distributed problems. One key aspect of agent-based system is coordinating agent actions to achieve coherent behavior. For example, in concurrent engineering (CE), it is necessary to ensure that the individual decision made by constituents in a design organization achieve overall organizational objectives (e.g., increase market share), while still allowing individuals to exploit their expertise. We believe CE is representative of many multi-agent problems, in that agent coordination must include facilities to support both solving a hierarchically decomposed problem, e.g., the contract net (Davis & Smith 1983), and interactions among peers (Bahler et al. 1995) as well.

One method to support problem decomposition is through task subcontracting (Davis & Smith, 1983). The process of subcontracting creates a hierarchical, decision-making organization. Coordination is accomplished by allowing general contractors, who have a global perspective, to provide direction to subcontractors, who have local expertise.

We believe that it is both practical and desirable to direct a subcontractor's actions by explicitly stating a preference structure that the agent must follow. Just as any contract describes a set of constraints that must be met for the contract to be fulfilled, a contract should include a preference structure that must be followed by a subcontractor in order to fulfill its obligations. Specifying a preference structure for a subcontractor does not require the general contractor to reveal all of its preferential knowledge to the subcontractor, only the subset of preferences that rank the implementation domain of the contracted subtask need be specified.

We are developing a concurrent-engineering tool, ACME (D'Ambrosio, Darr, & Birmingham 1996), which provides a framework for coordinating design agents based on contracting constraints and preferences among agents. Agent preferences are formally represented using a form of a utility function referred to as an imprecise multi-attribute value function. This function has the desirable property that the amount of work required to construct the function is significantly less than that normally associated with defining a multi-attribute utility function.

Consider the following example related to the design of a powertrain control system for an automobile. The project leader establishes contracts with several agents, including an electrical-system agent, and a software-development agent. The project leader's preferences are represented by a value function based on the component costs of the powertrain controller and the expected fuel economy. In general, these preferences provide only a partial order on a subordinate's decisions, and the subordinate is free to exploit its own expertise (preferences) in choosing among alternatives for which the supervisor is indifferent to.

In this example, the electrical system agent is responsible for selecting the necessary electrical components. This agent is primarily concerned with minimizing component costs, and the agent specifies an appropriate value function to represents its preferences. Since the contract between the project leader and the electrical agent includes the project leader's preferences, the electrical agent's decision making is not based on its value function alone, but on a lexicographic value function, where the first and most significant attribute is the value assigned by the supervisor's value function. Given that the supervisor's value function is based on fuel economy as well as cost, the electrical agent decisions will be made in a manner consistent with global preferences, as will all of the decisions made by the other agents in the design team.

The second attribute in the electrical agent's lexicographic value function is the value assigned by a group value function, that contains an attribute for the value assigned by each member of the design team, e.g., the electrical agent and the software agent. The group value function creates the necessary relationship among peers to ensure that the value of composite decisions is maximized in terms of the peer's stated preferences.

References

Bahler, D., et al. 1995. Mixed quantitative/qualitative method for evaluating compromise solutions to conflicts in collaborative design, *Artificial Intelligence for Engineering Design, Analysis and Manufacturing* 9:325-336.

D'Ambrosio, J.; Darr, T.; and Birmingham, W. 1996. Hierarchical Concurrent Engineering in a Multiagent Framework, *Concurrent Engineering: Research and Applications*, Forthcoming.

Davis, D., and Smith, R. 1983. Negotiation as a Metaphor for Distributed Problem Solving, *Artificial Intelligence* 20: 63-109.

Fast Discovery of Simple Rules

Pedro Domingos*
Department of Information and Computer Science
University of California, Irvine
Irvine, California 92717, U.S.A.
pedrod@ics.uci.edu
http://www.ics.uci.edu/~pedrod

The recent emergence of data mining as a major application of machine learning has led to increased interest in fast rule induction algorithms. These are able to efficiently process large numbers of examples, under the constraint of still achieving good accuracy. If e is the number of examples, many rule learners have $\Theta(e^4)$ asymptotic time complexity in noisy domains, and C4.5RULES has been empirically observed to sometimes require $\Theta(e^3)$ time. Recent advances have brought this bound down to $\Theta(e \log^2 e)$, while maintaining accuracy at the level of C4.5RULES's (Cohen 1995). Ideally, we would like to have an algorithm capable of inducing accurate rules in time linear in e, without becoming too expensive in other factors. This extended abstract presents such an algorithm.

Most rule induction algorithms employ a "separate and conquer" method, inducing each rule to its full length before going on to the next one. They also evaluate each rule by itself, without regard to the effect of other rules. This is a potentially inefficient approach: rules may be grown further than they need to be, only to be pruned back afterwards, when the whole rule set has already been induced. An alternative is to interleave the construction of all rules, evaluating each rule in the context of the current rule set. This can be termed a "conquering without separating" approach, by contrast with the earlier method, and has been implemented in the CWS algorithm.

CWS is outlined in pseudo-code in Table 1. All examples are initially assigned to the majority class. Each rule in CWS is associated with a vector of class probabilities computed from the examples it covers, and predicts the most probable class. Conflicts are resolved by summing the probabilities for all rules covering the test instance, and choosing the class with the highest sum. `Acc(RS)` is the accuracy of the rule set `RS` on the training set. This procedure would not be efficient if implemented directly, but, by avoiding the extensive redundancy present in the repeated computation of accuracies and class probabilities, the worst-case time complexity of CWS can be made linear in e and all other relevant parameters.

CWS has been extensively evaluated using benchmark problems, a large artificial dataset, and a detailed study on a large database related to process control on NASA's space shuttle. These studies show that, as expected, CWS's running time grows much more slowly with the number of examples than C4.5RULES's. CWS's rate of growth is linear in the artificial dataset (a noisy Boolean function), and $e \log e$ in the shuttle domain with 20% class noise, with the logarithmic factor due to processing of numeric attributes. C4.5RULES's time is approximately $e^2 \log e$ in the artificial database, and e^3 in the shuttle problem. CWS takes 11 hours on the full shuttle database, while C4.5RULES takes over two weeks. CWS is more accurate than C4.5RULES on the shuttle and artificial problems, and there is no significant difference on most benchmark datasets. CWS almost always produces simpler output than C4.5RULES, and hence, in principle, more easily understood results. This is an important consideration in many data mining problems, including the shuttle control one studied. In summary, this study indicates that CWS can be used to advantage when the underlying concept is simple and the data is plentiful but noisy.

Table 1: The CWS algorithm.

```
Let RS = EmptySet.
Repeat
   Add one active rule with empty body to RS.
   For each active rule R in RS,
      For each possible antecedent AV,
         Let R' = R with AV conjoined.
         Compute class probabilities for R'.
         Let RS' = RS with R replaced by R'.
         If Acc(RS') > Acc(RS)
            then replace RS by RS'.
      If RS' is still RS then deactivate R.
Until all rules are inactive.
Return RS.
```

References

Cohen, W. W. 1995. Fast Effective Rule Induction. In *Proceedings of the Twelfth International Conference on Machine Learning*, 115–123. Tahoe City, Calif.: Morgan Kaufmann.

*Partly supported by a PRAXIS XXI scholarship.

Multistrategy Learning: A Case Study

Pedro Domingos*
Department of Information and Computer Science
University of California, Irvine
Irvine, California 92717, U.S.A.
pedrod@ics.uci.edu
http://www.ics.uci.edu/~pedrod

Two of the most popular approaches to induction are instance-based learning (IBL) and rule generation. Their strengths and weaknesses are largely complementary. IBL methods are able to identify small details in the instance space, but have trouble with attributes that are relevant in some parts of the space but not others. Conversely, rule induction methods may overlook small exception regions, but are able to select different attributes in different parts of the instance space. The two methods have been unified in the RISE algorithm (Domingos 1995). RISE views instances as maximally specific rules, forms more general rules by gradually clustering instances of the same class, and classifies a test example by letting the nearest rule win. This approach potentially combines the advantages of rule induction and IBL, and has indeed been observed to be more accurate than each on a large number of benchmark datasets. However, it is important to determine if this performance is indeed due to the hypothesized advantages, and to define the situations in which RISE's bias will and will not be preferable to those of the individual approaches. This abstract reports experiments to this end in artificial domains.

Compared to rule induction algorithms, RISE should have an advantage when the concept to learn is best described by fairly specific rules, and vice-versa. If concepts are defined by Boolean DNF formulas, their degree of specificity can be measured by L, the average length of the disjuncts. Twenty artificial datasets were randomly generated for each value of L from 1 to 32. C4.5RULES was chosen for comparison. The average accuracies obtained are shown in Figure 1. They indicate that RISE's bias is indeed more appropriate when concepts are fairly to very specific, with the advantage increasing with specificity.[1] More general concepts were learned to a similar degree by both systems. We were unable to determine conditions where C4.5RULES's bias would be preferable to RISE's; corrupting the data with 10% and 20% class noise resulted in similar degradation for the two systems. Another surprising observation is that C4.5RULES's accuracy has an upward trend for length $\geq$ 14. This is due to

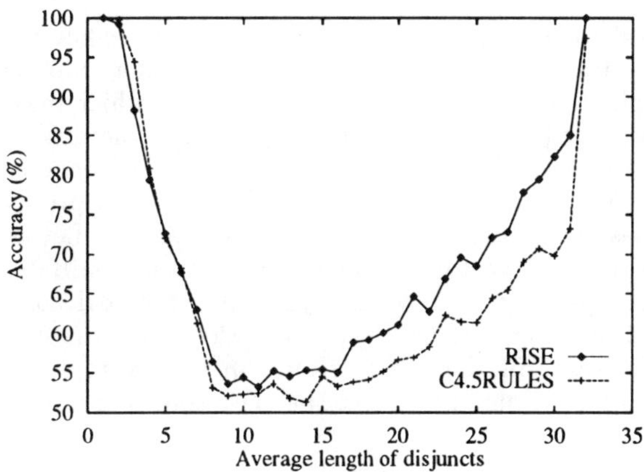

Figure 1: Accuracy as a function of concept specificity.

the fact that, as the concepts become very specific, it becomes easier to induce short rules for their negation, and C4.5RULES finds these.

Compared to IBL algorithms, RISE should have an advantage when some features are relevant in some parts of the instance space, but not in others. A natural measure of the extent to which this happens is D, the average number of different features for all pairs of disjuncts in the target concept description. Twenty mixed Boolean and numeric domains were generated at random for a succession of values of D, and the accuracy of RISE's feature selection method was compared with that of two methods commonly used in IBL, forward and backward selection. RISE's approach performed best throughout, with the advantage increasing with D. However, in separate studies it was observed to be at a disadvantage when each feature is either globally relevant or globally irrelevant, and the dataset is small and noisy.

Lesion studies were also conducted, showing that each of RISE's components is essential to its performance.

References

Domingos, P. 1995. Rule Induction and Instance-Based Learning: A Unified Approach. In *Proceedings of the Fourteenth International Joint Conference on Artificial Intelligence*, 1226–1232. Montréal: Morgan Kaufmann.

*Partly supported by a PRAXIS XXI scholarship.

[1] All accuracy differences for length $\geq$ 12 are significant at the 5% level.

Simple Bayesian Classifiers Do Not Assume Independence

Pedro Domingos* **Michael Pazzani**

Department of Information and Computer Science
University of California, Irvine
Irvine, California 92717, U.S.A.
{pedrod, pazzani}@ics.uci.edu
http://www.ics.uci.edu/~pedrod

Bayes' theorem tells us how to optimally predict the class of a previously unseen example, given a training sample. The chosen class should be the one which maximizes $P(C_i|E) = P(C_i)\,P(E|C_i)\,/\,P(E)$, where C_i is the ith class, E is the test example, $P(Y|X)$ denotes the conditional probability of Y given X, and probabilities are estimated from the training sample. Let an example be a vector of a attributes. If the attributes are *independent* given the class, $P(E|C_i)$ can be decomposed into the product $P(v_1|C_i)\ldots P(v_a|C_i)$, where v_j is the value of the jth attribute in the example E. Therefore we should predict the class that maximizes:

$$P(C_i|E) = \frac{P(C_i)}{P(E)} \prod_{j=1}^{a} P(v_j|C_i) \qquad (1)$$

This procedure is often called the *naive Bayesian classifier*. Here we will prefer the term *simple*, and abbreviate to *SBC*. The SBC is commonly thought to be optimal, in the sense of achieving the best possible accuracy, only when the "independence assumption" above holds, and perhaps close to optimal when the attributes are only slightly dependent. However, this very restrictive condition seems to be contradicted by the SBC's surprisingly good performance in a wide variety of domains, including many where there are clear dependencies between the attributes. In a study on 28 datasets from the UCI repository, we found the SBC to be more accurate than C4.5 in 16 domains, and similarly for CN2 and PEBLS. Other authors have made similar observations, but no interpretation has been proposed so far. Here we shed some light on the matter by showing that the SBC is in fact optimal even when the independence assumption is grossly violated, and thus applicable to a far broader range of domains than previously thought.

The key to this result lies in the distinction between classification and probability estimation. Equation 1 yields a correct estimate of the class probabilities only when the independence assumption holds; but for purposes of classification, the class probability estimates can diverge widely from the true values, as long as the maximum estimate still corresponds to the maximum true probability. For example, suppose there are two classes + and −, and let $P(+|E) = 0.51$ and $P(-|E) = 0.49$ be the true class probabilities given example E. The optimal decision is then to assign E to class +. Suppose also that Equation 1 gives the estimates $\hat{P}(+|E) = 0.99$ and $\hat{P}(-|E) = 0.01$. The independence assumption is violated by a wide margin, and yet the SBC still makes the optimal decision.

Consider the general two-class case. Let the classes be + and −, $p = P(+|E)$, $r = \frac{P(+)}{P(E)} \prod_{j=1}^{a} P(v_j|+)$, and $s = \frac{P(-)}{P(E)} \prod_{j=1}^{a} P(v_j|-)$. The SBC is optimal iff:

$$(p \geq \tfrac{1}{2} \wedge r \geq s) \vee (p < \tfrac{1}{2} \wedge r < s) \qquad (2)$$

The space U of values of (p, r, s) that correspond to valid probability combinations is a subspace of the unit cube $[0, 1]^3$, and its projection on all planes $p = k$ is the same. It is easily shown that Condition 2 holds in exactly *half* the total volume of U. In contrast, by the independence assumption the SBC would be optimal only on the line where the planes $r = p$ and $s = 1-p$ intersect. Thus the previously assumed region of optimality of the SBC is a second-order infinitesimal fraction of the actual one.

The SBC will be the optimal classifier in the entire example space iff Condition 2 holds for every possible combination of attribute values. For this reason, the fraction of all possible concepts on a attributes for which the SBC is optimal everywhere decreases exponentially with a, starting at 100% for $a = 1$. However, a similar statement is true for other learners, given a fixed training set size.

Testing Condition 2 directly for all combinations of values will generally be infeasible; see (Domingos & Pazzani 1996) for a number of more easily tested conditions. In summary, the work reported here demonstrates that the SBC has a far greater range of applicability than previously thought, and suggests that its use should be considered more often.

References

Domingos, P., and Pazzani, M. 1996. Beyond Independence: Conditions for the Optimality of the Simple Bayesian Classifier. In *Proceedings of the Thirteenth International Conference on Machine Learning*. Bari, Italy: Morgan Kaufmann. Forthcoming.

*Partly supported by a PRAXIS XXI scholarship.

CADI — An Intelligent, Multimedia Tutor for Cardiac Auscultation

Kurt D. Fenstermacher
Intelligent Information Laboratory
1100 E 58th Street
Chicago, IL 60637
e-mail: fensterm@cs.uchicago.edu

Cardiac auscultation is the difficult skill of listening to the human heart and using the sounds heard as clues in diagnosis. The CADI (*Cardiac Auscultation Diagnosis Instruction*) system is designed to tutor medical students and residents in both phases of auscultation: hearing the sounds and diagnosing illness based on what is heard. The system's design draws on the case-based teaching architecture (Schank 1991), which in turn is built on goal-based scenarios and case-based reasoning (Hammond 1989).

Cardiac auscultation is challenging because it requires both special listening skills and extensive domain knowledge. Teachers and students have found that the best way to learn this skill is to listen to hundreds of hearts with an experienced listener. Unfortunately, faculty time for teaching in medical schools is scarce, and experienced auscultators are rare.

Auscultation begins with listening, but the goal is diagnosis. But one must understand the underlying structures and causes of heart sounds before listening can be used as an aid to diagnosis. Thus, much of CADI's development will be devoted to a hypermedia textbook.

Goal-based scenarios are a formalization of the criteria needed to create effective "learning by doing" environments, particularly through the use of computer simulation; the theory is particularly appropriate for CADI's design, since it is partly based on research in medical problem-based learning (Barrow & Tamblyn 1980). Both theories emphasize the importance of placing the learning task in an authentic context.

We have observed that students need two things to become effective auscultators: a library of prototypical sounds and related heart conditions, and some method for comparing a current patient's sounds to those in the library. (There is evidence that complex auditory recall uses a schema-based mechanism which is similar to case-based reasoning (Bregman 1990).) Case-based reasoning captures both these phenomena. By listening to the new patient(s), we hope the student will develop a heightened awareness he can now bring to the original patient. We are currently researching the errors students make and developing case-based strategies to address each one.

By using a rich case representation, CADI will retrieve the most pedagogically appropriate cases for a particular student. In CADI , the retrieved case will not be the one most similar to the student's problematic case, but instead the most helpful from a teacher's view. In fact, the retrieved cases are likely to not be very similar in the traditional sense, but instead will differ in some key aspect.

Although case-based tutoring systems have been built before (Schank 1991), we are not aware of a case-based approach to tutoring a perceptual skill. By building a tutoring system to help students perceive better we hope to learn about the nature of perception. In addition, we claim that a successful case-based tutoring system is at least a partial validation of our assumption that auscultatory reasoning is case-based.

The key elements of the CADI environment are the extensive use of multimedia, realistic simulation of a plausible scenario and its case-based approach to teaching. Multimedia will offer students a better way to study the complex hemodynamic system. The realism of the environment will not only motivate students to learn, but also offer the necessary context to frame the learning task. When combined with its theoretical foundation, CADI provides a rich and effective environment for learning cardiac auscultation.

References

Barrow, H. S., and Tamblyn, R. M. 1980. *Problem-based learning: An Approach to Medical Education.* New York, NY: Springer Publishing.

Bregman, A. S. 1990. *Auditory Scene Analysis: The Perceptual Organization of Sound.* Cambridge, MA: MIT Press.

Hammond, K. J. 1989. *Case-Based Planning: Viewing Planning as a Memory Task.* Boston, MA: Academic Press.

Schank, R. C. 1991. Case-based teaching: Four experiences in educational software design. Technical Report 7, Institute for the Learning Sciences, Evanston, IL.

Integration of an Expert Teaching Assistant With Distance Learning Software

Steven P. Fonseca and Nancy E. Reed

Computer Science Department
University of California, Davis, CA 95616-8562
fonseca@ece.ucdavis.edu, nereed@ucdavis.edu

The Remote Teaching Assistant (RTA) software currently under development at UC Davis allows students and Teaching Assistants (TA's) to interact through multimedia communication via the Internet. To resolve the problem of TA unavailability and limited knowledge, an Expert Teaching Assistant (ETA) module is being developed. When TA's are not on-line, students in need of help consult ETA. The focus of this research is the development and integration of ETA with RTA, the establishment of an architecture suitable for use with education (the domain) in any sub-domain (course), and the creation of a mechanism usable by non-technical personnel to maintain knowledge bases.

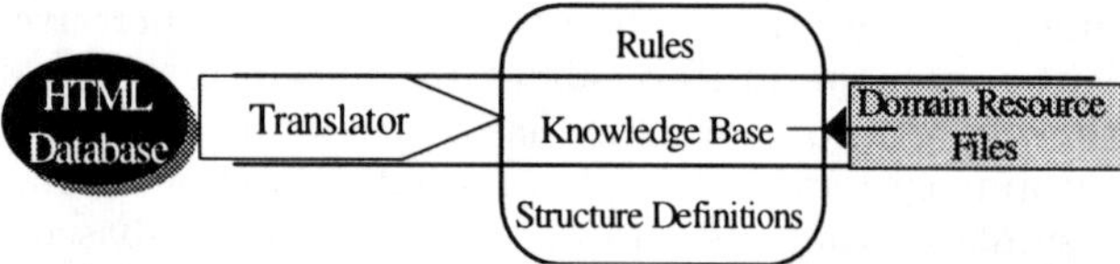

Figure 1: Basic System Architecture for the Expert TA.

The primary goal of ETA is to construct a set of Uniform Resource Locators (URL's) that index the most useful available web pages in the HTML database. To establish the relationship between information within the HTML documents, a small set of commands have been created that logically connect the information in the database. Pre-defined dependency types structure and chain the data objects. The translator reads two segments of an ETA header contained within comments in the HTML files and produces facts and rules that are compatible with the CLIPS inference engine. The first segment describes the nature of the document including the context and several other attributes. The second segment defines the data objects that inherit the attributes of the document and contain additional fields describing properties of the information. The HTML documents are structured for accuracy and ease of maintenance.

Periodically, the translator is invoked to generate or update the knowledge bases for all sub-domains. The translator scans all HTML files, produces CLIPS compatible code, and stores this for use by the inference engine. The translator organizes the CLIPS code, separating information by document and the scope it should have when the inference engine runs. Additional information is obtained from the domain resource files where rules that are sub-domain dependent and temporary relationships are kept.

In addition to the rules and facts generated by the translator, the knowledge base also contains knowledge applicable to all sub-domains. The inference engine executes two preliminary stages to prepare for a solution search and an iterative refinement stage to pinpoint possible solutions. Because students may have trouble describing their problem, ETA is designed to help students find a solution.

ETA is called by the RTA server when requested by a student using the student client. The server creates an instance of the ETA module dedicated to this student and acts as an intermediary for all future communication. During the first stage, ETA receives the sub-domain and a series of keywords entered by the student. These words are examined to ensure correct form and to eliminate any inadvertent errors. The goal of stage two is to generate additional pattern matches that are logically connected to the keywords provided by the student. Many different types of relationships may hold between pieces of information. Weakly related material is eliminated from the solution. The solution set is narrowed down by interactively prompting the user with a series of questions based on previous solution states, the initial keywords and stage two pattern matches, and the responses received to previous questions. The student client has a graphical user interface with dialog boxes, radio buttons, and other widgets available to obtain the user's responses. Upon reaching a solution set, ETA sends a ranked list of the URL's to the user. Each URL is paired with a description string that briefly describes the contents of the associated HTML document. Double clicking on this description invokes a browser to display the HTML document.

A prototype implementation of ETA was successfully integrated with RTA during the Fall of 1995 and tested in an introductory computer class at UC Davis. The knowledge base was composed of manually written rules and facts that linked a small database containing question and answer files, terms, and lecture notes. Development is ongoing for this course and others, including non-CS ones.

Self-Adaptation of Mutation Rates and Dynamic Fitness

Matthew R. Glickman* and **Katia P. Sycara**
School of Computer Science
Carnegie Mellon University
Pittsburgh, PA 15213-3891, USA
glickman+@cs.cmu.edu, katia@ri.cmu.edu

Abstract

In any search via artificial evolution, the likelihood of stagnation at local optima is determined by the particular choices of representation and search operators. Because the performance impact of these design choices is difficult to predict, it is an attractive option to let the representation and/or operators themselves evolve. However, effective evolution at this meta-level can be difficult to achieve for a number of reasons, including: (1) The complexity of the search space is increased; and (2) selection acts at the level of the fitness function and only indirectly at the meta-level, favoring variations only to the extent to which they are stochastically associated with fitness improvements. The question then becomes: Under what conditions is evolution of the representation and/or operators likely to be most effective?

To explore this question empirically, we've chosen to search for vectors of weights in an artificial neural network that minimize the sum-of-squared error (SSE) between the computed function and some simple target functions evaluated over a set of example inputs. As an instantiation of evolvable search operators, we've chosen to associate a *variable* mutation rate (*e.g.* as in Bäck 1991) with each weight, providing selection with the capacity to focus variation on specific subsets of the complement of weights.

While our results have quite generally favored the self-adaptation of per-weight mutation rates in the chosen domain, various experiments have indicated that they are most helpful at the point when only a small subset of the vector is ripe for evolutionary tuning. At the same time, it has been found that the variable rate scheme sometimes enhances the likelihood of the population stagnating at a premature local optimum. This effect appears to arise when the population finds its way to a local optimum steep and broad enough that the *expected fitness* of offspring will be greater the more strongly they resemble their parents. At this point, selection will tend to favor those individuals with the most conservative mutation rates, *i.e.* driving mutation rates toward zero, nestling the population snugly into the local optimum. These observations have led to the conjecture that meta-evolution may perform best when coupled with a dynamic fitness function that differentially favors reduced error in those regions of the target function where the population is performing worst (*e.g.* as in Rosin and Belew 1995). Such fitness functions might both exploit the ability to focus variation on an appropriate subset of the vector, as well as provide enough selective pressure to pop populations out of premature local optima.

Instead of minimizing the SSE, experiments have been conducted in which each individual is assigned a fitness score equal to the sum of its performance on each example point in the function divided by the population's total performance on the same example. Where f_i is the fitness of an individual i, e_{ij} is the error of individual i on example j (maximum value is 1), and with a population of size n:

$$f_i = \sum_j \frac{1 - e_{ij}^2}{n - \sum_k e_{kj}^2}$$

Initial results indicate that dynamism in the fitness function is an advantage, but not in the latter stages of the search, where it tends to inhibit fine-tuning. The best results have been achieved by starting search with the dynamic function, but switching to the static function once the average SSE drops below some pre-set threshold.

*Supported in part by an NSF Graduate Fellowship Award

References

Bäck, T. 1991. Self-adaptation in genetic algorithms. In *Proceedings of the First European Conference on Artificial Life.* MIT Press, 1992.

Rosin, C., and Belew, R. 1995. Methods for Competitive Co-Evolution: Finding Opponents Worth Beating. In Larry J. Eshelman (Ed.), *Proceedings of the Sixth International Conference on Genetic Algorithms*, pp. 373–380. Morgan Kaufmann, 1995.

Heterogeneous and Homogeneous Robot Group Behavior

Dani Goldberg

Brandeis University Computer Science Department
Volen Center for Complex Systems, Room 261
Waltham, MA 02254
dani@cs.brandeis.edu

When working with groups of robots it may be very difficult to determine what characteristics the group requires in order to perform a task most efficiently—i.e., in the least time. Some researchers have used groups of behaviorally differentiated robots—where the robots do not perform the same actions—and others have used behaviorally homogeneous groups. None of this research, however, explicitly compares the behavior of heterogeneous and homogeneous groups of robots to determine which performs a task more efficiently. The research described here makes such a comparison and aims at developing guidelines to aid in the design of the heterogeneous/homogeneous characteristics that will allow a group of robots to perform a task efficiently.

There are a number of issues that arise when one tries to define the homogeneous/heterogeneous nature of a group. These issues are mentioned in (Brooks 1991):

Individuality and Cooperation: Individuality deals with how the behaviors of the various *classes* of robots differ and how many classes of robots there are, while cooperation deals with how these classes interact.

Interference and Density Dependence: Any time more than one robot is present in a system there is the possibility that one will interfere with the actions of another. It is important to determine how many robots of each class, and how many total, produce the most efficient solution.

Communication: Communication may be used to help coordinate the actions of individual robots or the classes they belong to. It can therefore impact all of the previous issues.

Our research begins to explore some of these issues by implementing a hoarding task. The task requires the robots to search an 11 by 14 foot enclosure for *pucks* (small metal cylinders), collect them and bring them to a particular corner designated as *Home* (see figures). For this experiment we use four identical IS Robotics R2e robots.

One experiment is with a homogeneous group. All of the robots are behaviorally identical (i.e. they belong to the same class) and there is no explicit communication between them. Each robot searches for pucks while avoiding walls and other robots. When a robot finds a puck, it brings it Home, leaves it there, and continues searching for more pucks (see figure (a)). A robot may only enter the Boundary region if it has a puck. One might expect that, especially at the beginning of an experiment when there are a lot of pucks, that the probability of many of the robots simultaneously bringing a puck Home would be high. This would result in a lot of interference at Home as the robots attempt to drop off pucks. Our preliminary results seem to support this observation.

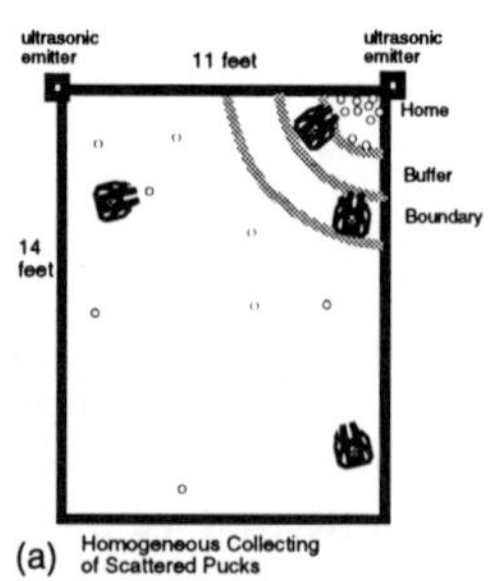

(a) Homogeneous Collecting of Scattered Pucks

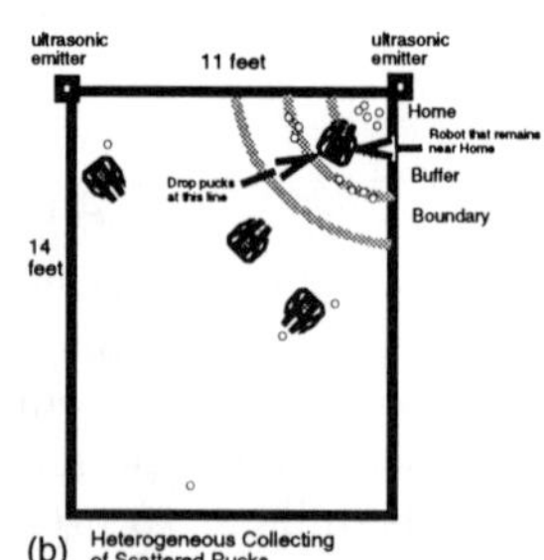

(b) Heterogeneous Collecting of Scattered Pucks

In order to lessen this interference we implement a heterogeneous hoarding behavior. Three of the robots, forming one class, collect pucks as above, but instead of bringing them Home they drop them at Boundary/Buffer line. The fourth robot, forming the second class, remains in the Home and Buffer regions, gathers the pucks left on the line, and places them at Home (see figure (b)). Preliminary results seem to indicate that the interference encountered with the homogeneous group is lessened in the heterogeneous group.

The research described above is still in progress. We are currently gathering data for these experiments, and designing other experiments to explore issues of heterogeneity and homogeneity more fully.

References

Brooks, Rodney A. 1991. Challenges for Complete Creature Architectures. In Proceedings of First International Conference on Simulation of Adaptive Behavior: From Animals to Animats, 434-443. Cambridge, Mass.: MIT Press.

Inducing design biases that characterize successful experimentation in weak-theory domains: TIPS

Vanathi Gopalakrishnan
Intelligent Systems Laboratory, University of Pittsburgh, Pittsburgh, PA 15260
vanathi@cs.pitt.edu

Experiment design in domains with weak theories is largely a trial-and-error process. In such domains, the effects of actions are unpredictable due to insufficient knowledge about the causal relationships among entities involved in an experiment. Thus, experiments are designed based on heuristics obtained from prior experience. Assuming that past experiment designs leading to success or failure can be recorded electronically, this thesis research proposes one method for analyzing these designs to yield hints regarding effective operator application sequences. This work assumes that the order in which operators are applied matters to the overall success of experiments. Experiment design can also be thought of as a form of planning, since it involves generation of a sequence of steps comprising of one or more operations that can change the environment by changing values of some of the parameters that describe the environment. Experiment design operators can therefore be thought of as plan operators at higher levels of abstraction. This thesis proposes a method for learning contexts within which applying certain sequences of operators has favored successful experimentation in the past.

The motivation for this thesis arose from study of experiment design in macromolecular crystallography. The goal of experiments in this domain is to obtain a good quality crystal of a macromolecule (protein/DNA/complex) so that it can be X-ray diffracted to yield the 3-D molecular structure. There is little understanding about how the large number of parameters (> 25) such as temperature, pH, and macromolecular concentration, interact and influence the growth of a particular macromolecular crystal. Yet, it is observed that some people are able to produce good quality crystals faster than others (crystal growing can take anywhere from a week to a few years). This observation seems to indicate that it is quite likely that these "good" crystallographers are using some *pet* solutions or other methodology that is helping them search this vast parameter space effectively and efficiently. We can refer to the different ways that crystallographers search the parameter space (by setting up appropriate experiments) as *design biases*.

It would be desirable to capture these design biases or preferences through knowledge engineering, via interviews with the experts. The caveat is that such knowledge tends to be very hard to convey verbally without reference to a specific protein or DNA molecule. Since the experiments are done over a long period of time, the most accurate record of the precise methodology used is found in the laboratory notebooks of individual crystallographers. We have found a way to capture the information found in laboratory notebooks electronically via an easy-to-use interface [1].

The Temporal Induction of Plan Sequence (TIPS) framework proposed in this thesis aims to provide a set of hints regarding operator application sequence for a particular problem posed by an experiment designer. The major component of TIPS is a symbolic inductive Rule Learner (Temporal-RL) that uses the method of *temporal specialization* to learn design biases from past cases of successful and failed experiment designs. Design biases are characterized by a context, followed by a set of temporal relationships (e.g., before, during) expressed among operators. Contexts refer to characteristics of the macromolecule (e.g., protein name, class, weight). The learned contexts are used for matching with the particular problem characteristics given by the user to TIPS.

Learning structured attributes is an open problem in machine learning. This thesis provides one method to deal with structured attributes such as steps in a plan. New symbolic learning representations are introduced for instance and concept description languages. These representations exploit the structured aspects of steps in experiment design. A symbolic inductive learner is augmented with capabilities to learn statistically significant relations between normal attributes (not structured) and structured attributes (steps and sequence of steps), with respect to the class of successful or failed experiment designs. The thesis also demonstrates that learning at different levels of abstraction by exploiting structures inherent in a domain can be efficient and meaningful.

Acknowledgements
I am extremely grateful to Prof. Bruce Buchanan for his guidance and contribution to this thesis idea. Thanks also to Prof. John Rosenberg and Dr. Patricia Wilkosz for being most helpful domain experts. This research is supported in part by funds from the W.M.Keck Center for Advanced Training in Computational Biology at the University of Pittsburgh, Carnegie Mellon University and the Pittsburgh Supercomputing Center, and also by NIH.

References

[1] Hennessy, D., Gopalakrishnan, V., Buchanan, B. G., Subramanian, D. Induction of rules for biological macromolecule crystallization. In *Proceedings of the Second International Conference on Intelligent Systems for Molecular Biology*, August 1994, pp. 179-187.

Belief Network Algorithms: a Study of Performance

Nathalie Jitnah
Department of Computer Science
Monash University
Clayton, VIC 3168, Australia
njitnah@cs.monash.edu.au

This abstract gives an overview of the work described in (Nicholson & Jitnah 1996). We present a survey of Belief Network algorithms and propose a domain characterisation system to be used as a basis for algorithm comparison and for predicting algorithm performance.

Belief Updating Algorithms

There are several algorithms for exact belief updating, for example, the polytree algorithm, clustering (Pearl 1988) or the Jensen tree method (Jensen, Lauritzen, & Olesen 1989). However, approximate methods are often preferred because the complexity of exact updating is NP-hard. Approximate updating is usually done by stochastic simulation (Pearl 1988). Variants include likelihood weighting, survival-of-the-fittest and Markov Chain Monte Carlo methods.

Another approach to complexity reduction is to approximate the model by simplifying the network. Some of the existing methods do this by state-space abstraction, removal of weak links, replacing small probabilities with zero and graph pruning. Such procedures may be applied individually or in combination.

Domain Characterisation

We characterise a problem by obtaining measurements, prior to each experiment, on the network as a whole and on instantiated and queried nodes. The measurements are then used for comparison of algorithm performance.

Measurements taken for the network relate to the numbers of nodes and arcs, the connectedness, path lengths, overall skewness of the conditional probability distributions (CPDs), sizes of the CPDs and the numbers of states of nodes. If using clustering or the Jensen method, we also record the clique network or the Jensen tree respectively.

For each instantiated or queried node, we record its location, the skewness of its CPD, its distance from root and leaf nodes, the clique network nodes or Jensen tree nodes which it belongs to. For the set of instantiated nodes, we record the size of the set, the distribution of evidence, the overall skewness of the CPDs, the total number of states and the probability of the evidence. For the set of queried nodes, we record the size of the set, the distribution of queries, the overall skewness of the CPDs and the total number of states. We also measure the distance between instantiated and queried nodes.

Implementation and Results

A range of problems are selected using various networks and evidence. We compare the time and accuracy of some exact and approximate algorithms on this range of problems. We also apply some model approximation procedures to the networks and evaluate the performance of the algorithms on the resulting models.

The results of our comparisons provide a means of predicting algorithm performance given a problem domain. Hence, the complexity issue can be tackled by designing efficient special-case solutions for particular problems, rather than by searching for general solutions.

References

Jensen, F.; Lauritzen, S.; and Olesen, K. 1989. Bayesian updating in recursive graphical models by local computations. Technical Report R 89-15, Institute for Electronic Systems, Dept of Mathematics and Computer Scence, University of Aalborg.

Nicholson, A., and Jitnah, N. 1996. Belief network algorithms: a study of performance using domain characterisation. Technical Report 96/249, in preparation, Department of Computer Science, Monash University.

Pearl, J. 1988. *Probabilistic Reasoning in Intelligent Systems.* San Mateo, Ca.: Morgan Kaufmann.

Proposed Interestingness Measure for Characteristic Rules

Micheline Kamber
School of Computing Science
Simon Fraser University
Burnaby, BC V5A 1S6, Canada
kamber@cs.sfu.ca

Rajjan Shinghal
Dept. of Computer Science
Concordia University
Montreal, QC H3G 1M8, Canada
shinghal@cs.concordia.ca

Introduction

Knowledge discovery systems can be used to generate rules describing data from databases. Typically, only a small fraction of the rules generated are of interest. Measures of rule interestingness are hence essential for filtering out useless information. Such measures have been predominantly objective, based on statistics underlying the discovered rules, or patterns. Examples include the J-measure (Smyth & Goodman 1992), rule strength (Piatetsky-Shapiro 1991), and certainty (Hong & Mao 1991). Although these measures help assess the interestingness of discriminant rules, they do not fully serve their purpose when applied to characteristic rules (Kamber & Shinghal 1996). Discriminant rules describe how objects of a class differ from objects of other classes. Such rules take the form $e \rightarrow h$, where e is the evidence (typically a conjunction of attribute-value conditions) and h is the hypothesis (predicting the class of objects satisfying e). Characteristic rules are of the form $h \rightarrow e$. They describe the characteristics common to all objects in a given class, although this constraint may be relaxed slightly in order to deal with real-world noisy data. Both types of rules can be of interest. We propose an interestingness measure for characteristic rules, based on the technical definition of sufficiency (Duda, Gaschnig, & Hart 1981).

Proposed Measure

The interestingness of characteristic rule $r = h \rightarrow e$ may be defined as the product of its utility and goodness (Smyth & Goodman 1992). Let $P(h)$ represent the utility of r, i.e., the probability that r will be used. The goodness of r can be assessed as a function of $Suf(r)$, the sufficiency of r, which measures the influence of h on e. This is defined as $Suf(r) = P(h|e)/P(h|\neg e)$, where the probabilities can be estimated from the given data (Duda, Gaschnig, & Hart 1981). Suf(r) lies in the range $[0, \infty]$. If Suf(r)$\rightarrow\infty$ then h invalidates $\neg e$, meaning $h \rightarrow e$ is certain. If $1<$Suf(r)$<\infty$, then the larger Suf(r) is, the more certain $h \rightarrow e$ is. If $0\leq$Suf(r)≤ 1 then r is invalid. We therefore propose the following interestingness measure for characteristic rule, r:

$$IC(r) = \begin{cases} (1 - 1/Suf(r)) \times P(h) & 1 < Suf(r) < \infty \\ 0 & \text{otherwise.} \end{cases}$$

IC(r) lies in the range [0,1] with 0 and 1 representing the minimum and maximum possible interestingness, respectively. Note that IC(r) increases monotonically with Suf(r).

Conclusions

To our knowledge, no interestingness measures exist for characteristic rules. We propose an interestingness measure for such rules based on sufficiency. The measure was applied to order a number of characteristic rules according to decreasing interestingness (not shown here due to limited space). Although further testing is required, the measure's performance was promising, placing the more complete and accurate rules towards the top of the list. Our present work focuses on using the measures to constrain the search space for characteristic rule discovery from databases.

Acknowledgments

We thank R. Hadley for very helpful feedback.

References

Duda, R.O., Gaschnig, J., & Hart, P.E. 1981. Model design in the Prospector consultant system for mineral exploration. In B.L. Webber & N.J. Nilsson, eds., *Readings in Artificial Intelligence*, 334–348, Tioga, Palo Alto, CA.

Hong, J. & Mao, C. 1991. Incremental discovery of rules and structure by hierarchical and parallel clustering. In G. Piatetsky-Shapiro & W. J. Frawley, eds., *Knowledge Discovery in Databases*, 177-194, AAAI/MIT Press, Menlo Park, CA.

Kamber, M. & Shinghal, R. 1996. Evaluating the interestingness of characteristic rules. Forthcoming.

Piatetsky-Shapiro, G. 1991. Discovery, analysis, and presentation of strong rules. In G. Piatetsky-Shapiro & W.J. Frawley, eds., *Knowledge Discovery in Databases*, 229-248, AAAI/MIT Press, Menlo Park, CA.

Smyth, P. & Goodman, R.M. 1992. An information theoretic approach to rule induction from databases. *IEEE Trans. on Knowledge and Data Engineering* 4(4):301–316.

A Transformational Analysis of the EBL Utility Problem

Jihie Kim and Paul S. Rosenbloom
Information Sciences Institute and Computer Science Department
University of Southern California
4676 Admiralty Way
Marina del Rey, CA 90292, U.S.A.
jihie@isi.edu, rosenbloom@isi.edu

Efficiency is a major concern for all problem solving systems. One way of achieving efficiency is the application of learning techniques to speed up problem solving. Accordingly, there has been considerable amount of research on applying explanation-based learning (EBL)(Mitchell, Keller, & Kedar-Cabelli 1986) techniques to problem solving. However, EBL is known to suffer from the *utility problem*, where the cost of using the learned knowledge overwhelms its benefit. We show that how the cost increase of a learned rule in an EBL system can be analyzed by characterizing the learning process as a sequence of transformations from a problem solving episode to a learned rule. The analysis of how the cost changes through the transformations can be a useful tool for revealing the sources of cost increase in the learning system. We focus on the Soar problem solving system which uses a variant of EBL called *chunking*(Rosenbloom *et al.* 1991). The chunking process has been decomposed into a sequence of transformations from the problem solving to a chunk (learned rule). By analyzing these transformations, we have identified a set of sources which can make the output chunk expensive. The set of sources and the proposed solutions are :

1. *Removing search control*: Ignoring search-control rules which constrained the problem solving can increase the cost. For example, PRODIGY/EBL (Minton 1993) and Soar ignore a large part of the search-control rules in learning to increase the generality of the learned rules. The consequence of this omission is that the learned rules are not constrained by the path actually taken in the problem space, and thus can perform an exponential amount of search even when the original problem-space search was highly directed (by the control rules). By incorporating search control in the explanation structure, the match process for the learned rule can focus on the path that was actually followed (Kim & Rosenbloom 1993).
2. *Eliminating intermediate rule firing (Unifying)*: In Soar, working memory is a set. Whenever two different instantiations create the equivalent working memory elements, they are merged into one. Eliminating this process in learning, and keeping equivalent set of partial instantiations separately can increase the cost. By preprocessing the partial instantiations, and merging the equivalent instantiations into one, this cost increase can be avoided. This could potentially be done either be grouping instantiations that generate the same working memory elements or by selecting one of them as a representative.
3. *Totally ordering the conditions (Linearize)*: Simplifying the structure of learned rule without considering the problem solving structure can increase the cost. By making the learning mechanism sensitive to the problem-solving structure, — i.e., by reflecting such structure in the match of the learned rule — we can avoid this source of expensiveness. The key thing that this requires is an efficient generalization for the match algorithm to interpret the non-linear structure (Kim & Rosenbloom 1996).

Based on the above analysis and the proposed potential solutions to the sources of expensiveness, we are currently working towards the specification and implementation of a variant of chunking which avoids any of these sources of extra cost. If it works, the cost of using a chunk should always be bounded by the cost of the corresponding problem solving. A similar transformational analysis should also be possible for any problem solving systems which use EBL techniques. As with the analysis of chunking, this analysis should identify sources of expensiveness in EBL, and help guide the design of safer EBL mechanisms(Kim & Rosenbloom 1995).

References

Kim, J., and Rosenbloom, P. S. 1993. Constraining learning with search control. In *Proc. 10th Int'l Conf. on Machine Learning*, 174–181.

Kim, J., and Rosenbloom, P. S. 1995. Transformation analyses of learning in Soar. Technical Report ISI/RR-95-4221, USC-ISI.

Kim, J., and Rosenbloom, P. S. 1996. Learning efficient rules by maintaining the explanation structure. In *Proc. 13th Nat'l Conf. on Artificial Intelligence (to appear)*.

Minton, S. 1993. Personal communication.

Mitchell, T. M.; Keller, R. M.; and Kedar-Cabelli, S. T. 1986. Explanation-based generalization – a unifying view. *Machine Learning* 1(1):47–80.

Rosenbloom, P. S.; Laird, J. E.; Newell, A.; and McCarl, R. 1991. A preliminary analysis of the soar architecture as a basis for general intelligence. *Artificial Intelligence* 47(1-3):289–325.

Controlling State-Space Abstraction in Bayesian Networks* (Abstract)

Chao-Lin Liu

Artificial Intelligence Laboratory, University of Michigan
1101 Beal Avenue
Ann Arbor, Michigan 48105
chaolin@umich.edu

Many applications require computational systems to respond to queries by a particular deadline. Failure to meet the deadlines may render the returned solution useless. Moreover, the deadlines of such time-critical applications are often uncertain at system design time. *Anytime algorithms* have been suggested to cope with these challenges by trading the quality of the solutions for the reactiveness of the systems at run time [1]. We have introduced an anytime evaluation algorithm [2] for a formalism commonly used in uncertain reasoning: Bayesian networks. Empirical results indicate that approximations of good quality can be obtained within a much shorter time than would be required to directly evaluate the networks by exact algorithms. Also the quality of the approximation improves with the allocated computational time on average.

Approximations of the desired solutions may be acquired by evaluating abstract versions of the given Bayesian networks, where the abstract networks ignore some of the distinctions between states of the variables, called *abstracted variables*. Reduction of the state spaces can dramatically cut down the computational time, at the expense of the quality of the solutions. When there is time for more computation, the evaluation algorithm recovers some of the ignored distinctions, and gets another approximation by evaluating the refined network. The algorithm iteratively evaluates refined abstract networks until stopped.

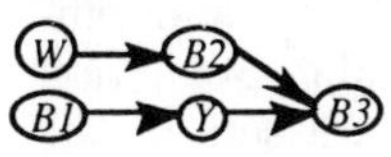

The structure of the Bayesian network has a special bearing on the quality of approximations K, defined based on the divergence between the true and the approximated distributions. Notice that larger K means worse quality. Specifically, we have shown that the quality of the approximated distribution of a set of variables that d-separates another set of variables from the abstracted variables is not better than that of the d-separated set. D-separation is a graphical property that implies conditional independence. Namely when variables in set X d-separate variables in set Y from the abstracted variables A given the instantiated variables, Y is conditionally independent of A. Consider the Bayesian network shown above. If we instantiate variable *B3* and abstract *B1*, then the qualities of the approximated marginal distributions of other variables have the relationship: $K_Y \geq K_{B2} \geq K_W$.

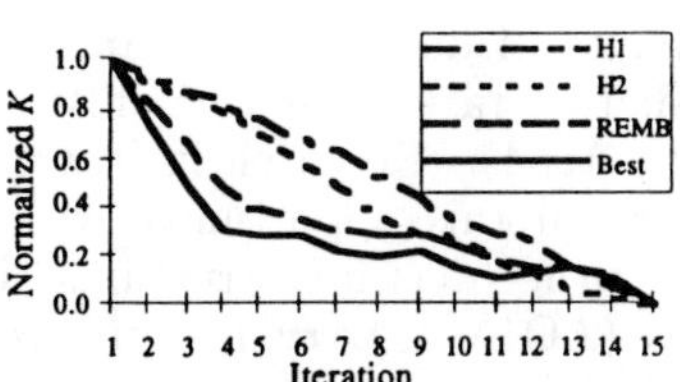

We are searching for the control methods of the state-space abstraction, aiming at improving performance profiles of the algorithm. In particular, we are exploring score functions for selecting the aggregated states to refine. The score functions compute the goodness of the aggregated states based on factors that are local to the aggregated states. It is hoped that the scores be highly correlated with the actual improvement of the approximation. Among the functions being investigated, the REMB function based on the relative entropy of the Markov boundary of the abstracted variable has demonstrated the best average performance in experiments. This is illustrated by the closeness of the REMB curve to the "Best" curve in the chart shown above. The "Best" curve is achieved by an ideal function that *always* lead to correct selection of the aggregated state to refine. Such a perfect capability is achieved in part by the evaluating the original network, and is *not* a practically achievable feature.

We have established a theorem that addresses the relationship between state-space abstraction and the quality of approximations. We also have limited, empirical results regarding control of state-space abstraction using a variety of heuristics. Future work will consider the usage of *value of information* in score functions. The goal is to establish strategies for controlling the state-space abstraction such that the algorithm provides the best performance possible.

References

[1] Boddy, M., and T. L. Dean. 1994. Deliberation scheduling for problem solving in time-constrained environments. *Artificial Intelligence* **67**: 245-285.

[2] Wellman, M. P., and C.-L. Liu. 1994. State-space abstraction for anytime evaluation of probabilistic networks. *Proceedings of the Tenth Conference on Uncertainty in Artificial Intelligence*, pp. 567-574.

---

* This work was supported in part by AFOSR Grant F49620-94-1-0027.

Ad Hoc Attribute-Value Prediction

Gabor Melli
Simon Fraser University
British Columbia, Canada, V5A 1S6
melli@cs.sfu.ca

The evolving ease and efficiency in accessing large amounts of data presents an opportunity to execute prediction tasks based on this data (Hunt, Marin, & Stone 1964). Research in learning-from-example has addressed this opportunity with algorithms that induce either decision structures (ID3) or classification rules (AQ15). Lazy learning research on the other hand, delay the model construction to strictly satisfy a prediction task (Aha, Kibler, & Albert 1991). To support a prediction query against a data set, current techniques require a large amount of preprocessing to either construct a complete domain model, or to determine attribute relevance. Our work in this area is to develop an algorithm that will automatically return a probabilistic classification rule for a prediction query with equal accuracy to current techniques but with no preprocessing requirements. The proposed algorithm, DBPredictor, combines the delayed model construction approach of lazy learning along with the information theoretic measure and top-down heuristic search of learning-from-example algorithms. The algorithm induces only the information required to satisfy the prediction query and avoids the attribute relevance tests required by the nearest-neighbour measures of lazy learning.

Given a data set in some domain, an attribute-value prediction query requests the prediction of an attribute's value for some partially described event drawn from this domain. Applicable classification rules for an attribute-value prediction query are shown to be based on the exponential number of combinations of the attribute-values specified in the query. DBPredictor performs an informed top-down search that incrementally specializes one attribute-value at a time to locate a maximally valued classification rule. In a sense the algorithm iteratively selects the next most relevant attribute-value for this query. If interrupted, the algorithm reports the best encountered classification rule to date. Given a query with n instantiated values the search is contained to $n + (n-1) + ... + 1 = n(n+1)/2$ evaluations. We use the information-theoretic J-Measure (Smyth & Goodman 1992) to evaluate the quality of a probabilistic classification rule.

A corresponding program based on DBPredictor has been developed to satisfy ad hoc attribute-value prediction queries against SQL-based relational database management systems. The performance and accuracy of DBPredictor is empirically tested against both real-world and synthetic data. Furthermore the results are contrasted to the ID3, AQ15, and ITRULE algorithms. DBPredictor commonly requires two orders of magnitude less processing than the other algorithms for a single query. Finally, as expected, DBPredictor's accuracy is equivalent to that of the other algorithms.

To exemplify the increased access to large amounts of information and the opportunities provided by this technique, an interactive version of the program has been placed on the World Wide Web. Users first choose the real-world database they want to query against, next they choose the attribute whose value will be predicted and finally, with the use of pull down menus, describe the event's instantiated attributes. Because of the inconclusive nature of most prediction queries based on real-world databases, the generated report provides a ranked distribution of the values to expect, rather than only the most likely value.

Several interesting future research directions are possible for DBPredictor. First, the search technique could be extended to support requests for more accurate classification rules. Finally the caching of discovered rules could be used to expedite future queries and eventually to better understand the underlying model of a large data set.

The DBPredictor algorithm's flexibility and efficiency can support ad hoc attribute-value prediction queries against large and accessible data sets of the near future.

References

Aha, D. W.; Kibler, D.; and Albert, M. K. 1991. Instance-based learning algorithms. *Machine Learning* 6:37–66.

Hunt, E. B.; Marin, J.; and Stone, P. J. 1964. *Experiments in Induction.* New York: Academic Press.

Smyth, P., and Goodman, R. M. 1992. An information theoretic approach to rule induction. *IEEE Transactions on Knowledge and Data Engineering* 4(4):301–316.

An Incremental Interactive Algorithm for Regular Grammar Inference

Rajesh Parekh and Vasant Honavar
Artificial Intelligence Research Group
Department of Computer Science
Iowa State University, Ames, IA 50011
{parekh|honavar}@cs.iastate.edu

Introduction

Grammar inference, a problem with many applications in pattern recognition and language learning, is defined as follows: For an unknown grammar G, given a finite set of positive examples S^+ that belong to L(G), and possibly a finite set of negative examples S^-, infer a grammar G^* equivalent to G. Different restrictions on S^+ and S^- and the interaction of the learner with the teacher or the environment give rise to different variants of this task. We present an interactive incremental algorithm for inference of a *finite state automaton* (FSA) corresponding to an unknown *regular grammar.*

Search Space

A set of positive examples (strings of the unknown language) is structurally complete if each production rule of the unknown grammar is used at least once in the generation of some string in the set. If S^+ is structurally complete, it implicitly defines a lattice (ω) of candidate grammars that is guaranteed to contain the target grammar. At the base of the lattice is the *maximal canonical automaton* (MCA) that accepts exactly the set S^+. Other elements of the lattice (ordered by the *grammar covers relation*) represent progressively more general languages i.e., supersets of S^+ and are generated by successively merging states of the MCA. This (exponential sized) search space can be concisely represented by two sets $\mathcal{S}$ and $\mathcal{G}$ which correspond to the most *specific* and most *general* FSA respectively.

A *version space* based technique is used to search the hypothesis space. FSA corresponding to two lattice elements (one from $\mathcal{S}$ and the other from $\mathcal{G}$) are compared for *equivalence*. If the two FSA are not equivalent, the shortest string y belonging to the symmetric difference of their languages is posed as a *membership query* to the teacher. Based on the teacher's response to the query the learner is able to prune the search space without eliminating the desired solution. For example, if the teacher's response to a query is *negative*, the FSA accepting the negative example and all FSA that cover it (and thus also accept the same negative example) are eliminated. This elimination is carried out implicitly by modifying the two sets $\mathcal{S}$ and $\mathcal{G}$ as needed. This interaction between the teacher and learner continues till the hypothesis space is reduced to one (or a set of equivalent) FSA. The resulting FSA is provably equivalent to the target FSA.

Incremental Algorithm

The incremental version of the algorithm relaxes the *structural completeness* assumption. The teacher may provide a few positive examples to start with. The learner performs candidate elimination by posing *safe membership queries* to the teacher. After seeing more positive examples, the learner incrementally updates the lattice to incorporate the new examples and continues with candidate elimination. Eventually, when the set of positive examples provided by the teacher includes a structurally complete set for the target FSA, no more lattice updates take place and all queries are treated as safe. The algorithm then converges to the target FSA. The necessary and sufficient conditions for guaranteed convergence of the algorithm to the correct solution are identified.

Future Directions

Promising directions for further research include: heuristics for informative query generation to speed up learning; inference of regular *tree grammars* and *attributed grammars*; empirical estimates of the expected case time and space complexity of the proposed grammar inference algorithm and its extensions.

References

Parekh R.G., and Honavar V.G. An Incremental Interactive Algorithm for Regular Grammar Inference. *Computer Science Department, Technical Report TR 96-03*, Iowa State University.

Constructive Neural Network Learning Algorithms

Rajesh Parekh, Jihoon Yang, and Vasant Honavar
Artificial Intelligence Research Group
Department of Computer Science
Iowa State University, Ames, IA 50011
{parekh|yang|honavar}@cs.iastate.edu

Introduction

Constructive Algorithms offer an approach for incremental construction of potentially minimal neural network architectures for pattern classification tasks. These algorithms obviate the need for an ad-hoc a-priori choice of the network topology. The constructive algorithm design involves alternately augmenting the existing network topology by adding one or more *threshold logic units* and training the newly added threshold neuron(s) using a stable variant of the *perceptron learning algorithm* (e.g., *pocket algorithm, thermal perceptron*, and *barycentric correction procedure*). Several constructive algorithms including *tower, pyramid, tiling, upstart*, and *perceptron cascade* have been proposed for 2-category pattern classification. These algorithms differ in terms of their topological and connectivity constraints as well as the training strategies used for individual neurons.

Multi-Category Pattern Classification

Several applications involve assigning patterns to one of M ($M > 2$) classes. The above constructive algorithms are known to converge to zero classification errors on a finite, non-contradictory, 2-category classification task. We have developed provably convergent multi-category extensions of the above constructive algorithms. Simulations on artificial and real world datasets have resulted in fairly compact networks. More recently, we have developed fast constructive algorithms that exhibit superior generalization.

Real world data sets often have continuous valued attributes. *Quantization* can be used to transform continuous valued patterns to an equivalent set of binary/bipolar valued patterns. Our experiments with quantization show that relatively difficult classification tasks can be transformed into simpler ones by effective quantization of the input space (albeit with the added expense of increased dimensionality in the pattern space).

Pruning Strategies

Network pruning involves elimination of redundant neurons and connections. With appropriate pruning strategies for constructive algorithms, it is possible to obtain smaller networks in terms of number of neurons and the number of connection weights. Smaller networks are known to possess better generalization ability. Pruning can be interleaved with the network construction phase or can take place once the entire network has been constructed. Some promising ideas on pruning include, removal of auxiliary neurons not contributing to the faithful representation of a layer in the tiling network; elimination of redundant daughter neurons in the upstart and cascade networks; retraining newly added output neurons in the tower and pyramid algorithms to improve classification accuracy at each successive layer. A systematic analysis of pruning strategies is a topic of ongoing research.

Current Research

Each constructive learning algorithm has a set of inductive and representational biases implicit in the design choices that determine where a new neuron is added and how it is trained. Our goal is to systematically characterize these biases and design constructive learning algorithms that can dynamically add, train, and prune neurons in a manner that is best suited to the needs of each individual classification task.

Acknowledgements

This research is partially supported by the NSF grant IRI-0409580 to Vasant Honavar.

References

Parekh, R., Yang, J., and Honavar V. (1995). Multi-category Constructive Neural Network Learning Algorithms for Pattern Classification, *Computer Science Department, Technical Report TR 95-15a*, ISU. (Refer http://www.cs.iastate.edu/~honavar/publist.html)

A Computational Model of Persistent Beliefs

Sunju Park

Artificial Intelligence Laboratory
The University of Michigan
Ann Arbor, MI 48109-2110
boxenju@eecs.umich.edu

The persistence of beliefs has been assumed in many research effotrs, either explicitly or implicitly, but a computational model is hard to find. For instance, in his well-known AOP article (Shoham 1993), Shoham suggests a formal language for beliefs and states that beliefs persist by default. The author writes $(Bel_A^3\ Bel_B^{10}\ Like(A,B)^7)$ means that at time *3* agent *A* believes that at time *10* agent *B* will believe that at time *7* *A* liked *B*. Shoham, however, does not elaborate on how to formally interpret the persistence of beliefs. Moreover, in his implemented agent language, AGENT-0, both the temporal aspect of beliefs (e.g., At time *t*, I believe ...) and the nested beliefs (e.g., I believe you believe I believe ...) have been omitted.

In this abstract, we summarize our work on developing a computational model of persistent beliefs, which supports both the temporal information and the nested belief model.

First, we propose a time-interval representation for nonambiguous interpretation of persistent beliefs. The main idea is rather simple: to have explicit lower and upper time-bounds when representing facts and beliefs.

The time-interval representation clarifies the meaning of persistence without tedious elaboration of each implied belief. For example, the time-interval representation, $(Bel_A^{[10\ \infty]}\ on(paper,\ table)^{[10\ \infty]})$, elaborates the *implied* persistence of the belief, $(Bel_A^{10}\ on(paper,\ table)^{10})$, without ambiguity. It is read as "Agent *A* believes at $t \geq 10$ that *on(paper,table)* will be true at $t \geq 10$". In addition, it can represent the history of beliefs, which was not possible in AOP.

Secondly, we have developed an algorithm for checking consistency between two beliefs. The basic idea is that *two beliefs are always compatible with each other unless all the following four conditions are satisfied.*

- Negated, same facts: Two beliefs (without any conjunction, disjunction, and deduction) can be potentially inconsistent only if they are about the same facts, one of which is negated.
- Same depth of nested beliefs: If the depth of two nested beliefs are different, they are always consistent.
- Beliefs of same agents: Two beliefs are always compatible if the agents holding two beliefs are different.
- Overlapping time-intervals: Only the overlap and subsume relations can have a potential for conflicts.

We have developed a consistency-checking algorithm between two beliefs, whose time complexity is $O(d)$, where d is the smaller nested depth between two beliefs. If we consider d as a large constant, the complexity is $O(1)$.

Thirdly, to incorporate a new set of beliefs into its old beliefs, the agent needs a belief-revision algorithm. At present, we consider two revision methods: one where new beliefs override old beliefs in the case of inconsistency, and the other where an agent chooses to believe the maximal number of consistent beliefs.

The former case is an extension of AGENT-0, since beliefs now can have temporal information and can be nested. The consistency-checking between two sets of beliefs will take $O((n+m)^2 \times d)$, where n and m represent the number of new beliefs and old beliefs, respectively.

On the other hand, the problem of finding the maximally consistent beliefs is transformed to the independent-set problem, which is NP-complete (Garey & Johnson 1979). If we assume internal consistency of the new belief set and of the belief DB, respectively, however, a polynomial-time algorithm can be possible (Park 1996).

Our research shows some promising early results. First, the interval-based representation is able to represent history and allows nonambiguous interpretation of persistent beliefs. Second, a computationally simple consistency-checking algorithm has been developed. Finally, although finding a maximally-consistent belief set is NP-complete, a polynomial-time revision algorithm is possible under the assumption of internal consistency.

In the future, we will work on relaxing our assumptions of not allowing disjunction and conjunction, and will develop a belief DB that supports basic operations, such as add, delete, update, and query (e.g., what the agent believes, believed, or will believe at time *t*).

This research has been funded in part by the Digital Libraries Initiative under CERA IRI-9411287.

References

Garey, M. R., and Johnson, D. S. 1979. *Computers and Intractability: A Guide to the Theory of NP-Completeness*: W. H. Freeman.

Park, S. 1996. Belief DB: A Computational Model for Persistent Beliefs. Forthcoming.

Shoham, Y. 1993. Agent-oriented Programming. *Artificial Intelligence* 60:51-91.

Contracting Strategy based on Markov Process Modeling

Sunju Park and Edmund H. Durfee

Artificial Intelligence Laboratory
The University of Michigan
Ann Arbor, MI 48109-2110
{boxenju, durfee}@eecs.umich.edu

One of the fundamental activities in multiagent systems is the exchange of tasks among agents (Davis & Smith 1983). In particular, we are interested in contracts among self-interested agents (Sandholm & Lesser 1995), where a contractor desires to find a contractee that will perform the task for the lowest payment, and a contractee wants to perform tasks that maximize its profit (payment received less the cost of doing the task). Multiple, concurrent contracts take place such that a contract may be retracted because of other contracts.

In our work, we are asking the question: What payment should a contractor offer to maximize its expected utility? If the contractor knows the costs of the agents and knows that the agent(s) with the minimum cost are available, then it can offer to pay some small amount above that cost. But the contractor usually will face uncertainty: it might have only probabilistic information about the costs of other agents for a task, and also about their current and future availability. A risk-averse contractor therefore needs to offer a payment that is not only likely to be acceptable to some contractee, but which also is sufficiently high that the contractee will be unlikely to retract on the deal as other tasks are announced by other contractors. A risk-taking contractor, on the other hand, may want to pay a little less and risk non-acceptance or eventual retraction.

This abstract defines the contractor's decision problem, and presents a contracting strategy by which the contractor can determine an optimal payment to offer.

The contractor's decision problem in the contracting process is to find a payment that maximizes its expected utility. The contractor's utility for the payment, ρ, is defined as $P_S \times U(Payoff_S(\rho)) + P_F \times U(Payoff_F(\rho))$, where $U(.)$ is the utility function, $P_{S/F}$ denote the probability of success (S) and failure (F) of accomplishing a contract, and $Payoff_{S/F}$ are the payoff of S and F, respectively, given ρ.

We have developed a four-step contracting strategy for the contractor to compute $P_{S/F}$ and $Payoff_{S/F}$ and thus to find the best payment to offer.

First, the contractor models the future contracting process stochastically as a Markov Process (MP). An example MP model is shown in Figure 1-(a). State *I* is the initial state, and state *A* is the announced state. State *C* is the contracted state, where the contractor has awarded the task to one of those who accepted its offer. State *S* and *F* are success and failure states, respectively. From *A*, the process goes to *C* if at least one agent accepts the offer. If no agent accepts the offer, the process goes to *F*. The process may go back to *I*, if there are some agents who can perform the task but are busy at the moment. If the contractee retracts the contractor's task (to do other more profitable task(s)), the process goes from *C* to *I*.

Second, the contractor computes the transition probabilities between the MP states. The transition probability from state *i* to state *j* is a function of many factors, such as the payment, the potential contractees' costs, the payments of other contracts, and so on.

Third, having the model and its transition probabilities, the contractor computes $P_{S/F}$ and $Payoff_{S/F}$. We have developed a theoretically-sound method of computing those values based on MP theory (Bhat 1972).

Finally, when $P_{S/F}$ and $Payoff_{S/F}$ are known, finding the optimal payment is an optimization problem. At present, the contractor uses a simple generate-and-test.

An example of a contractor's expected utility is plotted in Figure 1-(b). In this case, the contractor will receive the highest expected utility when it proposes a payment of 9.

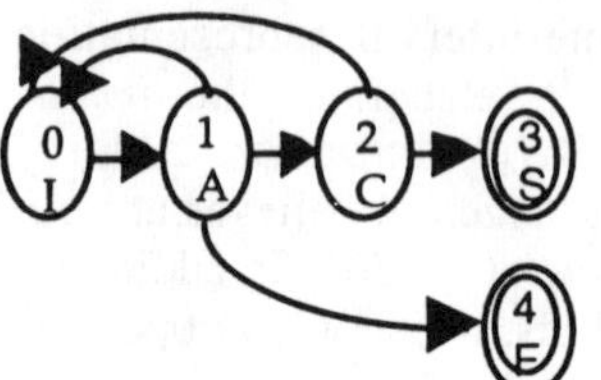

(a) Markov process model

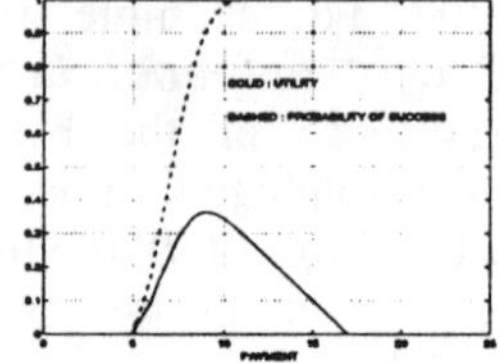

(b) Expected utility vs. payment

Figure 1: A Markov Process Model

We have applied our approach to cases with two tasks, and are currently building a *m*-task model.

This research has been funded in part by Digital Libraries Initiative under CERA IRI-9411287.

References

Bhat, U. 1972. *Elements of Applied Stochastic Processes*: John Wiley & Sons Inc.

Davis, R., and Smith, R. 1983. Negotiation as a Metaphor for Distributed Problem Solving. *AI* 20:63-109.

Sandholm, T., and Lesser, V. 1995. Issues in Automated Negotiation and Electronic Commerce: Extending the Contract Net Framework. In Proc. of ICMAS-95, 328-335.

Learning Procedural Planning Knowledge in Complex Environments

Douglas J. Pearson

Artificial Intelligence Laboratory
The University of Michigan, 1101 Beal Ave.
Ann Arbor, MI 48109, USA
dpearson@umich.edu, http://ai.eecs.umich.edu

Autonomous agents functioning in complex and rapidly changing environments can improve their task performance if they update and correct their world model over the life of the agent. Existing research on this problem can be divided into two classes. First, reinforcement learners that use weak inductive methods to directly modify an agent's procedural execution knowledge. These systems are robust in dynamic and complex environments but generally do not support planning or the pursuit of multiple goals and learn slowly as a result of their weak methods. In contrast, the second category, theory revision systems, learn declarative planning knowledge through stronger methods that use explicit reasoning to identify and correct errors in the agent's domain knowledge. However, these methods are generally only applicable to agents with instantaneous actions in fully sensed domains.

This research explores learning *procedural* planning knowledge through deliberate reasoning about the correctness of an agent's knowledge. As the system, IMPROV, uses a procedural knowledge representation it can efficiently be extended to complex actions that have duration and multiple conditional effects, taking it beyond the scope of traditional theory revision systems. Additionally, the deliberate reasoning about correctness leads to stronger, more directed learning, than is possible in reinforcement learners.

An IMPROV agent's planning knowledge is represented by production rules that encode preconditions and actions of operators. Plans are also procedurally represented as rule sets that efficiently guide the agent in making local decisions during execution. Learning occurs during plan execution whenever the agent's knowledge is insufficient to determine the next action to take. This is a weaker method than traditional plan monitoring, where incorrect predictions trigger the correction method, as prediction-based methods perform poorly in stochastic environments.

IMPROV's method for correcting domain knowledge is primarily based around correcting operator preconditions. This is done by generating and executing alternative plans in decreasing order of expected likelihood of reaching the current goal. Once a successful plan has been discovered, IMPROV uses an inductive learning module to correct the preconditions of the operators used in the set of k plans (successes and failures). Each operator and whether it lead to success or failure is used as a training instance. This *k-incremental* learning is based on the last k instances and results in incremental performance which is required in domains that are time-critical. K-incremental learning is stronger than traditional reinforcement learning as the differences between successful plans and failed plans lead to better credit assignment in determining which operator(s) were incorrect in the failed plans and how the operator's planning knowledge was wrong.

Actions are corrected by recursively re-using the precondition correction method. The agent's domain knowledge is encoded as a *hierarchy* of operators of progressively smaller grain size. The most primitive operators manipulate only a single symbol, guaranteeing they have correct actions. Incorrect actions at higher levels are corrected by changing the preconditions of the sub-operators which implement them. For example, the effects of a brake operator are encoded as more primitive operators which modify the car's speed, tire condition etc. IMPROV's correction method is recursively employed to change the preconditions of these sub-operators and thereby correct the planning knowledge associated with the brake operator's actions. This method allows IMPROV to learn complex actions with durations and conditional effects.

The system has been tested on a robotic simulation and in driving a simulated car. We have demonstrated that k-incremental learning outperforms single instance incremental learning and that a procedural representation supports correcting complex non-instantaneous actions. We have also shown noise-tolerance, tolerance to a large evolving target domain theory and learning in time-constrained environments.

MarketBayes: A Distributed, Market-Based Bayesian Network

David M. Pennock
Artificial Intelligence Laboratory, University of Michigan
1101 Beal Avenue
Ann Arbor, MI 48109-2110
dpennock@eecs.umich.edu

This paper presents initial work on a system called *MarketBayes*, a computational market economy where distributed agents trade in uncertain propositions. For any Bayesian network, we have defined a corresponding economy of goods, consumers and producers that essentially "computes" the same information. Although our research thus far has only verified the *existence* of a market structure capable of Bayesian calculations, our hope is that such a system may address a variety of interesting problems of distributed uncertain reasoning. For example, the economic framework should be well suited for *belief aggregation*, since the bids of numerous agents with varying beliefs, confidence levels and wealth are concisely "summarized" in the going prices of goods.

A Bayesian network structure consists of a set of related propositions with information about how the probabilities of the propositions depend on one another. In a MarketBayes economy, the goods to be bought and sold correspond to these propositions. If a proposition is true, the corresponding good is worth one "dollar"; if the proposition is false, it is worth nothing. Then if the proposition is uncertain, its worth should be exactly the probability that it is true (Hanson 1995), assuming risk neutrality. A MarketBayes economy is a set of goods along with a mix of consumers and producers that trade in these goods. After equilibrium is reached, the prices of the propositions should equal the probabilities that the propositions are true.

In a Bayesian network, links between propositions encode conditional probabilities. For example a single link from proposition A to proposition B is accompanied by the information $P(B|A) = k$ where k is some probability. The same equation can be rewritten as:

$$\Pr(AB) = k \Pr(A) \tag{1}$$

In a MarketBayes economy, the *consumers* effectively implement equations of the form (1). AB and A are propositions or goods, and the consumer's preference for AB is k times that of A. If the ratio of the prices $\Pr(AB)/\Pr(A)$ diverges from k, the consumer will buy or sell according to its preference, driving the ratio toward k.

In a Bayesian network, the laws of probability are inherent in the inference mechanism. In a MarketBayes economy, *producers* ensure that the laws of probability are not violated. For example, the following is an identity in probability theory:

$$\Pr(A) = \Pr(AB) + \Pr(A\bar{B}) \tag{2}$$

Equations of the form (2) are enforced by producers that have the technology to "transform" one A into one AB and one $A\bar{B}$, and vice versa. If the price $\Pr(A)$ diverges from the price $\Pr(AB) + \Pr(A\bar{B})$, a producer will transform one good into the other in order to capitalize on the potential profits—thus driving the two prices together. This type of producer is an *arbitrageur* since it capitalizes on inconsistencies between related prices.

We have found that consumers of the form (1) and producers of the form (2) are sufficient to encode any Bayesian network with binary propositions.

We have built the initial MarketBayes system on top of a distributed auction mechanism called WALRAS (Wellman 1993). Our next research goal is to better characterize any advantages that a market-based probabilistic reasoning mechanism may have over traditional Bayesian networks. We conjecture that the market system will offer a concise and principled way to aggregate beliefs of multiple distributed agents.

References

Hanson, R. D. 1995. Could gambling save science? Encouraging an honest consensus. *Social Epistemology* 9(1):3–33.

Wellman, M. P. 1993. A market-oriented programming environment and its application to distributed multicommodity flow problems. *Journal of Artificial Intelligence Research* 1:1–22.

The Kritzel System for Handwriting Interpretation *

Gaofeng Qian
The University of Texas at Dallas, Artificial Intelligence Lab
P. O. Box 830688, Richardson, Texas 75083-0688
gqian@utdallas.edu

Introduction

We present a new system for recognizing on-line cursive handwriting. The system, which is called the Kritzel System, has four features.

First, the system characterizes handwriting as a sequence of feature vectors. Second, the system adapts to a particular writing style itself through a learning process. Third, the reasoning of the system is formulated in propositional logic with likelihoods. Fourth, the system can be readily linked with other English processing systems for lexical and contextual checking.

System Structure

The Kritzel System is organized into three modules: Interpretation module, Partition module and Learning module.

The Interpretation module extracts local topological features along the pen trajectory, yielding a sequence of time-ordered feature vectors. By scanning the sequence against character templates, it identifies all possible characters and provides a confidence value for them. Using lexical and contextual checking, it selects reasonable words from these candidates.

The Partition module is invoked when the Interpretation module fails to provide the correct word. It asks the user for the exact word written, then partitions the handwriting into discrete segments which correspond to each character of the word.

Using the results of the Partition module, the Learning module analyzes the mistakes of the Interpretation module and adjusts the templates. The Learning module has three alternative ways to adjust the templates. Each of the alternatives is evaluated by a logic program and the best one is selected.

System Implementation

The Kritzel System is implemented in the C programming language. The logic programs are compiled by the Leibniz System.

The Interpretation module implements a five-layer decision pyramid. At layer 1, it reads X-Y coordinate values of the pen trajectory. At layer 2, it extracts local topological features such as maxima, minima, slope and curvature. This yields a sequence of time-ordered feature vectors. At layer 3, it does template matching to find all possible characters along the sequence. At layer 4, it figures out the relationships between each pair of those characters. At layer 5, it searches for the written word, using the Laempel System which performs lexical and contextual checking.

The Partition module is invoked when the result of the Interpretation module is incorrect. First, it locates the tall characters in the word. Then, using all feature vectors of the templates and a reasoning program, it searches for the remaining characters. The search is performed on each range separated by the already identified tall characters. If the word has not been fully segmented, it searches the possible ranges again using selected feature vectors of the characters.

The Learning module analyzes the mistakes made by the Interpretation module. For each mistake, it either does a monotone adjustment, or replaces an infrequently used template in the database, or adds a new template to the database. Monotone adjustment involves changing the thresholds or weights of some parameters of the feature vectors. By checking for conflicts with history and reasoning involving likelihoods, it selects the option which will improve the system the most.

Results To-Date

The Interpretation module, the Partition module and the Learning module have been developed. The system is under integration testing.

References

1. Leibniz System for Logic Programming, Version 4.0, Leibniz, Plano, Texas 75023, 1994
2. Laempel System, Version 1.1, University of Texas at Dallas, Richardson, Texas, 75083-0688, 1995

*Dissertation research supervised by Professor Klaus Truemper and supported in part by the Office of Naval Research under Grant N00014-93-1-0096.

SplitNet: A Dynamic Hierarchical Network Model

Jürgen Rahmel
University of Kaiserslautern, Centre for Learning Systems & Applications
PO Box 3049, 67653 Kaiserslautern, Germany
e-mail:*rahmel@informatik.uni-kl.de*

Graph Properties and Retrieval

We investigate the information that is contained in the structure of a topology preserving neural network. We consider a topological map as a graph G, propose certain properties of the structure and formulate the respective expectable results of network interpretation.

The scenario we deal with is the nearest-neighbor approach to classification. The problems are to find the number and positions of neurons that is useful and efficient for the given data and to retrieve a list L of m nearest neighbors (where m is not necessarily known in advance) for a presented query q that is to be classified.

First, we assume a complete storage of data records in the graph G, i.e. each data record is represented by a neuron, and a perfect topology preservation, which means that an edge between neurons N_i and N_j is in G iff $R_i \cap R_j \neq \emptyset$ where R_i denotes the Voronoi region of node v_i. Thus, the graph corresponds to the Delaunay triangulation of the nodes in G. For this situation, we can formulate an algorithm that is complete at any stage of its incremental retrieval.

Considering complete storage but imperfect topology preservation, we deal with a subgraph of the above mentioned Delaunay graph. We use a topographic function (Villmann et al. 1994) to measure the topology preservation and describe it by the characteristic number t^+ which is the size of the largest topological defect. We can reformulate the previous retrieval algorithm for this case and again its completeness can be shown. The efficiency of the algorithm depends exponentially on the value of t^+, so a good topology preservation of the network is needed.

However, if incomplete storage is investigated, we can show that we have to restrict the neuron distribution in the data space. If we use a quantizing method, we can minimize the probability of incompleteness of the retrieved list of nearest neighbors to a given query.

Guided by these insights, we developed the SplitNet model that provides interpretability by neuron distribution, network topology and hierarchy.

The SplitNet Model

SplitNet is a dynamically growing network that creates a hierarchy of topologically linked one-dimensional Kohonen chains (Kohonen 1990). Topological defects in the chains are detected and resolved by splitting a chain into linked parts, thus keeping the value of t^+ fairly low. These subchains and the error minimizing insertion criterion for new neurons (similar to the one presented in (Fritzke 1993)) provide the quantization properties of the network.

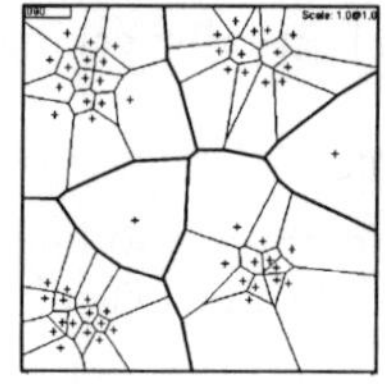

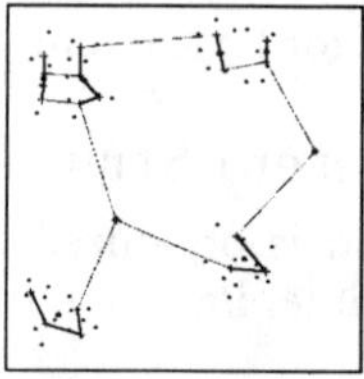

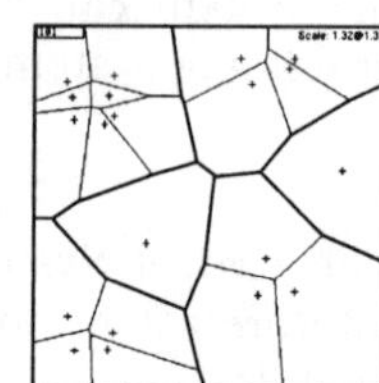

The figure depicts the behaviour of SplitNet for a two-dimensional sample data set (left). SplitNet develops a structure of interconnected chains (middle) and quickly approximates the decision regions of the data records as they appear in the Voronoi diagram (left and right, bold lines). The hierarchy cannot be seen from the figure, but on one hand speeds up the training remarkably and on the other hand provides an additional way of interpreting the grown structure. Different levels of generalization and abstraction are naturally observed.

References

B. Fritzke. Growing cell structures. Technical Report TR-93-026, ICSI, 1993.

T. Kohonen. The self-organizing map. *Proceedings of the IEEE*, 78(9):1464–1480, 1990.

Th. Villmann, R. Der, and Th. Martinetz. A new quantitative measure of topology preservation in Kohonen's feature maps. In *Proc. of the ICNN*, 1994.

Symbolic Performance & Learning in Continuous Environments

Seth O. Rogers

University of Michigan AI Lab
1101 Beal Avenue
Ann Arbor, MI 48109-2110 USA
srogers@eecs.umich.edu

Introduction

We present an approach which enables an agent to learn to achieve goals in continuous environments using a symbolic architecture. Symbolic processing has an advantage over numerical regression techniques because it can interface more easily with other symbolic systems, such as systems for natural language and planning. Our approach is to endow an agent with qualitative "seed" knowledge and allow it to experiment in its environment.

Continuous environments consist of a set of quantitative state variables which may vary over time. The agent represents goals as a user-specified desired value for a variable and a deadline for its achievement. To determine the correct action given the current situation and goals, the agent maps the numbers to symbolic regions, then maps these regions to an action. The learning task of the agent is to develop these mappings.

Performance and Learning

Our system, SPLICE (Symbolic Performance & Learning in Continuous Environments), incorporates a performance module and a learning module. The performance module applies the agent's knowledge to its situation. First the agent maps the numeric variables to hierarchical symbolic regions of varying generality, both for the perceived state and the agent's goals. Then the agent searches the action mappings from specific to general for a match with the symbolic situation and goals. If there is no matching action mapping, the agent uses a qualitative domain model to suggest an action. Finally the agent takes the suggested action.

For learning, the agent waits until the deadline, then evaluates the action's effect to create a new action mapping (a new condition and a new action). Failures may be caused either by overgeneral goal or state conditions. In the first case, the new condition is the most general goal not achieved by the action. In the second case, the new condition is the most general state region different from the situation when the action was first learned. The new action is the linear interpolation of the two closest results straddling the current goal.

Results

Since SPLICE does not explicitly represent domain law equations, it performs about as well in very complex nonlinear domains as simple domains. SPLICE was tested on three successively more detailed and complex automotive simulations. Figure 1 illustrates its performance where the agent is trying to find the right throttle setting for a desired speed. At first, the agent requires several attempts, but over time performance improves. The added detail and complexity of domains 2 and 3 does not slow the learning rate.

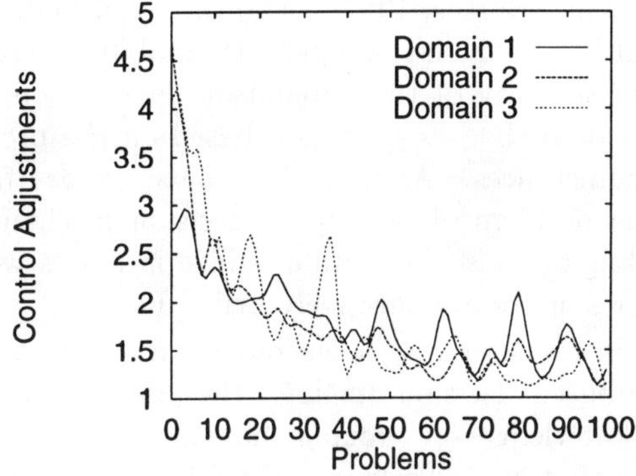

Figure 1: SPLICE performance in three domains.

Conclusion and Future Work

Instead of numerical techniques for adaptive control, SPLICE symbolically represents state variables and searches for mappings, allowing SPLICE to incorporate other symbolic systems, such as a qualitative reasoning module. Our current research has focussed on learning action mappings and left region mapping to a static binary division scheme. We are extending SPLICE in a number of dimensions, including multiple goals and hierarchical control structures. Our final objective is to demonstrate SPLICE in complex realistic environments, such as airplane flight.

Effects of local information on group behavior

Shounak Roychowdhury, Neeraj Arora, & Sandip Sen
Department of Mathematical & Computer Sciences,
University of Tulsa
600 South College Avenue, Tulsa, Ok 74104-3189.
e-mail: {roy,arora,sandip}@euler.mcs.utulsa.edu

Researchers in the field of Distributed Artificial Intelligence have studied the effects of local decision-making on overall system performance in both cooperative and self-interested agent groups (Bond & Gasser, 1988) . The performance of individual agents depends critically on the quality of information available to it about local and global goals and resources. Whereas in general it is assumed that the more accurate and up-to-date the available information, the better is the expected performance of the individual and the group, this conclusion can be challenged in a number of scenarios.

The populace in human societies tend to look for opportunities and search for better opportunities in their environment (Bartos, 1967) . The theory of migration in social behavior and occupational mobility suggests that the stability of the population depends on how an individual chooses its action based on the prevailing circumstances. As agent designers, we are faced with the problem of developing decision mechanisms that allow agent societies to stabilize in states where system resources are effectively utilized.

In this research, we focus on a particular aspect of distributed decision-making: the effect of limited global knowledge on group behavior. The research question that we are asking is the following: Can limited local knowledge be a boon rather than a bane in a multiagent system? To investigate this issue we use a resource utilization problem where a number of agents are distributed between several identical resources. We assume that the cost of using any resource is directly proportional to its usage. This cost can be due to a delay in processing of the task in hand, or a reduction in the quality of the resource due to congestion. Hence, there is a justified urge in agents to seek out and move to resource with lesser usage. Other researchers have shown that such systems can exhibit oscillatory or chaotic behavior where agents move back and forth between resources (Hogg & Huberman 1991; Kephart, Hogg & Huberman 1989) resulting in ineffective utilization of system resources. Whereas asynchrony, heterogeneous agent decision mechanisms, etc. has been suggested as possible means for solving the instability problem, our proposed solution of using locally differing global views is a novel mechanism to introduce asymmetry in group decisions that expedites group stability.

We have developed a decision mechanism to be used by individual agents to decide whether to continue using the same resource or to relinquish it in the above-mentioned resource utilization problem. We show that a spatially local view of an agent can be effectively used in a decision procedure that enable the system to quickly converge to a stable optimal global state (in terms of effective resource utilization). In addition, increasing the information available to an agent increases the time taken to reach the desired equilibrium state. We explain this phenomenon with a probabilistic analysis. This analysis also suggests a promising line of future work where adaptive agents use varying amounts of global information to further accelerate convergence.

References

Otomar J. Bartos. *Simple Models of Group Behavior.* Columbia University Press, New York, NY, 1967.

Alan H. Bond and Les Gasser. *Readings in Distributed Artificial Intelligence.* Morgan Kaufmann Publishers, San Mateo, CA, 1988.

Tad Hogg and Bernardo A. Huberman. Controlling chaos in distributed systems. *IEEE Transactions on Systems, Man, and Cybernetics*, 21(6), December 1991. (Special Issue on Distributed AI).

J. O. Kephart, T. Hogg, and B. A. Huberman. Dynamics of computational ecosystems: Implications for DAI. In Michael N. Huhns and Les Gasser, editors, *Distributed Artificial Intelligence*, volume 2 of *Research Notes in Artificial Intelligence.* Pitman, 1989.

Automated Formulation of Constraint Satisfaction Problems

Mihaela Sabin and **Eugene C. Freuder**

Department of Computer Science
University of New Hampshire
Durham, New Hampshire 03824, USA
mcs,ecf@cs.unh.edu

A wide variety of problems can be represented as constraint satisfaction problems (CSPs), and once so represented can be solved by a variety of effective algorithms. However, as with other powerful, general AI problem solving methods, we must still address the task of moving from a natural statement of the problem to a formulation of the problem as a CSP. This research addresses the task of automating this problem formulation process, using logic puzzles as a testbed. Beyond problem formulation per se, we address the issues of effective problem formulation, i.e. finding formulations that support more efficient solution, as well as incremental problem formulation that supports reasoning from partial information and are congenial to human thought processes.

A CSP is defined by a set of *variables* with their associated *domains of values* and a set of *constraints* which restrict the combinations of values allowed. The example in Fig. 1 shows a logic puzzle text and a corresponding constraint network representation. In CSP terms, associated with the introductory portion of the logic puzzle there are 8 variables, each variable with the same domain of values, the tower positions. All the variables are nodes in the constraint network with the values labeling them. Due to the structure of the problem (no two acrobats, as well as no two items, correspond to the same position in the tower), the CSP variables are partitioned into two *cliques*, `Acrobats` and `Items`, with disequality constraints (#) between every pair of variables in each clique (drawn as edges in the constraint network and marked as `initial` constraints in the figure).

The current implementation of the translation tool handles the translation of the clues into the CSP constraints. The translation scheme recognizes patterns such as *not*, *above* and *below*, that match logic puzzle clues in the input, and applies the translation rules to generate corresponding `clue` constraints. The figure shows the binary constraints as bold continuous lines, drawn as edges and labeled #, < and >, and the unary constraints as deleted (hashed) values.

More efficient CSP formulations are possible by exploiting the inherent structure of the problem (e.g. the two cliques in our example) or the semantics of the constraints. The enhanced translation scheme defines specialized consistency functions attached to each constraint. As we build the representation, with each clue parsed, corresponding local consistency can be performed that may add `inferred` constraints, examples of which are shown in the figure as bold, dotted lines. Postponing search as much as possible while locally propagating the available, partial information seems to reflect human problem solving behavior. The acquired reasoning power is encoded in the form of restricted domains and additional constraints which support more efficient problem solving.

Acknowledgments

This material is based on work supported by the National Science Foundation under Grant No. IRI-9207633 and Grant No. IRI-9504316 and on work supported by Digital Equipment Corporation. This work profited from discussion with Mohammed H. Sqalli. We thank Nancy Schuster and Dell Magazines for permission to reproduce material from *Dell Logic Puzzles*.

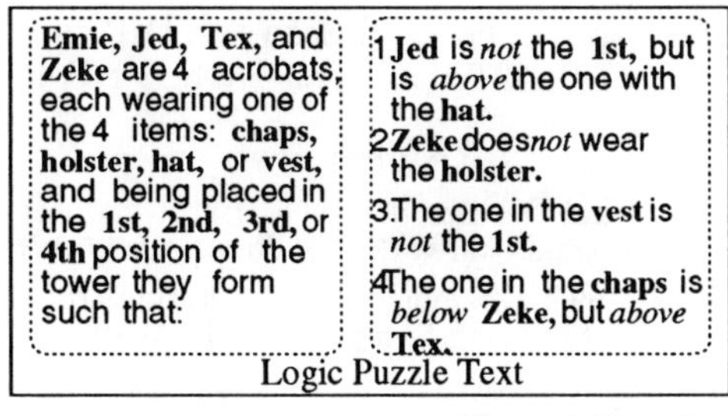

Logic Puzzle Text

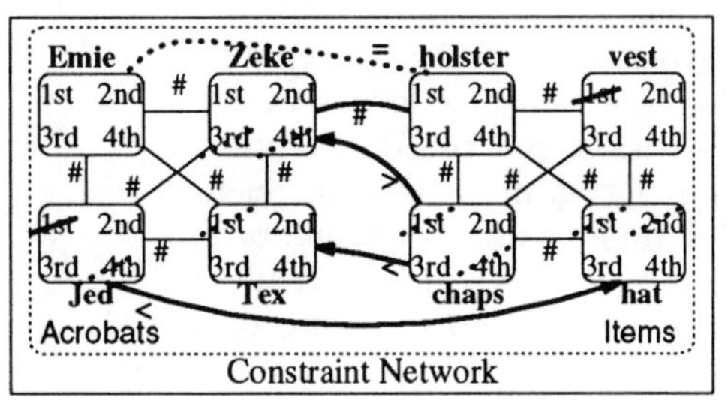

Constraint Network

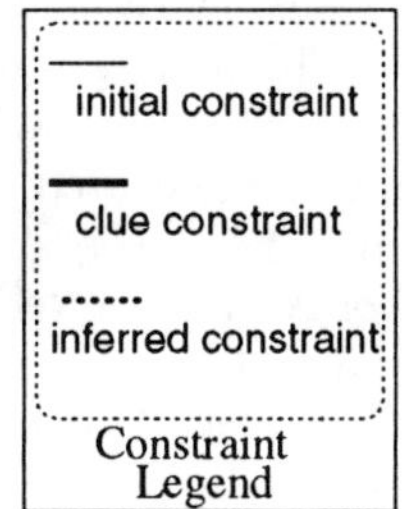

Constraint Legend

Figure 1. From logic puzzle statement to CSP formulation

Dynamic Constraint-based Planning in Trauma Management

Moninder Singh*

Dept. of Computer and Information Science
University of Pennsylvania, Philadelphia, PA 19104-6389
msingh@gradient.cis.upenn.edu

This research deals with planning in domains with dynamically changing, multiple, interacting goals. What distinguishes this work from reactive planners (e.g. (Firby 1987)) is the fact that the goals for which planning is done are *not known in advance*; rather, goals are formed and change rapidly during the planning process itself. Although planners that produce appropriate plans exist for such domains (Rymon *et al.* 1993), we want a planner that also provides a basis for explaining why some action is chosen over another or why some goal is no longer relevant etc., which is necessary for effective decision support (Gertner 1994).

I am developing an efficient, 3-level, dynamic constraint based planner for one such domain, trauma management. The three levels show how plans are naturally formed in this domain. The top level corresponds to goals, the second level corresponds to the various, alternative procedures that can be used to address these goals, while the third level corresponds to the actions that constitute these procedures. Different kinds of constraints are added at each level. For example, urgency constraints (e.g. "shock" must be treated first) hold between goals, while precedence constraints (e.g. perform IVP before arteriogram) hold at the action level. Constraints at higher levels are inherited by the lower levels. The network is dynamically updated by adding/deleting nodes and/or modifying constraints as goals are created, discarded or achieved. If an action/procedure cannot be done, or a goal cannot be addressed, the corresponding nodes are deactivated, but not removed. Then, if the situation changes later, the nodes are reactivated and again considered during the planning process. This structure, similar to dynamic constraint networks (Dechter *et al.* 1988), offers several distinct advantages.

First, by maintaining consistency and recording justifications for elimination/selection of actions, easy critiquing is facilitated. Consider a scenario involving, among others, the goals of treating a tension pneumothorax (TP) as well as ruling out a pericardial tamponade (PT) and a renal injury (RI) in a patient in shock. Urgency constraints are added requiring that TP, RI and PT be addressed before realizing other goals or performing time consuming actions. For treating the TP, a chest tube is the only option. However, making the network consistent and recording justifications not only causes a needle aspiration to be chosen for diagnosing the PT (over the normally preferred but lengthy ultrasound due to urgency constraints), but also enables the system to explain its choice.

*This work is funded by an IBM Cooperative fellowship.

Second, the three level structure with different, dynamic constraints at each level makes the planning process very efficient. In the above example, for ruling out a RI, an IVP is chosen over the normally preferred CT_scan (never done if patient in shock). Now, suppose that the planner considers scheduling an arteriogram to address a non-urgent goal. Although, precedence constraints require that an arteriogram precede an IVP, urgency constraints requiring the IVP to be performed first cause the arteriogram to be deactivated. This information is propagated upwards, thus deactivating all procedures involving an arteriogram. This causes alternative procedures to be chosen for all goals corresponding to the deactivated procedures; if there is no other procedure to satisfy some goal, the goal is left unaddressed. If planning is done using backtracking or a 'flat' constraint network, this would not be discovered until the later goals are planned for.

Third, the current plan can be easily modified to incorporate new information and/or goal changes, without re-planning from scratch. In the above example, assume that a chest tube relieves the shock. This causes the urgency constraints to be eliminated. Since nodes corresponding to the ultrasound, arteriogram and IVP (along with the relevant constraints) were only deactivated and not removed from the network, they are simply reactivated. This enables the planner to easily modify the current plan and schedule the ultrasound (preferred over needle aspiration) followed by an arteriogram (since CT_scan and IVP can now be done later) and a CT_scan (preferred over IVP).

References

Dechter, R. and Dechter, A. 1988. Belief maintenance in dynamic constraint networks. In *Proc. AAAI*, 178–183.

Gertner, A. 1994. Ongoing critiquing during trauma management. AAAI Spring Symp. on AI in Medicine.

Firby, R. J. 1987. An investigation into reactive planning in complex domains. In *Proc. AAAI*, 202–206.

Rymon, R., Webber, B., and Clarke, J. 1993. Progressive horizon planning. *IEEE Trans. on SMC* 23(6):1551–1560.

Blocking as a middle-ground for step-order Commitments in Planning

Biplav Srivastava
Advisor: Subbarao Kambhampati
Department of Computer Science and Engineering
Arizona State University, Tempe AZ 85287-5406
{biplav,rao}@asu.edu

Partial order planners commit only to the relative positions of the steps in the plan, and leave both their absolute positions as well as the relative distance between the different steps unspecified until the end of planning. Although this is seen as an advantageous feature of partial order planning, it can sometimes be a mixed-blessing. Because the relative distances between the steps are unspecified, any unordered step may be able to come between any existing steps and cause interactions and the planner may spend inordinate effort considering all possible interleavings of the subplans of the individual goals. This happens in cases where top-level goals are serializable but have long sub-plans which have internal interactions, plan-space planners would consider all simple-establishments and threats between steps of a the subplan of a top-level goal g_i (represented by P_{g_i}) and P_{g_j} which could affect its performance drastically. State-space planners, on the other hand, fix both the distance and position, and this is often more commitment than is needed, causing extensive backtracking (Barrett & Weld 1994).

We are investigating a middle ground between these two approaches, that we call "blocking" refinement. The essential idea is to work on individual subgoals one after another in LIFO fashion using the plan-space refinements. Once the complete subplan for one individual toplevel goal is constructed, the steps comprising that goal are "blocked" together by posting contiguity constraints between steps (Kambhampati & Srivastava 1995). To ensure completeness, we also leave the un-blocked version of the plan in the search space. Since no other steps can come between blocked steps, the planner will not waste time considering all possible interleavings of the subplans. Once all the top level goals are handled this way, any inter-block interactions between the blocked subplans are resolved (thereby implicitly sequencing the subplans of the individual goals). Notice that in contrast to partial order planning this approach fixes the distance between two steps in P_{g_i} but not the position of P_{g_i} with respect to P_{g_j}.

Variant of D^1S^2 domain			
Op	Prec	Add	Del
A_i (i odd)	I_i	M_i, he	hf
A_i (i even)	I_i	M_i, hf	he
B_i (i odd)	M_i, he	G_i	he
B_i (i even)	M_i, hf	G_i	hf

We implemented blocking on Universal Classical Planner (UCP). The implementation required distinguishing between inter-step, inter-block, and block-step conflicts in the plan and handling them at appropriate times. We tested the effectiveness of this approach in a variation of the D^1S^2 domain used in (Barrett & Weld 1994). Our domain contains a set of goals of the form g_i which can be achieved by action B_i. B_i in turn needs condition M_i given by action A_i. A_i also provides he to B_i, and B_i deletes he. Because of this latter condition, the subplans for individual toplevel goals will have many interactions, even though the overall plans are serializable. Figure 1 shows that blocking of steps of a top-level goal in a serializable domain improves performance over plan-space (PS) refinement. As UCP allows forward state-space (FSS) and means-ends analysis (MEA) refinements, we also tested them on this domain. Blocking not only visits lesser nodes than FSS, MEA and PS refinements, but also takes lesser time.

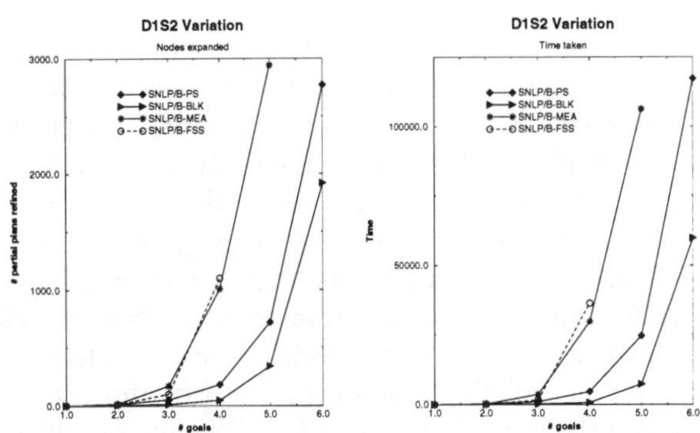

Figure 1: Plots illustrating the performance of blocking in D^1S^2 variation. Blocking performed the best among PS, Blocking, FSS and MEA

These results show the promise of the blocking refinement as a middle-ground between state-space and plan-space approaches in terms of step order commitment. In our future work, we will attempt to provide a better characterization of the classes of domains which could benefit from blocking, using theoretical and empirical analyses.

References

Barrett, A., and Weld, D. 1994. Partial order planning: Evaluating possible efficiency gains. *Artificial Intelligence* 67:71--112.

Kambhampati, S., and Srivastava, B. 1995. Universal classical planning: An algorithm for unifying state space and plan space planning approaches. *Current trends in AI Planning: EWSP 95, IOS Press.*

Experimentation-Driven Operator Learning

Kang Soo Tae
Department of Computer Science and Engineering
University of Texas at Arlington
Arlington, TX 76019, Box 19015
tae@cse.uta.edu

Expert-provided operator descriptions are expensive, incomplete, and incorrect. Given the assumptions of noise-free information and an completely-observable state, OBSERVER can autonomously learn and refines new operators through observation and practice (Wang 1995). WISER, our learning system, relaxes these assumptions and learns operator preconditions through experimentation utilizing imperfect expert-provided knowledge. Our decision-theoretic formula calculates a probably best state S' for experimentation based on the imperfect knowledge. When a robotic action is executed successfully for the first time in a state S, the corresponding operator's initial preconditions are learned as *parameterized S*. We empirically show the number of training examples required to learn the initial preconditions as a function of the amount of injected error. The learned preconditions contain all the necessary positive literals, but no negative literals.

Unless given a rule like *arm-empty* $\rightarrow \neg$*holding(X)*, a robot may believe a state, {(arm-empty), (holding *box)*}, to be possible due to unavoidable perceptual alias. The plan execution in this state is unreliable. To make a planner robust in a noisy state, WISER learns constraining negative preconditions by interconnecting two types of logic systems used in planning systems. The state representation uses two-value logic plus the Closed-World Assumption and the operator representation uses three-value logic. Let L represent all the predicates known to WISER and P the predicates true in S. By CWA, N, the predicates not true in S, is defined as $\{L - P\}$. WISER induces preconditions from $S^* = \{P \cup \neg N\}$, which prevent inconsistent actions in a noisy state.

Let the instantiated operators, iop_i and iop_j, be obtained from an operator *op* by instantiating each parameter of *op* to the same object respectively except that one parameter is instantiated to different objects of the same type, say a for iop_i and b for iop_j. iop_j is obtained by substituting b for a. In any state S, if the preconditions for iop_i and iop_j are both satisfied (or not satisfied) and their respective actions have the same (parameterized) effects on S, the two objects a and b are called *homogeneous* in terms of *op*. For example, if both *box1* and *box2* can be picked up by an agent, they are homogeneous to the PICKUP operator. Homogeneous objects of a type form an equivalence relation, partitioning the type into subtypes. If an object of a subtype is tested for the operator, no additional object of the subtype needs to be tested further.

WISER adopts the *abstract domain assumption* that every object in a type belongs to one and only one subtype. Therefore, we can experiment with an operator using only one object of a type for a parameter. This assumption drastically reduces the size of the search space. The abstraction of objects is inevitable in a real domain. The resulting representation is, however, inherently incomplete. The robot must be able to adjust its initial definitions, learned under the *abstract domain assumption*, in complex environments composed of heterogeneous objects by decomposing a type into many subtypes. The traditional approach, where a human-provided fixed type hierarchy is given, cannot handle this problem.

We handle this type classification problem using C4.5. Some unobservable predicates, such as *carriable(X)*, are used in classifying a type into subtypes. An object is described as a vector of observable features. The robot initially learns overly-general preconditions by assuming that every object of a box type is *carriable*. Experimentation acts as an environmental feedback and produces positive and negative training examples for [*carriable*] subtype of the box type. C4.5 selects the features to distinguish between positive and negative examples. The unobservable functional concept is represented by structural descriptions consisting of observable features, satisfying the operational criterion. We empirically demonstrate the learner's ability to generate more accurate definitions with each learning iteration.

References

Wang, X. 1995. Learning by observation and practice: An incremental approach for planning operator acquisition. In *Proceedings of the 12th International Conference on Machine Learning*.

Hybrid Knowledge- and Databases

Merwyn Taylor

Department of Computer Science
Univeristy of Maryland
College Park, MD 20742 USA
mtaylor@cs.umd.edu

In the modern era, databases have been created spanning many domains. However, these databases do not contain general knowledge about their respective domains. For example, whereas a medical database could contain an entry for a patient with some medical disorder, it would not normally contain taxonomic information about medical disorders, known causal agents, symptoms, etc. Collections of this sort of general information are usually called knowledge bases and powerful tools have been developed for querying these collections in complex and flexible ways. The research described in this abstract aims to develop methodologies for merging existing databases with knowledge bases, so that the power and flexibility of knowledge base technology can be applied to existing collections of data.[1]

In traditional DB's, queries are limited to those that do not reference general information about the domains in which the DB's are created. To support queries that reference such information, one can merge a DB created in some domain with a knowledge base of the domain to create a hybrid knowledge base / database. Merging a knowledge base with a database extends the range of queries that can be issued. In some cases, ad hoc queries can be simplified when applied to the hybrid KB/DB. Besides expanding the range of queries that can be issued, a hybrid KB/DB also lends itself to research in attribute oriented data mining techniques.

In this research, a frame based semantic network, Parka, developed by the PLUS group at the University of Maryland was used to facilitate the merger of a KB with a DB.

As an example, we are working with a medical database of about 20,000 OB/GYN patients. The DB is a single table with 70+ columns. Using the original DB, a user could query the DB to list all patients with a particular type of infection. But if the user wanted to query the DB to list all patients with infections known to be caused by any form of bacteria, the query would have to be expressed as a disjunction over all the infections that the user knows to be caused by bacteria. Since the DB does not contain a general concept of *bacteria,* the query would have to be constructed without any references to that term. Rather it would look something like:

select *patient*
from *ptable*
where *infection* = *'Peritonitis'* **OR**
infection = *'Pyelonephritis'* **OR ...**

This requirement limits the number of users that can issue interesting queries to those that have an extensive background in OB/GYN. With a hybrid KB/DB, a broader spectrum of users can issue interesting queries in a form much simpler than the one mentioned above. We have developed a hybrid OB/GYN KB/DB from the DB. (It contains 60,000 frames and 1.3 million assertions!) Figure 1 illustrates how the previous query can be expressed in a simpler form using Parka's Graphical Query By Example System.

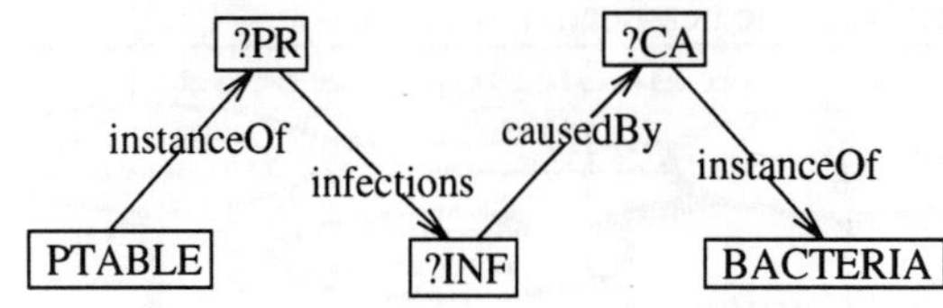

Figure 1: Sample Parka Query

In my current research I am developing general methodologies for merging DB's and KB's that allow this technique to be more widely applied. I am investigating techniques that automatically convert relational DB's to semantic networks by analyzing the schemas of relational DB's. I am also investigating techniques to automatically extract and integrate parts of existing KB's, such as NIH's medical term ontology, UMLS.

[1]This research was supported by AF contract F49609410422

Learning Models for Multi-Source Integration

Sheila Tejada Craig A. Knoblock Steven Minton
University of Southern California/ISI
4676 Admiralty Way
Marina del Rey, California 90292
{tejada,knoblock,minton}@isi.edu

Because of the growing number of information sources available through the internet there are many cases in which information needed to solve a problem or answer a question is spread across several information sources. For example, when given two sources, one about comic books and the other about super heroes, you might want to ask the question "Is Spiderman a Marvel Super Hero?" This query accesses both sources; therefore, it is necessary to have information about the relationships of the data within each source and between sources to properly access and integrate the data retrieved. The SIMS information broker captures this type of information in the form of a model. All the information sources map into the model providing the user a single interface to multiple sources.

Presently, models are manually constructed by human experts who are familiar with the data stored in the sources. Automation of this task would improve efficiency and accuracy, especially for large information sources. We have conducted preliminary work in automating model construction. There has been related work conducted in this area (Perkowitz & Etzioni, 1995), which has focused on learning the attributes of sources. Their approach assumes that it has an initial model of the information to be learned from the perspective sources.

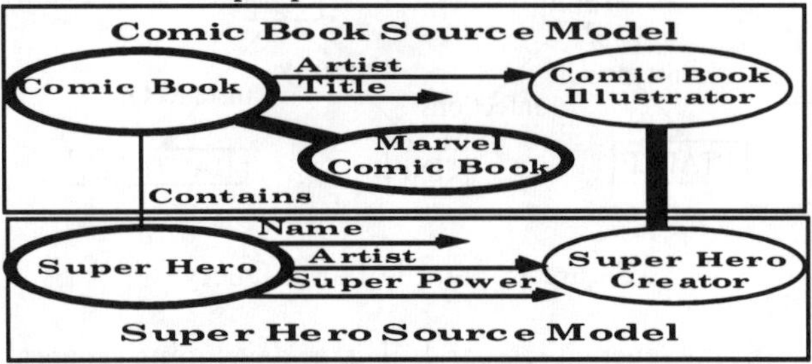

The diagram depicts a partial model of two sources. The ovals in the diagram represent classes of information and the lines describe the relationships between the classes. The two types of classes are basic classes and composite classes. Members of a basic class are single-valued elements, such as strings; while the members of a composite class are objects, which can have several attributes. **Comic Book Illustrator** and **Super Hero Creator** are basic classes; and **Comic Book**, **Marvel Comic Book**, and **Super Hero** are all represented as composite classes. Arrows represent the attributes of objects, and the thick lines represent the superclass/subclass relationships between classes.

Our approach to learning models examines all of the data to extract the relationships needed. Learning the model is an iterative process which involves user interaction. The user can make corrections or specify an information source to be added or deleted. The model proposed to the user is generated by heuristics we have developed to derive the necessary relationships from the data. These heuristics involve creating abstract descriptions of the data. We have assumed the data is stored as tables.

Properties of the data, such as type and range, are contained in an abstract description. For each column of data, an abstract description is computed. Each description corresponds to a basic class. For the basic class **Super Hero Creator** an example of an abstract description would be alphabetic strings with minimum length 8 and maximum 12. These descriptions are then used to help determine the superclass/subclass relationships that exist between the basic classes, like between **Comic Book Illustrator** and **Super Hero Creator**.

Potentially, all basic classes would need to be checked with every other basic class for a superclass/subclass relationship, but now only classes which have similar descriptions are tested. So, for example, the basic class **Super Hero Creator** would only be checked with other basic classes that contain alphabetic strings whose lengths are within the range specified in the abstract description. Our experimental results show that in every case using these restrictions reduced the running time and number of comparisions performed.

We are planning to apply statistical methods to assist in constructing the model, as well as integrating a natural language knowledge base into this process to help determine whether classes are semantically related. The relationships between the basic classes will be useful in the later steps of the modeling process which are to determine the relationships between composite class.

References

Ambite, J., Y. Arens, N. Ashish, C. Chee, C. Hsu, C. Knoblock, and S. Tejada. The SIMS Manual, Technical Report ISI/TM-95-428,1995.

Perkowitz, M. & Etzioni, O. Category Translation: Learning to Understand Information on the Internet. The International Joint Conference on Artificial Intelligence, Montreal, 1995.

Rabbi: exploring the inner world through stories

Marina Umaschi

MIT Media Laboratory
E15-320R, 20 Ames St.
Cambridge, MA 02139
marinau@media.mit.edu

In the oral tradition, stories were told by the elder sages in order to give indirect advice. Today most stories are told in order to entertain. While some research on storytelling systems has focused on drama/theater metaphors and adventure/mystery simulation games (Bates et al., 1995), my research emphasizes the counseling and self-awareness possibilities of storytelling.

I am exploring how storytelling systems can enable people to tell and listen to personal stories in order to learn about themselves. I am developing an authoring tool that allows children to create their own storytellers in order to start thinking about the complexity of meaning in communication.

In the light of this interest, I designed "Rabbi", a conversational storytelling system that simulates a rabbi with a repertoire of Hasidic stories to offer as indirect counsel. It approaches narrative through a psycho-social theory of discourse which looks not only at the linguistic structures of the text but also at the socio-cultural context in which the contract between teller and listener occurs. "Rabbi" uses rich interaction instead of complex matching and indexing techniques (Schank et al. 1981; Domeshek, 1992) to provide a meaningful experience for the user.

Research showed that the construction of emotional believable characters is requisite to maintain the suspension of disbelief (Weizenbaum, 1976; Bates, 1995). "Rabbi" constructs his "persona" through the conversational turns in order to set a socio-cultural context without limiting the interaction and breaking expectations.

System Design

The system parses user input and assigns prominence to keywords. To make the match with the Hasidic story, nouns and verbs in the user's story are augmented with synonyms, hyponyms and hypernyms found through WordNet (Miller et al 1993). Each Hasidic story in the data-base is indexed with a set of three descriptors: nouns, verbs and Commandments, that are weighted more heavily because they set up the story domain according to one of the universal values stated in the Ten Commandments. The conversational interaction is built around seven phases of an encounter with a rabbi (Schachter-Shalomi, 1991) :

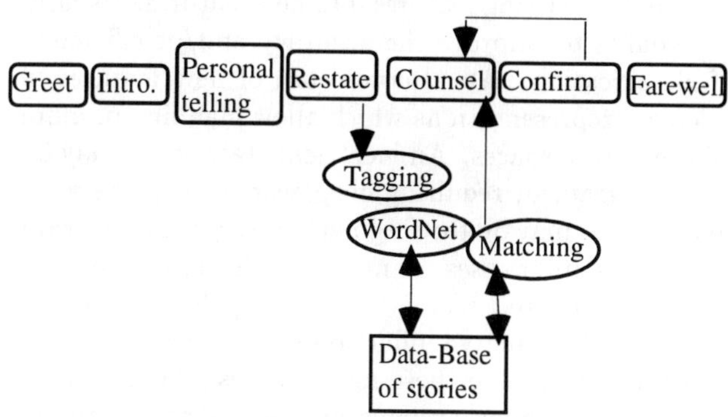

Conclusions

People using "Rabbi" expressed their need to tell personal stories. The fact that subjects found the Hasidic stories to be coherent with their own stories, in spite of the primitive matching technique, shows that given the appropriate socio-cultural context, construction of meaningful interpretation is possible. The system need not to be intelligent, but rather appears believable by projecting a personality to the user. Current work focuses on what kind of discourse structures the system should parse in order to abstract the point made by a personal story.

References

Bates, J. et al. 1995 *Interactive Story Systems: Plot & Character,*. In AAAI Working Notes Spring Symposium.
Domeshek, Eric. *"Do the right thing: a component theory for indexing stories as social advice"*. PHD Thesis Northwestern University, 1992.
Miller, G. et al. 1993.*WordNet: An On-line Lexical Database.* (paper found through ftp claritz.princeton.edu)
Schachter-Shalomi, Z. 1991 *Spiritual intimacy, a study of counseling in Hasidism*, NJ: Jason Aronson.
Schank, R. and Riesbeck, C. 1981 *Inside Computer Understanding.* Lawrence Elbaum.
Weizenbaum, J. 1976.*Computer power and human reason.* SF: Freeman and Co.

Constructive Induction of Features for Planning

Michael van Lent
Artificial Intelligence Laboratory
University of Michigan
1101 Beal Avenue
Ann Arbor, MI, 48109-2110
vanlent@umich.edu

Constructive induction techniques use constructors to combine existing features into new features. Usually the goal is to improve the accuracy and/or efficiency of classification. An alternate use of new features is to create representations which allow planning in more efficient state spaces. An inefficient state space may be too fine grained, requiring deep search for plans with many steps, may be too fragmented, requiring separate plans for similar cases, or may be unfocused, resulting in poorly directed search. Modifying the representation with constructive induction can improve the state space and overcome these inefficiencies. Additionally, since most learning systems depend on good domain features, constructive induction will compliment the action of other algorithms.

This abstract describes a system that uses constructive induction to generate new state features in the Tic-Tac-Toe (TTT) domain. The system generates features like win, block, and fork that are useful for planning in TTT. TTT has been chosen as an initial domain because it is simple, the features are well defined, and it is clear what domain knowledge has been added. Additionally, previous work on constructive induction in the TTT domain provides a starting point.

The CITRE system (Matheus & Rendell 1989) creates a decision tree with primitive TTT features (the contents of the board positions) and uses a binary *and* constructor to incrementally combine features selected to improve the decision tree. Domain knowledge filters out less promising features. CITRE minimally improves classification of board positions but cannot generate some types of planning features. Our system has fewer constraints and includes extensions that expand the space of constructible features. For example, n-ary conjunction (not binary) is used to combine existing features into more complex features and n-ary disjunction groups symmetrical versions of the same feature. Also, constructors are applied to all pairs of features, including a new "player to move" feature, without using domain knowledge as a filter.

The perfect "X win" feature is a disjunction of the 24 ways two X's in a row can appear in TTT. Each such row is represented by a conjunction of primitive features (e.g. *and* (pos11=X) (pos12=X) (to-move=X)). To construct new features, the system calculates the information gain of each existing feature. Due to the symmetry of TTT states, symmetrical features have equal information gains and the same parent primitive features and can be correctly grouped into disjunctions (e.g. *or* (pos11=X) (pos13=X) (pos31=X) (pos33=X)). Taking advantage of symmetrical features is one example of correcting a fragmented state space with constructive induction. The system then constructs more sets of features from the conjunction of elements of the disjunctive features (e.g. *and* (pos11=X) (pos12=X)). These sets of conjunctive features are again combined into symmetrical disjunctions by comparing information gain and parent features used. Conjunction and disjunction alternate, incrementally building complex features. This algorithm generates and selects features, such as win and block, which CITRE cannot generate. Win and block are each represented by 3 features covering the symmetries of the diagonal lines, the middle lines, and the outer lines. The fork and block-fork features are generated but criteria for selecting them need to be developed.

This constructive induction system creates useful features for planning in TTT. An immediate next step is to apply the system to more complex domains. Also, the present system inefficiently applies the conjunction constructor to all pairs of features. In the same way CITRE selects features to improve an existing decision tree, our system could use planning knowledge to direct its selection of features.

References

Matheus, C., and Rendell, L. 1989. Constructive induction on decision trees. In *Proceedings of the Eleventh International Joint Conference on Artificial Intelligence*, 645–650.

Agents Modeling Agents in Information Economies

José M. Vidal* and Edmund H. Durfee
Artificial Intelligence Laboratory, University of Michigan.
1101 Beal Avenue, Ann Arbor, Michigan 48109-2110
jmvidal@umich.edu

Our goal is to design and build agents that act intelligently when placed in an agent-based information economy, where agents buy and sell services (e.g. thesaurus, search, task planning services, etc.). The economy we are working in is the University of Michigan Digital Library (UMDL), a large scale multidisciplinary effort to build an infrastructure for the delivery of library services [2]. In contrast with a typical economy, an information economy deals in goods and services that are often derived from unique sources (authors, analysts, etc.), so that many goods and services are not interchangeable. Also, the cost of replicating and transporting goods is usually negligible, and the quality of goods and services is difficult to measure objectively: even two sources with essentially the same information might appeal to different audiences. Thus, each agent has its own assessment of the quality of goods and services delivered.

Our emphasis, therefore, is not on developing market mechanisms for traditional economies with interchangeable goods/services, but rather for those where each participant might be unique and inscrutable from the perspective of others. In order to make good decisions, an agent in such an economy must: (A) Determine exactly what services other agents provide and at what price. (B) Avoid agents whose services are not reliable or needed, and form teams with those that provide needed services. (C) Decide how much to charge and whom to target. We believe these can be accomplished if an agent builds models of how others appear to be assessing quality and/or establishing prices, and even how others are modeling others in these ways. Our previous work [1] considered such recursive models, and gave algorithms that trade-off the time costs of using the deeper recursive models versus the costs of taking a possibly inferior action. However, it assumed the agents already had correct deeper models of others.

The next problem to solve is how agents can acquire models of other agents. We have built agents that provide some useful services in the UMDL, but do not charge for them. As we incorporate the ability to buy and sell, the purchasing agents will have to make more complex decisions when deciding who to buy from, while the sellers will need to make decisions about how much to charge. Our research plan is to explore this economy, by expanding our agents into three types, based on their modeling capabilities. That is, we built agents that: (1) Do not build models of other agents. (2) Build one-level or "policy" models of other agents, based on observations of their behavior. (3) Build intentional/two-level models of others, which are composed of an intentional model of the agent being modeled, and the one-level models it has of others.

It should be clear that agents with no models of other agents cannot predict what others will do. Therefore, they either try to maximize their expected payoffs, given their ignorance of others' behaviors, or try to minimize their possible losses. Agents that are capable of building simple models are able to determine which agents have, in the past, delivered the best service. They have an advantage over agents that do not model and, in fact, are able to cheat them (i.e. deliver a lower quality service) and get away with it since, with no models, no records of their actions are kept. Agents with two-level models should be able to better predict what the competition will do (i.e. to "get inside their heads") giving them a small advantage over the competition. We are testing these assertions to determine exactly when it is advantageous to use deeper models. Preliminary results show correlations between the heterogeneity of the population, price volatility, and the benefits of using deeper models.

[1] J.M. Vidal and E.H. Durfee. Recursive Agent Modeling Using Limited Rationality. *ICMAS* 95.

[2] M. Wellman, *et.al.* Toward Inquiry-based Education through Interacting Software Agents. *IEEE Computer*. May 96.

*Supported by NSF/DARPA/NASA DL Initiative.

Optimal Factory Scheduling using Stochastic Dominance A*

Peter R. Wurman
Artificial Intelligence Laboratory
University of Michigan
1101 Beal Avenue
Ann Arbor, MI, 48109-2110
pwurman@umich.edu

Generating optimal production schedules for manufacturing facilities is an area of great theoretical and practical importance. During the last decade, an effort has been made to reconcile the techniques developed by the AI and OR communities. The work described here aims to continue in this vein by showing how a class of well-defined stochastic scheduling problems can be mapped into a general search procedure. This approach improves upon other methods by handling the general case of multidimensional stochastic costs.

We consider scheduling in a multi-product, single machine factory with sequence independent setup times. The machine processing and setup times are random variables. The factory is faced with a set of jobs that incur a late penalty if not completed by their deadlines. The optimization problem is to generate a static schedule that minimizes the expected penalty.

Given that factory performance is stochastic, it is easy to show that an optimal solution to a deterministic model using the expected run times will lead to sub-optimal schedules. Instead, we tackle the stochastic problem directly using an algorithm called Stochastic Dominance A* (Wellman, Ford, & Larson 1995). SDA* is designed for problems with path-dependent, stochastic operator costs. In SDA*, paths can be pruned only if their path cost is stochastically dominated by an already discovered path to the same state. For heuristics to be admissibile, the actual remaining cost must be stochastically dominated by the heuristic estimate. In addition, we impose a benign consistency condition to retain validity.

Our work extends SDA* to the scheduling problem. We formulate the problem as a state space search where the state is defined by the current inventory, the current machine setup, and the orders that have been filled. Three classes of operators are allowed. `Make` operators increment the inventory of the state. `Ship` operators decrement the inventory and change orders from unfilled to filled. `Setup` operators change the current product that can be built.

The path costs are defined by the pair <*time, penalty*>. We must keep the full probability distribution for the time attribute, but, assuming we are risk-neutral in penalty, it is sufficient to store only the expected value of the penalty. The `make` and `setup` operators increment only the time element of the path cost. The `ship` operator incurs a penalty as a function of the current time.

The definition of costs as a two-attribute structure requires some small elaborations to the SDA* algorithm. First, the priority queue is sorted by the estimated expected penalty of the paths. The estimated expected penalty is the sum of the penalty accumulated so far plus the heuristic estimate of the rest of the penalty. Second, paths can be pruned only if a path has already been found to the same state that dominates it in both time and penalty. This notion of dominance over multi-element costs is the same used in multi-objective A* (Stewart & White 1991).

To compare the algorithm's performance versus the deterministic model, we ran it on randomly generated problems where the number of orders and the total requested capacity were varied. We solved 400 such problems with both SDA* and A* using a deterministic model based on mean run and setup times. We found that in more than 70% of the problems, the solution found using SDA* had a lower expected cost than the deterministic solution applied to the stochastic data. We also found that the number of nodes expanded and the percentage of pruning between the stochastic and deterministic algorithms were very similar.

References

Stewart, B., and White, III, C. 1991. Multiobjective A*. *Journal of the Association for Computing Machinery* 38(4):775–814.

Wellman, M. P.; Ford, M.; and Larson, K. 1995. Path planning under time-dependent uncertainty. In *Proc. 11th Conf. on Uncertainty in AI*, 532–539.

Dynamic Map: Representation of Interactions between Robots

Christian Zanardi

GRPR, École Polytechnique de Montréal
P.O. Box 6079, succ. "Centre-ville",
H3C 3A7, Montréal, CANADA
email:zanardi@ai.polymtl.ca

Introduction

As robotics applications become more complex, the need for tools to analyze and explain interactions between robots has become more acute. We introduce the concept of Dynamic Map (DM), which can serve as a generic tool to analyze interactions between robots or with their environment. We show that this concept can be applied to different kinds of applications, like a predator-prey situation, or collision avoidance.

The Dynamic Map (DM)

For a dynamic system, represented by the state equation $\dot{x} = f(x, u, t)$, where x is the state of the system, u the control vector, and t time, T-reachable regions are commonly defined as the set of all states that can be reached within time T from a same initial position $x(0)$, with an acceptable control vector u. Although these regions indicate *which* points can be reached, they do not inform about (the *quality* of) the trajectories leading to these points. This information is provided by a goodness functional g—depending upon the task at hand—defined at each point of the T-reachable regions, and that must be maximized. We call this extension of the reachable regions Dynamic Map (DM) of the system.

Constructing and Using the DM With a simple model of a car-like robot, where the control is the steering angle, the Dynamic Map can be constructed along two methods. First, all points that can be reached are exhaustively generated using bang-bang controls, along with the value on the associated functional. Second, it is possible to contruct the map, using only "limits curves." The points on those curves are defined to be the external boundaries of reachable regions. It is then simple to generate the shape of the Dynamic Map based on those curves.

Ideally the goodness functional g should take into account important criteria such as presence of obstacles, energy consumption, and relative density of trajectories. Indeed, the values corresponding to points that belong to an obstacle should be negative in order to prevent trajectories to pass by them. Energy consumption is an important criteria, if a robot need to join periodically with an other to regain power. Since planned trajectories may have to change according to new environmental conditions while the initial goals remain, it would be important to know the relative density of trajectories leading to the neighboorhood of a point—*i.e.* the number of different trajectories leading to a similar position—as a mesure of confidence in the planned trajectory. Figure 1 presents an example of a DM, with such a functional—represented as shades of gray—for a car-like robot.

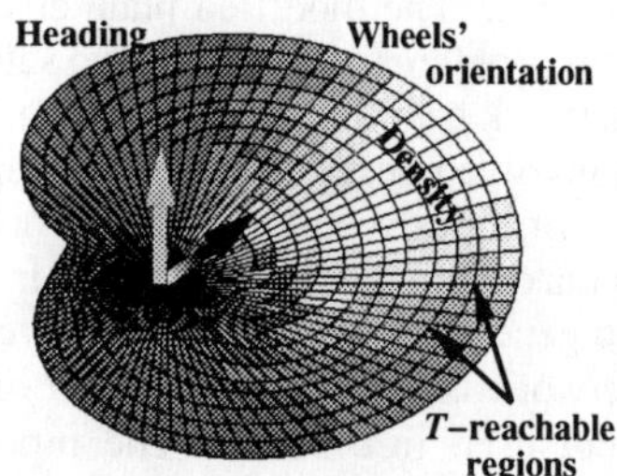

Figure 1: Example of DM

For example, if a mobile robot R is trying to evade its pursuer F, it would be safe to know *which* places R can reach before its adversary, and *how long* before F does. For such a problem, it is simply a matter of composing Dynamic Maps, *e.g.* through an addition. Thus, the robot will just have to combine an estimation of its adversary's map with its own, according to their relative pose. Then, using a simple maximization algorithm, the robot will be able to plan an evasion trajectory.

Conclusions

We presented here the Dynamic Map which is a tool to analyze interactions between mobile robots. One of the great advantages of the dynamic map—in a learning scheme context—is that it is built at the scale of the robot itself. Furthermore, it remains that the DM is a general concept that can be extended to a large number of dynamic systems, such as a robot manipulator.

Neural Network Guided Search Control in Partial Order Planning

Terry Zimmerman **Advisor: Subbarao Kambhampati**
Department of Computer Science and Engineering
Arizona State University, Tempe AZ 85287-5406
{zim@asu.edu}

The development of efficient search control methods is an active research topic in the field of planning (Kambhampati, Katukam, & Qu 1996). Investigation of a planning program integrated with a neural network (NN) that assists in search control is underway, and has produced promising preliminary results.

Project Overview: The UCPOP partial order planner (Penberthy & Weld 1992) was used in this project and the initial experiments were limited to "blocks world" problems with up to 3 blocks. Experimentation was done with several candidate sets of "partial plan" parameters or metrics in the search for one that is useful to the NN in discerning whether a partial plan is likely to evolve into a solution plan. This parameter set functions as the input vector to the NN.

The planning program was modified to automatically produce an input vector for every partial plan visited in its search process. When search is complete the program classifies each vector associated with plans lying on the solution path as positive examples and all other vectors generated as negative examples. The modified planner is run on a representative set of problems, generating two sets of input vectors -one for network training, one for testing.

The next project phase involved designing and training a NN using the training set of input vectors. The network should correctly classify a maximum number of its training vectors and still be able to generalize over vectors not yet presented. The trained network is subsequently tested on the set of input vectors **not** used in training. The input vector and/or network design is revisited if the trained network does not perform well in classifying these partial plan vectors.

The final phase is to develop a version of the UCPOP that incorporates the threshold function representing the successfully trained NN in such a manner that it can efficiently guide the planner's solution search. The performance of the modified planner on a variety of problems can then be compared with the original planner.

Current Design: The modified UCPOP program generated roughly 500 input vectors for training from 6 problems and 1000 testing vectors from a different 13 problems. UCPOP's default Best First Search (BFS) algorithm was used for search control during the input vector generation phase.

Designing a "good" candidate set of input parameters for the NN is a major (and ongoing) issue requiring careful analysis and iteration. But the process in itself provides interesting insight into the open question of the "goodness" of a partial plan. The candidate set on which the most extensive experimentation was performed contained 27 partial plan parameters:

- Number of nodes expanded at the current search stage
- Number of "refinements" in the current plan
- Number of unsatisfied subgoals on the goals queue
- 12 parameters that can take on 1 of 3 values representing whether each of the possible states for blocks (such as on(A B)) are present in the initial and/or goal state
- 12 related parameters indicating whether a series of (possibly temporary) causal links to the initial state has been established for each goal state literal

In this case the best performance was obtained with a multilayer feedforward network with 20 hidden nodes and one output node. The network was trained using a variation of the Gauss-Newton algorithm (Haykin 1994).

Results and Current Directions: When presented with the 1000 vectors from problems not trained on the NN correctly classifies 82% of them. That is, the trained NN exhibits a success rate of 82% in discriminating between those partial plans which will ultimately lie on the solution path and those which won't for plans created and visited by the planner during its solution search for test problems *not previously "seen" by the neural net.* This suggests the NN as configured has a "forecasting" capability that may be useful in improving the planner's search control.

Work is currently still underway on the last project phase discussed above, but initial attempts to use the "NN forecaster" in combination with UCPOP's BFS algorithm to provide search control have produced mixed results. It is apparent that UCPOP performance is very sensitive to how the NN forecasting is used to guide its search control. Various techniques for combining the BFS and NN guidance as well as methods for using the NN guidance alone are being investigated. There are also a number of interesting possibilities and techniques for improving the input vector with respect to partial plan parameters likely to be most useful to the neural network forecasting process.

References

Haykin, S. 1994. *Neural Networks -A Comprehensive Foundation.* Macmillan College Publishing, Inc. 215--217.

Kambhampati, S.; Katukam, S.; and Qu, Y. 1996. Failure driven dynamic search control for partial order planners: An explanation based approach. *Artificial Intelligence (forthcoming).*

Penberthy, J., and Weld, D. 1992. Ucpop: A sound, complete, partial order planner for adl. *Proceedings of KR-92* 103--114.

Eighth Innovative Applications of Artificial Intelligence Conference

Case Studies

EASy: Expert Authorizations System

Jonathan Altfeld
Senior Knowledge Engineer
Brightware, Inc.
1080 Holcomb Bridge Rd. Ste 300
Roswell, GA 30076
jonathan@brightware.com

Douglas E. Landon, Ph.D.
Senior Systems Analyst
Equifax Check Services
5301 W. Idlewild Ave.
Tampa, FL 33634
landon@packet.net

Charles J. Daniels
Lead Programmer/Analyst
Equifax Check Services
5301 W. Idlewild Ave
Tampa, FL 33634
repoman@cftnet.com

Abstract

Equifax Check Services provides retail merchants and other businesses with quality decisions concerning the acceptability, risk, or fraudulence of customer checks. The greatest percentage of these decisions are provided automatically through on-line links with point-of-sale terminals. When a transaction is suspect, a referral notice is generated directing the merchant to call one of Equifax Check Services' authorization centers for additional processing. This processing considers a wide variety of information unavailable through online processing, thereby giving consumers the greatest possible benefit of doubt prior to declining checks. These high-risk authorizations had historically been handled using a legacy mainframe system involving a high degree of manual intervention. Authorizations agents would complete a lengthy, rigorous training regimen, and be monitored as to their performance. Pursuit of service excellence caused Equifax, in conjunction with Brightware Corporation, to develop the Expert Authorization System (EASy), a rule-based solution for check authorizations that uses an innovative twist on a standard blackboard architecture. EASy was deployed and is used today by as many as 300 concurrent users. By encapsulating extensive domain knowledge, EASy has effectively eliminated authorization errors, provided consistent and replicable decisions, reduced elapsed time to a decision, and reduced the average agent training time from 4-6 weeks to 3 days.

Problem Description

The original check authorization system was Tandem-based, utilizing 3270 screens to provide authorization agents with various types of information. These Agents would enter some information, then page through several 3270 screens in order to accumulate a critical mass of information about the check-writer and the transaction. As this information built up, the agents would apply decision rules to specific circumstances and deliver an authorization decision. Agents were required to follow suggestions from the system, know when to ignore or override the system, and know when specific exceptions applied. Trained agents knew which screens to view in the appropriate order, and they knew how to scroll through historical information of various kinds to identify concerns which might affect an approval decision. Even with QA monitoring and established procedures, there was still agent variability in the approval process.

In addition, the existing system was experienced as being both difficult to learn and inflexible. From four to six weeks of extensive group and individual training was required. This was followed by a period of high QA monitoring to ensure proper decision making. Intermittent long-term QA monitoring was required to maintain high quality authorization decisions.

Since training required so much time and effort, coordinating the hiring, training, and QA monitoring schedule was a significant challenge, particularly during the holiday season, when the number of agents more than doubled.

Maintenance and reliability issues were concerns with the Tandem-based system. The legacy system had expanded over many years to account for new functionality and legal restrictions, utilizing expensive and increasingly outdated computing systems. Additionally, manpower was limited for Tandem support and was becoming increasingly more expensive. Continued software and hardware maintenance was producing diminishing returns on this system. Agents were using 286 model diskless PC's, which supported 3270 emulation into a Mainframe and a Tandem, and in some cases over a Novell LAN.

Objectives of the Expert Authorizations System

Equifax Check Services needed a way of standardizing authorization decisions as well as exception-handling. The complex nature of these decisions lent themselves perfectly to Expert System technology, and posed significant problems for a procedural and/or mainframe-based approach in designing a replacement system. A decision was made that there was little or no room for error, and a great need was realized for a malleable solution with more centralized control over authorization decision-making.

There were a number of objectives for the replacement authorization system, to include:

- Standardization and automation of all types of check authorization decisions across the entire agent pool.
- Migration from reliance on legacy mainframe systems to an open and cost-effective PC/LAN-based client-server solution.
- Replacement of a limited, inflexible system with an intelligent, more easily modifiable, and flexible system.
- Reduction in call times (i.e. time to make decisions).
- Reduction of training time, complexity, and costs, combined with improvement to the training process.
- Elimination of risk due to improper decisions.
- Enabling of customer-specific processing.

Previous Similar Work

At first glance, EASy needed to accomplish much of what had been accomplished with the American Express Authorizer's Assistant (AA) expert system, but with a few notable differences.

The following are some similarities between the AMEX AA and EASy:

- Both needed to apply business policies towards on-line incoming transactions in order to reach a faster, more consistent and reliable approval decision.
- Both worked in conjunction with authorizations agents in order to provide a human interface to their customers.
- Both systems handled the anomaly decisions through agent intervention.
- Both systems rely on alternative on-line systems to handle all of the straightforward decisions; this represents in both cases a significant percentage (a proprietary, variable number). Those transactions which require more attention are referred in both cases to AA and EASy, respectively.

The following are some differences between the two systems:

- AA is a credit granting system which extends credit, while EASy is a check authorizations system. No credit is granted because the intention in EASy is to guarantee the likelihood of existing funds availability through a combination of factors. AA already has a significant portfolio of information on their customers which originates with a credit application, and builds through repeated use of the card. EASy, by contrast, can have more or less information to work with, depending on the consumer's identification and the nature of the transaction.
- AA's customers are the consumers. EASy's customers are the merchants who require check guarantees for their customers (the consumers) payment.
- While AA requires flexibility and intelligence on the part of their agents, allowing decision-override capabilities under specific circumstances, all of EASy's check authorizations decisions occur within the expert system. The EASy agent guides the customer through providing appropriate information as EASy requests it, and relays the decision to the customer.

Application Description

The replacement system is called the Expert Authorizations System, or EASy. EASy processes from 4-6% of all transactions handled by Equifax Check Services, depending on the settings of certain business parameters. On-line transaction-based systems are called directly by retail point-of-sale terminals for the majority of decisions; most of these decisions are comparatively simple to make and usually result in immediate check approvals. Suspect transactions are referred with a request to contact an authorizations center.

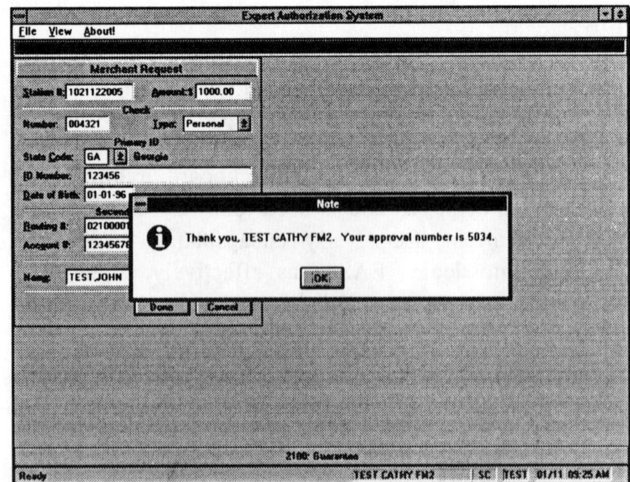

Figure 1: Approval Notification

When the merchant calls in to an authorizations center, an authorizations agent using EASy retrieves certain information about the merchant's customer (the consumer), and the check which caused the referral. This identification and transactional information is processed by EASy in combination with various types of information held at Equifax, and an authorization decision is returned.

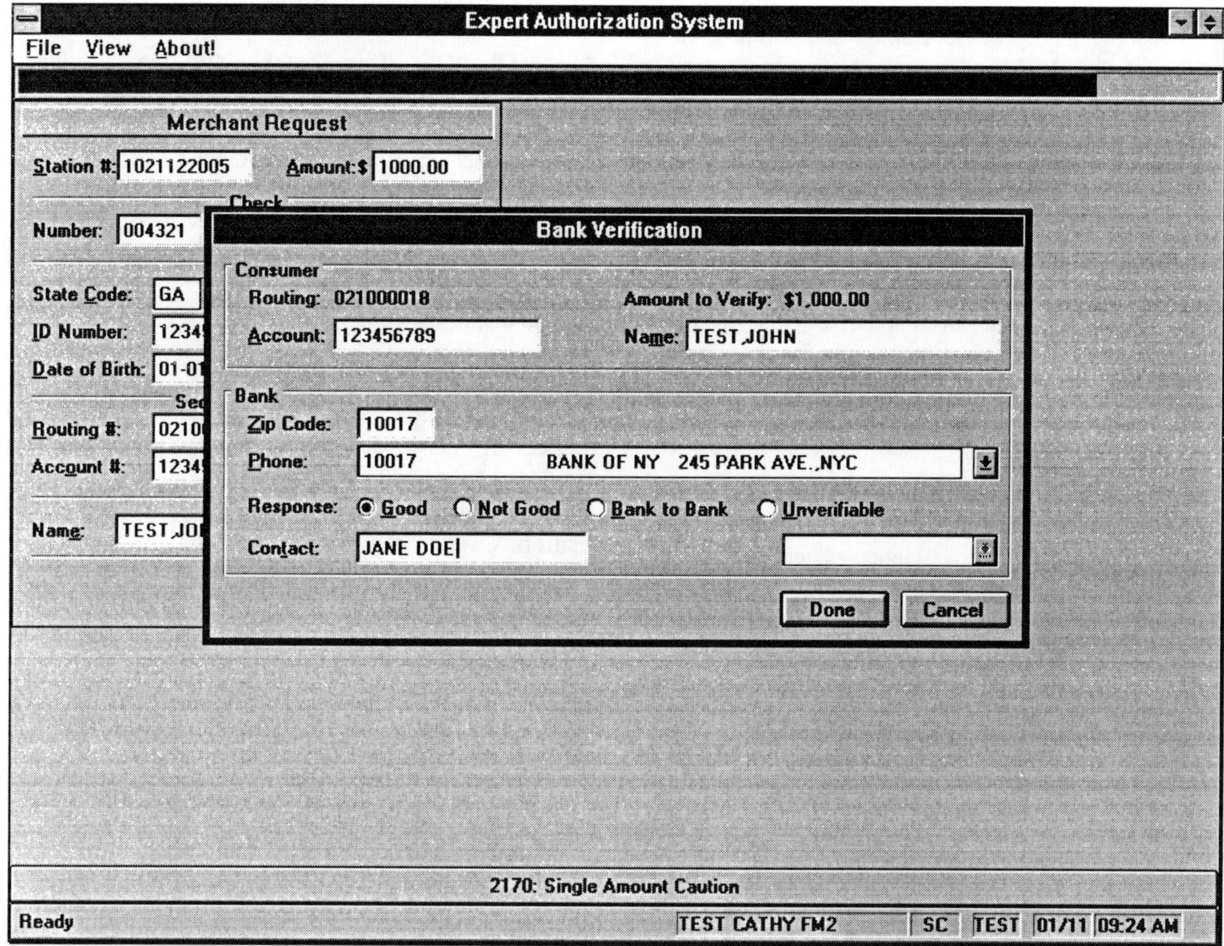

Figure 2 : In-Process Funds Verification

Figures 1-2 provide examples of some of EASy's graphical screens using fictitious data. Basic consumer information is entered by the agent through data request screens similar to that in Figure 1. The types of consumer data, and the order in which it is obtained, is controlled through rule firings in the EASy knowledge base.

As EASy progresses through its decision-making, it may request that the agent obtain additional data or perform certain actions. An example of the latter is shown in Figure 2, where EASy has requested that the agent obtain funds verification from a bank.

Once all the necessary information has been gathered and the processing completed, EASy will display an authorization decision as shown in Figure 2, which shows an example of an authorization approval message. There are a variety of approval, decline, and informational messages that can be displayed depending on the results of the decision process.

How the KB software solution fit these tasks

Both the problem domain and the expert knowledge embodied by the agents both through training and experience lent themselves clearly and immediately to a rule-based system. At a high level, the following activities occur over and over again at each agent's station:

- A new transaction arrives
- The system requests information
- Information is processed through a business model
- More information is obtained as needed
- More processing occurs
- A decision is rendered
- The system cleans up and refreshes itself

The basic function of obtaining data via indicators derived from a business model is a nearly classic description of a backward chaining expert system. The goal is an approve/decline authorization decision, and the system must request information to "prove" one or the other goal. However, reasoning forward from data provided by an agent is a more classic forward-chaining mechanism, thus also indicating an expert system approach. Additionally, because of a long history of developing and refining the business model for check authorizations, Equifax Check Services developed a robust set of "rules" governing what actions the agents should take to make a decision.

To capture these various aspects of authorization decision-making, a blackboard type of expert system architecture was designed, with the knowledge sources consisting of various cells of related rules that embodied the specific aspects of decision-making. The knowledge sources are activated using an innovative twist in the standard blackboard architecture that we refer to as rule phases. Further on we will describe how this differs from a classic ruleset approach.

EASy's User Platform

Each agent sits in front of a 486 or Pentium® PC running Microsoft® Windows® 3.1. Upon system boot-up, Windows starts up automatically, followed by EASy's agent login screen. Upon a validated login, agents can immediately begin taking calls.

These PC's locally run a Microsoft Visual Basic® application, a 32-bit ART**Enterprise*® application which operates on top of the Win32s libraries, a Microsoft Access® database, and a network layer to connect to the Equifax LAN. These applications are described in more detail in the next section.

EASy's Pseudo Three-Tier Environment

In addition to the expert system, EASy includes two additional software components, and represents a near-perfect model of a clear three-tier solution architecture. EASy's architecture differs from the purist definition of three-tier only in that the Graphical User Interface **(GUI)** and the Knowledge Base **(KB)** components sit on the same platform, a PC clone running Windows 3.1. The components are modified and/or maintained by different developers, and isolate areas of functionality, but they reside together and communicate back and forth with each other.

The EASy GUI. EASy's GUI was built using Microsoft Visual Basic 3.0. The Visual Basic GUI component contains neither knowledge nor transactional drivers. The extent of its intelligence is to check for some informational validity (i.e, that a number field actually contains a number). For its actions, it depends entirely on the EASy knowledge base.

The GUI utilizes static data stored in local databases implemented through Microsoft Access. Since an important quality parameter for authorization decisions is the average call time, the GUI also tracks and prominently displays call time durations.

The EASy KB. This {roughly 600-rule, 800-function} system was implemented using ART**Enterprise* from Brightware, Inc. All of the business knowledge which Equifax Check Services has developed over the course of its history about how to process checks resides here. The KB fully drives the GUI component, waits for data from the GUI, processes decisions or partial decisions, and then informs the GUI of either of those decisions or directs the GUI to display screens where the agent can enter additional data.

The EASy Database Layer. EASy makes use of numerous sources of data in determining consumer risk. This data resides within various databases maintained by Equifax Check Services. These operate or exist on numerous server platforms, including UNIX workstations and an IBM Mainframe system. Some of these servers are locally-based to the authorizations LAN, and some are remote. Concurrent on-line remote connections supporting Check Authorizations as well as other systems fully support all the required bandwidth problems posed by EASy.

Integrating EASy's Three Primary Components

Visual Basic **(VB)** integration with ART**Enterprise* was accomplished with functionality built into both the GUI and the KB components. On the KB component, functionality was designed to send either messages or requests to the GUI, at different times, for different purposes. The Log window shown in Figure 5 displays these flow-control instructional messages.

On the GUI component, a rudimentary token parser was built on top of a DDE server. Interestingly, the author of the GUI component wanted to improve maintenance issues and enhance communication across the DDE link. He therefore designed the VB DDE-Server's token parser to process a limited grammar modeled after ART*Script, the flexible scripting language within ART**Enterprise*. Thus, ART*Script could send DDE messages with any of a specified set of ART*Script commands, and they would be processed in the GUI component as though VB were an extension of ART**Enterprise*.[1]

In order to integrate the KB component with the Database component, specialized Equifax-proprietary

[1] ART**Enterprise* does contain an integrated platform-independent object-oriented GUI development tool. In mid-1993, Equifax was a beta-tester of ART**Enterprise* while they were moving forward with EASy's design. The EASy team needed to commit to a more functional and extensible GUI for EASy's Windows-based user platforms, where no portability was required. Visual Basic offered an immediate non-beta solution, and was readily integrated with ART**Enterprise*.

network message-passing calls were utilized to send information from the KB to multiple sources, and to request processing or information from any of multiple databases or external application processors. EASy's developers implemented this capability in Borland C®, using a Windows Dynamically Linked Library **(DLL)**, to which the KB would send calls.

Processing Residing Outside the KB

EASy relies on some processing which occurs on external application processors. In these cases, it sends a custom network request to return results for a particular job. Thus, it could be said that some of the application's knowledge resides outside the knowledge base. For example, EASy relies on external processing for the validation and analysis of consumer identification.

Additionally, EASy relies on external applications residing at various computers on the Check Services authorization Local Area Network [See Figure 3]. These external applications provide additional input to EASy regarding a variety of parameters that may affect the authorization decision. These parameters generally involve basic guidelines that are followed in an authorization decision and are derived from a combination of Equifax Check Services' business rules and agreements with merchants utilizing authorization services. These parameters and processes are external to EASy primarily because they are also used for the automatic electronic authorization processing.

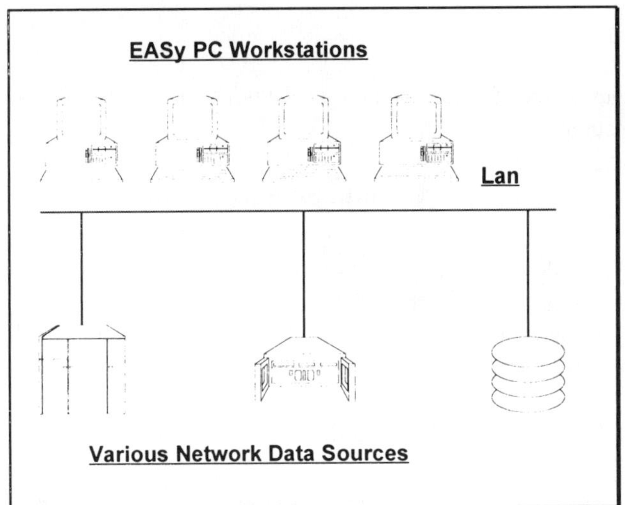

Figure 3: EASy LAN Topology

The types of information returned by these external processes provides EASy with initial information and status indicators for the current authorization transaction. These status indicators are prioritized by EASy and used as a basis for determining the order of processing of EASy's rule phases.

KB Design

Figure 4 illustrates the flow of the EASy KB process. The overriding structure of the KB is a traditional blackboard architecture. In order to organize the decision process the multiple mechanisms involved in the decision process were separated and implemented as independent sets of rules. Traditionally, using ART**Enterprise*, a grouped set of rules is linked using the ruleset mechanism. However, the ruleset mechanism was felt to be too restrictive for the EASy application for several reasons, including:

1. Check Authorizations management felt that custom processing options at a customer-specific level was a necessary future enhancement for EASy in order to deliver all proposed service enhancements; this was always envisioned as utilizing rule-set capabilities. It was determined that all possible custom rules for a given client would not easily be classified into singular areas of the knowledge base, and therefore should not be implemented as rule parameters.
2. It became obvious that different actions could occur within a given processing area, under the same conditions, depending on what might have occurred in the knowledge base beforehand. So the knowledge base at a micro level was non-deterministic, but was still deterministic at a macro level. Investigating further, two classifications could be made for particular rule-groups within the knowledge base. There were those that could be "called" at the *top level*, and those that could be "called" as *functions* of higher level knowledge base areas. The sequencing of certain rule-groups was critical to the decision process.

Based on the above reasons, rule groups became *phases* of a transaction. A deterministic set of all paths through these phases in any given transaction was mapped out, and mechanisms were created to allow orderly flow of a transaction through its phases. When rules and their corresponding exceptions needed to be able to fire under several different phases, their host phases could be enabled concurrently with other phases.

Like rulesets, phases were implemented with a simple control fact mechanism, but additional facts would be asserted in parallel. These would indicate which phase led to the current phase, how the current phase had been entered, and if the current phase was completed, indicating that control could be passed to another phase. This can not be fully viewed as procedural, because multiple phases can be concurrently enabled under known circumstances.

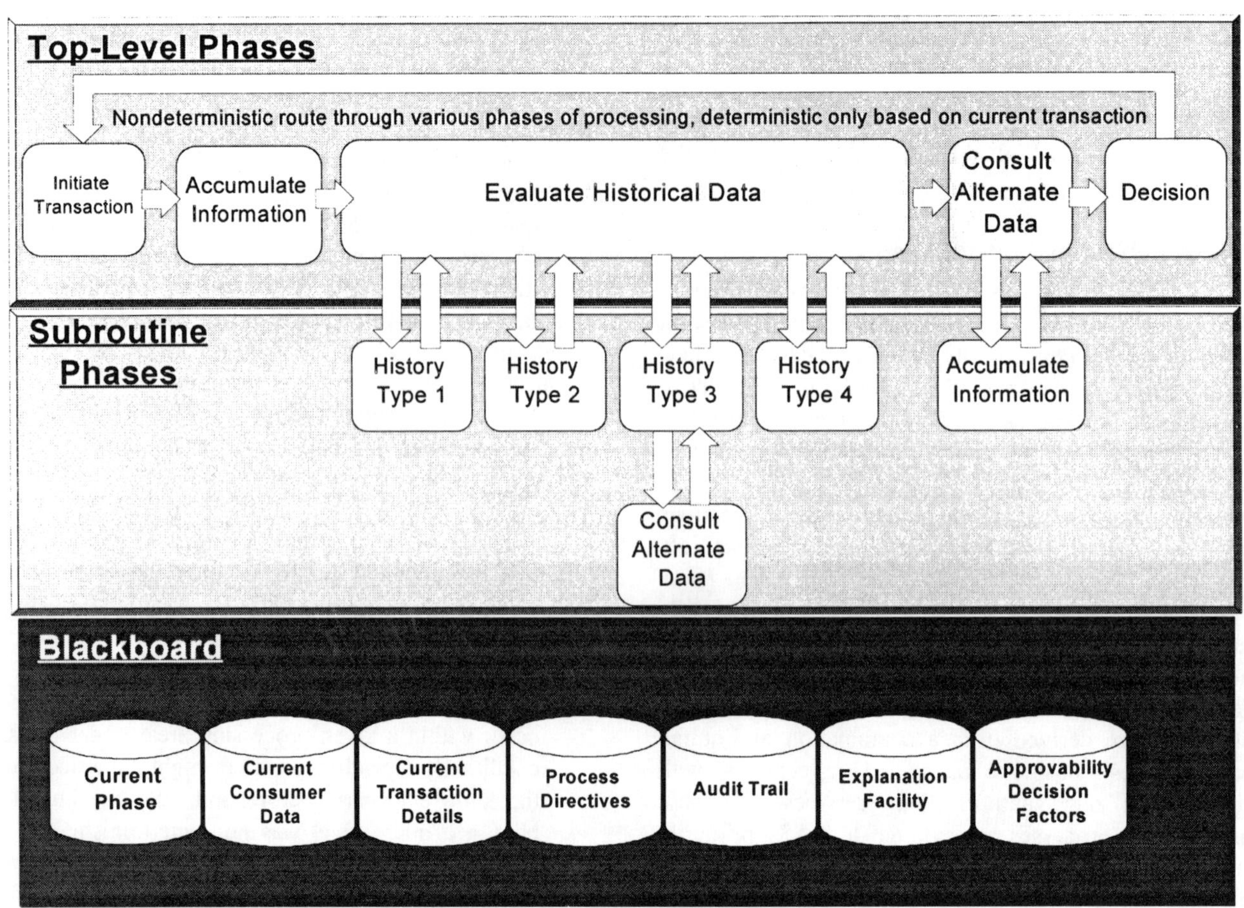

Figure 4: Phase Topology and Blackboard Architecture

Within each phase of processing, the EASy KB primarily uses forward-chaining, data-driven rules to accomplish its decisions in a classic non-deterministic fashion. However, as previously noted, one of the major features of the EASy KB is its ability to drive a user-interface and obtain additional data as needed, which is usually a function of backward-chaining rules.

The backward-chaining mechanism was directly implemented using a few simple rules that fired based on facts asserted within the forward-chaining phases. These facts were essentially goal facts which specified that certain types of information should be transferred to the GUI, and that the KB should wait for a response from the GUI. These GUI rules have the lowest priority in the KB. The KB behavior, in effect, is to process as much as it can on the current information, assert GUI goal facts if a rule determines that more information is needed, and then let the forward-chaining phases essentially run out of rule activations and allow the GUI rules to fire. The GUI then asserts the obtained data back into the KB, which in turn causes the forward-chaining, data-driven mechanism to resume.

Phases Mechanism and Topology

The following diagram illustrates the flow of phases and their relationship to the KB Blackboard.

Please note that in the following rule examples, all proprietary details have been left out.

A Phase Switch Initiation

```
(define-rule Switch-to-Phase-A
   "Recognize the switch moment for phase A"
   (phase current-phase & ~A)
   (transaction data one)
   (transaction data two)
   ...
=>
   (assert (switch-to phase A)
           (completed-phase ?current-phase))
)
```

In this generically defined rule, a firing would indicate that Phase A must be scheduled. It watches working memory to insure identify what phase is currently active. If the phase it wants to schedule (in this case A) can follow the currently active phase, and other conditions for phase entry are met, then the request to switch to the new phase is submitted by fact assertion. The Blackboard phase transition rules then retract the current phase gating fact [e.g. `(phase current-phase <phase-name>)`], and assert the necessary activation facts for the new phase. In a phase switch action, the current phase is considered completed and the new phase is considered active.

A Blackboard Phase-Switch rule

```
(define-rule PHASES:PHASE-SWITCH
  "Effect the transfer of phases"
  ?f1 <- (phase current-phase ?)
  ?f2 <- (phase switch-to     ?next)
  (phase-stack) ;empty stack, toplevel only
=>
  (retract ?f1 ?f2)
  (assert (phase current-phase ?next))
)
```

A follow-up rule-firing to the previously described example would be the standard Phase-Switch rule, shown immediately above, which effects all switches at the toplevel, regardless of their name/purpose. It is treated as being a Blackboard rule due to its applicability at any time throughout a transaction to any pair of phases.

An Intra-Phase Concluding Rule

```
(define-rule Sub-Call-Phase-A
  "Recognize the subroutine moment for A"
  (phase current-phase & ~A)
  (phase-stack $?SEQ
    &:(not (member$ A $?SEQ))) ;prevent loop
  (transaction data one)
  (transaction data two)
  ...
=>
  (assert (sub-call phase A))
)
```

In this rule, a firing would indicate that EASy should suspend the current phase for later re-activation, and enter Phase A much like a procedural subroutine. A decision from Phase A is required to assist the current phase with its own decision making. Note that a fact relation `(phase-stack...)` is maintained on the Blackboard, in order to store an ordered list of the current phase sub-calls. Localized facts used in the higher phases remain unused, with no matches, until their appropriate phase scope is re-activated.

Application Use and Payoff

Improvements in Agent Training

EASy has been fully deployed and in operation since February of 1995. During off-peak season, the minimum number of concurrent daytime users at all authorization sites is approximately 100. Given that the system operates 24 hours a day, 7 days a week, the total number of Authorizations Agent employees is higher.

During the height of peak season, the total number of transactions received by the on-line authorization system has reached 800,000 per day. On a peak day, up to 300 concurrent EASy users have taken 45,000 calls per day, where each call represents a transaction that has been referred from the on-line authorization system. Since the holiday shopping process ramps up substantially earlier than Thanksgiving, it takes time to ramp up the number of authorizations agents; training for peak used to be very costly.

As much as six weeks of training for each employee, using a methodology which required substantial individual attention, has been reduced to 3 days of group classes and supervision. As a result, EASy has reduced total training time by about *ninety per-cent* per year. This dramatic reduction in time, and therefore cost, has enabled EASy supervisory staff to more easily fill any openings caused by employee turnover during the peak season, and thereby maintain high levels of service throughout peak.

A residual but significant benefit of reduced training time is that agents can begin taking calls far earlier than before. This requires less training schedule management than before, because under EASy, extensive training courses do not need to be staggered over long periods of time. This directly and rapidly increases the productivity and consistency of decision-making in the authorizations department.

Enabling of Wider Service Offerings

Certainly an important future benefit is the enabling of customer-specific service offerings. The flexibility of the system provides for the incorporation of these specialized single-customer rule-sets in the short term. Work toward this area has already begun.

General System-Wide Benefits

Through the use of EASy, the time it takes to provide an authorizations decision has been slightly reduced, with significantly increased levels of confidence and reliability. However, EASy provides much more functionality than was available in the legacy system, and therefore some of the time savings of a KB implementation is given up to new processing and increased intelligence. This directly reduces the number of agents required during peak hours while providing shorter wait-times.

To help agents reduce their call times, they now have a color-coded timer bar running across the top of the Visual Basic GUI to indicate how much time has elapsed. At specific timer intervals the color changes from Green, through yellow and finally to Red. If a call that has extended into the red timer bar has not been resolved after a short while, the red timer bar begins flashing to provide additional impetus to complete the call.

Because of the reliability of EASy's standardized decision making, Equifax no longer must expend resources to transaction-process-monitor (TP Monitor) Check Authorizations that get routed to the authorizations center. Once the expert system has been validated by the experts and distributed to all the EASy stations, it needs no on-line monitoring. Should any issues arise, agents are able to report any problems or anomalies through their supervisory staff.

Application History

EASy Project History

EASy was designed and implemented to the point of deployment within 18 months, and has been deployed and fully operational since February of 1995.

EASy was implemented in stages, using an experimental approach to identify the best method of storing information, and the most optimal mechanisms for rule pattern-matching. Purity of design was originally sacrificed in order to provide proof of concept through rapid prototyping. This was done in order to provide continuous feedback as to the value and productivity of development within the rule-based paradigm.

The rapid-prototyping approach was combined with a modified spiral methodology, thereby providing for the effective inclusion of new developers on the project at any stage.

In practice, as EASy's multiple components approached completion, and testing/validation efforts rapidly increased, a waterfall methodology took precedence in order to validate new functionality and bug-fixes.

The following describes the major steps in EASy's development. The # of PC's refers to the total install base in a given time period, which is a superset of the total number of concurrent users at any given moment.

- **July 1993 - July 1994:** *Primary development effort. Resulted in 8 PC's running an early test version periodically under structured testing against real calls.*
    - *5 developers total, 3 at any one time.*
    - *0 Users.*
- **July 1994 - September 1994:** *Bug Fixing combined with an upgrade from ART*Enterprise 1.0.Beta to ART*Enterprise 1.0.General Availability. Resulted in 16 PC's running a newer test release of EASy, still under strict supervision but more frequently than before.*
    - *5 developers total, 3 at any one time.*
    - *0-16 Users, Alpha Release.*
- **October 1994 - December 1994:** *Calls were being taken on a regular basis on 16 PC's with a more stable and functional version. Development during this phase included some performance tuning, application re-engineering, and addition of new functionality.*
    - *4 developers total, 3 at any one time.*
    - *16-50 Users, Beta Release*
- **December 1994 - February 1995:** *A completion and cleanup of re-engineering effort; result is a new phased blackboard software architecture. and a new EASy which is deployed on 80 PC's locally, and 50 PC's at other locations.*
    - *3 developers concurrently.*
    - *50-130 Users, Initial Full Roll-out.*
- **February 1995 - April 1995:** *A concentrated period of enhancements and system stabilizing. Resulted in an unprecedented level of confidence in decision making. Peripheral results included the elimination of multiple extraneous KB mechanisms which had been built over time as patches, and not yet removed as part of the new phased architecture.*
    - *2 developers concurrently.*
    - *Full user deployment based on seasonal requirements.*
- **April 1995 - September 1995:** *Virtually eliminated reliance on legacy systems by adding to EASy the capability to interface with a new PC-based Authorizations System which provides suggestions for how to process transactions.*
    - *2 developers concurrently.*
    - *Full user deployment based on seasonal requirements.*
- **September 1995 - November 1995:** *During this period, developers and testers performed a "pre-season shake-out" in order to hammer out any rare but potential problems before the peak season arrived.*
    - *2 developers concurrently.*
    - *Full user deployment based on seasonal requirements.*

- **November 1995 - Present:** *Stable Operation, minimal risk. Equifax Management approval has been obtained to initiate an extensive feature-enhancement program.*
    - *2 developers concurrently.*
    - *Full user deployment based on seasonal requirements.*

How was EASy validated?

A parallel testbed system, using the same hardware as the production system but entirely different data paths, was developed to mirror the same capabilities available in the production system. Sample transactions could be run and recorded against the testbed system without any impact to production data or actual consumer transactions. The experts consulted by the Knowledge Engineers were the authorizations management and supervisory staff, which comprised the primary testing and validating group.

As either new functionality or bug fixes were coded, an update to a set of test PC's would occur. The experts would run real transactions which were known to be standard and/or boundary cases against the testbed EASy. If the system passed all the obvious tests designed to weed out problems, unstructured regression testing would occur. A set of standard unrelated transactions would be run to validate that existing functionality had not been broken. Those transactions had not been formalized largely because the experts could type in those transactions faster than developers could write them down.

Should any problems have missed detection by the experts, they were certainly found in production. Calls would be routed for particular problems to an agent who would complete the transaction manually, and a knowledge engineer could sit at that agent's PC, interrupt the production transaction, and call up ART**Enterprise*'s Command Interpreter to investigate the state of the problem. Usually the developer would immediately be able

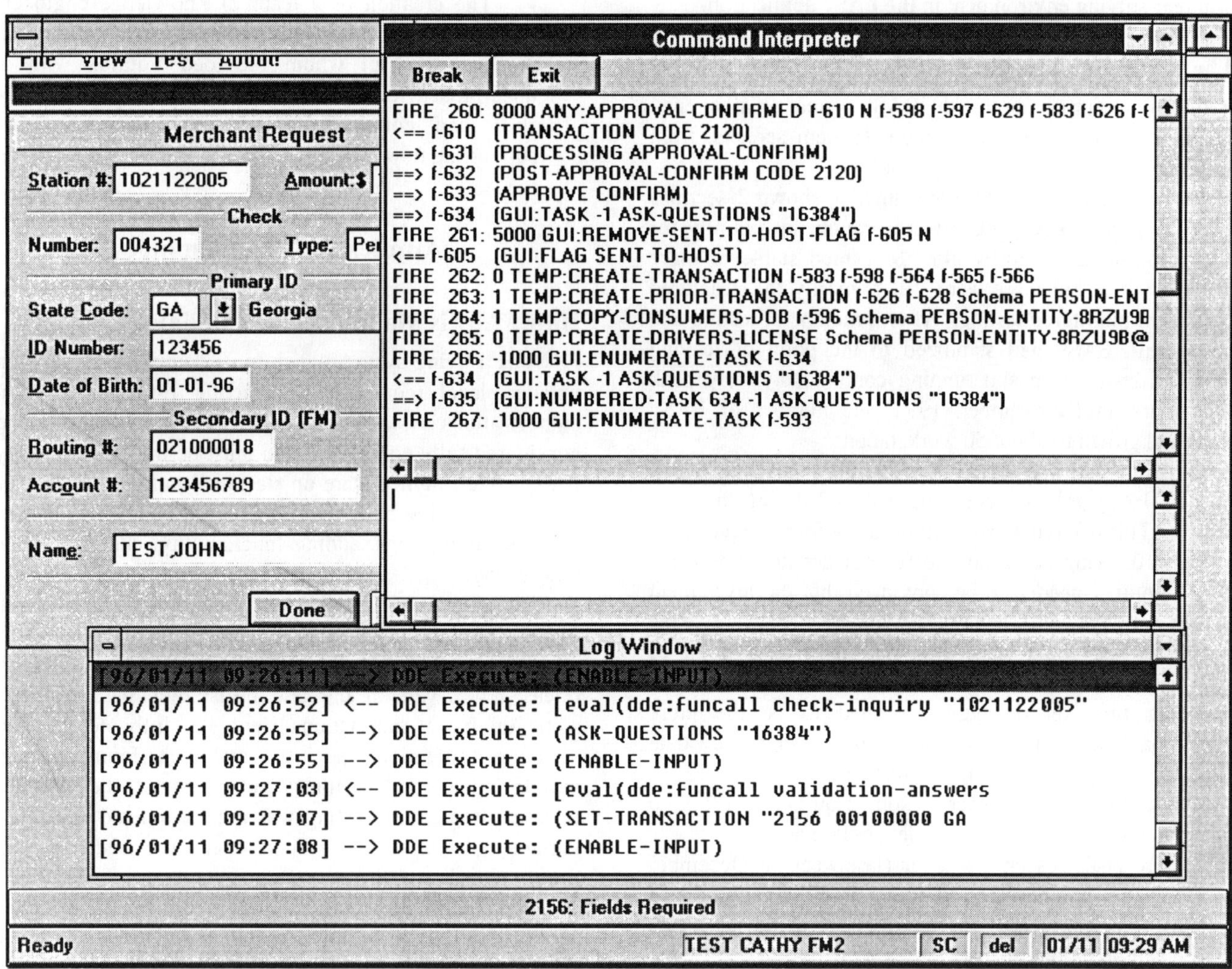

Figure 5: KB Development Environment

to tell what went wrong in the knowledge base or GUI. However, the transaction would always be completed such that the merchant received an appropriate decision, even if this required supervisory intervention.

ART*Enterprise* provides a highly customizable development environment. To simplify the development and maintenance of EASy, a specialized development environment was created by unlinking the GUI and other unused ART**Enterprise* tools, and adding functions and browsers that made rapid development and debugging of EASy code faster and easier. Figure 5 shows an example of a debugging session using a custom DDE message log window, and an enhanced Rule tracing facility.

With the modified bare KB studio, developers rapidly developed command-line functionality and skills for debugging EASy that allowed for rapid problem isolation.

Coupled with the visually minimal but significantly extended ART**Enterprise* environment, a special DDE Message log-window provided through the EASy GUI, enabled only for developers, makes for a very ideal problem-solving environment in the EASy application.

The EASy Deployment Process

It took six months to deploy the EASy system on all agents' stations as a replacement for their Tandem screens, from July, 1994 to January 1995.

To elaborate on the itemized timeline shown 2 sections prior, at first, 8 EASy PC's were brought up initially for testing purposes. Shortly after 8 seemed stable, 8 more were installed, but these were still primarily for structured periods of monitored testing. After 2 months of testing and debugging, EASy had stabilized to the point of leaving those 16 stations up and running continuously. By peak time (early-mid November, 1994) the number of EASy PC's had grown to about 50 workstations.

A policy had been issued by Equifax management that no new EASy releases could be installed during the peak season. This offered a prime opportunity for the developers to begin thinking about how to re-engineer the knowledge base. Equifax needed to be convinced that the investment in that activity would have clear payoffs. The knowledge engineers had found that they had reached a point of diminishing returns on working on bug-fixes. Thus spending time on debugging seemed to be the more questionable investment, as opposed to imposing a new data flow architecture on existing mechanisms.

Based on these and other reasons, Equifax gave the go ahead to complete the new knowledge-base architecture.

Before peak season was over (last week in December 1994), that re-engineering had begun, and by the middle of January, a re-engineered EASy was fully deployed across all the authorizations agents.

In the opinions of the authors of this paper, three elements contributed to the rapid completion and success of EASy's modification.

- The use of a knowledge-based paradigm had created within EASy the cellular groupings of data processing that automatically lent themselves to isolated rule-firing chains. Mechanisms that interoperated between these cells were easy to distinguish, clean up, and structure, such as control facts, absence of control facts, objects, and various types of consumer and merchant data.
- The use of ART**Enterprise* as the Expert System development tool, which provided the ability to extend development functionality, eliminate unrelated tools from the Studio, and provide run-time debugging capability. ART**Enterprise*/Windows allowed for integration of C code both directly and through DLL's, as well as setting up and maintaining DDE communication with the GUI component of the application.
- The creation of a team of knowledge engineers, GUI programmers, expert users and committed managers, all of whom provided Equifax with an unsurpassed level of aggregate knowledge, creativity, skill, and commitment to improving quality and supporting new technologies.

Application Maintenance

How EASy is Maintained and Updated

EASy is a living system which must comply with new and updated legal requirements affecting financial risk and authorizations systems. As a result, the system is never considered fully completed, and must be updated regularly. Knowledge Engineers are on staff at Equifax to update the EASy knowledge base, and they divide their time amongst updates, fixing bugs, adding functionality, and performing unit testing.

To achieve uniformity with respect to new system releases, Equifax's Quality Assurance manager maintains revision control and system update distribution. In order to release a new version, the new release must pass a variable suite of basic transactions, and be fully tested with boundary conditions against any bugs found through monitoring particular transactions against the previous release. Regression testing was not formalized due to the variable growth of the system over time under a rapid prototyping approach.

No hands-on distribution is necessary. To release a new version that has passed all compilation and testing steps, the QA manager sends the new software to a location on the LAN, and informs the supervisory staff for Authorizations that a special utility program for installing new versions of EASy can be run on each EASy station. This utility reconciles the current versions of all EASy applications and files with those found on the local PC.

The entire update process can be accomplished in less than an hour, assuming no errors were found during compiling and testing.

Who maintains EASy and how often?

Two full-time programmers/knowledge engineers maintain the system currently, alongside efforts to add/modify functionality. The users of the system are responsible for identifying any problems with the system, and their supervisors are responsible for determining what constitutes a user error vs. an actual system problem. Code modifications are made by knowledge engineers, tested against a testbed system, and agent supervisors then test the system in order to approve the code modifications prior to installation in the production environment.

Modifications to the system now occur once every 2 weeks, and these now encompass almost entirely new pieces of functionality, as opposed to bug-fixes.

Does EASy know more over time?

EASy must comply with changing state/local laws and Federal industry regulations, and so must be modified periodically to address such legal and regulatory concerns. Further, EASy has enabled the addition of new business knowledge that would have been difficult or impossible to implement with the legacy mainframe/Tandem based solution.

Does EASy's design ease/enable modification?

Several issues contribute to EASy being easily modifiable, including the choice of AI technology in general, the choice of ART**Enterprise* as the tool to provide that technology, and the choice of a phased blackboard architecture.

It was a central deliverable of the application to be able to change over time. The extent to which the system could be modified was proven during the phased architecture re-engineering process. In few other paradigms than a rule-based approach can you take a complete existing system with little structure and impose a clear structure in just over a month, automatically eliminating a significant number of bugs, without causing additional ones. In a procedural paradigm a rewrite would likely be required for the same level of modifications.

Future Plans

The current phasing architecture has provided EASy with a good deal of flexibility in dealing with the process of authorization decision making. The current phasing methodology is based on an underlying business model which could be more flexible in terms of what phases can fire and in what order. A fully non-deterministic approach would improve the ability to allow more variable authorization processing. To accommodate these requirements, the authorization business model is being sub-divided into its component processes. When this has been completed, an improved methodology for selecting custom authorization processing may be possible.

As might be imagined, this presents a variety of challenges for the current phase-based blackboard architecture. Although phases may be clearly considered as components, in hindsight, there are alternative ways to view a component-based authorizations decision which may be more applicable. For example, a specific customer may want components A, B, and D to be applied to their authorizations, skipping component C. This could present problems for both components B and D if component B, when viewed as a phase, wants to "naturally" transition to a phase (component) C. Also, component (phase) D may naturally require information normally supplied by component (phase) C. In the above example, a component may be required to process a transaction with incomplete information. A phasing architecture in this case may be required to schedule phases in a partially deterministic fashion based on customer requirements.

Work on these modifications to the EASy phase-based blackboard architecture has already begun. Equifax is re-examining the current business model to determine the extent to which partial information can be effectively applied in a component-based system, in order to reach a very clear (i.e. not partial) approval decision. As a result, the granularity of the components is also under review.

Summary

Through the Expert Authorizations System, Equifax Check Services has improved the quality of their existing services, and significantly enhanced their current and future services offerings. All of these benefits are now provided at lower cost to Equifax than the previous Tandem-based system could have allowed.

Since Equifax has shown EASy to numerous other departments, Expert System technology has received a high-level of buy-in and visibility. Other internal groups have begun exploring how to incorporate innovative AI approaches to improve their own productivity and quality.

In addition, through improved training quality, reduced training time and costs, and the user-friendly EASy environment, the authorizations department can now provide improvements in customer satisfaction.

Acknowledgments

The authors of this document would like to extend their hearty thanks to the following individuals who have been involved with EASy, in varying degrees, over the course of the project:

From Equifax: Greg Mallare, Margaret Fortson, Bill Overbay, Tim Prosser, Mike Hernandez, Cathy Reed, Lynda Patry, John Storch, and many others who have provided indirect but equally important assistance.

From Brightware: Bill Richer, Jeff Livesay, Kate Murphy, Greg Hadaller, Raj Rao

Special thanks go from Brightware to Greg Mallare and Margaret Fortson of Equifax, who were committed beta-testers and users of ART**Enterprise*/Windows from the earliest releases onward.

Trademark Acknowledgments

References

Dzierzanowski, J., Chrisman, K., MacKinnon, G., Klahr, P., 1989. The Authorizer's Assistant, A Knowledge-Based Credit Authorization System for American Express. *Proceedings of the 1989 Conference on Innovative Applications of Artificial Intelligence*, AAAI Press, Stanford, CA.

NEAR OPTIMAL OBJECTS PACKING THROUGH DIMENSIONAL UNFOLDING

Emilio Bertolotti, Enrico Castaldo, Gino Giannone

BULL HN, Italy
Via del Parlamento, 33 Borgolombardo, Mi, Italy 20098
Phone: + 39.2.6779.2054, Fax: + 39.2.6779.2515
EMail: frossill@eznet.it

Abstract

The efficient packing of regular shaped two dimensional objects is the core problem of several kinds of industry such as steel, thin-film and paper. This special kind of packing problem consists in cutting small rectangular stripes of different length and width from bigger coiled rectangles of raw material by combining them in such a way that trim loss is as low as possible. Previous attempts to apply "exact" discrete optimization techniques such as Simplex Partial Columns Generation, were not able to produce good cutting plans in large instances. We tackled this Roll Cutting Problem developing a new "dimension decomposition technique" that has been successfully experimented in a big steel industry first and then replicated in other steel and thin-film factories. This "unfolding" technique consists in splitting the overall search for good cutting plans in two separate graph search algorithms, one for each physical dimension of the rectangles. Searching individually in each dimension improves the overall search strategy allowing the effective pruning of useless combinations. Experimental evidence of how dimensional splitting strengthens the overall search strategy is given.

1. Introduction

The efficient packing of two dimensional objects affects the core business of several kinds of industry such as steel, thin film, paper and others. Normally, they have to cut small stripes of different length and width from bigger coiled rectangles of raw material by combining them in such a way that trim loss is as low as possible. This activity is crucial to their productivity, and thus highly relevant to their business. Dedicated experienced people normally apply naive methods to efficiently build sequences of cutting schema able to cover the overall set of workable commercial demands. Unfortunately, this packing problem is known to be hugely combinatorial even with tens of prototype rectangles of different sizes and the "stock cutting" industry suffers from its intractability. The "exact" computer discrete optimization techniques applied so far, such as Simplex Partial Columns Generation, were not able to deterministically produce good object packings in a reasonable response time. We tackled this Roll Cutting Problem devising a "dimensional decomposition" technique, we called 1D+1D heuristics, that has been successfully experimented in a big steel industry first (AST-ILVA) and then replicated in other factories. The technique is based on the co-operation of two separate graph search algorithms each one dedicated to a single dimension of the regularly shaped planar objects. Given m possible rectangular objects to cut from n available coils, then the "unfolding" of the two dimensions has the positive consequence to reduce the average time complexity of the resulting solution approach from an expected

$$\textit{Response-Time} = \textit{CONST} * (2^{n+m})$$

to a more attractive

$$\textit{Response-Time} = \textit{CONST} * (2^{n} + 2^{m})$$

where *CONST* is a common constant factor related to the speed of the machine. As a result, even if the complexity of the devised dimensional unfolding approach remains exponential, it is able to provide near optimal results in all real world cases faced so far. With the term near optimal we mean that ***optimal*** cutting plans can be ***exhaustively found in more that 95%*** of the cases within a reasonable response time (less than 120 seconds on a Pentium). This result is obtained through the dimensional unfolding which permits to avoid useless search. We practically demonstrated that the same basic 1D+1D technique applies to other kinds of cutting stock industry and is even suitable for parallel implementations whenever scale up factors require it. In fact, we applied 1D+1D to thin film industry (MANULI SpA) and also extended a critical pilot customer installation (MARCORA SpA) to exploit a parallel implementation. All these systems have been written in Common Lisp and now form a unique specialized platform named ROLL-CUTTER. Within the rest of the paper we will follow the steel industry study case to introduce the problem and the proposed solution. In section two, a precise description of the Roll Cutting Problem (RCP) together with the previously attempted Integer Linear Programming approaches are presented in some details. Section three introduces the 1D+1D decomposition and its strength in comparison with more classical 2D Implicit Enumeration Techniques. Feedbacks concerning the applications released so far are presented in section four. Section five discusses some of the implementation issues while section six gives an idea of how the ROLL-CUTTER platform is now going to be maintained and extended.

2. The Roll Cutting Problem

The overall objective of the Roll Cutting Problem (RCP) is to ensure the production of a sequence of *feasible* and *near optimal* cutting plans given a set of available coils and a set of workable commercial orders. To explain what this means, we will neglect any unnecessary detail concerning the chemical requirements and instead we will concentrate on the physical dimensions of the objects which constitute the core of the debated combinatorial problem. Figure 2.1 shows the basic dimensional parameters which completely describe all the involved entities: coils (*big coiled rectangles*) and commercial orders (*small rectangles or stripes*).

Coil χ_i of length Li and width Wi

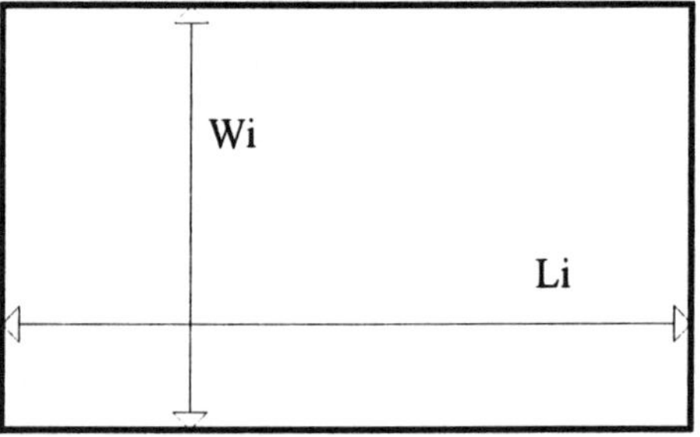

Order θ_j of length lj and width wj

Figure 2.1 Geometry of Coils & Stripes

Generally speaking, we have to manage two linear dimensions : Length and Width. However, to express the first linear dimension, we will use the weight C_i instead of length L_i since it renders the overall modelling simpler to formalize and closer to the way steel engineers describe the problem. Given the constant ν expressing the unitary weight of a given raw material, then length and weight are tied by the simple relation

$$C_i = L_i W_i \nu$$

The dimensional requirements of the rectangles, either coils χ_i and orders θ_j, will be thus completely defined through their weight C_i (c_j) and their width W_i (w_j). Conventionally, weight and width will be considered respectively as the first and the second dimension. Moreover, without loss of generality, we will always assume that all the coils have the same width W:

$$W_i = W \qquad i = 1,2,3,\ldots,n$$

In this way, each coil χ_i will be completely characterized just by its weight C_i.

Before describing what a *feasible* cutting plan is we have to explain first how orders must be cut out from coils, given the operational constraints of the cutting machines (slitters). Figure 2.2 shows an introductory example where three orders (θ_1, θ_2, θ_3) are cut out from two coils (χ_1, χ_2) of different weight.

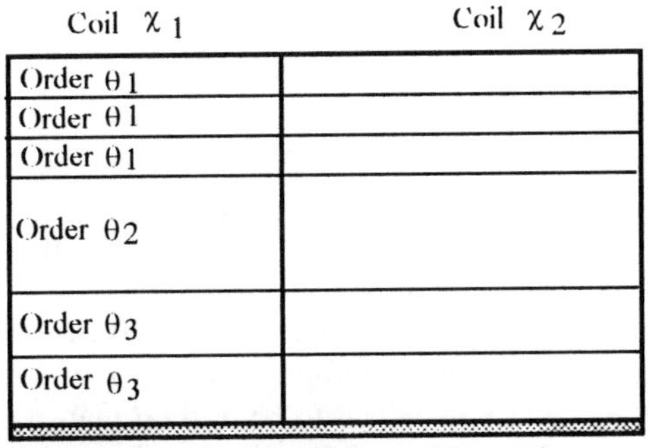

Coil χ_1	Coil χ_2
Order θ_1	
Order θ_1	
Order θ_1	
Order θ_2	
Order θ_3	
Order θ_3	

Figure 2.2 An introductory Example

Notice how coils can be bonded to reach the needed total weight while orders can be split in an arbitrary number of identical stripes to fulfil the available area W. This operational mode. is not limited to the steel industry. On the contrary, these "cutting rules" are quite common to all kinds of industries which must cut out planar objects of regular shape. In fact, these rules are tied to the cutting technology which is always the same no matter what the nature of the specific material to be cut is (steel, thin-film, paper, glass). Even when small sheets must be eventually obtained, this stripes cutting step is an unavoidable intermediate process Actually, there are other constraints, like the maximum weight allowed of each stripe, that discipline the feasibility of a cutting plan. However, even if these constraints are properly handled within our applications, we will not discuss them in the paper since they would inappropriately complicate the overall explanation.

Within each cutting plan the particular stripes configuration adopted is uniquely identified by the so called cutting pattern. A given cutting pattern determines the number of stripes for each order. The cutting pattern adopted in the example of figure 2.2 can be represented by the vector

$$\mathbf{Y} \equiv (y_1, y_2, y_3) \equiv (3, 1, 2)$$

By analogy, it is worth defining a coils pattern associated to a cutting plan. A coil pattern is represented through a binary vector **X** having one component for each available coil. A component's value is equal to 1 if the corresponding coil is used within the associated plan or 0 elsewhere. The coils pattern of the example is represented by the vector

$$\mathbf{X} \equiv (x_1, x_2) \equiv (1, 1)$$

Normally, a plan involves just a subset of the total available n coils and a subset of the total workable m orders. This means that some of the x_i and y_i will be equal to zero.

Tables 2.1, 2.2. show the weight and width values of the coils and orders used within the introductory example of figure 2.2

Coil	Width (inches)	Weight (pounds)	Pound per inch
χ_1	50	3500	70.0
χ_2	50	6000	120.0

Tab. 2.1 Coil Values of the Introductory Example

Order	Demanded Width (inches)	Demanded Weight (pounds)	Resulting Weight (pounds)
θ_1	5	2800 ±2%	2850
θ_2	16	3000 ±2%	3040
θ_3	8	3000 ±2%	3040

Tab. 2.2 Order Values of the Introductory Example

In this simple cutting plan the trim loss is three inches $(50 - [5 * 3] + 16 + [8 * 2] = 3)$. This means 570 pounds of wasted material and the plan would probably be considered not so good. Nevertheless, since human planners are normally dealing with tens of orders and coils, the huge number of combinations would have probably rendered the search for better plans a strenuous task.

2.1 Formal description of RCP

We are now in the position to precisely define what a *feasible* and *good* cutting plan is. Given n available coils and m workable orders then a feasible cutting plan P is defined by the couple

$$\mathrm{P} \equiv \{\mathbf{X}, \mathbf{Y}\}$$

where $\mathbf{X} \equiv (x_1, x_2, \ldots x_n)$ and $\mathbf{Y} \equiv (y_1, y_2, \ldots, y_m)$ are respectively a coils pattern and a cutting pattern such that the following $m + 1$ constraints hold

$$\frac{\sum_i^n x_i C_i}{W} y_j w_j \leq c_j + \delta_j \quad (j = 1 \ldots m) \qquad (2.1)$$

$$\sum_j^m y_j w_j \leq W \qquad (2.2)$$

2.1 ensures that for each order $j = 1, 2, 3, \ldots, m$ the planned weight does not violate the max. demand (*d_j is the max. allowed exceeding weight for the j-th order*). 2.2 guarantees that the total width W is never exceeded.

To plan the overall production demand, which comprehends m different commercial orders, what we should really build is a set {P} of feasible plans able to cover exactly the entire workload. This means we should find a set of plans {P} observing the following m constraints derived from (2.1) for $j = 1, 2, \ldots, m$.

$$c_j \leq \frac{\sum_i^n x_i C_i}{W} y_j w_j \leq c_j + \delta_j \qquad (2.3)$$

However, the problem of finding the overall set of covering plans is not of much interest to the scope of the paper for a couple of reasons. First of all, it must be necessarily solved in different ways according to the particular features of each specific case (e.g. *we were asked to solve it applying an order priority rule for a steel factory*). Moreover, there is a practical reason that makes this sort of global planning quite superfluous. In fact, only the next few *good* plans are really needed since the new incoming commercial orders and the new coiled material alter the possible combinations rendering earlier produced plans soon obsolete.

Thus, we will now continue to concentrate on the solution of a single *feasible* and *good* plan which is the real core aspect of RCP. In this framework the search for "the next" *feasible* and *good* plan will start from a chosen pivot order Oj. This pivot is the order that the human planner wants to be certain is inserted into the next plan. As already mentioned, the choice of the pivot order could be automatically done according to a priority rule (e.g. due-dates) or through a more exhaustive strategy which tries in turn all the orders as candidate pivots. Nevertheless, all these different ways to choose the next pivot can affect the overall computational complexity at most through a linear factor (*number of orders m*). The real source of *non-polynomial* complexity (2^{n+m}) remains the search for a single *feasible* and *good* plan once an arbitrary pivot order has been chosen.

Given a pivot order Oj several *feasible* cutting plans exist. These feasible plans are formed by all the couples {**X**,**Y**} observing the two equations (2.1) and (2.2). Before defining when a *feasible* plan P ≡ {**X**,**Y**} is judged to be a *good* plan we have to precisely define the optimization objectives used as selection criteria. These optimization objectives are the following

- Trim loss minimization :
  Min (TL (**Y**)).
- Maximize the usage of a given cutting pattern which is equivalent to minimize the number of knives changes :
  Max (KU (**X**)).

They can be formally expressed through the following relations

$$Min(TL(Y)) \equiv Min(W - \sum_j^m y_j w_j) \qquad (2.4)$$

$$Max(KU(X)) \equiv Max(\frac{\sum_i^n x_i C_i}{W}) \qquad (2.5)$$

The first objective (2.4) clearly expresses the minimization of trim loss. The second objective (2.5) is strongly tied to the minimization of the number of knife changes since maximizing the usage of the same pattern (KU(**X**)). In fact, according to the previous assumption, we are working on the search for "the next" single plan separately, so that pursuing the maximization of a plan weight, i.e. plan duration, implicitly minimize the frequency of knife changes.

We are now in the position to define when a *feasible* plan becomes a *good* plan. A candidate *feasible* plan P ≡ {**X**,**Y**} is a *good* plan if another *feasible* plan P' ≡ {**X'**,**Y'**} does not dominate P through the following dominance relationship

P' dominates P if and only if the following two conditions are jointly verified

$$TL(\mathbf{X'}) < TL(\mathbf{X}) \qquad \& \qquad (2.6)$$

$$KU(\mathbf{Y}') > KU(\mathbf{Y})$$

As normally happens with the use of dominant relationships, we have just identified a set of *good* plans instead of giving a definition of *the unique absolutely optimal* plan. In fact, the presence of multiple contrasting objectives would have rendered quite unnatural the definition of "plan optimality". In other words, between a plan with lower Trim Loss and a plan with lower Knife Changes, we cannot say which one is the best. Merging the two different objectives through a linear function would be quite an arbitrary decision. Anyway, the dominance relationship is known to be a powerful tool able to drastically prune outclassed solutions (Pearl 1985). Experimental results with real world data revealed how the dominant set formed by the resulting *good* plans has no more than five or six members. There are other external reasons, like overloading or underloading conditions affecting the cutting machines workload, that can help in making a more convenient selection amongst the *good* plans.

2.2 Revised Simplex approaches

Generally speaking, the RCP problem is within the family of two-dimensional regular shaped cutting stock problems which are known to be NP-hard (Dyckoff et al. 1984). This kind of problem has already been tackled through ILP partial columns generation approaches. This Revised Simplex method consists in generating only the columns suggested by the proper auxiliary knapsack problem solved at each step of the Simplex iteration (Gilmore & Gomory 1966). While the method works fine for 1D cutting stock problems, there are practical limitations that makes it difficult to apply to 2D real-world instances (Dyckoff et al. 1984). In fact, the ordinarily number of coils and orders to deal with are beyond the quantities normally handled though partial column generation. Moreover, the presence of multiple objectives and very specific constraints render the problem difficult to model through ILP approaches.

A flavour concerning the size of the potential search space is given considering the following simple formula. Being m the average number of available coils, n the average number of candidate orders and being $\overline{k}$ the average number of stripes per order, the potential number of possible cutting plans is proportional to the power-set of the coils times the power-set of the possible stripes, i.e.:

$$2^{(n+\overline{k}m)} \qquad (2.8)$$

Typical average values for n, m and $\overline{k}$ are respectively thirty, thirty and three.

3. 1D + 1D Decomposition

As already recognized (Dyckoff et al. 1984), the additional specific constraints and the particular structure found in this sort of problem may constitute a source of insuperable complexity for a general ILP modelization. By contrast, within a more tailored approach, these problem features can be exploited to render the modelization more tractable (Scutella' et al. 1995). Not surprising, a quite simple heuristic approach, based on a specialized greedy procedure, already demonstrated to produce fruitful results in a specific industrial roll cutting application (Ferreira 1990).

Pursuing the heuristic mainstream, we tackled the problem exploiting its structure to simplify the solution approach while avoiding degradation of the solution quality. More precisely, we have decomposed the overall two-dimensional cutting stock problem into two one-dimensional knapsack sub-problems we called : ***first-dimension-knapsack*** and ***second-dimension-knapsack***. A standard definition of the quite popular 0/1 knapsack problem is the following (Martello & Toth 1990).

Given n objects each one being defined through a given cost c_i and a given value v_i maximize the sum of v_i under the maximum capacity constraint expressed by a real value C which limits the sum of c_i' s.

We will see in which way both our sub-problems can be easily mapped into the knapsack modelization and what are the benefits of this straightforward decomposition.

3.1 First dimension sub-problem

Given a pivot order θ_p the ***first-dimension-Knapsack*** consists in the search for the possible combinations of coils which provides a *feasible* cutting plan just for this pivot order, disregarding the computation of the cutting patterns **Y** which would normally include other available orders to minimize trim loss. This knapsack problem can be formally stated as:

$$Max(\frac{\sum_i^n x_i C_i}{W}) \tag{3.1}$$

$$\sum_i^n \frac{x_i C_i}{W} \leq \frac{c_p + \delta_p}{y_p w_p} \tag{3.2}$$

Where 3.1, the knapsack value maximization, maps the objective of finding a coils combination **X** that maximizes the weight of the overall plan: (MAX (KU(**X**)) defined by 2.5.

Equation 3.2, the knapsack capacity constraint, guarantees that the coils combination **X** will never exceed the weight of the pivot order θ_p. Notice that this equation must be replicated for each possible number of stripes y_p. Since y_p ranges from 1 to (W / w_p) we have to actually solve a number of (W / w_p) knapsack instances. Being $\bar{k}$ the average number of stripes, to solve the first dimension sub-problem we have to solve $\bar{k}$ knapsack instances on the average (as already mentioned, the value k is certainly contained within the interval [1 . 20], while its average ranges from 2 to 5).

According to 3.1 and 3.2 a solution to the first dimension sub-problem is identified by the tuple **XS** defined as

$$\mathbf{XS} \equiv (\mathbf{X} \, . \, KU(\mathbf{X}) \, . \, y_p)$$

i.e. a coils pattern, its corresponding weight and a given number of stripes for the pivot order. Actually, we are interested in all the feasible patterns **X** observing the constraint 3.2. All these patterns will form the first dimension solutions set: {**XS**}. This set can be partitioned into y_p different sub-sets formed through the partition relationship

$$\{\mathbf{XS}\}_r \equiv \{\mathbf{XS} := \mathbf{XS} \text{ s.t. } y_p = r\}$$

Moreover, each sub-set can be ordered by decreasing values of weight, i.e. KU(**X**). The possibility to establish such a partitioning and ordering is crucial within the 1D+1D framework. In fact, it will allow to integrate the overall optimization of both the KU(**X**) and TL(Y) objectives simply through an efficient linear search as explained in 3.3.

3.2 Second dimension sub-problem

The goal of the second dimension sub-problem is to find a cutting pattern **Y**, *compatible* with a given first dimension solution, that minimizes Trim Loss. The term *compatible* means that each candidate pattern **Y** must take into account the y_p stripes of the pivot order θ_p that have already been inserted. Given a first dimension solution, identified by a tuple (**X**, KU(**X**), y_p), the ***second-dimension-knapsack*** problem can then be formally stated as:

$$Min(W - y_p w_p - \sum_j^{m-1} y_j w_j) \tag{3.3}$$

$$y_p w_p + \sum_j^{m-1} y_j w_j \leq W \tag{3.4}$$

Similarly to the first dimension sub-problem, equation 3.3 represents the objective of finding a cutting pattern **Y** which minimize the TL(**Y**) objective. Equation 3.4 guarantees that the solution patterns **Y** do not exceed the total width W. A solution to the second dimension sub-problem is identified through the tuple

$$\mathbf{YS} \equiv (\mathbf{Y} \, . \, TL(\mathbf{Y}) \, . \, y_p)$$

i.e. a cutting pattern, its corresponding trim loss and a given number of stripes of the pivot order.

Again, the set of feasible solutions {**YS**} can be partitioned into y_p different sub-sets in the same manner we have done for the {**XS**} set. Moreover, the objective TL(**Y**) induces a significant partial ordering on the each solution sub-set $\{\mathbf{YS}\}_r$.

3.3 1D+1D Integration

To see how the 1D+1D decomposition works on the introductory example of figure 2.2, when the pivot order is θ_1 and y_1 equals to three, let us build the corresponding first dimension and second dimension solutions

$$\mathbf{XS'} \equiv (\mathbf{X} \,.\, KU(\mathbf{X}) \,.\, y_1) \equiv ((1.1) \,.\, 190 \,.\, 3)$$

$$\mathbf{YS'} \equiv (\mathbf{Y} \,.\, TL(\mathbf{Y}) \,.\, y_1) \equiv ((3.1.2) \,.\, 3 \,.\, 3)$$

Suppose now that the following two new coils will become available :

Coil	Width (inches)	Weight (pounds)	Pound per inch
χ_3	25	1750	70.0
χ_4	25	3000	120.0

then we can add the following new solutions

$$\mathbf{XS''} \equiv ((0.\ 0.\ 1.\ 1) \,.\, 190 \,.\, 3)$$

$$\mathbf{YS''} \equiv ((3.\ 0.\ 1) \,.\, 2 \,.\, 3)$$

The solution sets become thus formed by:

$$\{\mathbf{XS}\}_3 \equiv \{((1.\ 1.\ 0.\ 0) \,.\, 190 \,.\, 3) \quad ((0.\ 0.\ 1.\ 1) \,.\, 190 \,.\, 3))\}$$

$$\{\mathbf{YS}\}_3 \equiv \{((3.\ 1.\ 2) \,.\, 3 \,.\, 3) \quad ((3.\ 0.\ 1) \,.\, 2 \,.\, 3)$$

Hereafter, we will see how the availability of the separated solutions sets $\{\mathbf{XS}\}_r$ and $\{\mathbf{YS}\}_r$ allow to efficiently build the set of the *good* cutting plans for the original entire RCP problem defined by equations 2.1, 2.2, 2.3, 2.4.

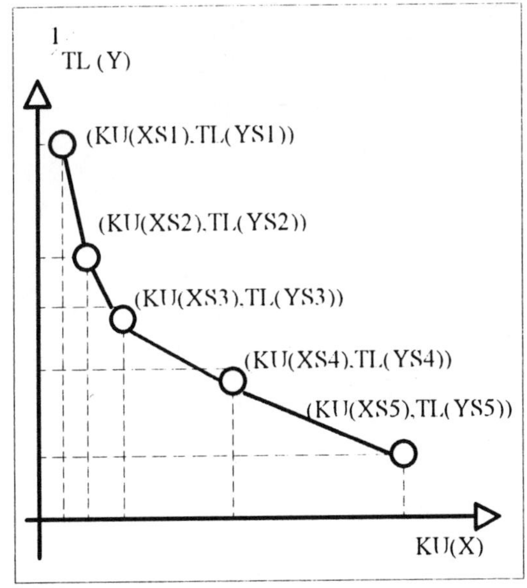

Figure 3.1 Dominance Frontier

According to the dominance relationship 2.6, to build the set of *good* cutting plans we have to find all the *dominant* cutting plans. In other words, we have to build the dominance frontier defined in the plan (KU(**XS**).TL(**YS**)) as shown in figure 3.1.

The following pseudo-procedure (***BUILD-D-***
Figure 3.1 Dominance Frontier
FRONTIER) can build precisely the dominance frontier in linear time. The procedure has as input the two collections of sets $\{\mathbf{XS}\}_r$. $\{\mathbf{YS}\}_r$ and the maximum number of stripes k_j of the given pivot order O_j.

```
(Function BUILD-D-FRONTIER ({XS} {YS} kj)
 ; Compute Dominance Frontier in D-frontier
  ; Init the Dominance Frontier
  (setq D-frontier nil)
  ; Cycle for each number of stripes i of
  ;  the given pivot order
  (Dotimes (r  kj)
    ; find coil pattern X with max KU
    (setq best-X
          (get-first-X  r  {XS}r ))
    ; find  cutting pattern with min TL
    (setq bets-Y
          (fget-first-Y  r  best-X  {YS}r  ))
    ; store the current solution
    (push (list best-X best-Y)
           D-frontier)))
```

Thanks to the partitioning and to the ordering of the partial solutions sets $\{\mathbf{XS}\}$ and $\{\mathbf{YS}\}$ the ***BUILD-D-FRONTIER*** can effectively build the dominance frontier in linear time. Being the number of steps within the ***BUILD-D-FRONTIER*** body equal to number of stripes k_j, its average time complexity is equal to $O(\bar{k}_j)$. To summarize, the complete set $\{P\}$ formed by the *feasible* and *good* solutions to the original RCP problem will be formed by <u>*all*</u> the couples

$$P = \{\mathbf{Y} \,.\, \mathbf{X}\}$$

belonging to the dominance set. With the 1D+1D heuristic decomposition, we have practically reduced the complexity of the problem from an expected

$$O(2^{(n+\bar{k}m)})$$

to a more affordable

$$O(2^n + 2^{\bar{k}m})$$

In fact, the solution is composed of two sequential steps : *first-dimension-knapsack* and *second-dimension-knapsack*. Time complexity of the first step is proportional to the power-set of the coils $O(2^n)$ while for the second step the time complexity is proportional to the power-set of the possible stripes $O(2^{\bar{k}m})$.

4. Application payoff

Three applications based on the 1D+1D heuristic have been already released to three different customers. Other customer projects are in progress. Table 3.1 shows 15 examples produced during one of the customer acceptance tests. Notice how ROLL-CUTTER produced expert level cutting plans in less than 120 seconds compared to the 1000 seconds taken by human experts.

The payoff of the released applications can be summarized by the following two results:

1) The quality of the cutting plans produced by the applications are comparable or even better than the cutting plans produced by experienced human beings. Particularly, the dominance set always includes the cutting plans that would have been produced by the top level experts.

2) The average processing time taken by the system to produce a set of dominant cutting plans is in the order of thirty seconds. Usually, human experts need from ten to sixty minutes to produce a good cutting plan.

ROLL-CUTTER is currently installed in three different factories :

- A service center whose main activity consists in cutting small coils from bigger ones. The system is integrated with the Manufacturing Information System which supplies the information concerning the commercial demands and the coils to program. The cutting programs formulated by the system are returned to the MIS once validated by the human operator. This kind of system integration applies to the other two ROLL-CUTTER installations as well.

Cutting Plan #	# Of orders inserted into the Plan	Total weight	# Of knives changes HUMAN EXPERT	% Trim Loss HUMAN EXPERT	TIME (SEC) HUMAN EXPERT	# Of knives changes ROLL CUTTER	% Trim Loss ROLL CUTTER	TIME (SEC) ROLL CUTTER
1	4	6797	4	2.64	> 1000	2	2.64	< 30
2	7	38924	6	0.89	> 1000	4	0.67	< 60
3	5	25000	3	1.33	> 1000	3	1.33	< 60
4	4	21000	3	2.30	> 1000	3	1.33	< 60
5	10	38000	5	0.76	> 1000	4	0.83	< 30
6	17	16300	6	0.82	> 1000	5	1.52	< 60
7	5	7700	2	4.79	> 1000	2	3.00	< 60
8	4	2600	2	2.00	> 1000	2	1.71	< 60
9	10	43100	6	0.76	> 1000	5	0.96	< 30
10	7	2280	2	1.33	> 1000	2	1.33	< 120
11	5	4620	2	0.75	> 1000	2	0.75	< 30
12	7	9000	3	3.27	> 1000	3	3.17	< 120
13	5	13300	5	3.62	> 1000	3	3.99	< 120
14	10	43100	6	0.76	> 1000	6	0.76	< 60
15	8	12100	4	1.15	> 1000	3	1.00	< 60

Tab. 3.1 Results taken from a Customer Acceptance Test

- A steel industry which direclty produces coils cutting them into smaller stripes. Within this context the auxiliary facilities provided by the system that allows fast selection / ordering of both coils and commercial demands have been particularly appreciated.

- The third site is concerned with thin-film production. In this case the performance of the system has been specifically stressed for a couple of reasons. First of all, the combinatorial facet of the problem was particularly relevant. Secondly, the system had to knock out a software program already used for several years from the human operators.

5. Implementations Issues

To implement the ROLL-CUTTER basic platform it took us two man years using Gold-Hill Common Lisp Developer running under Windows 3.11. We found the Lisp language specially helpful during the tuning of the knapsack search algorithms.

A variety of well studied exact and approximate algorithms to solve one-dimensional knapsack problems exist (Martello & Toth 1990). The two different one-dimensional knapsack problems. can be seen as two special instances of the general "value-independent-knapsack-problem" (also known as subset sum problem) where n objects characterized by different cost values c_i and a constant profit value v must be put into a knapsack without exceeding its capacity C. Toth's book devoted to 0/1 knapsack problems presents the well studied MTS algorithm which is based on tree search and dynamic programming techniques. In our implementation we followed this approach augmenting the basic tree search mechanism with heuristic criteria we derived from the specific nature of the problem.

Two different depth-first tree-search algorithms (DFTS) have been implemented. The two algorithms have a common depth-first strategy which provides the implicit enumeration mechanism on top of which two specialized heuristic search policy have been imposed. The features of such DFTS heuristics are the following

◊ First-dimension-DFTS features:

- Coils, which represents the knapsack objects, are pre-ordered by decreasing size (we verified how this ordering increases the pruning power).
- Lower values of y_j for the "pivot" order are tried first.

◊ Second-dimension-DFTS features:

- For each candidate order θ_j the number of stripes y'_j which allows to exactly match the demanded weight are tried first. This means to select first a number of stripes y'_j such that

$$c_j \le \frac{\sum_i^n x_i C_i}{W} y'_j w_j \le c_j + \delta_j$$

In this way the splitting of an order in different lots is avoided as much as possible.

6. Maintenance & Extensions

ROLL-CUTTER is in continuous evolution since its first customer installation which happened to be in January 1995. Within this evolution we are pursuing two main objectives:

- Continue to improve the performance of the basic 1D+1D decomposition technique

- Extend the application of the 1D+1D technique to other different cutting stock domains.

In the first direction we are currently developing, for a ROLL-CUTTER customer a parallel implementation of the 1D+1D algorithms. The implementation is based on a cluster of 586 PC's which co-operate during the building of the feasible solutions sets **{XS}**, **{YS}**. This improvement will allow us to tackle the production of cutting plans optimized throughout the overall orders portfolio.

Concerning the extension of the application domains we already successfully applied the 1D+1D technique to a different kind of industry : thin-film. Even if the basic technique is the same, this attempt generated some modification to the original ROLL-CUTTER platform. These needed modifications will bring us to generalize the overall ROLL-CUTTER shell. The idea is to have a unique platform providing the basic 1D+1D different decomposition mechanisms from which several more specialized platforms can be built. Other than Thin-film, another specialized platform is going to be derived for paper industry (glass industry is a good candidate too). Moreover, in the near term we intend to experiment the 1D+1D "unfolding" technique even with 3D placement problems (e.g. ships loading and unloading).

7 Conclusions

The 1D+1D problem decomposition allowed us to face a complex two dimensional cutting stock problem (RCP) reaching expert level performance. The method has produced exemplary results within several released applications. So far, we already demonstrated that the method is able to discover the complete set of dominant optimal solutions, 95% of the time, in a few seconds. It takes 15 minutes or more to build the "next" near optimal cutting plan to experienced human beings.

The ROLL-CUTTER platform on which all the released applications are based is now evolving in different directions. A parallel implementation of the 1D+1D technique to solve the global optimization of the overall cutting shop-floor is in progress. Moreover, we are generalizing the platform to facilitate the development of different applications addressing other industry sectors.

References

Albano, A. and Saluppo, G. 1980. *Optimal Allocation of Two-Dimensional Irregular Shapes Using Heuristic Search Methods.* IEEE Transaction on Systems, Man and Cybernetics. Vol. smc-10, No. 5, pp. 242-248.

Dyckoff, H. and Kruse, H. 1984. *Trim Loss and Related Problems.* The Int. Jl of Management Science. Vol. 13, No. 1 pp. 59-72.

Ferreira, J.S. 1990. *A two-phase Roll Cutting Problem.* European Journal of Operational Research. No. 44, pp. 185-196.

Gilmore, P.C. and Gomory, R.E. 1961. *A Linear Programming Approach to the Cutting Stock Problem.* International Business Machines Corporation, Research Center, Yorktown, New York, pp. 849-859.

Gilmore, P.C. and Gomory, R.E. 1966. *The Theory and Computation of Knapsack Functions.* International Business Machines Corporation, Yorktown Heights, New York, pp.1045-1074.

Ibarra, O.H. and Kim, C., 1975. *Fast approximation Algorithms for the Knapsack and Sum of Subset Problem.* Journal of the Association for computing Machinery. Vol. 22, No. 4 pp. 463-468.

Martello, S. and Toth, P., 1990. *0/1 Knapsack Problems: Algorithms and Computer Implementation.* John Wiley & Son Ltd.

Pearl J., eds. 1985. *Heuristics, Intelligent Search Strategies for Computer Problem Solving.* Addison-Wesley.

Scutella M.G.; Bertolotti E.; Castaldo E.; Gambale M.; 1995. *Cutting Stock: Hypergraphs and Decomposition techniques.* Dept. of Informatica, Pisa Univ.. Proceedings of the Conference: Models and Algorithms for Optimization Problems" (January 1995).

Sahni S., 1975. *Approximate Algorithms for the 0/1 Knapsack Problem.* Journal of the ACM. Vol. 22 No. 1 pp. 115-124.

Developing and Deploying Knowledge on a Global Scale

James Borron

Reuters America
360 Motor Parkway
Hauppauge, NY 11788
james.borron@reuters.com

David Morales

Reuters America
311 S. Wacker Dr., Suite 1000
Chicago, IL 60606
david.morales@reuters.com

Philip Klahr

Inference Corporation
100 Rowland Way
Novato, CA 94945
klahr@inference.com

Abstract

Reuters is a worldwide company focused on supplying financial and news information to its over 40,000 subscribers around the world. To enhance the quality and consistency of its customer support organization, Reuters embarked on a global knowledge development and reuse project. The resulting system is in operational use in the North America, Europe, and Asia. The system supports 38 Reuter products worldwide. This paper is a case study of the Reuters experience in putting a global knowledge organization in place, in building knowledge bases at multiple distributed sites, in deploying these knowledge bases in multiple sites around the world, and in maintaining and enhancing knowledge bases within a global organizational framework. This project is the first to address issues in multi-country knowledge development and maintenance, and multi-country knowledge deployment. These issues are critical for global companies to understand, address and resolve, in order to effectively gain the benefits of global knowledge systems.

Introduction

Reuters Holdings PLC supplies the global financial and news media communities with a wide range of products and services including:

- real-time financial data
- transaction systems for financial trading
- access to numerical and textual historical databases
- news
- graphics
- still photos and news video.

Reuters has 40,000 subscribers, 309,000 user accesses, and operates in 154 countries. Reuters information is accessed through a series of Reuter products. These products, and the real time data feeds, are supported through customer support help desks around the world.

While Customer Service Operations have been in place in Reuters for many years, it is only within the last few that help desks have risen to prominence in the company as a key competitive differentiator. There are three key areas in which Reuters competes:

- in the data and news content Reuters provides
- in the technology with which that data is delivered
- in customer service.

Providing outstanding customer support encourages customer loyalty, supports repeat business, and promotes a reputation for customer orientation. Within the last few years, Reuters has aggressively invested to provide significant improvements in its customer support organization and operations.

As the organic growth of help desks and technical support functions developed from local to continental initiatives, Reuters realized that a great deal of customer and technical support expertise was developing within the company which might effectively be reused. A global steering group was formed, and help desks in the United Kingdom and the Americas began exchanging staff and support materials. The idea of encoding and reusing knowledge is an extension of the initial effort to move people and their knowledge around the world.

Project History

In February, 1993, Reuters America (RAM) engaged Inference Corporation in a re-engineering study based on RAM's Chicago Customer Response Center to explore opportunities for significant improvements in customer support. Key findings of this study included:

- opportunities for improving inefficient internal systems
- an environment oriented around specialists, and not conducive to generalists
- issues in staff training and key competencies

- development of a strategy to preserve knowledge assets.

The strategy involved building knowledge systems using *Case-Base Reasoning* (CBR) [Kolodner, 1993]. Other customer support organizations had already reported successes in using CBR technology (as subsequently reported in IAAI conferences [Acorn & Walden, 1992; Nguyen et al., 1993; Hislop & Pracht, 1994]) and Reuters decided that CBR would be appropriate for developing knowledge systems for use in their help desks as well.

In June 1993, RAM launched its first case-base project. Initial tasks included:

- forming a project team
- initial authoring of a style guide
- agreeing on product domains to cover
- committing time for case authors (people building the case bases)
- developing an incentive program
- setting and achieving targets.

In December 1993, RAM deployed its first case base. It had approximately 1,200 robust cases. It had especially good response and feedback from new hires who were able to quickly use the tool to provide both self-training on an on-going basis, and an expert advisor to increase their competency and ability. The case base was also a strong source for infrequent and complex situations. As users learned the more routine situations, their use of the case base evolved to the more complex and unusual situations. This ability for users to come up to speed on the routine situations was significantly enhanced with the case-base tool.

There were, though, some difficult issues. Developing the case base required resources to *author* the knowledge.[1] Given the dozens of Reuter products available, the generation of knowledge bases would require a more critical mass of authors. The few authors that generated the initial 1,200 cases would be insufficient. Also important was that even though much expert knowledge existed in Chicago, there was significant expertise elsewhere at Reuters -- in London, Continental Europe, Asia, the Middle East and Africa. To exploit this knowledge was vital in generating complete and accurate case bases.

While RAM pursued CBR technology aggressively in 1993, other areas in Reuters were also pursuing CBR initiatives. Reuters United Kingdom and Ireland (UKI) was involved in CBR as early as mid-1992. UKI's principal focus in 1992 and 1993 had been on developing a call tracking and problem management system called CALLS. UKI used Inference International consultants to help build CALLS as well as to provide guidance on using and integrating CBR technology for problem resolution. Some initial case bases were built in UKI in the 1992-1993 timeframe which also helped RAM in its evaluation of CBR in early 1993. A third effort in CBR at Reuters was also simultaneously occurring the Reuters Middle East and Africa (MEA) organization. In particular, the South Africa help desk quickly and independently developed case bases to support their needs. Consultants from Syscon in South Africa supported this effort.

Given the three multiple CBR efforts at Reuters, and the distribution of expertise around the world, Reuters decided in February 1994 to form a Global Customer Support Steering Committee to organize a global case-base effort. Their initial objectives were to:

- consolidate the case-base projects in America, United Kingdom, and Africa
- increase domain coverage
- more effectively use the best resources for authoring worldwide
- establish a global funding mechanism
- organize a global management organization.

Interestingly, the idea of a distributed model for case authoring arose from the Chicago-based product experts' need to work from home. These experts needed isolation from the running of the day to day operation to be most productive. While at their desks, these senior-level experts are continually interrupted, as experts often are, and unable to devote the necessary time to writing good cases. Typically one writes a family of cases in one sitting, and continuous concentration is conducive to a well-designed case base.

As a result, expert authors were outfitted with home PCs and access to their supported products. In addition, they were given detailed instructions for writing cases in such a way that there would be no corruption to the database when their work was merged with the master case base file. From this experience, it dawned on the project team that cases could be written anywhere, whether 5 miles from

[1] We use the term *author* to describe the knowledge engineering/knowledge acquisition process. Authoring is the customary term used in the CBR customer support community. It provides a more concise active description of the entire process (acquiring the knowledge and encoding it). We discuss later the alternatives of having an expert author cases directly or having a knowledge engineer interview experts and then encode the knowledge.

downtown Chicago or 5,000 miles away!

Knowledge can be captured easily wherever it resides, and it was this conclusion that precipitated the drive toward a global case base.

By July 1994, a plan was established for an 18-month global project. This plan was approved by the Global Steering Committee, and the global project began in August 1994. The 18-month period can roughly be divided into three principal phases, each of 6-month duration:

> Phase 1: Project initiation and organization, formulate budget, establish global procedures, develop global style guide, generate initial knowledge base (combining and globalizing knowledge from three existing efforts), and prototype initial supporting software utilities.
>
> Phase 2: Complete first version of software utilities to support global procedures, solidify quality assurance procedures, expand knowledge building process (here focused on increasing the number of products/domains covered), provide initial user training, deploy and beta test initial versions of knowledge base, and compute return-on-investment metrics.
>
> Phase 3: Further expand knowledge building to a critical mass (now focused on increasing depth of knowledge for products/domains covered), complete second version of software utilities, quality test complete system, complete documentation (utilities, global procedures, training materials), and complete global rollout with more robust knowledge base.

Figure 1 provides an overview of the project timeline.

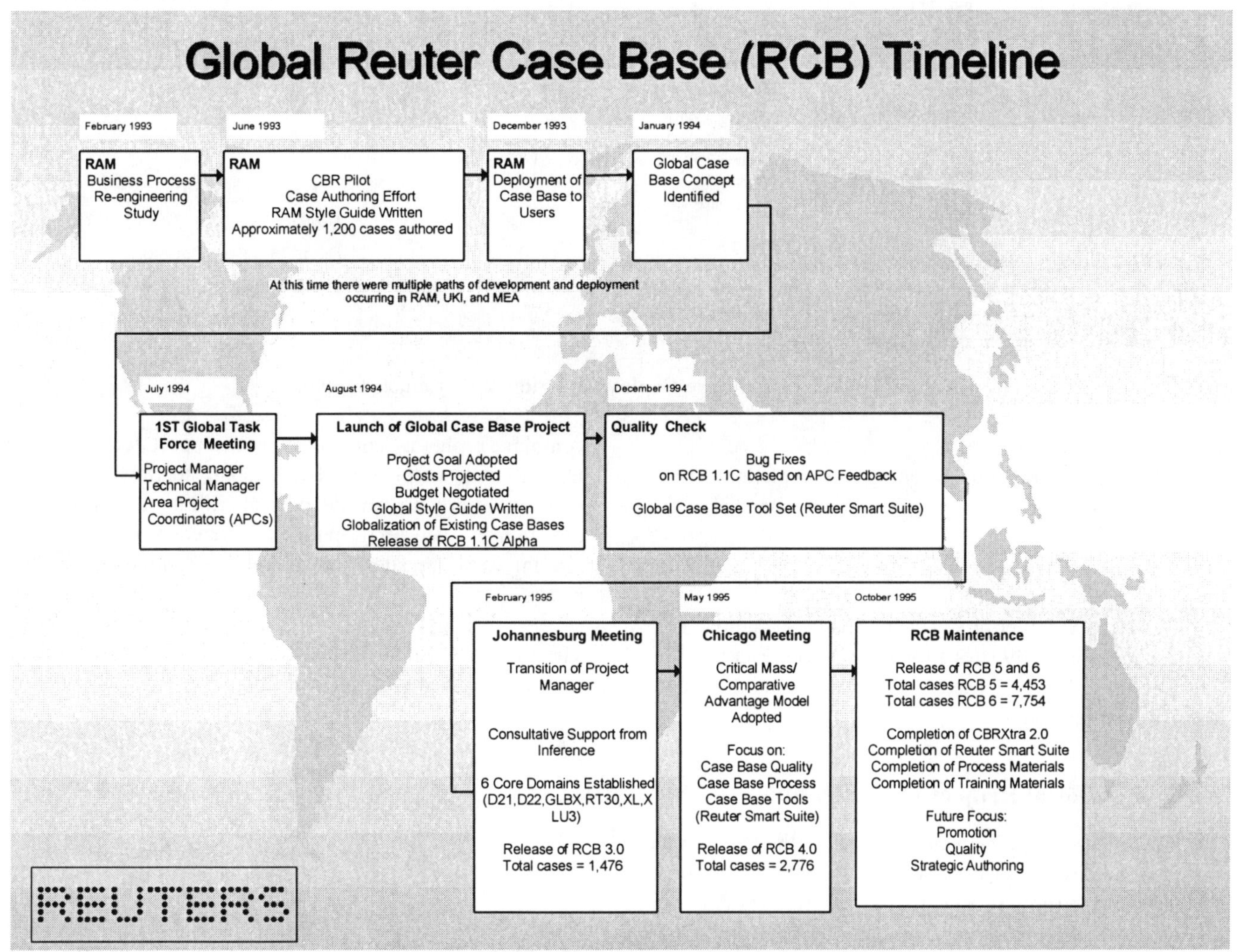

Figure 1. Global Reuter Case-Base Project Timeline.

The Reuter Case Base

The Reuter Case Base is a global knowledge base, created by Reuter staff, that grows with user interaction. It acts as a tool for Help Desk personnel in solving customer queries quickly, putting expertise at their fingertips.

UKI
Sites Installed: London
Area Project Coordinator:
Marcus Walia, London.
44-171-324-5222

RAM
Sites Installed:
Chicago, Stamford
Area Project Coordinator:
Mark Hanson, Chicago.
(312)-408-8633

RCEMA
Sites Installed:
Amsterdam Dusseldorf Kiev Moscow Vienna
Athens Frankfurt Luxembourg Munich Warsaw
Berlin Geneva Madrid Rome Zurich
Brussels Hamburg Milan Stuttgart
Area Project Coordinator:
Paul Cantini, Geneva.
41-022-718-2715

RA
Sites Installed:
Hong Kong, Kuala Lumpur,
Singapore, Tokyo
Area Project Coordinator:
Steven Sim, Singapore.
65-870-3157

Products Covered

Information
700 MRV
Adfin 2.2
Advanced Trader Workstation
Database Manager Server
Excel
Excel Utilities
FX Options
FxCalc 1.5
IDN Data
IDN Page Based Server
IDN SelectFeed Server
InsertLink
MarketLink
Personal Trader Workstation 3.0
Personal Trader Workstation 4.0
Reuter Bond Window
Reuter Graphics 2.0
Reuter Graphics 3.1
Reuter Link PC
Reuter Technical Analysis
Reuter Terminal 2.16
Reuter Terminal 3.0
ReuterMail
SelectFeed
SelectFeed Plus
Sink Distributor
Source Distributor
Telerate Digital Page Feed
Windows 3.1

News & Media
Multimedia Data Network/Client Receiver
News 2000
Newsfile
Reuter Company Newsyear

Transactions
Dealing 2000-1
Dealing 2000-2
Dealing 2000 Phase 2/Pre-Screen Pricing
Globex
Shipping 2000

The Global Site
Global Case Base Technical Manager
David Morales, Chicago.
(312)-408-8789

Figure 2. Reuter Case-Base Deployment Sites and Products Covered.

The 18-month effort is now reaching its completion. It has achieved all of its objectives. As of November 1995, the Reuter Case Base

- contains 7,754 cases
- covers 38 Reuter products and services (Figure 2)
- is installed in 29 sites around the world (Figure 2)
- is used by 190 users who are directly servicing Reuter customers.

Global Project Organization

The *Global Steering Committee* consists of the heads (vice president or director level) of customer support from each of the then five (now four) global areas: Reuters America (RAM), United Kingdom and Ireland (UKI), Reuters Asia (RA) Reuters Continental Europe (RCE), and Middle East and Africa (MEA) (RCE and MEA have since been combined), plus a senior customer support representative from Reuters corporate. The Global Steering Committee meets quarterly to review project milestones, issues and directions. Biweekly phone conference calls provide interim status updates and address immediate issues and needs.

The principal global organization structure includes five logically-defined job/skill positions:

- Global Project Manager
- Global Technical Manager
- Area Project Coordinators
- Domain Authors
- Case Authors

The *Global Project Manager* led the project and coordinated the development and deployment efforts in the five regions. This was certainly one of the more difficult challenges in the project. Not only are there significant time-zone differences among the five regions, but also differences in culture, in software development practices, in structure and management organization, and even in project objectives. In addition, from a knowledge perspective, there were also differences in operations and business practices which resulted in issues of "localization", i.e., differences in knowledge among the regions, which had to be factored in the knowledge development processes. Thankfully, foreign language issues were minimized. The standard language for financial information globally is English, and an English-only knowledge base was sufficient for current global deployments.[2]

The Global Project Manager was also responsible for managing the budget and all external consultants. Funding of the project was global, proportional to each region's revenue contributions to the company (e.g., a region contributing 20% of Reuter yearly revenues funded 20% of the project.) Thus, there were contributions required from all parts of the globe, both for financial funding and for case authoring. This approach insured appropriate management attention and buy-in worldwide, and minimized the common "not-invented-here" syndrome. Every region was participating.

The *Global Technical Manager* was responsible for supervising all technical aspects of the project, including:

- developing a single, standard global style guide for the knowledge base
- leading all software development efforts, including customizing the CBR Express authoring environment to support the Reuters style guide and building new utilities to support Reuters global procedures
- supervising technical deliverables of external consultants
- approving case bases for global distribution
- maintaining a central library (repository in Chicago) of global cases
- distributing global case bases and/or updates to the five regions worldwide
- technically supporting the five regions.

The *Area Project Coordinators* were responsible for the overall operation of their local region, including:

- managing the hardware and software infrastructure locally
- authoring knowledge bases (building case bases and supervising the domain authors and case authors)
- training authors and end users
- testing and approving locally-built knowledge bases
- transmitting knowledge bases to the central site in Chicago
- receiving global case bases and updates from Chicago and implementing them locally.

The *Domain Author* is the person responsible for a particular case base. Each case base contains cases relative to a particular product. This segmentation of knowledge based on product seemed the most natural at Reuters. Customer calls focused around the particular Reuter product the customer was using, and problems or issues associated with the product. A particular product case base was assigned for development to the particular region that had the most expertise in the product. The Domain Author is the individual assuming ownership (content, delivery, maintenance) of a product case base.

In some cases the Area Project Coordinator (APC) was also a Domain Author for one or more product domains. These added responsibilities for the APC varied and were based on the APC's workload and domain expertise.

A Domain Author could use multiple *Case Authors* to help author the knowledge in a particular case base. Again this was dependent on workload responsibilities and product expertise. Thus, many configurations were possible: an APC could fully author a small product case base, or could supervise a Domain Author who had several Case Authors to contribute the knowledge. The Domain Author is ultimately responsible for the knowledge content and organization within the assigned case base. That individual would accumulate cases from the Case Authors, look for redundancies, and ensure consistency and style.

This overall organization, while simple to present in terms of responsibilities, was very difficult to establish and manage. A principal issue that must be addressed in any such effort concerns reporting structure. APCs continued to report to their region's management structure, and not directly to the Global Project Manager nor the Global Technical Manager. Domain and Case Authors had phone responsibilities and allocation of their time for the global case-base project was done regionally, and not assigned

[2] Language issues are still a concern at Reuters -- in some areas (e.g., Japan), help desk operations are provided principally in the local language. Other unpublished non-Reuters CBR efforts have addressed the language issues (e.g., where support is provided in the local language only), and have set up translation processes to create multi-language knowledge bases. Issues of maintenance and updates are even more significant in these efforts.

globally. Thus, timetables and milestone dates were continually modified and various regions had peaks and valleys in terms of their productivity and commitments.

Added to this issue were some of the issues mentioned earlier: working with different cultures, with different work ethics, with different approaches to software development, with different business practices, etc. In view of these issues, the need to be realistic in deliverable time-scales and the need to remain flexible in achieving results were two very important lessons to be learned. An initial aggressive plan stalled when authors could not given sufficient time to build global cases; optimistic deadlines to produce working systems resulted in brittle and patchy knowledge bases; giving early incomplete case bases to end users created negative impressions that were hard to subsequently turnaround. Several times over the 18-month period, the project was almost killed due to missed deadlines and poor acceptance. Nevertheless at each decision point, these issues were evaluated and, each time, some progress occurred suggesting that the end goal could still be achieved. It was always important to continually focus on the original goals and objectives -- and each time they remained valid, and over time they seemed more and more within reach. Perseverance paid off.

CBR Technology

The use of case-based reasoning technology in the customer support arena has now been firmly established and reported on [Acorn & Walden, 1992; Nguyen et al., 1993; Hislop & Pracht, 1994]. The current Reuters project adds to these efforts in confirming the use of CBR as a viable technology to develop a *global* knowledge repository that can readily be built, maintained and reused. In the Reuters case, these CBR knowledge bases have been built in a distributed global environment and deployed in multiple countries. This environment, and its associated requirements, presented a whole new list of challenges and issues. But first we overview the technology used.

Briefly, for those unfamiliar with CBR technology, a CBR knowledge base consists of a set of past *cases* (situations, problems, inquiries) each of which contains a description and various features that define the situation and its uniqueness. Associated with each case is its applicable action or solution, i.e., given the defined situation, it is advisable to suggest the given solution.

Cases are aggregated into a *case base*, which is then used to search against in response to a new situation or problem. When a similar case is retrieved, it then forms the basis of a solution or response. Case bases evolve as new knowledge is entered or as modifications and updates occur to existing cases.

Case-based reasoning has been an active area of artificial intelligence research for over a decade [Riesbeck & Schank, 1989; Kolodner, 1993; Allen, 1994]. In the United States, ARPA sponsored-research in the mid to late 1980s served to establish CBR as an active research discipline [Kolodner, 1988; Hammond, 1989; Bareiss, 1991]. In Europe, a series of workshops helped formulate CBR research directions and highlighted opportunities for applications [Wess et al., 1994; Haton et al., 1995; Watson, 1995]. Worldwide, this has led to CBR's first international conference held in October 1995 [Veloso & Aamodt, 1995].

Applying CBR technology in the customer support help desk environment is a very appropriate use of the technology. A Reuter customer calls in with a problem or issue. The Reuter customer support representative tries to solve the problem with the help of the case base. The representative has a 486 PC (connected via a LAN to a server which stores the cases) and interacts with the case base to solve customer problems and answer various inquiries. The representative enters a description of the problem, and various features of the problem (entered through a question-answering dialog). Through a process of entering information, searching for relevant cases, and answering questions to help narrow the search, a solution is found. (If no solution is found the situation is then a candidate for a new case to be authored.) The representative then provides that solution to the customer.[3]

Reuters used off-the-shelf CBR products from Inference Corporation – CBR Express for building case bases, and CasePoint for deployment. These tools offer a combination of natural language entry and controlled searching. Every case usually has a textual description, much like an abstract of précis of the problem, describing the problem and its symptoms. When a user initiates a search, this system description alone often presents enough suggestions in the resultant set of possible solutions that the user can find the appropriate solution to use.

When the initial natural language search doesn't provide a

[3] There are now many examples of the use of CBR directly by customers for self help, where customers solve their own problems via a case base, for example, locally available on a CD-ROM, or remotely accessible through the Internet. These deployment strategies can have significant impact on reducing costs and increasing customer satisfaction.

useful result, the user can then begin answering the questions accompanying the first set of retrieved solutions. Each time a question is answered, the set of retrieved solutions is refined with more reasonable solutions. If no solution exists for a problem, this gradually becomes clear through the lack of a high-scoring matched case surfacing as a solution.

The rules for writing effective questions is defined by a *style guide*. At Reuters, the question and answer style definitions were devised by a team of people. The team approach was necessitated because of the breadth of the services offered by Reuters and the need to have all case studies end up in a single database at the conclusion of the project. When building questions/answer sets it is important to keep in mind all possible uses of the questions, so as to not build too many questions that might differ only in shades of meaning.

The difficulty in team approach is that many semantic arguments were endured, which could have been alleviated had only one individual defined the initial question/answer set. There was a great and ongoing debate about whether systems messages were error messages or informational messages, or whether all messages should be considered error messages. It was eventually determined that all messages are error messages (much to the dismay of former application programmers and system administrators on the initial authoring team who had a refined sense of computer messages). The point is that if the breadth of the case base can be understood by a single individual, it is probably more effective for that person to design the question/answer index and be given absolute authority to settle meaning disputes as they arise.

The Reuters style guide provided a single uniform template for cases, questions and actions. The GUI front-end to CBR Express was modified to create an authoring environment that enforced the Reuters style guide constraints. For example, all Reuter cases were required to contain the same two first questions "What product are you using?" and "What is the nature of your call?". The customized system, called CBRXtra, enforced this constraint for every new case generated by any author around the world. Another example of a style guide constraint is the requirement to put in a standardized product name as part of a case title (the product associated with the case). This customized interface created a consistent Reuters case template for use in authoring globally.

Given that case authoring was distributed around the world, various manual procedures were initially developed for correctly merging master case bases. However these manual procedures didn't always work correctly, as steps were skipped or not performed in the right order. On a few occasions authors' work was lost when files became corrupted. Subsequently, development began on the *Reuters Smart Suite* of utilities to automate the knowledge merging procedures making it impossible for authors to make case corrupting errors.

During the specification process of these utilities, some concern arose that what we were trying to do might in fact be impossible to achieve on a reliable basis. After a few days of horror that our assumptions were flawed, and through the persevering efforts of an analyst and the development team, all issues were ultimately resolved and it is now possible to write a case anywhere in the world at any time and have it merged into the Reuter Case Base.

The Reuters Smart Suite includes five utilities to support global authoring and distribution:

- *Smart Diverge* determines, for a recently modified case base (e.g., new cases added to a case base, or existing cases modified), those cases, question and actions that are new (and should be appended to the current global case base) and those that are modified/updated (and should replace those in the current global case base).

- *Smart Shred* eliminates unused questions and actions within a case base (locates defined questions and actions that never occur in any case, and discards them or puts them in separate file).

- *Smart Sort* sorts cases, questions and actions (e.g., by product domain), and cross references them.

- *Smart Collate* aggregates unresolved cases (i.e., situations for which a case was not found during search, and thus good candidates for new cases), into appropriate groups to send to particular regions in the world authoring case bases for those unresolves (i.e., determines to which Area Project Coordinator to send the individual unresolves). This utility is critical for the maintenance process to provide the information to the correct resource for knowledge authoring.

- *Architect* creates a tab-separated file showing the entire structure of a case base which can be printed or imported into Excel.

These customizations allowed Reuters to enhance and tune their authoring and distribution processes to support their requirements.

Global Knowledge Management

While the use of CBR on the help desk is no longer a technical or business innovation, developing a CBR knowledge base in a global framework did present some unique challenges that did require innovative solutions. Some of the management and organizational issues have already been discussed above. Here we address some of the issues and challenges of knowledge management and knowledge capture on a global level.

The issues Reuters faced, and we believe need to be addressed in any global knowledge effort, are grouped here into three primary areas: authoring, distribution and localization. While these issues are extensive, they are in no way insurmountable. We have interacted with other companies embarking on global knowledge efforts and each company solves these issues in different ways depending on their requirements, operations and business objectives. What is important is to recognize what the issues are, and the pros and cons of the various alternatives. We list here some of the more generic issues and how Reuters addressed them.

Knowledge Authoring

centralized vs. distributed

Certainly the easiest approach is to centralize the knowledge building process, i.e., in one central site with a group of knowledge engineers co-located in one area to share ideas, approaches, issues, etc. Management of the knowledge process is also simplified. At Reuters, however, expertise is distributed around the world and it was important to leverage all of that expertise into the most accurate and complete knowledge base possible.

segmentation of knowledge bases

Knowledge (case bases) is organized around Reuter products. Each product case base is assigned to (and owned by) a particular region who has responsibility for generating the case base, testing the case base, and maintaining the case base.

versions for different audiences

In developing case bases for global use, one needs to consider the users, most typically customer support telephone representatives - their skill level, mode of operation, and business practices. In other cases, users may be on the help desks of customers, or even customers directly (through case bases distributed to customers on CD-ROM, or available on the Internet). Case-base design needs to consider the end users and accommodate their (sometime conflicting) needs.

global knowledge vs. local knowledge

Ideally global case bases should contain information that is pertinent worldwide. In some cases, however, it may be important to include local information within global cases (see also the discussion in the Localization section below). For example in a 24-hour global support strategy (e.g., a London customer is connected to a London support center during office hours, but is connected to a U.S. support center in the evening, or to an Asia support center in the early morning hours before London is open), it might be important to give the correct local information to the customer (who may be on a different continent).

single global style vs. multiple styles

While Reuters created one global style for all cases worldwide, other efforts may require regional styles due to different business practices and requirements. The latter approach creates issues in translating case bases based on style (e.g., one region may enter detailed descriptions of problems and then focus in on a solution in a couple of confirmation questions; other regions may require leading the representative through a well-defined ordered question and answer dialog).

expert authoring vs. knowledge engineer authoring

Reuters has used both approaches due to workload constraints in various regions. In RAM, cases are authored by domain experts. The number of authors has varied between 6 and 12 authors who work between 4 to 8 hours per week authoring cases (the rest of the time they are on the phone solving customer problems). In UKI, 2 knowledge engineers (one being the UKI Area Project Coordinator) interviewed domain experts and created all the cases. Both approaches have been successful. The decision on which approach to adopt should be based on skill levels and time commitments of the people involved.

on-going maintenance

Case bases are maintained (authoring new cases and updating/modifying existing cases) using the same global organizational structure, i.e., the regions that built the case bases maintain them and optimally use the same domain and case authors to add and update the knowledge base. This process is facilitated by the Smart Collate utility described above to correctly identify the appropriate region to send new unresolved cases to author.

Knowledge Distribution

central library vs. distributed library

Reuters chose a central library to be a single repository for case bases. This seemed the best alternative to more readily manage the distribution of updates. The alternative is to have each region responsible for distributing their own case bases. In this alternative, regions would be getting updates on the varying (currently 38) case bases from multiple regions, necessitating more overhead in incorporating updates locally. With centralized distribution, updates are received from one site (Chicago).

distributing updates vs. whole case bases

Reuters global procedures allow distribution of updates (new or modified cases), and do not require sending whole case bases each time. Distributing updates is particularly recommended in those situations where local regions make local changes to cases (in which case you want to minimize their rework in making those local changes). In addition, communication bandwidth can significantly be reduced. On the other hand, in some cases, simply replacing a whole case base with another can be easiest if there are no local changes and communication bandwidth is not an issue.

frequency of updates

Ideally as soon as there is new knowledge, it should be distributed immediately. However, distributing updates requires testing the new release, packaging cases, transmission, and incorporating updates at the local level. While automating much of this process is desired and achievable, issues in version control and software management need to be considered in deciding on distribution frequency. Currently Reuters distributes updates twice each month.

foreign language translation (if required) before vs. after distribution

Foreign language translation requirements complicates the distribution process. Issues of sending whole case bases vs. updates, and frequency of distribution are all impacted. Translation could occur before distribution (centrally) or after distribution (locally). This depends on the particularly translation process used and who is designated to manage and control it. Cost and time issues can be significant as well, which would limit the turnaround time for issuing updates.

distribution format

Since Reuters has not yet established a worldwide standard for all databases, it chose to distribute cases as text files which are then read into each region's own environment to create a local database. Standardizing on a single database would allow database records to be distributed and thus further minimize the work required at the local level.

delivery mechanism

Various options exist here: ftp, e-mail, diskettes, CD-ROM, Internet. Initially distribution was done via diskettes and mail. This, of course, is cumbersome and slow. Reuters is moving toward electronic communication. Other options are being considered as case bases are being made available to other Reuter organizations and to outside customers.

extent to which the distribution process is automated

No surprise here - automate, automate, automate. The more that can be done computationally without human involvement the better. While Reuters has accomplished some of this through the Smart Suite (e.g., aggregating unresolved cases, determining what cases are new or modified, creating text files for distribution), much more is needed to make the whole process error-free, secure and shorter.

Localization

incorporating country-specific knowledge

Reuters allows individual regions to customize cases for their own use. (As mentioned above there may be good reasons for actually incorporating local knowledge within global cases.) Each region or country can have differing business practices (e.g., determining when to send out a field engineer), safety regulations (e.g., in allowing customers to replace parts or components on their own), legal issues, different cultures, etc. Cases are distributed to local sites as text files making it straightforward to edit cases, questions and actions. Local regions need to keep track of their changes, as additional updates sent from the global master site may impact cases modified for local use. New local cases can also be added regionally.

designing with localization in mind

If there are localization requirements, alternative case-base designs and distribution mechanisms need to be evaluated. For example, whether to distribute text files vs. compiled database records (i.e., CBR Express creates database tables for storing cases) -- it is easier for authors to work directly at the case-base level rather than at the database level for making local modifications. This is at the expense of efficiency (in distributing database records and index files directly).

Issues of standardizing on databases also factors in here. An example impact of localization relative to case-base design would be a design where authors creates global actions but allow local changes only through file attachments (and not through direct changes to the global cases and actions themselves). So a global action may specify that the customer should call another phone number, where the actual phone number is then stored in a local file. The global action is the same (to call in), but the local information is in a file created and maintained locally - the global action has the "hook" that allows the local action to be attached. The whole issue of localization needs to be understood, and requirements for localization need to be defined early on in the design process. Building global case bases and then seeing how local regions want to localize could be disastrous. The more localization required, the more complicated the design. At the extreme, if everything is localized, there is little reason to create global knowledge bases.

foreign language translation

This is a very important issue for every global effort. Reuter cases are all authored, distributed, and used in English (United Kingdom English was selected for worldwide use over American English). Issues of where translation is done (centrally, locally), when (before distribution, after distribution) and how (to what extent automated vs. manual translation, or even possibly authoring cases in multiple languages concurrently) all need to be addressed. Decisions need to be made on who maintains already translated cases, i.e., whether the local country should maintain a case base once translated, or continue to have updates translated and distributed from other sites.

different infrastructures or integration requirements

Again, understanding local requirements (and plans!) is critical - client computers, servers, networking, bandwidth, databases, etc. all need to be factored in for all the sites to be serviced. This infrastructure impacts system design and automation and distribution alternatives.

To note again, these issues all need to be considered in any global knowledge effort. Like any good software development effort, understanding all the requirements upfront is important. To the more common system requirements, we have added the knowledge requirements.

Benefits Achieved

Benefits from the Reuter Global Case Base Project have been significant. In some cases, however, exact measurements have been difficult to obtain. Processes have not been adequately established for accumulating statistics worldwide. Nevertheless, feedback both from existing numerical metrics as well as qualitative evaluations show improvements in numerous areas. A return-on-investment model has been established that focuses on four key benefit areas:

- *supporting first call clearance* (i.e., more calls are being resolved on the first call) -- the knowledge in the case base is providing an expert assistant to the phone agent, and that has enabled the agent to resolve more calls -- this saves escalation costs, repeat calls, and field visit costs.

- *lowered reliance on second-level technical support* saves experts' time in not having to deal with redundant problems and having to call back customers to provide the solutions.

- *reduction in field dispatches* – solving problems on the phone and avoiding field engineers having to visit customer sites saves $400-500 average for each site visit.

- *new hiring training reductions of 33%*; in addition, new hires become more productive more quickly than previously. Turnaround in help desk employees can be significant and this benefit alone justifies the project's cost.

While these benefits are measurable, many other very important benefits are much more difficult to measure. Yet these qualitative benefits often significantly outweigh the tangible benefits listed above:

- capturing and aggregating knowledge that is distributed worldwide into a single knowledge library that can then be distributed to any site around the world

- sharing this knowledge to other organizations besides customer support, e.g., to sales, marketing, and field service divisions

- providing consistency and high quality solutions worldwide

- enabling 24-hour service to any customer worldwide – with the same intelligent response and solution (processes to implement this strategy are currently in the planning phase; they involve automatic call transfer to other countries when local offices are closed.)

- enhanced customer satisfaction
- retention of customers, customer loyalty and repeat business.

In addition to deploying a global knowledge asset, the process of building the case base has also increased awareness of the discipline of problem solving among case authors. Some of the experts on the project commented that their methods and means of explanation to other less experienced staff improved because of the rigor of the authoring process. What seems intuitive and natural to a support expert when talking to someone directly experiencing a problem, is less natural when explaining to someone else or when trying to record that knowledge for later reuse.

When building cases, authors need to be precise about their meanings and the order of events in the troubleshooting process. Because of this care and attention in the case building process, authors themselves emerge more experienced in improving the efficiency with which they solve problems.

Finally, yet another very important benefit has resulted from the development of case bases – this time within the Reuters product development organization. Case bases are now being built and delivered simultaneous to new product launches. Not only are these case bases being built by the true product experts (those that designed and built the product), but this knowledge is being made available to the customer support organizations in time for them to use the knowledge base on the very first product call! The Reuter Bond Window product is the first Reuter product launched concurrently with a supporting case base. The release of case bases for products should become as commonplace as releasing product documentation.

Summary

The Reuter global case-base project is one of the very first projects to focus on building a knowledge base from expertise existing in many areas around the world. This knowledge is authored in multiple global regions and stored in a central master library. Knowledge is then distributed to multiple Reuter sites worldwide that need and want this knowledge. To support this enterprise, Reuters has established a global organization, global procedures, and supporting software to make this process effective. The project has now transitioned to an on-going maintenance process. Currently the system is in use in 29 sites by 190 users. The user base is expanding, not only into additional Reuter help desks, but also to other Reuter organizations. Product development is now building case bases to launch simultaneous with new product releases. Other plans under consideration include providing the knowledge base directly to customers' own help desks, providing the case base over the Internet, and leveraging the case base to provide 24-hour worldwide service to Reuter customers around the world.

Acknowledgments

There were many contributions from all over the globe. At various times in the project, the Global Steering Committee, which monitored and funded the project, included Phil Arnett (Reuters Corporate), Steve Arthers (Continental Europe, Middle East and Africa), Graeme Barbour (Asia), Marco Bernasconi (Continental Europe), Iian Burgess (Middle East and Africa), Steve Grigg (United Kingdom and Ireland), and Dan Rooney (America). Jim Borron, Chuck Schwartz, and Jack Bucsko were the principal project leaders at various times during the 18-month period. Phil Klahr provided global management and technical support. David Morales was the global technical manager. Area Project Coordinators included Paul Cantini (Continental Europe), Mark Hanson (America), Steven Sim (Asia), Andre Vanderschyff (Middle East and Africa), and Marcus Walia (United Kingdom and Ireland). External consultants included Ron Bewley, Doug Laney, Larry Mond, Steve Porvin, Savita Raj, Samir Rohatgi, and Mike Smith.

References

Acorn, T. L., and Walden, S. 1992. SMART: Support Management Automated Reasoning Technology for Compaq Customer Service. In *Innovative Applications of Artificial Intelligence 4, Proceedings of IAAI-92* (Scott & Klahr, eds.). Menlo Park, California: AAAI Press.

Allen, B. 1994. Case-Based Reasoning: Business Applications. *Communications of the ACM* 37(3):40-42.

Bareiss, E. R. (ed.) 1991. *Proceedings of the 3rd DARPA Case-Based Reasoning Workshop.* San Mateo, California: Morgan Kaufman Publishers.

Hammond, K. J. (ed.) 1989. *Proceedings of the 2nd DARPA Case-Based Reasoning Workshop.* San Mateo, California: Morgan Kaufman Publishers.

Haton, J. P., Keane, M., and Manago, M. (eds.) 1995. *Advances in Case-Based Reasoning, Proceedings of the*

Second European Workshop (EWCBR-94). Berlin: Springer-Verlag.

Hislop, C., and Pracht, D. 1994. Integrated Problem Resolution for Business Communications. In *Proceedings of the Sixth Innovative Applications of Artificial Intelligence Conference* (Byrnes & Aikins, eds.). Menlo Park, California: AAAI Press.

Kolodner, J. K. (ed.) 1988. *Proceedings of the 1st DARPA Case-Based Reasoning Workshop.* San Mateo, California: Morgan Kaufman Publishers.

Kolodner, J. 1993. *Case-Based Reasoning.* San Mateo, California: Morgan Kaufman Publishers.

Nguyen, T., Czerwinski, M., and Lee, D. 1993. Compaq QuickSource: Providing the Consumer with the Power of Artificial Intelligence. In *Proceedings of the Fifth Innovative Applications of Artificial Intelligence* (Klahr & Byrnes, eds.). Menlo Park, California: AAAI Press.

Riesbeck, C. K., and Schank, R. C. 1989. *Inside Case-Based Reasoning.* Hillsdale, New Jersey: Lawrence Erlbaum Associates.

Veloso, M., and Aamodt, A. (eds.) 1995. *Case-Based Reasoning Research and Development, Proceedings of the First International Conference on CBR (ICCBR-95).* Berlin: Springer-Verlag.

Watson, I. D. (ed.) 1995. *Progress in Case-Based Reasoning, Proceedings of the First United Kingdom Workshop.* Berlin: Springer-Verlag.

Wess, S., Althoff, K., and Richter, M. (eds.) 1994. *Topics in Case-Based Reasoning, Proceedings of the First European Workshop (EWCBR-93).* Berlin: Springer-Verlag.

An Intelligent System for Asset and Liability Assessment

Urs Bühler
Luca Bosatta
Swiss Bank Corporation,
57B Aeschenvorstadt,
Basel, Switzerland.
luca.bosatta@MHS.swissbank.com

Lawrence Poynter
Inference(CSE) GmbH,
Lise Meitner Strabe 3,
85716 Unterschleibheim, Germany.
lpoynter@inference.co.uk

Abstract

In the volatile and competitive banking market *Asset and Liability Management* (ALM) is becoming increasingly mission critical. Swiss Bank has built an intelligent system, called BALET (BALance sheet Estimation Tool), which supports this ALM process by automating the assessment of financial indicators. To provide alternative options, BALET simulates the possible effects of various economic trends. BALET's principal user is a company's chief financial officer or corporate treasurer who's goal is to propose options that directly reduce the organisation's operational financial exposure, particularly when associated with interest rate risk and fluctuations. BALET's architecture consists of intelligent agents which defines these options (the simulation agent), analyse the alternatives (the analysis agent), generate hedges (the hedging agent), explore various interest assumptions and their implications (the interest rate agent), and generate intelligent reports (the report agent). These agents operate over an object-oriented business model of a company's balance sheet. BALET is in operational use at Swiss Bank and over 12 of their customers.

Introduction

Asset and Liability Management (ALM) is one of the core strategic tasks of a modern company. The formal definition of the process is as follows:

> *The optimal structuring of the balance sheet in terms of financial return, whilst at the same time controlling the risks caused by the fluctuations of financial markets on this structure.*

Basically, the ALM manager needs to establish what the organisation is currently worth, and the risks that may threaten that value. The main risks of a balance sheet are as follows:

- **Interest Rate Risk** - Differences in an organisation's assets and liabilities result in exposure to interest rate fluctuations.
- **Currency Risk** - Changes in exchange rates can act to reduce organisational value.
- **Liquidity Risk** - To ensure liquidity, an organisation needs to maintain a predefined asset to liability ratio. This is of particular significance to Swiss banks where the required ratio is governed by law.

The most important and threatening risk is due to potential interest rate fluctuations. Correspondingly, the primary optimising objective is to control, or hedge, this factor by applying customised derivative instruments including swaps and options.

Swiss Bank has had great success in applying artificial intelligence technology to many of its operational activities, e.g., in credit evaluation [the CUBUS system presented at IAAI-91] and in mortgage lending [the MOCCA system presented at IAAI-92]. With this expertise and experience in hand, Swiss Bank undertook to develop an intelligent system (BALET) to support the more difficult ALM process. Prior to discussing BALET, we discuss the ALM process in more detail.

The Asset and Liability Management Process

The process of ALM should be viewed as a spiralling process with the discrete phases of *classification*, *analysis* and *optimisation*. At the conclusion of each optimisation phase, the ALM manager evaluates the forecasted risks and proposed hedging options, before determining whether or not to proceed with another loop of the spiral. The process completes when the ALM manager is content with the calculated level of risk and the structure of the balance sheet. The process has to be performed at regular intervals to ensure an accurate risk assessment as external market values change over time.

Classification Phase. The initial phase is concerned with classifying the financial data of the company into meaningful groups which then act as the basis for the calculation phase. The main data source is the balance sheet which has to be supplemented with derived values for those items that are either incomplete or unknown. For example, the future cashflow implications of balance sheet items with variable interest rates need to be calculated by integrating assumed future interest values. Each balance sheet item is classified according to its specific interest rate and maturity.

There are 3 main categories or classes for these financial items:

- **Fixed interest rates and known maturity**. Financial items in this class have no ambiguity, and correspondingly no risk. They need no additional information in order to compute present values.
- **Variable interest rate**. Financial items in this class are modelled by projecting a replicating portfolio of capital slices, each with a given maturity. Each slice is then assigned historical interest rate according to its particular maturity.
- **No interest rate**. Some balance sheet items eg. equities, have both unknown interest rates and maturites. Therefore the values for these two items has to be assumed.

Analysis Phase. The analysis phase is aimed at calculating all of the financial measures that are used as standard indicators of the balance sheet status. These indicators include the Net Present Value (total value of the balance sheet), the Interest Rate Risk profile (an indication of the exposure to interest rate risk) and Gap Analysis (an asset to liability comparison). Once these financial indicators have been calculated, they are displayed in a form that feeds into the optimisation phase.

Optimisation Phase. The ALM manager determines whether he needs to hedge his current position. He is particularly concerned about his exposure to interest rate risk, and given high exposure, is able to defend his position by applying certain derivative instruments. These derivatives e.g., swaps or options, are complex financial tools that need to be specifically configured to suit the requirements of the current situation. The configuration includes the start and finish dates, the amount, the rate and the maturity profile. When all of the derivative instruments have been defined they are integrated with the findings of the previous analysis phase to check that they have reduced the level of exposure. This phase is then repeated, tuning the derivative instrument configuration, until the overall position is considered by the ALM manager to be 'optimised'. In practice, this final optimisation may involve the ALM manager performing many iterations of this 'derivative tuning' before a satisfactory conclusion is reached.

This ALM process is complex. In order to perform each of its three phases well, a significant knowledge of financial assessment, risk analysis, and derivative tuning is required. This knowledge resides in ALM experts and thus represents an ideal domain for the application of artificial intelligence. In addition, as each phase of the process is calculation intensive, manual operation is both time consuming and often inaccurate. Developing an automated system that embodies ALM expert knowledge and automates the calculations represented a major opportunity at Swiss Bank. This intelligent system became known as BALET (BALance sheet Estimation Tool).

System Objectives

The main objectives of BALET were as follows:

- The complete ALM process should be automated by embedding and applying the knowledge required to calculate the required financial indicators.
- To support the user in the process of economic hypothetical reasoning. The tool should be equipped to integrate the results of its own calculations with the future economic assumptions of the user.
- To encapsulate the knowledge that is required to calculate hedging options.
- To operate within an environment of incomplete data. Where necessary, missing information is supplemented by data derived from a simulated economic model that is based on historical records.
- To optimise the derived economic position by proposing options to reduce the banks financial exposure. These options should include the definition of specific financial instruments, e.g., swaps, options, derivatives.
- To provide strategically powerful conclusions with relatively simple input. The tool should assume only limited user computing knowledge and should guide the user through the ALM process.
- The display of data should be flexible enough to allow the user to manipulate the display for views over different classes of balance sheet data.
- To generate user-modifiable reports.

BALET System Architecture

The architecture includes a collection of automated intelligent agents, where an agent is defined as a modular automated tool with a discrete operating task. We use the term *agent* because it suggests the analogy to human information workers, who are responsible for the production of information. As an analogy, consider the human workers in manufacturing, who instead of producing information, produce goods. Just as the production of goods has been largely automated by artificial agents (robots, machines), it is Swiss Bank's objective to automate financial information assessment, and to increase generally the level of automation in financial services. Thus, we consider the automated intelligent agents in the financial domain to be the 'information machines' of the information factory. We want these agents to be active, not just passive tools. From a production viewpoint they behave as human information entities, but operate in a more consistent and efficient manner.

The types of behaviour encapsulated within an agent is as follows:

- **Agent Triggers** Under what circumstances should this agent be initiated.
- **Data Requirements** The agent has a reference of all of the specific data that it requires to perform its task. If data is missing it is able to use its own mechanisms to assume data values. This is particularly used when forecasting forward interest rate curves, actual values are not available so BALET has to infer values based on its model of interest rate fluctuations.
- **Communication** Inter-agent communication is conducted via the global blackboard. Using this medium agents can post data that triggers other agents, or simply monitor the blackboard to await the command to execute.
- **Process Knowledge** - The detailed knowledge of how the specified task should be conducted. The hedging agent contains all of the knowledge that an expert financial practitioner would deploy to establish an optimal hedge.

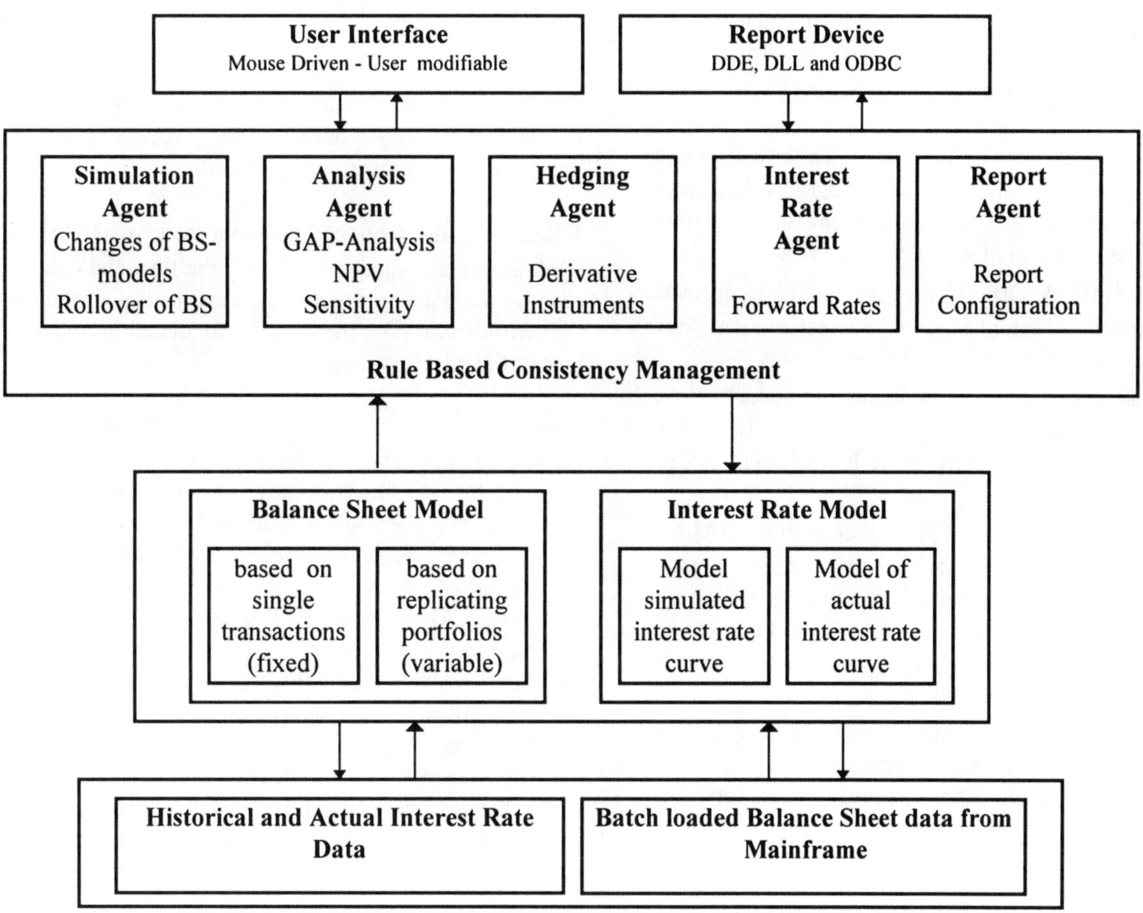

Figure 1. Balet System Architecture

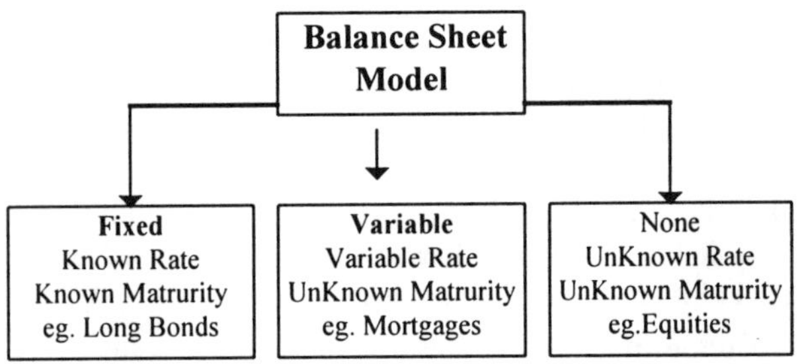

Figure 2 . Main Data Class Structure

This modularised agent approach has two main application maintenance benefits. First the autonomous nature of the agents with all of their embedded data requirements and behaviour localises the application debug process. Secondly the restricted inter-agent communication mechanism, via the blackboard, results in the uncomplicated deployment of agents as part of other agent-compliant applications. The interest rate forecasting agent could be re-deployed as part of an application that is designed to support the mortgage decision making process. The individual agents and their responsibilities include:

- **Analysis Agent** The core task of this agent is the calculation of the present values for each financial item in each balance sheet class. This includes Gap Analysis as well as the interest rate sensitivity. (See also Figure 3 and Figure 4.)
- **Hedging Agent** This agent helps in the definition and pricing of derivative instruments and integrates them into the balance sheet model. Its goal is to develop a 'perfect hedge' with the objective of no interest rate risk.
- **Interest Rate Agent** This agent provides, projects and calculates the different kinds of interest rates as they relate to par yield, zero coupon and forward rates.
- **Simulation Agent** The simulation component works together with the Interest Rate Agent. The simulation of an interest rate scenario is driven either by existing data or manually by a mouse.
- **Report Agent** Based on the actual session, BALET creates several different reports and writes them directly via a DDE channel into a Word document. Graphics are generated as postscript files. This kind of report generation guarantees highest flexibility in adding ones own comments to the standard reports produced.

In addition to defining and object-oriented agents, an object model of the balance sheet was developed to act as the framework for the simulation process. At the top level of abstraction the balance sheet item can be sub-divided into three main classes. (See Figure 2.)

The three main classes have much the same attribute structure but differ in their overall behaviour. Generally, calculations concerning fixed balance sheet items are performed without reference to items defined outside the bounds of the object encapsulated data. In contrast, variable balance sheet items need their own data supplemented with data from a secondary source. Supplementary data may correspond to data from other related objects or it may relate to calculated data that is passed by one of the BALET agents. This secondary data requirement is illustrated by the calculation of a mortgage cashflow involving not only the locally defined values of loan size and monthly charge, but also the simulated data for the replicating portfolios provided by the interest rate agent.

Rule-Based Consistency Management

One of the key objectives of BALET was to enable the user to experiment with potential financial scenarios. The system had to perform hypothetical reasoning. As part of this process a mechanism for maintaining the integrity of the blackboard was devised using ART**Enterprise* rules. Correspondingly, as the user decides to backtrack to an earlier assumption, so to BALET retracts all of the data and inferences that were generated after that assumption. This is what the BALET team refer to as rule-based consistency management.

System Operation

The operation of BALET was specifically modelled to follow the existing manual ALM processing phases of *classification*, *analysis* and *optimisation*.

Classification Phase. The initial task of BALET is to load the balance sheet and classify the financial data. Each item on the balance sheet is assigned to one of the classes that will dictate how the item is calculated and applied as part of the ALM process.

Analysis Phase This phase is aimed at calculating and displaying the various financial indicators that were required for the ALM process. As discussed earlier, the Net Present Value (NPV), Interest Rate Profile (exposure to risk), and GAP analysis (asset to liability comparison) are standard ALM measures.

The main GAP analysis window (Figure 3) represents time along the x-axis and assets (Akt) and liabilities (Pas) along the y-axis. Using a monthly base, BALET calculates all future cashflows and displays the maturity model of the balance sheet. A gap is defined as the situation where the amount due within a certain period on the asset side differs from the amount due on the liability side in the same period. The gaps of all time periods together provide the gap analysis.

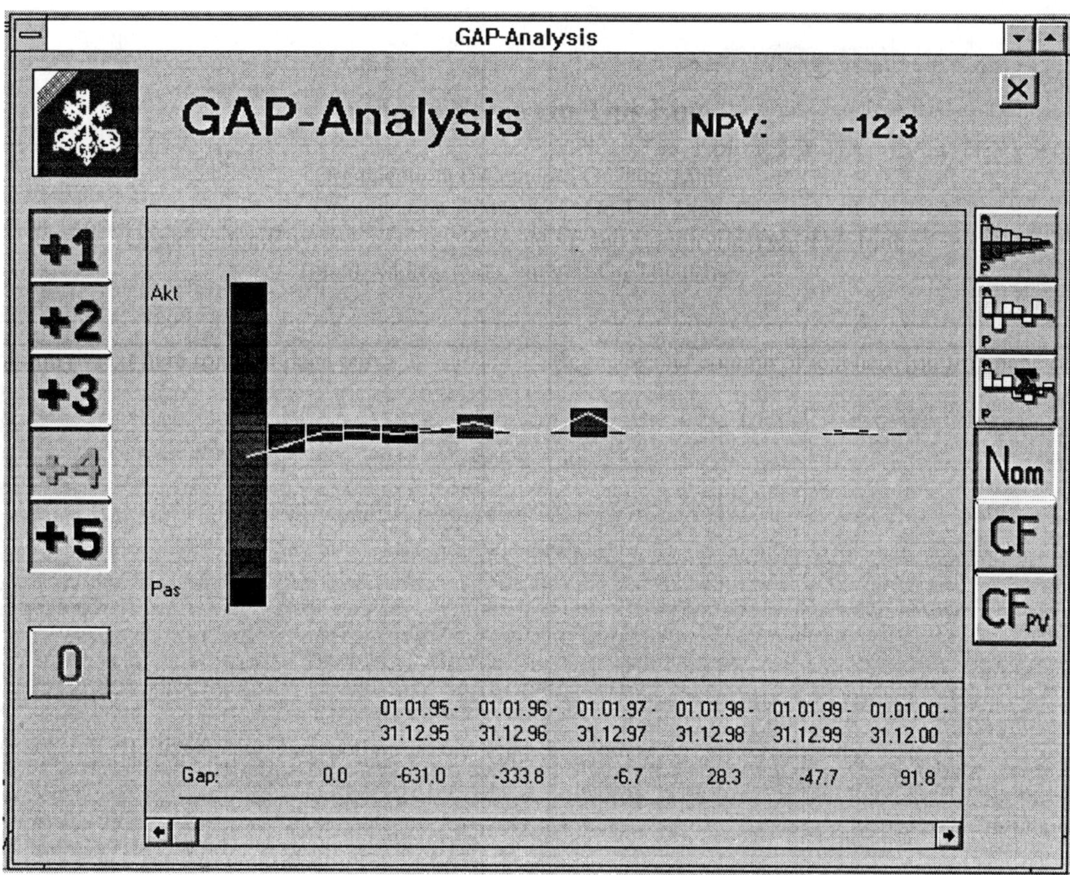

Figure 3. BALET GAP Analysis

The light-coloured single line on Figure 3 illustrates that the gap is initially negative, but moves towards the positive in the long term. The buttons on the left and right of the main GAP analysis display offer the user alternative views over the financial data. The numbers on the left control the display of items from specific classes. This enables the user to view the effect of GAP analysis on a subset of the balance sheet. The buttons on the right control the content of the data displayed, switching between the display of GAP, cash flow, and cumulative GAP. At the top of the window the balance sheet Net Present Value (NPV) is displayed. The exposure to interest rate risk is displayed in the Interest Rate Profile window. The example display in Figure 4 illustrates how the current balance sheet is exposed to interest rate fluctuations. If the interest rate were to increase 1% (100 basis points) the loses would be over **44 million** on the current position. If the interest rate remained constant then the loss/profit would be nil. A reduction in interest rate of 1% would improve the current position by **66 million**. The goal of the optimisation phase is to flatten the risk profile by deriving and applying hedging instruments.

The simulation of key economic factors can either be inferred by BALET's simulation agent or modified by the user. The user is able to define custom interest rate curves by hand using the mouse or by typing a list of numbers. Once these values have been entered, BALET recalculates the economic indicators that will have been affected by the changing forward interest rate assumption.

Optimisation Phase. The reduction of the interest risk exposure can be performed by creating derivative instruments and asserting them to the system. BALET's hedging agent generates an optimal hedge with swaps and integrates these with the existing balance sheet. After these swaps have been recalculated with the rest of the balance sheet the resultant exposure profile is illustrated by the light coloured line in Figure 4.

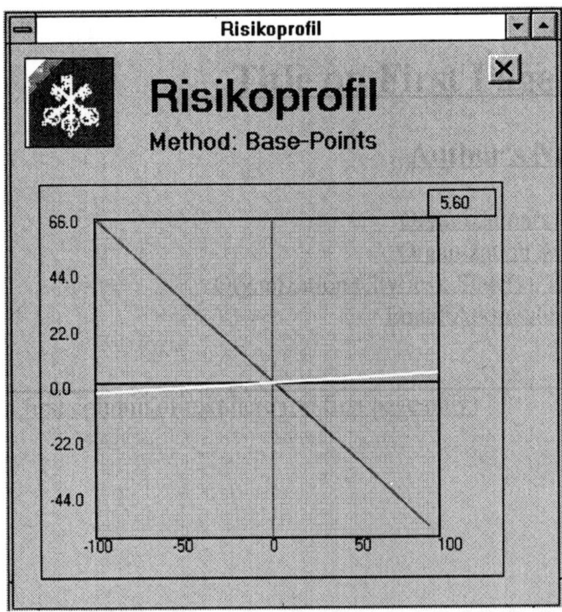

Figure 4. Interest Risk Profile

Note that the line runs from left to right horizontally almost along the zero exposure line. This flattening of the exposure line represents a balance sheet that has been optimally hedged. Fluctuations in the interest rate would have only a minimal effect on the net value of the balance sheet.

Application Payoff

The application is considered to be successfully deployed for the following reasons:

- **Early Return On Investment** The application has been so successfully received by Swiss Banks customers that they have been prepared to purchase licenses of the product. The revenues generated by these sales have already returned all of the initial development costs.
- **Corporate Financial Risk Reduction** BALET performs a significant role in the reduction of an organisation's exposure to interest rate risk. Depending on the size of the organisation, these losses can run into millions of dollars. The hedges that BALET proposes attempt to reduce the interest rate risk close to zero.
- **Improved Customer Service** The tool has supported the bank's front office process, advising its corporate clients on issues relating to ALM and risk management. The bank's customer relationship officers are able to present the findings of BALET on a portable computer at the customer's office. This innovative approach has improved, still further, the professional level of service that Swiss Bank delivers to its customers.

Platform and Resources

BALET is deployed on a Pentium PC with 32Mb of RAM. The tool was developed using the ART**Enterprise* development environment. The development lifecycle including beta testing and final production testing took 6 elapsed months involving approximately 10 man months of effort. From the user community the total manpower utilisation was less than two months to define the simulation models and test the working system.

Maintenance

BALET is strongly modularised (due to the agent-model architecture). The single agents are developed and updated independently and can be regarded as an enhancement of BALET's core. Correspondingly, the development of new more advanced agents, particularly within the hedging module, can be easily integrated into the core application. Updates in market data can be loaded by the user and are regularly provided by Swiss Bank on floppy disks. Delivery using the Internet is currently being considered.

Use

BALET has now been in operational use since February 1995 and new versions are being developed to integrate the additional features demanded by the current user base. BALET is operational and in use at Swiss Bank and over 12 of its customers. This number is steadily increasing as the tool is demonstrated to the banks customers.

Summary

BALET's automation of the Asset and Liability Management process has been enthusiastically received by both internal Swiss Bank users and customers alike. Its success is based on its ease-of-use, and on its automation of a task that is both complex and knowledge dependent. The conclusions are quickly delivered enabling the ALM manager to rapidly explore possible options while performing the difficult process of balance sheet optimisation.

References

Wenger, D. 1995 Financial Information Engineering. The Development of AI Agents. Ph. D. diss., University of Lausanne, Switzerland.

Inquiries

If you have any questions about the operation or availability of the BALET product then please contact.

Luca Bosatta,
Swiss Bank Corportation,
57B Aschenvorstadt,
Basel, Switzerland.

Localization of Troubles in Telephone Cable Networks

Chuxin Chen, Teresa L. Hollidge [1], and DD Sharma
Pacific Bell
2600 Camino Ramon, San Ramon, California 94583
cxchen@srv.PacBell.COM, thollidge@tibco.com, dxsharm@srv.PacBell.COM

Abstract

This paper describes an intelligent system which detects the location of troubles in a local telephone cable network. Such a task is very challenging, tedious, and requires human experts with years of experience and high analytical skills. Our system captures the expertise and knowledge required for this task, along with automated access to database systems, so that the system can help a human analyst to pin-point network trouble location more efficiently and accurately, ultimately reducing the cost of maintenance and repair. The system utilizes probabilistic reasoning techniques and logical operators to determine which plant component has the highest failure probability. This is achieved by building a topology of the local cable network, constructing a causal net which contains belief of failure for each plant component, given their current status, history data, cable pair distribution, and connectivity to other components. The Trouble Localization (TL) Module described in this paper is a crucial part of a larger system: Outside Plant Analysis System (OPAS) which has been deployed Statewide for over nine months at Pacific Bell PMAC centers. The TL system module utilizes AI and Object-Oriented technology. It is implemented in C++ on Unix workstations, and its graphical user interface is in an X Window environment.

Background

Pacific Bell has the largest and most complex telephone cable network in the state of California. The maintenance of this network is divided into two primary areas: reactive and proactive/preventative maintenance. Reactive maintenance is customer driven. For example, when a customer is experiencing trouble, they call for assistance and a technician is immediately dispatched to resolve the problem in the quickest way possible, which is not necessarily the most cost effective. Preventative maintenance is the ongoing repair and upkeep of the network which occurs prior to affecting customers. The trigger for preventative maintenance is based on several factors, but primarily recommendations from the technicians in the field and huge quantities of data regarding the maintenance and trouble history of each segment of the entire network. The ultimate goal of maintenance is to provide the customer with clear, continuous service and preventative maintenance is critical to achieve success.

The task of preventative/proactive maintenance for the entire network is distributed over five PMACs (Preventative Maintenance Analysis Centers) at various locations throughout the State. Obviously the cost of maintenance is very high and it is more effective to repair a troublesome network component *once* than to dispatch several technicians over time to patch and repatch the same trouble spot. Unfortunately, it isn't always easy to identify the exact location and cause of a particular source of trouble. It is a very time intensive, laborious manual task. If we are able to detect a problem early and identify the faulty device precisely, we are able to cost effectively manage the repair of the network facility before the customer is impacted.

The crucial task of a PMAC analyst is finding the exact location and root cause of telephone cable network troubles. Such a task is very challenging, tedious, and requires human experts with years of experience and analytical skills. An automated system with efficiency and precision will significantly reduce the maintenance cost and enhance customer service.

Problem Domain Description

The goal of preventive maintenance is to identify potential troubles before they affect a customer's telephone service. Indications of a degradation in the network are buried in several sources of information or databases. It is quite tedious and time consuming to retrieve this information, correlate potential symptoms, and derive a diagnosis. Even if this massive data mining task can be performed, one has to balance the cost of exhaustive diagnosis with the timeliness of identifying more serious troubles. In practice an analyst's attention is drawn to trouble based on information in a report called Program Scan. Every night an automated testing machine (called Predictor) tests the telephone network and collects the results in the Program Scan morning report.

Preventative maintenance often begins with a series of trouble indicators from Program Scan reports, in which trouble codes are associated with telephone cables and pairs. The type of trouble code represents the integrity of the line, ranging from Test OK, DC Fault, Open Circuit, Cross Talk, Ground, or Short.

Figure 1 depicts a sample telephone network, from an exchange (CO, the central office) to a customer's neighborhood, depicted by the letters A through H. The network from CO to a customer's house consists of many network elements such as the feeder cables (06, 36), cable splices in man holes (MH#2), a cross connect box (also called a B box, labeled X in Figure 1), distribution cable (0601), several splice points on the distribution cable, and terminal boxes A through H. When a Program Scan shows a trouble, in principle the trouble can be anywhere from

[1] Teresa L. Hollidge is now with TIBCO Inc., (formerly Teknekron Software Systems Inc.). Her e-mail address is thollidge@tibco.com.

the CO to the wires connecting terminal boxes to a customer's house. Much of this network is buried and not easily accessible for testing. The difficulty is to locate one cable pair (one line going to a customer's house) or a small group of cable pairs from a potentially large set of cable pairs (usually 3600) requiring attention and furthermore, to find the location of the trouble along that pair or pairs. Using Program Scan data it is easy to narrow down the defective cable pair range. However, to provide redundancy or to support growth, a cable pair may appear in multiple locations (though the telephone connection is only active in a single location). In this situation it is common for a trouble at one location to manifest itself at another location. When a single trouble manifests itself in multiple locations, it further complicates the diagnosis. In summary, the problem is to find the physical location of the trouble and the associated cable pair. For example, in Figure 1, the physical location of a trouble can be any one or more of the following: serving terminals A through H, the distribution cable (bounded by cable pair count), the splice junctions, the B box, feeder cable, or the central office (CO).

The analyst looks for patterns in the data and attempts to group the problems into network segments. He then retrieves related records from various legacy systems, such as an ACR report from LFACS (a type of cable record report from a legacy system which stores information about the physical outside plant), Repair History from MTAS (another legacy system which stores trouble repair history), and a Defective Pair report from LFACS. He may also search for related P3028 reports (which are written by technicians about observed conditions in the field), study the corresponding cable map, and even run other tests to gather further information. The goal is to pin-point the trouble location so that a technician can be dispatched for field testing. This process is slow, error-prone and tedious, requires special experience, knowledge, and analytical skills.

The reasoning process of an expert analyst is quite interesting. Normally, the analyst does not have all the relevant information available up front to support a proper diagnosis. As the analysis progresses, the analyst is driven towards various plausible causes and decides to collect information from various sources. The quality of information is often poor, forcing the analyst to seek other sources of information or derive partial conclusions. Formulating plausible hypothesis and collecting data to substantiate the hypothesis goes hand-in-hand - often the new data can rule out an earlier hypothesis or point towards a more appropriate hypothesis that subsumes many possible causes. For example, if many sets of cable pair coming from a B box show trouble then it is a plausible conclusion that the trouble is in the B box and not in the individual cable pair sets. It is obvious that the reasoning is inherently non-monotonic and the traditional backward chaining techniques (as used in MYCIN) are not appropriate. What is needed is a truth maintenance system reasoning engine with the power to handle probabilistic reasoning. Causal networks combined with Bayesian inference provides an appropriate framework for non-monotonic reasoning coupled with probabilistic reasoning. Given the heavy emphasis on conditional reasoning by expert analysts, poor quality of information in databases, and the non-monotonic nature of the reasoning, we found the Causal Network approach to be both elegant and scalable and selected it as a foundation for solving the trouble localization problem.

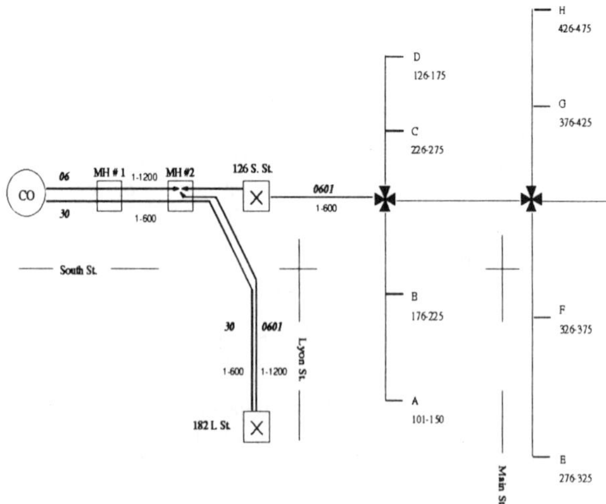

Fig. 1. An example of local telephone network.

System Architecture

The purpose of the Trouble Localization Module is to automate the physical and mental process of a PMAC expert, capture the expert's knowledge, and provide a useful tool for both new and experienced analysts. TL provides a way for the PMAC analyst to locate cable network troubles more efficiently and accurately.

The TL module utilizes Object-Oriented technology for knowledge representation and Artificial Intelligence methodology for reasoning and inference.

The major components of the TL module and its connections with OPAS Data Server are depicted in Figure 2. The functionality of the Data Server is to access the OPAS database, interface with Pacific Bell's legacy systems, and provide the TL module with its data retrieval and storage requirement.

The TL User Interface is an X Window based GUI, which allows the user to select a trouble list from legacy system reports, determine history range, run the trouble diagnosis, display the topology, causal net, and localization results, in addition to performing disk file manipulation tasks.

The TL system module consists of three major components:

1. Trouble Localization Specialist, which is responsible for generating the topology and the causal net, quantization of Program Scan and history data, and report creation.

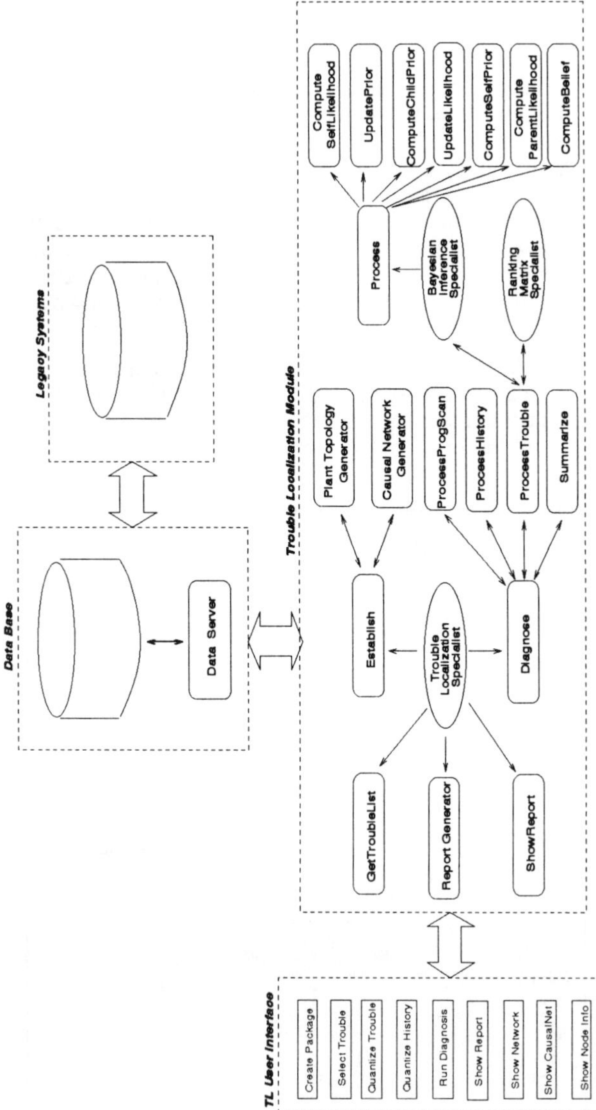

Fig. 2. TL system components and its connections to OPAS Data Server.

2. **Bayesian Inference Specialist**, whose function is processing the prior probability and likelihood of failure for each node and propagating the evidence throughout the causal net, and computing the final belief of failure for each plant component.

3. **Ranking Matrix Specialist**. which is responsible for activating logical operators and combining their results with the result from the Bayesian operator, and then generating the final trouble location ranking list.

Trouble Localization Strategy

The theoretical foundation of causal networks and its associated Bayesian operators is based on the book entitled *Probabilistic Reasoning in Intelligent Systems: Networks of Plausible Inference*, by Judea Pearl (Pearl 1988). The trouble localization task starts with the generation of a local plant topology graph which is very much like the hard copy cable map the PMAC analyst uses. Then another graph, a causal network, is constructed based on the plant topology. This graph takes consideration of the causal relationships among the different types of plant components, their history data, and Program Scan data.

The probability of failure is first calculated for each node, and more importantly, the evidence (belief of failure or non-failure) is propagated throughout the causal network according to certain rules. The value of belief in each node is then updated. When the causal network reaches its equilibrium state, i.e., no more evidence propagation needs to be performed, then the node with the highest probability of failure is the most likely the source of trouble.

The process starts with the creation of a trouble list which consists primarily of the Program Scan data. The cable and pair range of the data is determined by the user. Based on this input data, the TL module then requests several LFACS reports, parses them, and constructs a cable network topology. This network topology contains information on connectivity of the portion of the network of interest, as well as detailed information, including history, about each individual plant component.

In the next step, the TL module applies six operators to the given data. The first is the probabilistic reasoning (Bayesian) operator, and the remaining five are logical operators. A Causal Network is built based on the topology for applying Bayesian operator. It is a network of nodes, where each node contains state information (belief of failure) of a plant node. Two nodes are connected through a causal link, which means, the state of one node is the cause of the state of the other.

The belief of failure computed from the Causal Network is purely dependent on the Program Scan and history data, which is quantized to be used in the Bayesian inference procedure. Therefore, quantization of this data is also an important step of the process.

There are other factors which will influence the decision of which plant component is the “guilty one”. Thus, in addition to the Bayesian Operator which is based on a probabilistic model, five logical operators are created to fine tune the trouble localization process. These are:

(1) TDE (Total Damage Explained) operator, which calculates the percentage of total trouble coverage in a particular plant component;

(2) DWTC (Damage Within Total Count) operator, which calculates the percentage of trouble indicators within a total cable pair count of a particular plant component;

(3) Worker operator, which calculates the percentage of working lines within the total number of cable pairs in a serving terminal,

(4) Failure Type operator, which calculates a weight factor for a particular plant component, using the weight table for failure type and the type of trouble indicators observed, and

(5) Cluster operator, which calculates the number of clusters, cluster compactness, and overall cluster measure for F1 and F2 cables.

The Failure Measurement Matrix is generated from the output of these six operators. These outputs, normalized to values between 0 and 1, form the columns of the matrix, and the plant components, identified in the network topology, form the rows of the matrix. An ordering procedure will be designed to generate a final ranking list for plant components based on the total failure belief. Several schemes are being considered:

(1) Fixed ordering, in which the order of applying the operator's output in the ranking process is fixed before run-time,

(2) Dynamic ordering, in which the order is determined during the run-time with predefined rules, and

(3) Rule-based ordering, in which the order is determined using AI rule-based techniques.

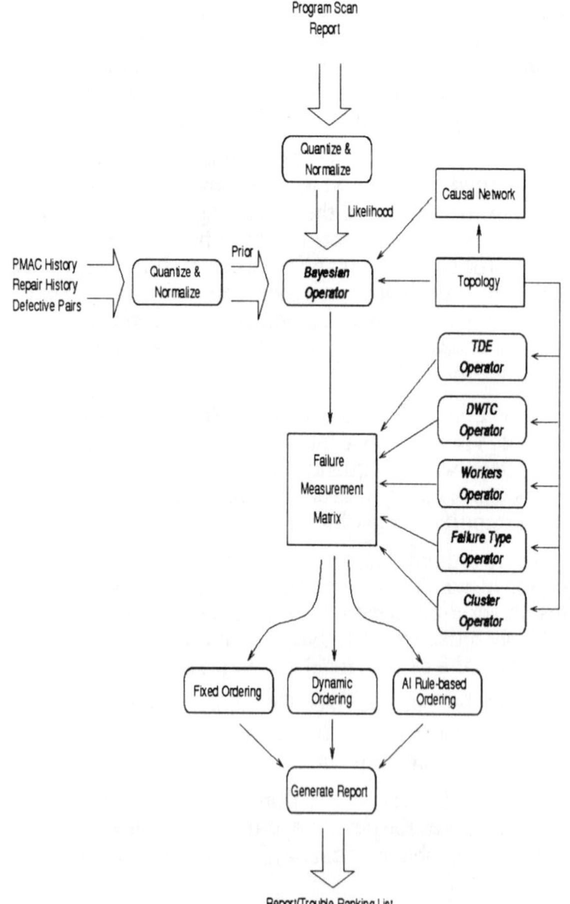

Fig. 3. The flow of control in TL module.

The following subsections further describe the processes within the TL module.

A. Construction of Network Topology

The goal of this procedure is to generate a network topology by issuing a request to the LFACS legacy system, receiving a report, parsing the report, and then building the topology. It is assumed that the PMAC analyst running the Trouble Localization module determines which wire center, cable, and pair range they want to examine. Using these as input data, several reports can be obtained to construct a network topology. Figure 4 shows an example, which is based on Figure 1 shown in the first section.

In the future we hope to streamline this process through direct access to the LFACS system. Currently we are constrained to parsing reports due to the proprietary nature of the LFACS database.

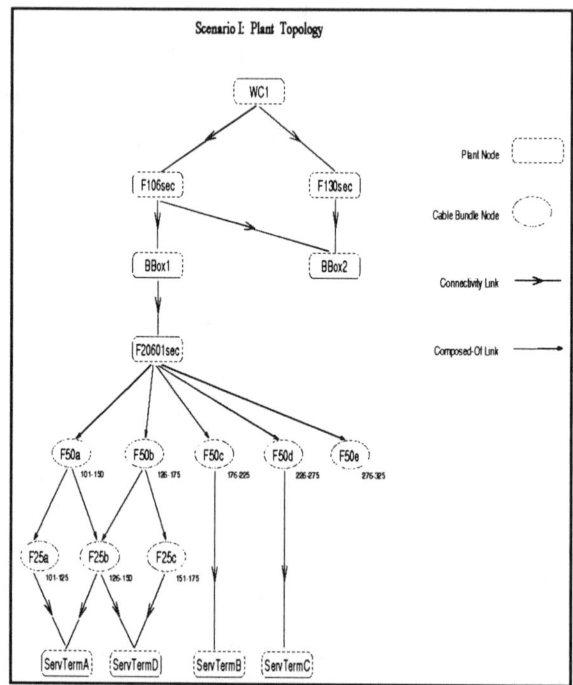

Fig. 4. An example of plant topology.

B. Construction of Causal Network

The Causal Network is built based on plant topology information. The graph nodes are classified into four categories:

- History Bayesian Nodes
- Plant Bayesian Nodes
- Cable Bundle Bayesian Nodes
- Program Scan Bayesian Nodes

The information in History nodes comes from three sources (from three databases):

- PMAC history,
- Repair history, and
- Defective pairs.

The information in Program Scan nodes comes from related program scan reports of corresponding cable and range. Processing is required to quantize, weight, and normalize this data so that an evidence vector may be computed for each node. The information in Plant and Cable bundle nodes is inherited from their counter parts in the plant topology.

The Causal Network (or sometimes referred as Bayesian Network) is constructed as a directed acyclic graph (DAG). The arrows in the graph represent causal influences of one node upon to another (Figure 5).

The functionality of the four different types of nodes (shown in Figure 6) in the Causal Network graph are:

- **History Node**

  This node contains the probability of repeated history failure of a particular plant component.

- **Program Scan Node**

  This node contains the evidence of current failure observed through Program Scan data, on a cable bundle.

- **Cable Bundle Node**

  This node contains the probability of failure within a specified range of the cable bundle.

- **Plant Component Node**

  This node contains the belief of failure regarding the particular plant component.

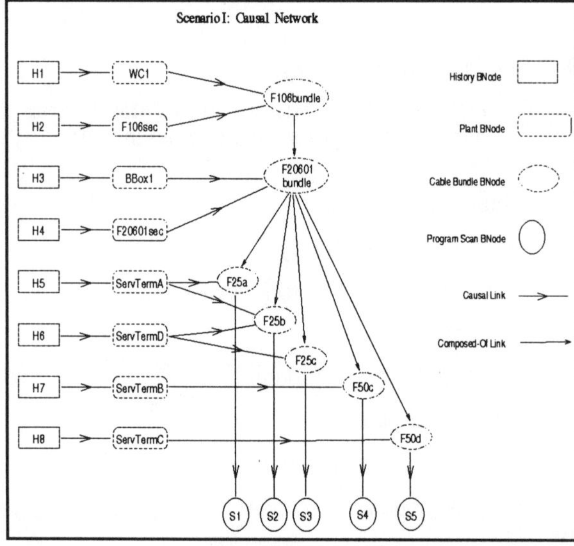

Fig. 5. The corresponding Causal Network to Figure 4.

In directed acyclic graphs, the relationship between any two nodes is defined as a parent-child relation. This is illustrated in Figure 7. The parent node is the one with a link arrow pointing away from it, and the child node is the one with a link arrow pointing towards it.

A Bayesian node x is characterized by its belief BEL(x), the prior probability, p, and the likelihood parameter, l. New information regarding a node is communicated to it by either changing the prior probability or the likelihood parameter. After receiving the new information, new values of appropriate parameter are computed and the evidence is propagated to other neighboring nodes.

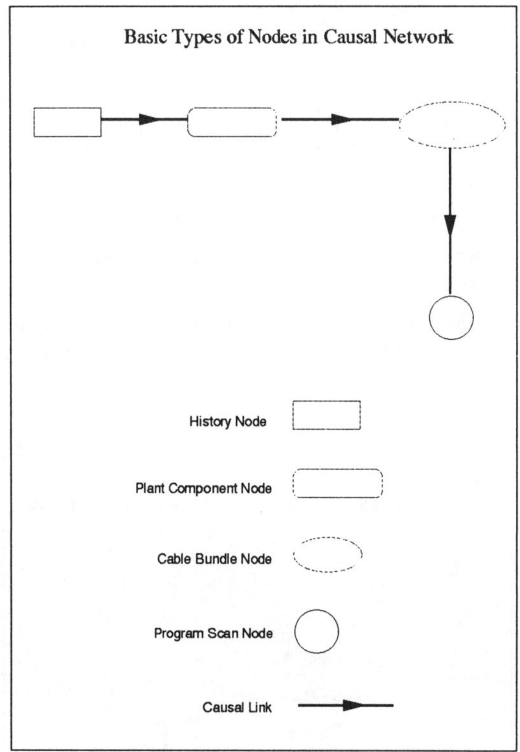

Fig. 6. Basic types of graph nodes.

The flow of propagation of evidence between a parent node and a child node is that the prior probability, π, is passed from the parent to the child, and likelihood, λ, is passed from the child to the parent.

In case of a network of nodes, the flow of propagation for each node becomes:

- Compute π
- Compute λ
- Compute BEL (belief)
- Propagate π to its child nodes

- Propagate λ to its parent nodes

where $BEL(x) = \alpha \bullet \pi(x) \bullet \lambda(x)$

α is a scaling factor,

$\pi(x) = \pi(u) \bullet M_{x|u}$,

$\lambda(x) = M_{y|x} \bullet \lambda(y)$,

and

$$M_{y|x} = P(Y = y|X = x)$$

$$= \begin{bmatrix} P(y_1|x_1) & P(y_2|x_1) & \cdots & P(y_n|x_1) \\ P(y_1|x_2) & P(y_2|x_2) & \cdots & P(y_n|x_2) \\ \cdot & \cdot & & \cdot \\ P(y_1|x_m) & P(y_2|x_m) & \cdots & P(y_n|x_m) \end{bmatrix}$$

is the conditional probability matrix.

The conditional probability matrix is especially useful when there are multiple parent and child nodes.

Further details on the computation of the parameters of a Bayesian node and propagation rules can be found in Ref. [1] (Pearl 1988).

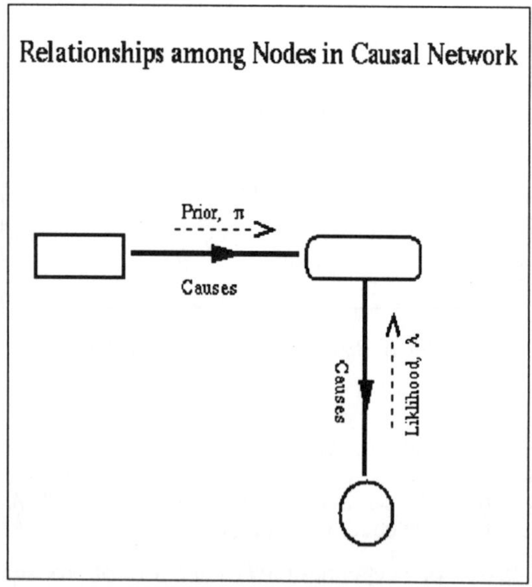

Fig. 7. Inter-node relationships.

C. Quantization of Program Scan Data

The goal of this procedure is to compute the values of likelihood in the Program Scan nodes of the Causal Network (Figure 8). The input data is obtained by running Program Scan, given the cable and its pair range, which provides the ver code, trouble message, and telephone number for each cable pair. The ver code is then mapped to a number between 0 and 1 based on a table look-up. The Program Scan data is divided into groups according to the cable pair range of Cable Bundle node, to which a Program Scan node is connected. Within a group, all values of mapped ver codes are summarized and normalized to calculate the likelihood vector for a particular Program Scan node.

D. Quantization of History Data

The history information related to a particular plant component is classified into three categories:

- PMAC History
- Repair History
- Defective Pair History

The information in each category is retrieved and processed, and a number between 0 and 10 is assigned. The number then is multiplied by a predetermined weight factor for that category. The resulting values from the three categories are summarized and normalized to a single value which is used to compute the prior (evidence) vector (Figure 9). This vector is stored in the corresponding History node in the Causal Network.

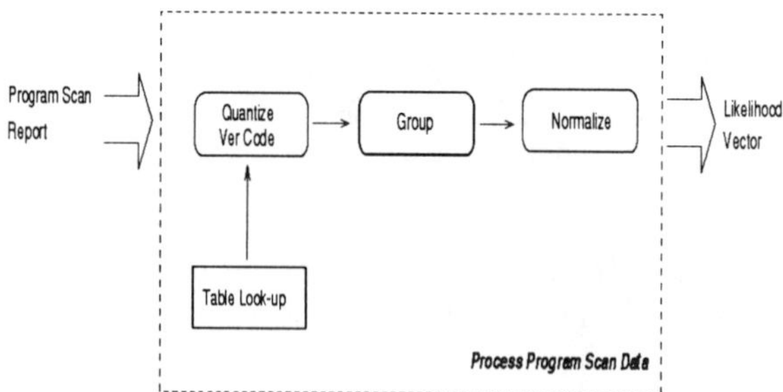

Fig. 8 Program Scan data quantization.

D.1 Quantize PMAC History

The source of PMAC History will be mainly from P3028 reports. These reports are classified into six different bins:

- Input file
- Closed; Construction job
- Pending status; No work needed but trouble found
- Closed; No trouble found
- Work in progress
- Closed; Work completed

The value of quantized PMAC history is then selected from a table.

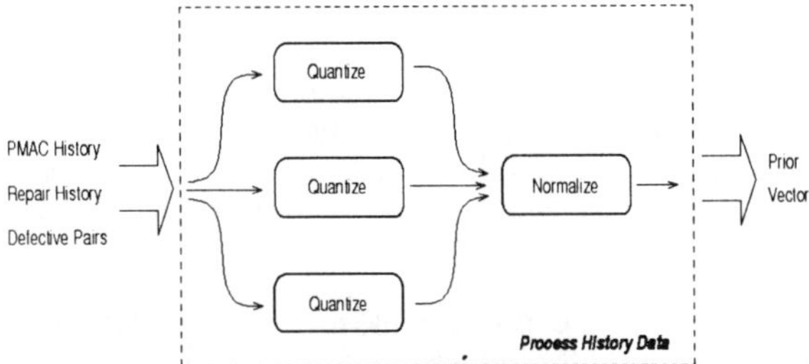

Fig. 9. History data quantization.

D.2 Quantize Repair History

The quantization method of repair history is based on predicting the behavior of repair needs of a particular plant component from its past records. By fitting a line or curve to a set of points located within time and percentage of repair axes, the future time at which the percentage of repair will exceed a certain fixed value (e.g., 10 %), can be determined (Figure 10). Using this time value, the quantization value is then computed based on a predefined function (Figure 11).

D.3 Quantize Defective Pair History

The quantization value for defective pairs is determined based on a simple function (Figure 12). The input data is expressed as a percentage within a cable. For example, if the following mapping function is used, then 20 % of defective pairs will result in value of 5 for the quantization.

D.4 Combine The Quantized Histories

The overall value of history quantization is calculated by multiplying each individual value by its corresponding weight factor, adding them together and then dividing by the sum of the weight factors.

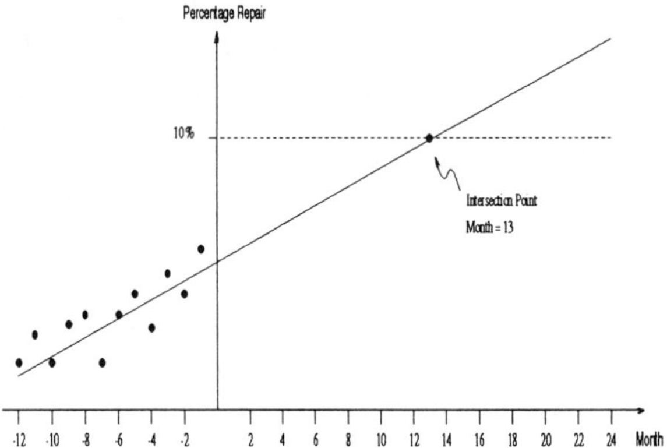

Fig. 10. Fitting a line to a set of points representing repair history.

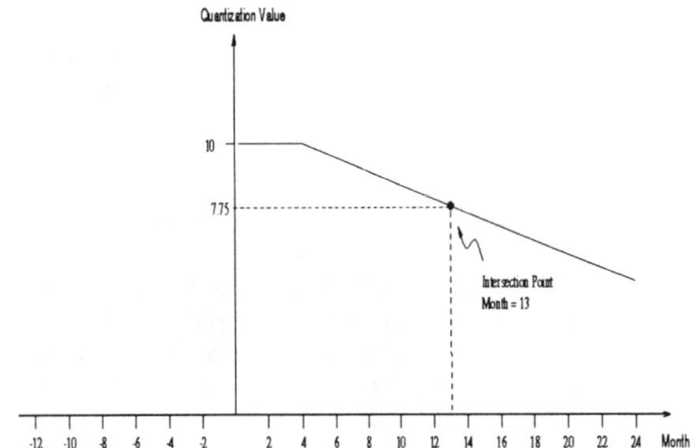

Fig. 11. Calculating the quantization value for repair history.

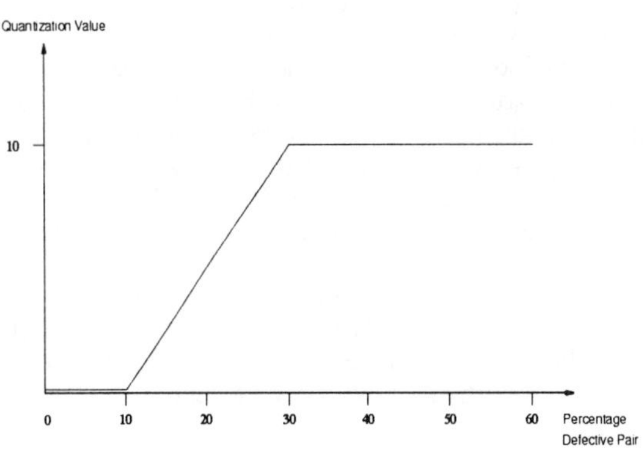

Fig. 12. Calculating the quantization value for defective pair history.

The final value of combined quantization is computed as:

Overall Value = (a * R + b * D + c * P) / (a + b + c)

where

a = Weight Factor of Repair History

b = Weight Factor of Defective Pair History

c = Weight Factor of PMAC History

R = Quantized Value of Repair History

D = Quantized Value of Defective Pair History

P = Quantized Value of PMAC History

System Implementation

The OPAS system is deployed in two centralized data

centers for use throughout the State of California by the five PMAC centers. Each data center contains all the communications links to the legacy systems and the data storage required for the OPAS system and the TL module. In essence, the OPAS database, which has been extended to support TL, acts as part of the knowledge base for the TL Module.

The TL Module is accessed by the PMACs through their workstations and is used primarily by analysts and engineers. The system is used on as-needed basis depending on the analysis requirements of the particular PMAC. As time progresses, we would expect that the TL Module would be used on a daily basis to help identify specific trouble areas of the network.

The expected payoff from the addition of TL to the OPAS system is tremendous. The primary purpose of TL is to locate the source of network trouble. By identifying the correct source of the problem without a site visit from a technician is a considerable cost savings. Prior to the develop of this system multiple site visits were required before a trouble could be identified and then repaired. Often the location of a trouble had been guessed and a technician dispatched only to discover that the trouble was elsewhere and the technician in the field was not qualified for that type of repair. With the addition of TL to OPAS we are able to dispatch the required resources to the site with the proper equipment and get the problem resolved before the customer is affected. In addition, since more network problems can be accurately located, the analysts and engineers in the PMAC are better able to plan for the repairs (i.e. schedule digging crews, allocate funding).

Scenario II: Plant Topology

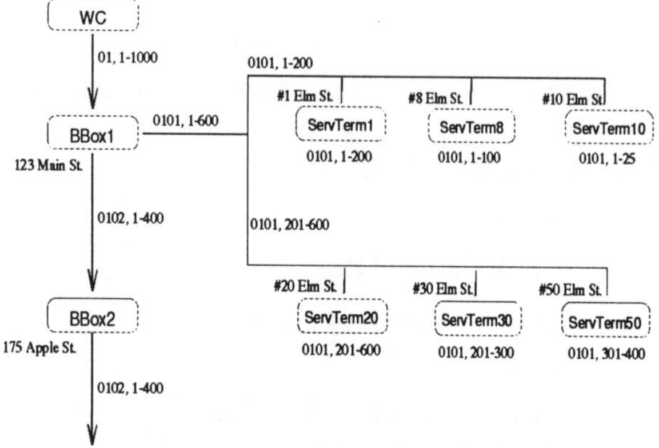

Fig. 13. Another example of local telephone cable network.

The other primary source of payoff is the reduction of the work load on the PMAC analysts. By providing the TL module, the PMAC analysts are able to bypass the horrendously tedious manual process of trouble localization analysis. Because the TL module is an automated process, the manual work is no longer necessary thereby speeding up the analysis process and freeing the PMAC analysts to work on larger projects. In addition, TL is of great benefit in several of the PMACs where the current staff do not have the extensive outside plant knowledge and analytical skills required to do trouble localization. TL provides them with expert analysis where none is currently available. Also, because it is fully automated, TL can provide the PMAC users with fully documented support for their analysis decisions, which can be reviewed by the PMAC staff for accuracy and training.

Overtime, we expect that the use of TL within the PMAC will build the knowledge of the existing staff in analysis and localization process. With the future development of an explanation facility for each step in the analysis process, users will learn the analysis steps required and will readily apply their knowledge. And as the knowledge of the user team increases they will be able to manipulate the current weights and operators to better suit their particular environment. And of course, since we are replacing a manual process with a primarily automated process, we expect the current work will be accomplished in a timely fashion.

Name	Description	Type	In Count	Out Count	Address
WC	wire center			01, 1-1000	
BBox1	x connect		01, 1-1000	0101, 1-600	123 Main St.
BBox2	x connect		01, 1-400	0102, 1-400	175 Apple St.
F1CBL01	F1 cable			01, 1-1000	
F2CBL01 01	F2 cable			0101, 1-600	
F2CBL01 02	F2 cable			0102, 1-400	
ServTerm 1	terminal	FIXED	0101, 1-200		#1 Elm St.
ServTerm 8	terminal	RA	0101, 1-100		#8 Elm St.
ServTerm 10	terminal	FIXED	0101, 1-25		#10 Elm St.
ServTerm 20	terminal	FIXED	0101, 201-600		#20 Elm St.
ServTerm 30	terminal	FIXED	0101, 201-300		#30 Elm St.
ServTerm 50	terminal	RA	0101, 301-400		#50 Elm St.

Table 1. Plant component information.

Development of the underlying TL system was undertaken by three individuals and took approximately 36 man-months. Currently a team of five is completing the work through full-deployment which is expected within six months. The development team relied heavily on their knowledge of AI, C++, database programming, user interface and system design. In addition, considerable effort has been spent with the domain experts to help the team understand the domain and to ensure that the system under construction would suit the needs of the users. The cost for the entire development of TL is estimated at $1.4 million.

Cable	Pair	Ver Code	Serving Terminal	CO Side Cable
0101	5	11	servTerm10	01:1
0101	6	11	servTerm8	01:2
0101	7	14	servTerm1	01:3
0101	12	14	servTerm8	01:4
0101	20	21	servTerm1	01:5
0101	21	21	servTerm10	01:6
0101	22	21	servTerm8	01:7
0101	23	21	servTerm1	01:8
0101	24	21	servTerm1	01:9
0101	25	11	servTerm1	01:10
0101	26	14	servTerm8	01:11
0101	27	21	servTerm8	01:12
0101	28	11	servTerm1	01:13
0101	50	11	servTerm1	01:14
0101	60	11	servTerm8	01:15
0101	75	11	servTerm1	01:16
0101	79	11	servTerm1	01:17

Table 2. The trouble list from Program Scan.

Application Results

The testing of TL module was conducted in two stages. The first one involved individual component testing, especially of the Bayesian Inference Specialist. Over sixty different scenarios were designed to verify the response and behavior of the causal net.

A point worth mentioning is that the object-oriented design approach allowed us to easily manipulate the input values and observe the output of each system component. The second testing stage involved the entire system. Figure 13 shows one of the scenarios.

Table 1 shows the plant information retrieved from the database.

Trouble Description: Table 2 shows that battery cross and ground trouble indicators occur on Cable 0101 between the pair range 1 to 100, in a random fashion. However, the troubles are mapped back to CO side cable, 01, from pair range 1 to 17, consecutively.

Desired Result from PMAC Analyst: F1 cable 01 is the most likely cause of the trouble, because of the cluster observed.

Actual Result from TL Module: It is displayed in Table 3, which shows a ranked list of plant components.

Reasoning by TL Module: Component [f1cable01] ranks the highest because it covers 100.% of troubles, and it has the highest value in Category [Cluster] of the Failure Matrix.

The above reasoning is generated by the Ranking Matrix Specialist. This result is consistent with the expectation of PMAC experts.

Rank	Name	TDE	Belief	DWTC	Worker	Cluster	Fail Type
1	f1cable01	1.000	0.000003	0.017	0.000	0.680	0.014
2	servTerm1	1.000	0.000895	0.085	0.529	0.091	0.043
3	servTerm8	1.000	0.001960	0.170	0.353	0.086	0.086
4	f2cable0101	1.000	0.000028	0.028	0.000	0.170	0.000
5	bbox1	1.000	0.000003	0.028	0.000	0.000	0.000
6	WC-ET	1.000	0.000000	0.000	0.000	0.000	0.000
7	servTerm10	0.588	0.006157	0.400	0.200	0.080	0.232
8	bbox2	0.000	0.000100	0.000	0.000	0.000	0.000
9	servTerm20	0.000	0.000001	0.000	0.000	0.000	0.000
10	servTerm50	0.000	0.000001	0.000	0.000	0.000	0.000
11	servTerm30	0.000	0.000001	0.000	0.000	0.000	0.000

Table 3. Ranking matrix generated by the TL module.

System Maintenance

Currently the TL Module and the OPAS system are being maintained by the developers and we are currently working on plans and procedures for moving the maintenance of the entire system to a maintenance organization within the company. The largest portion of the TL knowledge base is in the form of a large Oracle database which is within the OPAS system. The database draws data from the specified legacy systems as scheduled. Several of the legacy systems provide daily/hourly update and for others, data is requested on demand from the legacy system and the database is updated at that time.

Since the OPAS system is applied to the current copper cable network, the knowledge about the structure of the plant components will remain virtually unchanged. Thus the knowledge related to the plant itself does not need updating once it is established. Updates are required for the decision rules that govern the determination of ranking of faulty plant devices or components. In this regard, the system is expandable because the design of Ranking Matrix Specialist allows more operators to be added to the matrix.

Concluding Remarks

We have presented an intelligent system which utilizes object-oriented technology and a Bayesian network inference approach to solve real world problems. The system was designed to assist PMAC analysts but not to replace them; the system is to release the analysts from boring, tedious work and let people do their job in a more effective and accurate way. The system generates a ranked list of faulty components, but the final decision is made by the analyst. It is a decision support system where the user can change various parameters, try different scenarios, and compare different results to reach his conclusion.

Future development includes enabling the system with learning capability and diagnosis explanation capability. We hope to provide enhanced graphical output, so that the dispatched technician will have an annotated cable map to aid the repair and maintenance of the faulty component.

While this system was intended for the copper telephone cable network, we believe that the technology used here could be enhanced to support broadband networks.

Acknowledgment

The authors wish to thank Sam Allen for his expert advice, Ray Ronco and Tom Gill for their support, and all the OPAS team members for their assistance. The authors also thank the anonymous reviewers for their comments.

References

1. Judea Pearl, *Probabilistic Reasoning in Intelligent Systems: Networks of Plausible Inference,* Morgan Kaufmann Publishers, Inc., 1988.
2. Grady Booch, Object-Oriented Analysis and Design with Applications, The Benjamin/Cummings Publishing Company, Inc., 1994.
3. Todd E. Marques, *StarKeeper Network Troubleshooter: An Expert System Product,* AT&T Technical Journal, November/December 1988, pp 137-154.
4. DD Sharma and Teresa Hollidge, *OPAS Functional/ User Requirements,* Pacific Bell internal documents, August 1994.
5. Chuxin Chen and Teresa Hollidge, *OPAS Trouble Localization Module, Final Report,* Pacific Bell internal documents, January 1996.

Using Artificial Neural Networks to Predict The Quality and Performance of Oilfield Cements

P.V.Coveney, T.L.Hughes

Schlumberger Cambridge Research Ltd.,
High Cross, Madingley Road,
Cambridge CB3 0EL, U.K.
coveney@cambridge.scr.slb.com,
hughes@cambridge.scr.slb.com

P.Fletcher

Schlumberger Dowell,
Europe-Africa Technology Center,
Westhill Industrial Estate, Westhill,
Skene, Aberdeen, U.K.
fletcher@aberdeen.dowell.slb.com

Abstract

Inherent batch to batch variability, ageing and contamination are major factors contributing to variability in oilfield cement slurry performance. Of particular concern are problems encountered when a slurry is formulated with one cement sample and used with a batch having different properties. Such variability imposes a heavy burden on performance testing and is often a major factor in operational failure.

We describe methods which allow the identification, characterisation and prediction of the variability of oilfield cements. Our approach involves predicting cement compositions, particle size distributions and thickening time curves from the diffuse reflectance infrared Fourier transform spectrum of neat cement powders. Predictions make use of artificial neural networks. Slurry formulation thickening times can be predicted with uncertainties of less than ±10%. Composition and particle size distributions can be predicted with uncertainties a little greater than measurement error but general trends and differences between cements can be determined reliably.

Our research shows that many key cement properties are captured within the Fourier transform infrared spectra of cement powders and can be predicted from these spectra using suitable neural network techniques. Several case studies are given to emphasise the use of these techniques which provide the basis for a valuable quality control tool now finding commercial use in the oilfield.

Task Description

Cements are among the most widely used and the least well understood of all materials. While cements are often viewed as simple "low-tech" materials, they are in fact inherently complex over many length scales. The starting material, cement powder, is obtained by grinding cement clinker. The cement clinker is manufactured by firing limestone (providing calcium) and clay (providing silicon, aluminum and iron). Gypsum (calcium sulfate dihydrate) is then added to moderate the subsequent hydration process. After grinding the clinker and gypsum, the cement powder then consists of multi-size, multi-phase, irregularly-shaped particles ranging in size from less than a micrometer to slightly more than one hundred micrometers. When this starting material is mixed with water, hydration reactions occur which ultimately convert the water-cement suspension into a rigid porous material, which serves as the matrix phase for concrete, a cement paste-sand-rock composite.

The various chemical phases within the cement powder hydrate at different rates and interact with one another to form various reaction products. Some products deposit on the remaining unhydrated cement particle surfaces while others form as crystals in the water-filled pore space between cement particles. Moreover, some of the hydration products contain nanometer-sized pores, so that the size range of interest for these materials is from nanometers to hundreds of micrometers, or even centimeters if one includes the rock aggregates used in concrete. Due to these complexities, many questions remain unanswered in the science of cementitious materials. As with most materials of industrial importance, the key relationships between processing and underlying physicochemical properties must be elucidated in order to obtain better control over the material in use.

The most common application of cement is, of course, in building construction, where it has been used since at least Roman times. However, the work described here is concerned with another important application of cement - in the oil industry, where about three per cent of the world's annual cement output is deployed. Cement is used to line oil and gas wells, after drilling, by pumping a cement slurry between the well-bore and a steel casing inserted into the well, as shown in Figure 1. During placement, the cement displaces all the drilling fluid originally present from the drilling operation itself. The cement then sets to form a low-permeability annulus, which isolates the productive hydrocarbon-bearing zones of the well from the rest of the formations, from surplus water and from the surface.

Cement is used almost exclusively for oilfield cementing despite the fact that its performance is variable and not completely understood. Cement variability is observed between cements from different manufacturers, between different cement batches from the same manufacturer, and between samples from the same batch of cement that may have aged differently during storage. Because of all these problems, well cementing has remained until now more a black art than a science.

Various cement slurry properties, such as compressive strength development, permeability to oil and gas, and flow behavior need to be specified and controlled, taking into account the high temperature and pressure conditions prevailing downhole. For oilfield cement slurries, the *thickening time* plays a central role during slurry formulation since it is a measure of the time within which the cement is pumpable (American Petroleum Institute 1982). Experimentally, it is the time taken to reach a specified consistency as measured under defined conditions. Longer than required thickening times are a potential waste of drilling time and an inefficient use of expensive chemical additives. Operational problems due to short thickening times are especially dramatic since the cement may set prematurely in the casing or pumping equipment. Such major operating failures, or MOFs, may necessitate the complete re-drilling of a many-thousands-of-feet well-bore, and can cost between $1-2 million; less severe MOFs in which a limited amount of re-drilling is required typically cost around $0.6 million. Considerable and very time-consuming experimental effort is therefore devoted to precise control of slurry thickening times.

Application Description: The FTIR Spectra of Cements

In view of the overwhelming complexity of cement hydration, a valuable quality control tool would be a model predicting performance properties of a given cement sample prior to its use. However, the mathematical modeling of cement hydration based upon mechanistic understanding is still in its infancy (but see Coveney & Humphries 1996). The novel approach taken here is to dispense with detailed physicochemical characterisation of the cement particles in favour of methods based on a combination of statistics and artificial intelligence. Using this approach, cement composition and performance properties are correlated with a judiciously

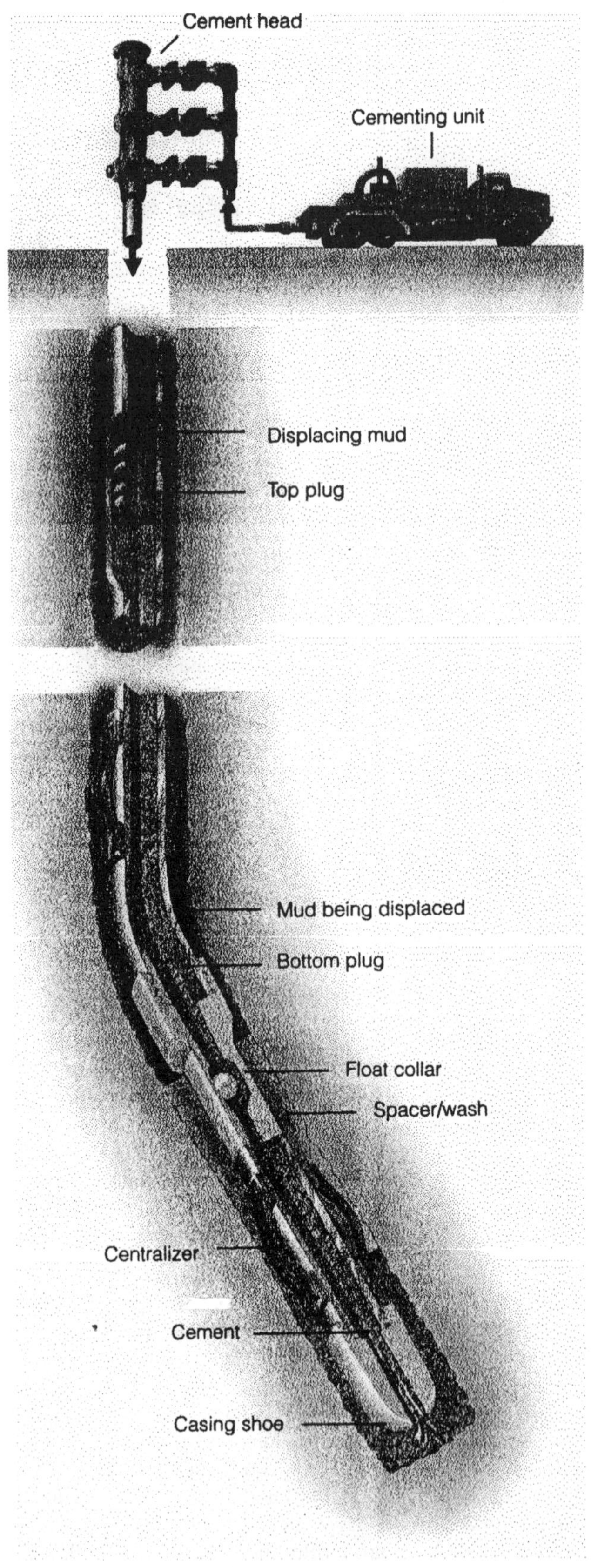

Figure 1: Cementing an oil well. The main objective of such well cementing is to provide complete and permanent isolation of the formation behind the steel casing previously placed in the borehole. The cement must be mixed to meet appropriate design parameters and is then pumped downhole, displacing all drilling mud from the annulus between casing and formation. Spacers or washes may be used along with top and bottom plugs to separate cement from drilling mud. Centralisers on the outside of the casing are used to keep the annular gap as even as possible.

chosen measurement which implicitly contains key information on cement composition, particle size distribution and surface chemistry. To give the method any chance of commercial success, this measurement has also to be relatively inexpensive and easy to perform on a routine basis.

The measurement chosen was based on the use of infrared spectroscopy, a common analytical technique used in the chemical sciences: it is well known that every chemical species has its own unique infrared spectrum. Indeed, chemists most commonly use this technique in a qualitative mode, by matching up spectral features in an unknown compound with previously recorded spectral data on known compounds available in look-up tables. An experienced chemist, working in a specified area of chemistry, can often identify a chemical by direct visual inspection of its infrared spectrum. A more specialized yet equally well established application is quantitative analysis of chemical mixtures, wherein measured spectra of unknown chemical composition are regressed against linear combinations of infrared spectra either of the pure chemical components or of mixtures of known chemical composition (Beebe & Kowalski 1987).

The particular variant used in this work is that of the Fourier Transform Infrared (FTIR) spectrum of dry cement powders, sometimes known as DRIFTS (Diffuse Reflectance Infrared Fourier Transform Spectroscopy), for reasons which we shall now describe. In this technique, white light radiation from a Michelson interferometer is focused on a compacted sample via a moving mirror. Radiation impinging on the sample undergoes two types of reflection. The first is *specular reflectance*, where the radiation is reflected from the sample surface as if from a mirror. The second is *diffuse reflectance* whereby a proportion of the radiation penetrates the sample and is reflected from particle surface to particle surface. At each reflection a degree of energy absorption occurs as indicated in Figure 2.

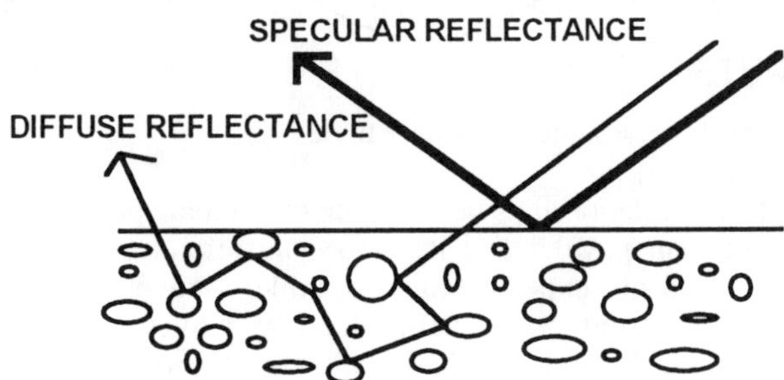

Figure 2: Schematic of the diffuse reflectance process

Energy is absorbed due to the vibration and stretching of chemical bonds in the molecules of the powder. The reflected light re-emerges from the sample and is collected by a second ellipsoidal mirror. The Fourier transform technique is used to convert the emergent radiation into a spectrum of absorbance versus frequency. The experimental method for collecting FTIR spectra of cement powders has been described elsewhere (Hughes *et al.* 1994, Hughes *et al.* 1995). The wavelength range of the mid infrared region of the electromagnetic spectrum is approximately 2.5×10^{-3}cm to 2.5×10^{-4}cm or 4000 to 400 wavenumbers, where wavenumbers are reciprocal wavelength in units of cm^{-1}.

Information Contained Within Cement FTIR Spectra

Particle Size. The extent of diffuse reflectance is inherently related to the particle size of the sample, but in a generally unknown manner. Large coarse particles allow the incident radiation to penetrate deeply into the sample thus increasing absorption. However, large particles show greater specular reflectance which distorts the frequency spectrum. As the particle size of a sample is reduced the depth of penetration and therefore absorption is less since more particles are present to reflect and limit the depth of penetration. Spectra are therefore distorted as a function of particle size although sample dilution in KBr minimises these effects. Accordingly, our spectral measurement is made with samples diluted to a concentration of 10% by weight in finely ground, infra-red inactive, potassium bromide.

Composition. To a good first approximation the FTIR spectrum of any multicomponent mineral assembly is a linear superposition of the spectra of the pure mineral components. In the case of oilfield cements, the American Petroleum Institute (API) lays down notional chemical composition specifications based on the so-called "Bogue" clinker phases: alite (tricalcium silicate), belite (dicalcium silicate), aluminate (tricalcium aluminate) and aluminoferrite (tetracalcium aluminoferrite). These Bogue phases, which themselves provide only an approximate chemical description, are traditionally by means of a linear transformation of the chemical composition of the clinker expressed in terms of its major oxides, which can be directly determined by other, more lengthy, non-infrared methods. Spectral features of the major Bogue cement chemical phases in the mid infrared are dominated by vibrations and stretching modes of water molecules which are located on mineral surfaces, within the sulfate and carbonate minerals and/or in calcium hydroxide. Within the mineral phases present, chemical bonds between silicon and oxygen, aluminium and oxygen, and iron and oxygen are also active in the mid infrared region. Despite the aforementioned complexities due to particle size distributions and the occlusion of minerals, it is established that linear statistical techniques can be used to correlate spectral characteristics with cement chemical composition, provided due care is taken in the sample preparation (Hughes *et al.* 1994, Hughes *et al.* 1995).

Other Spectral Attributes. Lack of crystallinity, impurities in minerals and pre-hydration have a more subtle effect on spectra, usually broadening absorbance peaks and shifting the frequencies at which absorbance occurs.

We may therefore assert with confidence that diffuse reflectance infra red spectra of cements contain information on the composition, particle size distribution and surface chemistry of the material, all of which influence cement hydration.

Methods for Predicting Cement Properties from FTIR Spectra

The Cement Properties Database

The methods we use for making quantitative predictions are based on establishing statistical correlations between cement infrared spectra and selected cement physicochemical parameters. Specifically, we were interested in seeking to establish unambiguous relationships between the infrared spectra and cement properties such as chemical composition, particle size distribution and thickening time. This required the construction of a database containing data on 158 oilwell cements collected worldwide. Our database is one of the most comprehensive currently available on oilfield cement properties. It contains the following standard physical and chemical data on each of the 158 cements:

- cement mineral composition expressed in weight per cent (wt%) of the following minerals: alite, belite, aluminate, ferrite, gypsum, the sulfates bassanite and syngenite, calcium hydroxide and calcium carbonate;
- cement oxide composition expressed in wt% of the following oxides: SO_3, Al_2O_3, Fe_2O_3, MgO, Na_2O, CaO, SiO_2, P_2O_5, TiO_2, CrO_2, MnO_2, ZnO and SrO_2;
- binned particle size distribution (PSD Bin), in volume fraction, and mean particle diameter, in microns, as measured by Cilas granulometry;
- weight loss on ignition, free lime content and insoluble residue;
- surface area as measured by Blaine's method ($cm^2\ g^{-1}$), which provides an estimate of the total surface area of cement particles;
- digitised thickening time curve for a neat cement slurry at 50 °C and solid /water ratio of 0.44;
- digitised thickening time curve for a slurry retarded with 0.2% D13 at 85 °C and solid/water ratio of 0.44;
- diffuse reflectance FTIR spectra recorded at 2 cm^{-1} resolution using a Nicolet 5DX spectrometer.

Modeling Techniques

The primary objective of this research was to construct models to predict cement properties from FTIR spectra as the sole input data. The most important cement information that one would hope to extract from infrared spectra are: (i) chemical composition according to the Bogue and oxide representations, (ii) particle size distribution, and (iii) thickening time profiles for neat and retarded cement slurries. Accordingly, five independent statistical models were constructed for the prediction from FTIR spectra of the following properties selected from the database:

Model [a]: the concentrations of the four API-specified Bogue minerals plus gypsum, syngenite, bassanite, calcium hydroxide and calcium carbonate;

Model [b]: the concentrations of the major oxides together with loss on ignition, free lime content and insoluble residue;

Model [c]: particle size distributions plus mean particle diameter;

Model [d]: digitised neat thickening time curves;

Model [e]: digitised retarded thickening time curves.

These models were subsequently used independently of one another.

It has previously been demonstrated that cement mineral compositions (model [a]) can be predicted from FTIR using linear statistical techniques (Fierens & Verhagen 1972, Hughes *et al.* 1994). A suitable procedure, described elsewhere (Sharf, Illman & Kowalski 1986, Martens & Naes 1989, Beebe & Kowalski 1987), is based on *partial least squares* (PLS). This technique is a variant on simple multiple linear regression which has the capacity to filter noise and redundant information from spectra prior to prediction. In this study PLS is used for the prediction of mineral compositions only. All other models make full use of artificial neural networks.

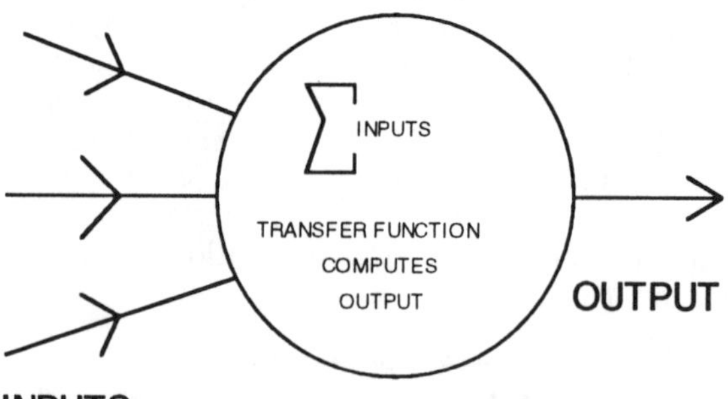

Figure 3: Schematic of a single node

The full relationships between the measurable properties of a cement powder and its slurry performance are not known and are expected to be complex; that is, highly nonlinear (Hunt 1986, Billingham & Coveney 1993, Bensted & Beckett 1993, Fletcher & Coveney 1995, Fletcher *et al.* 1995, Coveney & Humphries 1996). It is best, therefore, to choose a technique for finding such correlations which makes as few assumptions as possible regarding their nature. Artificial neural networks (ANNs) offer the possibility of finding input/output correlations of essentially arbitrary complexity, and consequently formed the basis for the artificial intelligence methods we used in this work. The main feature of the neural network methodology is that input/output information is correlated via a system of interconnected nodes (Rumelhart &

McClelland 1986, Lippmann 1987, Hush & Hornee 1993). These nodes, also called neurons, are the computational analog of nerve cells in the human brain. A single node is a processing element which combines a set of inputs to produce a single numerical output (Figure 3).

The strength of the output signal is given by a non-linear function called the transfer function. Commonly the transfer function is based on a weighted sum of the input signals. A complete neural network is constructed from an arrangement of individual neurons which link input data to output data via a network of arbitrary complexity. Within any architecture the strength of the signal received by any one node is a weighted sum of inputs sent by all the nodes to which it is connected. In the commonly used, supervised, feedforward, layered networks, nodes in an input layer first receive signals equal to the values of the external input data. This information is passed on in a non-linearly convolved fashion to nodes in an output layer representing output data (Figure 4). The network architectures and non-linear expressions are modified using a supervised training procedure such that input data is correlated with output data. In some networks there may be one or more layers of neurons connecting the input and output layers. These (hidden) layers add mathematical features to networks necessary to model complex relationships.

A fully trained artificial neural network is effectively a non-linear map between specified variables which is capable of filtering noise in the input data and has a predictive capacity, that is it is capable of making predictions for situations not previously encountered. The procedures for optimising artificial neural networks are described elsewhere (Masters 1993) and use goodness of fit criteria based on minimum residual prediction errors for test data.

Neural networks have the following valuable features:

- Respond with high speed to input signals
- Generalised mapping capabilities
- Filter noise from data
- Can perform classification as well as function modelling
- Can encode information by regression or iterative supervised learning

Some drawbacks of neural network methods are:

- They are data intensive
- Training is computationally intensive and requires significant elapsed wall clock time
- They have a tendency to overtrain if the network topology is not optimised, resulting in their mapping calibration data extremely well but becoming unreliable in dealing with new data
- Predictions are unreliable if extrapolated beyond the boundaries of the calibration data

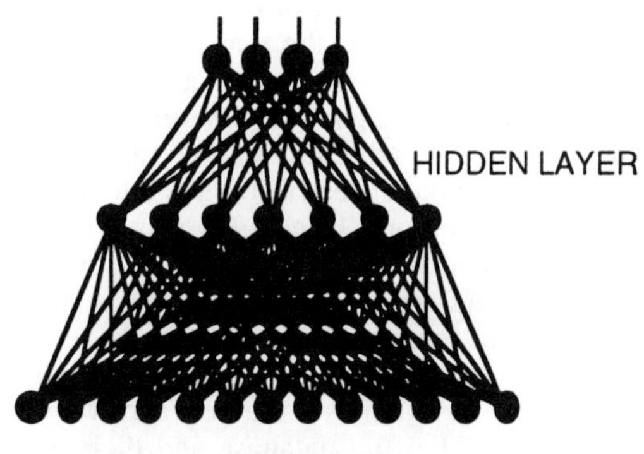

Figure 4: Schematic of an artificial neural network

There are many different types of neural networks which can be implemented to solve a wide range of complex non-linear problems. We originally worked with multi-layer perceptrons (MLP), comprised of three layers in which the number of nodes in the input and output layers were fixed by virtue of the mapping sought. Thus, the number of nodes in the input layer is equal to the number of individual pieces of data in a single cement input data record (also called an input vector), while the number of nodes in the output layer is equal to the number of separate parameters being predicted from the input vector. However, there are certain computational drawbacks to these MLP networks: finding the optimal number of nodes in the hidden layer is time consuming since network training by the backpropagation-of-errors algorithm is slow and, in addition, there is some possibility of the network becoming trapped in a local rather than the global error minimum.

The network type we found to be the most suitable for predicting cement properties employed Gaussian radial basis functions (Moody & Darken 1988, 1989) in a single hidden layer. We preferred these networks because their underlying learning algorithms are fast and, being based on linear algebra, they are guaranteed to find global optima. In radial basis function networks - also sometimes referred to as localised receptive field networks - the nodes in the hidden layer are of a different nature to those in a multi-layer perceptron: they are radial distribution functions which have centres and widths expressed in terms of the *n* dimensional space defined by the input data vectors. These Gaussian basis functions produce a non-zero response only when an input vector falls within a small, localised region of this *n* dimensional space centred on the mean and within the specified width of the basis function.

The process of constructing and optimising such networks involves several stages. First, an arbitrary number of Gaussian basis functions have to be selected. Their means and standard deviations (widths) are determined on the basis of the available data vectors to be used for training by a procedure such as *n* dimensional K-means clustering. This standard statistical procedure exploits the natural clustering of the input data in order to locate the means (that is, the centers) of the selected number of nodes such that their average Euclidean distances from all the input data vectors are minimised. The outputs from this arbitrarily chosen number of radial basis functions are then linearly correlated to the supplied target (output) vectors. The final stage of network optimisation is performed by systematically varying the number of clusters and overlap parameters to achieve an optimum fit to the training data.

For all types of ANN architecture employed and models constructed ([a] to [e] above), the networks were trained using a subset of the full database and their predictive capabilities evaluated using a completely independent test data set - that is, one containing data which had not been previously used by the network during training - selected randomly from the database. The importance of network optimisation and training in the construction of reliable and robust ANN models cannot be over stressed.

The extensive computation time for optimising even radial basis function neural networks becomes an issue when spectral data are used as input variables. A typical mid infra-red FTIR spectrum collected at 2 wavenumber resolution of the kind used here has approximately 2000 digitised points. Thus, in order to use FTIR spectra as input data for neural networks it was found necessary to first reduce the number of variables representing any spectrum. This was performed using the principal component method based on spectral eigenvector analysis and led to the useful information content in each spectrum being reduced to 35 principal components which allows network calibration and validation to be performed on PC's and workstations. For each of the models [b] to [e], the spectra were always reduced to 35 principal components although the optimum architectures were different for each model. More details of the theoretical basis of the modeling procedure are given elsewhere (Fletcher & Coveney 1996).

Predictive Capabilities of the Models

Model [a]: *Mineral Composition Predictions - PLS Model*

The expected uncertainties in mineral composition predictions have been described in detail elsewhere (Hughes *et al.* 1994, Hughes *et al.* 1995). They are summarised in Table 1, which lists the various chemical phases present, as well as the concentration ranges and associated uncertainties with which the phases are found (in weight per cent). As in all the models to be discussed, the quoted uncertainties refer to the imprecision of the model predictions compared with the known, experimentally measured values of the same quantities.

The predictions of the sulfate minerals (gypsum, bassanite and syngenite), calcium hydroxide, calcium carbonate, aluminate and ferrite are generally good and can be used to detect ageing of cements, as our later case studies show. The major uncertainties lie in the prediction of the individual silicate phases, although total silicates (alite + belite) is predicted well.

Component	*Concentration Range in wt%*	*Uncertainty/2σ in wt%*
Alite	42 - 70	± 5
Belite	4 - 35	± 5
Alite+Belite	70 - 82	± 1.5
Aluminate	0 - 15	± 1
Ferrite	5 - 20	± 1
Syngenite	0 - 3	± 0.6
Gypsum	0 - 6	± 0.6
Bassanite	0 - 6	± 0.6
$Ca(OH)_2$	0 - 3	± 0.1
$CaCO_3$	0 - 4	± 0.2

Table 1: Uncertainties in Model [a]

Model [b]: *Major Oxide Analyses - ANN Model*

Table 2 displays the cement chemical analysis represented more fundamentally in terms of the major oxides present, together with the concentration ranges and associated uncertainties with which these oxides occur.

Component	*Concentration Range in wt%*	*Uncertainty/2σ in wt%*
SO_3	1.5 - 4.0	± 0.2
Al_2O_3	3.0 - 7.0	± 0.3
Fe_2O_3	1.8 - 7.0	± 0.3
MgO	0.5 - 3.0	± 0.3
Total Alkalis	0.2 - 1.5	± 0.2
CaO	61 - 67	± 1
SiO_2	19.5 - 24	± 0.4
Insol. Res.	0 - 0.9	± 0.3
LOI	0.5 - 2.5	± 0.3
Free Lime	0.4 - 2.1	± 0.3

Table 2: Uncertainties in Model [b]

In all cases the oxides, weight loss on ignition (LOI), free lime and insoluble residue variables are predicted well, although the uncertainties are greater than expected errors on the measurements. The major uncertainties lie in the predictions of the concentrations of CaO and MgO. These arise from the fact that the variance in the levels of CaO and MgO is known to be small and the errors in prediction are proportionately large.

As with the mineral composition model [a], cement oxide compositions can be estimated with errors a little greater than those of the direct composition measurement itself, but general trends in chemical composition can be determined readily from both models.

Model [c]: *Particle Size Distribution Bins and Mean Diameter - ANN Model*

Figure 5 shows a typical particle size distribution prediction for an oilwell cement, while Table 3 lists its uncertainties.

In all cases the prediction errors are greater than the expected measurement errors although general trends are predicted well.

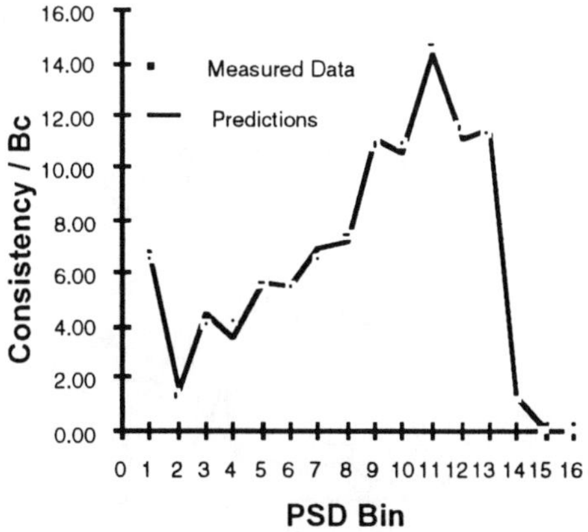

Figure 5: Measured and predicted particle size for a typical oilfield cement

Bin	*Diameter Range / μm*	*Uncertainty / 2σ in %*
1	0 - 1	± 1
2	1 - 1.5	± 1
3	1.5 - 3	± 1
4	2 - 3	± 1
5	3 - 4	± 1
6	4 - 6	± 1
7	6 - 8	± 1.2
8	8 - 1	± 1.2
10	16 - 24	± 1.2
11	24 - 32	± 1
12	32 - 48	± 1
13	48 - 64	± 1
15	96 - 128	± 1
16	128 - 192	± 1
Error on Mean Particle Diameter 2σ = ± 1μm		

Table 3: Uncertainties in Model [c]

Models [d] and [e]: *Thickening Time Curve Predictions - ANN Model*

Figure 6 shows predictions of the full digitised thickening time curves for the retarded and neat slurries for a typical oilfield cement. In this example the digitization simplifies the curve yet the general trends, including the point of departure and the actual thickening time, can be seen clearly.

The expected error limits for thickening time predictions for both neat and retarded formulations are shown in Table 4. These uncertainties are typically less than experimental thickening time measurement errors and thus support the use of FTIR as a rapid, quantitative predictor of cement slurry thickening times.

	Neat Slurry	*Retarded Slurry*
Mean Errors / Minutes	±16.0	±19.5
2σ / Minutes*	±31	±37
Mean % Error	±9.5	±10.6
Range of Fit / Minutes	50 - 350	50 - 450
**2σ indicates upper maximum expected errors*		

Table 4: Uncertainties for Thickening Time Predictions

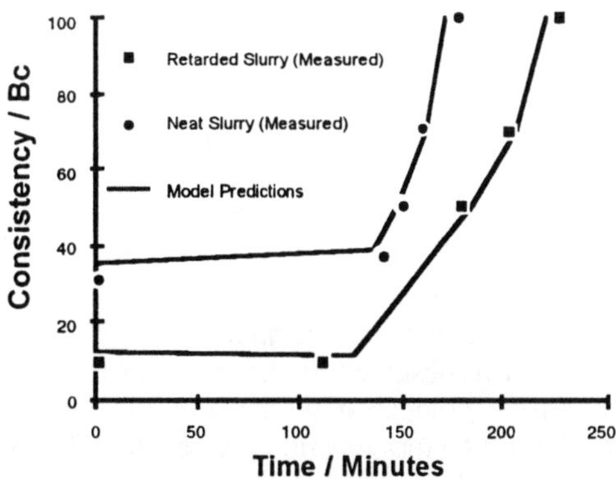

Figure 6: Measured and predicted thickening time curves for a typical oilfield cement. The upper continuous curve displays the ANN predictions for a neat slurry, while the continuous lower curve shows similar predictions for a retarded slurry.

Application Case Studies

The application offers two basic levels of interpretation. One is the qualitative assessment of cement FTIR spectral features. The other is the interpretation of quantitative predictions from the models. In this section, we provide a few examples of how this AI-based application works in commercial operations, where it has been deployed for more than 12 months.

Qualitative Interpretation

Qualitative interpretation involves identifying and comparing relevant features of cement spectra, without any reference to the AI-system. The simplest qualitative method is direct visual inspection of the spectra. This involves identifying the presence of specific components by the presence of characteristic absorbance bands and reference to the spectra of pure components provided in pre-existing look-up tables (Hughes *et al.* 1994, Hughes *et al.* 1995). The relative spectral changes may give indicators to changes in performance between batches. An alternative qualitative technique is spectral subtraction where one FTIR spectrum is subtracted from a second to leave a so-called residual spectrum which is used to identify differences in the spectra. This is particularly useful in the detection of contaminants.

Quantitative Interpretation

Quantitative interpretation involves predicting the composition, particle size distribution and performance properties of the cement using the artificial neural network based prediction modules. Most applications involve comparing the properties of one cement with another possibly suspect batch, using the cement FTIR spectra passed through our predictive models. Any statistically significant differences in composition or particle size distribution will indicate differences in performance. In some cases, such as the detection of aged cements, the changes in mineral compositions can indicate changes in performance. The performance predictions themselves can be used to support or confirm the qualitative interpretations. In some cases the compositional differences between cements are subtle and not easily interpreted. In these cases direct prediction of performance is informative.

Case A: *Detecting a Barite Contaminated Cement*

A cement sample was observed to yield an unexpectedly long thickening time compared with a normal cement taken from a different storage silo. A residual FTIR spectrum was obtained by subtracting the spectrum of the normal cement from that of the rogue cement. Figure 7 shows the residual spectrum compared with the spectrum of pure barite; the barite characteristics are confirmed by table look-up from existing databases. (No use of the AI-system is necessary for this application). The correspondence of spectral features confirmed the presence of barite in the rogue sample. Barite contamination leads to the slurry being over-retarded when the cement is used in a slurry formulated on the basis of an uncontaminated cement.

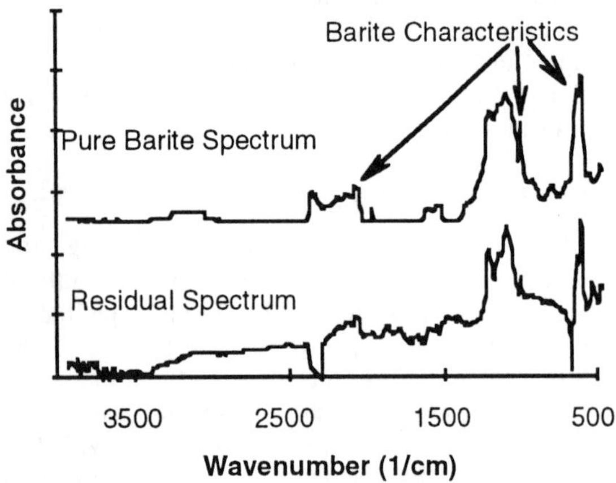

Figure 7: A Barite-Contaminated Cement

Case B: *Detecting an Aged Cement*

A cement from one storage silo was observed to show mixing and pumping problems and to yield a short thickening time compared to cement samples from other silos. The spectrum of the problem cement is shown in Figure 8, where it is compared with the spectrum of a normal cement. Enhanced syngenite features are visible in the spectrum of the problem cement; as in the case of the barite-contaminated sample, the spectral features characteristic of syngenite are confirmed by table look-up from existing databases.

The linear partial least squares composition model [a] predicted the syngenite content of the problem cement to be 2.7wt% compared with 0.9wt% for the normal cement. Ageing to form syngenite is consistent with the observed shortening of thickening times and pumping problems. The retarded slurry performance ANN model predicted the thickening time for the aged cement to be 50 minutes shorter than for the normal cement.

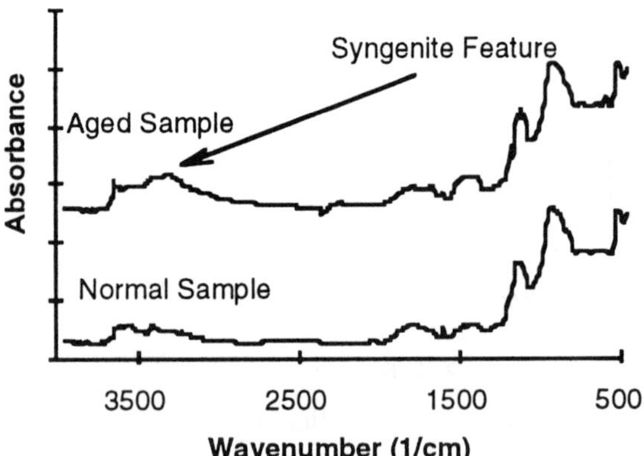

Figure 8: A Syngenite Aged Cement

Case C: *Identification of a Rogue Cement*

Figure 9 shows a retarded thickening time curve for an oilwell cement as predicted from its FTIR spectrum using our ANN model. The predicted data are compared to an average thickening time curve obtained from experimental measurements on five different batches of the same cement. An indication of the normal batch-to-batch variation due to storage is given by the two standard deviations limit. The rogue batch is identified as having a very short thickening time compared to the expected range for this cement and an unusually high initial consistency. This was subsequently confirmed experimentally. This example makes criticial use of the ANN-based performance prediction capability to identify a rogue cement without recourse to interpreting cement composition or particle size distribution which, on their own, are likely to provide ambiguous results. It will be recalled that premature setting of the slurry, as is the case here, would very likely lead to a costly major operating failure if such a cement were pumped in the field.

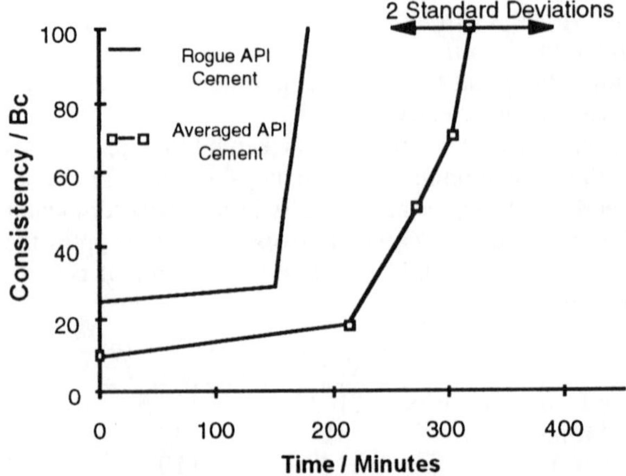

Figure 9: Thickening time curve predictions for a rogue oilfield cement

These case studies indicate the scope and power of prediction afforded by artificial neural networks. There remains the intriguing issue as to how these ANNs actually succeed in making correct composition and performance predictions from the compressed and convolved representation of cement FTIR spectra.

ANNs have been criticized at times since they appear to work like black boxes. However, the substantial quantity of knowledge they encode is available for more detailed interrogation and can be turned to very effective use in its own right. As an illustration, we mention in passing that we have constructed other ANN models which map chemical compositions and particle size distributions directly onto slurry thickening time curves (Fletcher & Coveney 1996). These networks may be used to investigate the sensitivity of, for example, changes in thickening time to changes in the values of input parameters, such as the amount of aluminum or iron in the cement, and so on. In some cases, these models have confirmed previously established qualitative trends known within the cementing community, such as the observation that increasing the iron content increases thickening times, while at the same time making these relationships more quantitative. But in many other instances, including for example the dependence on composition variables of the kick-off time and the subsequent rapidity of thickening following the usual quiescent period during which there is essentially constant slurry consistency (see Figures 6 and 9), no previous knowledge - either qualitative or quantitative - existed. Moreover, we have shown that a genetic algorithm can be used to invert the nonlinear forward mapping provided by such an ANN so as to furnish the precise physicochemical composition of a cement needed to deliver specified performance properties. This is particularly remarkable, since it implies that, in principle at least, it may one day be possible to tailor-make a cement to suite any particular application.

The cement quality assurance tool that we have described here is the result of the powerful combination of a modern AI technique (artificial neural networks) and the established laboratory measurement technique of FTIR spectroscopy. The integration of these two methodologies is achieved in routine use by passing the digitised output from an FTIR spectrometer into a 486 PC on which the trained ANNs reside. In this way, a single cement powder FTIR spectrum provides information simultaneously on cement chemical composition, particle size distribution and setting profile (including thickening time), together with a flag indicating the degree of statistical reliability to be expected from the predictions emanating from the AI device. This flag indicates whether or not a cement being analysed lies within the part of infrared parameter space on which the ANNs have been trained: if the former, the predictions are classified as reliable; if the latter, they are described as unreliable. As a consequence, one can record the FTIR spectrum of a cement powder and reliably predict its setting time in about fifteen minutes of real time, rather than waiting for more than four hours to observe when the slurry will actually set.

Our radial basis function neural network and other codes were home made, and were developed on Unix platforms. At the time when the method was transferred from Schlumberger Cambridge Research (SCR), where it had been developed, to Schlumberger Dowell's Europe-Africa Technology Center in Aberdeen, a decision was taken to port all codes to the Matlab commercial package, which is platform independent and was thus immediately accessible on a PC, the latter being the type of machine available in the field. This reduced the coding requirements of the commercial product to a minimum. It should be noted that our artificial neural network codes made no special use of Matlab's intrinsic features, nor did Matlab influence in any way our choice of network architecture: our work was completed prior to the availability of the Neural Network Toolbox within this package.

Application Use and Payoff

The cement quality control technique described here proved so successful in our research laboratories that a decision was made to turn it into a commercial product, called CemQUEST (for cement quality estimation). The technique is now being used in our Aberdeen regional field laboratories to detect and avoid cementing problems normally associated with cement quality and variability. The CemQUEST software can predict composition, particle size distribution and thickening times for certain cement slurry formulations directly from the FTIR spectrum.

The advantages of using CemQUEST compared with previous cementing practise are manifold. Obviously, there is the large time and manpower saving that accrues from predicting cement setting properties in this way. Other benefits include: (i) the avoidance of operational cementing failures due to batch to batch variation, ageing or cement contamination; (ii) improved efficiency of cement slurry formulation design through the identification of important slurry performance characteristics.

Since early 1995, CemQUEST has been in routine use within Schlumberger Dowell where it is part of the overall set of techniques employed for achieving improved cement slurry design and reliability on a daily basis. It has also attracted the attention of cement manufacturers and clients (oil companies) for whom cement quality control work is also now being done on a regular basis. CemQUEST is able to save around $3-5 million per year per client through its ability to detect potential major operating failures (MOFs) before they arise. The costs of slurry formulation are also reduced by CemQUEST: rapid screening and elimination of bad cements saves around 10% of the time taken by the lengthy process of formulation optimization. This translates to a savings of about $1000 per week per formulation in routine laboratory testing.

We expect additional benefits to arise with the passage of time for at least two reasons. The first will be due to the build up of a larger cement database, extending the domain of validity of the existing neural network models (which will require periodic retraining). A second reason will be due to an enhanced reputation for Schlumberger Dowell based on increasing reliability of its cementing jobs through use of the current product on a day-to-day basis.

Application Development and Deployment

The development of the CemQUEST prototype at Schlumberger Cambridge Research was the result approximately 12 person-years' effort, which commenced in 1991 and ended in mid-1993. The work involved coordinating a vast cement data collection exercise, with samples being sent from all areas of the world in which Dowell has cementing operations. This led to approximately 160 distinct cements, whose various physicochemical properties - chemical composition, particle size distribution, FTIR spectra, slurry thickening curves, etc. - had to be recorded. The reproducibility of all these measurements had to be investigated. This in itself required the cooperation of colleagues in our product center (then in St Etienne, France) and in Aberdeen. In addition, some of the chemical analysis work was performed externally at low cost. The samples needed careful storage in the absence of moisture and carbon dioxide to prevent alteration of cement properties with time, as these substances are readily absorbed by cement powders. The end result was a substantial cement database which was used for developing the final neural network models.

While data were being acquired, approximately three person-years of effort was devoted to an investigation of the feasibility of cement quality estimation using FTIR spectra linked to thickening time curves. The initial aim was to establish whether any of the cement data could be reliably used for such predictive purposes. When this was answered in the affirmative during late 1991 and early 1992, the target was to demonstrate that the same could be achieved on the basis of the single and easily performed FTIR powder measurement. The feasibility of doing this, fully confirmed during late 1992, opened the way to a commercially viable product. During 1993, about one person-year's effort was assigned to the development of the basic Matlab code for transfer to Aberdeen in mid 1993. One of the authors (PF) was transferred to Aberdeen, in part to ensure correct technical implementation of the product and to prepare for its commercialisation. This was seen to be important to guarantee a successful future for the product, since at that site there was previously only very limited expertise in the recording and interpretation of FTIR spectra.

Maintenance

Experience in the transfer of this product from research to operations showed that the key limitation is associated with the recording of FTIR spectra in field laboratories. Owing to the large size of the database and the technical issues involved in producing accurate predictive models, all of these models were developed in the research laboratory during 1992-93, using FTIR spectra recorded there. It was thus of paramount importance to ensure that FTIR cement spectra recorded in the field center on different spectrometers were closely coincident with the database spectra recorded in research. Clear guidelines for ensuring reproducible spectra had to be laid down by the research group.

Maintenance of the software and the database is now the responsibility of Aberdeen. To date, it has not proved necessary to update this knowledge base, owing to the rather wide representative coverage of the original cement data. However, data are being kept on all significant outlier cements detected by the reliability flag within the current AI system. Predictions of the physicochemical and performance properties of such outlier cements cannot be made reliably using the existing database and so at a future stage their measured FTIR spectra and performance properties will be added to supplement the dataset. When this is done, new ANN and other models will also need to be constructed and validated. This activity will be carried out entirely in Aberdeen, on a periodic basis.

Summary and Conclusions

Using artificial neural networks and conventional statistical methods, we have shown that the information in the FTIR powder spectra of cements can be used to predict composition, particle size distributions, and thickening time curves for simple slurries. This has established the FTIR measurement as a 'signature' for cement performance. The measurement can be used as a rapid technique for estimating cement quality and to detect batch to batch variability in cements. Specific case studies have demonstrated that the product can detect batch to batch variability between manufacturers as well as ageing and contamination of a given cement. It is thus capable of preventing the occurrence of very costly major operating failures in oilfield cementing operations. Under the name of CemQUEST, the application is finding successful commercial application within the oilfield.

Acknowledgments

PVC is grateful to Reid Smith for helpful comments and advice during the preparation of this paper.

References

American Petroleum Institute. 1982. *API Spec 10: Materials and Testing for Well Cements.* Dallas: American Petroleum Institute.

Beebe, K.R.; and Kowalski, B.R. 1987. An Introduction to Multvariate Calibration and Analysis. *Analytical Chemistry* 59: 1007A.

Bensted, J.; and Beckett, S.J. 1993. *Advances in Cement Research* 5: 111.

Billingham, J.; and Coveney, P.V. 1993. *Journal of the Chemical Society: Faraday Transactions* 89: 3021.

Coveney, P.V.; and Humphries, W. 1996. *Journal of the Chemical Society: Faraday Transactions* 92: 831.

Fierens, P.; and Verhagen, J.P. 1972. *Journal of the American Ceramic Society* 55: 306.

Fletcher P.; and Coveney P.V. 1995. *Advanced Cement Based Materials* 2: 21.

Fletcher P.; Coveney P.V.; Hughes T.; and Methven C.M. 1995. *Journal of Petroleum Technology* 47: 129

Fletcher, P.; and Coveney, P.V. 1996. Predicting Cement Composition and Performance with Artificial Neural Networks and FT-IR Spectroscopy. *The American Institute of Chemical Engineering Journal.* Forthcoming.

Hughes, T.L.; Methven, C.M.; Jones, T.G.J.; Pelham, S.E.; Fletcher, P.; and Hall,C 1995. *Advanced Cement Based Materials* 2: 91.

Hughes, T.L; Methven, C.M.; Jones, T.L.H; Pelham, S.E.; Vidick, B.; and Fletcher, P. 1994. *Offshore Technology Conference* 7582: 634.

Hunt L.P. 1986. *Cement and Concrete Research.* 16: 190.

Hush, D.R.; and Hornee, B.G. 1993 Progress in Supervised Neural Networks. *IEEE Signal Processing Magazine* 10: 8.

Lippmann, R.P. 1987 An Introduction to Computing with Neural Nets. *IEEE Signal Processing Magazine* 4: 4.

Martens, H.; and Naes, T. 1989. *Multivariate Calibration.* Chichester: Wiley.

Masters, T. 1993. *Practical Neural Network Recipes in C++.* New York: Academic Press.

Moody, J.; and Darken, C.J. 1988. Learning with Localised Receptive Fields. In Proceedings of the 1988 Connectionist Models Summer School, 133.

Moody J.; and Darken, C.J. 1989. *Neural Computation* 1: 281.

Rumelhart, D.E.; and McClelland J.J. eds 1986. *Parallel Distributed Processing: Explorations in the Microstructure of Cognition, Volume 1.* MIT Press.

Sharf, M.A.; Illman, D.L.; and Kowalski, B.R. 1986. *Chemometrix.* New York: Wiley Interscience.

Comet:
An Application of Model-Based Reasoning to Accounting Systems

Robert Nado, Melanie Chams, Jeff Delisio, and Walter Hamscher

Price Waterhouse Technology Centre
68 Willow Road
Menlo Park, CA 94025-3669
{nado chams delisio hamscher}@tc.pw.com

Abstract

An important problem faced by auditors is gauging how much reliance can be placed on the accounting systems that process millions of transactions to produce the numbers summarized in a company's financial statements. Accounting systems contain *internal controls*, procedures designed to detect and correct errors and irregularities that may occur in the processing of transactions. In a complex accounting system, it can be an extremely difficult task for the auditor to anticipate the possible errors that can occur and to evaluate the effectiveness of the controls at detecting them. An accurate analysis must take into account the unique features of each company's business processes. To cope with this complexity and variability, the Comet system applies a model-based reasoning approach to the analysis of accounting systems and their controls. An auditor uses Comet to create a hierarchical flowchart model that describes the intended processing of business transactions by an accounting system and the operation of its controls. Comet uses the constructed model to automatically analyze the effectiveness of the controls in detecting potential errors. Price Waterhouse auditors have used Comet on a variety of real audits in several countries around the world.

Auditors have the task of determining whether the financial statements of a company are a fair presentation of the company's financial position. An important problem faced by auditors is gauging how much reliance can be placed on the accounting systems that produce the numbers summarized in the financial statements. Accounting systems contain *internal controls*, procedures designed to detect and correct errors and irregularities that may occur in the processing of transactions. In a complex accounting system, it can be an extremely difficult task for the auditor to anticipate the possible errors that can occur, to determine their downstream effects in the accounting system, and to evaluate the effectiveness of the controls at detecting them. An accurate analysis must take into account the unique features of each company's business processes. To cope with this complexity and variability, the Comet system applies a model-based reasoning approach (cf. Hamscher *et al.*, 1992) to the analysis of accounting systems and their controls.

Comet supports the creation of hierarchical flowcharts that ultimately describe the processing of business transactions in terms of a set of primitive activities for operating on records and a set of controls for detecting and correcting errors that may occur in the processing. Using knowledge of the basic ways in which the primitive activities can fail, Comet finds potential failures that can occur in the accounting system and uses the structure of the flowchart to analyze the impact of those failures on the validity of the accounts. Comet then matches each potential failure to the set of controls capable of detecting it and evaluates the effectiveness of the controls in reducing the risk that the potential failure will go undetected. Finally, Comet ranks the controls with respect to their relative contribution to reducing the risk of undetected failures and selects a subset of key controls whose proper operation should be tested.

Task Description

In the United States, the SEC requires a yearly independent audit of the financial statements of public companies. Other countries have similar requirements. An accounting firm that is engaged to perform an audit of a public company has the task of issuing an opinion on whether the financial statements are a fair characterization of the financial position of the company and follow generally accepted accounting principles. The numbers that appear in the financial statements are typically the accumulated results of thousands, even millions, of detailed financial transactions in which the company has participated over the previous year.

There are two main approaches that can be taken to assessing the accuracy of financial statements. The *substantive* approach attempts to obtain evidence of the validity of financial statements by examining records of detailed transactions and applying analytical methods to gauge the reasonableness of the reported numbers. By contrast, the *systems-reliant* approach focuses not on verifying the numbers themselves but on assessing the adequacy of the accounting systems that produced the numbers. In taking a systems-reliant approach, an auditor looks at the internal controls that are in place in the accounting systems and evaluates their effectiveness in detecting and correcting errors that may occur in processing transactions.

For example, a company's "purchases and payables" system handles transactions involving the purchase of goods from suppliers. Such a system is designed to receive and record purchase orders, transmit them to suppliers, ensure that goods are received, payables recorded, and the supplier eventually paid for goods received. In auditing such a system, it is important to focus not so much on the computer system itself but on the business processes which it supports. A business process usually contains both manual and computerized steps and is partially performed by parties outside the company.

There are many things that can go wrong in a purchases and payables system. For example:

- An invoice may be received from a supplier for goods which were never ordered or received.
- The quantity or price of goods listed on the invoice may be incorrect, either due to an error at the supplier or because of an operator error in entering the invoice into the computer system.
- A fictional invoice may be entered into the system as part of an attempt to defraud.

In order to detect and correct such problems, a purchases and payables system should contain a number of internal controls. For example:

- Invoices that have been entered on to the computer system should be matched to corresponding purchase orders and records of goods received, with quantities and prices agreed. Although the matching process can be computerized, any discrepancies will generally need to be manually investigated and resolved.
- Access to the computer system for data entry should be restricted to authorized personnel by means of an appropriate security system.
- Data entry of an invoice should not be performed by the same person who later authorizes or reviews the invoice.

In practice, any given audit will combine elements of both the substantive and system-reliant approaches with the relative emphasis dependent on the particular characteristics of the business and its components. With large companies that have complex, computerized accounting systems processing vast numbers of transactions, the systems-reliant approach is becoming increasingly important, both to obtain adequate audit evidence and to reduce the cost of the audit. A specialized category of auditor, called a CIS (Computerized Information Systems) auditor[1], brings to bear skills in both accounting and systems analysis to carry out a systems-reliant audit approach.

In order to take a systems-reliant approach, a CIS auditor must obtain and document an understanding of how an accounting system processes business transactions and of the internal controls that are in place. In preparing this "model", the auditor may make use of available systems documentation from the client. However, systems documentation generally is not prepared from an audit point of view. It may explain how the system works in great detail, but generally does not contain adequate information on controls, does not have a business process focus, and omits the manual components of the business process. The auditor must supplement information obtained from documentation with observation of the system in operation and interviews with key personnel.

In determining the effectiveness of controls, it is important to distinguish the role of a control in the design of an accounting system from how well it is performed in practice. By analyzing the processes and data flows of an accounting system, an auditor attempts to determine those controls that play key roles in the prevention and detection of errors that may affect the validity of the financial statements. In order to obtain sufficient comfort that the system is actually operating as designed, the key controls need to be tested to ensure that they are being properly performed.

For complex accounting systems, a thorough and accurate controls evaluation is almost impossible to perform efficiently without some form of computer-based support. There are many different possible sources of error, some of which may be overlooked. It is extremely difficult to manually trace the effects of possible errors through the transaction processing to determine whether they are significant to the audit. There may be redundancy in the coverage of errors by controls, but detailed analysis is required to determine this with confidence. Because systems evolve rapidly, it is costly to determine the impact of system changes on controls effectiveness. Most importantly, human fallibility in the face of complex systems can lead to costly consequences.

Prior to Comet, CIS auditors have used a combination of flowcharting software and controls checklist software in their evaluation of controls. Commercial flowcharting software can be used to document major activities carried out in an accounting system but the result is not in a form that allows automated analysis. Checklist software is populated with libraries of controls that could be expected to be found in a client's system to address the major areas of risk. Although different libraries of controls can be

1. Variously called an EDP (Electronic Data Processing) auditor, or an ISRM (Information Systems Risk Management) auditor

developed for the major components of generic accounting systems as well as for different accounting software packages, it is difficult to tailor checklist software to reflect the varying characteristics of different industry sectors and the idiosyncratic aspects of a particular client's implementation. Furthermore, controls checklist software takes no advantage of the information captured in flowchart documentation.

The development of Comet was motivated by the intuition that an accounting system can be hierarchically decomposed into a structure that bottoms out in instances of a small set of primitive types of actions for processing records and for implementing internal control. Provided that the behavior of the primitive activity and control types can be suitably characterized, a model-based approach can be taken to the analysis of failures and their detection by internal controls. As a consequence, the auditor can concentrate on developing an accurate model of the accounting system under review, with Comet automating the more burdensome aspects of controls evaluation.

Application Description

Although model-based reasoning has been previously applied to financial domains, the models have generally consisted of equations and constraints representing the relationships between financial and microeconomic quantities [Bouwman, 1983, Hart *et al.*, 1986, Bridgeland, 1990, Hamscher, 1994]. Comet is novel in its application of a model-based approach to analyzing systems for processing financial records.

Basic Modeling Concepts

Accounting systems process records of business transactions through activities that create, use, alter, and store those records. Comet represents the processing performed by an accounting system as a hierarchically structured flowchart graph. The two most important kinds of nodes in a Comet flowchart are collection nodes and activity nodes. Collection nodes represent repositories of records, which may be in either paper or electronic form. Activities are represented hierarchically, starting with nodes representing activities at a high-level of abstraction and progressively decomposing them until nodes representing primitive activities are obtained.

Figure 1 shows the top-level flowchart of PURCHASE, a model of a simple Purchases and Payables accounting system. The top-level flowchart is intended to give a high-level overview of the system, indicating the major activities performed by the system, the relevant general ledger accounts, and important collections of records that are accessed and updated by the processing of a transaction. Activity nodes are distinguished by having a rectangular icon in their lower-left corner. Collection

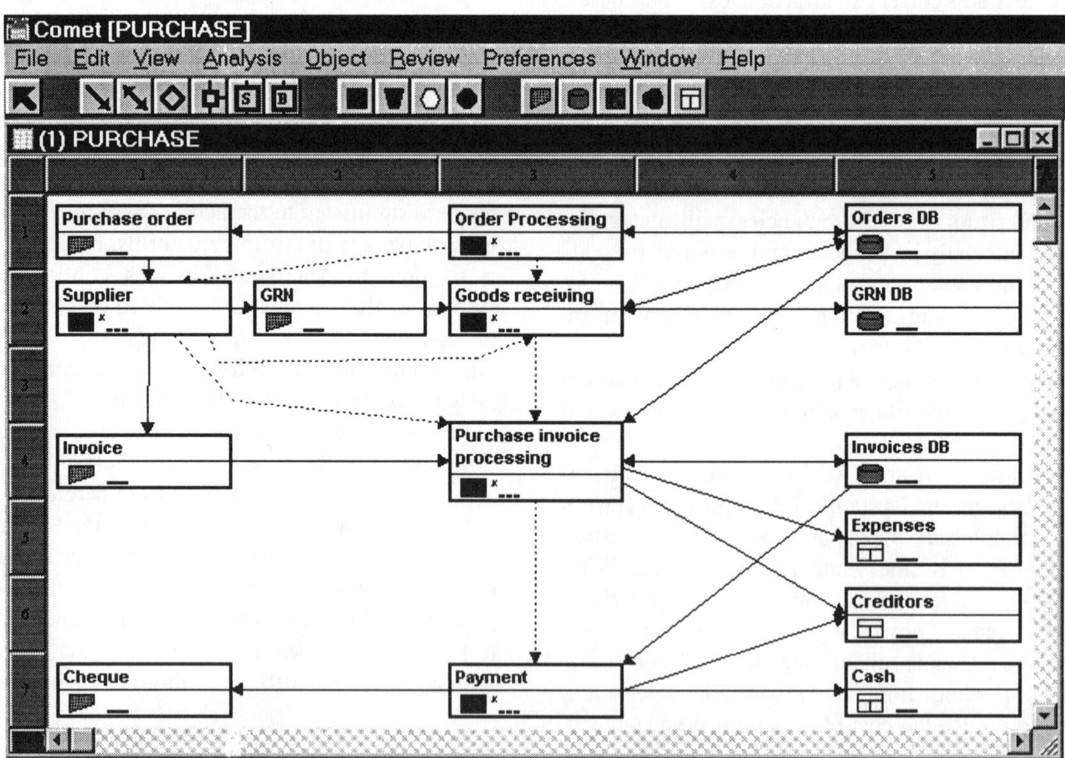

Figure 1: A Top-Level Flowchart

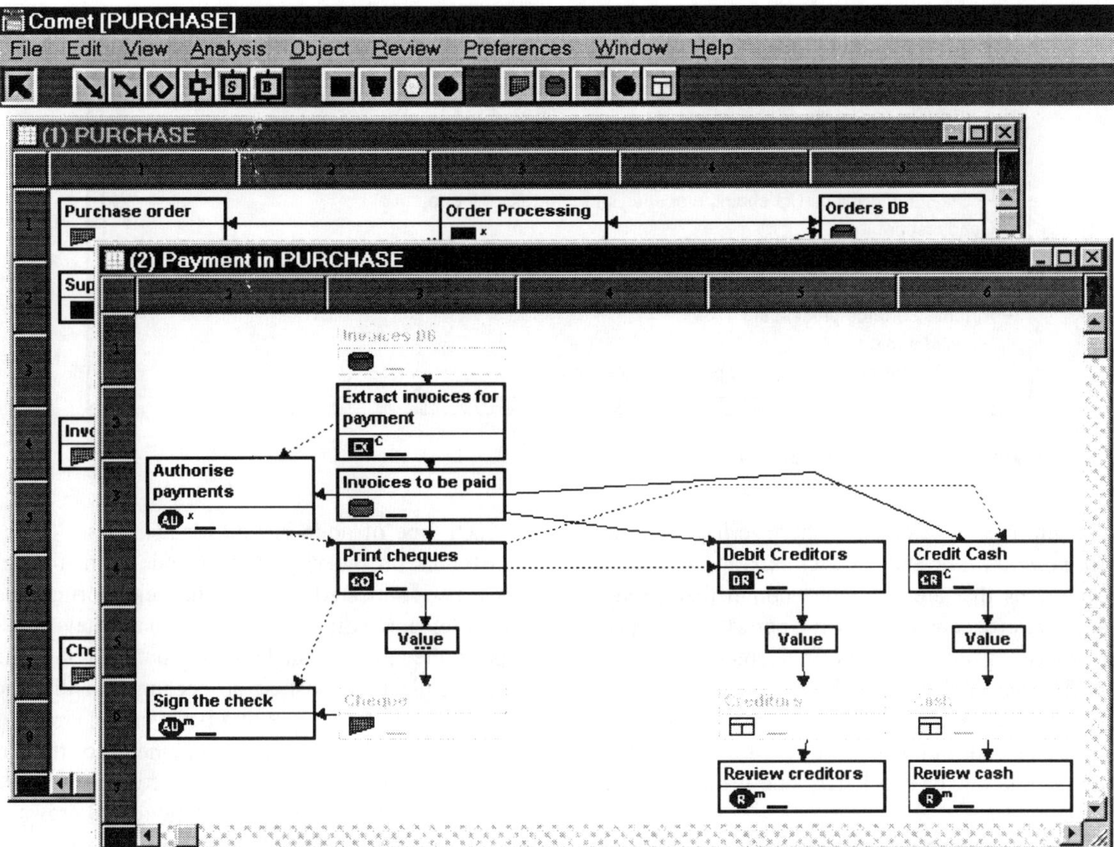

Figure 2: Expansion of the Payment Activity

nodes have a trapezoidal icon for paper records and a cylindrical icon for electronic records. Nodes representing general ledger accounts contain a "boxed T" icon. There are two kinds of arcs connecting nodes in the flowchart. The solid arcs represent data flow relationships between activities and collections. The dashed arcs represent precedence relationships between activities; the activity at the tail of a dashed arc must be completed before the activity at the head of the arc can proceed.

The *Order Processing* activity prepares a *Purchase order*, which is sent off to a *Supplier* to be filled and also recorded in the *Orders DB*. When the *Supplier* fills the order it sends a goods received note (GRN) and an invoice along with the goods. The *Goods receiving* activity records the GRN in the *GRN DB* and tries to match it up with a corresponding record in the *Orders DB*. The *Purchase invoice* activity records the invoice from the Supplier in the *Invoices DB* and compares it with the corresponding record on the *Orders DB*. If a matching order can be found, the *Purchase invoice* activity posts a credit to the *Creditors* account and a debit tc the *Expenses* account. The *Payment* activity periodically extracts invoices that are due for payment, prepares checks for payment to suppliers, debits the *Creditors* account, and credits the *Cash* account.

Since the top-level flowchart of PURCHASE gives a high-level overview of the system, it contains no primitive activities or controls. Each of the top-level activity nodes has a decomposition into a sub-flowchart that gives more detail about how that activity is performed. Figure 2 shows the flowchart for the decomposition of the *Payment* activity; it may be reached by double-clicking on the *Payment* node in the top-level flowchart. The nodes in Figure 2 that have dashed light-gray borders are called reference nodes; they refer to collections whose primary depiction is elsewhere in the flowchart. When an activity node is decomposed, each collection node to which it is directly connected has a reference node automatically created in the sub-flowchart. The reference nodes allow the input and output collections of the top-level activity to be referenced by the activities in the sub-flowchart.

Comet contains a predefined vocabulary of activity and control types, called *verbs*, that are used as a focal point for organizing the knowledge that Comet contains about accounting systems and their controls. Some verbs, such as *transfer*, *copy*, *create*, *merge*, *find*, *compute*, and *copy-field*, represent typical operations on records that are

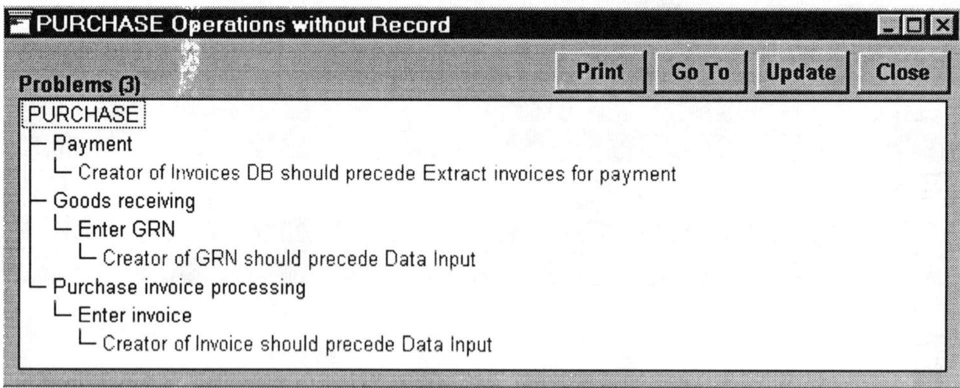

Figure 3: Example Review Dialog Box

treated as primitive by Comet. Other verbs, such as *maintain-standing-data* and *data-entry*, represent processing patterns that are common enough that Comet provides automatic decompositions for nodes using those verbs. For describing internal controls, Comet provides a set of control verbs, including *authorize*, *compare-agree*, *grant-access*, *reconcile*, and *review*. The verb associated with an activity or control node is indicated in the display of that node using a one or two letter code inside the icon in the lower-left corner.

Figure 2 contains four primitive activity nodes with the verbs *extract* (EX), *copy* (CO), *debit* (DR) and *credit* (CR). Figure 2 also contains four control nodes (the nodes with the circle icon) using two different control verbs, *authorize* (AU) and *review* (R). In addition to nodes representing collections, activities, and controls, Figure 2 contains three smaller, rectangular nodes, called selectors. Selector nodes are used to indicate the fields of records that are accessed or modified by activities. For example, the selector node between the *Debit Creditors* activity and the *Creditors* account indicates that the debits involve a field called *Value*.

Model-building Support

The analysis performed by Comet depends for its validity on the accuracy of the models that it operates on. Auditors attempt to verify the accuracy of a model by walking through the transaction processing steps specified in the model, checking for matching steps performed in the modeled system. Ideally, the walkthrough is performed by a person not involved in the model preparation. Although Comet cannot ensure that the models constructed by users are, in fact, accurate representations of the modeled accounting systems, Comet incorporates a number of tools to aid in the construction of models that are at least internally consistent and that contain enough detail to support Comet's analysis.

Each type of node has an associated set of declarative constraints on the ways that a node of that type may be correctly connected by arcs to neighboring nodes. For example, a Credit activity node must have exactly one input collection and at least one output collection. Every output collection must be an account. Finally, there must be selector nodes intervening between the Credit node and each of its output accounts giving the fields that are posted to the accounts. As the user edits a model, Comet monitors the constraints on each node and draws a red flag on those nodes whose constraints are not satisfied. For any node with a red flag, the user may obtain an explanation of the unsatisfied constraints.

Comet contains a number of review commands for examining the completeness and consistency of a model:

- Finding all nodes with violated syntactic constraints
- Finding all unexpanded generic activity nodes
- Finding control nodes that have been incompletely described
- Finding inconsistencies between the fields read from a collection node and the fields written to it
- Finding activity nodes that access records from a collection node without having a preceding activity node that creates records on the collection
- Finding inconsistencies between the inputs and outputs specified for an activity node and for its sub-flowchart

The results of the review commands are presented in the form of dialog boxes that allow convenient navigation to the points where problems occur in the model (cf. Figure 3).

Failure Generation and Propagation

Comet categorizes the errors and irregularities that can occur in an accounting system into three broad categories of failure corresponding to the focus on the processing of

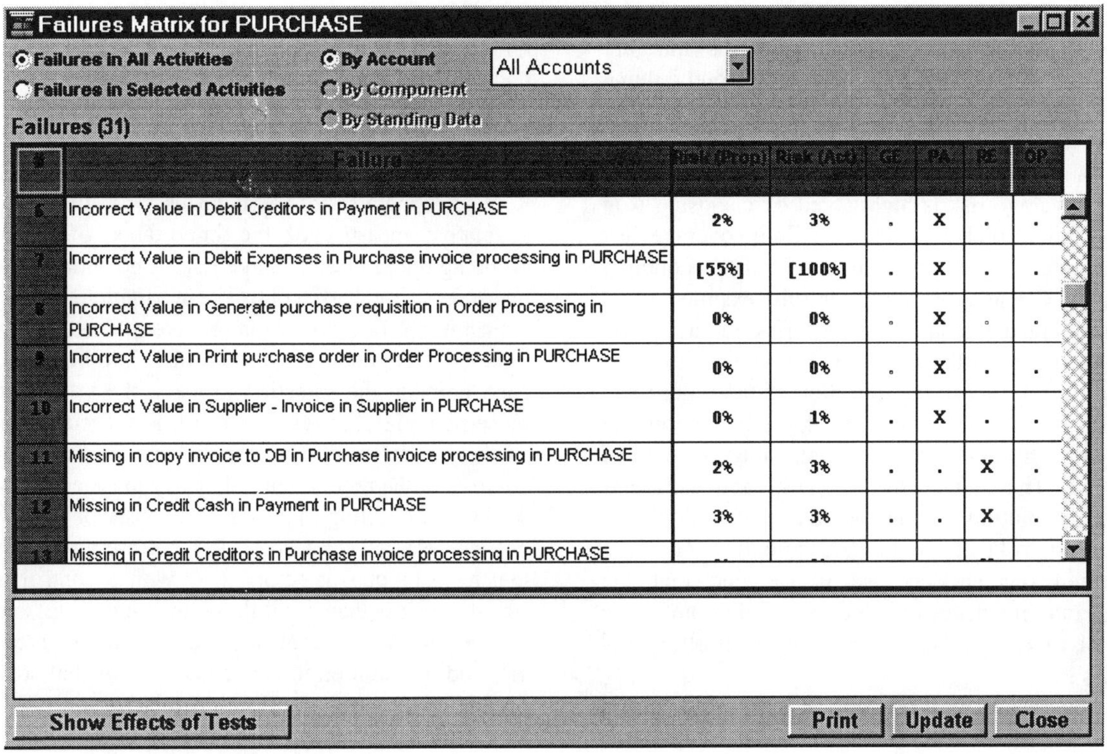

Failures Matrix for PURCHASE

Failures in All Activities | Failures in Selected Activities | By Account | By Component | By Standing Data | All Accounts

Failures (31)

#	Failure	Risk (Prop)	Risk (Act)	GE	PA	RE	OP
6	Incorrect Value in Debit Creditors in Payment in PURCHASE	2%	3%	.	X	.	.
7	Incorrect Value in Debit Expenses in Purchase invoice processing in PURCHASE	[55%]	[100%]	.	X	.	.
8	Incorrect Value in Generate purchase requisition in Order Processing in PURCHASE	0%	0%	.	X	.	.
9	Incorrect Value in Print purchase order in Order Processing in PURCHASE	0%	0%	.	X	.	.
10	Incorrect Value in Supplier - Invoice in Supplier in PURCHASE	0%	1%	.	X	.	.
11	Missing in copy invoice to DB in Purchase invoice processing in PURCHASE	2%	3%	.	.	X	.
12	Missing in Credit Cash in Payment in PURCHASE	3%	3%	.	.	X	.
13	Missing in Credit Creditors in Purchase invoice processing in PURCHASE						

Show Effects of Tests | Print | Update | Close

Figure 4: Failure Coverage Risks

records. A *missing* failure occurs when an activity that should have produced a record as output fails to do so. A *spurious* failure occurs when an activity produces an unauthorized or duplicate record as output. Finally, an *incorrect* failure occurs when an activity produces an incorrect value for a field in a record. An incorrect failure is associated with the name of the affected field. Each primitive activity type has associated with it the categories of failure to which it may give rise.

The first stage of Comet's analysis of a model generates the set of potential failures corresponding to each of the primitive activities in the model. Comet then determines which of the potential failures have audit significance. A failure has audit significance if its downstream effects in the flowchart model could cause any of several types of disagreement between the transactions that actually occurred and the way that they are recorded in the accounts. Comet works backwards in the flowchart from the account collections using a few fixed simple rules for the different primitive activity types to determine how failure effects on an output collection may be produced from failure effects on input collections. The result of this stage is to determine for each potential failure the impact that it may have, if any, on the validity of each account collection.

When constructed at a level of detail appropriate to the control evaluation task, a Comet model typically contains on the order of hundreds of primitive activities. Since each of these can fail only in a small number of ways, it is a tractable task to enumerate the set of potential failures and to determine their effects on the validity of accounts.

Control Evaluation

In order to evaluate the controls documented for an accounting system, Comet assesses for each potential failure with audit significance the likelihood that, if it occurs, it will not be detected by any control in the system. We call this likelihood, for a given failure, its *failure coverage risk*. To determine whether the potential failures are adequately covered by detecting controls, a CIS auditor using the system is required to associate with each account an *allowable risk level*. The allowable risk is the highest level of risk the auditor is willing to accept that any failure that occurs and is relevant to the account is not detected by any control.

Figure 4 shows a table generated by Comet of those potential failures generated for the PURCHASE model that have audit significance and the failure coverage risks that have been determined for them. Certain controls in a Comet model may be designated as proposed; proposed controls are used to explore the effects of recommending to the client that additional controls be added to the accounting system to address control weaknesses. The failures table in Figure 4 contains two columns listing failure coverage risks in percentage terms. The first column (Prop) gives the failure coverage risk taking into account both proposed controls and controls that are actually present in the modeled system; the second column (Act) takes into account only controls that are actually present. If a failure coverage risk is above the allowable risk level for one of the accounts that the failure affects, that failure coverage risk is highlighted by enclosing it in brackets. A failure with a bracketed failure coverage risk indicates a potential control weakness in the accounting system that the CIS auditor should carefully examine.

In determining the failure coverage risk for a failure, Comet first determines the set of controls in the flowchart model that are relevant to the detection of the failure and then assesses, for each relevant control, the likelihood that the control will fail to detect the failure, called the *control detection risk*. The failure coverage risk for a failure is determined by multiplying together the control detection risk for each control that could detect the failure. The risks are multiplied together because we assume that the controls operate independently, and for a failure not to be detected, all of the potentially detecting controls would have to miss it.

In assessing the control detection risk for a given control and potential failure, Comet takes into account three different factors -- control strength, control defeat, and control attenuation:

- Control strength is an assessment of the intrinsic effectiveness of the control, based on its type and how well it is performed. In Comet, the control strength is initially determined from the answers supplied by the modeler to a generic series of questions about how the control is performed. The control strength may be later adjusted as a result of testing the control.
- Control defeat is an assessment of the degree to which a control is rendered ineffective by problems with the maintenance of reference data upon which it depends. For example, a control cannot be relied upon if the maintenance process for a database of information that it employs has potential failures that are not sufficiently mitigated by controls.
- Control attenuation is a measure of the degree to which the effectiveness of a control is reduced by the distance in the flowchart between the control and the primitive activity whose failure it may detect. Control attenuation varies with the type of control and the types of the activities along the path from the control to the failing activity.

Key Controls Selection

A set of key controls is a subset of controls in the model that is sufficient to adequately mitigate the risk of all those potential failures that both have audit significance and are adequately mitigated by the full set of controls. Since placing reliance on a set of controls requires that the controls be tested for proper operation, testing costs can be reduced by choosing a minimal set of key controls. Unfortunately, the problem of finding a minimal set of key controls is a computationally intractable minimal set covering problem. Comet uses a greedy algorithm that works well in practice, but does not guarantee a minimal set.

In selecting a set of key controls for testing, Comet uses a relative measure of the importance of a control in reducing the failure coverage risk of potential failures; this measure is called control contribution. The control contribution for a control is relative to a set of failures, F, to be covered, and a set of controls, C, to be compared. At each point in the selection process, the set F consists of those potential failures whose risk is sufficiently mitigated (with respect to allowable risks) by the complete set of controls in the model, but not yet by those controls already selected for testing. The set C consists of those controls not yet selected for testing. If there are any failures in F that have unique detectors in C with a control detection risk that is less than 1, all these unique detectors are added to the set of key controls. Otherwise, the next control selected for addition to the key controls is that control with the highest control contribution relative to F and C. The algorithm terminates when the set F is empty or there are no controls in C with non-zero control contributions.

Performance

Comet has been successfully used by Price Waterhouse CIS auditors to construct and analyze models of complex client accounting systems. A representative example is a stock trading room system whose Comet model has a total of 934 nodes, including 217 primitive activities, 104 composite activities, 118 collections, and 139 controls. Comet's analysis produced 709 potential failures, of which 338 were found to have an impact on the validity of accounts and 68 were potential defeators of controls. Of these relevant failures, all but 17 were found to be adequately covered by the controls in the system. Comet found 60 controls to be key and therefore candidates for inclusion in a plan for testing controls. The total time required for the analysis was under 30 seconds on a 66Mz Pentium PC.

Application Use and Payoff

A Beta release of Comet has been used on a pilot basis by Price Waterhouse CIS auditors on a variety of real audits in several countries around the world, including Australia, Argentina, Brazil, India, Malaysia, Mexico, the U.S., the U.K., and much of Western Europe. The pilot audits have involved clients from a representative cross-section of different industries, including banking, insurance, oil and gas, manufacturing, and entertainment. The official 1.0 version of Comet was released this April.

The CIS audit partners and managers who have supervised the pilot audits believe, based on their experience, that use of Comet will lead to a significant improvement in auditor productivity. It is difficult at this point to reasonably estimate the size of the gain as a number of factors must be taken into account:

- The nature of the work performed changes with use of Comet. Business processes and their controls are documented to a greater level of detail and more rigorously than they would have been previously. This increases the documentation cost but the analysis performed by Comet allows the auditor to spend much less time anticipating possible errors and thinking about the controls available to detect and correct them. The increased detail and rigor of the models in conjunction with the analysis performed by Comet allows a greater reliance to be placed on controls with a comparable level of auditor effort.
- There is a nontrivial learning curve that applies to efficient use of Comet to model and analyze systems. Experience on the pilot audits suggests that it takes a typical user three to four jobs before they become truly proficient in the use of Comet. Part of what a user needs to learn through experience is the choice of an appropriate level of detail at which to model a system. Enough detail needs to be added to allow a useful Comet analysis to be performed; too much detail adds to the modeling cost without an additional payoff from the analysis.
- The cost of using Comet to model a system and its controls can be more effectively amortized over several years than previous methods of documenting the system. Comet is most appropriately used in a "year of change", either when a new or substantially updated system has been installed by the client or with a new client. In subsequent years, when minor system updates occur, the Comet model can be quickly updated and the impact of the changes on controls' effectiveness analyzed. This justifies somewhat greater initial modeling effort in the year of change as the work that needs to be performed in subsequent years is reduced.
- Use of Comet can reduce the cost of testing. Because of the difficulty of manually performing a thorough and precise evaluation of controls, there is a temptation to perform more detailed testing of transaction records than would be required if the controls work could be done more efficiently. Comet's ability to automatically generate lists of key controls also leads to more focused controls testing, as each control to be tested has been determined to make an important contribution to mitigating the risk of possible failures in the system.
- Comet's rigorous analysis can uncover both control weaknesses and control redundancies, leading to recommendations to the client that are a key value-added function of the audit.

Application Development and Deployment

In 1991, the Savile project was begun at the Price Waterhouse Technology Centre to examine the potential of applying a model-based approach to evaluating accounting systems and their internal controls. An initial prototype, also called Savile, was developed in Lucid Common Lisp running on a UNIX workstation to establish proof of concept. The record processing performed by an accounting system was described using an imperative programming language called SPLAT. Expressions in the SPLAT language were transformed into a causal network to support the evaluation of controls (Hamscher, 1992).

The CIS audit community within Price Waterhouse responded enthusiastically to the Savile prototype and resources were authorized to implement the Savile approach on the standard platform found in Price Waterhouse practice offices -- IBM PC clones running Microsoft Windows. In late 1992, work began on developing a more graphical form of representation for Savile models that would both support a highly interactive flowcharting system and support the analysis of failures and evaluation of controls. Franz Inc's Allegro Common Lisp for Windows was chosen as the implementation language to support rapid application development in the Windows environment.

Since early 1993, an average of three full-time programmers have worked on the development of Comet. In addition, the involvement of CIS auditors was critical to developing a system that matched the requirements of the CIS audit task. A senior CIS manager was assigned to the Price Waterhouse Technology Centre for two months in 1994, two months in 1995, and one month in 1996 to work intensively with the Comet developers to refine the system design.

CIS audit staff have developed a training course in the effective use of Comet in response to increasing worldwide demand. To date, approximately 20% of the total number of CIS auditors in Price Waterhouse firms worldwide have taken the course. In the European firm, all CIS auditors with more than one year of experience are being trained in the use of Comet and it is the recommended tool for use with relatively complex client systems.

Maintenance

As a model-based application, Comet does not contain a large knowledge base encoding expert experience in the domain of CIS audit. This eliminates the often difficult issues surrounding knowledge base update and maintenance. Rather, the behavior of Comet's analysis engine is a product of the properties of a small set of primitive activity and control types and the structure of the particular accounting system model being analyzed. The set of primitive activity and control types has been remarkably stable over the course of Comet's development and has been found adequate to model a large variety of different client systems encountered during the pilot audits.

After the official release of Comet, responsibility for evolutionary development will transfer from the R&D group in the Price Waterhouse Technology Centre to a Price Waterhouse organization responsible for supporting audit-related software.

Conclusion

Most applications of model-based reasoning have been to engineering domains. Comet applies model-based reasoning techniques to a new task domain, the analysis of the effectiveness of controls in accounting systems. Because of the complexity and variability to be found in realistic accounting systems, CIS auditors have difficulty evaluating controls to the level of detail required to place a high degree of reliance on systems when performing an audit of a company's financial statements. Comet allows a CIS auditor to focus on building a model that accurately describes the accounting system, then makes use of that model to automate the analysis of the adequacy of the controls for detecting potential errors in the system. Demand from the Price Waterhouse CIS audit community for deployment of Comet has been high because it is an effective tool in support of delivering high-quality audits to clients.

Acknowledgments

We would like to acknowledge the contributions of two Price Waterhouse CIS auditors who have been instrumental in the development and deployment of Comet. Pat Russell gave us early guidance on the issues of importance to CIS audit and has been a tireless champion of Comet within the firm. Robert Halliday worked intensively with us on key design issues and has been our day-to-day liaison with the CIS audit practice, giving us numerous suggestions on how to make Comet more useful to the CIS auditor.

References

Bouwman, M. J. 1983. Human diagnostic reasoning by computer: An illustration from financial analysis. *Management Science*, 29(6):653-672.

Bridgeland, D. M. 1990. Three qualitative simulation extensions for supporting economics models. In Proceedings of the Sixth Conference on Artificial Intelligence Applications, 266-273. Los Alamitos, Calif.: IEEE Computer Society Press.

Hamscher, W. C. 1992. Modeling Accounting Systems to Support Multiple Tasks: A Progress Report. In Proceedings of the Tenth National Conference on Artificial Intelligence, 519-524. Menlo Park, Calif.: AAAI Press/ The MIT Press.

Hamscher, W. C., Console, L., and de Kleer, J. eds. 1992. *Readings in Model-based Diagnosis*. San Francisco, Calif.: Morgan Kaufmann.

Hamscher, W. C. 1994. Explaining Financial Results. *International Journal of Accounting, Finance, and Management*, 3(1): 1-19.

Hart, P. E.; Barzilay, A.; and Duda, R. O. 1986. Qualitative reasoning for financial assessments: A prospectus. *AI Magazine*, 7(1):62-68.

Diagnosing Delivery Problems in The White House Information Distribution System

Mark Nahabedian & Howard Shrobe
MIT Artificial Intelligence Laboratory

Abstract:
As part of a collaboration with the White House Office of Media Affairs, members of the MIT Artificial Intelligence Laboratory designed a system, called COMLINK, which distributes a daily stream of documents released by the Office of Media Affairs. Approximately 4000 direct subscribers receive information from this service but more than 100,000 people receive the information through redistribution channels. The information is distributed via Email and the World Wide Web. In such a large scale distribution scheme, there is a constant problem of subscriptions becoming invalid because the user's Email account has terminated. This causes a backwash of hundreds of "bounced mail" messages per day which must be processed by the operators of the COMLINK system. To manage this annoying but necessary task, an expert system named BMES was developed to diagnose the failures of information delivery.

Background

In January 1993, the new Clinton administration committed itself to the use of electronic media such as Email (and later the World Wide Web) for making government information widely available to the public. A collaborative effort between the White House Office of Media Affairs, the MIT Artificial Intelligence Laboratory and others quickly created a workable framework for wide-scale distribution of a stream of daily documents originating in the Executive Office of the President. The document stream includes daily press briefings, speeches by the President and other officials, backgrounders, proclamations, etc. In addition, the stream of released information includes special documents such as the National Performance Review's reports on reinventing government, the proposed health care reform legislation, the yearly budgets, etc.

The Intelligent Information Infrastructure Project at the MIT Artificial Intelligence Laboratory created an information distribution server which functions as the focal point of the distribution chain. Documents are released from the Executive Office of the President through this system; they are sent from this system to a variety of archiving and retrieval systems around the country, to most on-line services (e.g. Compuserve, America Online), to about 4000 direct subscribers to the MIT server, and to a variety of other servers which further redistribute the documents. A survey of people connected to this distribution chain estimated that more than 100,000 people were receiving information through this medium.

Documents released through this service are coded with descriptive terms taken from two taxonomies: the first taxonomy categorizes the type of document (e.g. Press Release vs. Speech vs. Press Conference); the second taxonomy concerns content (e.g. Foreign Affairs, Domestic Affairs, Economy, Taxes). Subscribers to the service specify a personal profile consisting of combinations of the descriptive terms which characterize their interests; it is the servers job to guarantee that subscribers receive exactly those documents which match their profiles in a timely manner.

Users establish a subscription and modify their profiles by filling out electronic forms (using either Email or the World Wide Web) and submitting them to the server. The ease with which users can manage their profiles is an important measure of the quality of service delivered.

The Problem

The environment just described is open, large scale, and anarchic. The system services thousands of users at hundreds of sites in dozens of countries. Users may establish, modify and terminate subscriptions at any time. User Email addresses registered with the server may become invalid at any time; occasionally users cancel their subscriptions before this happens, but this is comparatively rare. Also, configuration problems at subscribers' sites make their Email addresses temporarily unreachable even though the addresses are valid.

Kinds of Mail Notification	Causes of Delivery Failure
Delivery Failure	User Not Found
Delivery Failure but still Trying	Host Not Found
Message Received	Mailer Configuration Problems
Message Opened	Temporary Mailer Resource Problem
Message Deleted	DNS Configuration Problem
"Vacation" Nortice	User Mailbox Full

In either of these cases, "bounced mail" messages are sent to the MIT server informing it of the inability to deliver a message to the invalid Email address. Most Email systems do not consolidate these bounced mail messages; if you send two messages to an invalid Email address, you receive back two bounced mail messages. The White House information stream typically includes as many as a dozen documents a day; with a subscription base of 4000 direct subscribers this leads to a rather large volume of bounced mail traffic each day (more than 100 messages). The failure to handle these messages and to update the subscription database accordingly, leads to a perception by the administrators of the receiving sites that they are being "spammed"[1] by the sending site; given that the sending site in this case is the White House, it is unacceptable to ignore the bounced mail traffic. A second class of problem arises when a user with a valid Email address attempts to terminate or modify a subscription without success; in this case, the perception is that the White House is spamming the subscriber personally, an even more unacceptable situation.

On the surface, it would seem that this problem is amenable to simple automation. However, the open, anarchic character of the Internet makes the problem quite complex: there are dozens of different mail servers, each with a unique "bounced mail" message format. In addition to the variety of Email servers speaking the Internet's native SMTP protocol [RFC821] there are also a large number of other protocol domains bridged to the Internet. These include UUCP, Bitnet, X.400 and a large number of proprietary Email systems (e.g. CC:mail, Microsoft Mail, etc.); bounced mail messages are often reformatted as they cross the bridge between protocol domains, sometimes losing information (and sometimes preserving information which is useless, such as one which directs the recipient to press the F1 key for more information). Within these other mail domains, the format of a mail address might be different from that used in the Internet; bounced mail messages from these domains often include their foreign format email address, rather than the Internet format address in our database.

A second set of complications arises from the variability of user's Email addresses. Many people have several Email addresses some of which are forwarded to another. Bounced mail messages in such cases often refer to the "forwarded to address" which isn't in our subscription database. Furthermore, people often subscribe using one address, switch to a second one as their primary address (forwarding the first one to the new address) and then more or less forget about the first address; attempts to modify the subscription using the new, primary address are then unsuccessful, because the system is unaware of the new address. Similarly, if the new address becomes invalid, then a bounced mail message will be sent to the server referring to the new address, which is unknown to the server.

In some mail systems (e.g. UNIX) users may direct their mail streams to shell scripts or other programs for processing. "Vacation programs" are a common example of this, they send back to the sender a message saying that the recipient is away and unlikely to respond soon. This is a courtesy when sent in response to a personal correspondence but when sent back to a bulk distributor like the White House server it shows up as part of the bounced mail stream. In addition, nothing prevents users from writing new mail handling programs, including incorrect ones; when such programs fail, the sender of the message (as opposed to the author of the buggy program) is usually sent a bounced mail message (in principle the postmaster at the receiving site should be sent this message, but principles and reality don't always correspond in this world).

A final complication, shown in Figure 1, arises because of the presence of redistributors. Redistributors are people or programs which receive the original message stream and then relay it to a set of subscribers known to the redistributor but not to the primary White House distribution server. Virtually any subscriber may independently decide to act as a redistributor of the document stream (for example, by establishing a mailing list). If an Email address on a redistributor's list becomes invalid, the redistributor should be notified; however, often the original source of the message (us) is notified instead. To get the behavior we

[1] *Spamming:* A colloquial term, now common in discussions about the Internet, which refers to the practice of filling up somebody's electronic mailbox with unwanted material, often advertisements, complaints or flames. Origin unknown.

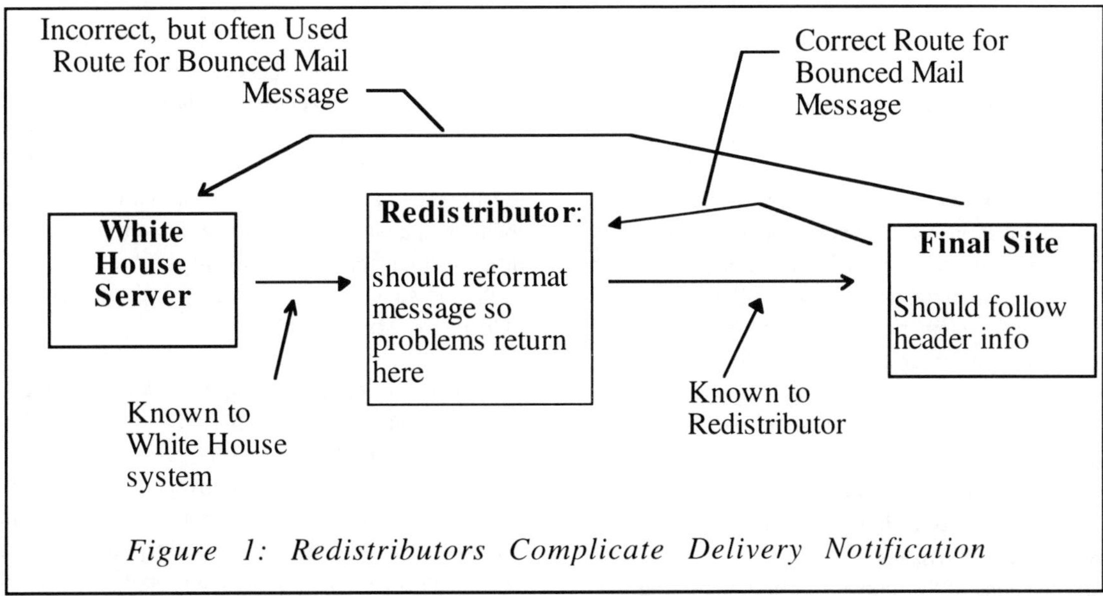

Figure 1: Redistributors Complicate Delivery Notification

desire, the redistributor should arrange for the headers of the redistributed message to identify it as the destination for problem reports; however, some redistributors fail to configure their mailer appropriately to achieve this behavior. This can also be caused by bugs in either the redistributor's software or in the Email server at the ultimate destination (e.g. failure to correctly interpret the headers) or both. COMLINK tries to distinguish redistributors from normal users by having different types of database entries for each; redistributor entries include an Email address for the administrator of the redistribution list. However, we rely on people to subscribe to COMLINK correctly and often people don't.

The problem of managing a large Email based distribution system in this environment has been recognized for some time [RFC1211]; however, to date the problem has been handled using one of two approaches:

Don't worry, be happy: In this approach, bounced mail messages are ignored. The sender builds up a rather large file of bounced mail messages which is periodically deleted. The destination sites receive many messages which are bounced, but this happens automatically. All told, a lot of resources are wasted, but nobody really cares because it's largely invisible. To be fair, most maintainers do from time to time examine a sampling of the bounced mail traffic and attempt to address the problems.

Big bag of tools to aid the administrator: A number of ad hoc tools are built to aid the system administrator in making sense of the bounced mail traffic [RFC1211]. These help the conscientious list administrator to solve difficult problems, but much of the work remains manual.

Given the high visibility of the White House distribution system and its role as an early experiment in using the Internet to improve government services, neither of these approaches was acceptable. Instead we decided to implement an expert system to aid in the handling of bounced mail and to help in managing other problems such as a user's inability to terminate or modify a subscription.

Structure of the System

The Bounced Mail Expert System (BMES) is a component of a larger system, called COMLINK, which is a substrate for building information distribution and group collaboration systems using Email, the World Wide Web and other Internet based transport protocols. At the core of COMLINK is an object oriented database which includes the following information:

<u>Subscribers</u>: Email address, personal name and subscriptions, date subscription started and date (if any) subscription turned off, whether this user is a redistributor.
<u>Network Hosts</u>: Subscribers at this host, upward and downward links in the domain name hierarchy, mail server type.
<u>Documents</u>: descriptive terms, release dates, subject, etc.
<u>Queued Tasks</u>: Time to execute the task, task type and arguments

BMES draws upon this information to help diagnose delivery failures.

BMES is a rule based diagnostic system driven by a file of bounced mail messages. Each message is a symptom of a failure in the delivery system. The user of BMES is the "postmaster" maintaining the White House COMLINK system. BMES's task is to discover, if possible, the reason why a mail message was bounced and if diagnosis is not possible to present meaningful information to the user and help in gathering more information. If diagnosis is successful, then the system rectifies the problem, usually by suspending a user's subscription.

For each message processed the system follows a standard pattern of processing:
Classification of the mailer which sent the message
Abstraction of the message to hide the syntactic differences between bounced mail messages.
Diagnosis of the cause of the delivery failure, including:
Heuristic generation of hypotheses
Interaction with administrators at remote sites.

The first task is Classification during which BMES matches features of the message against required features in the taxonomy of mailer types. In practice, the classification is done by a rather ad hoc set of rules which search for specific features in the headers and the first part of the body of the message. These features include characteristic substrings within particular headers or in specific locations within the body (usually the first several lines) of the message. These rules were determined based on the authors' observations of the bounce mail messages.

The system currently distinguishes 23 different types of mailers; these need not necessarily correspond to distinct pieces of mailer software, rather they correspond to the variety of distinct formats of bounced mail messages which we've observed. Some mailers have a rather broad range of configurability including the format of the bounced mail message to generate. We have no special knowledge of how the remote sites are being managed and so if two distinct hosts generate bounced mail messages which look different, we treat these as having been generated by distinct mailers even if this isn't necessarily the case.
New mailer types pop up occasionally, but this now happens rarely.

The second stage of processing is to Abstract the message, hiding the syntactic variability between the different formats of bounced mail messages but preserving their semantic commonality. For example, bounced mail messages typically contain a "transcript" which includes email addresses to which it was impossible to make a delivery, and an indicator of the cause of delivery failure. Similarly, most bounced mail messages contain a copy of the original message that couldn't be delivered. The original message includes a set of "**received**" headers [RFC822], each of which corresponds to a mail server in the chain of delivery; the header identifies the host which handled the message, the time of handing, and in some cases the user to whom the message was intended to be delivered. (Note that this is different than the destination in the "**to**" header [RFC822] of the message, which is typically a generic address such as "**Clinton-distribution**") .

Abstraction is effected using the object oriented programming techniques of CLOS [CLOS]. Once the classification stage has identified the mailer type, BMES constructs a CLOS object whose class corresponds to the type of the mailer. This object mediates the abstraction phase. We established a class hierarchy corresponding to the mailer types and an object-oriented protocol[2] that all mail messages must obey; the protocol consists of about a dozen methods. Each method in the protocol reflects an aspect of the common semantic content that any bounced mail message must contain. There is one method in the protocol which finds the transcript in the bounce message and a second one which maps over its failure descriptions, calling an action routine with the email address and a canonicalized version of the failure code. There are also protocol methods to locate the message text and then to map over the "**received**" headers [RFC822] contained in it. We use the class hierarchy to capture commonalities of message structuring. For example, the location within the bounced mail message and the encoding of the transcript and original message are idiosyncratic to each mailer, however several different mailers share the idea of partitioning the message body using the MIME standards [RFC1341] for structuring mail messages; however they may differ as to what fields they include. Therefore different classes implement the protocol methods differently, but where there is commonality this is captured by CLOS inheritance. All mailers which use MIME encoding, for example, are represented as subclasses of the common MimeStructured message class

[2] Here we use the term "protocol" in the same sense as in the "Meta-Object Protocol" [MOP] or the Joshua Protocol of Inference [Joshua], not in the sense of an Internet protocol such as SMTP [RFC822]. Fortunately, the object-model used here doesn't use the "message passing" metaphor or we would also have confusion between mail messages and messages being sent to objects.

The power of this approach is that it abstracts away the syntactic variability exhibited by the variety of bounced mail message formats, while highlighting their semantic commonality. Higher levels of the system can expect any mail message to contain standardized information and to behave in standard ways, without to be concerned with the underlying syntactic variability.

The next stage of processing is Diagnosis which involves deciding whether the failure is permanent and whether the recipient is actually known to the COMLINK system. If the address in the mail message is found explicitly in the COMLINK database, if the failure is due to the user's account being closed out (as opposed to a transient error) and if the user has an active subscription, then BMES cancels the subscription.

However, sometimes the bounced mail message reports an invalid address which is not present in the COMLINK database. At this point, the Heuristic Generation phase is entered. A small collection of heuristic candidate generation rules is used to suggest candidate addresses which are in the database and which might have led to mail being sent to the address reported in the message. For example the message might report a problem with "foo@ai.mit.edu"; in this case if "foo@w.ai.mit.edu" or "foo@mit.edu" are in the database, they would be good candidates for possible causes of the failure. A rule called Possible-User-at-Child-Host suggests the first. A second rule called Possible-User-at-Parent-Host suggest the second. An English paraphrase of the first rule is shown in Rule 1.

Let the name in the reported address be ?name-1
Let the host in the reported address be ?host-1
For each child ?child-host of ?host-1
If ?name-1@?child-host is the email address of an active subscriber ?sub-1
Then suggest that ?sub-1 is a possible cause of the delivery failure

Rule 1: Probable-User-is-Child-Host

Such candidate generation rules work by traversing COMLINK's map of the portions of the Internet domain name space for which it has subscribers. There are rules which suggest the superior domain (e.g. "mit.edu" is the superior of "ai.mit.edu"), any inferior domains (e.g. "w.ai.mit.edu" is an inferior of "ai.mit.edu"), and any sibling domains (e.g. "lcs.mit.edu" is a sibling to "ai.mit.edu") which the system knows about.

Most mailers attempt to deliver a message for several days when possibly transient problems are encountered; they deliver a failure message only after this elapsed time. Because of this long latency, bounced mail messages can continue to arrive for several days after a user's subscription has been canceled. If a bounced mail message refers to an Email address whose subscription has already been canceled, then the user of BMES is not bothered since the problem has already been handled; the message is presumed to have arisen during the period between the time when the Email address became invalid and when COMLINK was informed of this. This requires COMLINK to maintain an entry for users whose subscriptions have been canceled for a period of time after the cancellation; when BMES cancels a subscription, COMLINK creates a queued task entry in its database with a firing time of one month in the future. When this queued task runs it completely removes the user's account from COMLINK's database. However, during the intervening period, BMES can tell that it knows about this account and that it knows that it has already canceled the account's subscription.

Most messages are handled by the simple processing described above; however, there is usually a residual of harder problems left over. One cause of the residual problems is that many of the mailers provide minimally useful information in their bounced mail messages. In other cases, there is information provided but the bounced mail message refers to an Email address which isn't in the COMLINK database and none of the heuristics above lead to a known address either.

In almost all cases, this situation arises when the failing address is reached through an "indirection": Either the address is on the mailing list of a redistributor, or it is the target of a forwarding entry for some other Email address, or there is an MX[3] record [RFC974] involved. In these cases completely automatic processing isn't possible; there isn't enough information available to BMES to form a full diagnosis of the problem. Some of the required informa-

[3] MX records are part of the Internet Domain Name System; the MX record for a host specifies which machine should actually receive mail addressed to the original host.

tion is at a remote site and can be obtained only by communicating with an appropriate person at the remote site. It is a further complication that we don't actually know what remote site does have the information we need.

BMES can help make an educated guess: If it can find the original message included in the bounced mail message and if there are **received-from** headers in the original message, then the server mentioned in the header might have relevant information. In particular, any user at this server who is marked as a redistributor in the COMLINK database is a particularly useful candidate. Redistributor entries contain an Email address for the administrator of the redistribution list; BMES formats the first draft of a standard Email message to the maintainer asking if the failing address is known to the administrator of the list and, if not, requesting help in figuring out what else might be going wrong (the user is then offered the option of further editing the text of this message).

Another heuristic is to look for Email addresses similar to the failing one at each of the sites mentioned by the "received-from" headers and to then send to the postmaster at each of these sites a message explaining the problem and asking for help.

There are some techniques which we employ manually today which are subject to automation. One is used when there are a small number of users at the site which bounced the mail but when it still isn't possible to make a definitive identification of the invalid address (either because the bounced message doesn't contain an address or it contains one which doesn't match any entry in our database). In this case, we generate one message for each user in our database known at the site; this message explains that we are having delivery problems and asks for the user's help if possible. There are two useful outcomes: 1) One of the users knows what's going on and helps us fix it 2) One of these messages bounces, but since the bounced message has the specific user's address in it (which our normal messages lack since they are sent to the whole subscription list) we are now able to determine which address is invalid. This technique is analogous to techniques used in model-based trouble shooting where a new and maximally informative test is generated.

Application Payoff

This application is not a commercial venture and so payback in monetary terms is not a relevant metric for evaluation. BMES was created as a support tool within a collaboration between a research group at MIT and a line organization at the White House Office of Media Affairs. Each partner in this collaboration had their own goals: The participants from the Executive Office of the President wanted to make information routinely and reliably available to the public and to demonstrate the viability of the Internet as a model for the future National Information Infrastructure. The research group at MIT wanted to explore issues in computer supported collaborative work and in intelligent management of information. For both groups, management of the bounced mail problem is a necessary supportive task but one which cannot be allowed to consume valuable resources; in particular, neither group has substantial manpower to devote to the task. Therefore the relevant metric for evaluating the payback of the investment is in terms of the reduction of manpower contributions from the two groups. This in turn directly translates into the effectiveness of the system at handling bounced mail messages.

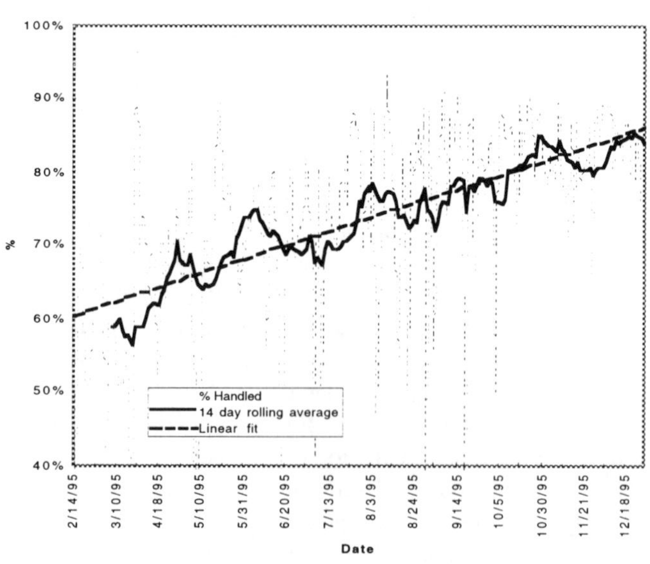

Figure 2: Effectiveness of BMES vs. Time

We have been collecting data on the effectiveness of BMES since early in its lifetime. Figure 2 shows this data for the bulk of calendar year 1995. During this period, 63,091 bounced mail messages were received. BMES was capable of automatically processing 48,031 of these message or 76% of the total. As can be seen from Chart 1, there is a great deal of temporal variability in the system's performance. It simply seems to be the case that some weeks we run into problems with sites whose mail servers provide less information; these weeks have lower overall performance. However, it is also noticeable that there is a long term trend of improvement in the system's performance. This is probably due to a combination two factors: 1) Over time, we have confronted most of the mailer types that exist and have built up useful heuristics for dealing with them. 2) Over time, there has probably been a stabilization of technology in the community and a switch to more robust and informative mailer software.

Over the whole lifetime of the project, the time per day put into bounced mail handling has declined from nearly 3 hours per day in calendar year 1993 to about 1/2 hour per day now. We would certainly like to drive this number down further, but the transformation so far has been a qualitative one: The three hours per day required at the start was simply not viable; today the task is annoying but well within scope.

File name	Chars	Lines	Defs
New-db-interface	2,180	69	10
User-rules	10,662	292	21
Zwei-msg	2,798	79	12
Understanding-bounced-mail	41,067	1,106	104
Zmail-commands	25,450	655	20
Mailer-vanilla-unix	10,308	256	11
Mailer-smailer	3,820	101	2
Mailer-compuserve	4,090	95	2
Mailer-mime	6,212	148	9
Mailer-mmdf	7,482	176	14
Mailer-pmdf	4,789	125	4
Mailer-mime-pmdf	5,810	163	6
Mailer-uucp	3,603	89	1
Mailer-uucp-warning	2,814	70	1
Mailer-ibm	3,352	86	3
Mailer-vines	3,130	79	2
Mailer-microsoft	4,894	124	4
Mailer-minos	2,724	71	3
Mailer-local-delivery-agent	5,242	127	6
Mailer-undeliverable	3,139	77	3
Mailer-cc	2,514	63	3
Mailer-aol	3,497	93	6
Mailer-lispm	4,825	122	4
Mailer-mercury	3,266	84	3
Mailer-ctstateu	3,324	80	2
Mailer-smtp	4,049	104	4
Mailer-ksgbbs	3,405	86	4
Bounced-mail-complaint-reply	1,882	51	5
Check-recipient	2,541	61	3
Simple-redirection	5,491	140	5
Relay-zmail-command	25,987	702	65
Total	214,347	5,574	342

Table 1: Code Distribution in BMES

Implementation

Both COMLINK and BMES are implemented within the Symbolics Genera environment, which runs both on Symbolics hardware and on Digital Equipment Corporation Alpha AXP workstations (using the Open Genera emulator software from Symbolics). BMES is integrated with Genera's ZMail[4] mail client which is built on an extensible substrate for complex mail handling applications. Much of the system relies on this substrate for low level processing such as mail file and header parsing, pattern matching and string searching. BMES itself is implemented in Joshua [Joshua] and makes extensive use of its Protocol of Inference to reason about the contents of the mail messages. BMES itself is invoked as a Zmail command which is applied to the mail file containing the bounced mail messages. When mail messages need to be sent to postmasters or users at remote sites, this is facilitated by use of ZMail's programmatic interface. Table 1 shows the component files in the system, including number of characters and lines of source text and number of definitions (rules, lisp functions, methods etc.).

Deployment and Maintenance History

Work on BMES was begun in the spring of 1993 as an adjunct to a predecessor system to COMLINK (called FORUM) which represented the first collaboration between the MIT AI Lab and the White House Office of Media Affairs. The bulk of BMES was completed by the summer of 1993. As COMLINK's development proceeded, a second version of BMES was developed by modifying the first version to take advantage of the extra information maintained by COMLINK. For a few months, COMLINK and FORUM were run in parallel while users were encouraged to switch their accounts over. During this period, both versions of BMES were run to manage problems from the two streams. The final cutover to COMLINK was completed in early 1995. Since that time, new features have been added to BMES as necessary.

It is interesting to note that BMES was literally developed and deployed simultaneously; it was an experience in evolutionary design of a complex software system. As soon as there was useful functionality, it was deployed and then enhanced during its ongoing operation.

[4] There are several other products named Zmail which are not related to the one included in the MIT Lisp Machine softare systems and its commercial offshoots such as Symbolics' Genera.

BMES is an unusual application: It is a component of the COMLINK system which supports thousands of users but there is only one user of BMES itself. That user is also the developer and maintainer. Currently, the bounced mail processing is done at MIT; however, we anticipate complete hand-off of the COMLINK system in the near future at which time, personnel in the Executive Office of the President will assume responsibility. As with much else about this application a crisp definition of deployment is not easy. A large population has received information from the White House for several years now and the management of Email delivery problems has been substantially automated as part of that task. It is true that the system is still operated by its developers, but that was the anticipated situation at the outset. Routine sustainable operation has been achieved and that has enabled other aspects of the project to proceed without undue drain on scarce personnel resources.

Future Work

Though BMES greatly reduces the effort required to process the mail backwash from a bulk electronic mail distribution, there is room for improvement. The addition of some form of reverse mapping of MX records would help to identify an address on the distribution list based on and address as determined from a bounce message. The domain name system does not provide such a mapping, so one would have to be constructed by iterating over all mail sites in the distribution database and doing a domain MX lookup for each one. Because of changes to the distribution database and to the DNS, this reverse mapping would need to be updated regularly.

As it is currently implemented, BMES is difficult to extend as new mailer types are discovered and as existing ones change. This difficulty is because the work of identifying mailer type is distributed over a number of ad-hoc parsers. As one adds a parser to recognize a new mailer type, one must be careful that this parser does not also recognize the messages of previously implemented mailer types. Perhaps reimplementing the parsers using a rule based parser generator would simplify the definition of mailer types.

The ideal solution to the problem of handling bounced mail would be the universal adoption of standards which specify how mail delivery status information is reported. If delivery failure notifications explicitly stated the reason for failure, and the failing address, as well as any addresses from which it might have been derived, then BMES could be replaced by a much simpler tool. Only one simple parser would be needed to extract the information from the bounce message. The system would require fewer, simpler rules for identifying the problem subscription. Recognizing the problem of numerous bounce mail formats, the Network Working Group of the Internet Engineering Task Force has recently proposed a set of standards [RFC1891, RFC1892, RFC1893, RFC1894] which specify how mailers should report delivery status. As sites upgrade their mailers to ones that adhere to these standards, there will be fewer and fewer bounce messages that will require a system like BMES to interpret.

References

[CLOS] "Common Lisp Object System Specification", Daniel G. Bobrow, Linda G. DeMichiel, Richard P. Gabriel, Sonya E. Keene, Gregor Kiczales, and David A. Moon
Sigplan Notices, 23(Special Issue), September 1988.

[RFC821] "SIMPLE MAIL TRANSFER PROTOCOL", Jonathan B. Postel, August 1982, Internet RFC 821.

[RFC822] "STANDARD FOR THE FORMAT OF ARPA INTERNET TEXT MESSAGES", David H. Crocker, August 13, 1982, Internet RFC 822

[RFC974] "Mail Routing and the Domain System", C. Partridge, January 1, 1986, Internet RFC 974.

[RFC1211] "Problems with the Maintenance of Large Mailing Lists", A.Westine and J. Postel, March 1991, Internet RFC 1211.

[RFC1341] "MIME (Multipurpose Internet Mail Extensions): Mechanisms for Specifying and Describing the Format of Internet Message Bodies", N. Borenstein, N. Freed, June 1992, Internet RFC 1341.

[RFC1891] "SMTP Service Extension for Delivery Status Notifications", K. Moore, January 1996.

[RFC1892] "The Multipart/Report Content Type for the Reporting of Mail System Administrative Messages", G. Vaudreuil, January 1996.

[RFC1893] "Enhanced Mail System Status Codes", G. Vaudreuil, January 1996.

[RFC1894] "An Extensible Message Format for Delivery Status Notifications",] K. Moore, January 1996.

[COMLINK] ``The Open Meeting: A Web-Based System for Conferencing and Collaboration," Hurwitz, Roger & John C. Mallery, Proceedings of The Fourth International Conference on The World-Wide Web, Boston: MIT, December 12, 1995.

[GENERA] **Genera Reference Manual,** Symbolics Inc.

[MOP] **The Art of the Metaobject Protocol,** Gregor Kiczales, Jim des Rivières, and Daniel G. Bobrow, MIT Press, 1991.

[Joshua] "Joshua:Uniform Access to Heterogeneous Knowledge Structures (or Why Joshing is better than Conniving or Planning), S. Rowley, H. Shrobe, R. Cassels, W. Hamscher, AAAI National Conference on Artificial Intelligence, 1987, Pages48-52.

[ZMAIL] **Editing and Mail Manual,** Symbolics Inc.

Settlement Analysis Expert (SAX) -- Modeling Complex Business Logic In The Development Of Enterprise Solutions

John C. Ownby

Frito-Lay, Inc.
7701 Legacy Drive
Plano, Texas 75024

Abstract:
SAX is a diagnostic system designed to search for inventory related errors in a large transaction base, propose solutions for correcting the errors, and extrapolate the identified errors into patterns of behavior. SAX uses a modular combination of backward-chaining rules and mathematical algorithms to replicate domain knowledge. The system was developed in two phases, with the error seeking phase deployed in 1990 and the pattern recognition phase in 1992. Today, the complete system is in production and provides expert diagnostics to 13,000 salespersons, 1,000 sales managers, and 60 clerical accounting employees.

Background:
Frito-Lay's sales force consists of approximately 13,000 route salespersons, with each salesperson responsible for ordering, managing, and selling an inventory of various snack products. Salespersons order and sell their products using a hand-held computer and telecommunicate their transactions to a central host each evening. These transactions are captured in an accounting system, which computes each salesperson's book inventory. Every four weeks each salesperson performs a physical inventory of all the products in their possession, and the accounting system compares each salesperson's physical inventory to their book inventory and identifies any overage or shortage condition.

Because of the high-volume nature of these routes, each salesperson can easily generate 100-200 separate transactions during a four-week time period, with each transaction encompassing any combination of up to 200 different products. Prior to the development of SAX these transactions were manually reviewed in an attempt to identify and correct errors causing overages and shortages. This activity was performed every four weeks by each of the 13,000 salespersons, 1,000 sales managers, and 60 clerical accounting employees, and was both complicated and time consuming.

Diagnostic Module:
SAX was developed in two phases. The diagnostic module (SAX-I) was designed to find errors within the transactions and identify a corrective action for the salesperson. The knowledge base was developed using a mainframe expert system shell and was built to replicate the expertise of a single individual who had fifteen years of domain experience. A rule-based system appeared to be the most natural approach, particularly since the expert was a very willing member of the team. The expert's knowledge was captured in a rule base containing 64 "chunks" of knowledge, expressed in 500 rules and applied against 1.7 million records of data every four weeks. SAX-I attempts to identify missing transactions, transactions containing errors, and transactions that indicate certain performance issues that need to be corrected.

The absence of a beginning inventory, for example, could indicate an error. The fact that this transaction is missing, however, could also indicate that the particular route is new, or that the route is a unique type of route that normally would not have an inventory of products on hand. So, when SAX-I detects a route that has a missing transaction, it then invokes the necessary logic to determine whether or not the route should have had such a transaction.

An example of an erroneous transaction would be a transaction that is a valid transaction for the route, but an error was made in the transaction's detail, such as an incorrect quantity or product code. When such an error is found, SAX-I searches the necessary transaction detail of potentially all other transactions on the route (and in some cases includes other routes' activity in its evaluation) and makes inferences based on relationships identified within the data. For example, SAX-I could identify one product code on a shipment transaction that contains a quantity that appears to be driving the over/short on that item for the entire route. If an error is made on a transaction between routes, SAX-I also checks the relationships on the other route to increase the certainty of it's inference.

FRITO-LAY, INC	SALES ACCOUNTING EXPERT	PAGE 1573
SAXP2000-01	SALESPERSON SETTLEMENT WORKSHEET	RUN DATE 02/05/92
TIME 03:14:12	AS OF PERIOD 01, 1992

ZONE 1 DIVISION 02 ROUTE 2604-006 NAME: JOHN Q. SMITH SSN: 123-45-6789

THE AUTOMATED SETTLEMENT ANALYSIS SYSTEM (SAX) HAS DETECTED A POSSIBLE ERROR IN THE FOLLOWING AREA. USE THIS INFORMATION AS A STARTING POINT TO IDENTIFY THE CAUSE OF YOUR OVER/SHORT BALANCE AND IDENTIFY ANY OUTSTANDING ERRORS IN NEED OF CORRECTION.

*PROBLEM: THE FOLLOWING REVERSE SHIPMENT CONTAINS UNUSUALLY LARGE QUANTITIES FOR SEVERAL PRODUCTS THAT ARE ALSO REPORTED AS OVERAGES ON YOUR ROUTE SETTLEMENT:

A. DOES THE REVERSE SHIPMENT DOCUMENT CONTAIN KEYING ERRORS (UPC OR QUANTITY)?
B. WAS THE REVERSE SHIPMENT GENERATED IN ERROR AND NOT VOIDED?
C. ARE ANY CHARGE DOCUMENTS MISSING ON THE SETTLEMENT (I.E. A SHIPMENT, TRANSFER-IN, ETC.)?

DOCUMENT #	DOCUMENT DATE	DOCUMENT AMOUNT
8965511	01/30/92	$(544.32)

FIGURE 1: SAX-1 OUTPUT IDENTIFIES SPECIFIC ERRORS & ISSUES WITHIN THE TRANSACTION BASE EVERY 4 WEEKS

In addition to finding missing and erroneous transactions, SAX-I also looks for and identifies certain performance issues. If SAX-I identifies a route that has an unusually high amount of stales, for example, it makes an exhaustive attempt to find a reason. If it can detect a probable cause for the high stales, it reports its findings to the route salesperson. If it cannot find a reason, it simply reports that a large number of stales occurred on the route.

Sax-I's logic is arranged hierarchically, in that it first attempts to prove a base hypothesis (i.e. there is a problem with high stales), then proceeds to refine the hypothesis based on all available pertinent facts (i.e. the high stales could be caused by stales occurring on the truck rather than in the store, or by mis-classification of another transaction as a stales transaction, or could be due to a keying error, etc.). For each hypothesis attempted, SAX-I remembers the last rule successfully fired, and formats the appropriate output text for reporting (***Figure 1***). Thus, SAX-I informs the salesperson in as much detail as possible the nature of the problem identified, as well as the appropriate corrective action.

Pattern Identification Module:

While SAX-I identifies transaction-related problems occurring within each four-week time period, the pattern identification module of SAX (SAX-II) is designed to identify patterns of behavior over a larger period of time. For example, certain patterns of errors can indicate that a salesperson needs training, or that write-off exposure exists, and in some cases can mean that a district-wide problem needs to be addressed.

SAX-II takes the output of SAX-I over a four month time frame, links it with other selected data elements, and employs a process of categorizing, scoring, selection, and analyses using hierarchical rules. Using 120 Level 1 rules (lowest level in the hierarchy), SAX-II categorizes

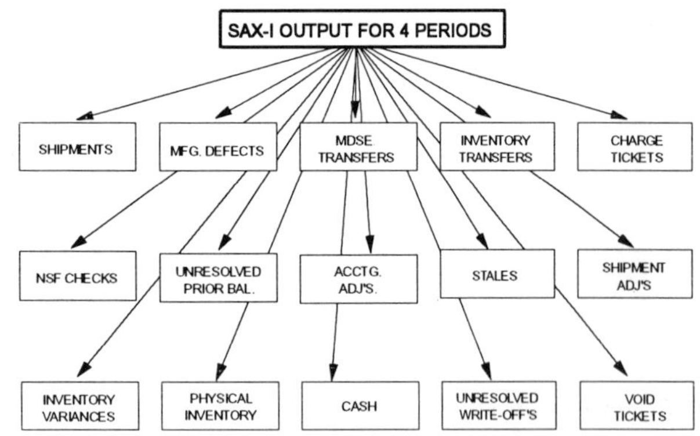

FIGURE 2: SAX-II CATEGORIES

the SAX-I rule firings as shown in ***Figure 2***. This categorization allows SAX-II to view the SAX-I output in terms of generic issues over time. In viewing shipment performance, for example, SAX-I can find any or all of the problems shown in ***Figure 3***.

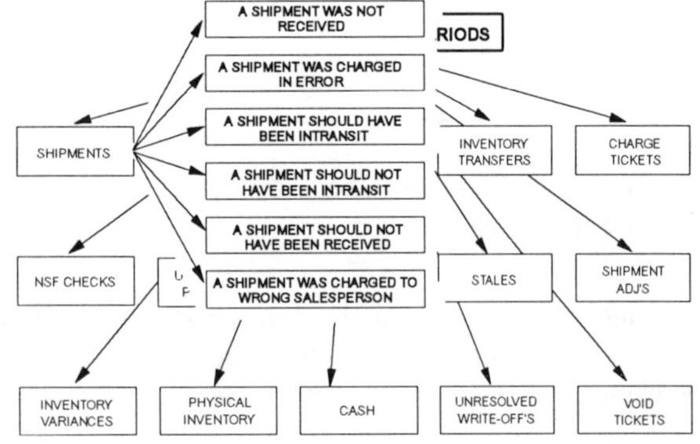

FIGURE 3: EACH CATEGORY CAN CONTAIN MULTIPLE ISSUES

Each of these error situations has a unique cause and subsequent corrective action that SAX-I addresses. For purposes of identifying patterns of behavior, however, SAX-II only needs to see that the salesperson has some form of recurring issue with processing shipments of merchandise. Therefore, SAX-II categorizes all shipment errors into one category.

After categorizing the SAX-I output, SAX-II then goes through a process of identifying and scoring frequency patterns found within each category. The frequency patterns are based on the categorized SAX-I rule firings, and assigned scores based on pre-defined patterns (***Figure 4***).

SCORE ASSIGNED	FREQUENCY PATTERN	EXPLANATION
1	CP	CURRENT PERIOD ONLY
2	CP+1P	CUR. PD. & IMMEDIATE PRIOR PD.
3	CP+2	CUR PD. & ANY 2 PRIOR PD'S.
4	CP+2P	CUR PD & 2 IMMEDIATE PRIOR PD'S.
5	CP+3	CUR PD & 3 PRIOR PERIODS

FIGURE 4: SAX-I FREQUENCY PATTERNS

After scoring, all categories with a defined frequency pattern will be selected for any salesperson with either a total score greater than a pre-defined threshold, or any salesperson that has one of five "special" conditions. These "special" conditions are patterns found that indicate further analyses and reporting is required, regardless of the salesperson's total score. For example, if a salesperson does not submit a physical inventory for two periods in a row, this lack of data could prevent other SAX-I rules from firing. Therefore, SAX-II would consider such a pattern as serious, regardless of the salesperson's total score, and select the route for analyses.

After scoring and selection is completed using SAX-II's Level I rule base, the output from Level 1 becomes the input for 400 Level II rules. The Level II rule base attempts to further refine the trends and patterns identified in Level I and, using a hierarchical structure, attempts to identify meaningful relationships using a combination of Level I rule firings and other selected raw data elements. For example, assume the Level I rule base fired the rules noted in ***Figure 5***.

The Level II rules take the inferences created in the Level I rules, and through a higher level of reasoning create new inferences. In this example, for instance, the Level II rules would determine that Rules 1270 & 1280 are related (Rule 1280 is actually identified the cause of the problem identified by Rule 1270), Rules 1350 & 1460 are related (the salesperson's outstanding NSF's are due to a customer problem), and Rules 1375, 1377, 1378 & 1380 are related (the salesperson has a growing shortage pattern, and no payroll action is being taken to reduce it).

From these Level II rules a new inference would be created indicating that the salesperson's growing shortage is probably being driven by customer NSF checks, and

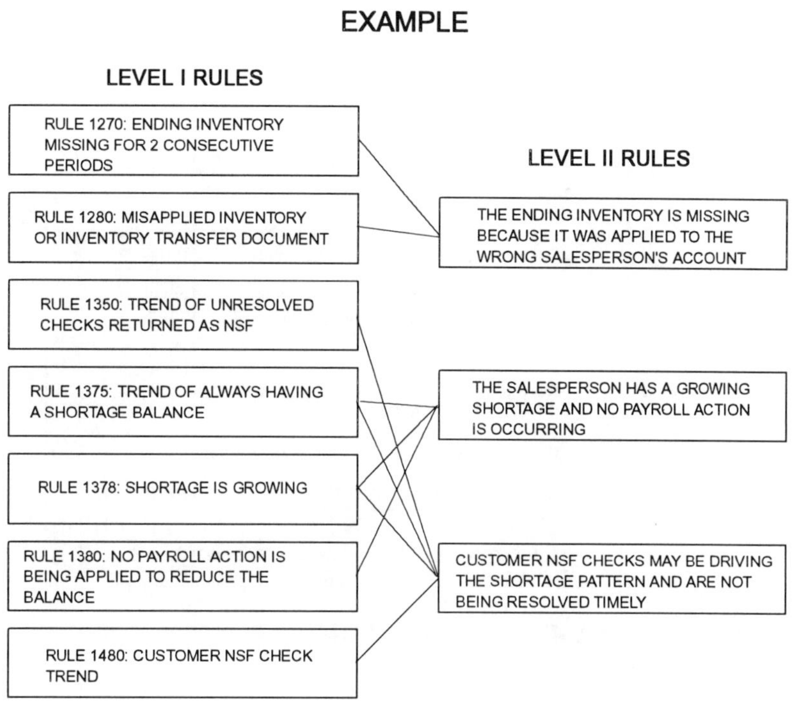

EXAMPLE

LEVEL I RULES

RULE 1270: ENDING INVENTORY MISSING FOR 2 CONSECUTIVE PERIODS

RULE 1280: MISAPPLIED INVENTORY OR INVENTORY TRANSFER DOCUMENT

RULE 1350: TREND OF UNRESOLVED CHECKS RETURNED AS NSF

RULE 1375: TREND OF ALWAYS HAVING A SHORTAGE BALANCE

RULE 1378: SHORTAGE IS GROWING

RULE 1380: NO PAYROLL ACTION IS BEING APPLIED TO REDUCE THE BALANCE

RULE 1480: CUSTOMER NSF CHECK TREND

LEVEL II RULES

THE ENDING INVENTORY IS MISSING BECAUSE IT WAS APPLIED TO THE WRONG SALESPERSON'S ACCOUNT

THE SALESPERSON HAS A GROWING SHORTAGE AND NO PAYROLL ACTION IS OCCURRING

CUSTOMER NSF CHECKS MAY BE DRIVING THE SHORTAGE PATTERN AND ARE NOT BEING RESOLVED TIMELY

FIGURE 5: LEVEL II INFERENCES DRAWN FROM LEVEL-I RULE FIRINGS

that although no inventory related issues were detected, the misapplication of the salesperson's inventory could be keeping such issues from surfacing -- the same conclusion that an overworked district manager could have reached, but only after pouring over boxes of sales tickets and shipment invoices for many days.

The Level II rules are linked to a text file, allowing each selected salesperson's patterns to be formatted and distributed to field sales managers (***Figure 6***). SAX-II eliminates much of the detailed research efforts required by providing the field manager with a concise summary of balance related behavioral issues that need to be addressed.

Validation:

The knowledge base was validated against live data. Each day, as new rules were added, a nightly cycle was run against live data. After successful validation by the expert resource, the systems output was then submitted to one-half of a test team provided by the user group. This half of the test team was charged with proving the output right or wrong.

The other half of the test team was not given the systems output, but was charged with working from the data to develop conclusions. These conclusions were then validated against the conclusions made by the system. This method of testing from the conclusions backward and from the data forward enabled the project team to significantly refine the logic used by the system.

Deployment:

SAX-I was initially developed using a mainframe expert system shell. Because of the vast amounts of input data required from other systems (approximately 1.7 million records every four weeks), the SAX-I rule base was translated into procedural code prior to deployment to shorten cycle times. Total development time (including knowledge acquisition, prototype development, testing, and preparation for production) was seven months, and staffed with a full time project team consisting of one knowledge engineer, two systems analysts, and one domain expert. The system was placed into production in August, 1990.

SAX-II was developed and deployed in a similar fashion. Total development time was 11 months, and was staffed with two knowledge engineers and one system analyst. The system was placed into production in January, 1992.

FRITO-LAY, INC SAXP30080 TIME 05:14:12	SETTLEMENT ANALYSIS EXPERT TREND ANALYSIS REPORT AS OF PERIOD 01, 1992	PAGE 926 RUN DATE 02/05/92

DISTRICT: 123	BALANCE FWD	TRENDS & PATTERNS
JOHN DOE	8,958.55 SH	GROWING LARGE SHORTAGE; PAYROLL ACTION HAS NOT BEEN TAKEN IN THE PAST TWO PERIODS
		DEVELOPING A TREND OF SUBMITTING CUSTOMER NSF CHECKS, WITH SOME NSF REMAINING UNRESOLVED
		THE ENDING INVENTORY HAS BEEN MISSING FOR TWO PERIODS IN A ROW, RENDERING THE HHC UNABLE TO ACCURATELY GENERATE INVENTORY VARIANCES
MARY SMITH	548.92 SH	GROWING LARGE SHORTAGE: PAYROLL ACTION HAS NOT RESOLVED THE BALANCE
		CONTINUAL PROBLEMS WITH LATE/MISSING CASH
		TREND OF HIGH STALES, WITH OVER 25% OF CURRENT PERIOD STALES REPORTED AS TRUCK STALES
		TREND OF UNRESOLVED CHARGE TICKET ADJUSTMENTS FOR THREE OF THE LAST FOUR PERIODS

FIGURE 6: EXAMPLE OF SAX-II OUTPUT

Although the systems were deployed using procedural code (to shorten the cycle times), the shell used in development was an essential tool in developing, testing, and refining the complex logic used by SAX in analyzing the transaction base.

Both systems have been in continuous production since their initial deployment, with the systems' output currently distributed to over 13,000 field salespersons and sales management personnel and 60 headquarters accounting personnel.

Is SAX Really AI?:

SAX-I was our first attempt at building an intelligent system, and we began the task with a somewhat "purist" approach, in that we intended to build the entire system within the expert system shell. Because of SAX-I's huge appetite for raw data (which is why we chose this task in the first place), reasoning over 1.7 million records within the shell was agonizingly slow, the cycle averaging roughly six CPU hours.

Rather than continue dimming the lights in the data center each time we ran SAX-I, we made a decision to experiment with pre-processing some of the incoming data elements by placing some of the easier rules into a module residing between the data and the shell. This was so successful that within a few months we made the decision to re-code the entire rule base into procedural code for the production system, and shortened the cycle time by 83%.

SAX-II was built and deployed using a similar approach. Even though the shell was not used in the final version of the production system, the use of knowledge based tools was critical in the development phase.

So, is SAX really an AI application? Our assessment after building, deploying, and living with both systems has led us to conclude that the AI in a system is not necessarily dependent upon the vehicle in which a system is developed or deployed, but is defined by the task the system performs. In the case of SAX-I & II, the systems replicate a highly complex reasoning process ***(Figure 7)*** that ultimately utilizes over 8 million records of raw data and answers the question of *"What does the data mean?,"* and *"What do you need to do about it?."* The AI in SAX is in the knowledge captured during the development phase and replicated by the systems' rules.

My guess is that over time the distinction between traditional systems and AI will become increasingly blurred. AI will become a widely accepted technique, and as AI techniques are embedded into traditional systems (using hopefully a variety of tools), AI will become more and more a part of mainstream system design.

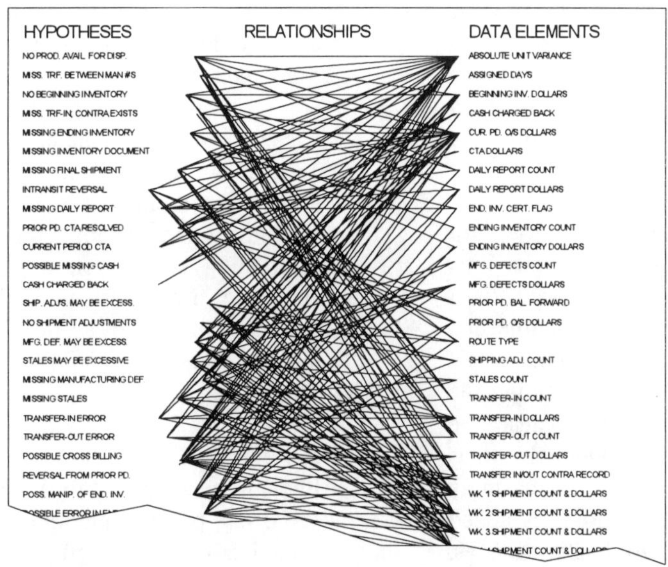

FIGURE 7: SAX REPLICATES A HIGHLY COMPLEX REASONING PROCESS

Innovative Aspects Of SAX:

The main innovative aspect of SAX-I & II comes from the complexity of the task performed ***(Figure 8)***. Working together, the two system modules efficiently turn over 8 million records of raw transactional data (sourced from a variety of systems) into roughly 6,000 concise and actionable conclusions. The input for SAX-I is raw data; the output is knowledge. The input for SAX-II is the *output of SAX-I*. Thus, the output for one expert system (SAX-I) becomes the input for another (SAX-II).

Maintenance:

As soon as we realized procedural code would be necessary to reduce cycle times, we took careful steps to ensure that SAX I & II would be maintainable. Variables, for example, that were shared by multiple rules were placed in user-maintainable tables (i.e. data aggregations

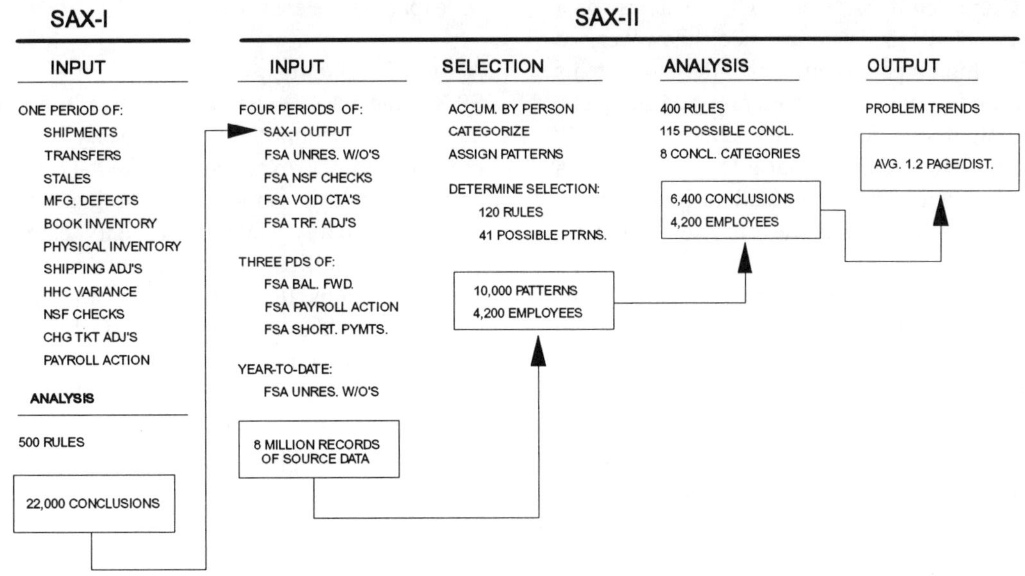

FIGURE 8: SAX TAKES 8 MILLION RECORDS OF RAW DATA AND TURNS IT INTO 6,000 CONCLUSIONS

that would be used repeatedly); algorithms were developed and re-used that enabled us to use fuzzy logic techniques in identifying transactions, such as mathematical relationships used to identify different data elements that "roughly offset" (a classic case of *"how tall is tall"*), and others that enabled SAX to determine the uniqueness of similar transactions.

Other algorithms were developed to allow for categorizing route types, dates, transaction types, etc. The definitions of these formulas were placed in a separate table and referenced by the system when needed to enable major reusable definitions to be maintained from a central system point. Thus far, maintaining the systems has not been difficult, however because the internal structure of the knowledge base is hierarchical, as our business continues to grow and become increasingly complex, we have to be vigilant as new logic is added over time. Should the business undergo drastic changes, we would probably have to consider re-development using the shell.

Learning's:

This system, particularly since it was our first attempt at replicating a difficult thought process, was a tremendous educational process. Some of our key learning's were:

- Traditional systems are usually designed two-dimensionally, in that most systems' ultimate output is expressed in some form of rows and columns, with summaries at various levels. Most business systems today (assuming they were well designed) were built with a high level of data integration. On the output side, however, a surprisingly high percentage of these systems resemble islands -- they may share raw data as inputs, but on the output side they are like strangers. Rarely does hindsight ever conclude that a low level of data integration within a highly integrated business process was a good idea -- the same is true of system outputs.

- As a business becomes increasingly "data rich," this overwhelming amount of data can cause it to simultaneously become "information poor" if the data is not efficiently converted into information. AI allows you to view your data multi-dimensionally, with an ultimate goal of identifying meaningful relationships. Therefore, AI opens the possibility of turning data into information by taking an integrated view of system outputs.

- Never underestimate the value of a willing domain expert. SAX-I was built to replicate a single person's knowledge, and not only was the expert willing, but was excited to play such an important role. SAX-II was more difficult, in that it represents a synthesis of several experts.

- Never underestimate human skepticism. As a general rule the average person accepts the concept of automated reasoning about as easy as they once accepted automated bank tellers. Focus on pre-selling and training before you deploy your system. We rolled the first system with little fanfare and subsequently had to spend a lot of effort getting people to understand and accept the power behind the system.

- Use every tool in your toolbox appropriately. Although the shell was invaluable in the development stage of the project, attempting to place the shell into production created lengthy cycle times. When we faced huge cycle times in the early stages of SAX-I, we looked at some fairly outrageous options before deciding upon using procedural code to replicate the shell's rule base. Our findings have prompted us to perhaps add a second set of conditions to the Turing Test: *"If a person in the next room can't tell what it's coded in, then ......"*

- Where transaction processing systems allowed us to eliminate the need for huge rooms filled with people punching numbers into calculators, AI can ultimately automate much of today's analytical tasks. Look around -- potential applications for automating human expertise are everywhere.

Acknowledgments:

SAX-I and SAX-II were the results of a number of highly talented and committed people. Mary McNeese provided critical domain expertise to SAX-I, and became so enthused with the possibilities she led the effort to build SAX-II. Audrey Holman not only came up with the solution to utilize procedural code, but spent many creative months figuring out how to replicate complex rules. Steve Shavel gave us a taste for where we could take these systems early on via his rapid prototyping expertise. Also, I would like to thank the numerous salespersons and district sales managers that provided valuable input to the team.

EZ Reader: Embedded AI for Automatic Electronic Mail Interpretation and Routing

Amy Rice and Julie Hsu
Brightware, Inc.

Anthony Angotti and Rosanna Piccolo
Chase Manhattan Bank, N.A.

Abstract

EZ Reader is an intelligent electronic mail (email) reader that employs a unique combination of rule-based parsing and case-based reasoning to automatically and with a high level of accuracy classify and respond to large volumes of incoming email. EZ Reader reduces the time and human resources required to handle incoming email by selecting responses and adding attachments and advice to each incoming message based on how previous similar messages were handled. The application, developed for Chase Manhattan Bank using Brightware, Inc.'s ART**Enterprise*® tool, answers emails automatically and decreases processing time for those requiring manual review. Phase I of EZ Reader was deployed in the first quarter of 1996, and handles up to 80% of incoming mail automatically, depending on message content. Later phases will enable automatic processing of a wider variety of messages. By dramatically reducing the effort associated with manual processing, EZ Reader will pay its own development costs within six months and will result in substantial, recurring dollar savings each year. This paper describes EZ Reader in detail, including its AI-based design, testing, implementation and development history.

Problem Description

Like other businesses that sought to expand access to their products and services through the Internet and other online channels[1], ChaseDirect, a unit of Chase Manhattan Bank N.A., Regional Bank, began to provide electronic banking services using phone and personal computer technology in 1995. Marketing campaigns advertised that email could be used to request information and services, opening a new electronic channel of communication with customers and prospects.

The success of its marketing campaigns created a challenge for ChaseDirect from the beginning to quickly and cost-effectively process email from multiple sources, including the Internet, Microsoft Money email, and another internal DOS-based money manager program with email capability. In addition to ChaseDirect's commitment to provide excellent, timely service to its customers, electronic commerce laws required the bank to respond to certain types of electronic correspondence within specific time frames. Although more than 80% of incoming messages were simple requests for product information, the staff often got backlogged and worked after hours and on weekends to keep up with the required analysis and responses. Faced with the huge projected increase in Internet email volume due to the planned introduction of a new World Wide Web server, as illustrated in Figure 1 below, ChaseDirect aggressively sought cost-effective, high-quality ways to process emails. This urgent business problem attracted attention from Chase's Regional Bank Knowledge Base (KB) technology team. The team's general charge was to apply artificial intelligence (AI) technology in key areas of the Regional Bank where appropriate to optimize operational decisions.

To address ChaseDirect's business problem, the Knowledge Base team created EZ Reader, an embedded AI application operating as an invisible layer between the Lotus Notes® email system and ChaseDirect. The application continuously retrieves incoming Internet email from Chase prospects and customers through an interface to Lotus Notes, and also acts as a filtering and routing

Contact information follows. *Amy Rice*: 301 Tresser Blvd., 13th floor, Stamford, CT 06901, rice@ brightware.com. *Julie Hsu*: 2010 Corporate Ridge, Suite 700, McLean, VA 22102, hsu@brightware.com. *Anthony Angotti*: One Chase Manhattan Plaza, 19th floor, New York, NY 10081, anthony.angotti@chase.com. *Rosanna Piccolo*: 15 E. 26th St. New York NY 10010, rosanna.piccolo@chase.com.

[1] Banks face significant threats to the retail banking franchise from advances in online banking (Taylor, Mehta & Wurster 1996)

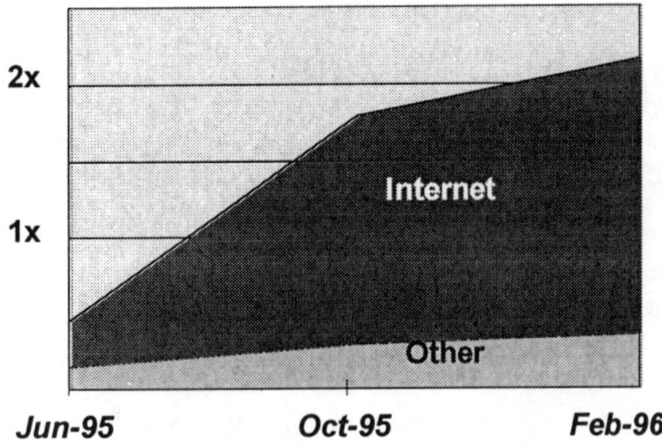

Figure 1. Projected Growth of Incoming Email by Source

mechanism, either replying to the email automatically or attaching a suggested response and referring the message for manual review. The KB team's overall business goal for EZ Reader was to reduce the number of emails that needed manual processing by more than 80%, with an accuracy rate of 95%. Other goals were to provide rapid turnaround time for return messages to customers and prospects and consistency in responses. EZ Reader's automated reasoning capabilities enabled ChaseDirect to reach these goals and significantly reduce the manual effort needed for email processing.

EZ Reader Design

The ChaseDirect email processing problem offered several clear opportunities for the implementation of automated reasoning.

AI in EZ Reader

The email review process involved complex reasoning. The process was distinctly knowledge-intensive; specialists applied domain-specific knowledge using heuristics based on knowledge of Chase products and services. The reliance on knowledge as a process component was evident as junior team members routinely relied upon the experience of their supervisor and other senior team members to explain how to classify ambiguous messages and formulate responses for new classes of messages. Finally, common reasoning tasks were reflected in the process output: *classification* of the email and *configuration* of a response from a limited set of prepared text modules.

EZ Reader's AI reasoning component is a data-driven forward-chaining rule parser operating in concert with case-based reasoning written in Brightware, Inc.'s ART**Enterprise,* a commercially successful knowledge-based application development tool. As described below, the Knowledge Base team considered and rejected several alternative software applications and tools for implementing the reasoning component of EZ Reader.

In-house procedural application languages such as COBOL could not handle the reasoning component of the email process because the input to the process was so complex and unpredictable. An approach of coding branches for each potential input using procedural methods alone would have been impractically complex. The Rete algorithm used by ART**Enterprise's* pattern matcher addressed this input complexity issue for EZ Reader. ART**Enterprise's* integrated rule scripting language, case-based and object modeling capabilities enabled automated reasoning to reverse or change conclusions drawn throughout sequential parsing and to disambiguate text while ignoring irrelevant portions, such as signature lines, without coding explicit subroutines.

Although input was in the form of natural language, the output was a simple classification based on the application of heuristic rules and experience. For this reason, syntactic analysis and interpretation, discourse analysis and pragmatic inferencing in commercial natural language processing (NLP) products such as SRA or Logicon, or augmented transition networks in custom developed applications such as the Intelligent Banking System (Sahin & Sawyer 1989) were viewed as providing only an pre-processor function to the classification reasoning task, and not providing a value-added output *per se*. This is illustrated by the fact that the ChaseDirect human email reviewers were able to classify a large majority of messages by using a relatively limited set of key linguistic clues that could be expressed as simple rules. Furthermore, when human reviewers had trouble identifying common linguistic clues in a particular message, they relied upon team experience to help them classify the message and configure or synthesize a response. Compared with the time to create rules and case structures in ART**Enterprise*, the time frame to fully analyze the semantics of the text interpretation domain and develop a comprehensive NLP module was deemed too long to meet business needs, and would have provided, at best, secondary functionality at greatly increased cost and technical complexity.

Fundamental technical requirements for an automated solution included compatibility with existing hardware and standards for run-time and network performance stability, scalability, vendor support and commercial viability. Widely-available shareware, proprietary intelligent programs specifically written for electronic forms processing (Compton & Wolfe 1993) and packaged email router/responder software such as Prolog-based

Mailbot™ (Daxtron Laboratories, Inc.) were rejected for these reasons. In contrast, the ART**Enterprise* tool had already been deployed in another application at Chase where broad functionality and customizability, product reliability and vendor support necessary for fielding commercial applications was previously validated.

Since the content, number and ordering of concepts in incoming emails was unpredictable, automatic processing could not easily be accomplished by conventional procedural programming techniques. The full-featured AI capabilities of the in-house knowledge-based development tool afforded a quickly implementable, one-tool technique for transforming the linguistic clues in emails to output classifications.

Process Flow

Figure 2. illustrates the flow of an email through the EZ Reader system as described below:

1. The customer sends an email to Chase Manhattan Bank's Internet address.
2. Chase's corporate email router passes the message from the domain server to ChaseDirect's Lotus Notes server.
3. EZ Reader periodically checks the inbox (a Lotus Notes mail database) for new mail. When a new email arrives in the inbox, EZ Reader retrieves the message and "interprets" it by performing rule-based parsing and case-based retrieval. The outcome of its interpretation is one of two possibilities:
   a) EZ Reader can respond to the email automatically. An automatic response, which is routed directly to the ChaseDirect outbox, consists of the original email and one or more attachments, or prepared replies, that are retrieved from a Lotus Notes repository of standard responses.
   b) EZ Reader cannot respond to the email automatically. It refers the email to ChaseDirect for human review and response. Before placing the email in the manual review inbox, EZ Reader assigns a category and priority to the message and suggests one or more standard replies based on message content. (Categories and priorities are described in more detail later.)
4. ChaseDirect specialists review and write responses to all messages referred by EZ Reader and place these electronic replies in the outbox.
5. Chase's corporate email router routes the message from ChaseDirect's Lotus Notes mail management system and places it in Chase's domain server for reply back through the Internet.
6. The customer receives ChaseDirect's email reply.

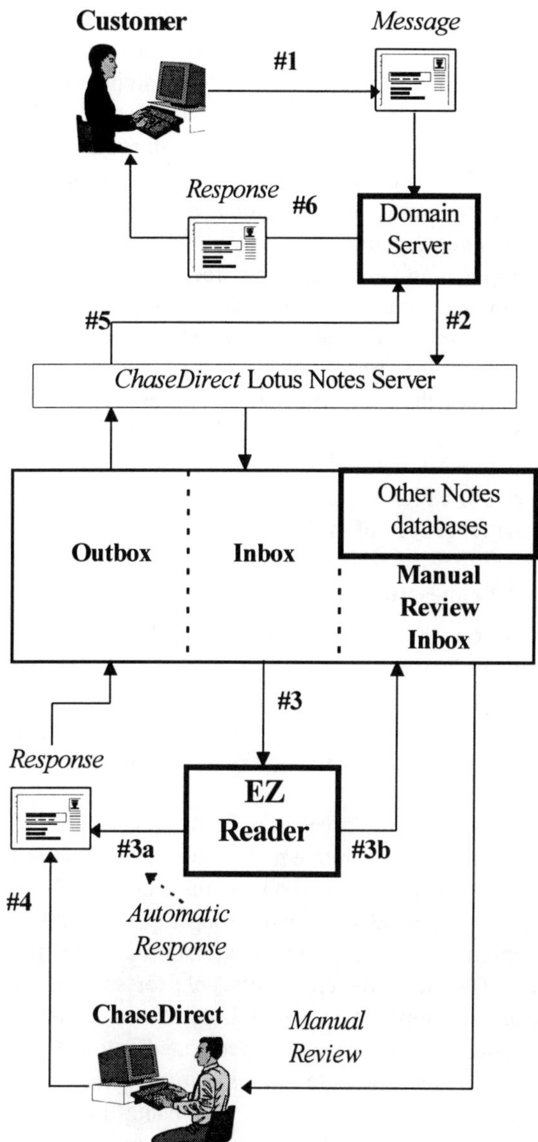

Figure 2. Email Path through ChaseDirect

EZ Reader Hybrid Knowledge Base Approach

EZ Reader's hybrid reasoning approach reflects the actual interpretation process used by human email reviewers in ChaseDirect. The application combines pre-processing rules for parsing and case-based retrieval with a domain-specific knowledge-base. Other text interpretation applications have successfully used a hybrid approach (Sahin & Sawyer 1989) (Goodman 1991). A hybrid AI design provided both a functional and manageable programmatic representation of the business knowledge and rules for email interpretation.

The combined rules and case-based approach was first evaluated after the team knowledge engineer observed and analyzed the ChaseDirect email interpretation process. Human email reviewers read each message from beginning to end while continuously evolving a final interpretation. The email reviewer recursively applied business knowledge to message content throughout the review. Reviewers modified their conclusions throughout the review, since an email contained any number of concepts in unpredictable order.

The application emulates the recursive nature of evolving interpretation by first detecting combinations of prominent words and patterns of text in any order throughout an incoming message, then setting object attribute values that both trigger and influence the case-based reasoning process. The application's case-based reasoning process then provides data to the rule-base to infer a classification by comparing the message content against the repository of messages in the case-base.

Internal Processing Flow

Within EZ Reader, program flow is controlled through the firing of declarative rules which trigger, monitor and control processing in the application programming interface (API), rule-base and case-base. Figure 3 depicts the knowledge-base processing flow, described in detail below.

Lotus Notes is Chase Manhattan Bank's corporate email standard; Chase's corporate email router routes emails to and from the Internet domain and Lotus Notes databases. Accordingly, EZ Reader was built to operate continuously and automatically in conjunction with Lotus Notes mail functions. The standard replies available for selection by EZ Reader are stored in a separate Lotus Notes database.

EZ Reader input and output is performed automatically through its connection to Lotus Notes, which was programmed via a Windows™ 3.1 API using the Vendor Independent Messaging (VIM) protocol and the API provided by Lotus Notes.

The EZ Reader API performs three important tasks:

1. It retrieves an email from the Lotus Notes inbox and returns it to EZ Reader.
2. It writes EZ Reader's output to either the manual review inbox (referral) or the outbox (auto-reply).
3. It marks the current email in the Lotus Notes inbox as read.

The API enables EZ Reader to send its output (the original message and EZ Reader's chosen response) to targeted Lotus Notes databases that can be viewed and edited by business users through a customized Lotus Notes interface that lists outputs by category. ChaseDirect business users have access to the Lotus Notes databases and all incoming emails within the Lotus Notes system, so EZ Reader does not interfere with Lotus Notes as the standard Chase platform for email-related word processing, archiving, reference, and reporting functions.

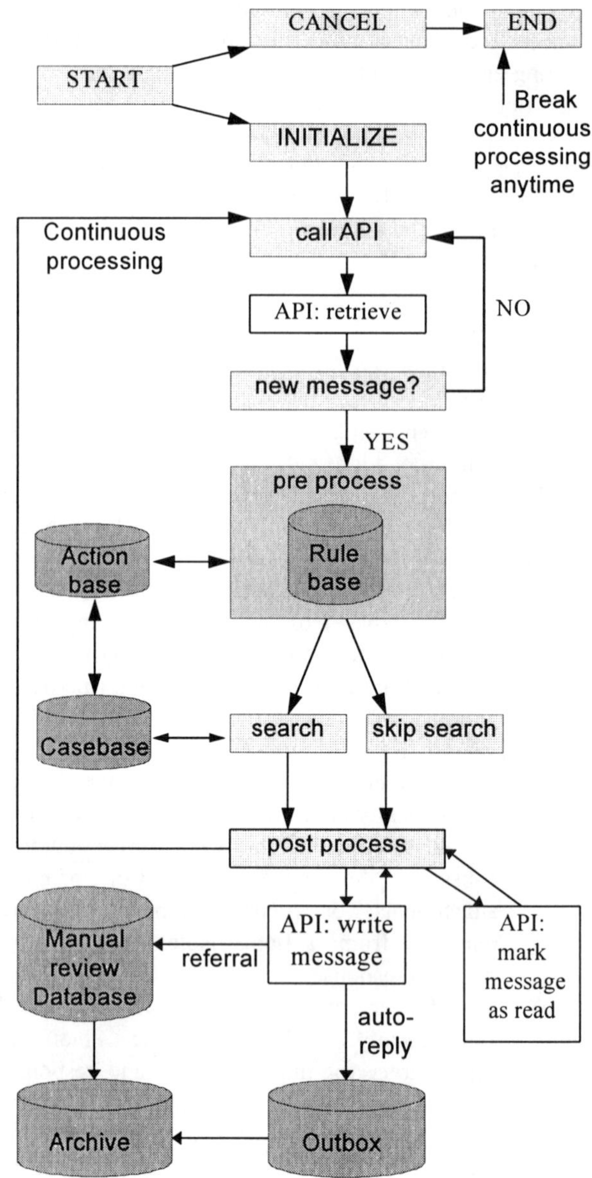

Figure 3. EZ Reader Internal Processing Flow

The API also contains functions to ensure transaction integrity in case of connectivity problems. Ordinary Lotus Notes processing tags a message as "read" when an unread mail message is opened for the first time and then closed. Typically, an API program that retrieves mail will mimic this action by marking a message as *read* immediately after retrieval. However, in EZ Reader, message marking is deferred until after the response has been sent to ensure that no data will be lost. For example, if the EZ Reader client machine loses its connection to the Lotus Notes server in the middle of processing an email, upon application restart, EZ Reader will again retrieve that email and attempt to complete processing.

AI Enables Email Classification

EZ Reader uses classification rules and case-based reasoning to assign a business category and priority to each incoming email. EZ Reader then uses the inferred classification to select and attach a standard response from the Lotus Notes database of standard responses.

Categories. Using AI techniques described in the following sections, EZ Reader classifies each incoming email based on total message content into any of the following three categories:

Automatic Response. EZ Reader assigns a category of *Automatic Response* to items that can be associated with a response from the Lotus Notes repository of standard responses and directly mailed back to the sender without manual review or revision.

Referral. EZ Reader assigns a category of *Referral* to messages that cannot be processed solely as automatic responses. EZ Reader then assigns a further sub-classification to the message to assist ChaseDirect staff with interpretation later. The sub-classifications reflect ChaseDirect's organization and operations, and are expected to change over time. Currently, there are two sub-categories for referred emails: Sales and Service, and 4 levels of priority.

Detected. EZ Reader assigns a category of *Detected* to emails that contain phrases or patterns that imply a particular manual handling procedure or interpretative aid for a referred message. In these cases, EZ Reader selects the appropriate remark to attach to incoming mail for manual review. Examples of Detected remarks include: "detected a phone number", "detected a foreign address".

Priority	Sub-Category: Service	Sub-Category: Sales
1	Fraud / lost cards	Promotional content (e.g., Microsoft Network)
2	Sensitive info (e.g., account number included)	Send Sign-Up Kit
3	Miscellaneous service	Multiple questions or lengthy messages
4	Comments, FYI	[none]

Table 1. Referrals - Categories and Priorities

Rule-base. EZ Reader uses rules to represent ChaseDirect business knowledge about how email content should be interpreted and handled. EZ Reader rules also control application processing flow.

EZ Reader's rules observe standard ART**Enterprise* syntax. These rules are represented in an IF-THEN format with a left hand side containing a set of conditions and a right hand side containing conclusions. The rules *fire* whenever the conditions set forth in the left hand side of the rule are met regardless of the sequencing of conditions. The general syntax of a rule follows.

```
RULE RULE-NAME:
  condition_1
  condition_2
    . . .
=>    ;; actions performed if all conditions are true
  action_1
  action_2
    . . .
```

An simple example of a rule for detecting foreign phone numbers is shown below. In this example, if the typical format of a foreign phone number is found in the message body (by calling a function called masked-member) or if other specified keywords are present, then all actions in the right-hand side of the rule will occur, including the printing of the text "Foreign Phone Number detected."

```
RULE foreign-phone
 (or
  (masked-member$ " +99 " ?message-body)
  (masked-member$ " +99-" ?message-body)
  (masked-member$ "(+99)" ?message-body)
  etc.
 )
  any other conditions...
=>
  (printout "Foreign phone number detected.")
  any other actions...
```

The left hand sides of the business knowledge rules in EZ Reader represent key linguistic clues that directly imply interpretive conclusions, including literals, wild card patterns, variables and segments, or choices of pattern sets. For example, one wild card pattern rule infers the presence of a foreign phone number by looking for patterns of text that resemble a phone number with a preceding plus sign. The inference of a foreign phone number is then used by the case-based search process to trigger an output classification.

Case-base. EZ Reader contains a case-base component that enables the application to emulate the reasoning of ChaseDirect staff when they use experience to determine how to handle an ambiguous email. When rule-base processing fails to clearly identify a classification for an ambiguous incoming email, EZ Reader attempts to find cases that closely resemble it. If a similar previous email is found, EZ Reader infers that the response used previously can be used (or adapted) for the incoming email.

Technically, the EZ Reader case-base is a searchable database of emails associated with specific actions and object instances stored within the EZ Reader application. It consists of an ART**Enterprise* object model of an email, called a Case. The Case object class contains attributes, or slots, for the important features of emails as defined by the knowledge used by ChaseDirect to interpret and respond to the messages. Initial attributes of the Case object include references to addresses, specific types of computers, investment options, etc. The Case object also includes control attributes such as a title for the case instance. Another attribute of the Case object lists the results associated with the case, serving to link the case-base with the rule-base and also to direct Lotus Notes to retrieve specific standard responses. Each actual email sample in the case-base is defined as an object instance.

Within the ART**Enterprise* development environment, an optimized case-base is prepared for searching by developer functions that create a case-base index, a highly optimized internal data structure that enables stored case and feature values to be matched very quickly with a an input case, called a *presented* case. EZ Reader searches the case-base assigning relative scores to each stored case based on the number of features, the mismatch of feature values and the absence of features as compared with the presented case using customizable case-based reasoning components supplied in the ART**Enterprise* tool.

Character matching with trigrams was chosen to drive case-base scoring in EZ Reader. A trigram is a 3-character sequence. For example, the word "CHASE" generates 7 consecutive trigrams: _ _ C; _ CH; CHA; HAS; ASE; SE_; E_ _. When character matching is used, the value of the character feature is broken up into consecutive trigrams, and the trigrams of a stored case are matched against the trigrams of the presented case. The degree of partial matching is based on the proportion of the trigrams in the presented case that match trigrams in the stored case. The trigram matching technique minimizes the importance of the order of the individual words in the incoming message.

Standard case-base scoring for the message text of an email (as for all text type features) is driven by ART**Enterprise's* default trigram character-matching algorithm:

$$\text{feature-weight}(f)_i = ((tx-tm)/tx)\ {}^{f}\text{mismatch}_i + (tm/tx)\ {}^{f}\text{match}_i$$

Where

- tm is the number of trigrams in common between the presented case and the stored case
- tx is the total number of trigrams in the presented case feature
- ${}^{f}\text{mismatch}_i$ is the mismatch weight of feature *f* for the i-th case
- ${}^{f}\text{match}_i$ is the match weight of feature *f* for the i-th case.

The standard algorithm works as follows: if the value in a feature of the stored email matches the value in the corresponding feature of the incoming email, the feature's match weight is add to the stored email's score. If the feature's value mismatches, the feature's mismatch weight, typically a negative value, is added to the score.

In EZ Reader, each attribute, or feature, used by the case-base was assigned a default match-weight and a customized mismatch-weight of zero. In EZ Reader, the mismatch-weight of zero leads to better differentiation of scores, because of the incidence of misspellings in incoming emails, combined with the well-bounded knowledge domain. The actual weight that any feature contributes is meaningful only within the context of a particular case and relative to the weights of other features. Since stored cases can contain different numbers of features, a presented case's raw score is normalized by dividing the raw score by the maximum possible match score for the case.

Mismatches are not entirely ignored by EZ Reader. Another factor in scoring cases in EZ Reader is that a global absence weight is assigned to selected stored cases throughout the case-base. The total contribution of the absence weight to a stored case's match score is calculated by multiplying the value by the number of features in the presented case which are not in the stored case. The total absence weight is then added into the raw match score for the case prior to normalization. The default absence weight is -1; EZ Reader utilizes an absence weight of 0 to reduce the impact of missing features.

The case-base process is dependent upon rules to derive its presented case feature values. In EZ Reader, rules fire before the case-based reasoning process to extract features or characteristics of the email that help distinguish the content of the message. Depending on the content of the message, any of the case-base search features may be set in the pre-processing rule phase. Any features set will then affect the scoring calculations performed by ART*_Enterprise's_ case-based reasoning engine. Drawing out salient characteristics of the message content using rules combined with inexact case-based retrieval allows for more powerful and precise email interpretation than simple keyword parsing or case-based retrieval based on message body only.

For example, if EZ Reader infers from incoming email text that the sender does not want to be telephoned by ChaseDirect, the rule for do-not-call-customer? fires and sets that attribute in the case to "Yes". Features set to "Yes" then contribute to the case-based search by adding weight for similar stored cases during case-base retrieval.

A sample of EZ Reader hybrid processing flow, including the interaction between rule firings and case-base matching, is set forth below. The importance of set attributes for the case-base search is clearly illustrated in these two examples.

Two sample instances of the object class:case are shown below:

CASE001:
title = "Sign-Up Kit request; Refer."
subject = "chase direct"
message text = "Please send me a
ChaseDirect sign-up kit.
My address is"
address? = "Yes"
action = refer:sign-up-kit,
detected:address,
auto:sign-up-ack

CASE002:
title = "Sign-Up Kit request/no address;
Auto Respond."
subject = "chase direct"
message text = "Please send me a
ChaseDirect sign-up kit."
action = chase-direct-std

Suppose ChaseDirect receives an email with the body of the message as follows:

Dear ChaseDirect,
Please send the ChaseDirect Sign-Up Kit
to my home address.
Thanks,
John Doe
123 Elm St.
NY, NY 10001

A rule for detecting an address will fire, resulting in setting the case attribute address? to "Yes." Next, EZ Reader will perform a search against the case-base, ranking CASE001 with a score higher than CASE002 because of the match on address?. The email will be referred because the sign-up kit must be sent out via postal mail, and the sender will receive an electronic acknowledgment that their request has been received and that it is being processed. The detected action simply aids the ChaseDirect staff in quickly determining important contents in the email. Next suppose another person requests the kit but does not include his postal address in the email, in which case the request cannot be fulfilled. The case-base search will result in CASE002 scoring higher and being selected over CASE001. The sender will then receive an automatic standard ChaseDirect response with instructions on how to receive the sign-up kit.

One of the main benefits of case-based retrieval is that the cases retrieved from the case-base do not have to match the criteria exactly (as in the message text attribute), but the desired precision of a match can be easily specified. This quality is important to the success of email interpretation. Because EZ Reader processes free-format text, it cannot simply rely on an exact match between the incoming message body and the message text attribute. As a consequence, some superfluous literals, such as the actual address of the message sender, were removed from message text attribute values during the case creation process. Since the case-based retrieval algorithm performs trigram matching on the message text feature, literals such as addresses can unintentionally affect a case-base match score.

In addition to the attribute-setting rules described above, EZ Reader's rule-base consists of several "action-setting" rules. The rules can detect information that a human reader may overlook. Some aspects of the customer's email reveal valuable information for ChaseDirect but do not necessarily contribute to the reply. For example, ChaseDirect keeps track of prospects' and customers' phone numbers. This information is important to ChaseDirect, but ChaseDirect does not necessarily want to respond to the customer in a different manner. EZ Reader can tag this email with a message about detecting a phone number, which will consequently be easily seen by staff members when manually reviewing the email.

The case-base currently contains over 300 cases; the introduction of more sample emails over time will enable EZ Reader to interpret a wider variety of messages, and increase precision through further case feature refinements.

Exception Message Handling. There are some messages that EZ Reader is not able to interpret[2], e.g., exception messages. The content of a exception message is ambiguous even for a knowledgeable person to interpret, for example, a message that contains only the word "Test". The EZ Reader application contains case examples of previously received exception messages, so it is able to forward them and all other uninterpretable messages to the Lotus Notes database for manual evaluation.

Error Processing. EZ Reader checks for errors both in its knowledge-base processing and in the API connection to Lotus Notes. Errors generated by the Lotus Notes API do not cause EZ Reader to terminate; instead, EZ Reader will continue trying to access Lotus Notes until a connection is made. For instance, if the Lotus Notes server is temporarily down, the API will send the relevant error message back to EZ Reader. EZ Reader then waits a few seconds before trying the connection again. In this manner, EZ Reader is self-monitoring and maintains maximum up-time.

Application Benefits

EZ Reader played a critical role in establishing ChaseDirect's ability to provide and maintain a responsive online marketing and service channel. The implementation of automated reasoning enabled process simplification, speed and consistency of responses, as described below.

EZ Reader increased the speed of response to the customer. EZ Reader eliminated manual intervention for a percentage of messages[3] and more than halved the time to process messages requiring manual intervention. The reduction in manual intervention allowed ChaseDirect to turn around email responses faster to customers. With a knowledge base processing speed of 1 message per second plus 2-5 seconds for Lotus Notes communications, EZ Reader reduced overall processing time by 6-8 minutes per message.

Another factor contributing to faster customer response was that the application was available on a 24-hour basis, allowing continuous processing of automatic response types of messages over a weekend when many customers tended to be active online.

EZ Reader enforced consistency of responses to customers. Before deployment of EZ Reader, ChaseDirect workers alternated the daily responsibility of reviewing emails. Each day, a different worker typically spent the whole work day manually reading and responding to email. Consistency of response was an important business consideration for ChaseDirect, and since quality of response was a function of knowledge and experience, responses frequently had to be checked by a supervisor. EZ Reader assured consistency of response because it automatically assigned prepared text depending on its singular interpretation of a message.

EZ Reader simplified the business process substantially. EZ Reader enabled ChaseDirect to reduce the number of manual steps and the effort needed to process its incoming email. A comparison of processing steps eliminated and modified by EZ Reader is outlined in Table 2 below.

Task	Before EZ Reader	After EZ Reader
Dial in to email system	one min. per access	eliminated
Read and analyze	one minute or more	eliminated
Print and annotate	up to one minute	eliminated
Select/Adjust response	five minutes or more	eliminated/ modified
Send email	up to one minute	modified
Archive original	up to one minute	modified
Delete from folder	up to one minute	modified
Enter into CMS[4]	avg: five minutes	no change

Table 2. Process Changes Enabled by EZ Reader

Application Maintenance

Currently, knowledge-base maintenance requires editing of cases, rules, and actions, all of which are in ART**Enterprise* syntax. One proposed technical enhancement to EZ Reader is to build a framework for maintenance in which business users could add and modify case objects, action objects, and even rules, through a GUI interface where the underlying ART**Enterprise* syntax of the objects is invisible to the maintainer.

Although specialized knowledge and skill sets are required to maintain EZ Reader today, the application is highly modular and object-oriented. The case-base and rule-base are independently structured. In addition, the

[2] around 5 percent of all messages

[3] see *Automatic Throughput Percentage* for a discussion of the effect of message content on average speed of response

[4] a contact management system used to track contacts with customers and prospects

design is general enough to be easily adapted to other domains, and code-level maintenance procedures are straightforward.

EZ Reader maintenance is required whenever certain business or technical environment changes occur. The following types of business changes usually require EZ Reader maintenance:

- A new or revised association between a type of message and its prepared response is required. For instance, if emails concerning a former marketing promotion need to be answered differently than they were originally, EZ Reader maintenance is performed. (Modifications to prepared response wording are performed through a Lotus Notes edit view.)
- A new type of message needs to be associated with a prepared response. For instance, if emails concerning a new marketing promotion need to be processed automatically, EZ Reader maintenance is performed.
- A new informational message needs to be generated by EZ Reader when it detects a particular type of incoming message, regardless of the response. For instance, if emails from current customers need to be flagged, EZ Reader maintenance is performed.

In addition to these knowledge-base maintenance scenarios, whenever a change in the technical environment around EZ Reader is planned, the application is assessed for required modifications and retested in the target environment. For example, because EZ Reader interfaces with Lotus Notes, if a new version of Lotus Notes is planned for installation, the EZ Reader / Lotus Notes API is tested and assessed for any relevant maintenance. In this case, because the connection to Lotus Notes is independent of the knowledge-base, only the API portion of EZ Reader requires retesting.

One person from the resident KB team at Chase is responsible for maintaining EZ Reader, among other duties. The team is trained in ART**Enterprise* as well as C language and Lotus Notes development. They also understand the business requirements of EZ Reader and are able to translate change requests into EZ Reader knowledge-base modifications.

No manual intervention is necessary for the day-to-day operation of EZ Reader. A local replica of the Lotus Notes databases resides on the development machine; these databases are used for testing and maintenance of the system. In addition, EZ Reader can be run in strictly manual mode in which it bypasses the API connection. Input data in this mode is retrieved from an external text file and allows for quick testing of the knowledge-base independent of the API.

Project History

Chase Manhattan Bank, Regional Banking, launched an initiative in 1995 to explore how artificial intelligence (AI) could help meet its business challenges. At that time, 12 applications were identified to leverage AI at Chase and EZ Reader is one of those implementations.

EZ Reader started with a concept paper written by members of Chase's Knowledge Base (KB) technology team, including Brightware consultants, in May 1995. Further development of functional specifications, cost analysis and presentations to management served to get approval for prototype development, which began in July 1995 and was finished in August. Development of a production system was granted approval in September 1995.

Beginning September 1995, EZ Reader production application development proceeded with one full-time technical developer and several part-time staff including four business analysts, three testing specialists, and numerous technical support personnel who specialized in Lotus Notes and the Chase email network.

The knowledge-base, consisting of the rule-base and case-base, were completed first, enabling user testing while the Lotus Notes API was being developed. Initial knowledge-base testing was performed in November, resulting in accuracy very close to our target level with throughput of one message per second. Further refinements increased the accuracy to our goal in December. Although the knowledge-base could have been deployed at this point in a semi-manual mode, management decided for a single integrated implementation after completion of the Lotus Notes API. The Lotus Notes API was completed, consolidated and tested with the knowledge-base a few weeks later.

EZ Reader was developed using ART**Enterprise* version 2.0b with the included Microsoft Win32s library, Visual C/C++ 1.5 and Lotus Notes version 3.0C all running on Windows™ 3.1. The application runs on a PC with an Intel-based 486/66MHz processor, 500MB of hard disk space and 32MB of RAM. The Lotus Notes server is an IBM 9595 running OS/2 version 2.1.1. with an Intel-based Pentium 122MHz processor, 2 hard disk drives of 500MB and 1GB, and 64MB of RAM.

Measuring EZ Reader Performance

EZ Reader was evaluated before implementation to ensure that ChaseDirect production approval criteria were met. To evaluate EZ Reader's performance, the team analyzed three measures: speed, accuracy and automatic throughput percentage. EZ Reader's performance on each measure is described below.

Speed. One essential success criterion for EZ Reader was that it reduce the total amount of time spent processing emails. The earliest tests of EZ Reader knowledge base demonstrated speed of one second or less for interpretation functions that manually took one minute or more. After Lotus Notes integration, an additional 3-5 seconds was required for each message. EZ Reader's Lotus Notes integration reduced the amount of time needed to attach and send responses where manual intervention was still required.

Accuracy. ChaseDirect was concerned that any software would be able to interpret messages with the required level of accuracy. The estimated accuracy level for manual processing was 98%. The team set EZ Reader's accuracy goal at a rate equal to that of 95% of the accuracy of manual processing.

The case-based reasoning logic in the EZ Reader knowledge-base was able to deliver a high level of accuracy. Its capability to rank the degree of similarity between incoming messages and previous messages in its case-base, combined with rules, results in a high level of accuracy.

Automatic Throughput Percentage. *Automatic throughput percentage* was a measure established by the team to evaluate the equilibrium between incoming message content and EZ Reader's knowledge base. It refers to the percentage of messages that can be processed without manual intervention. As more cases and rules are added to EZ Reader, the team expects to achieve an automatic throughput percentage of 80% or more.

During the early months of initial testing, the automatic throughput percentage varied from 20% to 80%. It fell when high volumes of messages with new, unexpected content were received. It also dropped when business requirements were implemented to refer additional types of messages. Based on a comparison of manual processing time with EZ Reader processing time, the automatic throughput percentage translates to significant productivity gains for each percentage point gained in automatic throughput.

Measures within Lotus Notes calculate and track the volume of messages by category (automatic or referral), date and sender email address. When a decreasing percentage of automatic throughput is detected, it alerts the business to the need to add new rules or examples to EZ Reader to enable it to recognize new types of messages sent by customers and prospects.

Knowledge Base Testing Method

To test EZ Reader's knowledge base, the team performed parallel testing to compare EZ Reader with manual processing, using the same messages both manually and through EZ Reader. The results from each were compared to assess the readiness of the EZ Reader knowledge-base for production.

Business analysts collected electronic copies of the actual incoming messages received during a two-week period as test bed data for the parallel test. EZ Reader developers used actual messages received by ChaseDirect as input data for testing EZ Reader. The testers fed the test bed messages electronically into EZ Reader in its native ART**Enterprise* development mode and printed the results. The printouts contained the incoming messages, the EZ Reader output classifications and the amount of time it took EZ Reader to process the message. The printouts also contained a blank formatted area that was used to record evaluation remarks.

Two reviewers from ChaseDirect who were not involved in the original manual processing stage analyzed the printouts. Where EZ Reader produced an incorrect category or response, the reviewer noted the expected response, and the error was reviewed by the EZ Reader team. Refinements to the case-base and rules were made and verified in subsequent abbreviated tests before the application was approved for production.

The Lotus Notes API and end-to-end network communications were thoroughly tested over a period of weeks using conventional systems testing techniques.

Summary

EZ Reader is an AI application that provides many tangible and intangible benefits to Chase Manhattan Bank as it seeks to maximize opportunities in the Internet market.

EZ Reader enabled ChaseDirect to eliminate the cost of overtime for email processing, helped meet customer expectations for service standards (such as response timeliness), provided for smoother implementation of ChaseDirect marketing programs and enabled unattended processing of email on weekends.

Since EZ Reader's knowledge base was developed for ChaseDirect, its initial utility was limited to email processing for that department. The following enhancements for EZ Reader are currently being considered:

- Add business knowledge for other business areas who choose to take advantage of World Wide Web communication with customers.
- Enable EZ Reader output to be addressed automatically to recipients throughout Chase via Lotus Notes.
- Automate the business knowledge maintenance functions of the application, i.e., enable ChaseDirect

business users to interact with EZ Reader to change how its knowledge base interprets messages and links them to responses.

- Provide the ability to automatically process incoming messages in Spanish or other languages, providing a potential global marketing advantage.
- Enable EZ Reader use of historical email and profile data to personalize EZ Reader processing.
- Link the contact management system to a process that adds customer knowledge from emails processed by EZ Reader.

Acknowledgments

ART**Enterprise®* is a registered trademark of Brightware, Inc., Novato, California. Lotus Notes® is a registered trademark of Lotus Notes Development Corporation. Microsoft® is a registered trademark and Microsoft Word for Windows™ and Windows™ are trademarks of Microsoft Corporation. Other names mentioned in this paper may be trademarks and are used for identification purposes only.

References

Compton, M. and Wolfe, S. 1993. Intelligent Validation and Routing of Electronic Forms in a Distributed Work Flow Environment. Technical Report, FIA-93-31, NASA Ames Research Center, Artificial Intelligence Research Branch.

Goodman, M. Prism. 1991. A Case-Based Telex Classifier. In Innovative Applications of Artificial Intelligence, Vol. 2: AAAI Press.

Sahin, K., and Sawyer, K. 1989. The Intelligent Banking System: Natural Language Processing for Financial Communications. In Innovative Applications of Artificial Intelligence: AAAI Press.

Taylor, D.; Mehta, B.; and Wurster, T. 1996. Online Delivery & the Information Superhighway; Searching for Retail Strategies. *Bank Management 72(1): 22-29.*

Intelligent Retail Logistics Scheduling

John Rowe, Keith Jewers

Office.RoweWJ, Keith.Jewers@js.btx400.co.uk
J. Sainsbury plc,
Stamford House,
Stamford Street,
London, SE1 9LL,
United Kingdom.
+44 (0) 171 921 6000
(Fax) +44 (0) 171 921 6178

Andrew Codd and Andrew Alcock

acodd, aalcock@inference.co.uk
Inference Corporation,
258 Bath Road,
Slough, Berkshire,
SL1 4DX,
United Kingdom.
+44 (0) 1753 771100
(Fax) +44 (0) 1753 771101

Abstract

The Supply Chain Integrated Ordering Network (SCION) Depot Bookings system automates the planning and scheduling of perishable and non-perishable commodities and the vehicles that carry them into J. Sainsbury depots. This is a strategic initiative, enabling the business to make the key move from weekly to daily ordering. The system is mission critical, managing the inwards flow of commodities from suppliers into J. Sainsbury's depots. The system leverages AI techniques to provide a business solution that meets challenging functional and performance needs. The SCION Depot Bookings system is operational providing schedules for 22 depots across the UK.

Problem Description

Business Context

J. Sainsbury is the United Kingdom's most well-established retailer with a market share of 11.7% of the UK food retail market and group annual sales of £12 billion (financial year 1995). J. Sainsbury has extensive assets with subsidiaries such as Shaws in the US and the Savacentre and Homebase chains in the UK.

Given J. Sainsbury's position in the retail market, the efficient and effective running of the supply chain for J. Sainsbury is critical to the mission of the organisation. The J. Sainsbury Logistics Purpose Statement is:

To manage the flow of goods from supplier to shelf, ensuring that the customer has the right product in the right place at the right time

To these ends J. Sainsbury's Logistics Group is committed to being World Class. The Group's Direction Principle is:

To be seen as the world's best Logistics team

In line with the Logistics mission, there has been a strong focus on developing a supply chain that leads the field in terms of providing highest quality service to the customer whilst reducing operating costs.

The Supply Chain Integrated Ordering Network (SCION) project is an element in the reengineering of the J. Sainsbury supply chain. SCION reengineers the ordering and booking processes of the depot replenishment links of the supply chain for perishable and non-perishable commodities. This is a move from a vertical to a horizontal supply chain. The SCION Depot Bookings system is a critical link in this chain as it is positioned with the forecasting and ordering links to its left and the distribution, warehousing and supplier links to its right in the supply chain.

Objectives of the Application

The SCION Depot Bookings system is categorised as a strategic enabler to enable the business to move from weekly to daily ordering. The business advantages of this move are reduced stock levels and greater flexibility in the placement of orders. Daily ordering enables the business to run with less stock in the supply chain yet provide higher levels of customer service. Daily ordering is the adoption of the idea from the manufacturing industry of Just In Time processing, i.e., making material available for a value adding activity in a process at the point in time it is required – not before nor after.

The SCION Depot Bookings system is a Business Process Automation system. The system automates the vehicle planning and scheduling processes.

The SCION Depot Bookings system is required to run for 22 warehouses and process between 100,000 and 200,000 pallets of non-perishable commodities to be placed on 5,000 to 10,000 vehicles per order cycle. The system is required to run in an operational window of two hours.

Application Description

Purpose. Under the daily ordering regime, an order to a supplier is defined as a vehicle with contents for a specific delivery time to a receiving slot on a shift of a depot. This should be contrasted with an order simply being a purchase order for a quantity of a commodity. The Depot Bookings system produces a schedule of orders for each of the 22 warehouses. The orders are sent via Electronic Data Interface protocols (E.D.I.) to J. Sainsbury's several thousand suppliers on the day of the bookings run.

The timescales under daily ordering are too restrictive for the business to have a global view of the schedule. This is because the time window for viewing the schedule is three hours. The volume of vehicles and their commodities is very high – up to 10,000 vehicles 200,000 pallets of commodities. These volumes have led the business down the process automation route to produce the Depot Bookings system. This gives the business control over the vehicles and contents by placing orders daily.

The schedule has a different view depending on from where in the business it is viewed. The schedule can be conceived in business terms as the composite of all the orders for a depot sent to suppliers as the result of a daily Depot Bookings run. Alternatively, the schedule can be viewed as all the vehicles going into a depot on any given day in response to the vehicle, its contents and delivery time generated by the Depot Bookings system. From a logistics controller's perspective, the schedule is those vehicles and commodities that belong to the suppliers that they manage.

Determine Vehicle Contents. The Determine Vehicle Contents process takes orders for commodities in the form of delivery units. A delivery unit is a pallet or part pallet of some commodity. The requirements of this process are:

- All delivery units on a vehicle belong to the same supplier or are transported by the same haulier
- The possible delivery days of each delivery unit assigned to the vehicle have some overlap
- There is a good mix of products on each vehicle
- The volume and weight of the delivery units assigned to a vehicle do not exceed the vehicle capacities
- To aggregate part pallet delivery units into full pallets, provided they are from the same supplier
- To balance filling vehicles with minimising the number of pallets delivered before their ideal delivery date
- Existing vehicles are 'topped up' before new vehicles are created
- The minimum number of vehicles is used.

Determine Day of Delivery. Once the contents of a vehicle have been determined, a day of delivery is assigned to each vehicle. This process takes into account:

- The depot capacities for the week in terms of pallets and vehicles
- The possible delivery days of each supplier and haulier
- The possible delivery days of each vehicle
- The spread of vehicle load sizes across the week
- The spread of suppliers' and hauliers' deliveries across the week.

Determine Booking Time. This process will assign a booking time to as many vehicles as capacity will allow using:

- Supplier/haulier delivery time preferences
- Supplier/haulier's imperative to the business
- The spread of vehicle load sizes across the day
- Depot shift and receiving slot capacities in vehicles and pallets.

Performance Requirement. Due to the strategic goal of the system to enable daily ordering, the SCION Depot Bookings system has to run in a very restrictive time window of two hours. This time window is determined by the business' operational timetable and as such is a hard requirement. The system is required to process of the order of 100,000 delivery units. This constitutes building and scheduling about 7,000 vehicles whilst observing the functional requirements stated above.

Software Design

The Software Solutions Architecture. The system has a three layered architecture, shown in Figure 1. The top layer of the system manages program flow. The middle layer, the 'solution level,' consists of designed subprocesses that perform meta-level processing over the model of the domain. The third layer is a model of the business domain.

The top level of system consists of forward chaining rules that govern program flow. Pattern matching is used to determine subprocess end points. When a given subprocess has completed the top level of the system fires a rule that sends a message causing the next subprocess to be performed.

The middle layer consists of solution service providers and subprocess objects. Solution service providers are subsystems or stand alone classes that perform a well-defined role in the generation of the solution. For example, the 'best-of-type class' is an abstract super-class that has as its role the determination of the 'best' slave object in a master-slave object pattern.

An example of a master-slave(s) relationship in the domain is the multiple-cardinality relationship between suppliers and their vehicles. A supplier will have many vehicles. The best-of-type class has knowledge of the interfaces of the master class and slave class. The 'best-of-type', that is the best slave in the master-slaves relationship, is determined by a method for the specific kind of best-of-type class. In the supplier-vehicles instance we may be interested in the biggest vehicle in terms of weight or volume, or we may be interested in the best-of-type in terms of the attachment of priority that the business places on the contents. 'Best-of-type' is particularly useful when considering compound properties of the slave class with multiple slaves instances.

Subprocess objects are typically specialised instances of a process manager abstract super-class. Specialisation consists of the knowledge of the representation of the problem domain and any methods required to provide the respective subprocess' services.

The approach taken was to model the business domain as classes of objects with relationships between classes.

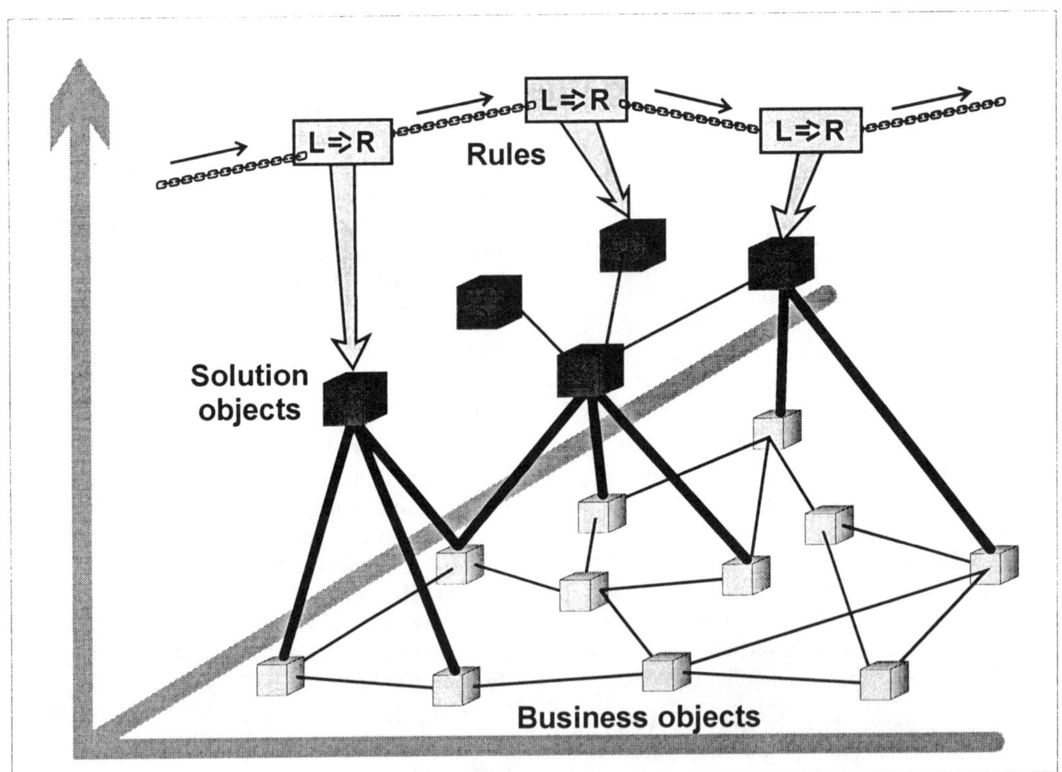

Figure 1. Three layered architecture

For example, a depot in the business is modelled as the 'depot' class, a depot's work shift is modelled as a 'shift' class, and a depot 'receiving-slot' has-a depot 'shift' class. Part of an object model is shown in Figure 2, and a class hierarchy in Figure 3. The classes in the business object model provide services modelled on the kind of information that is available about the real-world equivalents of the objects. For example, a receiving slot object could be sent a message asking what its pallet capacity is; the receiving slot would return the capacity.

Wherever possible and where appropriate the internal consistency of an object that is dependent on related properties of that object is maintained in a 'lazy' way. The use of objects to model the business domain gave us a representation that allowed us to build a 'referentially transparent' model of the objects in the domain, in terms of the objects' interfaces or services. Similarly, the use of objects enabled us to implement strategies like lazy evaluation for changes in dependent properties of an object.

AI Techniques Used

AI techniques are used throughout the system. They are leveraged most heavily in the 'Determine Booking Time' subsystem. In the 'Determine Vehicle Contents' and 'Determine Day of Delivery' subsystems the principal techniques used have been the representation and integration of rules and objects. Rules are used to manage the flow from subprocess to subprocess and Object Orientation is used to implement the subprocesses and to model the business enterprise.

The forward chaining of the production rules manages the process flow of the 'Determine Vehicle Contents' subsystem. When the state of the business object model indicates that there is no process currently operating, a production rule fires and initiates the next process in the bookings run by sending a message to the object responsible for the process.

Over the business object model four key processes drive the generation of booked vehicles for a day. The processes are termed 'targets', 'best-of-type', 'assignment', and 'constraint propagation'.

Targets. The target process manages all permissible supplier deliveries to all receiving slots on all shifts on a day.

The principle of least over commitment is a scheduling heuristic for putting filler objects into multiple container objects. The principle of least over-commitment for a set of containers and a set of fillers where each filler can go into some, but not all, of the containers is:

1. Calculate for each container the number of fillers that can go into it
2. Pick the container with the smallest number of fillers that can go into it and put a filler into it
3. Repeat 1. and 2. until there is either no space in the containers for the fillers or no fillers left.

This should be contrasted with naively putting fillers into containers without using the above. If we naively put fillers into containers simply on the basis of where the fillers would

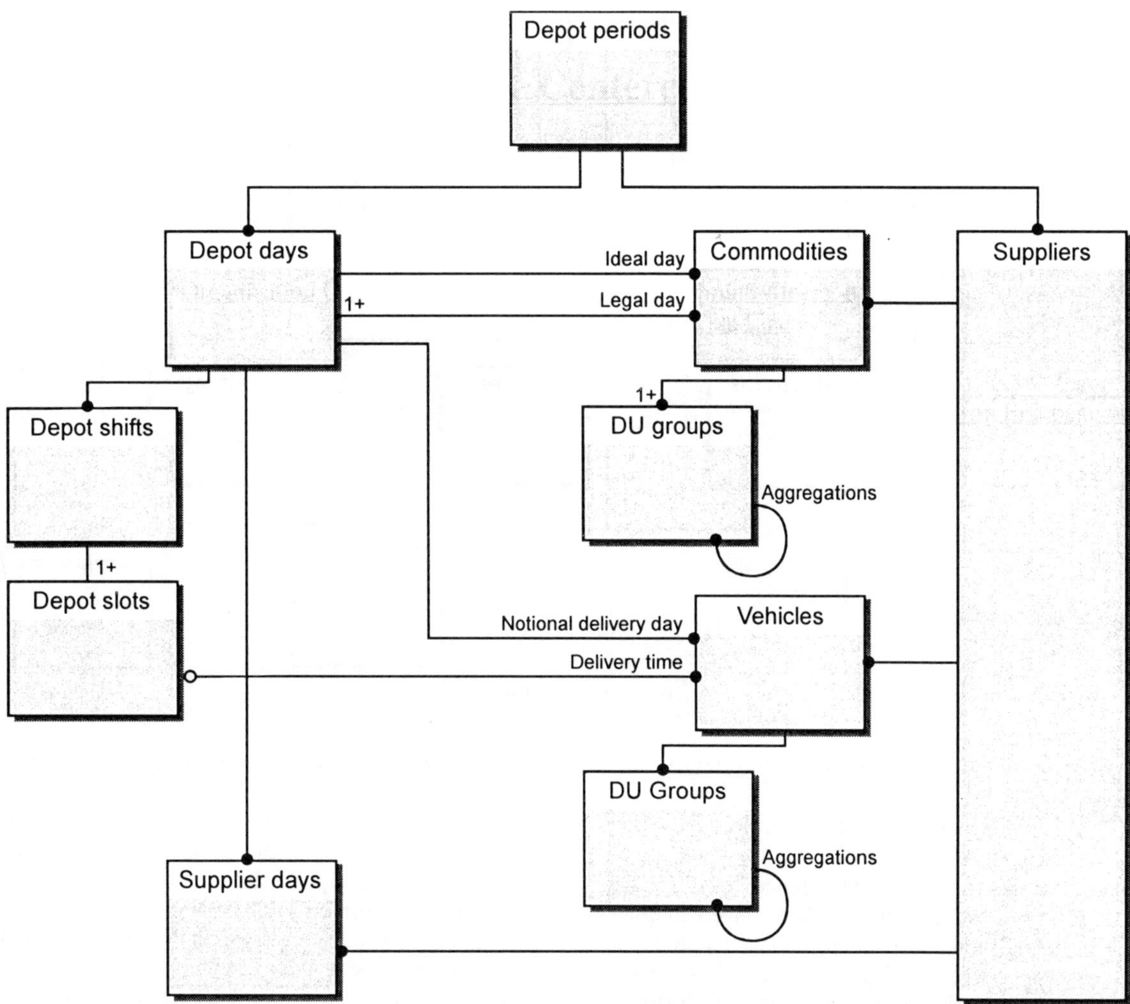

Figure 2. Object model

ideally like to go then we run out of capacity for the most over-committed containers and consume fillers that were permitted to go into less over-committed containers. This results in the most over-committed containers being full and the inability to fill the remaining containers as they are not permissible for the fillers remaining.

A supplier has a range of preferred times for delivery. This range is expressed by relationships from the supplier to the slot. There is a relationship for each preference for a receiving slot. The graph of all relationships to slots expresses all permissible deliveries into the depot on the day. A supplier will have a most preferred delivery time and a least preferred delivery time. A weighting algorithm proportionally distributes the number of pallets on vehicles with respect to suppliers preference for a delivery time. This information is termed the commitment value. The commitment value is stored on the relationships between the supplier and the receiving slots. The relationships are represented as linking objects. For a given receiving slot we can access all of the permissible linking relationships associated with the slot. This means that we can derive a value for the commitment for the receiving slot by aggregating deliveries the commitment values on them of the links into the receiving slot. The aggregation of commitment values on the linking objects into a slot gives us the commitment value for the receiving slot. The commitment value for a shift is the aggregation of slot commitment values.

Commitment only provides us with information about permissible deliveries to the depot. It does not give us any information about how the depot capacities are configured on the slots and shifts. This is built in by dividing the commitment for the slot or shift by the capacity of the slot or shift. This value is termed the over-commitment for the slot or shift. The targets process sets up the infrastructure so that the least over-committed shift be determined.

Best-of-type. Best-of-type uses a fitness function to determine the best child in a one:to:many parent-child relationship. The children are all of the same abstract type. Best-of-type provides meta-level information about the business object model. Best-of-type is employed where:

- The receiving slot is the parent and the preference links are the children

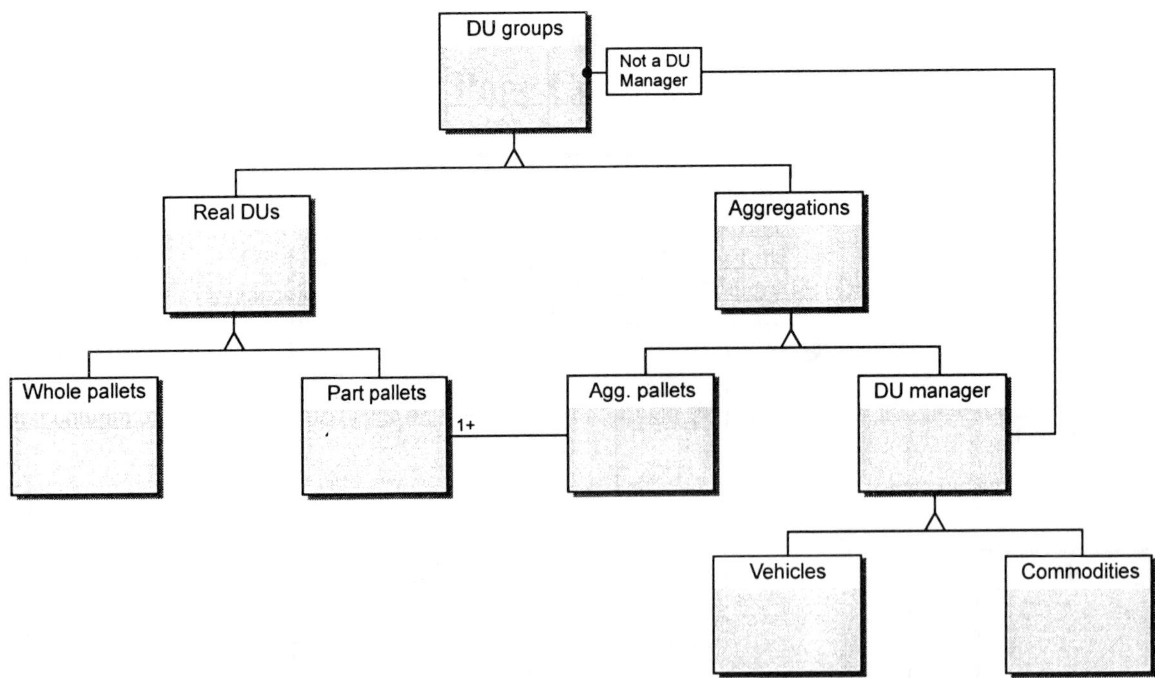

Figure 3. Class hierarchy

- Where the shift is the parent and where the slots are the children
- Where the depot day is the parent and where the shifts are the children.

The fitness function for the best preference link finds the best link by the following criteria: preference, supplier priority, commitment, vehicle size. The fitness function for the best slot uses the best-of-type for the link, over-commitment, and a weighting for assignments to each slot so far. The fitness function for the best shift uses the best slot and over-commitment for the shift. The criteria for the best-of-type were elicited from the business experts and refined through a prototyping process.

Best-of-type is implemented as an abstract super-class where specific best-of-types are specialisations of the best-of-type class.

Assignment. Assignment is implemented as the rule 'focus-decision-demand-spreading'. The rete algorithm manages the rules firing. The condition of the rule is the best-of-type for the relationship between the day and its shifts. The action of the rule is to traverse the business-object model finding the best-shift's best-slot, the best-slot's best-link and thus to the supplier. The supplier object provides the service of best vehicle. The best vehicle is the biggest vehicle that will fit within the constraints of the slot and shift capacity remaining for the best-slot and shift. This implements the packing heuristic of always placing the biggest fillers in a container before the smaller fillers. The best vehicle is assigned to the slot and given the slot's opening time as its time of delivery. The vehicle is written out to flat file to be updated to the database in a subsequent process.

Constraint Propagation. The business object model comprises related subsystems of objects. If a change is made to an object, any other class of object with dependent values must be modified. For example, if a vehicle is assigned to a slot then the slot's pallet and vehicle capacities are consumed. However, the slot's capacities are dependent on those of the shift and vice versa. As the value of the assignment is debited from the slot so we need to keep the object model consistent and debit the vehicle pallets from the shift's capacity and a vehicle from the shift's vehicle capacity. Similarly in an assignment the link from the supplier to the slot will close entailing the recalculations of the commitment values, over-commitment values and best-of-type.

The concept underlying constraint management using process classes is to encapsulate a process in an object. In this context, a process is understood as a sequence of operations toward some specific goal where the operations are distributed over the business object model. Complex processes can be built up by composition of processes. To be able to do this, a mechanism is required that enables the process to traverse the relationships between the codependent objects. These relationships will either be one:to:one relationships or one:to:many relationships. In traversing the business object model, the process object must be able to access the services of the business object and process the results of the accesses relative to the process' goal. This is implemented by an engine that traverses the object model, and a knowledge base of the classes and services that the engine must process. The engine and the template for the knowledge base are services of an abstract process class. The abstract-process-class with these services is the base class of any processes that are distributed across the business object model. The specialised process classes contain knowledge of their environment in terms of the map of classes and operations, and an intelligent traversal engine that allows them business process object to traverse the business object model whilst taking into account the state of the object model and not traversing dead paths through the object network. The process objects implement constraint propagation thus ensuring global consistency across the object model.

Booking for a Day. The constraint process objects are triggered by the assignment of a vehicle to a slot. They are sent a message as to the nature of the assignment and traverse the object model ensuring that the receiving slots' and shifts' capacities are modified accordingly, that receiving slots and shifts are closed if there is no more capacity available; that the supply group's links are constrained if there are no more vehicles to assign or if there is no capacity on the slots to which they are linked. When the processes have completed their modifications to the business object model, the targets are recalculated, best-of-types are reprocessed and the assignment rule refires. The cycle of constraint processes, targets, best-of-type and assignment continues until either there is no capacity left on the slots and shifts for permissible assignments or there are no vehicles left to assign. The output of this sequence of processes is a flat file of vehicles with contents and booking times. This file is subsequently loaded into a relational database and later that day the orders as vehicles with contents and delivery time are sent via E.D.I. to the suppliers.

Hardware and Software Environment

SCION Depot Bookings is written in ART-IM 2.5 R2, on the HP-UX 9 operating system, with an interface to Ingres written in C.

SCION runs in a group of HP-UX UNIX machines, comprising one H70 server and eight or more HP 9000/735 clients. This configuration is known as a 'snake farm' and is shown in Figure 4.

The snake farm shares an NFS directory, held on the server, across an Ethernet. The central data repository is an Ingres 6.4 RDBMS held on the server that can be queried by applications running both on the server and also on any client.

The H70 is a twin CPU mid-range machine with 512Mb RAM, optimised as a server; the 735's are smaller, single CPU machines with 80Mb RAM, optimised for processor speed. HP's TaskBroker job scheduling program is used to distribute jobs efficiently between clients and server and to manage the resources of the snake farm.

The SCION Depot Bookings operational data are chunked by depot, allowing parallelism across the clients during the two-hour window. TaskBroker controls the order in which depots are run, and best distributes the depots across the snake farm. This allows the SCION Depot Bookings scheduling solution to be easily scalable for different data volumes.

Applications Innovation and Business Significance

The system can claim innovation in the following ways:

- Use of Artificial Intelligence techniques to automate time-constrained business processes
- Integration of rules-based, object orientation and relational paradigms whilst leveraging Artificial Intelligence approaches to provide a business solution
- It is an enabler for J. Sainsbury's business strategy
- It is mission critical to J. Sainsbury's business
- It is a key component in a reengineered business process
- The system's scale – the system processes up to 200,000 delivery units, producing 10,000 vehicles for 22 depots
- The system's performance – the system runs in a two-hour time window whilst resolving a complex task and processing large volumes of data
- The system's technical architecture exploits concurrency to perform its function.

Project History

The lifecycle of the project can be divided into three phases: the development cycle, the continuous improvement cycle and the maintenance cycle.

The development cycle took place between Spring of 1993 and Spring of 1994. An evolutionary model was adopted for the systems development. This process was managed using a time box approach for each stage, each stage producing a system deliverable. The key system deliverables were:

- Conceptual Demonstrator: May 1993 – Jun 1993
- Prototype: Jun 1993 – Feb 1994
- Production Prototype: Mar 1994 – Jun 1994
- Production System: Jul 1994 – Nov 1994.

Each deliverable was seen as a stage in the evolution toward a solution that met all the business' requirements. The primary drivers for this approach were the management of business risk. In addition, the view of the development team was that all the successful complex systems that they were aware of had been 'grown' over time as opposed to a 'big bang' approach. At each stage J. Sainsbury Management had a tangible software deliverable that they could assess and to which they could offer feedback prior to moving forward.

The software development approach was for each stage cyclical. The software development cycles comprised:

- Domain Knowledge Acquisition
- Business Analysis
- Solution Design
- Software Logical and Physical Design
- Incremental Build
- Expert Verification

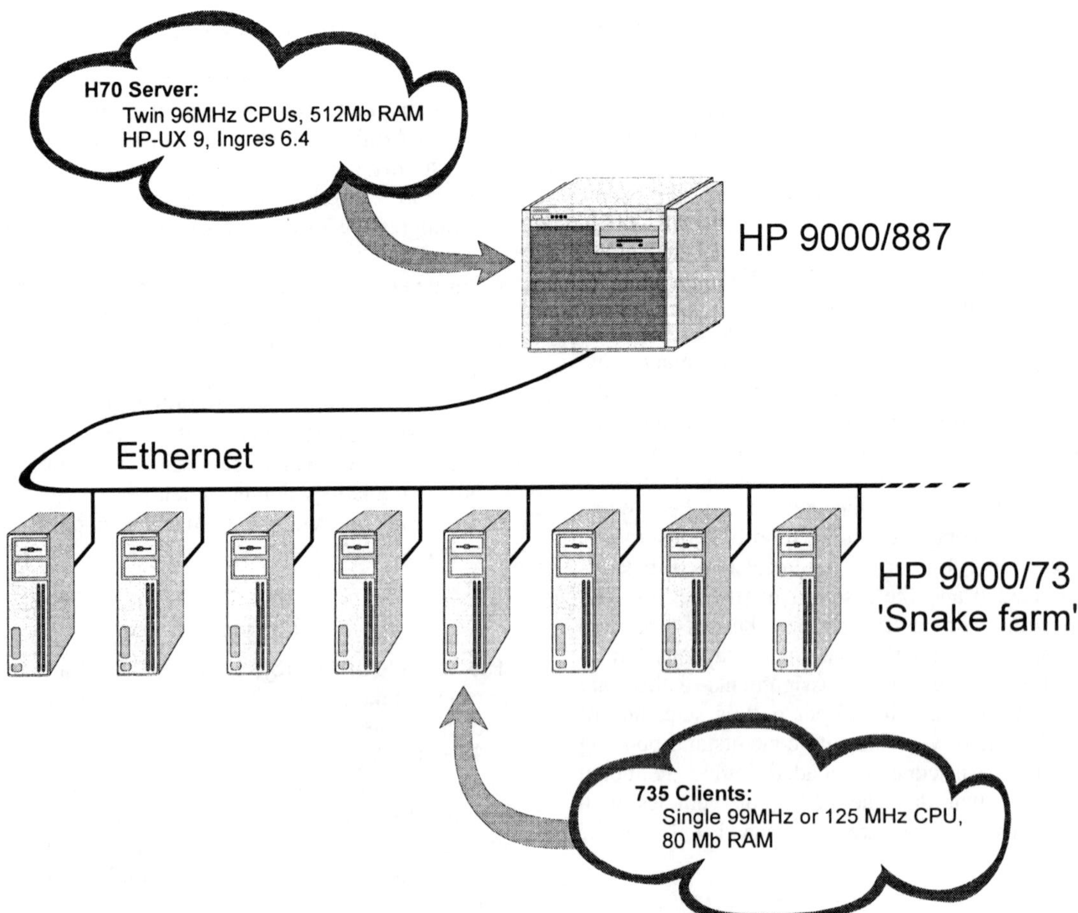

Figure 4. Hardware configuration

The evolutionary aspect of the lifecycle was implemented by significant design and code reuse between each stage of the lifecycle and the filtering out of approaches and mechanisms that were inefficient, non-robust or engendered high coupling. Considerable emphasis was placed on creativity in the design periods of a cycle.

The continuous improvement phase of the development cycle ran between January and November 1995 under a change management regime. The key driver for change for the system was the radical business process reengineering that occurred at organisational and process levels in J. Sainsbury. This manifested itself in requirements for enhancements, tuning of the quality of existing functionality, and a drive to reduce the system's run time. During this period, the run time was halved from two hours to one hour.

The support phase of the system commenced in January 1995 and will be ongoing for the life of the system. A two-tier model was adopted for the support of the system. This consists of primary support performed by J. Sainsbury, and secondary support performed by Inference.

Primary support comes into play if there is a system crash. The input data are manipulated at the database via SQL to remove the errant data that has caused the crash. The system is then restarted and run through to completion. Primary support requires no knowledge of the systems internal design or coding. An error recovery document contains the necessary knowledge and processes to resolve primary support problems. This document is supported by bespoke diagnostic tools.

Secondary support comes into play if a system crash cannot be resolved by manipulating the data. This entails accessing the system at the code level. This is performed by Inference staff with the requisite technical skills set and knowledge of the application's design and coding.

It should be noted that the system is very robust. The gearing of the development and implementation approaches have been such to ensure robustness. Evidence of this is that the SCION Depot Bookings system dealt with a 50% increase in data volumes over Christmas 1995 and ran within the operational time window. Nevertheless, due to the mission critical nature of the application, every effort has been made to put in place a practical workable support strategy.

Functional enhancements to the system are made by Inference consultants. The system has been engineered to be extensible. The use of Object Oriented approaches supports loose coupling within business object model and subprocess layers of the architecture. Similarly, the layers themselves are loosely coupled. Additional processes can be inserted into the system flow and subprocess layers of the system by adding rules or creating a specialised process class from the abstract super-class. As the business object model represents business reality, the business classes can evolve without jeopardising the internal structural coherence of the system.

System Validation

The functional requirements of the application were validated through three distinct processes: Firstly using the J. Sainsbury Business Experts within the project team; secondly by user acceptance testing by the business; thirdly by feedback from the incremental rollout of the system.

The first process consisted of two months of business rules' verification. During this period all conceivable operational scenarios were constructed by the Business Experts against which the system would be validated. The system was tuned where necessary for quality of results. When this process had been finished and signed off, the system was handed over to the business for user testing.

User testing started on one depot. The Logistics Group ran the system for one month in parallel with existing procedures, validating the results. Once a level of confidence in the system was gained, the system was incrementally rolled out a depot at a time until confidence was such that large numbers of depots could go live in one hit.

During this period the Business critically evaluated the system's output. In conjunction with operational readiness, the quality of output enabled the business to judge the speed of rollout of the system. This approach enabled the business to derive business benefit whilst simultaneously building confidence in the results of the system.

The performance requirement of the system was validated by two benchmarking exercises. These consisted of running the system against peak production data volumes on a production configured operating environment.

The robustness requirement of the system was validated by a stress testing exercise. This consisted of taking production data and randomising the data variables in their respective valid ranges. This process is ongoing as it periodically yields data conditions that throw the system. These are trapped and their resolution incorporated in the system.

Application Deployment and Use

The SCION project has been implemented in two phases: The automation of Depot Bookings under a legacy weekly ordering system, and then to migrate to the new SCION Ordering system that operates on a daily basis.

The goal of the first phase, to move all 22 depots onto the automated depot bookings process, was achieved by November 1995 (the first depot went live in October 1994). The rollout averaged three new depots moving to SCION Depot Bookings per calendar month.

The second phase is ongoing and represents a radical change to existing operating procedures and processes. There are currently six depots running under the daily ordering regime.

Application Payoff

System Benefits

The system is a strategic enabler. As such, the primary benefits of the system are realised across the whole of the supply chain. This occurs with the integration of the other key systems development programs and process reengineering that the J. Sainsbury Logistics Group are engaged in. Nevertheless, it is projected that the SCION project, comprising of SCION Ordering and Bookings, will produce benefits of more than £10 million in the next five years and return on investment in six months. This is primarily in the ability to improve the management of stock in the supply chain and improve customer service levels at the depots. Current stock levels and customer service levels as the result of SCION over the last year support these projections.

The other key benefits of the system are:

- Reduction in the amount of administration required to manage depot bookings, both at Head Office and for J Sainsbury's suppliers
- The Bookings system improves the utilisation of depot receiving resources
- It provides enhanced maintenance facilities for managing depot receiving capacities
- It supports new concepts critical to the reengineering of the supply chain
- It provides the business with control over the contents on vehicles hence supporting the management of transport costs.

Summary

The SCION Depot Bookings system automates the planning and scheduling of perishable and non-perishable commodities and the vehicles that carry them into J. Sainsbury depots. This is a strategic initiative, enabling the business to move to daily ordering. The system is mission critical, managing the inwards flow of commodities from suppliers into J. Sainsbury's depots. The system provides J. Sainsbury with control over the vehicles and goods coming into their depots. The Bookings system is written in ART-IM and makes extensive use of AI techniques that are used to provide the business with a solution that meets challenging functional and performance needs. The SCION Depot Bookings system is operational providing schedules for 22 depots across the UK.

References

Alexander C. (1979). *The Timeless Way of Building.* Oxford: University Press.

Hammer M. and Champy J. (1993). *Re-engineering the Corporation: A Manifesto for the Business Revolution.* NY HarperCollins.

Hart A. (1989). *Knowledge Acquisition for Expert Systems.* Reading, MA: Addison-Wesley

Jacobs S. (1992). What is business process automation? *Expert Systems Applications* August, 5-10.

Rumbough J., Blaha M., Premerlani W. *et al.* (1991). *Object-oriented Modelling and Design.* Englewood Cliffs, NJ: Prentice-Hall.

Winston P.H., (1992). *Artificial Intelligence.* Reading, MA: Addison-Wesley.

The NASA Personnel Security Processing Expert System

David Silberberg

The Johns Hopkins University Applied Physics Laboratory
Milton S. Eisenhower Research Center
Johns Hopkins Road
Laurel, MD 20723
(301) 953-6231
David.Silberberg@jhuapl.edu

Robert Thomas

NASA Headquarters
300 E Street, SW
Washington, D.C. 20546
(202) 358-2456
rthomas@hqops.hq.nasa.gov

Abstract

The NASA Personnel Security Processing Expert System is a tool that automatically determines the appropriate personnel background investigation required for a civil servant or contractor occupying a position of national security or public trust. It also instructs the personnel security processing staff to perform special checks based on a specific position.

The system is implemented using a rule-based expert system and a World Wide Web interface. The system design separates the user interface, knowledge base and control structure to simplify system evolution. When one subsystem is modified, the others are impacted minimally.

This system provides many benefits to the NASA Personnel Security Program. First, it frees the agency personnel security specialist from trouble-shooting and correcting all investigative problems. It also provides a learning tool for security processing staff at each installation. The system ensures that each installation security office is in compliance with all applicable laws, regulations and policies. Finally, eliminating overlapping, inappropriate and duplicative efforts to process employees saves many resources.

The system was deployed less than a year ago. To date, it saved $1.2 million of the $1.5 million agency-wide personnel security budget.

Problem Description

One of the mandates of the NASA Security Office is to ensure that the appropriate personnel background investigations are performed for civil servants and contractors occupying designated positions. Some of the common position duties require the development of or access to automated data processing systems, personnel reliability program information, national resource protection program facilities, and classified national security information. The level and type of background investigation required varies with the position and the employee. For instance, positions involving national security require screening at multiple levels to ensure that classified information is not compromised; the level depends on the sensitivity of the program and the employee's duties. Similarly, positions of public trust require screening at multiple levels commensurate with the amount of financial or resource damage that the employee potentially could cause. Other positions require specific background investigations mandated by the nature of the position, program and applicable laws. Finally, background investigations of employees who have had recent background investigations may reuse some of the information from the previous investigation, thus saving resources.

Currently, personnel security specialists at each NASA installation initiate the required investigations for applicants and employees at their respective centers. There are manuals, laws, executive orders, and federal regulations that stipulate the required background investigation to be conducted for each case. However, the manuals are not always utilized in an efficient manner to ensure compliance with current national policies pertaining to personnel security investigations. Therefore, applicants and employees are subject to being processed inappropriately, which may result in increased costs to the agency.

There is a formidable learning curve for new personnel security specialists. There are many positions and programs with unique requirements as well as laws, procedures and regulations that need to be understood and analyzed to determine the appropriate investigation level. Often, both new and experienced security specialists consult with the NASA personnel security expert at headquarters for guidance, direction and final arbitration on the appropriate background investigation. This process is costly and diverts the expert from other matters of national security.

To address these problems, we created an expert system with an interface available through the World Wide Web. An installation personnel security staff member loads the NASA Personnel Security Program home page (initial screen) and answers questions about the employee and position. The back-end expert system evaluates the questions, determines the appropriate background investigation for the position and employee, and displays the results and special instructions to the personnel security processing staff. If contradictory answers are entered, the user is encouraged to resolve the contradictions.

This paper describes the development of the NASA Personnel Security Processing Expert System. In the following sections, we describe the motivations for building an expert system available through the World Wide Web, the knowledge engineering process with respect to requirements gathering and rule acquisition, the system design, the user interface design, the structure of the expert system with special emphasis on the rule base, and the system's cost benefit to NASA. We also emphasize how the flexibility of the design approach made it easy to transition to a second version of the system. Finally, the conclusion describes the success of the system and future work anticipated.

Application Description

The following subsections discuss the alternatives considered and why a WWW-based expert system was chosen.

The Requirements

The NASA Security Office identified the need for an automated tool to aid in determining the appropriate background investigation. The system needed to capture knowledge of the applicable laws and regulations, and perform as well as the NASA personnel security expert. It also needed to ensure uniformity in investigation processing. Furthermore, the tool needed to be accessible by the NASA personnel security community on IBM-compatible PC's, Macintoshes and UNIX workstations. Finally, this system was a prototype effort and the budget was limited. Therefore, the system needed to be built with inexpensive software tools.

Why an Expert System

An *expert system* paradigm was chosen because it represents and reasons with knowledge of some specialist subject with a view to solving problems or giving advice. If the decision maker uses an expert system, it improves the decision maker's productivity. Also, if the decision maker is not yet an expert, an expert system can help the decision maker reach the level of an expert (Jackson 1990) (Luger 1993).

Issues of Expert Systems

Rule-based expert systems are appropriate for applications in which rules play a significant role. If the knowledge of the problem can not easily be expressed in terms of productions rules, than the expert system introduces overhead with little benefit. In our application, the information about what procedures apply was easily expressed in terms of rules.

Our application requires rules to be divided into *rule sets*, as will be explained later in the paper. There are two common ways to divide rules into sets. One is to write the software encapsulating the expert system shell in a procedural manner. The code loads a set of rules and calls the expert system shell to evaluate them. When an intermediate end state is reached, the code interprets the result, unloads the set of currently loaded rules, loads the set of new rules consistent with the result and calls the expert system shell to evaluate them. This process continues until the ultimate end state is reached. However, the software external to the expert system must be vested with some knowledge of the application. If the rule base changes or the method for determining appropriate rules is altered, this software must also be altered. One would like to separate completely the knowledge base from the control software so that the rules can be modified without recompiling the application.

Another alternative is to use *control rules* to determine when control passes from one rule set to another. For example, when all rules of a rule set have had the opportunity to fire, control rules fire to set facts indicating that another set of rules are ready to be considered. To ensure that the control rules fire after all other rules of a rule set have had the opportunity to fire, *salience* is utilized. The control rules are defined with the lowest salience in their rule set to ensure they fire last. This approach removes the control responsibility from the encapsulating program and places it on the rule set. This is good from the standpoint that the encapsulating code need not be altered and recompiled when the knowledge base is changed. However, the rules must have inherent control information as well as knowledge of the domain. This adds a level of complexity to the knowledge base and makes it more difficult to maintain.

The Expert System Platform

We implemented the system using the CLIPS 6.0 expert system shell (Giarratano 1993a) (Giarratano 1993b). CLIPS was developed by NASA at the Johnson Space Center.

Why the World Wide Web

The World Wide Web has been described as a wide-area hypermedia information retrieval initiative aiming to give universal access to a large universe of documents. The World Wide Web project provides users on computer networks with a consistent means to access a variety of media in a simplified fashion. Using a popular software interface browser to the Web such as Mosaic or Netscape, the user can access much information available through a multitude of network protocols (Boutell 1995a) (Boutell 1995b). The Web project has changed the way people view and create information — it has created the first true global hypermedia network (Hughes 1994).

The WWW consists of documents and links. Indexes are special documents which, rather than being read, may be searched. The result of such a search is another document containing links to the documents found. A network protocol called the HyperText Transfer Protocol, or HTTP, is used to allow a browser program to request a keyword search by a remote information server. The Web contains documents in many formats. Those documents, which are hypertext (real or virtual), contain links to other documents, or places within documents. All documents, whether real, virtual or indexes, look similar to the reader and are contained within the same addressing scheme. To follow a link, a reader clicks with a mouse (or types in a number if there is no mouse). To search an index, a reader gives keywords (or other search criteria). These are the only operations necessary to access the entire world of data (Berners-Lee 1994).

The Common Gateway Interface, or CGI, is an interface for running external programs, or gateways, under an information server. Currently, the supported information servers are HTTP servers. A gateway is really a program which handles information requests and returns the appropriate document or generates a document on-the-fly. With CGI, a server can serve information which is not in a form readable by the client (such as an SQL database), and act as a gateway between the two to produce something which clients can use (McCool 1993).

A requirement of the personnel screening application is that it be available to the security specialists at all NASA sites across the country. The specialists use a wide variety of platforms including UNIX workstations, IBM-compatible PC's and Macintoshes. An option would have been to write a program using products supported on all the platforms and distribute it to all sites. Certainly, upgrades and changes to the user interface and rule set would have been difficult to manage and maintain. Alternatively, we could have written the application using a client/server architecture with a proprietary interface package supporting the various platforms. While the rule set would have been easily managed, the user interface would not. Therefore, we chose to implement the system using the World Wide Web using the Common Gateway Interface. This simplifies the management of the user interface and the rule set in that it can be maintained at one location, while remaining accessible to a wide set of users and platforms. Furthermore, the costs of using these products are minimal.

Issues of the World Wide Web

A significant issue of the World Wide Web using the Common Gateway Interface protocol is that it is stateless. This means that once a request is processed by a server, the server program is terminated. If a user interface requires a series of screens for which to enter data, the program required to process the data of one screen knows nothing about the state of previous screen inputs. Generally, information passed from one screen state to another is crucial in user interfaces. Solutions to this problem are described later in the paper.

Another issue of developing World Wide Web interfaces is its limited user interface flexibility. Screens are created with a markup language, which provides a limited set of commands to represent common text, images and screen field formats on a Web browser. The most common markup language is the standard version of the HyperText Markup Language, or HTML; however, vendors and other software providers have created extensions to the standard HTML as well as other more powerful markup languages. While the features provided by the markup languages are limited, they did not significantly limit the development of our application.

Knowledge Acquisition

Our expert has been recognized in the area of background investigations at NASA for more than a decade. During his years of service, he has written several agency manuals and documents to formally express the rules of determining appropriate background investigations. However, these documents often were not read thoroughly by other security specialists. Therefore, he wrote a general questionnaire of approximately 50 questions to lead a personnel security officer through the expert's decision process. The responses would provide enough information to determine the correct background check in foreseeable circumstances. The questionnaire was also the vehicle by which the expert expressed his knowledge domain to the software engineer.

The initial interactions between the expert and the software engineer were driven by the expert. Much time was spent acquainting the software engineer with his world. The expert gave a complete overview of the personnel security level determination process, and placed the software engineer in the frame of mind of the expert.

During this time, much of the focus was placed on the questionnaire. The software engineer spent many hours asking about the meaning of the questions and their implications. Through the questions posed by the software engineer, the expert obtained a good sense of the structure of rules in an expert system and the models that were built to reflect the concepts. Slowly, as more questions were asked, the expert modified his questionnaire and the model of his own process. He refined his categorizations of the process which led to a refinement of the questions on the questionnaire. Both parties slowly developed insights into the other's world. The result of the process was a common structure, captured on paper, that defined the structure of the expert's thought process in an ontology that was understandable to the software engineer. The ontology was the interface between the expert and the software engineer (Farquhar et al. 1995).

System Design

In the development of a prototype system, what is initially conceived is not usually close to the end product. Therefore, the design of a successful prototype must account for the inevitable evolution of the system. The software engineer must design the system so that any change has minimal impact. Therefore, the system elements were divided into the interface, the underlying model and the control code. The interface is all the software and HTML files specific to the user interface display. The model is the expert system, which includes an inference engine and the knowledge base. The control code drives the interaction between the expert system and the user interface.

The expert system design also is divided into the model, the user interface and the control code. CLIPS has an X-based, C-callable and command-line interface. Its model is its knowledge base, and its control code is its inference engine.

The benefit of this approach is that the main aspects of the system are encapsulated. Generally, changes to the model do not affect the interface and changes to the interface do not affect the model. If control aspects need modification, neither the model nor the interface need to be altered. In practice, cosmetic changes to the interface require no modifications to the model. However, some changes to the interface require corresponding changes to the model. For instance, consider the case where a new question is added to a user interface screen to capture previously unaccounted for user knowledge. A corresponding rule is added to the model to process it. However, nothing in the paradigm of the user interface processing or expert system code needs modification. Also, the control code needs no modification in an instance such as this.

User Interface Approach

Two aspects of the user interface are described in this section. The first is the software structure of the user interface code. The second is the actual screen flow and design.

Software Structure

The user interface code was designed so that any change to the view and its interactions would only affect the view code and the HTML files. When the screen format changes, nothing else needs to be modified. If the screen captures new information to be interpreted by the expert system, then a corresponding modification is made to the rule base. However, no other part of the model requires modification.

The most common protocol for displaying files with a Web browser is the HyperText Transfer Protocol (HTTP). The Web browser, using the HTTP protocol, translates a Uniform Resource Locator (URL) to the IP (Internet Protocol) address of a computer and either a name of a file containing HTML code or a name of a server program which produces HTML code. A message is sent to the addressed computer requesting the file or the server program. The server either returns the contents of the fixed HTML file or an HTML stream generated by the server program for display on the browser. The protocol used for passing screen inputs to the server program is known as the Common Gateway Interface.

HTML that originates from a fixed file is relatively easy to debug. However, there is little flexibility for dynamic screen generation based on the user's inputs. HTML originating from a program is more difficult to debug because a server program can not be run in debug mode from the Web browser. If one attempts to debug the program on the server, one must run the program without a Web browser. The results is a stream of HTML text is written to the standard output device that can be not viewed with a Web browser. Despite the drawback of limited debugging capabilities, a server program offers maximum flexibility for dynamic screen generation.

To overcome these problems, screens in our application have fixed and variable areas. The fixed areas consist of text, images, and fields which always are visible when the screen is displayed. The variable areas are the portions of the screen that may be displayed depending on the user input. The screens exist as disk files; the fixed areas are written using standard HTML and the variable areas are written using macros embedded within HTML comment lines. When a disk file address is entered on a Web browser, it displays only the fixed portion of the screen. When our server program is addressed in the Web browser, it reads each line of HTML disk file and writes them to the standard output. When the server program encounters a macro, it creates the appropriate HTML based on the user input and inserts into the output stream.

When the developer debugs the fixed portion of the HTML code, the URL is displayed without executing the server code. The screen design and layout can be modified independent of the software that produces the variable section of the screen. When the variable portions of the screen need modification, the code can be modified independently of the fixed HTML. This strategy provides flexibility for debugging fixed and variable HTML files.

To overcome the stateless nature of the HTTP protocol, we carry information from screen to screen through HTML hidden fields. The hidden fields and corresponding values are embedded in the output stream of the next screen by the server program. When the user interacts with the next screen and selects the submit button, the values of the user selections are sent to the server along with the values of the hidden fields.

Screen Flow and Design

The interface of the initial version of the system was a single screen that resembled the initial questionnaire of approximately 50 questions. Because of its size, the user could view only four or five questions at a time, at most. After completing the questions in view, the user had to scroll down the questionnaire to answer subsequent questions. Also, the user had to complete the entire questionnaire before submitting the answers. Most of the security specialists were only mildly comfortable with computers; thus, the interface was somewhat intimidating. We realized that the interface had to be modified to make it usable by the community.

After re-examination of the questions, we realized that not all questions were appropriate for all employees or for all positions. We concluded that the questions needed to be categorized by employee and position type. In a sense, re-categorizing the questions meant re-categorizing the rules. We gathered old rules into new rule sets that categorized employees and position types. Then we modeled a new screen interaction according to the new rule sets.

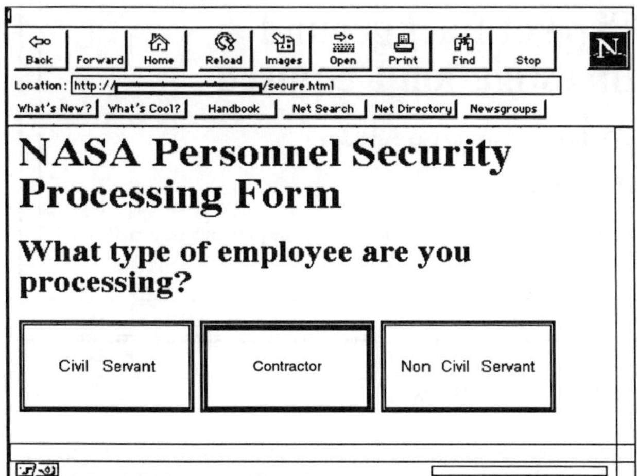

Figure 1. The Initial Screen

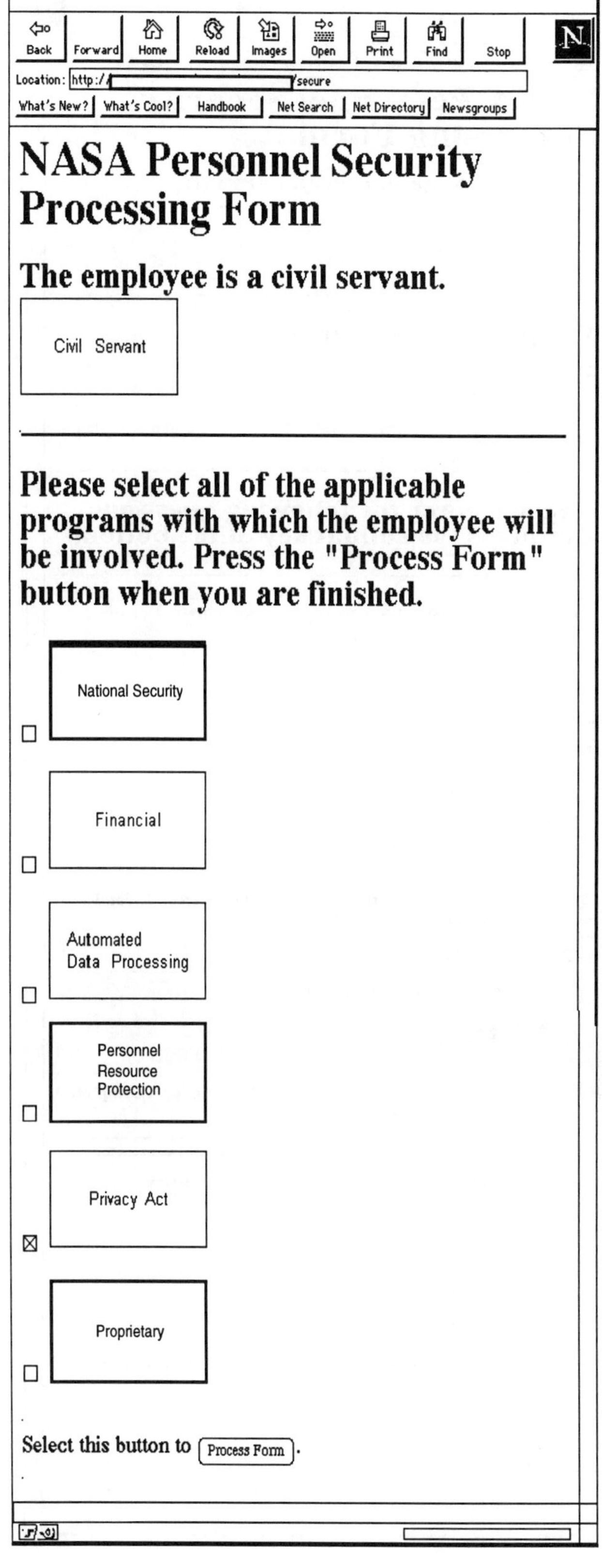

Figure 2. Selection of the Applicable Programs

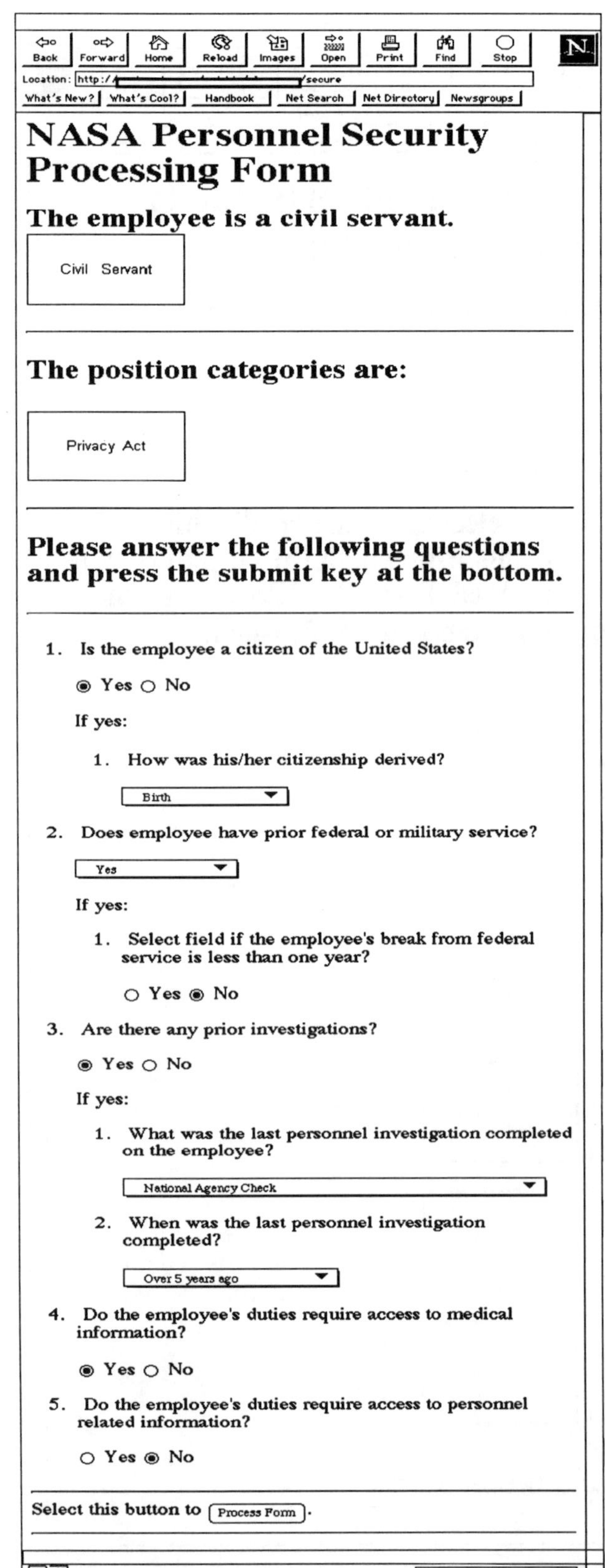

Figure 3. The Questionnaire

NASA positions are filled with civil servants, contractors and non civil servants (e.g., foreign nationals). There are many position types including positions of national security, automated data processing, financial management, child care, access to privacy act information, personnel resource protection, national resource protection, general services and general access to the site. Not all positions are available to each employee type. For example, civil servants are not hired to perform general services duties, and contractors are not hired to perform duties requiring access to proprietary information. Non civil servants must be escorted and will not have access to classified information.

The new interface is a series of three input screens. They are illustrated in Figs. 1, 2 and 3. The initial screen asks the user to select the type of employee being processed by "clicking" on a graphical icon representing the type of employee. The information is sent to the server, which calculates the positions appropriate for the selected employee type. The server returns a screen displaying the type of employee selected and a list of the potential duties that can be performed by that employee. Each duty is displayed with an icon and a check box. The user is asked to select all those duties that the particular employee being processed will perform. The user submits this form; the server calculates the appropriate questions applicable to the duties selected and displays a questionnaire to the user. This questionnaire may contain anywhere between two and ten questions, tailored to the duties selected. After answering the questions and submitting the form, the answers are sent to the server to calculate the correct background investigation. The server sends a screen back indicating the required background investigation and other checks that must be performed. This is illustrated in Figure 4.

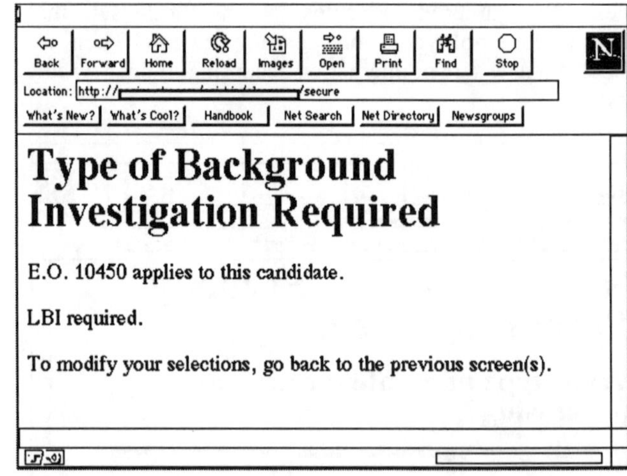

Figure 4. The Results

The new interface proved to be more user friendly. Users preferred to be presented with several short screens containing icons and a few questions rather than a long screen containing many questions. It was easier to use and faster to interact with. More fundamentally, the new approach gave the user clear understanding of the expert's process used to evaluate appropriate background investigations.

When the overall structure of the rules was examined, better rule classifications were determined. We took the classifications initially handled by the rules and transformed them into a graphical interaction to produce a new user interface. In a sense, we moved some of the knowledge base represented by the rules to the user interface. While it is not clear that this process can be formalized or generalized, it does provide an area for future exploration. Also, the nature of the user interaction itself provides insight into the expert's process and thus, serves as a learning tool for the users of the system. This functionality was previously accomplished by the rule base.

Expert System Rule Design

This section discusses the importance of rule categorization and the flexibility of our approach.

Rule Categorization

The initial knowledge acquisition process identified over 100 rules. They were categorized into rule sets that identify conflicting questionnaire responses, that inform users of special checks that must be performed, that determine the sensitivity of the position, and that determine the appropriate background investigation. In general, the rule sets are considered serially. In the first version of the system, the *Conflict* rules were very important for uncovering inconsistent responses to the 50+ questions with which users were faced. The new user interface presents the questions to the user in a limited and focused way. This dramatically reduces the amount of possible *Conflict* rules the system needs. In both user interface versions, *Special Checks* rules are important for highlighting official documents and other special checks required due to the uniqueness of the employee and/or position. The *Position Sensitivity* rules infer the sensitivity of the position based on a number of interdependent conditions specified by the user input. Finally, the *Background Investigation* rules infer the type of background check required based on the position sensitivity and the past security history of the employee.

A simplified subset of the rules appear in Figure 5 using the CLIPS syntax. For example, the first rule defined is the *prior-service* rule. The conditions that must be met to activate this rule are that the position type is a civil servant, the employee has a military or federal work history, and that there was no prior investigation. If the inference engine fires this rule, it takes the actions following the "=>" symbol. In this case, it creates a fact stating that a conflict exists and prints a corresponding message.

After the user completes the user interface questionnaire, the form fields and values are sent to the server. The server initializes the CLIPS expert system shell and sets the initial set of *facts* in accordance with the user interface responses. In the interaction presented in sample screen figures 1-3, some initial facts are that the position type is a civil servant (position-type "Civil Servant"), the employee has a military or federal work history (military-or-federal-

Conflicts

```
(defrule prior-service
   (position-type "Civil Servant")
   (military-or-federal-history Yes)
   (prior-investigation No)
 => (assert (conflict TRUE))
   (printout t "If there was prior
      military or federal history,
      there must have been a prior
      investigation.<p>"))
(defrule conflict-summary
   (declare (salience -100))
   (not (conflict TRUE))
 => (assert (inputs-OK TRUE)))
```

Special Checks

```
(defrule 10450-applies
   (inputs-OK TRUE)
   (position-type "Civil Servant")
 => (printout t "E.O. 10450 applies to
      this candidate.<p>"))
```

Position Sensitivity

```
(defrule medical-info-sensitivity
   (inputs-OK TRUE)
                (access-to-medical-info Yes)
 => (assert (public-trust-level Medium))
   (assert (national-security No))
   (assert (public-trust Yes))
   (assert (non-sensitive No)))
(defrule is-public-trust-rule
   (declare (salience -100))
   (inputs-OK TRUE)
   (not (sensitivity-conflict TRUE))
   (or (public-trust Yes)
      (and (national-security No)
      (public-trust Possible)))
 => (assert (is-public-trust TRUE)))
```

Background Investigation

```
(defrule public-trust-BI
   (is-public-trust TRUE)
   (position-type "Civil Servant")
   (public-trust-level High)
 => (printout t "BI required.<p>"))
(defrule public-trust-LBI
   (is-public-trust TRUE)
   (position-type "Civil Servant")
   (public-trust-level Medium)
 => (printout t "LBI required.<p>"))
```

Figure 5. Sample Rule Set

history Yes), (prior-investigation Yes), the position requires access to medical information (access-to-medical-info Yes) and the position does not require access to personnel information (access-to-personnel-info No). CLIPS operates on the facts by searching its rule base and *activating* all rules whose predicates match the set of facts. Our application first checks the rule set for conflicting facts and then processes special checks. Next, it determines the position sensitivity; and finally determines the appropriate investigation for the specified employee in the specified position. Each rule set contains *control rules* that fire only when all other rules in the set have had the opportunity to fire. When a control rule fires, it sets a *control fact* indicating that the processing of the current rule set is complete and the next appropriate set of rules can be considered.

In the knowledge base represented in Figure 5, the control fact (inputs-OK TRUE) indicates that all conflict rules have had the opportunity to fire, but that no conflicts exist. Similarly, the control fact (is-public-trust TRUE) indicates that all position sensitivity rules have had the opportunity to fire and that the position is one of public trust. Initially, only the *prior-service* and *conflict-summary* do not require the existence of control facts to fire. The *conflict-summary* rule is the control rule which is guaranteed to fire after all other rules in the conflicts rule set because it is declared with a lower salience. If facts are in conflict, the fact (conflict TRUE) is set; its existence prevents the *conflict-summary* rule from firing. If conflicts do not exist, *the conflict-summary* rule fires and produces the (inputs-OK TRUE) fact. This control fact is a predicate for all special checks and position sensitivity rules. In our example, there is no conflict in the user inputs. The control fact (inputs-OK TRUE) is set which permits the rules in the special checks and position sensitivity rule sets to be considered. When the *10450-applies* fires, a message containing embedded HTML code (<p> means start a new paragraph) is printed to the output stream, and thus to the Web browser. Also, when the *medical-info-sensitivity* fires, facts are set to indicate that the position is one of public trust. Finally, after all the rules in these sets have the opportunity to fire, the control rule *is-public-trust-rule* fires. It sets the *control fact* (is-public-trust TRUE) which, in turn, is the predicate for the background investigation rules *public-trust-BI* and *public-trust-LBI.* (BI stands for a particular investigation called Background Investigation; LBI stands for Limited Background Investigation). In our example, the rule public-trust-LBI fires and a message informing the user that an LBI is required is printed to the output stream, and thus to the Web browser.

Flexibility

The evolution from the first version (a questionnaire presented on a single page) to the second version (a more user friendly set of screens) required little modification to the rules. Only the rules made obsolete by the new user interface needed to change. Some of the original questions, and therefore some of the original rules, established a context identifying the type of employee and position. The second version established the employee and position type contexts via the user interface flow.

Application Use and Payoff

The system was deployed in July 1995. It is actively used by approximately 15-20 employees across 11 NASA field installations. The cost to produce the system was $60 thousand. Of the $1.5 million agency budget for personnel security investigations, it saved $1.2 million, or 80%, in less than one year. The head of personnel security for NASA used to spend 80% of his time helping personnel security specialists determine appropriate background investigations; now that the expert system is in use, he devotes less than 5% of his time to this activity. Personnel security specialists used to require several weeks to determine the appropriate background investigation for an employee; with the use of the expert system, they now complete their tasks in 10-15 minutes.

Soon, the White House Security Policy Board will issue new policies which will standardize security policies across all government agencies. We estimate that it will be trivial to incorporate the new rules into our system, thus saving $30 thousand in training costs for the personnel security specialists.

Conclusion

The system was well received by the user community and the NASA Security Office. It provides many benefits to the NASA Personnel Security Program. Since installation security staff were not utilizing manuals and applicable regulations appropriately, the Agency Personnel Security Specialist, or expert, was responsible for trouble-shooting and correcting all investigative problems. This tool saves the expert's time and allows him to pursue other pressing security issues. This system also provides a learning tool for security processing staff at each installation, by familiarizing them with the appropriate questions to ask when processing investigations. The system ensures that each installation security office is in compliance with applicable laws, regulations and policies. Finally, $1.2 million, or 80%, of the agency's budget was saved in less than a year by eliminating overlapping, inappropriate and duplicative efforts to process employees.

The system design provided flexibility. By separating the underlying model from the user interface, both were able to be developed and modified independently. This made system modification easy and fast.

The rules were classified into rule sets. Through the classification process, we were able to remove the rules that established context from the rule set and design the user interface to capture this knowledge in its presentation and screen flow. This clarified the user interface in that the users now understand the process of determining background investigations more clearly. Furthermore, it eliminated some of the rules established to perform classification.

Due to the system's success, plans are being developed to implement additional expert systems to aid in other areas of the NASA Security Program.

Acknowledgments

This work was performed for the NASA Security Office by Hughes STX. We would like to thank Rick Carr of the NASA Security Office and Frank Husson of Hughes STX for their support of this project. We would also like to thank Dr. Ralph Semmel and Marty Hall of the Johns Hopkins University Applied Physics Lab for their helpful review of this paper.

References

Berners-Lee, T. 1994. An Executive Summary of the World Wide Web.
http://www.w3.org/hypertext/WWW/Summary.html

Boutell, T. 1995b. What are WWW, Hypertext and Hypermedia*?*
http://sunsite.unc.edu/boutell/faq/hypertext.html..

Boutell, T. 1995c. "WWW FAQ Introduction: How Can I Access the Web?"
http://sunsite.unc.edu/boutell/faq/introaccess.html.

Farquhar, A., Fikes, R., Pratt, W., Rice, J. 1995. Collaborative Ontology Construction for Information Integration. Knowledge Systems Laboratory Department of Computer Science, KSL-95-63, Dept. of Computer Science, Stanford Univ.

Gruber. T. R. 1993. A Translation Approach to Portable Ontologies. *Knowledge Acquisition*, 5(2):199-220.

Giarratano, J.C. 1993a. *CLIPS User's Guild (CLIPS Version 6.0)*, NASA Lyndon B. Johnson Space Center.
Giarratano, J.C. 1993b. *CLIPS Reference Manual*, Vol. I and II, NASA Lyndon B. Johnson Space Center.

Hughes, K. 1994. Entering the World Wide Web - A Guide to Cyberspace.*" http://www.eit.com/web/www.guide.*

Jackson, P. 1990. *Introduction to Expert Systems.* Wokingham, England: Addison-Wesley Publishing Company.

Luger, G.F. 1993. *Artificial Intelligence Structures and Strategies for Complex Problem Solving*, Redwood City, California: The Benjamin/Cummings Publishing Company, Inc.

McCool, R. 1993. "CGI - Overview and Introduction."
http://hoohoo.ncsa.uiuc.edu/cgi/ .

KARMA:
Managing Business Rules from Specification to Implementation

Jacqueline Sobieski
Fannie Mae
3900 Wisconsin Avenue
Washington, DC 20016
(202) 752-4994
Fax: (202) 752-4205
sxujas@fnma.com

Srinivas Krovvidy
Brightware, Inc.
2200 Columbia Pike, #919
Arlington, VA 22204
(415) 899-9070 (x-508)
Fax: (202) 752-4205
krovvidy@brightware.com

Colleen McClintock and Margaret Thorpe
Tangram, Inc.
1155 Connecticut Avenue, #500
Washington, DC 20036
(202) 467-8539
colleen@tangram-inc.com and margaret@tangram-inc.com

Abstract

Fannie Mae is a congressionally chartered, shareholder-owned company and the nation's largest source of conventional home mortgage funds. Fannie Mae purchases and securitizes loans and is considered the leader in the secondary mortgage market. Because of its strong leadership role, Fannie Mae's policies for loan eligibility set the standard in the mortgage industry and applying these policies consistently and effectively is critical to Fannie Mae's mission and profitability.

Fannie Mae's policies for selling and servicing mortgage loans span the business functions of the secondary mortgage market and therefore are contained in many different software applications. Managing policy across multiple business applications became increasingly complex.

To meet these demands, Fannie Mae developed KARMA (Knowledge Acquisition and Rule Management Assistant) and the Business Rule Server to allow policy changes to be implemented quickly throughout its software application environment and to provide business users with direct ownership and management of Fannie Mae's policies in a way that seamlessly integrates policy into the software applications. KARMA is designed to support the management of these policies independent of the applications in which they are embedded. KARMA generates executable business rules which become part of the Business Rule Server. As a result, policy is managed centrally and no longer embedded in multiple applications. KARMA and the Business Rule Server have been running in production supporting the Cash Delivery application since July, 1995.

Background

Fannie Mae is a congressionally chartered, shareholder-owned company that was created in 1938 to provide liquidity to the U.S. housing market. It is the largest supplier of home mortgage funds, the nation's largest corporation in terms of assets, and the second largest borrower in the capital markets, next to the U.S. Treasury. Fannie Mae's corporate mission is to provide financial products and services that increase the availability of affordable housing for low-, moderate-, and middle-income Americans. It accomplishes this mission by channeling funds between primary market lenders that originate mortgages (commercial banks, savings institutions and mortgage companies) and capital market investors that purchase securities backed by those mortgages, thus helping create the secondary mortgage market.

In order to maintain the credit quality of their portfolio and the broad acceptance of their Mortgage-Backed Securities (MBS) by capital market investors, Fannie Mae must ensure that the loans that they purchase are of the highest quality. Fannie Mae accomplishes this through the establishment of underwriting guidelines and eligibility criteria, which must be adhered to by those lenders wishing to sell loans to Fannie Mae. Fannie Mae's business policies and procedural requirements are published in the Fannie Mae Selling and Servicing Guides, which are distributed to Fannie Mae customers in both electronic and paper form. For the purposes of this paper, business policy is defined as "business principles and guidelines, considered to be expedient, prudent or advantageous that are designed to influence and determine the decisions and actions of the business". The following is an example of a business policy from the Fannie Mae Selling Guide (FannieMae 1993):

> We will now accept second homes as the security for Two-Step adjustable-rate mortgages and for fixed-rate balloon mortgages -- as long as such mortgages are not subject to an interest rate buydown plan. The maximum allowable loan-to-value ratio for these mortgages will be 80% for purchase money transactions and 70% for limited cash-out transactions.

The Representation Problem

Within Fannie Mae, the English language is the primary means of specifying and communicating these business policies. Natural language, with its heavy dependence on domain knowledge, its ambiguity and its imprecision, works well for verbal and written communications between people with similar levels of knowledge (people within the same company, the same industry, etc.). However, when these policies become very complex, or when they are being communicated and interpreted with the goal of encoding them in computer systems, they must be translated into some sort of formal specification which can be checked for completeness and logical consistency prior to implementation. The existence of this type of specification increases the speed, efficiency and accuracy with which systems can be built and maintained. Without a formal specification, it becomes difficult to ensure that the business requirements are being accurately implemented in the software. In addition, as was the case at Fannie Mae, systems maintenance becomes an unwieldy process, unable to keep up with the rapidly changing business environment.

Like many corporations, Fannie Mae's computer systems execute on a variety of different hardware platforms and operating systems. They have been developed in a number of different programming languages and access different DBMSs. They have been developed using different methodologies, and the standards and procedures by which they are maintained often differ according to environment. Many of the legacy systems running at Fannie Mae today evolved over time based on changing business demands. These systems were not necessarily designed from the ground up to do the kind of processing that they are doing today. In many cases, individual systems have sprung up to accommodate narrow slices of business functions, rather than broader, integrated applications designed to handle an entire business function. As a result, the same business policies are often implemented in multiple applications, and coded in different programming languages, with no traceability back to a common set of requirements. This creates a real maintenance problem, as it is difficult to keep the various pieces of code current and synchronized with the business requirements, and almost impossible to keep them synchronized with each other.

Project Objectives

The mission of the Business Rule Services project was to develop the tools and techniques necessary to address the problems inherent in the representation of business policy at Fannie Mae. Specifically, we set out to accomplish the following:

I. Define a simple, English-like specification language for specifying business policies.
II. Create a single, shared repository where specified business policies can be stored, updated and accessed.
III. Give business users the ability to control and manage the specification and implementation of business policies.
IV. Eliminate the need for human interpretation and translation of specified business policies into executable code for implementation in computer systems.
V. Reuse Fannie Mae business policies reusable across multiple applications, and ensure that they are implemented consistently.

These objectives were accomplished through the development of the following set of related application components:

I. **Business Rule specification language** - a grammar-based representation for the specification of business policies
II. **Knowledge Acquisition & Rule Management Assistant (KARMA)** - a policy management application consisting of the following:
   - a GUI through which policy specifications can be defined and queried,

- a set of databases containing the policy specifications, their underlying models and all related metadata,
- a code generation component, which generates executable code directly from the policy specifications.

III. **Business Rule Server** - a knowledge base which provides software applications, acting as clients, with executable policy knowledge. KARMA generates the ART-IM rules which are executed in the Business Rule Server.

IV. **Data Translator** - a tool that enables sharing of data across software applications through the mapping of application data models to the data model upon which the business rules are based, the business object model.

Project Significance

Several AI applications have been successfully deployed in the mortgage industry over the past few years. The CLUES system (Talebzadeh et al. 1994) focused on automating the underwriting process. In CLUES, business policy is embedded within the knowledge base rules. GECCO (Bynum et al. 1995), is an automated compliance checker which checks loans against investor guidelines. This compliance checking is done at different stages in the mortgage loan processing pipeline. GECCO enabled different applications to use the same business policy by embedding the GECCO knowledge base in different applications. Our project differs from the above efforts in the following ways:

- **High-Level Knowledge Representation**

  Business policy is modeled as business rules in an English-like specification language that can be understood by business users. KARMA's business rule language is general enough to represent business rules in any policy related domain.

- **Knowledge Acquisition Tool**

  A knowledge acquisition tool, KARMA, was developed to define and manage these business rules, giving business users direct access to business policy implemented in the computer systems.

- **Automatic Code Generation**

  Executable business rules are automatically generated by KARMA from the business rule specification language.

- **Knowledge Server**

  Business Rules execute in a Business Rule Server which different applications, acting as clients to the Business Rule Server, can access.

- **Data Mapping**

  A data translation capability was developed from which data model translation code is generated from a high-level specification language to enable client applications to access the Business Rule Server regardless of their differing data models.

Overview of Application Components

These components, as illustrated in Figure 1, work together to provide an effective means of specifying and implementing Fannie Mae business policies. Business policies are conceived of and validated by the responsible business persons. They are then specified in the form of textual business rules using the KARMA Rule Editor. KARMA stores the logical representation of the business rule in the Business Rule database. Both the textual and the logical representation are based on an underlying data model which must first be defined through the KARMA Data Dictionary Editor, and stored in the Data Dictionary database. KARMA uses object-oriented and database technology to facilitate defining and managing business rules and uses AI technology to perform consistency checking on business rules and to generate executable business rules which become part of the Business Rule Server. The Business Rule Server is an ART-IM knowledge base which processes requests from client applications to execute the business rules. Since the client applications requiring access to the Business Rule Server may have different data models, the Data Translator translates the client application data into the data model used by the Business Rule Server. The following sections describe each application component in more detail.

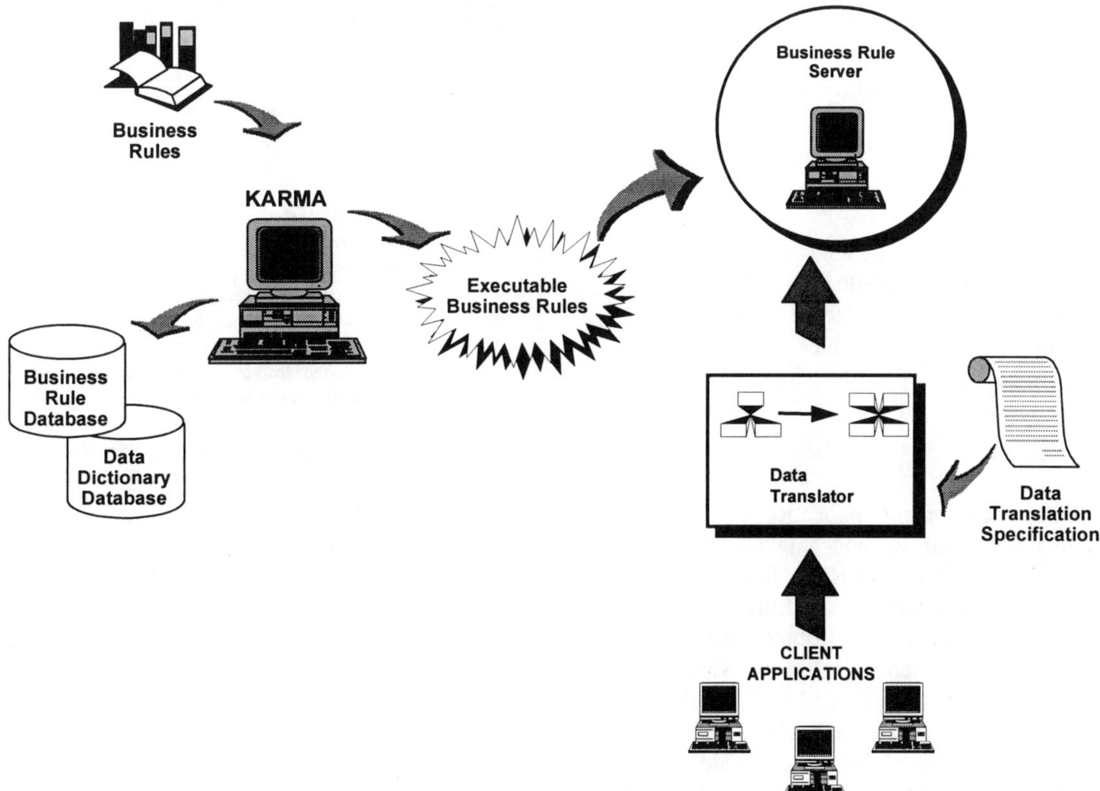

Figure 1. Application Component Overview

Business Rule Specification Language

The term "business rule" has become very popular over the last several years, particularly in the database and application development tool sectors of the software industry. It means different things to different people, but can be broadly defined as "an explicit statement stipulating a condition that must exist in a business information environment for information extracted from that environment to be consistent with business policy" (Appleton 1988). Business rules are usually described as discrete and atomic, implying that they represent the smallest units of business policy - that they cannot be broken down any further without losing their meaning. In the absence of a more precise industry definition, the term has been used to refer to everything from entity-relationship and attribute-domain constraints (which are traditional components of data models), to inference rules. There are a few researchers proposing business rule formalisms and categorization schemes, but it appears that more work will need to be done in this area before a common classification scheme will be complete and theoretically sound enough to gain general acceptance.

The term "business rule", as it is used within the context of this paper, actually refers to a very specific type of *fact constraint* - a *declarative* sentence that places restrictions on the relationships between people, places and things. These business rules do not include the simple data integrity constraints that are represented in traditional data models, instead they consist of the more complex and dynamic conditional business restrictions that are typically coded in computer programs. We created a specification language with a restricted vocabulary and relatively simple structures to precisely describe these business rules. In this artificial language, business rules consist of left-hand side and right-hand side clauses. Business rules may have one or more clauses ANDed together on the left-hand side but may only have a single clause on the right-hand side. This right-hand side clause restricts the value of a single attribute when the left-hand side conditions are satisfied. Therefore, business rules are represented as:

```
IF <clause>
AND <clause> .....
THEN <clause>
```

Where these clauses are of the following forms:

```
<Attribute> <Operator> <Attribute>
<Attribute> <Operator> <Value>
<Attribute> <Operator> <Attribute List>
<Attribute> <Operator> <Value List>
<Object> <Operator>
```

For example, in the business rule:

```
IF    Lien Type is Second Mortgage
THEN  Occupancy Status must be Principal
      Residence
```

The clause "Lien Type is Second Mortgage" is an `<Attribute>` `<Operator>` `<Value>` clause (Lien Type, is, Second Mortgage). The clause "Occupancy Status must be Principal Residence" is also an `<Attribute>` `<Operator>` `<Value>` clause.

The structure of the business rule lends itself naturally to knowledge representation as a production rule in a data-driven rule-based system and in fact, that is how the executable version of the business rules are represented. The Business Rule Server section describes this in more detail.

KARMA

KARMA is a policy management application developed to support the collection, analysis and implementation of business rules at Fannie Mae. KARMA has three main components: the Data Dictionary Editor, Rule Editor, and the Rule Browser. The objects and attributes available to create business rules are defined using the KARMA Data Dictionary Editor. Using the KARMA Rule Editor, business policy is formally specified in business rules using the English-like syntax described above. Rules defined in KARMA can be queried and browsed through the KARMA Rule Browser.

KARMA Data Dictionary Editor. The business object model is defined using the KARMA Data Dictionary Editor, shown in Figure 2. The user first defines an object, giving the object a name, and providing the business definition for the object. Any number of attributes can be defined for an object. For each attribute the user selects a data type, and provides the name and definition for the attribute. For enumerated data types, the user must define the set of enumerated values. The business object model defined using the Data Dictionary Editor is stored in a relational database, the Data Dictionary database. The objects, attributes and values stored in the Data Dictionary database are then available to be used in defining rules in the KARMA Rule Editor.

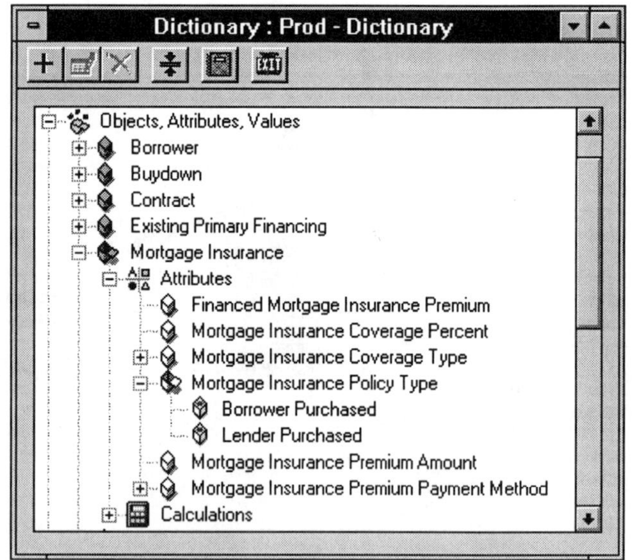

Figure 2. KARMA Data Dictionary Editor

KARMA Rule Editor. The KARMA Rule Editor, shown in Figure 3, allows users to define new rules and modify existing rules or rule properties. Once defined, rules are stored in the local MS-ACCESS Business Rule database or in the shared SYBASE Business Rule database. This allows users to keep a local copy of the Business Rules and Data Dictionary databases to work with during knowledge acquisition until they are ready to update the master Business Rules and Data Dictionary databases.

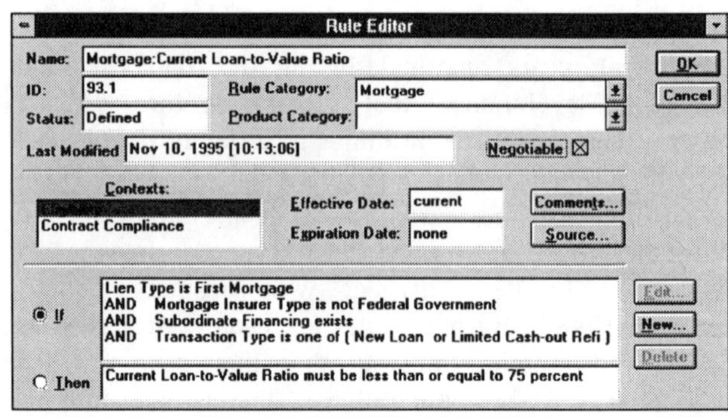

Figure 3. KARMA Rule Editor

The rule clauses are defined or modified through the KARMA Clause Editor, shown in Figure 4. The Clause Editor steps the user through the process of defining a rule clause by displaying only valid selections in the hierarchical list box control. A clause is defined to have the following structure `<Operand>` `<Operator>` `<Operand List>`. Valid selections are determined by the data type of the first operand selected. For each data type, a list of valid operators is defined in the Data Dictionary database. The valid operators for a data type are then made available in the KARMA Clause Editor when the first operand of a clause is selected. Once an operator is selected, the second operand or operand list of the clause is restricted by this operator. Multiple clauses can be defined for any given business rule.

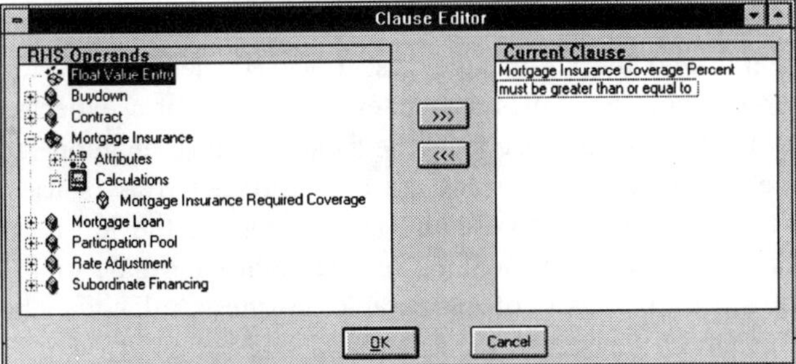

Figure 4. KARMA Clause Editor

KARMA Rule Browser. The KARMA Rule Browser, shown in Figure 5, displays all the rules defined in KARMA. Users can scroll through the rules defined in the Business Rule database. The rule text for the selected rule is displayed in the lower section of the Rule Browser. From the Rule Browser users can invoke the Rule Query capability which allows the user to specify criteria for which matching rules will be displayed in the Rule Browser. Rules displayed in the Rule Browser can also be sorted and printed.

Rulebase : MTCURR RULES

Id	Status	Name
81.1	Defined	VRM:Remaining Term
82.1	Defined	VRM:Mortgage Insurance Policy Type
83.1	Defined	VRM:Mortgage Insurance Policy Type
84.1	Defined	FRM:Product Line
85.1	Defined	VRM:Product Line
86.1	Defined	Mortgage:Financial Backing Type
87.1	Defined	Mortgage:Current Combined Loan-to-Value Ratio
88.1	Defined	Mortgage:Current Combined Loan-to-Value Ratio
89.1	Defined	Mortgage:Current Combined Loan-to-Value Ratio
90.1	Defined	Mortgage:Current Loan-to-Value Ratio
91.1	Defined	Mortgage:Current Loan-to-Value Ratio
92.1	Defined	Mortgage:Current Loan-to-Value Ratio
[illegible]	[illegible]	[illegible]
94.1	Defined	Mortgage:Current Loan-to-Value Ratio
95.1	Defined	Mortgage:Current Loan-to-Value Ratio
96.1	Defined	Mortgage:Energy Efficiency
97.1	Defined	Mortgage:Buydown Adjustment Frequency
98.1	Defined	Mortgage:Financed Mortgage Insurance Premium
99.1	Defined	Mortgage:FM Pool Participation Percent
100.1	Defined	Mortgage:FM Pool Participation Percent

IF Lien Type is First Mortgage
AND Mortgage Insurer Type is not Federal Government
AND Subordinate Financing exists
AND Transaction Type is one of (New Loan or Limited Cash-out Refi)
THEN Current Loan-to-Value Ratio must be less than or equal to 75 percent

Sort Query Edit View New Copy Delete

Figure 5. KARMA Rule Browser

Consistency Checking in KARMA. In order to fully support the business users in defining high-quality business rules, KARMA must ensure not only that the rule has a valid syntax but that it is consistent with other rules in the Business Rule database. These requirements are met through the GUI, which restricts users to creating rules using valid syntax, and the consistency checking component, which keeps users from defining rules which are inconsistent with rules that have already been defined.

KARMA's consistency checking implementation assumes that no nested conditions exist in the rules and that the consequents have only one literal and the antecedents have multiple literals with an "AND" connector. A unification based algorithm is used to perform consistency checking. The consistency checking capability identifies the following relationships among business rules: inferred rules, redundant rules, conflicting rules, and subsumed rules (Polat & Guvenir 1993).

For the verification of the rules, the comparison of the clauses is the primary operation. Let `C->lhs` be the left-hand side operand in the clause `C`, `C->op` be the operator in the clause `C` and `C-rhs` be the list of right-hand side operands in the clause `C`. Comparing two clauses C_1 and C_2 yields the following results with the respective substitution lists:

```
1.  C1 ≡ C2   if { C1->lhs = C2->lhs; C1->op =
                 C2->op; C1->rhs = C2->rhs }
                 SUB_LIST = {} or
              if { C1->lhs = C2->lhs; C1->op =
                 C2->op; C1->rhs ≠ C2->rhs }
                 SUB_LIST = UNIFY(C1->rhs =
                 C2-  >rhs )

2.  C1 ≡ ~C2  if { C1->lhs = C2->lhs; C1->op =
                 ~(C2->op); C1->rhs = C2->rhs }
                 SUB_LIST = {} or
              if { C1->lhs = C2->lhs; C1->op =
                 ~(C2->op); C1->rhs ≠ C2->rhs }
                 SUB_LIST = UNIFY(C1->rhs =
                 C2-  >rhs)

3.  C1 ⊂ C2   if { C1->lhs = C2->lhs, C1->op ⊆
                 C2->op; C1->rhs ⊆ C2->rhs }
                 SUB_LIST = UNIFY{C1->rhs ⊆
                 C2->rhs } or
              if { C1->lhs = C2->lhs, C1->op =
                 C2->op; C1->rhs ⊆ C2->rhs }
                 SUB_LIST = UNIFY{C1->rhs ⊆
                 C2->rhs } or
              if { C1->lhs = C2->lhs, C1->op ⊆
                 C2->op; C1->rhs = C2->rhs }
                 SUB_LIST = {}

4.  C1 ≠  C2
```

In each case, if SUB_LIST ≠ {}, then that list must consist of a consistent set of substitutions for each variable. Based on these relationships between clauses, any two rules R_i and R_j are compared as follows:

1. **IF** the right-hand side clause of Ri ≡ right-hand side clause of Rj with a consistent substitution list for unifying all the clauses on their left-hand sides **THEN** Ri and Rj are redundant.

2. **IF** the right-hand side clause of R_i ≡ ~right-hand side clause of R_j with a consistent substitution list for

unifying all the clauses on their left-hand sides **THEN** R_i and R_j are conflicting.

3. **IF** the right-hand side clause of $R_i \equiv$ right-hand side clause of R_j with a consistent substitution list for subsuming R_i's left-hand side clauses with those of R_j **THEN** R_i subsumes R_j.

4. **IF** the right-hand side clause of $R_j \equiv$ right-hand side clause of R_i with a consistent substitution list for subsuming R_j's left-hand side clauses with those of R_i **THEN** R_j subsumes R_i.

The left-hand side of a rule R_i subsumes that of R_j in the following cases:

- All the clauses in the left side of R_i have equivalent clauses in R_j and R_i has at least one more clause than R_j on its left side.
- At least one clause from the left-hand side of R_i subsumes those of R_j and the rest of the clauses from the left-hand side of R_i have equivalent clauses in the left-hand side of R_j.

Consistency checking in KARMA is implemented based on the above ideas. The results from the consistency checking have proven to be very valuable in the knowledge base verification. The output from KARMA consistency checking is shown in Figure 6.

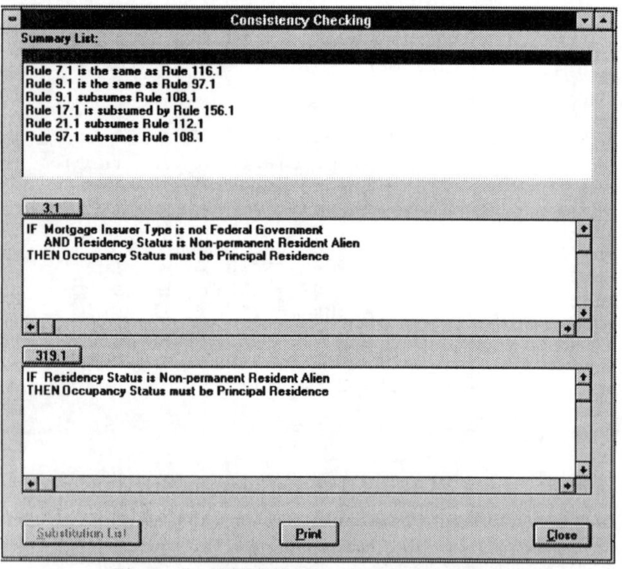

Figure 6. KARMA Consistency Checking

At the top of the Consistency Checking window, the summary results are displayed. The two rules for the selected result are displayed below the summary list.

Code Generation in KARMA. KARMA generates executable ART-IM rules for the Business Rule Server from the business rule representation stored in the Business Rule database. All code which is dependent upon the business rules is generated by KARMA. This means that there is no manual maintenance necessary for any application using the Business Rule Server when business policy changes.

In terms of rule generation, the business rule representation stored in the Business Rule database is the source and the knowledge base rule representation is the target; therefore, rules are generated in the form expected by the knowledge base from the database representation. In the knowledge base, rules are not represented as clauses. Rather, rules are represented as patterns on the left-hand side of the rule and actions on the right-hand side of the rule. In the case of executable business rules for the Business Rule Server, the right-hand side action is to create a violation message representing a policy violation.

The left-hand side patterns are simply conditions which are evaluated against the loan data. If all the conditions of the left-hand side are met, the rule fires and the violation message is created. For the rule:

```
IF    Lien Type is Second Mortgage
THEN  Occupancy Status must be Principal
      Residence
```

a violation of policy occurs when the Lien Type is Second Mortgage, and Occupancy Status is not Principal Residence. Notice that the THEN (right-hand side) clause of the business rule specification representation must be negated in the knowledge base representation when testing for a violation.

The ART-IM representation of the above rule is:

```
(defrule charter:occupancy-status-7-1
 (declare (salience 100 ))
 (schema ?mortgage-loan
    (instance-of mortgage-loan )
    (lien-type  ?lien-type &: (= ?Lien-Type
secondary-mortgage))
    )
 (schema ?property
    (instance-of property )
    (occupancy-status  ?occupancy-status
&:(NOT (= ?Occupancy-Status
             principal-residence)))
        )
  =>
 (generate-violation-message occupancy-
status-7-1)
 )
```

Rules are generated through the use of an intermediate representation (IR). A variant of BNF formalism is used to specify this IR. The variant is achieved by imposing certain restrictions to reduce the complexity of BNF. The use of an intermediate representation provides the flexibility to generate rules in any target language (not just ART-IM rules). Since ART-IM rules are generated through the IR, the knowledge base can be dealt with on a syntactic level allowing the business rules to be abstractly developed based on their knowledge composition rather that their detailed textual structure.

The IR is composed of three types of constructs:

- **Lexical Nodes**

  Lexical Nodes are atomic (they cannot be decomposed). They describe the syntactic elements on a character-by-character basis.

- **Repetition Nodes**

  Repetition Nodes are list nodes which specify one or more occurrences of a node of any type.

- **Construction Nodes**

  Construction Nodes are nodes which are composed of a fixed number of other nodes which may be lexical nodes, repetition nodes, or construction nodes.

The IR is defined using a grammar containing these three types of nodes, as shown in Figure 7. The IR contains the components needed to build the target business rules along with their associated unparsing schemes. Generation of the rules from the intermediate representation to the knowledge base representation is achieved by unparsing the intermediate representation. For example, at the highest level a business rule is specified in the IR as:

```
<eligibility_rule>: "(" <ruleheader> "\n"
<left_side> "\n=>\n" <right_side> ")"
```

So, an eligibility rule is composed of a `<ruleheader>`, a `<left_side>`, and a `<right_side>`. This is a construction node composed of three constructs. The character strings defined within quotes are terminal symbols, the other constructs are non-terminal symbols. During code generation, the strings are emitted before visiting each non-terminal node.

These constructs are defined at the next lowest level as:

```
<ruleheader> : "(defrule" <name>
"/n(salience " <salience>
")/n"
<left_side>: <pattern_list>

<right_side>: "(generate-violation-
message" ")"
```

The `<ruleheader>` is a construction node with two components, `<name>` and `<salience>`. The `<right_side>` is a lexical node. The `<left_side>` is a repetition node composed of several patterns.

The IR is implemented as a set of C++ classes representing the IR nodes. All IR classes are subclasses of the lexical, repetition, and construction node classes. During rule generation, the database representation is used to construct the IR classes. Once the IR classes are constructed, rules are generated by unparsing the IR nodes (Krovvidy & Wee 1988).

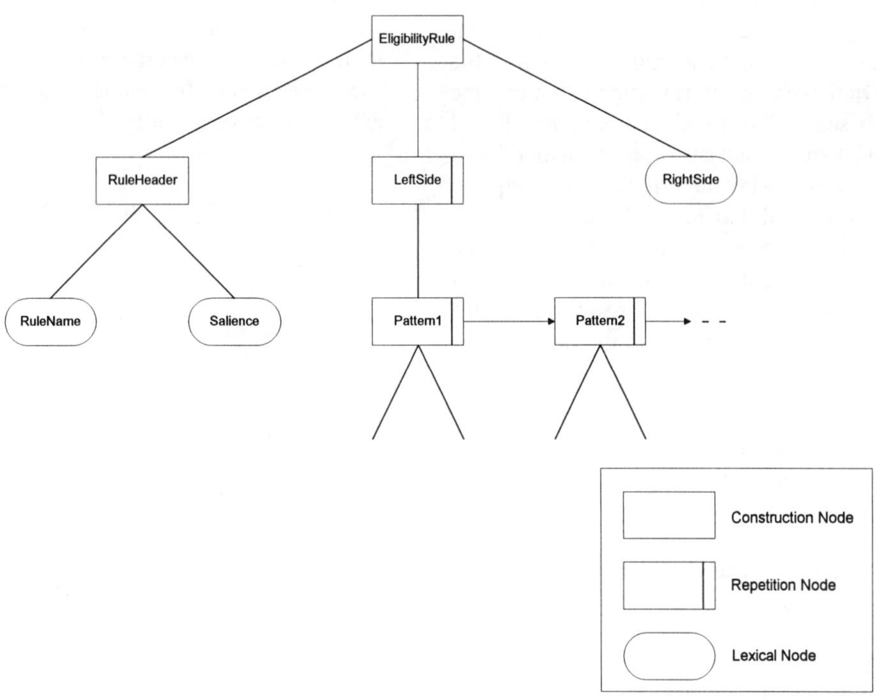

Figure 7. Intermediate Representation for Business Rules

Business Rule Server

The Business Rule Server is a client/server application capable of servicing multiple client applications simultaneously. The Business Rule Server makes Fannie Mae business policy available to applications as a service. Applications no longer need to contain these policies but instead can request access to them as a service from the Business Rule Server. Any application requiring the use of Fannie Mae business policy for compliance checking can send the loan data to the server with a request for loan validation. The server checks the loan for compliance with Fannie Mae policy and returns policy violations to the application. The complete compliance checking takes less than 0.5 seconds including network time.

The Business Rule Server consists of control structures written in ART-IM and C, an RPC based API developed using ONC RPC, executable business rules generated by KARMA, and data translation code generated by the Data Translator (explained in the next section). In order to request the loan validation service from the server, the client application first obtains the loan data to be passed to the server. Since the Business Rule Server only contains Fannie Mae business policy rules, data integrity checking and other system related editing must be performed by the client application before making a request to the Business Rule Server.

The API to the Business Rule Server is provided as a C library to the client application. Loan data is loaded into the data structures using the provided accessor functions and the server is invoked with an API call. Once the server receives the request and data, it translates the client application's source data into the data model defined in the KARMA Data Dictionary database (upon which the business rules are based). This translation is accomplished using the Data Translator. Translated data is mapped into the knowledge base along with the validate loan request. Inside the knowledge base all business rules are evaluated. Violated business rules produce violation messages which are returned to the client in a data structure. The client application can then retrieve violation messages using the provided accessor functions and process those violations.

Data Translator

The Data Translator was developed to enable applications with dissimilar data models to share data with the Business Rule Server, without modifying their data models. The Data Translator allows the Business Rule Server to be independent of data sources. There are many valid reasons why an application may not be able to modify their data model to match the data model upon which a particular set of business rules is based. Using the Data Translator, any application regardless of how its data is represented can request the services of the Business Rule Server. To facilitate a uniform access to the rule server, a translation layer was introduced between the client and the server and a data translation language was developed. This language is used by the client application team to specify the mapping of the data from their data model to the business rules data model. From these specifications, the Data Translator generates the required translation code. The data translation specification language currently supports the following features: object- based data models, conditional statements, assignment statements, multiple instances of objects, date arithmetic and local variables for complex mappings.

Data Translation Language (DTL) is defined using a context-free grammar. A complete set of DTL specifications consist of a source data model, a target data model and one or more translation rules to map the data from the source data model to the target data model. A sample data translation rule is specified as:

```
RefinanceRule
  {IF
    (ANY S-SpecialFeature:SpecialFeatureCode ==
    "refinance")
  THEN T-Mortgage_Loan:Refinance_Option =
    "Yes"};
```

The name of this rule is "RefinanceRule". The prefix S- corresponds to the objects from the source model and T- corresponds to the objects from the target model. This rule specifies that if there is an instance of the object SpecialFeature whose attribute SpecialFeatureCode has a value of "refinance", then the attribute "Refinance_Option" of the target object MortgageLoan is assigned a value of "Yes". These translation rules can include very complex logic. The code generation module of the Data Translator uses the same techniques as the generation of the executable business rules.

Application Development, Deployment and Maintenance

Development

Initially, the Business Rule Server and Rule Editor components of KARMA were prototyped in KBMS, an expert system shell by Trinzic Corporation (which has since been acquired by Platinum Technology). The English-like rule language of KBMS was well suited for business policy rules. At the end of 1993, an in-depth analysis of expert system shells on the market was performed. ART-IM by Inference Corporation (now Brightware) was selected for its powerful pattern matching capabilities and its embeddability. The Business Rule Server was prototyped as an ART-IM knowledge base imbedded in a C application during the first quarter of 1994. Following the prototype, Fannie Mae's Cash

Delivery application was selected as the first client application of the Business Rule Server because it was undergoing a major re-write.

The Cash Delivery application receives loans which Fannie Mae will purchase and hold in their portfolio. During the process of receiving the loans, known as the delivery process, loans are checked for compliance with Fannie Mae policy and contractual obligations. The business rules related to this process are applied by the Business Rule Server. The Cash Delivery application acts as a client application to the Business Rule Server, sending loans to the Business Rule Server for validation.

Knowledge Acquisition for the Cash Delivery application, during which all of the Fannie Mae business rules pertaining to cash delivery were acquired, took approximately six months with two full-time knowledge engineers and significant support of the business experts. During this Knowledge Acquisition phase, development on the Business Rule Server commenced. The Business Rule Server was developed using ART-IM and C under Solaris. The RPC capability was developed using ONC RPC. Development time for the Business Rule Server was approximately 15 months with two developers.

In July of 1994, a three month prototype of KARMA was completed using ART*Enterprise (A*E). Although A*E was valuable for rapid prototyping, the resource requirements and performance problems encountered with the early version used for the prototype prohibited using it for developing KARMA. Furthermore, the A*E rule language was inappropriate for the application, since KARMA is an event driven rather than a data driven system. Since KARMA is a procedural object-oriented application, Microsoft C++ under Windows NT was selected as the development environment for the production version. The Data Translator was also developed in Visual C++ under Windows NT using MKS Lex and YACC. KARMA and the Data Translator were developed by one full-time developer and one part-time developer over an 18 month period.

Deployment

Prior to production implementation, the Business Rule Server was tested by a dedicated testing team. The team consisted of three business users and one technical representative from the Business Rules team. Approximately 2600 test cases were created to test the 400+ business rules in the Business Rule Server. These test cases were carefully hand-crafted to test each business rule and the interdependencies among the business rules. Preparing the test cases took three business analysts two months to complete. Following the preparation of the test cases, three testing cycles were performed in which all cases were executed and all resulting problems were fixed. Testing was conducted over a three month period. During testing, the business analysts began developing a process for managing business rules through KARMA. KARMA introduced a powerful new capability that required new procedures to create a streamlined policy management process that could allow changes that previously had taken months to be implemented in days.

Following this testing, the Business Rule Server was moved to a production environment along with the Cash Delivery application to run in parallel with the old cash delivery application. This parallel production run lasted for approximately four months during which extensive analysis was performed to determine the impact of the Business Rule Server on cash loan purchasing. For example, would the Business Rule Server apply policy more strictly than the old cash delivery system? If so, were these good risk decisions or was the policy implemented too restrictively? Business users were presented an abundance of information about the loans that Fannie Mae was purchasing and specific reasons for those it chose to reject. KARMA and the Business Rule Server have had an important impact by providing business users with timely information combined with the ability to quickly react and adjust constraints to optimize business decision making.

The Cash Delivery application and Business Rule Server have been running in production since July of 1995. KARMA is being used to maintain all business policy related to cash purchasing.

Maintenance

KARMA was designed to enable quick decision-making related to policy. One of its key benefits is the ease with which the business rules can be maintained in the production Business Rule Server. All domain specific code for the Business Rule Server and the client API library is generated by KARMA and the Data Translator. In legacy systems, the turnaround time for implementing new policy frequently takes several months because so many different systems are impacted by a single business change. KARMA has accelerated the process to a maximum of several days for the Cash Delivery application. Business rules can actually be modified and re-generated in minutes; however, the production migration process can take several days. During the parallel production run, eight different rule changes were required and all were implemented in production in under three days. This benefit will be realized over and over again as new client applications use the Business Rule Server. Policy changes will be made in one place and become available to all impacted client applications simultaneously.

KARMA, the Data Translator, and the control structures of the Business Rule Server are maintained by the development team. Currently we are enhancing KARMA by adding more rule management capabilities and extending the rule language to provide additional language features. We are also preparing to support more client applications. As we acquire rules for these new domains, we are finding that many rules already existing in the Business Rule Server will be reused by these client applications.

Application Use and Payoff

The Business Rule Server is currently being used by a single Fannie Mae application, the Cash Delivery application. Use of the Business Rule Server has had an immediate and significant impact by improving the quality of information available to resolve policy issues for loans submitted to Fannie Mae for its Cash Portfolio business. The Business Rule Server has been processing an average of 1000 mortgage loans per day since it was implemented in production. Although the majority of the loans do not generate messages indicating policy violations, a significant portion of the loans do. These loans require special handling to review and resolve these policy violations in order to determine if Fannie Mae will purchase these loans. This review process is tedious and labor-intensive. The quality of the information supplied by the Business Rule Server has significantly aided this review process and is already resulting in reduced operational costs. In the future, use of the information provided by the Business Rule Server is expected to result in additional revenue for Fannie Mae.

In supporting Fannie Mae's Cash Delivery application, the Business Rule Server and KARMA have already provided Fannie Mae with important benefits, but the real payoff will result when other applications begin using these tools. Several strategic applications at Fannie Mae that require the use of policy information are currently preparing to use KARMA and the Business Rule Server. Without KARMA and the Business Rule Server, each application would have to develop and code to do their own policy checking. This code would be embedded in each application and therefore inaccessible to other applications. Policies in all these applications would need to be updated and maintained redundantly. The result would be high maintenance costs, the potential for inconsistent implementations of the same policies, and slower response to changes in the mortgage industry.

The Business Rule Server and KARMA not only eliminate these redundancies, but also provide new development projects with reduced development costs. New projects will require 70-80% less funding to develop the policy component of their application. Most of the costs associated with using KARMA and the Business Rule Server will be dedicated to knowledge acquisition to acquire new rules for the application (if they are not already available in the Business Rule Server). With KARMA and the Business Rule Server, business users can devote their resources to crafting the business policies rather than planning around lengthy implementations.

Lastly, KARMA is providing a powerful long-term benefit by making policy information in the form of business rules clear and unambiguous, easily modifiable and, most importantly, accessible to the business users. Business users can see exactly what business rules are currently implemented by querying KARMA from their desktops. They can also perform "what if" analysis to determine the impact of proposed policy changes as well as trend analysis to review the performance and impact of policies on loans that Fannie Mae has already purchased. The benefits to business users will accelerate as more business rules are acquired and defined in KARMA and new opportunities for using this knowledge emerge.

In summary, Fannie Mae is already finding its competitive position enhanced by using the Business Rule Server and KARMA. Fannie Mae can now respond quickly and efficiently to the changing economic conditions that are so prevalent in the mortgage industry today. Their policies can be easily modified and implemented to keep pace with new product developments and to proactively seek additional investment opportunities.

Acknowledgments

In addition to the authors, many individuals contributed to the successful development and deployment of KARMA and the Business Rule Server. The authors want to extend a special gratitude to Andrew Weiss for his continued support and guidance since the inception of this project. They also want to thank Peter Kopperman for directing this project and Bill Tucker, Brian Pannell and Paula Marlowe for their efforts in testing KARMA and the Business Rule Server. Finally, the authors want to express their thanks to Cathy Doman, Raza Hashim, Greg Close and Pete Silvestre for their ideas and development efforts and Carol Borchardt for providing the domain knowledge.

References

Appleton, D.S. 1988. Second Generation Languages. *Database Programming & Design* February 1988:48-54.

Bynum, S.; Noble, R.; Todd, C.; and Bloom, B. 1995. The GE Compliance Checker: A Generic Tool for Assessing Mortgage Loan Resale Requirements. In Proceedings of the Seventh Innovative Applications of Artificial Intelligence Conference, 29-40. Menlo Park, Calif: American Association for Artificial Intelligence.

Fannie Mae Selling Guide. 1993. Fannie Mae, Washington, DC.

Krovvidy, S., and Wee, W.G. 1988. Retargetable rule generation for expert systems. In Proceedings of the third international symposium on methodologies for intelligent systems, colloquia program 37-46.

Polat, F., and Guvenir, H.A.1993. UVT: A Unification-Based Tool for Knowledge Base Verification. *IEEE Expert* June 1993:69-75.

Talebzadeh, H.; Mandutianu, S.; Winner, C.F.; and Crane, L. 1994. Countrywide Loan Underwriting Expert System. In Proceedings of the Sixth Innovative Applications of Artificial Intelligence Conference, 141-152. Menlo Park, Calif: American Association for Artificial Intelligence.

The SIGNAL Expert System

Rolf Struve

SIGNAL Versicherungen
Joseph-Scherer-Straße 3
D-44121 Dortmund
Germany

Abstract

The SIGNAL insurance companies have developed an expert system for the support of its customer sales service. It was introduced at the end of 1993 and is currently used by approximately 500 customer service representatives. It involves a counseling system, which enables customer sales personnel to produce high-quality benefit analyses at the point of sale. It is not only an information system for the agent but involves the customer in an active role (through the implementation of sales talks, the conscious visualisation of facts, the generation of natural language explanations etc.). Thus, the customer is not faced with a fait accompli but is actively involved in solving the problem. To meet these requirements, several AI techniques are used, as described further below. The application has increased sales efficiency, optimized customer contact time and decreased training requirements. The system is developed with KEE (and reimplemented in Allegro CL/PC) and runs on notebooks with 8 MB RAM.

Introduction

The SIGNAL Insurance Group

The SIGNAL insurance companies with head office in Dortmund (Germany) offer insurance for both private and commercial requirements. Their product range includes a complete range of insurance products for private households (private health, accident and life insurance as well as transport, liability, household and building insurances) and mid-sized enterprises (insurance against work stoppages, environmental and asset damage, as well as industrial and professional liability insurances) whereby the emphasis is on insurance for individuals. In the private health insurance sector, SIGNAL is the fourth largest company on the market in Germany (measured in term of premium revenue, which last year came to DM 1,537 million in this insurance sector).

The SIGNAL insurance group, which was founded in 1907 and arose out of the merger of small, professionally oriented insurance companies, today has over 6,000 employees in its internal and external services and 52 branch offices all over Germany.

The sales agents are mainly group representatives who enjoy contractually agreed brokering exclusivity. The main job of the 3,500-plus customer service staff is the sale of its products (customer counseling, receipt of applications) and customer servicing (aftersales service).

The reaction to rising competition has been a tightening of the organizational structure, the introduction of profit centres, and a consistent customer and target group orientation. Today, this requires customer service personnel to be familiar with all business areas (segments) of the company.

The SIGNAL Agency System

The customer service personnel of the SIGNAL insurance companies is equipped with notebook computers running the 'SIGNAL Agency Package'. The system has two fundamental functions:

- It is an **information system** for customer representa-tives which supplies actual data (on assets, policy offers, deadlines, bill collection) and administers them (updating, selection and printing).
- It is a **reckoner** which allows customer representatives to compute premiums, draft offers etc.

In addition, work processes are supported within an agency, as for instance the invoicing of secondary customer representatives or financial accounting.

The Agency System is a tool for the customer representative. It frees the staff from routine jobs and saves time which can then be used on actual selling. Due to the interface used (character-based, small type size) and the lack of transparency of the system, user utilization is hardly possible and is not intended, in fact.

The SIGNAL Expert System

By contrast, the SIGNAL Expert System is a **counseling system** (used as part of the SIGNAL agency system) which supports the actual selling action at the point of sale while involving the customer in an active role.

Before describing the design of the system, we will by way of preparation explain a few points that are characteristic of insurance selling.

Problem Description

The Selling of Insurance

In contrast to tangible services, insurance is intangible in nature (i.e., it cannot be physically touched). In addition, it does not involve any direct ownership or property changes but covers an initially hypothetical risk.

For the selling of insurance, this means:

- insurance products are not visible and are therefore in need of special explanation (for example by showing the insurance benefits);
- the customer must actively participate in establishing the benefit category (by determining personal demand, through personal evaluation of risks, by taking a risk test);
- in general, the degree of possible standardization is low; the situation of each customer must be treated individually.

To deal with these aspects, which are crucial for the **counseling quality**, the customer service representatives must have a comprehensive knowledge which involves

- the SIGNAL products (in all insurance branches);
- acceptance and advertising guidelines (for example: Which persons may be offered SIGNAL health insurance? Does a waiting period need to be observed?);
- legal regulations (labour law, Insurance Control Law, Insurance Policy Law);
- tax aspects (e.g. what tax advantages does a capital insurance or a spouse's employment contract offer?);
- technical evaluation of a customer's insurance situation (Where do insurance gaps exist? Where should priorities be put?);
- the difference from competitors, which may come from abroad after the introduction of the domestic European market;
- the relationship to the media and to consumer associations
- the holding of sales meetings.

This knowledge must be constantly updated. In 1994 for example, there were considerable changes in the legal regulations in Germany (in social welfare legislation, in the Insurance Control Law and Insurance Policy Law).

Besides counseling quality, which is very knowledge-intensive, **service speed** plays an outstanding role in the selling of insurance. On the one hand, these two are the most urgent wishes of customers as a large number of surveys (Hübner & Selle 1995) has shown. On the other hand, from the view of the sales representatives and insurance companies, too, it is important to close a sale quickly and purposefully (to prevent offers from competitors from being considered and to ensure efficient insurance production).

In concrete terms, this demand means:

- reducing the number of customer visits necessary for making a sale (for the purpose of pension computations, to answer questions from customers, for a qualified benefit analysis etc.);
- correct filling out of application forms (between 20 and 50 percent (depending on the segments and sales channel) of all applications handed out are filled in wrongly or incompletely, possibly requiring queries with the customer; see (Hübner & Selle 1995));
- complete handing out of additional forms (doctor surveys, proof of income etc.);
- stemming the flood of paper (today, the sales kit of a customer representative includes: application forms, forms for doctors, pension record sheets, demand analysis sheets, tax tables, rate schedules, sales manuals, information brochures and specialized documentation).

Application Description

Objective and Conception of the System

To effectively support the sale of insurance in the areas mentioned above, the Board decided to offer a counseling system to its customer representatives in 1989, which enables the quick and efficient drawing up of high-quality benefit analyses at the point of sale.

The system differs in major areas from the traditional agency systems used in the insurance sector. Thus, it is not only a tool for the customer representative (as the conventional rate calculators and agency systems are) but a medium for communication with the customer: it supplies information to him (in which decisive factual situations are pointed out and described clearly and transparently), gives him opportunities for interaction (for the request of explanations, for inputting individual wishes and priorities, to control sequences) and aims at creating attention and interest (through a objective-oriented consultation and a certain entertainment value).

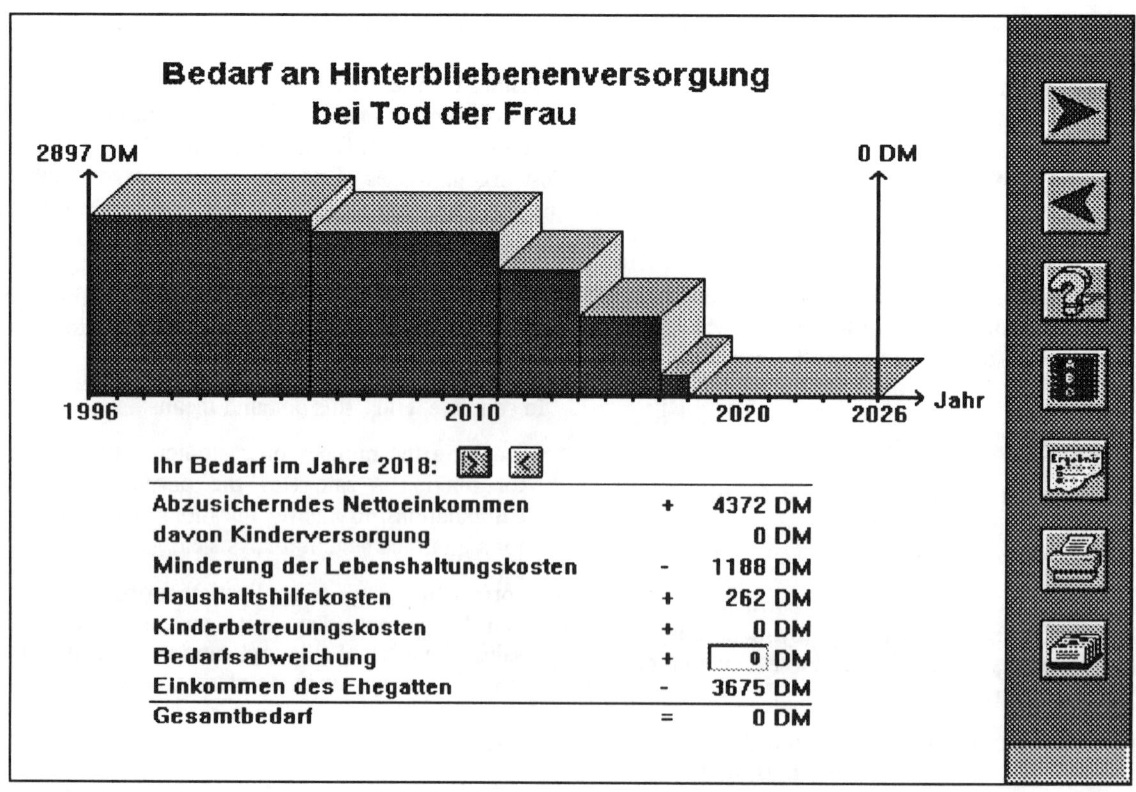

Figure 1: Progress of benefit gaps over time

The objective of using the counseling system is to involve the customer in an active role and to make the product 'insurance' understandable.

Toward this end serves:

- the implementation of a conclusive sales talk,
- the conscious visualization of factual circumstances (for example of progress of benefit gaps over time; Figure 1; Figure 2),
- explanation components in natural language (which may draw on a lexicon of technical insurance terms)
- elaborate problem solving components which allow individual wishes and priorities to be taken into consideration.

Thus, the customer is not faced with a fait accompli but is actively involved in solving the problem. This is important in order to strengthen the customer's readiness to sign.

The second emphasis during the development and the conception of the system is to make the knowhow of experts for sales meetings available on-the-spot. The Section 'The Selling of Insurance' lists the areas in which knowledge-based systems can support customer counseling.

Related Work

Systems to assist marketing were frequently presented in recent years at the IAAI-Conference, e.g. (Talebzadeh Mandutianu & Winner 1995), (Kleinert & Rao 1995) or (Carr et.al. 1994). By comparison to the expert system SIGNAL, these are all information systems for the sales staff, and not counseling systems, which actively include the customer in the use of the system.

Areas of Application

In terms of contents, the system executes a benefit analysis in the area of old-age and survival insurance and for protection from occupational and general disability. All the important aspects such as legal pension insurance, company old-age insurance or private pension are taken into consideration and referenced to the needs of the customer. Possible pension gaps are determined in their progress over time, graphically displayed and mentioned through explanation components using natural language. They may be concluded through a individual offer configuration (which also takes tax aspects and company old-age insurance into account). After a successful conclusion, it is possible to print out an insurance statement.

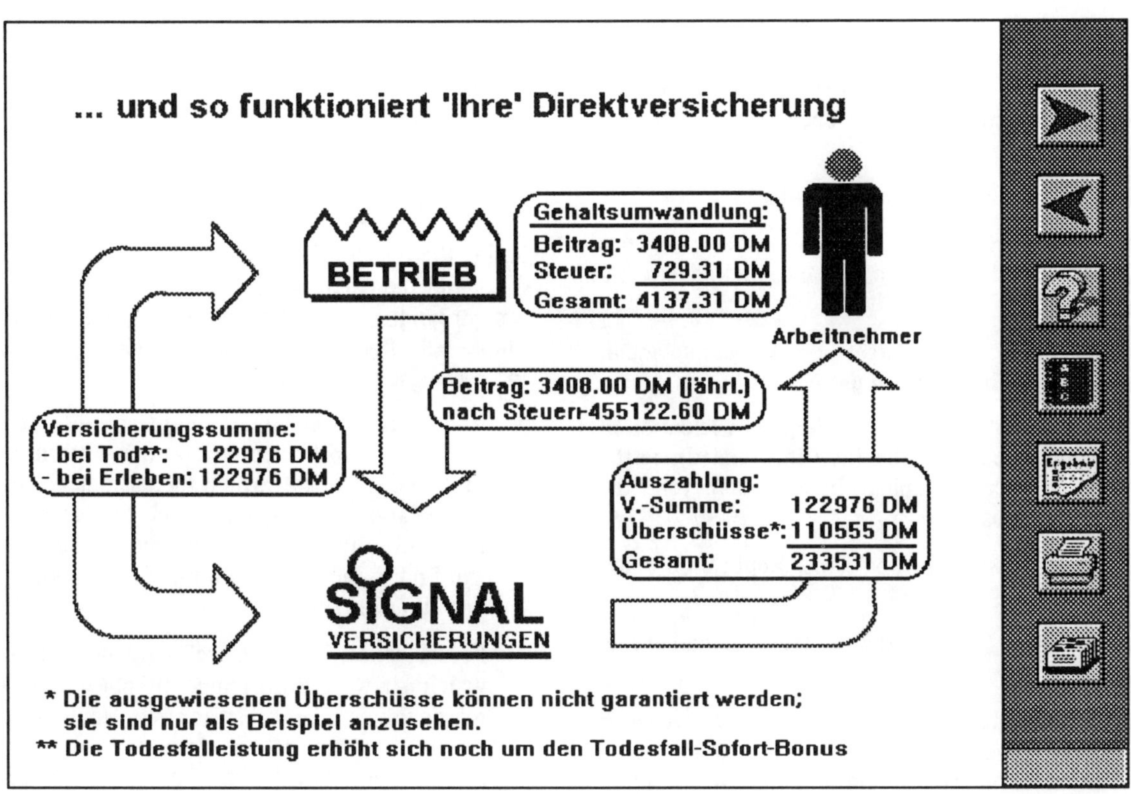

Figure 2: visualisation of insurance products

After completion and the execution of a field test in 1991, the system was supplemented by the requirement profile called 'Insurance in the Event of Illness'. The self-employed or employees can be counselled in price- or requirement-oriented sales talks whereby all relevant questions such as insurance exemption, family insurance or spouse employment contracts are addressed. A comprehensive explanation component supports the customer sales representatives when questions of maternal protection, health insurance in old age or similar are involved.

Architecture

When selecting a development tool for the project (in late 1989), an analysis of tools available on the market showed

that only the KEE expert system tool (from IntelliCorp) met all the demands made by the project. The flexible options of knowledge representation and knowledge processing as well as good graphic capabilities required to use a system in customer counseling with good PR effect, were decisive in opting for KEE.

All other expert system tools (such as ADS or Nexpert Object), which were suitable taking into account the target platforms (notebooks with 8 MB RAM) only had, at that time, very limited capabilities for graphic design and very much weaker forms of knowledge representation. They thus appeared to be less suitable for including the client in the use of the system and adequate modelling of the area of application.

KEE is one of the most advanced object-oriented expert system tools, which are available commercially. KEE is implemented as an extension to Lisp. The kernel of KEE is an object system with a rich functionality. Objects (or 'units' as they are called in KEE) are organized into knowledge bases and grouped into class-subclass-member hierarchies. An object is made up of slots, which represent the attributes of the object and which can store any piece of Lisp code. When new slots are created (or when values of existing slots are changed), these new slots and their values are immediately inherited by all the objects (subclasses and instances) below it. This 'dynamic inheritance' - which distinguishes KEE from other object-oriented tools - allows to update a knowledge base very efficiently. All components of the object system of KEE can be created, accessed, modified or deleted by KEE functions.

Special KEE units are rules, which can be used either forward chaining or backward chaining. You can as well mix forward and backward chaining in a single problem solution.

The object system of KEE allowed us to model the area of application in a natural way. The system has a blackboard architecture with 12 knowledge bases, of varying content, which represent the state-of-the-world or contain rule packages (the problem solving knowledge) or control the sequence with which the customer is given advice.

The first type includes knowledge bases

- on the products and tariffs of SIGNAL (insurance conditions and benefits, acceptance and advertising guidelines)
- on customer data (target group, employment, income and other personal data)
- on the needs of the customer (the family situation in the event of death or disability (time related), on the assets (property, capital investments), on the provision status etc.)
- on offers (cash value of gaps, application data, contract data).

The second type of knowledge bases contain rule packages

- to determine the need in the various insurance cases such as sickness, death or disability; for example this includes rules on determining the costs of living and to determine the expenses that can arise through children (child minding, child care, costs of a house help).
- on preparing offers (rules which lay down the strategies for preparing offers and control the optimization and revision of an offer)

Finally, there are knowledge bases, which control the sequence with which the customer is given advice (which contain strategic knowledge about qualified benefit analyses and requirement-oriented sales talks) and which administer the user interface (generation of forms and explanations, storage of results, etc.).

The application has more than 900 objects at the start of the session and several hundred units are created dynamically. The knowlege bases contain 135 rules.

Beside the object-oriented and rule-based programming styles we used in addition the functional style, which Lisp supports (to implement messages between objects; to define algorithms, which optimize the insurance offer, etc.).

Lisp has a powerful macro facility, which can be used to extend the basic language. We used this facility to implement a screen description language, which automatically generates objects, which represent the different screens, and which connects the input data with corresponding objects of the knowledge bases.

As a result, the knowhow put together by experts and residing in the program code is not implicit and dispersed but explicit and in declarative form, so that the knowledge can be called up in different situations and at different occasions (to generate explanations, to analyze customer situations, to take individual wishes and priorities into account, or for communication with the customer).

Further AI techniques used

Beside the object-oriented and rule-based programming styles and the extensive use of Lisp (which is the most popular language for AI programming) we used (in a simple but effective form) natural language processing and case-based reasoning.

- The system generates explanations (complete sentences with correct noun phrases and grammatical rules), which the customer can clearly understand. The module and the corresponding lexicon is implemented with source code, which you can find in the Lisp literature; e.g. in (Norvig 1992) and (Watson 1991).
- For objection handling we could not use a menu, which shows the customer all objections, he can reasonably make. Instead we implemented an interface, where he can formulate questions in a simple grammatical form. The questions are parsed and match against a database of cases (possible answers).

Performance

An important requirement was to deliver the expert system on notebooks with 8 MB RAM and an acceptable performance at the point of sale. This was a major challenge, because it was worldwide the first KEE application running on notebooks with 8 MB RAM. We met this requirement through a combination of application tuning and engineering work:

- KEE has an object-oriented graphics facility (with predefined classes of graphic primitives such as boxstrings or rectangles) , that makes it easy to craft interfaces from scratch, but which is very expensive in machine space and speed. To reduce this overhead we decided to reimplement the user interface on the basis of Common Windows, a low-level graphics tool built as an extension of Lisp.
- To reduce the overhead of the object-oriented representation of rules, we developed a compiler (written in Lisp), which translates KEE rules into (IF ... THEN ...) expressions of Lisp, and implemented a proper inference engine (from source code, which you can find e.g. in (Watson 1991)).
- We developed a compiler (written in Lisp) which translates the KEE object system (the features we needed; especially the 'dynamic inheritance'

described above) into Lisp data records (structures). The improvements in performance and space saving were considerable.

Application Development and Deployment

Project Development

When selecting a development tool for the project (in late 1989), an analysis of tools available on the market showed that only KEE met all the demands made by the project. The strength of KEE permits quick and practical implementation which is achieved at the expense of performance, though. To run the application on a laptop with 8MB RAM the application tuning and engineering work (described above) had to be done.

After the successful testing of the counseling system (in late 1992) it turned out that costs for software licenses had risen considerably. Another examination was made to determine the possibility of lowering the high investment costs for the introduction of the system. The examination showed that the tools had been available on the market since mid-1992 which permitted a substantially more cost-effective introduction of the system in the sales organization than was possible on the previous basis (development tool: KEE; operating system: Unix).

Allegro CL/PC (from Franz Inc.) was selected as tool for reimplementing the application under the DOS operating system. Thus the costs for UNIX and for the runtime licenses of KEE were eliminated. This was the main reason for reimplementing the system. In addition to this economic aspect, technical data processing reasons also played a part: IntelliCorp ceased to maintain and further develop KEE/PC, since KAPPA/PC became their strategic product on a PC basis; the integration into the SIGNAL agency system was considerably eased by Allegro CL (which runs under DOS).

The SIGNAL expert system was developed from SIGNAL (with two members of the computer division) and Insiders Co. It runs today on notebooks with 8 MB RAM and colour displays, using Windows 3.1 as operating system. It is fully integrated into the SIGNAL agency system (this includes the use of the database and maintenance system, and the use of existing COBOL programs).

The system was introduced to the customer sales service at the end of 1993 and is currently used by approximately 500 customer service representatives. This year, it will be made available to a further 400 agents and executive personnel.

Knowledge Acquisition

As an entry and basis for the project, a seminar on knowledge acquisition by Professor Otto Laske (University of Boston) was attended.

According to Laske, a differentiation is made between different types and areas of knowledge (which require different acquisition methods). A first area for obtaining knowledge was the 'working environment' of the sales staff (their work sequences, communication structures, documents and tools), which were analysed so as to develop a system that could actually be used in practice (which fits to the work processes).

To capture the domain knowledge, a basic delineation was made between competence and performance knowledge (these terms were introduced in the linguistics by (Chomsky 1965)). Competence knowledge is understood to be know-how, as noted down in books and pamphlets, e. g. knowledge about the SIGNAL products, and of legislative regulations. This type of knowledge was acquired in the project by studying documents and bibliography and by interviewing experts.

Competence knowledge can be used in different situations in different ways. The actual use in concrete situations is known as performance knowledge. In this project, this included carrying out qualified benefit analyses and holding associated sales talks. To obtain this knowledge, interviews were held (recorded on tape), role plays were carried out and sales staff were accompanied when they were giving advice to customers.

The most important media for obtaining knowledge was a special type of interview (the ethnographic interview), which had been developed by ethnography "as an explicit methodology designed for finding out both the explicit and tacit knowledge (you cannot talk about or express in direct ways)" (Spradley 1979). The features of the ethnographic interview include more than thirty kinds of ethnographic questions, for example:

- descriptive questions to start the knowledge acquistion and to keep the expert freely talking (e.g. 'grand tour questions' on a typical working day, or on characteristic problems)
- structural questions ("How many different types or possibilities are there?") and contrast questions ("What's the difference between ...?") to get a systematic completion of the domain knowledge.

In addition the ethnographic interview includes several important principles such as

- avoiding questions, which force the experts to give reasons (why questions), which contain a hidden judgemental component;

- the endeavour to make conclusions as to their importance through the use of terms and tools (the principle: Don't ask for meaning, ask for use);
- the repetition of statements by experts through words and formulations of the knowledge engineer (in contrast to normal conversations).

The ethnographic interview, which you can hardly find in any book about knowledge acquisition, proved to be very valuable.

Experience with the Development Tool

As the LISP programming language is not widely used in banking and insurance circles, a short comment on this development tool is in order. As before, LISP is the most important language for knowledge-based systems in the world and the first ANSI-standardized object-oriented language at all. Apart from the object system (CLOS), the design of the interface can also be programmed by an extension of LISP (common graphics) so that a unified syntax is available for the different programming tasks. The flexibility of LISP is well-known (see (Norvig 1992)).

Whilst special hardware for LISP was still being developed at the end of 80's (for example by Texas Instruments with the 'Explorer') and LISP was only available as an interpreted language on many systems, today LISP programs are developed, compiled and used just like any other software. As can easily be appreciated, they can perform just as well as C or C++ application packages of comparable complexity.

Maintenance

To be able to react quickly to changes in the statutory basis and the product range of SIGNAL, the sales staff receive a system update on floppy disk every three months. Since February 1996, the program and data services are also available on-line (ISDN). The necessary maintenance work (which consists in the simplest and most frequent cases of parameter alterations in the basic database) is carried out by the system developers.

Application Use and Payoff

The SIGNAL expert system permits competitive advantages by:

- ensuring high-quality individual counseling (throughout the insurance company)
- shortening process times from customer counseling up to the signing of the policy (by reducing the need for customer visits, through properly filled out application forms etc.)
- a consistent customer orientation by focussing on selected target groups and through the introduction of all-round counseling (instead of a branch-specific orientation)
- use as a training system (increasingly important due to greater product innovation and the present sales personnel turnover)

Conclusions

Lessons learned

The project shows that these advantages can by all means be realized but that more time for this is needed than was imagined by all those involved. The experience, gathered in this connection, shows that:

- It is crucial for the acceptance of the system that it does not replace but supports customer service personnel. Part of this is to ensure that the control and initiative remains with the customer representative and that the choices offered by the system can be changed or overwritten at any time.
- For the development of the system it was not sufficient (as has been suggested by literature on expert systems) that the knowledge of experts is gathered in interviews, case studies, role play etc. and represented by the system. In addition, comprehensive conceptual work was required (How to address the various target groups? What products are to be offered in which situations? How can the interfaces be designed with good PR effect?), which took up a fair amount of time.
- In training sessions it turned out to be important to provide training not of the contents of the program but of the practical application of the system. Next to the technical handling, this involves chiefly integration with the customer visit (When to turn on the laptop? How to place it so that everyone concerned can see the screen without inconvenience? How to hold computer-aided sales sessions?)
- 'Computer-aided selling' (CAS) requires a new selling approach from sales representatives which needs to be trained and tried out. Next to handling the system, a psychological difference to the previous selling practice also enters the picture. The representative no longer knows all the solutions in advance (and thus attempts to sell the matching product) but needs to work out a solution together with the customer and the counseling system

Summary

The expert system technology permits high-quality counseling systems to be drawn up, which are not only information systems for the agent but involve the customer in an active role.

The underlying technology is constantly developing further (which can only be intimated with terms like intelligent agents, help desks, case-based reasoning, neural networks; see (AAAI 1995)). In addition, there will be new possibilities offered by 'mobile computing' and multimedia (which will allow direct integration into the information and decision-making flow inside the company and new forms of advertising and interaction).

Our challenge of the future is to bring the power of these new technologies into harmony with the needs and the limits of our company.

Acknowledgements

We would like to thank the members of the SIGNAL project team, especially Werner Grigo, who is one of the principal developers; and all the sales representatives for their cooperation in knowledge acquisition.; and Dr. Uwe Gill (our development partner from Insiders Co.). We are particularly grateful to the management and Board of SIGNAL for their continued support throughout the entire project.

References

AAAI 1995. Proceedings of the Fourteenth International Joint Conference on Artificial Intelligence 1995. Menlo Park, Calif.: AAAI Press.

Carr, M.; Costello, C.;McDonald, K.; Cherubino D.; and Kemper, P, T. 1994. Embedded AI for Sales-Service Negotiation. In Proceedings of the Sixth Innovative Applications of Artificial Intelligence Conference, 141-152. Menlo Park, Calif.: AAAI Press.

Chomsky, N. 1965. *Aspects of the Theory of Syntax.* Cambridge, Mass.: The MIT Press.

Hübner, U., and Selle, H. 1995. *Die deutsche Versicherungswirtschaft: Strategien zur Zukunftsbewältigung.* Wiebaden: Gabler.

Kleinert, H.; and Rao, R.; 1995. SAMS: Strategic Account Management System. In Proceedings of the Seventh Innovative Applications of Artificial Intelligence Conference, 77-89. Menlo Park, Calif.: AAAI Press.

Laske, O. 1988. A Three-Phase Approach to Building Knowledge-Based Systems. *CCAI* 5 (2): 19-30.

Norvig, P. 1992. *Paradigms of Artificial Intelligence Programming.* Los Altos, Calif.: Morgan Kaufmann.

Spradley, J. P. 1979. *The Ethnographic Interview.* New York: Holt, Rinehart and Winston.

Talebzadeh, H.; Mandutianu, S.; and Winner C. F. 1995. Countrywide Loan-Underwriting Expert System. *AI magazine* 16 (1): 51-64.

Watson, M. 1991. *Common LISP Modules: Artificial Intelligence in the Era of Neural Networks and Chaos Theory.* New York: Springer.

Supporting Performance and Configuration Management of GTE Cellular Networks

Ming Tan, Carol Lafond, Gabriel Jakobson

GTE Laboratories Incorporated
40 Sylvan Road
Waltham, MA 02254
tan@gte.com, clafond@gte.com, gj00@gte.com

Gary Young

GTE Mobilnet
1350 Northmeadows Parkway
Rosewell, GA 30076
gyoung@GTEMC.sprint.com

Abstract

GTE Laboratories, in cooperation with GTE Mobilnet, has developed and deployed PERFFEX (PERFormance Expert), an intelligent system for performance and configuration management of cellular networks. PERFEX assists cellular network performance and radio engineers in the analysis of large volumes of cellular network performance and configuration data. It helps them locate and determine the probable causes of performance problems, and provides intelligent suggestions about how to correct them. The system combines an expert cellular network performance tuning capability with a map-based graphical user interface, data visualization programs, and a set of special cellular engineering tools. PERFEX is in daily use at more than 25 GTE Mobile Switching Centers. Since the first deployment of the system in late 1993, PERFEX has become a major GTE cellular network performance optimization tool.

Introduction

During the last 5–6 years, the number of cellular service customers in the United States has increased by 30% to 40% annually. In order to meet the demand and provide high-quality service at this growth rate, the cellular industry is making huge capital investments to build the required cellular infrastructures. However, this rapid build-up of cellular networks is not sufficient to solve all of the capacity and service quality problems. Cellular networks are extremely complex hardware and software systems. There is a need for constant surveillance, analysis of hundreds of system behavioral parameters, and tuning of tens of network configuration and radio equipment parameters.

Despite the existence of mathematical models of radio wave propagation, the process of configuring and tuning a cellular system remains an area requiring significant experience and experimentation. The task facing the performance engineers is to find an optimum solution in adjusting multiple conflicting characteristics such as coverage, signal strength, number of lost calls, and voice quality. The heuristic nature of the performance tuning process, the lack of precise solutions, and the incomplete and evolving content of the knowledge make cellular network performance analysis and tuning an ideal candidate for application of AI techniques.

PERFEX is an intelligent system for performance and configuration management of GTE cellular networks. PERFEX assists cellular network performance engineers in analyzing large volumes of cellular network performance and configuration data. It helps to locate performance violations, determines the potential causes of the violations, and provides intelligent suggestions about how to correct the occurring performance problems. The system combines expert cellular network performance tuning capability with data, network, and geographic map visualization. We found that data visualization and knowledge-based processing are complementary techniques of managing complex cellular networks. PERFEX is in daily use at more than 25 GTE Mobile Switching Centers (MCS).

Cellular network performance tuning is an integral part of the larger effort of operations support of cellular networks. These efforts include alarm/fault management, call traffic management, capacity planning, RF (radio frequency) propagation modeling, and others. Two systems in this category were described at the previous IAAI Conference: IMPACT (Jakobson, Weissman, and Goyal 1995) and AutoCell (Low et al. 1995). IMPACT is a knowledge-based network event correlation system used for real-time network surveillance and fault management. AutoCell is similar to PERFEX in its collection and display of network status and traffic data, but differs in its objectives and the methods used to implement those objectives. AutoCell collects cellular traffic data and uses heuristics to reassign channels among cells during unexpected high traffic demand or when there are faulty channels. PERFEX collects cellular network traffic and configuration data and uses a neural net to discover performance problems in the network, and then uses rules to generate expert advice on how to fine-tune the system parameters to improve performance.

The paper first introduces the cellular domain and the problems associated with cellular network performance optimization. It then describes the method that we have adopted for performance tuning, the PERFEX system itself, the system development and deployment experience, and the benefits of using PERFEX. It concludes with lessons learned and future enhancements. A more detailed description of the PERFEX approach can be found in (Tan and Lafond 1995, 1996).

Cellular Domain

A cellular network consists of a number of radio base stations, each responsible for covering a geographical service area called a cell. A mobile unit (portable or hand-held) communicates with the base station via a separate duplex voice channel. All base stations are linked by microwave, copper, or fiber transmission facilities to an MSC. The MSC coordinates the operation of the entire system, and serves as a connection point to the public switched telephone network. A set of control (setup) channels are reserved at each base station to help the mobile unit establish and monitor the quality of the voice communication.

Since there are a fixed number of RF frequencies allocated by the FCC (Federal Communications Commission) to cellular companies, there are a limited number of calls that one base station can support simultaneously. In order to provide greater capacity, the RF channels are reused by assigning the same frequencies to nonadjacent cells. Because the location of the base stations may not be evenly spaced (especially in urban areas) and the terrain covered may vary, these reused channels may overlap each other, causing interference or even dropped calls. For example, in order to decrease the interference factor, one can lower the power of the base station radios. However, this in turn reduces the coverage footprint, and the system may lose coverage in some portion of its service area. Therefore, voice quality has to be balanced with the need for coverage and capacity. When resources such as channels and trunks are limited, performance engineers must also take traffic patterns into consideration in order to optimize the distribution of these resources. These can be done only with a great deal of knowledge and expertise by adjusting system parameters at the cell sites.

As the cellular traffic grows and new cell sites are added or sectorized, adjustments must be made to neighboring sites, and the affected sites must be monitored for performance quality and tuned accordingly. For instance, a moving mobile unit's call should be handed over from one base station to another without dropping the call or losing the quality of the call. The candidate base stations for handoff are stored in a neighbor list. Performance tuning in this case involves updating neighbor lists and handoff thresholds so that calls are handed off smoothly between existing and new sites.

For these reasons, performance engineers continuously examine a large number of performance reports, check detailed handoff patterns, record power level measurements, and examine call processing failure messages to decide if there are problems in the network and how to solve them.

Problem Description

Monitoring system performance and tuning configuration parameters is a challenging task for most performance engineers. There are four major problems associated with the task: system dimension, incomplete knowledge, inter-dependency of parameters, and delayed feedback.

Practically, the system dimension problem translates into a data problem. There is a huge amount of data that performance engineers have to follow and understand. For example, a medium-size cellular network contains about 80–120 cell sites with about 200–300 antenna faces. It generates hourly more than one hundred peg counts of data per face. This data, combined with other peg counts of trunk and switch data, produces a constant flow of information which is very hard to follow and interpret. Consequently, it is not uncommon for network performance and radio field personnel to be unable to fine-tune the system in a timely manner.

The incomplete knowledge problem is due to the fact that cellular network performance optimization is a young and evolving domain. The performance data analysis and performance tuning knowledge is an evolving collection of heuristic rules, rules of thumb, and solutions often based on the intuition of performance engineers. Existing analytical relationships between the quality of service, such as the percentage of blocked calls, the system capacity, and signal strengths are sensitive to specific geographic, demographic, terrain, and other "nonanalytical" conditions. As a result, performance engineers often change system parameters on a "trial and error" basis.

Many configuration parameters are interdependent and have certain domain-specific constraints. Because of errors, ignorance, or improper use of tuning procedures, the performance engineers may fail to maintain these interdependencies and constraints. Yet, manual discovery of incorrectly set configuration parameters is a time-consuming task. This poses a serious threat to the system performance.

The delayed feedback problem is related to the fact that the cellular network, from the standpoint of performance tuning, is a "slow" system." The effects of the application of performance tuning actions may become apparent only after analyzing several hours of performance data. Therefore, incorrect tuning actions may have a long-lasting adverse effect on system performance before they can be discovered.

Performance Tuning Method

To address the problems mentioned above, PERFEX mimics the way a human expert performs the network performance tuning task. It also automates data preprocessing and configuration checking (see Figure 1).

Initially, hundreds of performance data counts describing the functioning of all cells, faces, links, and the different call processing components of the cellular switch are collected hourly and used to calculate a limited number, usually 20–25, of performance indicators. The performance indicators give an aggregated and quantifiable view of the state of the cellular network. Performance violations, such as call processing failures, incomplete handoffs, and blocked calls, are determined by comparing the performance indicators against performance quality thresholds. The performance quality thresholds, such as "the number of blocked calls should be less than two percent," can be changed by performance engineers.

After determining the performance violations, human experts typically examine all of the violations at one cell site and identify a problem category. The mapping from violations to problem categories varies depending on the cellular network configuration, the surrounding terrain, the nature of calling patterns, and other factors. PERFEX emulates this expert behavior by using neural networks. It identifies problem categories by using the trained neural network that maps multiple violations to categories. Currently, there are five problem categories: Interference, Coverage, Parameters, Resources, and Hardware. Each training case for the neural network contains a set of the values of violations and its associated problem categories. The training cases come from two sources: (1) expert-labeled specialized cases and (2) generic cases collected from field. For the expert-labeled cases, the problem categories are determined by the experts who take into account some nonquantifiable knowledge. The problem categories for the field collected cases are determined by

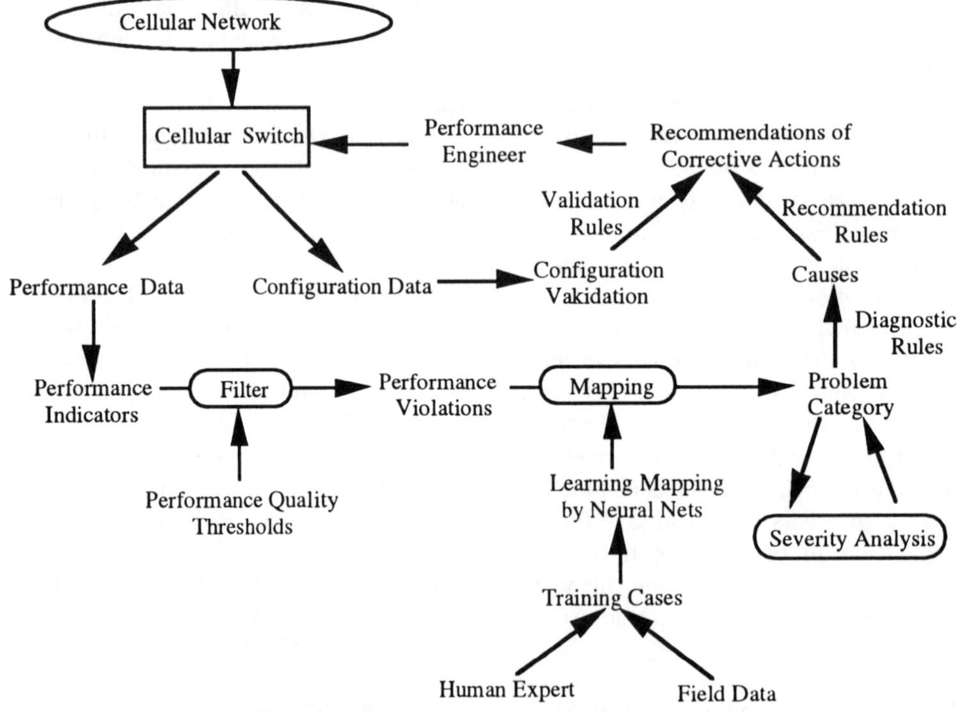

Figure 1. Performance Tuning Model

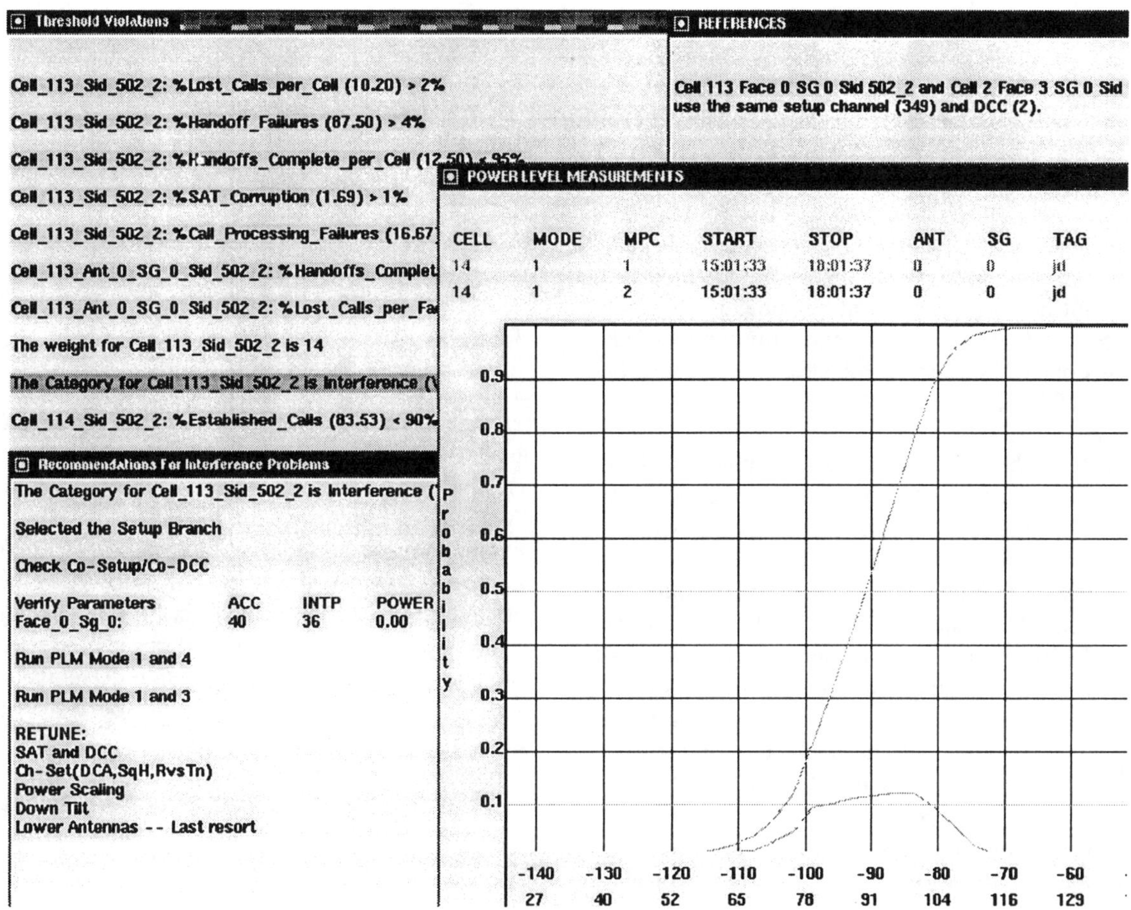

Figure 2. Multiple Violation Performance Tuning

using generic heuristics provided by human experts, which exclude any nonquantifiable knowledge. When running the neural network on new field cases, the correctness is about 90%, as judged against the generic heuristics. Results may be improved if the experts judge the correctness. The next step should be to add more specialized cases to the training set.

After the problem categories have been identified, a problem severity analysis is conducted to identify the cells with the most critical problems. For each cell and its corresponding problem category, PERFEX executes the corresponding diagnostic rules to further identify the causes. These rules can check additional performance data, scrub configuration data, verify handoff patterns, or execute special engineering tools to further analyze the problem. Finally, for the probable causes identified, PERFEX makes recommendations of corrective actions using recommendation rules. Examples of corrective actions include modifying dynamic power control parameters, reassigning handoff neighbors, scaling antenna power, down tilting the antenna, and adjusting access parameters. After corrective actions have been taken, the performance data must be closely monitored to recognize new problems and possible side effects of the actions.

Figure 2 illustrates the performance tuning process of PERFEX. The Threshold Violations window displays a list of violations associated with cell 113. Cell 113, with the highest calculated weight of 14 for the severity of violations, is ordered first. The predicted problem category for cell 113 is Interference. The Recommendations window displays several suggestions on how to fix the Interference problem:

- Check Co-Setup/Co-DCC
- Verify Parameters ACC (Access Threshold), etc.
- Run PLM (Power Level Measurements)
- Retune SAT (Supervisory Audio Tone), etc.

For example, the first recommendation suggests checking whether there are cells which have the same setup channel and digital color code (DCC) as cell 113 and whose signal strength is strong enough to interfere with cell 113. PERFEX finds that cell 2 meets those criteria and displays it on the References window. Therefore, either the setup channel or the digital color code of cell 113 should be modified to reduce the interference. The Power Level Measurement window shows the results of power level measurements performed as the second recommendation.

In parallel to the above-described main performance tuning loop, the network configuration data is collected daily and validated against incompleteness and inconsistency through a library of configuration scrub routines. The routines also flag configuration assignments that can potentially cause interference. The above performance tuning example actually calls one of those scrub routines to find a specific Co-Setup/Co-DCC offender.

It was clear from the beginning that traditional procedural approaches alone were insufficient to solve the problems facing the performance engineers. The mapping between performance problems and tuning recommendations is a nontrivial task of multiparameter optimization. No analytical methods existed to describe it. Initially we thought that PERFEX could be implemented exclusively as an expert system with tuning knowledge encoded as rules. As the system evolved, we realized that collecting cases for dynamic matching from performance violations to problem categories would be easier to update, and the lack of complete knowledge of how to map from multiple violations to problem categories could be compensated for by introducing a neural-net-based classification algorithm. On the other hand, the mapping from problem categories to recommendations is relatively static and has a standard procedure to follow. This knowledge is encoded as rules.

System Description

As a central process in PERFEX, performance tuning is supported by a variety of tools grouped into the following categories: Cellular Engineering Tools, Customization Tools, and Visualization Tools (see Figure 3).

Cellular Engineering Tools are used to examine the network in finer detail. They include PLM Graph, which displays histograms of the power levels measured from selected frequencies; Interference Measurement, which gives a quick estimate of the interference experienced by a certain mobile from multiple frequencies; Handoff Matrix, which displays all of the handoffs occurring between a selected set of cells and antennas; Call Processing Failure, which displays individual call failures in greater detail; and Configuration Scrub, which is used to detect the constraint and interdependency violations between multiple configuration parameters.

Typically, a user will run the performance tuning module on the most recent performance data and look at the cells with the most critical problems in the network. Sometimes

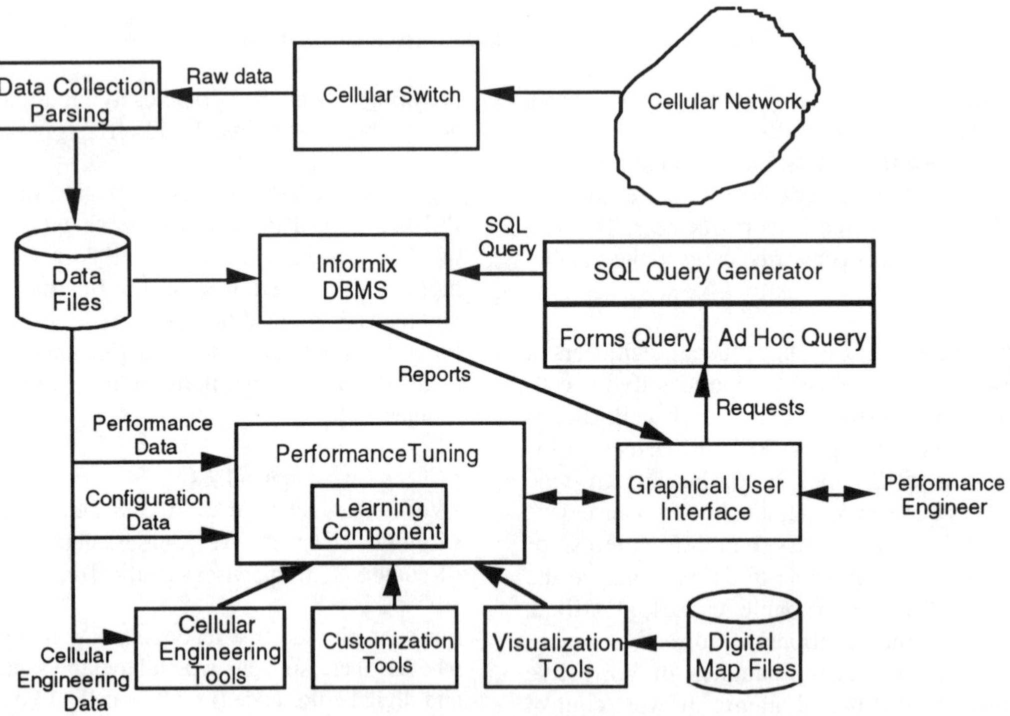

Figure 3. PERFEX Architecture

the advice includes a suggestion to run one of the Cellular Engineering Tools to get more corroborating evidence or to eliminate a possible cause. For example, the call processing failure tool can be used to isolate faulty radios at a specific cell site.

Customization Tools are used to adapt PERFEX for different regional installations and equipment. PERFEX provides domain specific editors to update cell site antenna and location information, and to modify thresholds for configuration data scrubs and performance calculations. The performance engineers can create their own performance reports, tables, and graphs with an easy graphical database interface. This interface includes a graphical query builder for ad hoc queries and a forms query interface for specializing previously defined ad hoc queries.

Visualization Tools are used to graph performance data, visualize data patterns, and picture cell sites overlaid on geographic maps. The PERFEX user interface contains a map of the cellular region with a graphical representation of each cell's antenna faces and server groups. Users can access historical data as well as the current day's data displayed as tables or graphs. A performance data trending graph allows users to examine the change of data over a period of time such as days, weeks, months, or years.

During the performance tuning process, a user can examine the individual performance counts supporting the conclusions, or bring up a trending graph to check for the duration and severity of the problem. Also a display of actual call handoff data patterns on the map can be used to update the neighbor lists of the problem cell. Figure 4 illustrates visualization of the handoff percentage data between a selected face (colored red on a color-monitor) and neighboring faces (colored yellow). The simultaneous display of a cellular network and color-coded patterns of network data help users to recognize performance and configuration problems.

PERFEX tools can also be used independently of the performance tuning process. For instance, they can be used to generate and print hardcopy reports for management, or create maps and tables for performance engineers for road testing the network.

A distinctive feature of the PERFEX design is the tight integration between its different information presentation forms, such as the map, tools, graphs, reports, and cell sites. Tight integration creates a uniform information space so users can easily navigate through the interface from one information presentation form to another.

All data in PERFEX is automatically collected, parsed, and stored in a uniform format so the most recent data, as well as the data from the previous days, weeks, or months, is available to the user and to all functional modules of the system. This dramatically reduces the time and knowledge required to manually gather this information from the switch.

Development, Deployment, and Maintenance

Development Schedule

Initial development of the PERFEX concept began in November 1992, and a proof of concept demonstration system was conceived by July 1993. During 1993, extensive knowledge acquisition sessions were conducted to collect and formalize performance tuning rules. By the end of the year, the first prototype system was completed, and in March 1994, PERFEX 1.0 was deployed for testing and evaluation in two GTE cellular markets. The prototype was well received by performance engineers. Several functional enhancements were suggested by the users, including additional data scrubs, cellular engineering tools, tools for performance trend analysis, and editors to customize the system violation thresholds, configuration, and data parsing routines. All changes were included in PERFEX 2.4, which was released by the end of 1994. By the middle of 1995, the system was operational at 12 GTE MSCs. In September 1995, a high-performance PERFEX system 2.9 was released, which significantly reduced raw performance data processing time. By the end of 1995, PERFEX 2.9 was installed at 25 centers, which covers the majority of GTE cellular service areas.

Implementation

The system is mainly written in Tcl/Tk (Ousterhout 1994), including the GUI, data processing routines, and some data visualization routines. Computationally intensive and time-critical components such as raw data parsers and digital map data processing routines are written in C. The database management system is Informix. The graphical query builder was initially developed by GTE Telecommunication Services, Inc., and modified by GTE Laboratories for PERFEX. PERFEX uses the Xerion Neural Network Simulator Version 3.1 (Van Camp 1993) for its neural network training and test. This simulator is also implemented in Tcl/Tk. The training cases and thresholds are stored in files, while recommendation rules are embedded in code. Training cases from the field are automatically generated, while the expert cases have to be collected by developers. The map information system uses U.S. Census Bureau data for generating geographic maps. PERFEX runs on a variety of UNIX platforms, including

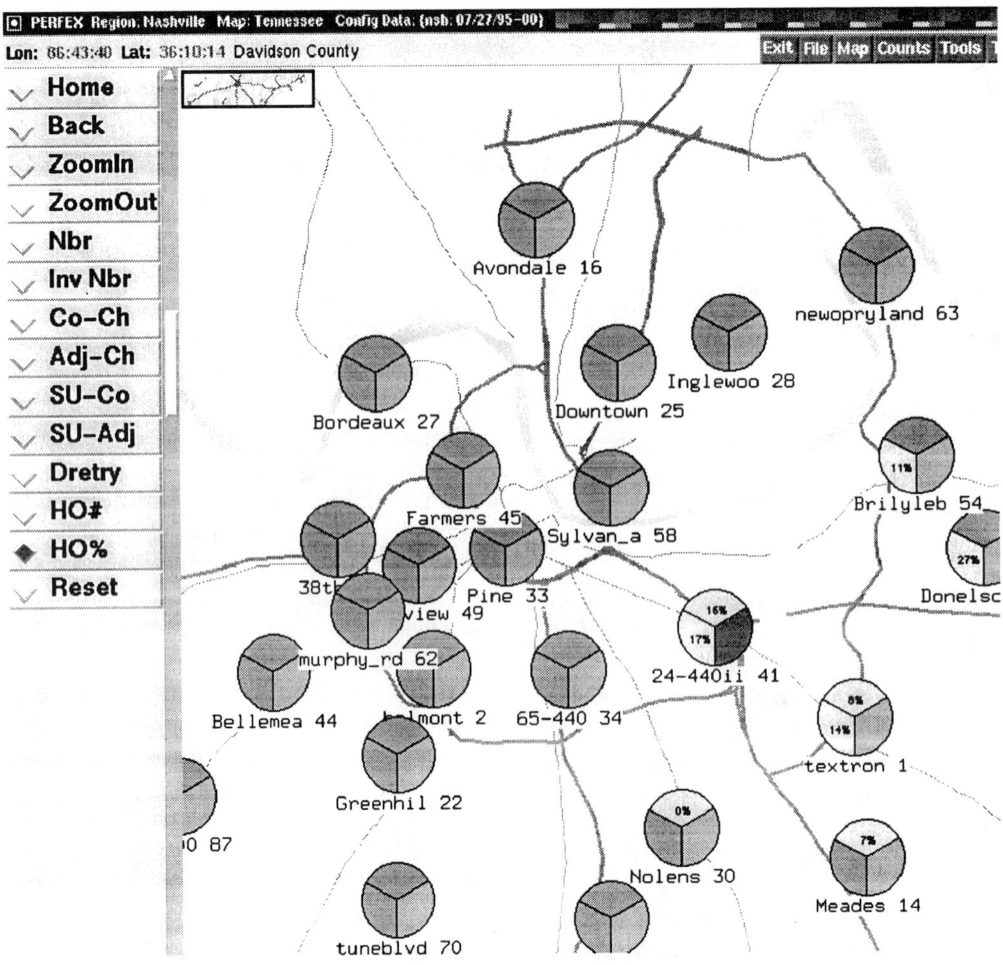

Figure 4. Display of Handoff Percentage Patterns

SUN, SGI, and Data General. The size of the code, including both Tcl/Tk and C, is about 90,000 lines.

Development Effort and Cost

At different stages of the project, 3–4 technical staff members from GTE Laboratories and 4–5 performance engineers from various GTE Mobilnet mobile switching centers took part in the system specification, knowledge acquisition, development, and deployment. The total project cost (including, hardware, software, and development) for the three-year effort was calculated at approximately $1.35M.

Maintenance

PERFEX is maintained by technical personnel from a GTE Mobilnet central office. This includes the tasks of maintaining the code, reporting bugs, installing new system releases, setting up data collection environments, and configuring hardware and software. PERFEX was designed to be easily maintainable. It accommodates changes in network configuration and tuning knowledge via format files and smart editors. GTE Laboratories is responsible for bug fixes and system enhancements. User training is currently provided by GTE Laboratories; in the near future, however, training will be provided by the GTE Mobilnet central office. So far, about 40 engineers have been trained to use the system.

Payoff

The five-year financial projection for PERFEX's payoff, a reflection of cost savings and revenue generation, totals over $12 million. The economic significance of PERFEX is a direct result of the technological benefits of PERFEX over the existing methods of cellular network configuration and performance management. The potential for increased revenues is derived from improved cellular system performance, increased customer base, and reduced customer turnover. The direct cost savings potential of PERFEX derives from several different sources: replacement of currently used third-party software, reductions in capital investment and user training, and reduced operational headcount. For the development and deployment of innovative technical solutions in support of GTE cellular services and for the cost savings and revenue generation, the PERFEX team won the highest GTE technical achievement award in 1995.

Lessons Learned and Future Enhancements

Initially, we underestimated the efforts needed to develop data collection, preprocessing, and other support functions needed in PERFEX. It gradually became apparent that many other components, such as cellular engineering tools, graphics, and DBMS-based reporting, would be necessary for the success of performance tuning. Particularly, the visual information presentation tools played an important role in creating the network management information space. Visualization significantly enhances the way performance engineers understand network configuration, recognize potential problems from performance data patterns, and undertake performance tuning actions. The tight seamless integration of different components was critical for our task because these components would not be used by performance engineers if access was inconvenient or required a separate process.

Future changes to the cellular networks include the addition of digital technology and the introduction of a different class of cellular switches. Both of these changes will require modifications to data formats, data interpretation, and network performance tuning and configuration knowledge.

Acknowledgments

We thank Cecil Glass, Mike Nail, Terry Dyson, and Chris Crowder from GTE Mobilnet for their contributions during the knowledge acquisition sessions, and the many GTE Mobilnet performance engineers for their feedback on PERFEX. Our thanks also go to Mark Weissman and Alan Lemmon for developing the map information system used in PERFEX. Finally, we thank our technical manager, Dr. Shri Goyal, for continuous support of this project.

References

Jakobson, G., Weissman, M., and Goyal, S. 1995. IMPACT: Development and Deployment Experience of Network Event Correlation Applications. In Proceedings of the 7th Innovative Applications of Artificial Intelligence Conference, 70–76, Montreal, Quebec.

Low, C., Tan, Y., Choo, S., Lau, S., and Tay, S. 1995. AutoCell — An Intelligent Cellular Mobile Network Management System. In Proceedings of the 7th Innovative Applications of Artificial Intelligence Conference, 114–124, Montreal, Quebec.

Ousterhout, J. 1994. *Tcl and the Tk Toolkit*. Reading, Mass.: Addison–Wesley.

Tan, M., and Lafond, C. 1995. PERFEX: An Intelligent Performance Tuning System for Cellular Networks. In Proceedings of the 7th International Conference on Wireless Communications, 299–307, Calgary, Canada.

Tan, M., and Lafond, C. 1996. PERFEX: A Cellular Performance Support Expert. In Proceedings of the 3rd World Congress on Expert Systems, 413–420, Seoul, Korea.

Van Camp, D. 1993. A Users Guide for the Xerion Neural Network Simulator, Department of Computer Science, University of Toronto.

Monitoring Frog Communities: An Application of Machine Learning

Andrew Taylor
Computer Science and Engineering
University of New South Wales
andrewt@cse.unsw.edu.au

Graeme Watson
Zoology
University of Melbourne
Graeme_Watson@muwayf.unimelb.edu.au

Gordon Grigg and **Hamish McCallum**
Zoology, University of Queensland
{ggrigg,HMccallum}@zoology.uq.edu.au

Abstract

Automatic recognition of animal vocalisations would be a valuable tool for a variety of biological research and environmental monitoring applications . We report the development of a software system which can recognise the vocalisations of 22 species of frogs which occur in an area of northern Australia. This software system will be used in unattended operation to monitor the effect on frog populations of the introduced Cane Toad.

The system is based around classification of local peaks in the spectrogram of the audio signal using Quinlan's machine learning system, C4.5 (Quinlan 1993). Unreliable identifications of peaks are aggregated together using a hierarchical structure of segments based on the typical temporal vocalisation species' patterns. This produces robust system performance.

Problem Description

Since the unfortunate introduction of the Cane Toad (*Bufo marinus*) to Australia, its abundance and continuing spread through northern Australia have been the cause of considerable concern. It is a voracious predator taking a wide range of prey. Cane Toads also possess poison glands which can kill unwary animals which attempt to prey on them. Although there is great public alarm at the effect Cane Toads are having or will have on Australia's native fauna, there is actually no conclusive data available establishing a detrimental effect on the population of a native species.

The reason is that censusing populations of most of Australia's native fauna is a difficult and expensive undertaking. Biologists have been unable to collect sufficient suitable data to properly address the question of the Cane Toad's impact on native fauna. This is very unfortunate as its make it difficult to determine the appropriateness, size and nature of efforts to control the Cane Toad.

The censusing of animals which make frequent distinctive vocalisations is more tractable but it is still expensive and time consuming. Australia's species of native frogs are one of the groups most likely to be affected by Cane Toads and can be aurally censused. However there are a number of problems with such an approach.

The most desirable study location is an area in front of the the advancing Cane Toads, allowing frog population censuses to be obtained before and after the Cane Toad's arrival. Unfortunately the main Cane Toad front is currently in a remote area of Australia's Northern Territory. This is an area whose weather is dominated by a wet season of monsoonal rains. Most of the frog species of the area are only active during this wet season so censuses must be conducted during this time.

Field work during the wet season is difficult as roads are often impassable and extreme heat and humidity is combined with intense irregular storms. The activity of most species is irregular, depending primarily on rainfall. Some species are active only during particular parts of the wet season. As a result short field trips to these areas are not a reliable method of censusing the frog populations. Continuous manual censusing through the wet season is not feasible so we have developed automatic methods which will be used to census frog populations at a number of sites through the wet season.

There are 22 frog species present in our study area. Their vocalisations range in length from less than 20 milliseconds to over a second. An example of the spectrogram of the vocalisation of a single frog can be seen in Figure 1.

Some species repeat their vocalisations incessantly, other species usually make only occasional isolated vocalisations. Many of the species tend to call in choruses with hundreds of individuals from a number of species present. There is also considerable background noise from insects, some species of which have vocalisations somewhat similar to some frog species.

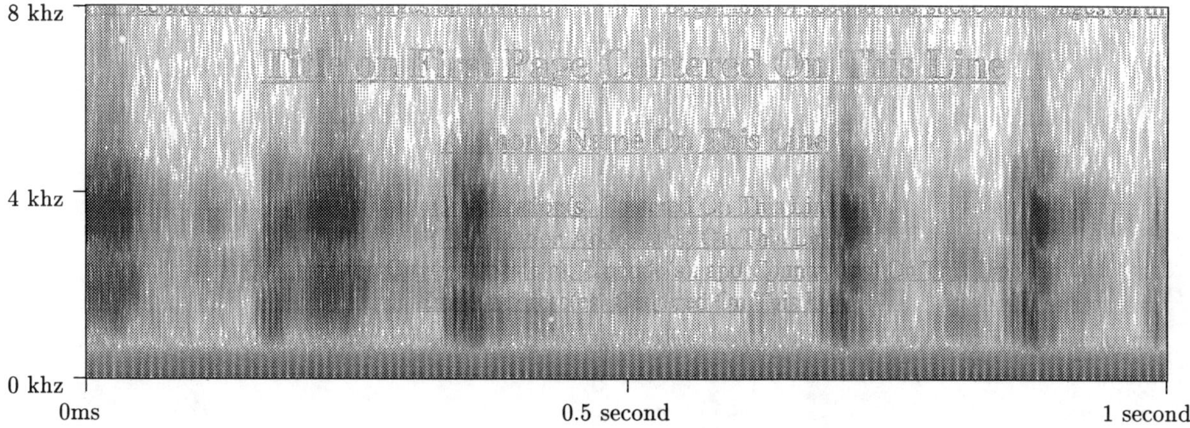

Figure 1: Spectrogram of a *Litoria nasuta* individual

Rain is another source of background noise which can not be ignored as some frog species call primarily during rain. An example of the spectrogram of a frog chorus recorded at our study site can be seen in Figure 2. The vocalisations of at least 11 individuals of 6 species of frog are apparent in this one second spectrogram. There is also noise from at least 3 species of insects present in the spectrogra. Figure 3 contains the spectrogram of a chorus with a similar species composition to Figure 2 but with a much larger number of individuals calling.

Most of the frog vocalisations function as an advertisement to other members of the same species and hence have evolved to be species-specific. Experiments on other frog species have shown a variety of properties can be used by frog species to recognise the vocalisations of their own species (Gerhardt 1988). These include call rate, call duration, amplitude-time envelope, waveform periodicity, pulse-repetition rate, frequency modulation, frequency and spectral patterns.

The vocalisations of some species have stereotypical properties which are apparently not used by members of that species for recognition (Gerhardt 1988). Little is known in these respects of the frog species in our study area. In any case the properties suitable for the wetware of a frog's hearing system and brains may not be the the best properties for our software and audio hardware.

Application Description

Automatic recognition of animal vocalisations would be valuable for a variety of biological research and environmental monitoring applications but it is an area which has seen little work and only preliminary results produced (Mills 1995), (Fristrup & Watkins 1995), (Taylor 1995).

One animal is an exception. There is a huge body of work devoted to distinguishing the complex vocalisations of *Homo sapiens.* This is usually termed speech recognition.

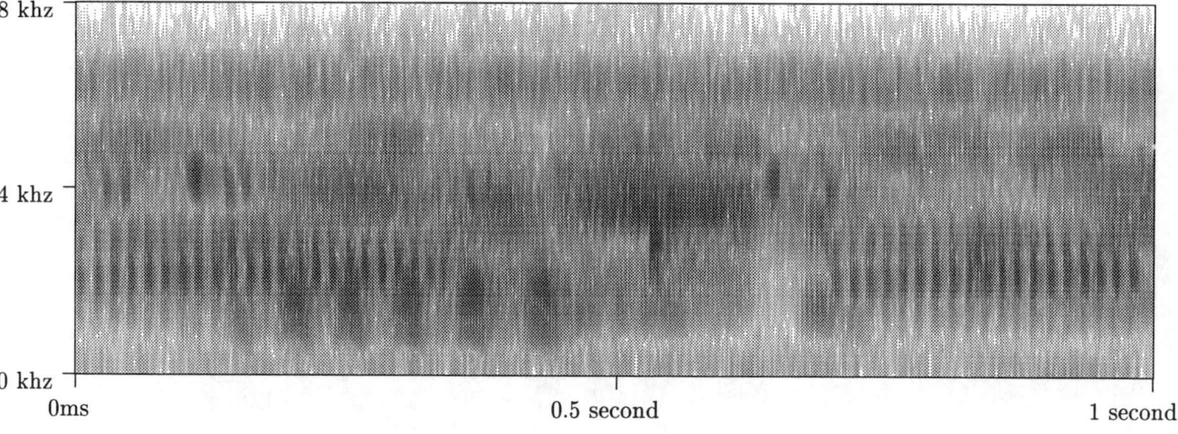

Figure 2: Spectrogram of a Frog Chrous

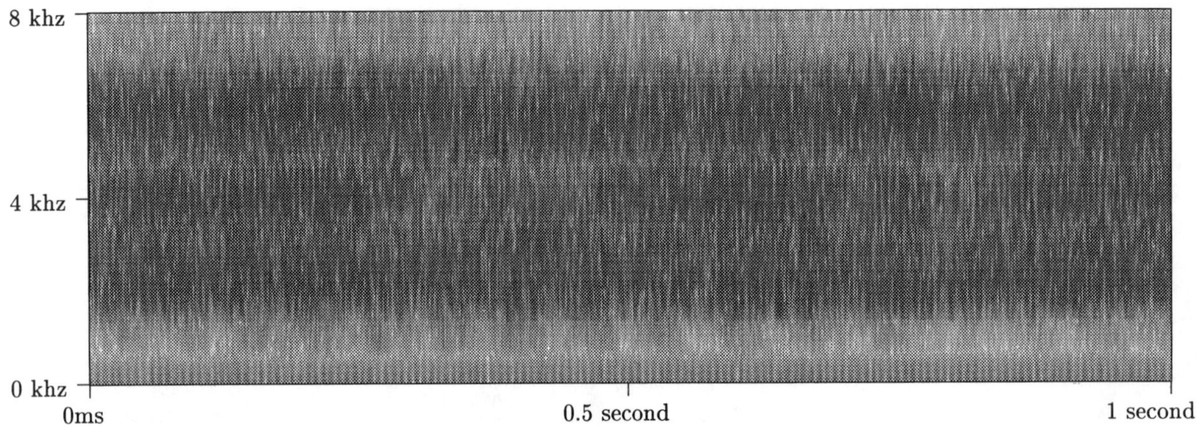

Figure 3: Spectrogram of a Frog Chorus

The frog vocalisations we wish to recognise are much simpler than those of humans. Their recognition would be an easy problem if it was conducted under similar conditions to that of most successfully deployed speech recognition systems: a single cooperative individual close to the microphone in a quiet environment (Deller, Proakis & Hansen 1993).

None of these conditions are met in our problem domain. Instead we must recognise simpler vocalisations but under much more difficult conditions.

Attributes

This has led us to adopt a different and simpler approach to that typically employed in speech recognition. Our system makes no attempt to segment or isolate individual vocalisations. It works entirely from the spectrogram of the incoming audio signal. A Fast Fourier Transform is used to produce a spectrogram of the signal with time-frequency pixels which are roughly 1 millisecond by 50 hertz.

Each time slice of the spectrogram is examined for pixels which contain more energy than any nearby (in frequency) pixels in the same time slice. There may be zero or more local peaks in a single time slice. If there are also local peaks at similar frequencies in several preceding and succeeding time slices then it is assumed the peak is part of a vocalisation and it is passed to the next stage of the system to be individually classified. Figure 4 contains a call with the local peaks marked.

Our system will examine each of the 40 local peaks in Figure 4 individually and classify it as belonging to a particular species. Information from the spectrogram surrounding the peak is used to constrcut attributes for classification. The information used includes the frequency of the peak, the relative frequency of nearby peaks in preceding and succeeding time slices and the relative height of pixels nearby in the same time slice and in preceding and succeeding time slices. There are a great number of way attributes might be constructed from this information.

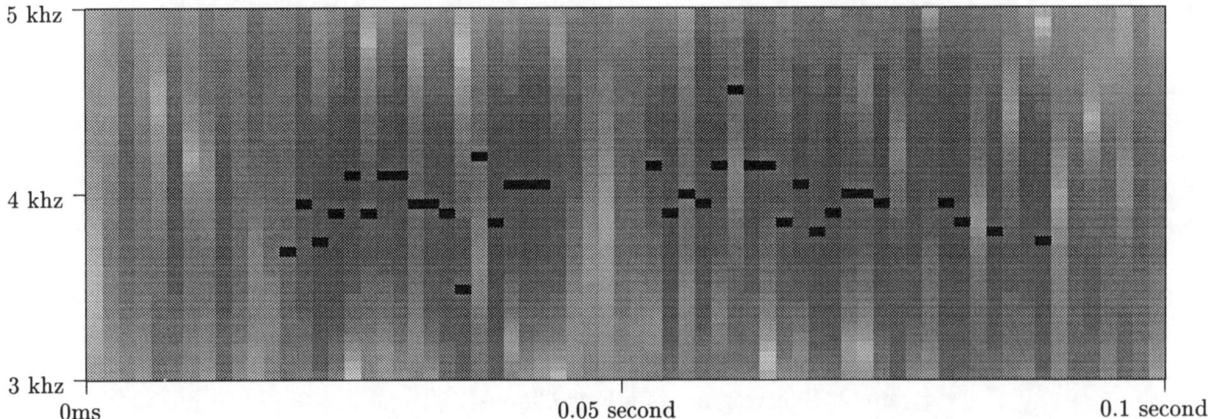

Figure 4: Local peaks of a *Litroia inermis* Call

During development we constructed a set of approximately 70 possible attributes and used a greedy search similar to what (John, Kohavi & Pfleger 1994) term *forward selection* to choose a subset of 15 of the attributes for the system to employ.

Training

Quinlan's machine learning system, C4.5 (Quinlan 1993), is used to construct the classifier. C4.5 is supervised learning system which, given a set of classified cases and a number of attributes for each case as training data, produces a decision tree to classify further cases. The training data for C4.5 was extracted from vocalisations of each of the 22 species in our study areas. These vocalisations were high quality recordings of single individuals. These had been gathered in previous biological research and were not from our study area. A number of vocalisations were selected manually from each recording for use in training. This ensured only vocalisations from the required species were present in each piece of raining data. These vocalisations totalled 5 to 20 seconds of sound for each species.

We also introduced as training data sounds from cricket species which occur in our study area. These have similar qualities to frog vocalisations and their explicit classifcation improved system performance.

The decision tree produced by C4.5 has approximately 5000 nodes. Here is a small fragment of the tree.

```
vert2 <= 18:
|   freq-4 <= -8: Uperoleia lithomoda
|   freq-4 > -8:
|   |   verta+vertb-vert <= 7: Litoria bicolor
|   |   verta+vertb-vert > 7 :
|   |   |   timef+4 <= 0: Uperoleia lithomoda
|   |   |   timef+4 > 0: Litoria caerulea
vert2 > 18 :
|   horiz <= -50: Litoria tornieri
|   horiz > -50: Uperoleia inundata
```

We automatically translate the decision tree to data suitable for inclusion in a C program.

The identifications of individual peaks is, of course, unreliable as effectively only a tiny fragment of sound is being examined. The error rate in local peak classifications approaches 50%.

Voting

Our system aggregates these unreliable identifications to produce reliable recognition of vocalisations. The model used is simple. If within a certain time period a threshold number of local peaks are identified as belonging to a given species then a vocalisation of that species is assumed to be present.

The obvious time period to choose is the typical length of the species' vocalisations. We could not obtain suitable system performance by attempting to recognise vocalisations within the typical period of some species' vocalisation, mainly because some species have very short vocalisations. We remedied this by adopting a hierarchical structure of time segments based on the typical temporal patterns of the species vocalisations.

For example, a species might have a vocalisation typically lasting 300 milliseconds containing a number of 30 millisecond "notes" and it might usually produce 4 or more vocalisations in 3 seconds. Our system models this with 3 levels of segments. The level 0 segments will be 30 milliseconds long. If a threshold number of local peaks occur in that time period then the species is regarded as present in that level 0 segment, in other words we assume we have recognised a single "note" belonging to the species.

The level 1 segment will be 300 milliseconds long. If a threshold number of level 0 segments are identified as containing the species within that time period then the species is regarded as present in the level 1 segment, in other words we assume we have recognised a single vocalisation of the species.

Similarly the level 2 segment will be 3 seconds long and a threshold number of level 1 segments will be required to regard the species as present in the level 2 segment and hence reliably identified.

In practice, it was only necessary to specify the three level hierarchy described above for a few species. For most species, a one or two level hierarchy was sufficient. These hierarchies are based on the typical calling patterns of an individual but, in practice, perform well even when multiple individuals are present. This temporal structure could, in principle, be acquired automatically by the system but, in practice, it was much easier to provide it manually.

It is much more desirable for our system to fail to recognise a vocalisation (a *false negative*) than to incorrectly indicate the vocalisation of a particular species is present (a *false positive*). It is crucial then to choose thresholds such that false positives are unlikely. Recent work in recognising individual humans from their vocalisations, usually termed speaker recognition, has examined similar problems at some length; for an overview see (Gish & Schmidt 1994). We were concerned the assumption involved in this work would not be sufficiently valid in our domain so we instead adopted an empirical process.

It is easy to provide large amounts of training data

which does not contain the vocalisations of a given species. This does require the time consuming manual extraction of vocalisations that positive training data does. The thresholds for a particular species are estimated by applying the local peak classifier to negative training data and examining how often peaks are (incorrectly) classified as belonging to the particular species.

Hardware Platform

Our monitoring stations are to be setup at the start of each wet season and dismantled four months later at the end of each wet season allowing the data to be collected. They use a rugged single board PC-compatible computer designed for industrial applications. The 25mhz Intel 486 CPU allows approximately 25% of incoming sound to be classified, i.e 15 seconds of sound takes approximately 1 minute to process. The speed is limited by the signal processing, not the call recognition. Power is supplied by a solar panel. Every 5 minute period, details of the frog species heard in that interval are logged to flash memory. The monitoring stations also log rainfall, temperature and humidity data. Data in flash memory should survive most modes of system failure.

Application Use

Our system will be deployed at 12 sites next wet season. We can report testing on field data. This wet season we collected 29 recordings of frog choruses in our study area. The recording ranged in length from 3 to over 30 minutes. An inexpensive dynamic microphone, similar to that employed in our stations, was used for these recordings. The recordings were made under as varied conditions as possible. The distance to the nearest frog varied from 2 to 70 metres. Significant amounts of noise are present in some recordings from insects, rain and human speech or other human activity.

At the time of each recording it was noted what species were present and these were placed into two categories: species which were conspicuous to the human ear and species which were not. Some species were placed in the second category because they made only a few isolated vocalisations during the time of the recording, others because their vocalisations were difficult to discern because they were distant or obscured by other species or both. Each recording contains 1 to 10 species. The number of species in each track placed in category 1 varies from 0 to 4.

In total the 29 recordings contain 9 different species which occur on at least one track in category 1. Another 7 species occur in the recordings but only as category 2. It was felt successful recognition of the category 1 vocalisations was a minimum requirement for our system.

System Performance

For all 29 recordings our system recognised the category 1 species with two exceptions. One species, *Uperoleia lithomoda* was never recognised. It has extremely brief vocalisations which sound like stones being clicked. A single *Uperoleia lithomoda* vocalisation, centred at 3 khz, can be seen just over 0.5 seconds into the spectrogram in Figure 2. We are currently investigating remedying this.

During our fieldwork collecting the recordings, it became apparent that it was very difficult for humans to separate the vocalisations of 3 of the species in our area. The frogs themselves of these species are also difficult to separate in the field. This makes collection of accurately labelled training and testing data difficult. In particular, even if you positively identify one species as dominating a chorus it is very difficult to exclude the presence of individuals of the other two species.

We have lumped these three species together in our system. Fortunately, this is acceptable for our project's purposes because of ecological similarities between these species. The lumped species was successfully recognised whenever it occurred in category 1.

System performance with category 2 species was varied. In approximately one third of cases category 2 species were recognised as being present in recordings. We are actively examining improving this performance. In one instance, a frog species was recognised as present even though the nearest individual was more than 70 metres distant. This exceeds the performance of the first author.

There were several misidentifications (i.e. *false positives*) of one species and one misidentification of a second species. We have since remedied this by modifying the temporal segements used for recognising these species.

We believe the above results demonstrate that the software component of our system will be successful.

Application Development and Maintenance

Application development has taken approximately two man months spread over 12 months. Some software from previous work was employed. The system could be trained for a new set of frogs in less than 1 day but performance evaluation and tuning would probably require up to a week.

We hope eventually to encapsulate and distribute the training software so biologists can construct their own identification systems. We also hope to apply the techniques to other taxa, including bats and cetaceans.

Acknowledgements

This work was supported by an Australian federal goverment grant. We thank the local land owners and the Northern Territory government for permitting our work.

References

J.R. Deller, J.G. Proakis, and J.H.L. Hansen. *Discrete-Time Processing of Speech Signals.* Macmillian, 1993.

K.M. Fristrup and W.A. Watkins. Marine animal sound classification. *Journal of the Acoustical Society of America*, 97(5):3369–3370, May 1995.

H.C. Gerhardt. Acoustic properties used in call recognition by frogs and toads. In Fritzsch et al., editor, *The Evolution of the Amphibian Auditory System*, pages 455–483. John Wiley, 1988.

H. Gish and M. Schmidt. Text-independent speaker identification. *IEEE Signal Processing Magazine*, pages 18–32, October 1994.

G.H. John, R. Kohavi, and K. Pfleger. Irrelevant features and the subset selection problem. In *Proceedings of the 11th International Conference on Machine Learning*, pages 121–129. Morgan Kauffman, 1994.

H. Mills. Automatic detection and classification of nocturnal migrant bird calls. *Journal of the Acoustical Society of America*, 97(5):3370–3371, May 1995.

J.R. Quinlan. *C4.5: Programs for Machine Learning.* Morgan Kauffman, 1993.

A.J. Taylor. Bird flight call discrimination using machine learning. *Journal of the Acoustical Society of America*, 97(5):3370–3371, May 1995.

AdjudiPro® 2.0

David Williams

Development Manager
United HealthCare Corporation
9705 Data Park Drive
Minnetonka, MN 55343
daw@uhc.com

Bradley C. Simons

Lead Knowledge Engineer
United HealthCare Corporation
5901 Lincoln Drive
Edina, MN 55436
bsimons@uhc.com

Joe Connolly

Lead Software Engineer
United HealthCare Corporation
9705 Data Park Drive
Minnetonka, MN 55343
jtc@uhc.com

Abstract

AdjudiPro, version 2.0, is the latest incarnation of United HealthCare's patented physician claims adjudication expert system (US patent # 5,359,509). Its core is an embedded expert system that contains the logic for processing 55% of all physician claim situations reviewed on United HealthCare's managed care system. Certain physician services are reviewed as part of the claims adjudication process to ensure that submitted charges meet contractual, and other guidelines. In 1995, nearly $20 million in gross savings was realized through use of this system. Since its initial deployment in 1991-1992, there has been a steep increase in AdjudiPro's processing volume. This increased demand created a number of issues that had to be addressed to ensure AdjudiPro's continued viability and growth. As a result, much of the past three years was spent rearchitecting AdjudiPro to meet the increasing load placed on it, while achieving acceptable throughput. AdjudiPro is now an essentially real-time application, processing claims twenty-four hours a day, seven days a week. This paper describes the current AdjudiPro application, and the key issues faced during the past three years.

Introduction

United HealthCare is a national leader in health care management, serving purchasers, consumers, managers, and providers of health care since 1974. The company serves over 40 million individuals through a broad continuum of health care products and services, including HMOs, point of service, preferred provider organizations (PPOs), and managed indemnity programs. United HealthCare also provides managed mental health and substance abuse services, utilization management, workers compensation and disability management services, specialized provider networks, third-party administration (TPA) services, employee assistance services, Medicare and managed care programs for the aged, managed Medicaid services, managed pharmacy, health care evaluation services, information systems, and administrative services.

This paper describes AdjudiPro®, a patented expert system (US patent #5,359,509, issued 10/94) developed at United HealthCare that is used in the physician claims adjudication process by many of United HealthCare's health plans. The initial production version of this application was described in a paper presented at IAAI in 1992. Although this paper describes the new version of this application, one of the goals of this paper is to describe major issues and challenges that arose as a result of the significant growth in AdjudiPro's impact to United HealthCare's business. Most of the major issues faced resulted from the overall design of the application, not from the expert system components themselves. Nevertheless, we feel that understanding and overcoming these issues were key to the ongoing success and growth of this application's use.

System Background

United HealthCare offers advanced health care management capabilities and contracting approaches layered upon a core claims administration process. Many of these capabilities are supported by United HealthCare's mainframe managed care system called COSMOS. This system supports the majority of the processes necessary for operating an HMO in today's marketplace. It is currently used to manage geographically dispersed HMOs with membership of more than 3 million.

COSMOS core claims administration is used to enter, adjudicate, pay, and store physician and hospital (facility) claims. Traditionally, United HealthCare increased COSMOS' capabilities through direct modification of COSMOS. However, in recent years many new features have been added by integrating other systems with COSMOS, both systems developed within United HealthCare and systems developed externally. AdjudiPro is one such application. Its design commenced in 1990, with implementation of the automatic claims update feature in mid-1992. Its goal was and is to improve

United HealthCare's claims adjudication process (i.e., determination of proper payment). In many cases, proper payment involves complex decision making that requires detailed knowledge of provider contracts, members' benefits, federal and state government regulations, and established billing practices. This decision process often requires the application of logic not easily programmed using a traditional, procedural approach. Traditionally, these types of payment decisions have been handled manually by expert personnel. It was for this reason that a knowledge based systems approach was selected for development of this automated adjudication process. In order to understand what AdjudiPro does, it is important to understand United HealthCare's overall claims adjudication process.

When a claim is received by COSMOS, a complex set of adjudication logic is applied. This process results in the claim being assigned one of two states -- payable (not necessarily as billed) or pended. A claim may be in a pended state for multiple reasons. Each of these reasons is called a review. Reviews are set whenever the claim, together with its associated historical claims and/or other factors, matches the criteria for the review. Associated with each review is a set of logic ("rules") and a priority. Application of the review's logic can alter the amount payable for the claim.

Reviews are processed in the order determined by the priorities of the reviews that match a claim. Reviews that have not yet been performed are termed open reviews, while processed reviews are closed reviews. The highest priority open review is called the next open review. In general, review priorities are grouped according to the "group" responsible for clearing the review. This is to simplify workflow issues and allow for timely payment of claims. Currently, review priorities are generally grouped as follows: 1) claims processor reviews, 2) AI reviews, and 3) medical analyst reviews. Claims processors are responsible for administrative types of reviews, such as verification of pre-authorization or referral. Medical analysts are RNs. This group is responsible for reviews that require clinical training and experience. Reviews processed by this group include determination of whether or not a submitted service is cosmetic or experimental. A review is considered an AI review when the majority of claims that pend to the review are automatically processed by AdjudiPro.

Once all reviews for a claim have been processed, the status of the claim is set to payable. Payable claims are paid periodically by a COSMOS checkwriting process, at which point the state of these claims is set to paid.

AdjudiPro's goal is to enhance the manual process described above, through full and partial automation of reviews. This applies both to existing fully manual reviews, as well as new reviews developed and implemented directly with AdjudiPro. Presently, AdjudiPro contains the logic to automatically resolve, fully or partially, nine existing reviews. AdjudiPro also contains the logic of 14 reviews that were implemented directly with AdjudiPro. As a result of this logic, AdjudiPro automatically resolves nearly 60% of all situations that pend for physician claims within the COSMOS system.

In most cases, logic for new reviews is sufficiently complete to allow near full automation of the review (i.e., > 99%). Overall, AdjudiPro resolves more than one million reviews per month, which is more than 97% of all the reviews it attempts to resolve. Any attempted review not automatically resolved is handled by a manual process similar to the one described above. However, in many of these cases, AdjudiPro is able to provide the claims processor or medical analyst with information (e.g., relevant claims history) that they would have otherwise been required to research manually.

Much of the success of AdjudiPro can be attributed to its close alignment with the business objectives of the organization. All systems developed at United HealthCare are required to meet one or more of the following four tenets -- the more that are applicable, the better. The systems must:

- Reduce the Medical Loss Ratio
- Reduce Selling, General and Administrative Expense
- Improve quality of medical care to our constituents, and
- Improve "time to market" for products

With the exception of a fair number of the reviews previously stated, the above description was the task accomplished and presented at the 1992 IAAI conference (Figure 1). However, since that time there have been several things that needed to be improved or implemented for this system to survive and prosper.

Problem Description

In September of 1992, three new reviews were added to AdjudiPro as part of the migration of an HMO, acquired by United HealthCare, from their existing managed care system to COSMOS. The addition of these reviews not only resulted in a dramatic rise in AdjudiPro cost savings, it demonstrated to United HealthCare business personnel that knowledge based systems approaches were viable. Moreover, it could be depended on as a tool to help meet key business objectives. The rapid completion of these three reviews, in a time span of just a few months, convinced many doubters of this technology.

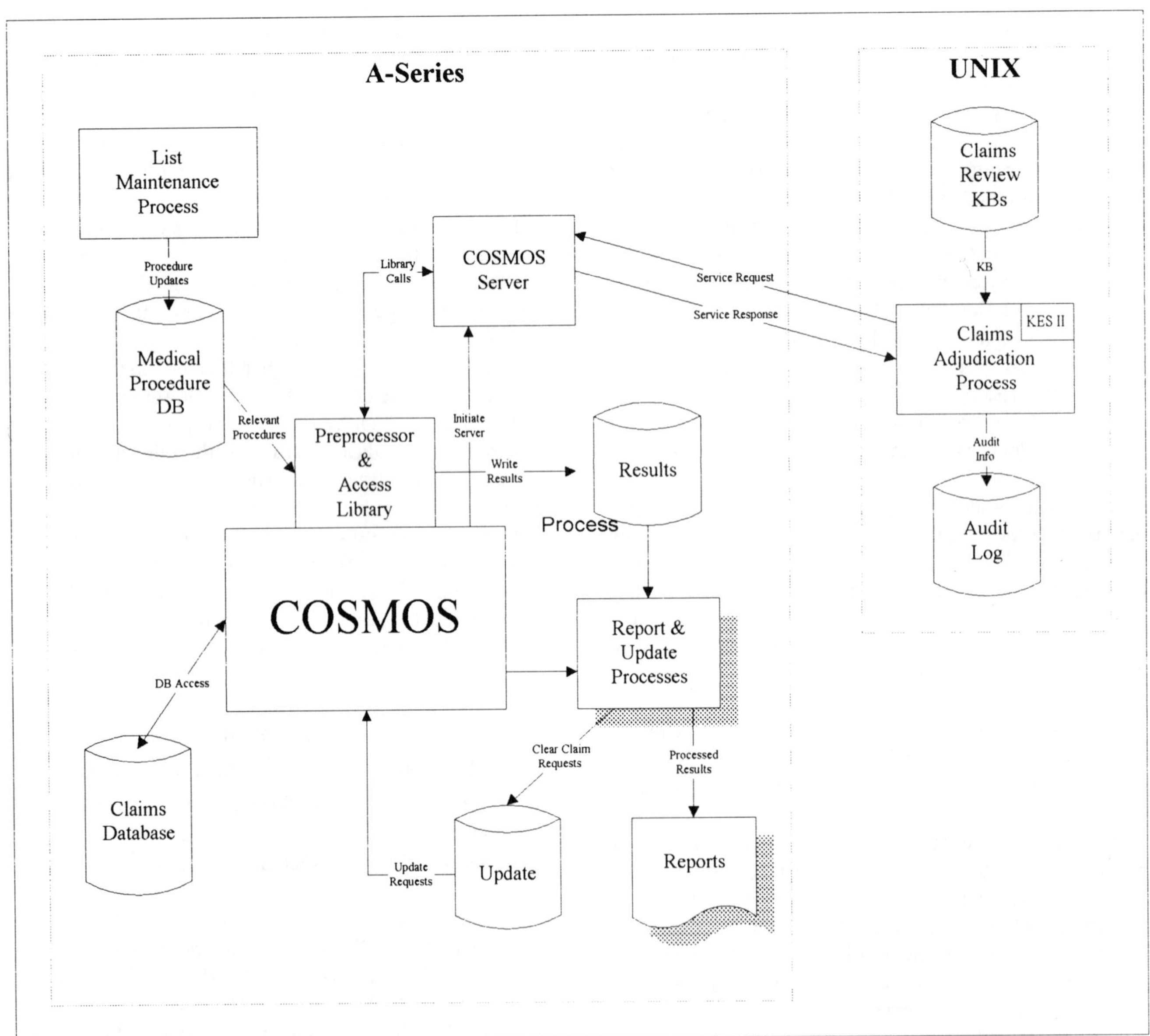

Figure 1

Following successful incorporation of these reviews, AdjudiPro entered a rapid growth phase in terms of both volume and return on investment (savings). From October of 1992 to October of 1993, review volume grew from 70,000/month to 450,000/month, while gross savings grew from $75,000/month to $900,000/month. It was around this time (October 1993) that some major issues arose. Although the business was generally convinced in the ability of AI technology to solve this problem, and was also increasingly impressed by the savings this application generated, business people were also increasingly concerned with the AdjudiPro's impact on claims throughput.

The original AdjudiPro system was a batch application that ran each review once a day. Reviews generally were run between midnight and 6 a.m., one job for each review for each health plan for each day. This created a problem with claims throughput, since reviews are required to be performed in a specific order and the way jobs were scheduled did not always allow every AdjudiPro review to be cleared in one night. In many cases, two to three days were required for all AdjudiPro processing of the claim to be completed. Since many of the reviews processed by AdjudiPro are reviews that were added to the overall adjudication process, this noticeably increased the average time to pay claims. There are often substantial financial penalties involved when the average time to pay claims is too long -- that is, when they exceed the performance guarantees specified in United HealthCare's contracts or in government regulations. Thus, this decrease in throughput was a key business concern. It was critical that AdjudiPro be redesigned to minimize its impact on claims throughput.

In the short run, increased throughput was achieved through careful scheduling of the time at which each review was run. In some cases, the frequency of execution of a review was also increased. In addition, the priority order for review processing was altered to simplify the scheduling effort. After several months work, AdjudiPro operations were tuned so that in most cases, AdjudiPro performed all its required processing for a claim within one day. However, the result of this rescheduling and increase in frequency of AdjudiPro jobs placed an increasing load on United HealthCare's Computer Operations Department. For each run of each review (for each of the twenty or so health plans using COSMOS), a job had to be scheduled on the mainframe and report distribution setup was required for each report recipient for each job. In other words, there were literally hundreds of AdjudiPro jobs scheduled daily on the mainframe. Each of these jobs required operational monitoring and support --a very undesirable situation.

Another issue that factored into the redesign of AdjudiPro was that the original design was beginning to have difficulty "keeping up" with the increasing claim volume. Finally, at about the same time (4Q93), United HealthCare made the decision to purchase Health Payment Review's Patterns of Treatment Plus™ software and incorporate it as a review within AdjudiPro. It was decided that this should not be done without a redesign of AdjudiPro to meet the claims department throughput needs. It was thus paramount to AdjudiPro's continued growth and perhaps survival that it be significantly redesigned.

Keep in mind that AdjudiPro was United HealthCare's first experience with knowledge bases systems technology. As a result, for the first three years the AdjudiPro development team focused on proving the viability of the technology. At United HealthCare, this meant using the technology to build an application that had a demonstrable return on investment. This led to sometimes choosing expediency in development over perfection in design. Had the initial development languished in analysis and design, funding for the system might have been cut.

In any case, the decision was made to focus resources on a major redesign in 1994. The goals of the redesign were twofold -- minimize the time for which a claim pends for AdjudiPro processing and minimize the impact of this application on Computer Operations. Since this was to be a major effort and the knowledge engineering staff had become aware of several shortcomings in the design of portions of the expert system core, it was also decided to incorporate modifications to the design of the expert system component (i.e., the knowledge base) as part of this project. Changes to AdjudiPro's overall architecture were largely completed by the end of 1994, at which time Patterns of Treatment Plus was incorporated in production, integrated with AdjudiPro. In 1995, further enhancements were completed and existing AdjudiPro reviews were converted to the new architecture, one by one, with the project completed in third quarter of 1995.

One of the major changes to the knowledge base was to redesign its class structure -- to more accurately reflect the underlying information, to facilitate maintenance of the existing rules, and to ease the addition of logic for the many new reviews scheduled for implementation. More extensive use of class inheritance was also incorporated at this time to simplify future maintenance by more clearly sharing elements of classes that were common to more than one review. Another goal was to modify the classes so that they not only mirrored United HealthCare's proprietary COSMOS environment, but so that they would be flexible enough to be used with other claims systems.

The other major enhancement to the knowledge base (KB) was the reorganization of its rules. AdjudiPro rules are actually contained in many separate sets of rules, or knowledge bases, with one knowledge base for each review. Until not that long ago, the knowledge base for a new review was created by copying and modifying the knowledge base of an existing review. As the number of reviews grew, this created a maintenance headache. Some KBs contained rules that were not applicable to that review, and many rules were duplicated across all of the KBs. As part of the redesign, all obsolete elements were removed from each KB. In addition, elements common to each KB were extracted and placed in files that could be shared. For example, rules common to multiple reviews were placed in files with .rul file extensions. Each KB that requires an element, references the common item where it belongs within the KB via a #include construct. Common elements are pulled into each KB prior to parsing the KB. One unexpected benefit of separating the common information into separate files was that it facilitated the use of AdjudiPro's data model, rules, and other elements by other applications.

Application Description

As noted above, AdjudiPro is a client/server, knowledge based system (i.e., expert system) that operates in tandem with COSMOS, United HealthCare's proprietary COBOL managed care system. AdjudiPro is primarily a UNIX application, but it includes several components that execute on the Unisys mainframe. The UNIX components execute on an IBM RS/6000 and the Unisys components execute on Unisys A-series mainframes.

AdjudiPro, version 2.0, transformed the application into a UNIX based client-server application. AdjudiPro only uses the Unisys mainframe as a data warehouse and a report distribution engine. All job and process management functions, plus creation of the report images, were migrated to UNIX. A Motif interface was also built to control and monitor AdjudiPro. This replaces the mainframe job scheduling described above. The application is now a data-driven, essentially real-time application. It is more flexible, tunable, and scaleable. A diagram of the system is shown in Figure 2. An overview of the AdjudiPro process is provided below, followed by a detailed description of the knowledge base component of the system.

AdjudiPro executes as a collection of Distributed Computing Environment (DCE) servers passing remote procedure calls (RPCs) amongst themselves and yet all functioning independently. These servers are constructed using a set of tools, Entera, supplied by Open Environment Corporation (OEC). One of the tools supplied by OEC is a production environment monitoring utility that verifies all servers are running, automatically restarting any servers that fail. Periodic UNIX cron jobs are executed to refresh the data upon which AdjudiPro is driven.

AdjudiPro consists of the following major components:

- UtoA Router: Provide access to Unisys data and services.
- COMS: Execute RPC's on Unisys.
- Claim Server: Obtain claim and process reviews.
- Knowledge Server: Execute adjudication logic on claim.
- Reviewable Claim Server: Provide access to reviewable claim list.

A detailed description of the AdjudiPro system flow of control is contained in the sections that follow but the basic steps include:

- Claim Server obtains next reviewable claim from Reviewable Claim Server.
- Claim Server obtains claim from COSMOS.
- Claim Server sends claim to Knowledge Server for adjudication.
- Claim Server sends request to modify COSMOS claim.
- Claim Server sends adjudication results to Report Server.

AdjudiPro's Unisys components are developed and maintained in XGEN, a fourth-generation language that generates COBOL. AdjudiPro's UNIX components (except for the KBs) are written in C. In addition, the client-server development relies heavily on the Entera tool set produced OEC. The Entera tools produce DCE compliant servers. Finally, the knowledge bases are built using SNAP's Object Modeler, version 6. SNAP is a development environment from Template Software. This Object Modeler component of SNAP is used for construction of AdjudiPro's embedded expert systems. Before describing each of AdjudiPro's components, as well as the relevant existing services used, a process (control) flow of the application will be provided.

AdjudiPro essentially operates in a continuous loop. Two basic functions are performed during each loop. The first is creation of the list of claims for which the next open review is a review processed by AdjudiPro. This list is known as the Reviewable Claims List (RCL) and its creation is controlled by the Reviewable Claims Server (RCS) described below. The RCL is stored in Sybase and is the list from which by the Claim Servers (CSs) operate.

The second step in each loop is the resolution of as many of the open reviews as possible, for all claims in the RCL. Each CS running extracts the highest priority claim in the list that has not been processed. The CS then attempts to resolve the claim's open, contiguous AdjudiPro reviews. (To be contiguous, two reviews must be next to each other in terms of priority.) This is done by a call to the appropriate Review Servers (RSs), each of which contains the full or partial logic for handling a single review. If the RS is unable to completely determine how to resolve a review, no further processing of this claim is done. The CS merely adds a record for the claim to the report file indicating that manual intervention is required. The CS then proceeds to the next claim in the RCL. If the Review Server fully resolves the review, the Claim Server checks if the next review on the claim is also an AdjudiPro review. If so, it continues processing of this claim as noted above. Otherwise, processing moves to the next available claim. Once all claims in the RCL have been processed, AdjudiPro rebuilds the RCL and begins anew.

Once a day, the logs and report information are copied from the working files to archive files. At this time, the report system is initiated. It is a collection of COBOL programs that generates reports for various user groups, including internal audit groups, claims processor groups and medical analyst groups. These last two groups use a "manual" report that lists claims reviewed by AdjudiPro that were not automatically cleared. The reports are distributed electronically to the Unisys system, allowing AdjudiPro to utilize the standard distribution system,

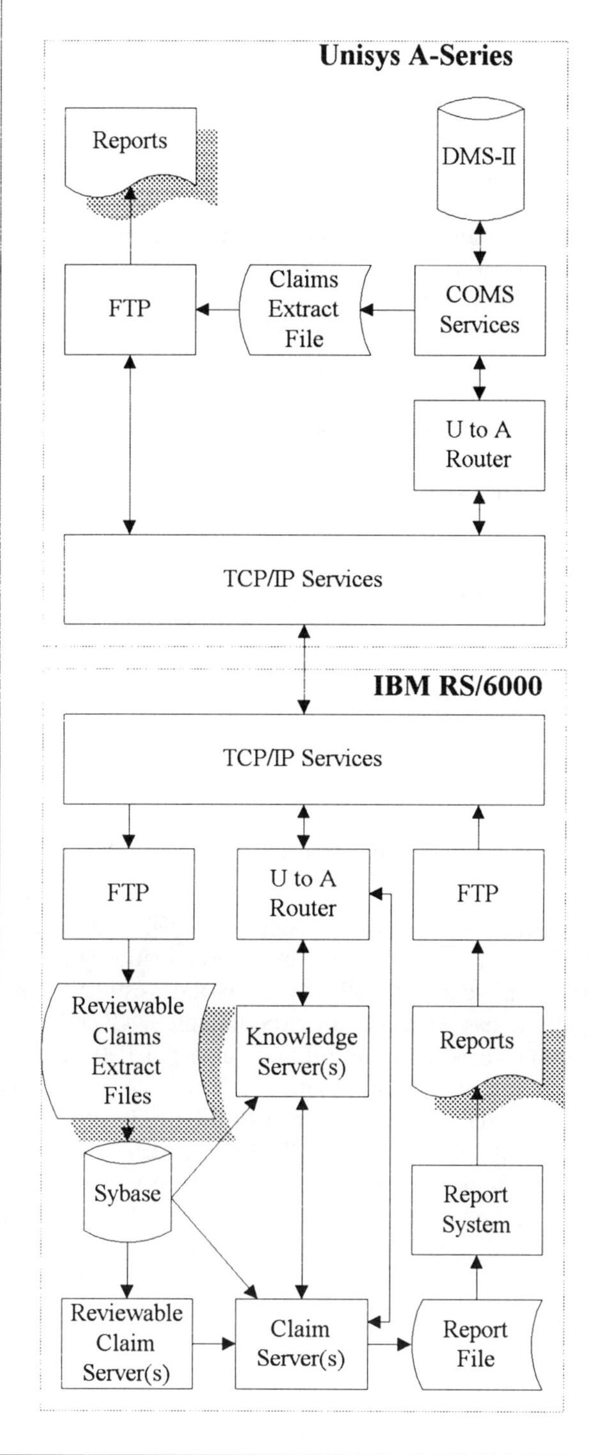

Figure 2

when appropriate. Reports are also moved electronically to some user groups, through United HealthCare's wide area network (WAN) and local area networks (LANs), to ease access to this information.

Unisys Components

As indicated in figure 2, a number of key systems and COSMOS services are utilized by AdjudiPro. The Unisys COSMOS system components used may be grouped into three categories - database services (DMS-II), transaction services (COMS), and communication services (TCP/IP, FTP, and the UtoA Router). The UtoA (UNIX to A-series) Router was developed to provide AdjudiPro and several other client-server applications access to COSMOS data. The UtoA Router provides access to COMS from remote hosts via standard TCP/IP sockets.

Reviewable Claim Server

The Reviewable Claim Server provides access to the reviewable claims Sybase table. The reviewable claims table contains all claims with an open AdjudiPro review. It is called by claim servers to get a claim to process.

Knowledge Server

The Knowledge Server is responsible for review adjudication. There are currently 23 AdjudiPro reviews. The logic for each review is in a SNAP knowledge base. Each Knowledge Server is a C program with an embedded SNAP component. The Knowledge Server initiates evaluation by the embedded KB by asserting the claim information and requesting payment advice. This results in a backward chaining process. This process proceeds until advice is determined or a situation is encountered for which the knowledge base has no internal knowledge source. In this situation, an external call is made to the Knowledge Server to retrieve the necessary information.

An example of how AdjudiPro can utilize other software applications is the Patterns review. Patterns of Treatment Plus is software tool used in the evaluation of the appropriateness of care. A DCE server, the Patterns Server, was developed that essentially included Patterns of Treatment Plus software as an embedded component. Claims that are put on review for appropriateness checking are then processed by having a knowledge server send the claims to the Patterns Server to obtain the Patterns of Treatment advice. In all other aspects, this review is handled by the knowledge server like all other reviews.

Specific information retrieved during the evaluation of a claim includes service authorization information, referral information, Sybase lookups, date computations, and claim history lookups. The claim history lookup is the most widely used lookup. Most AdjudiPro reviews attempt to reduce or deny payment of a claim. Most often this requires information about other procedures the member has had. The history lookup extracts all member claims for a specified period of time that match certain criteria. The period of time and criteria vary by review.

Knowledge Bases

The knowledge bases currently share 26 classes and 9 demons. The largest knowledge base is the one that contains the logic for processing the multiple surgical review. This review is performed whenever multiple surgical episodes are performed on the same patient in a single day. This KB currently contains 607 rules, as compared to 168 rules just three years ago. The total number of rules contained in the knowledge bases for AdjudiPro's 23 reviews is 2275. This is significantly more than the 461 rules that existed three years ago.

Within the knowledge bases, substantial class development has occurred since 1992. In order to accurately mirror COSMOS data model and to simplify maintenance and enhancement of AdjudiPro, a new set of classes that utilized inheritance was developed. In COSMOS, physician claims are stored with header information, plus up to four lines. Each of these lines details one service performed by a physician on a day. In addition, each claim has may have an infinite number of history claims to which it is related. However, the structure of the a claim and each of its related history claims is the same. This information was used to redefine AdjudiPro's data model. The initial version of AdjudiPro had four classes -- a claim class, a line class, a history claim class, and a history line class. Much of the information in the claim and line classes was identical.

For AdjudiPro 2.0, a tree structure was used for defining both the line and the claims classes. At the highest level there is a generic line class and a generic claim class. This is the first (root) level of the tree structure. These classes contain attributes that are common in all reviews for these data elements, for both historical and pending claims. The second level in the tree structure contains the review line class and the review claim class, which inherit the generic line class and the generic claim class, respectively. This second level is used to attach attributes to claims and lines that are specific to a review. Finally, at the third level of the tree structure contains the line class, the history line class, the claim class and the history claim class. The first two classes inherit the review line class, while the second two inherit the review claim class. This structure has provided a number of advantages, including the elimination of separate identical rules that existed in the previous version, one rule which processed lines and another which processed history lines. This is now accomplished by having a single rule that utilizes the review line class elements. Moreover, this structure maintains the capability for looping on only the lines of the claim pending payment, or looping on its history lines.

Claim Server

The Claim Server is responsible for overall AdjudiPro control. At activation, each Claim Server is provided a set of review criteria identifying for which claims the server is responsible. The Claim Server begins by requesting a reviewable claim from the Reviewable Claim Server. If a reviewable claim is found, the claim is obtained from COSMOS and passed to the appropriate Knowledge Servers. The Knowledge Servers to which the claim must be sent are determined based on the open reviews.

Each claim may have up to ten reviews, which must be cleared according to the priority order defined by COSMOS. As noted above, the next review to clear is referred to as the next open review. The Claim Server attempts to clear all contiguous AdjudiPro reviews. The processing of a claim stops when either all reviews are cleared, the open review is not cleared by the Knowledge Server, or the next open review is a non-AdjudiPro review.

Reports

The AdjudiPro reports are the only deliverable produced by the system. The necessity for reports is a concept inherited from COSMOS. Since AdjudiPro reports are intended for the same audience as COSMOS reports, AdjudiPro is designed to distribute reports via the mainframe. The reports are generated on UNIX and transferred to Unisys via FTP.

Application Payoff

AdjudiPro was initially developed in 1990, with initial production (non-update) in 1991. Automatic update of claims was added in 1992. Return-on-investment from AdjudiPro has exceeded all expectations. Overall, the project has a positive net present value ($4.1M), and an internal rate of return equaling 178%. AdjudiPro is currently used by all United HealthCare health plans (HMOs) that operate on the COSMOS system. Together these health plans provide managed care services to more than 2 million enrollees. AdjudiPro is used twenty-four hours a day, seven days a week to assist with COSMOS physician claims adjudication. Processing statistics and savings for AdjudiPro, since automatic update are shown below.

Year	Savings(Gross $)	Reviews Cleared
1992	500,000	250,000
1993	7,250,000	3,750,000
1994	11,750,000	8,000,000
1995	19,500,000	12,500,000

Application Development

AdjudiPro is currently supported and enhanced by a development staff of thirteen, including management, knowledge engineering, system development, customer support, and testing personnel. In addition, there are two key individuals on the business side of the house responsible for the ongoing maintenance and enhancement of this application. One of these users, the "AdjudiPro Specialist", resides in the group responsible for overall claims administration. The other user resides in the department responsible for development of medical policies that impact claims payment.

The actual redesign of AdjudiPro from version 1.0 to version 2.0 required approximately eighteen months to complete. The cost of this effort is approximately four full-time staff for 12 months. Ongoing enhancement and maintenance of this system is coordinated by the development staff and the AdjudiPro Specialist. This AdjudiPro Specialist is responsible for communication with internal business personnel impacted by AdjudiPro, scheduling of enhancements, training of users, communication with the health plans, etc. The development of new reviews typically involves discussions between the staff knowledge engineers and various business experts, including the AdjudiPro Specialist. The length of time for development of new reviews varies from a day or two to several months. Reviews and enhancements to the system go through a business priority setting process. Except for system errors and required enhancements, enhancements are prioritized according to their potential return on investment.

Maintenance

AdjudiPro is fully maintained, from a code perspective, by the development staff noted above. No interface has been built to allow users the ability to add, delete, or modify rules. Currently, thirty percent of staff hours are budgeted for maintenance of the application. However, as the system continues to grow, so does maintenance. Full-time staff are now budgeted for AdjudiPro maintenance activities.

There are two major sources of maintenance. The first is a yearly review and update of the logic to ensure the reviews take into account the yearly updates to CPT-4 (i.e., *Physicians' Current Procedural Terminology*, Fourth Edition). CPT-4 codes are the standard used within the United States for submitting claims for physician services. It is published by the American Medical Association and revised annually.

Generally, changes to established polices that result from the annual CPT-4 updates are not large. However, there have been a couple of instances where reviews needed to be rewritten from scratch. The reason for the major change has been a fundamental redefinition of an entire set of CPT-4 codes. Maintenance of CPT-4 code issues has been simplified by storing much of this information in lists external from the knowledge base. Updates to some of these lists are automatically generated using an electronic version of CPT-4. The second main source of maintenance is when reevaluation of existing policies occurs as the result of other regulatory changes, or a review of the policies following acquisition of another HMO.

Along with the previously stated maintenance, the AdjudiPro team is constantly receiving requests for enhancements. All enhancement requests are quantified in terms of a return and prioritized for inclusion in future releases of the system. All requests pass through the AdjudiPro Specialist, and are fully tracked and documented. In addition, they are annotated with information as development occurs, as acceptance testing is performed, and when the request is implemented. Management of this process and documentation is done by the AdjudiPro Quality Assurance and Customer Support staff that are part of the overall AdjudiPro development team.

Conclusion

AdjudiPro has proven the viability of the expert systems and AI technologies at United HealthCare. The completion of this new version of the system has resulted in an increasing demand for use of AdjudiPro by groups within United HealthCare. The environment has gone from one of caution and skepticism, to full support. As a result, funding for AdjudiPro and similar projects has increased dramatically.

Acknowledgments

The authors of this chapter would like to acknowledge the invaluable efforts of all the talented people who have been involved in the development and ongoing success of this application: all present and past memebers of the development team, the United HealthCare Medical Services Team, Group Service Administration Team, the Computer Operations group and management sponsors.

References

Kirschner, C.; Frankel, L.; Jackson, J.; Jacobson, C.; Kotowicz, G.; Leoni, G.; O'Heron, M.; O'Hara, K.; Reyes, D.; Rozell, D.; Willard, D.; Yacorella, S.; Younf, R.;

Zanutto, J. 1996. *Physicians' Current Procedural Terminology*. Chicago: American Medical Association.

PMIC. 1996. *International Classification of Diseases 9th Revision*. Los Angeles, CA.: Practice Management Information Corporation.

PMIC. 1996. *Health Care Financing Administration Common Procedure Coding System*. Los Angeles, CA.: Practice Management Information Corporation.

Template Software. 1989. *Training Manual: Knowledge Engineering System*. Herndon, VA.: Template Software.

Pederson, K. 1989. *Expert Systems Programming: Practical Techniques for Rule-Based Systems*. New York: Wiley.

Little, J.P.; Gingrich, M. 1992. AdjudiPro. In Proceedings of the Innovative Applications of Artificial Intelligence 4. Menlo Park, CA.: International Joint Conferences on Artificial Intelligence, Inc.

Knowles, A., "A Bargain at 15 Cents", *CIO Magazine*, February 1, 1996, pp. 42-44. International Data Group Publication.

HPR. 1995. *Patterns of Treatment Plus Knowledge Base Criteria*. Boston, MA: Health Payment Review, Inc.

Sybase. 1993. *Sybase: Reference Manual*. Emeryville, CA: Sybase.

OEC, 1996. *Entera Developer Package*. http://www.oec.com: Open Environment Corporation.

Openware. 1995. *XGEN 4GL: Reference*. Jacksonville, FL: Openware Technologies, Inc.

SSCFI: Autonomous Fault Isolation in Communications Circuits

Ralph Worrest, Roland Zito-Wolf[1], Hongbin Wang, Shri Goyal
Integrated Intelligent Systems Department
GTE Laboratories, Incorporated
40 Sylvan Road
Waltham, MA 02254 USA
rworrest,rzito-wolf,hwang,sgoyal@gte.com

Abstract

SSCFI[2] is a rule-based expert system that diagnoses problems in a wide variety of "special circuits," that is, telephone circuits other than regular switched business and residential lines. Special circuits are significantly more complex than regular circuits, and hence more difficult to diagnose. SSCFI diagnoses problems by recursively partitioning the circuit until the responsible fault is isolated. SSCFI selects which circuit to work on, reads its design, selects and initiates analog and digital tests via remotely-activated test equipment, interprets the results of each test in the context of the circuit design, and when done, writes out a detailed description of the problem found and routes it to the party responsible for its repair. SSCFI is entirely autonomous in operation.

SSCFI has become an essential element of GTE's special circuit maintenance operations. It has been in service since 1991 and has been in operation at all GTE's US sites since 1994. SSCFI testing saves millions of dollars annually and significantly improves the uniformity of testing and quality of the resulting diagnoses.

This paper discusses the domain, architecture, and development of the SSCFI system, and the key factors and techniques that made it successful. Lastly, two current projects building on SSCFI's expertise are discussed -- interactive test assistance and automatic design database cleanup.[12]

Problem Description

GTE is a major provider of telecommunications services, with over 20 million customer circuits. Of these, roughly 1 million are "special circuits," which includes any telephone circuit except a normal residential or business connection -- bank ATM, foreign-exchange, off-premise extension, high-capacity, hard-wired, or otherwise customized circuits (GTE, 1990). Special circuits are significantly more complex than regular circuits and typically span multiple central offices (COs). Maintenance of these circuits is a significant problem because locating faults in geographically extensive circuits is labor-intensive and slow -- possibly requiring the cooperation of technicians at multiple central offices as well as repair personnel in the field -- and because repair time requirements for special circuits are significantly more stringent than for regular circuits. Consequently, GTE has equipped many special circuits with remote testing capability, allowing circuits to be diagnosed from centralized testing centers.

When a customer reports trouble on a special service circuit, the customer service representative enters the raw problem data into a workflow system, the Trouble Administration System (TAS). A *trouble ticket* is created which represents that problem. The ticket is then routed to a Special Service Control Center (SSCC). SSCC personnel test circuits using several remote test systems, including SAS™, SARTS™, AUTOTEST 2™, and REACT 2000™. The tester first verifies the reported problem and then isolates the fault as much as possible, ideally localizing the fault to a specific location to which a technician can be dispatched. He then writes his observations and conclusions onto the TAS trouble ticket and instructs TAS to dispatch it to (that is, to place it in the work queue of) the party responsible for repair or further diagnosis. Possible dispatch locations for faults include: a central office, the outside plant associated with a specific CO, and the customer premises.

Fault isolation is a kind of diagnosis, differing in that the primary goal is to isolate the fault to within a particular organization's area of responsibility (e.g., a particular CO), rather than to a particular faulty component. This reflects the practical tradeoff that while it is important that the tester make as specific a diagnosis as possible, it is even more important that the ticket be routed as quickly as possible, which implies that the number of tests performed be minimized.

[1] Address correspondence to: rzito-wolf@gte.com, (617)466-2470, FAX (617)466-2960

[2] Pronounced "scuffy"

Automated Fault Isolation

While remote testing significantly improved the repair process, the large volume of work at the SSCCs required several hundred test personnel and was a major expense. There were also problems with testing quality, due to the wide variation in tester expertise and the large number of special circuit configurations, and with testing time, due to the need to access multiple systems per diagnosis. Reducing testing time is especially important because over the past few years the allowable time-to-repair has been reduced from 4 hours to 1-3 hours, depending on the circuit type.

GTE's answer to this problem was to automate the fault isolation process. SSCFI (Special Service Circuit Fault Isolation) diagnoses troubles reported in a wide variety of GTE special service circuits. SSCFI operates similarly to a human tester in the SSCC environment (see Figure 1). SSCFI polls the TAS work queues for trouble tickets, selecting the highest-priority trouble among the unassigned work. If additional design information is required, SSCFI accesses the CNAS II design database to obtain it. SSCFI then invokes one or more remote test system(s) to verify and isolate the fault. Lastly, SSCFI writes a summary of its conclusions (its *remarks*) onto the TAS ticket and dispatches it.

SSCFI is a model-based expert system (Davis & Hamscher, 1992). It reads the target circuit's design to generate an internal circuit model; it then selects tests with the goal of maximizing diagnosis quality and minimizing test time. SSCFI has specialized knowledge about circuit types, testing, and diagnosis, and can currently test most types of special circuits, both analog and digital. Unlike many expert systems, SSCFI operates *on-line* and *autonomously*. SSCFI is responsible for determining when it cannot successfully test a circuit, perhaps due to an unsupported configuration or lack of test access, and referring it to a human tester. SSCFI is able to recognize test-equipment and other system-level problems and page an appropriate human to get them resolved.

One current limitation is that SSCFI must rely on the automated systems for all its input, whereas human testers often work cooperatively with field personnel to resolve difficult troubles. When SSCFI cannot access a circuit, requires a test assist, or cannot satisfactorily isolate a fault, it dispatches the trouble to SSCC human personnel. In such cases, SSCFI attempts to summarize in its remarks whatever results it has been able to obtain, to help whomever next works on the ticket.

SSCFI has become an essential component of GTE's special circuit maintenance operations. It has been in operation at all GTE's special-service testing centers since 1994. SSCFI currently performs more than 40,000 circuit diagnoses per year; this number will continue to rise as SSCFI's knowledge of circuit types, area-specific practices, and testing methods is expanded.

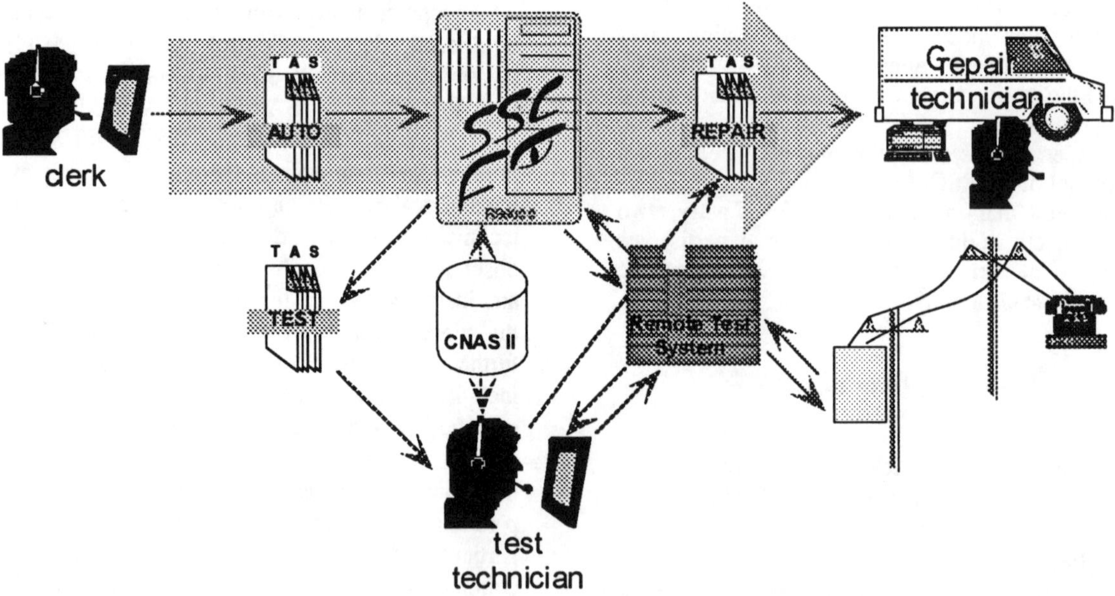

Figure 1: SSCFI's Work environment

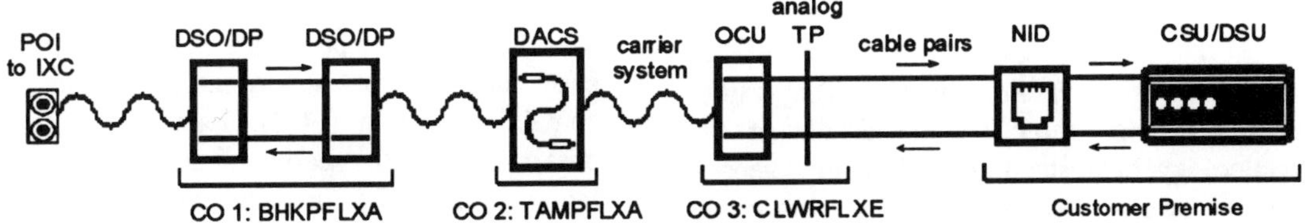

Figure 2: A Typical Point-to-POI Digital (DDS) Circuit

Problem Example

Figure 2 illustrates a typical low-speed digital (DDS service) circuit. The left side is the *A-end* or *top*; the right side the *Z-end* or *bottom*. At the A-end is a POI, a *point of interconnect*, indicating that beyond this point the circuit is provided by another telephone company. At the Z-end is a CSU/DSU (a customer's modem), making this a *point-to-POI* circuit. (When both ends of a circuit terminate at customer equipment, it is called *point-to-point*.) From the POI to the Office Channel Unit (OCU), the circuit is multiplexed onto high-bandwidth digital carrier systems. A signal can pass through multiple offices on digital carrier systems. Carriers can be connected at intermediate offices through a digital cross-connect system (a DCS) as in TAMPFLXA, or via back-to-back channel units (DSO/DPs) as in BHKPFLXA. DCS interconnects provide digital test access to the circuit. From the OCU in CLWRFLXE to the CSU/DSU at the customer's site, the circuit is a dedicated 4-wire circuit (transmit and receive *pairs*). An analog test point is generally included in this section to allow analog tests of each pair.

In digital circuits each piece of equipment has an addressable identity and can be individually looped back, that is, put into an echoing mode to verify signal transmission to the device and back. In this circuit, it is possible to separately loop the OCU, the NID, the CSU, the DSU, and each DSO/DP, all from the DCS test point. Faults are isolated primarily through differential loopback tests, plus analog measurements on the local loop. In contrast, analog-circuit fault isolation relies about equally on loopbacks and continuity tests.

To make it easier to distinguish between failures in GTE's and the customer's equipment, GTE generally provides a loopable *network interface device* (NID) -- at the customer site. If a tester can loop the NID but not the CSU/DSU beyond it, then the problem is most likely the customer equipment; if he cannot loop the NID, its a GTE fault. Without a NID, it is difficult to remotely distinguish between GTE and customer problems.

This domain has several challenging features:

- There is great variety in equipment behaviors and circuit configurations.
- The circuit design is generally not fully known, as the design records are neither complete nor fully reliable. For example, it happens that DDS circuit designs are unreliable as to whether a NID is present. This information is important when the tester is unable to loop any equipment at the customer's site. If the tester can't be sure a NID is present, then field personnel must be dispatched to the customer in many cases that are actually the customer's problem. The human testers determine if a NID is present (when it fails to loop) by the impedance signature observed from *analog* testing.
- The test equipment can be misconfigured or unreliable. Analog test points are often wired with the pairs swapped or the ends of the circuit reversed. Testers must recognize such conditions and compensate.

Why a Rule-Based Approach?

This domain has several features that suggest a rule-based approach.

- *Much of the experts' knowledge is procedural* -- situation-specific rules such "when you see an X fault in local circuit configuration Y, do test Z" -- which are highly amenable to expression in rules. The experts' primary diagnostic method is successive division of the circuit based on simple causal knowledge. They also use significant amounts of heuristic knowledge about the properties of specific circuit types and components.

Rule-base programming allowed us to express the experts' diagnostic procedures directly. It facilitated the construction of an initial system and incremental expansion of its competence. It also turned out to be a major factor in making the system's operation and results *understandable* – to both the technicians who implement SSCFI's repair recommendations and the testing experts who evaluate them.

• *Detailed circuit modeling is not required.* The testing experts generally do not know all the details of the underlying technology, but instead make do with a general models of each class of component. The component modules are purchased from third parties, meaning that their internal operation is generally proprietary, poorly-documented, and subject to change. In addition, the circuit model isn't fully known beforehand. The tester's model of the circuit can change as testing proceeds and additional evidence is accumulated.

• *The primary goal of testing is to get the circuit back into operation.* It is desirable but not necessary that testing be optimal or that the diagnosis be exact. For example, it is faster to replace suspect components than to try to identify a precise fault etiology.

SSCFI Architecture and Operation

SSCFI runs on RS6000 workstations under the AIX™ operating system. Each RS6000/580 supports 5-6 testers running simultaneously, plus various daemon processes handling administrative monitoring and control for the testers on that machine. Each SSCFI tester is capable of handling about 10-12 tickets per day.

Each tester is composed of two processes, the diagnostic process (the Knowledge Base, or KB, process) and a communications control process (the COMM process), which communicate via shared files and semaphores. The KB process controls the diagnostic session. It contains the knowledge about interpreting circuit designs, running tests, isolating faults, and describing results. The KB process is written in Brightware Corp.'s ART-IM™ (Brightware, 1988), a rule-based language. It currently includes about 1200 rules, 600 facts, 900 initial data structures, and 1600+ functions.

The COMM process is comprised of ExpecTerm scripts for requesting test operations and gathering data from each of the systems that SSCFI interfaces with. Expect (Libes, 1991) is an extension of the Tcl scripting language (Osterhout, 1994) for communicating with interactive processes; ExpecTerm is a further extension for interfacing with screen-oriented protocols. The COMM process's task is to manage the details of interaction with systems having terminal-oriented interfaces; it incorporates a minimum of testing and testing systems knowledge and so will not be discussed further here.

Diagnostic Algorithm

SSCFI's diagnostic procedure is outlined in Figure 3. The basic data structure used to control diagnosis is the fault-containing section (FCS). Each FCS specifies a fault observation and the section of the circuit within which the fault occurred. FCSs are used to reason explicitly about the problem-solving state (cf. NEOMYCIN: Clancey, 1988).

1. Select a ticket to work on. SSCFI prioritizes the pending tickets based on class of service and commitment time. An initial FCS covering the entire circuit is created for the reported fault.

2. Fetch and parse circuit design. SSCFI uses its design knowledge to fill in missing information and to check the design for consistency.

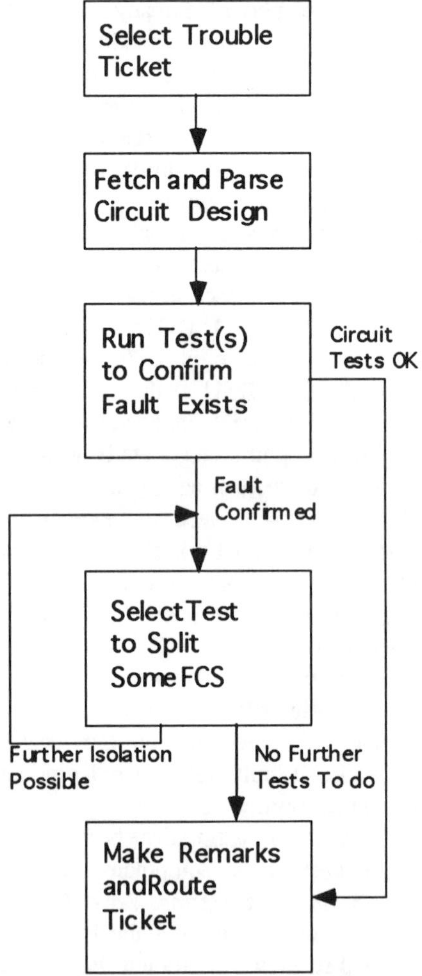

Figure 3: SSCFI's Diagnostic Algorithm

```
Auto results: LOOPBACK-FAILURE to A-END DSO/DP 2.

The reported trouble (DATA FAILURE) could be explained by:
  {1} LOOPBACK-FAILURE to A-END DSO/DP 2;
  {2} LOOPBACK-FAILURE to Z-END NID.

Discharge Summary:
  From SSCFI to BHKPFLXA: Please check {1},
    then route to CLWRFLXE (work loc: ACSC, dac: 8004).
  From SSCFI to CLWRFLXE: Please check {2}.

The above remarks are based on testing from the A-end DSO/DP 2 to the Z-end NID.

Summary of known good sections of the circuit:
  {4} LOOPBACK-OK to A-END DSO/DP 1 from DACS 1264-24 in TAMPFLXA
  {5} LOOPBACK-OK to Z-END OCU from DACS 1264-24.
```

Figure 4: SSCFI's Diagnostic Remarks for the Example Problem

3. Confirm the fault. SSCFI selects an initial test or set of tests that exercises as much of the circuit as possible, based on the type of circuit, availability of test access, and the type of trouble reported. If the circuit tests OK, the ticket is routed to a customer representative or a test technician; else SSCFI tries to isolate the fault(s).

4. Isolate the fault. While some unexplored FCS F exists, do:

- Select and run a set of tests that can potentially split F into sub-regions;
- Interpret test results and create a new FCS for each fault observed;
- Determine if any new FCS explains F;
- If F is now explained or no further subtests exist, mark F explored;

SSCFI performs tests to split each FCS until no further split is possible and worthwhile. SSCFI has knowledge suggesting appropriate tests to run to isolate each fault type, given the local circuit context and conditions; how to interpret the readings generated by the test and identify new faults; how to recover from bad or inconsistent test results, and so forth.

5. Generate remarks. The last step is to write out a description of the faults found and any other related information, and to route the ticket. Related information includes any additional information that might help localize the fault further, a statement of what part of the circuit was covered by the tests performed, and any miscellaneous observations or problems encountered during testing, such as test system problems, and non-explaining or minor faults.

Diagnosis Example

We now illustrate the diagnostic procedure in the circuit of Figure 1. In this example, both the farthest DSO/DP and the NID at the customer interface are faulty. (For brevity, details of fault selection and design interpretation are omitted.)

Confirming the fault. SSCFI first selects a test access point. Since this is a point-to-POI circuit, the DCS closest to the POI is selected; if it were point-to-point then any DCS point would be acceptable. SSCFI verifies the configuration of the DCS and takes a data sample; certain data codes are diagnostic of test equipment failure. If the DCS were misconfigured or faulty, SSCFI would notify the system administrator and look for an alternate DCS point.

SSCFI then confirms the fault by looping the end equipment in each direction. This is done with the "DDS macro" provided by the REACT test system, which performs loopbacks of all the customer-end devices -- the OCU, NID, CSU, and DSU -- in one operation. In this circuit the NID is faulty, so the DDS macro test in the customer (Z) direction returns "good" to the OCU and "failure" to all farther devices. In the A direction, the DDS macro fails to loop anything.

Fault Isolation. A latching loopback in the A direction to the furthest DSO/DP is attempted and fails. SSCFI then tries to loop back the nearer DSO/DP, which succeeds, meaning that the furthest DSO/DP has failed. Toward the Z-end, the differential between the loopbacks to the OCU and NID indicates that the fault must be contained in the section of the circuit from OCU to NID. There is an analog test point in this FCS, from which SSCFI performs analog measurements (voltage, resistance, and capacitance) in both directions. The resistance across each pair is in the 1K range, and the capacitances are normal. This indicates that equipment is connected and that the pairs are good to the NID, reducing the FCS to the NID itself. At this point, no further tests suggest themselves, so fault isolation is complete.

Remarks Generation. SSCFI's findings for this circuit are shown in Figure 4. The first line states the primary fault to be repaired. The second paragraph lists all faults found that explain the reported trouble and were not a consequence of some more specific fault. (If incidental faults were found, that is, faults that did not account for the reported trouble, they would be listed separately.) The third section indicates in detail how SSCFI suggests the ticket be routed, here, to the DSO/DP failure first and then to the NID failure in the field. Expressions in braces are references to previously mentioned test results.

SSCFI then explicitly states what portion of the circuit it believes it has tested, and lastly lists results documenting the part of the circuit that tested OK. Information beyond the primary diagnosis is provided for several reasons: it increases user confidence in the reliability of SSCFI's diagnoses, it makes the results more useful in complex cases such as multiple faults, and it facilitates retesting after repair.

Development History and Status

Initial knowledge acquisition for SSCFI began in September, 1989, focusing on analog testing in the South (Florida) region. It involved several weeks of expert interviews, from which a design and initial implementation were generated. The knowledge was then intensively refined for several months through expert review of SSCFI's performance on real cases. Only in this way could we elicit the tacit knowledge used in performing the task, knowledge that experts typically do not think to mention unless asked. Knowledge tuning continued for another 6-12 months of prototype operation until the knowledge update rate leveled off.

The first operational system was completed in May 1991, for selected voice circuits; full testing of analog voice and data circuits was achieved that October, followed by a significant period of tuning and further knowledge acquisition. SSCFI was extended to operate in the West (California) region in 1993, and countrywide by mid-1994. This effort involved a significant restructuring of the test-request mechanisms to accommodate an additional test system (SAS). Digital testing knowledge acquisition began in mid-1994, involving 3 weeks of interviews, 6 months of intensive refinement, and 6 months of tuning in the field. Testing of DDS-class circuits was operational by mid-1995.

Over the last three years significant improvements in the knowledge, efficiency, and success rate of the system have been achieved. SSCFI's success rate is now about 90%, up from 65% in 1992, and continues to improve; average test time has been reduced from 35-40 minutes to around 25 minutes under full system load. We expect to reach 20-minute testing in 1996 though hardware upgrades and replacement of the current terminal-emulation-based interfaces to external systems with program-to-program interfaces (APIs).

Maintenance

SSCFI's knowledge base is constantly evolving. Expert users perform regular reviews of cases with incorrect diagnoses, failed test requests, or excessive test time. This generates a steady stream of "bug" reports (about 1 per day). Of these, about 25% are due to new situations of various kinds -- design syntax variations, new or changed test system error messages, or unusual circuit configurations. Another 25% are minor enhancements worth doing as time permits. In addition, detailed reviews are conducted yearly. New releases are generated every 4-6 months.

Release testing is a major issue. Our release process includes a regression suite of over 200 cases, with more being added all the time. Regression testing has been very effective in exposing bugs and errors in the code.

There are several reasons for the continued knowledge base changes. One is that there is a lot of minor variation among cases and new variations are always turning up. This tends to level off over time. A second reason is that the users keep coming up with ideas for improvements, which we try to incorporate as much as possible. A third reason is that the domain is in constant flux. We are regularly confronted with changes in circuit equipment behavior, test system interface operation, and operational requirements such as workflow policies. This is the most serious maintenance problem.

Evaluation

SSCFI is regarded by the SSCC as a major success. SSCFI currently handles about 90% of the auto-testable circuits reporting troubles each day -- over 40,000 trouble reports per year. (Auto-testable circuits are those with remote test access, about half of GTE's special circuits.) When SSCFI is unavailable in a testing region, the SSCC testing staff are hard pressed to cope with the workload. Development required about 25 man-years; over the next 5 years, SSCFI is expected to return at least 7 times its development cost.

SSCFI is also recognized for significantly improving the overall quality of specials testing. SSCFI receives high marks from experienced testers for its thoroughness of testing and clarity of explanation. With the speed enhancements mentioned above, SSCFI will in most cases be faster than human testers as well, an important factor in the increasingly competitive telecommunications marketplace. The success of the system has prompted other organizations to develop automated specials diagnosticians, but to our knowledge no comparable system is currently available, commercially or otherwise.

Lessons Learned

Why is it Successful? There are several reasons for SSCFI's success.

SSCFI's domain and task environment are well-suited to a heuristic approach. The domain is one where the experts rely more on heuristic procedures derived from experience and simple causal models than on detailed knowledge of component behavior, which is varied and constantly changing. Computationally, the task is not too complex – a divide-and-conquer approach works in the majority of cases.

There is a wide distribution of skill levels among the testing staff. The term "expert system" is something of a misnomer: SSCFI has been successful in its target task because it brings a uniform and reliable level of competence to the testing task, rather than because it has achieved strictly "expert" performance.

Errors are not fatal in this domain. SSCFI makes accurate diagnoses most of the time, and can recognize and route most circuits it cannot handle, but it is only a program and errors still occur. The impact of diagnostic errors is limited because the SSCC's repair workflow separates diagnosis from repair. Every tester's diagnosis and routing is subject to revision by the technician in the field. This is a major reason why SSCFI can run autonomously. Running in an "advisor" or "assistant" mode would require that humans remain in the loop and would substantially reduce the cost benefits of the system.

No sophisticated user interface was required. SSCFI runs autonomously, so it was possible to focus on the core competence without being sidetracked by the substantial issues of providing user-friendly interfaces, of interactive explanation, and the like. Now that the system's value is established, we intend to explore the added value of interactive testing. The key point here is that the current interest in interactive operation is motivated by the tangible value of providing greater access to SSCFI's proven expertise, rather than the speculative one of providing a clever "assistant."

Significant effort went into maintaining sponsor and user interest. Developers maintained constant contact with both groups. The importance of this point should not be underestimated. The domain is one of continual small changes. The developers need to be aware of changes in technology, operational practice, management, and policy, preferably in advance. There need to be regular reviews of the system with the operational people involved to be sure that their needs and expectations are met. Several other development projects of a similar sophistication in the authors' experience failed to be established as an integral part of operations because they were unable to adjust their goals and schedules in response to such changes in operational requirements.

Managing Large Rule-Bases. The distributed structure of rule-bases facilitates incremental development but confounds modular design. Extensive use was made of state variables to partition and sequence rule subsets along functional boundaries; without this modularization the system would be unmaintainable. State sequencing also provides a simple way to implement closed-world assumptions ("if no rule has yet concluded X, then conclude Y") and replaced many uses of the computationally expensive "logical" construct (assertions which maintain their dependency information).

A second critical issue is optimization, which was essential to the viability of SSCFI. The literature on rule-base optimizations tends to focus on the join section of the RETE network (e.g., Giarratano & Riley, 1993; Brightware, 1988) where extremely costly errors are possible. Our experience is that, except for the occasional gross blunder, the greatest gains came from optimizing pattern (alpha) nodes (cf. the "average growth effect," Acharya, 1994) and reducing the number of individual RETE update calls (e.g., by batching updates).

What is the Task Expertise? As has been the case for many other "expert" systems, a significant portion of

SSCFI's knowledge relates to other than its nominal area of expertise, that is, diagnosis. The largest such body of knowledge regards the parsing and structure of designs. SSCFI routinely needs to adjust for erroneous or missing data and to infer missing components, such as the NID problem discussed above. Other problems include missing test points, incorrect test benchmark data, and undocumented equipment substitutions.

A second area of knowledge regards the testing equipment, which is not always reliable or properly configured. SSCFI had to be taught to distinguish failures of the testing process itself from those of the circuit under test, as the human testers do. This yielded a significant incidental benefit -- by routing explicit notifications of these problems directly to system administrators via their pagers, SSCFI has improved the testing environment for both human and automated testers.

Future Directions

SSCFI development is a ongoing process. A maintenance organization has been engaged to take over the ongoing tasks of user support, bug fixes, policy changes, release testing and management, and minor enhancements. This will enable us to focus on several significant enhancements in the coming year: extension to higher-speed digital services (T1/T3), continued knowledge tuning and enhancement, and direct (API) interfaces to the workflow and testing systems.

Perhaps the most significant change will be the implementation of an interactive interface to SSCFI which will allow it to be used on-line as either a diagnostic expert or an intelligent repair assistant, in addition to its current autonomous mode. Interactive operation will extend the system's usefulness in several ways: it will give SSCFI access to additional observations about circuit state and function via the repair technician; SSCFI will be able to offer explanations of its diagnoses at various levels of detail; and SSCFI will provide active test assistance to the technicians in the field. In particular, SSCFI will provide technicians a uniform abstract interface to the underlying circuit test systems.

We are also exploring applying SSCFI's accumulated design-parsing knowledge to the problem of automatic design database cleanup. Database quality is a large and chronic problem, in spite of several costly efforts to address it. It is prohibitively costly to update the designs by hand, but automated methods -- cross-comparing data from multiple databases, combined with explicit testing for verification -- have great potential.

Conclusions

SSCFI was the first fully integrated, on-line operations support system at GTE to use knowledge-based technology. Many competent knowledge-based systems have failed to achieve user acceptance; SSCFI has been successful because it successfully captured the testers' expertise in a form that can be deployed *cost-effectively* throughout the organization, resulting in both substantial monetary savings and significant improvement in testing quality.

Acknowledgments

Many people have contributed significantly to this project. We wish to acknowledge the financial and organizational support of Clark Erskine, Bob Abe, Linda Whittaker, and Jim Crutchfield. We thank Gene Nordgren, John Hernandez, Tony Leto, William Mattil, Joe Dwyer, and Mike Warren for many spent hours patiently explaining to us the details of special circuits and testing. Hank Henning deserves especial thanks for his multiple contributions to SSCFI's acceptance as a legitimate and valuable tool: as California SSCFI administrator, National SSCFI Coordinator and advocate, and testing expert. Mike Sullivan, Brad Orner, Hansel Wan, and Mark Weissman contributed significantly to the design and implementation of SSCFI. We thank Rick Alterman for his comments on an earlier draft of this paper.

References

Acharya, A. 1994. Scaling up production systems: Issues, approaches, and targets. *Knowledge Engineering Review*, 9(1): 67-72.

Brightware Corp. 1988. ART-IM Programming Language Reference.

Clancey, William J. 1988. Acquiring, Representing, and Evaluating a Competence Model of Diagnostic Strategy. In Chi, M.; Glaser, R.; and Farr, M. editors, *The Nature of Expertise*, 343-418.

Davis, R. and Hamscher, W. C. 1992. Model-based reasoning: Troubleshooting. In Hamscher, W.; Console,

L.; and De Kleer, J. editors, *Readings in Model-Based Diagnosis*, 3-24. Morgan Kaufmann, San Mateo CA.

Giarratano, J. and Riley, G. 1993. *Expert Systems: Principles and Programming*. PWS Publishing Company, Boston.

GTE Services Corporation 1990. GTE Technical Interface Reference Manual.

Libes, D. 1991. Expect: Scripts for controlling interactive processes. *Computing Systems*, 4(2), University of California Press, Berkeley, CA.

Osterhout, J. 1994. *Tcl and the Tk toolkit*. Addison-Wesley, Reading, MA.

Roth, Emilie M. and Woods, David D. 1989. Cognitive task analysis: An approach to knowledge acquisition for intelligent system design. In Guida, G. and Tasso, C. editors, *Topics in Expert System Design*, 233-264. Elsevier Science Publishers B.V.

Invited Talks

The BOEING 777 - Concurrent Engineering and Digital Pre-Assembly

Bob Abarbanel

Advanced Design Systems, Research & Technology,
Boeing Information & Support Serv
PO Box 3707, MS 7L-40
Seattle, WA 98124-2207
Email: abar@boeing.com

Abstract

The processes created on the 777 for checking designs were called "digital pre-assembly". Using FlyThru(tm), a spin-off of a Boeing advanced computing research project, engineers were able to view up to 1500 models (15000 solids) in 3d traversing that data at high speed. FlyThru(tm) was rapidly deployed in 1991 to meet the needs of the 777 for large scale product visualization and verification. The digital pre-assembly process has had fantastic results. The 777 has had far fewer assembly and systems problems compared to previous airplane programs. Today, FlyThru(tm) is installed on hundreds of workstations on almost every airplane program, and is being used on Space Station, F22, AWACS, and other defense projects. It's applications have gone far beyond just design review. In many ways, FlyThru is a Data Warehouse supported by advanced tools for analysis. It is today being integrated with Knowledge Based Engineering geometry generation tools.

Data Mining and Knowledge Discovery in Databases: Applications in Astronomy and Planetary Science

Usama M. Fayyad*

Microsoft Research
One Microsoft Way
Redmond, WA 98052-6399
fayyad@microsoft.com
http://www.research.microsoft.com/research/dtg

* Author is also affiliated with:
Machine Learning Systems Group
Jet Propulsion Laboratory
California Institute of Technology
http://www-aig.jpl.nasa.gov/mls

Abstract of Invited Talk

Overview of the Topic

Knowledge Discovery in Databases (KDD) is a new field of research concerned with the extraction of high-level information (knowledge) from low-level data (usually stored in large databases) [1]. It is an area of interest to researchers and practitioners from many fields including: AI, statistics, pattern recognition, databases, visualization, and high-performance and parallel computing. The basic problem is to search databases for patterns or models that can be useful in accomplishing one or more goals. Examples of such goals include:

- prediction (e.g. regression and classification),
- descriptive or generative modeling (e.g. clustering),
- data summarization (e.g. report generation), or
- visualization of either data or extracted knowledge (e.g. to support decision making or exploratory data analysis).

KDD is a process that includes many steps. Among these steps are: data preparation and cleaning, data selection and sampling, preprocessing and transformation, data mining to extract patterns and models, interpretation and evaluation of extracted information, and finally evaluation, rendering, or use of final extracted knowledge. Note that under this view, *data mining constitutes one of the steps of the overall KDD process*. The other steps are essential to make the application of data mining possible, and to make the results useful. Within data mining, methods for deriving patterns or extracting models originate from statistics, machine learning, statistical pattern recognition, uncertainty management, and database methods such as on-line analysis processing (OLAP) or association rules [2].

The process is typically highly interactive and may involve many iterations before useful knowledge is extracted from the underlying data. This talk will give an overview and summary of the rapidly growing field of KDD, and then focus on two specific applications in scientific data analysis to illustrate the potential, limitations, challenges, and promise of KDD. An overview of the KDD process is given in [3].

Science Data Analysis

Today's science instruments are capable of gathering huge amounts of data, making traditional human-based comprehensive analysis an infeasible endeavor. This has been a primary motivation to develop tools to automate science data analysis tasks. The talk will describe efforts to develop a new generation of data mining systems where users specify what to search for simply by providing the system with training examples, and letting the system automatically learn what to do. The system would then automatically sift through the data and catalog objects of interest for analysis purposes.

The learn-from-example approach is a natural solution to a problem we call the *query formulation problem* in the exploration and analysis of image data [4]: How does one express a query for objects that are typically only recognized by visual intuition? Translating human visual intuition to pixel-level algorithmic constraints is a difficult problem. By asking the user to simply "show" the system examples of objects of interest, then let the system figure out how to formulate the appropriate query, we believe the problem can be surmounted in certain circumstances.

Two applications at JPL will be used to illustrate the learning techniques and their effects. The first targets automating the cataloging of sky objects in a digitized sky survey consisting of three terabytes of image data and containing on the order of two billion sky objects. The Sky Image Cataloging and Analysis Tool (SKICAT) [5] allows for automated and accurate classification, enabling the automated cataloging of an estimated two billion sky objects, the majority of which being too faint for visual recognition by astronomers. This represents an instance where learning algorithms solved a significant and difficult scientific analysis problem. Several new results in astronomy have been achieved based on the SKICAT catalog [6]. Recent results of the application of SKICAT to help in discovery of new objects in the Universe include the discovery of 16 new high-redshift quasars: some of the furthest and oldest objects detectable by today's instruments [7].

The second system we describe is called JARtool (JPL Adaptive Recognition Tool) [8]. JARtool is being initially developed to detect and catalog an estimated one million small volcanoes (< 15km in diameter) visible in a database consisting of over 30,000 images of the planet Venus. The images were collected by the Magellan spacecraft using synthetic aperture radar (SAR) to penetrate the permanent gaseous cloud cover that obscures the planet's surface in the optical range.

Work at JPL's Machine Learning Systems Group continues to extend data mining techniques to automate analysis in other areas of science including: cataloging of Sun spots, remote-sensing detection of earthquake faults [9], spatio-temporal analysis of atmospheric data, and others (see http://www-aig.jpl.nasa.gov/mls/ for live descriptions of ongoing work).

Other Applications

Although this talks focuses on applications in science data analysis, we believe these techniques to be applicable to a wide range of problems and have little to do with the fact that the data happens to be images. Potential applications include medical imaging, automated inspection and diagnosis in manufacturing, decision support systems, database marketing, and summarization/visualization of large databases. Coverage of applications in science data analysis is given in [10]. Coverage of industrial applications of KDD is provided in [11].

Beware the Hype

While it is true that in many situations some simple data mining work can result in great successes, this by no means justifies the public perception that data mining can be used to solve all analysis problems. The fundamental problems in the field are far from being solved. The basic problem in KDD is one of statistical inference from a finite set of data. Issues of model overfitting and justification of findings remain as major challenges. Many models are extractable from data (in fact infinitely many models from a finite data set). Most of these are likely to be due to spurious correlations and random chance (simply because the data is finite, and computation is limited). See [12] for a critique and warnings of pitfalls. Hence, any derived predictions and any inference of causality information from data is to be taken with a fairly huge helping of salt. Furthermore, effective techniques for incorporating the necessary prior knowledge about an application into a data mining algorithm to help the automated system avoid some of the basic traps are still lacking.

The fact that initial successes exist should be taken as encouraging signs that this new and emerging field holds some promise to address the daunting problems of information overload facing modern society.

Information Resources

A good starting point to get a summary of what has been done in this field is to start with [1] and [13]. Appendix 1 of [1] by Kloesgen and Zytkow provides a glossary of terminology used in KDD, while Appendix 2 by Piatetsky-Shapiro provides pointers to various resources. The next source of information is to follow up on the following resources on the internet and the world-wide web:

- http://www-aig.jpl.nasa.gov/kdd95/ is the homepage of the First International Conference on Knowledge Discovery and Data Mining (KDD-95); The homepage of KDD-96 is at http://www-aig.jpl.nasa.gov/kdd96. Information on the new journal for this field: *Data Mining and Knowledge Discovery* can be obtained at http://www.research.microsoft.com/research/datamine.
- http://info.gte.com/~kdd/ is the *Knowledge Discovery Mine* maintained by Gregory Piatetsky-Shapiro at GTE Laboratories. This site serves as a collecting point of information directly relevant to KDD, including tools available free on-line, commercial products, pointers to many other relevant groups and organizations, as well as a repository of all back issues of *KDD Nuggets.*
- *KDD Nuggets:* is a moderated mailing list that serves as the main forum of communicating with or receiving news of interest to the KDD community (kdd-request@gte.com).

Acknowledgments

The applications described in this talk were conducted while the author was still with the Jet Propulsion Laboratory, California Institute of Technology, under a contract with the National Aeronautics and Space Administration.

Collaborators on the SKICAT work at Caltech and Palomar Observatory include S.G. Djorgovski and Nick Weir. We also thank Reinaldo DeCarvalho and Julia Kennefick (Caltech), Joe Roden, John Loch, Maureen Burl, Scott Burleigh, Jennifer Yu, and Alex Gray (JPL).

JARtool work is in collaboration with Padhraic Smyth (JPL), Michael Burl and Pietro Perona (Caltech), and Jayne Aubele and Larry Crumpler (Brown University). We also thank Maureen Burl, Joe Roden, Victoria Gor, and Michael Turmon (JPL).
Program management of this work at NASA was under the direction of Melvin Montemerlo (Code XS), and at JPL under direction of David Atkinson and Richard Doyle.
In my overview coverage of data mining and KDD, I have borrowed material from my co-authors on [3]: Gregory Piatetsky-Shapiro and Padhraic Smyth.

References

[1] Fayyad U.; Piatetsky-Shapiro, G.; Smyth, P.; and Uthurusamy, R. (Eds.) 1996. *Advances in Knowledge Discovery and Data Mining.* Cambridge, Mass.: MIT Press/AAAI Press.

[2] Agrawal, A.; Mannila, H.; Srikant, R.; Toivonen, H.; and Verkamo, I. 1996. "Fast Discovery of Association Rules", in *Advances in Knowledge Discovery and Data Mining.* Fayyad U.; Piatetsky-Shapiro, G.; Smyth, P.; and Uthurusamy, R. (Eds.), Cambridge, Mass.: MIT Press/AAAI Press.

[3] Fayyad U.; Piatetsky-Shapiro, G.; and Smyth, P. 1996. "From Data Mining to Knowledge Discovery: An Overview", in *Advances in Knowledge Discovery and Data Mining.* Fayyad U.; Piatetsky-Shapiro, G.; Smyth, P.; and Uthurusamy, R. (Eds.), Cambridge, Mass.: MIT Press/AAAI Press.

[4] Fayyad, U. and Smyth P. 1995. "The Automated Analysis, Cataloging, and Searching of Digital Libraries: A Machine Learning Approach", in *Digital Libraries, Lecture Notes in Computer Science 916,* N.R. Adam, B.K. Bhargava, and Y. Yesha (Eds.) Berlin: Springer-Verlag.

[5] Fayyad U.; Djorgovski, S.G.; and Weir, N. 1996. "Automating the Analysis and Cataloging of Sky Surveys", in *Advances in Knowledge Discovery and Data Mining.* Fayyad U.; Piatetsky-Shapiro, G.; Smyth, P.; and Uthurusamy, R. (Eds.), Cambridge, Mass.: MIT Press/AAAI Press.

[6] Weir, N.; Djorgovski, S.G.; and Fayyad, U.M. 1995. "Initial Galaxy Counts From Digitized POSS-II", *Astronomical Journal*, 110-1:1-20.

[7] Kennefick, J.D.; De Carvalho, R.R.; Djorgovski, S.G.; Wilber, M.M.; Dickinson, E.S.; Weir, N.; Fayyad, U.; and Roden, J. (1995). "The Discovery of Five Quasars at z>4 using the Second Palomar Sky Survey", *Astronomical Journal*, 110-1:78-86.

[8] Burl, M.C.; Fayyad, U.; Perona, P.; Smyth, P.; and Burl, M.P. (1994). "Automating the Hunt for Volcanoes on Venus", in *Proc. of Computer Vision and Pattern Recognition Conference (CVPR-94),* pp. 302-308, IEEE Computer Society Press.

[9] Stolorz, P. and Dean, C. 1996. "Quakefinder: A Scalable Datamining System for Detecting Earthquakes from Space", submitted to *Second International Conf. on Knowledge Discovery and Data Mining*. AAAI Press.

[10] Fayyad, U.; Haussler, D.; and Stolorz, P. 1996. "Science Applications", special issue on Data Mining and Knowledge Discovery, *Communications of the ACM,* forthcoming.

[11] Brachman. R.J.; Khabaza, T.; Kloesgen, W.; Piatetsky-Shapiro, G.; and Simoudis, E. 1996. "Industrial Applications of Data Mining and Knowledge Discovery", in *Proc. Of the Second International Conference on Knowledge Discovery and Data Mining (KDD-96),* Menlo Park, Calif.: AAAI Press.

[12] Glymour, C.; Madigan, D.; Pregibon, D.; and Smyth, P. 1996. "Statistics and Data Mining", special issue on Data Mining and Knowledge Discovery, *Communications of the ACM,* forthcoming.

[13] Piatetsky-Shapiro, G. and Frawley W. (1991). *Knowledge Discovery in Databases*. Cambridge, MA: MIT Press.

Index